CLYMER®

MERCURY/MARINER

OUTBOARD SHOP MANUAL

4-90 HP FOUR-STROKE • 1995-2000

The world's finest publisher of mechanical how-to manuals

INTERTEC PUBLISHING

P.O. Box 12901, Overland Park, KS 66282-2901

FIRST EDITION
First Printing February, 2001

Printed in U.S.A.

ISBN: 0-89287-754-5

Library of Congress: 00-111867

Technical photography by Mark Rolling.

Technical illustrations by Michael Rose and Robert Caldwell.

Technical assistance provided by Larry Compton, Plano Marine Service, Plano, Texas.

Cover photography courtesy of Mercury Marine, Fond du Lac Wisconsin.

PRODUCTION: Greg Araujo.

0886892

CLYMER PUBLICATIONS

Intertec Directory & Book Division

Chief Executive Officer Timothy M. Andrews

President Ron Wall

Vice President, Directory & Book Division Rich Hathaway

The following books and guides are published by Intertec Publishing.

CLYMER SHOP MANUALS
Boat Motors and Drives
Motorcycles and ATVs
Snowmobiles
Personal Watercraft

ABOS/INTERTEC/CLYMER BLUE BOOKS AND TRADE-IN GUIDES
Recreational Vehicles
Outdoor Power Equipment
Agricultural Tractors
Lawn and Garden Tractors
Motorcycles and ATVs
Snowmobiles and Personal Watercraft
Boats and Motors

AIRCRAFT BLUEBOOK-PRICE DIGEST
Airplanes
Helicopters

AC-U-KWIK DIRECTORIES
The Corporate Pilot's Airport/FBO Directory
International Manager's Edition
Jet Book

I&T SHOP SERVICE MANUALS
Tractors

INTERTEC SERVICE MANUALS
Snowmobiles
Outdoor Power Equipment
Personal Watercraft
Gasoline and Diesel Engines
Recreational Vehicles
Boat Motors and Drives
Motorcycles
Lawn and Garden Tractors

Contents

Quick Reference Data

MAINTENANCE INTERVALS

Before each use	Check and correct engine oil level. Check the condition of the propeller. Check for tight engine mounting fasteners. Check the fuel system for leakage. Check for proper operation of the lanyard stop switch. Inspect the steering linkage for looseness or binding. Inspect the steering system for loose fasteners.
After each use	Flush the cooling system. Clean all external gearcase and drive shaft housing surfaces.
Once a year or every 100 hours of usage	Change the engine oil. Clean or replace the engine oil filter.* Service the water pump. Lubricate the swivel tube and clamp brackets. Lubricate the steering system components. Lubricate the throttle and shift linkages. Lubricate the propeller shaft splines. Clean and inspect the spark plugs. Clean or replace the fuel filter. Inspect the gearcase and power head anodes. Change the gearcase lubricant. Lubricate the upper drive shaft splines. Check the tightness of all external fasteners. Inspect all fuel lines and hoses for defects. Inspect the thermostat for damage or corrosion. Adjust the valve clearance. Check control cable adjustments.* Inspect the timing belt for deterioration or damage.* Adjust the carburetor(s). Check the power trim fluid level.* Check the battery condition.* Clean carbon deposits from the engine. Check the ignition timing.
Every 3 years or every 300 hours of usage	Change the engine oil. Replace the engine oil filter. Replace the water pump impeller. Lubricate the swivel tube and clamp brackets. Lubricate the steering system components. Lubricate the throttle and shift linkages. Lubricate the propeller shaft splines. Clean and inspect the spark plugs. Clean or replace the fuel filter. Change the gearcase lubricant. Lubricate the upper drive shaft splines. Check the tightness of all external fasteners. Inspect all fuel lines and hoses for defects. Replace the thermostat. Adjust the valve clearance. Check control cable adjustments.* Inspect the timing belt for deterioration or damage.* Adjust the carburetor(s). Check the power trim fluid level. * (continued)

MAINTENANCE INTERVALS (continued)

Every 3 years or every 300 hours of usage (continued)	Check the battery condition.* Clean carbon deposits from the engine. Check the ignition timing. Inspect the gearcase and power head anodes. *
* This maintenance item does not apply to all models.	

ENGINE OIL CAPACITY (approximate)

Model	Capacity
4 -6 hp	15 fl oz. (450 ml)
9.9 and 15 hp	1 qt. (0.95 L)
25-50 hp	3 qt. (2.84 L)
75 and 90 hp	5 qt. (4.73 L)

GEARCASE CAPACITY

Model	Capacity
4-6 hp	6.5 fl oz. (195 ml)
9.9 and 15 hp	
Standard gearcase	6.8 fl oz. (200 ml)
Optional gearcase	7.8 fl oz. (230 ml)
25 hp	14.9 fl oz. (440 ml)
30 and 40 hp	
Standard gearcase	14.9 fl oz. (440 ml)
Optional gearcase	22.5 fl oz. (655 ml)
50 hp	
Standard gearcase	14.9 fl oz. (440 ml)
Optional gearcase	22.5 fl oz. (655 ml)
75 and 90 hp	22.5 fl oz. (665 ml)

SPARK PLUG SPECIFICATIONS

Model	Spark Plug	Gap
4-6 hp	NGK DCPR6E	0.035 in. (0.9 mm)
9.9 hp		
Serial No. OH000057-prior	NGK DPR6EA-9	0.035 in. (0.9 mm)
Serial No. OH000058-on	NGK CR6HS	0.024-0.028 in. (0.6-0.7 mm)
15-50 hp	NGK DPR6EA-9	0.035 in. (0.9 mm)
75 and 90 hp	NGK LFR5A-11	0.043 in. (1.1 mm)

RECOMMENDED FULL THROTTLE ENGINE SPEED

Model	Engine Speed (rpm)
4-6 hp	4500-5500
9.9 and 15 hp	4500-5500
25-40 hp	5500-6000
50 hp	5500-6000
75 and 90 hp	5000-6000

IGNITION TIMING

Model	Specification
4 and 5 hp	
High speed timing	24°-26° BTDC
9.9 hp	
Serial No. OH000057-prior	
800 rpm and below	5° BTDC
2800-3300 rpm	30° BTDC
Serial No. OH000058-on	
800-900 rpm	4°-6° BTDC
2500-3000 rpm	34°-36° BTDC
15 hp	
800 rpm and below	5° BTDC
2800-3300 rpm	30° BTDC.
25 hp	
800 rpm and below	
ECU part No. 855311	10° BTDC
ECU part No. 856058/856190	5° BTDC
6000 rpm	30° BTDC
30 and 40 hp	
800 rpm	10° BTDC
6000 rpm	28° BTDC
50 hp	
Closed throttle (idle)	5° BTDC
2500-3000 rpm	35° BTDC
75 and 90 hp	
800 rpm	5° ATDC
6000 rpm	18° BTDC

CLYMER®

MERCURY/MARINER

OUTBOARD SHOP MANUAL

4-90 HP FOUR-STROKE • 1995-2000

Introduction

This Clymer shop manual covers service, maintenance and repair of 4-90 hp four-stroke Mercury and Mariner outboard motors manufactured from 1995-2000. Coverage is provided for outboard motors designed for recreational use only; commercial models are not covered in this manual.

Step-by-step instructions and hundreds of illustrations guide you through tasks ranging from routine maintenance to complete overhaul.

This manual can be used by anyone from a first time owner to a professional technician. Easy-to-read type, detailed drawings and clear photographs provide all the information need to complete the procedure correctly.

Having a well-maintained outboard motor will increase your enjoyment of your boat as well as ensuring your safety offshore. Keep this shop manual handy and use it often. Performing routine, preventive maintenance will save time and money by helping prevent premature failure and unnecessary repairs.

Chapter One

General Information

This detailed, comprehensive manual contains complete information on maintenance, tune-up, repair and overhaul. Hundreds of photos and drawings guide you through every step-by-step procedure.

Troubleshooting, tune-up, maintenance and repair are not difficult if you know what tools and equipment to use and what to do. Anyone not afraid to get their hands dirty, of average intelligence and with some mechanical ability, can perform most of the procedures in this book. See Chapter Two for more information on tools and techniques.

A shop manual is a reference. You want to be able to find information fast. Clymer books are designed with you in mind. All chapters are thumb tabbed and important items are indexed at the end of the book. All procedures, tables, photos, etc., in this manual assume that the reader may be working on the machine or using this manual for the first time.

Keep this book handy in your tool box. It will help you to better understand how your machine runs, lower repair and maintenance costs and generally increase your enjoyment of your marine equipment.

MANUAL ORGANIZATION

This chapter provides general information useful to marine owners and mechanics.

Chapter Two discusses the tools and techniques for preventive maintenance, troubleshooting and repair.

Chapter Three describes typical equipment problems and provides logical troubleshooting procedures.

Following chapters describe specific systems, providing disassembly, repair, assembly and adjustment procedures in simple step-by-step form. Specifications concerning a specific system are included at the end of the appropriate chapter.

NOTES, CAUTIONS AND WARNINGS

The terms NOTE, CAUTION and WARNING have specific meanings in this manual. A NOTE provides additional information to make a step or procedure easier or clearer. Disregarding a NOTE could cause inconvenience, but would not cause damage or personal injury.

A CAUTION emphasizes areas where equipment damage could result. Disregarding a CAUTION could cause permanent mechanical damage; however, personal injury is unlikely.

A WARNING emphasizes areas where personal injury or even death could result from negligence. Mechanical damage may also occur. WARNINGS *are to be taken seriously.* In some cases, serious injury or death has resulted from disregarding similar warnings.

TORQUE SPECIFICATIONS

Torque specifications throughout this manual are given in foot-pounds (ft.-lb.) and either Newton meters (N•m) or meter-kilograms (mkg). Newton meters are being adopted in place of meter-kilograms in accordance with the International Modernized Metric System. Existing torque wrenches calibrated in meter-kilograms can be used by performing a simple conversion: move the decimal point one place to the right. For example, 4.7 mkg = 47 N•m. This conversion is accurate enough for mechanics' use even though the exact mathematical conversion is 3.5 mkg = 34.3 N•m.

ENGINE OPERATION

All marine engines, whether 2- or 4-stroke, gasoline or diesel, operate on the Otto cycle of intake, compression, power and exhaust phases.

4-stroke Cycle

A 4-stroke engine requires two crankshaft revolutions (4 strokes of the piston) to complete the Otto cycle. **Figure 1** shows gasoline 4-stroke engine operation. **Figure 2** shows diesel 4-stroke engine operation.

2-stroke Cycle

A 2-stroke engine requires only 1 crankshaft revolution (2 strokes of the piston) to complete the Otto cycle. **Figure 3** shows gasoline 2-stroke engine operation. Although diesel 2-strokes exist, they are not commonly used in light marine applications.

FASTENERS

The material and design of the various fasteners used on marine equipment are not arrived at by chance or accident. Fastener design determines the type of tool required to work with the fastener. Fastener material is carefully selected to decrease the possibility of physical failure or corrosion. See *Galvanic Corrosion* in this chapter for more information on marine materials.

Threads

Nuts, bolts and screws are manufactured in a wide range of thread patterns. To join a nut and bolt, the diameter of the bolt and the diameter of the hole in the nut must be the same. It is just as important that the threads on both be properly matched.

The best way to determine if the threads on two fasteners are matched is to turn the nut on the bolt (or the bolt into the threaded hole in a piece of equipment) with fingers only. Be sure both pieces are clean. If much force is required, check the thread condition on each fastener. If the thread condition is good but the fasteners jam, the threads are not compatible.

Four important specifications describe every thread:

a. Diameter.
b. Threads per inch.
c. Thread pattern.
d. Thread direction.

Figure 4 shows the first two specifications. Thread pattern is more subtle. Italian and British

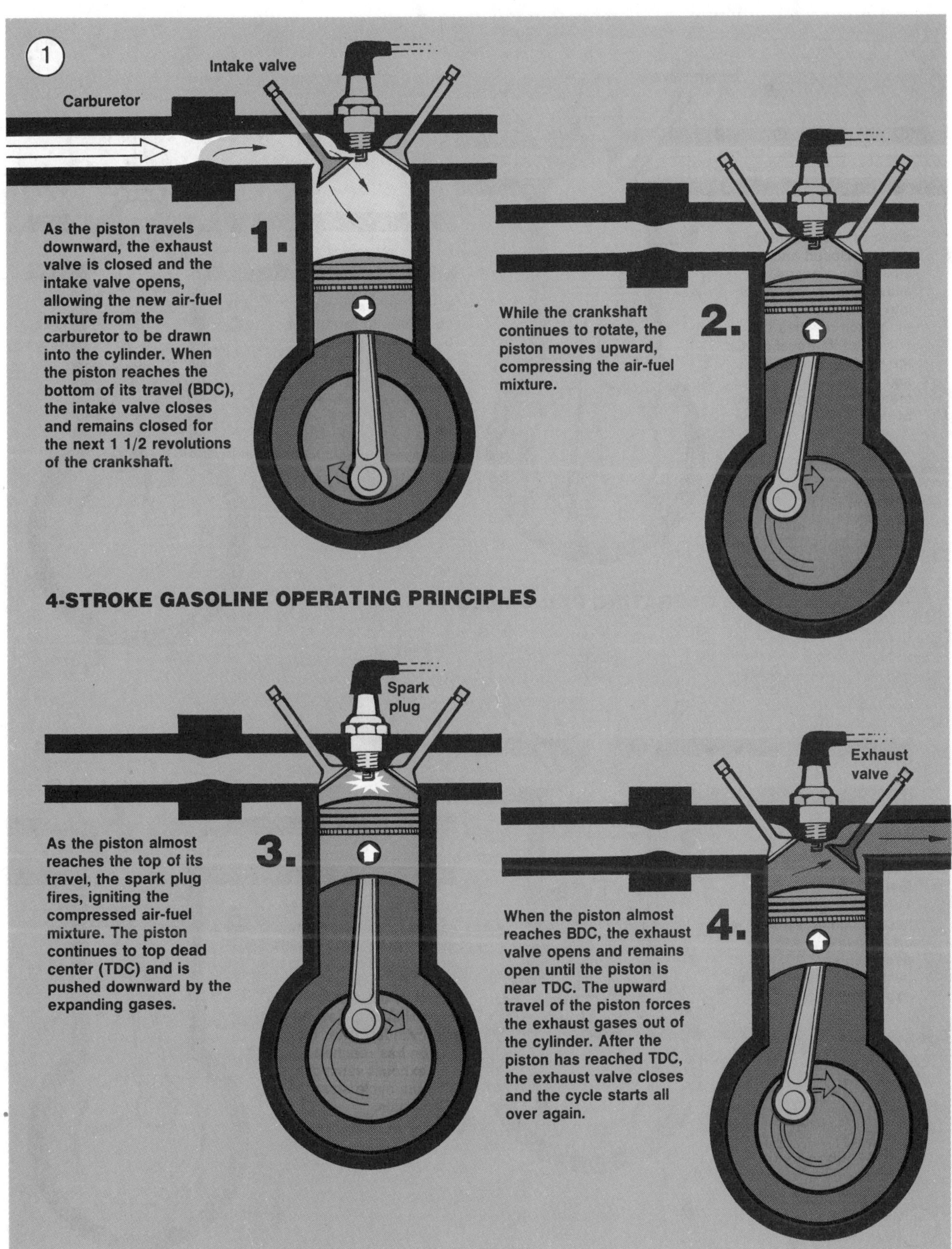
1
Intake valve
Carburetor
1.
As the piston travels downward, the exhaust valve is closed and the intake valve opens, allowing the new air-fuel mixture from the carburetor to be drawn into the cylinder. When the piston reaches the bottom of its travel (BDC), the intake valve closes and remains closed for the next 1 1/2 revolutions of the crankshaft.
2.
While the crankshaft continues to rotate, the piston moves upward, compressing the air-fuel mixture.
4-STROKE GASOLINE OPERATING PRINCIPLES
Spark plug
3.
As the piston almost reaches the top of its travel, the spark plug fires, igniting the compressed air-fuel mixture. The piston continues to top dead center (TDC) and is pushed downward by the expanding gases.
Exhaust valve
4.
When the piston almost reaches BDC, the exhaust valve opens and remains open until the piston is near TDC. The upward travel of the piston forces the exhaust gases out of the cylinder. After the piston has reached TDC, the exhaust valve closes and the cycle starts all over again.

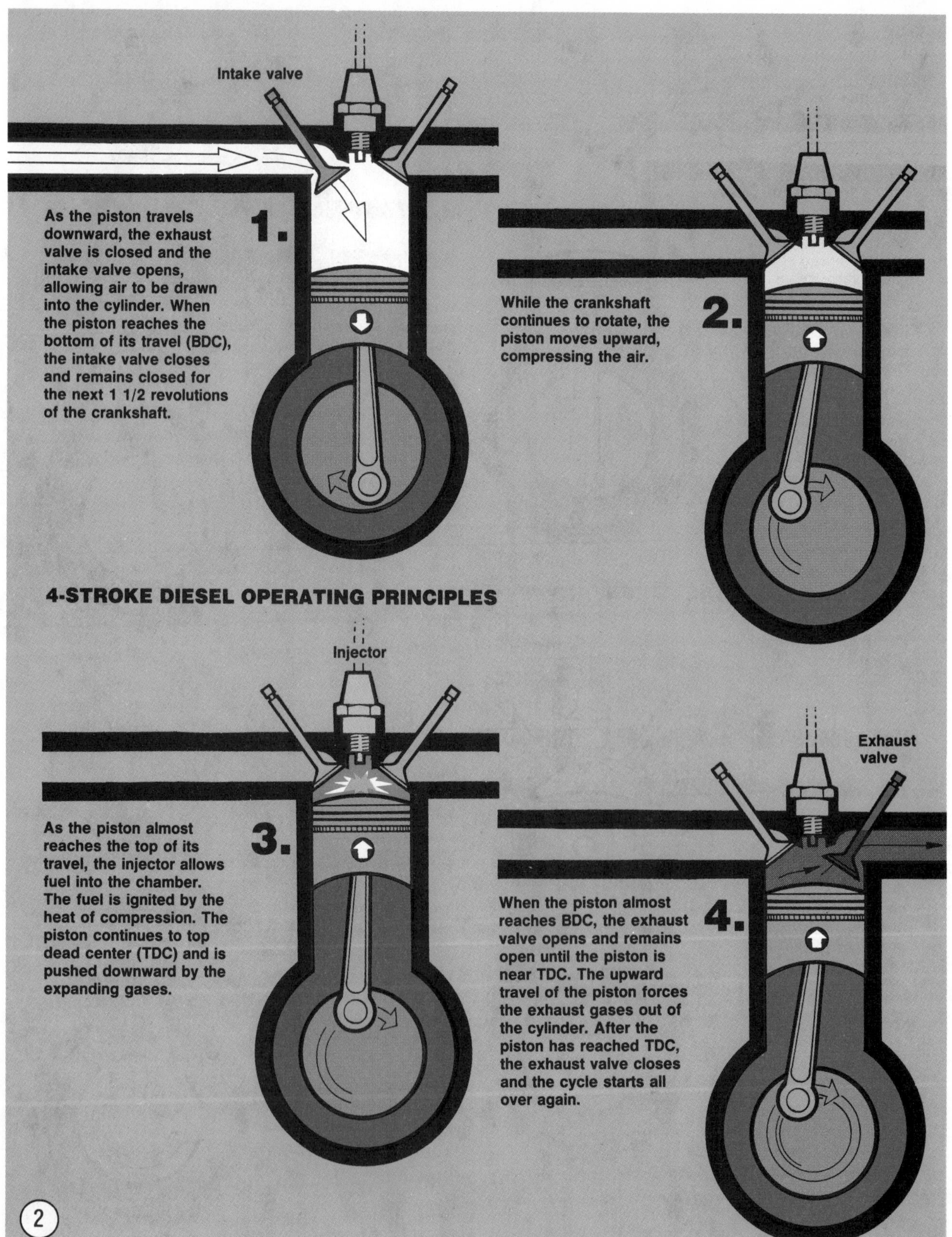
Intake valve
1.
As the piston travels downward, the exhaust valve is closed and the intake valve opens, allowing air to be drawn into the cylinder. When the piston reaches the bottom of its travel (BDC), the intake valve closes and remains closed for the next 1 1/2 revolutions of the crankshaft.
2.
While the crankshaft continues to rotate, the piston moves upward, compressing the air.
4-STROKE DIESEL OPERATING PRINCIPLES
Injector
3.
As the piston almost reaches the top of its travel, the injector allows fuel into the chamber. The fuel is ignited by the heat of compression. The piston continues to top dead center (TDC) and is pushed downward by the expanding gases.
Exhaust valve
4.
When the piston almost reaches BDC, the exhaust valve opens and remains open until the piston is near TDC. The upward travel of the piston forces the exhaust gases out of the cylinder. After the piston has reached TDC, the exhaust valve closes and the cycle starts all over again.
2

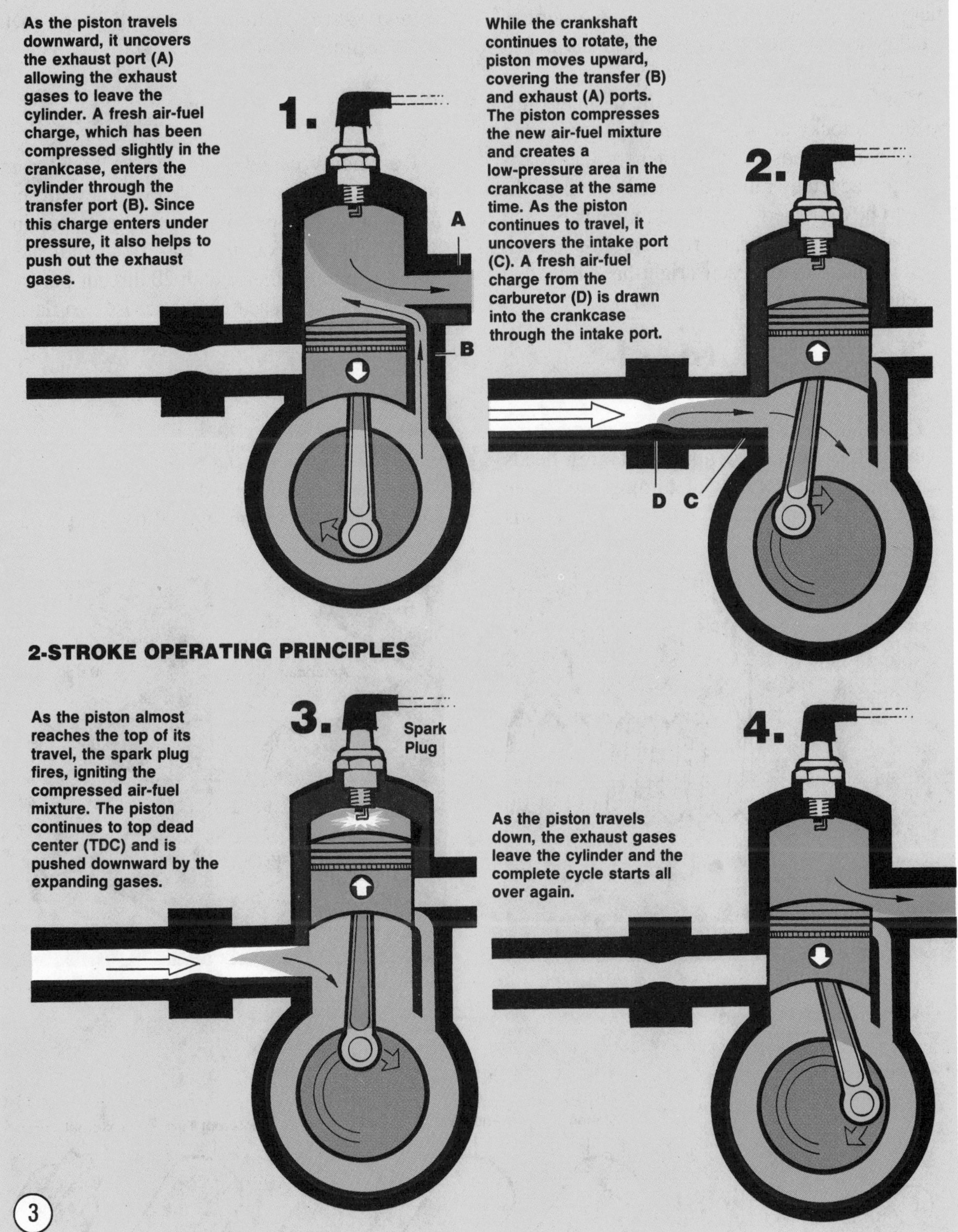
As the piston travels downward, it uncovers the exhaust port (A) allowing the exhaust gases to leave the cylinder. A fresh air-fuel charge, which has been compressed slightly in the crankcase, enters the cylinder through the transfer port (B). Since this charge enters under pressure, it also helps to push out the exhaust gases.
1.
A
B
While the crankshaft continues to rotate, the piston moves upward, covering the transfer (B) and exhaust (A) ports. The piston compresses the new air-fuel mixture and creates a low-pressure area in the crankcase at the same time. As the piston continues to travel, it uncovers the intake port (C). A fresh air-fuel charge from the carburetor (D) is drawn into the crankcase through the intake port.
2.
D
C
2-STROKE OPERATING PRINCIPLES
As the piston almost reaches the top of its travel, the spark plug fires, igniting the compressed air-fuel mixture. The piston continues to top dead center (TDC) and is pushed downward by the expanding gases.
3.
Spark Plug
4.
As the piston travels down, the exhaust gases leave the cylinder and the complete cycle starts all over again.
3

standards exist, but the most commonly used by marine equipment manufacturers are American standard and metric standard. The threads are cut differently as shown in **Figure 5**.

Most threads are cut so that the fastener must be turned clockwise to tighten it. These are called right-hand threads. Some fasteners have left-hand threads; they must be turned counterclockwise to be tightened. Left-hand threads are used in locations where normal rotation of the equipment would tend to loosen a right-hand threaded fastener.

Machine Screws

There are many different types of machine screws. **Figure 6** shows a number of screw heads requiring different types of turning tools (see Chapter Two for detailed information). Heads are also designed to protrude above the metal (round) or to be slightly recessed in the metal (flat) (**Figure 7**).

Bolts

Commonly called bolts, the technical name for these fasteners is cap screw. They are normally described by diameter, threads per inch and length. For example, 1/4-20 × 1 indicates a bolt 1/4 in. in diameter with 20 threads per inch, 1 in. long. The measurement across two flats on the head of the bolt indicates the proper wrench size to be used.

Nuts

Nuts are manufactured in a variety of types and sizes. Most are hexagonal (6-sided) and fit

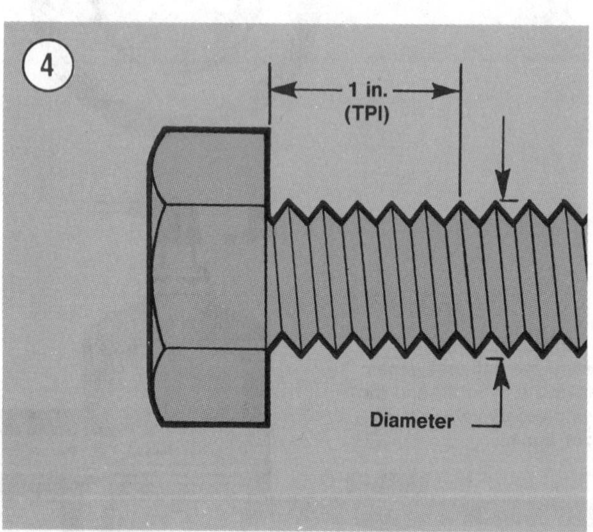

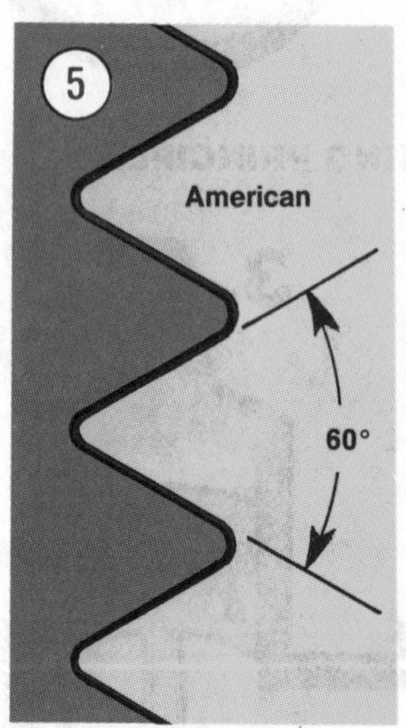

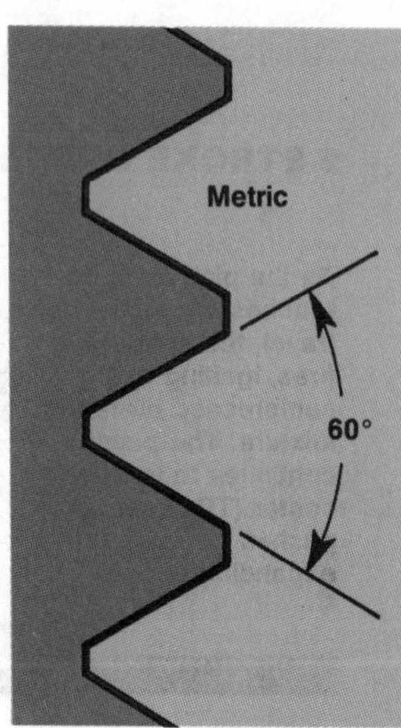

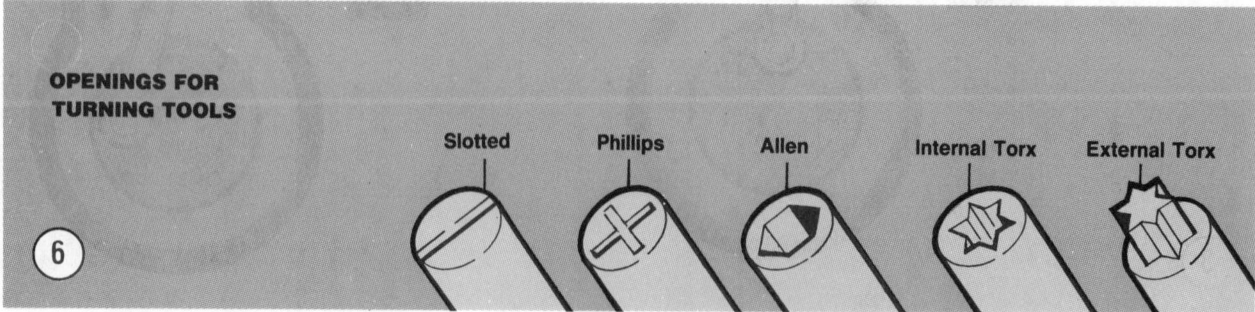

on bolts, screws and studs with the same diameter and threads per inch.

Figure 8 shows several types of nuts. The common nut is usually used with a lockwasher. Self-locking nuts have a nylon insert that prevents the nut from loosening; no lockwasher is required. Wing nuts are designed for fast removal by hand. Wing nuts are used for convenience in non-critical locations.

To indicate the size of a nut, manufacturers specify the diameter of the opening and the threads per inch. This is similar to bolt specification, but without the length dimension. The measurement across two flats on the nut indicates the proper wrench size to be used.

Washers

There are two basic types of washers: flat washers and lockwashers. Flat washers are simple discs with a hole to fit a screw or bolt. Lockwashers are designed to prevent a fastener from working loose due to vibration, expansion and contraction. **Figure 9** shows several types of lockwashers. Note that flat washers are often used between a lockwasher and a fastener to provide a smooth bearing surface. This allows the fastener to be turned easily with a tool.

Cotter Pins

Cotter pins (**Figure 10**) are used to secure special kinds of fasteners. The threaded stud

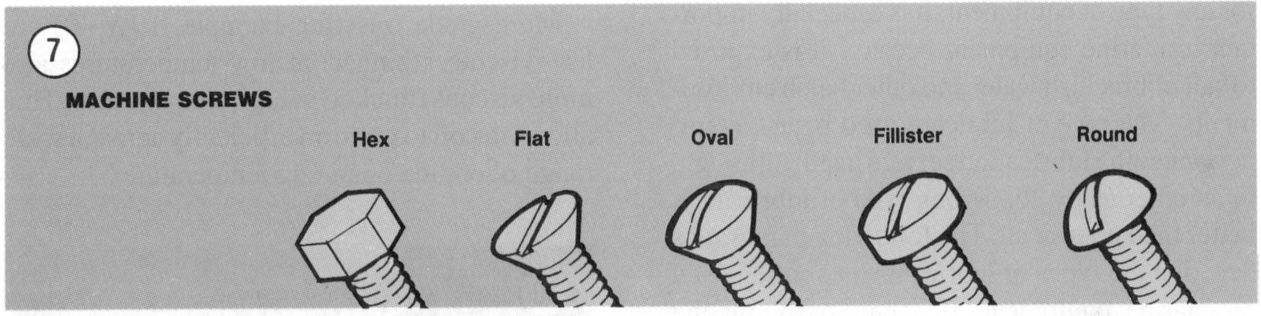

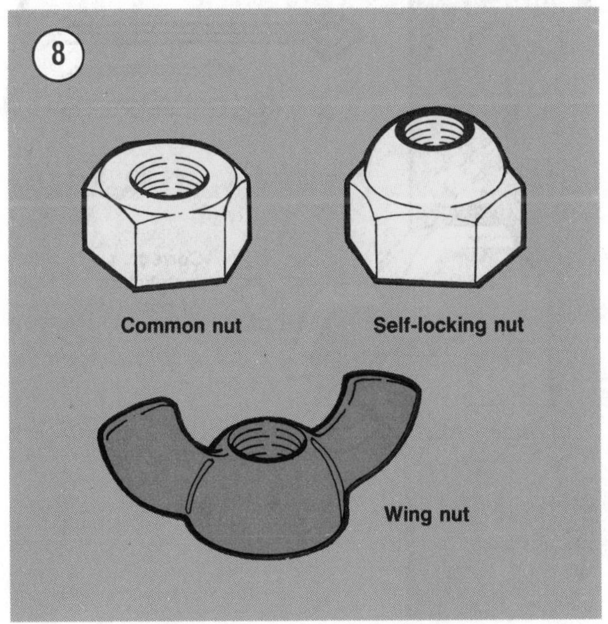

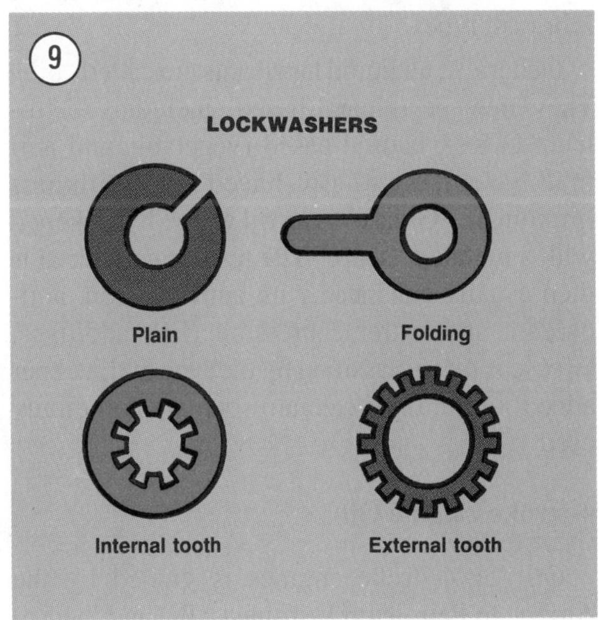

must have a hole in it; the nut or nut lock piece has projections that the cotter pin fits between. This type of nut is called a "Castellated nut." Cotter pins should not be reused after removal.

Snap Rings

Snap rings can be of an internal or external design. They are used to retain items on shafts (external type) or within tubes (internal type). Snap rings can be reused if they are not distorted during removal. In some applications, snap rings of varying thickness can be selected to control the end play of parts assemblies.

LUBRICANTS

Periodic lubrication ensures long service life for any type of equipment. It is especially important to marine equipment because it is exposed to salt or brackish water and other harsh environments. The *type* of lubricant used is just as important as the lubrication service itself; although, in an emergency, the wrong type of lubricant is better than none at all. The following paragraphs describe the types of lubricants most often used on marine equipment. Be sure to follow the equipment manufacturer's recommendations for lubricant types.

Generally, all liquid lubricants are called "oil." They may be mineral-based (including petroleum bases), natural-based (vegetable and animal bases), synthetic-based or emulsions (mixtures). "Grease" is an oil which is thickened with a metallic "soap." The resulting material is then usually enhanced with anticorrosion, antioxidant and extreme pressure (EP) additives. Grease is often classified by the type of thickener added; lithium and calcium soap are commonly used.

4-stroke Engine Oil

Oil for 4-stroke engines is graded by the American Petroleum Institute (API) and the Society of Automotive Engineers (SAE) in several categories. Oil containers display these ratings on the top or label (**Figure 11**).

API oil grade is indicated by letters, oils for gasoline engines are identified by an "S" and oils for diesel engines are identified by a "C." Most modern gasoline engines require SF or SG graded oil. Automotive and marine diesel engines use CC or CD graded oil.

Viscosity is an indication of the oil's thickness, or resistance to flow. The SAE uses numbers to indicate viscosity; thin oils have low numbers and thick oils have high numbers. A "W" after the number indicates that the viscosity testing was done at low temperature to simulate cold weather operation. Engine oils fall into the 5W-20W and 20-50 range.

Multi-grade oils (for example, 10W-40) are less viscous (thinner) at low temperatures and more viscous (thicker) at high temperatures. This allows the oil to perform efficiently across a wide range of engine operating temperatures.

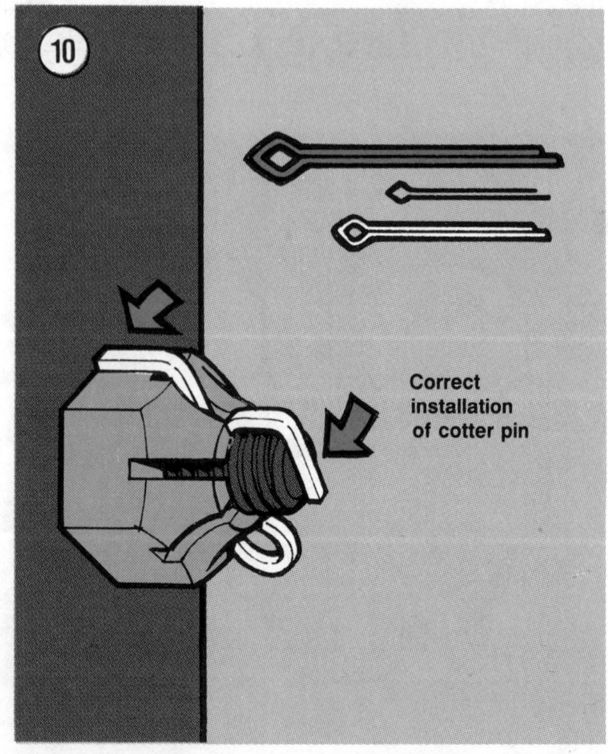

2-stroke Engine Oil

Lubrication for a 2-stroke engine is provided by oil mixed with the incoming fuel-air mixture. Some of the oil mist settles out in the crankcase, lubricating the crankshaft and lower end of the connecting rods. The rest of the oil enters the combustion chamber to lubricate the piston, rings and cylinder wall. This oil is then burned along with the fuel-air mixture during the combustion process.

Engine oil must have several special qualities to work well in a 2-stroke engine. It must mix easily and stay in suspension in gasoline. When burned, it can't leave behind excessive deposits. It must also be able to withstand the high temperatures associated with 2-stroke engines.

The National Marine Manufacturer's Association (NMMA) has set standards for oil used in 2-stroke, water-cooled engines. This is the NMMA TC-W (two-cycle, water-cooled) grade (**Figure 12**). The oil's performance in the following areas is evaluated:

a. Lubrication (prevention of wear and scuffing).
b. Spark plug fouling.
c. Preignition.
d. Piston ring sticking.
e. Piston varnish.
f. General engine condition (including deposits).
g. Exhaust port blockage.
h. Rust prevention.
i. Mixing ability with gasoline.

In addition to oil grade, manufacturers specify the ratio of gasoline to oil required during break-in and normal engine operation.

Gear Oil

Gear lubricants are assigned SAE viscosity numbers under the same system as 4-stroke engine oil. Gear lubricant falls into the SAE 72-250 range (**Figure 13**). Some gear lubricants are multi-grade; for example, SAE 85W-90.

Three types of marine gear lubricant are generally available: SAE 90 hypoid gear lubricant is designed for older manual-shift units; Type C gear lubricant contains additives designed for electric shift mechanisms; High viscosity gear lubricant is a heavier oil designed to withstand the shock loading of high-performance engines or units subjected to severe duty use. Always use a gear lubricant of the type specified by the unit's manufacturer.

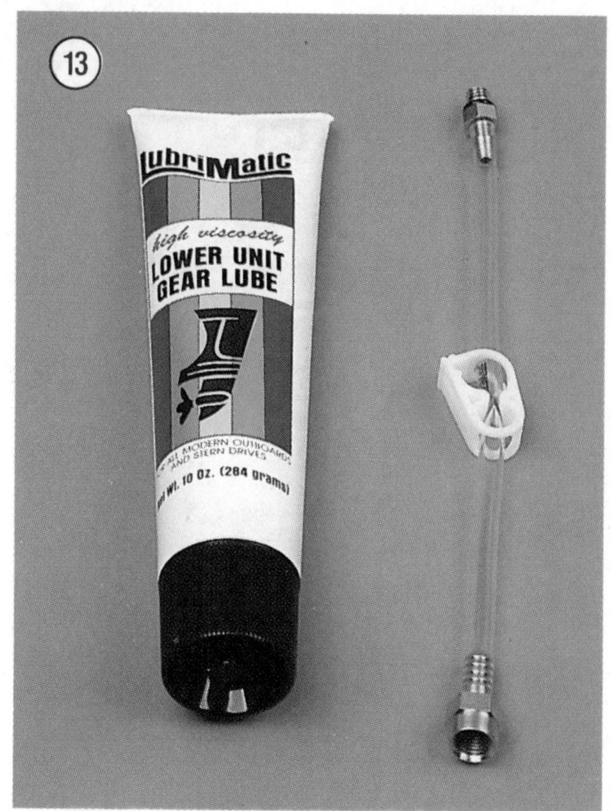

Grease

Greases are graded by the National Lubricating Grease Institute (NLGI). Greases are graded by number according to the consistency of the grease; these ratings range from No. 000 to No. 6, with No. 6 being the most solid. A typical multipurpose grease is NLGI No. 2 (**Figure 14**). For specific applications, equipment manufacturers may require grease with an additive such as molybdenum disulfide (MOS^2).

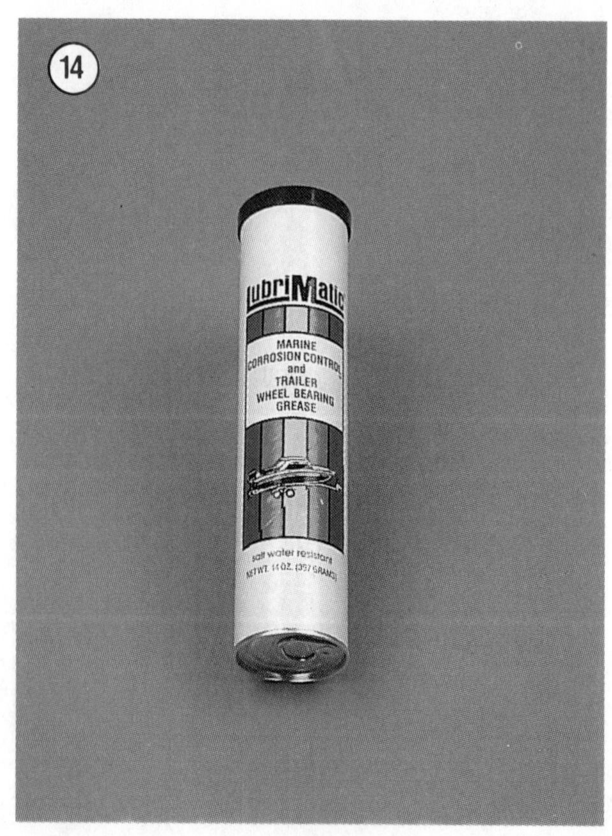

GASKET SEALANT

Gasket sealant is used instead of pre-formed gaskets on some applications, or as a gasket dressing on others. Two types of gasket sealant are commonly used: room temperature vulcanizing (RTV) and anaerobic. Because these two materials have different sealing properties, they cannot be used interchangeably.

RTV Sealant

This is a silicone gel supplied in tubes (**Figure 15**). Moisture in the air causes RTV to cure. Always place the cap on the tube as soon as possible when using RTV. RTV has a shelf life of one year and will not cure properly when the shelf life has expired. Check the expiration date on RTV tubes before using and keep partially used tubes tightly sealed. RTV sealant can generally fill gaps up to 1/4 in. (6.3 mm) and works well on slightly flexible surfaces.

Applying RTV Sealant

Clean all gasket residue from mating surfaces. Surfaces should be clean and free of oil and dirt. Remove all RTV gasket material from blind attaching holes because it can create a "hydraulic" effect and affect bolt torque.

Apply RTV sealant in a continuous bead 2-3 mm (0.08-0.12 in.) thick. Circle all mounting holes unless otherwise specified. Torque mating parts within 10 minutes after application.

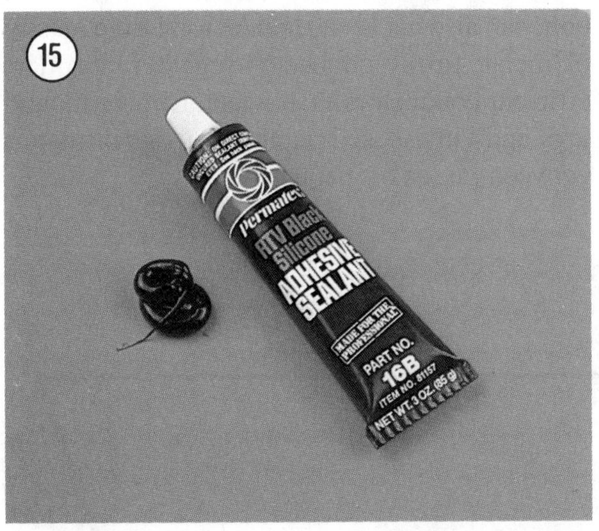

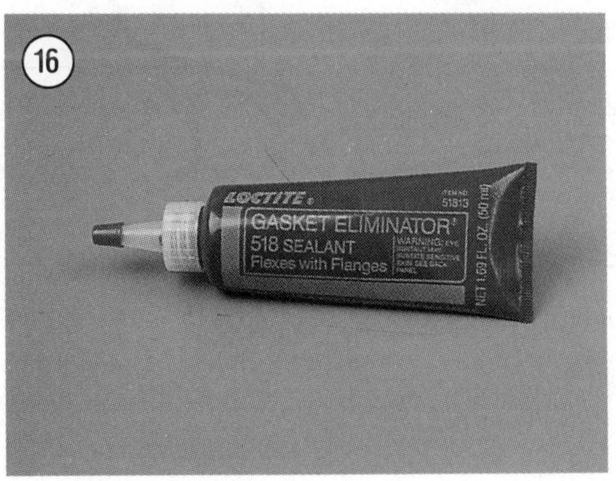

Anaerobic Sealant

This is a gel supplied in tubes (**Figure 16**). It cures only in the absence of air, as when squeezed tightly between two machined mating surfaces. For this reason, it will not spoil if the cap is left off the tube. It should not be used if one mating surface is flexible. Anaerobic sealant is able to fill gaps up to 0.030 in. (0.8 mm) and generally works best on rigid, machined flanges or surfaces.

Applying Anaerobic Sealant

Clean all gasket residue from mating surfaces. Surfaces must be clean and free of oil and dirt. Remove all gasket material from blind attaching holes, as it can cause a "hydraulic" effect and affect bolt torque.

Apply anaerobic sealant in a 1 mm or less (0.04 in.) bead to one sealing surface. Circle all mounting holes. Torque mating parts within 15 minutes after application.

GALVANIC CORROSION

A chemical reaction occurs whenever two different types of metal are joined by an electrical conductor and immersed in an electrolyte. Electrons transfer from one metal to the other through the electrolyte and return through the conductor.

The hardware on a boat is made of many different types of metal. The boat hull acts as a conductor between the metals. Even if the hull is wooden or fiberglass, the slightest film of water (electrolyte) within the hull provides conductivity. This combination creates a good environment for electron flow (**Figure 17**). Unfortunately, this electron flow results in galvanic corrosion of the metal involved, causing one of the metals to be corroded or eaten away by the process. The amount of electron flow (and, therefore, the amount of corrosion) depends on several factors:

a. The types of metal involved.

b. The efficiency of the conductor.

c. The strength of the electrolyte.

Metals

The chemical composition of the metals used in marine equipment has a significant effect on the amount and speed of galvanic corrosion. Certain metals are more resistant to corrosion than others. These electrically negative metals are commonly called "noble;" they act as the cathode in any reaction. Metals that are more subject to corrosion are electrically positive; they act as the anode in a reaction. The more noble metals include titanium, 18-8 stainless steel and nickel. Less noble metals include zinc, aluminum and magnesium. Galvanic corrosion becomes more severe as the difference in electrical potential between the two metals increases.

In some cases, galvanic corrosion can occur within a single piece of metal. Common brass is a mixture of zinc and copper, and, when immersed in an electrolyte, the zinc portion of the mixture will corrode away as reaction occurs between the zinc and the copper particles.

Conductors

The hull of the boat often acts as the conductor between different types of metal. Marine equipment, such as an outboard motor or stern drive unit, can also act as the conductor. Large masses of metal, firmly connected together, are more efficient conductors than water. Rubber mountings and vinyl-based paint can act as insulators between pieces of metal.

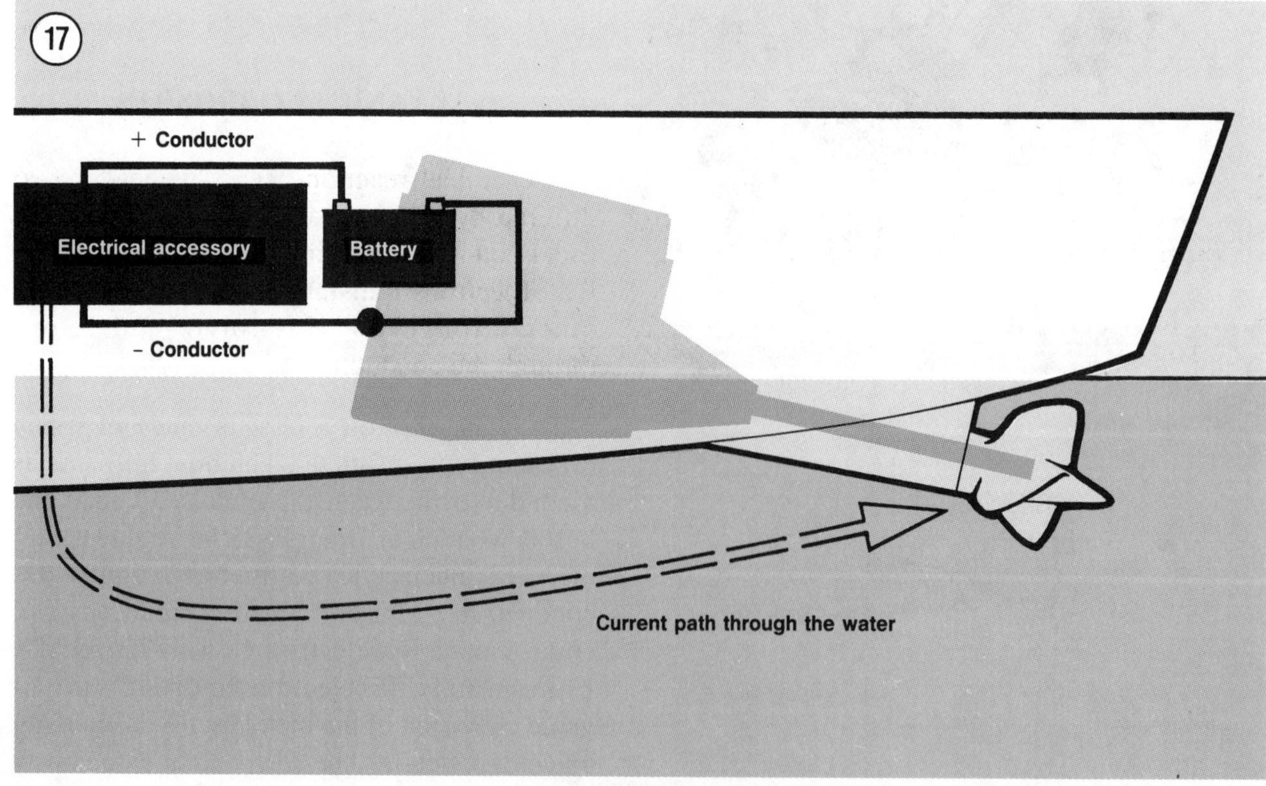

Electrolyte

The water in which a boat operates acts as the electrolyte for the galvanic corrosion process. The better a conductor the electrolyte is, the more severe and rapid the corrosion.

Cold, clean freshwater is the poorest electrolyte. As water temperature increases, its conductivity increases. Pollutants will increase conductivity; brackish or saltwater is also an efficient electrolyte. This is one of the reasons that most manufacturers recommend a freshwater flush for marine equipment after operation in saltwater, polluted or brackish water.

PROTECTION FROM GALVANIC CORROSION

Because of the environment in which marine equipment must operate, it is practically impossible to totally prevent galvanic corrosion. There are several ways by which the process can be slowed. After taking these precautions, the next step is to "fool" the process into occurring only where *you* want it to occur. This is the role of sacrificial anodes and impressed current systems.

Slowing Corrosion

Some simple precautions can help reduce the amount of corrosion taking place outside the hull. These are *not* a substitute for the corrosion protection methods discussed under *Sacrificial Anodes* and *Impressed Current Systems* in this chapter, but they can help these protection methods do their job.

Use fasteners of a metal more noble than the part they are fastening. If corrosion occurs, the larger equipment will suffer but the fastener will be protected. Because fasteners are usually very small in comparison to the equipment being fastened, the equipment can survive the loss of material. If the fastener were to corrode instead of the equipment, major problems could arise.

Keep all painted surfaces in good condition. If paint is scraped off and bare metal exposed, corrosion will rapidly increase. Use a vinyl- or plastic-based paint, which acts as an electrical insulator.

Be careful when using metal-based antifouling paints. These should not be applied to metal parts of the boat, outboard motor or stern drive unit or they will actually react with the equipment, causing corrosion between the equipment and the layer of paint. Organic-based paints are available for use on metal surfaces.

Where a corrosion protection device is used, remember that it must be immersed in the electrolyte along with the rest of the boat to have any effect. If you raise the power unit out of the water when the boat is docked, any anodes on the power unit will be removed from the corrosion cycle and will not protect the rest of the equipment that is still immersed. Also, such corrosion protection devices must not be painted because this would insulate them from the corrosion process.

Any change in the boat's equipment, such as the installation of a new stainless steel propeller, will change the electrical potential and could cause increased corrosion. Keep in mind that when you add new equipment or change materials, you should review your corrosion protection system to be sure it is up to the job.

Sacrificial Anodes

Anodes are usually made of zinc, a far from noble metal. Sacrificial anodes are specially designed to do nothing but corrode. Properly fastening such pieces to the boat will cause them to act as the anode in *any* galvanic reaction that occurs; any other metal present will act as the cathode and will not be damaged.

Anodes must be used properly to be effective. Simply fastening pieces of zinc to your boat in random locations won't do the job.

You must determine how much anode surface area is required to adequately protect the equipment's surface area. A good starting point is provided by Military Specification MIL-A-818001, which states that one square inch of new anode will protect either:

a. 800 square inches of freshly painted steel.
b. 250 square inches of bare steel or bare aluminum alloy.
c. 100 square inches of copper or copper alloy.

This rule is for a boat at rest. When underway, more anode area is required to protect the same equipment surface area.

The anode must be fastened so that it has good electrical contact with the metal to be protected. If possible, the anode can be attached directly to the other metal. If that is not possible, the entire network of metal parts in the boat should be electrically bonded together so that all pieces are protected.

Good quality anodes have inserts of some other metal around the fastener holes. Otherwise, the anode could erode away around the fastener. The anode can then become loose or even fall off, removing all protection.

Another Military Specification (MIL-A-18001) defines the type of alloy preferred that will corrode at a uniform rate without forming a crust that could reduce its efficiency after a time.

Impressed Current Systems

An impressed current system can be installed on any boat that has a battery. The system consists of an anode, a control box and a sensor. The anode in this system is coated with a very noble metal, such as platinum, so that it is almost corrosion-free and will last indefinitely. The sensor, under the boat's waterline, monitors the potential for corrosion. When it senses that corrosion could be occurring, it transmits this information to the control box.

The control box connects the boat's battery to the anode. When the sensor signals the need, the control box applies positive battery voltage to the anode. Current from the battery flows from the anode to all other metal parts of the boat, no matter how noble or non-noble these parts may be. This battery current takes the place of any galvanic current flow.

Only a very small amount of battery current is needed to counteract galvanic corrosion. Manufacturers estimate that it would take two or three months of constant use to drain a typical marine battery, assuming the battery is never recharged.

An impressed current system is more expensive to install than simple anodes but, considering its low maintenance requirements and the excellent protection it provides, the long-term cost may actually be lower.

PROPELLERS

The propeller is the final link between the boat's drive system and the water. A perfectly

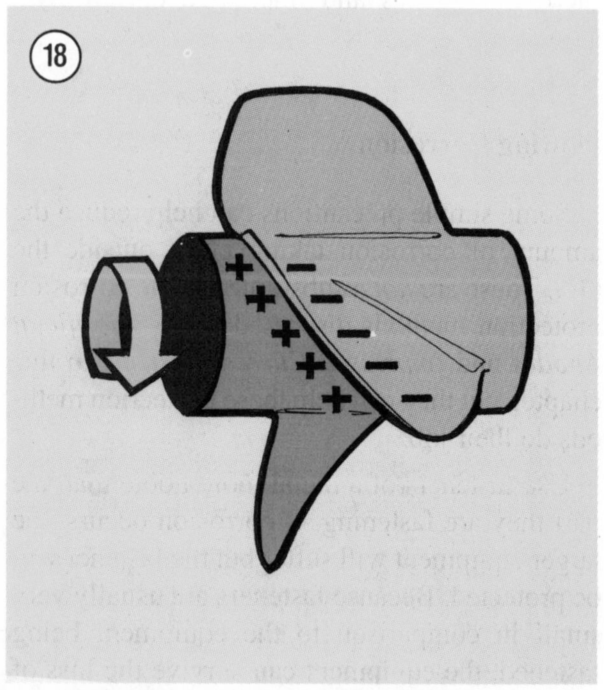

maintained engine and hull are useless if the propeller is the wrong type or has been allowed to deteriorate. Although propeller selection for a specific situation is beyond the scope of this book, the following information on propeller construction and design will allow you to discuss the subject intelligently with your marine dealer.

How a Propeller Works

As the curved blades of a propeller rotate through the water, a high-pressure area is created on one side of the blade and a low-pressure area exists on the other side of the blade (**Figure 18**). The propeller moves toward the low-pressure area, carrying the boat with it.

Propeller Parts

Although a propeller may be a one-piece unit, it is made up of several different parts (**Figure 19**). Variations in the design of these parts make different propellers suitable for different jobs.

The blade tip is the point on the blade farthest from the center of the propeller hub. The blade tip separates the leading edge from the trailing edge.

The leading edge is the edge of the blade nearest to the boat. During normal rotation, this is the area of the blade that first cuts through the water.

The trailing edge is the edge of the blade farthest from the boat.

The blade face is the surface of the blade that faces away from the boat. During normal rotation, high pressure exists on this side of the blade.

The blade back is the surface of the blade that faces toward the boat. During normal rotation, low pressure exists on this side of the blade.

The cup is a small curve or lip on the trailing edge of the blade.

The hub is the central portion of the propeller. It connects the blades to the propeller shaft (part of the boat's drive system). On some drive systems, engine exhaust is routed through the hub; in this case, the hub is made up of an outer and an inner portion, connected by ribs.

The diffuser ring is used on through-hub exhaust models to prevent exhaust gases from entering the blade area.

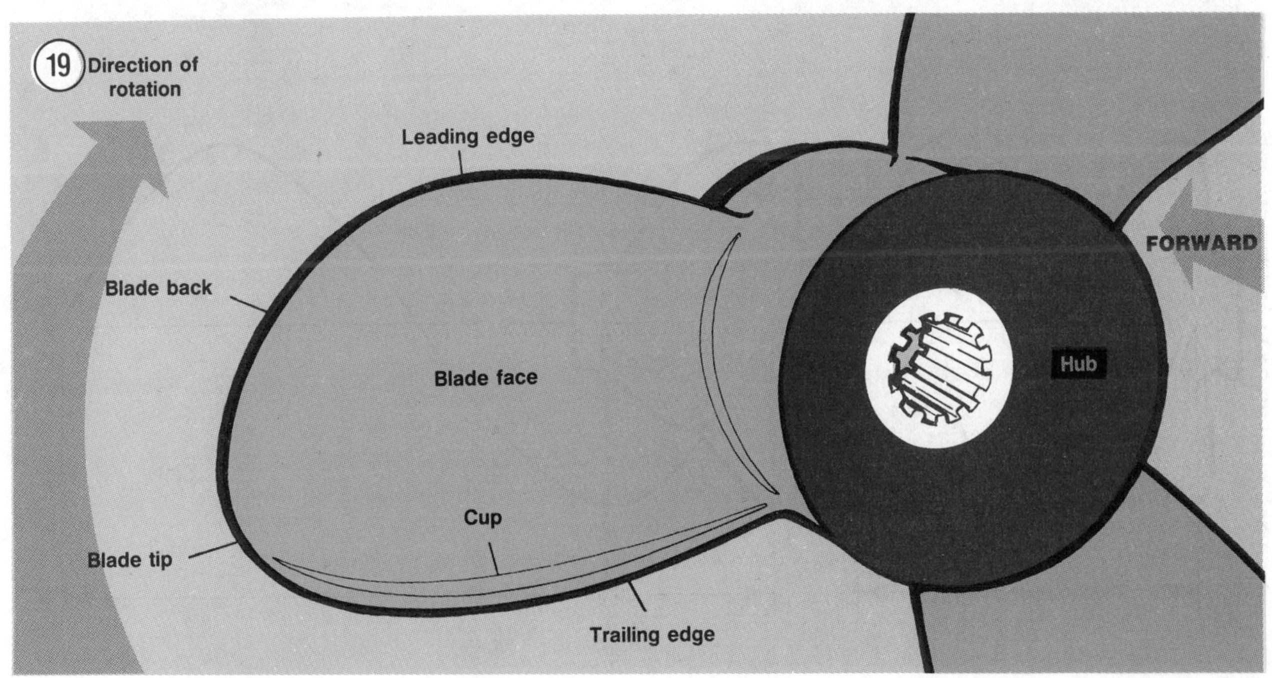

Propeller Design

Changes in length, angle, thickness and material of propeller parts make different propellers suitable for different situations.

Diameter

Propeller diameter is the distance from the center of the hub to the blade tip, multiplied by 2. That is, it is the diameter of the circle formed by the blade tips during propeller rotation (**Figure 20**).

Pitch and rake

Propeller pitch and rake describe the placement of the blade in relation to the hub (**Figure 21**).

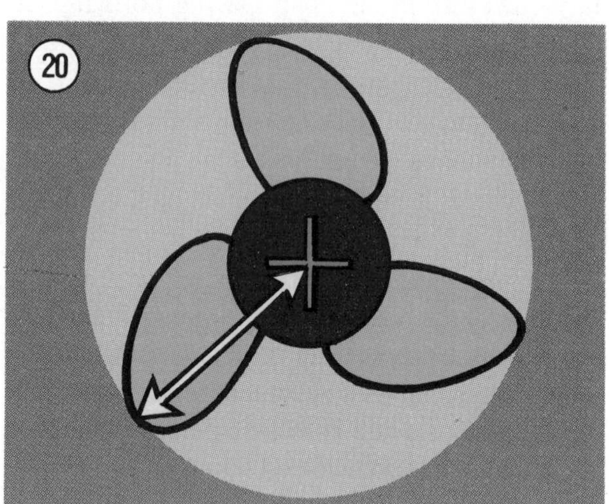

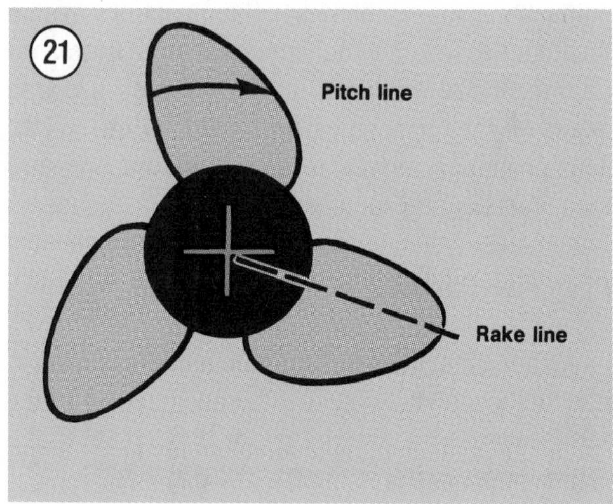

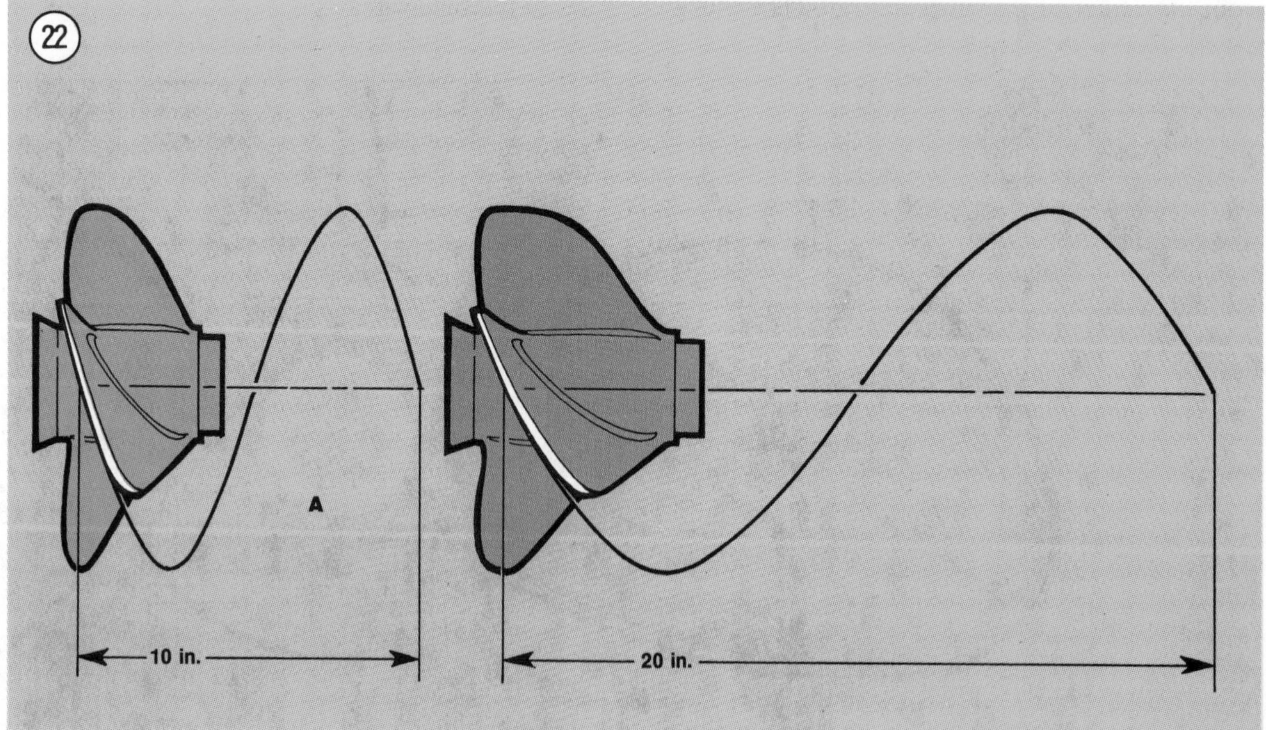

Pitch is expressed by the theoretical distance that the propeller would travel in one revolution. In A, **Figure 22**, the propeller would travel 10 inches in one revolution. In B, **Figure 22**, the propeller would travel 20 inches in one revolution. This distance is only theoretical; during actual operation, the propeller achieves about 80% of its rated travel.

Propeller blades can be constructed with constant pitch (**Figure 23**) or progressive pitch (**Figure 24**). Progressive pitch starts low at the leading edge and increases toward to trailing edge. The propeller pitch specification is the average of the pitch across the entire blade.

Blade rake is specified in degrees and is measured along a line from the center of the hub to the blade tip. A blade that is perpendicular to the hub (A, **Figure 25**) has 0° of rake. A blade that is angled from perpendicular (B, **Figure 25**) has a rake expressed by its difference from perpen-

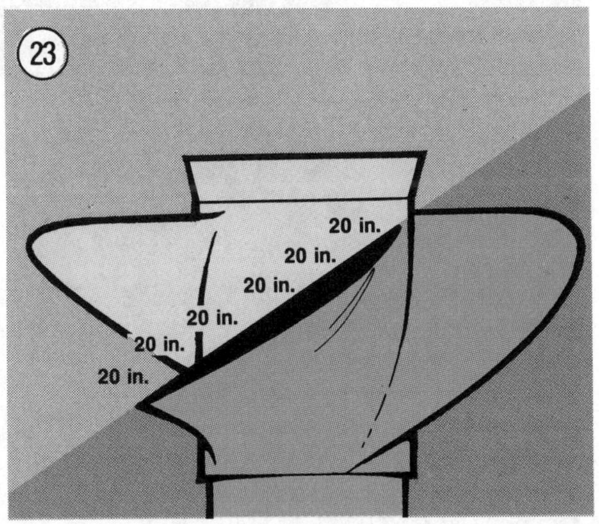

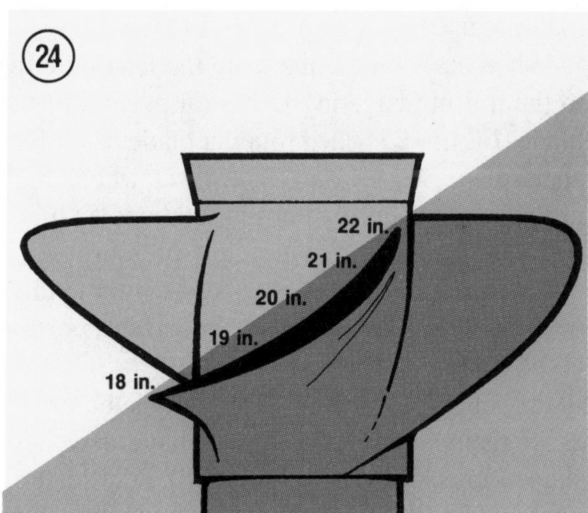

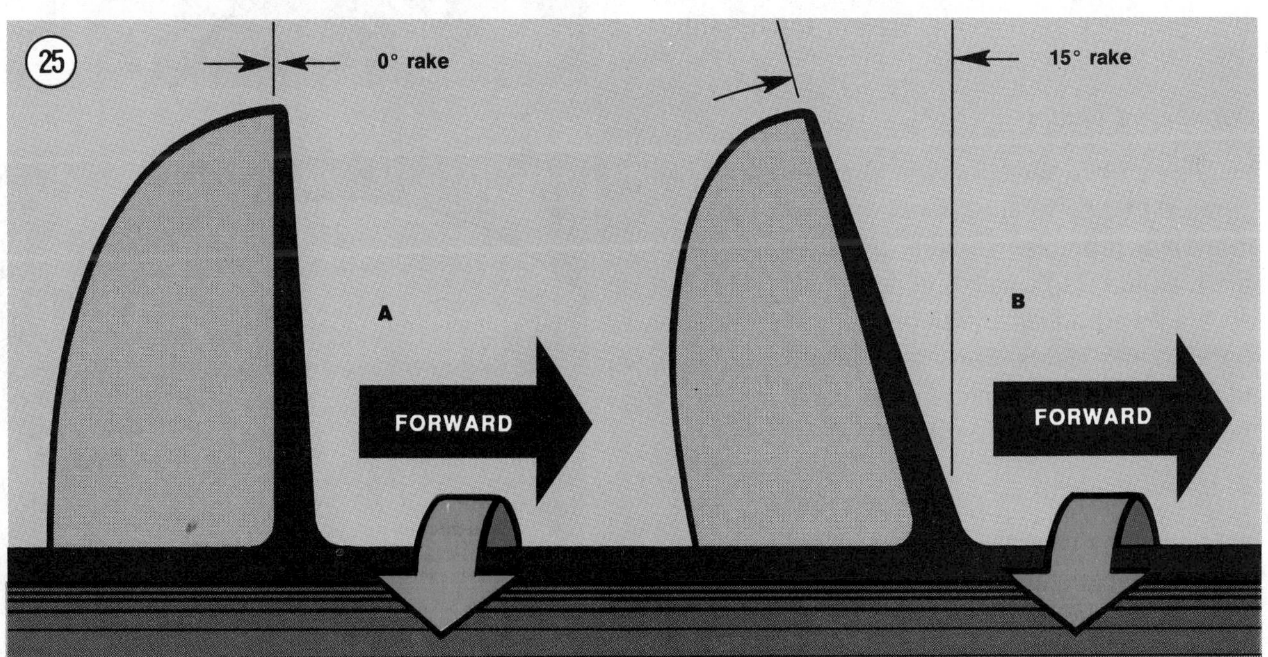

dicular. Most propellers have rakes ranging from 0-20°.

Blade thickness

Blade thickness is not uniform at all points along the blade. For efficiency, blades should be as thin as possible at all points while retaining enough strength to move the boat. Blades tend to be thicker where they meet the hub and thinner at the blade tip (**Figure 26**). This is to support the heavier loads at the hub section of the blade. This thickness is dependent on the strength of the material used.

When cut along a line from the leading edge to the trailing edge in the central portion of the blade (**Figure 27**), the propeller blade resembles an airplane wing. The blade face, where high pressure exists during normal rotation, is almost flat. The blade back, where low pressure exists during normal rotation, is curved, with the thinnest portions at the edges and the thickest portion at the center.

Propellers that run only partially submerged, as in racing applications, may have a wedge-shaped cross-section (**Figure 28**). The leading edge is very thin; the blade thickness increases toward the trailing edge, where it is the thickest. If a propeller such as this is run totally submerged, it is very inefficient.

Number of blades

The number of blades used on a propeller is a compromise between efficiency and vibration. A one-blade propeller would be the most efficient, but it would also create high levels of vibration. As blades are added, efficiency decreases, but so do vibration levels. Most propellers have three blades, representing the most practical trade-off between efficiency and vibration.

Material

Propeller materials are chosen for strength, corrosion resistance and economy. Stainless steel, aluminum and bronze are the most commonly used materials. Bronze is quite strong but

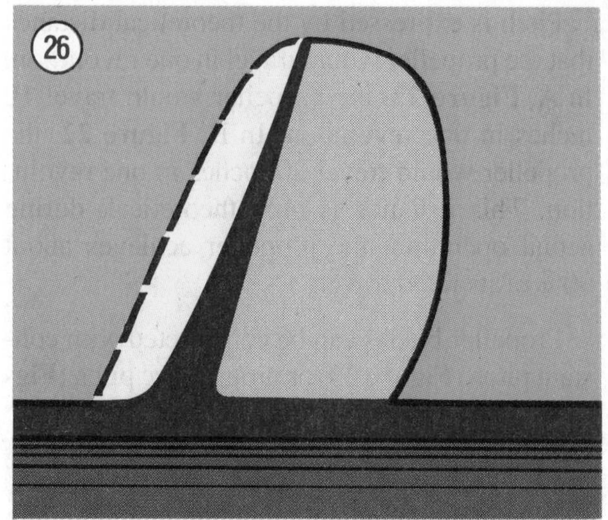

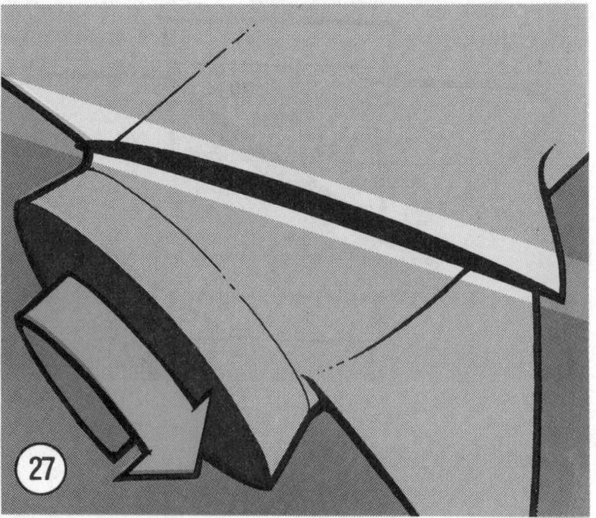

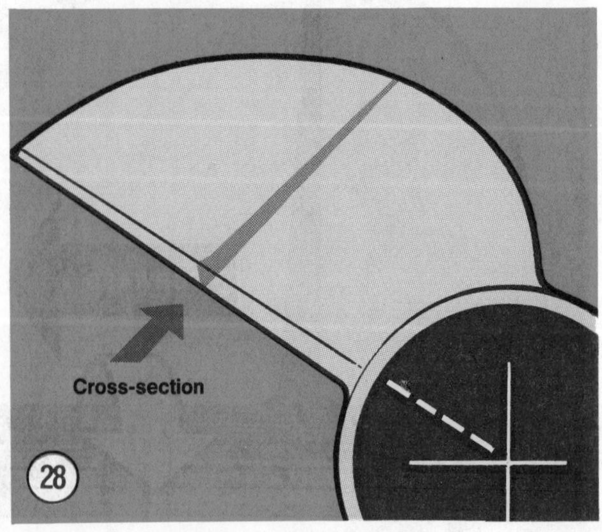

rather expensive. Stainless steel is more common than bronze because of its combination of strength and lower cost. Aluminum alloys are the least expensive but usually lack the strength of steel. Plastic propellers may be used in some low horsepower applications.

Direction of rotation

Propellers are made for both right-hand and left-hand rotation although right-hand is the most commonly used. When seen from behind the boat in forward motion, a right-hand propeller turns clockwise and a left-hand propeller turns counterclockwise. Off the boat, you can tell the difference by observing the angle of the blades (**Figure 29**). A right-hand propeller's blades slant from the upper left to the lower right; a left-hand propeller's blades are the opposite.

Cavitation and Ventilation

Cavitation and ventilation are *not* interchangeable terms; they refer to two distinct problems encountered during propeller operation.

To understand cavitation, you must first understand the relationship between pressure and the boiling point of water. At sea level, water will boil at 212° F. As pressure increases, such as within an engine's closed cooling system, the boiling point of water increases—it will boil at some temperature higher than 212° F. The opposite is also true. As pressure decreases, water will boil at a temperature lower than 212° F. If pressure drops low enough, water will boil at typical ambient temperatures of 50-60° F.

We have said that, during normal propeller operation, low-pressure exists on the blade back. Normally, the pressure does not drop low enough for boiling to occur. However, poor blade design

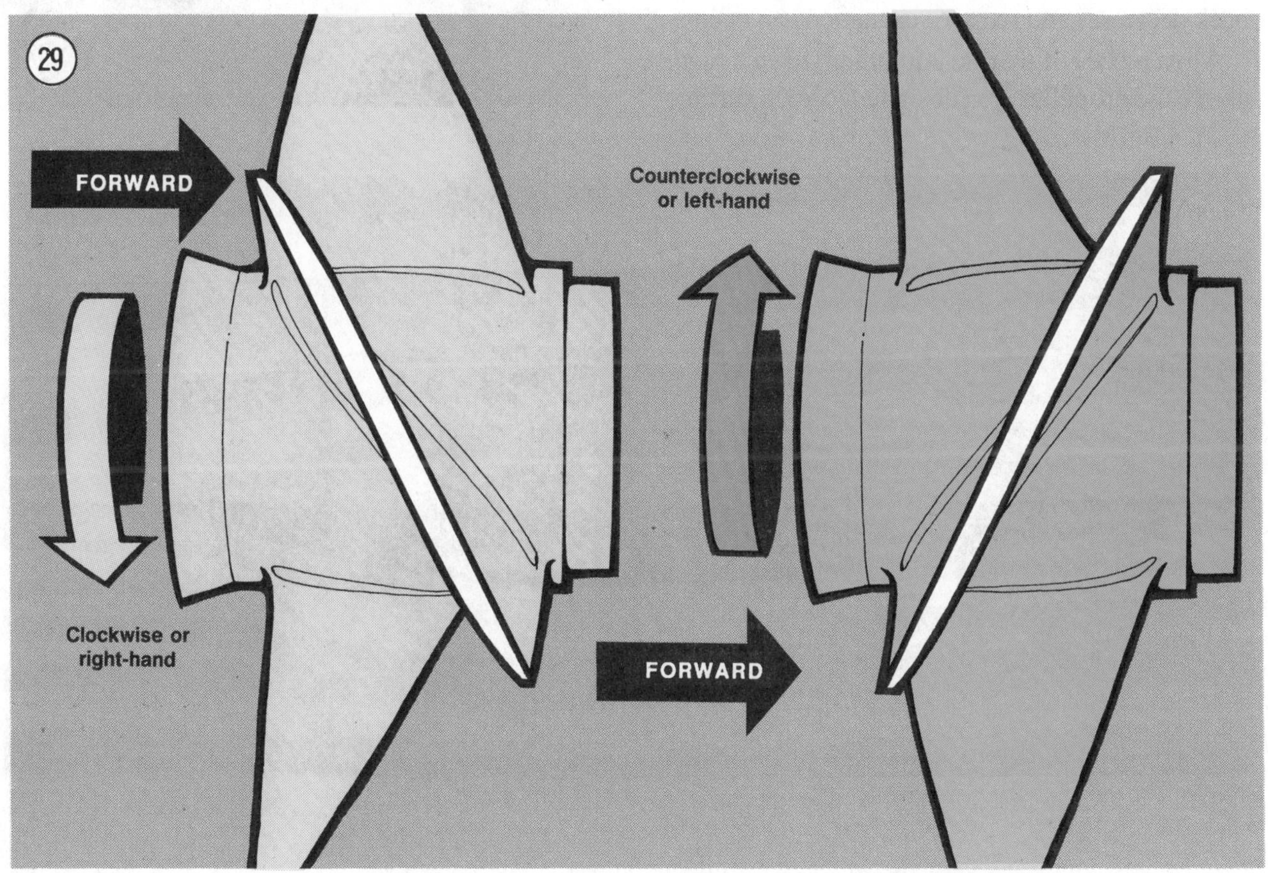

or selection, or blade damage can cause an unusual pressure drop on a small area of the blade (**Figure 30**). Boiling can occur in this small area. As the water boils, air bubbles form. As the boiling water passes to a higher pressure area of the blade, the boiling stops and the bubbles collapse. The collapsing bubbles release enough energy to erode the surface of the blade.

This entire process of pressure drop, boiling and bubble collapse is called "cavitation." The damage caused by the collapsing bubbles is called a "cavitation burn." It is important to remember that cavitation is caused by a decrease in pressure, *not* an increase in temperature.

Ventilation is not as complex a process as cavitation. Ventilation refers to air entering the blade area, either from above the surface of the water or from a through-hub exhaust system. As the blades meet the air, the propeller momentarily over-revs, losing most of its thrust. An added complication is that as the propeller over-revs, pressure on the blade back decreases and massive cavitation can occur.

Most pieces of marine equipment have a plate above the propeller area designed to keep surface air from entering the blade area (**Figure 31**). This plate is correctly called an "antiventilation plate," although you will often *see* it called an "anticavitation plate." Through hub exhaust systems also have specially designed hubs to keep exhaust gases from entering the blade area.

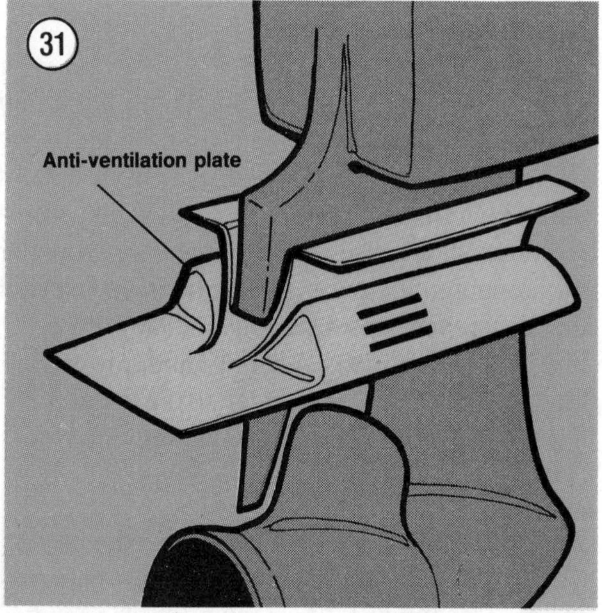

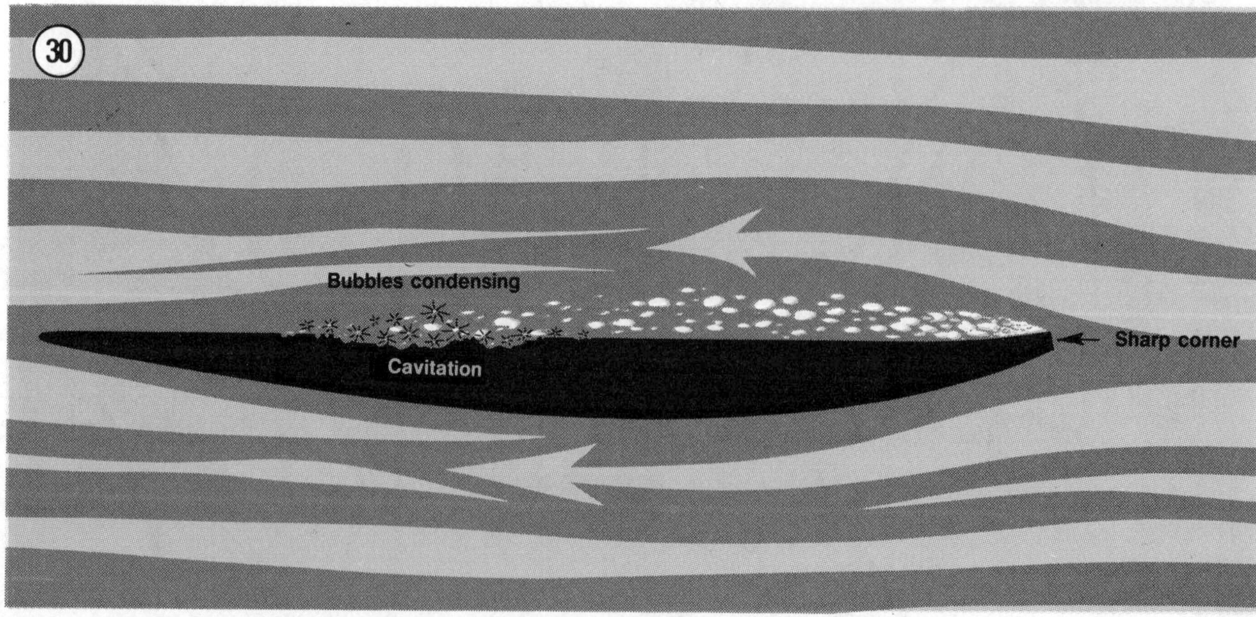

Chapter Two

Tools and Techniques

This chapter describes the common tools required for marine equipment repairs and troubleshooting. Techniques that will make your work easier and more effective are also described. Some of the procedures in this book require special skills or expertise; in some cases, you are better off entrusting the job to a dealer or qualified specialist.

SAFETY FIRST

Professional mechanics can work for years and never suffer a serious injury. If you follow a few rules of common sense and safety, you too can enjoy many safe hours servicing your marine equipment. If you ignore these rules, you can hurt yourself or damage the equipment.

1. Never use gasoline as a cleaning solvent.
2. Never smoke or use a torch near flammable liquids, such as cleaning solvent. If you are working in your home garage, remember that your home gas appliances have pilot lights.
3. Never smoke or use a torch in an area where batteries are being charged. Highly explosive hydrogen gas is formed during the charging process.
4. Use the proper size wrenches to avoid damage to fasteners and injury to yourself.
5. When loosening a tight or stuck fastener, think of what would happen if the wrench should slip. Protect yourself accordingly.
6. Keep your work area clean, uncluttered and well lighted.
7. Wear safety goggles during all operations involving drilling, grinding or the use of a cold chisel.
8. Never use worn tools.
9. Keep a Coast Guard approved fire extinguisher handy. Be sure it is rated for gasoline (Class B) and electrical (Class C) fires.

BASIC HAND TOOLS

A number of tools are required to maintain marine equipment. You may already have some of these tools for home or car repairs. There are also tools made especially for marine equipment repairs; these you will have to purchase. In any case, a wide variety of quality tools will make repairs easier and more effective.

Keep your tools clean and in a tool box. Keep them organized with the sockets and related drives together, the open end and box wrenches together, etc. After using a tool, wipe off dirt and grease with a clean cloth and place the tool in its correct place.

The following tools are required to perform virtually any repair job. Each tool is described and the recommended size given for starting a tool collection. Additional tools and some duplications may be added as you become more familiar with the equipment. You may need all standard U.S. size tools, all metric size tools or a mixture of both.

Screwdrivers

The screwdriver is a very basic tool, but if used improperly, it will do more damage than good. The slot on a screw has a definite dimension and shape. A screwdriver must be selected to conform with that shape. Use a small screwdriver for small screws and a large one for large screws or the screw head will be damaged.

Two types of screwdriver are commonly required: a common (flat-blade) screwdriver (**Figure 1**) and Phillips screwdrivers (**Figure 2**).

Screwdrivers are available in sets, which often include an assortment of common and Phillips blades. If you buy them individually, buy at least the following:

a. Common screwdriver—5/16 × 6 in. blade.
b. Common screwdriver—3/8 × 12 in. blade
c. Phillips screwdriver—size 2 tip, 6 in. blade.

Use screwdrivers only for driving screws. Never use a screwdriver for prying or chiseling. Do not try to remove a Phillips or Allen head screw with a common screwdriver; you can damage the head so that the proper tool will be unable to remove it.

Keep screwdrivers in the proper condition and they will last longer and perform better. Always keep the tip of a common screwdriver in good condition. **Figure 3** shows how to grind the tip to the proper shape if it becomes damaged. Note the parallel sides of the tip.

Pliers

Pliers come in a wide range of types and sizes. Pliers are useful for cutting, bending and crimping. They should never be used to cut hardened objects or to turn bolts or nuts. **Figure 4** shows several types of pliers.

Each type of pliers has a specialized function. General purpose pliers are used mainly for holding things and for bending. Locking pliers are used as pliers or to hold objects very tightly, like a vise. Needlenose pliers are used to hold or bend small objects. Adjustable or slip-joint pliers can

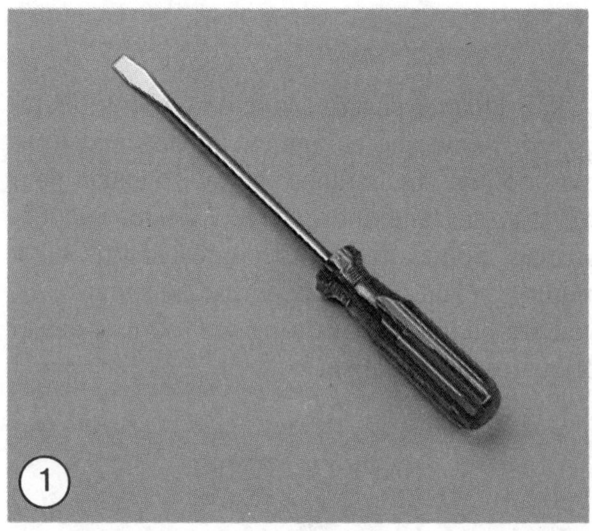
1

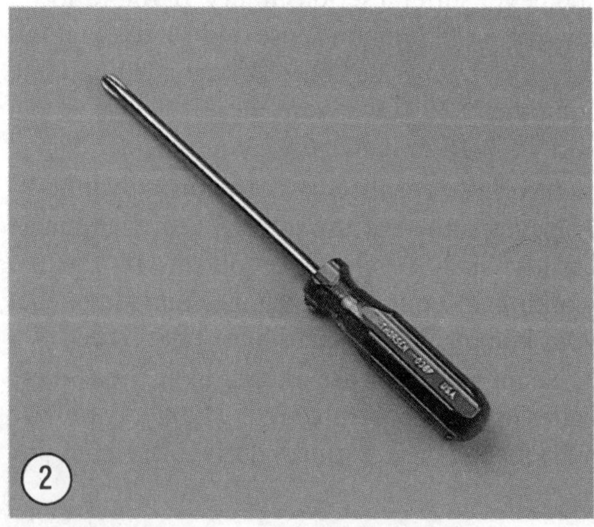
2

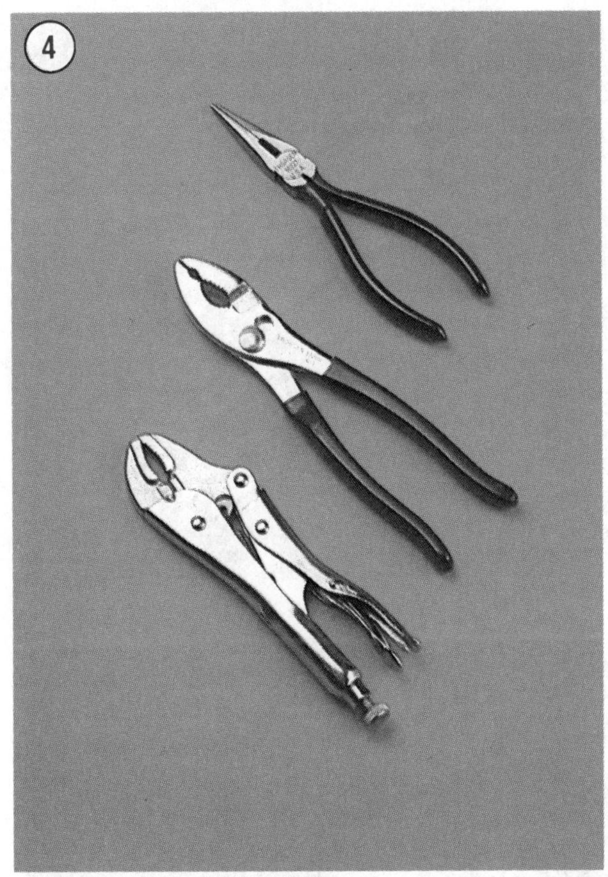

be adjusted to hold various sizes of objects; the jaws remain parallel to grip around objects such as pipe or tubing. There are many more types of pliers. The ones described here are the most commonly used.

Box and Open-end Wrenches

Box and open-end wrenches are available in sets or separately in a variety of sizes. See **Figure 5** and **Figure 6**. The number stamped near the end refers to the distance between two parallel flats on the hex head bolt or nut.

Box wrenches are usually superior to open-end wrenches. An open-end wrench grips the nut on only two flats. Unless it fits well, it may slip and round off the points on the nut. The box wrench grips all 6 flats. Both 6-point and 12-point openings on box wrenches are available. The 6-point gives superior holding power; the 12-point allows a shorter swing.

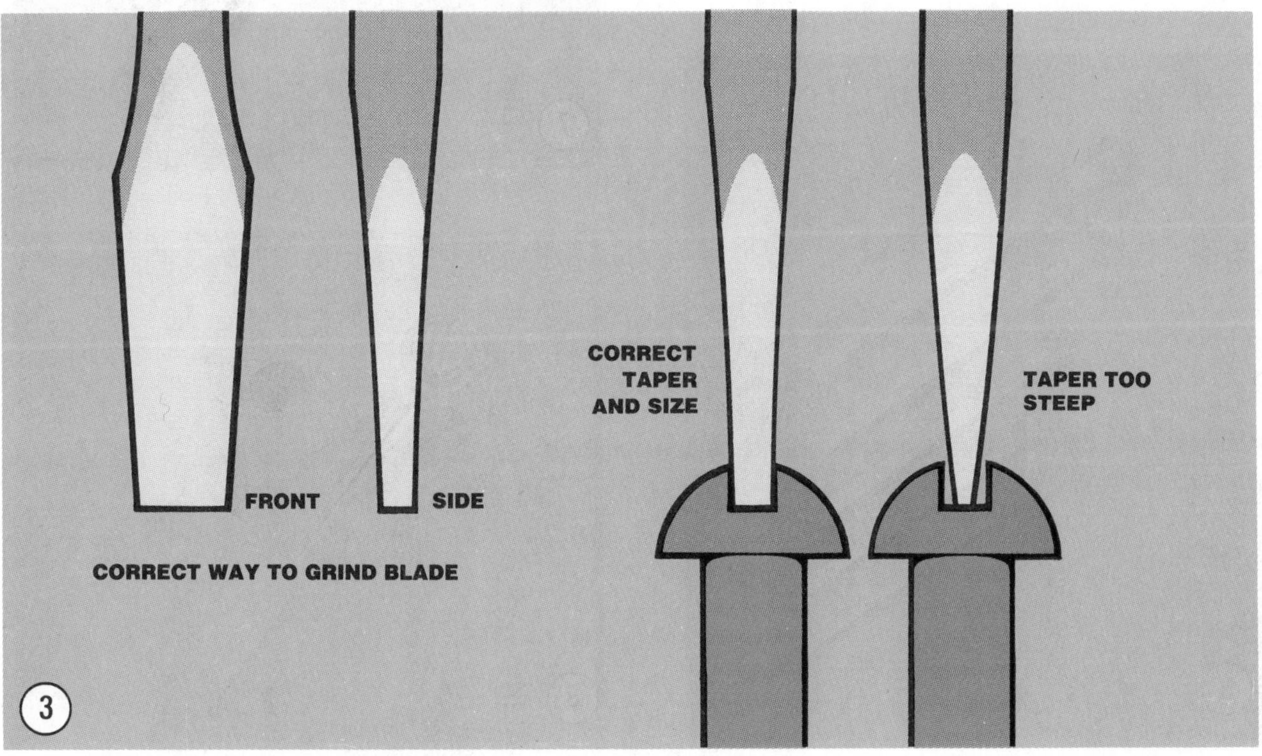

Combination wrenches, which are open on one side and boxed on the other, are also available. Both ends are the same size.

Adjustable Wrenches

An adjustable wrench can be adjusted to fit nearly any nut or bolt head. See **Figure 7**. However, it can loosen and slip, causing damage to the nut and maybe to your knuckles. Use an adjustable wrench only when other wrenches are not available.

Adjustable wrenches come in sizes ranging from 4-18 in. overall. A 6 or 8 in. wrench is recommended as an all-purpose wrench.

Socket Wrenches

This type is undoubtedly the fastest, safest and most convenient to use. See **Figure 8**. Sockets, which attach to a suitable handle, are available with 6-point or 12-point openings and use 1/4, 3/8 and 3/4 inch drives. The drive size indicates

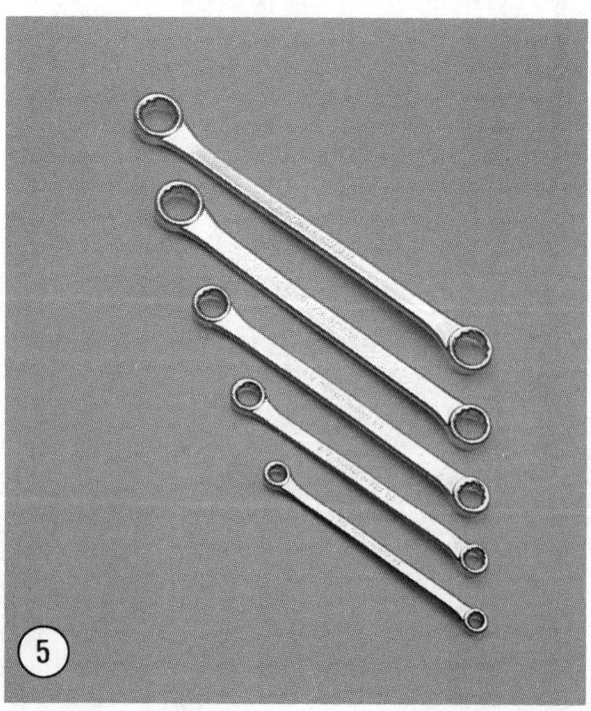

5

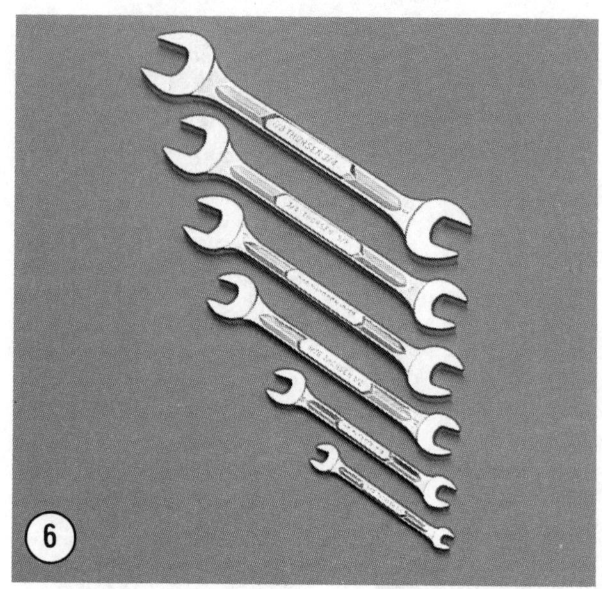

6

7

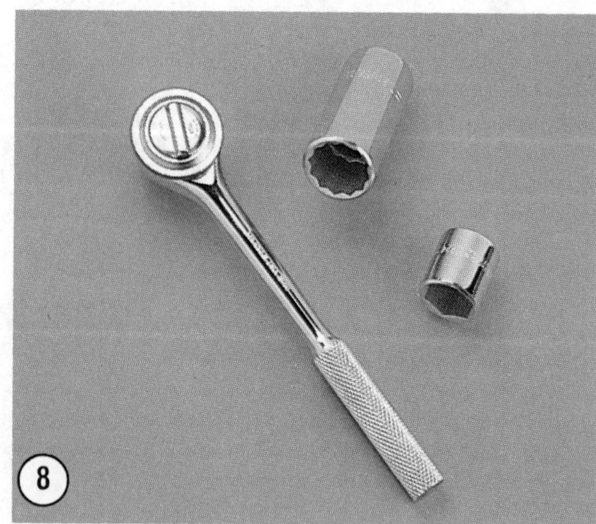

8

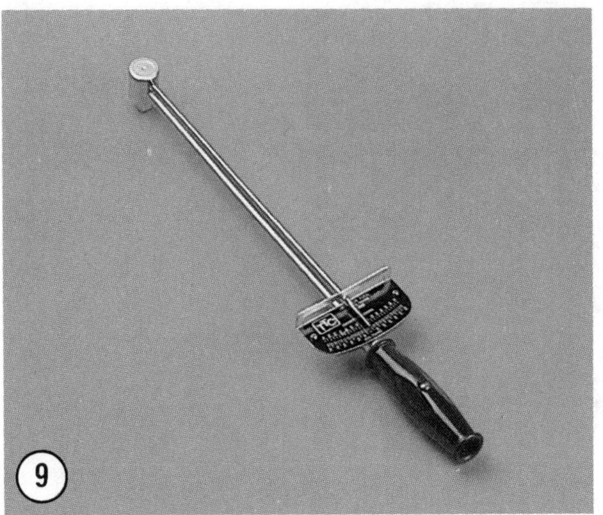

9

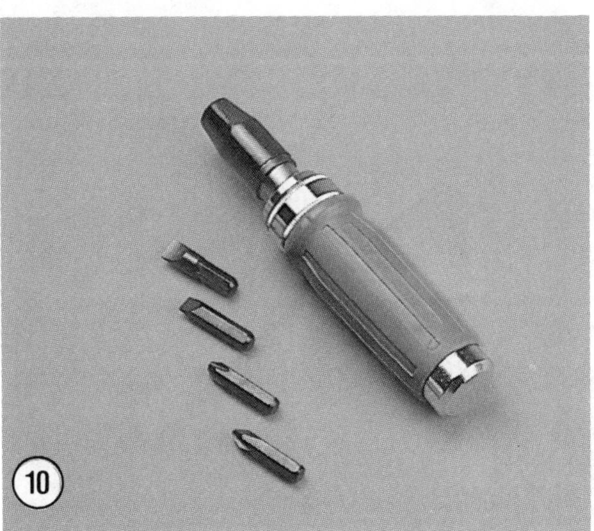

10

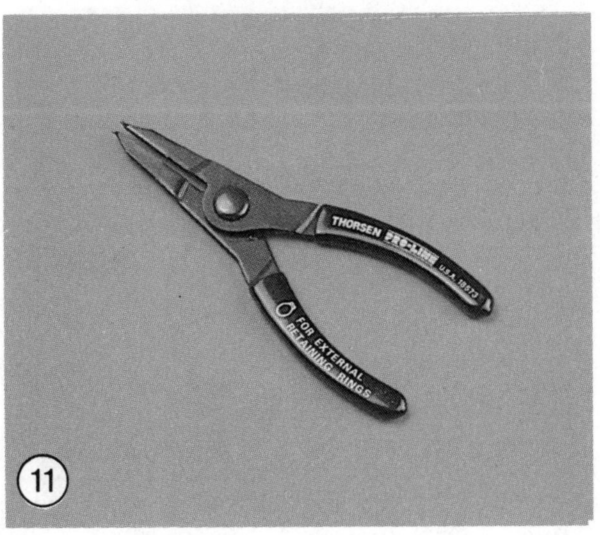

11

the size of the square hole that mates with the ratchet or flex handle.

Torque Wrench

A torque wrench (**Figure 9**) is used with a socket to measure how tight a nut or bolt is installed. They come in a wide price range and with either 3/8 or 1/2 in. square drive. The drive size indicates the size of the square drive that mates with the socket. Purchase one that measures up to 150 ft.-lb. (203 N•m).

Impact Driver

This tool (**Figure 10**) makes removal of tight fasteners easy and eliminates damage to bolts and screw slots. Impact drivers and interchangeable bits are available at most large hardware and auto parts stores.

Circlip Pliers

Circlip pliers (sometimes referred to as snap-ring pliers) are necessary to remove circlips. See **Figure 11**. Circlip pliers usually come with several different size tips; many designs can be switched from internal type to external type.

Hammers

The correct hammer is necessary for repairs. Use only a hammer with a face (or head) of rubber or plastic or the soft-faced type that is filled with buckshot (**Figure 12**). These are sometimes necessary in engine tear-downs. *Never* use a metal-faced hammer as severe damage will result in most cases. You can always produce the same amount of force with a soft-faced hammer.

Feeler Gauge

This tool has either flat or wire measuring gauges (**Figure 13**). Wire gauges are used to measure spark plug gap; flat gauges are used for all other measurements. A non-magnetic (brass) gauge may be specified when working around magnetized parts.

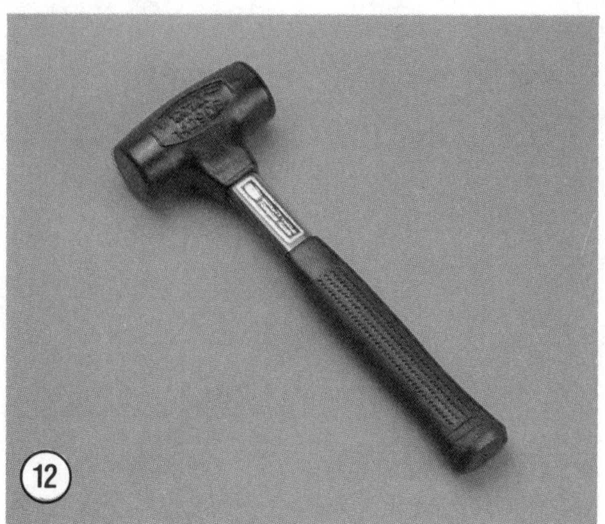

12

Other Special Tools

Some procedures require special tools; these are identified in the appropriate chapter. Unless otherwise specified, the part number used in this book to identify a special tool is the marine equipment manufacturer's part number.

Special tools can usually be purchased through your marine equipment dealer. Some can be made locally by a machinist, often at a much lower price. You may find certain special tools at tool rental dealers. Don't use makeshift tools if you can't locate the correct special tool; you will probably cause more damage than good.

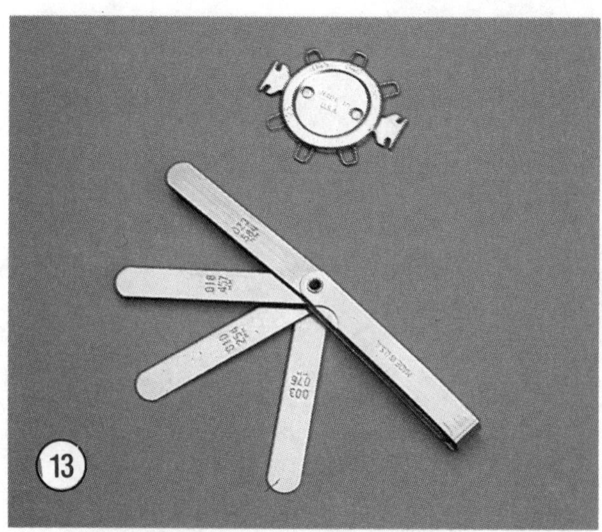

13

TEST EQUIPMENT

Multimeter

This instrument (**Figure 14**) is invaluable for electrical system troubleshooting and service. It combines a voltmeter, an ohmmeter and an ammeter into one unit, so it is often called a VOM.

Two types of multimeter are available, analog and digital. Analog meters have a moving needle with marked bands indicating the volt, ohm and amperage scales. The digital meter (DVOM) is ideally suited for troubleshooting because it is easy to read, more accurate than analog, contains internal overload protection, is auto-ranging (analog meters must be recalibrated each time the scale is changed) and has automatic polarity compensation.

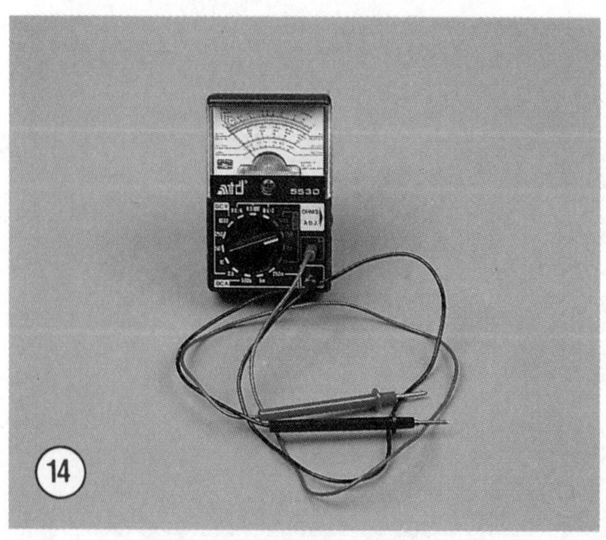

14

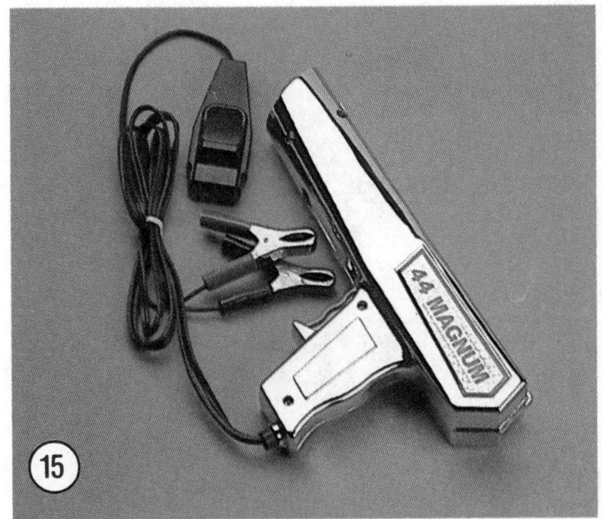

15

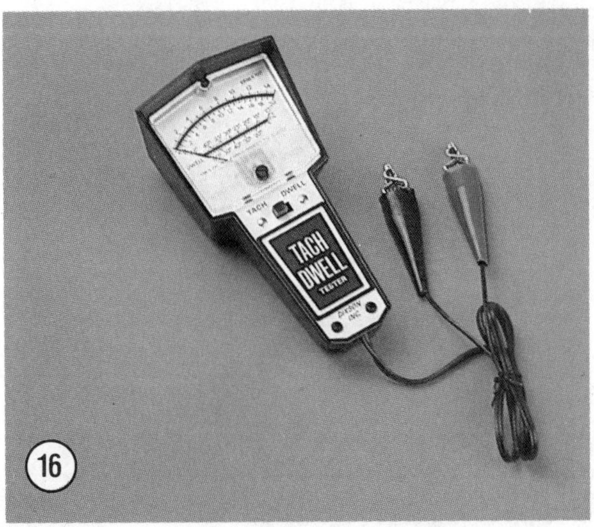

16

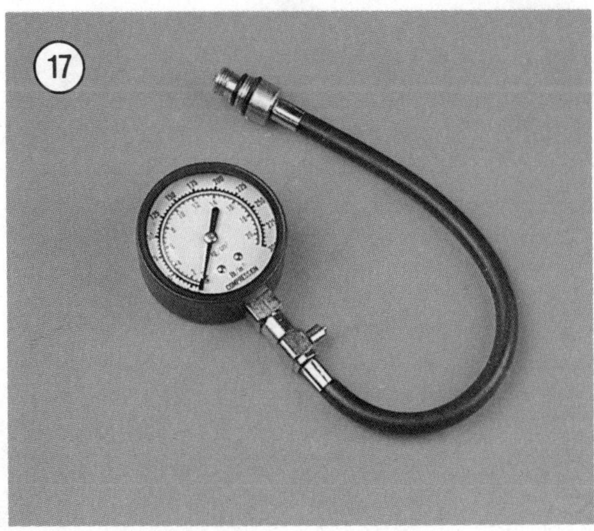

17

Strobe Timing Light

This instrument is necessary for dynamic tuning (setting ignition timing while the engine is running). By flashing a light at the precise instant the spark plug fires, the position of the timing mark can be seen. The flashing light makes a moving mark appear to stand still opposite a stationary mark.

Suitable lights range from inexpensive neon bulb types to powerful xenon strobe lights. See **Figure 15**. A light with an inductive pickup is best because it eliminates any possible damage to ignition wiring.

Tachometer/Dwell Meter

A portable tachometer is necessary for tuning. See **Figure 16**. Ignition timing and carburetor adjustments must be performed at the specified idle speed. The best instrument for this purpose is one with a low range of 0-1000 or 0-2000 rpm and a high range of 0-6000 rpm. Extended range (0-6000 or 0-8000 rpm) instruments lack accuracy at lower speeds. The instrument should be capable of detecting changes of 25 rpm on the low range.

A dwell meter is often combined with a tachometer. Dwell meters are used with breaker point ignition systems to measure the amount of time the points remain closed during engine operation.

Compression Gauge

This tool (**Figure 17**) measures the amount of pressure present in the engine's combustion chamber during the compression stroke. This indicates general engine condition. Compression readings can be interpreted along with vacuum gauge readings to pinpoint specific engine mechanical problems.

The easiest type to use has screw-in adapters that fit into the spark plug holes. Press-in rubber-tipped types are also available.

Vacuum Gauge

The vacuum gauge (**Figure 18**) measures the intake manifold vacuum created by the engine's intake stroke. Manifold and valve problems (on 4-stroke engines) can be identified by interpreting the readings. When combined with compression gauge readings, other engine problems can be diagnosed.

Some vacuum gauges can also be used as fuel pressure gauges to trace fuel system problems.

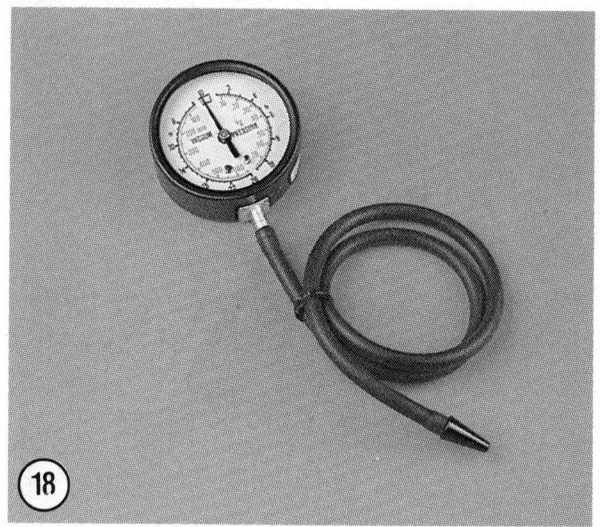

18

Hydrometer

Battery electrolyte specific gravity is measured with a hydrometer (**Figure 19**). The specific gravity of the electrolyte indicates the battery's state of charge. The best type has automatic temperature compensation; otherwise, you must calculate the compensation yourself.

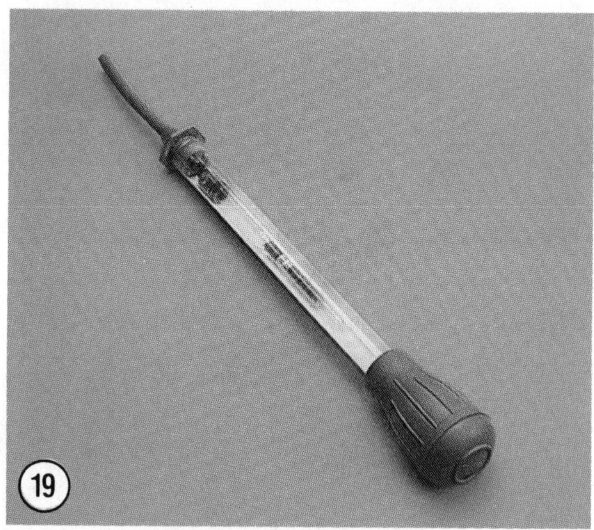

19

Precision Measuring Tools

Various tools are needed to make precision measurements. A dial indicator (**Figure 20**), for example, is used to determine run-out of rotating parts and end play of parts assemblies. A dial indicator can also be used to precisely measure piston position in relation to top dead center; some engines require this measurement for ignition timing adjustment.

Vernier calipers (**Figure 21**) and micrometers (**Figure 22**) are other precision measuring tools used to determine the size of parts (such as piston diameter).

Precision measuring equipment must be stored, handled and used carefully or it will not remain accurate.

20

SERVICE HINTS

Most of the service procedures covered in this manual are straightforward and can be performed by anyone reasonably handy with tools.

It is suggested, however, that you consider your own skills and toolbox carefully before attempting any operation involving major disassembly of the engine or gearcase.

Some operations, for example, require the use of a press. It would be wiser to have these performed by a shop equipped for such work, rather than trying to do the job yourself with makeshift equipment. Other procedures require precise measurements. Unless you have the skills and equipment required, it would be better to have a qualified repair shop make the measurements for you.

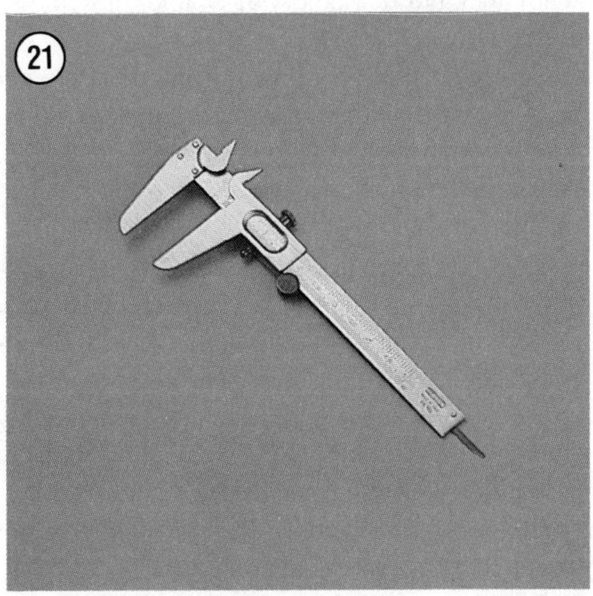

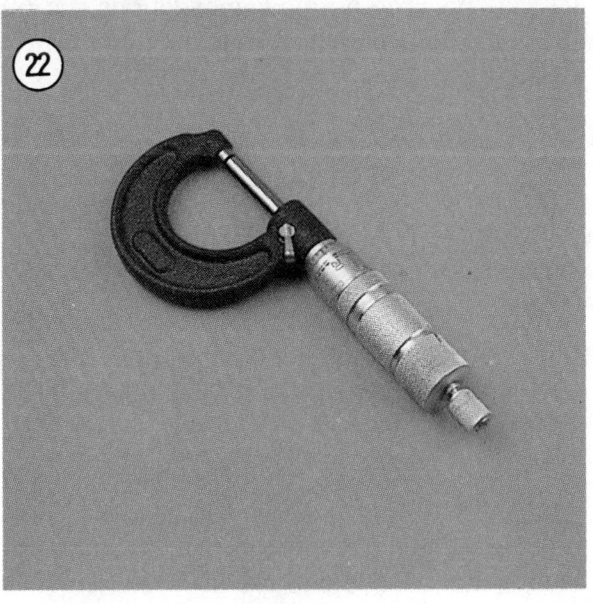

Preparation for Disassembly

Repairs go much faster and easier if the equipment is clean before you begin work. There are special cleaners, such as Gunk or Bel-Ray Degreaser, for washing the engine and related parts. Just spray or brush on the cleaning solution, let it stand, then rinse away with a garden hose. Clean all oily or greasy parts with cleaning solvent as you remove them.

WARNING
Never use gasoline as a cleaning agent. It presents an extreme fire hazard. Be sure to work in a well-ventilated area when using cleaning solvent. Keep a Coast Guard approved fire extinguisher, rated for gasoline fires, handy in any case.

Much of the labor charged for repairs made by dealers is for the removal and disassembly of other parts to reach the defective unit. It is frequently possible to perform the preliminary operations yourself and then take the defective unit in to the dealer for repair.

If you decide to tackle the job yourself, read the entire section in this manual that pertains to it, making sure you have identified the proper one. Study the illustrations and text until you have a good idea of what is involved in completing the job satisfactorily. If special tools or replacement parts are required, make arrangements to get them before you start. It is frustrating and time-consuming to get partly into a job and then be unable to complete it.

Disassembly Precautions

During disassembly of parts, keep a few general precautions in mind. Force is rarely needed to get things apart. If parts are a tight fit, such as a bearing in a case, there is usually a tool designed to separate them. Never use a screwdriver to pry apart parts with machined surfaces (such as cylinder heads and crankcases). You will mar the surfaces and end up with leaks.

Make diagrams (or take an instant picture) wherever similar-appearing parts are found. For example, head and crankcase bolts are often not the same length. You may think you can remember where everything came from, but mistakes are costly. There is also the possibility you may be sidetracked and not return to work for days or even weeks. In the interval, carefully laid out parts may have been disturbed.

Cover all openings after removing parts to keep small parts, dirt or other contamination from entering.

Tag all similar internal parts for location and direction. All internal components should be reinstalled in the same location and direction from which removed. Record the number and thickness of any shims as they are removed. Small parts, such as bolts, can be identified by placing them in plastic sandwich bags. Seal and label them with masking tape.

Wiring should be tagged with masking tape and marked as each wire is removed. Again, do not rely on memory alone.

Protect finished surfaces from physical damage or corrosion. Keep gasoline off painted surfaces.

Assembly Precautions

No parts, except those assembled with a press fit, require unusual force during assembly. If a part is hard to remove or install, find out why before proceeding.

When assembling two parts, start all fasteners, then tighten evenly in an alternating or crossing pattern if no specific tightening sequence is given.

When assembling parts, be sure all shims and washers are installed exactly as they came out.

Whenever a rotating part butts against a stationary part, look for a shim or washer. Use new gaskets if there is any doubt about the condition of the old ones. Unless otherwise specified, a thin coat of oil on gaskets may help them seal effectively.

Heavy grease can be used to hold small parts in place if they tend to fall out during assembly. However, keep grease and oil away from electrical components.

High spots may be sanded off a piston with sandpaper, but fine emery cloth and oil will do a much more professional job.

Carbon can be removed from the cylinder head, the piston crown and the exhaust port with a dull screwdriver. *Do not* scratch either surface. Wipe off the surface with a clean cloth when finished.

The carburetor is best cleaned by disassembling it and soaking the parts in a commercial carburetor cleaner. Never soak gaskets and rubber parts in these cleaners. Never use wire to clean out jets and air passages; they are easily damaged. Use compressed air to blow out the carburetor *after* the float has been removed.

Take your time and do the job right. Do not forget that the break-in procedure on a newly rebuilt engine is the same as that of a new one. Use the break-in oil recommendations and follow other instructions given in your owner's manual.

SPECIAL TIPS

Because of the extreme demands placed on marine equipment, several points should be kept in mind when performing service and repair. The following items are general suggestions that may improve the overall life of the machine and help avoid costly failures.

1. Unless otherwise specified, use a locking compound, such as Loctite Threadlocker, on all bolts and nuts, even if they are secured with lockwashers. Be sure to use the specified grade

of thread locking compound. A screw or bolt lost from an engine cover or bearing retainer could easily cause serious and expensive damage before its loss is noticed.

When applying thread locking compound, use a small amount. If too much is used, it can work its way down the threads and stick parts together that were not meant to be stuck together.

Keep a tube of thread locking compound in your tool box; when used properly, it is cheap insurance.

2. Use a hammer-driven impact tool to remove and install screws and bolts. These tools help prevent the rounding off of bolt heads and screw slots and ensure a tight installation.

3. When straightening the fold-over type lockwasher, use a wide-blade chisel, such as an old and dull wood chisel. Such a tool provides a better purchase on the folded tab, making straightening easier.

4. When installing the fold-over type lockwasher, always use a new washer if possible. If a new washer is not available, always fold over a part of the washer that has not been previously folded. Reusing the same fold may cause the washer to break, resulting in the loss of its locking ability and a loose piece of metal adrift in the engine.

When folding the washer, start the fold with a screwdriver and finish it with a pair of pliers. If a punch is used to make the fold, the fold may be too sharp, thereby increasing the chances of the washer breaking under stress.

These washers are relatively inexpensive and it is suggested that you keep several of each size in your tool box for repairs.

5. When replacing missing or broken fasteners (bolts, nuts and screws), always use authorized replacement parts. They are specially hardened for each application. The wrong 50-cent bolt could easily cause serious and expensive damage.

6. When installing gaskets, always use authorized replacement gaskets *without* sealer, unless designated. Many gaskets are designed to swell when they come in contact with oil. Gasket sealer will prevent the gaskets from swelling as intended and can result in oil leaks. Authorized replacement gaskets are cut from material of the precise thickness needed. Installation of a too thick or too thin gasket in a critical area could cause equipment damage.

MECHANIC'S TECHNIQUES

Removing Frozen Fasteners

When a fastener rusts and cannot be removed, several methods may be used to loosen it. First, apply penetrating oil, such as Liquid Wrench or WD-40 (available at any hardware or auto supply store). Apply it liberally and allow it penetrate for 10-15 minutes. Tap the fastener several times with a small hammer; do not hit it hard enough to cause damage. Reapply the penetrating oil if necessary.

For frozen screws, apply penetrating oil as described, then insert a screwdriver in the slot and tap the top of the screwdriver with a hammer. This loosens the rust so the screw can be removed in the normal way. If the screw head is too chewed up to use a screwdriver, grip the head with locking pliers and twist the screw out.

Avoid applying heat unless specifically instructed because it may melt, warp or remove the temper from parts.

Remedying Stripped Threads

Occasionally, threads are stripped through carelessness or impact damage. Often the threads can be cleaned up by running a tap (for internal threads on nuts) or die (for external threads on bolts) through threads. See **Figure 23**.

Removing Broken Screws or Bolts

When the head breaks off a screw or bolt, several methods are available for removing the remaining portion.

If a large portion of the remainder projects out, try gripping it with vise-grip pliers. If the projecting portion is too small, file it to fit a wrench or cut a slot in it to fit a screwdriver. See **Figure 24**.

If the head breaks off flush, use a screw extractor. To do this, centerpunch the remaining portion of the screw or bolt. Drill a small hole in the screw and tap the extractor into the hole. Back the screw out with a wrench on the extractor. See **Figure 25**.

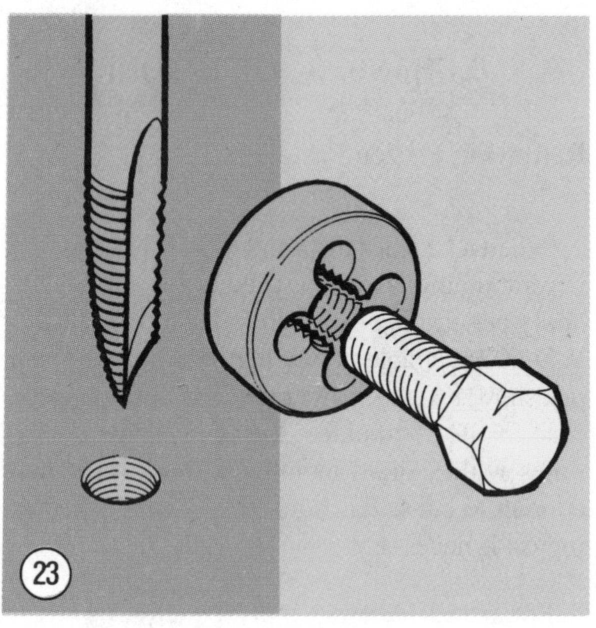
23

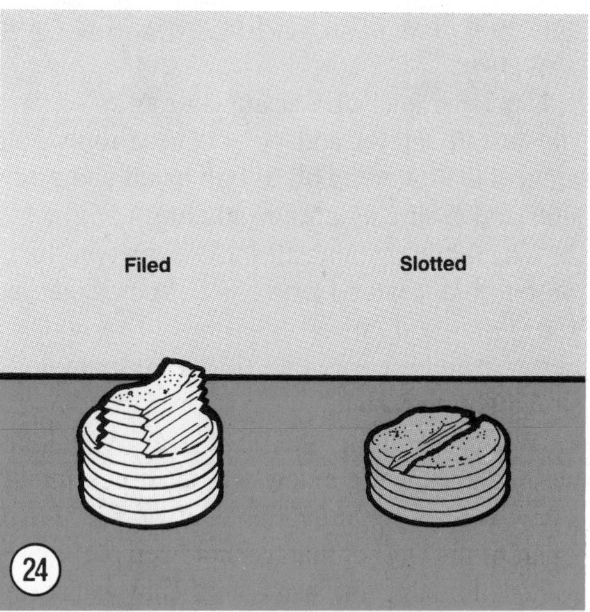

24

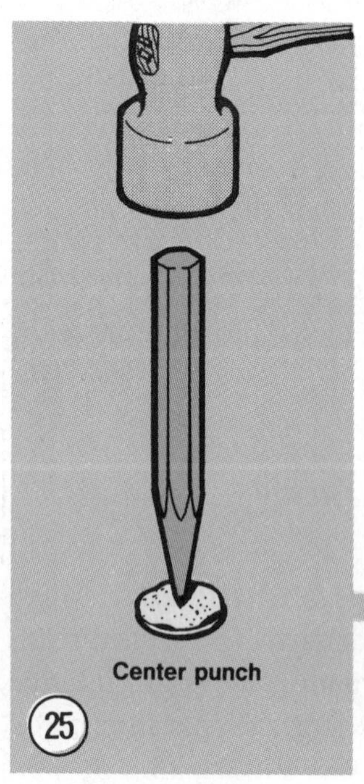

25

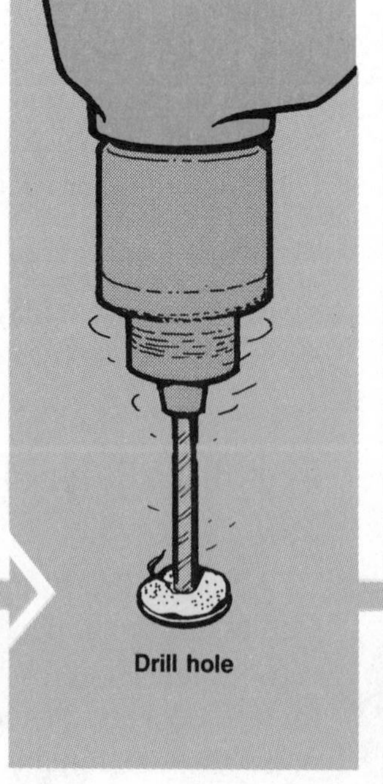

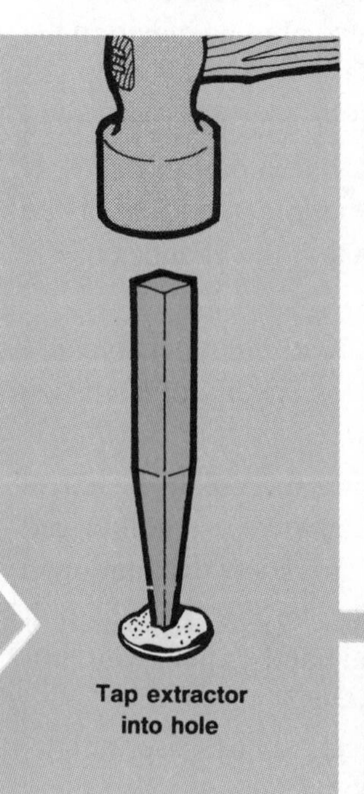

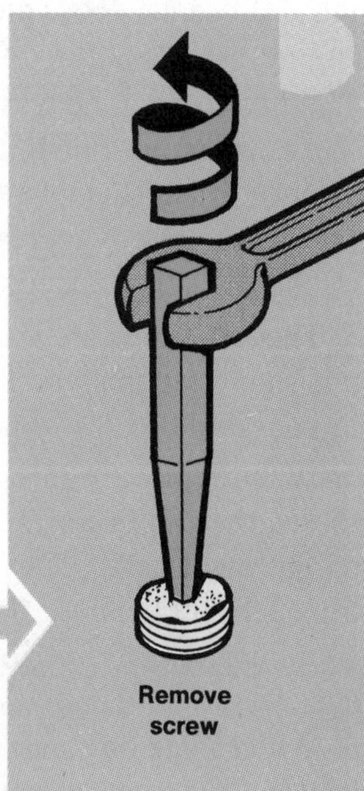

3

Chapter Three

Troubleshooting and Testing

Modern outboard engines are quite reliable when compared to earlier models. They provide impressive performance, better fuel economy and greater reliability than those produced just a few years ago. However, as reliable as outboards are, problems can and eventually do occur. This chapter provides the information required to pinpoint the source of most operational problems.

If a problem occurs, perform a quick visual inspection before attempting any involved testing procedures. Look for leaking fluid, disconnected wires or damaged components. Refer to *Preliminary Inspection* in this chapter for a list of other items to check.

Troubleshooting instructions help determine which system is causing a malfunction. Additional testing pinpoints which components of the system are faulty.

Test specifications and other relevant specifications are provided in **Tables 1-26**. **Tables 1-26** are located at the end of this chapter.

Outboard Engine Identification

It is absolutely essential that the outboard engine is correctly identified before performing any testing, maintenance or repairs. Test specifications and repair instructions may vary by model, production year, engine characteristics and unique serial number. Information stamped onto the serial number tag (**Figure 1**) provides this information. Engine weight, maximum engine speed and power output specifications are also listed on the serial number tag.

Serial Number Tag Location

On 4-6 hp models the serial number tag is affixed to the top side of the tilt bracket directly under the tiller handle bracket (**Figure 2**). Steer the engine fully starboard to provide the best view of the tag. In addition, the serial number is stamped into a plug (**Figure 3**) located on the port side of the power head.

On 9.9-90 hp models the serial number tag is located on the rear side of the starboard clamp bracket (**Figure 4**). In addition the engine serial number is stamped into a plug (**Figure 3**) affixed to the lower starboard side of the power head.

The serial number tag lists the model designation (3, **Figure 5**). In this example the engine is a 9.9 EL. The

model designation provides more than the rated horsepower output of the engine. To better meet the application, many engines are produced in different versions for a given horsepower. Variations include the starting system used (**Figure 6**), drive shaft length, tiller or remote control, and power trim. Refer to *Engine characteristics* (in this chapter) for additional information.

On all 1998-on models, the horsepower and kilowatt rating is listed on the serial number tag (5 and 9, **Figure 5**). The horsepower rating is listed in the model name portion (3, **Figure 5**) of the serial number tag. In this example the engine is rated at 9.9 hp.

The model year is listed on the serial number tag (2, **Figure 5**) directly above the model name. Specifications or test/repair instructions may change during the model year. Should this occur, the serial number is used to identify the affected engines.

The year of production is listed at the lower right of the serial number tag (7, **Figure 5**). Do not assume the year model and year of production are the same.

NOTE

Electric starting kits, power trim kits, different gearcase sizes and other items may be installed on the outboard. These changes are not reflected in the serial number tag. Should testing or repair be required on these add-on kits, refer to the specifications and instructions for similar models with the selected equipment factory installed.

Engine Characteristics

Mercury and Mariner outboards are produced with many variations of each horsepower rating. Variations exist in drive shaft length, starting system used, type of control system, trim systems and other engine components.

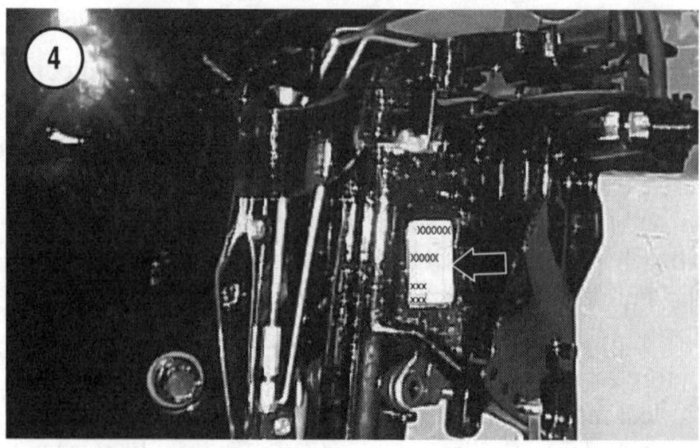

The test and repair requirements may also vary with the engine characteristics.

Engine characteristic identification is easily accomplished referring to the model name portion of the serial number tag (3, **Figure 5**). In this example the engine is a 9.9 EL. The 9.9 indicates the horsepower of the engine. The letter code to the right of the horsepower indicates the characteristics or version of engine. The EL (3, **Figure 5**) in this example indicates the engine is equipped with electric start and a long drive shaft length. Refer to **Table 4** to match the model codes to the outboard's version or characteristics.

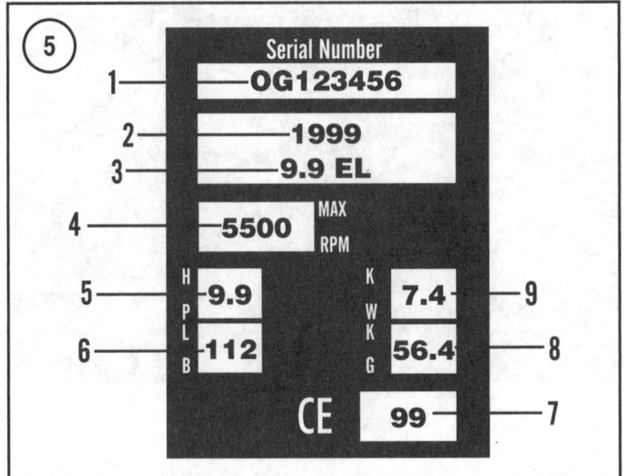

Serial number

The engine's serial number is listed on the serial number tag (1, **Figure 5**). It identifies the outboard from other outboards of the same model. In many states this number is used to register or title the outboard. Record this number and place it in a secure place. In the event that the outboard is lost or stolen this number provides accurate identification of the outboard.

In the example in **Figure 5**, the first digit is O followed by a letter code, then six numbers. The numbers increase sequentially as engines are produced. The letter code increases alphabetically when all combinations are used. In theory, the serial number following OG999999 would be OH000000, then OH000001 and so on. Because the serial number identifies the outboard motor, always supply it when purchasing replacement parts.

Engine weight

All boats have a maximum weight capacity listed on the boat rating tag. The weight of all passengers, gear, fuel ,tanks and the engine must be considered prior to loading or operating the boat. Never load the boat beyond its rated capacity. To determine the total weight, refer to the engine weight on the serial number tag. The engine weight without fuel or tanks is listed in pounds (6, **Figure 5**) and kilograms (8).

TROUBLESHOOTING TEST EQUIPMENT

Most troubleshooting and testing can be performed using easily available test equipment. Examples of the equipment used include the multimeter, vacuum/pressure gauges, compression tester, and the gearcase pressure tester.

Most of these tools and equipment can be purchased from a local automotive parts store. Contact a tool supplier if unable to purchase them locally.

To ensure safe and accurate test results, read and understand all test precautions and instructions before using any of the test equipment.

Multimeter

The expanded use of advanced electronic control systems have resulted in increased use of a multimeter (**Figure 7**) when troubleshooting the outboard. A thorough understanding of the proper use of the multimeter is essential for accurate troubleshooting and component testing.

Two basic types of multimeters are available—analog (**Figure 7**) and digital (**Figure 8**).

The main parts of an analog multimeter include the meter face (A, **Figure 9**), needle (B, **Figure 9**), selector (C, **Figure 9**) and test leads (D, **Figure 9**).

Values are determined by reading the position of the needle on the meter face. If the needle (**Figure 10**) aligns

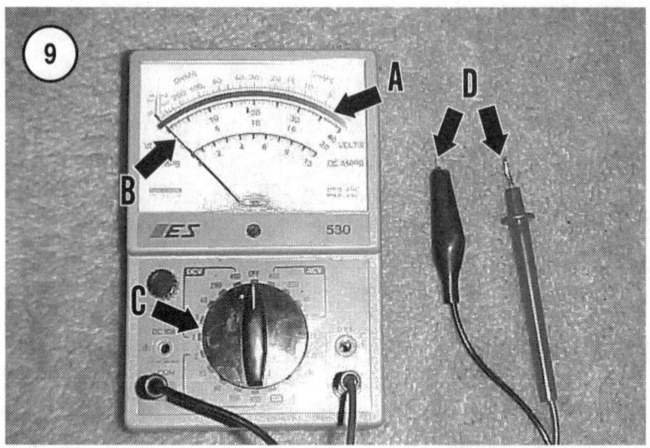

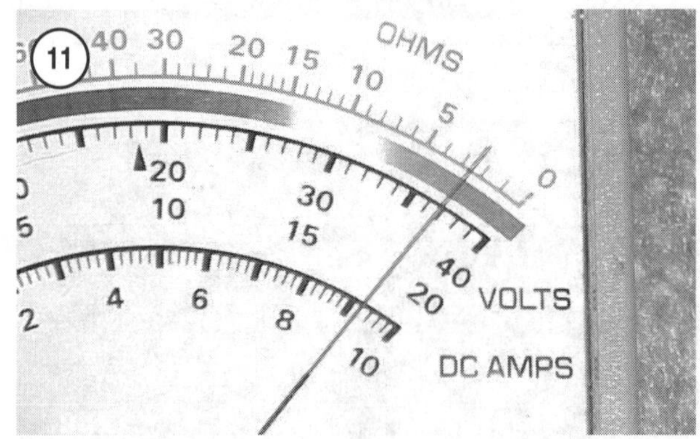

with the 10 mark indicates a value of 10 ohms. If the needle (**Figure 11**) is positioned midway between the second and third marks indicates a value of 2.5 ohms.

The main parts of a digital multimeter are the display screen (A, **Figure 12**), selector (B, **Figure 12**) and test leads (C, **Figure 12**).

The value measured with a digital meter is displayed on the screen (A, **Figure 12**). Digital meters are usually easier to read than an analog meter.

Use a digital meter if the test specifications are very low in value or the specification lists a number. to the right of the decimal point. For an example a value of 1.59 volts is indicated in **Figure 13**. In most cases a digital multimeter provides more accurate readings than an analog multimeter when low ranges are required.

Be aware that some testing cannot be accurately performed using a digital multimeter. In these cases an analog multimeter must be used.

As with analog meters, selection of the proper function is required prior to performing any testing. Most digital multimeters are *auto scaling* and selection of the proper scale or range is not required. Refer to *Function Selection* in this chapter to determine the correct function to select.

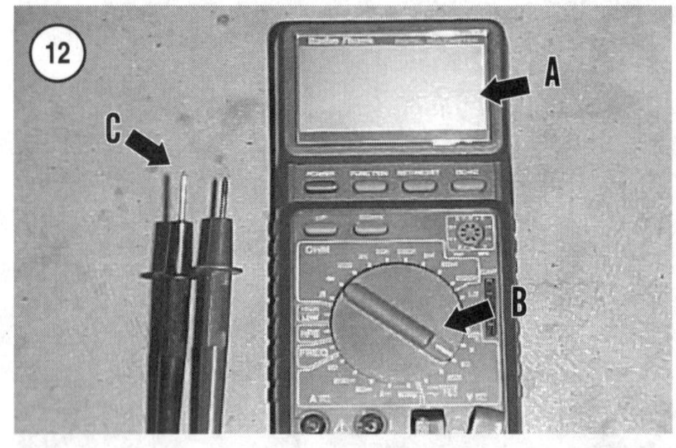

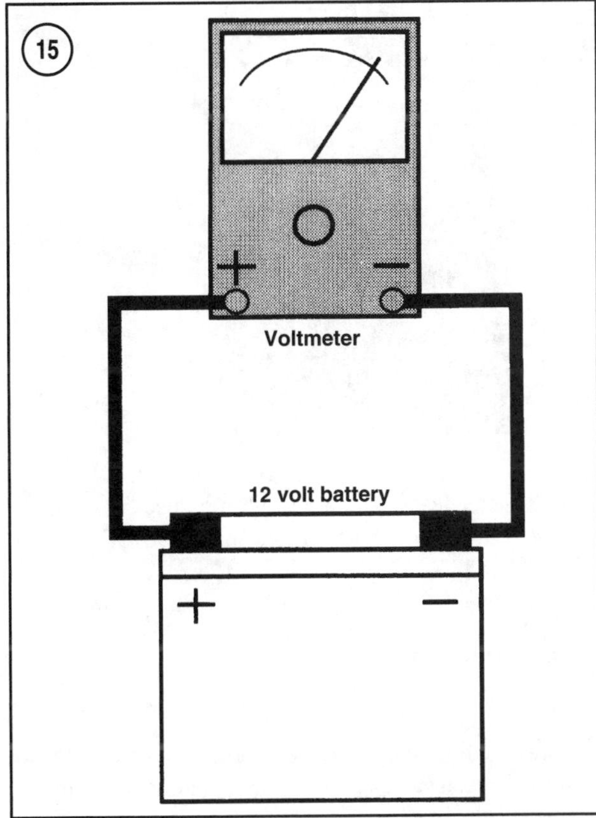

Refer to *Scale or Range Selection* in this chapter to determine the correct scale or range to select.

Always identify the test lead polarity prior to performing any test. The negative (–) meter test lead is usually black and the positive (+) meter test lead is usually red.

The positive and negative lead connections are usually marked on the meter to identify the correct polarity of the test leads. A positive (+) (A, **Figure 14**) mark is used for the positive or red test lead. A negative (–) (B, **Figure 14**) mark or common indicates the connection for the negative or black test lead. Be certain that the test leads are connected with correct polarity to ensure accurate test results.

CAUTION
Make certain all test lead connections are clean prior to performing any test. Dirty or corroded leads and connections lead to inaccurate test results and the replacement of good parts.

Voltage

Voltage is best described as the pressure of the electrical current in a wire. It can be compared to the water pressure present in a garden hose when the water valve is turned on. Electrical pressure or voltage can be measured using a voltmeter as water pressure can be measured using a water pressure gauge. Both DC (direct current) and AC (alternating current) can be measured with most meters.

DC or direct current describes electrical current flowing in one direction in a circuit

WARNING
Use extreme caution when working around batteries. Never smoke or allow sparks to occur around batteries. Batteries produce explosive hydrogen gas that can explode and result in injury or death. Never make the final connection of a circuit to the battery terminal as an arc may occur and lead to fire or explosion.

A common test using a DC voltmeter is the battery voltage test. Connect the positive meter lead to the positive terminal of a battery and the negative meter lead to the negative terminal (**Figure 15**).

This type of connection is commonly referred to as a parallel connection. Carefully follow all test instructions to ensure safety and accurate test results.

Use DC voltage measurements to test the starting, charging, trim, electrical sensors and other components on the outboard.

AC (alternating current) describes current flowing in both direction in a wire.

A common test using the AC volts function is an ignition charge coil output. Typically the positive meter test lead connects to a charge coil lead and the negative lead connects an engine ground or other point on the engine (**Figure 16**). This type of connection is best described as a parallel connection. In most cases voltage is measured without removing existing connections.

Carefully follow all test instructions to ensure safety and accurate test results. Use AC voltage measurements

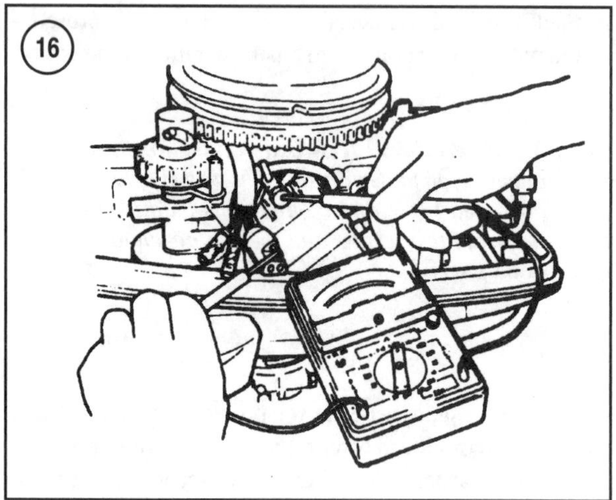

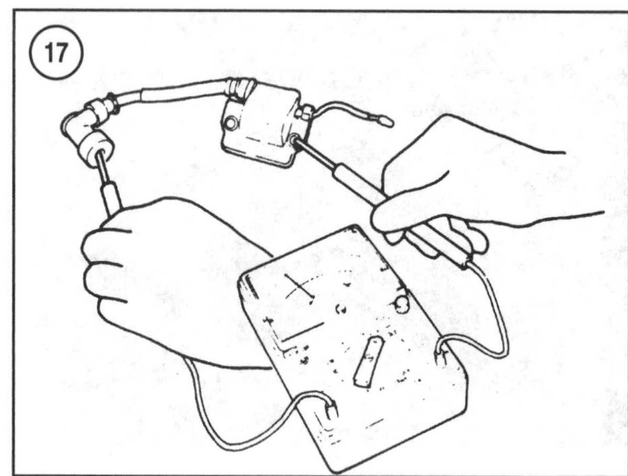

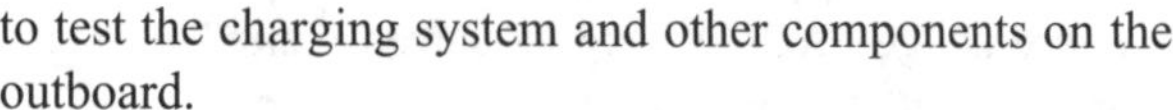
to test the charging system and other components on the outboard.

CAUTION
Use only the AC voltage or DVA function of the meter when measuring AC voltage. Some meters are capable of measuring the RMS voltage and are useful for some marine generator applications. Voltage measurements can vary considerably when using the RMS scale instead of the standard AC voltage or DVA scale. Use the AC voltage scale unless the test specifications indicate the RMS scale.

Resistance

Resistance is the resistance to current flow in a circuit. The length of the wire, size of the wire and the type of material a wire is constructed can affect current flow.

The longer the circuit the greater the resistance to current flow. The size and type of material used in the circuit, temperature of the circuit and the presence of corrosion on the contacts can affect electrical current flow.

Higher temperature generally increases resistance. In many cases the test specifications list a given temperature. Measure the resistance at normal room temperature unless a specific temperature is listed.

The unit used to measure resistance is the *ohm*. The higher the resistance the greater the ohms reading.

To measure resistance, isolate (disconnect) the circuit or component from the remainder of the system. Then connect the ohmmeter between each end of the circuit or to specified points on the component (**Figure 17**). Usually, polarity is not important during a resistance test; however, certain tests, like checking a diode, require that the ohmmeter leads be connected in a specific polarity. Always follow the instructions closely.

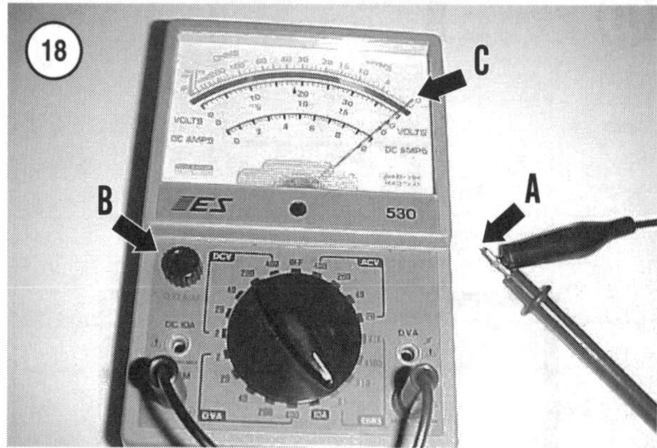

Ohmmeter Calibration

Always calibrate or zero an analog ohmmeter prior to performing resistance tests. Failure to calibrate the meter usually results in inaccurate measurements.

1. Connect the positive meter lead to the negative lead (A, **Figure 18**).

2. Rotate the adjusting knob (B, **Figure 18**) until the needle perfectly aligns with the 0 on the meter face (C, **Figure 18**). Clean the test leads or replace the meter batteries if unable to calibrate the meter. Do not move the adjusting knob during the test.

3. Calibrate the meter each time a different scale is selected and prior to performing any resistance test.

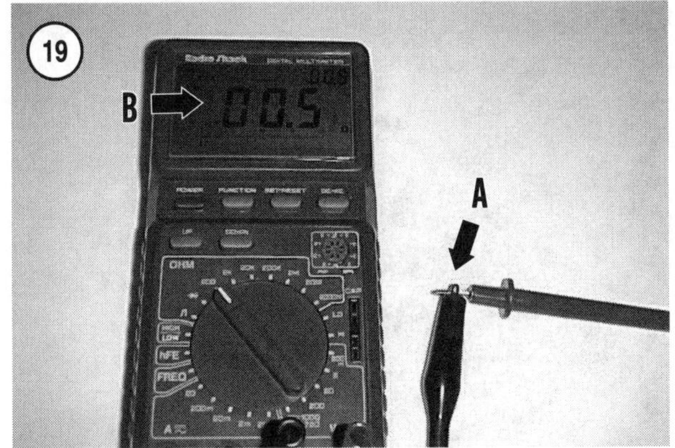

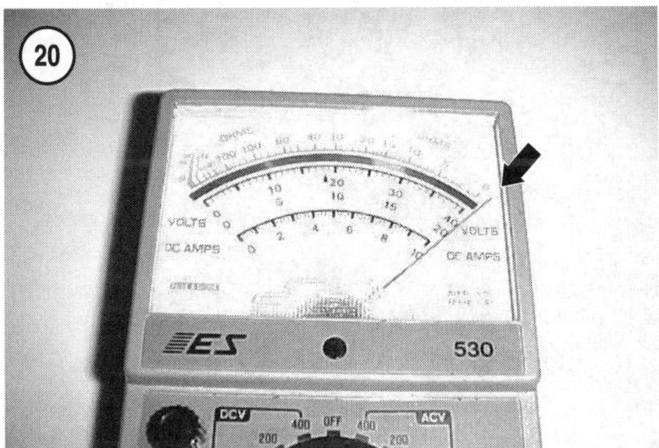

Ohmmeter Internal Resistance Test (Digital Ohmmeter)

Check the internal resistance prior to performing a resistance test using a digital ohmmeter. Failure to check and compensate for the internal resistance usually results in inaccurate resistance measurements.

1. Connect the positive meter lead to the negative lead (A, **Figure 19**).

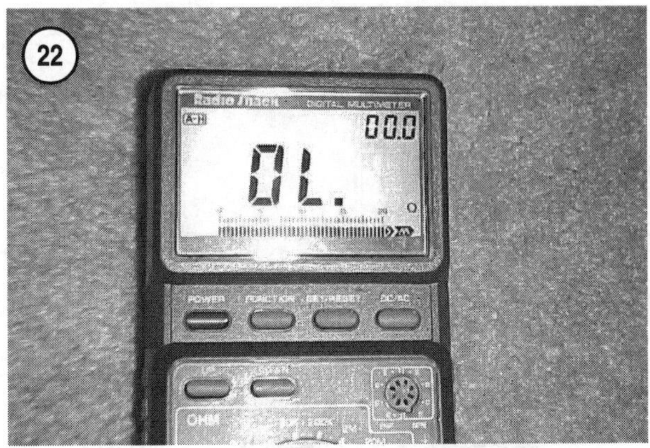

2. Switch the meter on. Record the resistance indicated on the meter display (B, **Figure 19**).
3. Subtract the displayed value from the resistance measurement obtained during the test.
4. The result is the resistance of the circuit or component minus the internal resistance of the ohmmeter.

Continuity Test

A continuity test determines the integrity of a circuit or component. A broken wire or open circuit has no continuity; a complete circuit has continuity. Continuity can be checked using an ohmmeter or a self-powered test lamp. Using an ohmmeter, a low resistance reading, usually 0 ohm, indicates continuity (**Figure 20**). An infinity reading (**Figure 21** or **Figure 22**) indicates no continuity. Also, some digital ohmmeters are equipped with a continuity test function (**Figure 23**) providing an audible or visual signal if continuity is present. Using a self-powered test lamp, continuity is indicated if the test lamp glows. If the lamp does not glow, no continuity is present.

The circuit or component must be isolated or disconnected from any other circuit to check continuity.

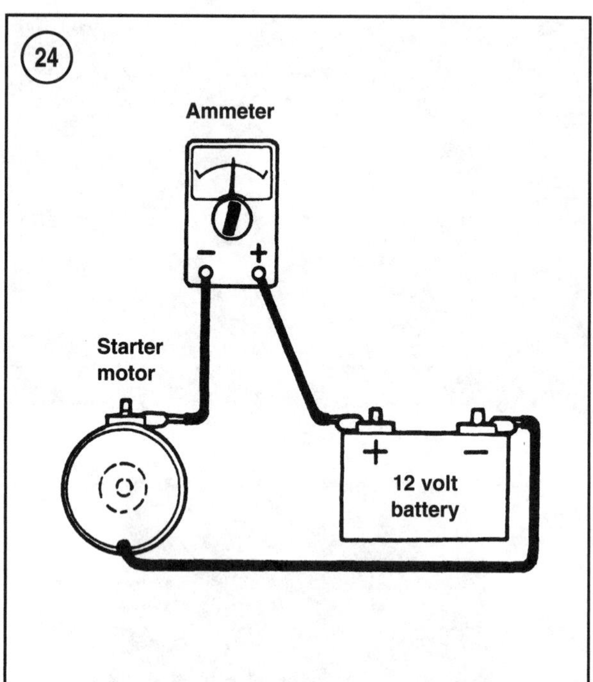

Amperage

Amperes (amps) are the unit used to measure current flow in a circuit or through a component. Current is the actual flow of electricity. The more current that flows, the more work that can be accomplished. However, if excessive current flows through a wire, the wire will overheat and possibly melt. Melted wires are caused by excessive current, not excessive voltage.

Amperes are measured using an ammeter attached in a series connection. **Figure 24** illustrates a starter motor current draw test using an ammeter connected in series. Amperage measurement requires that the ammeter be spliced into the circuit in a series connection. Always use an ammeter that can read higher that the anticipated current flow to prevent damage to the meter. Connect the red lead of the ammeter to the electrical source and the black lead to the electrical load.

Peak Voltage

Some meters are capable of reading peak electrical pulses. Many ignition system components produce AC voltage pulses of very short duration. The standard voltmeter is incapable of accurately measuring these short duration electrical pulses. Special circuits in a peak-reading voltmeter capture the maximum voltage produced during the short duration electrical pulses. The peak voltage produced is displayed on the meter. Peak voltage usually is

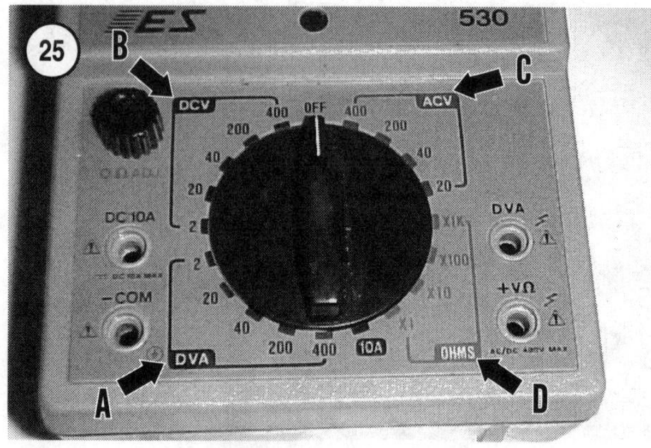

displayed on the selector (A, **Figure 25**) if the meter has this capability.

Diode Testing

A diode is a device that performs like an electrical check valve. The diode allows electrical current to flow easily in one direction and provides resistance when the current attempts to flow in the opposite direction.

To test a diode, connect an ohmmeter or self-powered test lamp to the diode, note the meter (or lamp), then reverse the leads. If the diode is good, it will allow current to flow one direction (continuity) and block the flow in the other direction (no continuity).

NOTE
*It is difficult to determine the polarity of a diode because the internal polarity of many ohmmeters is different. However, some meters have a diode test function **(Figure 26)** that can determine the diode polarity. Regardless of polarity, consider a diode good if it has continuity in one direction and no continuity in the other.*

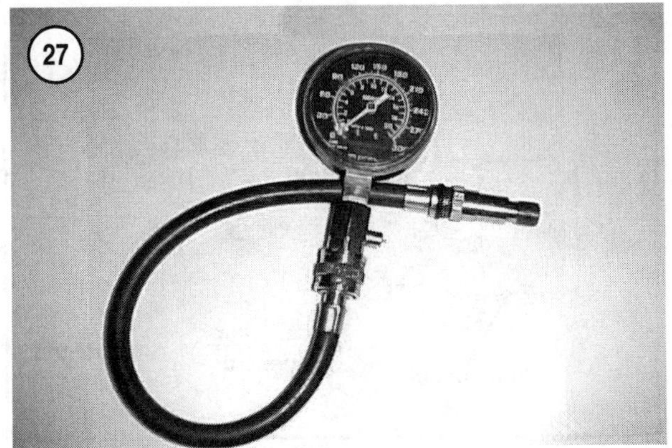

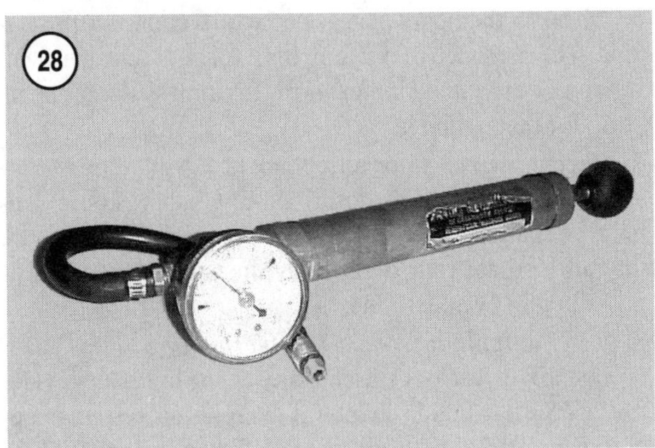

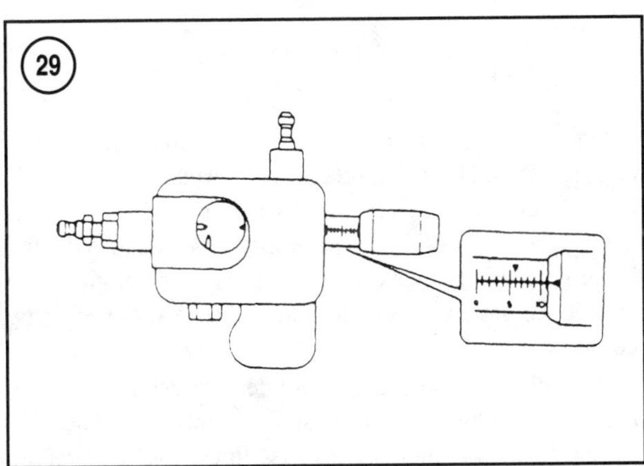

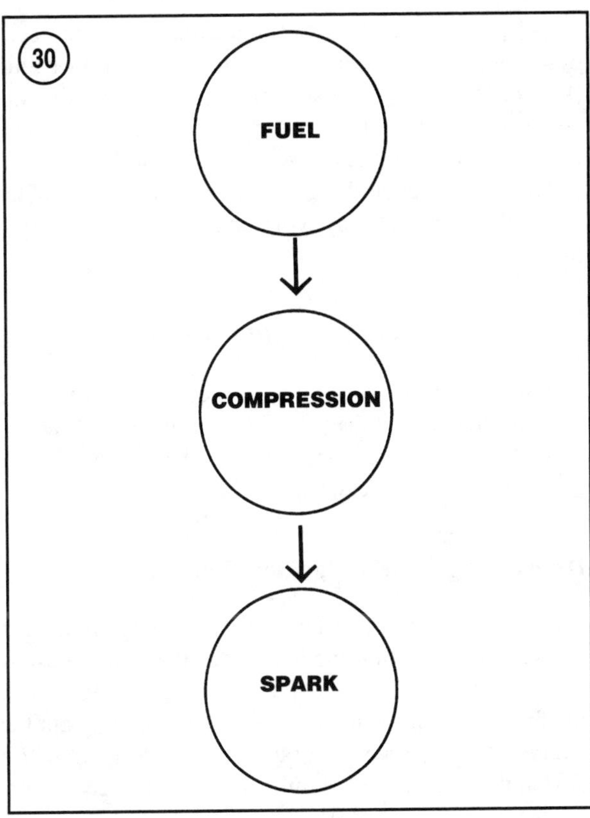

Compression Tester

Use a compression tester (**Figure 27**) to measure the pressure that builds in the combustion chamber at a specified cranking speed. Compression testers are available at most automotive supply stores and tool suppliers. Use a gauge capable of reading pressure up to 16.0 kg/cm^2 (226.0 psi).

Gearcase Pressure Tester

Use a gearcase pressure tester (**Figure 28**) to find the source of water or lubricant leakage from the gearcase and other components. These are considered specialty tools and are not generally available from automotive supply stores. They can be purchased through many tool suppliers. Specific instructions on the use of these testers are provided in this chapter.

Spark Gap Tester

Use a spark gap tester (**Figure 29**) to determine if spark is present at the spark plug lead. Spark gap testers are available from a variety of sources including tool suppliers and automotive parts stores. Testers are available to accommodate a single cylinder engine or multiple cylinders. Some models have an adjustable spark gap (**Figure 29**) and are useful with some brands of outboards that have minimum spark gap test.

Operating Requirements

The three basic requirements for an internal combustion engine to run include a fresh supply of fuel and air in the proper proportion, adequate compression in the combustion chamber and a source of ignition at the proper time (**Figure 30**). If any of these requirements are missing the engine will not run. If any of these requirements are weak the engine may not run properly.

Additional troubleshooting instructions and troubleshooting tips are listed by symptoms in the following section.

STARTING DIFFICULTY

If starting the engine is difficult, the problem may be with the engine or it may caused by an improper starting procedure. The owner's manual is the best source for the proper starting instructions.

Determining a Fuel or Ignition Fault

It can be difficult to determine if a starting problem is related to fuel, ignition or other causes. It is usually easiest to first verify that the ignition system is operating. Check the fuel system if the ignition system is operating but the engine will not start or starting is difficult. Refer to *Spark Test* in this chapter to determine if spark is present at the spark plugs.

WARNING

High voltage is present in the ignition system. Never touch any wires or electrical components while running the engine or performing a test. Never perform ignition system tests in wet conditions.

Spark Test

This test checks for ignition system output at the spark plug connector. A spark gap tester is required to perform this test.

1. Disconnect the spark plug leads from all cylinders. Remove the spark plugs (Chapter Four) from all cylinders.
2. Remove the propeller from the gearcase as described in Chapter Nine.
3. Connect the ground lead (**Figure 31**) of the spark gap tester to a suitable engine ground such as a cylinder head bolt.
4. Connect the spark plug connector (**Figure 31**) for one cylinder to the appropriate terminal on the spark gap tester. On adjustable spark gap testers adjust the gap to approximately 1/4 in. (6.35 mm).
5. Connect all remaining spark plug leads to a suitable engine ground. Shift the engine into neutral. Place the tester away from the spark plug openings.

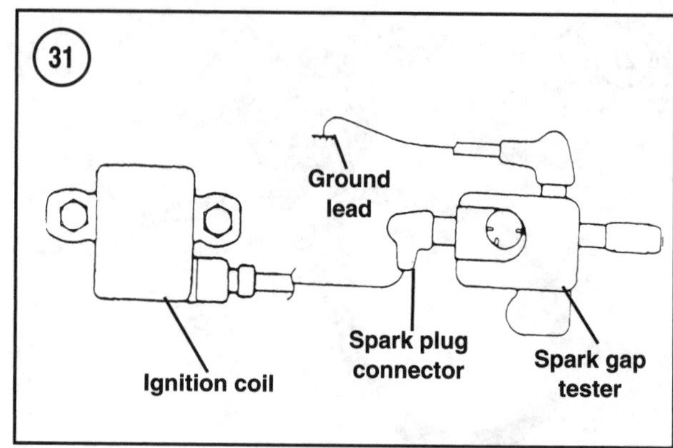

6. Observe the spark gap tester while cranking the engine. The presence of a strong blue spark at the spark gap tester while cranking indicates the ignition system is operating for that cylinder.
7. Repeat Steps 3-6 for all cylinders. Clean, gap and install the spark plugs as described in Chapter Four. Connect the spark plug leads to the correct spark plugs. Ensure that all lead are routed correctly. Install the propeller as described in Chapter Nine.
8. Refer to *Ignition System Troubleshooting* in this chapter if spark is weak or missing any of the cylinders. Refer to *Fuel System* in this chapter if the ignition system is operating properly but the engine is difficult or impossible to start.

Fuel System

Fuel related problems are common with most outboard engines. Gasoline has a relatively short shelf life and become stale within a few weeks under some conditions. This gasoline work fine in an automobile because the fuel is consumed in a week or so. Because marine engines may sit idle for several weeks at a time the gasoline often becomes stale.

As fuel evaporates, a gummy deposit usually forms in the carburetor or other fuel system components. These deposits may clog fuel filters, fuel lines, fuel pumps and small passages in the carburetor.

Fuel stored in the fuel tank tends to absorb water vapor from the air. Over time, this water separates from the fuel then settles to the bottom of the fuel tank. Water in the fuel tank can lead to the formation of rust in the fuel tank. These contaminants block fuel filters and other fuel system passages. Inspect the fuel in the fuel tank when the engine refuses to start and the ignition system is not at fault. An unpleasant odor usually indicates the fuel has exceeded its shelf life and should be replaced.

32

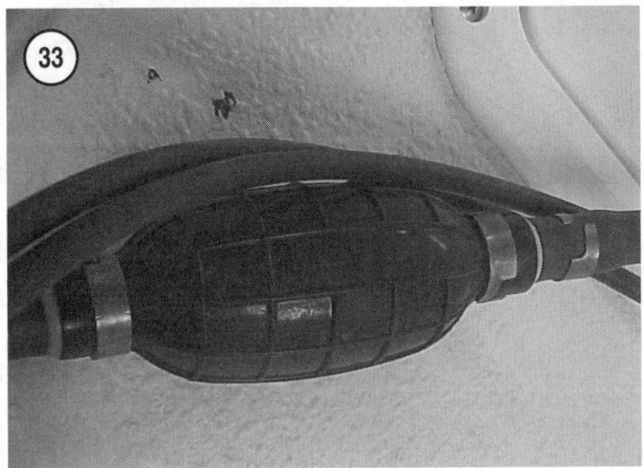

33

WARNING
Use extreme caution when working with the fuel system. Fuel is extremely flammable and if ignited can result in injury or death. Never smoke or allow sparks to occur around fuel or fuel vapor. Wipe up any spilled fuel at once with a shop towel and dispose of the shop towel in an appropriate manner. Check all fuel hoses, connections and fittings for leakage after any fuel system repair.

Fuel Inspection

Check the condition of the fuel if the engine has been stored for some time and refuses to start. All models covered in this manual are equipped with float bowl drains (**Figure 32**) on the individual carburetors. Refer to Chapter Six to locate the float bowl drain plugs.

To inspect the fuel, slide a container under the bowl drain plug. Pump the primer bulb (**Figure 33**) until it becomes firm. Slowly remove the plug and allow all fuel to drain from the float bowl. Inspect the drain plug gasket for torn or damaged surfaces. Replace the gasket if necessary. Pour the fuel sample into a clear container. Install the drain plug and gasket. Securely tighten the screw then promptly clean up any spilled fuel.

34

Inspect and carefully smell the fuel. An unusual odor, debris, cloudy appearance or the presence of water indicates a problem with the fuel. If any of these conditions are noted, dispose of all the fuel in an environmentally friendly manner. Contact a local marine dealership or automotive repair facility for information on the proper disposal of the fuel.

Clean and inspect the entire fuel system if water or other contamination is in the fuel. If the float bowl(s) is empty, check all hoses and connections for loose or damaged fittings. If the hoses and connections are in good condition, clean and inspect the carburetor(s).

If no fuel can be drained from the float bowl check the fuel tank for fuel and check all hoses and connections for loose or damaged fittings. Typically the fuel inlet needle is stuck closed or plugged with debris.

Faulty Choke Valve or Electrothermal Valve

A faulty choke solenoid (**Figure 34**) or binding choke valve linkage can result in hard starting of a cold or warm engine. Check for proper operation of the choke valve if the engine starts hard and all other fuel system components operate correctly.

All 25-75 hp and 9.9 hp (serial No. OH000058-on) models are equipped with an electrothermal valve (**Figure 35** and **Figure 36**).

On 50 hp models, the plunger portion of this valve holds the throttle open slightly during cold starting or running conditions. The resulting faster idle speed helps prevent stalling and allows for quicker warm up.

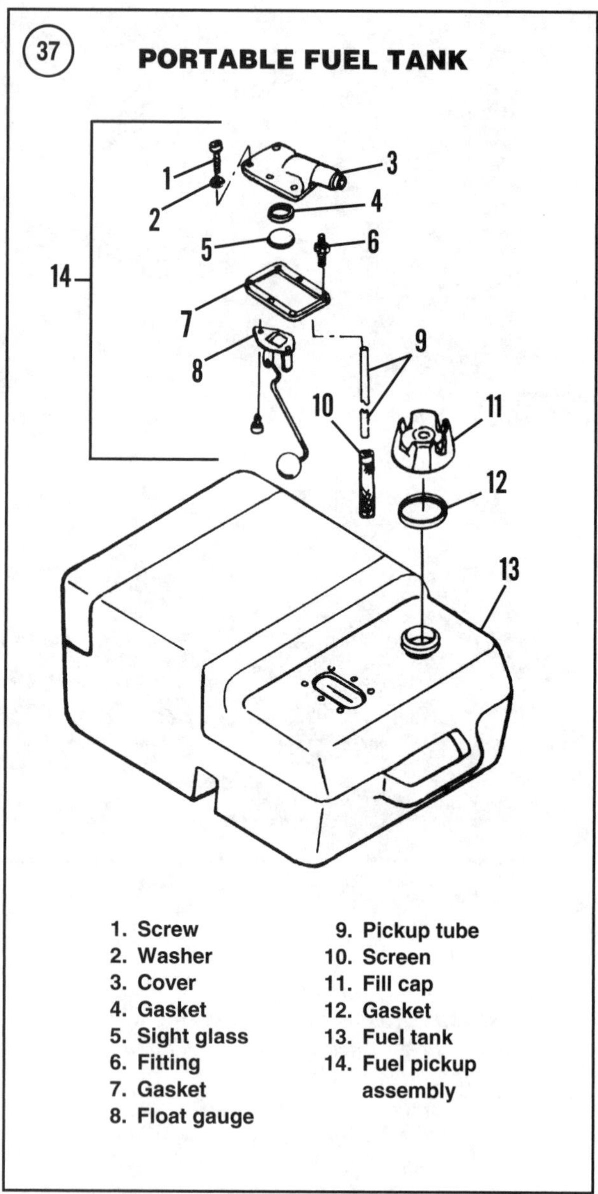

On other models, this component provides additional fuel to the engine during cold start and warm up. Additional fuel is supplied using a connection of the valve to passages within the carburetor. The additional fuel helps prevent stalling and allows for quicker warm up. In addition circuits within the ignition system advance the ignition timing during cold running condition to enhance cold running characteristics.

A malfunction of this component can cause hard starting, stalling or excessive exhaust smoke. Refer to *Fuel System Component Testing* in this chapter for choke solenoid and electrothermal valve test instructions.

Fuel tank And Fuel Hose Testing

A faulty fuel tank, fuel hose or related components can restrict fuel flow or allow air to enter the fuel flowing to the engine. In either case, the engine will misfire due to inadequate fuel delivery. In most instances the misfire occurs only at higher engine speeds as the fuel flow is adequate for low speed operation.

Most outboards use portable fuel tanks (**Figure 37**). This arrangement allows easy tank removal for filling, cleaning and inspection. Some larger boats are equipped with built in fuel tanks that are not easily removed for service or cleaning. Often times major structural components of the boat must be removed to access the tank.

The most effective method to determine if the fuel tank is faulty is to temporarily run the engine on a known-good fuel tank. Ensure the tank used for testing had good fuel hoses, fresh fuel and secure fuel hose connections. Ensure the inside diameter of the fuel hose and fuel fittings of the test fuel tank is 6.4 mm (1/4 in.) or larger. Using hose that is too small can result in a continued engine malfunction.

A problem with the fuel, fuel tank pickup, fuel hoses, primer bulb, fuel tank vent or antisiphon device on built-

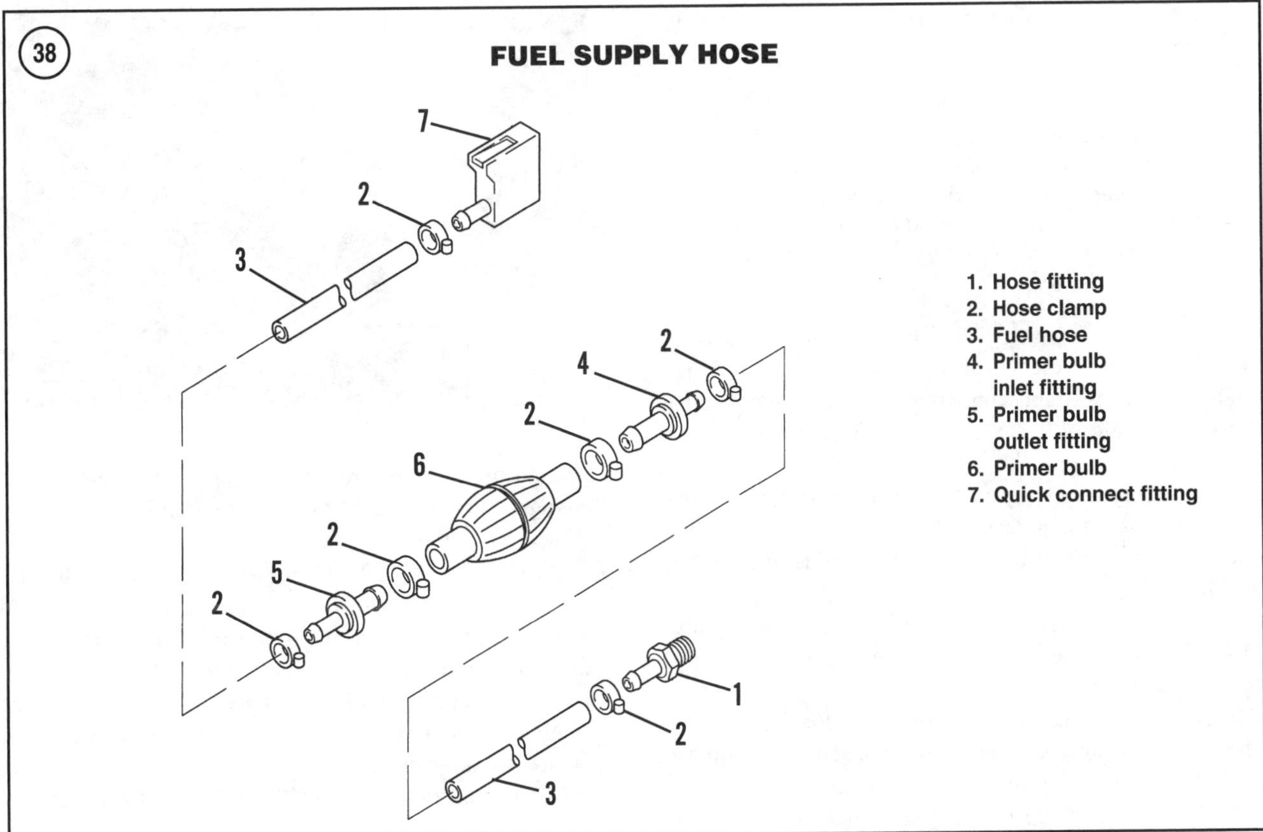

in tanks is indicated if the engine performs properly on a known-good fuel tank and hose.

A fault with fuel system, ignition system, or other engine component is likely if the malfunction persists with the good fuel tank. Refer to **Table 2** and **Table 3** to determine which components to test, adjust or inspect.

NOTE

The engine must be run at full throttle for several minutes to accurately check for a fuel tank related fault. Smaller engines (25 hp and lower) can be run at high speeds in a test tank. With larger engines, it is usually necessary to run the engine at high engine speeds while under actual running conditions.

Fuel Tank Pickup

The fuel tank pickup (14, **Figure 37**) draws fuel from near the bottom of the fuel tank. Most applications use a simple tube extending from the cover (3, **Figure 37**) to near the bottom of the fuel tank. Some fuel tanks are equipped with a screen or filter (10, **Figure 37**) to capture debris present in the fuel tank. This filter may become obstructed with debris and restrict fuel flow. Debris can block the tube type fuel tank pickup as well.

Partial disassembly of the fuel tank is necessary to inspect the fuel tank pickup. Refer to Chapter Six for portable fuel tank inspection and repair instructions.

With applications using a built-in fuel tank, inspection of the fuel tank pickup is usually much more difficult. Accessibility to the fuel tank and its components may be limited. On some boats seating, storage areas and even the structure of the boat must be removed to access the fuel tank.

Contact the boat manufacturer for information on the repair and a source for replacement parts of a built-in fuel tank.

Fuel Supply Hoses

A faulty fuel supply hose (**Figure 38**) can result in fuel leakage, cause a fuel restriction or allow air to enter the fuel supply. Visually inspect all fuel hoses for cracks or a weathered appearance. Pinch the fuel hose until collapsed then release it. Replace the fuel hose if it is difficult to squeeze, excessively soft or tends to stick together on the internal surfaces. Replace the fuel hose if any leakage is detected.

CAUTION
Avoid using couplings or other patching methods to repair a damaged fuel hose. The coupling or patch may result in restricted fuel flow and lead to fuel starvation. A temporary repair usually fails and results in a fuel or air leak.

To check for an internal fuel hose restriction, disconnect the hose from the fuel tank and the engine. On 75 and 90 hp models, the fuel supply hose must be disconnected from the fitting on the hose exiting from the front and lower engine covers.

Thoroughly drain any fuel from the hose into a container. Direct the engine end of the hose into a container then pump the primer bulb to remove residual fuel. Refer to **Figure 38**.

1A. On 4-50 hp models, remove the fuel hose clamps from the engine end of the fuel hose. Carefully pull the quick connector from the fuel hose.

1B. On 75 and 90 hp models, remove the fuel hose clamp then carefully pull the fuel hose from the connector on the hose leading into the front and lower engine covers.

2. Remove the clamp then carefully pull the fuel hose from the tank fitting (1, **Figure 38**). Remove the clamps then pull the primer bulb and check valves as an assembly from the fuel line. Refer to *Primer bulb* in this section to test the primer bulb.

3. Direct one end of the disconnected hose to a clear area and use compressed air to blow through the hose. Replace the hose if air does not flow freely through it. An internal restriction is usually caused by deteriorated internal surfaces.

4. Inspect all fuel hoses from the tank to the carburetors if any restriction is found.

5. Replace all fuel hose clamps during assembly. Check the entire fuel system for fuel leaks and correct them before operating the engine. Refer to Chapter Six for primer bulb installation instructions.

Quick Connect Fittings

Quick connect fittings (**Figure 39**) are used on 4-50 hp models to connect the fuel tank hose to the engine. On these models, the female end of the connector clamps to the fuel hose leading to the fuel tank. The male end of the connector attaches to the lower engine cover. It connects within the engine cover to the fuel filter and fuel pump. Some fuel tanks use a quick connect fitting at the fuel tank end. This allows removal of the fuel tank without disconnecting the fuel line from the engine. As the connectors engage, internal check valves unseat and allow fuel to flow through the connector.

On 75 and 90 hp models the fuel hose connects directly to the hose leading to the fuel filter using a fitting and clamps. The clamps must be removed from the fitting to disconnect the fuel supply hose from the engine.

Disconnect the fuel hose connector by depressing the small lever and carefully pulling the female connector from the engine connector.

Connect the quick connect fitting to the engine connector as follows:

1. Align the pin on the engine connector (A, **Figure 39**) with the smaller hole (B) in the female connector.

2. Depress the lever on the quick connector and firmly push the connectors together. Hold the connector in position then release the lever.

3. Ensure the lever engages over the ridge on the engine mounted connector. Gently tug on the fuel supply hose to check for a secure connection.

A problem with the connector can result in fuel leakage, air leaks and in some cases a fuel restriction. If air leakage is present at the fitting at the engine or fuel tank, the fuel pump draw air into the fuel hose. This condition can result in insufficient fuel for the engine. In most cases the symptoms worsen at higher engine speeds. In most, but not all, cases a fuel leak is detected at the connection points when the primer bulb is pumped.

Have an assistant operate the engine while the fuel starvation symptoms are present. Carefully press the connector tightly against the connection point and hold it in position. A problem with the connector is evident if the symptoms cease within a few minutes. The problem is generally due to a worn or damaged seal or clamp. Replace both connectors (**Figure 39**) if a defect is indicated in either connector.

Worn or damaged component and the presence of debris can result in an internal fuel restriction the connector.

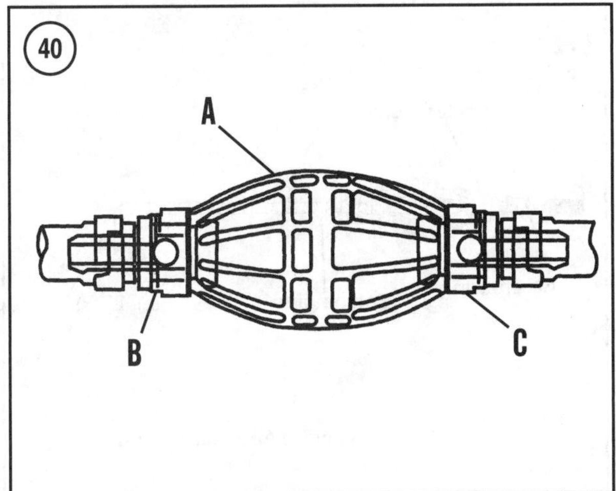

To check for a restriction, run the engine with the fuel hose temporarily connected directly to the fuel pump. Refer to Chapter Six to identify the fuel pump inlet. Carefully squeeze the primer bulb and check for fuel leaks. Correct any leaks before running the engine. Run the engine and check for proper operation. Replace both connectors if the symptoms disappear. Always check for and correct any fuel leaks prior to operating the engine.

If a fuel restriction is present at the tank side connectors the primer bulb tends to collapse at higher engine speeds. In most cases the problem is with the hose end connector and replacement is required.

Primer Bulb

The primer bulb (**Figure 33**) is a hand operated fuel pump integrated into the fuel supply hose. It serves as a means to fill the carburetor float bowl(s) with fuel prior to starting the engine..

Pump the primer bulb only if the engine has not been used for several hours. Excessive pumping can create a potential flooding condition.

Never use excessive force when pumping the primer bulb. Gently squeeze the primer bulb until it becomes firm indicating that the carburetor float bowl is filled.

The major components of the primer bulb include the bulb (A, **Figure 40**), inlet check valve (B) and outlet check valve (C).

A malfunctioning primer bulb can lead to an inability to prime the fuel system or can cause a restriction in the fuel system. Hard starting, poor performance or engine stalling are the typical symptoms. Most failures of the primer bulb are the result of defective check valves at the engine or fuel tank side of the bulb.

A blocked check valve will cause insufficient fuel delivery to the engine. If the restriction is on the tank side, the bulb will collapse during engine operation. If a check valve fails to seat properly, the bulb will not become firm when the float bowl(s) are full.

Fuels available today may contain ingredients that tend to cause deterioration of many of the fuel system components including the primer bulb. Squeeze the primer bulb until fully compressed then release it. Replace the primer bulb if it tends to stick together on the internal surfaces when released. Thoroughly inspect the fuel hose and other fuel system components if this condition is noted. Prior to replacing the primer bulb, pressure test it following the instructions listed in this section.

WARNING

Use extreme caution when working with the fuel system. Fuel is extremely flammable and if ignited can result in serious injury or death. Never smoke or allow sparks to occur around fuel or fuel vapor. Wipe up any spilled fuel at once with a shop towel and dispose of the shop towel in an appropriate manner. Check all fuel hoses, connections and fittings for leakage after any fuel system repair. Correct all fuel leakage before returning the engine to service.

Primer bulb pressure test

Test the primer bulb check valves using a hand operated vacuum pump available at most automotive parts stores and through most tool suppliers.

1. Disconnect both ends of the fuel line connecting the fuel tank to the engine. Remove and discard the clamps (2, **Figure 38**) at both fuel line connections to the primer bulb. Position the primer bulb over a container and pull both fuel lines from the primer bulb.
2. Squeeze the primer bulb until fully collapsed. Replace the primer bulb if it does not freely expand when released. Replace the primer bulb if it is cracked, weathered or is hard to squeeze.
3. Use the *arrow* on the primer bulb (**Figure 41**) to determine the engine side of the bulb. The arrow points toward the engine side. Connect a hand operated pressure pump (**Figure 41**) to the fuel tank side fuel connection. Clamp the hose securely to the primer bulb hose fitting. Gently squeeze the hand operated pump. Air must exit the engine side (**Figure 41**) as the pressure pump is operated. Replace the primer bulb assembly or check valves if it does not operate as specified.
4. Connect the hand operated vacuum pump to the engine side fuel connection (**Figure 42**). Clamp the pump hose

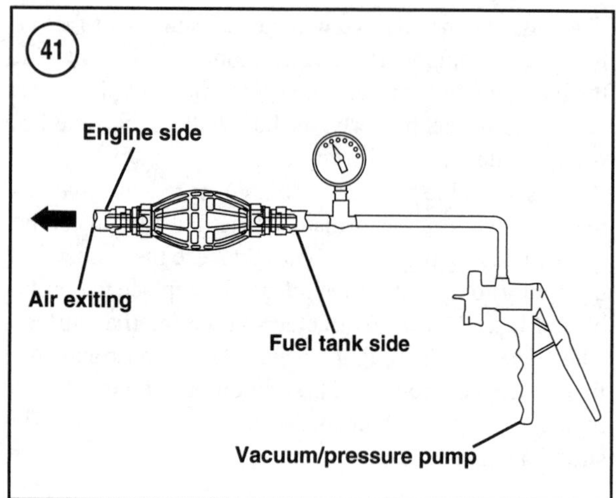

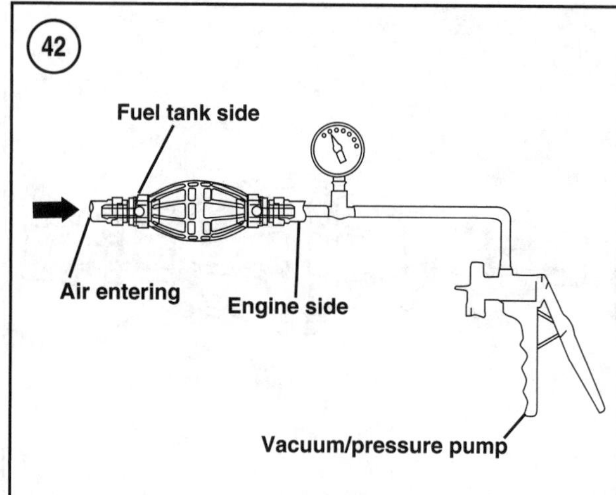

securely to the primer bulb fuel fitting. *Gently* pump the vacuum pump lever. Air must enter the fuel tank side hose fitting (**Figure 42**) as the pump is operated. If not, replace the primer bulb assembly or check valves.

5. Connect the pressure pump hose to the fuel tank side fuel connection (**Figure 41**). Block the engine side fitting with a finger. Submerge the primer bulb in water. *Gently* pump the hand operated pressure pump enough to achieve a few pounds of air pressure inside the bulb. Replace the primer bulb assembly if air bubbles are detected. Thoroughly dry the primer bulb after testing.
6. Install the primer bulb as described in Chapter Six.

Fuel Tank Vent

Fuel tank venting is required for fuel to flow from the fuel tank to the engine. Inadequate venting allows a vacuum to form in the tank as fuel is drawn from the tank. With continued running the vacuum becomes strong enough to prevent the fuel pump from drawing fuel from the tank. Fuel starvation occurs when the supply of fuel is less than the engine demands. Fuel starvation usually results in decreased power or surging at higher engine speeds. Fuel starvation can also occur at lower speeds causing the engine to stall and not restart.

The vent for a portable tank is incorporated into the fill cap. This allows closing of the vent to prevent fuel spillage when carrying the fuel tank.

The vent system for a built-in fuel tank includes a vent hose at the fuel tank, the vent hose and the hull mounted vent fitting (**Figure 43**). This type of venting system is always open. It is not uncommon for insects to obstruct the vent passages with a nest or their bodies.

If inadequate fuel tank venting is suspected, loosen the fuel tank fill cap (**Figure 43**) slightly to allow the tank to vent. Clean and inspect the fuel tank vent hose and all fittings on built-in fuel tank applications if the fuel starvation symptoms disappear shortly after the cap is loosened.

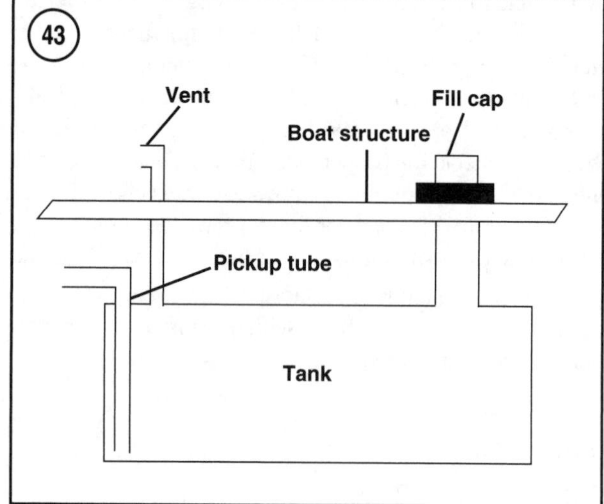

Check the position of the vent screw on the fill cap with applications using portable fuel tanks. Replace the fill cap if the screw is fully open but fuel starvation still occurs.

Antisiphon Devices

An antisiphon device prevents fuel from siphoning from the tank if a leak occurs in the fuel line between the tank and engine. An antisiphon valve is generally used on applications with a built-in fuel tank. The most common type is a spring loaded check valve located at the fuel pickup hose fitting. Other types are the manual valve and solenoid activated valve. Antisiphon devices are an important safety feature and should be bypassed.

CAUTION
Never run an outboard without providing cooling water. Use either a test tank or flush/test device. Always remove the propeller before running the engine on a flush/test device.

The most effective way to test for a faulty antisiphon device if so equipped is using a process of elimination. Run the engine using a portable fuel tank connected directly to the engine fuel pump. Perform this test under actual running conditions. A fault is indicated with the fuel tank pickup, fuel hoses, primer bulb, fuel tank vent or antisiphon device if the engine performs properly while connected to the portable fuel tank. If all fuel hose components are in good condition the malfunction is likely caused by a blocked or faulty antisiphon device. Remove and replace the antisiphon device following the instructions provided with the new component.

Replacement of the antisiphon device requires removal of the fuel hose and possibly the fuel tank pickup. Inspect the faulty valve prior to installing the new one. Clean the fuel tank if significant amounts of debris is found in the antisiphon device or fuel tank pickup. Debris in the fuel tank will usually cause a repeat failure. Inspect all fuel system hoses and filters for blockage if debris is in the fuel tank, fuel tank pickup or antisiphon device. Always correct any fuel system leakage prior to returning the engine to service.

NOTE
Some antisiphon devices can be cleaned instead of replaced. Thoroughly inspect the device for worn, damaged or corroded components. Replace the valve if in questionable condition.

Fuel Pump Test

Failure of the fuel pump (**Figure 44**) can result in inadequate fuel delivery to the engine (fuel starvation), fuel leakage or in some rare cases excessive fuel pressure.

A graduated container suitable for holding fuel and a stopwatch can be used to check the volume of fuel delivered during a specific time frame. This test delivers accurate results however is time consuming and the potential for dangerous fue leakage is always present.

An easier, faster and effective means to check the fuel pump is to have an assistant operate the engine under actual running condition. Vigorously pump the primer bulb when fuel starvation symptoms occur. Thoroughly inspect the fuel pump if the symptoms disappear when pumping the primer bulb. Refer to Chapter Six for fuel pump removal, inspection and repair.

NOTE
Always inspect all fuel filters before testing the fuel system.

Carburetor Testing

The carburetor (**Figure 45**) meters air and fuel to the engine. Movement of the throttle plate in the carburetor controls the air flow into the engine. Air flowing through the carburetor causes fuel flow from the carburetor into the engine. Sized passages in the carburetor control the rate of fuel flow at a given engine speed and throttle opening.

A problem with the carburetor can result in hard starting, rough idle or an inability to run at idle speed. Other symptoms include rough operation and hesitation during acceleration. Poor performance at higher engine speeds and spark plug fouling are other common symptoms.

CAUTION
Always correct problems with the fuel, fuel tank and the fuel pump prior to troubleshooting the carburetor(s).

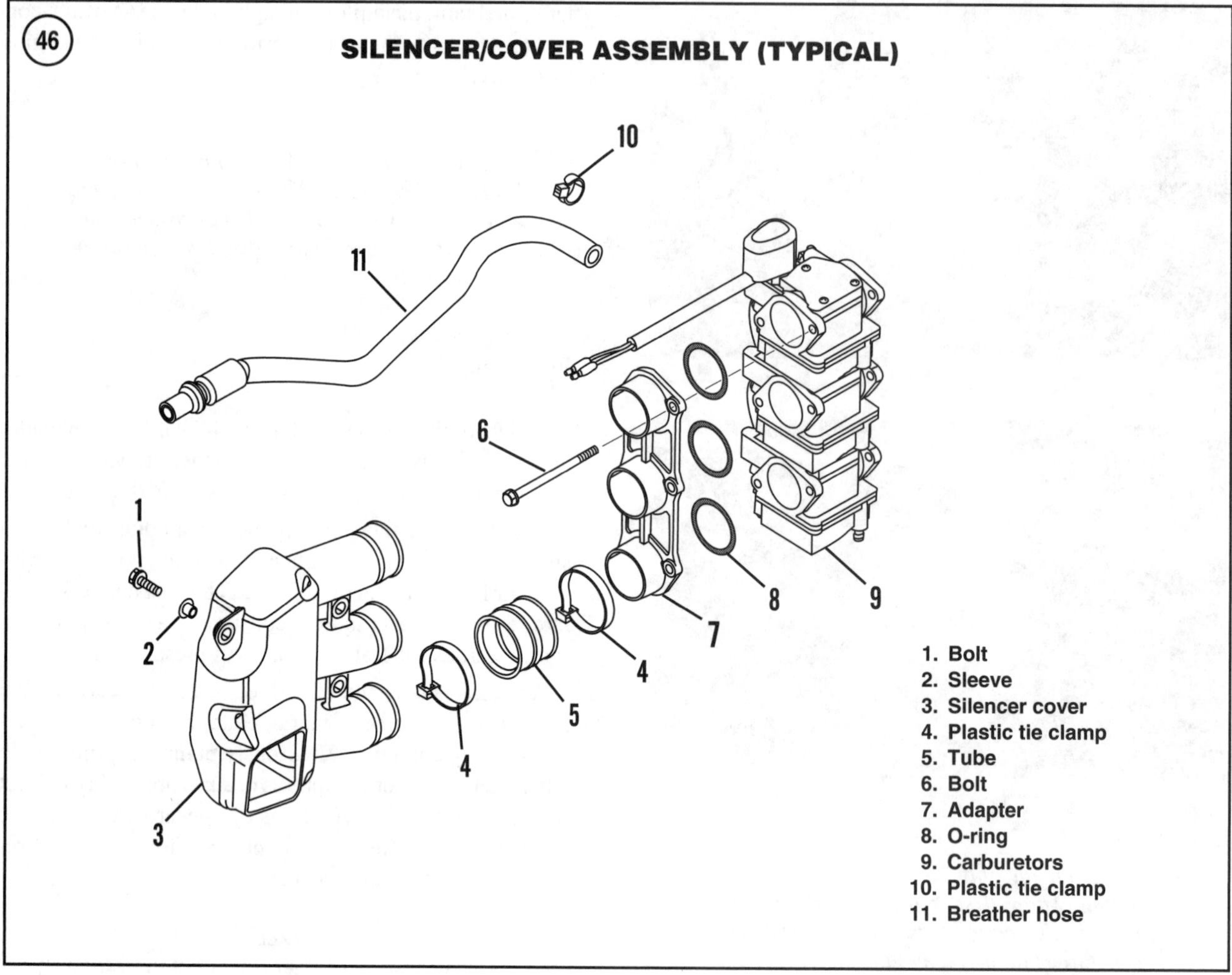

This section provides troubleshooting tips and instructions to help isolate the cause of most carburetor related problems.

1. If hard starting, rough idle or stalling at idle occurs, check the following:
   a. Choke valve malfunction.
   b. Electrothermal valve malfunction.
   c. Flooding carburetor.
   d. Improper carburetor adjustment or synchronization.
   e. Plugged carburetor passages.
2. If rough operation at various engine speeds is noted, check the following:
   a. Improper carburetor adjustment or synchronization.
   b. Choke valve malfunction.
   c. Electrothermal valve malfunction.
   d. Plugged carburetor passages.
   e. Improper float adjustment.
3. If a hesitation is present during acceleration, check the following:
   a. Faulty or misadjusted accelerator pump.
   b. Improper carburetor adjustment or synchronization.
   c. Plugged carburetor passages.
   d. Improper float adjustment.
   e. Flooding carburetor.
   f. Choke valve malfunction.
   g. Electrothermal valve malfunction.
   h. Incorrect propeller.
4. If spark plug fouling or excessive exhaust smoke occurs, check for the following:
   a. Choke valve malfunction.
   b. Electrothermal valve malfunction.
   c. Improper carburetor adjustment or synchronization.
   d. Flooding carburetor.
   e. Plugged carburetor passages.
5. If poor performance at higher engine speeds is occurs, check the following:
   a. Plugged carburetor passages.
   b. Choke valve malfunction.

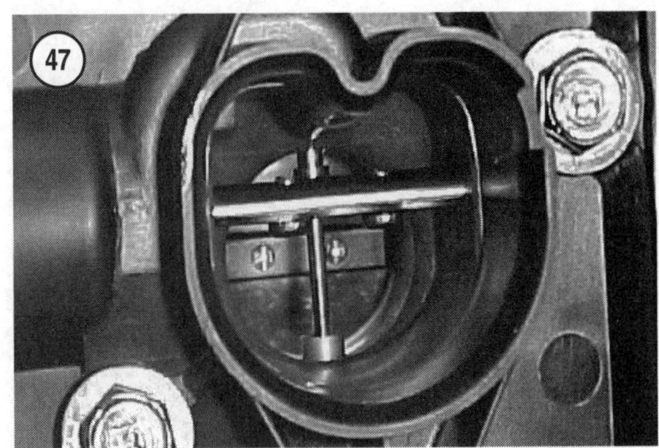
47

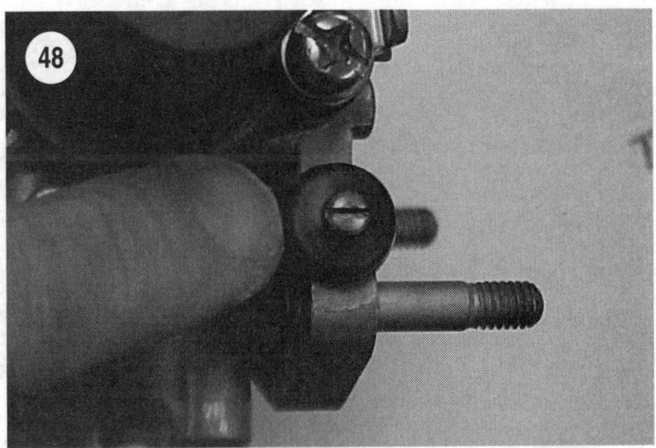
48

c. Improper carburetor adjustments or synchronization.

6. If the engine stalls when the throttle is returned to idle position:

a. Faulty or improperly adjusted dashpot.

b. Improper carburetor adjustment or synchronization.

WARNING

Use extreme caution when working with the fuel system. Fuel is extremely flammable and if ignited can result in injury or death. Never smoke or allow sparks to occur around fuel or fuel vapors. Wipe up any spilled fuel at once with a shop towel and dispose of the shop towel in an appropriate manner Check all fuel hoses, connections and fittings for leaks after any fuel system repair. Correct all fuel system leakage before returning the engine into service.

Flooded Carburetor

A flooded carburetor is generally the result of debris in the needle valve or possibly a worn or damaged needle valve and seat. A misadjusted, damaged or fuel saturated float can also cause carburetor flooding. The result allows excessive amounts of fuel to enter the engine causing stalling or poor low speed operation. In many cases the engine performs satisfactory at higher engine speeds as the engine is able to burn the excess fuel.

Removal of the silencer cover (3, **Figure 46,** typical) followed by visual inspection of the carburetor verifies a flooding condition in most cases. Inspection requires removal of the silencer/cover from the carburetor.

CAUTION

On models 9.9 hp (serial No. OH000058-on), 25 hp, 75 and 90 hp models the silencer cover can be removed without loosening the carburetor mounting bolts. On all other models the silencer cover mounting screws also retain the carburetors to the engine. The carburetors along with gaskets or O-rings can be damaged or fall from position with these bolts removed. Support the carburetors prior to removing the silencer cover/carburetor mounting bolts. Reinstall the mounting bolts after lifting the silencer cover from the carburetor(s). Support the carburetor and install the silencer cover after testing. Do not run the engine with the silencer cover removed.

1. Refer to Chapter Six and remove the silencer cover (3, **Figure 46,** typical).
2. Open the choke valve on models so equipped and look into the front opening of the carburetor (**Figure 47**) while gently squeezing the primer bulb. The presence of fuel flowing from the carburetor opening indicates a flooding condition.
3. Should a flooding condition be detected, remove and repair the affected carburetor as described in Chapter Six.
4. Clean all spilled fuel with shop towels. Install the silencer cover (3, **Figure 46** typical) as described in Chapter Six. Correct any fuel leakage before running the engine.

Incorrect Carburetor Adjustment

Improper carburetor adjustment can result in stalling at idle speed, rough running at idle and/or mid range engine speeds, hesitation during acceleration and excessive exhaust smoke.

All 4-15 hp models are equipped with a single carburetor (**Figure 45**). Adjustment on these models is limited to the idle speed and the pilot screw. Pilot screws (**Figure 48**) are used on 4, 5 and some later 9.9 hp models. Earlier

9.9 hp and all 15 hp models use calibrated low speed fuel orifices and adjustment is not required.

All 25-90 hp models are equipped with multiple carburetors (**Figure 49**). Adjustment on these models is limited to idle speed, carburetor synchronization and dashpot adjustment.

Earlier 50 hp models (prior to 1998) and some non-EPA 75-90 hp models are equipped with pilot adjustment screws. Pilot screws adjust the amount of fuel flowing into the low speed passages. Models without pilot screws use calibrated low speed fuel orifices and adjustment is not required.

Adjust the pilot screw as described in Chapter Five.

On multiple carburetor models, the carburetor throttle plates (**Figure 50**) must open and close at exactly the same time. If not, the engine will idle and run roughly. Carburetor synchronization screws are used on all 25-90 hp models (**Figure 51**). They allow adjustment of the throttle plate opening for each individual carburetor.

On 25-90 hp models, synchronize the carburetors as described in Chapter Five. Refer to **Table 2** and **Table 3** for other items to check if rough operation continues after adjustment.

Improper pilot screw adjustment results in hard starting, stalling at idle, excessive exhaust smoke, hesitation/bogging on acceleration or rough idle. In most cases the symptoms are present at lower engine speeds only.

Choke valve (**Figure 52**) and accelerator pump (**Figure 53**) linkage adjustments are required on some models. Misadjustment can cause hard starting, hesitation during acceleration, stalling at idle and poor performance. Refer to *Choke valve malfunction* in this section for testing instructions.

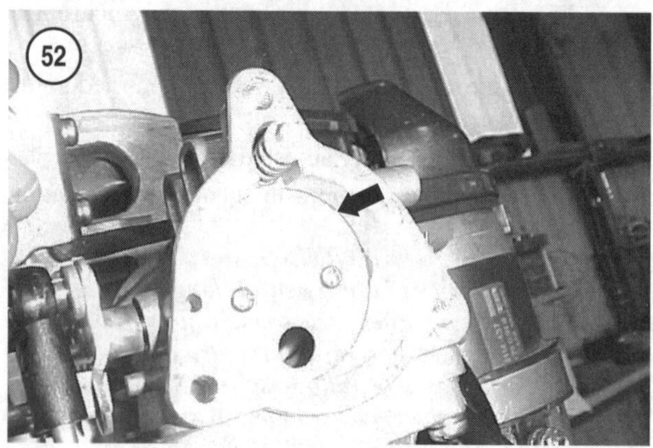

Faulty or Misadjusted Accelerator Pump

A faulty or misadjusted accelerator pump usually causes hesitation during rapid acceleration. Typically the engine performs properly during slow acceleration. Rapid acceleration causes an instantaneous pressure change within the intake manifold. This pressure change causes a momentary decrease in fuel delivery from the carburetor(s) and a potential for hesitation or stalling. The accel-

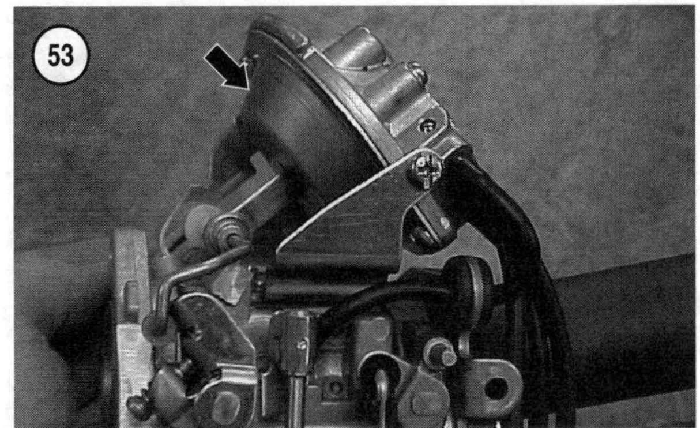

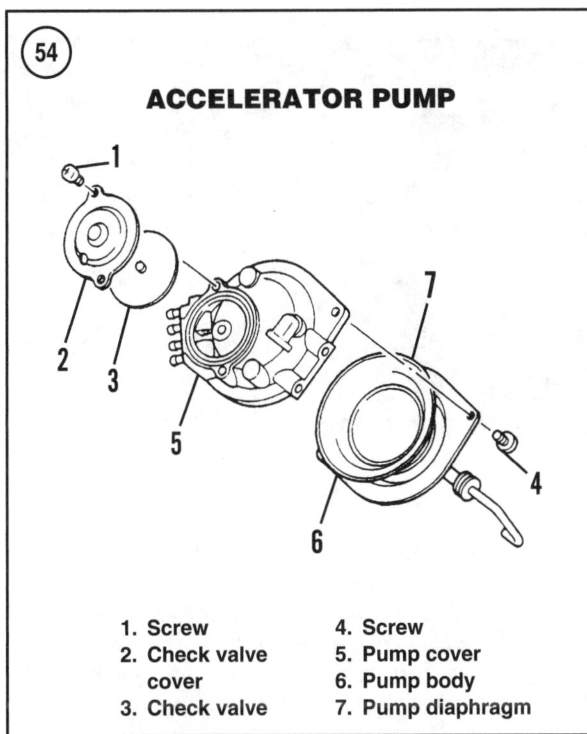

erator pump provides additional fuel to the engine during rapid acceleration.

On 50 hp models, the accelerator pump mounts to the top carburetor (**Figure 53**). Rapid movement of the accelerator pump linkage moves the diaphragm (7, **Figure 54**) in the accelerator pump body. This causes air to flow rapidly through the hoses connected to the carburetors. Rapid flow of air into the carburetor passages provides additional fuel flow into the engine. A disc type valve (3, **Figure 54**) controls air flow into and out of the accelerator pump cavity. During a slower rate of acceleration, the air flowing into the carburetor passages is not rapid enough to cause additional fuel flow. During slower rates of acceleration, the pressure change in the intake manifold is gradual. Special fuel passages in the carburetor provide the fuel needed during slow acceleration.

On 75 and 90 hp models the dashpot provides the accelerator pump function. Refer to *Faulty or misadjusted dashpot* in this chapter for additional information.

On other models, the accelerator pump is integrated into the carburetor (**Figure 55**). Using an internal plunger and check valves, additional fuel is provided to the engine during rapid acceleration. The design of the pump limits the amount of fuel delivered during slower acceleration.

Adjust the accelerator pump linkages if hesitation occurs during rapid acceleration. Refer to Chapter Five for adjustment instructions.

Disassemble, clean and inspect the accelerator pump if symptoms continue after adjustment.

Plugged Carburetor Passages

Plugged jets, passages, orifices or vents in the carburetor can result in excessive fuel (rich condition) or inadequate fuel (lean condition) delivery. Typical symptoms of plugged carburetor passages include difficult starting, surging or misfiring at higher engine speeds or hesitation during acceleration. The symptoms can occur at any engine speed depending on the location and extent of the blockage. With plugged low speed passages the engine may run roughly or stall at idle speed yet run good at higher engine speeds.

Remove, clean and inspect the carburetors if all other fuel system components such as fuel , fuel tank and fuel pump are in good condition, but these symptoms are present. Complete carburetor removal, cleaning, inspection and assembly are covered in Chapter Six.

CAUTION
Continued operation with a lean fuel condition can lead to piston damage and power head failure.

Air Leakage at the Carburetor Mounting Surfaces

Air leakage at the carburetor mounting surface (**Figure 56**, typical) causes air to be drawn into the engine along with the air/fuel mixture. The resulting dilution of the air/fuel mixture causes the engine to operate under an excessively lean condition.

Typical symptoms of an air leak include:

1. A hissing or squealing noise emanating from the engine.
2. Rough idle characteristics.
3. Hesitation during acceleration.
4. Poor high speed performance.
5. Spark plug overheating (Chapter Four).

A common method to locate the leakage is using a spray type lubricant such as WD 40. With the engine running at idle speed, carefully spray the lubricant onto the carburetor mating surface (**Figure 56**). If a leak is present the lubricant is drawn into the engine at the point of leakage. Any change in the idle characteristic indicates leakage at the carburetor mounting surfaces.

Remove the carburetor, spacer if so equipped, and gaskets as described in Chapter Six if leakage is detected. Inspect the gasket surfaces. Replace any seals, gaskets or O-rings the carburetor or intake manifold when they are disturbed. Even small tears or nicks allow sufficient air leakage to cause an engine malfunction.

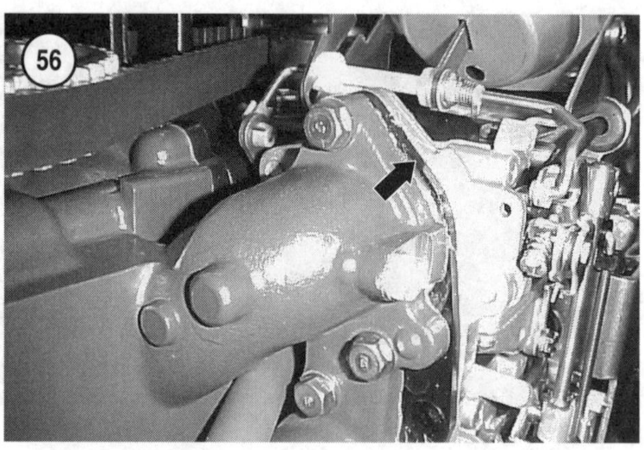

Altitude Adjustments

When operating the outboard motor at high elevation, it is usually necessary to change the carburetor main jets and readjust the carburetors. Higher elevation generally decreases the amount of fuel required for proper operation. Contact a Mercury or Mariner outboard dealer in the area where the engine is operated for jet change or adjustment recommendations. Be aware that carburetor adjustments beyond the factory recommendation may cause damage to the engine.

All 1998-on models have an emissions information decal on the flywheel cover or silencer cover. The information on this decal supersedes other adjustment specifications. Unless specifically recommended by the engine manufacture, do not adjust the outboard outside of the specifications listed on this decal.

CAUTION
Carburetor adjustment or jet changes return the engine to its original settings is required if the engine is later operated at a lower altitude. Internal engine damage can occur if the engine is run at lower altitudes with the higher altitude fuel adjustments.

CAUTION
On 50 hp models, perform choke valve testing only on a completely coolded down engine. These models are equipped with a choke temperature switch that prevents operation of the choke solenoid once the engine reaches operating temperature.

Choke Valve Test

The choke valve provides the additional fuel required to start a cold engine. It restricts air flow into the carburetor opening when activated. Restricting the air flow causes additional fuel to flow into the engine while starting.

This valve pivots on the shaft located at the front opening of the carburetor. When activated it blocks the opening at the front of the carburetor (**Figure 52**) causing a decrease in air and an increase in fuel delivered to the engine.

A malfunctioning choke valve can cause hard starting, rough idle, spark plug fouling or poor performance. The cause is usually sticking or binding linkage or control

58

59

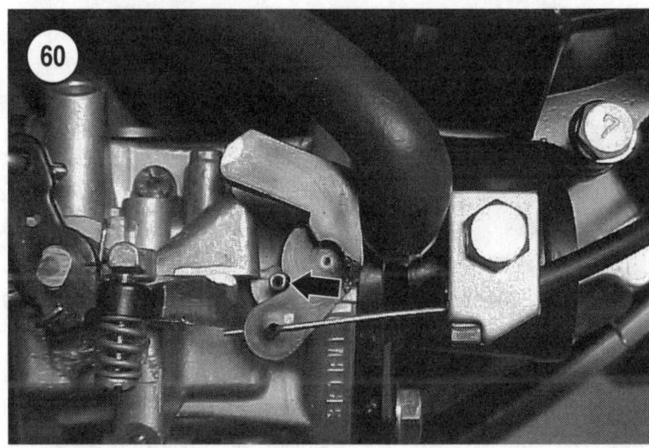
60

mechanism. In some instances the choke solenoid is faulty.

All electric start 9.9 hp (prior to serial No. OH000058), 15 hp and 50 hp models are equipped with a solenoid type motor (A, **Figure 57**) to activate the choke valve. Electric current from the choke switch integrated into the ignition key switch is directed to the choke solenoid. The current flowing through the solenoid causes a magnetic field to form. This magnetic field moves the choke plunger (B, **Figure 57**) and connected linkage. Movement of the linkage causes the choke valve to pivot and block the carburetor opening (**Figure 52**).

When the switch is released the field collapses allowing a spring on the choke valve shaft to open the choke valve (**Figure 58**).

All manual start 4, 5, 9.9 (prior to serial No. OH000058) and 15 hp models are equipped with a manual operated choke valve. To operate the choke simply pull the choke knob (**Figure 59**) out.

Electric start models

Check the operation of the choke valve and solenoid as follows:

1. Remove the silencer/cover (3, **Figure 46**, typical) from the front of the carburetor. Reinstall the carburetor mounting bolts to retain the carburetor during testing.
2. Place the key switch in the RUN position.
3. Note the position of the choke valves. The valves must be fully open.
4. Have an assistant push the key switch IN. The choke valves should now be fully closed (**Figure 52**).
5. If the choke system does not function as described, proceed as follows:
   a. Thoroughly clean all choke linkage and pivot points.
   b. Check for bent linkage and repair or replace as required.
   c. Test the choke solenoid as described under *Choke Solenoid Resistance* in this chapter.
   e. Adjust the choke linkage as described in Chapter Five.
   f. Install the silencer cover.

Manual start models (4-6 hp)

1. Push the choke knob to the fully IN position (**Figure 59**).
2. Note the alignment of the spring stop and choke lever. The spring stop should be aligned with the notch in the choke lever as shown in **Figure 60**.
3. Pull the choke knob outward until fully extended.
4. The spring stop should now be aligned with the highest cam surface of the choke lever (**Figure 61**).
5. If necessary, adjust the choke cable or linkage as described in Chapter Five.

Manual start models (9.9 and 15 hp)

Check for correct manual choke operation as follows:

1. Push the choke knob fully inward (**Figure 59**).
2. With the choke knob fully in, the choke lever (**Figure 62**) should contact the stop on the carburetor.
3. Pull the choke knob outward until fully extended.
4. The tab on the choke lever should contact the stop (B, **Figure 61**) on the carburetor.
5. Adjust the choke as described in Chapter Five if necessary.

Choke Solenoid Resistance (All Models Except 50 hp)

NOTE
The choke solenoid can be tested without removing it from the power head. Remove the solenoid only if necessary to access the solenoid wires.

1. Disconnect the negative battery cable from the battery. Disconnect both choke solenoid (**Figure 63**) wires from the engine harness.
2. Connect an ohmmeter between the solenoid wires and note the resistance. Replace the solenoid (Chapter Six) if its resistance is not as specified in **Table 13**.
3. Reconnect the solenoid black wire to the engine harness.
4. Connect the ohmmeter between the solenoid blue wire and a good engine ground. Continuity should be present between the blue wire and ground. If not, check the black wire for a clean, tight connection and make sure the solenoid is securely mounted.

Choke Solenoid Resistance (50 hp Models)

1. Disconnect the cables from the battery. Disconnect both choke solenoid wires (**Figure 64**) from the main engine harness.
2. Connect the positive ohmmeter lead to the blue wire leading to the choke solenoid and the negative meter lead to the black wire.
3. Replace the solenoid if its resistance is not as specified.
4. Test the choke temperature switch, ignition key switch and associated wiring if the choke fails to operate yet the choke resistance is correct. Test instructions for the choke temperature switch and ignition switch are provided in this chapter.
5. Clean the wire harness terminals then connect the solenoid wire terminals to the engine wire harness. Clean the terminals then connect the cables to the battery.

Choke temperature switch test

The choke temperature switch prevents operation of the choke solenoid once the engine reaches normal operating

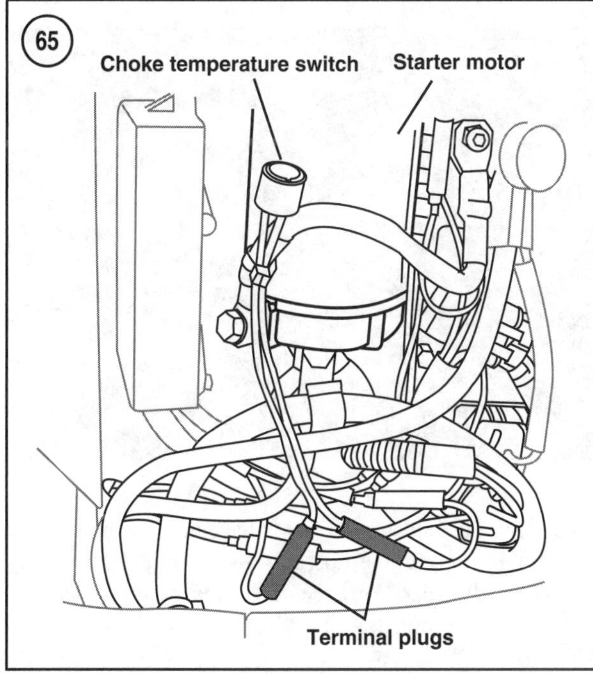

temperature. This component is used on late 50 hp models. A retrofit kit (mercury part No. 87-852420A 1) is available to install on older units experiencing warm engine starting difficulty.

A faulty switch can allow the choke to operate even if the engine is warm. Choke operation with a warm engine can cause flooding and hard starting.

A faulty switch can prevent operation of the choke when the engine is cold.

The switch clamps to the large cable leading to the starter motor (**Figure 65**). The switch opens when the surrounding air temperature reaches approximately 110° F (44° C). Test specifications for the switch are not available. However, the switch can be tested for basic operation using an ohmmeter and portable hair or heat gun.

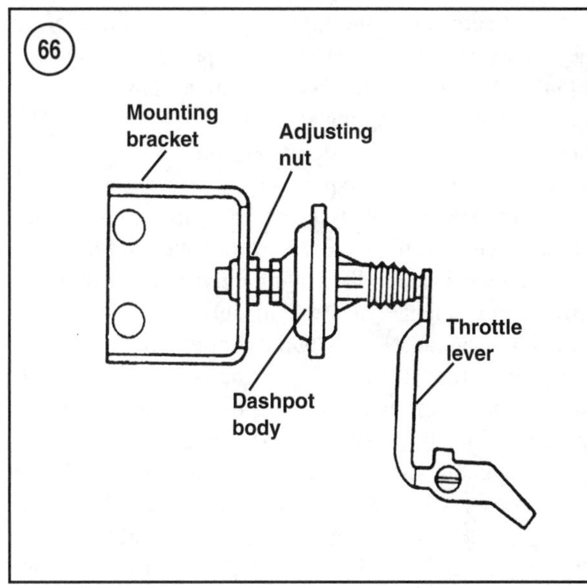

1. Disconnect both cables from the battery. Cut the plastic tie strap retaining the choke temperature switch to the starter cable.
2. Disconnect the wires connecting the switch to the engine harness. Lift the switch from the engine and place it in a refrigerator or other cool area.
3. Remove the switch from the refrigerator and place it on a work surface. Ensure the work surface is at normal room temperature.
4. Connect the positive ohmmeter lead to the blue/yellow wire and the negative lead to the blue wire.
5. The meter should indicate continuity with the switch cold.
6. Warm the choke temperature switch using a heat gun or hair dryer while observing the ohmmeter.
7. The switch should open when its temperature reaches approximately 110° F (44° C).
8. Replace the choke temperature switch if it does not function as specified.
9. Reconnect the switch to the engine harness. Connect the battery cables to the battery.

Faulty or misadjusted dashpot

Rapid closing of the throttle can cause engine stalling under certain conditions. A dashpot (**Figure 66**) is utilized on all 50-90 hp models to prevent a rapid closing of the throttle plates. The diaphragm in dashpot body traps air as the throttle is opened. The dashpot plunger contacts the throttle as the throttle returns to idle position. A cushion effect occurs as the diaphragm moves the trapped air through a calibrated orifice. The cushion effect created by the diaphragm allows the engine speed to stabilize before the throttle returns to the normal idle position.

On 50 hp models, the dashpot plunger is moved outward by an internal spring as the throttle is opened. The plunger contacts the throttle linkage only when the throttle is placed near the idle position.

On 75 and 90 hp models the dashpot linkage (A, **Figure 67**) connects directly to the throttle linkage. This arrangement allows instant diaphragm movement with rapid throttle movement. On these models the dashpot also functions as an accelerator pump. Rapid throttle opening causes air to rush from the dashpot housing to the individual carburetors through dedicated hoses. This rush of air causes additional fuel delivery to the engine. During slow throttle opening additional fuel is not delivered as the air flows to the carburetors at a slower rate. A check valve is integrated into the hoses connecting to the carburetors. It prevents air and fuel from flowing toward the dashpot during deceleration.

Failure of the dashpot is almost always the result of a damaged or leaking diaphragm. On 50 hp models it is difficult to check for a problem with the diaphragm. On these models, adjust the dashpot as described in Chapter Five. Replace the dashpot if stalling during rapid deceleration and correct adjustment is verified.

On 75 and 90 hp models, test for a leaking diaphragm as follows:

1. Disconnect both cables from the battery.
2. Advance the remote control lever to the full throttle position. Carefully pull the hose (B, **Figure 67**) from it fitting on the dashpot.
3. Block the opening in the fitting with a finger. Have an assistant move the remote control lever to the idle position while observing the throttle linkage (A, **Figure 67**).
4. Replace the dashpot if the throttle linkage extends to the idle position when the throttle is moved.
5. Observe the throttle linkage when removing a finger from the opening in the fitting.
6. Replace the dashpot if the linkage fails to return to the idle position when the opening in the fitting is uncovered.
7. Slide the hose onto the fitting on the dashpot (B, **Figure 67**).
8. Clean the terminals and connect the cables to the battery.

Electrothermal Valve Malfunction

NOTE
*The electrothermal valve will not operate properly unless the throttle is **closed** while starting the engine. Refer to the owner's manual for the engine starting procedure.*

Failure of the electrothermal valve can cause hard starting, rough cold engine operation, stalling at idle speed, excessive idle speed or excessive exhaust smoke at idle and low engine speeds.

On 9.9 hp models (serial No. OH000058-on) the electrothermal valve mounts to the top side of the carburetor (**Figure 68**). It provides additional fuel to the engine during cold start and warm up. The additional fuel flows directly into the engine through passages in the carburetor.

On 25-40 hp models the electrothermal valve mounts in a recess provided in the top carburetor (**Figure 69**). It provides additional fuel to the engine during cold start and warm up using passages in the carburetor.

On 50 hp models the electrothermal valve mounts to the side of the intake manifold (**Figure 70**). It provides for a faster idle speed during cold start and engine warm up. Using a moveable plunger it holds the throttle slightly open when the engine is cold. As the engine runs the plunger gradually closes allowing the throttle to return to the normal idle position.

On 75 and 90 hp models an electrothermal valve (**Figure 71**) is affixed to both the top and No. 3 carburetors. They provide additional fuel to the engine during cold start and warm up using internal passages and external hoses. The top electrothermal valve provides additional fuel for the top and No. 2 cylinders. The electrothermal valve mounted to the No. 3 carburetor provides additional fuel for the No. 3 and No. 4 cylinders.

On 25-40 hp models, electric current is supplied to the electrothermal valve using a dedicated power source coil under the flywheel. Movement of the flywheel magnets next to this coil produces AC current.

On 75 and 90 hp models, current is supplied to the electrothermal valve by the battery charge coil via wires connected to the engine control unit.

Heat is produced as this current passes through a coil inside the electrothermal valve. This heat is conducted to a wax pellet in the valve. When heated, the wax pellet expands and moves the plunger portion of the valve outward. Movement of the plunger causes the additional fuel or higher idle speed to gradually cease. The amount of heat produced in the electrothermal valve is directly related to run time, engine speed and the engine temperature

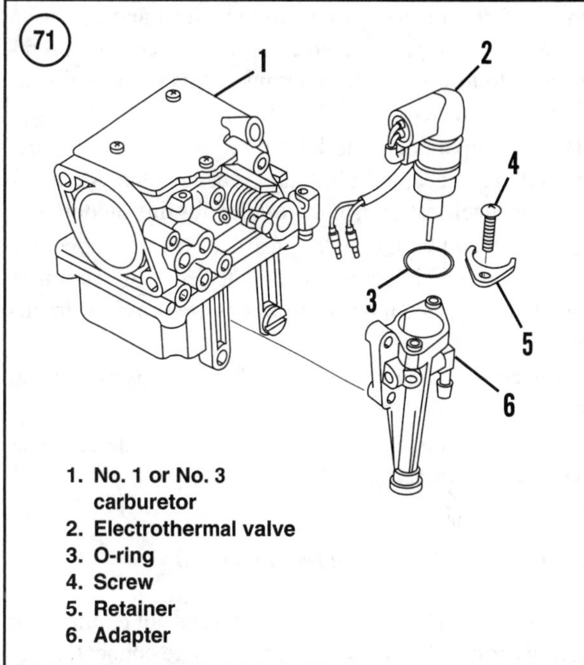

1. No. 1 or No. 3 carburetor
2. Electrothermal valve
3. O-ring
4. Screw
5. Retainer
6. Adapter

gain during warm up. After switching the engine off, the electrothermal valve cools along with the engine. When cool the plunger moves to a position providing additional fuel or faster idle speed. This allows for automatic temperature compensation and smoother cold engine operation.

Failure of the electrothermal valve can be caused by a failure of the power source coil, failure of the internal heat producing coil or a failure to generate plunger movement. Testing of the valve involves checking for coil heating, coil resistance testing, power source resistance testing and checking for plunger movement. Check for coil heating then perform the additional testing as indicated.

Electrothermal valve coil heating test

This test requires running the engine on a test tank or under actual running conditions. Perform this test only on a cold flushing device, in an engine.

1. Attach a flushing device to the gearcase as described in Chapter Four.
2. On 50 hp models, carefully pull the insulated cover from the electrothermal valve (**Figure 72**).
3. Have an assistant start the engine. Touch the body of the electrothermal valve and note the presence of heat as the engine runs.
4. A gradual increase in valve temperature should occur as the engine runs. It make take a few minutes before noticing increasing heat.

5A. On 9.9 hp (serial No. OH000058-on) and 25-40 hp models, test the power source coil resistance and coil resistance following the instructions in this section if heating is not detected.

5B. On 50 hp models check for plunger movement as described in this chapter if heating is not detected. A coil resistance specification is not provided for this model.

5C. On 75 and 90 hp models, test the coil resistance and charging system if heating is not detected. Coil resistance and charging system test instructions are provided in this chapter.

6. Check for plunger movement if symptoms persist and coil heating is detected.

7. On 50 hp models, carefully slide the insulated cover over the electrothermal valve.

Electrothermal valve coil resistance test

Removal of the electrothermal valve is not required for testing provided there is access to the wire connectors for the valve. For accurate test result, use a digital ohmmeter for this test.

1. Disconnect both cables from the battery if so equipped. Refer to the wiring diagrams located at the end of the manual to identify the electrothermal valve wires.
2. Note the wire routing and connection points then carefully disconnect the electrothermal valve wires from the engine wire harness.
3. Connect the meter to the wires in **Table 12**.
4. Compare the resistance with the specification in **Table 12**. Replace the electrothermal valve as described in Chapter Six if resistance is not as specified.
5. On 75 and 90 hp models, repeat Steps 2-5 for the remaining electrothermal valve.
6. Clean the terminals then connect the cables to the battery if so equipped.

Power source coil resistance test

The power source coil for the electrothermal valve is integrated into the stator assembly (**Figure 73**). The coil is located beneath the flywheel on all models. Removal of the coil is not required for testing provided there is access to the wires. To ensure accurate test results use a digital ohmmeter when testing this component.

1. Disconnect both cables from the battery.
2. Refer to the following information to identify the wire colors leading to the power source coil.
   a. On 9.9 hp models (serial No. OH000058-on), the coil wires are black.

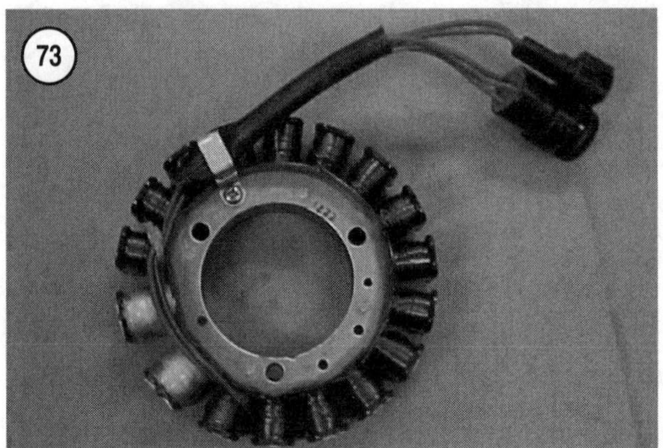

   b. On 25, 30 and 40 hp models, the coil wires are yellow/black.
   c. On 75 and 90 hp models, the coil wires are black and blue.
3. Disconnect the power source from the engine wire harness.
4. Connect the ohmmeter to the power source coil wires indicated in **Table 14**.
5. Compare the resistance with the specification in **Table 15**. Replace the power source coil if the resistance is not as specified. Power source coil removal and installation instruction is covered in Chapter Seven.
6. Connect the power source coil to the engine wire harness.
7. Clean the terminals and connect the cables to the battery if so equipped.

Electrothermal valve plunger movement test

WARNING

Use extreme caution when working around batteries. Never smoke or allow sparks to occur in or around a battery. Batteries pro-

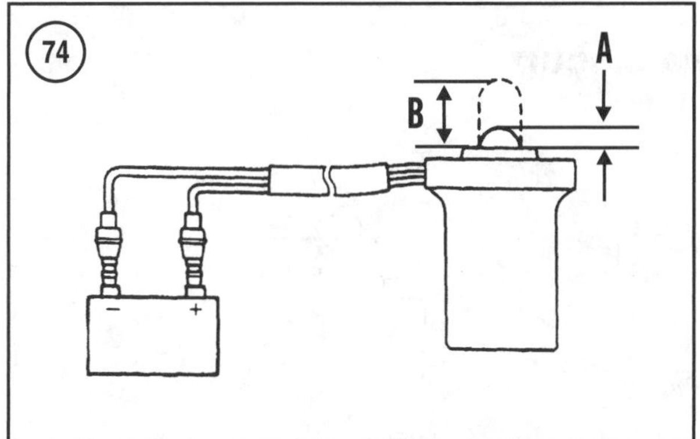

duce explosive hydrogen gas that can explode and result in injury or death. Never make the final connection of a circuit to the battery terminal as an arc may occur leading to fire or explosion.

This test checks for electrothermal valve movement when applying a power source. A fully charged battery, jumper wires and a small ruler are required to perform this test.

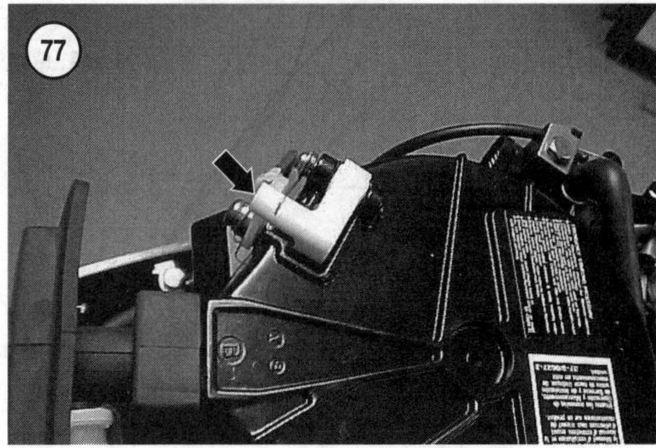

1. Refer to Chapter Six and remove the electrothermal valve from the engine.
2. Measure the plunger extension at the points indicated (A, **Figure 74**). Record the measurement.
3. Using a jumper lead connect one lead of the electrothermal valve to the positive terminal of a fully charged battery (**Figure 74**).
4. Using a jumper lead connect other lead of the electrothermal valve to the negative terminal of a fully charged battery (**Figure 74**).
5. Maintain the connections for 5-7 minutes continue at Step 6.
6. With all leads connected to the battery measure and record the plunger extension at the points indicated in B, **Figure 74**.
7. Compare the measurement in Step 2 with measurement in Step 6. Replace the electrothermal valve if no difference in measurement is indicated.
8. Install the electrothermal valve as described in Chapter Six.

STARTING SYSTEM

All 4-6 hp models are equipped with a manual starter (**Figure 75**). A manual or electric starter (**Figure 76**) is available on all 9.9-40 hp models. All 50-90 hp models are equipped with an electric starter.

Manual Starter

Binding, slipping or roughness when the rope is pulled indicates a possible problem with the manual starter. A faulty or maladjusted neutral start mechanism (**Figure 77**) can prevent the starter from operating. Binding, slipping or failure to engage the flywheel is usually caused by contamination or broken or excessively worn components. If necessary, repair the manual starter as described in Chap-

(78)

TYPICAL STARTING CIRCUIT

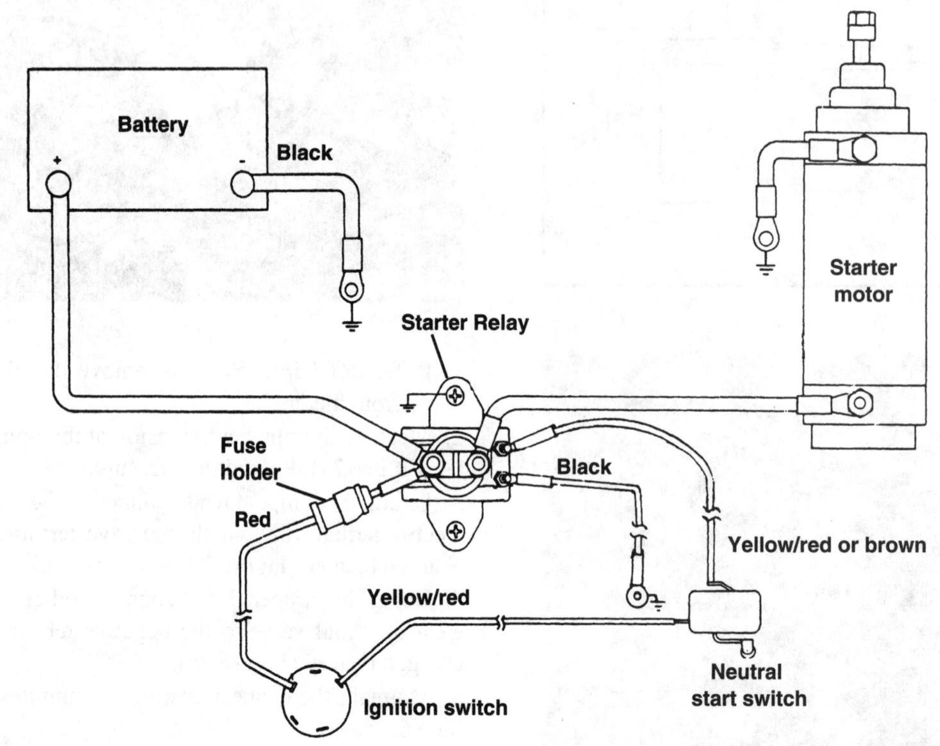

Battery
+
-
Black
Starter motor
Starter Relay
Fuse holder
Red
Black
Yellow/red or brown
Yellow/red
Neutral start switch
Ignition switch

ter Ten. Neutral start mechanism adjustment is covered in Chapter Five.

Electric Start Models

The major components of the electric starting system (**Figure 78**) include the battery, ignition switch, starter motor, starter relay, neutral start switch and associated wiring.

The starter motor (**Figure 76**) is similar in design to those used on automotive applications. Its mounting location allows the starter drive (**Figure 79**) to engage the flywheel ring gear during operation. A neutral switch prevents the starter motor from operating when the engine is shifted into forward or reverse gear.

The starter motor is capable of producing substantial torque, but only for a short time without overheating. To be able to produce the required torque, the starting system requires a fully charged battery that is in good condition. Weak or undercharged batteries are the leading cause of starting system problems. Battery maintenance and testing are covered in Chapter Seven.

(79)

Electric starter operation

Operation of the starter circuit begins at the ignition switch (**Figure 78**) or starter button on tiller control models. This switch or button connects to the positive terminal of the battery. When the switch is activated, current travels from the ignition switch or starter button through the neutral start switch to the starter relay. One large terminal of the starter relay connects to the positive terminal of the

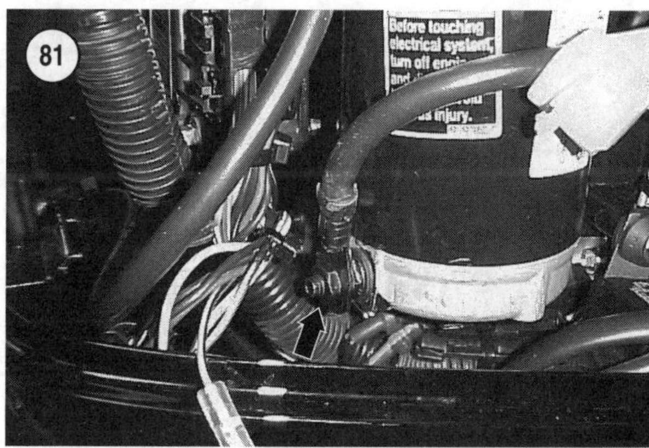

battery. The other large terminal connects to the starter motor. The starter motor (**Figure 76**) mounts and is grounded to the cylinder block.

Activation of the starter relay occurs when current is applied to it from the ignition switch or starter button. When activated, internal switching connects both large terminals (**Figure 80**) to one another. Essentially the starter relay connects the battery positive terminal to the starter motor. This allows remotes switching of the current flow required by the starter motor using the shortest practical wire length. The inertia effect combined with the helical armature shaft causes the starter drive to move upward and engage the flywheel ring gear.

Releasing the ignition switch or starter button deactivates the starter relay and current flow to the starter motor stops. The spring above the starter drive gear (**Figure 79**) pushes the drive gear away from the flywheel and the starter motor stops spinning. Accumulated dirt or grease can prevent the starter drive gear from engaging or disengaging the flywheel ring gear. Clean and lubricate the armature shaft as described in Chapter Four.

The neutral start switch allows current flow to the starter relay only when the engine is in neutral. The neutral start switch opens the circuit when forward or reverse gear is selected preventing activation of the starter relay.

CAUTION

Never operate the starter motor for over 10 seconds without allowing at least 2 minutes to cool. Operating the electric starter motor with an undercharged battery can result in starter motor overheating and subsequent failure.

Starter Motor Cranking Voltage Test

WARNING

Use extreme caution when working around batteries. Never smoke or allow sparks to occur in or around batteries. Batteries produce explosive hydrogen gas that can explode and result in injury or death. Never make the final connection of a circuit to the battery terminal as an arc may occur leading to fire or explosion.

This test measures the voltage delivered to the starter motor while cranking the engine. A voltmeter is required to check the voltage. A seized gearcase or power head must be ruled out before repairing or replacing any starting system components.

1. Remove the propeller following the instruction listed in Chapter Nine. Shift the engine into neutral. Reconnect the battery cables after removing the propeller.
2. Connect the positive meter lead to the large terminal at the starter motor (**Figure 81**).
3. Connect the negative meter lead to a suitable engine ground.
4. Disconnect all spark plug leads and connect them to a suitable engine ground. Observe the voltmeter while operating the starter motor.
5. Repair or replace the starter motor if the voltage is 9.5 volts or greater but the engine does not crank or cranks slowly. Refer to Chapter Seven for starter motor repair or replacement.
6. A voltage of less that 9.5 indicates a faulty battery, wires or connections, ignition switch, starter button on tiller control models or neutral start switch. Refer to Chapter Seven and test the battery if low voltage in indicated.
7. Test all starting system components as described in this chapter.
8. Disconnect both battery cables and install the propeller.

Starter Relay Test

Two separate tests are required to properly test the relay. The first test checks for voltage at the starter relay as the start switch or button is activated.

The second test is a functional test to verify proper internal switching. Perform this test if test results indicate correct voltage at the relay. Use a multimeter, short jumper wires and a fully charged battery to perform the functional test.

On 9.9 and 15 hp models, the starter relay is mounted to a bracket at the front port side of the power head just forward of the starter motor.

On 25-40 hp models, the starter relay is mounted to the port side of the power head between the starter motor and oil filter.

On 50 hp models, the starter relay is mounted to a bracket on the front side of the power head at the port side of the starter motor.

On 75 and 90 hp models, the starter relay is mounted to the front of the power head directly above the trim system relays.

Relay voltage test

WARNING
Use extreme caution when working around batteries. Never smoke or allow sparks to occur in or around batteries. Batteries produce explosive hydrogen gas that can explode and result in injury or death. Never make the final connection of a circuit to the battery terminal as an arc may occur and lead to fire or explosion.

1. Disconnect both cables from the battery. Remove the spark plugs (Chapter Four) and connect the spark plug leads to a suitable engine ground.
2. Remove the propeller as described in Chapter Nine and reconnect the cables to the battery.
3. Connect the negative voltmeter lead to a suitable engine ground. Move the insulated cover aside to access the battery positive cable attached to the starter relay (**Figure 82**). Note the voltmeter and touch the positive voltmeter lead to the battery cable.
   a. Battery voltage should be noted.
   b. If less than battery voltage is noted, check for defective battery cables, loose or corroded connections.
4. Disconnect the starter relay exciter wire from the starter relay as follows:
   a. On 9.9, 15 and 50 hp models, disconnect the brown relay wire from the yellow/red wire.

   b. On 25-40 hp models, remove the small nut then lift the yellow/red wire from the starter relay.
   c. On 75 and 90 hp models, disconnect the brown relay wire from the brown wire of the engine wire harness.
5. Reconnect the cables to the battery. Connect the voltmeter to the engine wire harness as follows.
   a. On 9.9-50 hp models, connect the positive test lead to the disconnected yellow/red wire. Connect the negative test lead to the starter mounting bolt (**Figure 83**).
   b. On 75 and 90 hp models, connect the positive test lead to the disconnected brown wire. Connect the negative test lead to the starter mounting bolt (**Figure 83**).
6. Note the meter reading without activating the starter button or ignition key switch. The correct meter reading is 0 volts with the starter button or ignition key switch at rest. A faulty starter button, ignition key switch or wire harness is indicated if voltage is detected.
   a. On remote control models, place the ignition key switch in the ON position. Do not select the start position. Note the meter reading. A faulty ignition

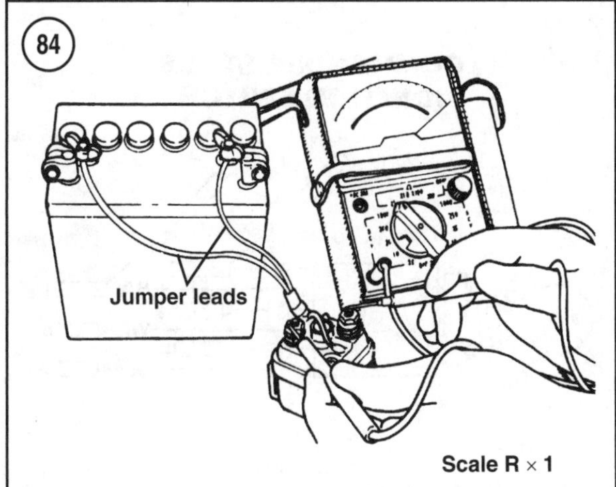

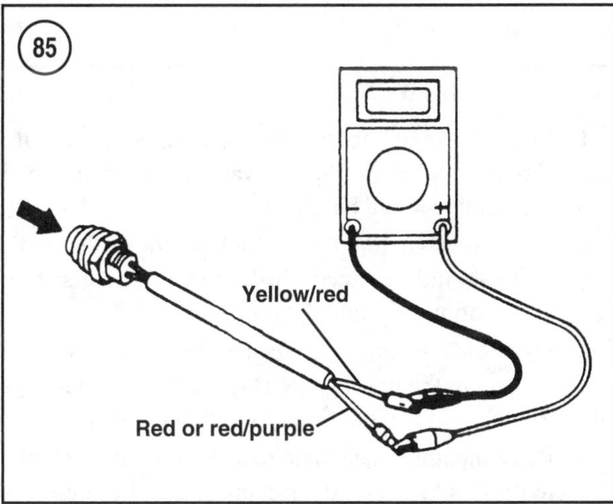

switch, wire terminal or wire harness is indicated if voltage is detected. Test the ignition switch as described in this section. Refer to *Fuses And Wire Harness* in this chapter if the ignition switch is in working condition.

7. Observe the meter reading as an assistant operates the starter button or places the ignition switch in the START position. The correct test result is 12 volts or higher as the button or switch is activated.

   a. Test the wire harness fuses for missing, loose or blown fuses if no voltage is noted. Refer to *Fuses and Wire Harness* in this chapter.

   b. Test the neutral start switch, starter button and ignition switch if less than battery voltage is measured.

8. Disconnect the cables from the battery and install the propeller as described in Chapter Nine.

9. Reconnect the brown or yellow/red wire to the starter relay wire or terminal. Install the spark plugs and spark plug leads. Reconnect the cable to the battery.

Starter relay functional test

An ohmmeter, fully charged battery and short jumper leads are required to test the starter relay. Refer to the wire diagrams located at the back of the manual to identify starter relay.

1. Disconnect both cables from the battery. Remove the starter relay as described in Chapter Seven.
2. Place the electric starter relay on a suitable work surface far away from any flammable substance.
3. Connect the positive meter lead securely to one of the larger diameter terminals (**Figure 84**) on the relay. Connect the negative meter lead securely to the other larger diameter terminal (**Figure 84**). The correct result is no continuity.
4. Connect one end of a jumper lead to the black wire or either of the smaller diameter wire terminals of the relay (**Figure 84**). Connect the other end of this jumper lead securely to the negative terminal of a fully charged 12 volt battery (**Figure 84**).
5. Connect one end of a jumper lead to the positive terminal of the 12-volt battery. Touch the other end of the jumper lead to the brown wire terminal or the remaining small diameter terminal of the relay and note the ohmmeter. The ohmmeter should now indicate continuity and an audible click should be heard.
6. Replace the starter relay if it does not perform as described.

Starter Button Test (Tiller Control Models)

A starter button is used on 9.9-25 hp models equipped with a tiller handle. Button removal is not required for testing if there is access to the starter button wires. Refer to the wiring diagrams at the back of the manual to identify the starter button wires.

1. Disconnect the cables from the battery.

2A. On 9.9-25 hp models, disconnect both start button wires from the engine harness and neutral start switch.

2B. On 50 hp models, remove the cover from the transom mounted switch panel. Disconnect the red/purple and yellow/red wires from the starter button.

3. Connect the ohmmeter to the starter button as follows:

   a. On 9.9 and 15 hp models, connect the positive lead to the red wire leading to the starter button and the negative lead to the yellow/red wire (**Figure 85**).

b. On 25 hp models, connect the positive lead to the red/purple wire terminal leading to the starter button and the negative lead to the yellow/red wire (**Figure 85**).

c. On 50 hp models, connect the positive lead to the red/purple wire leading to the starter button and the negative lead to the yellow/red wire.

4. Push the starter button and note the ohmmeter. Continuity should now be present.

5. Replace the starter button as described in Chapter Seven if it fails to operate as described. If the starter button is in good condition, but the starting system fails to operate, test the neutral start switch as described in this chapter.

Ignition Switch Test

The ignition switch is mounted in the remote control on most models. Some models have the ignition switch mounted in the dash of the boat. On 30 and 40 hp models this switch is integrated into a transom mounted switch and button panel.

Access to the switch wires is required for testing. On dash mounted models, remove the ignition switch from the dash to allow access to the wires.

On 30 and 40 hp models, remove the cover from the transom mounted switch and button panel to access the wires.

On remote control models, remove and partially disassemble the control box to access the wires. Refer to Chapter Twelve for remote control box disassembly and assembly.

1. Disconnect both cables from the battery terminals. Shift the engine into neutral.

2. Disassemble the remote control assembly enough to gain access to the ignition switch wires. Disconnect all wires leading to the ignition switch.

3. Connect the positive ohmmeter lead to the black wire terminal leading to the ignition switch and the negative lead to the black/yellow wire key switch (**Figure 86**).

a. With the ignition switch in the OFF position, the ohmmeter should indicate continuity.

b. Place the ignition switch to the ON position. The meter should indicate no continuity. Push the switch inward and note the ohmmeter. No continuity should be noted.

4. Connect the positive meter lead to the red switch wire and the negative meter lead to the yellow/black wire (**Figure 86**).

a. With the switch OFF, the meter should indicate no continuity.

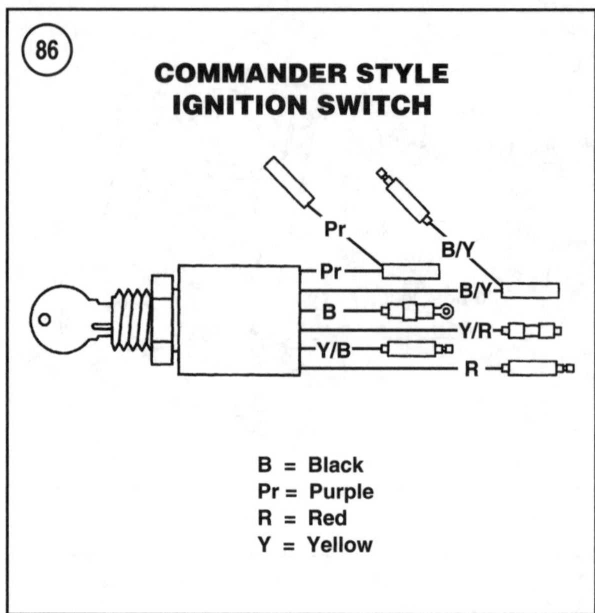

b. Place the switch in the ON position. No continuity should be present. Push inward on the switch and continuity should be noted.

c. Place the switch in the START position. No continuity should be noted. Push inward on the switch and continuity should be noted.

5. Connect the positive meter lead to the red wire and the negative lead to the purple wire (**Figure 86**). With the ignition switch OFF, no continuity should be noted.

a. Place the ignition switch in the ON position. Continuity should be noted. Push inward on the key. Continuity should be noted.

b. Place the ignition switch in the START position. Continuity should be noted. Push inward on the key. Continuity should be noted.

6. Connect the positive meter lead to the red wire and the negative lead to the yellow/red wire (**Figure 86**). With the ignition switch OFF, no continuity should be noted.

a. Place the ignition switch in the ON position. No continuity should be noted. Push inward on the key. No continuity should be noted.

b. Place the ignition switch in the START position. Continuity should be noted. Push inward on the key. Continuity should be noted.

7. Connect the positive meter lead to the red wire and the negative lead to the black wire (**Figure 86**). With the ignition switch OFF, no continuity should be noted.

a. Place the ignition switch in the ON position. No continuity should be noted. Push the key inward. No continuity should be noted.

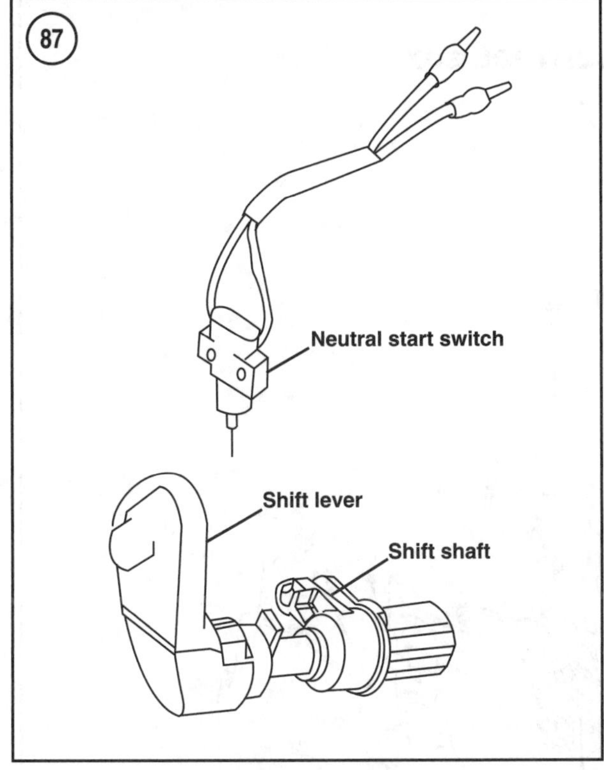

b. Place the ignition switch in the START position. No continuity should be noted. Push the key inward. No continuity should be noted.

8. Replace the ignition switch if it fails to operate as described.

Neutral Start Switch

The neutral start switch (**Figure 87** or 6, **Figure 88**) prevents operation of the starter motor when either forward or reverse gear is engaged. On tiller control 9.9-25 and 50 hp models and all remote control models, it opens the circuit connecting the starter button or ignition switch to the starter relay when activated. On tiller control 30 and 40 hp models the switch opens the ground circuit for the starter relay when activated.

A defective neutral start switch can prevent starter motor operation when in neutral or allow starter operation when forward or reverse gear is selected.

All tiller control models utilize an engine mounted neutral start switch (**Figure 87**). Activation of the switch occurs from direct contact with the shift selector shaft. All remote control models use a remote control mounted neutral start switch (6, **Figure 88**). Activation of the switch occurs from direct contact of the switch with the shift gear (10, **Figure 88**).

Removal of the switch is not required for testing purposes, however it is necessary to access the switch wires. With models using a remote control mounted ignition key switch, removal and partial disassembly of the remote control is usually required to access the wires. With most applications using a dash mounted ignition switch, the wires extend from the bottom or side of the remote control.

Refer to Chapter Twelve for remote control disassembly and assembly. Refer to the wire diagrams located at the back of this manual to identify the neutral start switch wires.

Tiller control models

On most models, the neutral start switch is mounted to the lower front starboard side of the power head. The switch is mounted into the shift lever housing on 9.9 and 15 hp models with the optional front mounted shift lever.

1. Place the shift lever into NEUTRAL. Activate the starter button or ignition key start position for a few seconds only. Correct operation results in operation of the starter motor.

2. Place the shift lever into FORWARD gear. Activate the starter button or ignition key start position. Correct operation prevents operation of the starter motor.

3. Repeat Step 1 and Step 2 with the shift lever in REVERSE.

4. Perform Steps 5-10 if incorrect operation is noted in Steps 1-3.

5. Disconnect both cables from the battery.

6. Shift the engine into NEUTRAL.

7. Disconnect the black neutral start switch wires from the yellow/red, black or brown engine harness wires.

8. Connect the ohmmeter between the two black wires leading to the neutral start switch. With the engine in neutral, the ohmmeter should indicate no continuity.

9. Shift into FORWARD or REVERSE and note the meter. Continuity should be noted when shifted into gear.

10. If the neutral start switch does not function as described, adjust the shift linkage as described in Chapter Five. Replace the switch (Chapter Seven) if it fails to operate properly after adjusting the shift linkage.

Remote control models

The neutral switch is designed to prevent starting system operation if the shift lever is in FORWARD or REVERSE gear. The starting system should operate normally when the shift lever is in NEUTRAL. If the neutral

88

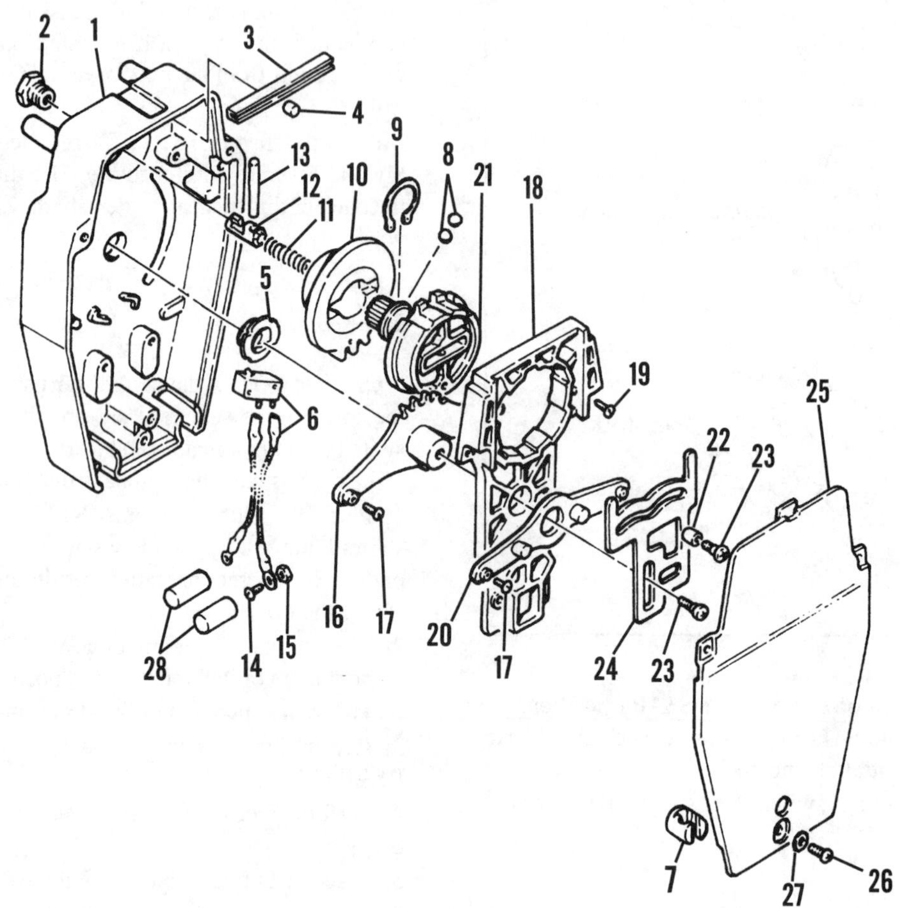

1. Housing
2. Handle lock bolt
3. Detent spring
4. Detent roller
5. Bushing
6. Neutral start Switch
7. Cable anchor
8. Steel balls
9. C-clip
10. Shift gear
11. Shift lock-out spring
12. Shift lock-out shaft
13. Pin
14. Screw
15. Nut
16. Shift arm
17. Screw
18. Support housing
19. Screw
20. Throttle arm
21. Main handle shaft
22. Throttle plate roller
23. Shoulder screw
24. Throttle plate
25. Rear cover
26. Cover screw
27. Washer
28. Insulator

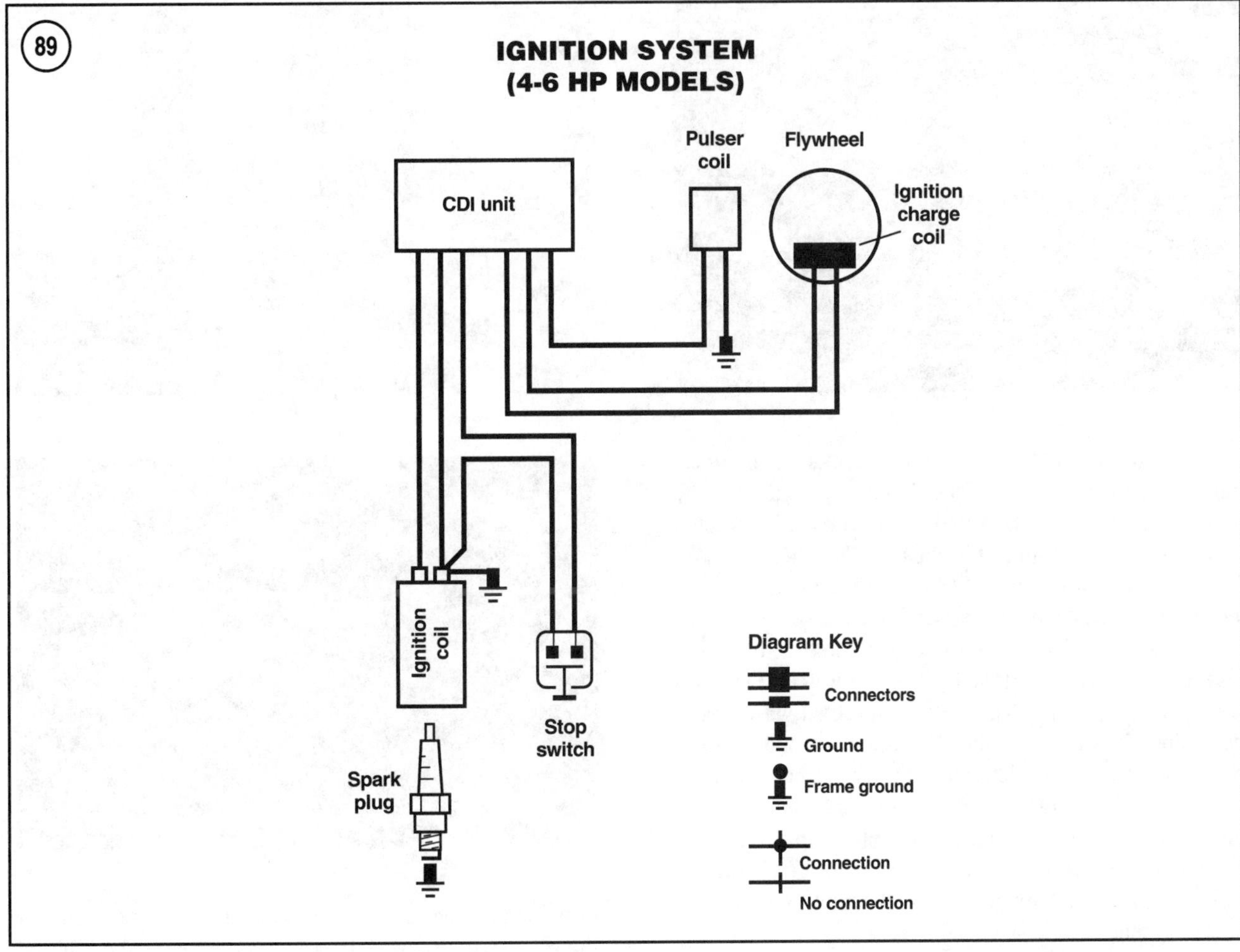

start switch does not operate as described, test the switch as follows.

1. Disconnect both cables from the battery.

2A. *Dash-mounted ignition switch*—Disconnect the two yellow/red wires from the ignition switch.

2B. *Remote control mounted ignition switch*—Remove the rear cover (25, **Figure 88**) as described in Chapter Twelve. Disconnect the yellow/red neutral start switch wires from the wire harness.

3. Connect an ohmmeter between the yellow/red wires.

4. With the shift lever in NEUTRAL, continuity should be noted.

5. While observing the ohmmeter, shift into FORWARD, then REVERSE gears. No continuity should be noted with the shift lever in the FORWARD or REVERSE position.

6. Replace the neutral start switch if it does not perform as described. See Chapter Twelve.

IGNITION SYSTEM

Outboard engines consistently run at a higher speed than most internal combustion engines. This places a greater burden on the ignition system and other engine systems. Proper engine operation is only possible when the ignition system is operating correctly. Spark must be generated at the plugs several thousand times per minute and each spark must occur at exactly the right time.

This section provides a brief description on the various systems used on Mercury and Mariner outboard motors followed by testing instructions for the various components.

Operation (4-6 hp Models)

Electrical current to operate this system is provided by the flywheel and the ignition charge coil. A wiring diagram is provided in **Figure 89**.

90

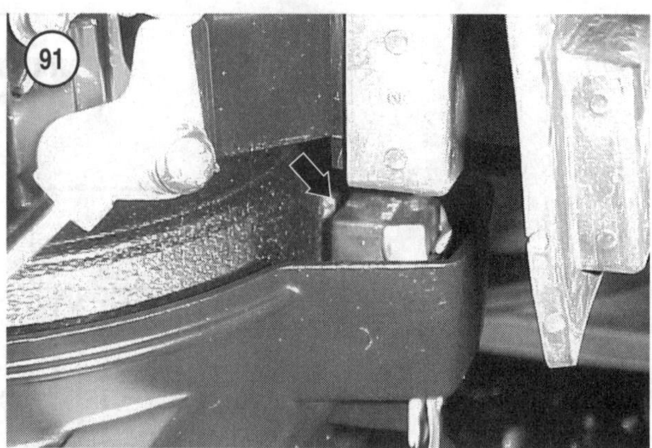
91

Alternating current (AC) is generated as the magnets mounted to the inner ring of the flywheel pass next to the ignition charge coil (**Figure 90**). This current is directed via wires to the CDI unit (**Figure 89**). The CDI unit converts this alternating current (AC) to direct current (DC) and stores it in a capacitor for later release.

A low voltage electrical pulse is generated as the raised boss on the outer ring of the flywheel (**Figure 91**) passes next to the pulser coil. This pulse is directed via wires to the timing circuits within the CDI unit. This pulse allows the timing circuits to determine the crankshaft position relative to TDC. This also allows the CDI unit to accurately compute engine speed. Using the input from the pulser coil, the timing circuits compute the correct time to initiate a spark at the plug. Timing adjustments are not required on these models.

At the computed time these circuits turn on an SCR (silicon controlled rectifier) inside the CDI unit. When turned on this switch directs the electrical current stored in the capacitor to the ignition coil (**Figure 92**). As this current flows through the primary winding in the coil a much higher voltage is developed in the secondary coil winding. This high voltage current is directed to the spark plug through the spark plug lead. The voltage supplied to the spark plug is high enough to jump the plug gap under most operating conditions.

The CDI unit provides automatic spark advancement with increasing engine speed.

This type of ignition system is commonly referred to as a double fire system as the spark plug fires once per flywheel revolution. A spark occurs as the piston is nearing the top of its compression stroke and when the piston is nearing the top of its exhaust stroke. The additional spark is essentially wasted as no or very little fuel remains in the combustion chamber during the exhaust stroke.

When activated, the stop switch directs the current stored in the capacitor to an engine ground. This grounding of the capacitor prevents it from storing the current

92

produced by the ignition charge coil. No spark occurs at the plug as very little current is available for the ignition coil.

This system is extremely reliable and except for routine spark plug cleaning and inspection requires very little maintenance. Problems with this system are usually related to loose or corroded wire connections or a faulty stop circuit.

Operation (9.9 hp [Serial No. OH000057-Prior] and 15 hp Models)

Electrical current to operate this system is provided by the flywheel and the ignition charge coil (**Figure 90**). A wiring diagram is provided in **Figure 93**.

Alternating current (AC) is generated as the magnets mounted to the inner ring of the flywheel pass next to the ignition charge coil (**Figure 93**). This current is directed via wires to the engine control unit (**Figure 93**). The engine control unit converts this alternating current to direct current (DC) and store it in a capacitor for later release.

93

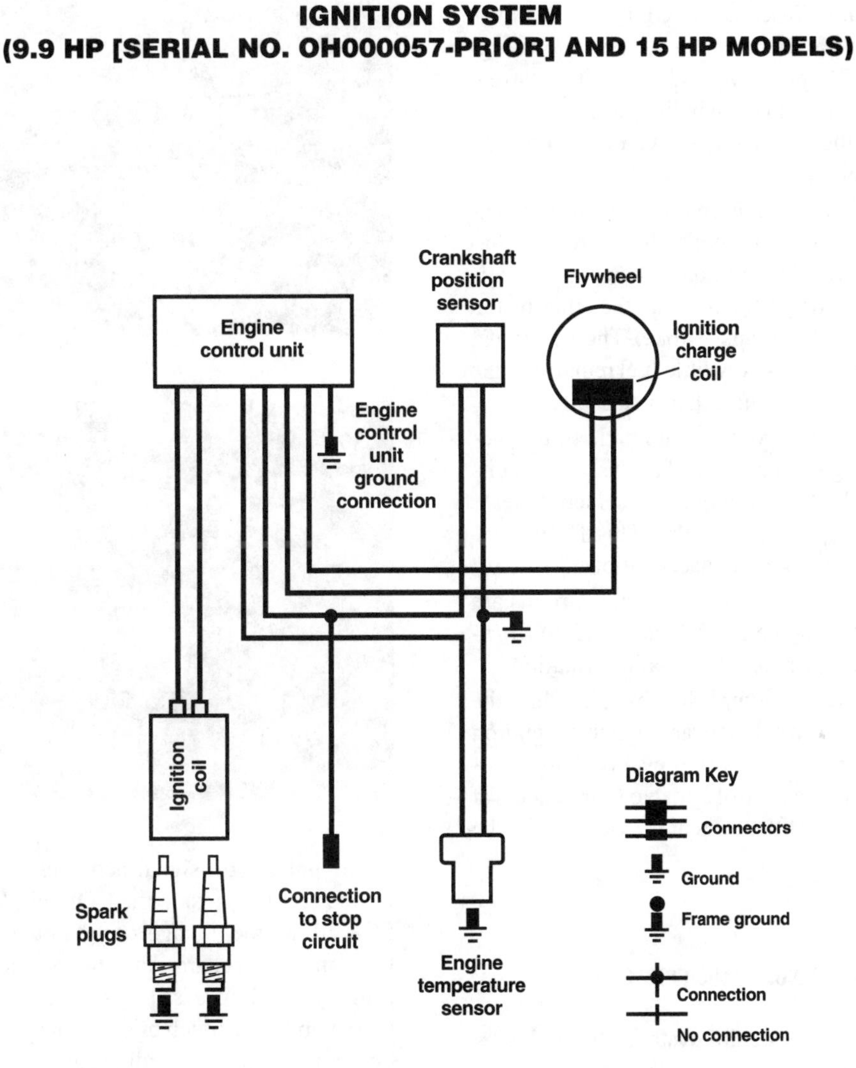

IGNITION SYSTEM
(9.9 HP [SERIAL NO. OH000057-PRIOR] AND 15 HP MODELS)

Crankshaft position sensor
Flywheel
Engine control unit
Ignition charge coil
Engine control unit ground connection
Ignition coil
Spark plugs
Connection to stop circuit
Engine temperature sensor
Diagram Key
Connectors
Ground
Frame ground
Connection
No connection

94

The crankshaft position sensor mounts under the flywheel (**Figure 94**) and aligns with the teeth around the periphery of the flywheel (**Figure 95**). An electric pulse is generated as the flywheel teeth pass the crankshaft position sensor. The width and spacing of the teeth produce a varying pulse as the flywheel rotates. The pulse is directed to the engine control unit, which uses the varying pulses to determine crankshaft position relative to TDC, determine engine speed and initiate spark at the correct time. Using this input the engine control unit calculates the correct ignition timing. Because the engine control unit controls the spark timing, ignition timing adjustment is not required.

At the correct time, the crankshaft position sensor signal activates an SCR (silicon controlled rectifier) inside the engine control unit. When activated, the SCR allows the current stored inside the capacitor to flow into the ignition coil (**Figure 96**) primary winding. As the current flows through the coil primary winding, a much higher voltage develops in the coil secondary windings and is directed to the spark plugs.

This type of ignition system is commonly referred to as a double fire system as both spark plugs fire simultaneously for each flywheel revolution. When one piston is nearing the top of its compression stroke the other piston is nearing the top of its exhaust stroke. The additional spark is essentially wasted as very little fuel remains in the combustion chamber during the exhaust stroke.

The engine control unit provides automatic timing advance with increasing engine speed. These same circuits provide an increased rate of timing advancement when a rapid rise in engine speed is detected. This feature enhances performance during rapid acceleration.

Low oil pressure and overspeed protection circuits are also integrated into the engine control unit. Refer to *Warning Systems* in this chapter for additional information.

Stopping the engine is accomplished by grounding the wire leading to the stop switch, lanyard switch or ignition key switch. Grounding of this wire prevents charging of the capacitor in the engine control unit. No spark occurs at the plugs as none or very little current is available for the ignition coil.

Operation (9.9 hp Models [Serial No. OH000058-On])

Electrical current to operate this system is provided by the flywheel and the ignition charge coil. A wiring diagram is provided in **Figure 97**.

Alternating current (AC) is generated as the magnets mounted to the inner ring of the flywheel pass next to the ignition charge coil (**Figure 98**). This current is directed to the CDI unit (**Figure 97**). The CDI unit converts this alternating current to direct current (DC) and stores it in an internal capacitor for later release.

A low voltage pulse is generated as the magnets mounted to the outer ring of the flywheel (**Figure 99**) pass next to the pulser coil. This pulse is directed to the timing circuit inside the CDI unit. This pulse allow the timing circuit to determine the crankshaft position relative to TDC and allows the CDI unit to accurately compute engine speed. Using the input from the pulser coil, the timing circuit determines the correct time to initiate spark at the plugs. Timing adjustment is not required on this model.

The pulser coil signal activates an SCR (silicon controlled rectifier) inside the CDI unit. When activated, the SCR allows the voltage stored in the capacitor inside the CDI unit to discharge into the ignition coil (**Figure 96**) primary winding. As the voltage flows through the primary winding, a much higher voltage develops in the ignition coil secondary windings and is directed to the spark plugs.

This type of ignition system is commonly referred to as a double fire system as both spark plugs fire simultaneously for each flywheel revolution. When one piston is nearing the top of its compression stroke the other piston is nearing the top of its exhaust stroke. The additional spark is essentially wasted as very little fuel remains in the combustion chamber during the exhaust stroke.

The CDI unit provides automatic timing advance with increased engine speed. The same circuits provide an increased rate of timing advancement when a rapid rise in engine speed is detected. This feature enhances performance during rapid acceleration.

Low oil pressure and overspeed protection functions are also integrated into the CDI unit. Refer to *Warning Systems* in this chapter for additional information.

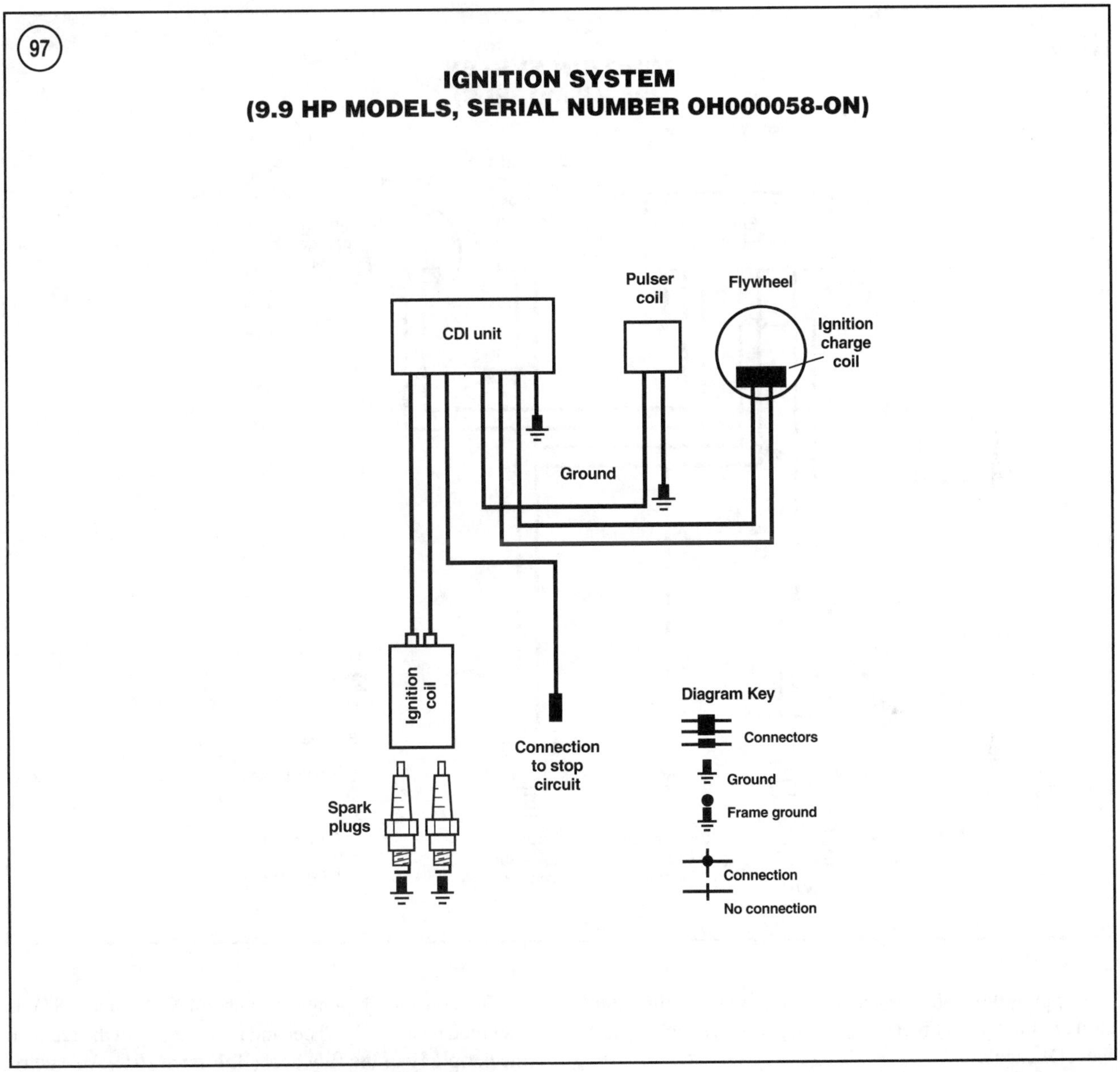

97

IGNITION SYSTEM
(9.9 HP MODELS, SERIAL NUMBER OH000058-ON)

CDI unit
Pulser coil
Flywheel
Ignition charge coil
Ground
Ignition coil
Connection to stop circuit
Spark plugs

Diagram Key
Connectors
Ground
Frame ground
Connection
No connection

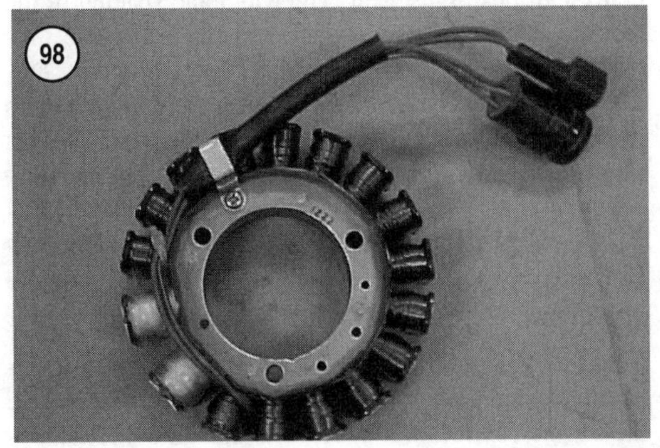

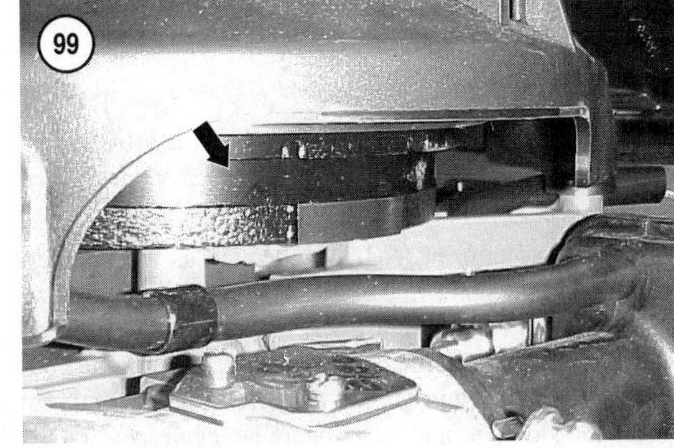

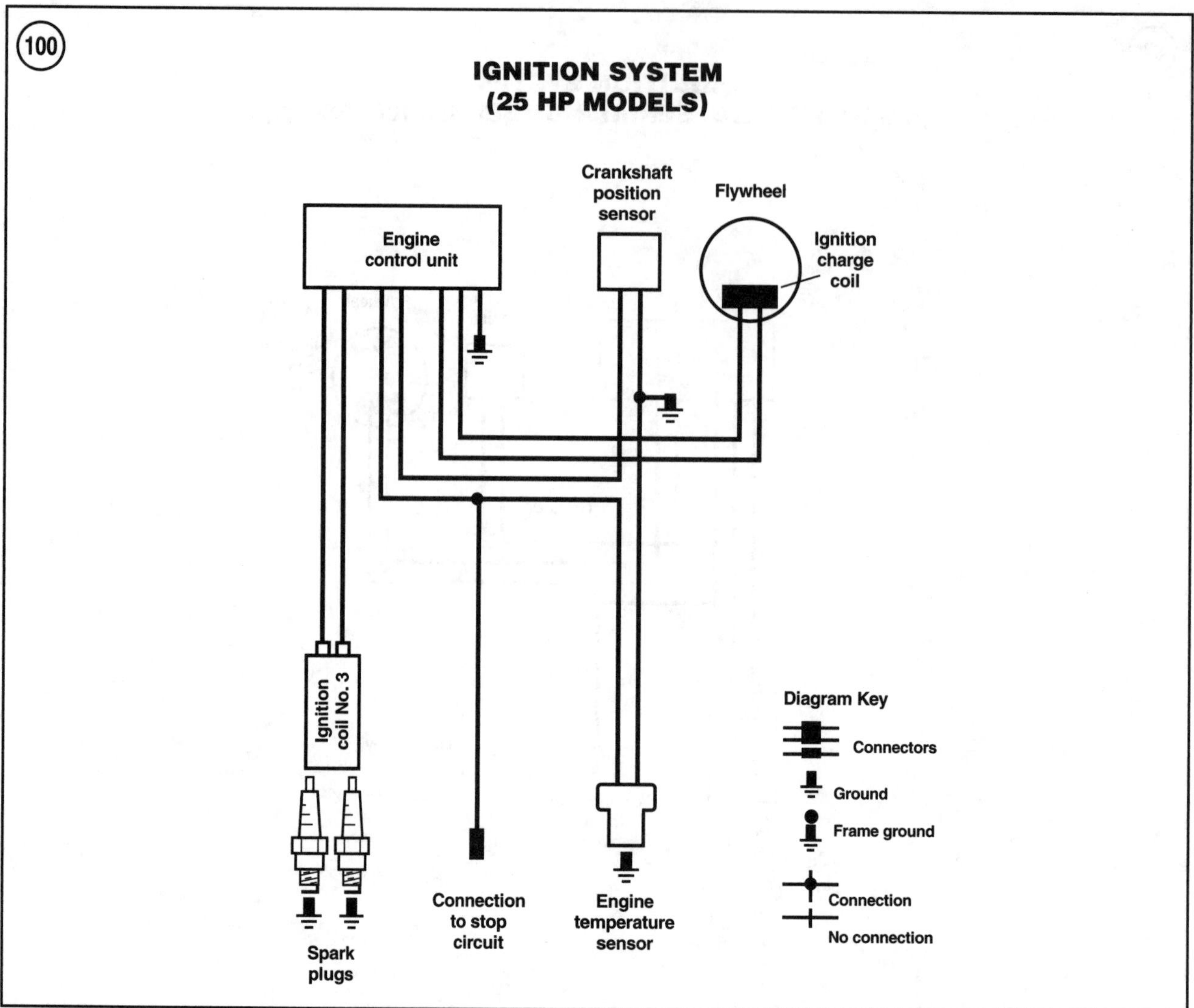

Stopping the engine is accomplished by grounding the stop circuit, which prevents the charge coil from charging the CDI capacitor.

Operation (25 hp Models)

Electrical current to operate the system is provided by the flywheel and the ignition charge coil. A wiring diagram is provided in **Figure 100**.

Alternating current (AC) is generated as the magnets mounted to the inner ring of the flywheel pass next to the ignition charge coil (**Figure 98**). This current is directed to the engine control unit (**Figure 100**). The engine control unit converts this alternating current to direct current (DC) and stores it in a capacitor for later release.

The crankshaft position sensor (A, **Figure 101**) is mounted near the flywheel and is aligned with the teeth on the periphery of the flywheel (B, **Figure 101**). An electrical pulse is generated as the flywheel teeth pass near the crankshaft position sensor. The width and spacing of the teeth produce a varying pulse spacing as the flywheel rotates. This pulse is directed to the engine control unit (**Figure 100**). The varying pulses allow the timing circuits to determine the crankshaft position relative to TDC. This input also allows the engine control unit to accurately compute engine speed. Using input from the crankshaft position sensor, the engine control unit compute the correct time to initiate spark at the plugs. Ignition timing adjustment is not required on this model.

At the correct time, the crankshaft position sensor signal activates an SCR (silicon controlled rectifier) inside the engine control unit. When activated, the SCR allows

the current stored inside the capacitor to flow into the ignition coil (**Figure 96**) primary winding. As the current flows through the coil primary winding, a much higher voltage develops in the coil secondary windings and is directed to the spark plugs.

This type of ignition system is commonly referred to as a double fire system as both spark plugs fire simultaneously for each flywheel revolution. When one piston is nearing the top of its compression stroke the other piston is nearing the top of its exhaust stroke. The additional spark is essentially wasted as very little fuel remains in the combustion chamber during the exhaust stroke.

An engine temperature sensor (**Figure 102**) is utilized on this model. It provides a varying resistance value to the engine control unit that corresponds to the varying engine temperature. This allows changes in ignition timing to enhance cold engine running characteristics. This input is also used by the engine control unit to activate the overheat warning system.

The engine control unit provides automatic timing advance with increased engine speed. This also helps prevent engine stalling by advancing the timing if the idle speed drops below 615 rpm. Another function of the timing circuit provides an increased rate of timing advancement when a rapid rise in engine speed is detected. This enhances performance during rapid acceleration.

Low oil pressure and overspeed protection circuits are also integrated into the engine control unit. Refer to *Warning Systems* in this chapter for additional information.

Stopping the engine is accomplished by grounding the stop circuit, which prevents the charge coil from charging the CDI capacitor.

Operation (30 and 40 hp Models)

Electrical current to operate this system is provided by the flywheel and the ignition charge coil. An ignition system wiring diagram is provided in (**Figure 103**).

Alternating current (AC) is generated as the magnets mounted to the inner ring of the flywheel pass next to the ignition charge coil (**Figure 98**). The current is directed to the engine control unit (**Figure 104**) which converts the alternating current to direct current (DC) and stores it in a capacitor for later release.

The crankshaft position sensor (A, **Figure 101**) is mounted near the flywheel and is directly aligned with the teeth on the periphery of the flywheel (B, **Figure 101**). An electrical pulse is generated as the teeth pass near the crankshaft position sensor. The width and spacing of the teeth produce a varying pulse as the flywheel rotates. This pulse is directed to the engine control unit (**Figure 104**). The varying pulses allow the timing circuit to determine the position of each of the three pistons relative to the top of their stoke. This input also allows the engine control unit to accurately determine engine speed. Using input from the crankshaft position sensor, the timing circuit computes the correct time to initiate spark for the individual cylinders. Ignition timing adjustments is not required on these models.

At the correct time, the crankshaft position sensor signal activates an SCR (silicon controlled rectifier) for the appropriate cylinder. When activated, the SCR allows the voltage stored in the capacitor inside the CDI unit to flow into the ignition coil (**Figure 105**) primary winding. As the voltage flows through the primary winding, a much higher voltage develops in the ignition coil secondary winding and is directed to the spark plugs.

This type of ignition system is commonly referred to as a double fire system as each spark plug fires once per flywheel revolution. A spark occurs as each piston is nearing the top of its compression stroke and when each piston is nearing the top of its exhaust stroke. The additional spark is essentially wasted as very little fuel remains in the combustion chamber during the exhaust stroke.

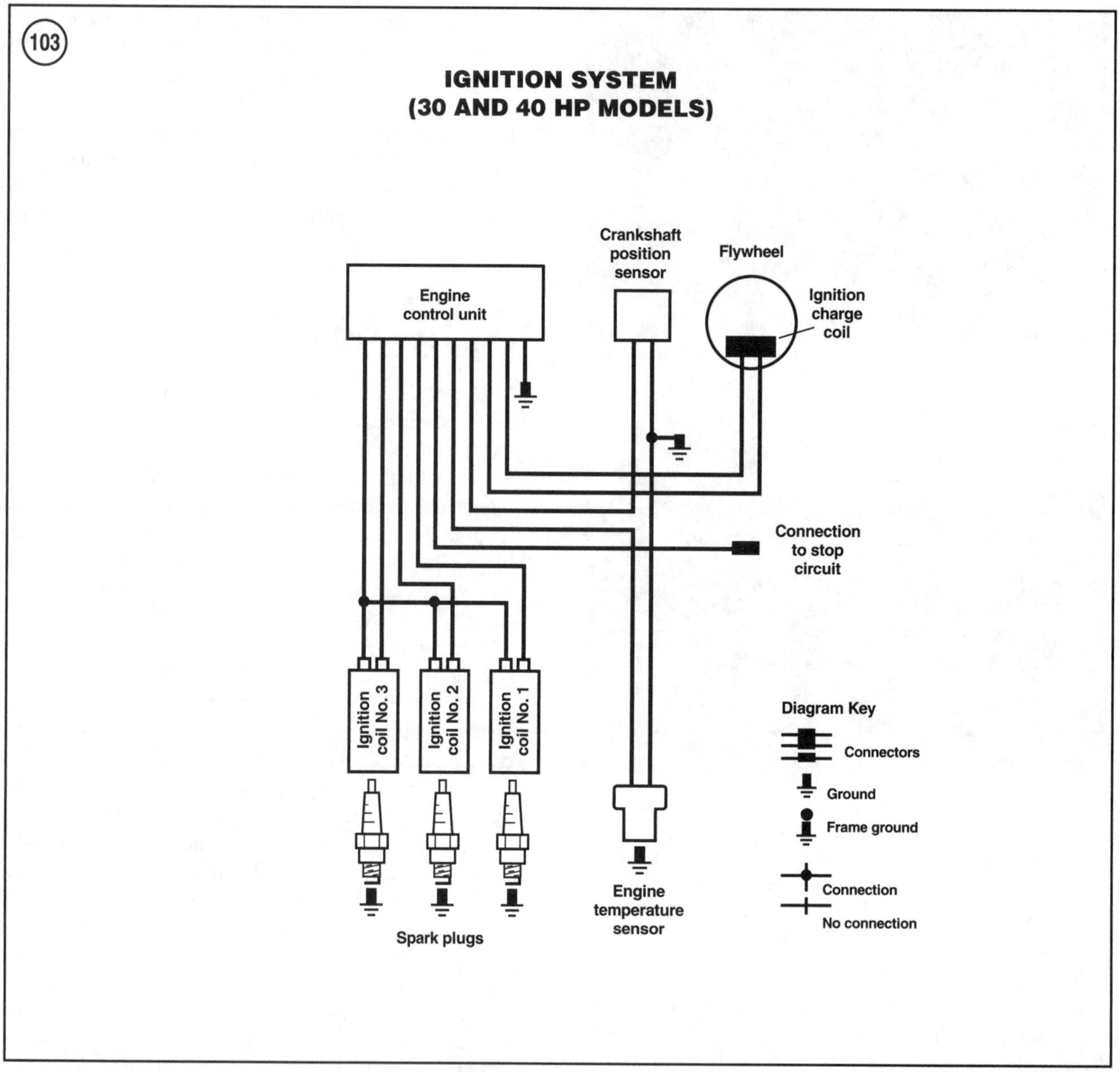

103

IGNITION SYSTEM (30 AND 40 HP MODELS)

Engine control unit

Crankshaft position sensor

Flywheel

Ignition charge coil

Connection to stop circuit

Ignition coil No. 3

Ignition coil No. 2

Ignition coil No. 1

Spark plugs

Engine temperature sensor

Diagram Key

Connectors

Ground

Frame ground

Connection

No connection

104
⚠ WARNING
Avoid possible serious injury or death from unexpected acceleration.
Required start-in-gear protection device must be in control box.

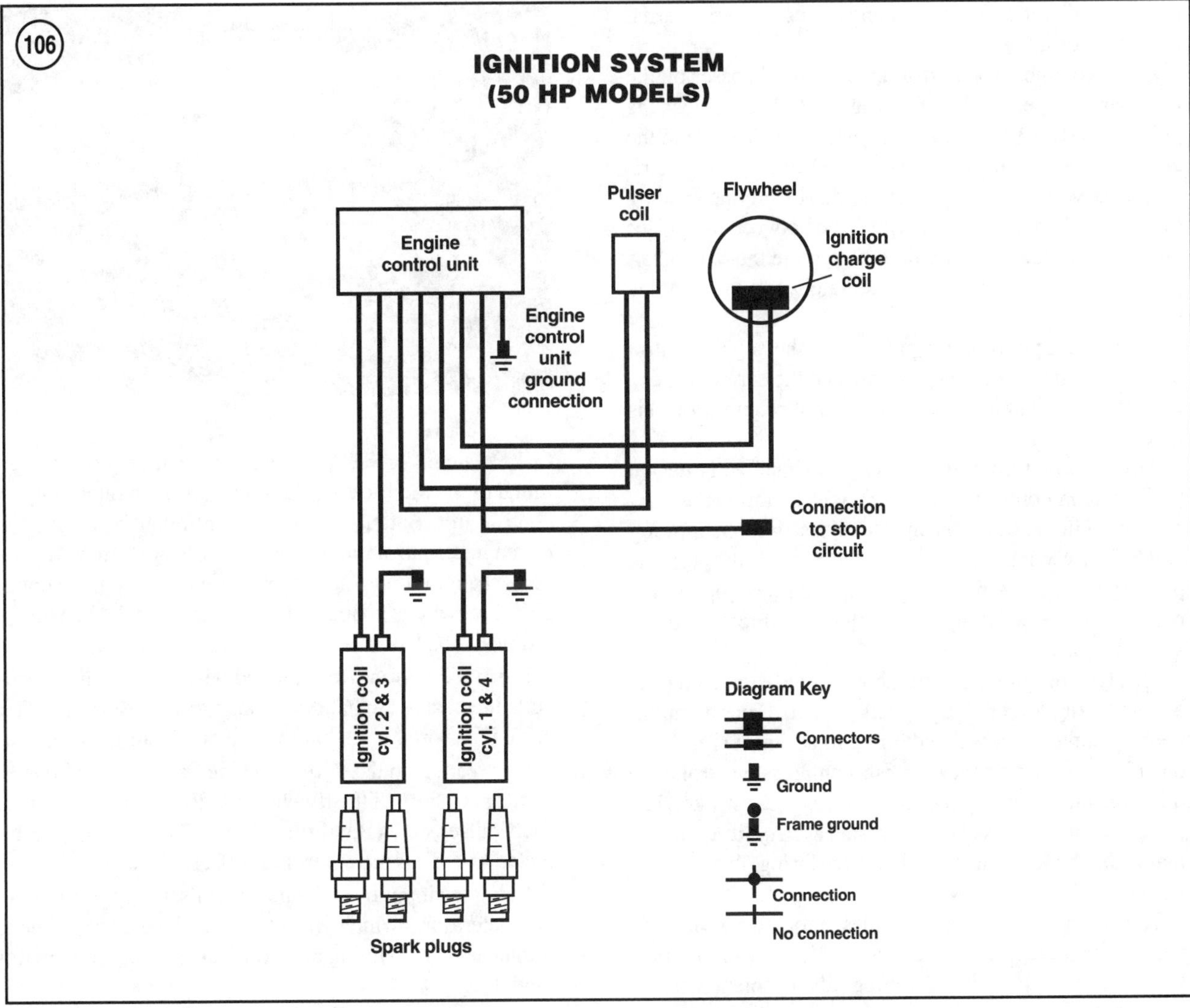

An engine temperature sensor (**Figure 102**) is utilized on this model. It provides a varying resistance value to the engine control unit that corresponds to engine temperature. This allows changes in ignition timing to enhance cold engine running characteristics. This input is also used by the engine control unit to activate the overheat warning system.

The engine control unit provides automatic timing advance with increased engine speed. This also helps prevent engine stalling by advancing the timing if the idle speed drop below 615 rpm. Another function of the timing circuit provides an increased rate of spark advancement when a rapid rise in engine speed is detected. This enhances performance during rapid acceleration.

Low oil pressure and overspeed protection circuits are also integrated into the engine control unit. Refer to *Warning Systems* in this chapter for additional information.

When activated, the stop switch, lanyard switch or ignition switch grounds the stop circuit. Grounding the stop circuit prevents the charge coil from charging the CDI capacitor, which disables the ignition system and stops the engine.

Operation (50 hp Models)

Electrical current to operate this system is provided by the flywheel and the ignition charge coil. An ignition wiring diagram is provided in **Figure 106**.

Alternating current (AC) is generated as the magnets mounted to the inner ring of the flywheel pass next to the ignition charge coil (**Figure 98**). This current is directed to the engine control unit which converts this alternating current to direct current (DC) and stores it in an internal capacitor for later release.

A low voltage pulse is generated as raised bosses on the periphery of the flywheel (A, **Figure 107**) pass near the pulser coil (B, **Figure 107**). The pulses are directed to the engine control unit. The elapsed time between the electrical pulses varies with engine speed due to varying spacing of the raised bosses. The varying time between the pulses allow the engine control unit to determine the crankshaft position relative to TDC and accurately compute engine speed.

Using the input from the pulser coil, the engine control unit determines which plugs to fire and the correct time to initiate spark. Timing adjustment is not required on this model.

At the correct time, the pulser coil signal activates an SCR (silicon controlled rectifier), which causes the voltage stored in the CDI capacitor to release into the ignition coil primary winding. As the voltage flows through the primary winding, a much higher voltage develops in the coil secondary winding. This voltage is directed to the spark plugs.

This type of ignition system is commonly referred to as a double fire system. Cylinders 1 and 4 fire simultaneously and cylinders 2 and 3 fire simultaneously. When one piston is nearing the top of its compression stroke the other piston is nearing the top of its exhaust stroke. The additional spark is essentially wasted as very little fuel remains in the combustion chamber during the exhaust stroke.

The engine control unit provides automatic timing advance with increased engine speed. This same circuit provides an increased rate of timing advancement when a rapid rise in engine speed is detected. This feature enhances performance during rapid acceleration.

Low oil pressure and overspeed protection circuits are also integrated into the engine control unit. Refer to *Warning Systems* (in this chapter) for additional information.

When activated, the stop switch, lanyard switch or ignition switch grounds the stop circuit. Grounding the stop circuit prevents the charge coil from charging the CDI capacitor, which disables the ignition system and stops the engine.

Operation (75 and 90 hp Models)

An ignition system wiring diagram is provided in **Figure 108**. These models utilize a direct current (DC) powered capacitor discharge type ignition system. The battery and charging system provides the electric current to operate the system. Two separate wires supply battery voltage

to the system. A red wire connects the battery positive terminal of the rectifier/regulator to a terminal on the engine control unit. Battery voltage is continuously supplied to the engine control unit using this wire. A white wire connects the ignition switch stop circuit to the engine control unit. This wire is connected to engine ground when the ignition switch is in the OFF position.

Electrical current from the red wire powers special circuits increasing the battery voltage to 165-200 volts. This current is stored in an internal capacitor for later release.

Low voltage pulses are developed as the raised bosses on the periphery of the flywheel (A, **Figure 109**) pass near each pulser coil (B, **Figure 109**). These pulses are directed to the engine control unit (**Figure 104**).

Using the input from the pulser coils, the engine control unit determines which plugs to fire and the correct time to initiate a spark. Timing adjustment is not required on this model.

At the correct time, the pulser coil signal activates an SCR (silicon controlled rectifier), which causes the voltage stored in the CDI capacitor to release into the ignition coil primary winding. As the voltage flows through the primary winding, a much higher voltage develops in the coil secondary winding. This voltage is directed to the spark plugs.

This type of ignition system is commonly referred to as a double fire system. Cylinders 1 and 4 fire simultaneously and cylinders 2 and 3 fire simultaneously. When one piston is nearing the top of its compression stroke the other piston is nearing the top of its exhaust stroke. The additional spark is essentially wasted as very little fuel remains in the combustion chamber during the exhaust stroke.

These models are equipped with a throttle position sensor (**Figure 110**). The sensor is mounted to the port side of the bottom carburetor. A coupling to the carburetor throttle shaft (**Figure 111**) allows the sensor shaft to rotate as

108

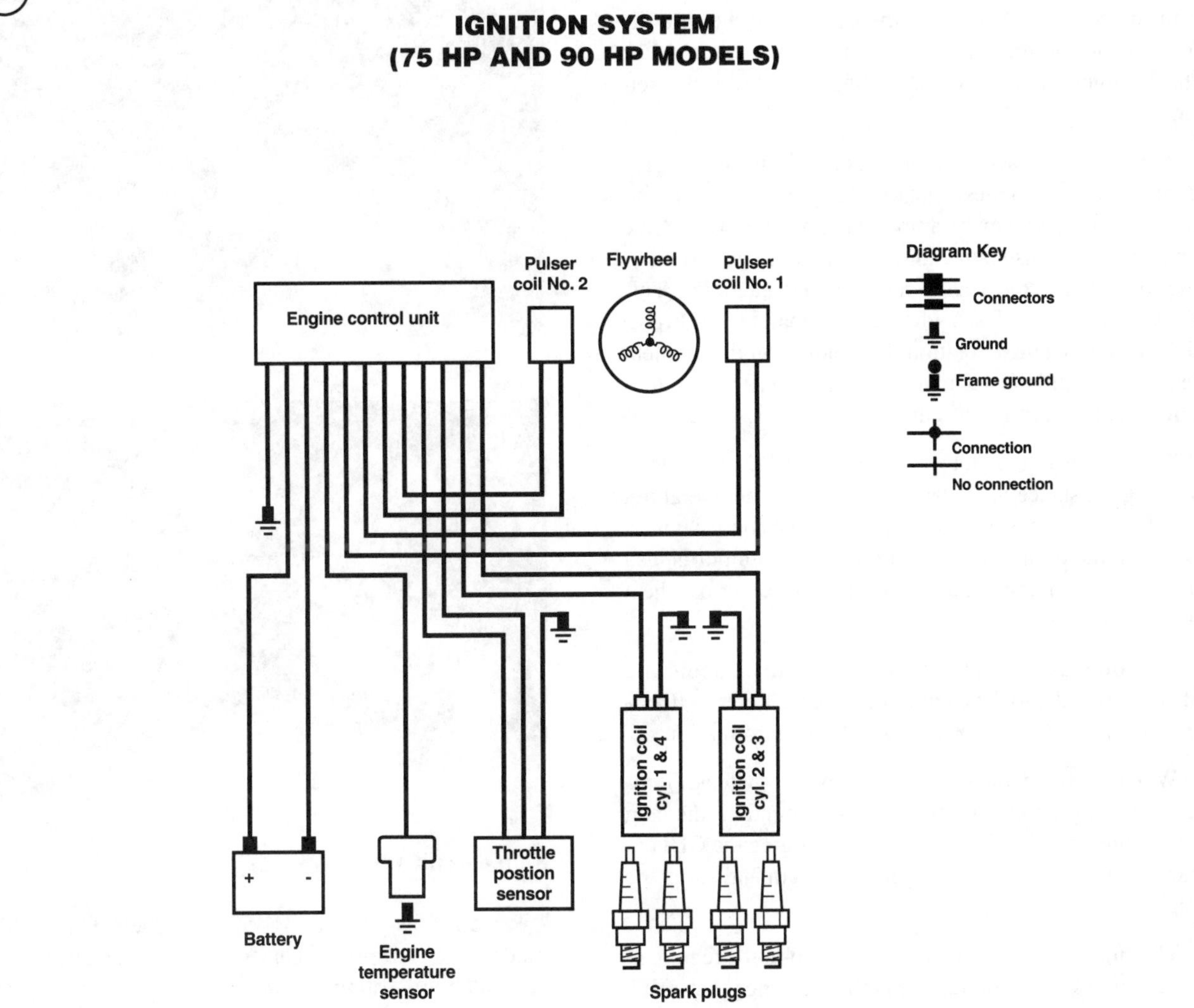

IGNITION SYSTEM
(75 HP AND 90 HP MODELS)

Engine control unit

Pulser coil No. 2

Flywheel

Pulser coil No. 1

Diagram Key

Connectors

Ground

Frame ground

Connection

No connection

Ignition coil cyl. 1 & 4

Ignition coil cyl. 2 & 3

Battery

Engine temperature sensor

Throttle postion sensor

Spark plugs

the throttle opens and closes. A varying voltage signal from the throttle position sensor allows the engine control unit to accurately determine the position of the throttle. The engine control unit uses this information to calculate the optimum ignition timing settings for all throttle settings.

A temperature sensor is incorporated into the engine control unit. It provides input to the engine control unit indicating the approximate ambient temperature within the engine cover. This feature allows changes in ignition timing to enhance cold engine running characteristics. This feature provides a faster idle (approximately 1100 rpm) during cold engine operation. Depending on the ambient temperature, this faster idle speed can occur for up to 5 minutes after starting the engine.

The engine temperature sensor (**Figure 112**) provides a varying resistance value based upon engine temperature. Input from the sensor is used by the engine control unit to compute the optimum ignition timing. This input is also used by the engine control unit to activate the overheat warning system.

Low oil pressure and overspeed protection circuits are also integrated into the engine control unit. Refer to *Warning Systems* in this chapter for additional information.

When activated, the stop switch, lanyard switch or ignition switch grounds the stop circuit. Grounding the stop circuit prevents the charge coil from charging the CDI capacitor, which disables the ignition system and stops the engine.

The engine control unit provides a limp-home feature in the event of sensor failure. The ignition timing is set at 10° BTDC if the input from the throttle position or engine temperature sensor extends beyond the normal operating ranges. This feature allows for continued engine operation at reduced power output.

Ignition Component Test Sequence

Always refer to *Troubleshooting Preparation* in this chapter prior to performing any testing. Many times ignition problems are the result of dirty, loose, corroded or damaged wire connections. Wasted time and the replacement of good components results from not performing these preliminary steps.

Refer to **Table 2** to determine the component or system requiring testing. Testing instructions for these components or systems is provided in this chapter.

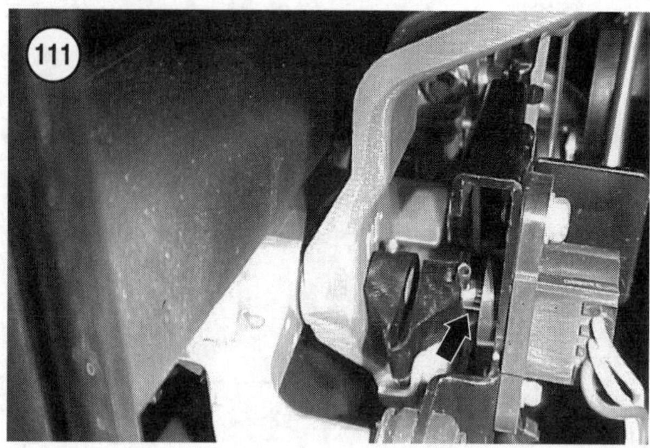

Stop Circuit Test

Perform this test on all 4-50 hp models. On 75-90 hp models refer to *Ignition On Circuit* in this chapter for stop and on circuit testing.

A faulty stop circuit usually results in an inability to start the engine. Starting is difficult as the fault prevents proper charging of the capacitor in the CDI or engine control unit.

In some cases the engine will start yet suffer an ignition misfire at various engine speeds. A partial short to ground in this circuit prevents the capacitor from being its fully charged. This fault prevents adequate voltage to the ignition coil and spark plug. Generally a higher voltage is required to fire the plugs at higher engine speeds. This fault is usually evident at higher engine speeds.

A faulty stop circuit can also result in an inability to switch the engine off.

The stop circuit includes the ignition switch, stop button, lanyard switch and associated wiring.

Refer to *Spark Test* in this chapter to determine if spark is present prior to testing the stop circuit. A problem with the stop circuit is unlikely if spark is present at the spark

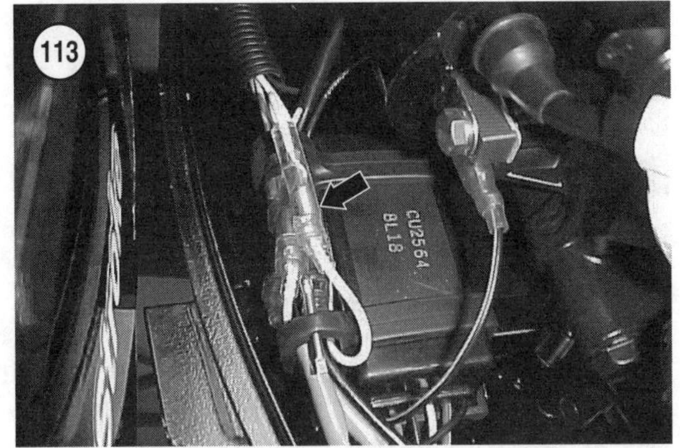
CU2564
8L18

113

Avoid possible serious
injury or death from
unexpected acceleration.
Required start-in-gear
protection device must
be in control box.

114

115

plug(s), however testing may indicate a partial short or intermittent problem. Perform all tests without running the engine.

1. Disconnect both cables from the battery.
2. Isolate the stop circuit from the CDI or engine control unit as follows.
   a. On 4-6 hp models, disconnect the brown stop circuit wire (**Figure 113**) from the wire leading to the CDI unit.

116

117

   b. On 9.9 and 15 hp models, unplug the black/yellow wire from the white wire leading to the CDI or engine control unit.
   c. On 25-40 hp models, gently push down on the locking tab of the engine control unit connector (**Figure 114**). Pull straight out on the connector to free it from the engine control unit. On 25 hp models, refer to *Crankshaft Position Sensor Test* in this section for instructions then disconnect the sensor wires from the engine wire harness.
   d. On 50 hp models, unplug the tiller or remote control wire harness (**Figure 115**)from the lower port side of the power head.
3. Connect the ohmmeter to the engine wire harness as follows:
   a. On 4-6 hp models, connect the positive lead to the brown wire leading to the stop switch and the negative lead to the coil mounting bolt (**Figure 116**).
   b. On 9.9 and 15 hp models, connect the positive lead to the disconnected black/yellow wire terminal and the negative lead to a suitable engine ground (**Figure 117**).

c. On 25 hp models, touch the positive lead to the No. 13 terminal in the disconnected engine control unit connector (**Figure 118**). Number marks are provided on the side of the connector. Ensure this terminal connects to the red/white wire leading to the connector. Connect the negative lead to a suitable engine ground (**Figure 117**).

d. On 30 and 40 hp models, connect the positive lead to the No. 8 terminal in the disconnected engine control unit connector (**Figure 118**). Number marks are provided on the side of the connector. Ensure this terminal connects to the black/yellow wire leading to the connector. Connect the negative lead to a suitable engine ground (**Figure 117**).

e. On 50 hp models, connect the positive lead to the black/yellow wires (**Figure 119**) in the harness connector leading to the remote or tiller control. Connect the negative lead to a good engine ground.

4. Place the ignition switch if so equipped in the ON position. Ensure the lanyard switch, if so equipped, is in the RUN position.
5. The ohmmeter should indicate no continuity.
6. Place the ignition switch (if so equipped) in the OFF position or push the stop switch. Now continuity should be noted.
7. Place the ignition switch (if so equipped) in the ON position. Observe the ohmmeter and pull the lanyard from the lanyard switch. The ohmmeter should indicated continuity when the lanyard switch is tripped.
8. If the stop circuit does not function as described, test the ignition switch, stop switch or lanyard switch as necessary. If the switch(es) are in good condition, inspect the stop circuit for an open or shorted circuit or loose or corroded connections.
9. If all stop circuit components function correctly, but the ignition system does not have spark, test the charge coil, pulser coil, crankshaft position sensor and ignition coil(s) as necessary.

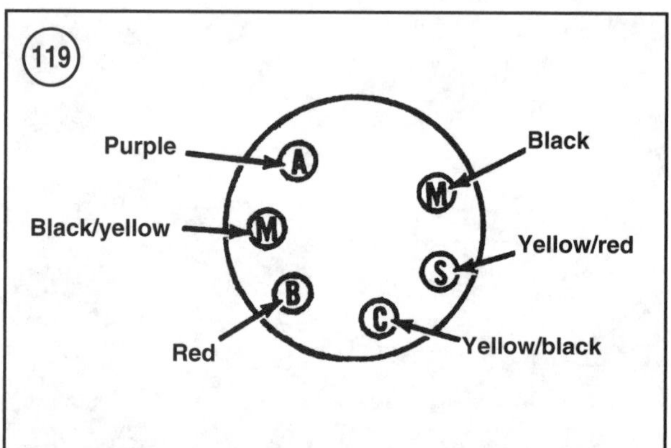

Lanyard Switch Test

The lanyard switch (**Figure 120**) is mounted in the remote control or dash panel on all remote control models. On tiller control models, the lanyard switch is mounted to the front side of the lower engine cover or to the tiller handle bracket. On 4-6 hp models a single switch (**Figure 121**) provides both stop and lanyard switch functions.

On remote control models, partial disassembly of the remote control is required to access the wires. Refer to Chapter Twelve to remove the remote control from its mounting location. Disassemble the remote control enough to access the lanyard switch wires. Refer to the wire diagrams located at the back of the manual to identify the lanyard switch wires.

1. Disconnect both battery cables from the battery terminals.
2. Disconnect both lanyard switch wires from the engine harness or remote control wiring harness.
3. Connect the positive lead to the black/yellow or brown wire leading to the switch and the negative lead to the black wire leading to the switch.

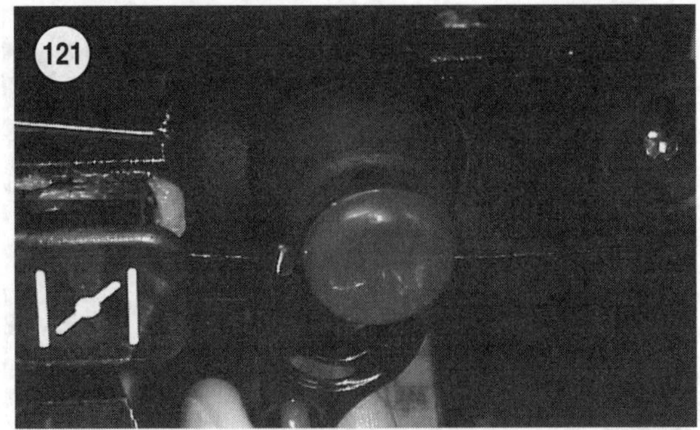

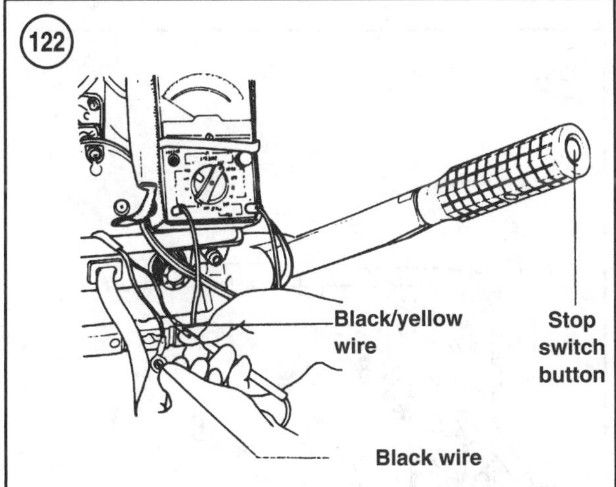

4. Place the lanyard cord connector over the switch. On remote control and 9.9-50 hp models, toggle the switch to the RUN position.

5. Observe the meter reading. No continuity should be noted.

6. Pull the lanyard from the lanyard switch while observing the meter. Continuity should be noted as the lanyard releases from the switch.

7. Replace the lanyard switch if it does not operate as described.

Stop Switch Test

On 4-6 hp models the stop and lanyard switch functions are integrated into a single switch. The switch is located at the front side of the lower engine cover (**Figure 121**). The stop function activates as the red button on the switch is pushed in.

On 9.9-50 hp models the stop switch button is mounted to the very end of the tiller control grip (**Figure 122**). The

stop function activates as the red button on the end of the grip is pushed in.

1. Disconnect both battery cables at the battery terminals.

2. On 4-6 hp models, disconnect the brown and black wires from the stop/lanyard switch wires.

3. On 9.9-50 hp models, disconnect the black/yellow and black stop switch wires from the harness.

4A. On 4-6 hp models, connect the positive ohmmeter lead to the brown wire leading to the switch) and the negative lead to the black wire leading to the switch. Place the lanyard in position under the red button (**Figure 121**).

4B. On 9.9-50 hp models, connect the positive lead to the black/yellow wire leading to the switch and the negative lead to the black wire leading to the switch.

5. The meter should indicate no continuity.

6. Observe the meter and push in the red stop button. The meter should indicate continuity as the button is depressed.

7. If the stop switch fails to operate as described, first inspect all wires and connections. If the wiring and connections are in acceptable condition, replace the stop switch. Refer to Chapter Eleven for tiller removal and installation.

Ignition ON Circuit Test

An ignition ON circuit is used on 75 hp and 90 hp models. This test checks for proper voltage to the engine control unit ON circuit and the stop circuit. Use a voltmeter and ohmmeter to perform this test. Refer to the wiring diagrams located at the end of the manual to identify the ignition circuit wires. Test for battery voltage at the circuits as follows:

1. Disconnect both cables from the battery. Remove the propeller as described in Chapter Nine. Shift the engine into FORWARD gear.

2. Push the locking tabs up (**Figure 123**) then remove the electrical component cover (**Figure 124**).

3. Disconnect the lower engine harness (A, **Figure 125**) from the engine control unit (C). This connector contains the blue, black, white and red wires. Connect the battery cables to the battery.
4. Select the DC volts function on the multimeter. Select the 20 or 40 volt scale on the meter.
5. Connect the positive voltmeter lead to the red wire terminal in the connector leading to the engine wire harness. Connect the negative lead to a suitable engine ground (**Figure 117**).
6. Note the meter reading. The meter should indicate 12 volts or more. Check for a faulty ignition switch, blown fuse or damaged wire if an incorrect reading is noted.
7. Disconnect both cables from the battery. Place the ignition switch in the OFF position.
8. Connect the positive ohmmeter lead to white wire terminal in the connector leading to the engine wire harness. Connect the negative lead to a suitable engine ground (**Figure 117**). Note the meter reading. The meter should indicate continuity.
9. With the test leads still connected as described in Step 8 place the ignition switch in the ON position. The meter should now indicate no continuity.
10. A faulty ignition switch, lanyard switch or wire harness is indicated if an incorrect test result is noted in Step 8 or Step 9.
11. Connect the harness connector to the engine control unit. Carefully snap the electrical component cover onto its retaining slots. Ensure the locking tabs fully engage the slots.
12. Install the propeller and connect the cables to the battery.

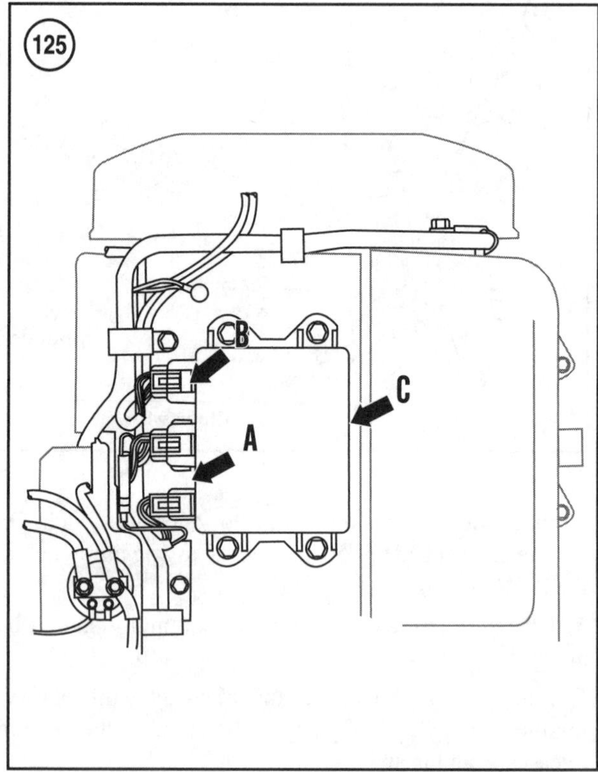

Ignition Switch Test

Refer to *Starting System* in this chapter for ignition switch test instructions.

Ignition Charge Coil Test

The ignition charge coil provides the electric current to power the ignition system on all 4-50 hp models. A defective ignition charge coil generally results in a no spark condition. On occasion the only symptom is an ignition misfire at higher engine speeds. In some rare instances the misfire occurs only at lower engine speeds.

Testing the coil involves the use of a multimeter to measure the resistance of the coil winding. Fairly high resistance values are present due to the long wire used to create this coil. Ambient temperature has a significant effect on resistance readings when long wires are tested. Perform this test at 68° F (20° C). Ignition charge coil resistance specifications are listed in **Table 5**.

The ignition charge coil is located under the flywheel and removal of the flywheel is required should it need replacement. Resistance measurements can be performed without removing the flywheel provided that the ignition charge coil wires are accessible. Refer to the wire diagrams located at the back of the manual to identify the ignition charge coil wires.

1. Disconnect both cables from the battery if so equipped.
2. Disconnect the charge coil from the engine wire harness. If necessary, refer to the appropriate wiring diagram

and make sure the wires lead to the charge coil under the flywheel (**Figure 126**).

3. Connect the meter to the wires listed in **Table 6**. Ensure the test leads connect to the wires leading to the ignition charge coil and not the engine wire harness.
4. Record the resistance value for each connection. Compare the resistance with the specifications listed in **Table 5**.
5. Replace the ignition charge coil if the resistance is not as specified. Refer to Chapter Seven for ignition charge coil removal and installation.
6. Connect the ignition charge coil to the engine wire harness. Ensure the wires route in a manner preventing them from contacting any moving components.

7 Connect the cables to the battery. Install the electric component cover onto the engine.

Pulser Coil Test (9.9 [Serial No. OH000058-On] and 50-90 hp Models)

A pulser coil is used on 4, 5, 9.9 (serial No. OH000058-on) and all 50-90 hp models. The pulser coil is mounted near the periphery of the flywheel (**Figure 127**). Twin pulser coils are used on 75 and 90 hp models. Always test both pulser coils if a fault is suspected.

Bear in mind that a defective flywheel trigger magnet may cause intermittent pulser coil operation and an ignition misfire. Corrosion or debris on the magnet or pulser coil can interfere with the pulser coil operation. Replace the flywheel if cracks or other damage to the magnets is noted. Clean grease or oily deposits from the flywheel magnet using a light solvent or carburetor cleaner. Carefully scrape thick paint from the magnet surfaces using a dull knife.

Most faults can be readily detected by performing a resistance test. On 75 and 90 hp models an additional test is required to verify correct operation of the pulser coil. Refer to *Pulser Coil Peak Output* in this section for test instructions.

Refer to the wire diagrams located at the end of the manual to identify the pulser coil wires.

NOTE

It is not necessary or recommended to remove the pulser coil from the engine for testing. Remove the pulser coil only if necessary for access to the wires. Pulser coil removal and installation are covered in Chapter Seven.

1. Disconnect both battery cables from the battery.
2. Disconnect the pulser coil from the wire harness. Clean the wire terminals prior to testing.
3. Connect the ohmmeter to the wires listed in **Table 6**. Record each resistance measurement. Repeat the test for all pulser coils on the engine.
4. Compare the resistance with the specification listed in **Table 6**. Replace the pulser coil if the measured resistance is beyond the specification. Pulser coil removal and installation are provided in Chapter Seven.
5. Connect the pulser coil wires to the engine wire harness. Ensure the wires route in a manner preventing them from contacting the flywheel or any moving components.
6. Connect the cables to the battery.

Pulser Coil Peak Output Test (75 and 90 hp Models)

Perform this test on 75 and 90 hp models. This test requires that the engine be run at specified speed ranges under actual conditions. Have an assistant operate the boat during the test. A special test harness (Mercury part No. 91-804771), shop tachometer and a meter capable of measuring peak voltage are required.

1. Disconnect both cables from the battery. Push up and in on the locking tabs (**Figure 123**) and lift the electrical component cover (**Figure 124**) from the of the power head.
2. Disconnect the engine upper harness (B, **Figure 125**) from the engine control unit (C).
3. Connect the test harness to the engine harness plug and to the engine control unit (**Figure 128**).
4. Connect the positive meter lead to the white/yellow wire of the test harness and the negative meter test lead to the white wire test harness wire.
5. Route the test leads and harness away from any moving components.
6. Attach the shop tachometer to the engine following its manufacturer's instructions. Connect the cables to the battery.
7. Have an assistant operate the engine at the speeds indicated in **Table 16**. Record the voltage output for each speed range.
8. Stop the engine. Connect the positive meter lead to the white/red wire of the test harness and the negative meter test lead to the white wire of the test harness. Repeat Steps 4-7 to test the remaining pulser coil.
9. Compare the recorded readings with the specifications listed in **Table 16**. If an incorrect meter reading is noted in Step 7 replace the appropriate pulser coil.
10. If an incorrect meter readings are noted in Step 7 and step 8, clean all debris or contaminants from the flywheel magnet. Repeat the test. Replace both pulser coils if incorrect readings persist. A faulty flywheel is likely if the incorrect meter readings and the ignition misfire persist after replacing the pulser coils.
11. Disconnect the test leads and test harness from the engine. Connect the engine harness (B, **Figure 125**) to the engine control unit.
12. Carefully serial snap the electrical component cover onto its retaining slots. Ensure the locking tabs fully engage the slots. Connect the cables to the battery.

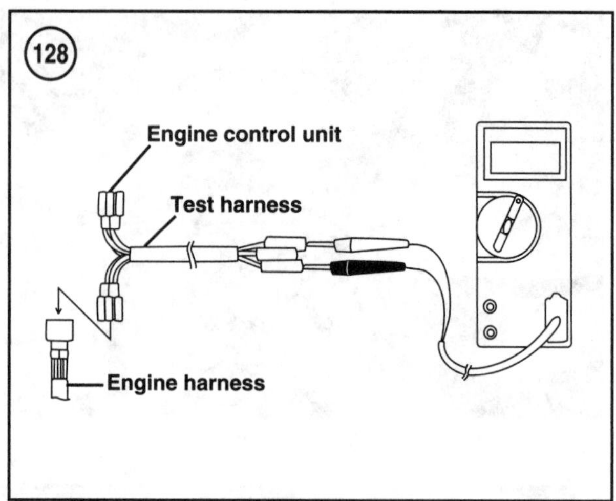

Crankshaft Position Sensor Test (9.9 [Prior to Serial No. OH000058] and 15-40 hp Models)

The crankshaft position sensor is mounted next to the flywheel directly aligned with the bosses protruding from the flywheel. It provides timing input to the engine control unit. A defective crankshaft position sensor generally results in no spark at the coil. At times a sensor malfunction can occur randomly and result in intermittent ignition misfire.

A buildup of oil, grease or other contamination can cause the crankshaft position sensor to malfunction. If allowed to build to a sufficient thickness the deposits prevent the sensor from detecting the passing of the flywheel bosses. Clean excessive oil, grease or other deposits from the crankshaft position sensor and the flywheel bosses with a light solvent.

To operate correctly, the crankshaft position sensor must be mounted a specified distance from the flywheel bosses (**Figure 129**). Refer to Chapter Seven to adjust the sensor air gap.

Removal of the sensor is not required for testing if there is adequate access to the sensor wires. Refer to the wire diagrams located at the end of the manual to identify the sensor wires. Resistance readings increase at higher temperature and decrease with lower temperatures. To ensure accurate results perform all testing at approximately 68° F (20° C).

1. Disconnect both cables from the battery. Disconnect the sensor from the engine wire harness.
2. Connect the ohmmeter to the wires specified in **Table 11**. Connect the test leads to the wires leading to the crank-

shaft position sensor (**Figure 130**) not the engine wire harness.

3. Record the measured resistance. Compare the resistance with the specification listed in **Table 11**.
4. Replace the crankshaft position sensor if the resistance is not as specified. Refer to Chapter Seven for sensor removal and installation instructions.
5. Connect the sensor to the engine wire harness. Route the wires in a manner preventing them from contacting moving components. Connect the cables to the battery.

Engine Control Unit Peak Output

Perform a control unit peak output test on 75 and 90 hp models. The test measures the peak voltage delivered to the ignition coils. An accurate tachometer, test harness (Mercury part No. 91-804771) and a voltmeter capable of measuring peak voltage is required.

1. Disconnect the battery cables from the battery. Push up and in on the locking tabs (**Figure 123**), then remove the electrical component cover (**Figure 124**).
2. Disconnect the engine upper harness (B, **Figure 125**) from the engine control unit.
3. Connect the test harness to the engine wire harness plug and engine control unit as shown in **Figure 128**.
4. Connect the positive meter lead to the white/blue wire test harness terminal. Connect the negative lead to the white wire.
5. Select the peak volt function on the meter.
6. Route the test leads and harness away from any moving components. Clamp them as necessary to ensure the test leads maintain secure contact to the test harness during engine operation.
7. Attach the shop tachometer to the engine following its manufacturer's instructions. Connect the cables to the battery.
8. Have an assistant operate the engine at the speeds indicated in **Table 15**. Record the voltage readings for each speed range.
9. Stop the engine. Connect the positive meter lead to the white/green wire terminal of the test harness and the negative lead to the white wire terminal of the test harness.
10. Have an assistant operate the engine at the speeds indicated in **Table 15**. Record the voltage readings for each speed range.
11. Compare the meter readings with the specifications listed in **Table 15**.
    a. Test the ignition coil for cylinders No. 2 and No. 3 if the voltage readings in Step 8 are above the specification listed in **Table 15**.
    b. Test the ignition coil for cylinders No. 1 and No. 4 if the voltage readings in Step 10 are above the specification listed in **Table 15**. Follow the test instructions provided in this section.
    c. Test the pulser coil resistance and peak output if the voltage readings in Step 8 or Step 10 are below the specification listed in **Table 15**. Follow the test instructions provided in this section.
12. Test the battery charging coil and voltage regulator if the pulser coils test correctly but incorrect test results are noted in Step 8 and Step 10. Refer to *Charging System* in this chapter.
13. A faulty fuse, wire harness or engine control unit is indicated if the pulser coils, ignition coil and charging system test correctly but the misfire persists. Check the fuses and wire harness before replacing the engine control unit. Refer to *CDI or Engine Control Unit* in this section for additional information.
14. Disconnect both cables from the battery. Disconnect the test leads and test harness from the engine. Connect the engine harness connector (B, **Figure 125**) to the engine control unit.
15. Carefully serial snap the electrical component cover onto its retaining slots. Ensure the locking tabs fully engage the slots. Connect the cables to the battery.

Ignition Coil Test

Resistance testing checks for open circuits or short circuits in the primary and secondary windings of the ignition coil.

The wire length used for the primary winding of the ignition coil is relatively short and the resistance readings are fairly low. A much longer length of wire is used in the secondary winding and the resistance readings are relatively high. To ensure accurate test result use a digital ohmmeter. In the vast majority of cases a fault within the ignition coil surfaces when the resistance is tested. Ignition coil test specifications are listed in **Table 7** and **Table 8**. Make all resistance tests at approximately 68° F (20° C) to ensure accurate test results.

Bear in mind that a resistance test only indicates a short or open circuit. Faults within the coil may result in internal arcing that prevents a strong blue spark at the spark plug. If an internal short is present a clicking noise emanates from the coil while attempting to start the engine may be noted. Use a spark test tool to check for a good strong blue spark as the engine is cranked. Refer to *Spark Test* in this chapter for instructions on using a spark test tool. Test both the primary and secondary resistance for each coil on the engine.

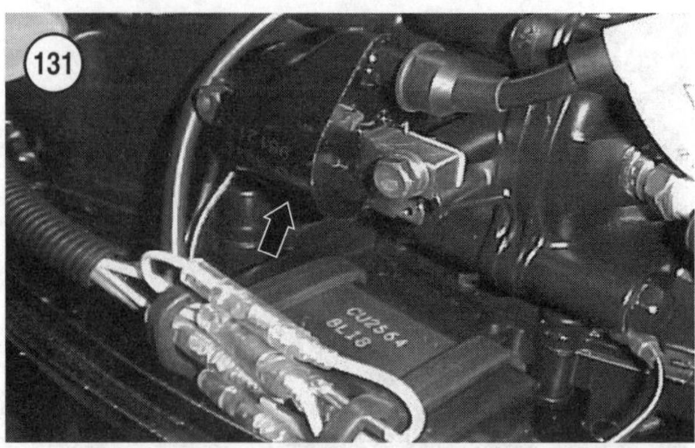

Primary Resistance Test (4-6 hp Models)

Removal of the ignition coil (**Figure 131**) is not required for testing provided there is access to its wire terminals. Refer to Chapter Seven if coil removal is required.

1. Remove the spark plug from the engine.
2. Carefully pull the single wire connector from its terminal on the ignition coil (**Figure 132**).
3. Touch the positive ohmmeter lead to the wire terminal (**Figure 133**) on the side of the ignition coil and the negative lead to the laminated section of the ignition coil (**Figure 134**)
4. Record the resistance and compare the meter reading with the specifications in **Table 7**.
5. Replace the ignition coil if its primary resistance is beyond the specification in **Table 7**. Refer to Chapter Seven for coil removal and installation.
6. Connect the single wire to its terminal on the ignition coil (**Figure 132**). Install the spark plug and spark plug wire.

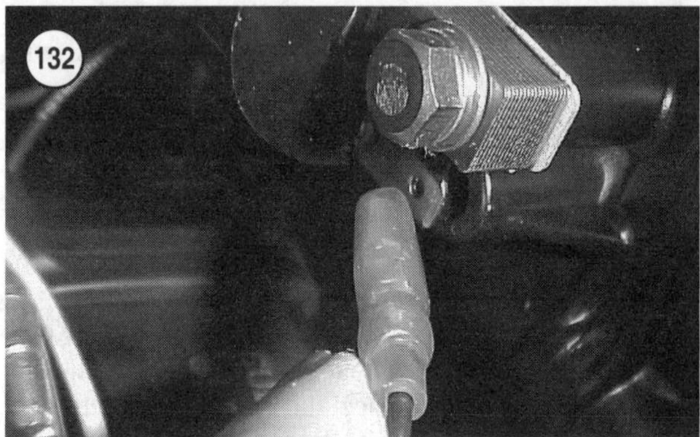

Primary Resistance Test (9.9-25 and 50-90 hp Models)

Removal of the ignition coil is not required for testing provided there is access to its wire terminals. Refer to Chapter Seven if coil removal is required.

1. Disconnect both cables from the battery.
2. The mounting location for the ignition coil varies by the model. Locate the ignition coil using the following information.
   a. On 9.9 and 15 hp models, the ignition coil is mounted on port side of the power head near the No. 2 spark plug (**Figure 135**).

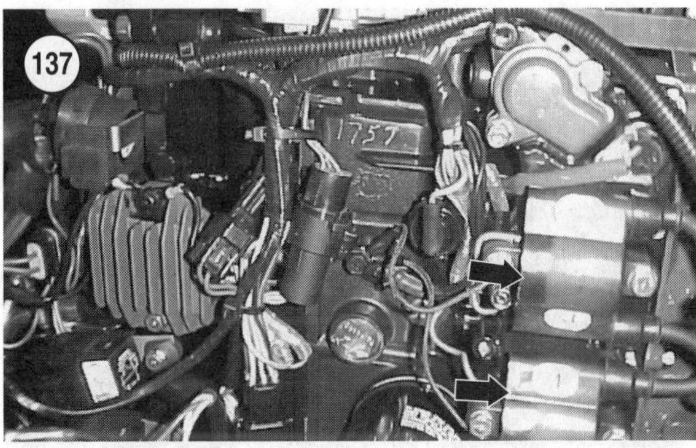

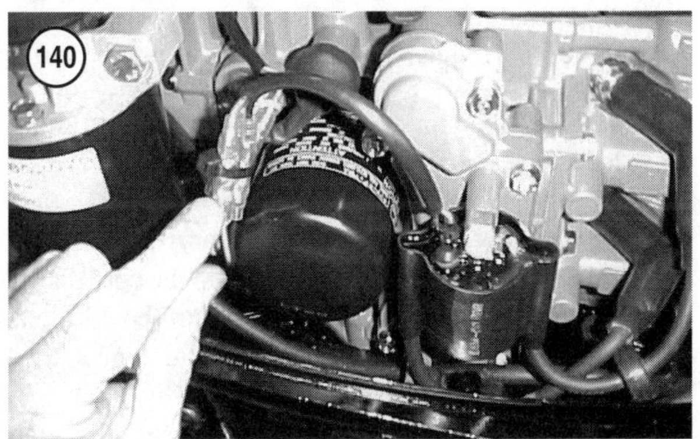

b. On 25 hp models, the ignition coil is mounted on the rear side of the power head below the yellow oil fill cap (**Figure 136**).

c. On 50 hp models, both ignition coils are mounted on the port side of the power head (**Figure 137**).

d. On 75 and 90 hp models, the ignition coils are mounted on the starboard side of the cylinder head (**Figure 138**) to the left of the oil filter.

3. Trace the small wires from the ignition coils to the engine wire harness (**Figure 139**) or (**Figure 140**).

4. Unplug the ignition coil wires from the engine wire harness.

5. Connect the ohmmeter lead to the terminals specified in **Table 7**. Record the measured resistance. On 50-90 hp models, repeat the test for the remaining ignition coil. Record the test results.

6. Compare the test results with the specification listed in **Table 7**. Replace the ignition coil if its resistance is beyond the listed specification. Refer to Chapter Seven for ignition coil removal and installation.

7. Connect the ignition coil wires to the engine wire harness.

8. Connect the cables to the battery.

Primary Resistance Test (30 and 40 hp Models)

Removal of the ignition coil is not required for testing provided there is access to its wire terminals. Refer to Chapter Seven when coil removal is required.

1. Disconnect both cables from the battery.
2. The three ignition coils are mounted on the port side of the cylinder head (**Figure 141**) to the left of the oil filter.
3. Unplug the ignition coil wires from the engine wire harness.
4. Connect the ohmmeter between the terminals listed in **Table 7**. See **Figure 142.** Repeat for the remaining coils.
5. Compare the resistance to the specification in **Table 7**. Replace the coil (**Figure 143**) if its resistance is not as specified. Refer to Chapter Seven for ignition coil replacement.

Secondary Resistance Test (4-6 hp Models)

Removal of the ignition coil is not required for testing provided there is access to its wire terminals. Refer to Chapter Seven if coil removal is required. A resistor is integrated into the spark plug cap (**Figure 144**) on these models. The spark plug cap must be removed prior to testing the coil.

1. Locate the ignition coil on the lower port side of the engine (**Figure 131**).
2. Carefully pull the single wire connector from the ignition coil (**Figure 132**). Carefully twist the spark plug cap counterclockwise to unthread it from the spark plug lead (**Figure 145**).
3. Touch the positive meter lead to the wire terminal (**Figure 133**) on the side of the ignition coil. Touch the negative lead to the wire inside the spark plug lead.
4. Record the resistance and compare the reading with the specification in **Table 8**.

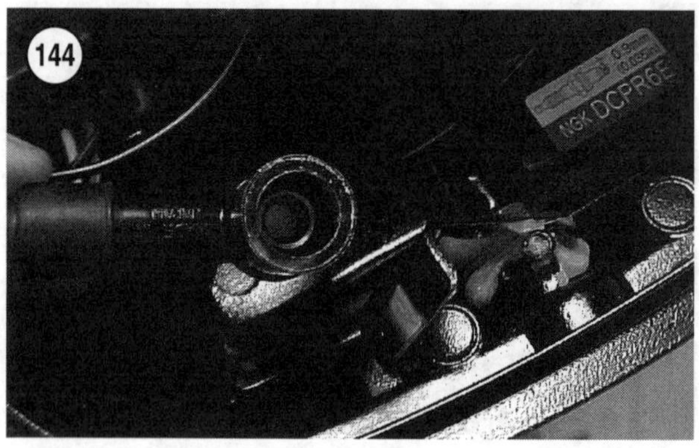

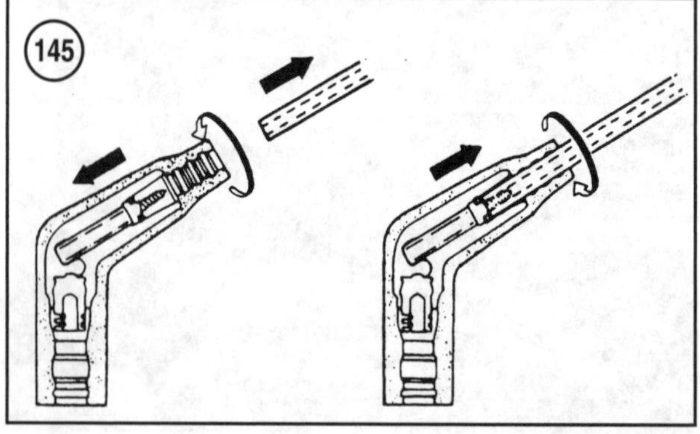

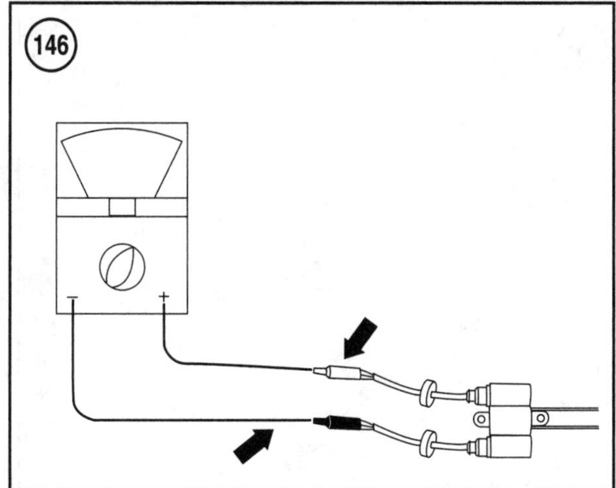

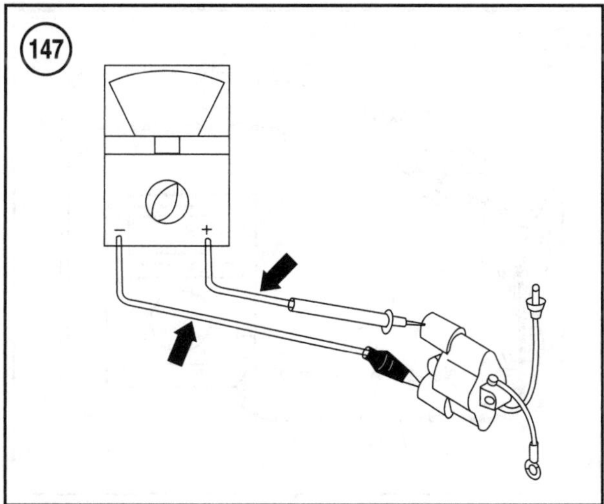

5. Replace the ignition coil if the secondary resistance is not as specified. Refer to Chapter Seven for coil removal and installation.

6. Thread the spark plug cap onto the spark plug lead (**Figure 145**). Connect the single wire to its terminal on the ignition coil (**Figure 132**).

Secondary Resistance Test (9.9-25 and 50-90 hp Models)

Removal of the ignition coil is not required for testing provided there is access to its wire terminals. Refer to Chapter Seven if coil removal is required. A resistor is integrated into the spark plug cap (**Figure 144**) on these models. The spark plug cap must be removed prior to testing the coil. On 50-90 hp models, test each ignition coil separately.

1. Disconnect both cables from the battery.

2A. On 9.9 and 15 hp models, the ignition coil is mounted to port side of the power head and near the No. 2 spark plug (**Figure 135**).

2B. On 25 hp models, the ignition coil is mounted on the rear side of the power head below the yellow oil fill cap (**Figure 136**).

2C. On 50 hp models, both ignition coils are mounted to the port side of the power head (**Figure 137**).

2D. On 75 and 90 hp models, the ignition coils are mounted to the starboard side of the cylinder head (**Figure 138**) to the left of the oil filter.

3. Trace the small wires from the ignition coils to the engine wire harness (**Figure 139** or **Figure 140**).

4. Unplug the ignition coil wires from the engine wire harness.

5A. On 9.9-50 hp models, carefully twist the cap counterclockwise to unthread it from the spark plug lead (**Figure 145**).

5B. On 75 and 90 hp models, carefully twist the spark plug lead counterclockwise near its connection to the ignition coil to unthread it from the ignition coil.

6. Connect the meter test lead to the ignition coil as follows:
   a. On 9.9-25 hp models, touch the positive test lead to the wire inside one of the spark plug leads (**Figure 146**). Touch the negative lead to the wire inside the other spark plug lead. Ensure each test lead is inserted deep enough to fully contact the wire.
   b. On 75 and 90 hp models, touch the positive lead to the threaded spark plug wire connector in the ignition coil (**Figure 147**) and the negative lead to the other threaded spark plug wire connector.

7. Record the measured resistance. On 50-90 hp models, repeat the test for the remaining ignition coil.

8. Compare the resistance with the specification in **Table 8**. Replace the ignition coil if its resistance is beyond the specification. Refer to Chapter Seven for ignition coil removal and installation.

9. Connect the ignition coil wires to the engine wire harness.

10. Connect the cables to the battery.

Secondary Resistance Test (30 and 40 hp Models)

Removal of the ignition coil is not required for testing provided there is access to its wire terminals. Refer to Chapter Seven if coil removal is required. A resistor is integrated into the spark plug cap (**Figure 144**) on these models. The spark plug cap must be removed prior to testing the coil.

1. Disconnect both cables from the battery.
2. The ignition coils are mounted to the port side of the cylinder head (**Figure 141**) to the left of the oil filter.
3. Trace the small wires from the ignition coil to the engine wire harness (**Figure 142**).
4. Unplug the ignition coil wires from the engine wire harness.
5. Carefully twist the cap counterclockwise to unthread it from the spark plug lead (**Figure 145**).
6. Test lead connections are listed in **Table 8**. Touch the positive meter lead to the wire inside the spark plug lead (**Figure 148**). Ensure the test lead is inserted deep enough to fully contact the wire. Connect the negative lead to the specified wire terminal inside the connector (**Figure 142**).
7. Record the resistance and repeat Steps 3-6 for the remaining two coils.
8. Compare the test results with the specification in **Table 8**. Replace the ignition coil if its resistance is beyond the listed specification. Refer to Chapter Seven for ignition coil removal and installation.
9. Connect the ignition coil wire connector to the engine wire harness. Route the wires in a manner preventing them from contacting any moving components.
10. Connect the cables to the battery.

NOTE
On 30 and 40 hp models, the spark plug cap resistance specification is indicated by the letter and number code on the side of the cap.

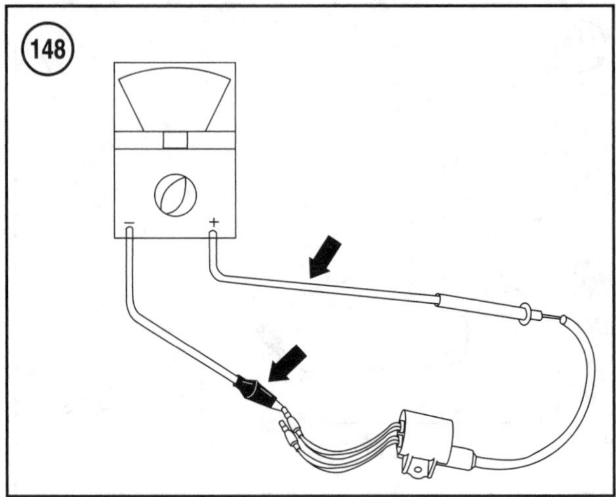

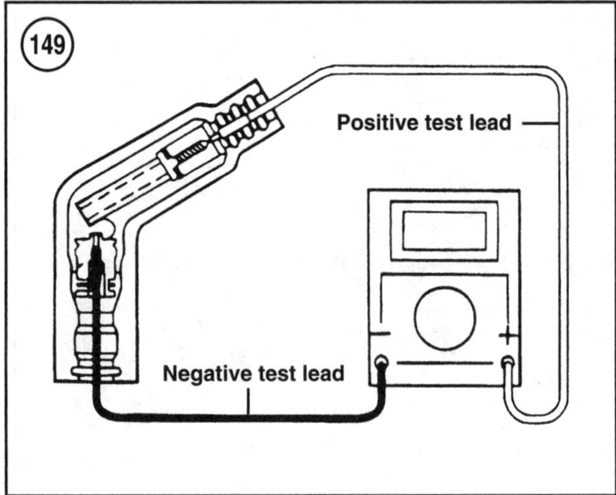

Spark Plug Cap Test

Perform this test on 4-50 hp models only. A resistor is integrated into the cap to reduce electrical interference from the ignition system. Spark plug cap resistance specifications are provided in **Table 9**.

On 75 and 90 hp models, the spark plug cap does not contain a resistor. Refer to *Spark Plug Lead Test* in this chapter.

A defective spark plug cap can result in a no start condition or an ignition misfire at higher engine speeds. Inspect the cap for corrosion or a weathered appearance. If defects are noted replace all of the spark plug caps and the wires. Defective wires or caps may allow arcing around the cap while cranking or running the engine.

1. Disconnect both cables from the battery.
2. Carefully twist the cap counterclockwise to unthread it from the spark plug lead (**Figure 145**).
3. Connect the ohmmeter to the spark plug cap as shown in **Figure 149**. Repeat for the remaining spark plug caps.
4. Compare the resistance to the specification in **Table 9**. Replace the plug cap if its resistance is not within the specification.

Spark Plug Lead Test

Inspect the spark plug lead for cracks in the insulation, abraded surfaces or a weathered appearance. Defective insulation allows arcing to the cylinder block or other surfaces. This condition results in an ignition misfire and creates a potentially hazardous condition.

On 4-50 hp models, the spark plug lead is integrated into the ignition coil. Replace the ignition coil and lead assembly if necessary. Attempts to remove the lead will damage the ignition coil or lead and cause an ignition coil failure.

On 75-90 hp models the spark plug lead is threaded onto the ignition coil. This allows replacement of the lead.

The amount of lead resistance varies by the cylinder in which the lead connects. Always mark the cylinder number on the lead and coil prior to removal. Test the resistance on these models as follows:

1. Disconnect both cables from the battery.
2. Carefully twist the spark plug lead counterclockwise near the ignition coil (to unthread it from the ignition coil.
3. Connect an ohmmeter to each end of the spark plug lead and note the resistance and the cylinder from which the lead was removed. Repeat for each spark plug lead.
4. Replace the spark plug lead if its resistance is not as specified in **Table 10**.
5. Twist the spark plug clockwise to reinstall it.

Engine Temperature Sensor Test

An engine temperature sensor (**Figure 150**) is used on 25-40 hp and 75-90 hp models. It provides a varying resistance value to the engine control unit. This varying resistance value allows the engine control unit to determine the approximate engine temperature. This input allows the engine control unit to alter the ignition timing and enhance cold start and cold engine running characteristics.

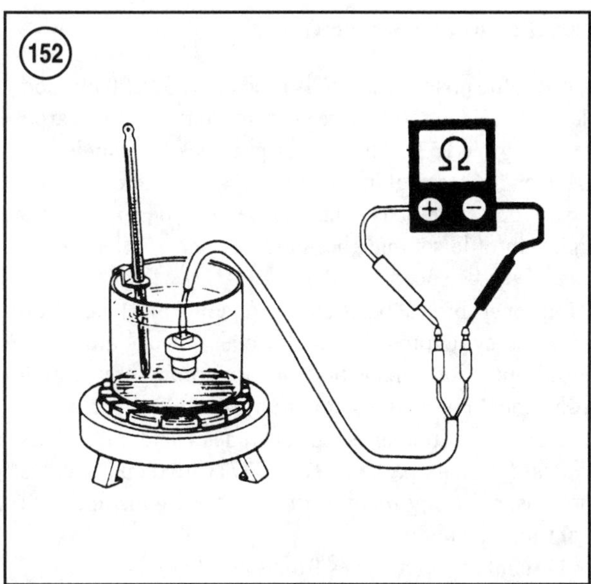

The input from the engine temperature is also used by the engine control unit to determine when to activate the overheat warning system.

Testing this sensor requires a container of water that can be heated and a liquid thermometer. Use a digital or an accurate analog ohmmeter to read the resistance at the specified temperatures.

1. Refer to Chapter Seven and remove the engine temperature sensor from the power head.

2A. *25 hp models*—Connect the ohmmeter between the two tan/black sensor wires.

2B. *30 and 40 hp models*—Connect the ohmmeter between the two black sensor wires.

2C. *75 and 90 hp models*—Connect the ohmmeter between the two sensor terminals (**Figure 151**).

3. Suspend the sensor in a container of water that can be heated (**Figure 152**). Ensure the sensor does not touch the bottom or sides of the container and the tip of the sensor is completely below the water surface.
4. Add cold water or heat the container until the water temperature reaches the temperatures specified in **Table 19**. Record the resistance at each temperature.
5. Compare the resistance reading with the specification listed in **Table 19**. Replace the engine temperature sensor if incorrect meter readings are noted.
6. Install the engine temperature into the power head following the instructions in Chapter Seven. Connect the engine wire harness to the engine temperature sensor. Route the wires away from moving components or the spark plug leads.

Throttle Position Sensor Test

A throttle position sensor is used on 75 and 90 hp models only. It is mounted to the port side of the bottom carburetor (**Figure 153**). This sensor provides a voltage value to the engine control unit that changes with throttle opening. A defective sensor can cause poor performance at higher throttle settings, hesitation during acceleration or excessive idle speed.

Improper throttle position sensor adjustment can cause the same symptoms as a faulty one. Always adjust the throttle position sensor prior to performing any testing. Adjustment instructions are provided in Chapter Five.

A digital voltmeter, shop tachometer and special test harness (mercury part No. 91-805773) are required to test the sensor. Testing requires running the engine under actual running conditions.

1. Disconnect both cables from the battery.
2. Trace the wire harness extending from the throttle position sensor to the engine wire harness connector (**Figure 154**). Disconnect the throttle position sensor from the engine wire harness.
3. Connect the test harness to the throttle position sensor and engine wire harness as shown in **Figure 155**.
4. Select the DC volts function on the digital voltmeter.
5. Connect the positive meter lead to the red wire terminal of the test harness and the negative lead to the orange wire terminal of the test harness.
6. Route the test leads and harness away from any moving components. Clamp them as necessary to ensure the test leads maintain secure contact with the test harness during engine operation. Connect the cables to the battery.
7. Start the engine and allow it to run at idle speed until warmed to normal operating temperature.
8. With the engine warm and running at idle speed, the voltmeter should indicate 4.75-5.25 volts. If not, inspect for a faulty wiring harness, poor connection or defective engine control unit. Stop the engine and disconnect the voltmeter. Do not remove the test harness.
9. Next, connect the positive voltmeter lead to the pink test harness wire and the negative lead to the orange test harness wire.
10. Connect a tachometer to the engine. Route all test leads away from moving components.

NOTE

Perform Steps 11-13 with the boat in the water in forward gear. Observe the voltmeter while an assistant operates the throttle.

11. Start the engine and slowly advance throttle to 850 rpm. The throttle position sensor voltage should be 0.68-0.82 volt. If not, adjust the throttle position sensor as described in Chapter Five. Replace the sensor if it cannot be correctly adjusted.

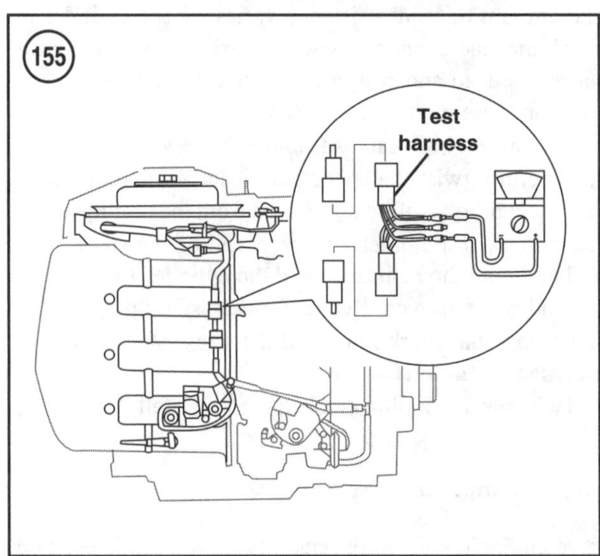

12. Slowly advance the throttle while observing the voltmeter. A steady increase in the voltage must be noted. Re-

156
CU2564
8L18

157
WARNING

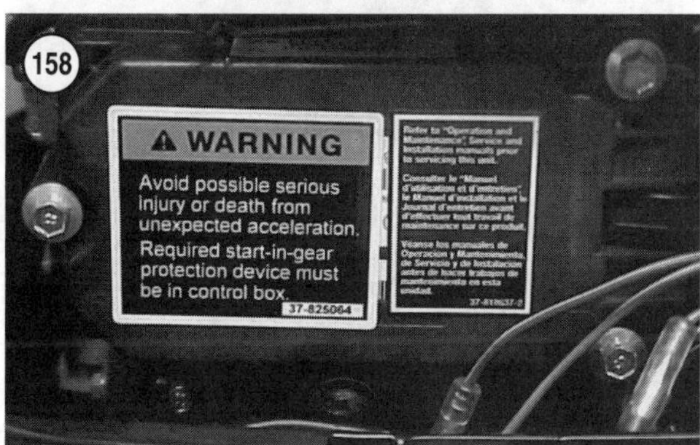
158
WARNING
Avoid possible serious injury or death from unexpected acceleration.
Required start-in-gear protection device must be in control box.
37-825064

159
WARNING
Avoid possible serious injury or death from unexpected acceleration.
Required start-in-gear protection device must be in control box.

160
QUICKSILVER
DIGITAL
DIAGNOSTIC
TERMINAL

place the throttle position sensor (Chapter Seven) if the voltage is erratic.

13. Slowly close the throttle while observing the voltmeter. A steady decrease in voltage must be noted. Replace the throttle position sensor (Chapter Seven) if the voltage is erratic.

CDI and Engine Control Unit

A faulty CDI or engine control unit can cause a no start condition, irregular idle, ignition misfire or incorrect speed limiting. See **Figure 156** (4-6 hp)**, Figure 157** (9.9, 15 and 50 hp) and **Figure 158** (75 and 90 hp). In some rare cases a fault can cause incorrect warning system operation. Refer to *Warning Systems* in this chapter for additional information on warning system operation and test instructions.

Test the CDI or engine control unit following a process of elimination. Test all other components of the ignition system as described in this chapter. Replace the CDI unit or engine control unit only after ruling all other components. Faulty wires or connectors cause far more ignition problems than a defective CDI or engine control unit.

All 25-40 hp models have a connection plug (**Figure 159**) for the DDT (digital diagnostic terminal). The DDT (**Figure 160**) displays data from the engine control unit. This data lists the engine speed and coolant temperature. Using a timing light you can verify if actual ignition timing and the displayed timing are the same. A difference in the timing indicates faulty crank shaft sensor position or engine control unit. This cost of this tool exceeds the cost of the total ignition system components. Most ignition problems can be solved without using the tool. If electing to purchase this tool (part No. 91-823686a 2) it can be ordered from a Mercury or Mariner dealership. A test cartridge and special harnesses are also required. Refer to the instructions provided with the tool for all test instructions.

Faulty Flywheel

The flywheel (**Figure 161**) can result in an ignition misfire or erratic ignition timing. These faults are generally caused a buildup of grease or other contamination on the flywheel magnets. A cracked or damaged flywheel magnet (**Figure 162**) can cause similar symptoms. Inspection of the flywheel magnets requires it be removed from the power head. Flywheel removal and installation are provided in Chapter Eight.

Clean the flywheel using a light solvent. The use of strong solvents can damage the adhesive bonding the magnets to the flywheel on some models. Wipe iron dust or small metallic particles from the magnets using a lightly oiled shop towel.

161

162

WARNING SYSTEMS

The warning system alerts the operator in the event of a cooling or lubrication system failure.

Another feature of the warning system provides engine overspeed control. Should the engine reach or exceed a designated engine speed, the CDI unit or engine control unit initiates an ignition misfire to reduce the engine speed.

Continued operation with the warning system activated can lead to serious and expensive engine damage. Refer to *Warning System Operation* prior to testing any components. This section provides a brief description how the system operates and the components used. Refer to *System/Component Testing* in this chapter for warning system test instructions.

163

Warning System Operation (4-6 hp Models)

These models use a system to alert the operator if low oil pressure occurs. An overheat warning system is not used on these models. Inspect the water stream (**Figure 163**) to monitor the cooling system on these models. Glance at the water stream frequently during engine operation. A weak water stream indicates a cooling system malfunction. Continued operation of the engine with inadequate cooling results in costly engine damage.

The low-oil pressure indicator light (**Figure 164**) mounts to the front side of the lower engine cover. The oil pressure switch (**Figure 165**) controls the light and the ignition charge coil provides the current to operate the system. If the oil pressure is above a predetermined value, the contacts inside the switch remain open. If the oil pressure drops below the predetermined level, the switch closes and activates the warning system. Intermittent flickering of the light is normal at idle speed.

The CDI unit (**Figure 156**) provides overspeed protection. If engine speed exceeds a predetermined value, the CDI unit causes an ignition misfire to lower engine speed. Normal operation resumes when the engine speed is reduced to below the predetermined level.

Warning System Operation (Tiller Control 9.9 and 15 hp Models)

These models use a system to alert the operator if of low oil pressure occurs. An overheat warning system is not used on these models. Inspect the water stream (**Figure 163**) to monitor the cooling system. Glance at the water stream frequently during engine operation. A weak water stream indicates a cooling system malfunction. Continued operation with inadequate cooling results in costly engine damage.

The oil pressure indicator light (**Figure 164**) is mounted to the front side of the lower engine cover. Continued operation with low oil pressure results in costly damage to the power head. Control of the light is provided by the oil pressure switch (**Figure 166**). Electric current to operate the system is provided by the CDI or engine control unit (**Figure 157**).

On 9.9 hp (prior to serial No. OH000058) and all 15 hp models, both terminals of the oil pressure light connect to the to the engine control unit. Current from the ignition system is directed to the oil pressure light by the engine control unit. During normal operation the oil pressure light illuminates a green glow indicating adequate oil pressure. Contacts inside the oil pressure switch remain open provided adequate oil pressure is applied to the switch. The contacts n the switch close if the oil pressure drops below a set pressure. Closing the contacts provides a connection to ground. This connection to ground allows the current to flow to engine ground instead of the light. Without current the light does not illuminate indicating insufficient oil pressure.

On 9.9 hp models (serial No. OH000058-on) one terminal of the of the oil pressure light is connected to engine ground. The other terminal is connected to the CDI unit and the oil pressure switch. Contacts in the oil pressure switch remain open provided adequate oil pressure is applied to the switch. During normal operation current flows from the CDI unit through the oil pressure light to engine ground. As this current flows through the light it illuminates a green glow indicating adequate oil pressure. Should the oil pressure drop below a preset value the contacts in the oil pressure switch close providing a connection to ground. This connection to ground allows the current to flow to engine ground instead of the light. Without electrical current flow the light does not illuminate indicating insufficient oil pressure.

The CDI or engine control unit detects low oil pressure using the oil pressure switch. Power reduction is initiated by the CDI or engine control unit if low oil pressure is detected. A reduction in ignition timing advance or ignition misfire prevents the engine speed from exceeding 2000 rpm if low oil pressure occurs.

The oil pressure light does not illuminate immediately upon starting the engine. Adequate oil pressure is usually not present for the first few seconds of operation. Intermittent flickering of the light is a normal occurrence idle. Flickering of the light at higher engine speeds is not normal and indicates low oil pressure. Never operate the engine unless the light illuminates within a few second of starting the engine.

Overspeed protection is provided automatically by the CDI unit. An ignition system misfire occurs at a preset value to limit the engine speed. Normal ignition system operation resumes when the throttle is reduced enough to drop the engine speed below the preset value. Overspeed control specifications and the recommended wide-open throttle engine speeds are provided in **Table 25**.

Warning System Operation (Remote Control 9.9 and 15 hp Models)

These models use a system to alert the operator in the event of low oil pressure. An overheat warning system is not used on these models. Inspect the water stream (**Figure 163**) to monitor the cooling system. Glance at the water stream frequently during engine operation. A weak water stream indicates a cooling system malfunction. Continued operation of the engine with inadequate cooling results in costly engine damage.

A dash mounted low oil pressure light is used on these models. Continued operation with low oil pressure results in costly damage to the power head. Control of the light is provided by the oil pressure switch (**Figure 166**). Electric current to operate the system is provided by a connection to the ignition switch.

On 9.9 hp (prior to serial No. OH000058) and all 15 hp models, one terminal of the oil pressure light connects to the to the engine control unit. The other terminal of the light connects to the ignition switch. During normal operation the low oil pressure light remains off indicating adequate oil pressure. Contacts inside the oil pressure switch remain open provided adequate oil pressure is applied to the switch. The contacts in the switch close if the oil pressure drops below a preset pressure. Closing the contacts allows the current to flow through the low oil pressure light to ground. The current flow through the light causes it to illuminate indicating inadequate oil pressure.

On 9.9 hp models (serial No. OH000058-on) one terminal of the low oil pressure light is connected to the ignition switch. The other terminal is connected to the CDI unit and the oil pressure switch. Contacts in the oil pressure switch remain open provided adequate oil pressure is applied to the switch. During normal operation the low oil pressure light remains off. A diode in the circuit to prevents current from flowing to the low oil pressure from the CDI unit. Should the oil pressure drop below a preset value the contacts in the oil pressure switch close. Closing the contacts allows the current to flow from the ignition switch to the low oil pressure light to engine ground. The current flow through the light causes it to illuminate indicating inadequate oil pressure.

The CDI or engine control unit detects low oil pressure using the connection to ground through the oil pressure switch. Power reduction is initiated by the CDI or engine control unit if low oil pressure is detected. A reduction in ignition timing advance or an ignition misfire prevents the engine speed from exceeding 2000 rpm when low oil pressure is detected.

The low oil pressure light illuminates when the ignition switch is place in the ON position. This light may illuminate for a few seconds after starting the engine. Adequate oil pressure is usually not present for the first few seconds of operation. Intermittent flickering of the light is a normal occurrence at idle speeds. Flickering of the light at higher engine speeds is not normal and indicates low oil pressure. Never operate the engine unless the light switches off within a few seconds of starting the engine.

Overspeed protection is provided automatically by the CDI or engine control unit. An ignition system misfire occurs at a preset value to limit the engine speed. Normal ignition system operation resumes when the throttle is reduced enough to drop the engine speed below the preset value.

Warning System Operation (Manual Start 25 hp Models)

This model alerts the operator if low oil pressure or an overheated power head occurs.

The oil pressure switch (**Figure 166**) controls the low oil pressure warning system. If sufficient oil pressure is present, the contacts inside the switch remain open. If the oil pressure falls below a predetermined level, the contacts close and activate the warning system.

The engine control unit monitors engine temperature using the engine temperature sensor (**Figure 167**) and activates the warning horn if the engine overheats. **Table 17** lists the temperatures at which the overheat alarm switches on and off.

Using an internal diode the warning horn driver provides a DC voltage supply to the warning horn. AC current from the power source coil powers the warning horn driver. Should low oil pressure or overheating occur, the engine control unit switches on the warning horn driver and warning horn. The engine control unit connects the tan/light blue wire leading to the warning horn and driver to the engine ground. This connection completes the circuit required to switch on the warning horn driver and warning horn.

An overheated engine causes the horn to sound continuously. The horn sounds until the engine speed drops below 1000 rpm and the temperature drops below the temperature specified in **Table 17**.

Low oil pressure causes the horn to sound a repeating one second signal. This signal continues until the engine is switched off.

The engine control unit initiates power reduction when either overheating or low oil pressure occurs. A reduction in ignition timing advance and ignition misfire prevents the engine speed from exceeding 2000 rpm when activated.

Overspeed protection is provided automatically by the engine control unit. An ignition system misfire occurs at a preset value to limit the engine speed. Normal ignition system operation resumes when the throttle is reduced enough to drop the engine speed below the preset value. Overspeed control specifications and the recommended wide-open throttle engine speeds are provided in **Table 25**.

Warning System Operation (Electric Start 25-40 hp Models)

Low oil pressure and overheat warning systems are used on these models. The power source coil provides the current to operate the warning systems. A warning horn mounted in the tiller arm bracket or remote control alerts the operator if the engine overheats or if low oil pressure occurs.

The oil pressure switch (**Figure 166**) controls the low oil pressure warning system. The oil pressure switch remains open if sufficient oil pressure is present. If oil pressure falls to a predetermined value, the oil pressure switch closes and activates the warning horn.

The engine temperature sensor (**Figure 167**) provides input to the engine control unit. The engine control unit initiates an alarm if overheating is detected. **Table 17** lists the temperatures in which the overheat alarm switches on and off.

An overheated engine causes the horn to sound continuously. The horn sounds until the engine speed drops below 1000 rpm and the temperature drops below the temperature specified in **Table 17**.

A low oil pressure condition causes the horn to sound a repeating one second horn on horn off signal.

This signal continues until the engine is switched off.

Never operate the engine with the warning horn sounding or with illuminated warning lights. Continued operation results in costly damage to the power head and other engine components.

The engine control unit initiates power reduction when either overheating or low oil pressure occurs. A reduction in ignition timing advance or an ignition misfire prevents the engine from exceeding 2000 rpm when either condition is detected. Normal operation resumes when the fault is corrected.

Overspeed protection is provided automatically by the engine control unit. An ignition system misfire occurs at a preset value to limit the engine speed. Normal ignition system operation resumes when the throttle is reduced enough to drop the engine speed below the preset value. Overspeed control specifications and the recommended wide-open throttle engine speeds are provided in **Table 25**.

Warning System Operation (Manual Start 30 and 40 hp Models)

These models alert the operator if low oil pressure or an overheated power head occurs. Electrical current to operate the system is provided by the ignition charging coil and the engine control unit. A warning horn provided alerts the operator should either condition occur.

The low oil pressure warning system is controlled by the oil pressure switch (**Figure 166**). The oil pressure switch remains open provided adequate oil pressure is applied to the switch. Should the oil pressure drop below a preset value the switch closes and activates the warning system.

The engine temperature sensor (**Figure 167**) provides input to the engine control unit. The engine control unit initiates an alarm if overheating is detected. **Table 17** list the temperatures in which the overheat alarm switches on and off.

An overheated engine causes the horn to sound continuously. The horn sounds until the engine speed drops below 1000 rpm and the temperature drops below the temperature specified in **Table 17**.

A low oil pressure condition causes the horn to sound a repeating one second signal. This signal continues until the engine is switched off.

Never operate the engine with the warning horn sounding. Continued operation results in costly damage to the power head and other engine components.

The engine control unit initiate power reduction when either overheating or low oil pressure is detected. A reduction in ignition timing advance or an ignition misfire prevents the engine speed from exceeding 2000 rpm when either condition is detected. Normal operation resumes when the fault is corrected and the warning horn ceases.

Overspeed protection is provided automatically by the engine control unit. An ignition system misfire occurs at a preset value to limit the engine speed. Normal ignition system operation resumes when the throttle is reduced enough to drop the engine speed below the preset value. Overspeed control specifications and the recommended wide open throttle engine speeds are provided in **Table 25**.

Warning System Operation (50 hp Models)

This model alerts the operator if low oil pressure occurs or the power head overheats. Electrical current to operate the system is provided by the ignition switch and engine control unit. The ignition charge coil provides the current to operate the warning circuit in the engine control unit (**Figure 157**).

A warning horn alerts the operator should either condition occur.

Control of the low oil pressure warning system is provided by the oil pressure switch (**Figure 166**). The oil pressure switch remains open provided adequate oil pressure is applied to the switch. Should the oil pressure drop below a preset value, the oil pressure switch closes and activates the warning system.

The engine temperature switch (**Figure 168**) mounts directly to the cylinder head in direct contact with the water jacket and is connected to the engine control unit. During normal operation the switch remains closed. Should the engine temperature reach a preset temperature, the switch opens and initiates a warning.

The warning horn sounds when either overheating or low oil pressure is detected and continues until the fault is corrected and the engine is switched off.

Never operate the engine with the warning horn sounding. Continued operation results in costly damage to the power head and other engine components.

The engine control unit initiate power reduction when either overheating or low oil pressure is detected. A reduction in ignition timing advance or an ignition misfire prevents the engine speed from exceeding 2000 rpm when

either condition is detected. Normal operation resumes when the fault is corrected and the warning horn ceases.

Overspeed protection is provided automatically by the engine control unit. An ignition system misfire occurs at a preset value to limit the engine speed. Normal ignition system operation resumes when the throttle is reduced enough to drop the engine speed below the preset value. Overspeed control specifications and the recommended wide open throttle engine speeds are provided in **Table 25**.

Warning System Operation (75 and 90 hp Models)

This model alerts the operator if low oil pressure occurs or if power head overheats. Electrical current to operate the system is provided by a connection to the on circuit of the ignition key switch. The charging system provides the current to operate the warning system control unit (**Figure 158**). A warning horn alerts the operator should either condition occur. An optional warning light kit is available to provide a visual warning.

Control of the low oil pressure warning system is provided by the oil pressure switch (**Figure 166**). The oil pressure switch remains open provided adequate oil pressure is applied to the switch. Should the oil pressure drop below a preset value, the oil pressure switch closes and activates the warning system.

The engine temperature sensor (**Figure 151**) provides input to the engine control unit. The engine control unit initiates an alarm if overheating is detected. **Table 17** lists the temperatures in which the overheat alarm switches on and off.

The engine control unit sounds the horn if overheating or low oil pressure is detected. The horn sounds until the throttle is returned to the idle position and the fault is corrected.

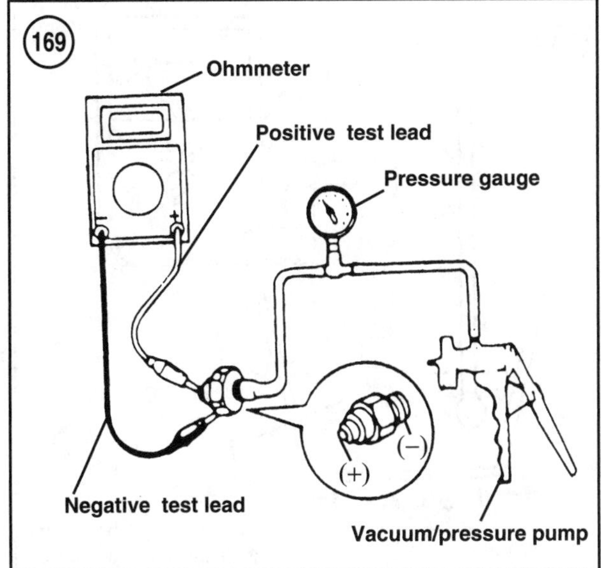

On models with the optional warning lights, battery voltage is provided to the warning lights by the ignition switch. The engine control unit provides the connection to ground for the overheat and low oil pressure warning lights. This connection to ground completes the circuit required to illuminate the lights.

Never operate the engine with the warning horn sounding or with illuminated warning lights. Continued operation results in costly damage to the power head and other engine components.

The engine control unit initiates power reduction if either overheating or low oil pressure is detected. The engine control unit switches off the ignition to selected cylinders and retards the ignition timing to limit the engine speed to 3000 rpm if either condition is detected. Normal operation resumes when the throttle is returned to idle position and the faults are corrected.

Overspeed protection is provided automatically by the engine control unit. A controlled ignition system misfire occurs at a preset values to limit the engine speed. Normal ignition system operation resumes when the throttle is reduced enough to drop the engine speed below the preset value. Overspeed control specifications and the recommended wide-open throttle engine speeds are provided in **Table 26**.

Warning System Tests

Refer to *Cooling System* in this chapter to check the cooling system operation if overheating is detected. Refer to *Power Head* in this chapter to check the engine oil pressure if low oil pressure is detected.

Test the all applicable warning system components if a warning alarm occurs and a cooling or lubrication system fault has been ruled out. Refer to *System Operation* in this section to determine which components are used.

3

Oil pressure switch test

Testing the oil pressure switch requires an ohmmeter and a vacuum/pressure pump. Purchase the vacuum/pressure pump from a local automotive parts or tool supply store. Test the switch as follows:

1. Remove the oil pressure switch from the power head as described in Chapter Seven.
2. Carefully slide an appropriately sized hose over the fitting side of the oil pressure switch (**Figure 169**). Apply a clamp over the connection to ensure accurate test results. Do not apply pressure at this time.
3. Connect the positive ohmmeter lead to the wire on the oil pressure switch (**Figure 169**) and the negative lead to body of the switch.
4. Note the reading on the ohmmeter. The correct test result is continuity.
5. Observe the ohmmeter and the pressure gauge while slowly applying pressure to the switch. Record the pressure gauge reading when the meter reading changes to no continuity.
6. Relieve the pressure then repeat Step 5 several times to ensure an accurate result.
7. Compare the pressure reading with the specification listed in **Table 18**. Replace the oil pressure switch if the meter readings do not change at the indicated pressures.
8. Remove the test leads and pressure/vacuum pump from the oil pressure switch. Clean all hose material from the threaded section of the switch.
9. Install the oil pressure switch as described in Chapter Seven.

Engine temperature switch test

CAUTION
Suspend the overheat switch so only the overheat switch is below the surface of the water. An inaccurate reading will occur if the test leads contact the water.

This component is used on 50 hp models only. The engine temperature switch is designed to switch ON at a predetermined temperature and switch OFF at a slightly lower temperature. This switch signals the engine control unit that overheating is occurring. The engine temperature switch (**Figure 168**) mounts to the cylinder head in direct contact with the water jacket.

One engine temperature switch lead is connected to the engine ground. This switch will not operate correctly if this connection is faulty. The other lead is connected to the engine control unit.

Test the engine temperature switch using a container of water that can be heated, an ohmmeter and a liquid thermometer.

1. Disconnect both cables from the battery.
2. Remove the overheat switch as described in Chapter Seven.
3. Fill the container with cool tap water and suspend the tip of the overheat switch in the water (**Figure 170**). Ensure the switch does not contact the bottom or sides of the container. Place a liquid thermometer in the container with the overheat switch shown in **Figure 170**.
4. Connect the ohmmeter between the two overheat switch wires. The meter should indicate continuity.
5. Begin heating and gently stirring the water while observing the ohmmeter. Record the temperature when the ohmmeter switches from continuity to no continuity. This temperature should be approximately 131° F (55° C) Discontinue the test if the water boils before the ohmmeter changes.
6. Allow the water to cool and record the temperature at which the ohmmeter changes from no continuity to continuity. This temperature should be approximately 104° F (40° C).
7. Replace the overheat switch if it does not perform as described.

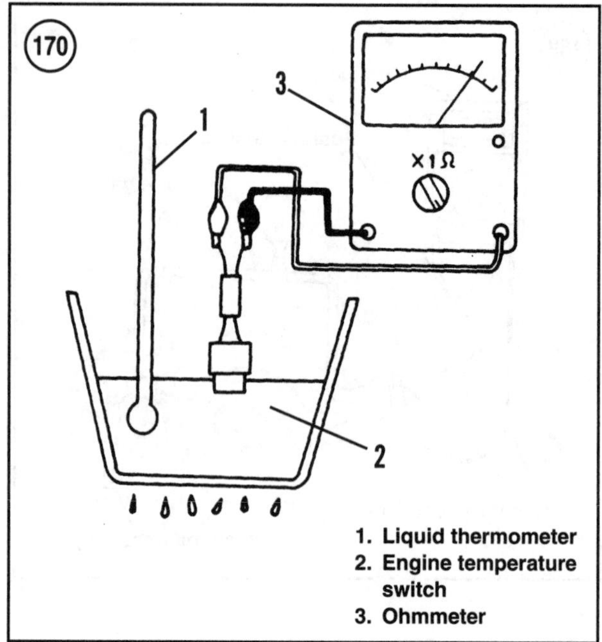

1. Liquid thermometer
2. Engine temperature switch
3. Ohmmeter

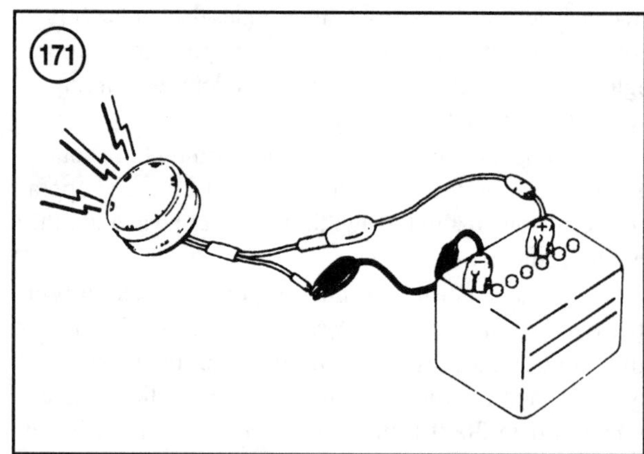

Engine temperature sensor test

This component is used on 25-50 hp and 75-90 hp models. It provides input for both the timing control and warning systems. Test the engine temperature sensor as described under *Ignition System* in this chapter.

Warning horn test

A warning horn is mounted inside the remote control, below the tiller arm bracket or behind the dashboard. Access to both wires is required to test the warning horn. Refer to Chapter Twelve to access the leads inside the remote control. Connect the leads of the horn to a battery using jumper leads (**Figure 171**). Replace the warning horn if it fails to emit a loud warning.

CAUTION

A controlled delay is incorporated into the warning circuit on some models. It prevents activation of the warning system due to residual heat (warm engine starting) or low oil pressure at start up. The length of the delay is dependent upon the engine temperature during start up. When making connections to initiate an alarm signal, maintain the test connections for one minute before determining test results.

Warning horn driver test

A warning horn driver is used only on manual start 25 hp models. Check for proper operation of the warning horn driver as follows:

1. Check and correct the engine oil level as described in Chapter Four. Operate the engine on a flush test adapter see *Flushing The Engine* in Chapter Four.

2. Disconnect the light blue wire from the oil pressure switch (**Figure 172**).
3. Using a jumper wire, connect the light blue wire to a suitable engine ground. The warning horn should sound shortly after making the connection. Switch the engine off.
4. Test the warning horn as described in this section if the horn fails to sound.
5. A faulty warning horn driver, engine control unit or wire harness is indicted if the horn operates correctly but the horn does not sound in Step 3.
6. Check all warning system wires and connectors before replacing the warning horn driver or engine control unit. Replace the warning horn driver if no faults are found with the wiring.

Oil pressure light test

NOTE
Some models use an LED type oil pressure light. Test lead polarity can affect the test results with this type of light. Before condemning the light, reverse the 9 volt battery connection points. Replace the light if it still fails to illuminate.

This component is used on 4-15 hp tiller control models. An optional low oil pressure light may be installed on some electric start 25-40 hp models. Check the light for basic operation using jumper leads and a 9-volt battery. Refer to the wiring diagrams located at the end of the manual to identify the wires used for the light.
1. Disconnect both cables from the battery, when so equipped.
2. Disconnect both oil pressure light wires from the engine harness.
3. Using suitable jumper lead connect the 9 volt battery to the oil pressure light as follows.
   a. On 4-6 hp models, connect the positive terminal of the battery to the white wire of the oil pressure light. Connect the negative terminal of the battery to the light green wire.
   b. On tiller control 9.9 hp (prior to serial No. OH000058) and 15 hp models, connect the positive terminal of the battery to the yellow/red wire of the oil pressure light. Connect the negative terminal of the battery to the pink wire.
   c. On 9.9 (prior to serial No. OH000058) and 15 hp remote control models, connect the positive terminal of the battery to the tan/black wire of the oil pressure light. Connect the negative terminal of the battery to the tan/white wire.
   d. On 9.9 hp (serial No. OH000058-on) manual start models, connect the positive terminal of the battery to the yellow/red wire of the oil pressure light. Connect the negative terminal of the battery to the black wire.
   e. On 9.9 hp (serial No. OH000058-on) electric start models, connect the positive terminal of the battery to the brown/black wire of the oil pressure light. Connect the negative terminal of the battery to the brown/white wire terminal. Do not connect the battery to the wire leading to the diode.
   f. On 25-40 hp models with the optional low oil pressure warning light. Connect the positive terminal of the battery to the purple wire of the oil pressure light. Connect the negative terminal of the battery to the black wire.
4. The light should glow when the battery is connected. If not, replace the bulb.

Diode test

This component is used on 9.9 hp (serial No. OH000058-on) manual start models. A faulty diode can allow false operation of the oil pressure light. Test the diode using an ohmmeter. Refer to the wiring diagrams located at the end of the manual to identify diode wires.
1. Trace the brown/white wire from the oil pressure light to the diode. Disconnect the diode from the engine and oil pressure light harness.

NOTE
The diode is a one-way check valve for electricity. It should allow current to pass in one direction, but not the other direction.

2. Connect the ohmmeter between the two diode wires. Note the meter, then reverse the ohmmeter leads and again note the meter.

3. The meter should indicate continuity with the meter connected one way and no continuity when the leads are reversed.
4. Replace the diode if it does not function as described.

CDI or engine control unit

Check all wire and connections if the switches or sensors are in good condition. Replace the CDI or engine control unit if all other warning system components operate correctly but a false alarm persists. Bear in mind that far more false alarms are caused by faulty wire connections than a defective CDI or engine control unit. Thoroughly inspect all applicable wires and terminals before replacing the CDI or engine control unit. CDI and engine control unit removal and installation are provided in Chapter Seven.

Overspeed protection system test

The CDI or engine control unit controls the overspeed protection system. It initiates an ignition misfire to prevent power head damage from excessive engine speed.

A malfunctioning overspeed protection system can cause a misfire to occur while running within the recommended speed range. Conversely, a malfunction may allow engine speed above the recommended range without activating the system. **Table 25** lists the recommended engine speeds for all models. Also listed is the speed at which overspeed control should activate.

To test the system, connect an accurate tachometer and run the engine at wide-open throttle in a test tank or on the water. Replace the CDI or engine control unit if the engine speed exceeds the maximum limit without activating the overspeed protection system. If a misfire occurs while running within the recommended speed range, first test all fuel and ignition system components. If all fuel and ignition system components are functioning correctly, replace the CDI or engine control unit.

CHARGING SYSTEM

The battery charging systems provide electric current to operate various components on the engine such as the trim and engine control systems. It also provides current to operate electric devices on the boat such as navigational lighting, radios, depth finders and live well pumps. Another duty of the charging system is charging the onboard batteries. Charging system components include the flywheel, battery charging/lighting coil, rectifier/regulator, fuses, wiring and the battery.

173

174

This section provides information on the various system used, how they operate and system testing instructions.

All electric start models are equipped with a regulated battery charging system. An optional lighting coil kit may be installed on 4, 5, 9.9 (prior to serial No. OH000058) and 15 hp models. Later 9.9 hp (serial No. OH000058-on) and all 25-40 hp manual start models are equipped with lighting coils. The lighting coil allows for operation of normal navigational lighting. A special harness connects the navigational lights directly to the lighting coil.

An optional rectifier kit may be installed on 4-6 hp models. It provides unregulated battery charging capability when added to the lighting coil option.

An optional battery charging kit may be installed on manual start 9.9-40 hp models. This kit includes a rectifier/regulator and the wire harnesses to connect these components to the battery and lighting coil. It provides a regulated battery charging capability.

Charging System Operation

When the engine is running the magnets located along the inner ring of the flywheel (**Figure 173**) pass next to the lighting or battery charging coil (**Figure 174** or **175**). Al-

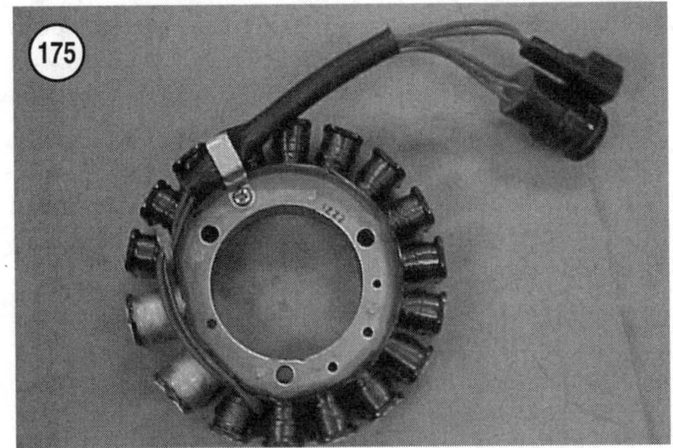

175

176

ternating current (AC) is created as the magnetic lines of force from the flywheel mounted magnets pass through the lighting or battery charging coil. This alternating current is not suitable for charging the battery or operating many engine electrical components. A rectifier or rectifier/regulator (**Figure 176**) converts the AC to direct current (DC) providing battery charging capability. The rectifier/regulator limits the output of the charging system to prevent overcharging the battery. Overcharging can damage the battery and some electrical component on the engine. Models using a rectifier have relatively low charging system output and overcharging of the battery is unlikely with normal operation. Continued high speed operation while using a small capacity battery may allow overcharging on rectifier equipped models.

System Testing

A malfunctioning charging system generally results in an undercharged battery. Many newer boats are equipped with numerous electrical components including electric trolling motors, depth finders, communication radios, stereo systems, live well pumps, lighting and other electrical

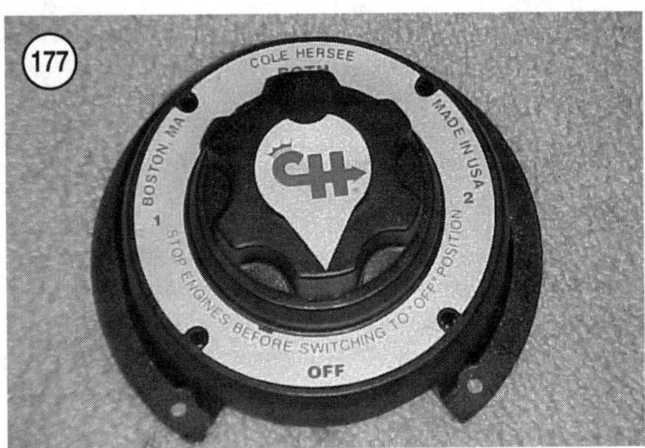

177

accessories. Many times the current required to operate these accessories exceeds the output of the charging system resulting in an undercharged battery.

The installation of an auxiliary battery and a switching device (**Figure 177**) may be required to power these accessories. These devices separate the batteries and prevent electrical accessories from discharging the engine cranking battery. They also allow in most cases charging of multiple batteries while underway. Follow the manufacturer's instructions when installing these switching devices.

Some engines are equipped with a dash mounted tachometer. The signal to operate the tachometer is provided by the charging system. In almost all instances the charging system is providing some battery charging capacity if the tachometer registers engine speed. However a fault can allow tachometer operation even though the charging system is performing well below its maximum efficiency.

Perform the *System Output Test* to determine if the charging system is operating. Testing the individual components of the charging system should identify the faulty components. Test all of the charging system components. In many instances more than one component has failed.

On models using a lighting coil only, test the lighting coil if the navigational lighting fails to operate. A faulty wire, terminal or light is likely if the coil operates correctly.

On models with battery charging capability, refer to *Charging System Output Test* in this chapter for testing instructions.

Overcharging is almost always the result of a faulty rectifier/regulator on models so equipped. An overcharge condition can also result from a faulty battery or corroded terminals and wiring. Refer to Chapter Seven if the rectifier/regulator operates correctly but overcharging is occuring. Always clean the terminals and correct any problems with wiring or connections prior to testing the charging system.

WARNING
Use extreme caution when working around batteries. Never smoke or allow sparks to occur around batteries. Batteries produce explosive hydrogen gas that can explode and result in injury or death. Never make the final connection of a circuit to the battery terminal as an arc may occur and lead to fire or explosion.

CAUTION
Never remove or disconnect the battery cables or any lead of the charging system while the engine is running. Permanent damage to the charging system components usually occurs when these cables or leads are disconnected.

WARNING
Stay clear of the propeller shaft while running an outboard on a flush/test device. Remove the propeller before running the engine to help avoid serious injury. Disconnect all spark plug leads and both battery cables before removing or installing the propeller.

CAUTION
Never run an outboard without providing cooling water. Using a test tank or flush/test device. Remove the propeller before running the engine on a flush/test device. Use a test propeller to run the engine in a test tank.

Charging System Output Test

This test requires the use of a voltmeter and a flush/test device or test tank. Always inspect the battery terminals, all wire terminals, plugs and other charging system connections for corrosion, debris or damaged terminals. Correct all defects prior to performing this test. Refer to Chapter Four to run the engine using a flush/test device or a test tank.

1. Switch all electrical accessories OFF.
2. With the engine OFF, connect the voltmeter to the battery. Record the battery voltage.
3. Start the engine, run at idle speed and note the voltage. The voltage should be at least 0.2 volt greater than the voltage recorded in Step 2.
4. Next, throttle up to approximately 2000 rpm and note the voltmeter. The voltage should again be at least 0.2 volt greater than the voltage recorded in Step 2.
5. Repeat Step 3 and Step 4 with all onboard accessories turned on one at a time. If the voltage drops below 0.2 volt more than the voltage recorded in Step 2, the charging system is likely functioning correctly; however, the accessory load may exceed the capacity of the charging system.
   a. The charging system output is correct if the running voltage is 0.2 volt (or more) greater than the battery voltage recorded in Step 2.
   b. If the voltage increases less than 0.2 volt, test the rectifier or rectifier/regulator and battery charge coil as described in this chapter.
   c. If the charging voltage exceeds 13.8 volts, the charging system is overcharging. First, check the charging system wiring for damaged wires or loose or corroded connections. If the wiring and connections are in acceptable condition, replace the rectifier/regulator as described in Chapter Seven.

Battery Charging/Lighting Coil Resistance Test

This test requires an ohmmeter and with some models some short jumper leads. Refer to the wire diagram located at the end of the manual to identify the coil wire. **Table 20** provides the resistance specifications and the meter test lead connection points.

Removal of the battery charging/lighting coil is not required provided there is access to the wires. Refer to Chapter Seven if coil removal is required.

1. Disconnect both cables from the battery.
2. Disconnect the battery charging/lighting coil from the engine wire harness.
3. Connect the ohmmeter to the battery charging/lighting coil wires indicated in **Table 20**. Record the meter reading for each test lead connection.
4. Compare the meter readings with the specifications listed in **Table 20**. Replace the battery charging/lighting coil if the resistance is beyond the listed specification. Refer to Chapter Seven for removal and installation.
5. Connect the battery charging/lighting coil to the engine wire harness. Ensure the wires route in a manner preventing them from contacting any moving components.
6. Connect the battery cables to the battery.

Rectifier Test

A rectifier is used on 4-6 hp models equipped with the optional lighting coil and battery charging coil. An ohmmeter is required to test this component.

1. Disconnect both cables from the battery.
2. Trace the yellow/red wire from the battery charging coil under the flywheel to the yellow wire to the rectifier.

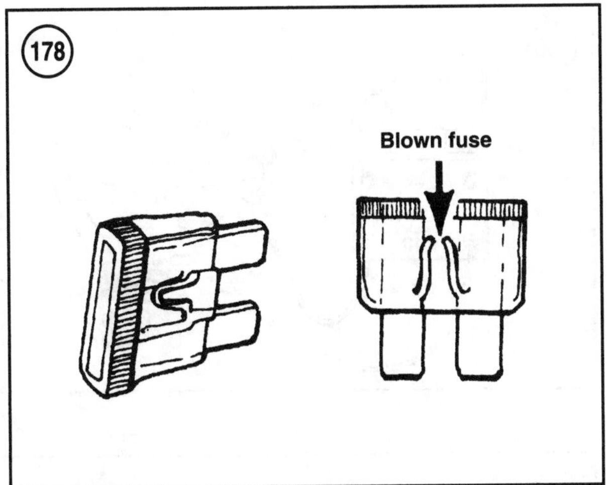

3. Disconnect the yellow and red wires from the rectifier.

4. Connect the positive ohmmeter lead to the yellow wire and the negative lead to the red wire. Note the meter reading.

5. Reverse the ohmmeter leads and note the meter reading.

6. The readings in Step 4 and Step 5 must be opposite (continuity in one step and no continuity in the other step. Replace the rectifier if both readings are continuity or if both are no continuity.

Rectifier/Regulator Test

Removal of the rectifier/regulator (**Figure 176**) is not required provided there is adequate access to the wire terminals. Rectifier/regulator removal and installation is covered in Chapter Seven.

All test specifications are provided in **Table 21**.

1. Disconnect both cables from the battery.

2. Disconnect the rectifier/regulator from the engine wire harness.

3. Connect the meter test leads to the rectifier/regulator terminals indicated in **Table 21**. Record the meter readings at test lead connection.

4. Compare the meter readings with the specifications listed in **Table 21**. Replace the rectifier/regulator if any incorrect readings are noted. Rectifier/regulator removal and installation instructions is covered in Chapter Seven.

5. Carefully route the wires while connecting the rectifier/regulator wires to the engine wire harness.

6. Connect the cables to the battery.

FUSES

Fuses protect the wiring harness and electric components from damage if an overloaded or shorted circuit occurs. Refer to the wire diagrams located at the end of the manual to determine fuse usage for the all models.

All 4-6 hp models with the optional lighting coil and battery charging coil rectifier are equipped with a single 10 amp fuse. This fuse is located in the wire red wire connecting the rectifier to the positive terminal of the battery. A fault with this fuse prevents charging of the battery.

All 9.9 and 15 hp models with electric start are equipped with a single 20 amp fuse. This fuse is located in the red wire connecting the starter relay to the voltage regulator. A fault with this fuse prevents operation of the starter motor and choke solenoid.

All 25-50 hp models with electric start are equipped with a single 20 amp fuse. This fuse is located in the red and red/purple wire connecting the starter relay to the remote control or tiller control harness. A fault with this fuse prevents operation of the starter relay and all dash mounted instruments or warning lights. A fault with this fuse also prevents charging of the battery and operation of trim system switches.

Two fuses are used on 75 and 90 hp models. A 30 amp fuse in located in the red wire connecting the rectifier/regulator to the starter relay. A fault with this fuse prevents charging of the battery and operation of all dash mounted instruments, the electric starter motor and the switches for the trim system. A 20 amp fuse is located along red wire connecting the rectifier/regulator to the ignition switch. A fault with this fuse prevents operation of the starter, all dash mounted instruments and the switches for the trim system.

WARNING

Never replace a fuse without thoroughly checking the wire harness for defects. Never install a fuse with a capacity greater than the original fuse.

Fuse Testing

A blown fuse (**Figure 178**) can usually be identified with a visual inspection. However, a fuse can appear to be in good condition, but still not have continuity. Therefore, it is good practice to check the continuity of all fuses using an ohmmeter anytime an electrical problem is encountered.

Refer to the wiring diagrams at the back of this manual to determine the number and location of fuses. If an elec-

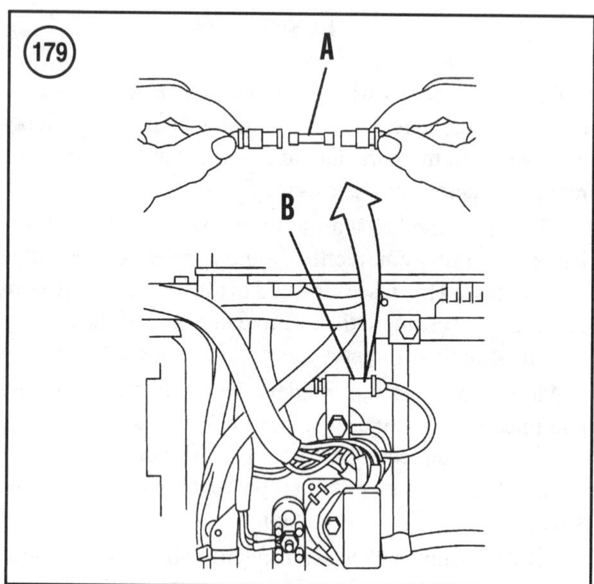

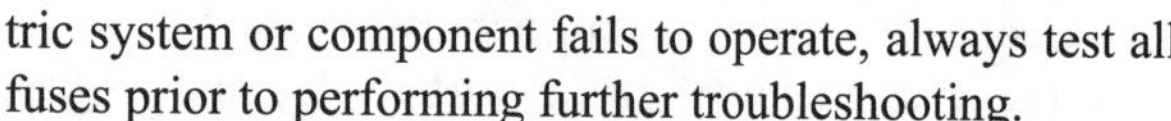

tric system or component fails to operate, always test all fuses prior to performing further troubleshooting.

1. Disconnect both cables from the battery.
2. On models using a 10 amp fuse, carefully pull the fuse (A, **Figure 179**) from its cylindrical holder (B).
3. On models using 20 and/or 30 amp plug-in type fuses (**Figure 178**), carefully pull the cover from the fuse holder. Grasp the back of the fuse and pull it out to remove it.
4. Connect the ohmmeter to each fuse terminal and note the meter.
5. If the fuse is good, the ohmmeter will indicate continuity.
6. No continuity means the fuse has failed and must be replaced. Note that a fuse failure is usually the result of a shorted or overloaded circuit. Inspect all engine and instrument wires for damaged insulation, chafing, loose or corroded connections or other damage. Repair damaged wiring or poor connections prior to replacing the fuse.

Wire Harness Test

Due to the harsh marine environment that boats operate in, wiring harness problems are common. Corroded or damaged wires or connections can cause electrical or ignition system components to malfunction. Electrical problems can also occur intermittently making troubleshooting extremely difficult.

If an electrical malfunction occurs and testing indicates that all individual components are functioning properly, suspect the wiring harness. Test the harness for continuity using an ohmmeter after disconnecting all components from the harness (**Figure 180**).

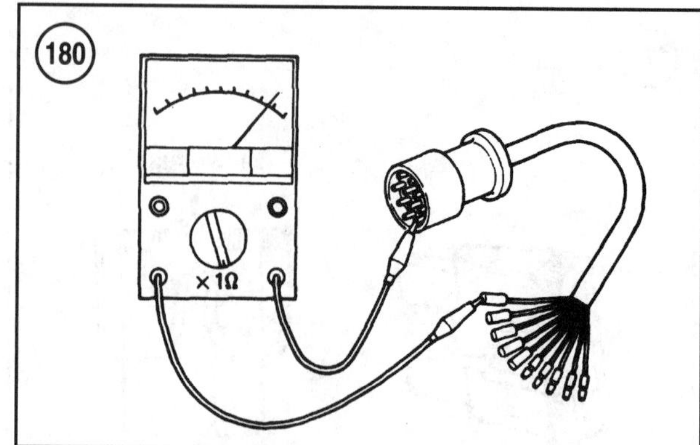

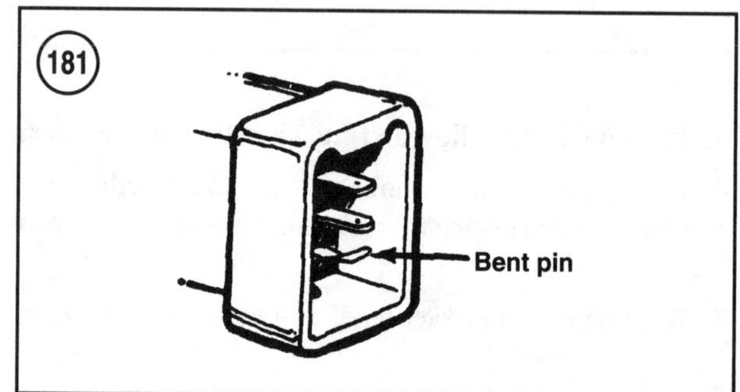

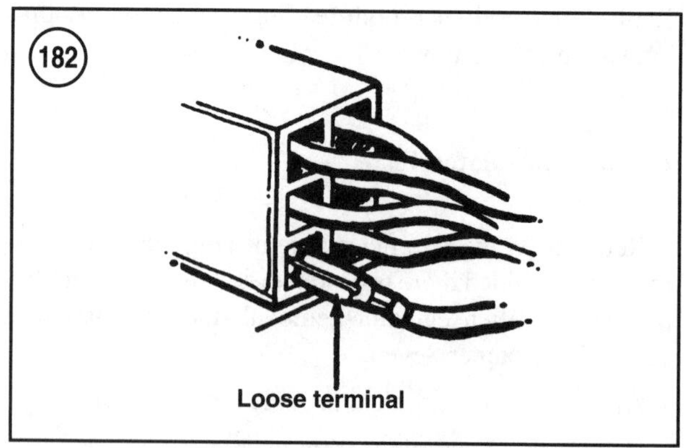

Most wiring harness problems occur at the connectors and plugs. Inspect the connectors for bent pins (**Figure 181**) and loose terminals (**Figure 182**). Make sure the connectors lock together securely (**Figure 183**). Loose connectors are a major cause of intermittent electrical problems. To test the wiring harness, proceed as follows:

1. Disconnect both cables from the battery.
2. Mark all wire terminals connected to the wire harness. Note the wire routing then disconnect all wires from the harness.

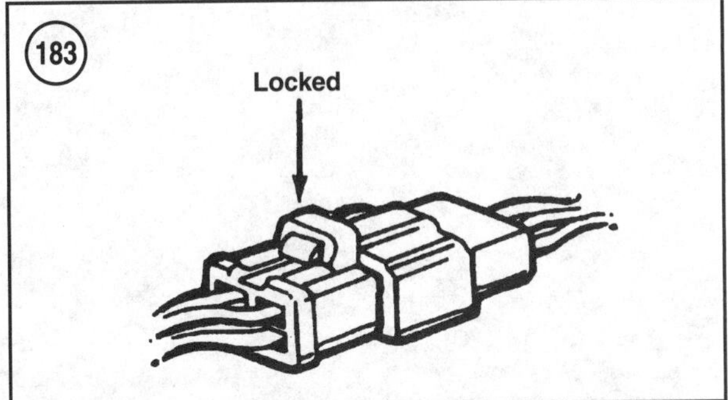

3. Refer to the wire diagrams located at the end of the manual to identify the wire color to connector pin locations. Connect the meter test leads to the pins as indicted in **Figure 180**.
4. Note the meter reading. The correct test is continuity.
5. Note the meter reading while twisting, bending and pulling on the wire harness. A fault is indicated if the meter reading changes to no continuity. Often intermittent faults are found this way.
6. Repeat Steps 3-5 for the remaining wires in the harness.
7. Connect all components to the engine wire harness. Route all wires in a manner preventing them from contacting any moving components. Prior to connecting them ensure all ground terminals for the wire harness are clean and securely attached to the wire harness.
8. Clean the terminals then connect the cables to the battery.

POWER HEAD

All 9.9-90 hp models utilize an overhead camshaft (**Figure 184**). The use of an overhead camshaft reduces engine weight compared to a cylinder block mounted camshaft. The overhead camshaft design provides a less complex valve train and allows for easier adjustments and repairs.

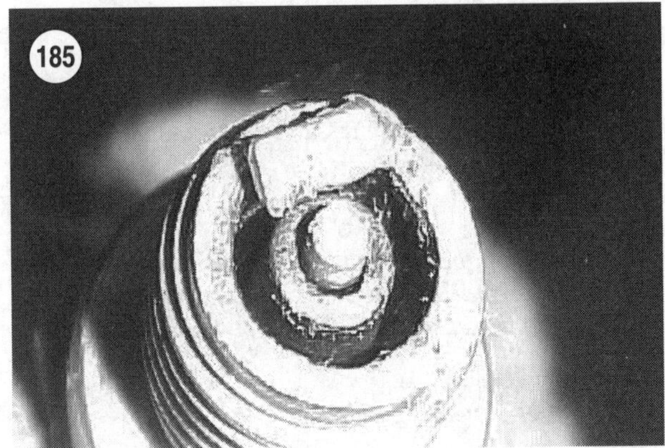

This section provides troubleshooting tips and testing instructions to pinpoint most power head related failures. Compression and oil pressure testing are also provided in this section.

Engine Noises

Some power head noise is generated during normal engine operation. A ticking noise or a heavy knocking noise intensifying when accelerating is a reason for concern.

If suspecting a worn or damaged component is the cause of an engine noise, consider having a professional technician listen to the engine. In many cases only the trained ear of the technician can determine what component has failed.

Power head repairs can be costly and time consuming. Investigate all noises thoroughly before disassembling the power head.

A broken or loose bracket or fastener can cause a noise that is easily mistaken for an internal power head failure.

Ticking noise

The ticking noise is common when valve adjustment is required or a valve train component has failed. Adjust the valves as described in Chapter Four then listen to the engine.

A ticking noise can also result from a damaged piston. Inspect the spark plugs for damage or aluminum deposits (**Figure 185**). Complete power head disassembly and repair is required if metal deposits are found on the spark plug. Perform a compression test as described in this chapter. Remove the cylinder head and inspect the valves, gaskets, pistons and cylinders if low compression is revealed. Cylinder head removal and installation are provided in Chapter Eight.

See *Valve Train Failure* in this section for additional information if the spark plugs and compression are good, but the ticking noise persists.

CAUTION
Running the engine with an abnormal noise may result in increased damage dramatically increasing the cost of repairs.

Whirring or squealing noise

A whirring or squealing noise is usually related to a problem with main or connecting rod bearings. Often the noise becomes louder if the throttle is abruptly reduced to idle from a higher speed.

Sometimes the cylinder creating the noise can be identified using a mechanic's stethoscope (**Figure 186**). Touch the tip of the probe to the power head while listening. Compare the noise emanating from one area of the power head, cylinder head or crankcase, with the noise from the same area but different cylinder. A noise common to one cylinder only indicates a problem with its connecting rod bearing. A noise common to all cylinders indicates a problem with crankshaft main bearings. Test the oil pressure see *Oil Pressure Test* in this chapter to determine if the noise is caused by insufficient lubrication. Be aware that the timing belt and pulleys can generate a fair amount of noise. Use the stethoscope (**Figure 186**) to ensure the noise is emanating from the power head before proceeding with a power head repair.

WARNING
Use extreme caution when working on or around a running engine. Never wear loose fitting clothing. Take all necessary precautions to ensure no one gets near the flywheel or drive belts. Never allow anyone near the propeller or propeller shaft while the engine is running.

Knocking noise

Use a mechanic's stethoscope to determine if the noise is emanating from the power head or elsewhere. The noise will be more pronounced in the crankcase area if a problem exists in the crankshaft and connecting rods. Special insulated pliers are available allowing spark plug lead removal while running the engine. The noise may lessen when the spark plug lead is removed on the suspected cylinder. This procedure is difficult to do and may result in damage to the electrical system. Ground the spark plug

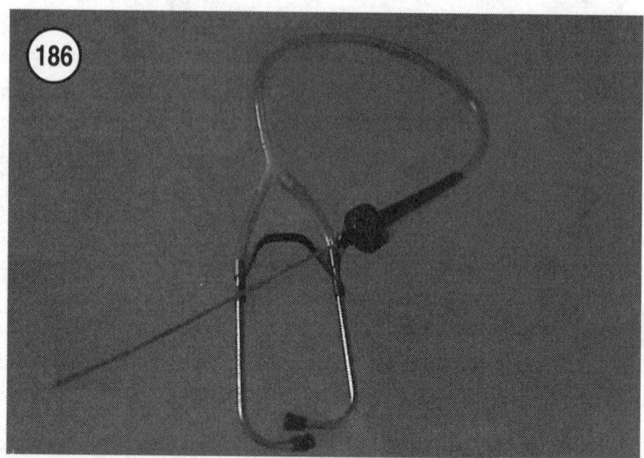
186

187

promptly to reduce the chance of damage to ignition system. Another method of isolating the cylinder is to remove one spark plug lead and attach it to an engine ground. Start the engine and listen to the noise. Install the spark lead and repeat the process for another cylinder. If the noise is less when one lead is grounded when compared with another, that cylinder is suspect. The stethoscope method of isolating cylinders is more effective for an amateur technician.

Always perform an oil pressure test if a knocking noise is detected. Knocking noise combined with low or unstable oil pressure generally indicates fault with the crankshaft main and/or connecting rod bearings. Refer to *Oil pressure test* in this chapter.

Bearing failure causes metal particles to accumulate in the oil pan. These particles are picked up by the oil pump where they are deposited in the oil filter. Inspect the oil filter if bearing failure is suspected. Remove the filter as described in Chapter Four. Cut open the filter and inspect the filter element. Bearing failure is likely if a significant amount of metal debris is found.

188

189

190

Lubrication System

A lubrication system failure can result in catastrophic power head failure. Lubrication system failure leads to scuffed pistons (**Figure 187**), excessive wear of valve train components (**Figure 188**) and eventual power head failure.

Failure of the lubrication system results from the following common causes:

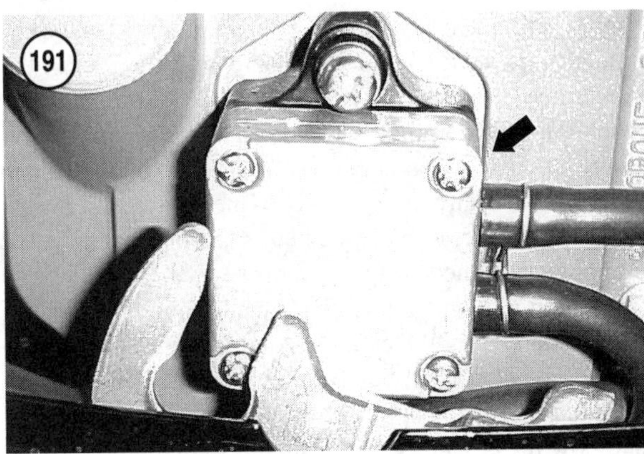
191

1. Incorrect oil level.
2. Oil leakage or high oil consumption.
3. Using contaminated, diluted or wrong type of oil.
4. Failure of the oil pump system.

CAUTION

Damage can occur in a matter of seconds if the lubrication system fails. To help prevent serious engine damage, slow down and stop the engine at once if low oil pressure is indicated by the warning system.

Incorrect oil level

Incorrect oil level can result from improperly filling the engine or improperly checking the engine oil level.

Too high of an oil level allows the crankshaft and other components to agitate the oil and cause the formation of bubbles or foam. This foamy oil may cause a drop in oil pressure and lead to activation of the low oil pressure warning system. In some cases the oil pressure can remain above the low oil pressure activation point yet the engine will still suffer from inadequate lubrication.

Oil level check and oil filling instructions are provided in Chapter Four.

Oil leakage or high oil consumption

A rapid drop in oil level can result from oil leakage or from high oil consumption. In most cases oil leakage is easily detected and corrected. Common leakage points are at the rocker cover area (**Figure 189**), oil filter mounting surface (**Figure 190**), fuel pump mounting surface (**Figure 191**) or crankcase mating surfaces. Finding the point of leakage can be difficult. Air flowing around the power head often distributes a thin film of oil on all external surfaces. To locate the point of leakage, carefully clean the engine using a shop towel and degreasing agent. Run the engine until it reaches operating temperature. Turn the engine off then wipe a white towel across all surfaces of the power head. Oil leakage is readily detected on the towel when the leakage point is contacted. Pinholes or casting flows may cause leakage to occur at other points on the power head. Many times simply tightening fasteners corrects oil leakage. Replace gaskets, seals or other effected components if the leakage continues.

All engines consume some oil while running. Some of the oil lubricating the cylinders and valves is drawn into the combustion chamber and subsequently burned. Oil consumption rates vary by model, condition of the engine and how the engine is used. Engines with high operating hours or engines with worn internal components generally burn much more oil than new or low hour engines. Damage to the piston and cylinders from detonation or preignition can cause increased oil consumption. New or recently rebuilt engine generally consume oil during the break-in period. After the break-in period the oil consumption should return to normal.

A typical symptom of excessive oil consumption is a blue smoke coming from the exhaust during hard acceleration or high speed operation. Inspection of the spark plug usually reveals fouling or an oily film on the spark plug.

Perform a compression test if smoking or an oil fouled plug is noted. Worn or damaged components will generally cause a low compression reading. Compression test instructions are provided in this section.

On 4-6 hp models the oil pan is integrated into the cylinder block. On all 9.9-75 hp models the oil pan is located in the drive shaft housing. Oil leakage from the gearcase or the presence of water in the oil can also occur if the oil pan is leaking. Power head removal is required to access the oil pan and the power head mounting adapter. Refer to Chapter Eight for power head removal and installation. Drive shaft housing removal and installation is covered in Chapter Eleven.

Contaminated, diluted or wrong type of oil

Contaminants enter the engine oil during normal operation. Dirt or dust enters the engine along with the air used during normal operation. Other particles form during the combustion process. Dirt, dust and other particles are captured by the lubricating oil and circulated throughout the engine. Most of the larger particles are captured in the oil filter (except 4-6 hp models). Smaller particles circulate through the engine with the lubricating oil. Frequent oil changes flush these particles from the oil before they reach high concentrations. High concentrations of these particle cause increased wear of internal power head components.

During normal operation, unburned fuel and water vapor accumulate the lubricating oil. Oil also absorbs heat from the engine during operation. This heating causes the unburned fuel and water to evaporate from the oil and form crankcase vapor. The crankcase ventilation system (**Figure 192**) returns the vapor to the combustion chamber where they burn or exit through the exhaust.

A faulty fuel system can dramatically increase the amount of unburned fuel in the oil. High levels of unburned fuel may not evaporate quickly enough to prevent oil dilution.

Failure to reach normal engine operating temperature prevents the fuel and water vapor from evaporating. Failure to reach normal operating temperature is generally caused by a faulty or improperly installed thermostat or water pressure relief valve (75 and 90 hp models).

Wipe a sample of the oil from the dipstick between your finger and thumb. Compare the thickness of the oil with a sample of new oil. Smell the oil then check for a white or light color residue.

A very thin feel, fuel smell in the oil or white residue indicates oil dilution. Test the cooling and fuel system, as described in this chapter, if oil dilution is indicated.

Using the wrong grade, type or weight of oil can lead to increased engine wear and/or complete power head failure. Poor quality oil may not provide the level of protection required by the engine. Using the wrong type of oil usually leads to severe power head damage. Never use two-stroke outboard oil in a four-stroke outboard. Using the improper weight of oil can prevent correct oil circulation during cold engine operation or allow excessive thinning of the oil at higher temperatures. Oil recommendations are provided in Chapter Four.

Failure of the lubrication system

Failure of the lubrication system results in rapid wear of internal components and eventual power head seizure. Causes of oil pumping system failure include:

1. Worn, damaged or broken oil pump components.
2. Worn or damaged crankshaft or connecting rod bearings.
3. A blocked, damaged or loose oil pickup tube or screen.
4. A faulty or stuck oil pressure relief valve.

Failure of the lubrication system causes a loss of oil pressure and activation of the low oil pressure warning system. Continued operation results in rapid wear of internal components followed by eventual power head seizure. Check the oil pressure if the warning system activates and low oil level is ruled out as the cause. Refer to *Oil Pressure Testing* in this section.

Detonation

Detonation damage is the result of the heat and pressure in the combustion chamber becoming too great for the fuel that is used. Fuel normally burns a controlled rate during normal combustion. The fuel explodes violently if the heat and pressure become too high. These violent explosions in the combustion chamber cause serious damage to internal engine components. The piston typically suffers the brunt of the damage. Detonation usually occurs only at higher engine speeds or during heavy acceleration. A pinging noise from the power head accompanied by a loss of power is often noted when detonation is occurring. Inspect the spark plug if detonation damage is suspected. Aluminum deposits or a melted electrode (**Figure 193**) indicate probable detonation damage. Perform a compression test to determine the extent of damage to the power head. Repair the power head if low compression is indicated. Correct the causes of detonation to prevent additional power head damage or repeat failures.

Conditions that promote detonation include:

1. Using a fuel with too low of an octane rating.
2. Excessive carbon deposits in the combustion chamber.
3. Overheating of the engine.
4. Using the incorrect propeller or overloading the engine.
5. Excessively lean fuel delivery.
6. Over-advanced ignition timing.

Preignition

Preignition is caused by a glowing object inside the combustion chamber causing early ignition. The flame from the early ignition collides with the flame front initiated by the spark plug. A violet explosion occurs as these flame fronts collide. The piston suffers the brunt of the damage caused by this explosion. Inspect the spark plug and perform a compression test if pre-ignition is suspected. Aluminum deposits on the spark plug are likely when preignition has occurred. Repair the power head if low compression is revealed. Correct the causes of preignition to prevent additional power head damage or repeat failures.

Conditions that promote pre-ignition include:

1. Excessive carbon deposits in the combustion chamber.
2. Using the wrong hear range of spark plug.
3. Overheating of the engine.

Engine Seizure

Power head seizure results from failure of internal power head components. This can occur at any engine speed. Should the failure occur at higher engine speeds the engine may abruptly stop or gradually slow down and stall. Typically the seizure is caused by a crankshaft, connecting rod or piston failure. Although not as common , power head seizure also occurs from a failure of the valve train components. Power head seizure prevents the manual or electric starter from cranking the engine. Major repair is almost always required when power head seizure occurs.

Bear in mind that failure of the gearcase can also prevent flywheel rotation. Before suspecting the power head, remove the gearcase. Gearcase removal and installation are provided in Chapter Nine.

Oil in the cylinders can hydraulically lock the cylinders and prevent flywheel rotation. Refer to *Oil in the Cylinders* in this section if the engine is seized after storage or transport. Manually attempt to rotate the flywheel with the gearcase removed. Repair the gearcase if the flywheel can be rotated. Remove then repair the power head the seizure persists. Power head removal, repair and installation instructions are provided in Chapter Eight.

Water Entering the Cylinder

Water can enter the cylinder from a number of areas including:

1. Water entering the carburetor opening.
2. Water in the fuel.
3. Leaking exhaust covers or gaskets.
4. Leaking cylinder head gaskets.
5. Leaking water jackets in the cylinder block.
6. Leaking water jackets in the cylinder head.

The typical symptom is rough running particularly at idle. The engine may run correctly at higher speed as a

(193)

SPARK PLUG CONDITION

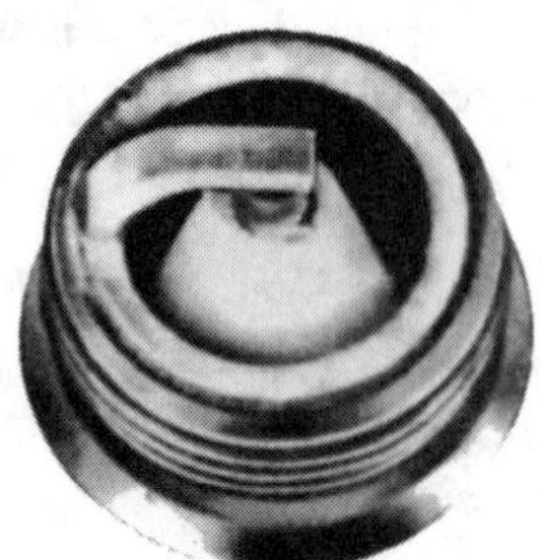

NORMAL

- Identified by light tan or gray deposits on the firing tip.
- Can be cleaned.

GAP BRIDGED

- Identified by deposit buildup closing gap between electrodes.
- Caused by oil or carbon fouling. If deposits are not excessive, the plug can be cleaned.

OIL FOULED

- Identified by wet black deposits on the insulator shell bore and electrodes.
- Caused by excessive oil entering combustion chamber through worn rings and pistons, excessive clearance between valve guides and stems or worn or loose bearings. Can be cleaned. If engine is not repaired, use a hotter plug.

CARBON FOULED

- Identified by lack, dry fluffy carbon deposits on insulator tips, exposed shell surfaces and electrodes.
- Caused by too cold a plug, weak ignition, dirty air cleaner, too rich a fuel mixture or excessive idling. Can be cleaned.

LEAD FOULED

- Identified by dark gray, black, yellow or tan deposits or a fused glazed coating on the insulator tip.
- Caused by highly leaded gasoline. Can be cleaned.

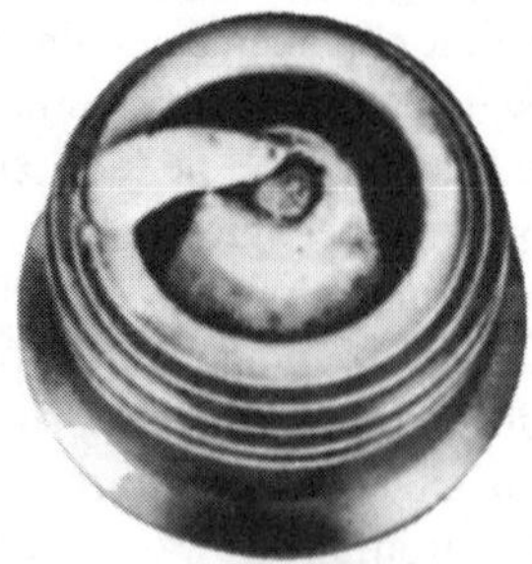

WORN

- Identified by severely eroded or worn electrodes.
- Caused by normal wear. Should be replaced.

FUSED SPOT DEPOSIT

- Identified by melted or spotty deposits resembling bubbles or blisters.
- Caused by sudden acceleration. Can be cleaned.

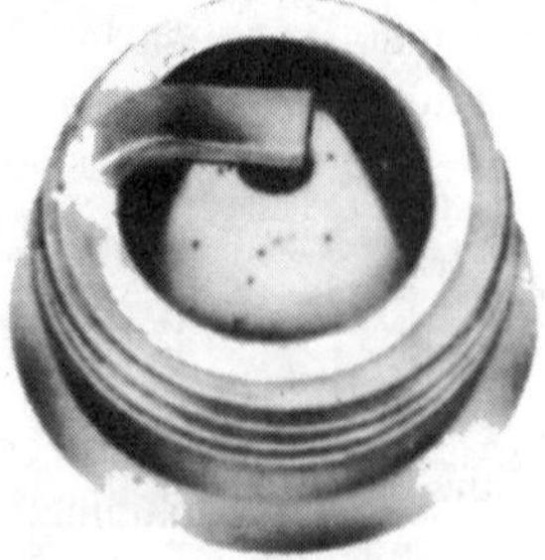

OVERHEATING

- Identified by a white or light gray insulator with small black, gray or brown spots and with a burnt appearance of electrodes.
- Caused by engine overheating, wrong type of fuel, loose spark plugs, too hot a plug or incorrect ignition timing. Replace the plug

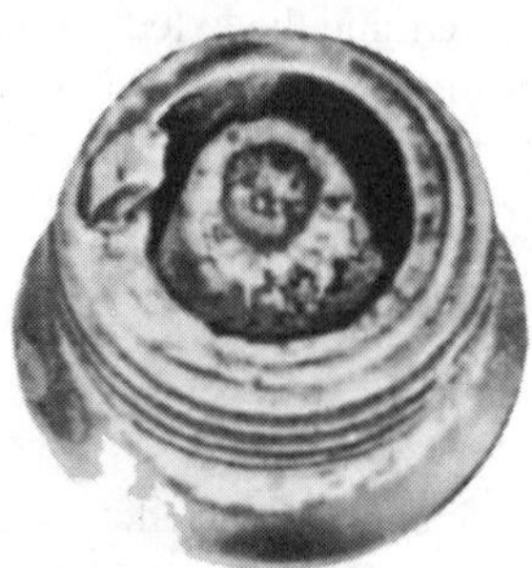

PREIGNITION

- Identified by melted electrodes and possibly blistered insulator. Metallic deposits on insulator indicate engine damage.
- Caused by wrong type of fuel, incorrect ignition timing or advance, too hot a plug, burned valves or engine overheating. Replace the plug

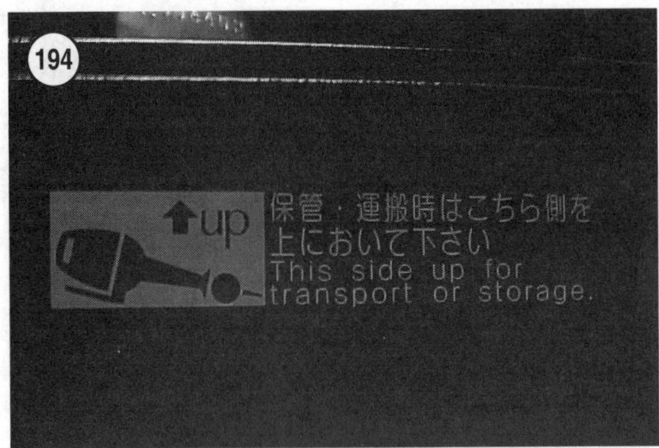
194
up
保管：運搬時はこちら側を
上において下さい
This side up for
transport or storage.

small amount of water may not prevent normal combustion at higher speeds.

Water in the cylinder is almost always verified upon removal and inspection of the spark plug. Water remaining on the plug, a white deposit or very clean appearance indicates water is entering the cylinder.

Water marks or the presence of water in the silencer cover indicates water is entering the engine through the carburetor openings. This condition results from submersion, mounting the engine too low on the boat or a mounting location subjecting the engine to a considerable amount of water spray.

Water in the fuel allows water to enter the cylinders along with the incoming air. Inspect the fuel in the carburetor bowl for the presence of water as described this chapter.

Leaking exhaust covers and/or gaskets allow water to enter the cylinders from the exhaust passages. High performance four stroke engines typically have an aggressive camshaft lift and duration creating a fair amount of valve overlap. Valve overlap allows reverse exhaust flow under certain condition. Reverse exhaust flow may increase the chance of water entering the cylinder through the exhaust valve if water is present in the exhaust passages. Leaking exhaust cover gaskets allow water into the exhaust passages. Correct leaking exhaust cover gaskets if external leakage is detected or water is found in the cylinder. Exhaust cover removal, inspection and installation are provided in Chapter Eight.

A leaking cylinder head gasket results from a failure of the gasket that seals the cylinder head to the cylinder block. Damage to the gasket is likely if the engine has overheated. Symptoms of a leaking head gasket include:

1. Water in the oil.
2. Water entering the cylinder(s).
3. Overheating (particularly at higher engine speeds).
4. Rough running (particularly at lower engine speeds).
5. External water or exhaust leakage at the cylinder head-to-cylinder block mating surfaces.

Perform a compression test if any of these symptoms are noted. Bear in mind that cylinder head gasket leakage is not always verified by a compression test. Typically slightly lower compression is noted on two adjoining cylinders. Only removal and inspection of the gasket and mating surfaces verifies a gasket failure.

Remove the cylinder head and inspect the cylinders and piston domes if water is entering the cylinders and external causes such as water in the fuel or silencer cover are ruled out. Compare the appearance of the affected cylinder with other cylinders on the engine except 4-6 hp models. Cylinders suffering from water intrusion usually have significantly less carbon deposit on the piston and cylinders. Rusting or corrosion of the valves, valve seats, cylinders and piston dome is common when this condition is occurring. A complete power head repair is required if rusting or pitting is noted on the cylinders or piston domes. Refer to Chapter Eight for cylinder head removal and installation instructions.

Leaking water jackets in the cylinder block or cylinder head can be difficult to find. Casting flaws, pinholes and cracks may or may not be visible. Replacement of the cylinder block and/or cylinder head is required if water is entering the cylinder and no visible defects in the gaskets can be found. Continued operation with water intrusion results is power head failure.

Oil Entering the Cylinders

Oil entering the cylinders is almost always the result of improper storage of the engine. When positioned improperly, oil from the crankcase or oil pan can flow past the piston rings and enter the combustion chambers. This can lead to a seized or hydraulically locked engine, fouled spark plugs, low oil level and high oil consumption. The preferred position for the engine is in the upright position. Remote control models must be stored in the upright position. Small tiller control engines are often transported or stored on their side.

Place the engine with the tiller handle side down when they must be transported or stored lying down. On tiller control models, a decal (**Figure 194**) is placed on the side of the lower engine cover to indicate the correct storage position.

Remove and inspect the spark plugs if oil in the cylinders is suspected. Attach the spark plugs leads to a suitable engine ground. Place a shop towel over the spark plug holes and slowly rotate the flywheel to blow the oil from the cylinders. Correct the oil level as described in Chapter Four. Install the spark plugs and leads. Run the engine to check for proper operation. Inspect the spark plugs after running the engine, as subsequent spark plug fouling is likely. Refer to Chapter Four for spark plug maintenance.

Timing Belt

CAUTION
Attempts to start the engine with improper valve timing or a broken timing belt can lead to damaged valves, pistons and other power head components.

Failure of the timing belt (**Figure 195**) will result in an inability to start the engine, rough running or poor performance.

A broken timing belt prevents valve operation and operation of the fuel and oil pumps. This prevents any chance of starting the engine.

An excessively worn timing belt may allow the belt to jump over one or more of the teeth on the crankshaft pulley. This results in improper valve timing causing rough operation and poor performance.

Inspect the camshaft timing marks (**Figure 196**) as determined in Chapter Five. Perform a compression test if poor performance continues after correcting the broken timing belt or incorrect valve timing. Inspect the condition of the timing belt as described in Chapter Four.

Sticking, Worn or Damaged Valves

Sticking, worn or damaged valves cause low compression, rough operation, poor performance and/or backfiring.

Corrosion or heavy carbon deposits can cause valves (**Figure 197**) to stick in the open position. Valves can become bent or damaged from contacting the top of the piston or foreign objects in the combustion chamber.

Any of these conditions result in an inability to fully close the affected valve. Rough operation at lower engine speed is common with a sticking, worn or damaged valve. Backfiring occurs when a leaking valve allows the burning fuel to enter the intake manifold or exhaust passages. Backfiring from the intake usually is the result of a stuck, worn or damaged intake valve. Backfiring from the exhaust is usually the result of a stuck, worn or damaged exhaust valve.

Perform a compression test if any the listed symptoms are noted.

Improper valve adjustments can cause the same symptoms as sticking, worn or damaged valves. Check the valve adjustment before disassembling the power head. Valve adjustment is provided in Chapter Five.

If backfiring is noted, run the engine with one spark plug lead at a time grounded. The backfire will stop when the spark plug lead is grounded on the affected cylinder. Remove the cylinder head and inspect the valves and valve seats (**Figure 198**) when backfiring and low compression are evident on the same cylinder and improper valve adjustment is ruled out.

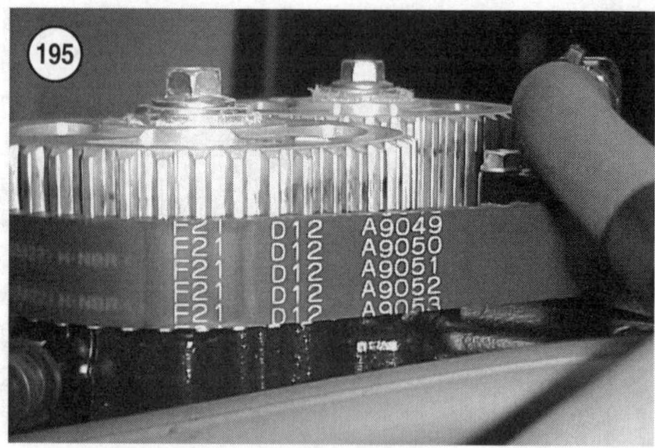

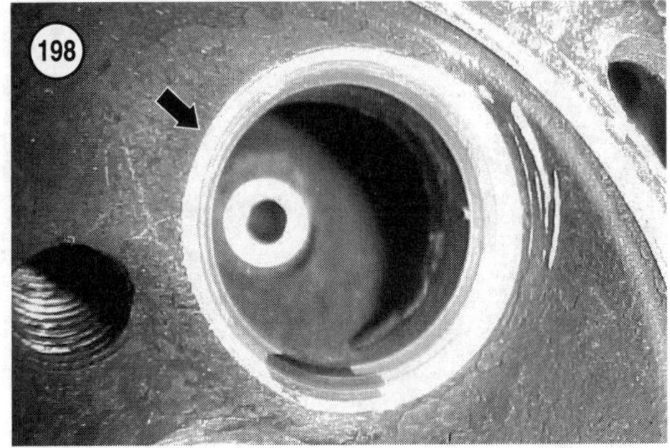

Sticking valves are often the result of improper long term storage, water entering the cylinders or submersion of the engine. Using the wrong type of oil, improper fuel system operation or lugging the engine all contribute to increased deposits or wear of the valve and seat area.

Oil recommendations are provided in Chapter Four. Prevent lugging by selecting the correct propeller for the given engine and boat combination. Refer to Chapter One for propeller selection.

Worn Valve Guides

Worn valve guides prevent consistent closing of the valves. A compression test usually does not verify an excessively worn valve guide because the valve tends to seat normally at cranking speed. Continued operation with worn valve guides will cause the valve seats to wear unevenly with the resultant low compression.

High oil consumption, fouled spark plugs and blue exhaust smoke during deceleration are typical symptoms of excessively worn valve guides and valve stem seals. Only disassembly of the cylinder head and subsequent measurement can confirm excessively worn valve guides. Refer to Chapter Eight.

Camshaft Failure

Failure of any of the camshaft lobes (**Figure 199**) can cause the same symptoms as a sticking or damaged valve. Removal of the rocker arm cover (**Figure 189**) on all except 4-6 hp models allows inspection of the camshaft lobes. Rocker arm cover removal and installation is covered in Chapter Eight. Inspect the camshaft lobes for excessive wear as described in Chapter Eight.

Excessively worn camshaft lobes are generally the result of improper valve adjustment, using the incorrect type, grade or weight of oil, a high number or operating hours and or oil dilution. Valve adjustment is covered in Chapter Five.

Rocker Arm Failure

Failure of a rocker arm results in loss of power and a ticking noise from the affected cylinder. Loss of compression results if failure holds the corresponding valve open. Removal of the rocker arm cover (**Figure 189**) allows inspection of the rocker arm (**Figure 200**) and related components. Replace broken or worn rocker arms and components following the instructions provided in Chapter Eight. Ensure all remnants of the failed components are removed from the cylinder head or oil pan prior to operating the engine. Catastrophic power head failure can result should these components contact other moving components. Perform a compression test after repair to check for potential damage to other components.

Oil Pressure Test

WARNING

Stay clear of the propeller shaft while running an outboard on a flush/test device. Remove the propeller before running the engine to help avoid serious bodily injury or death. Disconnect all spark plug leads and both battery cables before removing or installing the propeller.

CAUTION
Never run an outboard without first providing cooling water. Use either a test tank or flush/test device. Remove the propeller before running the engine on a flush/test device. Use a suitable test propeller to run the engine in a test tank.

An oil pressure gauge (**Figure 201**), T-fitting adapter and a shop tachometer are required to perform an oil pressure test. Perform the test while running the engine under actual operating conditions. Test 15 hp and smaller engines in a test tank.

Test the oil pressure at the threaded opening for the oil pressure switch. Mounting locations, removal and installation instructions for the oil pressure switch are provided in Chapter Seven.

Use an adapter (**Figure 202**) with the same threads as the oil pressure switch on the male and female ends. One of the female ends must have the same thread size and pitch as the oil pressure gauge. Oil pressure gauges and threaded adapters are available from most automotive parts stores. Tighten the adapters securely before running the engine.

Test the oil pressure as follows:

1. Run the engine in a test tank or on a flush/test adapter until it reaches normal operating temperature.
2. Refer to Chapter Seven and remove the oil pressure switch (**Figure 203**).
3. Install the male end of the adapter into oil pressure switch opening. Securely tighten the adapter.
4. Install the oil pressure switch into one of the female opening of the adapter. Securely tighten the oil pressure switch.
5. Install the threaded adapter of the oil pressure gauge (**Figure 201**) into the remaining female opening of the adapter. Securely tighten all fittings. Secure the oil pressure gauge hose to prevent it from contacting any moving components.
6. Following the manufacturer's instructions, attach the shop tachometer to the engine.
7. Refer to **Table 25** to determine the correct speed to run the engine. Start the engine and immediately correct any oil leakage at the gauge and adapter fittings.
8. Shift the engine into forward gear. Observe the oil pressure gauge and advance the throttle to the specified engine speed (**Table 24**). Record the oil pressure. Return the engine to idle speed for a minute then switch if off.

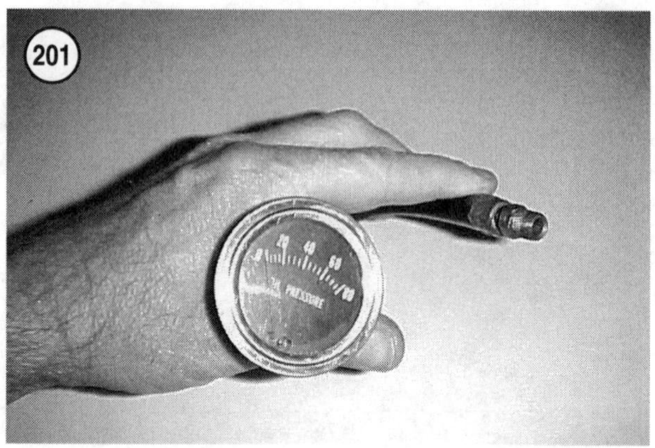

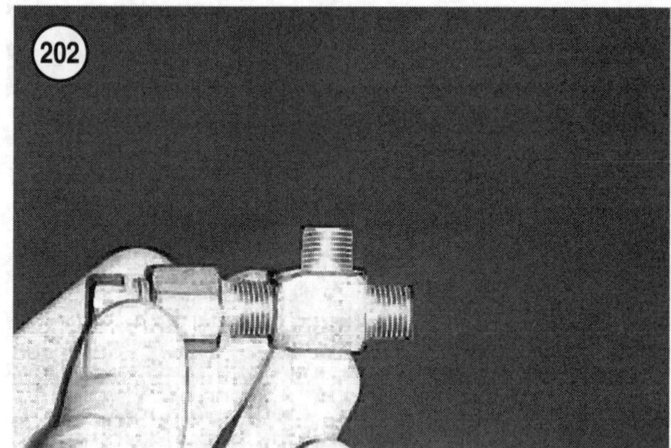

9. Compare the oil pressure reading with the specification listed in **Table 24**. Oil pressure below or above the listed specification indicates a problem with the oil pumping system.
   a. Low oil pressure indicates low oil level, damaged or blocked pickup tube, worn or broken oil pump components or worn crankshaft or connecting rod bearings. Inspect the oil pump and related components as described in Chapter Eight.

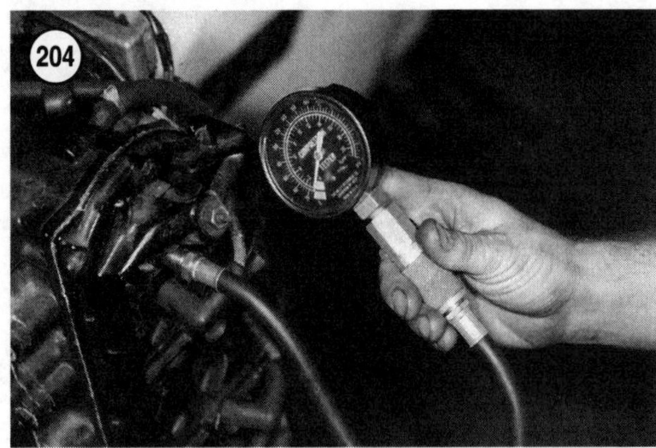

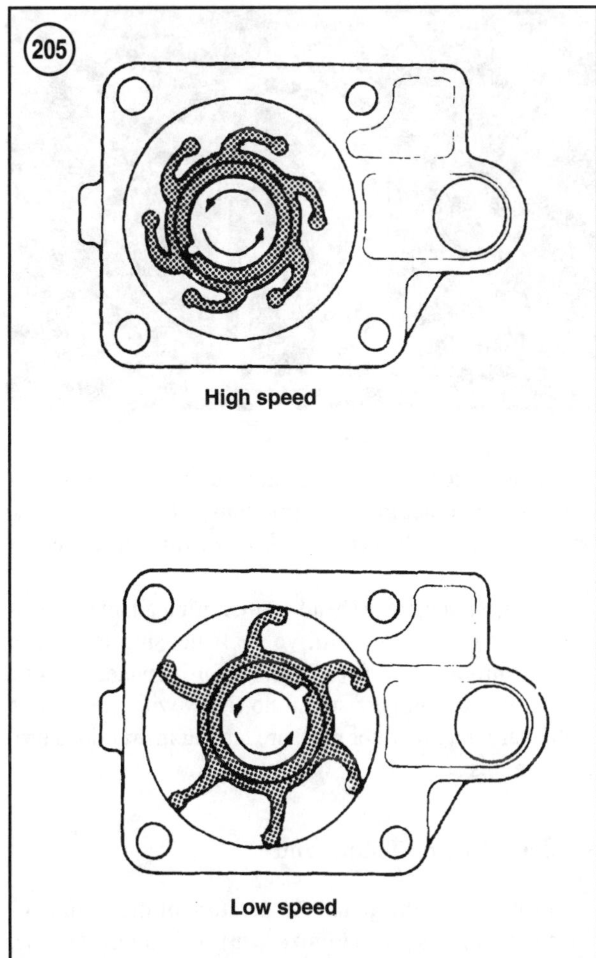

b. High oil pressure indicates a stuck or faulty oil pressure relief valve. Remove and inspect the valve following the instructions provided in Chapter Eight.

10. Remove the shop tachometer, oil pressure gauge and adapter. Install the oil pressure switch following the instructions provided in Chapter Seven.

Compression Test

NOTE

*A compression relief mechanism is utilized on 4-6 and 25-40 hp manual start models to reduce starting effort. This mechanism prevents accurate compression testing as it holds the exhaust valves open at cranking speeds. Refer to **Table 26** to determine which models are so equipped.*

A good quality compression gauge and adapter are required for accurate compression testing. They are available at automotive parts stores and from tool suppliers. A small can of engine oil may also be required.

1. Remove all spark plugs and connect the spark plug leads to a suitable engine ground (clean cylinder head bolts).
2. Install the compression gauge into the No. 1 spark plug hole (**Figure 204**). Securely tighten the hose adapter. Position the throttle in the wide-open position during testing.
3. Stand clear of the remaining spark plug openings during testing. Observe the compression gauge and operate the manual or electric starter. Crank the engine a minimum of five revolutions at normal cranking speeds. Record the compression reading.
4. Repeat Step 2 and Step 3 for the remaining cylinders. Record all compression readings.
5. Compare the recorded readings with the specifications listed in **Table 26**. Perform Step 6 if any of the readings are below the listed specifications.
6. The compression must be within the specification in **Table 26**. In addition, the compression must not vary more than 10 percent between cylinders.
7. If low compression is noted, squirt approximately 1 teaspoon of clean engine oil into the cylinder through the spark plug hole. Rotate the engine several revolutions to distribute the oil in the cylinder, then repeat Step 2 and Step 3.
   a. If the compression increases significantly, the piston rings and cylinder are excessively worn.
   b. If the compression does not increase, the compression leakage is the result of a worn valve face or seat.

COOLING SYSTEM

Water is pumped into the power head by the gearcase mounted water pump (**Figure 205**). The water is pumped to the exhaust area of the power head then the cylinder block and heads where it absorbs heat from the power head. The water exits the power head near the power head mounting surface and travels out through the drive shaft housing. As it flows out the drive shaft housing it absorbs heat from the oil pan. All models are equipped with a thermostat (**Figure 206**). Their use helps maintain a minimum power head temperature by restricting exiting water until the minimum temperature is reached. All 75 and 90 hp models are equipped with a water pressure relief valve. This valve allows additional water to exit when the cylinder block pressure reaches a set value. Cylinder block water pressure increases with increasing water pump speed. This valve allows for additional water flow through the power head at higher engine speeds.

A stream is visible at the rear of the lower motor cover when water is exiting the power head. The fitting for the stream commonly becomes blocked with debris and ceases flowing. Clean the passage with a stiff wire. Inspect the cooling system if the water stream is still not present.

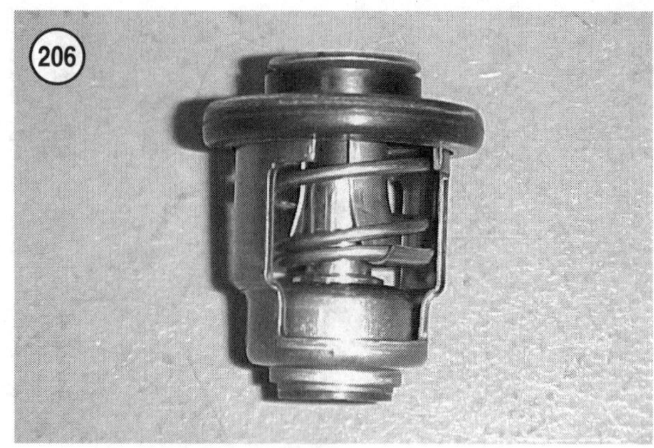

Cooling System Inspection

Inspect the cooling system if the gauge overheats, the warning horn sounds or the water stream is not present at the rear of the engine. Overheating is the result of insufficient water flowing through the power head or it fails to absorb heat as it flows. Overheating causes activation of the warning system on 25-90 hp models. All 4-15 hp models are not equipped with overheat warning system. The lack of a water stream, unusual odors or the presence of steam from the exhaust indicates overheating. Poor idle quality or stalling at idle may also occur with overheating.

Most overheating problems are directly related to excessive wear or failure of water pump components. Inspect and correct any faults found in the water pump prior to inspecting any other cooling system components. Refer to Chapter Nine for water pump inspection and repair instructions.

Inspect the water pressure relief valve on 75 and 90 hp models and test the thermostat if overheating persists after water pump inspection. Thermostat testing is provided in this section.

Inspect the cooling system passages (**Figure 207**) for debris and deposit buildup if no faults can be found with the water pump, thermostat and water pressure valve. Removal of the cylinder head and exhaust cover may be required to access these water passages. Water flow may be restricted by rocks, pieces of the water pump, sand, shells or other debris. Salt, calcium or other deposits can form in the cooling passages and restrict water flow. The other problem with deposit buildup is the insulating quality of the deposit prevents the water from absorbing the heat from the power head. Use a cleaner specifically designed to dissolve this type of deposit. Make sure the cleaner used is suitable for use on aluminum material. Always follow the manufacturer's instructions when using these products. These cleaners are usually available at marine specialty stores.

Leakage at the power head-to-mounting adapter can allow water to exit to the drive shaft housing instead of flowing through the power head. Perform a water pressure test if overheating persist and no faults with the cooling system are noted. Water pressure testing instructions provided in this section.

Verifying Engine Temperature

Always verify the actual temperature of the engine using thermomelt sticks (**Figure 208**) before testing other cooling system components. Thermomelt sticks resemble crayons and are designed to melt at a specific temperature. The melting temperatures are listed on the side of the stick or its label.

Hold the sticks against the cylinder head near the temperature sender or overheat switch. On 4-15 hp models not equipped with at an overheat alarm hold the stick near the spark plug mounting area. Try to check the tempera-

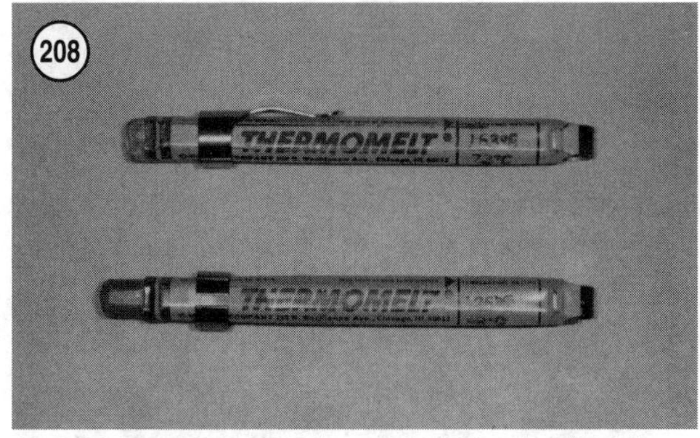

208

209

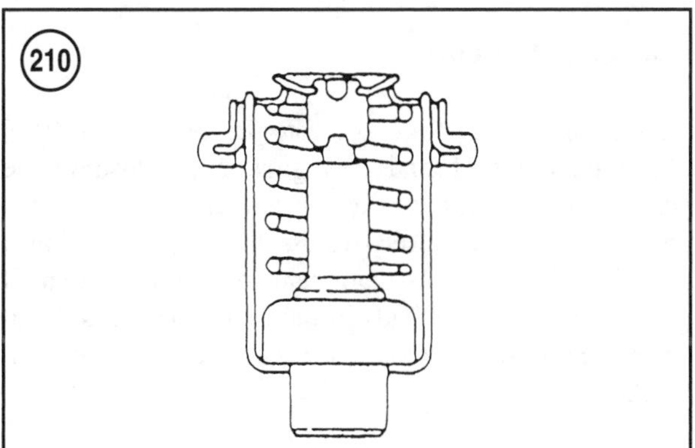

210

ture immediately after or during the suspected overheat condition. Hold different temperature sticks to the power head to determine the temperature range the engine is reaching. Stop the engine if the temperature exceeds 195° F (90°C). Normal water temperature is 140-190° F (60-88° C). Perform a cooling system inspection if higher than normal temperature is noted. Test the temperature sender or switch if an alarm or gauge is indicating overheating but the thermomelt sticks indicate normal temperature. Troubleshooting an overheating problem using a flush/test attachment is difficult if not impossible. Water supplied by the flushing adapter tends to mask problems with the cooling system. Perform this test with the engine in the water under actual operating conditions. On 4-15 hp models test the cooling system in a suitable test tank.

Thermostat Test

Test the thermostat if the engine is overheats or is running too cool. A thermometer, piece of string and a container of water that can be heated are required.

1. Remove the thermostat as described in Chapter Eight. Suspend the thermostat into the container of water with the string tied to the thermostat as shown in **Figure 209**.
2. Place the liquid thermometer in the container and begin heating the water. Observe the temperature of the water and the thermostat while heating the water.
3. Note the temperature at which the thermostat begins to open (**Figure 210**). Replace the thermostat if the water begins to boil prior to the thermostat opening.
4. Cease heating the container then observe the thermostat and the thermometer. Note the temperature at which the thermostat just begins to close.
5. Compare the opening and closing temperatures with the specifications listed in **Table 23**. Replace the thermostat if incorrect opening or closing temperatures are noted.
6. Install the thermostat as described in Chapter Eight.

Water Pressure Testing

CAUTION
The same type of plug is used for water and oil passages. Never operate the engine with an oil passage test plug removed. The correct plug opening leads into the water jacket or directly inside of the thermostat cavity.

NOTE
Some models are available with an optional gearcase. Water pressure test specifications are dependent on the size of gearcase used. Refer to the information in Chapter Nine to correctly identify the gearcase.

A water pressure gauge, shop tachometer, barb type fitting and a length of hose is required to test cooling system water pressure. Purchase the water pressure gauge and shop tachometer from a local automotive parts store or tool supplier. The gauge must be capable of reading 2-25 psi (14-172 kPa).

Select the correct size of barb fitting after removing the plug (**Figure 211**) from the cylinder block. The fitting must be the correct size and thread pitch as the plug.

On most models the water pressure test port is located near the thermostat cover. On other models this port is located on the cylinder head. Some production runs are not equipped with a water pressure test port.

Inspect the plug after removal.

1. Remove both cables from the battery.
2. Remove the test port plug (**Figure 211**). Probe the opening with a small wire to ensure it leads into a water jacket.
3. Carefully thread the barb type fitting into the test port opening. Securely tighten the fitting.
4. Slide and appropriately sized hose over the fitting. Secure the hose to the fitting with a hose clamp.
5. Direct the free end of the hose into a container. Connect the cables to the battery.
6. Connect the water pressure gauge to the free end of the hose. Clamp the hose to the hose.
7. Monitor the tachometer and water pressure gauge as an assistant operates the engine at the speeds listed in **Table 22**.
8. Compare the pressure readings with the specifications listed in **Table 22**.
   a. A faulty water pump, water tube connection, water pressure relief valve, stuck thermostat (open) or power head adapter gasket is indicated if a low pressure reading is noted.
   b. A faulty water pressure relief valve (75 and 90 hp models only), a stuck thermostat (closed) or water jacket blockage is indicated if excessive water pressure is noted.
9. Disassemble and inspect the cooling system if incorrect pressure gauge readings are indicated. Refer to Chapter Eight for power head related components. Refer to Chapter Nine for gearcase related components.
10. Remove the barb fitting and pressure gauge from the plug opening. Coat the thread with a light coat of gasket sealing compound then carefully thread the plug into its opening. Securely tighten the plug.
11. Start the engine then immediately inspect the plugs. Remove, reseal then reinstall the plug(s) if leakage is noted.

GEARCASE

Gearcase problems are generally leakage and failed components and usually are the result of striking underwater objects or insufficient maintenance.

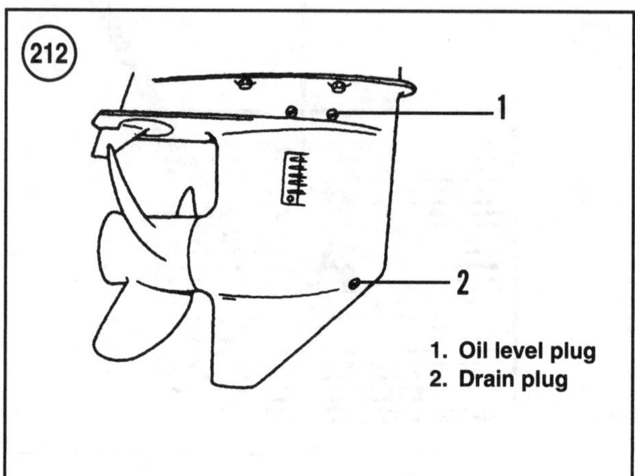

Inspecting the Lubricant

Refer to Chapter Nine to locate the gearcase oil level and drain plugs (1 and 2, **Figure 212**). Position the gearcase in a vertical position. Do not remove the oil level plug (1, **Figure 212**). Remove the drain plug and allow a thimble full of gearcase lubricant to flow onto a small piece of cardboard. Quickly install the drain plug. Refer to Chapter Four to check and correct the gearcase lubricant level.

Water in the Gearcase

Under certain conditions a small amount of water may find its way into the gearcase lubricant. Pressure test the gearcase to determine the source of water intrusion. Refer to *Pressure Testing* in this chapter. Failure to correct the leakage eventually leads to extensive damage to the internal components. Continued neglect will cause complete failure of the gearcase. Partial disassembly of the gearcase is needed to inspect the internal components for damaged.

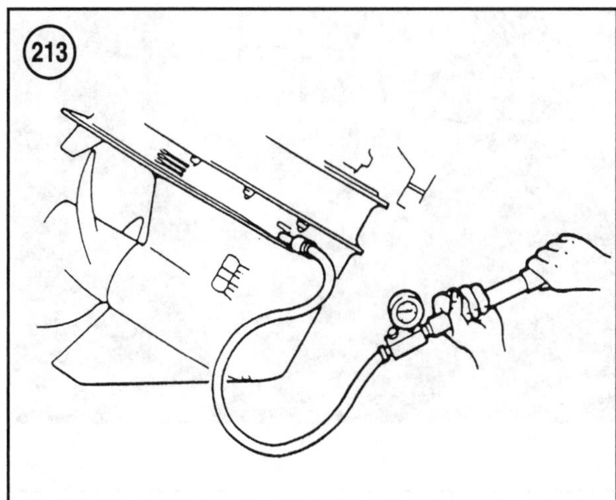

Refer to Chapter Nine for gearcase disassembly, inspection and assembly.

Lubricant Leakage

The presence of gearcase lubricant on the exterior or around the gearcase indicates a need to pressure test and find the source of leakage. Refer to *Pressure Testing* in this chapter. Failure to correct the leakage results in gear and bearing damage. Continued neglect will cause complete gearcase failure. Refer to Chapter Nine for gearcase disassembly, inspection and assembly.

Pressure Testing

A suitable gearcase pressure tester is required to perform this test. Air pressure is applied to the internal cavities of the gearcase. The pressure gauge indicates if leakage is present. The entire gearcase can be submerged in water to check for the presence of bubbles to help determine the point of leakage.

1. Thoroughly drain the gearcase as described in Chapter Four. Refer to Chapter Nine and remove the gearcase from the engine.
2. Install the pressure tester fitting into the oil level plug opening (**Figure 213**). Install the drain plug in the lower threaded opening. Securely tighten the lower plug and the pressure tester fitting.
3. Slowly apply pressure to the gearcase (**Figure 213**). Push, pull and turn all shafts while observing the pressure gauge as the pressure is slowly increased. Stop applying pressure when it reaches 100 kPa (14.5 psi).
4. Submerge the gearcase with the pressure applied if the unit will not hold this pressure for at least 10 seconds. Replace the seal or seal surface at the location where bubbles appear. Refer to Chapter Nine for gearcase repair instructions.
5. Slowly bleed the air out of the gearcase. Fill the gearcase with the recommended lubricant as described in Chapter Four.

Metal Contamination in the Lubricant

Fine metal particles form in the gearcase during normal usage. The gearcase lubricant may have a *metal flake a*ppearance when inspected during routine maintenance. The fine metal particles tend to cling to the end of the drain plug. Carefully apply some of the material to the forefinger and thumb and rub them together. If any of the material is large enough to feel between the finger and thumb, disassemble and repair the gearcase as described in Chapter Nine.

Gearcase Vibration or Noise

Normal gearcase noise is barely noticeable over normal engine noise. The presence of rough growling noises or a loud high pitched whine is reason for concern. These noises usually are caused by failed or damaged internal components. Inspect the gearcase lubricant for metal contamination if abnormal noises are noted. In almost all cases, inspection of the gearcase lubricant will determine if gearcase components have failed.

Knocking or Grinding Noise

A knocking or grinding noise coming from the gearcase is likely caused by damaged gears of other components in the gearcase. Damaged gears typically create a substantial amount of larger metal particles. This type of failure usually results in damage to most internal components and complete repair is needed. Refer to Chapter Nine for gearcase repair.

High Pitch Whine

If a high pitch whine is present it normally indicates a bearing problem or the gears are running out of alignment. The only way to verify a faulty gear or bearing is to disassemble the gearcase and inspect all components. Refer to Chapter Nine for gearcase repair.

Gearcase Vibration

Vibration in the engine can originate in the gearcase. In almost all cases the vibration is due to a bent propeller shaft or damaged propeller. The propeller can appear to be in perfect condition yet be out of balance. The best way to solve propeller vibration is to have the propeller checked at a reputable propeller repair shop. Another option is to simply try a different propeller.

Always check for a bent propeller shaft if vibration is present. Check the propeller shaft as described in Chapter Nine. A bent propeller shaft is usually caused by impacting underwater objects while underway. In many cases other damage occurs to the gearcase.

Never operate the engine if severe vibration is present. Vibrating or out of balance components place added stress to the gears, bearings and other engine components. Operating the engine with excessive gearcase vibration can seriously compromise the durability of the entire outboard motor.

WARNING
Remove all spark plug leads and disconnect both battery cables before working around the propeller.

Propeller Hub Slippage

The prop hub is installed in the propeller to cushion the shifting action and help absorb the shock of minor impact. When the propeller hub fails it spins inside the bore. Make a reference mark on the propeller shaft aligned with a reference mark on the prop. Operate the boat to verify the slippage. After removing the engine from the water, compare the reference marks. Have the prop repaired if the reference marks are not aligned after running the engine.

Shifting Difficulty

Hard shifting or difficulty when engaging the gear is usually the result of improper shift cable adjustment. Refer to Chapter Five and adjust the shift cables and linkage. Gearcase removal, disassembly and inspection is required if shifting problems are not corrected with adjustments. Refer to Chapter Nine for gearcase repair.

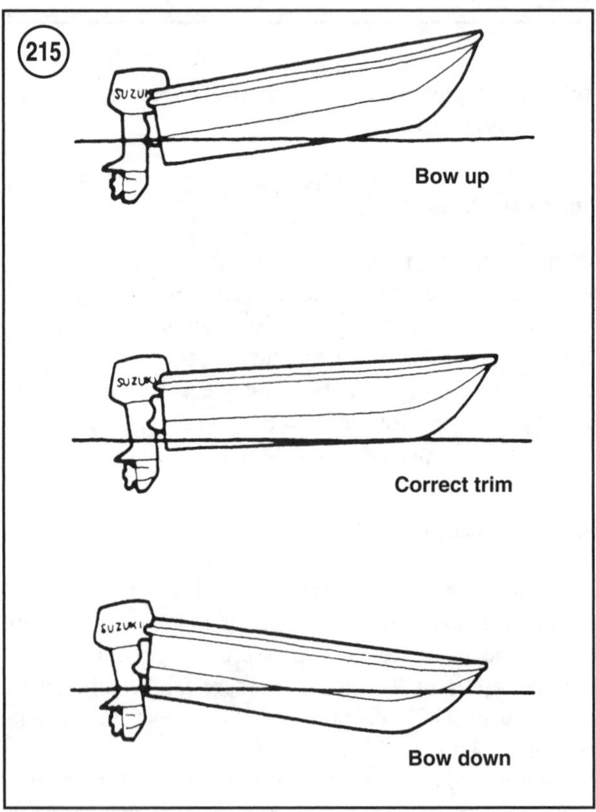

TRIM SYSTEM

This section covers troubleshooting manual and hydraulic assist trim systems (**Figure 214**).

Operating the boat with the engine tilted out tends to raise the bow of the boat. This bow-up trim (**Figure 215**) may increase boat speed by reducing the amount of water contacting the hull. Tilting the engine out may also cause excessive bow lift and result in reduced visibility for the driver during acceleration. The propeller is positioned progressively closer to the water surface as the engine is tilted out and may allow the propeller to draw in surface air (ventilate). Ventilation causes the propeller to lose its grip on the water and causes the engine speed to increase with no increase in thrust.

Operating the boat with the engine tilted in tends to lower the bow of the boat. This bow-down trim (**Figure 215**) tends to improve rough water ride and reduces ventilation during acceleration. Be aware that tilting the engine in generally reduces boat speed and can contribute to a dangerous handling condition (bow steer) on some boats.

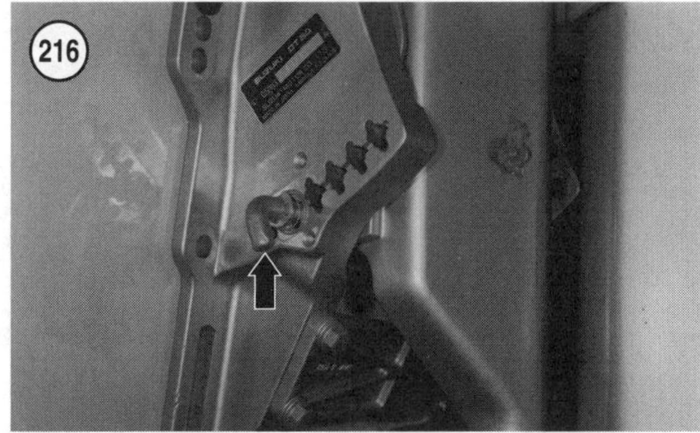
216

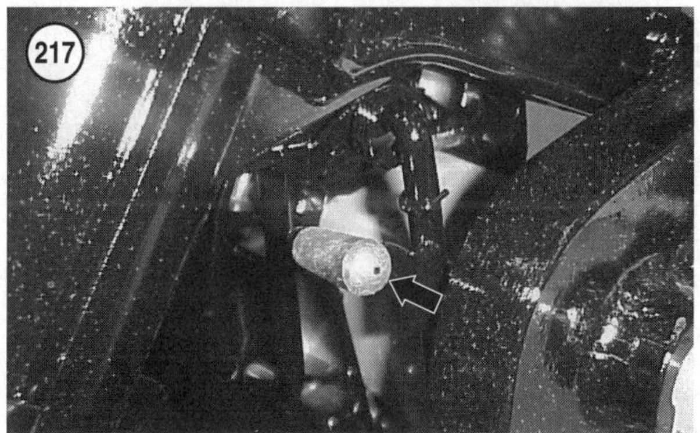
217

218

219

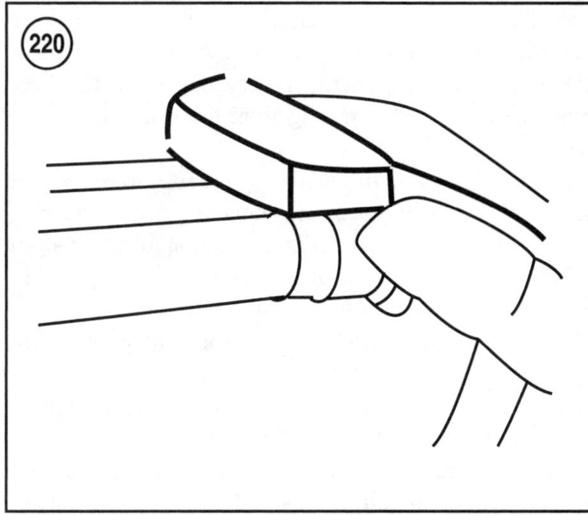
220

The correct trim angle is a compromise between the best acceleration and top speed. The angle chosen must not be high enough to cause a rough ride or low enough that handling suffers. The correct trim angle (**Figure 215**) is 3-5° from the water line on most applications.

Trim System (4-15 hp models)

Changing the tilt angle is accomplished by changing the position of the tilt pin (**Figure 216**) in the clamp brackets. A special mechanism (**Figure 217**) allows tilting of the engine beyond the normal operating range for low speed operation in shallow water. Never operate the engine at higher engine speeds in the shallow water range.

The reverse hold-down mechanism (**Figure 218**) grasps the tilt pin during reverse operation. This prevents reverse thrust from raising the motor from the water.

A steering friction mechanism (**Figure 219**) is used to reduce arm fatigue caused by steering torque. Tightening the friction adjusting screw or moving the lever on 9.9-15 hp models (**Figure 220**) applies a load to the swivel tube. This load helps reduce the effort required to hold the engine on course at higher engine speeds.

Trim System (25 hp models)

Changing the tilt angle is accomplished by changing the position of the tilt pin (**Figure 216**) in the clamp brackets or operating the optional power trim system (**Figure 221**).

On non-trim models, a special mechanism (**Figure 217**) allows tilting of the engine beyond the normal operating range for low speed operation in shallow water. Never operate the engine at higher engine speeds in the shallow water range. The reverse hold down mechanism (**Figure 218**) grasps the tilt pin during reverse operation. This prevents the engine from raising from the water due to reverse propeller thrust.

A steering friction mechanism (**Figure 220**) is used on non trim models to reduce arm fatigue cause by steering torque. Moving the lever (**Figure 220**) applies a load to swivel tube. This load helps reduce the effort required to hold the engine on course at higher engine speeds.

All electric start models are available with power trim. The major components of this system include a bidirectional electric motor (A, **Figure 221**), hydraulic pump (B) and hydraulic cylinder (C).

A pair of relays (**Figure 222**) control electric motor/pump rotational direction and fluid movement within the system. Switch the relays by operating the trim switch (**Figure 223**).

Operating the trim in the up direction causes fluid to flow into the up side or up cavity of the single trim cylinder by the hydraulic pump. The pressure exerted onto the piston inside the cylinder causes it to tilt the engine outward. Valves in the trim system prevent the engine from tilting beyond a set amount unless the engine speed is below approximately 2000 rpm. This is accomplished by limiting the pressure in the hydraulic cylinder at higher tilt ranges. The pressure is limited to the point the hydraulic cylinder cannot offset the propeller thrust created at higher engine speeds. The pressure is high enough to allow full outward tilting at lower engine speeds. This feature helps prevent over trimming of the engine at higher speeds yet allow full outward tilting for shallow water operation or placing the engine into the trailer position.

Operating the trim system in the down direction causes fluid to flow to the down side of the hydraulic cylinder. The pressure exerted onto the piston in the cylinder causes it to pull the engine inward. Tilt-in limit bolts (**Figure 224**) are installed into holes in both sides of the clamp bracket. They prevent an excessive tilt-in angle causing handling problems on some boats. Move the bolts to holes closer to the transom different holes if additional tilt in is desired. Move the bolts to holes away from the transom if undesirable handling characteristics are noted when the engine is operated in the full-in position. Install these bolts in the same holes on each clamp bracket.

Fluid remaining in the cylinders after stopping the pump effectively locks the cylinder in position. This helps the engine maintain its trim setting and holds the engine down when in reverse.

Pressure relief valves located in the piston provide a shock control system in the event of underwater impact. It allows fluid to move from the down to the up side of the

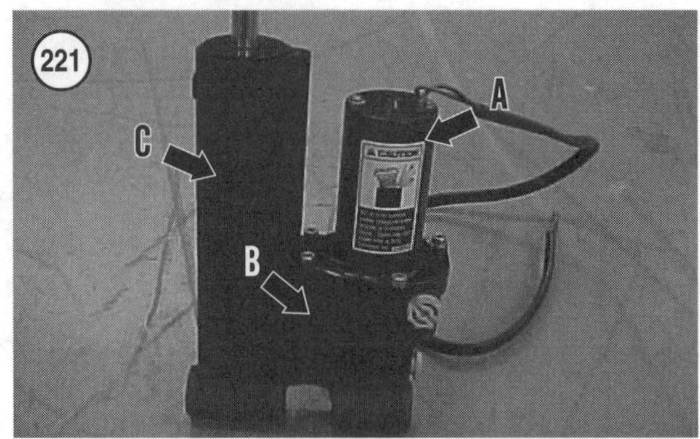

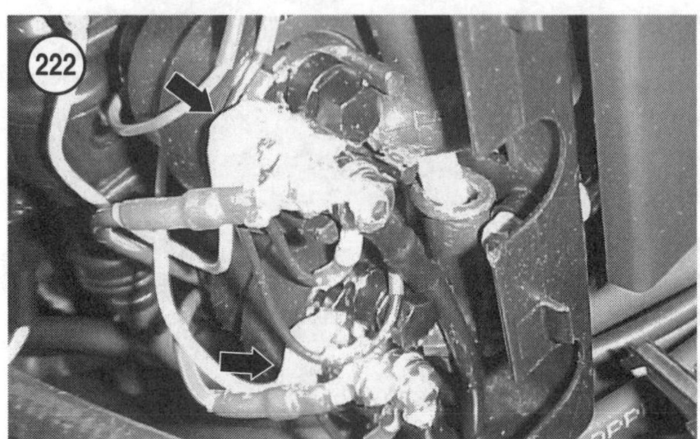

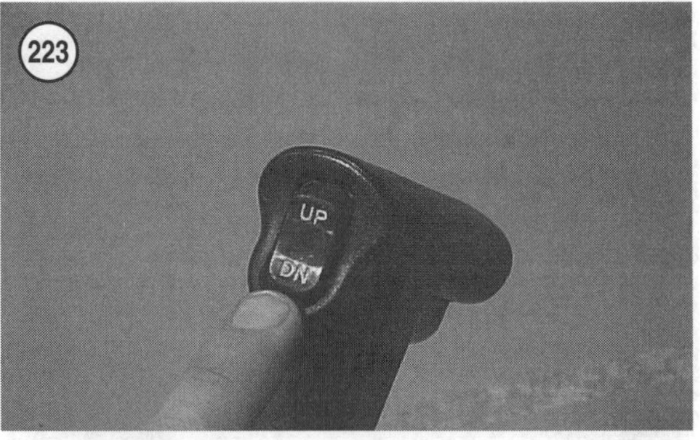

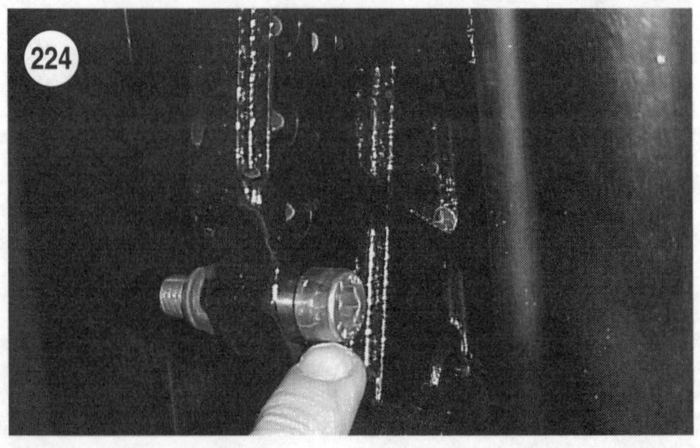

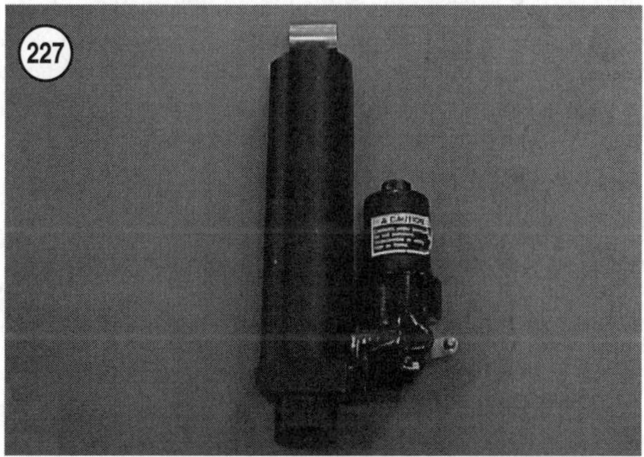

cylinder upon impact. This controlled fluid flow allows outward engine movement at a much slower and safer rate. Bear in mind this system only helps minimize the impact damage and cannot totally prevent damage to the engine.

The manual relief valve is located through an opening in the starboard clamp bracket (**Figure 225**). It allows manual tilting or lowering of the engine if the trim motor

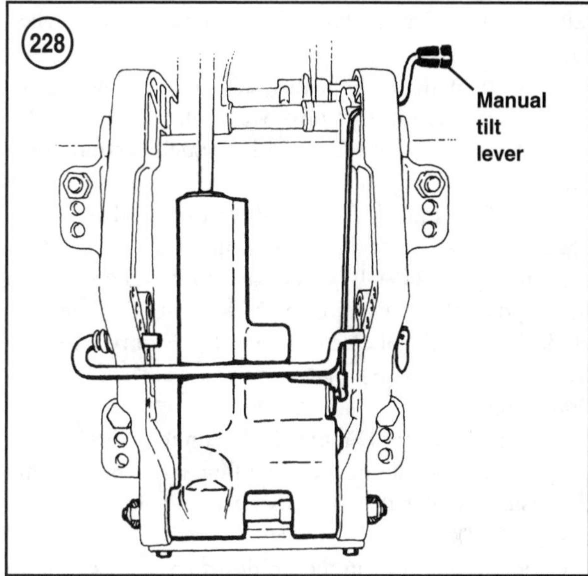

or pump fails. To activate the manual relief valve slowly rotate the valve three complete turns counterclockwise. Manually raise or lower the engine to the desired position then have an assistant securely tighten the manual relied valve.

The fluid fill/level check plug (**Figure 226**) is located on the rear facing side of the manifold. This mounting location allows access only with the engine in the full tilt up/out position. Never remove the fluid fill/level check plug with the engine lowered. Fluid filling and level check instructions are provided in Chapter Four. Refer to Hydraulic Components Troubleshooting *in this chapter for additional information.*

Trim System (30-90 hp Models)

These models are equipped with either a manual hydraulic tilt system or a power trim system.

All 30-50 hp non trim models are equipped with a manual hydraulic tilt system (**Figure 227**). This system mounts between the clamp brackets and provides assistance when tilting the engine for trailering or beaching. The system is controlled by a lever (**Figure 228**). Placing the lever in the tilt range allows fluid flow into and out of both chambers in the cylinder. This allows manual movement as desired. The pressure required to move the engine up or out is reduced by applying pressure to the fluid. This is accomplished using pressurized nitrogen gas stored in the accumulator. Placing the lever in the locked position closes the valves preventing fluid from flowing into and out of the hydraulic cylinder. This helps the engine maintain its trim setting and holds the engine down or in when running in reverse.

Early 50 hp models are equipped with the same type of trim system used on all 25 hp models with power trim. Refer to the information for the 25 hp models for additional information.

Later 50 hp models, 30 and 40 hp trim models and all 75and 90 models are equipped with the later style trim system (**Figure 229**). It is identified by its yellow fill cap (C, **Figure 229**). The major components of this system include a bidirectional electric motor (A, **Figure 229**), the hydraulic cylinder (B), manual release valve and the hydraulic pump.

A pair of relays (**Figure 222**) control electric motor/pump rotational direction and fluid movement within the system. Switch the relays by operating the trim switch (**Figure 223**).

Operating the trim in the up direction causes fluid to flow into the up side or up cavity of the single trim cylinder by the hydraulic pump. The pressure exerted onto the piston in the cylinder causes it to tilt the engine outward. Valves in the trim system prevent the engine from tilting beyond a set amount unless the engine speed is below approximately 2000 rpm. This is accomplished by limiting the pressure in the hydraulic cylinder at higher tilt ranges. The pressure is limited to the point the hydraulic cylinder cannot offset the propeller thrust created at higher engine speeds. The pressure is high enough to allow full outward tilting at lower engine speeds. This feature helps prevent over trimming of the engine at higher speeds yet allow full outward tilting for shallow water operation or placing the engine into the trailer position.

Operating the trim system in the down direction causes fluid to flow to the down side or cavity of the hydraulic cylinder. The pressure exerted onto the piston in the cylinder causes it to pull the engine inward. Tilt in limit bolts (D, **Figure 229**) installed in holes in both sides of the clamp bracket prevent an excessive tilt in angle. An excessive tilt in angle can cause handling problems on some boats. Move the bolts to holes closer to the transom different holes if additional tilt in is desired. Move the bolts to holes away from the transom if undesirable handling characteristics are noted when the engine is operated in the full in position. Install the bolts in the same holes on each clamp bracket.

Fluid remaining in the cylinders after stopping the pump effectively locks the cylinder in position. This helps the engine maintain its trim setting and holds the engine down when running in reverse.

A pressure relief valve located in the piston in the hydraulic cylinder provides a shock control system in the event of underwater impact. It allows fluid to move from

the down to the up side of the cylinder during the impact. This controlled fluid flow allows outward engine movement at a much slower and safer rate. Bear in mind this system only helps minimize the impact damage and cannot totally prevent damage to the engine.

The manual relief valve, located through an opening in the starboard clamp bracket (**Figure 225**), allows manual tilting or lowering of the engine. To activate the manual relief valve slowly rotate the valve three complete turns counterclockwise. Manually raise or lower the engine to the desired position then have an assistant securely tighten the manual relied valve.

The fluid fill/level check plug (C, **Figure 229**) is located on the rear side of the manifold. This mounting location allows access only with the engine in the full tilt up/out position. Never remove the fluid fill/level check plug with the engine lowered. Fluid filling and level check instructions are provided in Chapter Four. Refer to Hydraulic Components Troubleshooting *in this chapter for additional information.*

Hydraulic System Troubleshooting

Common hydraulic malfunctions include:

1. The engine will not move up.
2. The engine will not move down.
3. The engine leaks down from a full tilt position.
4. The engine leaks down when underway.
5. The engine trails out when slowing down.
6. Hydraulic fluid leaks from the system.

The engine will not move up or down

A low fluid level, defective manual relief valve, hydraulic pump, trim system check valve or hydraulic cylinder is indicated if the electric motor operates, but the trim system fails to operate. Check the fluid level as described

in Chapter Four. Inspect the manual relief valve following the instructions provided in Chapter Eleven. A faulty hydraulic pump, hydraulic cylinder or trim system check valve is likely if the fluid level is correct and manual relief valve check correctly.

The engine leaks down or trails out

A faulty manual relief valve, trim system check valve, hydraulic cylinder or hydraulic pump is indicated if the trim system moves up and down , but fails to maintain its position. Check the manual relief valve as described in Chapter Eleven. A faulty trim system check valve, hydraulic cylinder or hydraulic pump is likely if the manual relief valve is in good condition. Disassemble and inspect the entire trim system following the instructions in Chapter Eleven. Replace the hydraulic pump if the symptoms continue.

Fluid leaks from the system

The presence of fluid does not always indicate a leak from the trim system. Check the fluid level as described in Chapter Four. A film of fluid and a low fluid level indicates leakage. Clean all debris from the external surfaces of the trim system. Use care when using pressurized water. Water can enter the system if pressurized water is directed against the seal surfaces.

After a thorough cleaning, operate the system through several full up to full down cycles. Wipe a clean shop towel over the seals and all surfaces of the trim system to check for leakage. Reseal or replace any components found.

Trim System Electrical Testing

The major electrical components of the trim system are the electric motor, trim relays, trim position sender and the trim switches. This section provides test instructions for the electric trim system components.

The electric trim motor (**Figure 230**) is provided with a blue and green wire. Current flow to the electric trim motor is controlled by the trim relays (**Figure 222**) and the trim switches (**Figure 231**).

When UP trim or tilt direction is selected the up trim relay activates. It connects the blue trim motor wire to the positive battery terminal of the starter relay (A, **Figure 232**) The green lead of the electric motor is connected to the engine ground by the down relay.

When the down direction is selected the down trim relay activates. It connects the green trim motor wire to the positive battery terminal of the starter relay. The blue trim motor wire is connected to the engine ground by the up relay. This switching of terminals causes the electric motor to reverse direction.

Battery voltage is supplied to the trim switch using a red/purple wire connecting the trim switch to the ignition switch or starter relay. When the switch is toggled to the UP direction, the red/purple wire connects to the light blue or blue/white wire. This wire is connected to the wire harness to the UP relay (**Figure 232**). When the switch is toggled to the DOWN direction the red/purple wire to the light/green or green/white wire. This wire is connected to the down relay.

Internal switching occurs when electrical current from the trim switch is applied to the selected relay. This internal switching causes this relay to supply voltage to the electric motor. The other relay remains deactivated and supplies the connection to ground for the electric motor. This connection to ground opens when a relay is activated. Both relays must make the proper internal connection for the electric motor to operate. This twin relay arrangement is used on all power trim models.

A fuse (**Figure 232**) is provided in the circuit that connects the positive battery terminal to the main engine har-

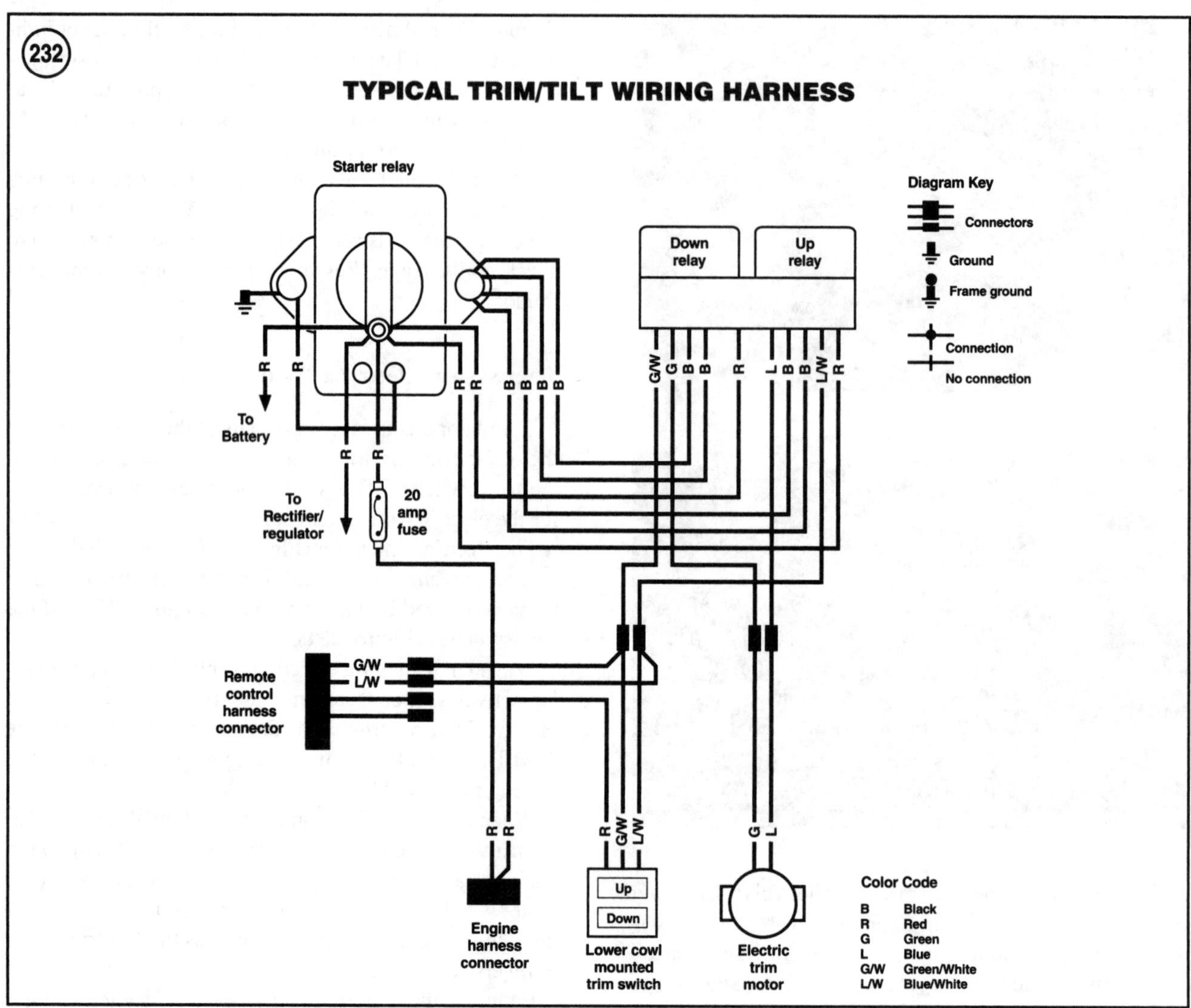

ness. One terminal of the fuse connects to the wire leading to the starter relay (**Figure 232**). The other terminal of the fuse connects to the wire leading to the ignition switch (**Figure 232**). A faulty fuse prevents battery current from reaching the trim switch. It prevents operation of the electric starter motor or gauges. On 75 and 90 hp models, a pair of fuses protects the trim and ignition circuits. A faulty 20 amp fuse prevents operation of the remote control-mounted switch yet allow operation of the engine cover mounted trim switch. Refer to the wire diagrams in the back of the manual to locate this fuse in the engine wire harness. Test this fuse if the electric trim motor fails to operate. Refer to *Fuse Testing* in this chapter.

Test for correct switching at the relays if the trim pump does not operate when both the UP and DOWN direction is selected. Perform this test before testing or replacing any electrical trim system components.

Relay operation

Perform this test before testing other trim system electrical components.

1. Remove the propeller as described in Chapter Nine.

2. Connect the negative lead of a voltmeter to a good engine ground. With the positive lead, probe the red wires leading to each relay (**Figure 232**). Battery voltage should be present at the red wires. Check for a broken wire, blown fuse or loose or corroded connections if battery voltage is not noted.

3. Disconnect the blue and green trim motor wires from the trim relay wiring harness. (**Figure 232**).

4. Connect the positive voltmeter lead to the blue wire and negative lead to the green wire.

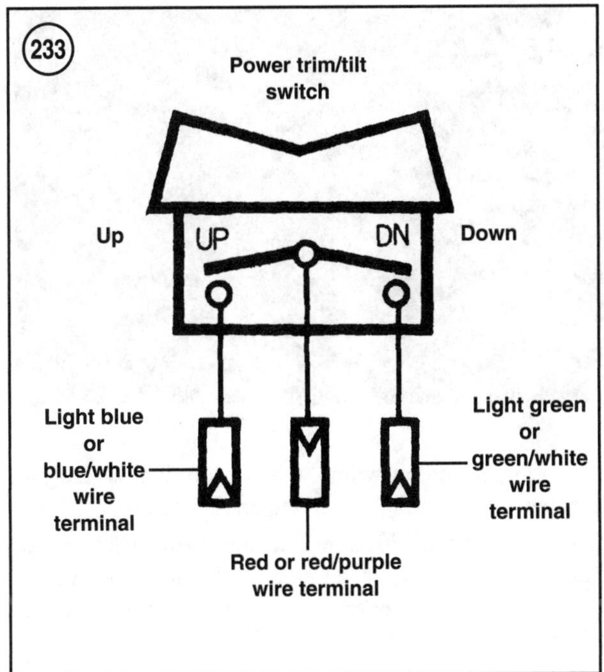

5. Observe the meter and toggle the trim switch to the UP position. Battery voltage should be noted. If battery voltage is noted, the UP relay is functioning correctly.
6. Connect the positive voltmeter to the green wire and the negative lead to the blue wire.
7. Observe the meter and toggle the trim switch in the DOWN direction. Battery voltage should be noted. If battery voltage is noted, the DOWN relay is operating correctly.
8. Connect the positive voltmeter lead to the blue or blue/white wire to the UP relay (**Figure 232**) and negative meter lead to the UP relay black relay wire.
9. Push the trim switch to the UP direction. Battery voltage should be noted. If not, first make sure the black wire has continuity to engine ground, then test the trim switch as described in this chapter. Also inspect the trim switch connector for loose or corroded terminals.
10. Connect the positive voltmeter lead to the green or green/white wire to the DOWN relay and the negative meter lead to the down relay black wire.
11. Push the trim switch to the DOWN position and note the meter. Battery voltage should be present. If not, test the trim switch as described in this chapter. Also inspect the trim switch for loose or corroded terminals.
12. Disconnect the negative battery cable from the battery.
13. Disconnect the trim motor wires from the relay harness. Connect the ohmmeter between the blue wire leading to the UP relay a good engine ground. Continuity must be present. If no continuity or very high resistance is noted, inspect the wires for loose or corroded connections. If the wiring and connections are in acceptable condition, replace the UP relay as described in Chapter Eleven.
14. Connect the ohmmeter between the green wire leading to the DOWN relay and a good engine ground. Again, continuity must be noted. If no continuity or very high resistance is noted, inspect the wires for loose or corroded connections. If the wiring and connections are in acceptable condition, replace the DOWN relay as described in Chapter Eleven.

Trim switch test

A three-position switch (**Figure 223**) controls the trim/tilt system. For operator convenience some models have an additional switch mounted in the lower engine cover (**Figure 231**). Testing instructions are similar regardless of the switch location. This rocker type switch is spring loaded toward the center or off position. Use the switch to activate either the UP or DOWN relay by toggling the switch to the desired position. Battery voltage is applied to the switch by a wire from the ignition switch or starter relay. Check the fuse or wire harness if voltage is not present on the wire before replacing the switch.

1. Disconnect both cables from the battery.
   a. When testing the remote control-mounted trim switch, disassemble the remote control as necessary to access the trim switch wires. See Chapter Twelve.
   b. When testing the lower engine cover-mounted trim switch, refer to the wire diagrams located at the end of the manual to identify the switch wires.
   c. When testing a dash mounted trim switch, remove the switch from the dash.
2. Disconnect all three wires from the wire harness, control harness or engine harness.
3. Connect the ohmmeter between the red or red/purple wire and the light blue or blue/white wire leading to the switch. With the switch in the OFF position, no continuity should be noted.
4. Toggle the switch to the DOWN position. No continuity should be present. Toggle the switch to the UP position. The ohmmeter should now indicate continuity. Replace the switch if it fails to operate as described.
5. Connect the ohmmeter between the red or red/purple wire and the light green or green/white wire (**Figure 233**). With the switch in the OFF position, no continuity should be noted. Toggle the switch to the UP position. No continuity should be present. Toggle the switch to the DOWN position. Continuity should be now be present. Replace the switch if it fails to operate as described.

Trim position sensor testing

All 75 and 90 hp models can be equipped with the optional trim gauge kit. This kit allows the operator to monitor the engine trim position at the control station. A gauge and sensor (**Figure 234**) mounted to the clamp bracket provide this feature. Rotation of the upper pivot pin moves the rotor portion of the sender. A potentiometer in the sender sends a varying voltage signal to the gauge. Voltage supplied to the dash mounted gauge increases as the engine is trimmed up decreases.

A failure to operate is due to a faulty sensor, gauge wiring or connections. Improper adjustments or installation of the upper pivot pin can also prevent correct operation of the sensor. Adjustment instructions are provided in Chapter Five. Upper pivot pin installation is provided in Chapter Eleven.

Inspect the wiring and connections before replacing the sensor or gauge. Test the sensor as follows:

1. Disconnect the purple, black and brown/white wires from the trim gauge.
2. Select the DC volts function on the multimeter. Select the 20 or 40 volt scale on the meter.
3. Connect the positive meter lead to the purple wire. Connect the negative lead to the black wire.
4. Place the ignition key switch in the ON position. Do not start the engine. Observe the meter reading. A faulty battery, ignition key switch, wire or terminal is likely if less than battery voltage is noted on the meter.
5. Connect the positive lead to the brown/white wire. Connect the negative lead to the black wire. Observe the meter reading while operating the trim system to the full up and down positions..
6. Correct operation results in a smooth increase and decrease in voltage as the trim sensor is operated. Place the ignition switch in the OFF position.
7. Replace the trim position sensor if all wiring and the trim position sensor are in good condition, but the gauge fails to operate.

Table 1 STARTING SYSTEM TROUBLESHOOTING

Symptom	Causes	Corrective Action
Electric starter does not operate	Engine not in neutral	Shift into neutral
	Weak or discharged battery	Fully charge and test battery
	Dirty or corroded terminals	Thoroughly clean battery terminals
	Blown fuse in wire harness	Check all fuses
	Faulty neutral start switch	Test neutral switch operation
	Faulty starter button or switch	Test starter button or switch
	Faulty starter relay	Test starter relay
	Dirty or loose starter wires	Clean and tighten wire connections
	Faulty starter motor	Repair starter motor
	Improperly installed starter	Check for proper installation
	Improperly installed wires	Check for proper wire installation

(continued)

Table 1 STARTING SYSTEM TROUBLESHOOTING (continued)

Symptom	Causes	Corrective Action
Starter engages flywheel but rotates slowly	Weak or discharged battery	Fully charge and test battery
	Dirty or corroded battery terminals	Thoroughly clean battery terminals
	Loose or faulty starter wires	Clean, tighten and repair wire connections
	Faulty starter motor	Repair starter motor
	Improperly installed starter	Check for proper installation
	Engine is in gear	Check and correct shift system
	Water or oil in the cylinder(s)	Remove and inspect spark plug(s)
	Seized power head	Check for power head seizure
	Seized gearcase	Check for gearcase failure
Starter engages flywheel but flywheel does not rotate	Weak or discharged battery	Fully charge and test battery
	Dirty or corroded battery terminals	Thoroughly clean battery terminals
	Loose or faulty starter wires	Clean, tighten and repair wire connections
	Faulty starter motor	Repair starter motor
	Improperly installed starter	Check for proper installation
	Seized gearcase assembly	Check for gearcase failure
	Seized power head	Check for manual flywheel rotation
	Water in the cylinders	Check for water in the cylinders
	Oil in the cylinders	Remove and inspect the spark plugs
	Faulty starter motor	Repair starter motor
Noisy starter operation	Dirty or dry starter drive	Clean and lubricate starter drive
	Improperly installed starter	Check for proper installation
	Worn or dry starter bearings	Repair starter motor
	Corroded or damaged flywheel gear	Check condition of flywheel gear teeth
	Worn or damaged starter drive	Check condition of starter drive
	Internal power head damage	Check for problem in power head
	Internal gearcase damage	Check for problem in gearcase

Table 2 IGNITION SYSTEM TROUBLESHOOTING

Symptom	Causes	Corrective Action
Will not start	Lanyard switch activated	Check lanyard switch position
	Shorted stop circuit	Test stop circuit
	Faulty ignition charge coil	Test ignition charge coil
	Faulty ignition coil	Test ignition coil
	Faulty CDI unit	See CDI unit (Chapter Three)
	Faulty pulser coil	Test pulser coil
	Misadjusted throttle position sensor	Adjust as required (Chapter Five
	Faulty throttle position sensor	Test throttle position sensor
	Faulty crankshaft position sensor	Test the crankshaft position sensor
	Faulty CDI or engine control unit	See engine control unit (Chapter Three)
Dies at idle speed	Shorted stop circuit	Test stop circuit
	Faulty ignition charge coil	Test ignition charge coil
	Faulty ignition coil	Test ignition coil
	Faulty CDI unit	See CDI unit (Chapter Three)
	Faulty pulser coil	Test pulser coil

(continued)

Table 2 IGNITION SYSTEM TROUBLESHOOTING (continued)

Symptom	Causes	Corrective Action
Dies at idle speed (continued)	Misadjusted throttle position sensor	Adjust as required (Chapter Five)
	Faulty throttle position sensor	Test throttle position sensor
	Faulty crankshaft position sensor	Test crankshaft position sensor
	Faulty engine temperature sensor	Test engine temperature sensor
Idle speed too high	Improper idle speed adjustment	Adjust as required
	Faulty CDI unit	See CDI unit (Chapter Three)
	Engine in warm up mode	Check thermostat operation
	Faulty engine temperature sensor	Test engine temperature sensor
	Misadjusted throttle position sensor	Adjust as required (Chapter Five)
	Faulty throttle position sensor	Test throttle position sensor
	Faulty crankshaft position sensor	Test crankshaft position sensor
	Faulty pulser coil	Test pulser coil
Hesitation during acceleration	Faulty CDI unit	See CDI unit (Chapter Three)
	Faulty ignition charge coil	Test ignition charge coil
	Faulty ignition coil	Test ignition coil
	Overheated engine	Check overheat switch
	Misadjusted throttle position sensor	Adjust as required (Chapter Five)
	Faulty throttle position sensor	Test throttle position sensor
	Faulty crankshaft position sensor	Test crankshaft position sensor
	Faulty pulser coil	Test pulser coil
	Faulty engine temperature sensor	Test temperature sensor
Poor high speed performance	Overheat or low oil condition	See Warning Systems (Chapter Three)
	Wrong propeller installed	Verify wide-open throttle engine speed
	Faulty rev limit circuit	See CDI unit (Chapter Three)
	Partially shorted stop circuit	Test stop circuit
	Faulty ignition charge coil	Test ignition charge coil
	Faulty ignition coil	Test Ignition coil
	Faulty CDI unit	See CDI unit (Chapter Three)
	Faulty pulser coil	Test pulser coil
	Faulty crankshaft position sensor	Test crankshaft position sensor

Table 3 FUEL SYSTEM TROUBLESHOOTING

Symptom	Causes	Corrective Action
Engine will not start	Old or contaminated or fuel	Supply the engine with fresh fuel
	Fuel pump malfunction	Check for proper pump operation
	Plugged carburetor jets	See Plugged Carburetor Jets (Chapter Three)
	Improper carburetor adjustment	Check carburetor adjustment (Chapter Five)
	Blocked fuel filter	Check all fuel filters
	Closed fuel tank vent	Check for closed vent
	Air leakage in the fuel hoses	Check fuel hoses
	Faulty primer bulb	Test primer bulb
	Fuel leaking from system	Check for fuel leakage
	Flooding carburetor	Check for flooding carburetor
	Improper choke operation	Check for proper choke operation
	Faulty electrothermal valve	Test the electrothermal valve
Rough idle	Old or contaminated fuel	Supply the engine with fresh fuel
	Fuel pump malfunction	Check for proper pump operation

(continued)

Table 3 FUEL SYSTEM TROUBLESHOOTING (continued)

Symptom	Causes	Corrective Action
Rough idle (continued)	Plugged carburetor jets	See plugged carburetor jets (Chapter Three)
	Improper carburetor adjustment	Check carburetor adjustment (Chapter Five)
Air leakage in the fuel hoses	Check fuel hoses	
	Flooding carburetor	Check for flooding carburetor
	Improper choke operation	Check for proper choke operation
Engine dies at idle speed	Old or contaminated or fuel	Supply the engine with fresh fuel
	Fuel pump malfunction	Check for proper pump operation
	Plugged carburetor jets	See Plugged Carburetor Jets (Chapter Three)
	Improper carburetor adjustment	Check carburetor adjustment
	Blocked fuel filter	Check all fuel filters
	Closed fuel tank vent	Check for closed vent
	Air leakage in the fuel hoses	Check fuel hoses
	Fuel leaking from system	Check for fuel leakage
	Flooding carburetor	Check for flooding carburetor
	Improper choke operation	Check for proper choke operation
	Incorrect idle speed adjustment	Adjust idle speed (Chapter Five)
	Misadjusted throttle position sensor	Adjust sensor (Chapter Five)
	Faulty primer bulb	Test primer bulb
Idle speed too high	Improper carburetor adjustment	Check carburetor adjustment
	Improper idle speed adjustment	Adjust as required
	Improperly adjusted throttle cable	Check cable adjustment
	Binding throttle linkage	Check linkage
	Incorrect idle speed adjustment	Adjust idle speed (Chapter Five)
	Faulty electrothermal valve	Test electrothermal valve
Bogging on acceleration	Faulty accelerator pump	Check accelerator pump
	Old or contaminated or fuel	Supply the engine with fresh fuel
	Fuel pump malfunction	Check for proper pump operation
	Plugged carburetor jets	See Plugged Carburetor Jets (Chapter Three)
	Improper carburetor adjustment	Check carburetor adjustment
	Blocked fuel filter	Check all fuel filters
	Closed fuel tank vent	Check for and correct closed vent
	Air leakage in the fuel hoses	Check fuel hoses
	Fuel leaking from system	Check for fuel leakage
	Flooding carburetor	Check for flooding carburetor
	Improper choke operation	Check for proper choke operation
	Misadjusted throttle position sensor	Adjust sensor (see Chapter Five)
	Faulty electrothermal valve	Test electrothermal valve
Misfire at high engine speed	Old or contaminated or fuel	Supply the engine with fresh fuel
	Fuel pump malfunction	Check for proper pump operation
	Plugged carburetor jets	See Plugged Carburetor Jets (Chapter Three)
	Blocked fuel filter	Check all fuel filters
	Closed fuel tank vent	Check for and correct closed vent
	Air leaks in the fuel hoses	Check fuel hoses
	Fuel leaking from system	Check for fuel leakage
	Improper choke operation	Check for proper choke operation
	Faulty primer bulb	Test primer bulb
Excessive exhaust smoke	Improper carburetor adjustment	Check carburetor adjustment
	Fuel leaking from system	Check for fuel leaks
	Flooding carburetor	Check for flooding carburetor
	Improper choke operation	Check for proper choke operation

Table 4 ENGINE CHARACTERISTICS

Letter Codes	Characteristics
M	Manual starter Standard shaft
E	Electric starter Standard shaft
ML	Manual starter Long shaft
EL	Electric starter Long shaft
MXL	Manual starter Extra long shaft
EH	Electric starter Tiller handle control
ELH	Electric starter Long shaft Tiller handle control
ELPT	Electric starter Long shaft Power trim
ELHPT	Electric starter Long shaft Tiller handle control Power trim

Table 5 IGNITION CHARGE COIL RESISTANCE SPECIFICATIONS

Model	Positive test lead	Negative test lead	Ohms
4-6 hp	White wire terminal	Black/red wire terminal	95-134
9.9 hp			
(serial No. OH000057 and prior)	Brown wire terminal	Blue wire terminal	270-410
(serial No. OH000058-on)	Brown wire terminal	Blue wire terminal	280-420
15 hp	Brown wire terminal	Blue wire terminal	270-410
25-40 hp	Green/white wire terminal	White/green wire terminal	660-710
50 hp	Brown wire terminal	Blue wire terminal	272-408

Table 6 PULSER COIL RESISTANCE SPECIFICATIONS

Model	Positive test lead	Negative test lead	Ohms
4-6 hp	Red/white wire terminal	Black wire terminal	149-243 *
9.9 hp			
(serial No. OH000058-on)	White/red wire terminal	Black wire terminal	168-252
50 hp	White/red wire terminal	White/black wire terminal	396-594
75 and 90 hp	White/black wire terminal	Black wire terminal	445-545
	White/red wire terminal	Black wire terminal	445-545

Table 7 IGNITION COIL PRIMARY RESISTANCE

Model	Positive test lead	Negative test lead	Ohms
4-6 hp	Wire terminal on the coil	Coil laminations	0.02-0.38
9.9 hp			
Serial No. OH000057-prior	Orange wire terminal	Black wire terminal	0.16-0.24
Serial No. OH000058-on	Orange wire terminal	Black wire terminal	0.08-0.22
15 hp	Orange wire terminal	Black wire terminal	0.16-0.24
25 hp	Orange wire terminal	Black wire terminal	0.08-0.70
30 and 40 hp	Black/white wire terminal	Black wire terminal	0.08-0.70
50 hp	Orange wire terminal	Black wire terminal	0.10-0.70
75 and 90 hp	Black/white wire terminal	Black wire terminal	0.078-0.106

Table 8 IGNITION COIL SECONDARY RESISTANCE

Model	Positive test lead	Negative test lead	Ohms
4-6 hp	Wire terminal on the coil	Spark plug lead	3000-4000[1]
9.9 hp			
Serial No. OH000057 and prior	No. 1 spark plug lead	No. 2 spark plug lead	3900-5900[1]
Serial No. OH000058-on	No. 1 spark plug lead	No. 2 spark plug lead	13000-16000[1]
15 hp	No. 1 spark plug lead	No. 2 spark plug lead	3900-5900[1]
25 hp	No. 1 spark plug lead	No. 2 Spark plug lead	3500-4700[1]
30 and 40 hp	Spark plug lead	Black wire terminal	2720-3680[1]
50 hp	Spark plug lead	Spark plug lead	3500-4700[1]
75 and 90 hp	Plug lead terminal	Plug lead terminal	3500-4700[2]

1: Perform this test with the spark plug caps *removed* from the plug lead.
2: Perform this test with the spark plug lead *removed* from the coil.

Table 9 SPARK PLUG CAP RESISTANCE

Model	Ohms
4-6 hp	3500-5200
9.9 hp	
Serial No. OH000057-prior	3500-5200
Serial No. OH000058-on	4900-5100
15 hp	3500-5200
25 hp	3500-5200
30 and 40 hp	
VDFP marking	0
VD05FP marking	3500-5200
50 hp	3500-5200
75 and 90 hp*	–

*Spark plug cap resistance specifications are not provided for these models. Refer to *Checking Spark Plug Lead Resistance* in Chapter Three.

Table 10 SPARK PLUG LEAD RESISTANCE

Model	Ohms
75 and 90 hp	
Cylinder No. 1	4500-10700
Cylinder No. 2	3300-8000
Cylinder No. 3	3700-8900
Cylinder No. 4	4300-10200

Table 11 CRANKSHAFT POSITION SENSOR RESISTANCE*

Model	Positive test lead	Negative test lead	Ohms
9.9 hp			
Serial No. OH000057			
and prior	Green/white wire terminal	Black wire terminal	230-350
15 hp	Green/white wire terminal	Black wire terminal	230-350
25-40 hp	Red wire terminal	White wire terminal	300-350

*Perform this test at 68° F (20° C).

Table 12 ELECTROTHERMAL VALVE RESISTANCE

Model	Positive test lead	Negative test lead	Ohms
9.9 hp			
Serial No. OH000058-on	Black wire terminal	Black wire terminal	4.8-7.2
25-40 hp	Yellow wire terminal	Yellow wire terminal	15-25
75 and 90 hp	Green/white wire terminal	Black wire terminal	15-25

Table 13 CHOKE SOLENOID RESISTANCE*

Model	Positive test lead	Negative test lead	Ohms
9.9 hp			
Serial No. OH000057-prior	Blue wire terminal	Black wire terminal	3.2-4.8 *
15 and 50 hp	Blue wire terminal	Black wire terminal	3.2-4.8 *

* Perform this test at 68° F (20° C).

Table 14 POWER SOURCE COIL RESISTANCE (Electrothermal valve power source)

Model	Positive test lead	Negative test lead	Ohms
9.9 hp			
Serial No. OH000058-on	Black wire terminal	Black wire terminal	0.24-0.50
25-40 hp	Yyellow/black wire terminal	Yellow/black wire terminal	6.7-7.1

Table 15 CDI UNIT PEAK OUTPUT TEST

Model	Positive test lead	Negative test lead	Peak volts
75 and 90 hp	Black/white wire terminal	Black wire terminal	165-190 at cranking speed
			175-200 at 1500 rpm
			175-200 at 3500 rpm
	Black/orange wire terminal	Black wire terminal	165-190 at cranking speed
			175-200 at 1500 rpm
			175-200 at 3500 rpm

Table 16 PULSER COIL PEAK OUTPUT TEST

Model	Positive test lead	Negative test Lead	Peak volts
75 and 90 hp	White/red wire terminal	Black wire terminal	2.8-3.4 at cranking speed
			6.5-7.8 at 1500 rpm
			10.5-12 at 3500 rpm

(continued)

Table 16 PULSER COIL PEAK OUTPUT TEST (continued)

Model	Positive test lead	Negative test Lead	Peak volts
75 and 90 hp (continued)	White/black wire terminal	Black wire terminal	2.8-3.4 at cranking speed 6.5-7.8 at 1500 rpm 10.5-12 at 3500 rpm

Table 17 OVERHEAT WARNING ACTIVATION SPECIFICATIONS

Model	Switching temperature
25 hp	
switch on	194° F (90° C)
switch off	188° F (87° C)
30 and 40 hp	
switch on	192° F (89° C)
switch off	183° F (84° C)
50 hp	
switch on	131° F (55° C)
Open circuit	
switch off	104° F (40° C)
Closed circuit	
75 and 90 hp	
switch on	140° F (60° C)
switch off	118° F (48° C)

Table 18 OIL PRESSURE SWITCH SPECIFICATIONS*

Model	Switching-on pressure
4-6 hp	2.8-4.2 psi (19.3-29 kPa)
9.9 and 15 hp	2.5 psi (17 kPa)
25 hp	2.5 psi (17 kPa)
30 and 40 hp	1.5-3 psi (10.3-20.7 kPa)
50 hp	2.9 psi (17 kPa)
75 and 90 hp	2.9 psi (19.9 kPa)

* Test the oil pressure switch at 68° F (20° C).

Table 19 ENGINE TEMPERATURE SENSOR SPECIFICATIONS

Model	Temperature	Ohms
25-40 hp	32° F (0° C)	3200
	40° F (7° C)	2300
	60° F (16° C)	1500
	90° F (32° C)	720
	120° F (49° C)	380
	150° F (66° C)	200
	180° F (82° C)	120
	212° F (100° C)	80
75 and 90 hp	32° F (0° C)	5790
	68° F (20° C)	2450
	104° F (40° C)	1500

Table 20 BATTERY CHARGING COIL RESITANCE*

Model	Positive test lead	Negative test lead	Ohms
4-6 hp	Yellow/red wire terminal	Yellow/red wire terminal	0.31-0.47
9.9 hp			
Serial No. OH000057-prior			
6 amp system	Green wire terminal	Green wire terminal	0.48-0.72
10 amp system	Green wire terminal	Green wire terminal	0.24-0.36
Serial No. OH000058-on			
6 amp system	Green wire terminal	Green wire terminal	0.73-1.09
	White/green wire terminal	Black wire terminal	0.96-1.44
10 amp system	Green wire terminal	Green wire terminal	0.91-1.37
	White/green wire terminal	Black wire terminal	0.96-1.44
15 hp			
6 amp system	Green wire terminal	Green wire terminal	0.48-0.72
10 amp system	Green wire terminal	Green wire terminal	0.24-0.36
25-40 hp			
6 amp system	Yellow wire terminal	Yellow wire terminal	0.9-1.1
15 amp system	Yellow wire terminal	Yellow wire terminal	0.22-0.24
50 hp	Green wire terminal	Green wire terminal	1.2-3.2
75 and 90 hp	White wire terminal	White wire terminal	0.32-0.48

* Take all measurements at 68° F (20° C)

Table 21 RECTIFIER AND RECTIFIER REGULATOR SPECIFICATIONS

Model	Positive test lead	Negative test lead	Specification
4-6 hp	Red wire terminal	Yellow wire terminal	No continuity
	Yellow wire terminal	Red wire terminal	Continuity
9.9 hp (serial No. OH000057-prior) and 15 hp (serial No. OG590000-on)			
6 amp system	Black wire terminal	Green/white wire terminal	0.30-0.80 ohm
	Black wire terminal	Green wire terminal	030-0.80 ohm
	Black wire terminal	Red wire terminal	0.65-2.0 ohm
	Green/white wire terminal	Green wire terminal	No continuity
	Green/white wire terminal	Red wire terminal	0.30-0.80 ohm
	Green/red wire terminal	Green/white wire terminal	No continuity
	Green/red wire terminal	Red wire terminal	0.30-0.80 ohm
	Red wire terminal	Green/white wire terminal	No continuity
	Red wire terminal	Green wire terminal	No continuity
10 amp system	Black wire terminal	Green/white wire terminal	0.30-0.80 ohm
	Black wire terminal	Green wire terminal	0.30-0.80 ohm
	Black wire terminal	White/green wire terminal	No continuity
	Black wire terminal	Red wire terminal	0.65-1.20 ohm
	Green/white wire terminal	Black wire terminal	1.0 ohm or more
	Green/white wire terminal	Green wire terminal	1.2 ohm or more
	Green/white wire terminal	White/green wire terminal	No continuity
	Green/white wire terminal	Red wire terminal	0.30-0.80 ohm
	Green wire terminal	Black wire terminal	1.0 ohms or more
	Green wire terminal	Green/white wire terminal	1.2 or more
	Green wire terminal	White/green wire terminal	No continuity
	Green wire terminal	Red wire terminal	030-0.80 ohm
	White/green wire terminal	Black wire terminal	1.2 ohms or more
	White/green wire terminal	Green/white wire terminal	0.30-0.80 ohm
	White/green wire terminal	Green wire terminal	1.5 ohms or more
	White/green wire terminal	Red wire terminal	0.65-1.30 ohm
	Red wire terminal	Black wire terminal	No continuity

(continued)

Table 21 RECTIFIER AND RECTIFIER REGULATOR SPECIFICATIONS (continued)

Model	Positive test lead	Negative test lead	Specification
9.9 hp (serial No. OH000057-prior) and 15 hp (serial No. OG590000-on) 10 amp system (continued)	Red wire terminal	Green/white wire terminal	No continuity
	Red wire terminal	Green wire terminal	No continuity
	Red wire terminal	White/green wire terminal	No continuity
Serial No. OH000058-on	Black wire terminal	Green/white wire terminal	0.30-0.80 ohm
	Black wire terminal	Green wire terminal	0.30-0.80 ohm
	Black wire terminal	White/green wire terminal	No continuity
	Black wire terminal	Red wire terminal	0.65-0.95 ohm
	Green/white wire terminal	Black wire terminal	0.50-1.80 ohm
	Green/white wire terminal	Green wire terminal	0.75-2.0 ohm
	Green/white wire terminal	White/green wire terminal	No continuity
	Green/white wire terminal	Red wire terminal	0.30-0.80 ohm
	Green wire terminal	Black wire terminal	No continuity
	Green wire terminal	Green/white wire terminal	No continuity
	Green wire terminal	White/green wire terminal	No continuity
	Green wire terminal	Red wire terminal	0.30-0.80 ohm
	White/green wire terminal	Black wire terminal	0.75-2.0 ohm
	White/green wire terminal	Green/white wire terminal	0.30-0.80 ohm
	White/green wire terminal	Green wire terminal	0.95-2.0 ohm
	White/green wire terminal	Red wire terminal	0.65-1.07 ohm
	Red wire terminal	Black wire terminal	No continuity
	Red wire terminal	Green wire terminal	No continuity
	Red wire terminal	Green wire terminal	No continuity
	Red wire terminal	White/green wire terminal	No continuity
25 hp	Red wire terminal	Yellow wire terminal[1]	100-400 ohms
	yellow wire terminal[1]	Red wire terminal	40,000 ohms or more[2]
	Rectifier/regulator housing	Yellow wire terminal[1]	15,000 ohms or more
	Gray wire terminal	Rectifier/regulator housing	10,000-50,000 ohms
30 and 40 hp	Red wire terminal	Yellow wire terminal[1]	100-400 ohms
	Yellow wire terminal[1]	Red wire terminal	20,000 ohms or more[2]
	Rectifier/regulator housing	Yellow wire terminal[1]	8000-15,000 ohms
	Gray wire terminal	Rectifier/regulator housing	10,000-50,000 ohms
50 hp	Black wire terminal	Green wire terminal[1]	0.3-0.8 ohm
	Black wire terminal	Green/white wire terminal	0.3-0.8 ohm
	Black wire terminal	Red wire terminal	0.8-1.3 ohm
	Green wire terminal[1]	Black wire terminal	No continuity
	Green wire terminal	Green wire terminal	No continuity
	Green wire terminal[1]	Green/white wire terminal	No continuity
	Green wire terminal[1]	Red wire terminal	0.3-0.8 ohm
	Green/white wire terminal	Black wire terminal	No continuity
	Green/white wire terminal	Green wire terminal[1]	No continuity
	Green/white wire terminal	Red wire terminal	0.3-0.8 ohm
	Red wire terminal	Black wire terminal	No continuity
	Red wire terminal	Green wire terminal[1]	No continuity
	Red wire terminal	Green/white wire terminal	No continuity
75 and 90 hp	Red wire terminal	Green wire terminal[1]	100-300 ohms
	Red wire terminal	Green/white wire terminal[1]	100-300 ohms
	Green wire terminal[1]	Red wire terminal	No continuity
	Green/white wire terminal[1]	Red wire terminal	No continuity
	Black wire terminal	Green wire terminal[1]	No continuity
	Black wire terminal	Green/white wire terminal[1]	No continuity
	Green wire terminal[1]	Black wire terminal	100-300 ohms
	Green/white wire terminal[1]	Black wire terminal	100-300 ohms

1. Perform test using *each* same color wire.
2. No continuity should be noted when the second yellow wire terminal is selected.

Table 22 WATER PRESSURE SPECIFICATIONS

Model	Pressure
4-6 hp	
1300 rpm	2.3-3.6 psi (16-25 kPa)
5000 rpm	8-15 psi (55-104 kPa)
9.9 and 15 hp	
Standard Gearcase	
950 rpm	0.5-1.5 psi (3.4-10.4 kPa)
5000 rpm	5-7 psi (35-48 kPa)
Optional gearcase	
950 rpm	1-4 psi (6.9-28 kPa)
5000 rpm	6-9 psi (41.4-62.1 kPa)
25 hp	
800 rpm	2-4 psi (14-28 kPa)
6000 rpm	12-17 psi (83-117 kPa)
30 and 40 hp	
Standard Gearcase	
800 rpm	2-4 psi (14-28 kPa)
6000 rpm	12-17 psi (83-117 kPa)
Optional gearcase	
800 rpm	2-4 psi (14-28 kPa)
6000 rpm	10-15 psi (69-103 kPa)
50 hp	
Standard Gearcase	
750 rpm	2-4 psi (14-28 kPa)
6000 rpm	12-17 psi (83-117 kPa)
Optional gearcase	
750 rpm	2-4 psi (14-28 kPa)
6000 rpm	10-15 psi (69-103 kPa)
75 and 90 hp	
1000 rpm	5 psi (34.5 kPa)
6000 rpm	20.5 psi (141.5 kPa)

Table 23 THERMOSTAT SPECIFICATIONS

Model	Specifications
4-6 hp	
Initial opening temperature	122°-129° F (50°-54° C)
Fully opened temperature	145°-153° F (63°-67° C)
Valve opening height	0.12 in. (3 mm)
9.9-50 hp models	
Initial opening temperature	136°-143° F (58°-62° C)
Fully opened temperature	158° F (70° C)
Valve opening height	0.12 in. (3 mm)
75 and 90 hp	
Initial opening temperature	140° F (60° C)
Fully opened temperature	158° F (70° C)
Valve opening height	0.12 in. (3 mm)

Table 24 OIL PRESSURE SPECIFICATIONS

Model	Pressure
4-6 hp	
1300 rpm	4 psi (27.5 kPa)
5000 rpm	21 psi (144.5 kPa)
Relief valve opening	31-40 psi (213-275 kPa)
	(continued)

Table 24 OIL PRESSURE SPECIFICATIONS (continued)

Model	Pressure
9.9 and 15 hp	
3000 rpm	30-40 psi (206-275 kPa)
Relief valve opening	55-64 psi (378-440 kPa)
25-50 hp	
3000 rpm	30-40 psi (206-275 kPa)
75 and 90	
850 rpm	46.5 psi (320 kPa)
Relief valve opening	71 psi (488 kPa)

Table 25 OVERSPEED SYSTEM SPECIFICATIONS

Model	Maximum recommended engine speed (rpm)	Overspeed prevention (rpm)
4-6 hp	4500-5500	5700-6100
9.9 hp		
Serial No. OH000057-prior	4500-5500	5700
Serial No. OH000058-on	4500-5500	5850
15 hp	4500-5500	5850
25-40 hp	5500-6000	6200-6250
50 hp	5500-6000	6120-6280
75 and 90 hp	5000-6000	6200-6350

Table 26 COMPRESSION SPECIFICATIONS

Model	Compression ratio	Cylinder compression
4 and 5 hp	8.5:1	36-50 psi (247-343 kPa) 99-127 psi (681-874 kPa)[1]
9.9-15 hp	9.3:1	185-190 psi (1273-1308 kPa)
25 hp	9.8:1	180-210 psi (1238-1445 kPa)[2]
30 and 40 hp	9.8:1	180-210 psi (1238-1445 kPa)[2]
50 hp	9.8:1	170-190 psi (1169-1306 kPa)
75 and 90 hp	9.6:1	138 psi (950 kPa) (minimum)

1. Normal compression measurements with the decompression mechanism *disabled*
2. A compression relief mechanism used on *manual start models* prevents compression testing.

Chapter Four

Lubrication, Maintenance and Tune-up

When operating properly, the Mercury or Mariner outboard provides smooth operation, reliable starting and excellent performance. Regular maintenance and frequent tune-ups keep it in good shape and running great. This chapter provides the information necessary to perform all required lubrication, maintenance and tune-up on the Mercury or Mariner four stroke outboard.

During operation certain components and fluids in the engine wear or become contaminated. Unless these components and fluids are renewed, engine performance, reliability and engine life diminish. Performing routine lubrication, maintenance and tune-ups help ensure the outboard performs as it should and delivers a long and trouble free life.

Table 1 lists the maintenance items and intervals for all engine systems and components. Maintenance intervals are also provided in the Quick Reference Data section at the front of the manual. **Tables 2-5** provide lubricant capacities, spark plug recommendations and timing specifications. **Table 6** lists tightening specifications for maintenance related fasteners. **Tables 1-6** are located at the end of this chapter.

LUBRICATION AND MAINTENANCE

Lubrication is the most important maintenance item for any outboard. The outboard simply will not operate without proper lubrication. Lubricant for the power head, gearcase and other areas helps prevent wear, guards against corrosion and provides smooth operation of turning or sliding surfaces.

Outboards operate in a corrosive environment and often require special types of lubricants. Using the wrong type of lubricant can cause serious engine damage or substantially shorten the life of the engine. Special pumps and lubricants (**Figure 1**) are required to perform many of the maintenance items. These pumps are available from most automotive parts stores. The lubricants are available from most marine suppliers or marine dealerships.

Before Each Use

As specified in **Table 1**, certain items must be checked before each use. Following these recommendations help identify and correct conditions leading to a dangerous

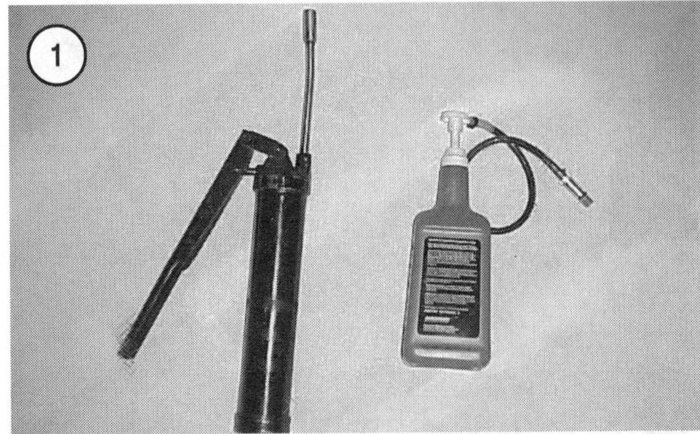

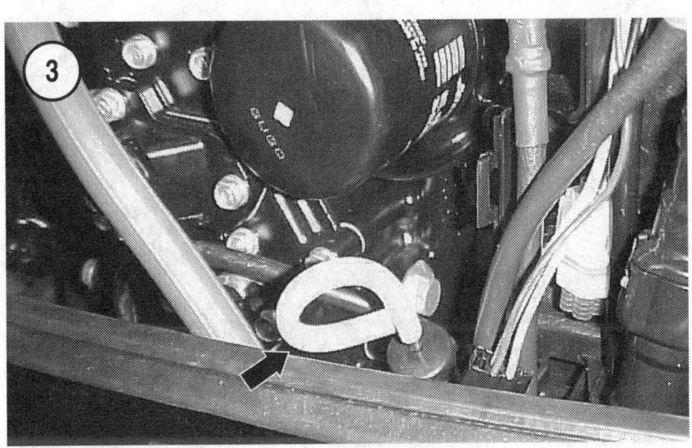

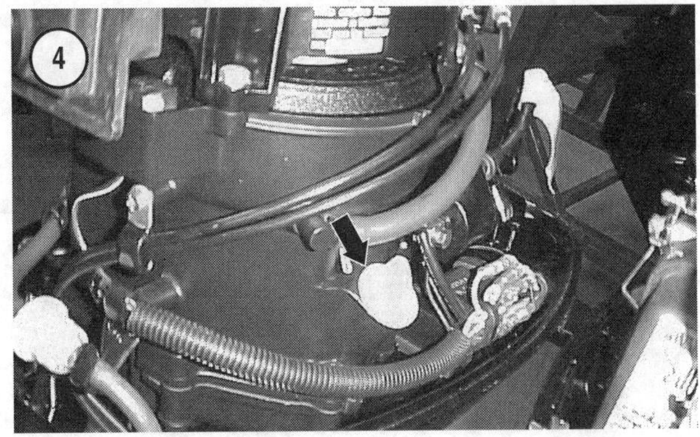

lack or control or damage to the engine. This section provides instructions for performing the following inspections:

1. Checking the oil level.
2. Checking the propeller.
3. Checking the engine mounting bolts/screws.
4. Checking the fuel system for leakage.
5. Checking the steering system for looseness or binding.
6. Checking the cooling system.
7. Checking the operation of the lanyard or stop switch.

CAUTION

Never run the engine with the oil level over the full mark on the dipstick. Over filling can result in foaming of the oil and inadequate lubrication of internal components.

Checking the oil level

To prevent serious damage to the power head always check the engine oil level before starting the engine. To avoid overfilling the oil, wait until the engine has been switched off for 30 minutes or more. This allows the oil in the power head time to drain into the oil pan. Always check the oil level with the engine in a vertical position (**Figure 2**). The location and type of oil dipstick (**Figure 3**) varies by model. A yellow handle on most models allows easy identification of the dipstick.

On 4-6 hp models, the combination oil fill plug and dipstick is located on the lower port side of the power head (**Figure 4**).

On 9.9 and 15 hp models, the dipstick is located on the lower starboard side of the power head just below the intake manifold (**Figure 5**).

On 25-40 hp models, the dipstick (**Figure 6**) is located on the lower port side of the power head to the right of the oil filter.

On 50 hp models, thedipstick (**Figure 7**) is located on the lower port side on the power head and directly below the ignition coils.

On 75 and 90 hp models, the dipstick (**Figure 3**) is located on the lower starboard side of the power head below the oil filter.

Check the oil level as follows:

1. Place the engine in the vertical position (**Figure 2**) with the ignition switched off.
2. Remove the dipstick from the engine as follows:
   a. On 4-6 hp model, twist the dipstick/oil fill plug counterclockwise to unthread it from its opening.
   b. On 9.9, 15, 75 and 90 hp models, pull straight up on the dipstick to pull it from its opening.
   c. On 25-50 hp models, pull up on the end of the locking lever to release the locking mechanism. Pull the dipstick from its opening.
3. Wipe the dipstick with a clean shop towel.
4. Insert the dipstick fully into its opening. Do not engage the locking mechanism.
5. Pull the dipstick from the engine and note the oil level relative to the *max and add* marks on the dipstick (**Figure 8**). Inspect the oil for the presence of water, milky appearance, or significant fuel odor. Refer to *Power Head* in Chapter Three if any of these conditions are noted.
6. If necessary, add oil until the level is even with the full mark. Do not overfill the engine. It is preferable for the oil level to be slightly low than overfilled. If the engine is overfilled, drain the excess oil as described under *Changing the Oil* in this chapter.
7. Install the dipstick by reversing the removal procedure.

Checking the propeller

Inspect the propeller for cracked, damaged or missing blades (**Figure 9**). Operation with a damaged propeller results in decreased performance, excessive vibration and increased wear. Straighten small bent areas using locking pliers. Repair small nicks using a metal file. To prevent an out of balance condition, do not remove excessive amounts of material from the propeller. Have the propeller repaired at a reputable propeller repair shop if significant damage is noted.

To check for a bent propeller shaft, disconnect the battery cables and spark plug leads, then place the engine in NEUTRAL. Spin he propeller while observing the propeller shaft (**Figure 10**). If the shaft wobbles noticeably, the propeller shaft is bent and must be replaced. See Chapter Nine.

6

7

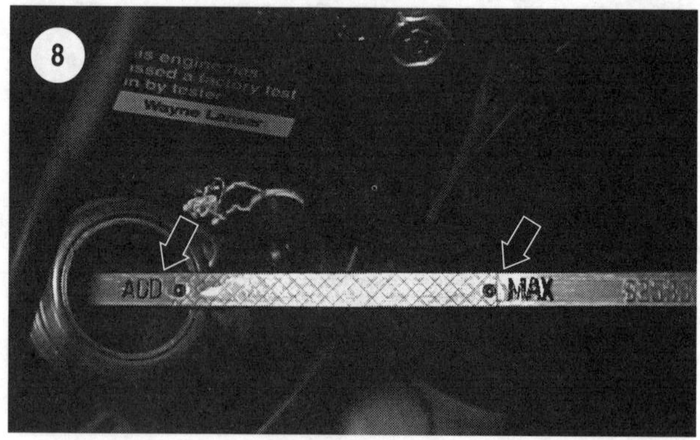

8

9

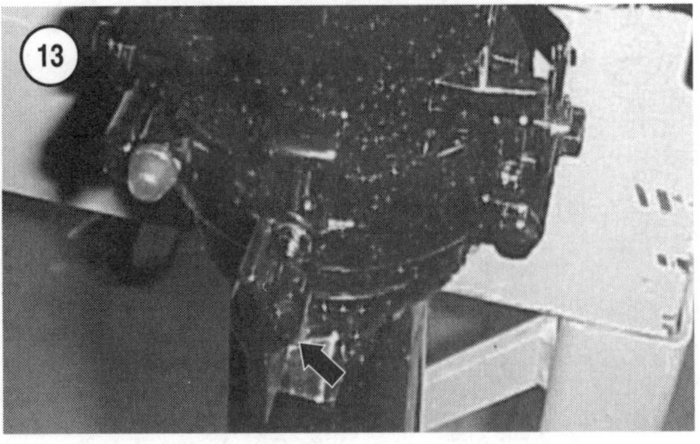

Checking the mounting bolts and screws

WARNING

Operating the engine with loose clamp screws or engine mounting bolts can result in serious bodily injury, death and loss of the engine. Always check and tighten all mounting bolts or screws before operating the engine.

Tiller control 4-6 hp models are attached to the boat transom using lever type clamp screws (**Figure 11**). Tiller control 9.9-40 hp models are attached to the boat transom using both lever type clamp screws (**Figure 11**) and through the transom mounting bolts (**Figure 12**).

Check and tighten all through the transom mounting bolts and lever type clamp screws before operating the outboard.

Checking the fuel system for leakage

Observe all fuel hoses, hose connections and the carburetor and squeeze the primer bulb. Correct the source of leakage prior to starting the engine.

After starting the engine check for the presence of a sheen on the water surface around the engine and fuel odor. Stop the engine and inspect the fuel system for leakage if either of these conditions are noted.

Fuel system repair is covered in Chapter Six.

Checking the steering system

Check the operation of the steering components prior to starting the engine.

On tiller control models, move the tiller handle to the full port and starboard limits. Note the presence of looseness or binding. A loose tiller arm, tiller arm bracket or engine mounts is indicated if looseness is noted. A misadjusted or faulty steering friction system (**Figure 13**) is indicated if binding is noted.

On remote control models, rotate the steering wheel to the clockwise and counterclockwise limits. Note the presence of binding or excessive slack as the wheel changes direction. A faulty steering cable, faulty helm or damaged midsection components are indicated if binding is noted. Midsection repair instructions are provided in Chapter Eleven.

Correct the causes of looseness or binding before operating the outboard.

4

Checking the cooling system

Check for the presence of the water stream immediately after starting the engine. A stream of water (**Figure 14**) exiting the lower back area of the engine indicates the water pump is operating. This stream may not appear for the first few seconds of operation especially at idle speed. Stop the engine and check for cooling system if the stream fails to appear. Refer to *Cooling System* in Chapter Three. Never run the engine if it is overheating or the water stream fails to appear.

Checking the lanyard or stop switch

Check the operation of the lanyard or stop switch before getting underway. Press the stop button or switch the ignition OFF on remote key switch models. Start the engine then pull the lanyard cord from the lanyard switch (**Figure 15**). If the engine fails to stop, operate the choke, disconnect the fuel line or squeeze the fuel line until the engine stalls. Repair the faulty stop circuit before restarting the engine. Test instructions for the stop circuit are provided in Chapter Three.

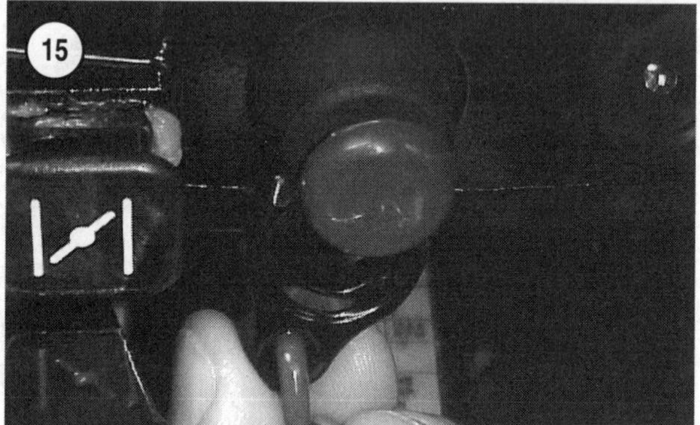

After Each Use

As specified in **Table 1** certain maintenance items must be performed after each usage. Observing these requirements can dramatically reduce corrosion of engine components and extend the life of the engine. Topics covered in this section include:

1. Flushing the cooling system.
2. Cleaning debris or contaminants from the engine surfaces.
3. Checking for propeller or gearcase for damage.

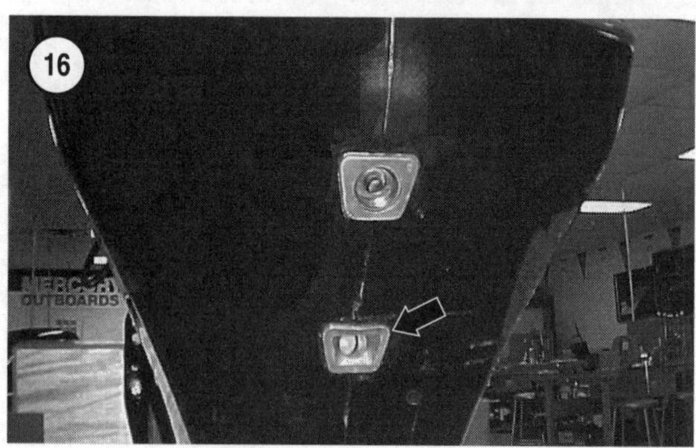

Flushing the cooling system

Flush the cooling system after each use to prevent corrosion and deposit buildup in the cooling passages. This is even more important if the engine is run in salt, brackish or polluted water.

Some models are equipped with a power head flush fitting (**Figure 16**) at the rear of the lower motor cover. This fitting allows connection of a garden hose for flushing the power head cooling passages. Connect the hose to this fitting then run water through the power head for approximately five minutes. Never run the engine while using the power head flush fitting.

On engines stored on a trailer or boat lift, flush the engine using a flush/test adapter (**Figure 17**). These adapters

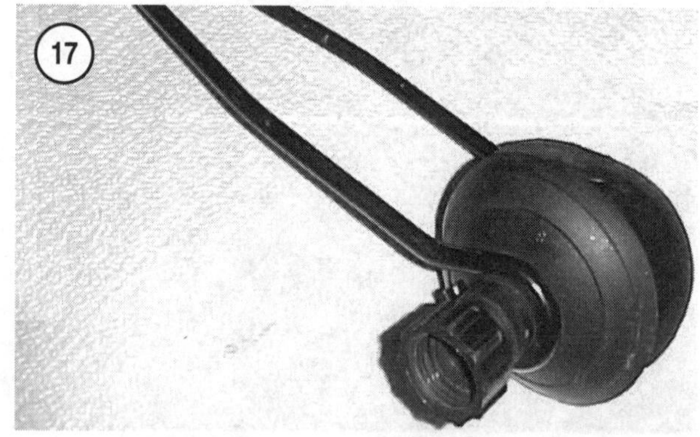

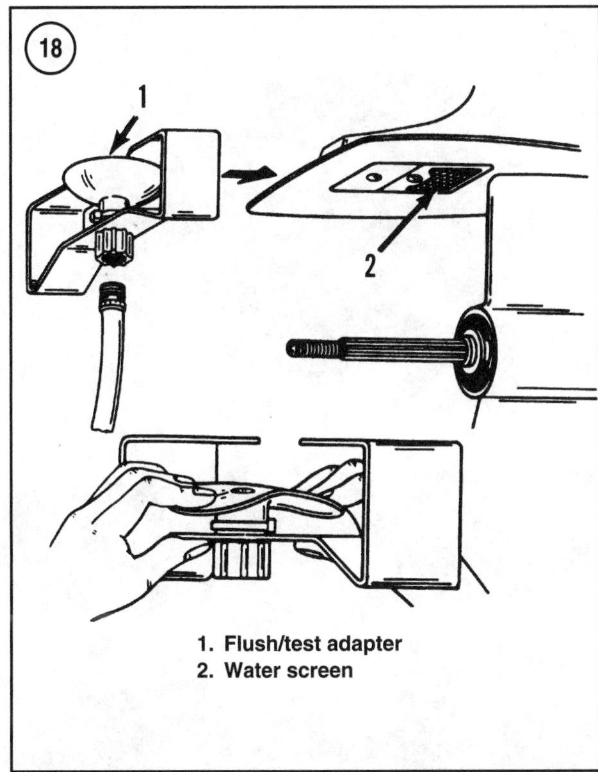

1. Flush/test adapter
2. Water screen

are available from marine dealerships or marine supply stores. This method is preferable as it flushes the entire cooling system. The engine can be flushed by operating it in a suitable test tank filled with clean water.

The type of flush adapter used is determined by the location of the water screens. Most smaller engines have the water screen (2, **Figure 18**) located under the antiventilation plate. Larger engines have the water screens located on the side of the gearcase (**Figure 19**). Some models have water screens on the side of the gearcase and an auxiliary water pickup tube located under the antiventilation plate. This feature provides cooling water to the power head should the side mounted pickup become blocked. Use the adapters for the side mounted screen on these models.

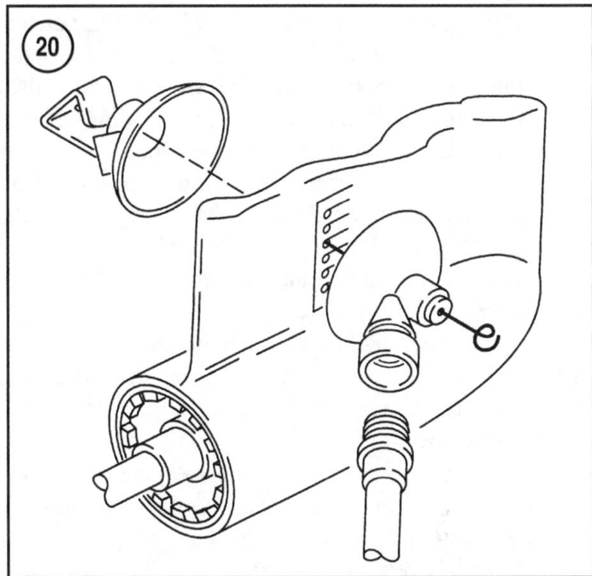

Use the slide-on flush test adapter (**Figure 17**) or a two piece flush/test adapter (**Figure 20**) on all models with side mounted water screens. The two piece design is preferred over the slide-on type because it will not slip out of position during engine operation. Purchase the two piece adapter (part number 44357A 2) from a Mercury or Mariner dealership.

NOTE

Water may exit the auxiliary water pickup opening while running the engine on flush test adapter. This is normal. To ensure adequate engine cooling, use full water pressure and never run the engine at high speed using a flush adapter.

Flush the cooling system as follows:

1. Remove the propeller as described in Chapter Nine.
2. Carefully attach the flush adapter to the engine.
   a. On models using an antiventilation plate mounted adapter, connect the garden hose to the adapter. Collapse the cupped portion of the adapter then slide top side of the adapter over the top side of the antiventilation plate. Center the cup over the water screens then release the cup.
   b. If using the slide-on type flush adapter, connect the garden hose to the adapter. Starting at the front edge of the gearcase, slide the cups onto each side of the gearcase. Position the cups over the water screens (**Figure 19**).

c. If using the two piece adapter (**Figure 20**), connect the garden hose to the adapter. Squeeze the clamp plate on the opposite from the hose connection then pull the cup from the wire. Slide the wire with the cup attached through the water screen openings (**Figure 20**). Squeeze the clamp plate enough to pass the wire through the cup and both sides of the clamp plate. Press both cups and the wire loop firmly against the gearcase then release the clamp plate.

3. Turn the water on. Make certain that the flush adapter is firmly positioned over the water screen. Start the engine and run at a fast idle in neutral until the engine reaches full operating temperature.

4. Continue to run the engine until the water exiting the engine is clear and the engine has run for a minimum of 5 minutes. Monitor the engine temperature. Stop the engine if it begins to overheat or water is not exiting the water stream fitting.

5. Bring the engine back to idle for a few minutes then stop the engine. Remove the flush adapter. Install the propeller as described in Chapter Nine. Allow the engine to remain in the vertical position for a few minutes to allow complete draining of the cooling system.

Cleaning the engine

Clean all dirt or vegetation from all external engine surfaces after each use. This important maintenance item helps reduce corrosion, reduces wear on gearcase and trim system seals and allows easier inspection for worn or damaged components.

Never use strong cleaning solutions or solvent to clean the outboard motor. Mild dish soap and pressurized water does an adequate job of cleaning most debris from the engine. To prevent damaged or contaminated power head components, never direct water towards any openings on the engine cover. Avoid directing the spray from a high pressure nozzle or pressure washer directly at any opening, seals, plugs, wiring or wire grommets. The water may bypass seals and contaminate the trim system, electric trim motor or trim fluid reservoir.

Rinse the external surfaces with clean water to remove any soap residue. Wipe the engine with a soft cloth to prevent water spots.

ROUTINE MAINTENANCE

Always keep a log of maintenance items performed and when they were done. Try to log the number of running hours after each use. Without a maintenance/running hours log or a dash mounted hour meter (**Figure 21**) it is almost impossible to accurately determine the hours of usage. Be aware that a dash mounted hour meter may run when the key switch is ON and the engine not running. Note this event in the maintenance log should it occur.

Table 1 lists the required maintenance items and maintenance schedules. Some maintenance items do not apply to all models. The type of control system, starting system, and trim system used determines the engines unique maintenance requirements. Perform all applicable maintenance items listed in **Table 1**.

WARNING.
Use extreme caution when working with or around fuel. Never smoke around fuel or fuel vapors. Make sure no flame or source of ignition is present in the work area. Flame or sparks can ignite the fuel or vapor resulting in fire or explosion.

NOTE
Fuel has a relatively short shelf life. Fuel begins to lose some of its desirable characteristics in as little as 14 days. Use the fuel within a few weeks after purchase.

Fuel Requirements

Always use a major brand fuel from a facility that sells a large amount of fuel. Fuels available today have a relatively short shelf life. Some fuels begin to lose potency in as little as 14 days. This should be considered when purchasing fuel for the outboard.

All models are designed to use unleaded fuel. Use regular grade fuel with an average octane rating of 87 or higher for all models. This fuel should meet the requirements for the engine when operated under normal operating conditions. Premium grade fuel offers little advantage over regular fuel under most operating condition. Premium fuel is not recommended by the manufacturer for use in all models covered in this manual.

Purchase fuel from a busy fuel station. They usually have a higher turnover of fuel, giving you a better opportunity to purchase fresh fuel. Always use the fuel well before it becomes old or stale. Refer to *Storage* in this chapter for information on fuel additives.

WARNING.

Use extreme caution when working with or around fuel. Never smoke around fuel or fuel vapor. Make sure no flame or source of ignition is present in the work area. Flame or sparks can ignite the fuel or vapor resulting in fire or explosion.

CAUTION

Never run the outboard on old or stale fuel. Engine damage could result from using deteriorated fuel. Varnish-like deposits form in the fuel system as fuel deteriorates. These deposits block fuel passages and result in decreased fuel delivery. Decreased fuel delivery causes a lean condition in the combustion chamber. Damage to the pistons, valves and other power head components result from operating the engine with an excessively lean fuel mixture.

Fuel Filter Inspection

Inspect or replace the fuel filter at the intervals specified in **Table 1**. An inline fuel filter (**Figure 22**) is used on all models covered in this manual. It is constructed of translucent material allowing visual detection of contamination inside the tiller.

This filter is located in the fuel hose connecting the quick connector fitting (**Figure 23**) or fuel tank connector to the fuel pump (**Figure 24**).

Direct a beam of light into the filter body to allow easier detection of debris. Replace the fuel filter if debris is noted inside the filter body. Fuel filter removal and is provided in Chapter Six.

NOTE

Some boats are equipped with large spin on type fuel filters. Most of these provide water separating capabilities. They are located between the primer bulb and fuel tank on most applications. Service these units when servicing other fuel filters on the engine. Replacement filter elements for this type of filter are available from marine dealerships and marine supply stores. Follow the filter manufactures instructions to remove or install this type of filter.

CAUTION

Never use nondetergent oil or two stroke outboard motor oil in a four stroke outboard. Its use will not provide adequate lubrication of the internal engine components. Operating the engine without adequate lubrication results in severe power head damage or engine seizure.

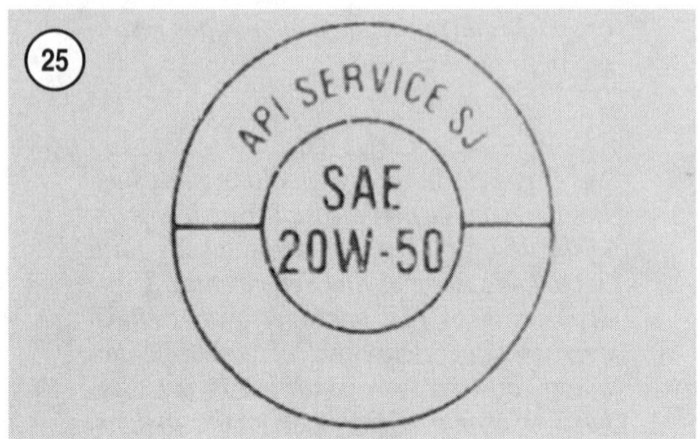

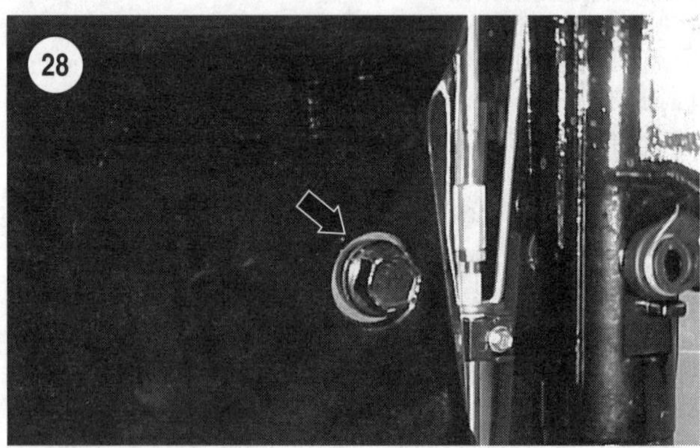

Engine Oil Requirements

Mercury Marine recommends using Quicksilver 4-cycle marine oil or a premium quality four-stroke oil in all Mercury or Mariner four stroke outboards. Quicksilver oil is available at a local Mercury or Mariner dealership. Premium quality four-stroke is available from automotive parts stores and many other sources.

Always use a good grade of oil in the four stroke outboard. Look for the API classification emblem (**Figure 25**) on the oil container when selecting oil for the engine. This label lists the service classification of the oil. Use only oil meeting or exceeding one the following service classifications: SH, SG, SF, CF-4, CE, CD or CDII.

Oils with a 10W-30 viscosity rating are recommended for use in all air temperature operating ranges. Oils with a 25W-40 viscosity rating are acceptable for use provided the air temperature exceeds 40° F (4° C). The oil viscosity rating is listed on the API classification emblem (**Figure 25**). Engine oil capacities are provided in **Table 2**.

The oil filter traps dirt, debris and other contaminants during engine operation. Always replace the filter or clean the screen when changing the oil. If the filter is not changed, contaminated oil remaining in the filter will immediately flow into the fresh oil upon start up. Oil filter change and filter cleaning instructions are provided in this section.

Oil Drain and Fill Locations

On 4-6 hp models, the oil drain fitting (**Figure 26**) is located on the front port side of the engine. Move the tiller handle upward to access the fitting. The combination oil fill cap/dipstick (**Figure 27**) is located on the front port side of the power head.

On 9.9 (prior to serial No. OH000058) and 15 hp models, the oil drain fitting (**Figure 28**) is located on the starboard side of the drive shaft housing. The oil fill cap (**Figure 29**) is located on the rocker arm cover near the fuel pump.

On 9.9 hp models (serial No. OH000058-On) the oil drain fitting is located under a cover (**Figure 30**) mounted to the rear side of the drive shaft housing. The oil fill cap (**Figure 29**) is located on the rocker arm cover near the fuel pump.

On 25-50 hp models, the oil drain fitting is located on the port side of the drive shaft housing (**Figure 31**). The oil fill cap (**Figure 32**) is located on the rocker arm cover near the fuel pump.

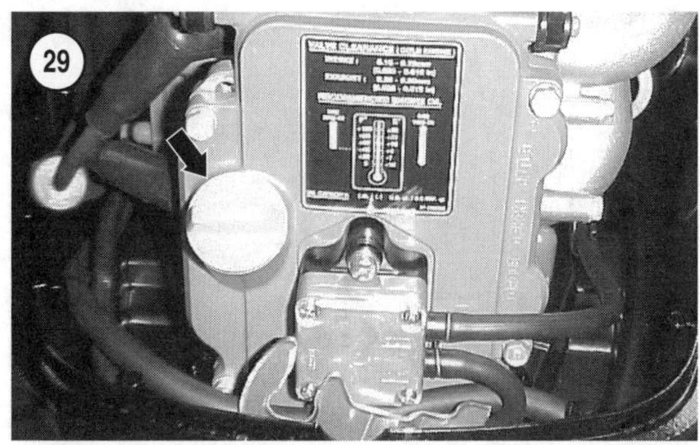

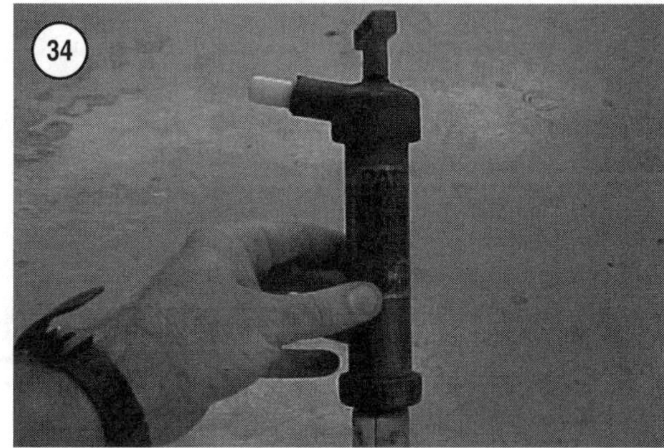

On 75 and 90 hp models, the oil drain fitting is located on the port side of the drive shaft housing (**Figure 30**). The oil fill cap (**Figure 33**) is located on the upper end of the rocker arm cover above the fuel pumps.

Pumping the Oil From the Engine

The oil can be pumped from the oil pan or crankcase on applications where the boat is stored in the water or if the drain plug is difficult to access. Hand operated pumps (**Figure 34**) or electric motor operated pumps (**Figure 35**) are available from most marine dealerships or marine supply stores.

On 4-15 hp models, insert a tube into the dipstick tube to remove oil through the dipstick opening. The tube must reach the bottom of the crankcase to remove all of the oil.

On 25-90 hp models, attach the pump directly to the threads on the dipstick tube. On these models the dipstick tube length is sufficient to pump all of the oil from the oil pan.

Pump the oil from the engine as follows:

1. Disconnect both cables from the battery.
2. Place the engine in the vertical position. Remove the dipstick from the engine.

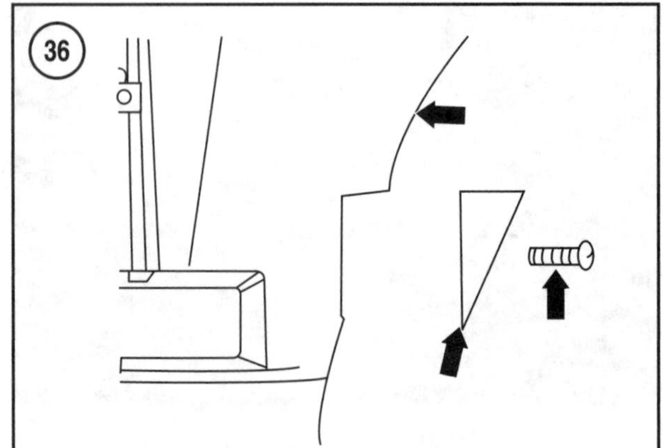

3. On 4-15 hp models, insert the small diameter tube of the oil pump into the dipstick tube until it contacts the bottom of the crankcase or oil pan.
4. On 25-90 hp models, install the sealing washer onto the threaded adapter of the oil pump. Carefully thread the adapter onto the dipstick.
5. Operate the pump until all oil is remove. Stop the oil pump for a few minutes to allow any remaining oil to drain to the bottom of the oil pan or crankcase.
6. Operate the pump to remove any remaining oil. Remove the oil pump from the dipstick. Dispose of the used oil in an environmentally responsible manner.
7. Refill the engine with oil as described in this chapter.

Draining the Oil

1. Remove both battery cables from the battery.
2. On 4-6 hp models, move the tiller handle upward to access the oil drain fitting.
3. On 9.9 hp models (serial No. OH000058-on), remove the screw then pull the oil drain cover (**Figure 36**) from the rear portion of the drive shaft housing.
4. Position the engine as follows:
   a. On 4-6 hp models, tilt the engine up slightly.
   b. On 9.9 hp (prior to serial No. OH000058) and 15 hp models, tilt the engine to the full up position then engage the tilt lock mechanism. Position the engine toward the starboard direction enough to direct the oil drain fitting downward (**Figure 37**).
   c. On 9.9 hp (serial No. OH000058-on), place the engine in the upright or vertical position (**Figure 38**).
   d. On 25-90 hp models, tilt the engine to the full up position then engage the tilt lock mechanism. Position the engine toward the port direction enough to direct the oil drain fitting downward (**Figure 39**).
5. Remove the oil drain fitting from the engine.

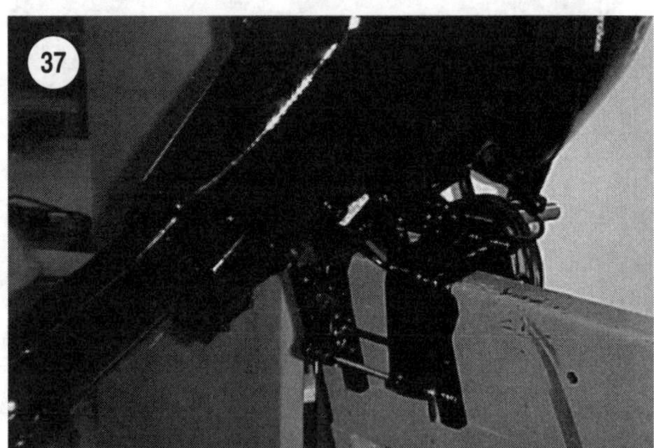

6. Inspect the sealing washer or O-ring on the oil drain fitting for worn, torn or damaged areas. Replace as required. Lubricate the seal or O-ring with a light coating of engine oil.

7. Install the drain fitting after all the oil has drained from the engine. Securely tighten the oil drain fitting on 4-6 hp models. On 9.9-90 hp models tighten the oil drain fitting to the specification provided in **Table 6**. Refill the engine with oil as described in this chapter.

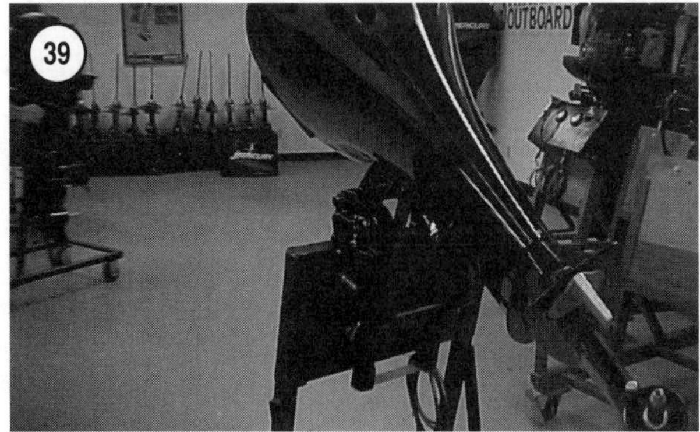

39

40

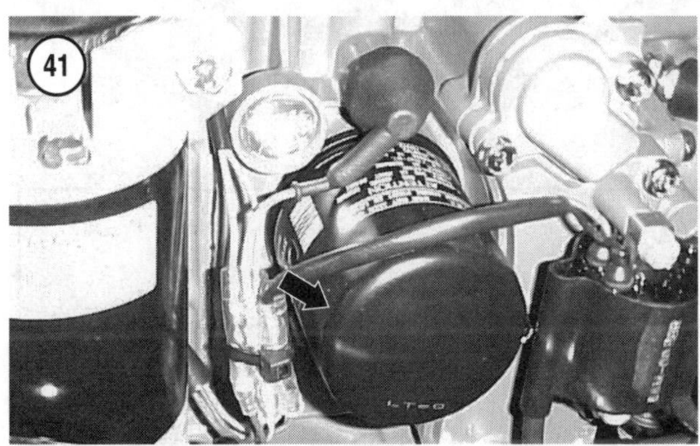

41

42

43

Filling the Oil

Refer to **Table 2** to determine the quantity of oil required.

1. Place the engine in the upright or vertical position (**Figure 38**). Clean the external surfaces then remove the oil fill cap from the cylinder block or rocker arm cover.
2. Using a suitable funnel, slowly pour approximately 75% of the oil capacity into the oil fill opening.
3. Check the engine oil level as described in this chapter. Add oil to the opening in small quantities until the oil level just reaches the max marking on the dipstick. Do not overfill the engine oil. Drain excess oil if necessary.
4. Install the oil fill cap.

Changing the Oil Filter

All 25-90 hp models utilize a spin-on type oil filter. Some 9.9 and 15 hp models are equipped with a serviceable oil screen. Refer to *Cleaning the oil screen* in this chapter. Purchase a new filter from a local Mercury or Mariner dealership prior to starting this operation. A suitable oil filter removal tool (**Figure 40**) is required to remove the oil filter. Mercury marine offers a filter removal tool (parts No. 91-802653). A tool is also available from most automotive parts stores and tool suppliers.

Oil will drain from the engine when the filter is removed. Fashion a suitable oil filter drain pan from a used plastic oil container. Cut the container to a depth allowing it to slide directly under the filter.

On 9.9 and 15 hp models except models with an oil screen, the oil filter (**Figure 41**) is located on the lower port side of the power head.

On all 25-50 hp models the oil filter (**Figure 42**) is located on the lower port side of the power head.

On 75 and 90 hp models the oil filter (**Figure 43**) is located on the lower starboard side of the power head below the electric starter motor.

1. Remove both battery cables from the battery.

44

45

2. Using compressed air, blow all debris from area of the oil filter. Place a small container under the oil filter. Place a shop towel under the oil filter if unable to fit a container under the filter.

3. Using an oil filter removal tool, loosen the oil filter one turn counterclockwise, then remove the filter.

4. Inspect the oil filter for the presence of the gasket (**Figure 44**). Remove the gasket from the cylinder block if not found on the oil filter. Dispose of the oil filter in an environmentally responsible manner.

5. Carefully clean the oil filter mating surface (**Figure 45**). Apply a light coat of engine oil to the sealing ring on the new oil filter (**Figure 44**). Thread the oil filter onto the cylinder block fitting until the sealing ring just contacts the mating surface (**Figure 45**). Using the oil filter removal tool, tighten the filter (**Figure 46**) to the specification listed in **Table 6**. Turn the oil filter a minimum of ¾ turn clockwise after the sealing ring contacts the mating surface.

6. Check the oil level as described in this chapter. Correct the oil level as required.

7. Clean the terminals then connect the cables to the battery.

8. Correct oil leaks immediately after starting the engine.

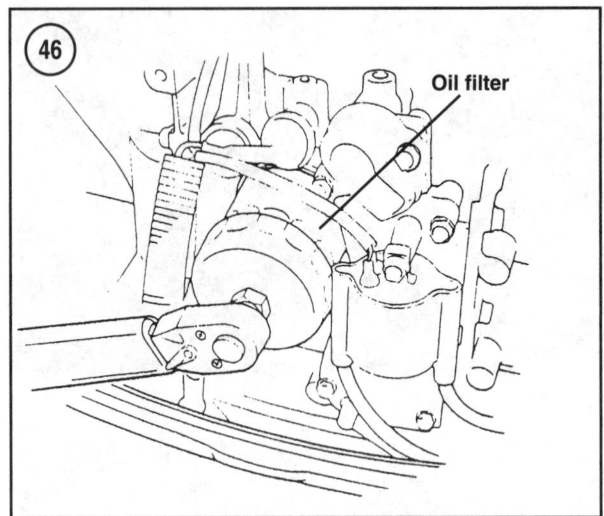

46

47

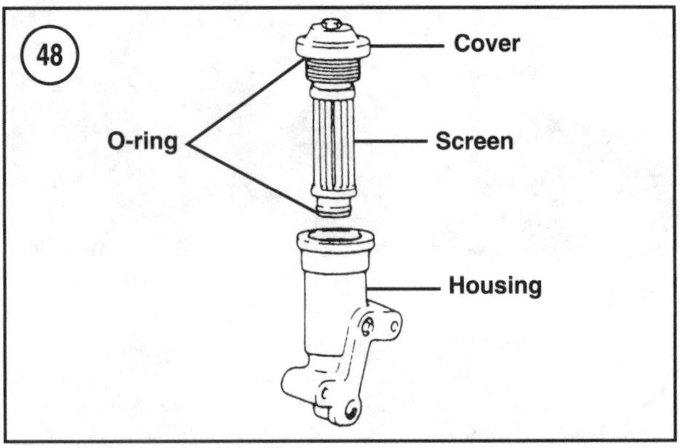

48

Cleaning the Oil Screen

Some early model 9.9 and 15 hp models are equipped with an oil screen instead of a spin-on oil filter. Clean the screen at the intervals listed in **Table 1**.

1. Disconnect both cables from the battery.

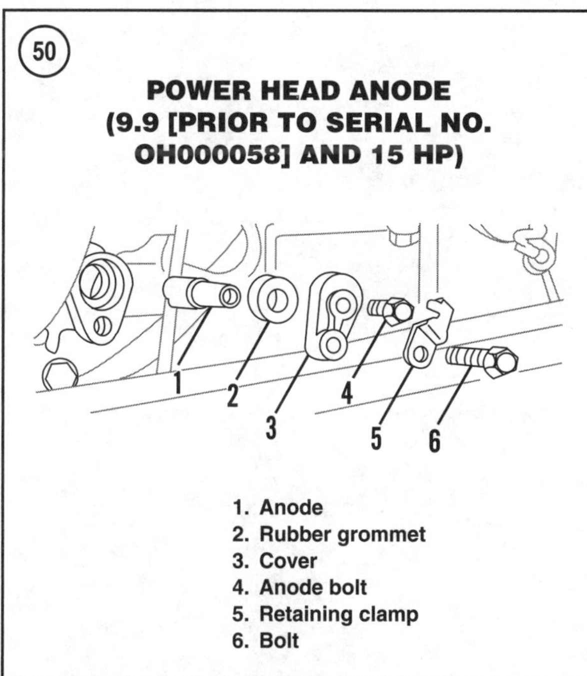

POWER HEAD ANODE
(9.9 [PRIOR TO SERIAL NO. OH000058] AND 15 HP)

1. Anode
2. Rubber grommet
3. Cover
4. Anode bolt
5. Retaining clamp
6. Bolt

2. Remove the oil screen cover (**Figure 47**) from the rear starboard side of the power head.

3. Lift the cover and oil screen from the screen housing (**Figure 48**). Cover the opening to prevent contamination of the oil. Inspect both O-rings on the screen and cover for worn, cut or damaged areas. Replace the O-rings if any defects are noted.

4. Thoroughly clean the screen using a suitable solvent. Blow all solvent from the screen using compressed air.

5. Inspect the filter screen for torn, corroded or damaged areas. Replace the screen if any damage is noted.

6. Lubricate the O-rings with a light coat of engine oil. Seat the O-rings into their respective grooves at the bottom of the screen and the filter cover.

7. Carefully insert the oil screen into its housing (**Figure 48**). Do not dislodge the O-rings during installation. Thread the cover into the oil screen housing. Tighten the cover to the specification in **Table 6**.

Removing Carbon Deposits

On many models the carbon must be removed from the combustion chamber at regular intervals. Excessive carbon deposits can increase engine compression and promote detonation. To help prevent serious power head damage, decarbon the engine at the intervals listed in **Table 1**.

Special fuel additives and sprays (**Figure 49**) are very effective at removing most carbon deposits. These additives and sprays are most effective when used on a regular basis. They are available from most Marine dealerships and Marine supply stores. These products are either added to the fuel or sprayed into the carburetor opening during engine operation. Always follow the manufacturer's instructions when using these products.

Remove stubborn or heavy carbon deposits by manually scraping from the pistons and combustion chambers. Cylinder head removal, cleaning and installation are provided in Chapter Eight.

Prevent heavy carbon deposits by using good quality fuel and oil. Use the correct propeller for the engine and boat combination (Chapter One). Check and correct all applicable carburetor adjustments to minimize carbon deposits.

Anodes

Anodes are used to help counteract corrosion damage to the power head cooling passages. The anode is constructed of a material more corrosively active than the cylinder head or cylinder block material. Essentially the anodes sacrifice themselves to protect the power head. Regular inspection and replacement helps ensure continued protection against corrosion damage.

All 4-6 hp models are not equipped with power head anodes.

All 9.9 (serial No. OH000057-prior) and 15 hp models, are equipped with a single anode located beneath a retaining clamp and cover (**Figure 50**) on the lower starboard side of the cylinder block.

All 9.9 hp models (serial No. OH000058-on) are equipped with a single anode mounts to a special plug (**Figure 51**) located beneath the rocker arm cover.

All 25-50 hp models are equipped multiple anodes mounted beneath a cover on the port side of the cylinder

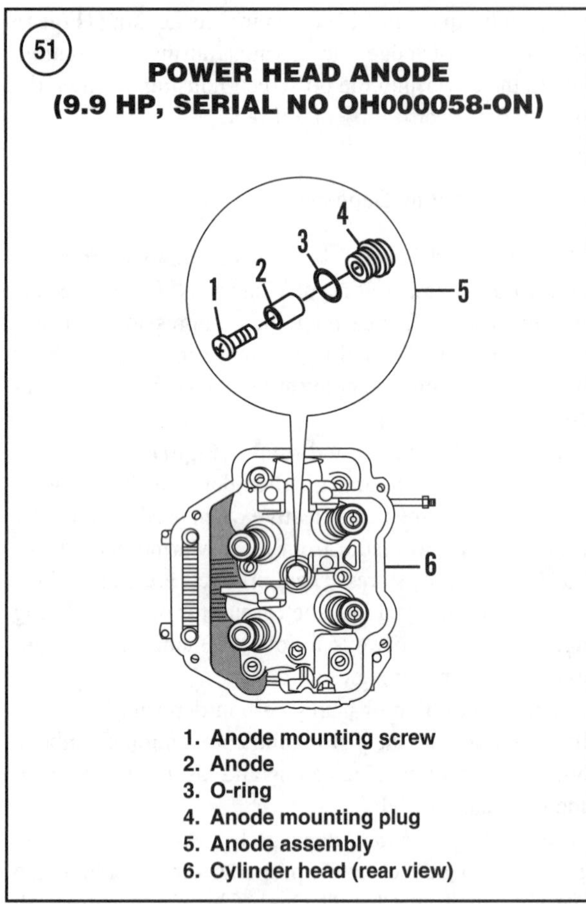

head (**Figure 52**). An anode is located near each spark plug.

All 75 and 90 hp models are equipped with a pair of anodes mounted to special covers (**Figure 53**) located beneath the spark plug cover.

Inspect and/or replace the anode as follows:

1. Disconnect both cables from the battery.
2. On 9.9 (serial No. OH000057-prior) and 15 hp models remove the anode as follows:
   a. Remove the bolt (6, **Figure 50**) and retainer (5) from the starboard side of the cylinder block.
   b. Carefully pry the anode cover from the cylinder block.
   c. Using needlenose pliers, carefully pull the anode (1, **Figure 50**) and rubber grommet (2) from the cylinder block.
3. On 9.9 hp models (serial No. OH000058-on), remove the anode as follows:
   a. Remove the rocker arm cover as described in Chapter Eight.
   b. Unthread the anode assembly (5, **Figure 51**) from the cylinder head (6).

56

57

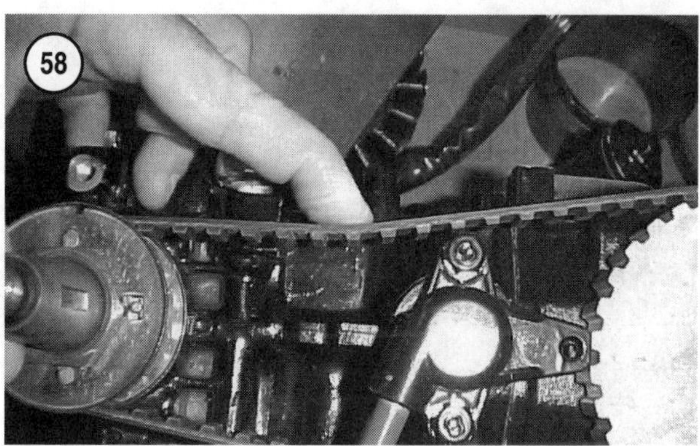
58

c. Clamp the anode assembly in a vice with soft jaws.
d. Remove the screw (1, **Figure 51**) from the anode mounting plug.
e. Remove the anode (2, **Figure 51**) and O-ring (3) from the mounting plug.

4. On all 25-50 hp models remove the anodes as follows.
   a. Remove the retaining screw then lift each anode cover (**Figure 54**) from the cylinder head.
   b. Using needlenose pliers if necessary, carefully pull the anodes and rubber grommets (**Figure 55**) from the cylinder head.
   c. Remove the rubber grommet from the anodes.

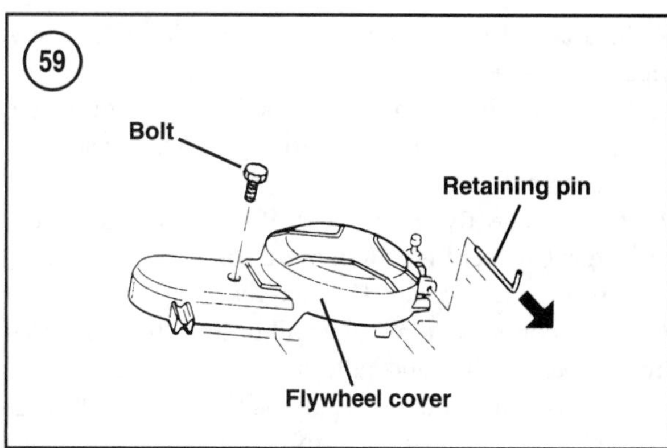
59

5. On 75 and 90 hp models, remove the anodes as follows:
   a. Remove the spark plug cover as described in Chapter Eight
   b. Carefully loosen and remove each anode cover mounting bolt (**Figure 56**).
   c. Carefully pry the cover loose then lift it and the anode from the cylinder head (**Figure 57**).
   d. Remove the single bolt then pull the anode and rubber grommet from the anode cover.
6. Clean all corrosion or contaminants from the anode surfaces using a wire brush. Do not damage the rubber grommet contact surfaces.
7. Inspect the anode for deep pitting or cracked surfaces.
8. Replace the anode if deep pitting is noted or if 50% or more of the anode has corroded away.
9. Inspect the rubber grommet or O-ring type seals for worn or damaged areas. Replace the rubber grommet or O-ring if defects are noted.
10. Thoroughly clean the anode mounting surface or opening.
11. Installation is the reverse of removal noting the following:
   a. To maintain corrosion protection, do not apply any paint or protective coatings to the anode or mounting bolts.
   b. Tighten all anode mounting bolts and retainers to the specification listed in **Table 6**.
   c. Inspect all anode covers for water leakage after start up. Correct all leakage at once.

Timing Belt and Pulleys

Inspect the timing belt (**Figure 58**) for damage or excessive wear at the intervals listed in **Table 1**. Removal of the manual starter or flywheel cover (**Figure 59** Typical) is required to access the timing belt and pulleys. Flywheel cover removal and instructions are provided in Chapter

Eight. Manual starter removal and installation are provided in Chapter Ten.

1. Disconnect both cables from the battery. Remove the spark plugs then connect the spark plug leads to a suitable engine ground.
2. Remove the flywheel cover, if so equipped, as described in Chapter Eight. Remove the manual starter, if so equipped, as described in Chapter Ten.
3. Using compressed air, blow all dust or loose material from the timing belt and pulleys.
4. On 9.9-25 hp models, push in on the timing belt (**Figure 58**) to check the amount of belt deflection. Replace the timing belt if it deflects 10 mm (0.39 in.) or more with pressure from your finger.
5. Thoroughly inspect the timing belt (**Figure 60**). Replace the timing belt if any of the following conditions are noted.
   a. Any oil soaked surfaces.
   b. Deformed or bulging areas.
   c. Worm timing belt cogs.
   d. Cracks or wear on the flat side of the belt.
   e. Cracked or missing timing belt cogs.
   f. Worn edges on the top or bottom side of the timing belt.
6. Inspect both the crankshaft and camshaft pulleys for worn cogs (**Figure 61**) and damage or corrosion. Replace the pulleys if worn or damaged. Replace the pulleys if corroded surfaces cannot be cleaned by polishing them with crocus cloth. Pulley removal and installation are provided in Chapter Eight.
7. Install the flywheel cover as described in Chapter Eight. Install the manual starter (Chapter Ten).
8. Install the spark plugs and leads. Clean the terminals then connect the cables to the battery.

60

61

Hoses and Clamps

Inspect all fuel and breather hoses and clamps at the intervals listed in **Table 1**.

Carefully squeeze all hoses to check their flexibility. Inspect the entire length of all fuel and breather hoses. Noting the presence of leakage, weathered, burned or cracked surfaces.

Replace fuel lines that are hard or brittle, when leaking or have a spongy feel. Use only the recommended hose available from a Mercury or Mariner dealership. Other fuel hoses available at auto parts stores may not meet the demands placed upon them or may not meet coast guard requirements.

Replace all fuel and breather hoses if defects are noted in any of them.

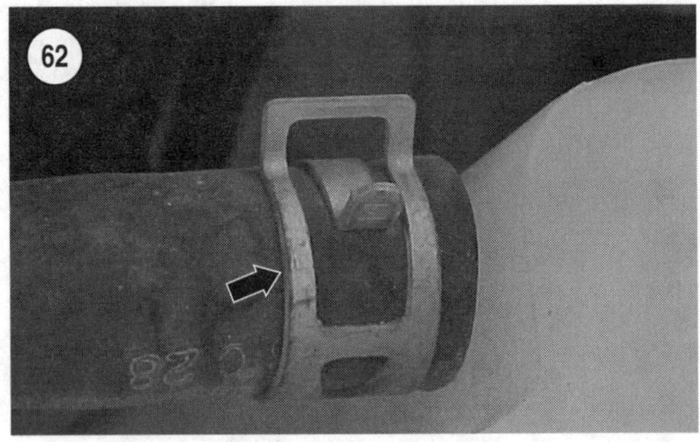
62

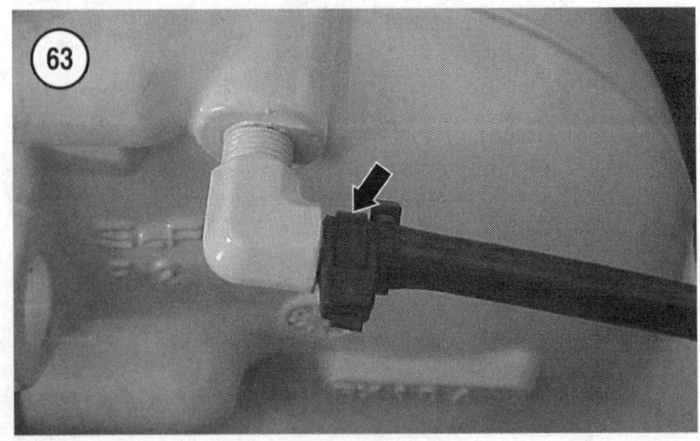
63

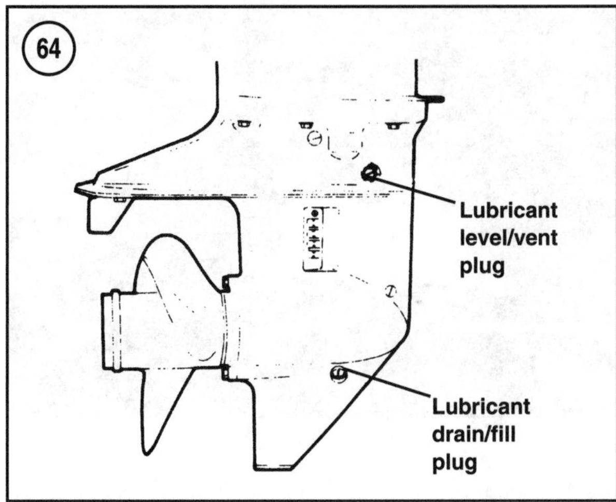

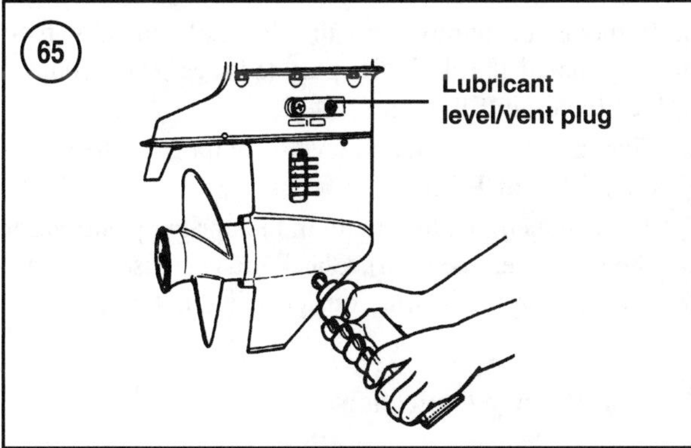

Inspect the spring clamps (**Figure 62**)for corrosion or damage. Remove and replace plastic tie clamps (**Figure 63**) if are brittle.

Carefully tug on the fuel lines to ensure a tight fit at all connections. Check for loose plastic tie clamp or faulty spring type clamp if a loose fitting is noted.

Thermostat Inspection

Inspect the thermostat at the intervals listed in **Table 1**. Thermostat removal, inspection and installation instructions are provided in Chapter Eight. To prevent overheating or oil dilution problems, replace a faulty or damaged thermostat.

Gearcase Lubricant

CAUTION
Never use automotive gearcase or transmission lubricant in the gearcase. These types of lubricants are usually not suitable for marine applications. The use of other than recommended lubricants can lead to increased wear and corrosion of internal components.

Use Mercury or Mariner gearcase lubricant or a good quality SAE 90 marine gearcase lubricant that meets GL5 specifications. Read the information on the container to ensure it meets this specification before using it in the outboard. **Table 3** lists the *approximate* gearcase lubricant capacity for the Mercury or Mariner four stroke outboard. All 9.9-50 hp models are available with an optional gearcase. Gearcase identification is provided in Chapter Nine.

CAUTION
Prevent gearcase damage due to incorrect gearcase lubricant level. Remove all correct gearcase oil level plugs when checking or changing the gearcase lubricant. Some 50 hp models and all 75 and 90 hp models are equipped with two oil level plugs. Remove both plugs when checking the lubricant level, draining the gearcase lubricant and filling the gearcase lubricant.

Checking the gearcase lubricant

Check the gearcase lubricant level and condition at the intervals listed in **Table 1**. Some models have two oil level/vent plugs. Refer to Chapter Nine to identify the lubricant plug locations.

1. Position the engine in the vertical position for at least a hour before checking the lubricant.
2. Position a suitable container under the gearcase. Slowly remove the drain/fill plug (**Figure 64**) and allow a small sample, a teaspoon or less, of fluid to drain from the gearcase. Quickly replace the drain/fill plug and tighten it securely. Refer to Chapter Three if water or a milky appearance is noted in the fluid sample.
3. Rub a small amount of the fluid sample between finger and thumb. Refer to Chapter Three if the lubricant feels gritty or metal particles are present.
4. Remove the level/vent plug(s) (**Figure 64**). The lubricant level should be even with the bottom of the threaded level/vent plug opening.
5. Perform the following if the lubricant level is low:
   a. Remove the lubricant drain/fill plug then quickly install the lubricant pump hose or tube into the opening.
   b. Add lubricant into the drain/fill plug opening (**Figure 65**) until fluid flows from the level/vent plug (**Figure 65**).

c. A leak is likely if over 1 oz. (30mL) of lubricant is required to fill the gearcase. Pressure test the unit following the instructions provided in Chapter Three.
d. Install the level/vent plug then tighten it securely.
e. Remove the lubricant pump hose or tube then quickly install the lubricant drain/fill plug.

6. Tighten the lubricant drain/fill and level/vent plugs to the specification **Table 6**.
7. Allow the gearcase to remain undisturbed in a shaded area for one hour then check the lubricant level. Top off the lubricant as necessary.

CAUTION
Inspect the sealing washers on all gearcase plugs. Replace missing or damaged sealing washers to prevent water or lubricant leakage.

NOTE
A small amount of very fine particles are usually present in the gear lubricant. These fine particles form during normal gearcase operation. Their presence does not necessarily indicate a problem. However, the presence of large particles indicates a potential problem within the gearcase.

Changing the gearcase lubricant

Change the gearcase lubricant at the intervals listed in **Table 1**. **Table 3** lists the approximate gearcase lubricant capacity. All 9.9-50 hp models are available with an optional size gearcase. Refer to in Chapter Nine to identify the gearcase.

Some models use two level/vent plugs. On these models, remove both plugs during the gearcase draining and filling procedure.

1. Place a suitable container under the gearcase. Remove the drain/fill plug from the gearcase (**Figure 64**). Remove the level/vent plugs (**Figure 64**).
2. Take a small sample of the gearcase lubricant and inspect as described under *Checking the gearcase lubricant* in this section. Refer to Chapter Three if any problems are noted with the fluid.
3. Allow the gearcase to drain completely. Tilt the engine to position the drain/fill opening to its lowest point to ensure the gearcase drains completely. After draining, place the engine in the upright position.
4. Use a pump type dispenser or squeeze tube then *slowly* pump gearcase lubricant into the drain plug opening (**Figure 65**). Continue to fill the gearcase until lubricant flows out the level/vent plug openings (**Figure 65**) Without removing the pump or tube from the drain/fill opening, install the level/vent plug into the opening. Securely tighten the level plug.

5. Remove the pump from the drain/fill opening then quickly install the drain/fill plug (**Figure 64**). Securely tighten the drain/fill plug.
6. Tighten the drain/fill and level/vent plugs to the specification listed in **Table 6**.
7. Allow the engine to remain in the upright position for one hour (shaded location). Check the gearcase lubricant level following the instructions provided in this chapter.

Gearcase Anode Inspection

Sacrificial anodes (**Figure 66** typical) are used on all models to lesson corrosion damage to exposed gearcase surfaces. The anode material is more corrosively active than the other exposed engine components. Essentially the anodes sacrifice themselves to protect the engine from corrosion damage.

These anodes are mounted to an exposed portion of the gearcase. Refer to the exploded drawings in Chapter Nine to identify the anode mounting arrangement. Some models are equipped with clamp bracket anodes. Clean and inspect these anodes at the same intervals as the gearcase anodes.

Clean and inspect the gearcase anodes at the intervals listed in **Table 1**. Inspect and clean the anodes more often if the engine is run or stored in salt, brackish or polluted water. Use a stiff blush to clean deposits and other material from the anode. Replace the anode when it has lost 40 percent or more of its material. Never paint or cover the anode with a protective coating. Doing so dramatically decreases its ability to protect the engine. Clean the mounting area thoroughly before installing a new anode. The anode must contact a bare metal surface to ensure a proper connection.

67

68

Inspect the anode mounting area if corrosion is noted on engine, but the anode is not experiencing corrosion. It is likely that corrosion or contamination is preventing the anode from making adequate contact with the mounting surface. Clean the area thoroughly if this condition is noted.

Water Pump and Impeller Inspection

Inspect the water pump impeller at the intervals listed in **Table 1**. During use, certain components of the water pump wear. Inspect the water pump impeller and related water pump components to help ensure reliable operation of the cooling system. Water pump impeller inspection instructions is covered in Chapter Nine.

Propeller Shaft

Lubricate and inspect the propeller shaft at the interval listed in **Table 1**.

1. Remove the propeller as described in Chapter Nine.
2. Observe the propeller shaft for wobbling while spinning the propeller shaft. Replace the propeller shaft if any wobbling is detected. Propeller shaft replacement is provided in Chapter Nine.
3. Using a suitable solvent and a shop towel, clean the propeller shaft splined section, propeller nut threads and tapered section.
4. Inspect the propeller nut, thrust washer and spacers for wear, cracks or damage. Replace all defective or worn components.
5. Apply a generous coat of water-resistant grease to the splined section of the propeller shaft.
6. Install the propeller as described in Chapter Nine.

Swivel and Tilt Tube Lubrication

Lubricate the pivot points of the swivel and tilt tubes at the intervals listed in **Table 1**.

Pump water-resistant grease into all fittings on the swivel tube (**Figure 67**) and tilt tube (**Figure 68**). Continue to pump until the old grease is expelled from between the pivot points.

Steering System Components

CAUTION

The steering cable must be in the retracted position before grease is injected into the fitting. The cable can become hydraulically locked when grease is injected with the cable extended. Refer to the cable manufacturer's instructions for the type and frequency of lubrication

Some steering cables are provided with a grease fitting. Regular lubrication of the steering cable and linkage dramatically increase their service life. Pump water-resistant grease into the grease fitting until a slight resistance is felt. Avoid overfilling the steering cable with grease. Apply grease to the sliding surfaces and pivot points of all steering linkage and pivot points. Cycle the steering to full port and full starboard several times to distribute the lubricant.

WARNING

Always wear suitable eye protection, gloves and protective clothing when working around the power trim/tilt system. The fluid in the trim system is under pressure. Loosen all valves and reservoir plugs slowly and allow any internal pressure to slowly subside.

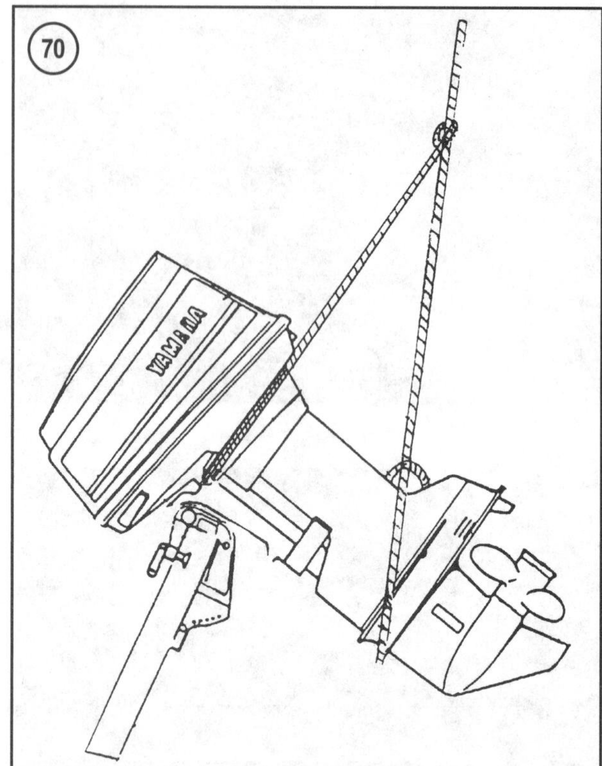

Trim System Fluid Level Check

Check the trim fluid level at the intervals specified in **Table 1** or if a low fluid level is suspected of causing a trim system malfunction.

Use only Quicksilver power trim and steering fluid (part No. 92-190100A12) in all power trim systems.

Access to the manual relief valve (**Figure 69**) is required when checking the fluid level. The manual relief valve opening is located on the starboard clamp bracket on all models. Use a large screwdriver to prevent damage to the slotted portion of the valve. The engine must be secured in the full tilt position to access the trim system fill plug. Use an overhead lift (**Figure 70**) or use other methods to support the engine while checking and filling the fluid level. Do not rely solely on the tilt lock mechanism to support the engine. Two different types of systems are used on four stroke models. On either type the trim system fill cap (**Figure 71** and **72**) is located on the aft side of the pump portion of the trim system. The fluid in the reservoir may be under pressure. Always remove the reservoir plug slowly and allow the pressure to gradually subside.

1. Operate the trim/tilt system or open the manual relief valve and move the engine to the full up position. Securely tighten the manual relief valve.
2. Secure the engine in position with an overhead cable or other reliable method (**Figure 70**). Use compressed air to clean the fill cap area. Place a suitable container under the trim system to capture any spilled fluid.
3. Slowly remove the fill cap from the trim system pump or reservoir.
4. The fluid level should be even with the fill cap opening. Use a toothpick or other suitable tool to gauge the depth of the fluid.
5. Add fluid until its level is even with the bottom of the fill cap opening (**Figure 73**). Clean the fill cap and carefully thread it onto the reservoir. Securely tighten the fill cap.

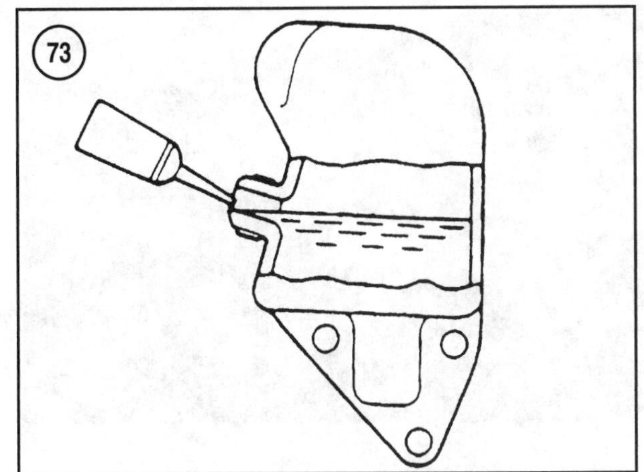

73

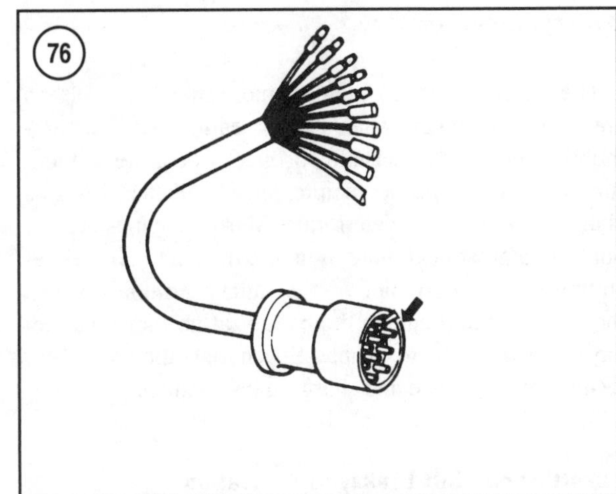

76

74

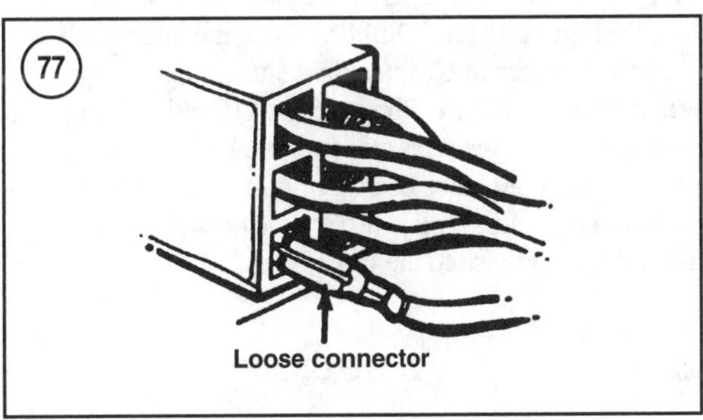

77

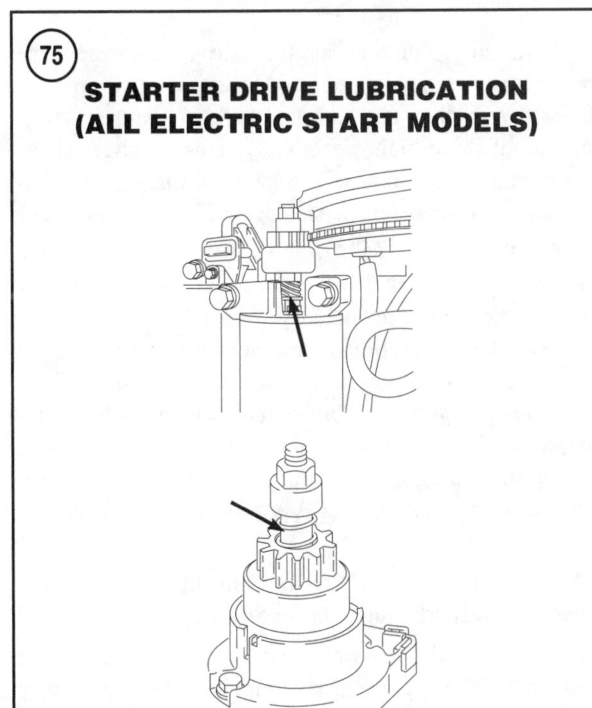

75

STARTER DRIVE LUBRICATION (ALL ELECTRIC START MODELS)

6. Remove the overhead cable or supporting blocks and lower the engine. Run the trim system to the full up and full down position several times to purge air from the internal passages.

Electric Starter Motor Maintenance

Clean the starter motor terminals (**Figure 74**) and apply water-resistant grease to the starter drive (**Figure 75**) at regular intervals. Refer to Chapter Seven for starter motor removal, disassembly and assembly.

Wiring Inspection

Periodically inspect the main harness connector (**Figure 76**) for contaminated or faulty pin connections (**Figure 77**). Carefully scrape contamination from the contacts. Apply a light coat of water-resistant marine grease to the main harness plug and terminals to seal out moisture and prevent corrosion. Inspect the entire length of all wires and harness for worn, burnt, damaged or bare insulation. Repair or replace the wire harness as required.

Battery Inspection

The cranking battery requires more maintenance than any other component related to the engine. Unlike automobiles, boats may set idle for weeks or more without running. Without proper maintenance the battery loses its charge and begins to deteriorate. Marine engines are exposed to a great deal more moisture than automobiles resulting in more corrosion on the battery terminals. Clean the terminals and charge the battery at no more than 30 day intervals. Refer to Chapter Seven for complete battery testing, maintenance and charging instructions.

Throttle and Shift Linkage Lubrication

Apply water-resistant grease to all pivot points of the throttle (**Figure 78**) and shift linkage at the intervals listed in **Table 1**. Refer to Chapter Five and Chapter Six to determine the location of the shift and throttle linkage. A small amount of grease is all required. Use just enough to lubricate the connector or pivot point. Use a penetrating corrosion prevention oil if difficult access prevents properly applying grease to the linkage.

TUNE UP

A complete tune up involves a series of adjustments, tests, inspections and parts replacements to return the engine to original factory specifications. Only a complete tune up delivers the expected performance, economy and durability. Perform all operations listed in this section for a complete engine tune up.

1. Compression test.
2. Spark plug replacement.
3. Valve adjustment.
4. Carburetor adjustment.
5. Check the ignition timing.
6. Test run the outboard.

Compression Test

No tune up is complete without a compression test. An engine with low or weak compression on one or more cylinders simply cannot be properly tuned. Perform a compression test before replacing any components or performing any adjustments. Correct the cause of low compression before proceeding with the tune up. Compression test instructions are provided in Chapter Three.

78

79

Spark Plugs

All Mercury and Mariner four stroke outboards use breakerless ignition systems. These systems produce higher energy than conventional breaker point systems. Benefits of these higher energy systems is longer spark plug life and less chance of spark plug fouling. Nevertheless, spark plugs operate in a harsh environment and eventually require cleaning or replacement.

Replacement spark plugs must be of the correct size, reach and heat range to operate properly. Many of the later engines have a spark plug recommendation decal located inside the lower engine cover near the rear side of the power head (**Figure 79**). On 75 and 90 hp models the decal is attached to the rocker arm cover or spark plug cover. Use the spark plug listed on this decal. Refer to the spark plug recommendations in **Table 4** if unable to locate or read this decal.

All four stroke models covered in this manual use a conventional spark plug (**Figure 80**).

Inspection of the spark plug can reveal much about the condition of the engine. Inspection gives the opportunity to correct problems before expensive engine damage oc-

curs. Remove the spark plugs and compare them to the ones shown in **Figure 81**.

Be sure to correct any engine problems prior to installing new spark plugs.

Spark plug removal

On 75-90 hp models the spark plugs are positioned under the rocker arm cover. Remove the cover to access them. Remove all five retaining bolts (**Figure 82**) then lift the spark plug cover from the rocker arm cover. On these models a long extension and thin-walled socket is required to remove or install the spark plugs. On all other models the spark plugs are located on the rear port side of the cylinder head.

Mark the cylinder number on the spark plug leads before removing them from the spark plugs. Use compressed air to blow debris from around the spark plugs before removing them. Apply a penetrating oil to the threaded section and allow it to soak if the plug is corroded at the threads.

On occasion the aluminum thread in the cylinder heads are damaged during spark plug removal. This condition can be effectively repaired without removing the cylinder head by installing a special threaded insert. Have a reputable marine repair shop perform this repair unless familiar with this operation and have access to the necessary tools.

Clean the spark plug holes in the cylinder head with a thread chaser (**Figure 83**). These are available at most automotive parts stores. Thread the chaser by hand into each spark plug hole. Several passes may be required to remove all carbon or corrosion deposits from the threaded hole. Blow all debris from the holes with compressed air.

Spark plug inspection

Remove the plugs and compare them to the plugs shown in **Figure 81**. Spark plugs can give a clear indication of problems in the engine sometimes before the symptoms occur. Additional inspection and testing may be required if an abnormal spark plug condition is noted. Refer to Chapter Three for troubleshooting instructions.

NOTE

Use only resister type plugs on 30 and 40 hp models. Using nonresistor type spark plugs can cause electrical interference affecting the operation of the engine control unit. Look for the R mark on the side of the spark plug insulator to verify resistor type plugs.

Spark plug cleaning

Although cleaning and adjusting the gap on the plugs usually corrects most spark plug related problems, replacement is highly recommended. Spark plugs are inexpensive and new ones offer a considerably longer life than a cleaned and gapped plug.

If the spark plugs must be reused, clean the plug using a wire brush and solvent to dissolve the deposits. Special spark plug cleaning devices are available that use a forced abrasive blast to remove stubborn deposits.

Remove all debris from the plug with compressed air prior to installation.

Spark plug gap adjustment

Use a gap adjusting tool (**Figure 84**) to adjust the spark plug gap. Never tap the plug against a hard object to close the gap. The ceramic insulator can crack and break away. Gapping tools (**Figure 84**) are available at most auto parts stores. They allow correction of the gap without damaging the plug.

1. Refer to **Table 4** to determine the correct spark plug gap.
2. Check the gap using a wire feeler gauge (**Figure 85**) of the same thickness as the recommended gap. The gauge should pass between the electrodes (**Figure 86**) with a slight drag.
3. Open the gap and set the gap if the gauge cannot be inserted.
4. Inspect the spark plug for parallel electrode surfaces (**Figure 86**). Carefully bend the electrode until the surfaces are parallel and the gap is correct.

(81)

SPARK PLUG CONDITION

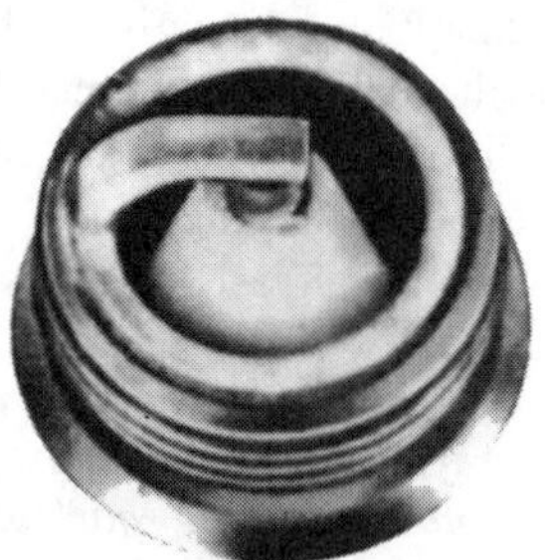

NORMAL

- Identified by light tan or gray deposits on the firing tip.
- Can be cleaned.

GAP BRIDGED

- Identified by deposit buildup closing gap between electrodes.
- Caused by oil or carbon fouling. If deposits are not excessive, the plug can be cleaned.

OIL FOULED

- Identified by wet black deposits on the insulator shell bore and electrodes.
- Caused by excessive oil entering combustion chamber through worn rings and pistons, excessive clearance between valve guides and stems or worn or loose bearings. Can be cleaned. If engine is not repaired, use a hotter plug.

CARBON FOULED

- Identified by lack, dry fluffy carbon deposits on insulator tips, exposed shell surfaces and electrodes.
- Caused by too cold a plug, weak ignition, dirty air cleaner, too rich a fuel mixture or excessive idling. Can be cleaned.

LEAD FOULED

- Identified by dark gray, black, yellow or tan deposits or a fused glazed coating on the insulator tip.
- Caused by highly leaded gasoline. Can be cleaned.

WORN

- Identified by severely eroded or worn electrodes.
- Caused by normal wear. Should be replaced.

FUSED SPOT DEPOSIT

- Identified by melted or spotty deposits resembling bubbles or blisters.
- Caused by sudden acceleration. Can be cleaned.

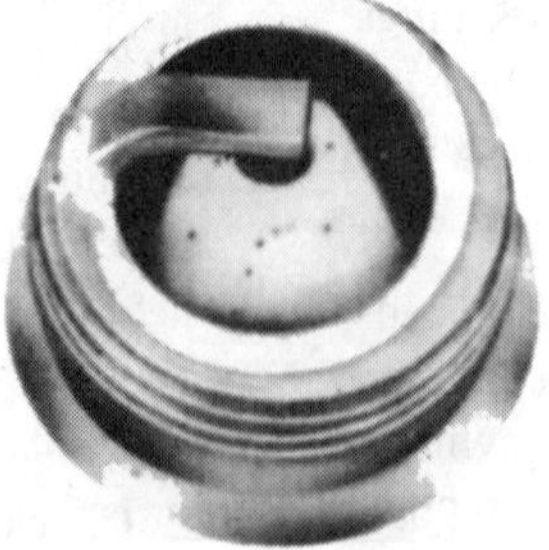

OVERHEATING

- Identified by a white or light gray insulator with small black, gray or brown spots and with a burnt appearance of electrodes.
- Caused by engine overheating, wrong type of fuel, loose spark plugs, too hot a plug or incorrect ignition timing. Replace the plug

PREIGNITION

- Identified by melted electrodes and possibly blistered insulator. Metallic deposits on insulator indicate engine damage.
- Caused by wrong type of fuel, incorrect ignition timing or advance, too hot a plug, burned valves or engine overheating. Replace the plug

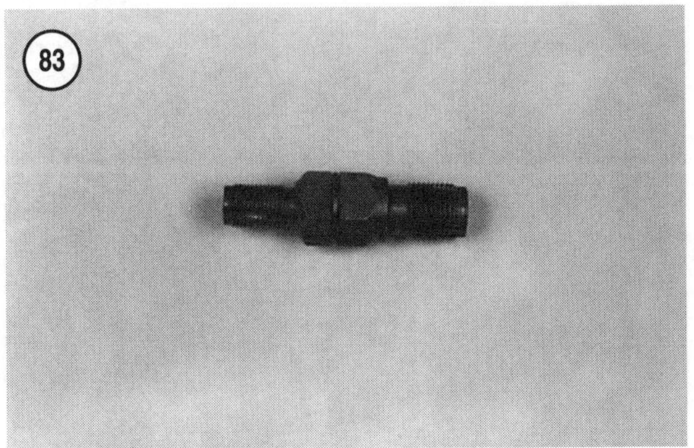

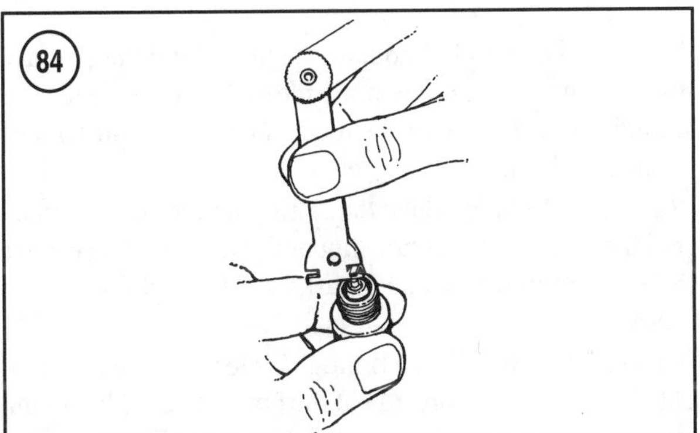

NOTE
*Some spark plug brands require the terminal end be installed prior to installation. Thread the terminal onto the spark plug as indicated in **Figure 87**.*

Spark plug installation

1. Apply a very light coat of light oil to the spark plug threads and thread them in by hand. Use a torque wrench and tighten the spark plugs to the specification in **Table 6**.

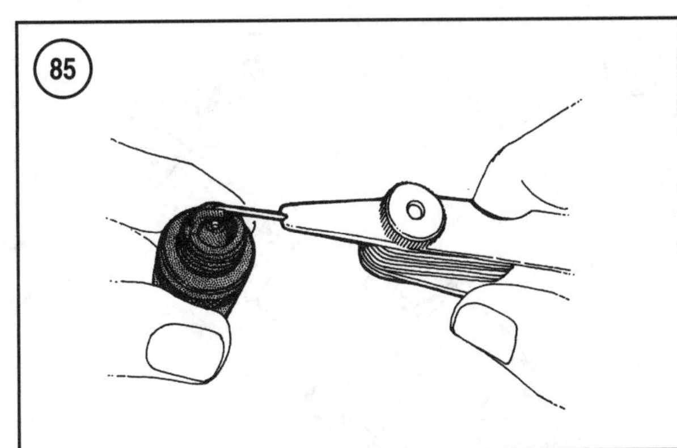

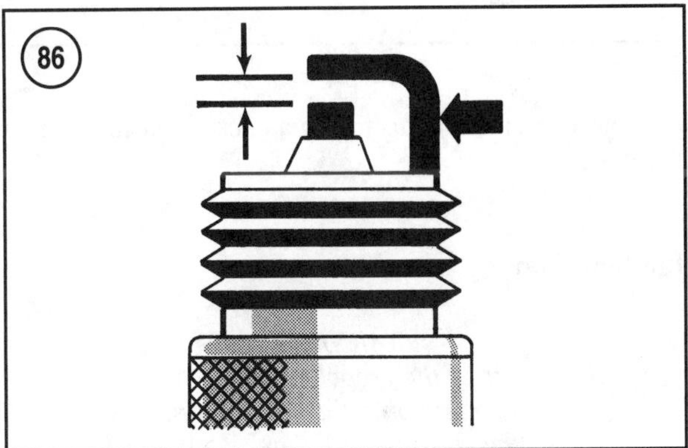

2. Apply a light coating of corrosion preventative oil (silicone lubricant) to the inner surfaces of the spark plug cap. Carefully slide the cap over the correct spark plug. Snap the connector fully onto the spark plug.
3. Clean the terminals and connect the battery cables to the battery.

Valve Adjustment

Excessive clearance causes valve system noise and may increase wear on some valve train components. Insufficient clearance can result in rapid wear of valve train components, reduced power and rough engine operation. Check then correct valve adjustments at the intervals specified in **Table 1**. Valve adjustment is covered in Chapter Five.

Carburetor Adjustment

Proper carburetor adjustment is essential for smooth and efficient operation. Carburetor adjustment includes carburetor synchronization (30-90 hp models) and idle speed adjustment. Some models also require pilot screw adjustment. To ensure correct operation, perform all ap-

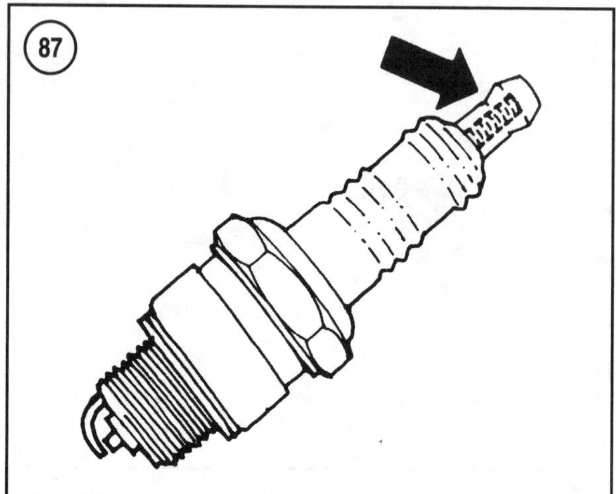

plicable carburetor adjustments as described in Chapter Five.

Ignition Timing

WARNING
Stay clear of the propeller shaft while running an engine on a flush/test adapter. Remove the propeller before running the engine to avoid injury or death. Disconnect all spark plug leads and disconnect the battery before removing or installing the propeller.

CAUTION
Never run the engine without first providing cooling water. Use either a test tank of flush/test adapter. Remove the propeller before running the engine.

The ignition timing is fixed on all models and provides automatic spark advance. Although ignition timing adjustment is not required, check the timing after performing a tune-up to verify that the ignition system functions correctly. Checking the ignition timing requires an accurate shop tachometer and a strobe type timing light.

1. Connect the shop tachometer to the engine following the manufacturer's instructions.

2. Connect the pickup of the timing light to the No. 1 spark plug lead.

3. Start the engine and allow it to run at idle speed until it reaches normal operating temperature.

4A. On 4-6 hp models, the timing marks are cast into the cylinder block (**Figure 88**) directly above the dipstick. The timing reference mark is located on the flywheel.

4B. On 9.9 and 15 hp models, the timing pointer (**Figure 89**) is located at the upper port side of the power head. The timing reference marks are located on the circumference of the flywheel.

4C. On 25-40 hp models, the timing pointer is integrated into the manual starter housing or flywheel cover (**Figure 90**). The timing reference marks are located on the flywheel.

4D. On 50 hp models the timing pointer (**Figure 91**) is located on the upper port side of the power head. The timing reference marks are located on the circumference of the flywheel.

4E. On 75 and 90 hp models, the timing pointer is located at the front and top side of the power head. It is visible through a window in the flywheel cover (**Figure 90**). The timing reference marks are located on the flywheel.

5. Refer to **Table 5** to identify the ignition timing and the specified speeds. Have an assistant operate the engine at the specified speed while directing the timing light at the timing pointer, window or timing mark. Record the timing mark aligning with the pointer or reference mark.

6. Compare the ignition timing with the specification listed in **Table 5**. A faulty CDI or engine control unit or

other ignition system component is likely if incorrect timing is indicated. On 75 and 90 hp models, test and adjust the throttle position sensor before replacing the engine control unit.

7. Test all ignition system components (Chapter Three) if ignition timing is incorrect.

Test Running the Outboard

Operate the engine on a flush/test device or in a test tank to ensure correct starting and idling prior to water testing the boat. Connect a shop tachometer to the engine. Follow the manufacturer's instructions when attaching the tachometer to the engine. Have an assistant operate the boat while noting the idle speed. Refer to Chapter Five to adjust the idle speed.

Note the tachometer reading at wide-open throttle. Perform this test with the average load in the boat. Operate the tilt/trim system, if so equipped, to the correct trim position. Record the maximum engine speed then refer to Chapter Three to determine the correct engine operating range for the engine. Check the propeller for damage or incorrect pitch if the engine speed is not within the recommended speed range. Refer to Chapter Three the correct propeller is installed but the engine fails to reach the recommended speed range. Check all fuel system, ignition system and timing adjustments.

Try a rapid acceleration and run the engine at various speed ranges. Refer to Chapter Three if rough operation is noted at any speed range or hesitation occurs during rapid acceleration.

4

SUBMERSION

If the engine has been subjected to complete submersion three factors need to be considered. Was the engine running when the submersion occurred? Was the engine submerged in salt, brackish or polluted water? How long has the engine been retrieved from the water?

Complete disassembly and inspection of the power head is required if the engine was submerged when running. Internal damage to the power head (bent connecting rod) is likely should this occur. Refer to Chapter Eight for power head repair instructions.

Many components of the engine suffer the corrosive effects of submersion in salt, brackish or polluted water. The symptoms may not occur for some time after the event. Salt crystals form in many areas of the engine and promote intense corrosion in that area. The wire harness and its connections are usually damaged very quickly. It is difficult to remove all of the salt crystals from the harness connectors. Replace the wire harness and clean all electrical connections to ensure a reliable repair. The starter motor, relays and any switch on the engine usually fail if not thoroughly cleaned of all salt residue.

Retrieve and service the engine as soon as possible. Vigorously wash all debris from the engine with freshwater after retrieval. Complete power head disassembly and inspection is required when sand, silt or other gritty material is noted inside the engine cover. Refer to Chapter Eight for power head repair instructions.

Service the engine quickly to ensure it is running within two hours after retrieval. Submerge in a tank of clean freshwater if the engine cannot be serviced within a two hour time frame. This is especially important if the engine was submerged in salt, brackish or polluted water. This protective submersion prevents exposure to air and decreases the potential for corrosion. This will not preserve the engine indefinitely. Service the engine within a few days after beginning protective submersion.

Completely disassemble and inspect the power head internal components if the engine was not serviced in a timely manner.

Perform the following steps as soon as the engine is retrieved from the water.

1. Remove the engine cover and vigorously wash all material from the engine with freshwater. Completely disassemble and inspect the power head if sand, silt or gritty material is present inside the engine cover.
2. Dry the exterior of the engine with compressed air. Remove thel spark plugs and ground all spark plug leads. Remove the propeller as described in Chapter Nine.
3. Drain all water and residual fuel from the fuel system. Remove any water from the carburetor cover. Replace all fuel filters on the engine. See Chapter Seven
4. Drain the oil from oil pan or crankcase. Position the engine with the spark plugs openings facing down. Remove the rocker arm cover as described in Chapter Eight.
5. Slowly rotate the flywheel clockwise as viewed from the flywheel end by the recoil starter or manually on electric start models to force the water from the cylinders. Rotate the flywheel several times noting if the engine is turning freely. Completely disassemble and inspect power head if interference is noted.
6. Position the engine with the spark plug openings facing up. Pour approximately one teaspoon of engine oil into each spark plug opening. Repeat Step 5 to distribute the oil in the cylinders.
7. Disconnect all electrical connections and inspect the terminals. Dry all exterior surfaces and wire connectors with compressed air. Remove, disassemble and inspect the electric starter motor as outlined in Chapter Seven.
8. Clean the rocker arm and rocker arm cover. Install the rocker arm cover (Chapter Eight).
9. Replace the oil filter and fill the engine with fresh oil. Clean and install the spark plugs. Reconnect all wire harnesses and battery terminals.
10. Provide the engine with a fresh supply of fuel. Start the engine and run it at a low speed for a few minutes. Refer to Chapter Three for troubleshooting instructions if the engine cannot be started. Stop the engine immediately and investigate if unusual noises are noted. Allow the engine to run at low speed for a minimum of 30 minutes to dry any residual water from the engine. Promptly investigate any unusual noises or unusual running conditions.
11. On manual start models, disassemble and inspect the manual starter. See Chapter Ten.
12. Change the engine oil again and clean or replace the oil filter. Perform all maintenance items listed in **Table 1**.

Storage

The objective when preparing the engine for long term storage is to prevent corrosion or deterioration during the storage period. Recommissioning prepares the engine for operation after storage.

All major systems require some preparation before storage. If done correctly the engine should operate properly after recomminishing.

Perform any maintenance that becomes due during the storage period. Maintenance requirements are listed in **Table 1**. These requirements generally include the following:

1. Change the gearcase lubricant .
2. Check the fluid in the hydraulic tilt or trim system.
3. Lubricate the propeller shaft.
4. Remove and maintain the battery as described in Chapter Seven.
5. Check all electrical harnesses for corrosion or faulty connections.
6. Lubricate all steering, throttle and control linkage.
7. Lubricate all pivot and swivel shafts on the midsection of the engine.
8. Change the engine oil and clean or replace the oil filter.
9. Check the condition and clean all sacrificial anodes.

Serious problems can be avoided if the fuel system is properly prepared for storage. Drain as much fuel from the fuel tank as possible. Clean or change all fuel filters on the engine prior to storage.

Clean the exterior of the gearcase, drive shaft housing and swivel brackets to remove vegetation, dirt or deposit buildup.

Wipe down the components under the cover and apply a good corrosion preventative spray. Corrosive preventative sprays are available from most marine dealerships and marine supply stores. Flush the cooling system following the instructions in this chapter.

Treat the internal power head components with a storage sealing agent (**Figure 92**). This step can prevent corrosion inside the power head during the storage period.

Use a fuel stabilizer to help prevent the formation of gum or varnish in the fuel system during the storage period. Be aware some additives may adversely affect some fuel system components if mixed incorrectly. Deteriora-

tion of hoses, check valves and other nonmetallic components may occur. Never mix these additives at a rate greater than specified on the label.

1. Remove the silencer cover from the carburetors as outlined in Chapter Six.
2. Run the engine at idle speed in a test tank or on a flush/test adapter for 10 minutes or until the engine reaches operating temperature.
3. Raise the engine speed to approximately 1500 rpm. Spray the storage sealing agent into all carburetor openings. Try to spray the agent evenly into all carburetors on multiple carburetor engines. Spray in 5-10 second intervals. Continue to spray the agent into the engine until heavy smoking from the exhaust is noted. This indicates the agent has passed through the engine. Stop the engine at this point.
4. Remove the engine from the test tank or remove the flush/test adapter. Remove each spark plug and spray the sealing agent into each spark plug hole. Crank the engine a few times to distribute the sealing agent.
5. Check the engine oil level and correct as required. Drain each carburetor float bowl. Disconnect the fuel hose from the fuel tank and route it to a container suitable for holding fuel. Slowly pump the primer bulb to move residual fuel in the fuel hoses to the float bowl for drainage. Install the drain plugs and securely tighten them. Disconnect the fuel hose from the engine. Treat any remaining fuel in the fuel tank with fuel stabilizer.
6. Apply a light coat of engine oil to the threads and install the spark plugs. Store the engine in the upright position. Check the speedometer opening at the leading edge of the gearcase (**Figure 93**) and other water drains on the gearcase for the presence of debris. They must be clear to ensure water is not trapped in the cooling system. Clean them with a small piece of wire and compressed air.
7. Inspect the water stream fitting on the lower engine cover (**Figure 94**) for the presence of debris. Blow through the opening with compressed air to ensure it is clear. Remove stubborn debris with a small piece of stiff wire.
8. Disconnect the battery cables. Refer to Chapter Seven for battery storage instructions.

4

Recommissioning

Perform all required maintenance It is wise to service the water pump and replace the impeller as described in Chapter Nine. This vital component may deteriorate during extended storage.

Change or correct all lubricant levels. Supply the engine with fresh fuel.

Install the battery on models so equipped as instructed in Chapter Seven. Supply cooling water and then start the engine. Run the engine at low speed until the engine reaches operating temperature. Check for proper operation of the cooling, electrical and warning systems and correct as required. Refer to Chapter Three for troubleshooting if a problem is noted.

Corrosion Prevention

Reducing corrosion damage is a very effective way to increase the life and reliability of an outboard motor. Corrosion damage can affect virtually every component of the engine.

Corrosion is far more prevalent if the engine is operated in salt or heavily polluted water. Serious damage to the engine is certain if steps are not taken to protect the engine. A simple and effective way to reduce corrosion in the power head cooling passages is to always flush the cooling system after running the engine. Refer to *After Each Use* in this chapter.

Use a corrosion preventative spray on the external engine components to substantially reduce corrosion damage to engine wiring, terminals, exposed fasteners and other components. Regular use is highly recommended if the engine is operated in salt laden or polluted water. Corrosion preventative sprays are available from most marine dealerships or marine supply stores.

Inspect all gearcase and power head anodes at more frequent intervals if the engine is operated in a corrosive environment. Special electronic equipment is available using current from the battery to offset galvanic corrosion. The current draw from these systems is relatively low. Regular charging of the battery or operation of the engine easily recharges the battery. Consider installing this type of system if the boat is stored in the water for extended periods of time. The cost of the system may very well be less than the cost of repairing corrosion damage. These systems are available from most marine dealerships and marine supply stores.

Never connect the boat accessories to AC shore power. The potential for remarkably rapid corrosion of engine components exist under this circumstance. Disconnect the cables from the battery or remove the battery from the boat for charging.

Special isolators are available that allow charging the battery or connections to shore power without promoting rapid corrosion. Contact a marine dealership or marine supply store for information on isolators.

Ensure all grounding wires (**Figure 95**) on the gearcase, midsection and power head are attached and making a good connection at their terminal. Failure to maintain the ground connections prevents the sacrificial anodes from protecting the ungrounded components.

Table 1 MAINTENANCE INTERVALS

Before each use	Check the engine oil level. Check the condition of the propeller. Check for tight engine mounting fasteners. Check the fuel system for leakage. Check for proper operation of the lanyard stop switch. Inspect the steering linkage for looseness for binding. Inspect the steering system for loose fasteners.
After each use	Flush the cooling system. Clean all external gearcase and drive shaft housing surfaces.
Once a year or every 100 hours of usage	Change the engine oil. Clean or replace the engine oil filter.* Service the water pump. Lubricate the swivel tube and clamp brackets. Lubricate the steering system components. Lubricate the throttle and shift linkages. Lubricate the propeller shaft splines. Clean and inspect the spark plugs. Clean or replace the fuel filter. Inspect the gearcase and power head anodes. Change the gearcase lubricant. Lubricate the upper drive shaft splines. Check the tightness of all external fasteners. Inspect all fuel lines and hoses for defects.

(continued)

Table 1 MAINTENANCE INTERVALS (continued)

Once a year or every 100 hours of usage (continued)	Inspect the thermostat for damage or corrosion. Adjust the valve clearance. Check control cable adjustment.* Inspect the timing belt for deterioration or damage.* Adjust the carburetor(s). Check the power trim fluid level.* Check the battery condition.* Clean carbon deposits from the engine. Check the ignition timing.
Every 3 years or every 300 hours of usage	Change the engine oil. Replace the engine oil filter.* Replace the water pump impeller. Lubricate the swivel tube and clamp brackets. Lubricate the steering system components. Lubricate the throttle and shift linkages. Lubricate the propeller shaft splines. Clean and inspect the spark plugs. Clean or replace the fuel filter. Change the gearcase lubricant. Lubricate the upper drive shaft splines. Check the tightness of all external fasteners. Inspect all fuel lines and hoses for defects. Replace the thermostat. Adjust the valve clearance. Check control cable adjustment.* Inspect the timing belt for deterioration or damage.* Adjust the carburetor(s). Check the power trim fluid level.* Check the battery condition.* Clean carbon deposits from the engine. Check the ignition timing. Inspect the gearcase and power head anodes.*

*This maintenance item does not apply to all models.

Table 2 ENGINE OIL CAPACITY (approximate)

Model	Capacity
4-6 hp	15 fl. oz. (450 ml)
9.9 and 15 hp	1 qt (0.95 L)
25-50 hp	3 qt (2.84 L)
75 and 90 hp	5 qt (4.73 L)

Table 3 GEARCASE CAPACITY

Model	Capacity
4-6 hp	6.5 fl. oz. (195 ml)
9.9 and 15 hp	
Standard gearcase	6.8 fl. oz. (200 ml)
Optional gearcase	7.8 fl. oz. (230 ml)
25 hp	14.9 fl. oz. (440 ml)
30 and 40 hp	
Standard gearcase	14.9 fl. oz. (440 ml)
Optional gearcase	22.5 fl. oz. (655 ml)

(continued)

Table 3 GEARCASE CAPACITY (continued)

Model	Capacity
50 hp	
Standard gearcase	14.9 fl. oz. (440 ml)
Optional gearcase	22.5 fl. oz. (655 ml)
75 and 90 hp	22.5 fl. oz. (665 ml)

Table 4 SPARK PLUG SPECIFICATIONS

Model	Spark plug	Gap
4-6 hp	NGK DCPR6E	0.035 in. (0.9 mm)
9.9 hp		
Serial No. OH000057-prior	NGK DPR6EA-9	0.035 in. (0.9 mm)
Serial No. OH000058-on	NGK CR6HS	0.024-0.028 in. (0.6-0.7 mm)
15-50 hp	NGK DPR6EA-9	0.035 in. (0.9 mm)
75 and 90 hp	NGK LFR5A-11	0.043 in. (1.1 mm)

Table 5 IGNITION TIMING

Model	Specification
4 and 5 hp	
High speed timing	24°-26° BTDC
9.9 hp	
Serial No. OH000057-prior	
800 rpm and below	5° BTDC
2800-3300 rpm	30° BTDC
Serial No. OH000058-on	
800-900 rpm	4°-6° BTDC
2500-3000 rpm	34°-36° BTDC
15 hp	
800 rpm and below	5° BTDC
2800-3300 rpm	30° BTDC.
25 hp	
800 rpm and below	
ECU part No. 855311	10° BTDC
ECU part No. 856058/856190	5° BTDC
6000 rpm	30° BTDC
30 and 40 hp	
800 rpm	10° BTDC
6000 rpm	28° BTDC
50 hp	
Closed throttle (idle)	5° BTDC
2500-3000 rpm	35° BTDC
75 and 90 hp	
800 rpm	5° ATDC
6000 rpm	18° BTDC

Table 6 TIGHTENING TORQUE

Fastener location	ft-lb.	in-lb.	N•m
Spark Plug(s)			
4-6 hp	13	156	17

(continued)

Table 6 TIGHTENING TORQUE (continued)

Fastener location	ft-lb.	in-lb.	N•m
Spark plug(s) (continued)			
9.9 hp			
Serial No. OH000057-prior	13	156	17
Serial No. OH000058-on	9	108	12
15 hp	13	156	17
25-90 hp	20	240	27
Oil Filter			
9.9 and 15 hp			
Screen type filter	13	159	18
Spin type filter	–	70	8[1]
25-40 hp	–	70	8[1]
50-90 hp	13	156	17[1]
Gearcase plugs			
4-6 hp[2]	–	–	–
9.9-90 hp	–	60	7
Oil Drain Plug			
9.9 hp			
Serial No. OH000057-prior	18	210	24
Serial No. OH000058-on	–	70	8
15 hp	18	210	24
25-40 hp	17	207	23
50 hp	17	207	23
75 and 90 hp	17	212	24
Power head anode cover			
9.9 hp (serial No. OH000057-prior)	–	44	5
15 and 25 hp	–	44	5
30-90 hp	–	70	8
Anode retaining plate			
9.9 hp (serial No. OH000057-prior)	–	70	8
15 hp	–	70	8
75 and 90 hp	–	70	8
Anode mounting plug			
9.9 hp (serial No. OH000058-On)	–	156	18

1. Approximate minimum tightening torque. Tighten the filter until its gasket contacts the mounting base then tighten an additional 3/4 to 1 turn.
2. Tightening torque specifications are not provided for this model. Securely tighten the drain and fill plug.

Chapter Five

Synchronization and Adjustments

This chapter covers adjustment for all systems on the outboard motor. Included are fuel system adjustment, valve adjustment, shift and throttle cable and linkage adjustment, neutral start mechanism adjustment and power trim/tilt system adjustment. **Tables 1-4** list adjustment and tightening specifications. **Tables 1-4** are located at the back of this chapter.

FUEL SYSTEM ADJUSTMENTS

The following fuel system adjustments are covered in this section.

1. Throttle position sensor.
2. Pilot screw.
3. Idle speed.
4. Dashpot.
5. Accelerator pump.
6. Choke valve.
7. Carburetor synchronization.

Throttle Position Sensor Adjustment

Throttle position sensor adjustment is required only on 75 and 90 hp models. Adjust the throttle position sensor as follows:

1. Disconnect both cables from the battery.
2. Locate the sensor (**Figure 1**) on the lower port side of the engine. Place the throttle in the idle position.
3. Loosen both sensor screws (**Figure 2**) just enough to allow rotation of the sensor body.
4. Rotate the sensor body clockwise direction until the screws reach the end of the adjusting slot. Hold the sensor in this position, then securely tighten both screws.
5. Clean the terminals and connect the cables to the battery.

Pilot Screw Adjustment

NOTE

On late models, the pilot screws are covered with an aluminum plug. Remove the plug and pilot screw only if necessary for cleaning the carburetor passages. Afterward, adjust the pilot screw using the same instructions as for carburetors without the plugs. After adjusting the pilot screw, install a new plug.

Pilot screw adjustment is required on 4-6 hp models (serial No. OH000058-on) and 1995-1997 50 hp models.

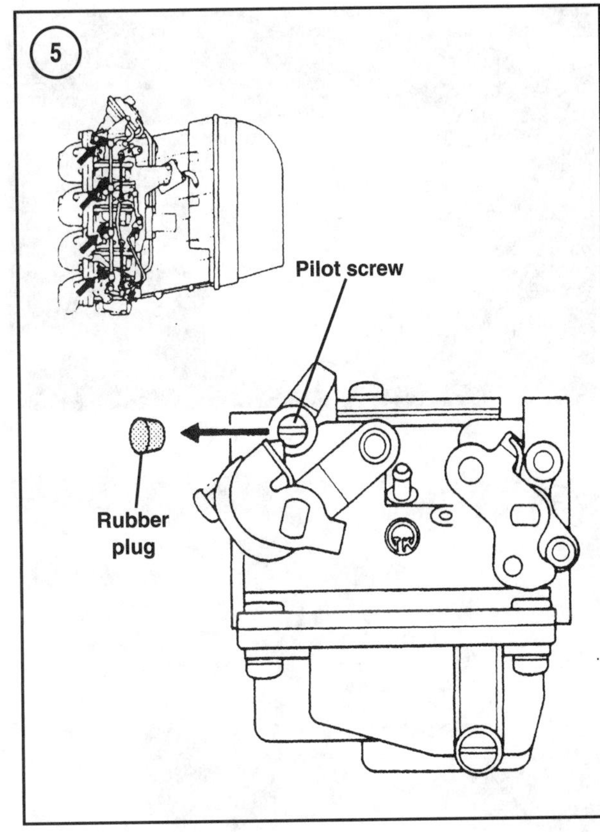

5

1. Refer to **Figure 3** (4-6 hp), **Figure 4** (9.9 hp [serial No. OH000058-on]) and **Figure 5** (1995-1997 50 hp) for pilot screw locations.
2. On 50 hp models, remove the rubber plug (**Figure 5**) using a scribe or small screwdriver.
3. Gently turn the pilot screw clockwise until it lightly seats. Do not force the screw into its seat or the seat and screw will be damaged.
4. Back out the screw the number of turns specified in **Table 1**.

Idle Speed

This section covers idle speed adjustment for 4-25 hp models. On 30-90 hp models, the idle speed is set during the synchronization process. Refer to *Carburetor Synchronization* in this chapter. To properly adjust idle speed, the boat must be in the water, with the correct propeller installed.

1. Attach an accurate tachometer to the power head following its manufacturer's instructions.
2. Start the engine and run at idle speed until warmed to normal operating temperature.

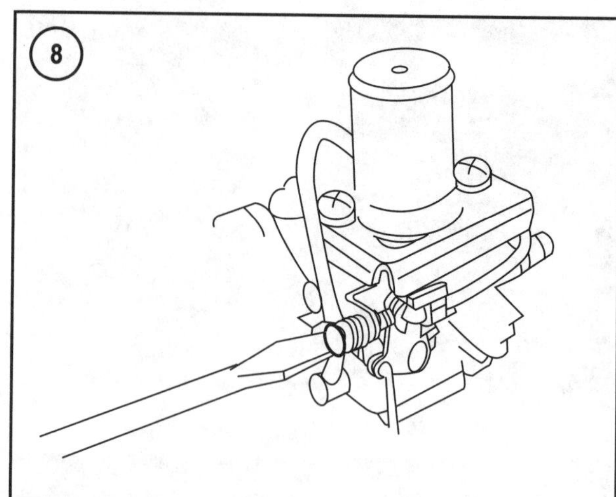

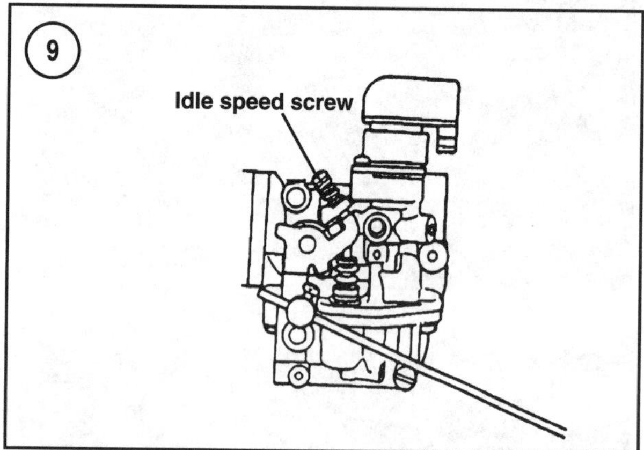

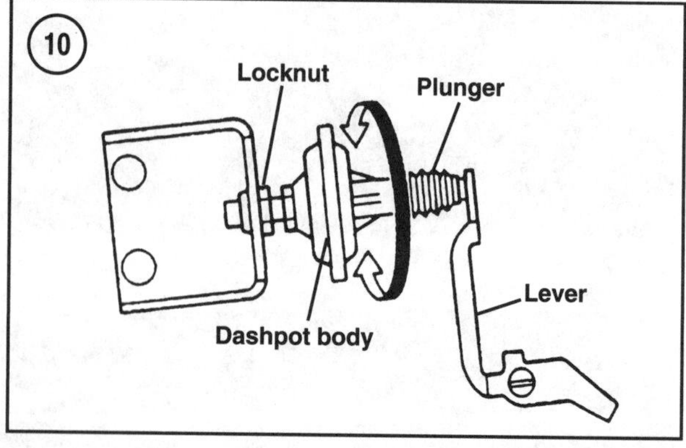

3. To identify the idle speed screw, refer to **Figure 6** (4-6 hp, **Figure 7** (9.9 hp [prior to serial No. OH000058]), **Figure 8** (9.9 hp [serial No. OH000058-on]) and **Figure 9** (25 hp).
4. With the engine running at idle speed in NEUTRAL, adjust the speed to the midrange of the *idle speed* specification in **Table 2**.
5. Next, shift into FORWARD gear, allow the engine speed to stabilize and note the idle speed. Adjust the speed as required to obtain the midrange of the *in-gear* specification in **Table 2**.

Dashpot Adjustment (50 hp Models)

1. Connect an accurate shop tachometer to the engine following the instructions provided with the tachometer.
2. Operate the engine until it reaches operating temperature. Shift the engine into NEUTRAL.
3. Locate the dashpot (**Figure 10**) on the lower starboard and toward the rear of the power head.
4. Observe the tachometer reading and pull the plunger against the lever. Ensure the plunger is fully extended. Correct adjustment causes the engine speed to reach 1650-1750 rpm.
5. If adjustment is required, loosen the jam nut (**Figure 10**) the rotate the dashpot body until the correct adjustment is attained. Securely tighten the locknut then repeat Step 4.

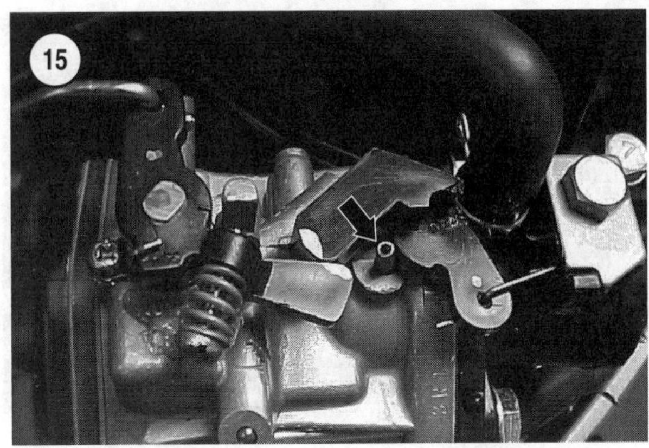

6. Remove the shop tachometer.

Accelerator Pump Adjustment

1. Move the throttle from idle to wide-open throttle and back to idle while observing the accelerator linkage.
2. At idle, the free play in the linkage must be as small as possible without binding or holding the throttle open.
3. If adjustment is required, loosen the jam nut (A, **Figure 11**) and rotate the adjusting nut (B) until a slight free play is present in the linkage.
4. Make sure the adjusting nut engages the linkage by at least six threads. Hold the adjusting nut and securely tighten the jam nut.

Choke Valve Adjustment

4-6 hp models

1. Push the choke knob (**Figure 12**) in.
2. Loosen the bolt on the cable retainer (**Figure 13**). Push in on the choke knob.
3. Position the choke lever until the stop spring aligns with the notch on the lever. (**Figure 14**). Hold the lever against the stop and securely tighten the bolt (**Figure 13**).
4. Pull out on the choke knob and inspect the choke lever. The lever should align with the choke lever as indicated in **Figure 15**. Loosen the bolts and readjust the cable as required. Ensure the choke lever reaches its full open and full choke positions after adjustments.

9.9 (prior to serial No. OH000058) and 15 hp models

1. Disconnect both cables from the battery if so equipped.
2. Push in on the choke knob (**Figure 12**).

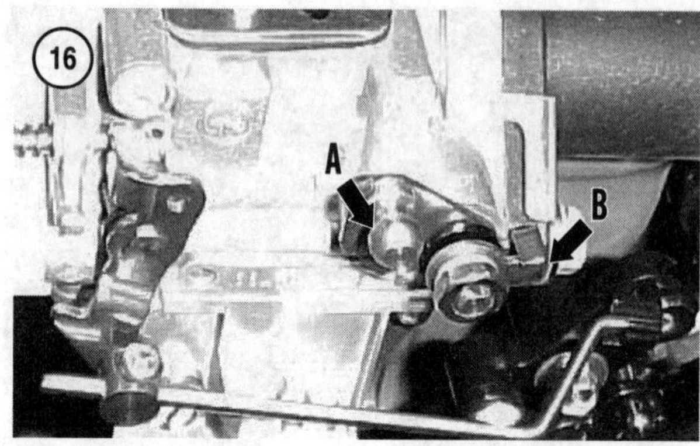

3. Carefully pry the choke linkage from the choke lever (A, **Figure 16**). Rotate the lever counterclockwise to fully open the choke valve. Rotate the connector on the linkage until it aligns with the choke lever (A, **Figure 16**) with the choke knob pushed in.
4. Snap the linkage onto the connector. Observe the lever while pulling out on the choke knob. The choke lever should just contact the stop lever (B, **Figure 16**). Push in on the choke knob. Verify that the choke returns to the off position. Readjust as required.
5. Clean the terminals and connect the cables to the battery if so equipped.

50 hp models

1. Disconnect both cables from the battery.
2. Loosen the adjusting screw for the choke linkage (**Figure 17**).
3. Measure the ambient air temperature. Move the linkage up or down to set the gap (**Figure 17**) for the given temperature.
   a. Set the gap at approximately 0.080 in. (2.0 mm) at 41° F (5° C).
   b. Set the gap at approximately 0.110 in. (2.8 mm) at 68° F (20° C).
   c. Set the gap at approximately 0.137 in. (3.5 mm) at 86° F (30° C).
   d. Set the gap at approximately 0.212 in. (5.4 mm) at 104° F (40° C).
4. Hold the linkage at the specified gap then securely tighten the screw (**Figure 17**).
5. Back the adjustment screw (**Figure 18**) out until two threads protrude from the support. Push down on the choke linkage until the choke lever on the No. 1 carburetor contacts the stop (**Figure 18**).
6. Hold down lightly on the choke linkage during screw adjustment. Turn the adjustment screw in until it just contacts the lever (**Figure 18**).

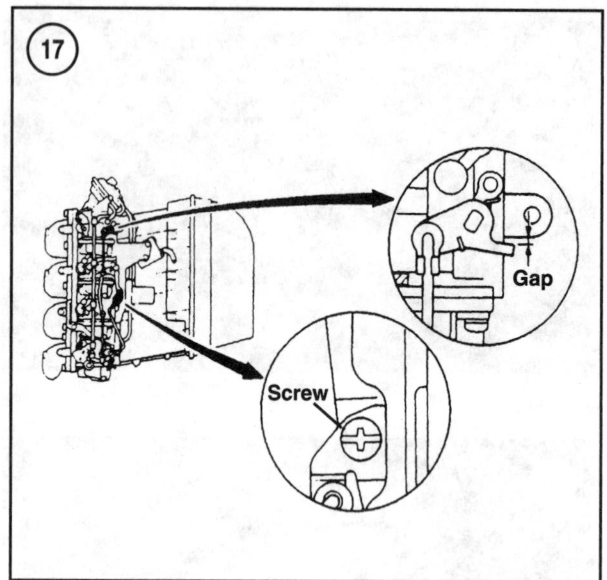

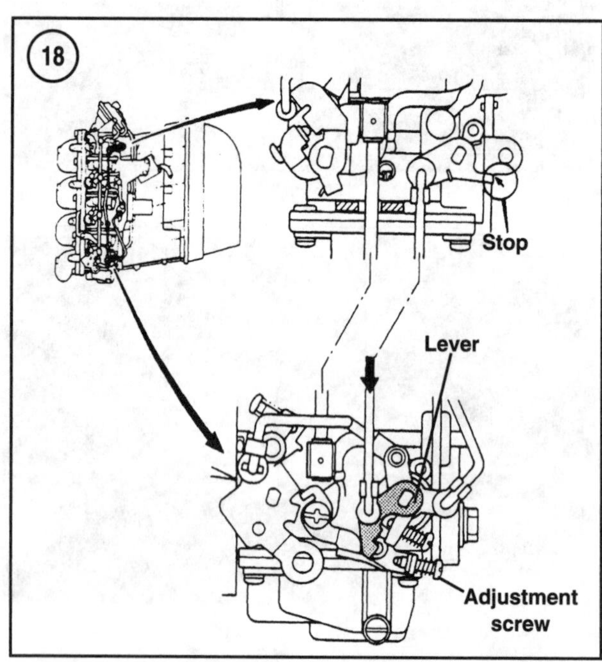

7. Push down on the choke linkage (**Figure 19**). Measure the gap between the No. 4 carburetor choke lever and the adjusting screw (**Figure 19**).
8. Turn the adjusting screw in or out to attain the gap for the current ambient air temperature.
   a. Set the gap at approximately 0.118 in. (3.0 mm) at 50° F (10° C).
   b. Set the gap at approximately 0.080 in. (2.0 mm) at 68° F (20° C).

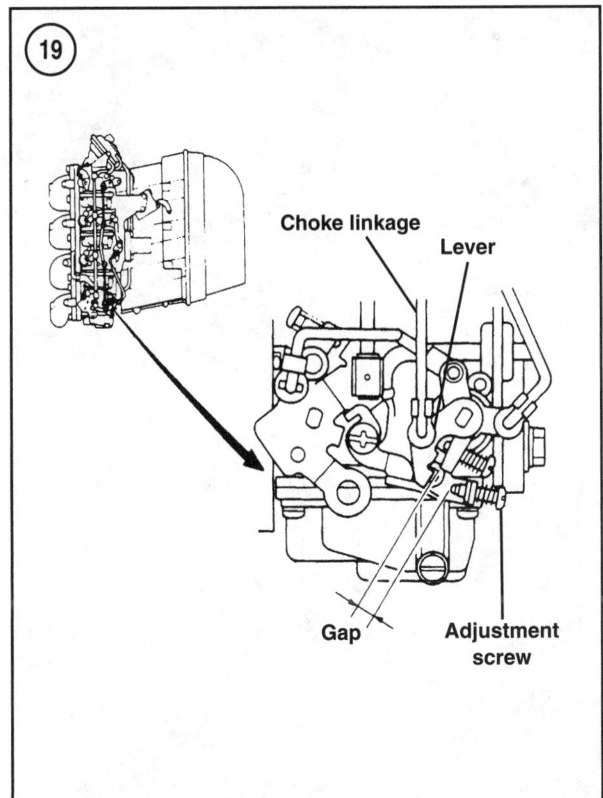

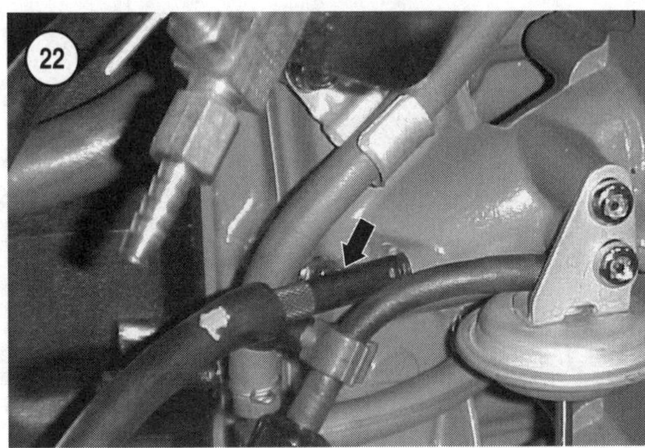

c. Set the gap at approximately 0.040 in. (1.0 mm) at 77° F (25° C).

d. Set the gap at approximately 0.027 in. (0.7 mm) at 86° F (30° C).

9. Clean the terminals and connect the cables to the battery.

WARNING
Use extreme caution if working on or around a running engine. Stay clear from the flywheel, timing belt and pulleys.

Carburetor Synchronization

This section provides carburetor synchronization and idle speed adjustments for 30-90 hp models. An accurate shop tachometer and carburetor synchronization gauge set (**Figure 20**) are required for these adjustments. Adapters included with the gauge set usually fit the plug openings in the intake runner. Remove the plug (**Figure 21**) from the intake runner and compare the plug diameter and thread pitch with the adapters. Purchase the correct size adapters as required.

Some models require certain hoses to be pinched shut during synchronization. Use small locking pliers for this purpose.

Adjustments must be made under actual running conditions. Attempts to perform these adjustments using a flush/test device will result.

30 and 40 hp models

1. Remove all three synchronization port plugs (**Figure 21**) from the intake runners. Thread the adapters (**Figure 22**) into all three ports. Connect the gauge set hoses to the adapters. Mark the intake runner number for each connection on the gauge set.

2. Attach an accurate shop tachometer to the engine following its manufacturer's instructions.
3. Start the engine and allow it to run at fast idle until it reaches normal operating temperature.
4. Using small locking type pliers (**Figure 23**), pinch shut the single gray hose on the top carburetor (**Figure 24**).
5. Pinch the gray hose shut (**Figure 25**) connecting the top carburetor to the second carburetor. On earlier models an additional gray hose connects the second carburetor to the bottom carburetor. Pinch this hose shut if so equipped.
6. Shift the engine into NEUTRAL. Rotate the idle speed screw (**Figure 26**) until the engine reaches exactly 1000 rpm.
7. Observe the reading on the gauge for the bottom and second carburetor along with the tachometer. Slowly turn the synchronization screw (**Figure 27**) on the second carburetor until the gauge readings are equal. Stop immediately and adjust the idle speed (Step 6) if the engine speed changes during adjustment. Continue adjusting the screw until equal gauge readings are attained with the engine speed at 1000 rpm.
8. Observe all three gauge readings and the tachometer while adjusting the synchronization screw (**Figure 27**) for the top carburetor. Slowly turn the synchronization screw until all three readings are equal. Stop immediately and adjust the idle speed (Step 6) if the engine speed changes during adjustment. Continue adjusting until all three gauge readings are equal with an engine speed of 1000 rpm.
9. Advance the engine speed to 2500 rpm then slowly return to idle. Check the gauge and tachometer readings. Readjust if required.
10. Adjust the idle speed (**Figure 26**) to the specification in **Table 2**. Shift the engine into FORWARD gear. Allow the engine speed to stabilize then check the idle speed in gear. Adjust the idle speed in neutral to the higher or lower side of the specification to attain the correct.
11. Remove the adapters from the intake runners. Inspect the sealing washers on the plugs for damage. Replace the

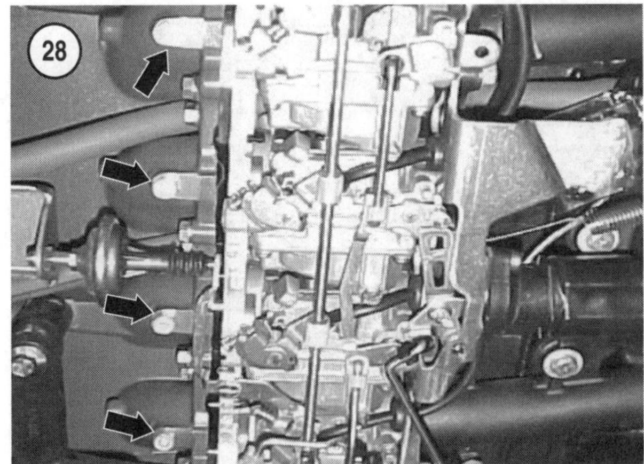

washers if damage is noted. Install and securely tighten the plugs (**Figure 21**).

12. Remove the locking pliers from the electrothermal valve hoses and remove the tachometer.

50 hp models

1. Remove all four synchronization port plugs (**Figure 28**) from the intake runners. Thread the adapters (**Figure 22**) into all four ports. Connect the gauge hoses to the adapters. Mark the intake runner number for each connection on the gauge set.
2. Attach an accurate shop tachometer to the engine following its manufacturer's instructions.
3. Start the engine and allow it to run at fast idle or until it reaches normal operating temperature.
4. Shift the engine into NEUTRAL gear. Rotate the idle speed screw (**Figure 29**) and adjust the screw until the engine reaches exactly 1000 rpm.
5. Observe the reading on the gauge for the bottom and No. 3 carburetor along with the tachometer. Slowly turn the synchronization screw (**Figure 30**) on the No. 3 carburetor until the gauge reading for the No. 3 carburetor indicates 1 cm less vacuum than the bottom carburetor. Stop immediately and adjust the idle speed (Step 4) if the engine speed changes during adjustment. Continue adjusting the screw until the specified vacuum difference is attained with the engine at 1000 rpm.
6. Observe the reading on the gauge for the bottom and No. 2 carburetor along with the tachometer. Slowly turn the synchronization screw (**Figure 30**) for the No. 2 carburetor until the gauge reading for the No. 2 carburetor indicates 2 cm less vacuum than the reading for the bottom carburetor. Stop immediately and adjust the idle speed (Step 4) if the engine speed changes during adjustment. Continue adjusting the screw until the specified vacuum difference is attained with the engine at 1000 rpm. Check and adjust the No. 3 gauge reading as required (Step 5).
7. Observe the reading on the gauge for the bottom and top carburetor along with the tachometer. Slowly turn the synchronization screw (**Figure 30**) for the top carburetor until the gauge reading for the top carburetor indicates 3 cm less vacuum than the reading for the bottom carburetor. Stop immediately and adjust the idle speed (Step 4) if the engine speed changes during adjustment. Continue adjusting the screw until the specified vacuum difference is attained with the engine at 1000 rpm. Check the gauge reading and if required adjust the synchronizer screw for the No. 3 and No. 2 carburetors (Step 5 and Step 6).
8. Advance the engine speed to 2500 rpm then slowly return to idle. Check the gauge and tachometer readings. Readjust if required.
9. Adjust the idle speed screw (**Figure 29**) until the idle speed reaches the speed indicated in **Table 2**. Have an assistant operate the boat then shift the engine into forward gear. Allow the engine speed to stabilize then check the idle speed in forward gear. Adjust the neutral gear idle speed to the higher or lower side of the specification to attain the correct idle speed in forward gear. Turn the engine off.

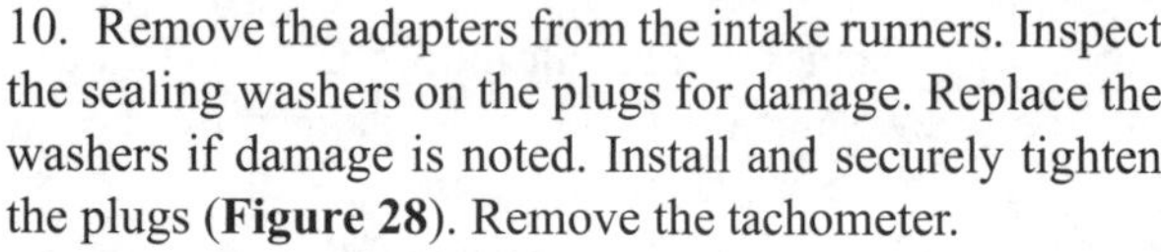
10. Remove the adapters from the intake runners. Inspect the sealing washers on the plugs for damage. Replace the washers if damage is noted. Install and securely tighten the plugs (**Figure 28**). Remove the tachometer.

75 and 90 hp models

1. Remove all four synchronization port plugs (**Figure 31**) from the intake runners. Thread the adapters (**Figure 22**) into all three ports. Connect the gauge set hoses to the adapters. Mark the intake runner number for each connection on the gauge set.
2. Attach an accurate shop tachometer to the engine following its manufacturer's instructions.
3. Start the engine and allow it to run at fast idle until it reaches normal operating temperature.
4. Shift the engine into NEUTRAL. Rotate the idle speed screw (**Figure 32**) and adjust the screw until the engine reaches exactly 1000 rpm.
5. Observe the reading on the gauge for the bottom and No. 3 carburetor along with the tachometer. Slowly turn the synchronization screw (Figure 33) for the No. 3 carburetor until both vacuum gauge readings are equal. Stop immediately and adjust the idle speed (Step 4) if the engine speed changes during adjustment. Continue adjusting the screw until equal gauge readings are attained with the engine at 1000 rpm.
6. Observe the gauge readings for cylinders 2-4 and the tachometer while adjusting the screw for the No. 2 carburetor. Slowly turn the synchronization screw (**Figure 33**) until all three vacuum readings are equal. Stop immediately and adjust the idle speed (Step 4) if the engine speed changes during adjustment. Continue adjusting until all three gauge readings are equal with an engine speed of 1000 rpm.

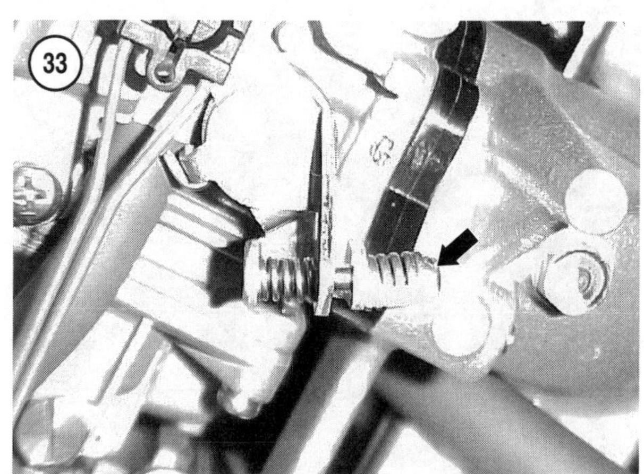

7. Observe the gauge readings for cylinders 1-4 and the tachometer while adjusting the screw for the top carburetor. Slowly turn the synchronization screw (**Figure 33**) until all four vacuum readings are equal. Stop immediately and adjust the idle speed (Step 4) if the engine speed changes during adjustments. Continue adjusting until all four gauge readings are equal with an engine speed of 1000 rpm.
8. Advance the engine speed to 2500 rpm then slowly return to idle. Check the gauge and tachometer readings. Readjust if required.
9. Adjust the idle speed screw (**Figure 32**) to the specification in **Table 2**. Shift the engine into forward gear. Allow the engine speed to stabilize then check the idle speed in forward gear. Adjust the idle speed in neutral to the higher or lower side of the specification to attain the correct in-gear idle speed. Turn the engine off.
10. Remove the adapters from the intake runners. Inspect the sealing washers on the plugs for damag. Replace the washers if damage is noted. Install and securely tighten the plugs (**Figure 31**). Remove the tachometer.

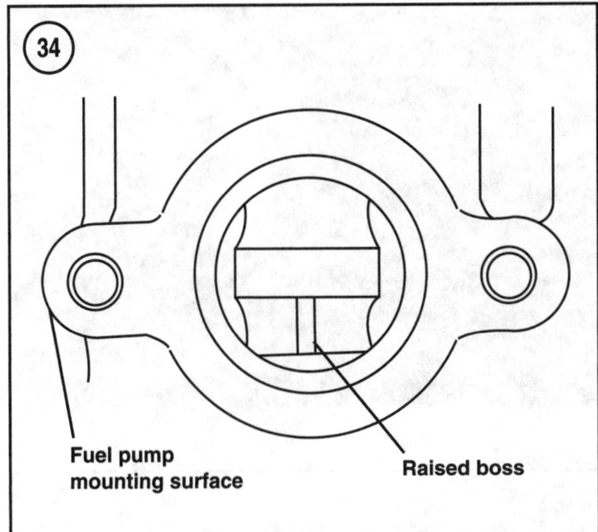

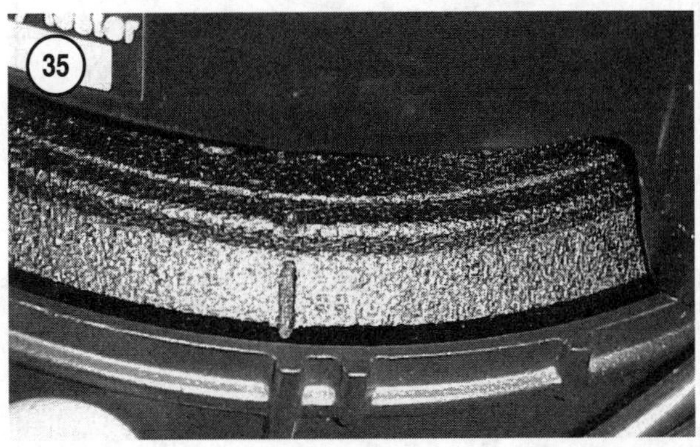

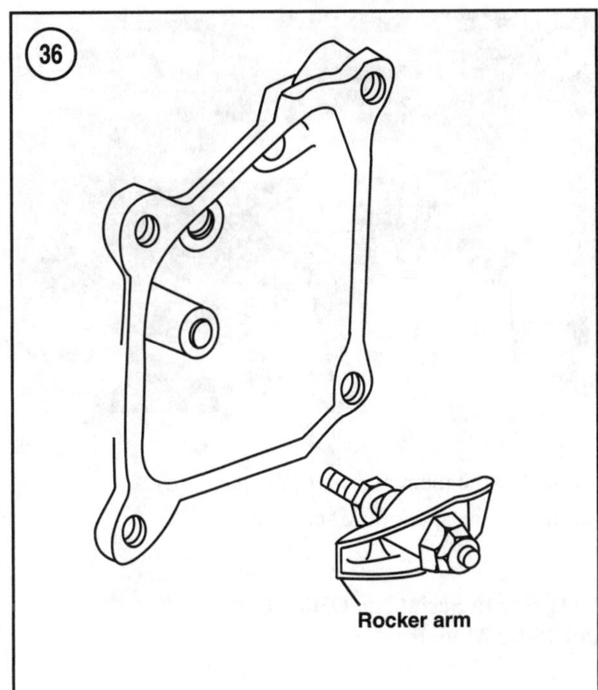

VALVE ADJUSTMENT

Adjust the valves at the intervals specified in Chapter Four. Excessive valve lash causes excessive valve train noise and wear. Insufficient lash will cause poor performance and damaged valves and valve seats.

4-6 hp Models

1. Remove the spark plug and connect the spark plug lead to a suitable engine ground.
2. Remove the manual starter as described in Chapter Ten.
3. Remove the rocker arm cover as described in Chapter Eight.
4. Remove the fuel pump as described in Chapter Six.
5. Look into the fuel pump opening while rotating the flywheel clockwise from the flywheel end. Stop when the a raised boss on the camshaft (**Figure 34**) is visible in the fuel pump opening.
6. Rotate the flywheel until the raised boss on the flywheel aligns with the longer raised mark on the cylinder block (**Figure 35**). Ensure the raised boss on the camshaft is still visible (Step 5). This step positions the crankshaft and camshaft at TCD (top dead center).
7. Slip feeler gauges between the rocker arm (**Figure 36**) and the valve stem. The feeler gauge that slips between the components with a slight drag indicates the valve clearance. Record the clearance for both valves. Compare the measurements with the specifications provided in **Table 3**.
8. Adjust the intake and exhaust valves if incorrect clearance is noted:
   a. Loosen the rocker arm nut on the end of the rocker arm stud.
   b. Check the clearance with feeler gauges while turning the adjusting nut located beneath the rocker arm nut. Turn the adjusting nut clockwise to decrease the valve clearance and counterclockwise to increase the clearance.
   c. Continue until the clearance is within the specification provided in **Table 3**.
   d. Hold the adjusting nut and tighten the rocker arm nuts to the specification provided in **Table 4**.
   e. Check the clearance after tightening the rocker arm nut.
9. Install the rocker arm cover (Chapter Eight).
10. Install the fuel pump (Chapter Six).

5

11. Install the manual starter (Chapter Ten).
12. Install the spark plug and lead.

9.9 (Prior to Serial No. OH000058) and 15 hp Models

1. Disconnect both cables from the battery if so equipped. Remove the spark plugs then connect the spark plug leads to a suitable engine ground.
2. On manual start models, remove the manual starter as described in Chapter Ten.
3. On electric start models, remove the flywheel cover as described in Chapter Eight.
4. Remove the rocker arm cover as described in Chapter Eight
5. Place the crankshaft and camshaft in the TDC position for cylinder No 1 as follows:
   a. Observe the timing pointer (**Figure 37**) while rotating the flywheel clockwise. Stop when the timing pointer aligns with the line next to the O mark.
   b. Inspect the camshaft timing mark alignment. The TDC position for No. 1 cylinder occurs when the *1* and triangle marks align with the triangle mark on the cylinder block (**Figure 38**). Rotate the flywheel exactly one revolution clockwise if the *2* mark aligns with the triangle.
   c. Ensure the flywheel mark and pointer align. Ensure the No. 1 camshaft pulley marking and triangle marks align. Rotate the flywheel as required. Remove the timing belt and reposition the camshaft pulley if required. Refer to Chapter Eight.
6. **Figure 39** shows the intake and exhaust rocker arms for the No. 1 cylinder. Slip feeler gauges between the rocker arm and the valve stem (**Figure 40**). The feeler gauge that slips between the components with a slight drag indicates the valve clearance. Record the clearance for both valves. Compare the clearances with the specifications provided in **Table 3**.

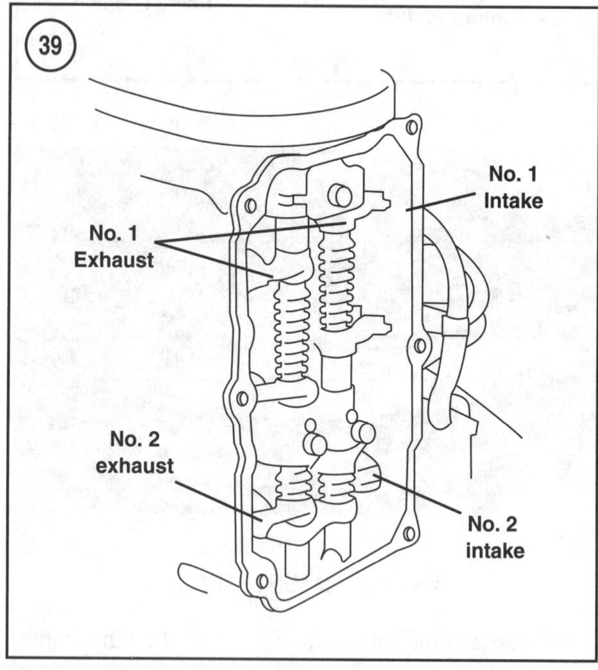

7. Adjust the valves clearance as follows:
   a. Loosen the rocker arm nut on the valve stem end of the rocker arm.
   b. Check the clearance with a feeler gauge while turning the adjusting screw (**Figure 40**). Turn the adjusting screw clockwise to decrease the valve clearance and counterclockwise to increase the clearance.
   c. Continue until the clearance is within the specification provided in **Table 3**. Adjust both valves.
   d. Hold the adjusting screws and tighten the rocker arm nuts to the specification in **Table 4**.

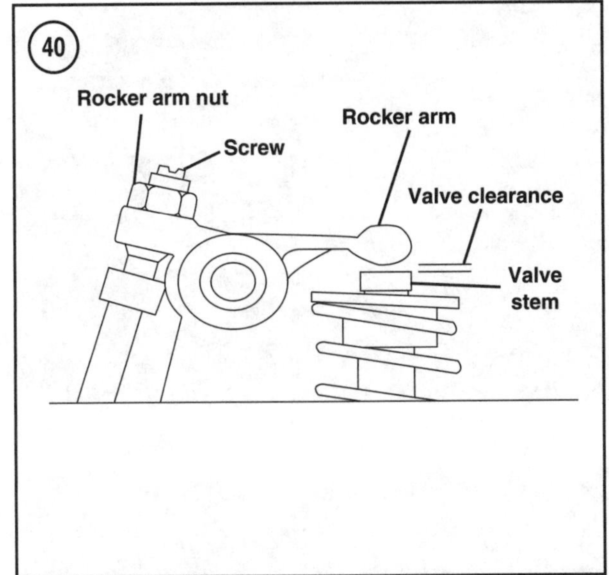

8. Place the flywheel and camshaft at TDC for the No. 2 cylinder as follows:
   a. Observe the timing pointer (**Figure 37**) while rotating the flywheel in the clockwise direction. Stop when the timing pointer aligns with the line next to the *0* mark.
   b. Inspect the camshaft timing mark alignment. The TDC position for No. 2 cylinder occurs when the *2* and triangle mark aligns with the triangle mark on the cylinder block (**Figure 41**). Rotate the flywheel exactly one revolution clockwise if the *1* mark aligns with the triangle.
   c. Ensure the flywheel mark and pointer align. Ensure the No. 2 camshaft pulley and triangle marks align.
9. Slip feeler gauges between the rocker arm and the valve stem (**Figure 40**). The feeler gauge that slips between the components with a slight drag indicates the valve clearance. Record the clearance for both valves. Compare the recorded clearances with the specifications provided in **Table 3**.
10. Adjust the valves if incorrect clearance is noted:
   a. Loosen the rocker arm nut on the valve stem end of the rocker arm.
   b. Check the clearance with a feeler gauges while turning the adjusting screw (**Figure 40**). Turn the adjusting screw clockwise to decrease the valve clearance and counterclockwise to increase the clearance.
   c. Continue until the clearance is within the specification provided in **Table 3**. Adjust both valves.
   d. Hold the adjusting screws and tighten the rocker arm nuts to the specification in **Table 4**.
11. Install the rocker arm cover (Chapter Eight).
12. On electric start models, install the flywheel cover (Chapter Eight).
13. On manual start models, install the manual starter (Chapter Ten).
14. Install the spark plugs and leads. Clean the terminals and connect the cables to the battery if so equipped.

5

9.9 hp Models (Serial No. OH000058-On)

1. Disconnect both cables from the battery if so equipped. Remove the spark plugs then connect the spark plug leads to a suitable engine ground.
2. On manual start models, remove the manual starter as described in Chapter Ten.
3. On electric start models, remove the flywheel cover as described in Chapter Eight.
4. Remove the rocker arm cover as described in Chapter Eight
5. Check the TDC (top dead center position for the crankshaft when removing or installing the timing belt or when suspecting incorrect alignment. Position the crankshaft at TDC as follows:

NOTE

The flywheel must be removed to view the timing mark on the cylinder block. However, the flywheel must be placed back onto the crankshaft to turn the engine and to compare the timing marks on the flywheel with the timing pointer in the following steps. Be sure to align the flywheel key and key slot when placing the flywheel on the crankshaft.

   a. Remove the flywheel as described in Chapter Eight.
   b. Rotate the crankshaft until the raised boss on the crankshaft pulley plate aligns with the raised boss

on the cylinder block (**Figure 42**). If necessary, place the flywheel onto the crankshaft and use it to turn the crankshaft.

6. Place the crankshaft and camshaft at TDC for cylinder No 1 as follows:
   a. Inspect the camshaft timing mark alignment. The TDC position for No. 1 cylinder occurs when the *1* mark and raised boss aligns with the raised boss on the cylinder block (**Figure 43**). Rotate the flywheel exactly one revolution clockwise if the *2* mark aligns with the bosses.
   b. Ensure the flywheel mark and timing pointer align and the No. 1 camshaft pulley mark aligns with the raised boss on the cylinder block. Remove the timing belt and reposition the camshaft pulley if required. Refer to Chapter Eight.
7. Slip feeler gauges between the rocker arm and the valve stem (**Figure 40**). The feeler gauge that slips between the components with a slight drag indicates the valve clearance. Record the clearance for both valves. Compare the clearances with the specifications provided in **Table 3**.
8. Adjust the valves as follows:
   a. Loosen the rocker arm nut on the valve stem end of the rocker arm.
   b. Check the clearance with a feeler gauge while turning the adjusting screw (**Figure 40**). Turn the adjusting screw clockwise to decrease the valve clearance and counterclockwise to increase the clearance.
   c. Continue until the clearance is within the specification provided in **Table 3**. Adjust both valves.
   d. Hold the adjusting screws and tighten the rocker arm nuts to the specification in **Table 4**.
9. Place the flywheel and camshaft at TDC for the No. 2 cylinder as follows:
   a. Rotate the flywheel until the *2* mark and raised boss on the camshaft pulley aligns with the raised boss on the cylinder block (**Figure 44**).
10. Slip feeler gauges between the rocker arm and the valve stem (**Figure 40**). The feeler gauge that slips between the components with a slight drag indicates the valve clearance. Record the clearance for both valves. Compare the clearances with the specifications provided in **Table 3**.
11. Adjust the valves as follows:
   a. Loosen the rocker arm nut on the valve stem end of the rocker arm.
   b. Check the clearance with a feeler gauge while turning the adjusting screw (**Figure 40**). Turn the adjusting screw clockwise to decrease the valve clearance and counterclockwise to increase the clearance.
   c. Continue until the clearance is within the specification provided in **Table 3**. Adjust both valves.
   d. Hold the adjusting screws and tighten the rocker arm nuts to the specification provided in **Table 4**.
12. Install the flywheel and rocker arm cover following the instructions provided in Chapter Eight.

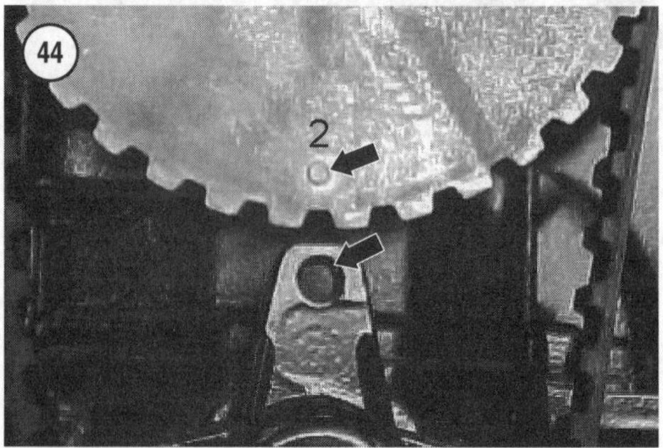

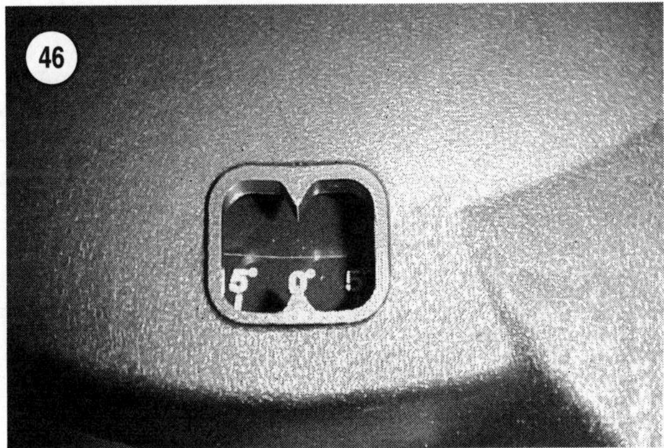

13. On electric start models, install the flywheel cover (Chapter Eight).
14. On manual start models, install the manual starter (Chapter Ten).
15. Install the spark plugs and leads. Clean the terminals and connect the cables to the batter if so equipped.

25 hp Models

1. Disconnect both cables from the battery if so equipped. Remove the spark plugs then connect the spark plug leads to a suitable engine ground.
2. On manual start models, remove the manual starter as described in Chapter Ten.
3. On electric start models, remove the flywheel cover as described in Chapter Eight.
4. Remove the rocker arm cover as described in Chapter Eight
5. Place the crankshaft and camshaft at TDC (top dead center) position for cylinder No 1 as follows:
   a. Rotate the flywheel clockwise then place the flywheel cover or manual starter onto the cylinder block to allow use of the timing pointer (**Figure 45**).

   b. Continue until the *0* mark aligns with the pointer (**Figure 46**).
   c. Remove the flywheel cover or manual starter.
6. Inspect the camshaft timing mark alignment. The TDC position for No. 1 cylinder occurs when the triangle mark on the camshaft pulley aligns with the raised triangle on the cylinder block (**Figure 38**). Rotate the flywheel exactly one revolution clockwise if the raised circle on the pulley aligns with the triangle mark on the cylinder block.
8. Ensure the flywheel and timing pointer align and the raised triangle on the camshaft pulley and cylinder block align. Remove the timing belt and reposition the camshaft pulley if required. Refer to Chapter Eight for instructions.
8. Slip feeler gauges between the rocker arm and the valve stem (**Figure 40**). The feeler gauge that slips between the components with a slight drag indicates the valve clearance. Record the clearance for both valves. Compare the recorded clearances with the specifications provided in **Table 3**.
9. Adjust the valves as follows:
   a. Loosen the rocker arm nut on the valve stem end of the rocker arm.
   b. Check the clearance with a feeler gauge while turning the adjusting screw (**Figure 40**). Turn the adjusting screw clockwise to decrease the valve clearance and counterclockwise to increase the clearance.
   c. Continue until the clearance is within the specification provided in **Table 3**. Adjust both valves.
   d. Hold the adjusting screws and tighten the rocker arm nuts to the specification provided in **Table 4**.
10. Place the flywheel and camshaft at TDC for the No. 2 cylinder as follows. Rotate the flywheel until the raised circle on the camshaft pulley aligns with the triangle marking on the cylinder block (**Figure 47**).
11. Slip feeler gauges between the rocker arm and the valve stem (**Figure 40**). The feeler gauge that slips between the components with a slight drag indicates the

valve clearance. Record the clearance for both valves. Compare the recorded clearances with the specifications provided in **Table 3**.

12. Adjust the valves as follows:
    a. Loosen the rocker arm nut on the valve stem end of the rocker arm.
    b. Check the clearance with a feeler gauge while turning the adjusting screw (**Figure 40**). Turn the adjusting screw clockwise to decrease the valve clearance and counterclockwise to increase the clearance.
    c. Continue until the clearance is within the specification provided in **Table 3**. Adjust both valves.
    d. Hold the adjusting screws and tighten the rocker arm nuts to the specification provided in **Table 4**.
13. Install the rocker arm cover (Chapter Eight).
14. On electric start models, install the flywheel cover (Chapter Eight).
15. On manual start models, install the manual starter (Chapter Ten).
16. Install the spark plugs and leads. Clean the terminals then connect the cables to the battery, if so equipped.

30 and 40 hp Models

1. Disconnect both cables from the battery, if so equipped. Remove the spark plugs then connect the spark plug leads to a suitable engine ground.
2. On manual start models, remove the manual starter as described in Chapter Ten.
3. On electric start models, remove the flywheel cover as described in Chapter Eight.
4. Remove the rocker arm cover as described in Chapter Eight
5. Place the crankshaft and camshaft at TDC for cylinder No. 1 as follows:
    a. Temporarily place the flywheel cover or manual starter onto the cylinder block. Make a reference mark on the power head that aligns with the approximate position of the timing pointer (**Figure 45**). Remove the flywheel cover or manual starter.
    b. Rotate the flywheel clockwise until the *0* mark aligns with the reference mark.
    c. Temporarily install the flywheel cover or manual starter to check the actual pointer and flywheel mark alignment. Repeat until the *0* mark aligns with the pointer (**Figure 46**).
    d. Remove the flywheel cover or manual starter. Inspect the camshaft timing mark alignment. The camshaft is at TDC for the No. 1 cylinder if the No. 1 mark and the triangle mark on the camshaft pulley aligns with the raised mark on the cylinder block (**Figure 38**). Rotate the flywheel exactly one revolution if a raised circle with a number mark (**Figure 48**) aligns with the triangle mark.
    e. Verify alignment of the flywheel mark and timing pointer and alignment of the raised triangle on the camshaft pulley and mark on the cylinder block. If the alignment is not correct, remove the timing belt and reposition the camshaft pulley as required. Refer to Chapter Eight.
6. **Figure 49** shows the rocker arms for the No. 1 cylinder. Slip feeler gauges between the rocker arm and the valve stem (**Figure 40**). The feeler gauge that slips between the components with a slight drag indicates the valve clearance. Record the clearance for both valves. Compare the clearances with the specifications provided in **Table 3**.
7. Adjust the valves as follows:
    a. Loosen the rocker arm nut on the valve stem end of the rocker arm.

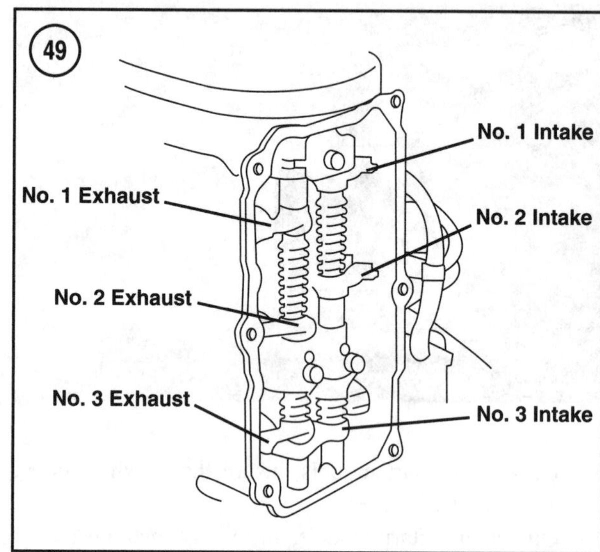

b. Check the clearance with a feeler gauge while turning the adjusting screw (**Figure 40**). Turn the adjusting screw clockwise to decrease the valve clearance and counterclockwise to increase the clearance.

c. Continue until the clearance is within the specification provided in **Table 3**. Adjust both valves.

d. Hold the adjusting screws and tighten the rocker arm nuts to the specification provided in **Table 4**.

8. Place the flywheel and camshaft at TDC for the No. 2 cylinder as follows. Rotate clockwise the flywheel 2/3 of a revolution and until the No. *2* and triangle mark on the camshaft pulley aligns with the triangle marking on the cylinder block (**Figure 41**).

9. Slip feeler gauges between the rocker arm and the valve stem (**Figure 40**). The feeler gauge that slips between the components with a slight drag indicates the valve clearance. Record the clearance for both valves. Compare the recorded clearances with the specifications provided in **Table 3**.

10. Adjust the valves as follows:

a. Loosen the rocker arm nut on the valve stem end of the rocker arm.

b. Check the clearance with a feeler gauge while turning the adjusting screw (**Figure 40**). Turn the adjusting screw clockwise to decrease the valve clearance and counterclockwise to increase the clearance.

c. Continue until the clearance is within the specification provided in **Table 3**. Adjust both valves.

d. Hold the adjusting screws and tighten the rocker arm nuts to the specification provided in **Table 4**.

11. Place the flywheel and camshaft at TDC for the No. 3 cylinder as follows. Rotate clockwise the flywheel 2/3 of a revolution and until the No. *3* and triangle mark on the camshaft pulley aligns with the triangle mark on the cylinder block (**Figure 50**).

12. Slip feeler gauges between the rocker arm and the valve stem (**Figure 40**). The feeler gauge that slips between the components with a slight drag indicates the valve clearance. Record the clearance for both valves. Compare the clearances with the specifications provided in **Table 3**.

13. Adjust the valves as follows.

a. Loosen the rocker arm nut on the valve stem end of the rocker arm.

b. Check the clearance with a feeler gauges while turning the adjusting screw (**Figure 40**). Turn the adjusting screw clockwise to decrease the valve clearance and counterclockwise to increase the clearance.

c. Continue until the clearance is within the specification provided in **Table 3**. Adjust both valves.

d. Hold the adjusting screws and tighten the rocker arm nuts to the specification provided in **Table 4**.

14. Install the rocker arm cover (Chapter Eight).

15. On electric start models, install the flywheel cover (Chapter Eight).

16. On manual start models, install the manual starter (Chapter Ten).

17. Install the spark plugs and leads. Clean the terminals then connect the cables to the battery, if so equipped.

50 hp Models

1. Disconnect both cables from the battery. Remove the spark plugs then connect the spark plug leads to a suitable engine ground.

2. Remove the flywheel cover as described in Chapter Eight.

3. Remove the rocker arm cover as described in Chapter Eight

4. Place the crankshaft and camshaft at TDC (top dead center) for cylinder No 1 as follows:

a. Rotate the flywheel until the timing pointer aligns with the mark next to the *0* mark (**Figure 51**).

b. Inspect the camshaft pulley marks. If positioned at TDC for the No. 1 cylinder, the *1* and the raised triangle mark will be aligned with the triangle mark on the cylinder block (**Figure 52**).

c. If the *4* mark and the triangle on the flywheel align with the triangle on the cylinder block, rotate the flywheel exactly one turn clockwise.

d. Ensure the *0* mark on the flywheel and the pointer align and the No. *1* and triangle on the camshaft pulley align with the cylinder block mark before adjusting the valves. Remove the timing belt and correct any minor timing mark misalignment. Refer to Chapter Eight for instructions.

5. **Figure 53** shows the intake and exhaust rocker arms for the No. 1 cylinder . Slip feeler gauges between the rocker arm and the valve stem (**Figure 40**) for arms. The feeler gauge that slips between the components with a slight drag indicates the valve clearance. Record the clearance for all four valves. Compare the clearances with the specifications provided in **Table 3**.

6. Adjust valves as follows:

a. Loosen the rocker arm nut on the valve stem end of the rocker arm.

b. Check the clearance with a feeler gauge while turning the adjusting screw (**Figure 40**). Turn the adjusting screw clockwise to decrease the valve clearance and counterclockwise to increase the clearance.

c. Continue until the clearance is within the specification provided in **Table 3**. Adjust both valves.

d. Hold the adjusting screws and tighten the rocker arm nuts to the specification provided in **Table 4**.

7. Position the crankshaft and camshaft a TDC No. 4 cylinder as follows:

a. Rotate the flywheel clockwise exactly one revolution. Ensure the timing pointer and marks align as shown in **Figure 51**.

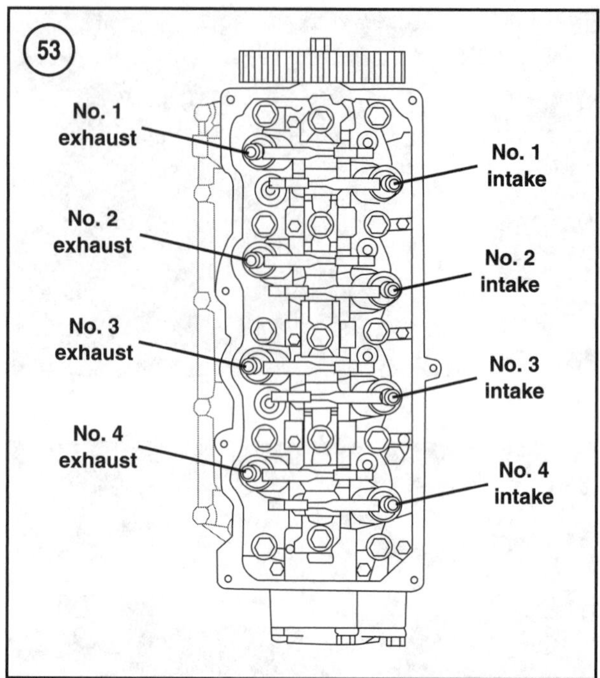

b. The No. *4* and raised triangle mark on the camshaft pulley should align with the triangle mark on the cylinder block (**Figure 54**).

8. Slip feeler gauges between the rocker arm and the valve stem (**Figure 40**). The feeler gauge that slips between the components with a slight drag indicates the valve clearance. Rrecord the clearance for all four valves. Compare the clearances with the specifications provided in **Table 3**.

9. Adjust the valves as follows:

a. Loosen the rocker arm nut on the valve stem end of the rocker arm.

b. Check the clearance with a feeler gauges while turning the adjusting screw (**Figure 40**). Turn the adjusting screw clockwise to decrease the valve

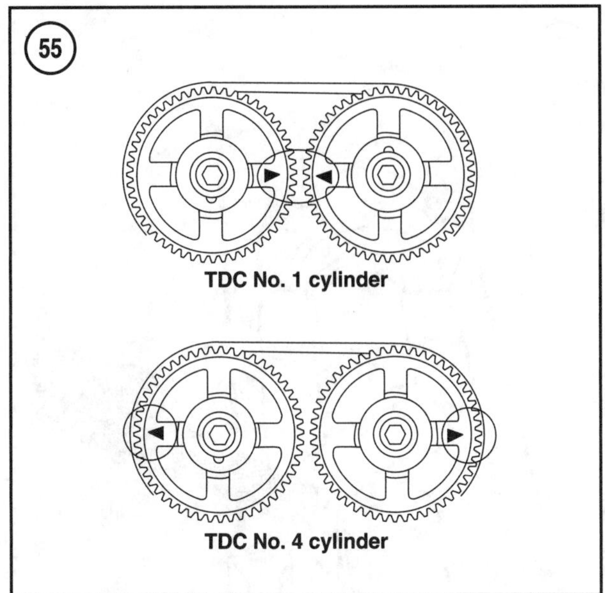

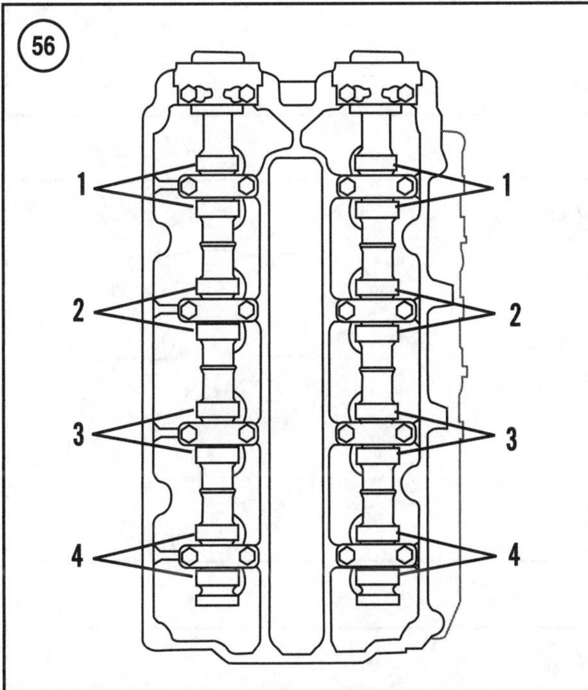

clearance and counterclockwise to increase the clearance.

c. Continue until the clearance is within the specification provided in **Table 3**. Adjust both valves.

d. Hold the adjusting screws and tighten the rocker arm nuts to the specification provided in **Table 4**.

10. Install the flywheel and rocker arm covers (Chapter Eight).

11. Install the spark plug and leads. Clean the terminals then connect the cables to the battery.

75 and 90 hp Models

1. Disconnect both cables from the battery. Remove the spark plugs then connect the spark plug leads to a suitable engine ground.
2. Remove the flywheel cover as described in Chapter Eight.
3. Remove the rocker arm cover as described in Chapter Eight
4. Place the crankshaft and camshaft TDC (top dead center) for cylinder No 1 as follows:
   a. Rotate the flywheel clockwise then temporarily place the flywheel cover onto the cylinder block to allow use of the timing pointer (**Figure 45**).
   b. Continue until the *0* mark aligns with the pointer (**Figure 46**).
   c. Remove the flywheel cover.
5. Place the camshaft pulley in the No. 1 TDC position as follows:
   a. Inspect the alignment of the marks on the camshaft gears (**Figure 55**). The marks directly align with the camshafts at TDC for No. 1 cylinder.
   b. Rotate the flywheel exactly one revolution if the marks point in opposite directions (**Figure 55**). Rotate the flywheel just enough to correct camshaft mark alignment. Remove and reinstall the timing belt if unable to align the camshaft mark and the flywheel timing pointer at the same time. Refer to Chapter Eight for instructions.
6. Refer to (**Figure 56**) to locate the following valve pads and camshaft lobes (**Figure 57**).
   a. Both No. 1 intake valve pads and lobes.
   b. Both No. 2 intake valve pads and lobes.
   c. Both No. 1 exhaust valve pads and lobes.

5

d. Both No. 3 exhaust valve pads and lobes.

7. Insert feeler gauges between the valve pad and the camshaft lobe (**Figure 58**). Select the feeler gauge passing between the lobe and pad with a slight drag. (**Figure 59**). Record each camshaft-to-valve pad clearance.

8. Rotate the flywheel exactly one revolution and until the camshaft pulley markings face in opposite directions (**Figure 55**). This places the crankshaft and camshafts in the No. 4 TDC position.

9. Refer to (**Figure 56**) to locate the following valve pads and camshaft lobes (**Figure 57**).

a. Both No. 3 intake valve pads and lobes.

b. Both No. 4 intake valve pads and lobes.

c. Both No. 2 exhaust valve pads and lobes.

d. Both No. 4 exhaust valve pads and lobes.

10. Insert a feeler gauge between the valve pad and the camshaft lobe (**Figure 58**). Select the feeler gauge passing between the lobe and pad with a slight drag (**Figure 59**). Record each camshaft-to-valve pad clearance.

11. Rotate the flywheel exactly one revolution clockwise to place the engine in the No. 1 cylinder TDC position.

12. Compare the clearance with the specifications provided in **Table 3**. Adjust the valves as follows:

a. Remove the camshaft and pulleys as described in Chapter Eight.

b. Using the notch (**Figure 60**) for access, carefully pry the valve pad from its location.

c. Measure the thickness of the valve pad near the outer edge.

d. Select a pad of the thickness required to correct the clearance. Pads are available in varying thickness from a Mercury or Mariner dealership. Install a thicker pad to decrease or thinner pad to increase the valve clearance.

e. Perform these steps valve as necessary.

f. Install the camshafts and pulleys (Chapter Eight).

13. Install the flywheel and rocker arm covers (Chapter Eight).

14. Install the spark plug and leads. Clean the terminals and connect the cables to the battery.

CABLES AND LINKAGE

This section provided adjustment instructions for shift/throttle cables and linkages. Adjustment instructions for the reverse hold down mechanism, trim tab, neutral start mechanism and trim position sender are also included.

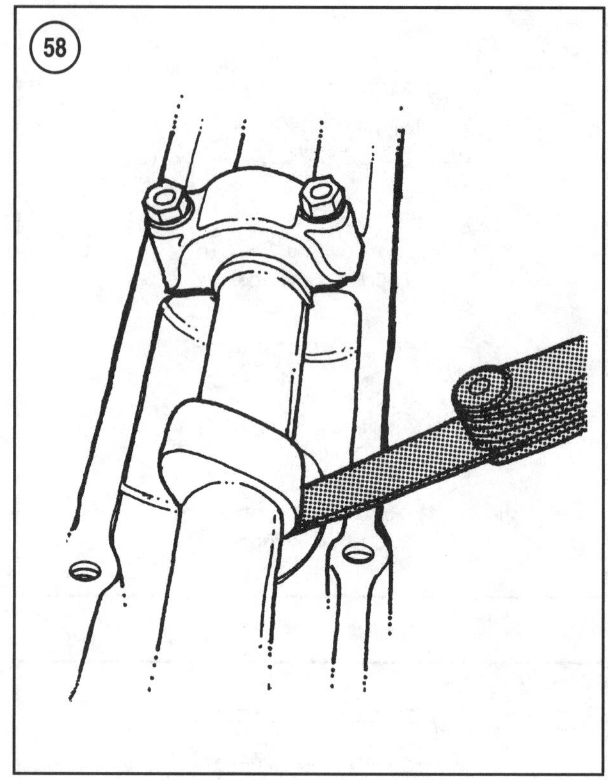

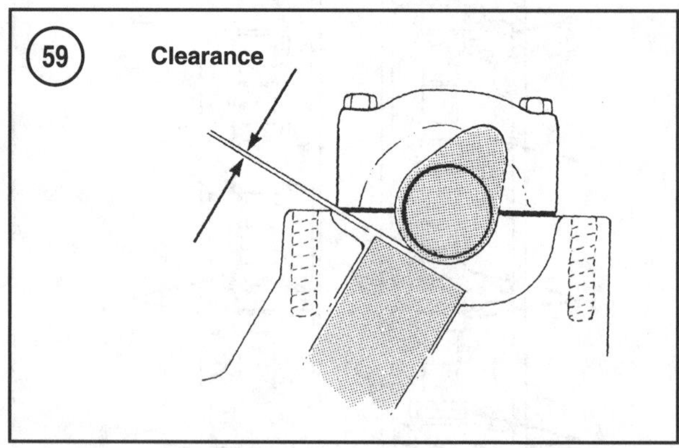

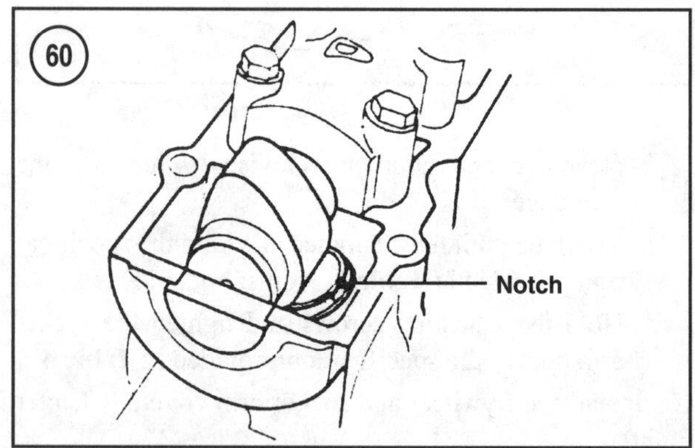

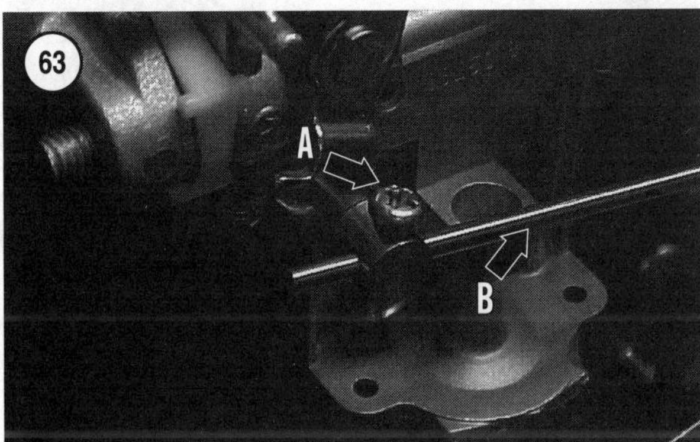

Throttle Cables and Linkage

This section provides general adjustment instructions for the throttle cables and linkages. Instructions for both tiller and remote control are included. Refer to the instructions for the type of control system used.

Throttle Cable Adjustment (Tiller Control Models)

5

1. Disconnect both cables from the battery if so equipped.
2. Turn the tiller throttle grip to the idle position.
3. Locate the cable attaching points at the throttle wheel, throttle cam or throttle lever.
   a. On 4-6 hp models, the cables attach to the throttle wheel (**Figure 61**) on the top side of the cylinder block.
   b. On 9.9 and 15 hp models the cables attach to the throttle wheel on the lower starboard side of the power head.
   c. On 25 hp models, the cables attach to the throttle lever on the lower starboard side of the power head.
   d. On 30 and 40 hp models, the cables attach to a bracket and throttle cam on the rear starboard side of the power head.
   e. On 50 hp models, the cables attach to a bracket and throttle lever on the lower starboard rear side of the power head.
4. Loosen all cable adjusting and locking nuts. Adjust the cables as follows:
   a. On 4-6 hp models, adjust the nuts until the slack is just removed and the throttle lever is just touching the stop (**Figure 62**).
   b. On 9.9 and 15 hp models. Loosen the screw (A, **Figure 63**) then gently push the throttle linkage (B, **Figure 63**) toward the front of the engine until the looped end contact the boss on the throttle wheel. Adjust the nuts (**Figure 61**) until the slack in the cable is just removed. Hold the linkage in position then tighten the screw (A, **Figure 63**).
   c. On 25 hp models, adjust the nuts on the throttle cables until the mark or notch on the throttle cam aligns with the center of the throttle roller (**Figure 64**).
   d. On 30 and 40 hp models, adjust the cables until all slack is just removed and a 1/16 in. (1/6 mm) gap is present between the throttle lever and the oval boss behind the lever.
   e. On 50 hp models, gently push the carburetor throttle linkage toward the idle position. Adjust the cables until all slack is just removed and a 1/8 in. (3.2 mm) gap is present between the throttle lever and the oval boss behind the lever.

5. Securely tighten all cable attaching and locking nuts.

6. Turn the throttle grip to full throttle and back to idle several times. While moving the throttle check for free throttle movement, full throttle range and a consistent return to idle. Perform additional adjustments if binding, inconsistent idle return or lack of full range is detected.

7. Clean the terminals and connect the cables to the battery if so equipped.

8. Correct any throttle control malfunctions before returning the engine to service.

Throttle Cable Adjustment (Remote Control Models)

1. Disconnect both cables from the battery if so equipped. Position the throttle in the idle position.

2. Adjust the throttle cable as follows:
   a. On 9.9 and 15 hp models, loosen the screw (A, **Figure 63**) until the throttle linkage (B) slides freely within the adjustment boss. Attach the throttle cable to the throttle lever. Ensure the throttle linkage extends a minimum of 0.28 in. (7 mm) beyond the adjusting boss, then securely tighten the screw (A, **Figure 63**).
   b. On 25 hp models, rotate the cable barrel until the mark or notch on the throttle cam aligns with the center of the throttle roller (**Figure 64**).
   c. On 30 and 40 hp models, rotate the cable barrel until a 1/16 in. (1.2 mm) gap is present between the throttle cam and the oval-shaped boss.
   d. On 50 hp models, gently push the carburetor throttle linkage toward the idle position. Adjust the cable barrel until a 1/8 in. (3.2 mm) gap is present between the throttle and the oval-shaped boss behind the lever.

3. On 75 and 90 hp models, rotate the throttle cable until the tip on the throttle cam aligns with the throttle shaft (A, **Figure 65**). Ensure the roller aligns with the cam opening as indicated in B, **Figure 65**.

4. Attach the cable barrel and cable end to the engine. Ensure all cable retainers are securely fastened.

5. Advance the remote control to full throttle and back to idle several times. While moving the throttle, check for free throttle movement, full throttle range and a consistent return to idle. Perform additional adjustments if binding, inconsistent idle return or lack of full range is detected.

6. Clean the terminals and connect the cables to the battery if so equipped.

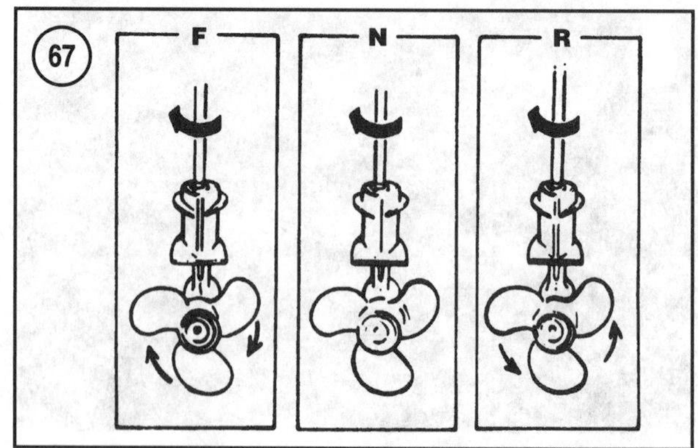

Shift Adjustment (Tiller Control Models)

1. Place the shift selector lever in the NEUTRAL position.

2. Disconnect both cables from the battery if so equipped.

3. On 4-6 hp models, remove the rubber grommet from the starboard side of the gearcase to access the shift shaft clamp bolt (**Figure 66**). Loosen the bolt and move the lower shift shaft up or down until the propeller spins freely in both directions (**Figure 67**). Ensure the shift se-

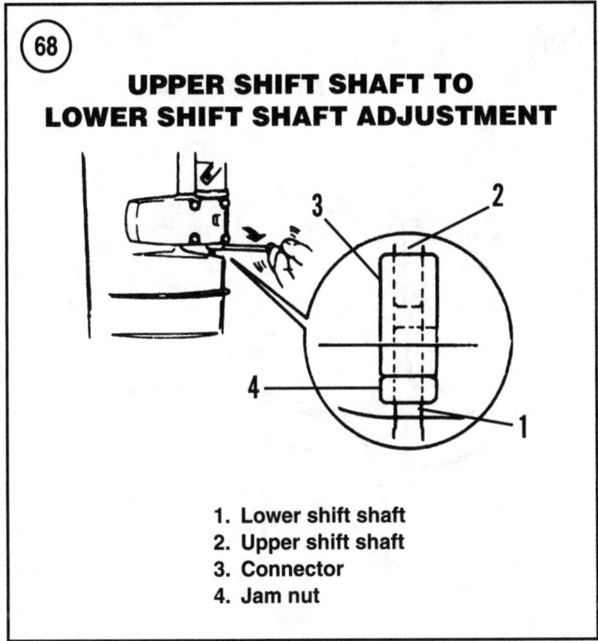

1. Lower shift shaft
2. Upper shift shaft
3. Connector
4. Jam nut

lector aligns with the neutral mark. Without moving either shift shaft up or down securely tighten the shift shaft clamp bolt. Install the rubber grommet into the opening.

4. On 9.9-25 hp models and 30-50 hp models with the standard gearcase, locate the shift shaft connector and jam nut (**Figure 68**). Loosen the jam nut then unthread the connector from both shift shafts. Move the lower shift shaft up or down until the propeller spins freely in both directions (**Figure 67**). Without moving either shift shaft up or down thread the connector onto the lower shift shaft. Hold the connector with a wrench and securely tighten the jam nut.

NOTE
If improper shift operation is evident on 30-50 hp models equipped with the optional gearcase, the shift shafts may be misaligned or damaged. Remove the gearcase (Chapter Nine) and check for proper alignment of the upper and lower shift shafts.

5. Check shift operation as follows:
   a. The propeller must turn freely in both directions when the gearcase is in NEUTRAL.
   b. Shift into FORWARD gear. The propeller must not turn counterclockwise.
   c. Shift into REVERSE gear. The propeller must not turn clockwise.
6. If the shift operation is not as specified, readjust the linkage as required.

Shift Adjustment (Remote Control Models)

1. Disconnect both cables from the battery. Remove the spark plugs then connect the spark plug leads to a suitable engine ground. Place the remote control in the NEUTRAL position.
2. Disconnect the shift cable from the engine.
3. Push the shift linkage lightly toward the reverse gear direction. Do not push hard enough to engage reverse. Use just enough pressure to take all slack from the linkage. Keep the linkage in this position until the cable is attached.
4. Lightly push the end of the cable toward the barrel to remove all slack from the cable. Rotate the barrel until the cable attaches with the linkage positioned as described in Step 3. This provides a slight pre-load towards reverse gear and reduces the chance of unintentional shifting into forward gear.
5. Attach the shift cable to the shift linkage and barrel retainer. Secure all fasteners.
6. Check for proper adjustment as follows:
   a. Place the remote control lever in the forward gear position as while rotating the propeller counterclockwise. Correct adjustment results in no counterclockwise rotation as forward is selected.
   b. Have an assistant place the remote control lever in the neutral gear position. Correct adjustment results in free propeller rotation in either direction as neutral gear is selected.
   c. Have an assistant place the remote control lever in the reverse gear position while rotating the propeller in the clockwise direction. Correct adjustment results in no clockwise rotation as reverse gear is selected.
7. Readjust the shift linkage if incorrect clutch engagement or disengagement is noted
8. Install the spark plug(s) and lead(s). Clean the terminals then connect the cables to the battery, if so equipped.
9. Check for correct and predictable shift selection when the engine is started. Correct faulty adjustments before operating the engine.

Reverse Hold Down Mechanism Adjustment

On 4-6 hp models, an extension on the shift shaft makes direct contact with the reverse lock hooks. Failure of the hook to engage the tilt pin when shifted into reverse or release when shift into forward indicates bent, damaged or excessively worn components.

On all other models, adjust the mechanism as follows:

1. Disconnect both cables from the battery if so equipped.

5

2. Shift the engine into REVERSE gear. Loosen the bolt and nut on the reverse lock adjusting clamp. Move the adjusting clamp toward the mechanism until the reverse lock hooks fully engage the tilt pin. Securely tighten the bolt and nut.
3. Observe the reverse lock hooks and tilt pin as while shifting the engine into NEUTRAL. The hooks must disengage the tilt pin. Sufficient clearance must exist between the hooks and pin to prevents unintentional engagement. Readjust the clamp to achieve the clearance.
4. Clean the terminals and connect the cables to the battery (if so equipped).
5. Check for correct reverse hold down operation using very low throttle settings. Readjust the mechanism if required.

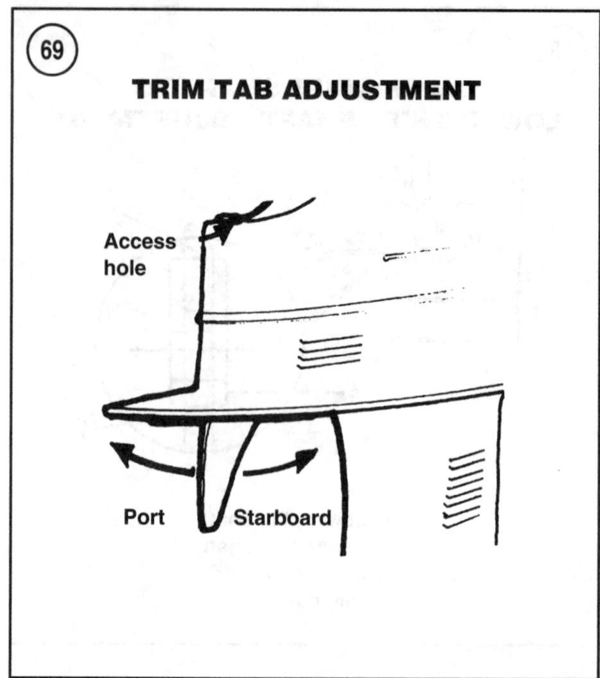

Trim Tab Adjustment

Water test the boat with an average load onboard. When running at planning speed, note if the boat tends to steer in one direction or the other. If so, the steering effort can be neutralized by adjusting the trim tab.
1. Loosen the trim tab retaining bolt. On some models the bolt in located just forward of the trim tab fin.
2. If the engine steers or pulls in the port direction, pivot the rear trailing edge of the trim tab slightly toward the port side (**Figure 69**) . If the engine steers or pulls in the starboard direction, pivot the rear trailing edge of the trim tab slightly toward the starboard side (**Figure 69**).
3. Securely tighten the trim tab bolt.
4. Additional adjustment may be required to further reduce steering pull.

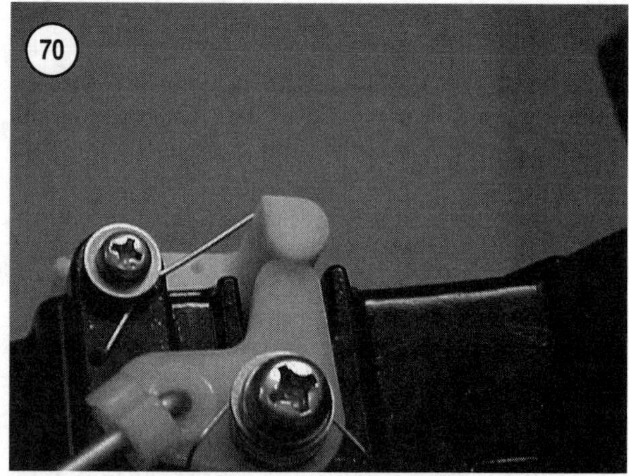

Neutral Start Mechanism Adjustment (4-6 hp Models)

1. Remove the spark plug then connect the spark plug leads to a suitable engine ground. Shift the engine into NEUTRAL.
2. The lever should align with the cam as indicated (**Figure 70**). Improperly installed, damaged or worn linkage is indicated if incorrect alignment is noted.
3. Shift the engine into FORWARD gear then attempt to pull the manual starter. Correct operation prevents starter rotation in forward gear.
4. Shift the engine into REVERSE gear then attempt to pull the manual starter. Correct operation prevents starter rotation in reverse gear.
5. Disassemble, inspect and reassemble the mechanism and linkage if incorrect operation is noted. Refer to Chapter Ten.
6. Check for proper neutral start operation and correct any faults before operating the engine.
7. Install the spark plug and lead.

Neutral Start Mechanism Adjustment (9.9 hp [Serial No. OH000057-Prior] and 15 hp Models)

1. Remove the spark plugs then connect the spark plug leads to a suitable engine ground. Shift the engine into NEUTRAL.
2. Loosen the jam nut (**Figure 71**).

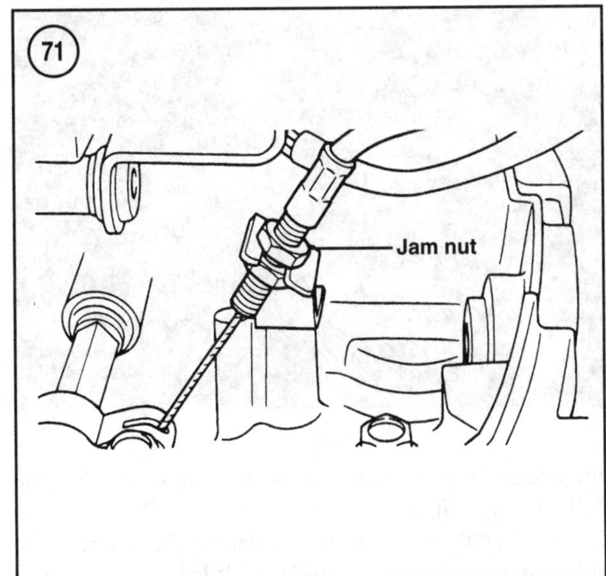

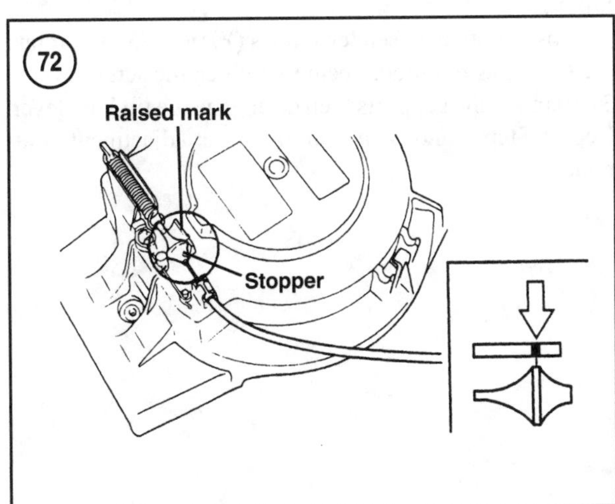

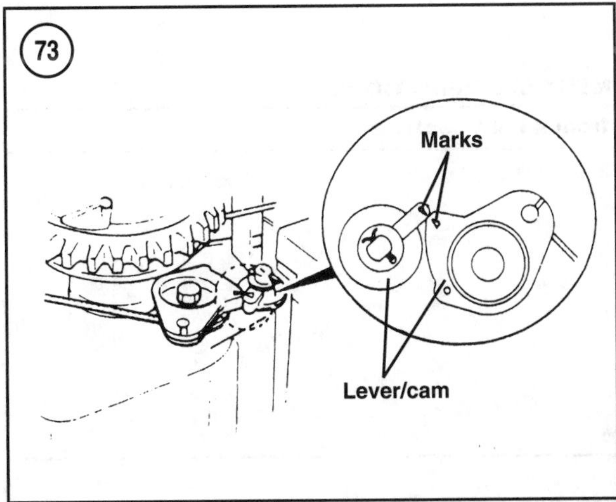

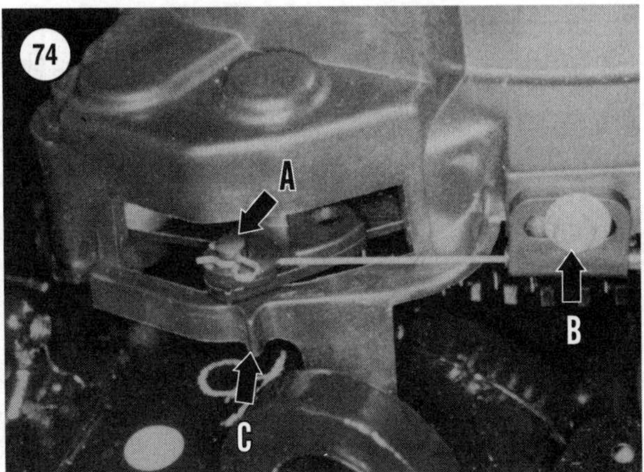

3. Turn the lower adjusting nut until the stopper aligns with the raised mark on the starter housing as indicated in **Figure 72**.

4. Securely tighten the jam nut.

5. After adjustment, the starter must not operate while in FORWARD or REVERSE gear. The starter must be able to operate only while in NEUTRAL.

Neutral Start Mechanism (9.9 hp Models [Serial No. OH000058-On])

1. Remove the spark plugs then connect the spark plug leads to a suitable engine ground. Shift the engine into neutral gear. Locate the mechanism on the top and port side of the manual starter.

2. Loosen the jam nut (**Figure 71**).

3. Turn the lower adjusting nut until the marks on the lever and cam align as indicated in **Figure 73**.

4. Securely tighten the jam nut.

5. After adjustment, the starter must not operate while in FORWARD or REVERSE gear. The starter must be able to operate only while in NEUTRAL.

Neutral Start Mechanism (25-40 hp Models)

1. Remove the spark plug then connect the spark plug leads to a suitable engine ground. Shift the engine into neutral gear.

2. Loosen the cable clamp screw (B, **Figure 74**). Move the cable until the cable pivot (A, **Figure 74**) aligns with the raised mark (C, **Figure 74**) on the starter housing.

3. Hold the cable in this position then securely tighten the cable clamp screw (B, **Figure 74**).

4. After adjustment, the starter must not operate while in FORWARD or REVERSE gear. The starter must be able to operate only while in NEUTRAL.
5. Install the spark plugs and leads. Check for correct operation before putting the engine into service.

NOTE
Gauge resistance, battery voltage, wire length and sender resistance may prevent the gauge from reaching both the fully up and down readings. Synchronize the sender to the fully down position only.

Trim Position Sender Adjustment

NOTE
Gauge resistance, battery voltage, wire length and sender resistance may prevent the gauge from reaching both the fully up and down readings. Synchronize the sender to the fully down position only.

A trim position sender is used on 75 and 90 hp models. Adjust the sender as follows:
1. Observe the trim gauge while trimming the engine to the fully down position. The gauge should indicate that the engine is fully down just as the engine reaches the fully down position.

2. To adjust the trim position sender, tilt the engine to the fully up/out position. Engage the tilt lock lever and use blocks or an overhead cable to prevent the engine from falling.

Loosen both trim sender screws (**Figure 75**) and rotate the sender as required. Securely tighten the screws.
3. Remove the supports then disengage the tilt lock lever. Repeat Step 1 and Step 2 until correct adjustment is attained.

Table 1 PILOT SCREW ADJUSTMENT SPECIFICATIONS

Model	Turns out from a light seat
4-6 hp	2-1/2 to 3-1/2
9.9 hp	
Serial No. OH000057-prior*	–
Serial No. OH000058-on	2 to 3
15 hp*	–
25-40 hp*	–
50 hp	
1995-1997	2-1/2
1998-on*	–
75 hp	2 to 3
90 hp	1-1/2 to 2-1/2
*These models are not equipped with adjustable pilot screws.	

Table 2 IDLE SPEED SPECIFICATIONS

Model	Idle speed (rpm)
4-6 hp	
Neutral	1250-1350
Forward gear	1050-1150
9.9 and 15 hp	
Neutral	900-1000
Forward gear	800-900
25 hp	
Neutral	800-850
Forward gear	750-800
30 and 40 hp	
Neutral	875-925
Forward gear	775-825
50 hp	
Neutral	800-850
Forward gear	700-750
75 and 90 hp	
Neutral	825-875
Forward gear	775-800

Table 3 VALVE ADJUSTMENT SPECIFICATIONS*

Model	Clearance
4-6 hp	
Intake valve	0.002-0.005 in. (0.05-0.12 mm)
Exhaust valve	0.004-0.007 in. (0.10-0.17 mm)
9.9 hp	
Serial No. OH000057-prior	
Intake valve	0.006-0.010 in. (0.15-0.25 mm)
Exhaust valve	0.008-0.012 in. (0.20-0.30 mm)
Serial No. OH000058-on	
Intake valve	0.006-0.008 in. (0.15-0.20 mm)
Exhaust valve	0.008-0.010 in. (0.20-0.25 mm)
15 hp	
Intake valve	0.006-0.010 in. (0.15-0.25 mm)
Exhaust valve	0.008-0.012 in. (0.20-0.30 mm)
25-50 hp	
Intake valve	0.006-0.010 in. (0.15-0.25 mm)
Exhaust valve	0.010-0.014 in. (0.25-0.35 mm)
75 and 90 hp	
Intake valve	0.007-0.009 in. (0.17-0.23 mm)
Exhaust valve	0.012-0.014 in. (0.31-0.37 mm)

* Specification with the engine at 68° F (20° C).

Table 4 TIGHTENING TORQUE

Fastener location	ft-lb.	in-lb.	N·m
Rocker arm nut			
4-6 hp	7.5	90	10
9.9 hp			
Serial No. OH000057-prior	10	120	14
Serial No. OH000058-on	–	70	8
15 hp	10	120	14
25-50 hp	10	120	14

Chapter Six

Fuel System

This chapter covers removal, repair and installation of all fuel system components. Topics covered in this chapter include:

1. Servicing the fuel system.
2. Fuel tank.
3. Fuel hoses and connectors.
4. Fuel filters.
5. Primer bulb.
6. Fuel pump.
7. Silencer cover and carburetors.
8. Intake manifold.
9. Dashpot and accelerator pump.
10. Choke solenoid.
11. Electrothermal valve.

Tightening torque and other fuel system specifications are provided in **Tables 1-4**. **Tables 1-4** are located at the end of this chapter.

Refer to *Servicing The Fuel System* in this chapter prior to removal and disassembly of any fuel system component. This section provides information to ensure a safe, reliable and effective repair.

Refer to the instructions for the selected component or system.

WARNING

Use caution when working with the fuel system. Never smoke around fuel of fuel vapors. Make sure no flame or source of ignition is present in the work area. Flame or sparks can ignite fuel or vapor resulting in a fire or explosion.

Servicing the Fuel System

Always use gloves and eye protection when working with the fuel system. Take all necessary precautions against fire or explosion. Always disconnect the battery cables *before* servicing any outboard.

Pay close attention when removing and installing components especially carburetors to avoid installing them in the wrong location during assembly.

Capture fuel from disconnected hoses or fittings using a small container or clean shop towel. Try to use a clear container as it allows a visual inspection of the fuel. Clean the fuel tank and all other fuel delivery components if water or other contamination is noted in the fuel.

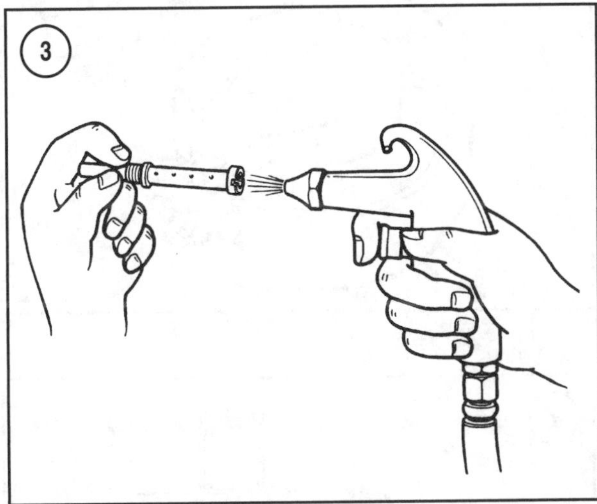

Drain all fuel from the carburetor using the float bowl drain (**Figure 1**). Refer to *Carburetors* in this chapter for diagrams that help locate the bowl drain screw.

Inspect all hoses for leakage or deterioration when servicing the fuel system. Damaged fuel hoses pose a safety hazard. In addition, pieces of deteriorated or damaged hoses can break free and block fuel passages in the system. Refer to *Fuel Hoses* in this chapter.

On multiple-carburetor (**Figure 2**) engines, disassemble and assembler *one* carburetor at a time. Some models have fuel and air jet sizes calibrated to the cylinder in which they supply fuel. Refer to *Carburetor* in this chapter for additional instructions.

Gaskets, Seals and O-rings

To avoid potential fuel or air leakage, replace all seals and O rings anytime a fuel system component is removed from the engine. To avoid excessive down time and the potential for contamination, have the required gasket or repair kit on hand prior to removal and disassembly of the component(s).

To ensure a safe and reliable repair use only factory recommended replacement parts. Some commonly available seals or O-rings are not suitable for contact with fuel.

Cleaning Carburetors and Other Components

The most important step in carburetor or fuel pump repair is the cleaning process. Use only solvents suitable for use on carburetors. Some cleaning agents can damage fuel system components. Spray type carburetor cleaners are available at most auto parts stores. They effectively remove most stubborn deposits. Avoid using any solvents not suitable for aluminum.

Remove all plastics or rubber components from the fuel pump, carburetor or filter assembly before cleaning them with solvent. Gently scrape away gasket material with a scraper. Never scrape away any metal from the component. Use a stiff part cleaning brush and solvent to remove deposits from the carburetor bowl. Never use a wire brush as thee sealing surfaces can quickly become damaged. Blow out all passages and orifices with compressed air (**Figure 3**). A piece of straw from a broom works well to clean small passages. Never use stiff wire for this purpose as the wire may enlarge the size of the passage possibly altering the carburetor calibration. Allow components to soak in the solvent for several hours if the deposits are particularly difficult to remove.

Use great care and patience when removing fuel jets and other threaded or pressed in components. Clean the passage without removing the jet if it cannot be removed without causing damage. Carburetor fuel jets are easily damaged.

One small particle in the carburetor can compromise the cleaning process. Continue to clean until *all* deposits and debris are removed.

Inspection

Place all components on a clean surface as they are removed from the carburetor and cleaned. Arrange these components in a manner consistent with the provided illustrations. This saves time and help ensure the parts are installed in the correct location.

Inspect the inlet needle for wear or deterioration (**Figure 4**). Replace the inlet needle unless its tip is perfectly cone shaped.

Inspect the inlet needle seat for grooved or damaged surfaces. All 4-50 hp models utilize a press-fit needle seat. On these models the carburetor must be replaced if the seat is damaged. Carburetor flooding is likely if a worn or faulty inlet needle or seat is used.

Inspect the tip of the pilot screw on models so equipped for wear or damage (**Figure 5**). Damage to the tip usually occurs from improper seating of the screw during adjustment. In many instances the seat for the tip is also damaged. Damage to the screw or seat will cause rough idle or improper off idle engine operation. Replace the screw or carburetor when worn or faulty components are noted.

Inspect the float (**Figure 6**, typical) for wear or damage. Some floats are made of a translucent material allowing the detection of fuel within the float.

Push a thumbnail gently against the material on non-translucent floats. A leaking or saturated float is indicated if fuel appears at the thumbnail contact area. Replace the float if visibly damaged, leaking or saturated. Check the float for free movement while moving on the float pin. Replace the float if it does not move freely.

Adjust the float level settings (**Figure 7**) prior to assembling the carburetor. Use an accurate ruler or a caliper with depth reading capability. Set the float *exactly* as specified to help ensure proper carburetor operation. Specific instructions are provided in the carburetor disassembly and assembly instructions. Float level specifications are provided in **Table 1**.

Move the throttle lever (**Figure 8**) from closed to wide-open throttle. Remove the throttle plate and repeat this step if binding or rough operation is noted. Continued binding indicates a bent throttle shaft. If free movement is noted with the plate removed a misaligned or damaged throttle plate is indicated. Apply a suitable thread locking compound and stake all throttle plate retaining screws to prevent loosening.

Fuel Jets

Fuel jets (**Figure 9**) meter the fuel flow through various passages in the carburetor. They along with other components allow the carburetor to deliver the precise amount of

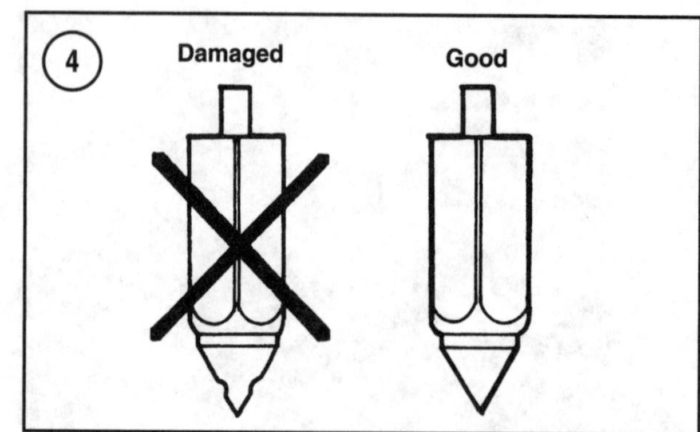

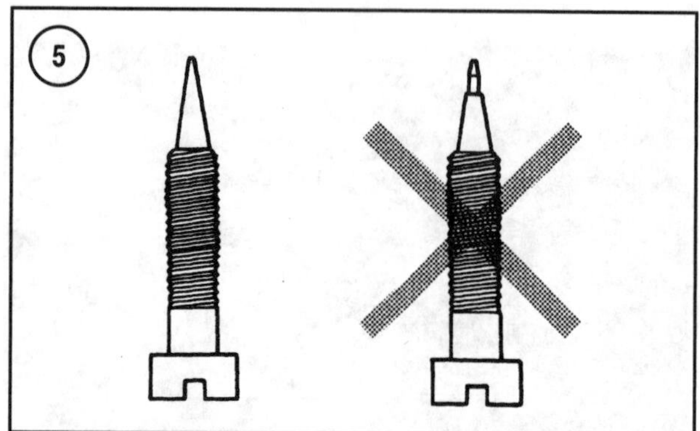

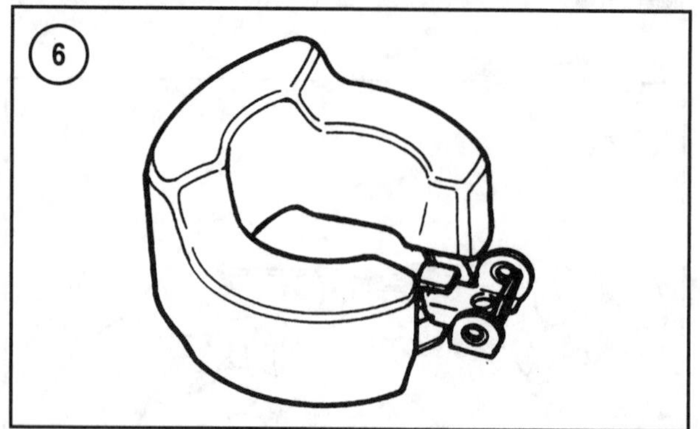

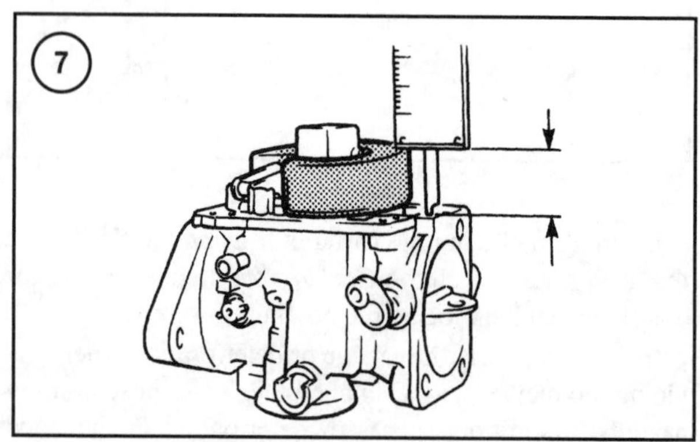

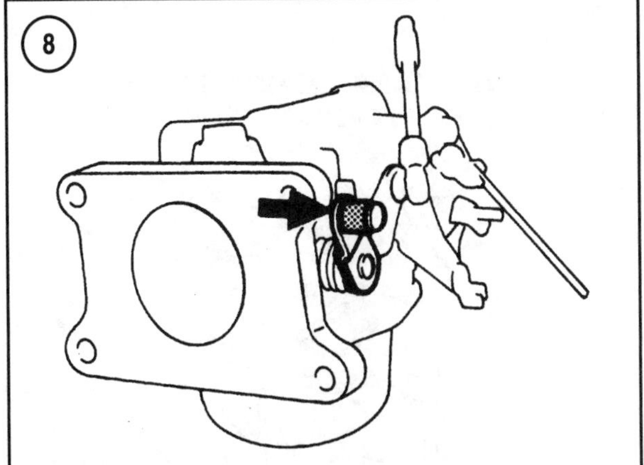

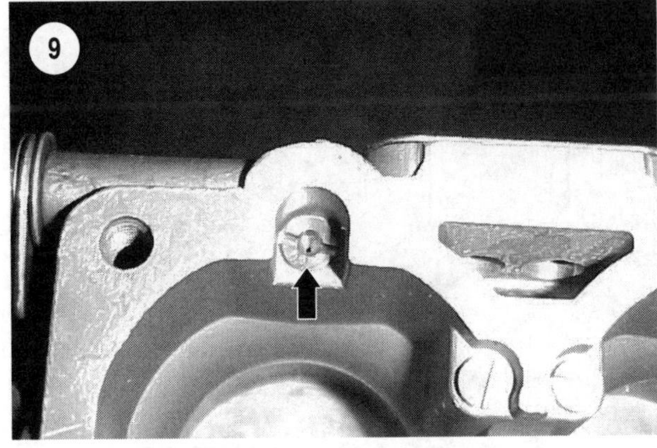

fuel needed for the engine. Fuel jet sizes vary by model and carburetor location on the engine. Fuel jets normally have a number stamped on the side or end. Note the fuel jet number and location in the carburetor prior to removal. Reinstall the fuel jets and other carburetor components to the correct location.

Purchase replacement jets at a Mercury or Mariner dealership or a carburetor specialty shop. For proper engine operation, replacement jets must have the same size and shape of opening as the original fuel jets. Improper engine operation, increased exhaust emissions or potentially serious power head damage can result from using incorrect fuel jets.

Using the engine at higher elevation (5000 ft. [1524 m]) may require alternate fuel jets to achieve optimal engine operation. If necessary, contact a Mercury or Mariner dealership in the area with a similar elevation for recommended jet changes.

Never install a damaged jet in the carburetor. The fuel or air flow characteristics may be altered. Altering the fuel and air flow can cause an engine malfunction or potentially serious power head damage.

Fuel Tank

Two types of fuel tanks are used with Mercury and Mariner four stroke outboards. They include portable fuel tanks (**Figure 10**) and built-in fuel tanks.

Most models use the original portable fuel tank that came with the engine. They have the Quicksilver name molded into the body of the fuel tank (some models use a decal). Purchase any required parts for these fuel tanks from a local Mercury or Mariner dealership.

Be aware that portable fuel tanks are manufactured by several different companies. The engine may be equipped with any one of them. The types of components used, cleaning and repair instructions are similar for all brands of fuel tank. Refer to reputable marine repair shop or marine dealership if parts are needed for other brands of fuel tanks.

Built-in fuel tanks usually located slightly forward of the boat transom. On some boats the fuel tank is mounted further forward or under the deck or floor. Fortunately, tank access panels are installed in most boats. These panels allow access to fuel line fittings and the fuel level sender assembly. Removal of upholstery or major boat structures may be required if the tank requires removal. Proper long term storage and fuel system inspection is more important with built in fuel tanks. Long term storage and fuel system inspection are provided in Chapter Four.

Portable fuel tank cleaning and inspection

Portable remote fuel tanks may require periodic cleaning and inspection. Inspect the remainder of the fuel system for potential contamination if water is found in the tank. The tank used on the engine may differ in appearance and component usage from the illustration (**Figure 10**).

1. Remove the fuel tank cap and seal (11 and 12, **Figure 10**) from the fuel tank. Carefully pour the fuel from the tank into a suitable container.

2. Remove the screws retaining the connector/adapter (3, **Figure 10**) to the fuel tank. Carefully lift the fuel gauge and float (8 and 15, **Figure 10**) from the tank. Never force the assembly as damage may occur. Rotate or tilt the assembly as required for removal. Remove and discard the gasket (7, **Figure 10**) located between the connector/adapter and fuel tank.

3. Check for free movement of the float arm on the fuel gauge assembly (8, **Figure 10**). Replace the assembly if binding cannot be corrected by bending the float arm into the correct position.

4. Inspect the float (15, **Figure 10**). Replace the float if any physical damage is noted or it appears to be saturated with fuel.
5. Carefully pull the screen and pickup tube (9 and 10, **Figure 10**) from the fitting (6). Clean the tube and screen using a suitable solvent. Dry them with compressed air. Inspect the screen for torn or damaged surfaces. Inspect the pickup tube for cracks or deterioration. Replace the screen or tube if defects are noted.
6. Remove the fitting (6, **Figure 10**) from the connector/adapter (3). Carefully push the window and seal (4-6, **Figure 10**) from the connector/adapter. Clean the fitting and all passages of the connector/adapter using a suitable solvent.
7. Add a small amount of solvent to the fuel tank. Block the gauge/pickup opening with a shop towel. Install the fuel tank cap. Shake the tank to distribute the solvent throughout the tank. Empty the solvent and dry the tank with compressed air.
8. Inspect the internal and external tank surfaces. Repeat Step 7 if debris remains in the tank. Inspect the tank for cracks, damage or softened surfaces. Replace the tank if any defects are noted or a possible point of leakage is suspected.
9. Assembly is the reverse of disassembly:
   a. Clean all debris from the gasket surfaces.
   b. Install a new gasket (7, **Figure 10**) between the connector/adapter and the fuel tank.
   c. Install a new seal (4, **Figure 10**) between the window and the connector/adapter.
   d. Do not bend the fuel gauge rod during installation into the fuel tank.
10. Check for and correct any fuel leakage as soon as it is detected.

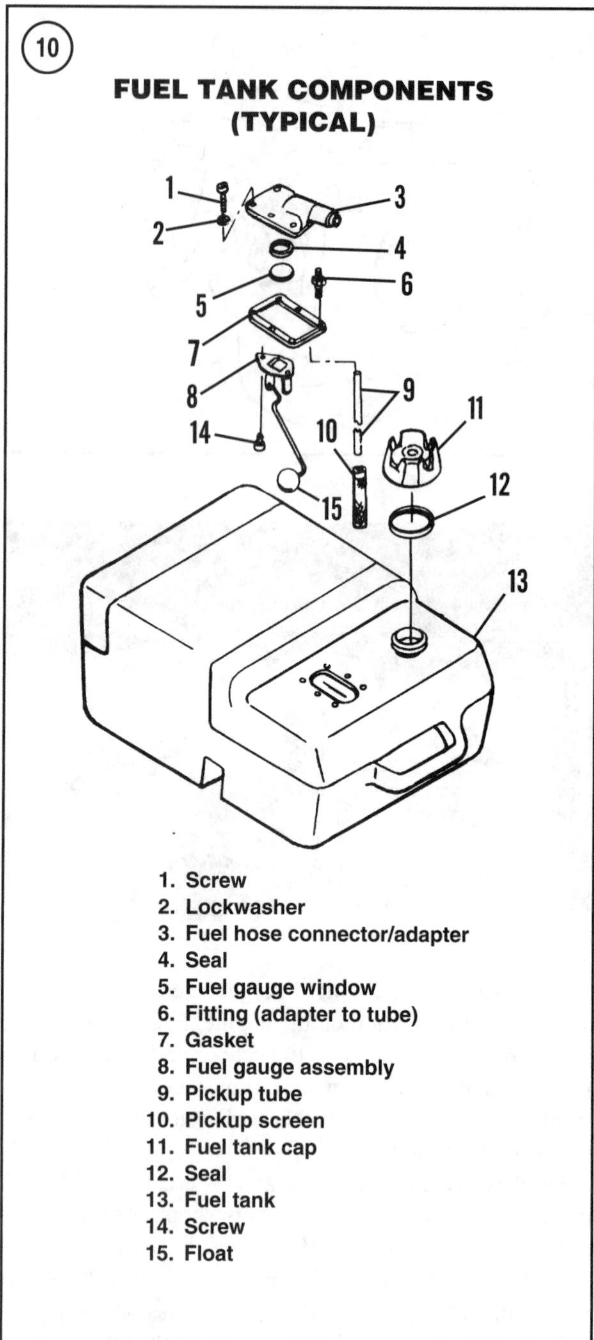

1. Screw
2. Lockwasher
3. Fuel hose connector/adapter
4. Seal
5. Fuel gauge window
6. Fitting (adapter to tube)
7. Gasket
8. Fuel gauge assembly
9. Pickup tube
10. Pickup screen
11. Fuel tank cap
12. Seal
13. Fuel tank
14. Screw
15. Float

Built-In fuel tank cleaning and inspection

The only components that can be serviced without major disassembly of the boat are the fuel pickup, fuel level sender and antisiphon device. These components are available from most marine dealerships and marine supply stores. Removal and inspection instructions vary by the model and brand of fuel tank. Contact the tank manufacturer or boat manufacturer for specific instructions. Correct any fuel leakage before filling the tank or operating the engine.

Fuel Hoses

Refer to **Figures 11-14** for fuel system diagrams.

Use only Mercury or Mariner replacement hoses or hose that meets US Coast Guard requirements for marine applications. Never install a fuel hose smaller in diameter than the original hose.

Inspect all fuel hoses and replace hoses that are sticky, spongy, hard and brittle or have surface cracks. Replace hoses that are split on the ends. Do not cut off the split end and reconnect the hose. The hose will split again and

11

FUEL SYSTEM (4-25 HP)

Carburetor
Fuel pump
Quick connector
Fuel filter

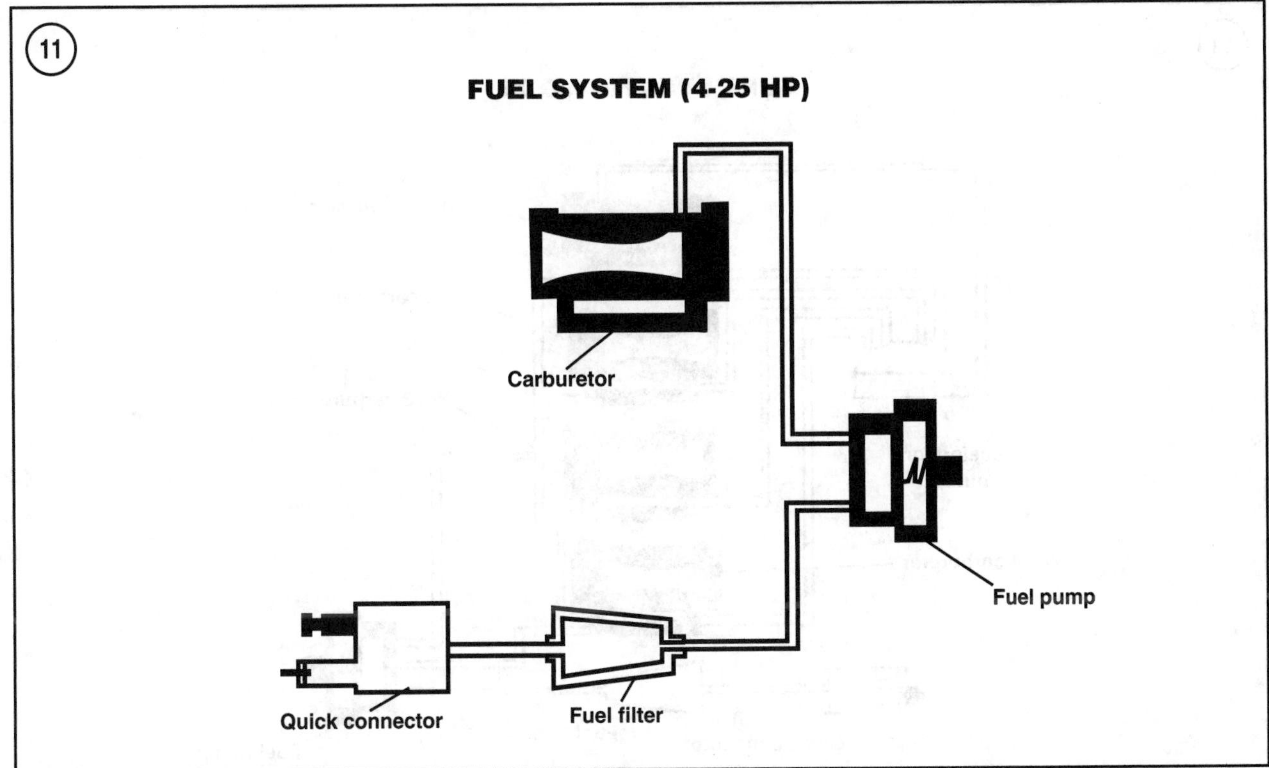

12

FUEL SYSTEM (30 AND 40 HP)

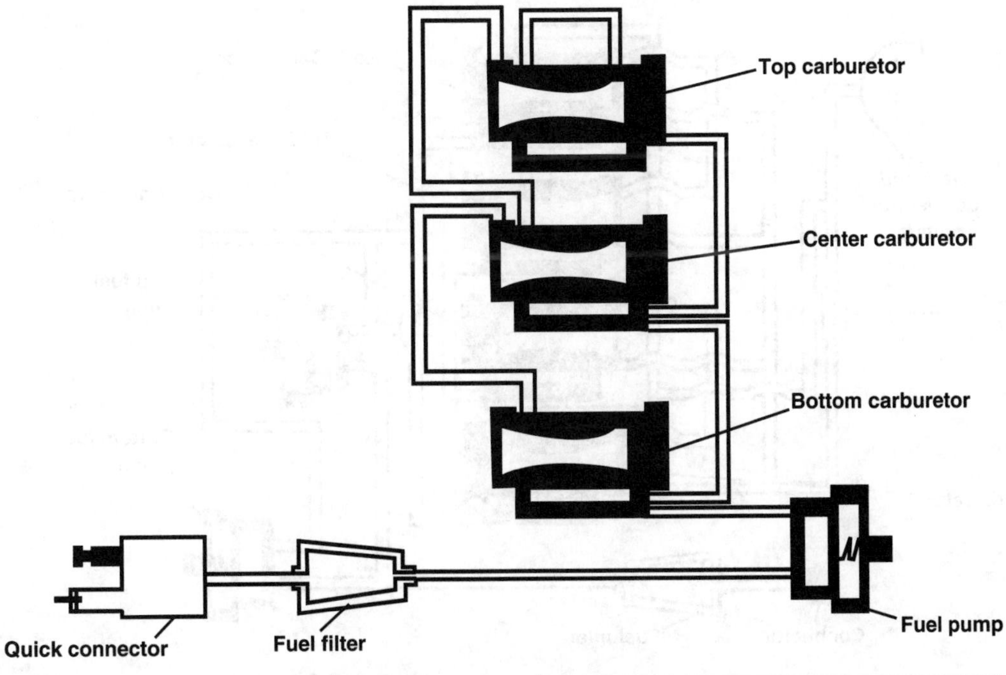

Top carburetor
Center carburetor
Bottom carburetor
Fuel pump
Quick connector
Fuel filter

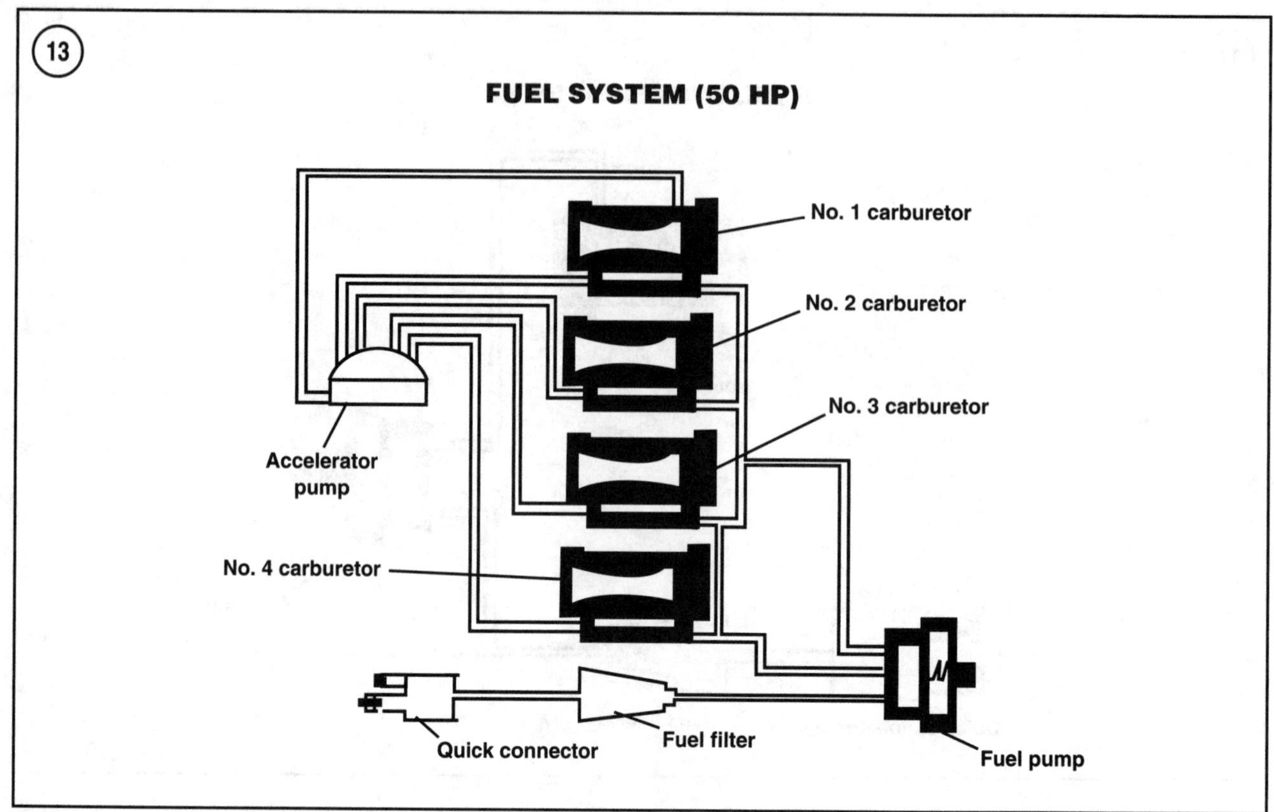
13
FUEL SYSTEM (50 HP)
No. 1 carburetor
No. 2 carburetor
No. 3 carburetor
Accelerator pump
No. 4 carburetor
Quick connector
Fuel filter
Fuel pump

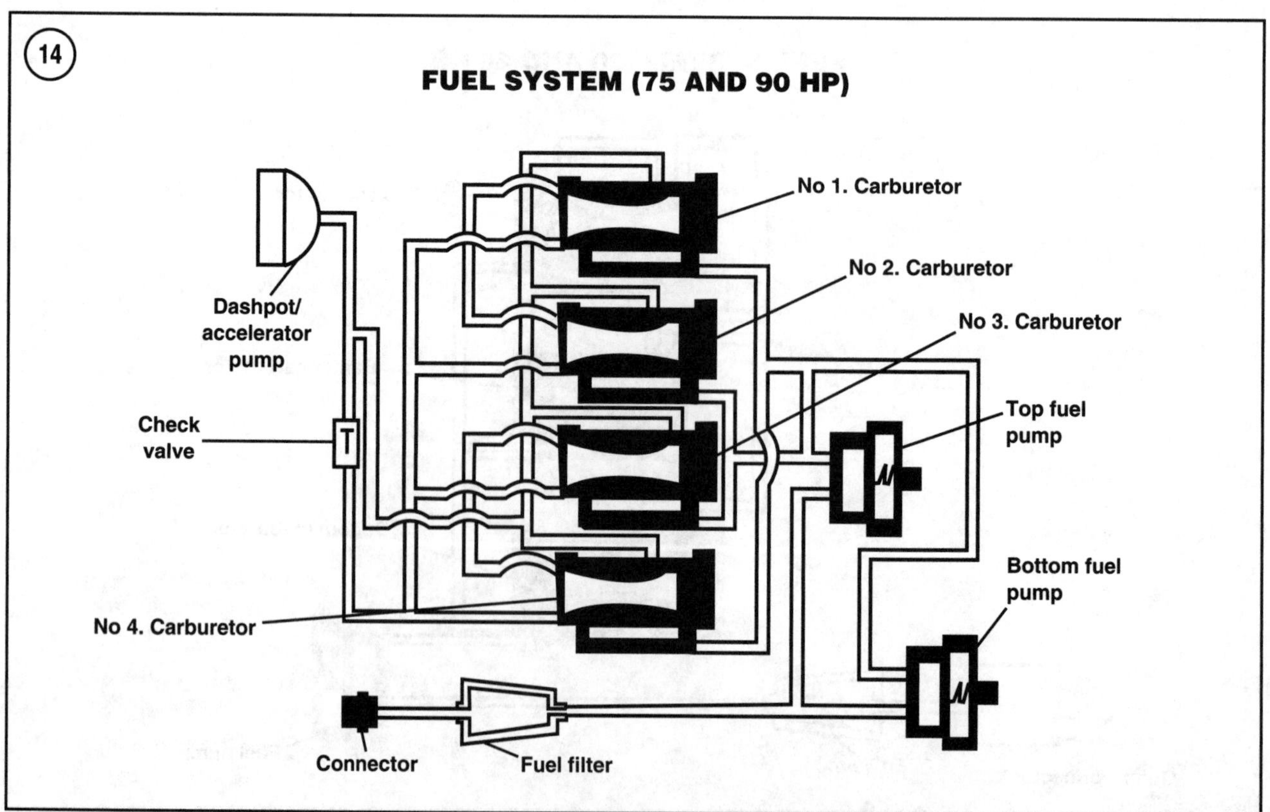
14
FUEL SYSTEM (75 AND 90 HP)
No 1. Carburetor
No 2. Carburetor
No 3. Carburetor
Dashpot/ accelerator pump
Top fuel pump
Check valve
T
Bottom fuel pump
No 4. Carburetor
Connector
Fuel filter

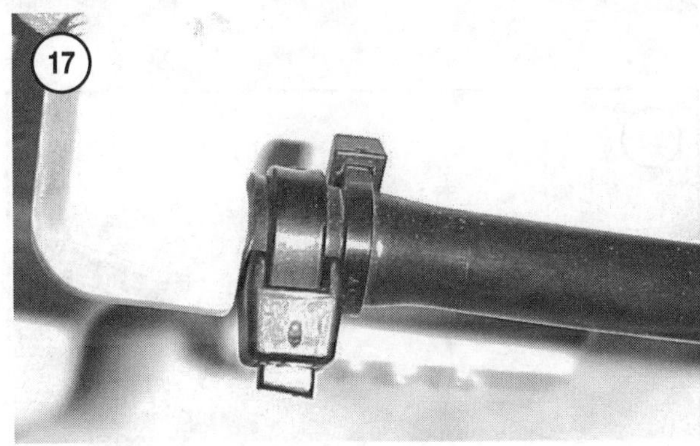

cause a potentially dangerous fuel leak. To avoid hose failure or interference with other components, never install a shorter or longer hose than the original. When one fuel hose on the engine requires replacement others likely have similar defects. Replace all fuel hose on the engine to ensure a reliable repair.

Fuel Hose Connectors

The fuel delivery hose used with a portable fuel tank connects to the engine using a quick connector (**Figure 15**). The clamps used to secure fuel hoses include the spring clamp (**Figure 16**) and plastic tie clamp (**Figure 17**). Always replace clamps with the same type to ensure a leak-free connection. The wrong clamp can cause fuel leakage or physical interference with other components.

When replacing the quick connector on the fuel tank hose end, remove and discard the hose clamp from the connector. Pull the fuel hose from the connector. Slide the hose onto the new connector, install a new hose clamp and tighten it securely.

When replacing the connector at the engine end (**Figure 18**), remove the screw or spring clip retaining the quick connector to the lower engine cover. Pull the connector and its grommet from the lower engine cover. Remove the plastic tie clamp then carefully pull the connector from the fuel hose. Drain the fuel from the hose. Carefully slide the hose over the fitting of the new connector. Install a new clamp over the hose and fitting. Securely tighten the clamp. Place the quick connector and grommet into position on the lower engine cover. Install the screw or clip onto the connector and securely tighten the retaining screw.

Remove the spring clamps (**Figure 16**) by squeezing the ends together pliers while carefully moving the clamp away from the fitting. Replace the clamp if corroded, bent, deformed or if it has lost spring tension.

The plastic tie clamp (**Figure 17**) must be cut to be removed. Some plastic tie clamps are not suitable for fuel system applications and may fail. Use only the Mercury or Mariner parts for hose clamps. After placing the clamp into position, pull the end through the clamp (**Figure 19**) until the hose is securely fastened and will not rotate on the fitting. Avoid pulling the clamp too tight as the clamp may be damaged, then loosen or fail. Cut any excess length of clamp with side cutters or scissors.

WARNING

Fuel leakage can lead to fire or explosion causing injury, death or destruction of property. Always and correct fuel leakage after any repair is made to the fuel system.

6

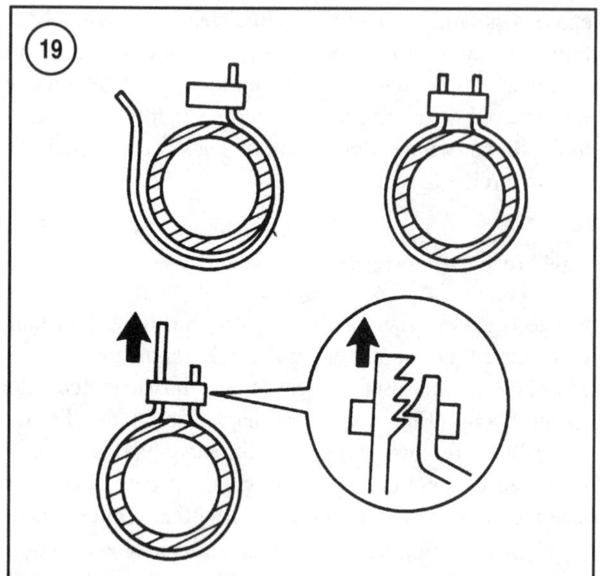

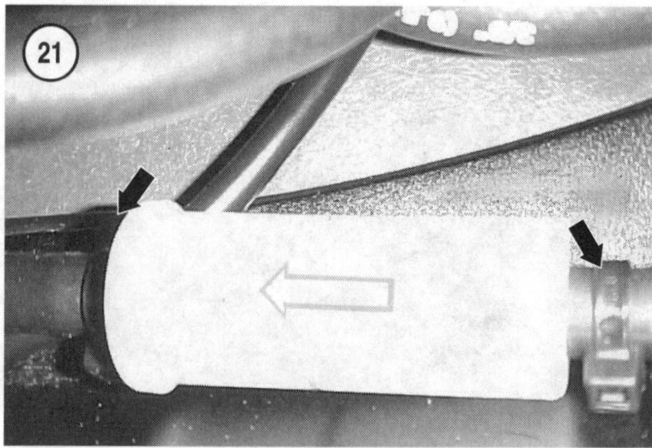

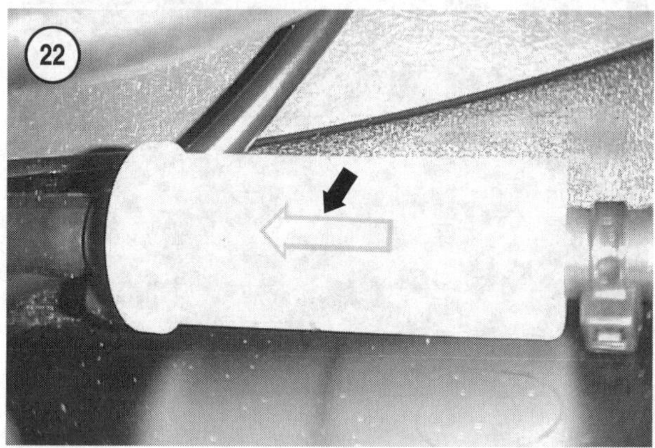

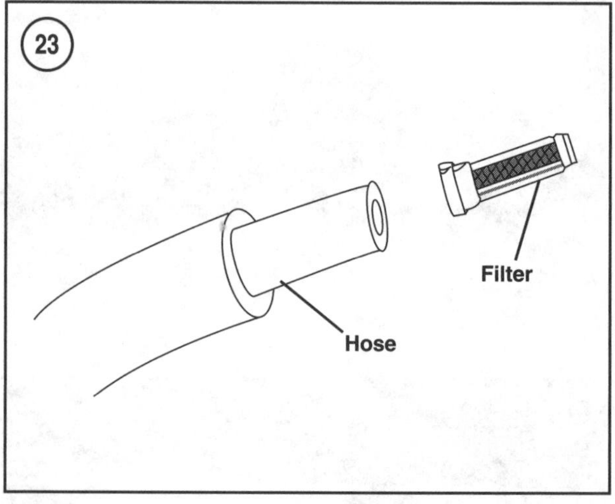

Fuel Filter Replacement

An inline fuel filter (**Figure 20**) is used on all models covered in this manual.

1. Disconnect both cables from the battery if so equipped.
2. Note the location then remove any plastic locking clamps preventing the removal of filter.
3. Place a suitable container or shop towels under the fuel filter to capture spilled fuel.
4. Move spring type hose clamps, if so equipped, away from the fuel hose fittings. Carefully remove the plastic locking clamps, if so equipped, from the hoses at each end of the fuel filter (**Figure 21**).
5. Using a blunt screwdriver, push each hose away from filter body. Drain any residual fuel from the hoses. Clean up any spilled fuel at once.
6. Note the arrow on the replacement filter (**Figure 22**). Carefully slide each fuel hose fully over its fitting. Ensure the arrow on the filter body faces the hose leading to the fuel pump.
7. Carefully slide the spring type hose clamps, if so equipped, over their respective fittings on the filter. Install new plastic clamps, if so equipped, over each hose and filter fitting. Tighten each clamp securely.

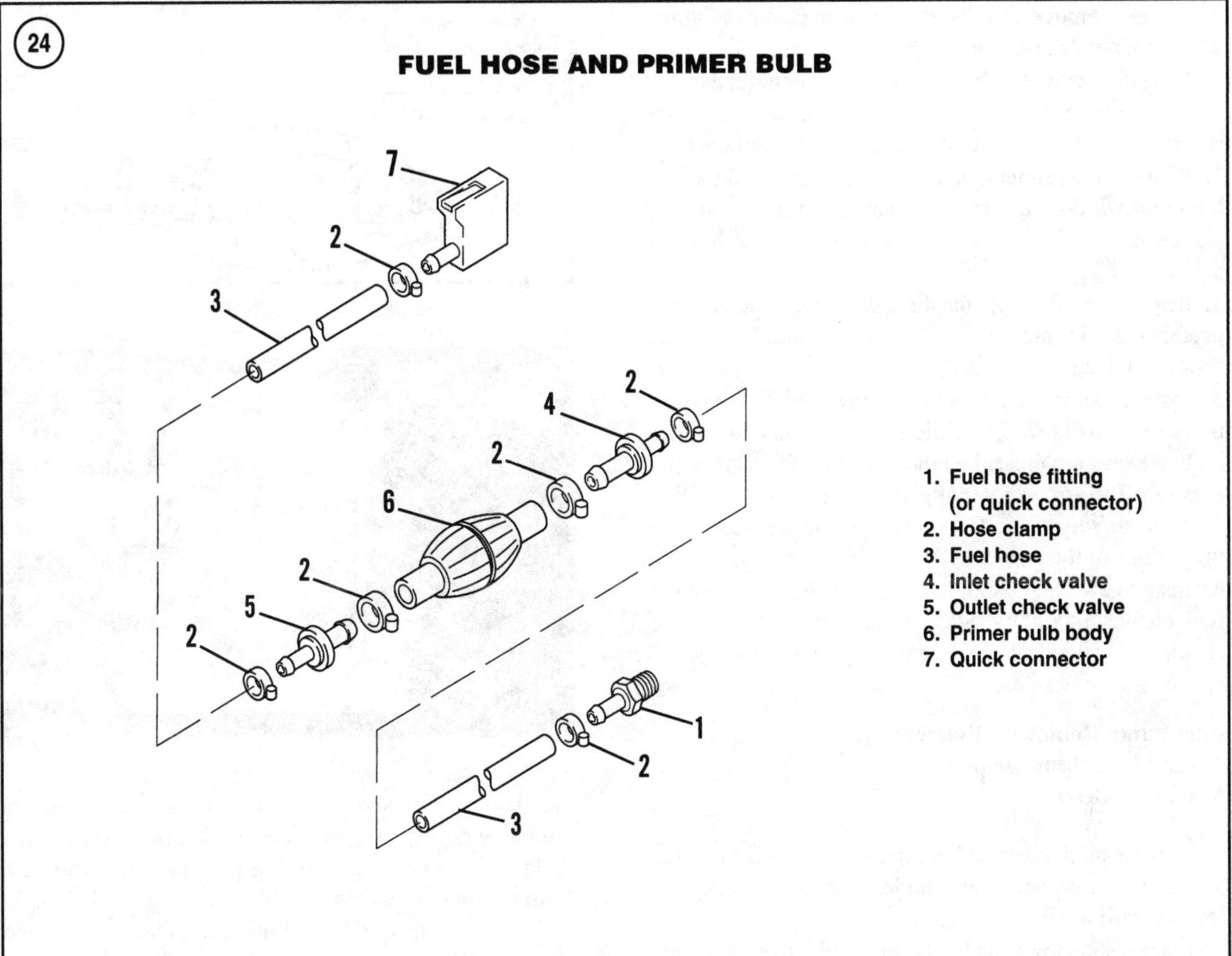

8. Place the filter into its original location within the lower engine cover. Install new plastic locking type clamps to replace those removed in Step 2. Ensure the hoses and filter route in a manner preventing them from contacting any moving components.
9. Observe the fuel filter and other fuel system components while pumping the primer bulb. Correct the cause of fuel leakage if present.
10. Clean the terminals and connect the cables to the battery, if so equipped.

Filter inside fuel hose

The 75 and 90 hp models use filters inside the hoses that connect the fuel pump to each carburetor (**Figure 23**). Push the filter from the carburetor end of the hose using a piece of stiff wire. Clean the hose using a suitable solvent. Carefully slide the filter open end toward the fuel pump into the hose end. Push the filter until it is positioned midway in the length of the hose.

WARNING

Fuel leakage can lead to fire and explosion with injury, death and destruction of property. Check for and correct fuel leaks after any repair to the fuel system.

Primer Bulb Removal and Installation

The primer bulb (**Figure 24**) is located in the fuel hose connecting the fuel tank to the engine. Primer bulb testing instructions are provided in Chapter Three.

1. Disconnect the quick connector from the engine. On 75 and 90 hp models, remove the clamp then slide the fuel tank hose from the coupling in the fuel hose leading into the engine cover. Drain any residual fuel into a suitable

container. Remove and discard the hose clamps (**Figure 24**) at both ends of the primer bulb.

2. Note the arrow (**Figure 25**) on the primer bulb, then remove the primer bulb from the fuel hoses. Drain any fuel remaining in the primer bulb into a suitable container.

3. Squeeze the primer bulb until fully collapsed. Replace the bulb if it does not freely expand when released. Replace the bulb if it is weathered, cracked or is hard to squeeze.

4. Inspect the fuel hoses for wear, damage, weathered appearance or the presence of leakage. Replace both fuel hoses if defects are noted.

5. Installation is the reverse of removal. Note the direction of flow (**Figure 25**) while installing the new primer bulb. Arrows are present on the new bulb for correct orientation. The arrows must align with the direction of fuel flow *toward the engine*. Carefully slide the fuel hoses onto the fittings of the primer bulb.

6. Install new fuel clamps at the primer bulb. Ensure the fuel clamps fit tightly. Squeeze the primer bulb while checking for fuel leakage. Correct any fuel leaks.

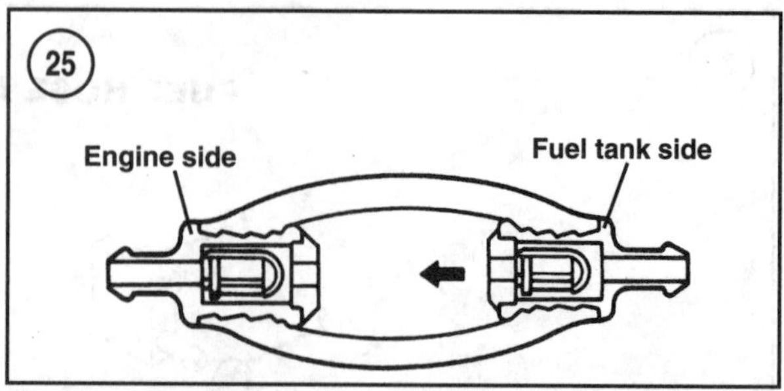

Fuel Pump Removal, Disassembly, Assembly and Installation (4-6 hp models)

On these models the fuel pump (**Figure 26**) is mounted to the starboard side of the cylinder block and directly below the carburetor.

1. Place a shop towel under the fuel pump to capture any spilled fuel. Mark each hose and the fuel pump to ensure correct installation.

2. Move each hose clamp away from its respective hose fitting. Using a blunt screwdriver, carefully push each hose off of its respective hose fitting. Capture any residual fuel in a suitable container.

3. Support the fuel pump while loosening then removing both screws (**Figure 26**) from the fuel pump. Pull the fuel pump away from the cylinder block. Direct the fittings into a suitable container then drain all fuel from the pump. Place the pump on a clean work surface. Remove the O-ring from the mounting cover or cylinder block. Clean the mounting surfaces. Stuff a small shop towel into the opening to prevent contamination of the crankcase.

4. Remove the four screws (10, **Figure 27**) retaining the mounting cover (9) to the fuel pump body (1).

5. Carefully pry the body from the cover. Do not use excessive force or scratch any mating surfaces.

6. Push in on the plunger (12, **Figure 27**) while pushing in on the diaphragm (7, **Figure 27**). Rotate the diaphragm 90° to release it from the plunger. Carefully pull the diaphragm, gaskets and spring (6-8, **Figure 27**) from the mounting cover (9). Discard the gasket (6, **Figure 27**).

7. Pull the plunger and spring (11 and 12, **Figure 27**) from the mounting cover.

8. Remove both screws (5, **Figure 27**) then lift the cover (4), valve (3) and stopper (2) from the pump body(1).

9. Inspect the diaphragm for ripped, creased or stretched surfaces. Replace the diaphragm if any defects are noted.

10. Inspect the check valve for wear or damage. Replace the check valve if it is not in perfect condition.

11. Clean the fuel pump body, springs, plunger and mounting cover using a suitable solvent. Dry all surfaces using compressed air. Direct air through both fuel hose fittings to clear debris.

12. Inspect the fuel pump body and mounting cover for corroded or damaged surfaces. Replace defective components. Inspect both springs for corrosion or damage. Replace if any defects are noted. Inspect the plunger for wear or corrosion. Replace the plunger if defects are noted.

13. Install the clear plastic check valve stopper (2, **Figure 27**) onto the fuel pump body. Align the notch in the stop with the tab on the fuel pump body.

14. Install the check valve (3, **Figure 27**) onto the fuel pump body. Ensure the check valve rests on the stopper and its notch aligns with the tab on the fuel pump body.

15. Place the cover (4, **Figure 27**) onto the check valve. Align the notch on the bottom side of the cover with the

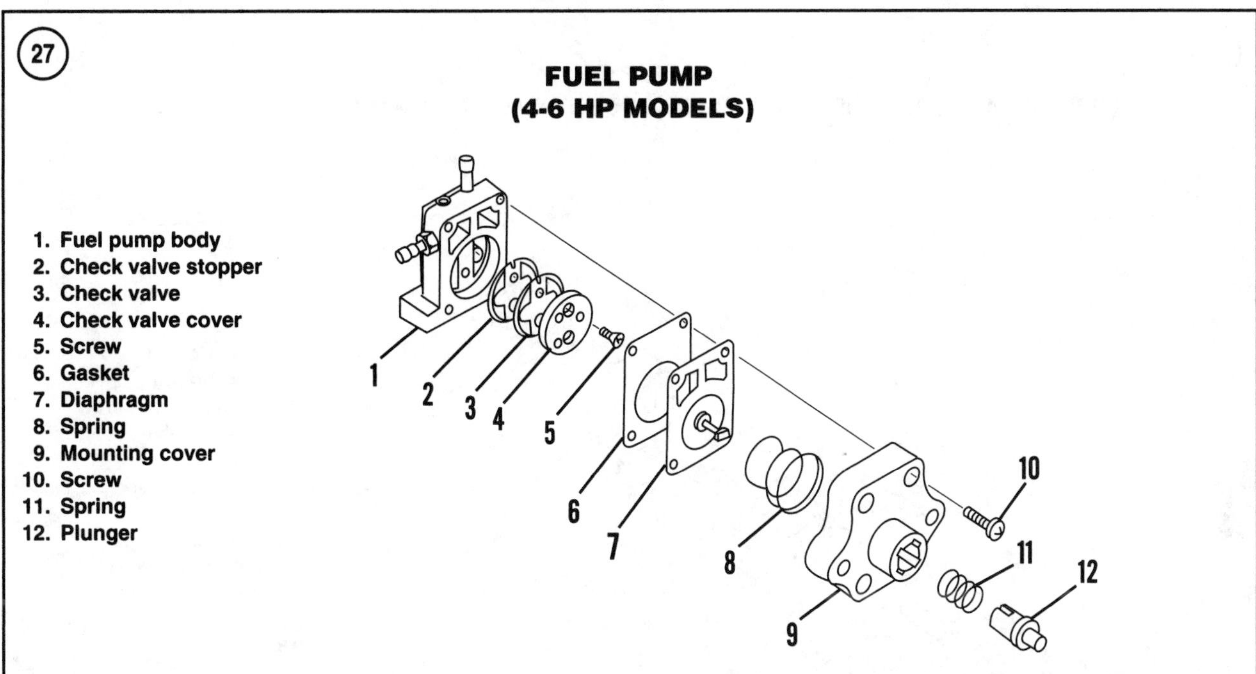

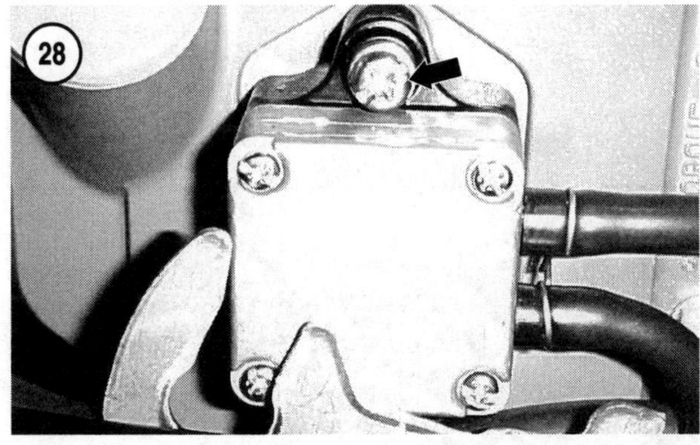

tab on the fuel pump body. Install both screws and securely tighten them.

16. Install the smaller spring (11, **Figure 27**) into its opening on the mounting cover (9). Install the plunger (12, **Figure 27**) into the mounting cover (9) with the recess facing the spring (11).

17. Install the larger spring (8, **Figure 27**) onto the mounting cover (9) with the larger diameter side facing the cover. Slide the arm of the diaphragm (7, **Figure 27**) through the spring (8) and the opening of the mounting cover. Push in on the plunger (12, **Figure 27**) while aligning the diaphragm arm with the recess in the plunger. Rotate the diaphragm 90° after the tab fully enters the recess (in the plunger).

18. Release the plunger and diaphragm. Correct installation prevents these components from separating. Align the screw holes in the diaphragm with the screw holes in the mounting cover. Install a new gasket (6, **Figure 27**). Align the center of the opening in the gasket with the metal backing for the diaphragm arm.

19. Install the fuel pump body onto the mounting cover, gasket and diaphragm. Align the check valve cover (4, **Figure 27**) with the opening of the gasket (6). Check for pinching, misalignment or creasing of the gasket and diaphragm.

20. Hold the fuel pump body (1, **Figure 27**) in firm contact with the mounting cover (9) while installing all four screws (10). Securely tighten the screws.

21. Lubricate the O-ring with engine oil and slide it over the protrusion on the mounting cover. Carefully insert the fuel pump onto the cylinder block with the longer side of the pump facing down. Install both mounting screws (**Figure 26**) and securely tighten them.

22. Slide both fuel hoses onto their respective fittings. Position each clamp over the hoses and fittings. Inspect all fuel hose connections and squeeze the primer bulb. Correct any fuel leakage.

Fuel Pump Removal, Disassembly, Assembly and Installation (9.9 [Prior to Serial No. OH000058] and 15 hp Models)

The fuel pump (**Figure 28**) is mounted to the rocker arm cover.

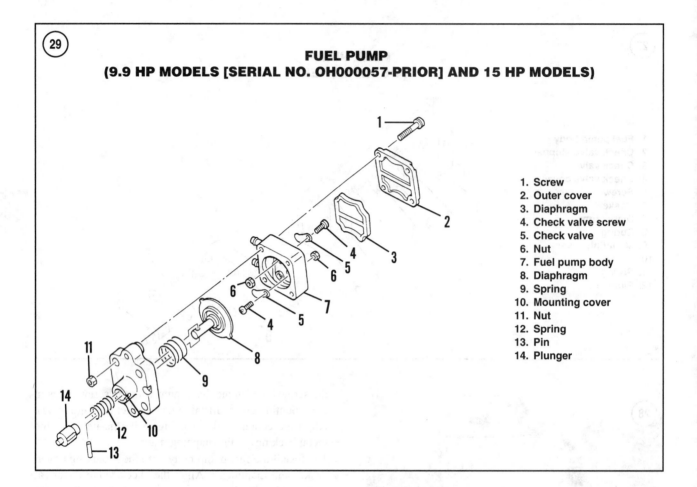

29

FUEL PUMP
(9.9 HP MODELS [SERIAL NO. OH000057-PRIOR] AND 15 HP MODELS)

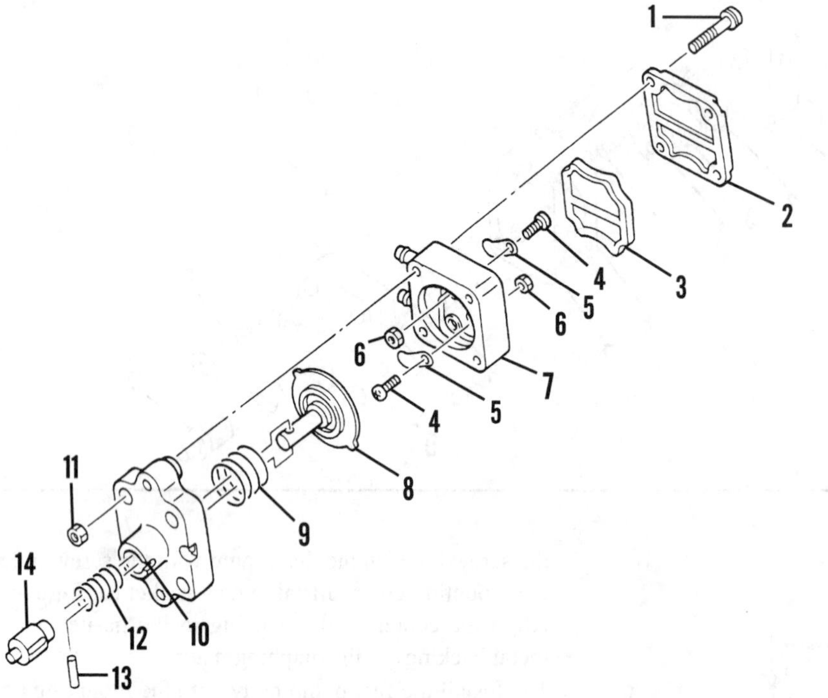

1. Screw
2. Outer cover
3. Diaphragm
4. Check valve screw
5. Check valve
6. Nut
7. Fuel pump body
8. Diaphragm
9. Spring
10. Mounting cover
11. Nut
12. Spring
13. Pin
14. Plunger

1. Disconnect both cables from the battery if so equipped.

2. Place a shop towel under the fuel pump to capture any spilled fuel. Mark each hose and the fuel pump to ensure correct installation.

3. Move each hose clamp away from its respective hose fitting. Using a blunt screwdriver, carefully push each hose off of its hose fittings. Capture any residual fuel in a suitable container.

4. Remove the screws (**Figure 28**) from the fuel pump. Pull the fuel pump away from the cylinder block. Direct the fittings into a suitable container then drain all fuel from the pump. Place the pump on a clean work surface. Remove the O-ring from the mounting cover or cylinder block. Inspect the O-ring for crushed, cut or damaged surfaces. Replace the O-ring if these or other defects are noted. Clean the mounting surfaces. Stuff a small shop towel into the opening to prevent contamination of the crankcase.

5. Remove the four screws (1, **Figure 29**) retaining the cover (2) and mounting cover (10) to the fuel pump body (7). Remove the four nuts (11, **Figure 29**) from their recess in the mounting cover (10).

6. Lift the cover from the fuel pump body (**Figure 30**). Lift the diaphragm from the fuel pump body (**Figure 31**). Lift the fuel pump body from the mounting cover and spring diaphragm (**Figure 32**).

7. Push in on the plunger (14, **Figure 29**) while pushing in on the diaphragm and spring (8 and 9, **Figure 29**). Rotate the diaphragm (8, **Figure 29**) until the pin (13) aligns with the notch in the mounting cover (10). Pull the pin

31

32

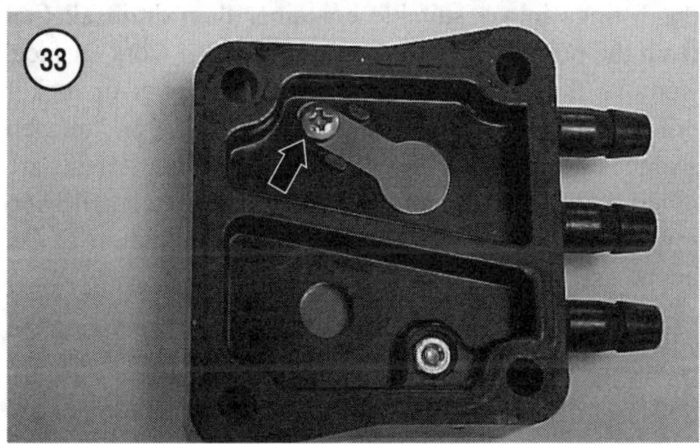

33

(13, **Figure 29**) from the diaphragm arm. Carefully pull the diaphragm, plunger and spring from the mounting cover.

8. Remove the screws (**Figure 33**) and lift both check valves (5, **Figure 29**) from the fuel pump body (7). Remove both nuts (6, **Figure 29**) from their recess in the fuel pump body (7).

9. Inspect both diaphragms for ripped, creased or stretched surfaces. Replace the diaphragms if any defects are noted.

10. Inspect the check valve for worn, cracked or broken surfaces. Replace the check valves if defects are noted.

11. Clean the fuel pump body, springs, plunger and both covers using a suitable solvent. Dry all surfaces using compressed air. Direct air through both fuel hose fittings to clear debris.

12. Inspect the fuel pump body, both covers, springs and plunger for excessive wear, corrosion or other damage. Replace all defective components.

13. Place both nuts (6, **Figure 29**) into their respective recess in the fuel pump body (7). Place each check valve in position on the fuel pump body.

14. Install the screws (**Figure 33**) into the check valve and nuts. Securely tighten them.

15. Install the smaller spring (12, **Figure 29**) into its opening on the mounting cover (10). Install the plunger (14, **Figure 29**) into the mounting cover (10) with the smaller diameter side facing out.

16. Install the larger spring (9, **Figure 27**) onto the mounting cover (10) with the larger diameter side facing the cover. Slide the arm of the diaphragm (8, **Figure 29**) through the spring (9) and the opening of the mounting cover.

17. Push in on the plunger (14, **Figure 29**) while pushing in on the diaphragm. Rotate the diaphragm until the hole in the diaphragm arm aligns with the notch in the mounting cover (10). Insert the pin (13, **Figure 29**) through the notch and into its opening in the diaphragm arm. Release the plunger and diaphragm.

18. Rotate the diaphragm until its screw holes align with the screw holes in the mounting cover.

19. Place the fuel pump body (7, **Figure 29**) onto the mounting cover. Align the screw holes in the fuel pump body with the holes in the mounting cover and diaphragm (**Figure 32**).

20. Install the outer diaphragm (3, **Figure 29**) onto the fuel pump body (**Figure 31**). Install the cover (2, **Figure 29**) onto the outer diaphragm. Align the screw holes in the diaphragm and cover. Check for pinching, misalignment or creasing of the diaphragms.

21. Insert all four nuts (11, **Figure 29**) into their recess in the mounting cover. Hold the cover in firm contact with the fuel pump body and mounting cover while installing all four screws (1, **Figure 29**). Tighten the screws in a crossing pattern to the specification in **Table 4**.

22. Lubricate the O-ring with engine oil and slide it over the protrusion on the mounting cover. Carefully install the fuel pump onto the cylinder block. Install both mounting screws (**Figure 28**) into the fuel pump and rocker arm cover. Evenly tighten both screws to the specification in **Table 4**.

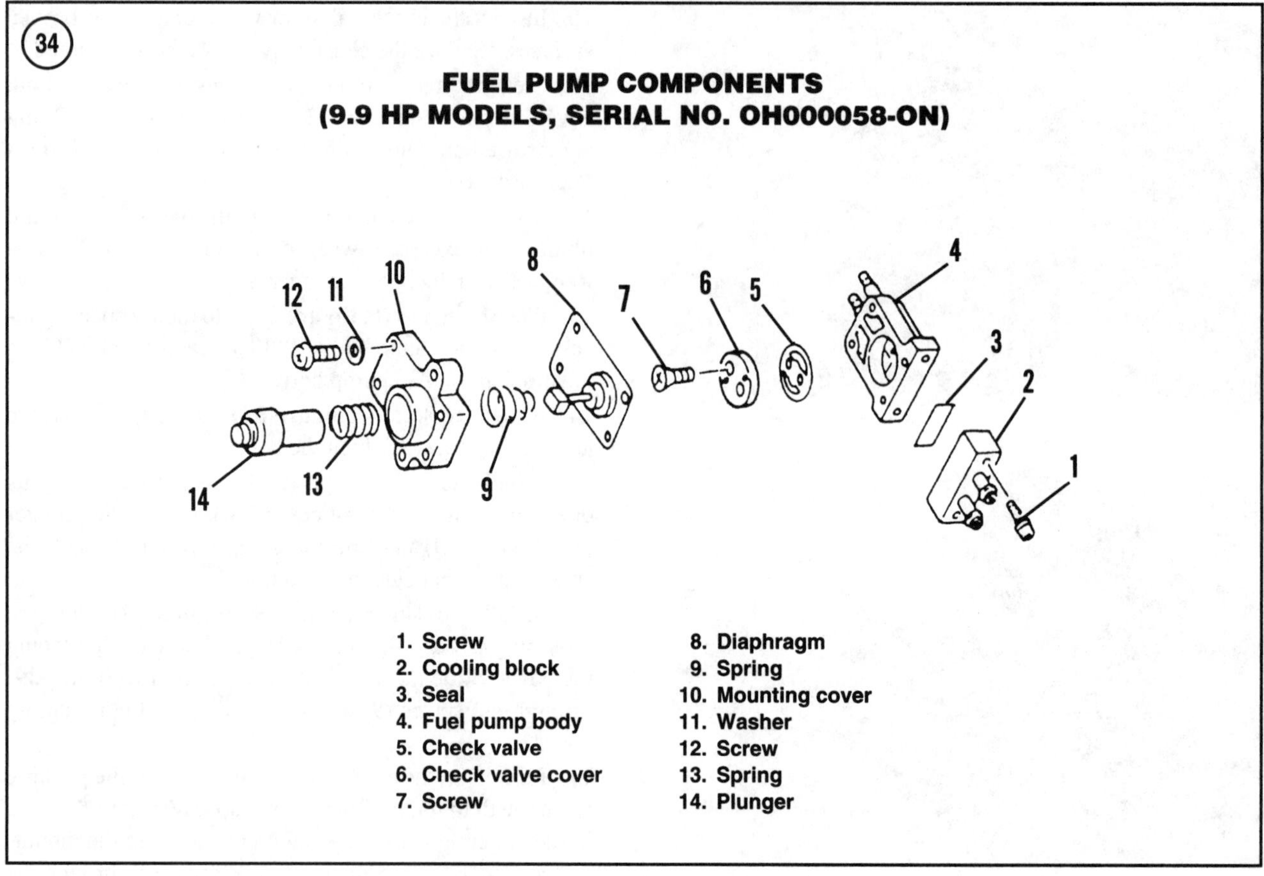

23. Slide both fuel hoses onto their respective fittings. Position each clamp over the hoses and fittings. Inspect all fuel hose connections while squeezing the primer bulb. Correct any fuel leaks.
24. Clean the terminals and connect the cables to the battery if so equipped.

Fuel Pump Removal, Disassembly, Assembly and Installation (9.9 hp Models [Serial No. OH000058-On])

The fuel pump is mounted to the rocker arm cover.

1. Disconnect both cables from the battery if so equipped.
2. Place a shop towel under the fuel pump to capture any spilled fuel. Mark each hose and the fuel pump to ensure correct installation. On models so equipped, remove both screws (1, **Figure 34**) and pull the cooling block (2) and seal (3) away from the fuel pump.
3. Move each hose clamp away from its fitting. Using a blunt screwdriver, carefully push each hose off of its fittings. Capture any residual fuel in a suitable container.
4. Remove both screws (**Figure 26**) from the fuel pump. Pull the fuel pump away from the cylinder block. Direct the fittings into a suitable container then drain all fuel from the pump. Place the pump on a clean work surface. Remove the O-ring from the mounting cover or rocker arm cover. Inspect the O-ring for crushed, cut or damaged surfaces. Replace the O-ring if these or other defects are noted. Clean the mounting surfaces. Stuff a small shop towel into the opening to prevent contamination of the crankcase.
5. Remove the four screws (11, **Figure 34**) retaining the mounting cover (10) to the fuel pump body (4).
6. Carefully pry the body from the cover. Do not use excessive force or scratch any mating surfaces.
7. Push in the plunger (14, **Figure 34**) while pushing in the diaphragm (8, **Figure 34**). Rotate the diaphragm 90° to release it from the plunger. Carefully pull the diaphragm and spring (9, **Figure 34**) from the mounting cover (10). Remove the gasket from the diaphragm. Discard the gasket.
8. Pull the plunger and spring (13 and 14, **Figure 34**) from the mounting cover.
9. Remove both screws (7, **Figure 34**) then lift the cover (6) and check valve (5) from the pump body (4).

10. Inspect the diaphragm for ripped, creased or stretched surfaces. Replace the diaphragm if any defects are noted.
11. Inspect the check valve for wear or damage. Replace the check valve if is not in perfect condition.
12. Clean the fuel pump body, springs, plunger and mounting cover using a suitable solvent. Dry all components using compressed air. Direct air through both fuel hose fittings to clear debris.
13. Inspect the fuel pump body and mounting cover for corrosion or other damage and replace if necessary. Inspect both springs and plunger for corrosion or damage.
14. Install the check valve (5, **Figure 34**) onto the fuel pump body. Align the notch in the check valve with the tab on the fuel pump body.
15. Place the cover (6, **Figure 34**) onto the check valve. Align the notch on the bottom side of the cover with the tab on the fuel pump body. Install both screws and securely tighten them.
16. Install the smaller spring (13, **Figure 34**) into its opening on mounting cover (9). Install the plunger (14, **Figure 34**) into the mounting cover (10) with the recess facing the spring (13).
17. Install the larger spring (9, **Figure 34**) onto the mounting cover (10) with the larger diameter side facing the cover. Slide the arm of the diaphragm (8, **Figure 34**) through the spring (9) and the opening of the mounting cover. Push in on the plunger (14, **Figure 34**) while aligning the diaphragm arm tab with the recess in the plunger. Rotate the diaphragm 90° after the tab fully enters the recess in the plunger.
18. Release the plunger and diaphragm. Correct installation prevents these components from separating. Align the screw holes in the diaphragm with the screw holes in the mounting cover. Install a new gasket onto the diaphragm. Align the center of the opening in the gasket with the metal backing for the diaphragm arm.
19. Install the fuel pump body onto the mounting cover, gasket and diaphragm. Align the check valve cover (6, **Figure 34**) with the opening of the gasket. Check for pinching, misalignment or creasing of the gasket and diaphragm. Correct as required.
20. Hold the fuel pump body (4, **Figure 34**) in firm contact with the mounting cover (10) while installing all four screws (10) and washers (11). Tighten the screws in a crossing pattern to the specification in **Table 4**.
21. Lubricate the O-ring with engine oil and slide it over the protrusion on the mounting cover. Remove the shop towel from the opening. Carefully insert the fuel pump onto the cylinder block with the longer side of the pump facing down. Install both mounting screws **(Figure 26)** and securely tighten them.
22. Position the seal and cooling block (2 and 3, **Figure 34**) in contact with the fuel pump mating surface. Install both screws (1, **Figure 34**) and securely tighten them.
23. Slide both fuel hoses onto their respective fittings. Position the clamps over the hoses and fittings. Inspect all fuel hose connections while squeezing the primer bulb. Correct any fuel leaks.

6

Fuel Pump Removal, Disassembly, Assembly and Installation (25-90 hp Models)

One fuel pump is used on 25-50 hp models and is mounted on the rocker arm cover. Two fuel pumps (**Figure 35**), mounted on the rocker arm cover, are used on 75 and 90 hp models. Always service both pumps on models so equipped.

1. Disconnect both cables from the battery if so equipped. On 75 and 90 hp models, remove the spark plug cover as described in Chapter Eight.
2. Place a shop towel under the fuel pump to capture any spilled fuel. Mark each hose and the fuel pump to help ensure correct connections upon installation.
3. Move each spring type hose clamp away from it respective hose fitting. Using a blunt tip screwdriver, carefully push each hose off of its respective hose fittings. Capture any residual fuel in a suitable container.
4. Support the fuel pump and remove both screws (**Figure 28**) from the fuel pump. Pull the fuel pump away from the cylinder block. Direct the fittings into a suitable container then drain all fuel from the pump. Place the pump on a clean work surface. Remove the O-ring from the mounting cover or cylinder block. Inspect the O-ring for crushed, cut or damaged surfaces. Replace the O-ring if these or other defects are noted. Clean all debris or contaminants from the mounting surfaces and stuff a small shop towel into the opening to prevent contamination of the crankcase.

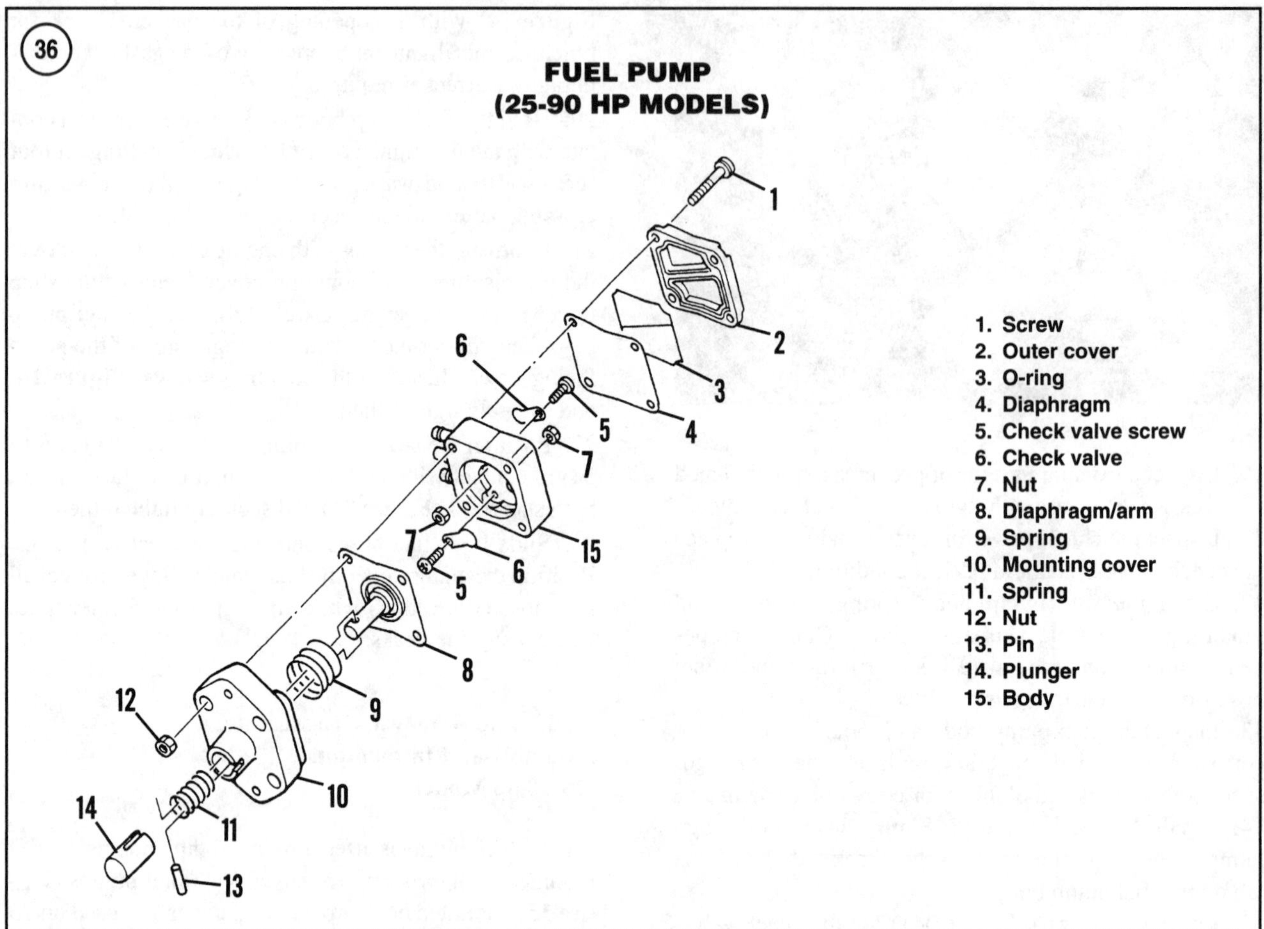

5. Remove the four screws (1, **Figure 36**) retaining the outer cover (2) and mounting cover (10) to the fuel pump body (15). Remove all four nuts (12, **Figure 36**) from their recess in the mounting cover (10).

6. Lift the cover from the fuel pump body (**Figure 30**). Pull the O-ring from the outer cover (**Figure 37**). Inspect the O-ring for worn, pinched or deteriorated surfaces. Replace the O-ring if defects are noted. Lift the diaphragm from the fuel pump body (**Figure 31**). Lift the fuel pump body from the mounting cover and spring diaphragm (**Figure 32**).

7. Push in on the plunger (14, **Figure 36**) while pushing in on the diaphragm (8, **Figure 3**) and spring (9). Rotate the diaphragm (8, **Figure 36**) until the pin (13) aligns with the notch in the mounting cover (10). Pull the pin (13, **Figure 36**) from the diaphragm arm. Carefully pull the diaphragm, plunger and springs from the mounting cover.

8. Remove the screws (**Figure 33**), then lift both check valves (6, **Figure 36**) from the fuel pump body (15). Remove both nuts (7, **Figure 36**) from their recess in the fuel pump body (15).

9. Inspect both diaphragms for ripped, creased or stretched surfaces. Replace the diaphragms if any defects are noted.

10. Inspect the check valve for worn, cracked or broken surfaces. Replace the check valves if defects are noted.

11. Clean the fuel pump body, springs, plunger and both covers using a suitable solvent. Dry all components using compressed air. Direct air through both fuel hose fittings to clear debris.

12. Inspect all components for corrosion or other damage and replace as necessary.

13. Place both nuts (7, **Figure 36**) into their respective recess in the fuel pump body (15). Place each check valve into position on the fuel pump body.

14. Install both screws (**Figure 33**) into the check valves and nuts. Securely tighten them.

15. Install the smaller spring (11, **Figure 36**) into its opening on the mounting cover (10). Install the plunger (14, **Figure 36**) into the mounting cover (10) with the smaller diameter side facing out.

16. Install the larger spring (9, **Figure 36**) onto the mounting cover (10) with the larger diameter side facing the cover. Slide the arm of the diaphragm (8, **Figure 36**) through the spring (9) and the opening of the mounting cover.

17. Push in on the plunger (14, **Figure 36**) while pushing in on the diaphragm. Rotate the diaphragm until the hole in the diaphragm arm aligns with the notch in the mounting cover (10). Insert the pin (13, **Figure 36**) through the notch and into its opening in the diaphragm arm. Release the plunger and diaphragm.

18. Rotate the diaphragm until its screw holes align with the screw holes in the mounting cover.

19. Place the fuel pump body (15, **Figure 36**) onto the mounting cover. Align the screw holes in the fuel pump body with the holes in the mounting cover and diaphragm (**Figure 32**).

20. Install the outer diaphragm (4, **Figure 36**) onto the fuel pump body (**Figure 31**). Install the O-ring (3, **Figure 36**) into its groove in the outer cover (**Figure 37**). Install the cover (2, **Figure 36**) onto the outer diaphragm. Align the screw holes in the diaphragm and cover. Check for pinching, misalignment or creasing of the diaphragms. Correct as required.

21. Insert all four nuts (11, **Figure 29**) into their recess in the mounting cover. Hold the cover in firm contact with the fuel pump body and mounting cover and install all four screws (1, **Figure 36**). Tighten the screws in a crossing pattern to the specification in **Table 4**.

22. Lubricate the O-ring with engine oil and slide it over the protrusion on the mounting cover. Remove the shop towel from the opening. Install the fuel pump onto the cylinder block and install both mounting screws (**Figure 28**). Evenly tighten both screws to the specification in **Table 4**.

23. Slide both fuel hoses onto their fittings. Position the clamps over the hoses and fittings. Inspect all hose connections while squeezing the primer bulb. Correct any fuel leaks.

24. On 75 and 90 hp models, install the spark plug cover as described in Chapter Eight. Clean the terminals and connect the cables to the battery if so equipped.

Silencer Cover, Carburetor and Intake Manifold Removal and Installation

If only the silencer cover or carburetor(s) require removal, perform only the steps necessary to remove them. Reverse the removal steps to reinstall the components.

4-6 hp models

1. Remove the spark plug then connect the spark plug lead to a suitable engine ground.

2. Remove the manual starter (**Figure 38**) as described in Chapter Ten.

3. Slide the clamp from the fitting and disconnect the breather hose (**Figure 39**) from the silencer cover.

4. Place a small container or shop towel under the fuel hose fitting (A, **Figure 40**), then carefully pull the fuel hose from the side of carburetor. Drain fuel remaining in the hose into a suitable container. Clean up any spilled fuel at once.

5. Loosen the bolt (B, **Figure 40**) and remove the choke cable from the choke lever.

6. Support the carburetor while removing both bolts, sleeves and washers (11-13, **Figure 41**). Pull the silencer cover (10, **Figure 41**) from the carburetor (6).

7. Pull the carburetor (6, **Figure 41**) slightly away from the manifold (1), then remove both gaskets and the insulator (3-5, **Figure 41**).

8. Tilt the carburetor enough to slip the throttle cable from the throttle lever (C, **Figure 40**).

9. Carefully scrape all gasket material from the carburetor, insulator and manifold mating surfaces. Clean the mating surfaces using a suitable solvent.

10. Clean the silencer cover using a suitable solvent.

11. Remove the bolts and lift the manifold from the cylinder head. Stuff a shop towel into the cylinder head opening to prevent contamination from entering the engine. Carefully scrape all gasket material from the cylinder head and manifold. Remove the shop towel from the opening.

12. Place a new gasket on the manifold mating surface. Place the intake manifold onto the cylinder head. Install the bolts and tighten them evenly to the specification in **Table 4**.

13. Tilt the carburetor enough to insert the throttle cable into its opening on the throttle lever (C, **Figure 40**). Position the silencer cover onto the front of the carburetor. Insert the sleeves, bolts and washer (11-13, **Figure 41**) through the silencer cover and carburetor mounting flanges.

14. Place the new gasket (5, **Figure 41**) over the bolts and in contact with the carburetor mounting flange. Install the insulator and the other new gasket (3 and 4, **Figure 41**) onto the bolts.

15. Hold the carburetor in position against the manifold (1, **Figure 41**) while threading the bolts (13) into the manifold. Securely tighten the bolts.

16. Slip the choke cable into its opening on the choke lever. Securely tighten the bolt (B, **Figure 40**).

17. Slide the breather tube (7, **Figure 41**) and clamp (8) onto its fitting to the silencer cover. Slide the fuel hose (14, **Figure 41**) and clamp (15) onto the carburetor fuel fitting (A, **Figure 40**).

18. Install the manual starter following the instructions provided in Chapter Ten. Observe the carburetor and all fuel fittings while squeezing the primer bulb. Correct the cause of fuel leakage as noted.

19. Install the spark plug and lead.

20. Perform all applicable carburetor adjustments following the instructions provided in Chapter Five.

9.9 (serial No. OH000057-prior) and 15 hp models

1. Disconnect both cables from the battery if so equipped.

2. Loosen the screw (A, **Figure 42**) and slide the throttle linkage from the carburetor throttle lever. Carefully pry the manual or electric choke linkage from the choke lever (B, **Figure 42**).

3. Pull the breather hose (5, **Figure 43**) from its fitting on the silencer cover (6).

4. Place a small container or shop towel under the fuel fitting (A, **Figure 40**) and carefully pull the fuel hose (10, **Figure 43**) from the carburetor.

5. Drain fuel remaining in the hose into a suitable container. Clean up any spilled fuel at once.

6. Support the carburetor while removing both bolts, sleeves, washer and the plate (1-4 **Figure 43**) from the silencer cover. Pull the silencer cover (6, **Figure 43**) from the carburetor (9). Remove the O-ring (7, **Figure 43**) from the silencer cover. Inspect the O-ring for worn, flattened or damaged surfaces. Replace the O-ring if defects are noted.

7. Pull the carburetor (6, **Figure 43**) away from the intake manifold (14) and remove both gaskets and the insulator (10-13, **Figure 43**) from the manifold or carburetor.

8. Remove the bolts, washers and wire clamps (15-17, **Figure 43**) then carefully pry the intake manifold (14) from the cylinder head. Insert shop towels into the cylinder head opening to help prevent contamination from entering the engine. Carefully scrape the gasket (18, **Figure 43**) from the intake manifold and cylinder head mating surfaces.

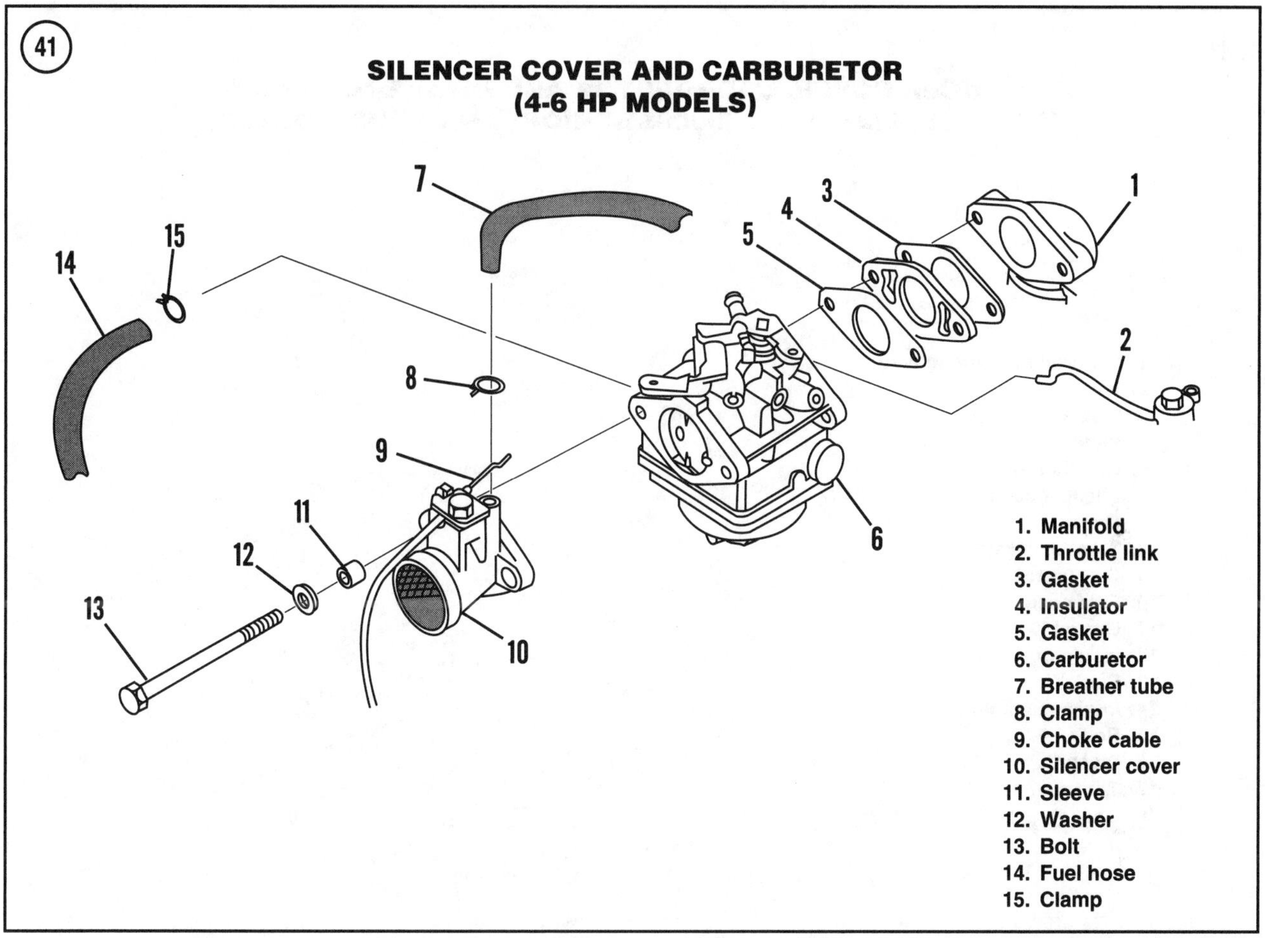

41

SILENCER COVER AND CARBURETOR (4-6 HP MODELS)

1. Manifold
2. Throttle link
3. Gasket
4. Insulator
5. Gasket
6. Carburetor
7. Breather tube
8. Clamp
9. Choke cable
10. Silencer cover
11. Sleeve
12. Washer
13. Bolt
14. Fuel hose
15. Clamp

42

9. Carefully scrape all gasket material from the carburetor, insulator and intake manifold mating surfaces. Clean the mating surfaces using a suitable solvent. Stuff a shop towel into the cylinder head openings to prevent contamination from entering the engine.

10. Clean the silencer cover and intake manifold using a suitable solvent.

11. Remove the shop towels then install a new gasket (18, **Figure 43**) onto the cylinder head. Ensure the alignment pins fit into their gasket openings. Place the intake manifold onto the gasket and cylinder head. Ensure the alignment pins engage their respective holes then install the bolts, wire clamps and washers. Evenly tighten the bolts to the specification in **Table 4**.

12. Apply a light coat of oil to the O-ring (7, **Figure 43**) and install it on the silencer cover.

13. Insert the sleeves, bolts, washers and plate (1-4, **Figure 43**) through the silencer cover and carburetor mounting flanges.

14. Place the new gasket (11, **Figure 43**) on the carburetor mounting flange. Install the insulator (12, **Figure 43**) then the other new gasket (13) onto the bolts.

15. Hold the carburetor in position against the intake manifold (14, **Figure 43**) while threading the bolts (13) into the mounting flange. Tighten the carburetor mounting bolt (1, **Figure 43**) to the specification in **Table 4**.

16. Carefully snap the choke linkage onto its connector to the choke lever (B, **Figure 42**). Slide the throttle linkage

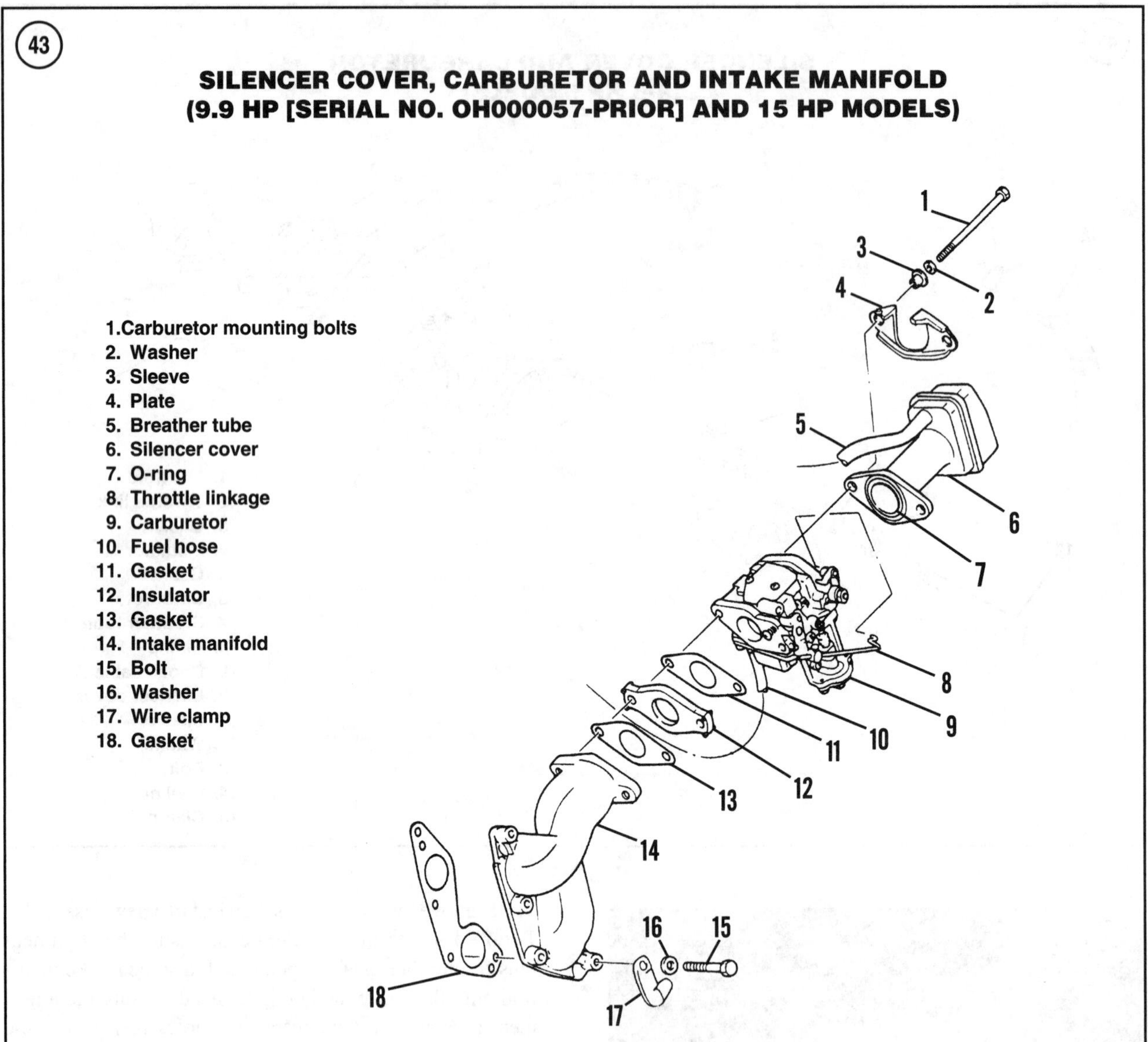

into the throttle lever. Securely tighten the screw (A, **Figure 42**).

17. Slide the breather tube (5, **Figure 43**) onto its fitting on the silencer cover (6). Slide the fuel hose and clamp (10, **Figure 43**) onto the carburetor fuel fitting (A, **Figure 40**).

18. Observe the carburetor and all fuel fittings while squeezing the primer bulb. Repair any fuel leakage.

19. Clean the terminals and connect the cables to the battery if so equipped.

20. Perform all applicable carburetor adjustments as described in Chapter Five.

9.9 hp models (serial No. OH000058-On)

1. Disconnect both cables from the battery if so equipped.
2. Carefully pry the throttle linkage from the throttle lever. Do not damage the plastic linkage connector.
3. Disconnect the electrothermal valve wires on the top side of the carburetor from the engine wire harness.
4. Place a small container or shop towel under the fuel hose fitting (24, **Figure 44**) then pull the fuel hose from the carburetor. Drain fuel remaining in the hose into a suitable container. Clean up any spilled fuel at once.
5. Remove both screws (3, **Figure 44**) the pull the silencer cover (2) and gasket (5) from the carburetor. Pull the screen (1, **Figure 44**) from the silencer cover.

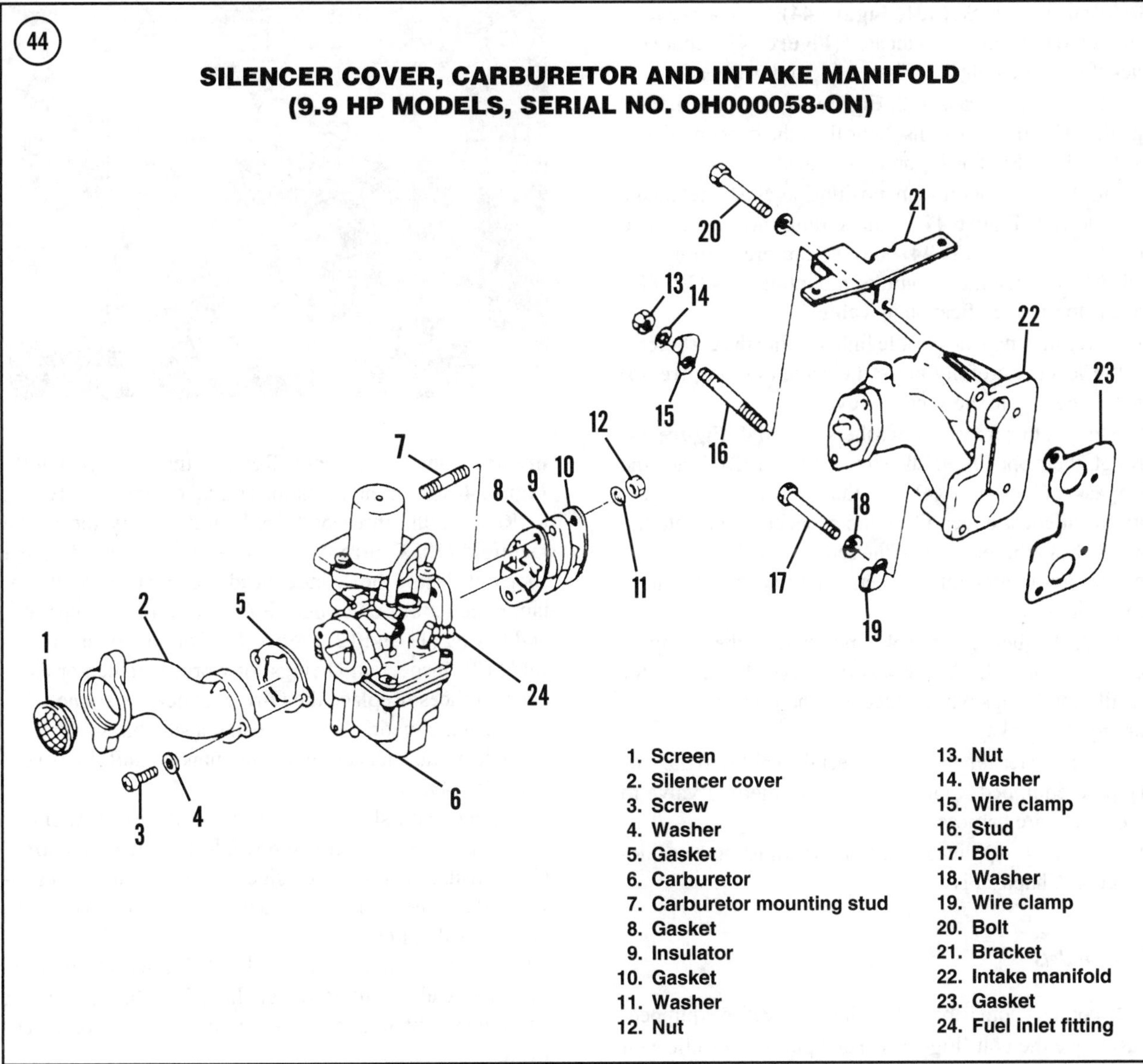

6. Support the carburetor while removing both nuts (11, **Figure 44**) from the mounting studs (7). Carefully pull the carburetor (6, **Figure 44**) from the intake manifold (22).

7. Remove the gaskets and insulator (8-10, **Figure 44**) from the carburetor.

8. Remove the bolt (20, **Figure 44**) then pull the bracket (21) for the breather chamber from the intake manifold. Remove the nuts, washers and wire clamps (13-15, **Figure 44**) then remove the bolts and wire clamps (17-19, **Figure 44**) from the intake manifold. Carefully pry the intake manifold (22) from the cylinder head.

9. Insert shop towels into the cylinder head openings to help prevent contamination from entering the engine. Carefully scrape the gasket (23, **Figure 44**) from the intake manifold and cylinder head mating surfaces.

10. Carefully scrape all gasket material from the carburetor, insulator and intake manifold mating surfaces. Clean the mating surfaces using a suitable solvent.

11. Clean the silencer cover and intake manifold using a suitable solvent.

12. Install a new gasket (23, **Figure 44**) onto the cylinder head. Place the intake manifold onto the gasket and cylinder head. Install all bolts, nuts, wire clamps and washers (13-19, **Figure 44**). Securely tighten all nuts and bolts following a crossing pattern.

13. Install the bracket (21, **Figure 44**) for the breather chamber to the intake as indicated (**Figure 44**). Secure the bracket with the bolt (20, **Figure 44**) and washer.

14. Place the new gasket (8, **Figure 44**) over the mounting studs (7). Install the insulator then the other new gasket (9 and 10, **Figure 44**) onto the studs.

15. Hold the carburetor in position against the intake manifold (22, **Figure 44**) while sliding the washers and nuts (11 and 13, **Figure 44**) onto the carburetor mounting studs (7). Tighten the carburetor mounting nuts (12, **Figure 44**) to the specification in **Table 4**.

16. Carefully snap the throttle linkage onto the carburetor throttle lever. Carefully press the screen (1, **Figure 44**) into its opening in the silencer cover (2).

17. Slide both screws and washers (3 and 4, **Figure 44**) through their opening in the silencer cover (2). Place the new gasket (5, **Figure 44**) over the screws and in contact with the silencer cover. Place the silencer cover onto the front of the carburetor. Align the screws with their holes in the carburetor and thread them in by hand. Securely tighten the screws.

18. Slide the fuel hose and clamp fully onto the fitting on the carburetor (24, **Figure 44**). Observe the carburetor and all fuel fittings while squeezing the primer bulb. Repair any fuel leakage.

19. Clean the terminals and connect the cables to the battery if so equipped. Connect the electrothermal valve to the engine wire harness.

20. Perform all applicable carburetor adjustments as described in Chapter Five.

25 hp models

1. Disconnect both cables from the battery if so equipped.
2. Remove the bolt (**Figure 45**) and pull the throttle cam away from the intake manifold (10, **Figure 46**).
3. Pull the breather hose from its fitting on the side of the silencer cover (3, **Figure 46**).
4. Place a small container or shop towel under the fuel hose fitting (A, **Figure 40**). Cut the hose clamp, then carefully pull the fuel hose from the carburetor.
5. Drain fuel remaining in the hose into a suitable container. Clean up any spilled fuel at once. Disconnect both yellow electrothermal valve wires from the engine wire harness.
6. Support the carburetor while removing bolts, and sleeves (1 and 2, **Figure 46**) from the silencer cover. Pull the silencer cover and O-ring (3 and 4, **Figure 46**) from the carburetor.
7. Pull the carburetor and insulator (6 and 8, **Figure 46**) from the intake manifold (10). Remove the O-ring (7, **Figure 46**) from the insulator. Remove the other O-ring (9, **Figure 46**) from the insulator or intake manifold (10).

45

8. Remove the three bolts and carefully pry the intake manifold (10, **Figure 46**) from the cylinder head. Insert shop towels into the cylinder head opening to prevent contamination from entering the engine. Pull the separator and O-ring (11 and 12, **Figure 46**) from the intake manifold (10). Inspect all O-rings for worn, flattened or damaged surfaces. Replace the O-rings if defects are noted.
9. Clean the mating surfaces using a suitable solvent.
10. Clean the silencer cover and intake manifold using a suitable solvent.
11. Remove the shop towels then install the separator and O-ring (11 and 12, **Figure 46**) into the intake manifold (10). Ensure the contoured side of the separator faces inward. Place the O-rings (7 and 9, **Figure 46**) into position on the insulator (8).
12. Install the intake manifold (10, **Figure 46**) onto its cylinder head mounting flange. Install all three mounting bolts then tighten them evenly to the specification in **Table 4**.
13. Insert the sleeves and bolts (1 and 2, **Figure 46**) and (1-4, **Figure 43**) the silencer cover. Place the O-ring (4, **Figure 46**) into position on the silencer cover (3).
14. Slide the bolts of the silencer cover through the carburetor mounting flanges. Install the insulator (8, **Figure 46**) onto the bolts and position as indicated in **Figure 46**.
15. Hold the silencer cover, carburetor and insulator in position against the intake manifold (10, **Figure 46**) while threading the bolts (1) into the intake manifold. Tighten the carburetor mounting bolt (1, **Figure 46**) to the specification in **Table 4**.
16. Position the throttle cam onto the intake manifold. Securely tighten the bolt (**Figure 45**). Ensure the cam rotates freely upon installation.
17. Slide the breather tube onto its fitting on the silencer cover (3, **Figure 46**). Slide the fuel hose onto the carbure-

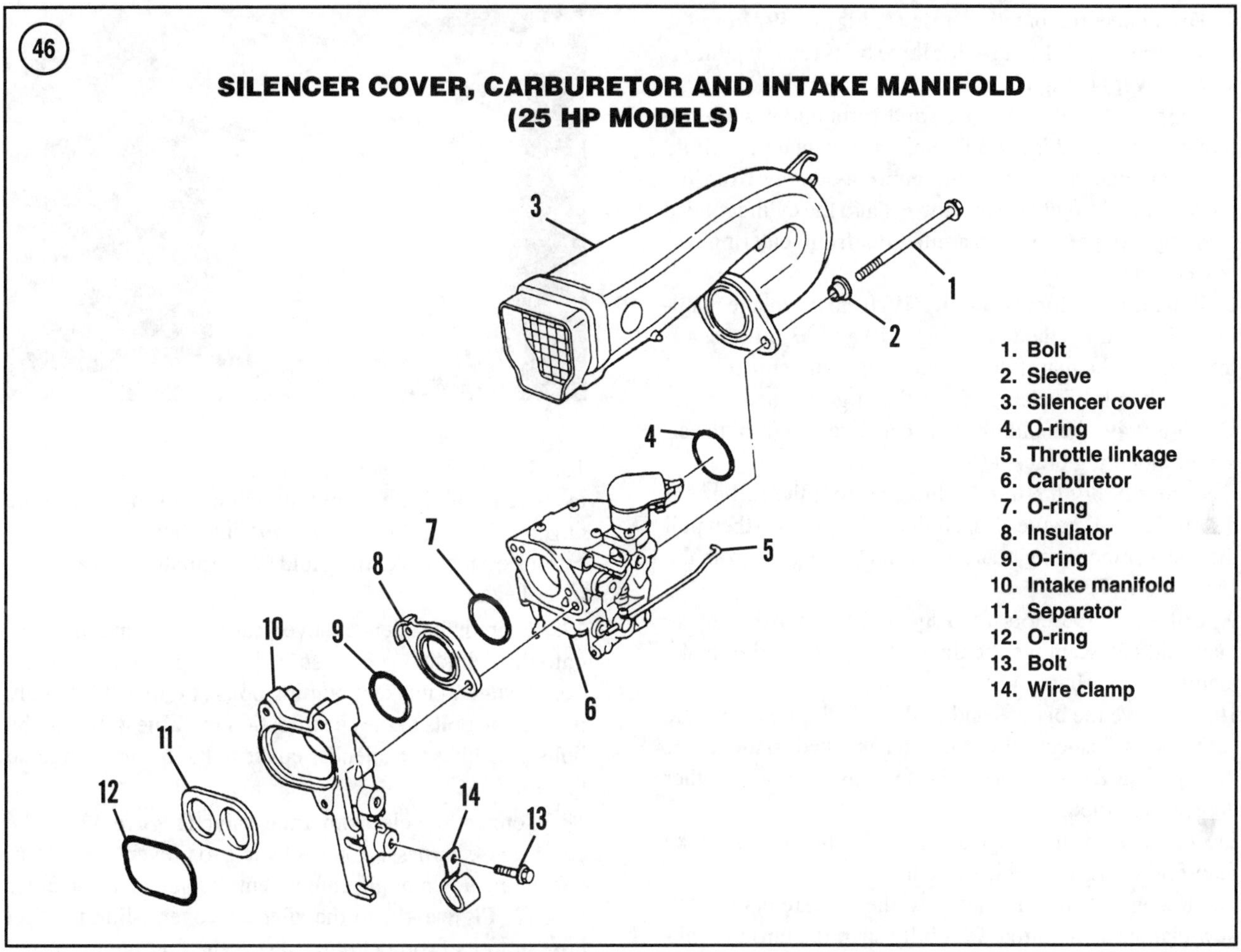

46

SILENCER COVER, CARBURETOR AND INTAKE MANIFOLD (25 HP MODELS)

1. Bolt
2. Sleeve
3. Silencer cover
4. O-ring
5. Throttle linkage
6. Carburetor
7. O-ring
8. Insulator
9. O-ring
10. Intake manifold
11. Separator
12. O-ring
13. Bolt
14. Wire clamp

47

tor fuel fitting (A, **Figure 40**). Install a new hose clamp over the fitting.

18. Observe the carburetor and all fuel fittings while squeezing the primer bulb. Correct any fuel leakage. Connect both yellow wires to the engine wire harness.

19. Clean the terminals and connect the cables to the battery if so equipped.

20. Perform all applicable carburetor adjustments as described in Chapter Five.

30 and 40 hp models

NOTE

Mark the mounting location on each carburetor prior to removing them. Improper fuel calibration or problems with linkage or hose connections are likely if carburetors are installed in the wrong locations.

1. Disconnect both cables from the battery if so equipped.
2. Disconnect the electrothermal valve wires (**Figure 47**) from to the engine harness.
3. Put a small container under the outlet fitting on the fuel pump (**Figure 48**). Remove the clamp then carefully pull the fuel hose from the fitting. Drain all fuel from the disconnected hose.

4. Disconnect the breather hose (2, **Figure 49**) from the silencer cover (1). Remove the three bolts retaining the silencer cover (1, **Figure 49**) to the cylinder block.
5. Support the silencer cover and carburetors while removing all bolts (**Figure 50**) retaining the intake manifold to the cylinder head. Pull the entire assembly from the powerhead. Stuff clean shop towels into the cylinder head openings to prevent contamination from entering the power head.
6. Pull the insulator (11, **Figure 49**) from the intake manifold (9). Remove the six O-rings (10 and 13, **Figure 49**) from the intake manifold, insulator or cylinder head.
7. Cut the plastic clamps from the large diameter hoses (3, **Figure 49**) then pull the silencer cover (1) from the silencer mounting bracket (5).
8. Carefully pry the throttle linkage from the carburetor throttle lever. Remove all six bolts (4, **Figure 49**) then pull the silencer mounting bracket (5) and O-rings (6) from the carburetors (7).
9. Lift the carburetors (7, **Figure 49**) from the intake manifold (9). Remove the three O-rings from the intake manifold or carburetors.
10. Remove the clamps and pull the fuel hoses from the carburetors. Inspect all O-rings for pinched, flattened or damaged surfaces. Replace the O-rings if these or other defects are noted.
11. Clean from the silencer cover, insulator and intake manifold using a suitable solvent.
12. Reconnect the fuel hoses to the carburetors. Install new clamps as required. Carefully snap the throttle linkage onto the carburetor throttle lever. Apply a light coating of engine oil to them, then place the O-rings (8, **Figure 49**) onto their respective locations on the intake manifold (9).
13. Place the carburetor onto the intake manifold. Ensure the O-rings remain in position and the carburetor bores align with the intake openings. Apply a light coating of engine oil to them, then place the O-rings (6, **Figure 49**) into their respective opening on the silencer mounting bracket (5). Place the silencer mounting bracket onto the carburetor openings. Ensure the O-rings remain in position and the silencer bracket openings align with the carburetor bores.
14. Install the six bolts (4, **Figure 49**) through the silencer mounting bracket and carburetor mounting flanges. Ensure all O-rings remain in position and evenly tighten the bolts to the carburetor mounting specification in **Table 4**.
15. Slide the large hoses (3, **Figure 49**) over their respective connections on the silencer mounting bracket (5). Install new plastic clamps over the connections. Securely tighten the clamps.

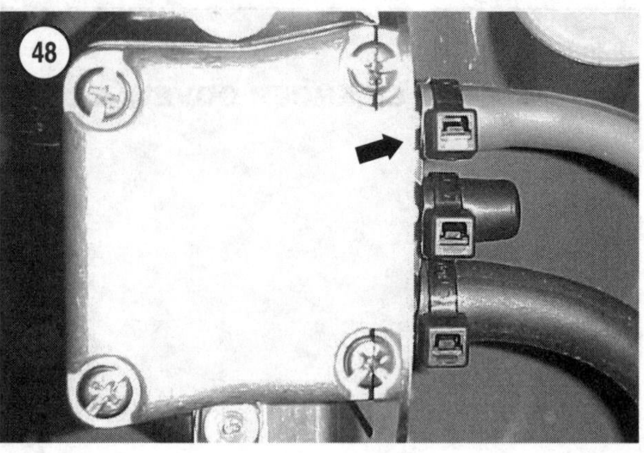

16. Remove the shop towels from the cylinder head openings. Lubricate them with engine oil then place the O-rings (8, 10 and 13, **Figure 49**) onto their respective locations on the intake manifold (9), insulator (11) and cylinder head.
17. Position the silencer cover, carburetors, and insulator onto the cylinder head. Ensure all O-rings remain in position. Install all intake mounting bolts (**Figure 50**). Evenly tighten the bolts to the specification in **Table 4**. Install the bolts attaching the silencer cover bolts. Securely tighten the bolts.
18. Connect the electrothermal valve (**Figure 47**) to the engine wire harness. Route all wires to prevent them from contacting any moving components. Connect the breather tube (2, **Figure 49**) to the silencer cover. Slide the fuel hose onto its fitting (**Figure 48**) at the fuel pump. Install new hose clamps then securely tighten them.
19. Observe the carburetor and all fuel fittings while squeezing the primer bulb. Correct any fuel leakage.
20. Clean the terminals and connect the cables to the battery if so equipped. Perform all applicable carburetor adjustments as described in Chapter Five.

50 hp models

CAUTION
Mark the mounting location on each carburetor prior to removal. Improper fuel calibration or problems with linkage or hose connections are likely if carburetors are installed in the wrong locations.

1. Disconnect both cables from the battery if so equipped.
2. Disconnect the electrothermal valve (**Figure 51**) and choke solenoid (**Figure 52**) from the engine wire harness.
3. Put a small container under the outlet fittings on the fuel pump (**Figure 53**). Remove the clamp then carefully

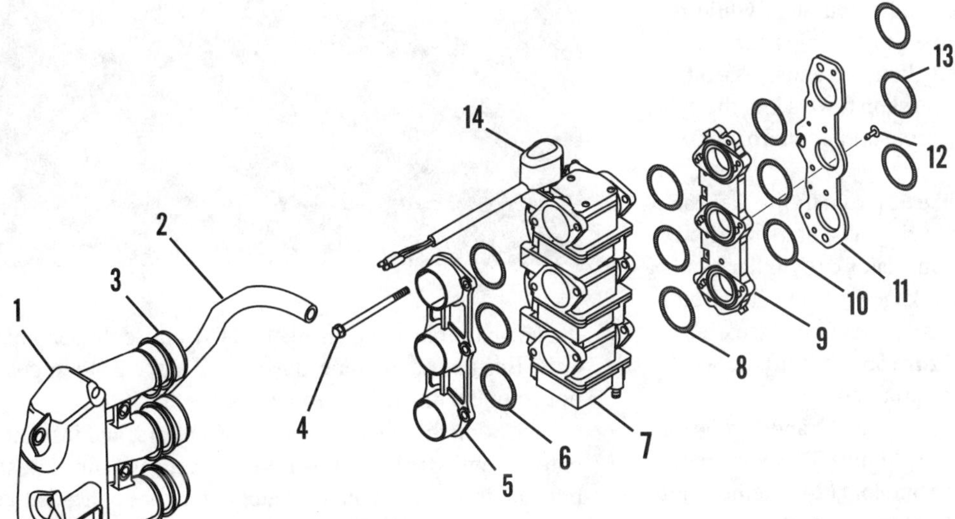
49
SILENCER COVER, CARBURETOR AND INTAKE MANIFOLD
(30 AND 40 HP MODELS)
1
2
3
4
5
6
7
8
9
10
11
12
13
14
1. Silencer cover
2. Breather tube
3. Large diameter hose
4. Carburetor mounting bolt
5. Silencer mounting bracket
6. O-ring
7. Carburetors
8. O-ring
9. Intake manifold
10. O-ring
11. Insulator
12. Plug
13. O-ring
14. Electrothermal valve

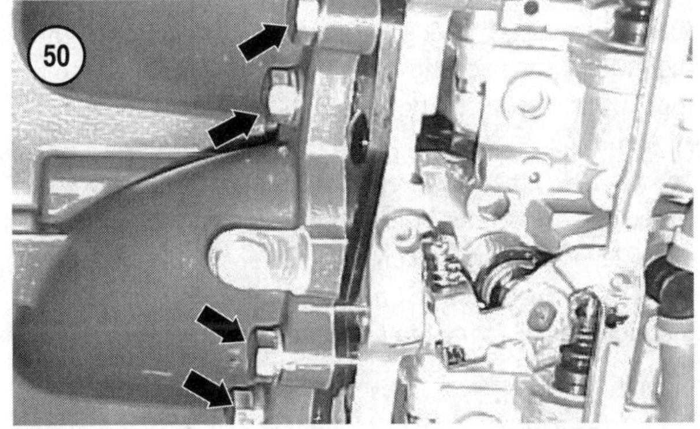
50

52

51

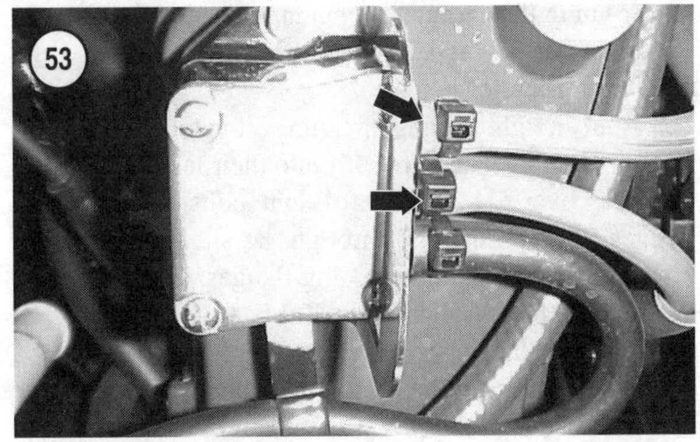
53

pull both outlet hoses (**Figure 53**) from their fitting. Drain all fuel from the disconnected hose.

4. Remove both bolts (**Figure 54**) retaining the silencer cover (1, **Figure 55**) to the cylinder block.

5. Support the silencer cover and carburetors while removing the eight bolts (**Figure 56**) retaining the intake manifold to the cylinder head. Pull the entire assembly from the power head. Stuff clean shop towels into the cylinder head openings to prevent contamination from entering the power head.

6. Pull the insulator (16, **Figure 55**) from the intake manifold (13). Remove the eight O-rings (14 and 18, **Figure 55**) from the intake manifold, insulator or cylinder head.

7. Carefully pry the throttle linkage from the carburetor throttle lever. Disconnect the fuel hoses from the carburetors. Remove the screws (9, **Figure 55**), then lift the accelerator pump (10) from the top carburetor.

8. Remove the eight bolts and sleeves (2 and 3, **Figure 55**) then lift the silencer cover (1, **Figure 55**) and silencer mounting plate (7) from the carburetors (24). Remove all eight O-rings (5 and 8 **Figure 55**) from the silencer cover or silencer mounting plate. Lift the carburetors (24, **Figure 55**) from the intake manifold (13). Remove all four O-rings (12, **Figure 55**) from the intake manifold or carburetors.

9. Inspect all O-ring for pinched, flattened or damaged surfaces. Replace the O-rings if these or other defects are noted. Clean the silencer cover, insulator and intake manifold using a suitable solvent.

10. Reconnect the fuel hoses to the carburetors. Install new clamps as required. Carefully snap the throttle linkage onto the carburetor throttle lever. Apply a light coating of engine oil to them, then place the O-rings (12, **Figure 49**) onto their locations on the intake manifold (13). Place the carburetor onto the intake manifold. Ensure the O-rings remain in position and the carburetor bores align with the intake openings.

11. Apply a light coating of engine oil to them, then place the O-rings (8, **Figure 55**) into their openings on the carburetors (24). Place the silencer mounting bracket (7, **Figure 55**) onto the carburetor openings. Ensure the O-rings remain in position and the silencer bracket openings align with the carburetor bores.

12. Apply a light coating of engine oil to them then place all four O-rings (5, **Figure 55**) into their locations on the silencer cover (1). Install all eight bolts, washers and sleeves (2-4, **Figure 55**) through the silencer mounting bracket and carburetor mounting flanges. Evenly tighten the bolts to the specification in **Table 4**.

13. Remove the shop towels from the cylinder head openings. Lubricate them with engine oil then place the O-rings (14 and 18, **Figure 55**) onto their locations on the intake manifold (13), insulator (16) and cylinder head (19). Ensure the aligning pins (15, **Figure 55**) are positioned in the intake manifold (13).

14. Position the silencer cover, carburetors, and insulator onto the cylinder head. Ensure all O-rings remain in position and the holes in the insulator and cylinder head align with the pins (15, **Figure 55**). Install the eight intake mounting bolts (**Figure 56**). Evenly tighten the bolts to the specification **Table 4**. Install the bolts (**Figure 54**) attaching the silencer cover. Securely tighten the bolts.

15. Connect the electrothermal valve (**Figure 51**) and choke solenoid (**Figure 52**) to the engine wire harness. Slide the fuel hoses onto their fittings (**Figure 53**) on the fuel pump. Install new hose clamps then securely tighten them. Install the accellerator pump (10, **Figure 55**) to the top carburetor. Securely tighten its mounting screws (11, **Figure 55**).

16. Observe the carburetor and all fuel fittings while squeezing the primer bulb. Correct any fuel leakage.

17. Clean the terminals and connect the cables to the battery if so equipped. Perform all applicable carburetor adjustments as described in Chapter Five.

CAUTION
Mark the mounting location on each carburetor prior to removal. Improper fuel calibration or problems with linkage or hose connections are likely if carburetors are installed in the wrong locations.

75 and 90 hp models

1. Disconnect both cables from the battery.

2. Disconnect both electrothermal valve (**Figure 57**) wires to the engine wire harness. Put a small container under the outlet fittings on each fuel pump (**Figure 58**). Remove the clamp and carefully pull both outlet hoses from their fittings. Drain all fuel from the disconnected hose.

55

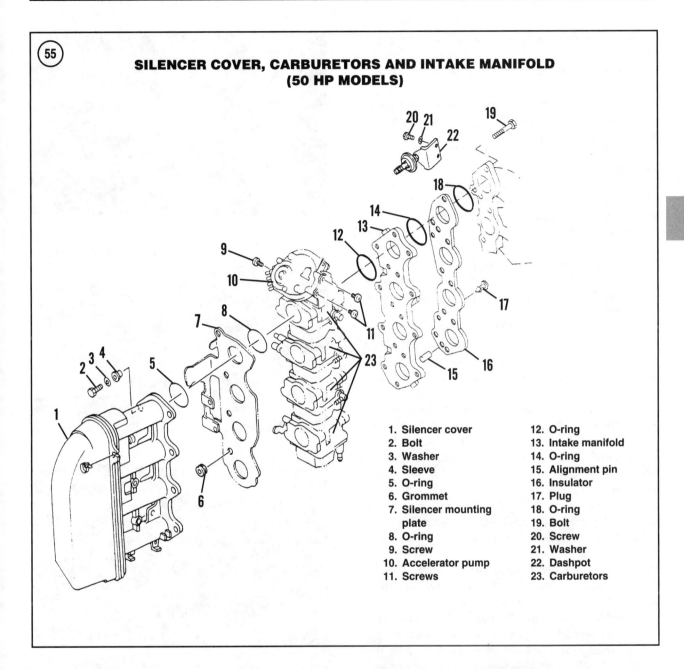

SILENCER COVER, CARBURETORS AND INTAKE MANIFOLD (50 HP MODELS)

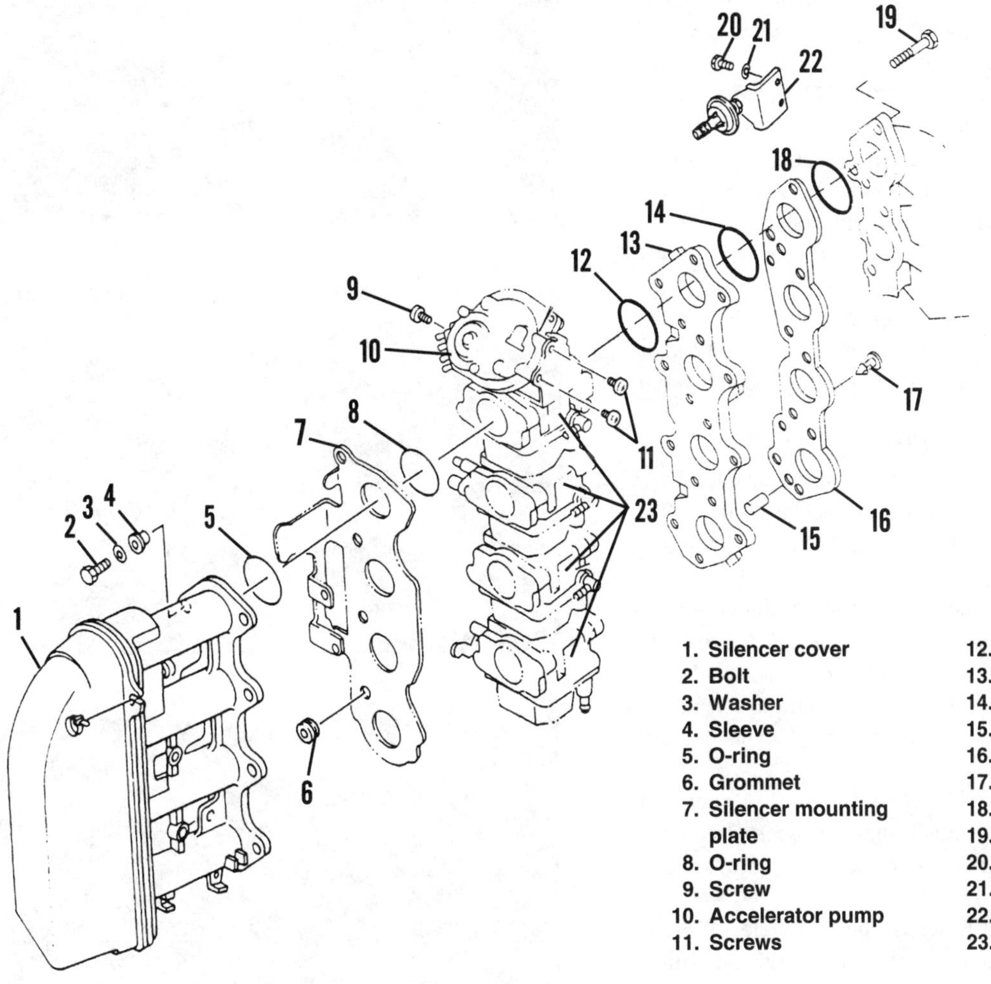

1. Silencer cover
2. Bolt
3. Washer
4. Sleeve
5. O-ring
6. Grommet
7. Silencer mounting plate
8. O-ring
9. Screw
10. Accelerator pump
11. Screws
12. O-ring
13. Intake manifold
14. O-ring
15. Alignment pin
16. Insulator
17. Plug
18. O-ring
19. Bolt
20. Screw
21. Washer
22. Dashpot
23. Carburetors

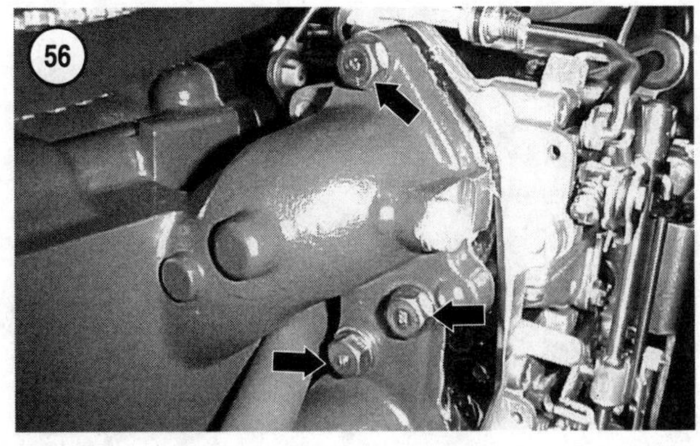

3. Disconnect the throttle position sensor (**Figure 59**) wire from the engine wire harness. Remove both bolts (**Figure 60**) and pull the throttle lever and linkage away from the carburetors. Remove the bolt (**Figure 61**) and pull the throttle cam and roller away from the intake manifold. Disconnect the dashpot (9, **Figure 62**) linkage from the bottom carburetor linkage.
4. Remove the three bolts (1, **Figure 62**) retaining the silencer cover to the cylinder block. Support the silencer cover and carburetors while removing the five bolts (16, **Figure 62**) from the intake manifold. Disconnect the breather tube (21, **Figure 62**) from the silencer cover.
5. Pull the entire assembly from the power head. Stuff clean shop towels into the cylinder head openings to prevent contamination from entering the power head. Remove the gasket (19, **Figure 62**) from the cylinder head or intake manifold (13). Carefully scrape all gasket material from the mating surfaces.
6. Remove the eight bolts (**Figure 63**), then lift the silencer cover from the carburetors (7, **Figure 62**). Remove the four spacers (5, **Figure 62**) from the carburetors. Remove the eight O-rings (4 and 6, **Figure 62**) from the carburetors or spacers.
7. Pull the insulators (**Figure 64**) from the intake manifold. Remove the eight O-rings (14 and 18, **Figure 55**) from the intake manifold, insulator or cylinder head.
8. Carefully pull the throttle linkage from the carburetor throttle lever (**Figure 65**). Disconnect the fuel hoses from the carburetors.
9. Inspect all O-rings for pinched, flattened or damaged surfaces. Replace the O-rings if these or other defects are noted. Clean the silencer cover, insulators and intake manifold using a suitable solvent.
10. Reconnect the fuel hoses to the carburetors. Install new clamps as required. Carefully snap the throttle linkage onto the carburetor throttle lever.
11. Apply a light coating of engine oil to them, then place the O-rings (8 and 11, **Figure 62**) onto their locations on each insulator (10). Place the insulators onto the intake manifold (13). Ensure the O-rings remain in position and the insulator bores align with the intake openings.
12. Install each carburetor. Ensure the O-rings remain in position.
13. Apply a light coating of engine oil to them, then place the eight O-rings (4 and 6, **Figure 62**) into the spacers (5). Align the silencer cover (20, **Figure 62**) with the spacers.
14. Install the eight bolts (2, **Figure 62**) through the silencer cover (20), spacers (5) and carburetor (7) mounting flanges. Ensure all O-rings remain in position. Evenly tighten the bolts to the specification in **Table 4**.
15. Remove the shop towels from the cylinder head openings. Ensure the alignment pins (12 and 19, **Figure**

62

SILENCER COVER, CARBURETORS AND INTAKE MANIFOLD (75 AND 90 HP MODELS)

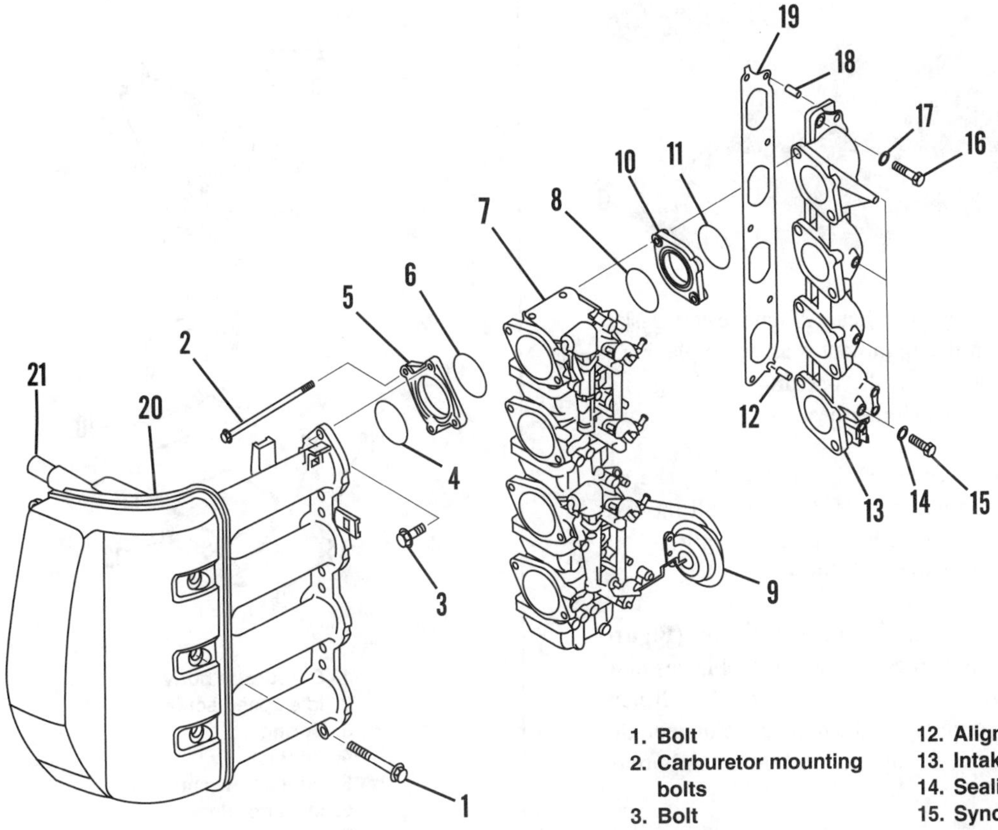

1. Bolt
2. Carburetor mounting bolts
3. Bolt
4. O-ring
5. Spacer
6. O-ring
7. Carburetors
8. O-ring
9. Dashpot
10. Insulator
11. O-ring
12. Alignment pin
13. Intake manifold
14. Sealing washer
15. Synchronizing port plug
16. Bolt
17. Washer
18. Alignment pin
19. Gasket
20. Silencer cover
21. Breather tube

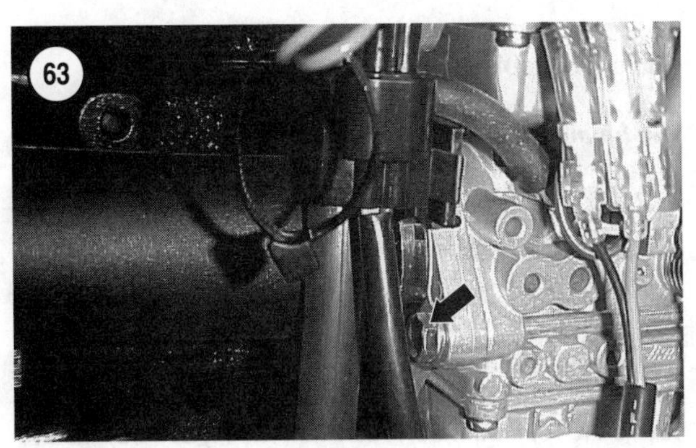
63

64

62) are in place on the cylinder head. Align the new gasket (19, **Figure 62**) with the alignment pins while placing it on the cylinder head. Align the openings in the gasket with the openings in the cylinder head.

16. Place the silencer cover, carburetors and intake assembly in position on the cylinder head. Install the five manifold attaching bolts (16, **Figure 62**). Evenly tighten the bolts to the specification in **Table 4**.

17. Connect the both electrothermal valve wires (**Figure 57**) to the engine wire harness. Slide the fuel hoses onto their fittings (**Figure 58**) on the fuel pump. Install new hose clamps then securely tighten them. Connect the dashpot (9, **Figure 62**) linkage to the bottom carburetor lever.

18. Install the throttle linkage and lever into position next to the bottom carburetor. Install both bolts through the rubber mounting grommets (**Figure 60**). Securely tighten the bolts. Align the throttle roller with the throttle cam as shown in **Figure 61**. Install the mounting bolt (**Figure 61**). Securely tighten the bolt. Connect the throttle position sensor (**Figure 60**) wire to the wire harness.

19. Observe the carburetor and all fuel fittings while squeezing the primer bulb. Correct any fuel leakage.

20. Clean the terminals and connect the cables to the battery. Perform all applicable throttle position sensor and carburetor adjustments as described in Chapter Five.

CAUTION

Always replace damaged carburetor fuel jets. Seemingly insignificant damage to a jet can have a profound effect on fuel delivery. Adverse effects to performance, emissions and engine durability can result from using of damaged carburetor fuel jets.

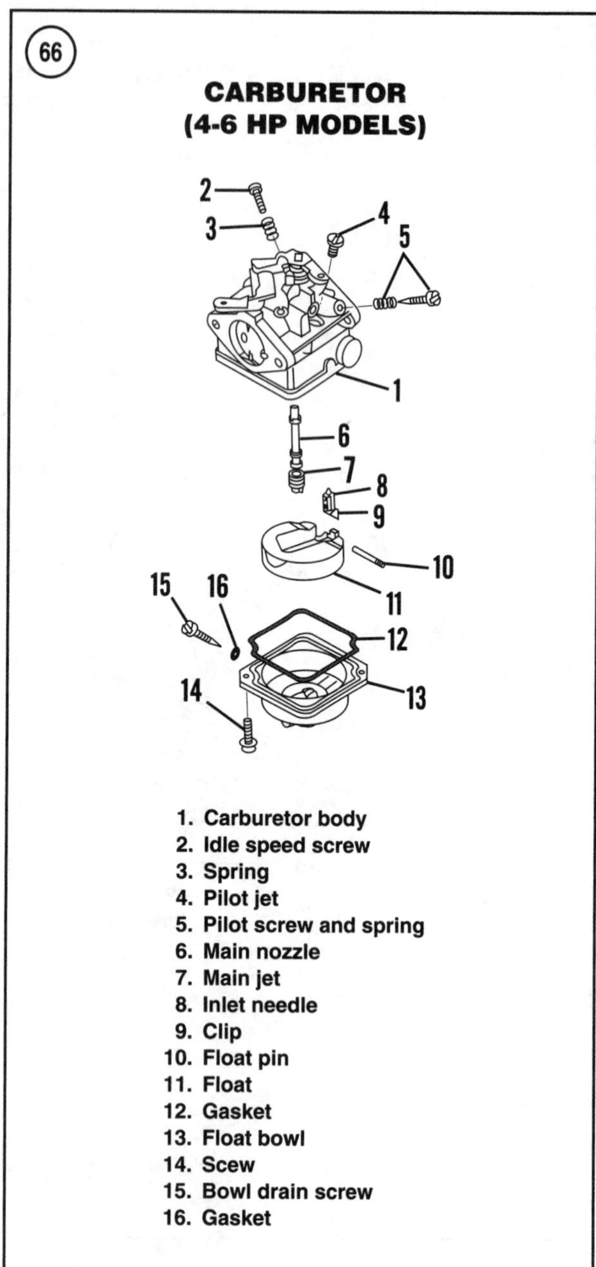

CARBURETOR (4-6 HP MODELS)

1. Carburetor body
2. Idle speed screw
3. Spring
4. Pilot jet
5. Pilot screw and spring
6. Main nozzle
7. Main jet
8. Inlet needle
9. Clip
10. Float pin
11. Float
12. Gasket
13. Float bowl
14. Scew
15. Bowl drain screw
16. Gasket

Carburetor Disassembly/Assembly

4-6 hp models

Refer to **Figure 66** to assist with component identification and orientation.

1. Remove the carburetor from the engine as described in this chapter.
2. Remove the drain screw and seal (15 and 16, **Figure 66**) then drain all residual fuel from the carburetor. Remove the four float bowl screws (14, **Figure 66**) then re-

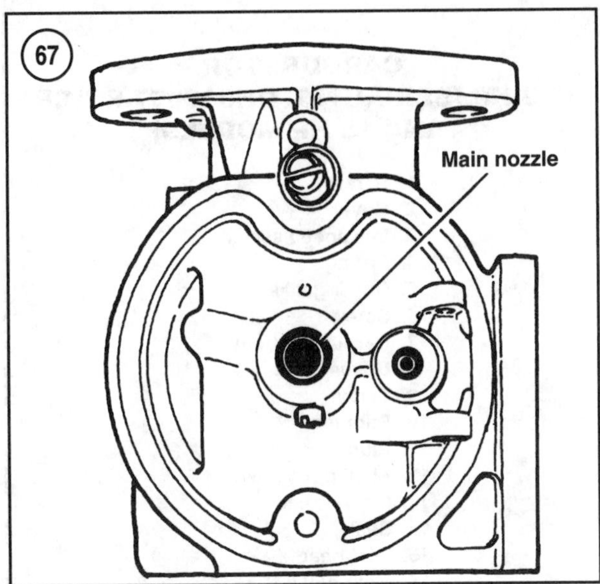

move the float bowl (13) and gasket (12) from the carburetor.

3. Carefully drive the float pin (10, **Figure 66**) toward the fuel hose fitting side of the carburetor to remove it carburetor. Lift the float (11, **Figure 66**) and inlet needle (8) from the carburetor.

4. Using a suitable screwdriver, remove the main fuel jet (7, **Figure 66**) from the carburetor. Insert a screwdriver into the throttle bore opening and push the main nozzle (**Figure 67**) down and out of the carburetor.

5. Remove the pilot jet (4, **Figure 66**), pilot screw (5) and idle speed screw (2) from the carburetor.

6. Clean and inspect all carburetor components as described in this chapter.

7. Assembly is the reverse of disassembly while noting the following:

   a. Install the float pin from the fuel hose fitting side of the carburetor. The ribbed side of the pin must fit in the pin mounting boss. Slide the needle clip (9, **Figure 66**) over the tab on the float (11).
   b. Adjust the float level as described in this section.
   c. Turn the pilot screw in until it just contacts its seat. Back the screw out the number of turns listed in **Table 2**. Turn the idle speed screw in until the throttle plate is slightly open.
   d. Push the main nozzle fully into its opening (**Figure 67**). Ensure the double ridged side faces the main jet.
   e. Install new gaskets, seals and O-rings during assembly. Securely tighten all jets and screws.

8. Install the carburetor as described in this chapter.

9.9 (serial No. OH000057-prior) and 15 hp models

Refer to **Figure 68** to assist with component identification and orientation.

1. Remove the carburetor from the engine as described in this chapter.

2. Remove the drain screw (26, **Figure 68**) and drain all residual fuel from the carburetor. Remover the four float bowl screws (25, **Figure 68**) and remove the float bowl (24) and gasket (22) from the carburetor.

3. Pull the valve (28, **Figure 68**) from the carburetor and lift the screen (23) from its opening. Remove the screw (**Figure 69**), then lift the float (18, **Figure 68**), float pin (17) and inlet needle (15) from the carburetor.

4. Remove the screw (32, **Figure 68**) from the accelerator pump cover (31). Remove the three screws (32, **Figure 68**) and pull the accelerator pump cover (31) from the float bowl (24). Pull the pump diaphragm and spring (29 and 30, **Figure 68**) from the float bowl.

5. Using needlenose pliers, remove the spring clip (19, **Figure 68**) from the accelerator pump bore. Pull the cap and plunger (20 and 21, **Figure 68**) from the bore.

6. Using a suitable screwdriver, remove the main fuel jet and seal (14 and 16, **Figure 68**) from the carburetor. Insert a screwdriver into the throttle bore opening then push the main nozzle (**Figure 67**) down and out of the carburetor.

7. Pull the plug (11, **Figure 68**) from the carburetor and remove the pilot jet (10). Remove the screw (9, **Figure 68**), then lift the cover (8) from the carburetor. Remove both screws (1, **Figure 68**) and lift the cover (2) from the carburetor. Remove the idle speed screw and spring (3 and 4, **Figure 68**).

8. Clean and inspect all carburetor components as described in this chapter.

9. Assembly is the reverse of disassembly while noting the following.

   a. Clean the screen (23, **Figure 68**) prior to assembly.
   b. Adjust the float level as described in this section.
   c. Install new gaskets, seals and O-rings during assembly.
   d. Push the main nozzle fully into its opening (**Figure 67**). Ensure the side with the small holes is positioned nearest the float bowl.
   e. Turn the idle speed screw in until the throttle plate is slightly open.

10. Install the carburetor as described in this chapter.

9.9 hp models (serial No. OH000057-on)

Refer to **Figure 70** to assist with component identification and orientation.

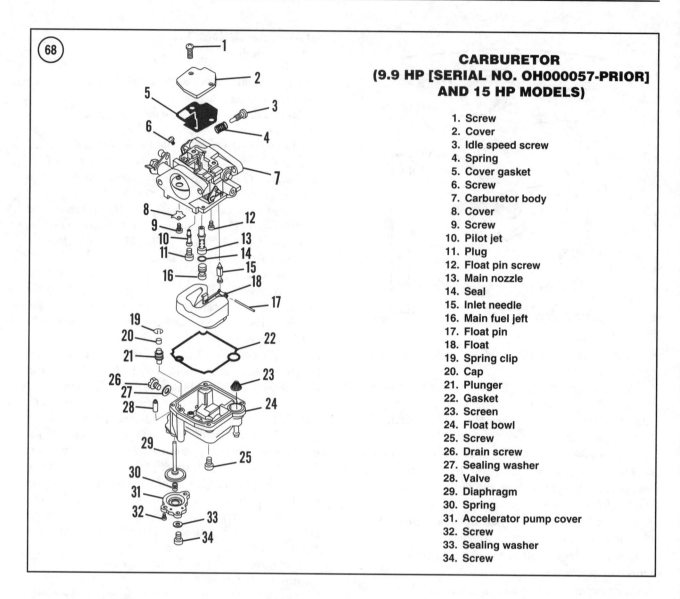

68

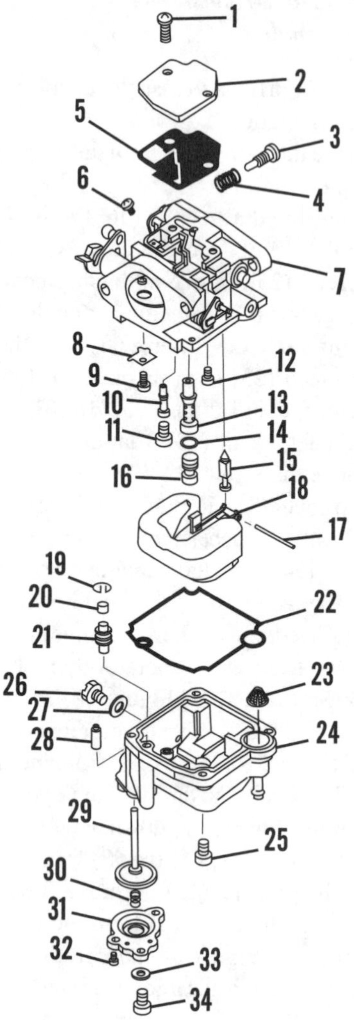

CARBURETOR (9.9 HP [SERIAL NO. OH000057-PRIOR] AND 15 HP MODELS)

1. Screw
2. Cover
3. Idle speed screw
4. Spring
5. Cover gasket
6. Screw
7. Carburetor body
8. Cover
9. Screw
10. Pilot jet
11. Plug
12. Float pin screw
13. Main nozzle
14. Seal
15. Inlet needle
16. Main fuel jeft
17. Float pin
18. Float
19. Spring clip
20. Cap
21. Plunger
22. Gasket
23. Screen
24. Float bowl
25. Screw
26. Drain screw
27. Sealing washer
28. Valve
29. Diaphragm
30. Spring
31. Accelerator pump cover
32. Screw
33. Sealing washer
34. Screw

1. Remove the carburetor from the engine as described in this chapter.

2. Remove the drain screw and gasket (37, **Figure 70**) then drain all residual fuel from the carburetor. Remove the screws and washer (1 and 2, **Figure 70**), then lift the electrothermal valve (4, **Figure 70**) and bracket (3) from the carburetor. Pull the O-ring (5, **Figure 70**) from the carburetor or electrothermal valve. Replace the O-ring when removed.

3. Remover the four float bowl screws (30, **Figure 70**), then remove the float bowl (28) and gasket (26) from the carburetor. Remove the screws (41, **Figure 70**), then lift the cover (39) from the float bowl. Remove the diaphragm and spring (31 and 32, **Figure 70**) from the float bowl.

4. Pull the float pin (17, **Figure 70**) from its mounting bosses. Lift the float (25, **Figure 70**) and inlet needle (19)

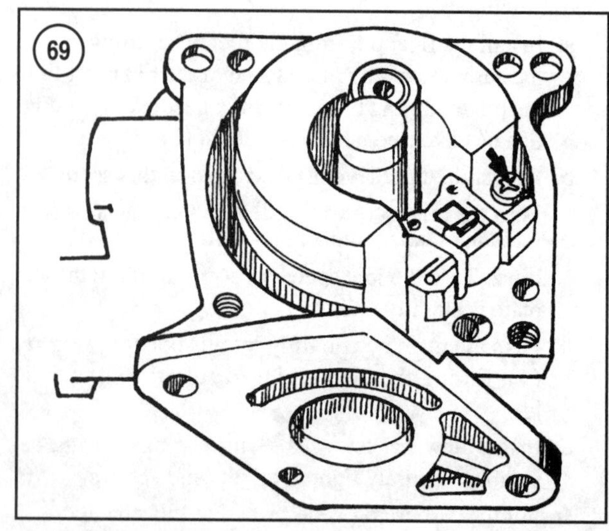

(70)

CARBURETOR COMPONENTS (9.9 HP MODELS, SERIAL NO. OH000058-ON)

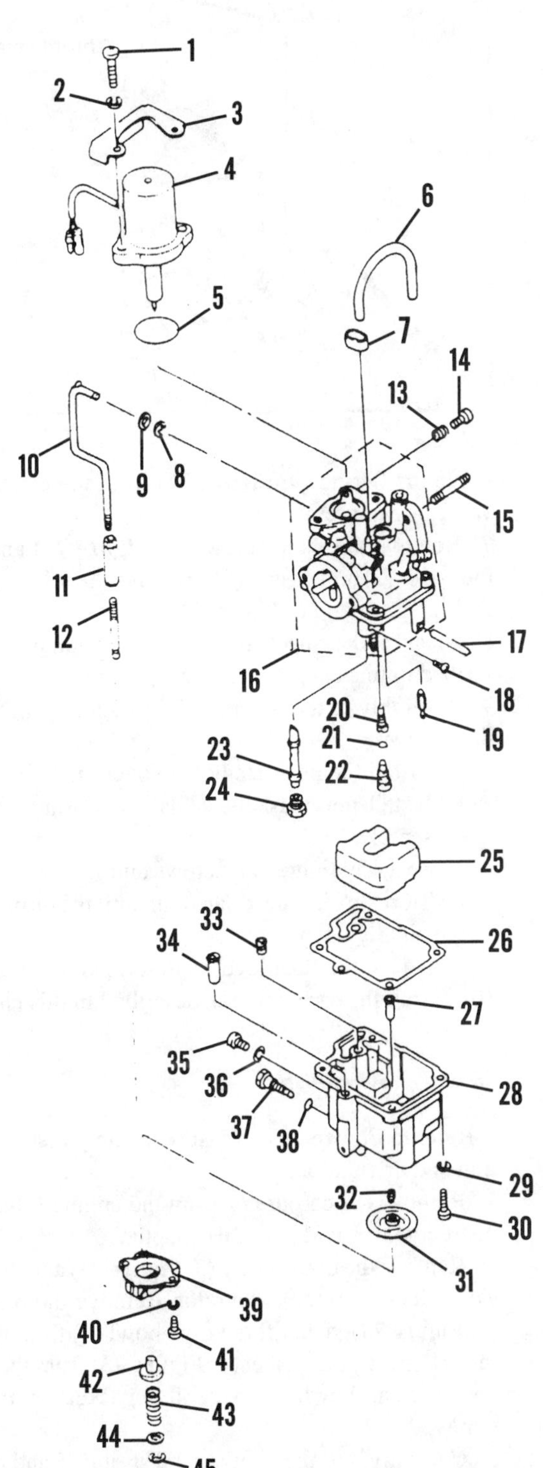

1. Screw
2. Washer
3. Bracket
4. Electrothermal valve
5. O-ring
6. Hose
7. Clamp
8. Clip
9. Washer
10. Accelerator pump linkage
11. Shaft
12. Linkage
13. Spring
14. Idle speed screw
15. Mounting stud
16. Carburetor body
17. Float pin
18. Nozzle retaining screw
19. Inlet needle
20. Pilot screw
21. Gasket
22. Plug
23. Main nozzle
24. Main fuel jet
25. Float
26. Gasket
27. Screen
28. Float bowl
29. Washer
30. Screw
31. Diaphragm
32. Spring
33. Starter jet
34. Valve
35. Screw
36. Gasket
37. Drain screw
38. Gasket
39. Accelerator pump cover
40. Washer
41. Screw
42. Plug
43. Spring
44. Washer
45. Clip

from the carburetor. Using a suitable screwdriver, remove the main fuel jet (24, **Figure 70**) from the carburetor. Remove the main nozzle retaining screw (18, **Figure 70**). Insert a screwdriver into the throttle bore opening and push the main nozzle (**Figure 67**) down and out of the carburetor.

5. Remove the clamp (7, **Figure 70**), then pull the hose (6) from the carburetor. Remove the idle speed screw and spring (13 and 14, **Figure 70**). Remove the clip (8, **Figure 70**) and remove the accelerator pump linkage from the throttle linkage.
6. Clean and inspect all carburetor components as outlined this chapter.
7. Assembly is the reverse of disassembly while noting the following.
   a. Adjust the float level as described in this section.
   b. Install new gaskets, seals and O-rings during assembly.
   c. Push the main nozzle fully into its opening (**Figure 67**). Position the notch in the throttle bore as shown in **Figure 71**.
   d. Turn the idle speed screw in until the throttle plate is slightly open.
8. Install the carburetor following the instructions provided in this chapter.

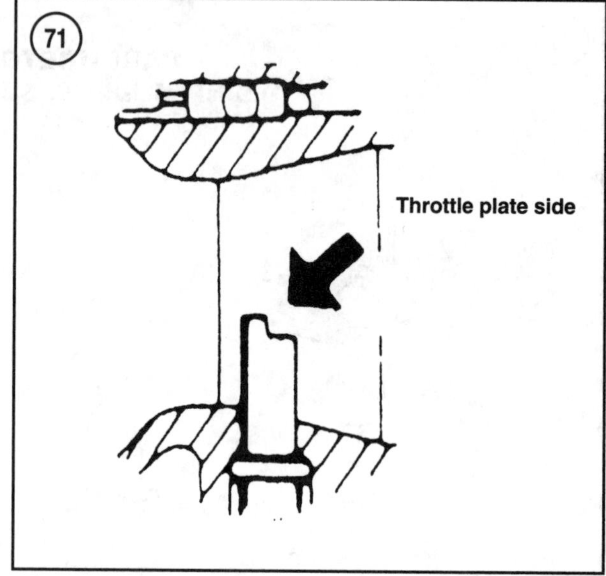

25 hp models

Refer to **Figure 72** to assist with component identification and orientation.

1. Remove the carburetor from the engine as described in this chapter.
2. Remove the drain screw (31, **Figure 72**) and drain all residual fuel from the carburetor. Remove the four screws (30, **Figure 72**) and lift the float bowl (29) from the carburetor. Remove the gasket (24, **Figure 72**) from the carburetor or float bowl. Replace the gasket anytime it is removed.
3. Carefully pull the plunger and spring (25 and 26, **Figure 72**) from the float bowl. Remove the screw (**Figure 69**), then lift the float (19, **Figure 72**), float pin (20) and inlet needle (18) from the carburetor.
4. Using a suitable screwdriver, remove the main fuel jet (17, **Figure 72**) from the carburetor. Insert a screwdriver into the throttle bore opening and push the main nozzle (**Figure 67**) down and out of the carburetor.
5. Carefully remove the plug (15, **Figure 72**), then remove the pilot jet from the carburetor. Pull the accelerator pump rod and boot from the carburetor body.
6. Remove the screw (10, **Figure 72**) and remove the electrothermal valve (4, **Figure 72**) and bracket (11). Remove the O-ring (9, **Figure 72**) from the electrothermal valve or carburetor.
7. Remove the three screws (1, **Figure 72**) and remove the cover (2) and gasket (3). Remove the idle speed screw and spring (5 and 6, **Figure 72**).
8. Clean and inspect all carburetor components as described in this chapter.
9. Assembly is the reverse of disassembly while noting the following.
   a. Install the inlet needle clip over the float tab.
   b. Install new gaskets, seals and O-rings during assembly.
   c. Securely tighten all screws and jets.
   d. Turn the idle speed screw in until the throttle plate is slightly open.
   e. Adjust the float level as described in this section.
10. Install the carburetor as described in this chapter.

30 and 40 hp models

Refer to **Figure 73** to assist with component identification and orientation.

1. Remove the carburetor from the engine following the instructions provided in this chapter.
2. Remove the drain screw (3, **Figure 73**) and drain all residual fuel from the carburetor. Remove the four screws (2, **Figure 73**), then lift the float bowl (1) from the carburetor. Remove the gasket (8, **Figure 73**) from the carburetor or float bowl. Replace the gasket anytime it is removed.
3. Carefully pull the plunger and spring (5 and 6, **Figure 73**) from the float bowl. Remove the screw (**Figure 69**)

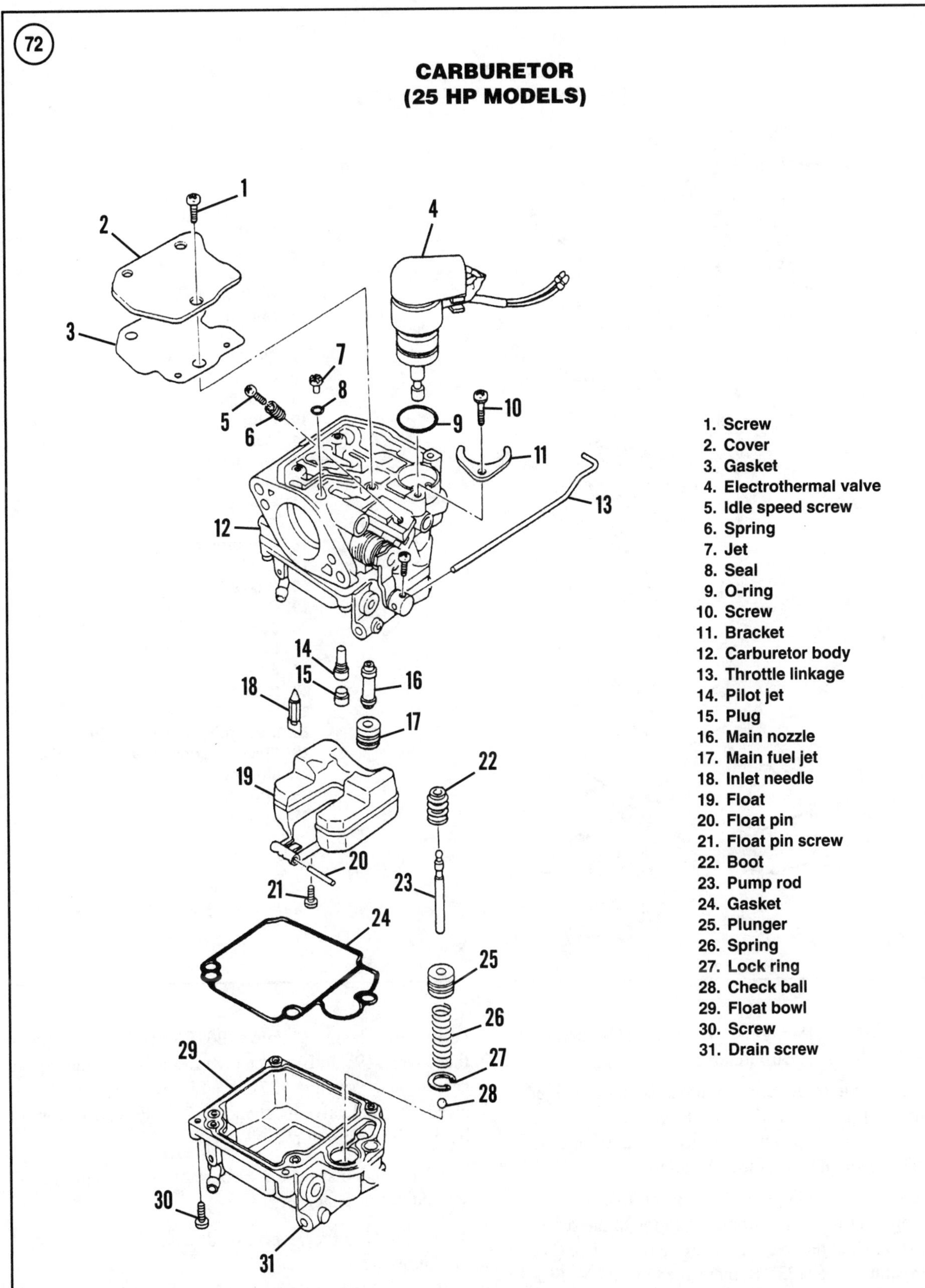
72
CARBURETOR
(25 HP MODELS)
1. Screw
2. Cover
3. Gasket
4. Electrothermal valve
5. Idle speed screw
6. Spring
7. Jet
8. Seal
9. O-ring
10. Screw
11. Bracket
12. Carburetor body
13. Throttle linkage
14. Pilot jet
15. Plug
16. Main nozzle
17. Main fuel jet
18. Inlet needle
19. Float
20. Float pin
21. Float pin screw
22. Boot
23. Pump rod
24. Gasket
25. Plunger
26. Spring
27. Lock ring
28. Check ball
29. Float bowl
30. Screw
31. Drain screw

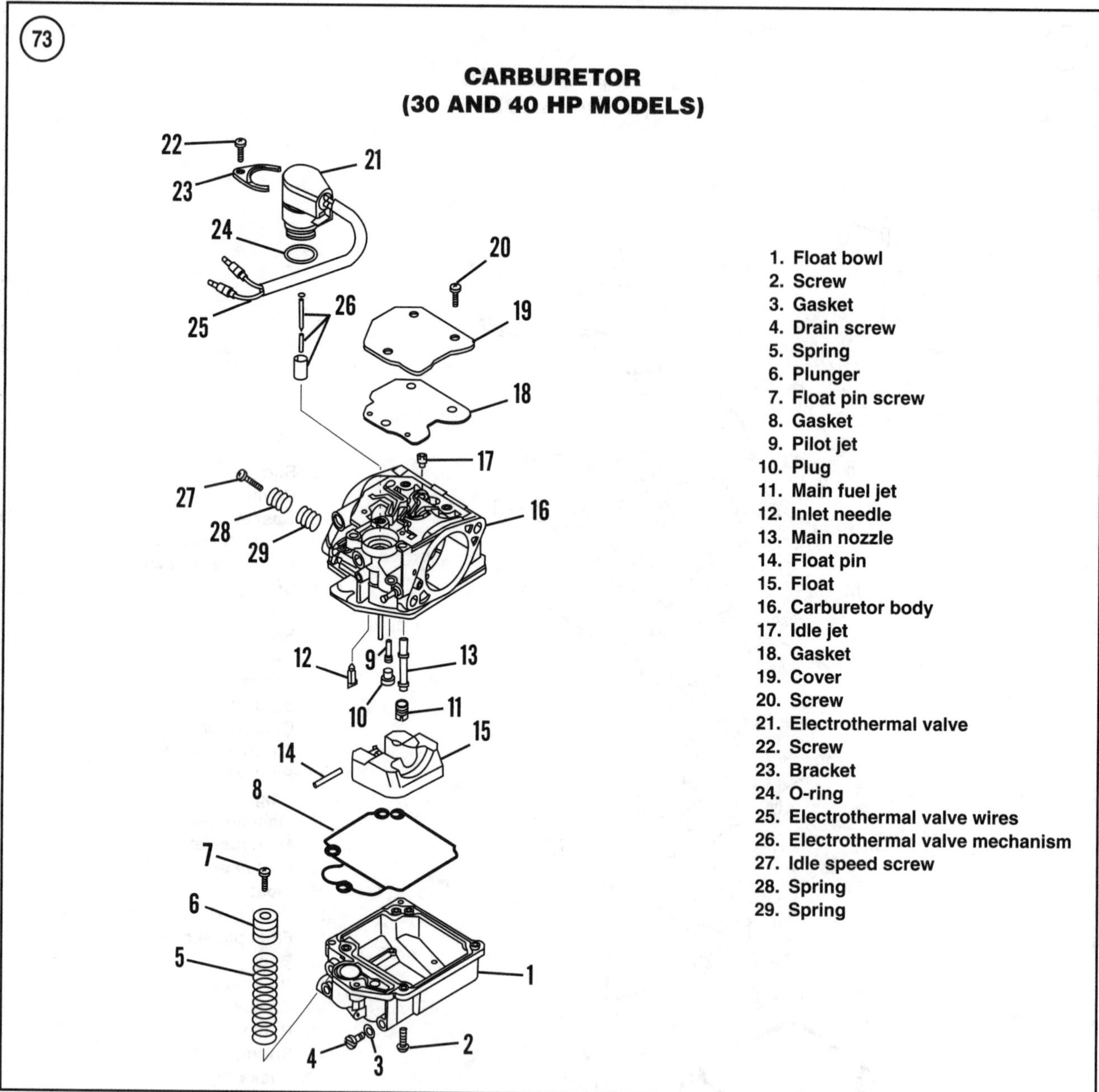

and remove the float (15, **Figure 73**), float pin (14) and inlet needle (12) from the carburetor.

4. Using a suitable screwdriver, remove the main fuel jet (11, **Figure 73**) from the carburetor. Insert a screwdriver into the throttle bore opening and push the main nozzle (**Figure 67**) down and out of the carburetor.

5. Carefully pry out the plug (10, **Figure 73**), then remove the pilot jet from the carburetor. Remove the screw (22, **Figure 73**) and remove the electrothermal valve (21, **Figure 73**) and bracket (23). Remove the O-ring (24, **Figure 73**) from the electrothermal valve or carburetor.

6. Remove the three screws (20, **Figure 73**) and remove the cover (19) and gasket (18).Remove the idle speed screw and spring (27-29, **Figure 73**). Pull the electrothermal valve mechanism (26, **Figure 73**) from its bore in the carburetor.

7. Clean and inspect all carburetor components as described in this chapter.

8. Assembly is the reverse of disassembly while noting the following:

   a. Install the inlet needle clip over the float tab.

74

CARBURETOR (50 HP MODELS)

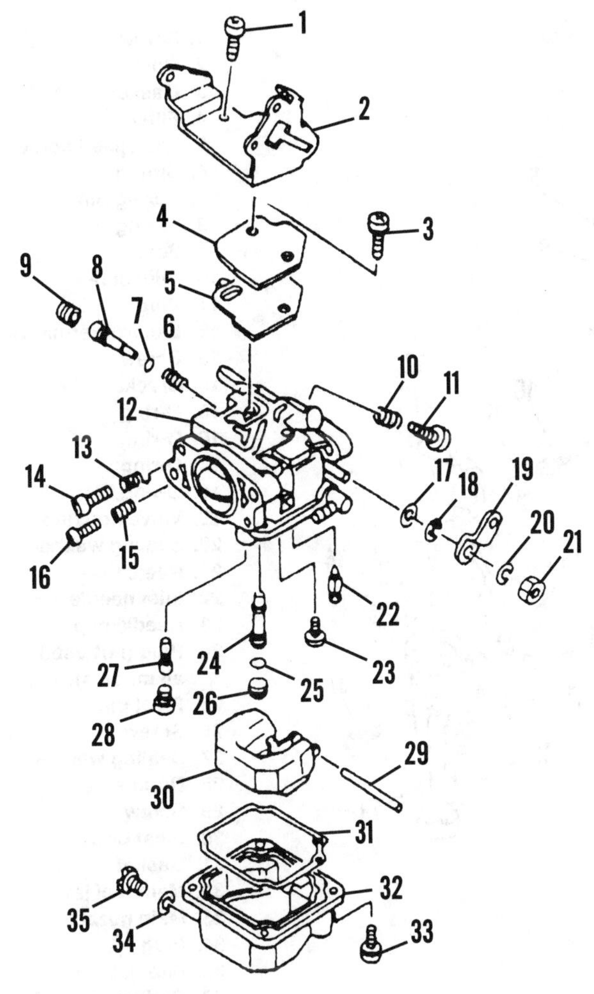

1. Screw
2. Accelerator pump bracket
3. Screw
4. Cover
5. Gasket
6. Spring*
7. Seal*
8. Pilot screw*
9. Plug
10. Spring
11. Screw
12. Carburetor body
13. Spring
14. Screw
15. Spring
16. Screw
17. Washer
18. Clip
19. Throttle lever
20. Clip
21. Nut
22. Inlet needle
23. Float pin screw
24. Main nozzle
25. Seal
26. Plug
27. Pilot jet
28. Main fuel jet
29. Float pin
30. Float
31. Gasket
32. Float bowl
33. Screw
34. Sealing gasket
35. Drain screw

*Do not remove this component when reference No. 9 is used.

b. Install new gaskets, seals and O-rings during assembly.

c. Securely tighten all screws and jets.

d. Turn the idle speed screw in until the throttle plate is slightly open.

e. Adjust the float level as described in this section.

9. Install the carburetor as described in this chapter

50 hp models

Refer to **Figure 74** to assist with component identification and orientation.

1. Remove the carburetor from the engine following the instructions provided in this chapter.
2. Remove the drain screw (34, **Figure 74**) then drain all residual fuel from the carburetor. Remove the four screws (33, **Figure 74**) and lift the float bowl (32) from the carburetor. Remove the gasket (31, **Figure 74**) from the carburetor or float bowl. Replace the gasket anytime it is removed.
3. Remove the screw (**Figure 69**) and remove the float (30, **Figure 74**), float pin (29) and inlet needle (22) from the carburetor.
4. Using a suitable screwdriver, remove the plug and gasket (25 and 26, **Figure 74**) from the carburetor. Insert a

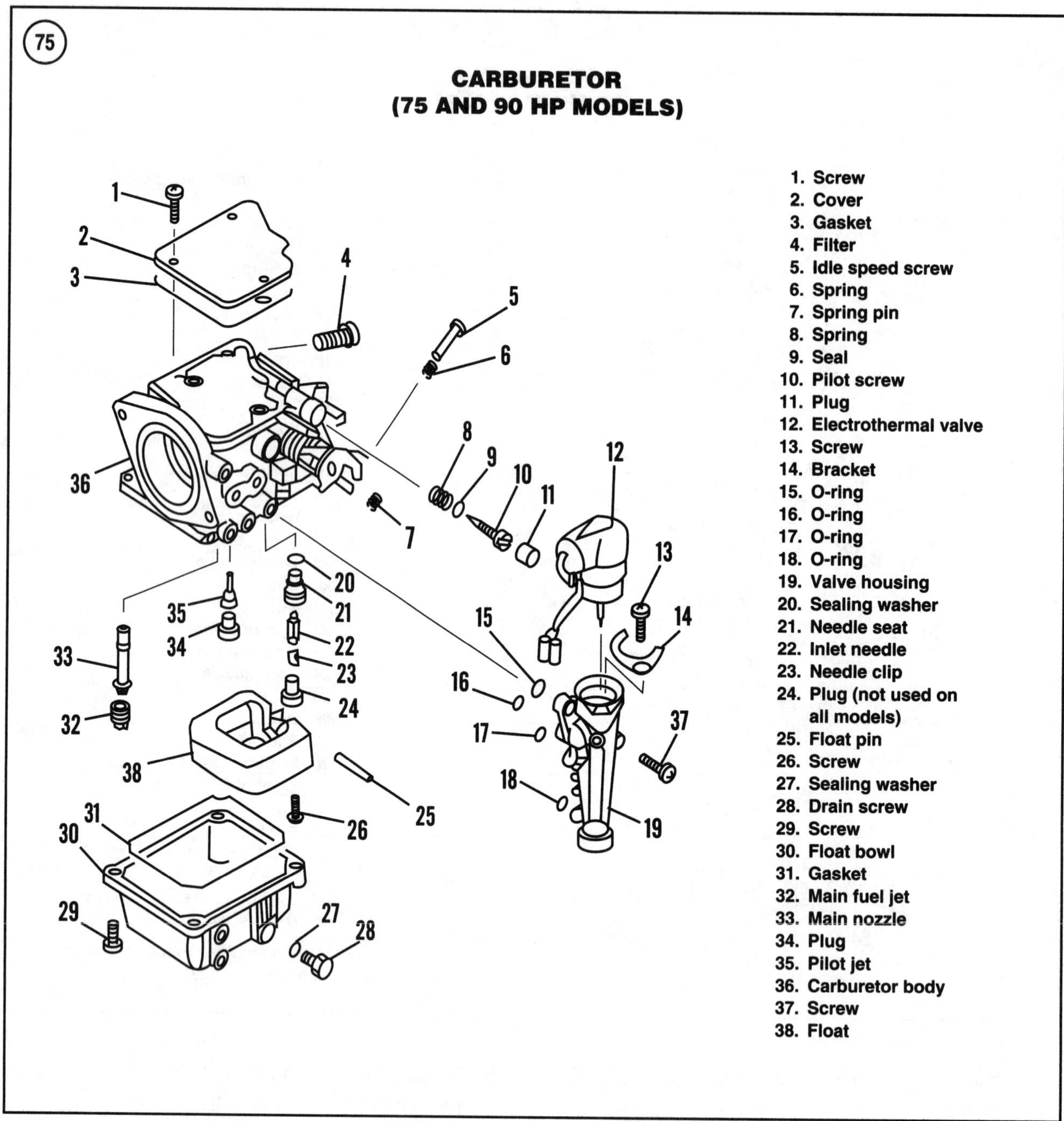

screwdriver into the throttle bore opening and push the main nozzle (**Figure 67**) down and out of the carburetor.

5. Using a suitable screwdriver remove the main fuel jet (28, **Figure 74**) and pilot jet (27) from the carburetor. Remove the pilot jet from the carburetor.

6. Remove the screws (1, **Figure 74**) and lift the accelerator pump bracket from the carburetor. Remove both screws (3, **Figure 74**) and remove the cover (4) and gasket (5) from the carburetor.

7. Clean and inspect all carburetor components as described in this chapter.

8. Assembly is the reverse of disassembly while noting the following.

   a. Install the inlet needle clip over the float tab.

   b. Install new gaskets, seals and O-rings during assembly.

   c. Securely tighten all screws and jets.

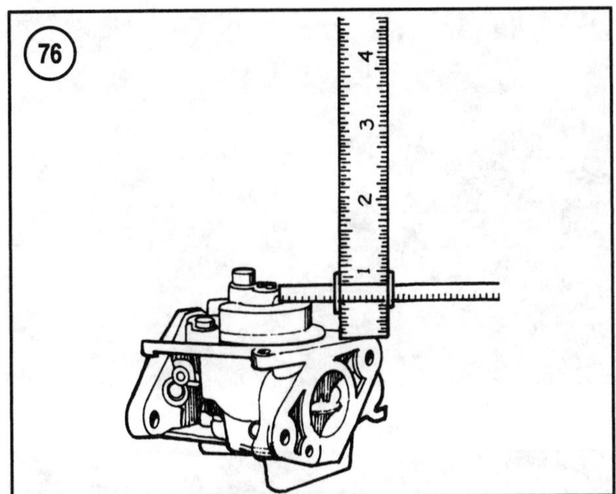

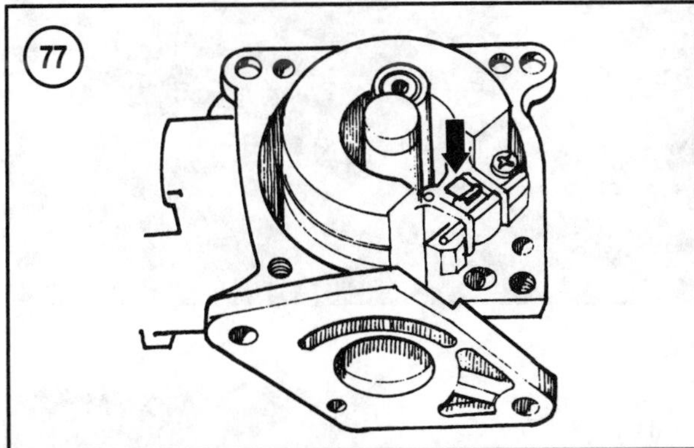

d. Turn the idle speed screw in until the throttle plate is slightly open.

e. Adjust the float level following the instructions in this section.

9. Install the carburetor following the instructions this chapter.

75 and 90 hp models

Refer to **Figure 75** to assist with component identification and orientation.

1. Remove the carburetor from the engine following the instructions in this chapter.
2. Remove the drain screw (27, **Figure 75**) and drain all residual fuel from the carburetor. Remove the four screws (29, **Figure 75**), then lift the float bowl (30) from the carburetor. Remove the gasket (31, **Figure 75**) from the carburetor or float bowl. Replace the gasket anytime it is removed.
3. Remove the screw (**Figure 69**) and remove the float (38, **Figure 75**), float pin (25) and inlet needle (22) from the carburetor. Using a large screwdriver, remove the inlet needle seat (21, **Figure 75**) and gasket (20).
4. Using a suitable screwdriver, remove the main fuel jet (32, **Figure 75**) from the carburetor. Insert a screwdriver into the throttle bore opening and push the main nozzle (**Figure 67**) down and out of the carburetor. Carefully pry out the plug (34, **Figure 75**) from the carburetor then remove the pilot jet (35).
5. Remove the three screws (1, **Figure 75**) and lift the cover (2) and gasket (3) from the carburetor. Remove the idle speed screw and spring (5 and 6, **Figure 75**) from the carburetor. Remove the screw (13, **Figure 75**) and remove the electrothermal valve (12) and bracket (14) from the carburetor. Remove the O-ring from the electrothermal valve. Replace the O-ring anytime it is removed.
6. Remove the screws (37, **Figure 75**) and pull the valve housing (19) from the side of the carburetor. Remove the four O-rings (15-18, **Figure 75**) from the carburetor or valve housing.
7. Clean and inspect all carburetor components following the instructions in this chapter.
8. Assembly is the reverse of disassembly while noting the following.
   a. Install the inlet needle clip over the float tab.
   b. Install new gaskets, seals and O-rings during assembly.
   c. Securely tighten all screws and jets.
   d. Turn the idle speed screw in until the throttle plate is slightly open.
   e. Adjust the float level following the instructions in this section.
9. Install the carburetor following the instructions in this chapter.

6

Float Adjustment (Except 50 hp Models)

CAUTION
Never force the float toward the carburetor. Allow the float to just rest on the inlet needle when measuring the float height. Remove the float and bend the tab with needlenose pliers. Never bend the float arm with it installed on the carburetor.

1. Assemble the inlet needle and float onto the carburetor. Ensure the needle clip is positioned over the float tab.
2. Turn the carburetor upside down (**Figure 76**). Allow the tab on the float (**Figure 77**) to just rest on the inlet needle.

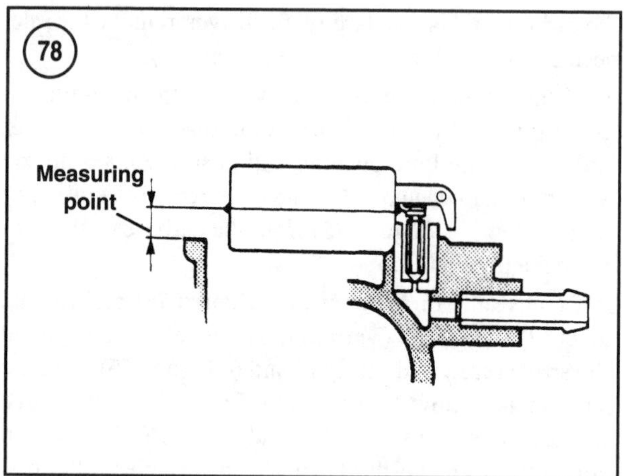

3. Measure the distance from the carburetor body to the bottom surface of the float (**Figure 76**). Compare the measurement with the specification listed in **Table 1**.
4. Bend the metal tab (**Figure 77**) up or down until the specified measurement is attained.

Float Adjustment (50 hp Models)

1. Assemble the inlet needle and float onto the carburetor. Ensure the needle clip is positioned over the float tab.
2. Turn the carburetor upside down (**Figure 76**). Allow the tab on the float (**Figure 77**) to just rest on the inlet needle.
3. Measure the distance from the carburetor to middle of the float (**Figure 78**). Compare the measurement with the specification listed in **Table 1**.
4. Bend the metal tab (**Figure 77**) up or down until the specified measurement is attained.

Dashpot Removal/Installation (50 hp Models)

The dashpot is mounted on the rear starboard side of the power head. Remove and install the dashpot as follows:
1. Disconnect both cables from the battery.
2. Remove both screws (**Figure 79**) and lift the dashpot and bracket from the intake manifold. Count the number of threads exposed on the adjustment bolt (**Figure 80**).
3. Loosen the jam nut, then remove the dashpot from the bracket. Thread the replacement dashpot onto the bracket until the same number of threads are exposed (Step 2). Securely tighten the jam nut.
4. Install the dashpot and bracket in position on the intake manifold. Install both mounting screws (**Figure 79**). Securely tighten the screws.

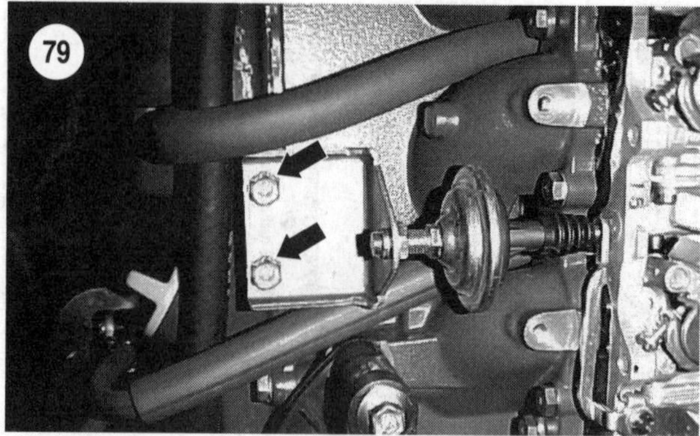

5. Clean the terminals and connect the cables to the battery if so equipped. Adjust the dashpot following the instructions in Chapter Five.

Dashpot Removal/Installation (75 and 90 hp Models)

The dashpot is mounted to the lower rear port side of the power head (**Figure 81**). Remove and install the dashpot as follows.
1. Disconnect both cables from the battery.

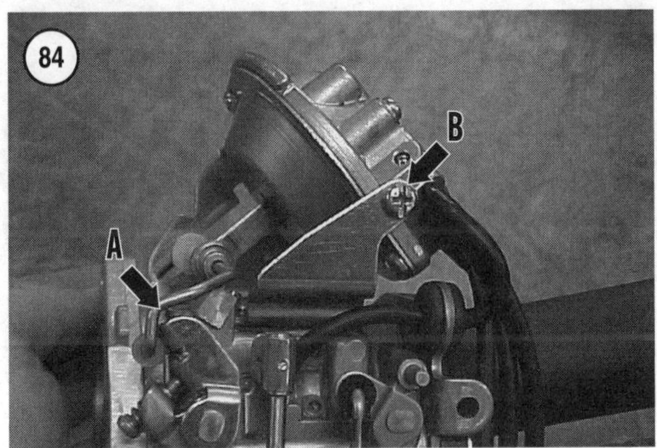

2. Disconnect the dashpot linkage from the throttle lever (**Figure 81**). Remove both screws (**Figure 82**) and lift the dashpot from the intake manifold.
3. Connect the dashpot linkage to the throttle lever (**Figure 81**). Install the dashpot and bracket in position on the intake manifold. Install and tighten both mounting screws (**Figure 82**).
4. Connect the cables to the battery if so equipped. Adjust the dashpot following the instructions in Chapter Five.

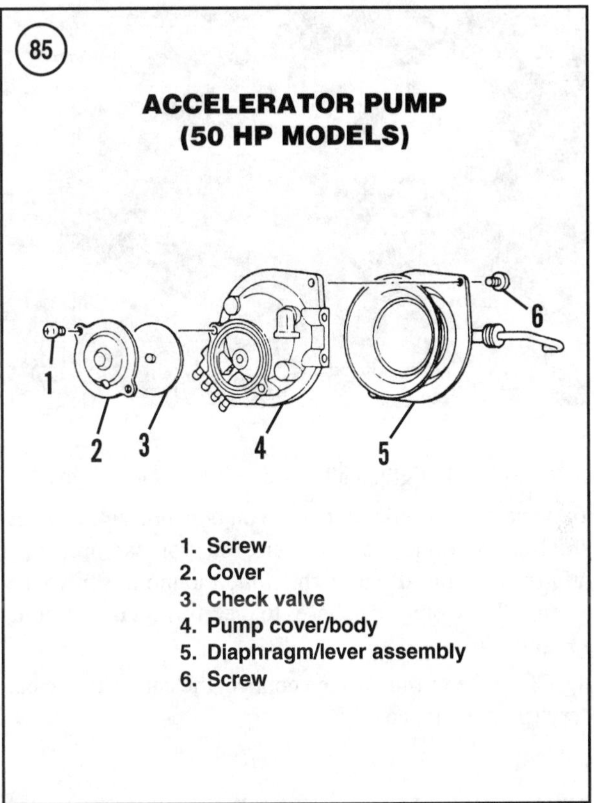

Accelerator Pump Removal/Installation (50 hp Models)

This section provides removal, repair and installation instructions for the accelerator pump assembly (**Figure 83**) used on all 50 hp models. Other models utilize a carburetor mounted accelerator pump. Refer to *Carburetors* in this chapter for repair instructions involving the accelerator pump on other models.

1. Disconnect both cables from the battery.
2. Disconnect the pump linkage (A, **Figure 84**) from the throttle lever on the top carburetor. Note the routing and connection points then remove each hose from the accelerator pump. Remove the mounting screws (B, **Figure 84**) and lift the accelerator pump from its mounting bracket.
3. Remove both screws (1, **Figure 85**) and lift the cover (2) and check valve (3) from the pump. Remove both screws (6, **Figure 85**), then lift the pump cover (4) from the diaphragm (5).
4. Clean all components with a mild solvent such as kerosene. Inspect the diaphragm/lever for holes and excessive wear. Inspect the check valve for wear, cracks or damage. Replace any damaged components.
5. Assembly is the reverse of disassembly.
   a. Assemble the components as shown in **Figure 85**.

6

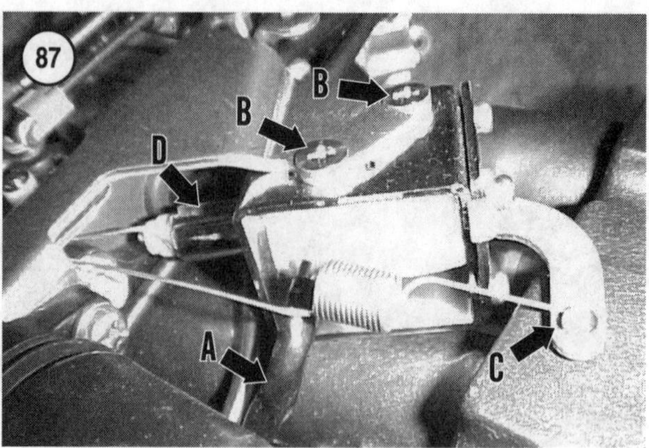

b. Securely tighten all screws.

6. Install the accellerator pump onto its bracket. Connect the linkage to the throttle lever of the top carburetor (A, **Figure 84**). Install and tighten the mounting screws (B, **Figure 84**). Connect all hoses to their fittings on the pump (**Figure 86**).

7. Clean the terminals then connect the cables to the battery (if so equipped).

Choke Solenoid Removal/Installation (9.9, 15 and 50 hp Models)

A choke solenoid (**Figure 87**) is used on electric start 9.9 and 15 hp and all 50 hp models.

Remove and install the choke solenoid as follows:

1. On 50 hp models, Remove the silencer cover, carburetors and intake manifold as an assembly following the instructions in this chapter.
2. Disconnect the choke solenoid (A, **Figure 87**) from the engine wire harness.
3. Disconnect the spring from the lever (C, **Figure 87**). Remove the mounting screws (B, **Figure 87**) and lift the solenoid from the solenoid plunger (D).
4. Clean the solenoid plunger and plunger opening in the solenoid using a corrosion preventative spray such as WD 40.
5. Installation is the reverse of removal while noting the following:
   a. Route all wires in a manner away from moving components.
   b. Guide the choke plunger into the solenoid opening during installation.
   c. Check for proper choke operation after installation. Refer to Chapter Three for testing instructions.

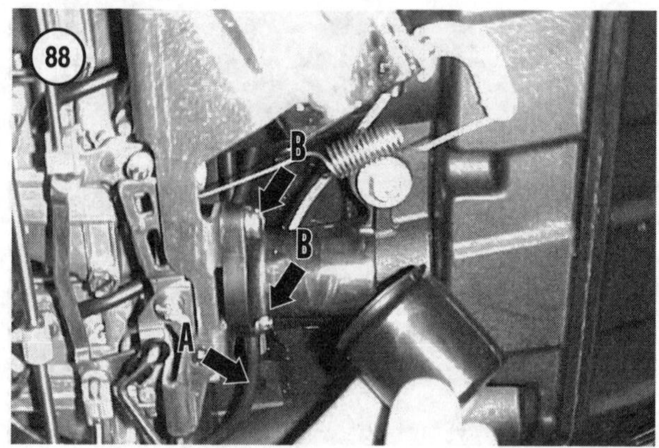

6. Clean the terminals then connect the cables to the battery if so equipped.

Electrothermal Valve Removal/Installation (50 hp Models)

On 50 hp models remove and install the electrothermal valve as follows:

1. Disconnect both cables from the battery.
2. Disconnect the electrothermal valve (A, **Figure 88**) from the engine wire harness.
3. Remove the cover from the valve (**Figure 88**). Remove both mounting screws (B, **Figure 88**) and lift the electrothermal valve from its mounting bracket.
4. Installation is the reverse of removal while noting the following:
   a. Mount the valve with the wires exiting the valve on the lower side.
   b. Securely tighten the mounting screws.
   c. Route all wires away from moving components.
   d. Install the cover to help ensure correct operation of the valve.
5. Connect the cables to the battery if so equipped.

Table 1 FLOAT HEIGHT

Model	Measurement
4-6 hp	0.35-0.39 in. (9-9.9 mm)
9.9 hp	
Serial No. OH000057-prior	0.57-0.65 in. (14.5-15.5 mm)
Serial No. OH000058-on	0.96-1.04 in. (24.4-26.4 mm)
15 hp	0.57-0.65 in. (14.5-16.5 mm)
25-40 hp	0.47-0.63 in. (11.9-16 mm)
50 hp	0.37-0.41 in. (9.5-10.5 mm)
75 and 90 hp	0.51-0.59 in. (13-15 mm)

Table 2 INITIAL PILOT SCREW SETTING

Model	Turns out from a light seat
4 and 5 hp	2-1/2 to 3-1/2
9.9 hp	
Serial No. OH000057-prior*	–
Serial No. OH000058-on	2 to 3
15 hp*	–
25-40 hp*	–
50 hp	
1995-1997	2-1/2
1998-on*	–
75 hp	2 to 3
90 hp	1-1/2 to 2-1/2

*These models are not equipped with adjustable pilot screws.

Table 3 CARBURETOR JET SPECIFICATIONS

Model	Jet number/size
4 hp	
Main jet	70
Pilot jet	40
5 hp	
Main jet	70
Pilot jet	42
6 hp	
Main jet	75
Pilot jet	45
9.9 hp	
Serial No. OH000057-prior	
Main jet	68
Pilot jet	45
Serial No. OH000058-on	
Main jet	86
Pilot jet	48
Enrichner jet	0.024 in. (0.61 mm)
15 hp	
Main jet	104
Pilot jet	45
25 hp	
Main jet	115
Pilot jet	50
Idle jet	45
30 and 40 hp	
Main jet	98

(continued)

Table 3 CARBURETOR JET SPECIFICATIONS (continued)

Model	Jet number/size
30 and 40 hp (continued)	
Pilot jet	38
Idle jet	42
50 hp	
Main jet	112
Pilot jet	42
75 hp	
Main fuel jet	112
Main air jet	115
Pilot fuel jet	45
Pilot air jet	85
90 hp	
Main fuel jet	128
Main air jet	75
Pilot fuel jet	42
Pilot air jet	85
Mid range jet	40

Table 4 TIGHTENING TORQUE

Fastener location	in.-lb.	N•m
Silencer/cover		
50 hp		
Front bolts	50	5
Side bolts	75	8
75 and 90 hp		
Front bolts	70	8
Side bolts	159	18
Intake manifold		
4-6 hp	70	8
9.9 and 15 hp	70	8
25-40 hp	75	9
50 hp	70	8
75 and 90 hp	159	18
Carburetor mounting		
9.9 hp (serial No. OH000057-prior)	88	10
15 hp	88	10
25 hp	75	9
30-90 hp	70	8
Fuel pump cover		
9.9 hp (serial No. OH000057-prior)	13	1.5
15 hp	13	1.5
75 and 90 hp	27	3
Fuel pump mounting		
9.9 and 15 hp	70	8
25-50 hp	75	9
75 and 90 hp	70	8
Choke bracket		
9.9 hp (serial No. OH000057-prior)	70	8
15 hp	70	8

Chapter Seven

Electrical and Ignition System

Tables 1-5 provide tightening torque specifications for electrical and ignition components, electric starter motor specifications, battery requirements, battery state of charge and battery capacities. **Tables 1-5** are located at the end of this chapter

BATTERY

Batteries used in marine applications are subjected to far more vibration and pounding action than automotive applications. Always use a battery designated for marine application (**Figure 1**). These batteries are constructed with thicker cases and plates than typical automotive batteries. This allows them to better handle the marine environment.

Use a battery meeting or exceeding the cold cranking amperage requirements for the engine. Cold cranking amperage requirements are provided in **Table 3**. Some marine batteries list *marine/deep cycle* on the label. Deep cycle batteries are constructed to allow repeated discharge and charge cycles. These batteries are excellent for powering accessories such as trolling motors. Always charge deep cycle batteries at a low amperage rate. They are not generally designed to be charged or discharged at a rapid rate. Rapid charging rates can significantly reduce the life of deep cycle batteries.

Table 5 lists the usage hours capacity for both 80 and 105 amp-hour batteries. Approximate recharge times are listed as well. Deep cycle batteries can be used as the starting battery providing they meet the cold cranking amperage requirements for the engine.

Loose or corroded cable connections cause many problems in marine applications. Use cable connectors securely crimped or molded to the cable. Avoid the use of temporary or emergency clamps for normal usage. They are prone to corrosion and do not meet the Coast Guard requirements for terminal connections.

Use a cover on the positive (+) terminal post. They are available at marine dealerships.

Make sure the battery is securely mounted in the boat to avoid dangerous acid spills or electrical arcing that can cause a fire. The most common types of battery mounting include the bracket mounted to the floor of the boat with a support across the top of the battery (**Figure 2**). The other common type of battery mounting is the battery case and cover enclosing the battery and securing it to the boat structure (**Figure 3**). When properly installed either of these methods provide secure mounting and protection for the terminals.

Mount the battery in a location allowing easy access for maintenance. Ensure the battery terminals are not able to contact any component in the mounting area. The rigorous marine usage can cause shifting of the battery during use.

WARNING
When mounting a battery in a boat constructed of aluminum take extra precaution to ensure the battery is securely mounted to eliminate the possibility of the battery contacting metal components. Electrical arcing can result in fire or explosion if a fuel source is present. Injury, death or damage to property can occur. Batteries produce explosive gasses that can ignite when arcing is present.

WARNING
Always wear gloves and protective eye wear when working with batteries. Batteries contain a corrosive and dangerous acid solution. Never smoke or allow any source of ignition to be near a battery. Batteries produce explosive gases that can ignite and result in an explosion if a source of ignition is present.

Battery Inspection

Inspect the battery case for cracks, leakage, abrasion and other damage when the battery is removed for charging. Replace the battery if any questionable condition exists. During normal usage a corrosive deposit forms on the top of the battery. These deposits may allow the battery to discharge at a rapid rate as current can travel through the deposits from one post to the other.

CAUTION
Never allow the water and baking soda solution to enter the battery solution through the vent caps. The acid solution becomes neutralized and causes permanent damage to the battery.

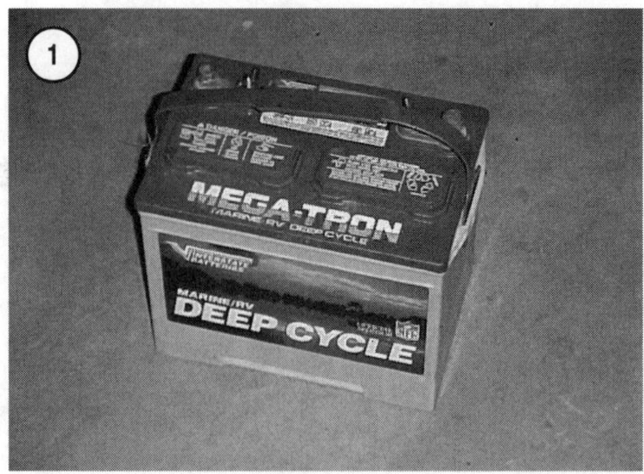

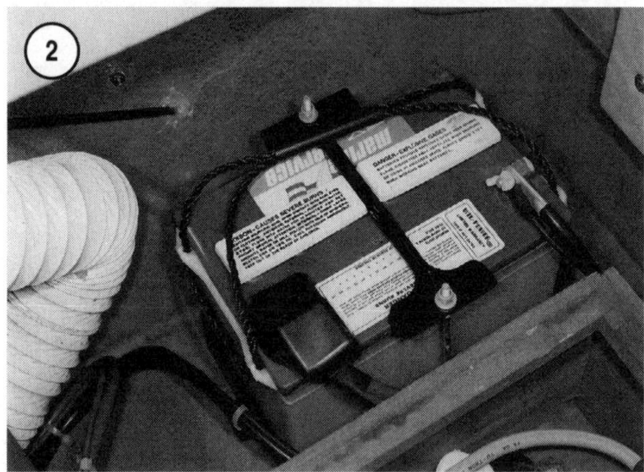

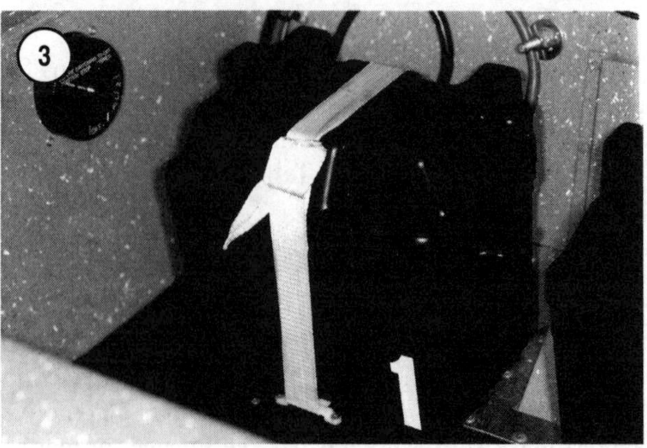

Make sure the battery caps are properly installed. Remove the battery from the boat and carefully wash loose material from the top of the battery with clean water. Use a solution of warm water and baking soda along with a soft bristled brush to clean deposits from the battery (**Figure 4**). Wash the battery again with clean water to remove all of the baking soda solution from the battery case.

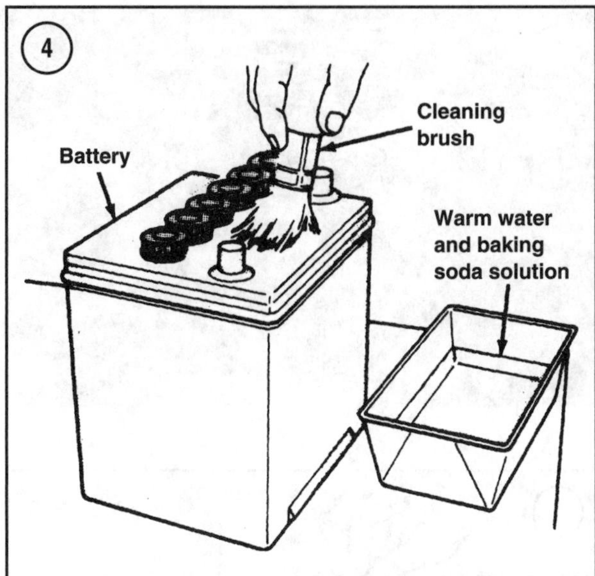

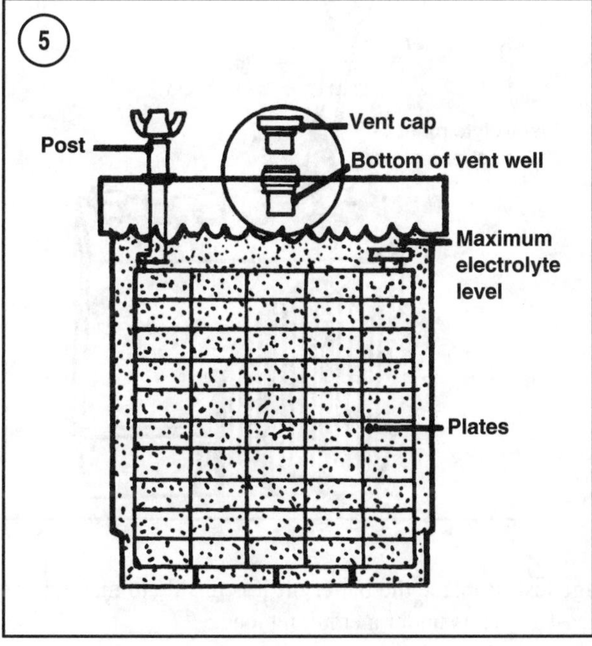

CAUTION
Never overfill the battery. The electrolyte may expand due to the heat created from charging and overflow from the battery.

Check the electrolyte level on a regular basis. Heavy usage or usage in warm climates increases the frequency for adding water to the battery. Carefully remove the vent caps (**Figure 5**) and inspect the electrolyte level in each cell. The electrolyte level should be 3/16 in. (4.8 mm) above the plates yet below the bottom of the vent well

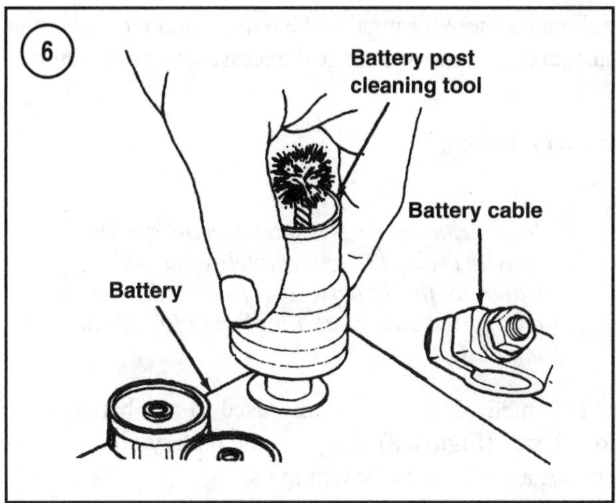

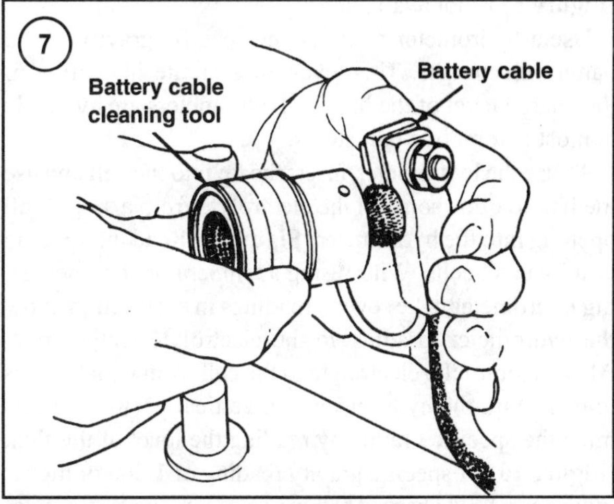

(**Figure 5**). Use distilled water to fill the cells to the proper level. Never use battery acid to correct the electrolyte level. The acidic solution becomes too strong and leads to damaged or deteriorated plates.

Clean the battery terminals at regular intervals or anytime the terminal is removed. Use a battery cleaning tool available at most automotive part stores to remove corrosion and deposits. Remove the terminal and clean the post (**Figure 6**). Rotate the tool on the post until the post is clean. Avoid removing too much material from the post or the terminal may not attach securely to the post.

Use the other end of the tool to clean the cable end terminal. Clean flat spade type connectors and the attaching nuts with the wire brush end of the tool (**Figure 7**).

Apply a coat of petroleum gel or other corrosion preventative to the battery posts and cable terminals. Tighten the fasteners securely. Avoid using excessive force when

7

tightening these terminals. The battery and terminals can sustain considerable damage if excessive force is applied.

Battery Testing

NOTE
Inaccurate readings result when the specific gravity is checked immediately after adding water to the battery. To ensure accuracy charge the battery at a high rate for 15-20 minutes.

Two methods are commonly used to test batteries. A load tester (**Figure 8**) measures the battery voltage as it applies a load across the terminals.

Perform a *Cranking Voltage Test* following the instructions in this section to check the battery if a load tester (**Figure 8**) is not available.

Use a hydrometer to check the specific gravity of the battery electrolyte. This gives an accurate indication of the charge level of the battery. Hydrometers are available at most automotive part stores.

To use the hydrometer, insert the tip into the cell and use the ball to draw some of the electrolyte from a single cell opening into the hydrometer (**Figure 9**). Read the specific gravity in all cells. When using a temperature compensating hydrometer, take several readings in each cell to allow the hydrometer to adjust to the electrolyte temperature. Always return the electrolyte to the cell from which it was drawn. With the hydrometer in a vertical position, determine the specific gravity by reading the level of the float (**Figure 10**). A specific gravity reading of 1.260 or higher indicates a fully charged battery. Compare the hydrometer readings with the information in **Table 4** to determine the state of charge. Always charge the battery if the specific gravity varies more than 0.050 from one cell to another.

NOTE
Add 0.004 to the reading for every 10° above 80° F (25° C) when the hydrometer is not a temperature compensating model. Subtract 0.004 from the reading for every 10° below 80° F (25° C).

Cranking Voltage Test

Check the battery condition by measuring the voltage at the battery terminals while cranking the engine. Connect the positive meter lead to the positive battery terminal. Connect the negative meter test lead to a suitable engine ground. Measure the voltage while cranking the engine (**Figure 11**). Fully charge the battery if the voltage drops below 9.6 volts while cranking. Repeat the cranking voltage test. Replace the battery if it is unable to maintain at least 9.6 volts under a cranking load.

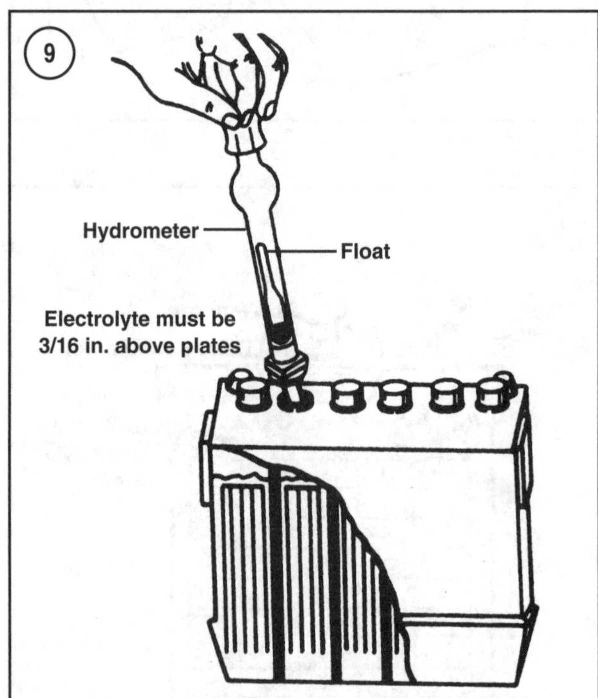

Battery Storage

Batteries lose some of the charge during storage. The rate of discharge increases in a warm environment. Store the battery in a cool, dry location to minimize the loss of charge. Check the specific gravity every 30 days and charge the battery as required. Perform the maintenance on the battery case and terminals as described in this section. Refer to *Battery Charging* in this section for battery charging times.

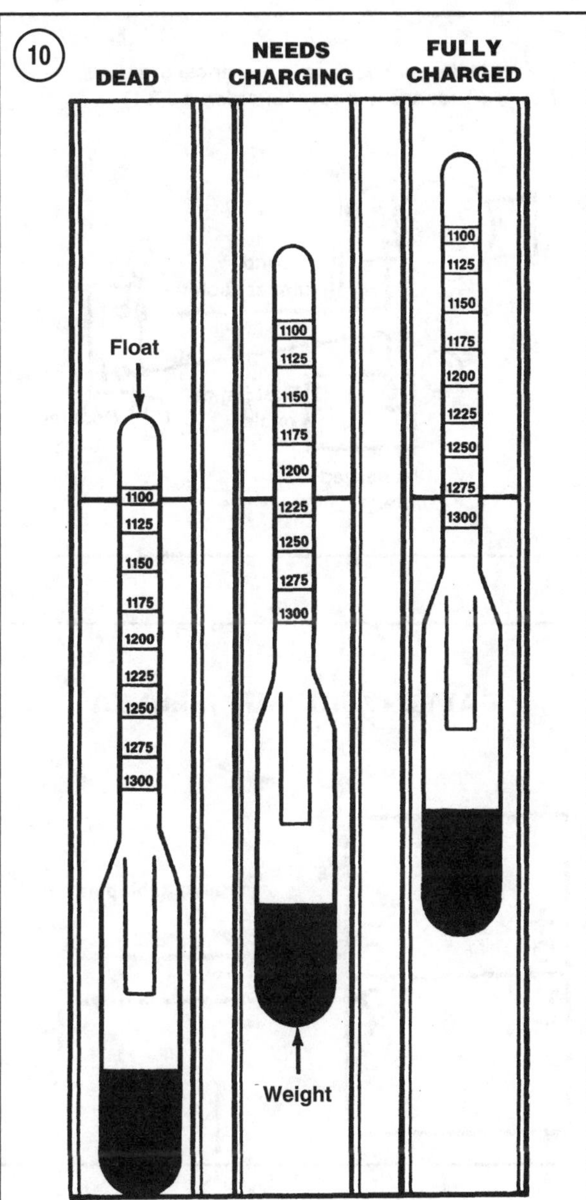

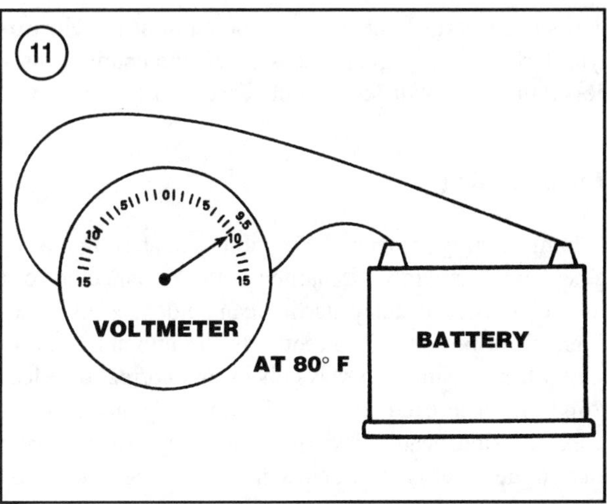

Battery Charging

WARNING
Batteries produce explosive hydrogen gas. Charge the battery in a well-ventilated area. Wear eye protection and suitable gloves when working around batteries. Never smoke or allow any source of ignition in the area where batteries are stored or charged. Never allow any noninsulated components to contact the battery terminals as arcing can occur and ignite the hydrogen gas. The battery can explode resulting in serious injury, death or damage to property.

Always remove the battery from the boat to charge it. Batteries produce explosive hydrogen gas while charging. This explosive gas can remain in the area long after the charging process is complete. In addition to the explosion hazard, the gas causes accelerated corrosion in the area around the battery compartment. Removing the battery also allows easier inspection and cleaning.

WARNING
Use extreme caution when connecting any wires to the battery terminals. Avoid making the last connection at the battery terminal. Explosive hydrogen gas in and around the battery may ignite and lead to an explosion resulting in injury, death or damage to property.

Connect the battery charger to the battery *before* plugging the charger in or switching the charger ON. This important step can help prevent dangerous arcing at the terminals. Connect the battery charger cables to the proper terminals on the battery. Plug the charger into its power supply and select the 12-volt setting.

Charging the battery at a slow rate (lower amperage) results in a more efficient charge and helps prolong the life of the battery. With a severely discharged battery it may be necessary to charge the battery at a higher amperage rate for a few minutes before starting the lower rate charge. A severely discharged battery may not allow the charging to begin without first *boost* charging at a high rate.

Battery charging time varies by the battery capacity and the state of charge. Typical battery charging times are provided in **Table 5**. Check the specific gravity often and halt the charging process when the battery is fully charged. Severely discharged batteries may require as long as eight hours to recharge. Check the temperature of the electrolyte during the charging process. Halt the charging process if the electrolyte temperature exceeds 125° F (53° C).

Jump Starting

Jump starting provides the capability of starting the engine with a severely discharged battery connected to a fully charged one. Jump starting can be dangerous, however, if not performed correctly. Never attempt to jump start a frozen battery. Always check and correct the electrolyte level in each battery before making any connection. A significant risk of explosion exists if the electrolyte level is at or below the top of the plates. Always use a good pair of jumper cables with clean connector clamps. Keep all clamps totally separated from any metallic or conductive material. Never allow the clamps to contact other clamps.

Follow Steps 1-6 when making jumper cable connections.

1. Connect the jumper cable clamp to the positive terminal of the discharged battery (1, **Figure 12**).
2. Connect the same jumper cable clamp to the positive terminal of the fully charged battery (2, **Figure 12**).
3. Connect the second jumper cable to the negative terminal of the fully charged battery (3, **Figure 12**).
4. Connect the second jumper cable remaining clamp to a good engine ground, such as the starter ground cable (4, **Figure 12**).
5. Make sure the cables and clamps are positioned so they will not or interfere with moving components.
6. Start the engine then remove the cables in the exact reverse of the connection order (Steps 1-4).

12 and 24 Volt Electric Trolling Motors

Many fishing boats are provided with an electric trolling motor requiring 24 volts to operate. Two or more batteries are necessary for this application. A series battery connection (**Figure 13**) provides 24 volts for the trolling motor.

A series connection provides the approximate total of the two batteries (24 volts). The amperage provided is the approximate average of the two batteries.

Connect the trolling motor batteries in a parallel arrangement (**Figure 14**) if the trolling motor requires 12 volts to operate.

The voltage provided is the approximate average of the two batteries (12 volt). The amperage provided is the approximate total of the two batteries.

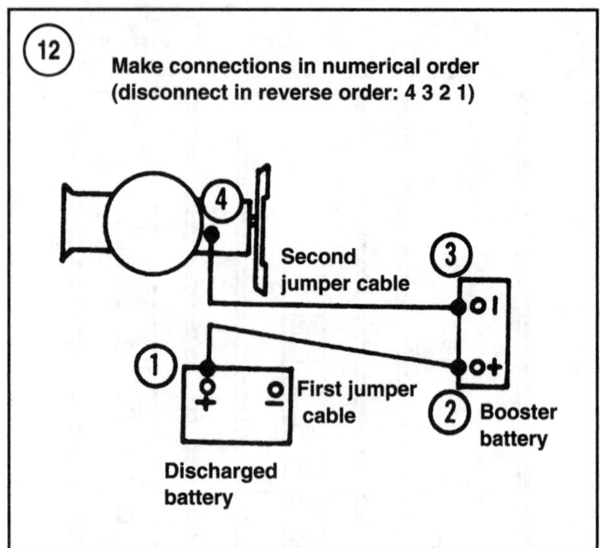

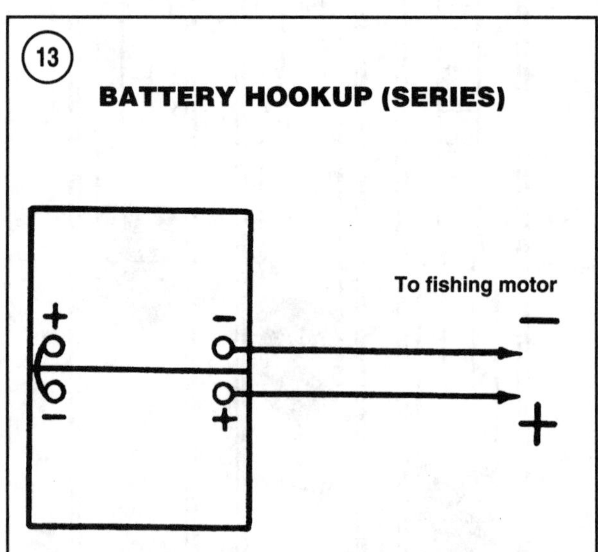

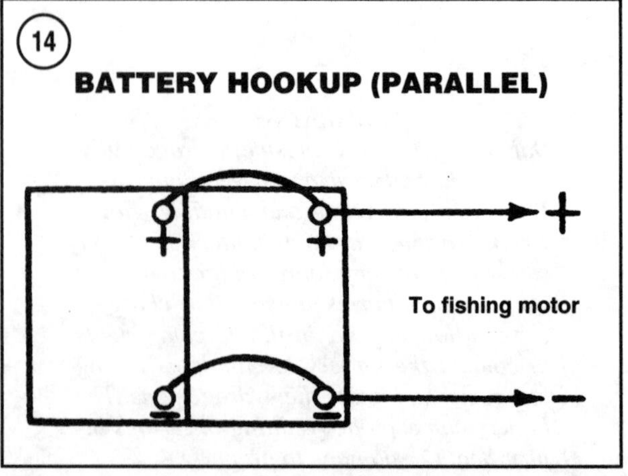

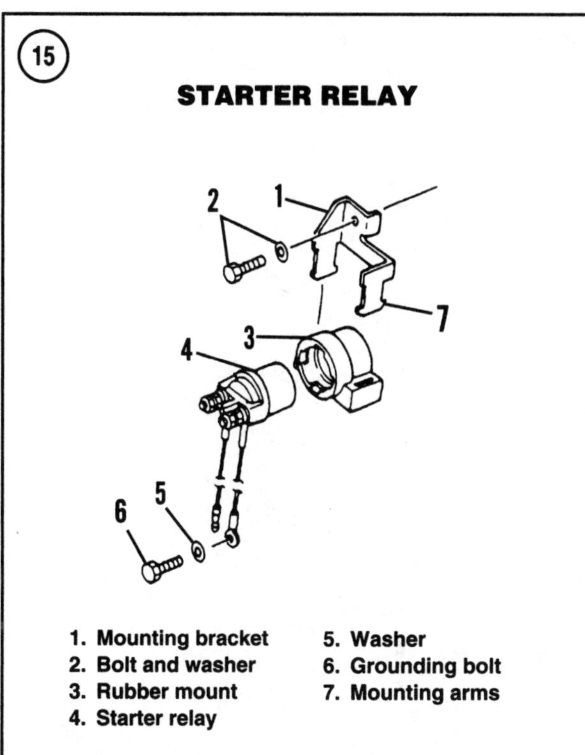

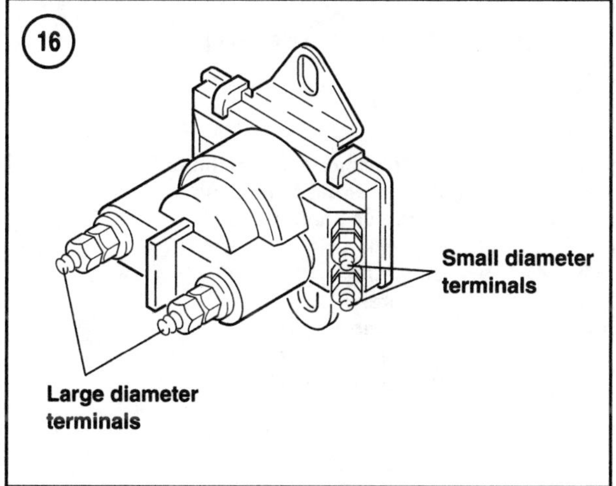

STARTING SYSTEM

This section provides removal, inspection and installation of the following components:

1. Starter relay.
2. Starter solenoid.
3. Ignition key switch.
4. Electric starter motor.
5. Neutral start switch.
6. Starter button.

In addition this chapter provides complete electric starter motor repair instructions.

Starter Relay Removal/Installation

Two different starter relays are used. All 9.9, 15, 50, 75 and 90 hp models utilize a rubber-mounted starter relay (**Figure 15**). This relay is retained by a snug fit in the rubber mount. The rubber mount is secured by a snug fit of the arms (7, **Figure 16**) in the mounting bracket (1). On 25-40 hp models, the relay is attached to a metal mounting bracket. Bolts, washers and grommets attach the relay to the power head.

To identify the starter relay, refer to the wire diagrams located at the back of the manual. Identify the wire color used for the relay. In all cases the relay is mounted near the electric starter motor. Refer to the instructions for the type of relay used on the selected model.

Rubber-mounted starter relay

1. Disconnect both cables from the battery.
2. Disconnect both larger diameter wires from the relay. Disconnect the smaller diameter wires from the engine wire harness or engine ground.
3. Carefully tug the starter relay (4, **Figure 15**) from the rubber mount (3).
4. Inspect the mount for damage or deterioration. Remove the mount by carefully tugging it from the mounting bracket. Replace the mount by slipping the elongated openings over the mounting arms (7). Ensure the arms pass completely through the elongated openings and the hooked ends engage the openings.
5. Slide the relay (4, **Figure 15**) fully into its opening in the rubber mount. Fit the lip on the opening over the outer edge of the relay.
6. Connect one large wire terminal over each large terminal of the relay. Securely tighten the terminal nuts. Ensure the wire terminals do not touch the other terminal or other components.
7. Connect one of the smaller diameter wires to the engine wire harness. Connect the other smaller diameter wire to the engine wire harness or engine ground. Route all wires away from contacting moving components.
8. Connect the cables to the battery. Check for proper starting system operation.

Bracket mounted starter relay

1. Disconnect both cables from the battery.

2. Disconnect the large diameter wires (**Figure 16**) from the starter relay. Remove the small screws and disconnect both small wires from the starter relay.
3. Remove the mounting bolts, washers, spacers and grommets and remove the relay from the power head. Clean the relay mounting surfaces.
4. Install the relay and all fasteners, spacers and grommets. If so equipped, reattach the ground wire to the relay mounting bolt.
5. Reattach the wires to the relay. Route all wires away from moving components.
6. Connect the battery cables to the battery and check starting system operation.

Starter Solenoid Removal (75 and 90 hp)

1. Remove the starter motor following the instructions in this chapter. Remove the larger nut retaining the short cable to the starter solenoid. Disconnect the cable from the starter solenoid.
2. Remove both bolts (1, **Figure 17**) and lift the starter solenoid (9) from the starter motor housing (2).
3. Pull the starter lever (4, **Figure 17**) from the starter motor housing (2). Pull the lever spring (5, **Figure 17**) from its mounting holes in the starter solenoid (9).
4. Remove both screws (6, **Figure 17**) then, lift the cover (7) from the starter solenoid (9).

Solenoid Test

1. Remove the solenoid from the starter motor following the instructions in this section.
2. Connect an ohmmeter between the two large solenoid terminals. The ohmmeter should indicate no continuity.
3. Clamp the solenoid into a vise with soft jaws. Using a jumper wire, connect the black/white solenoid terminal to the positive terminal of a12-volt battery.
4. Observe the ohmmeter while attaching a jumper wire from the negative terminal of the battery to an unpainted surface of the solenoid. Continuity should be present and the solenoid shaft should extend rapidly when the jumper wire is attached.
5. Replace the solenoid if fails to operate as described.

Solenoid Installation

1. Align the screw and spring holes in the cover (7, **Figure 17**) with their matching holes in the solenoid (9). Install and securely tighten both screws (6, **Figure 17**). Install both ends of the spring into the cover and solenoid as indicated in **Figure 17**.

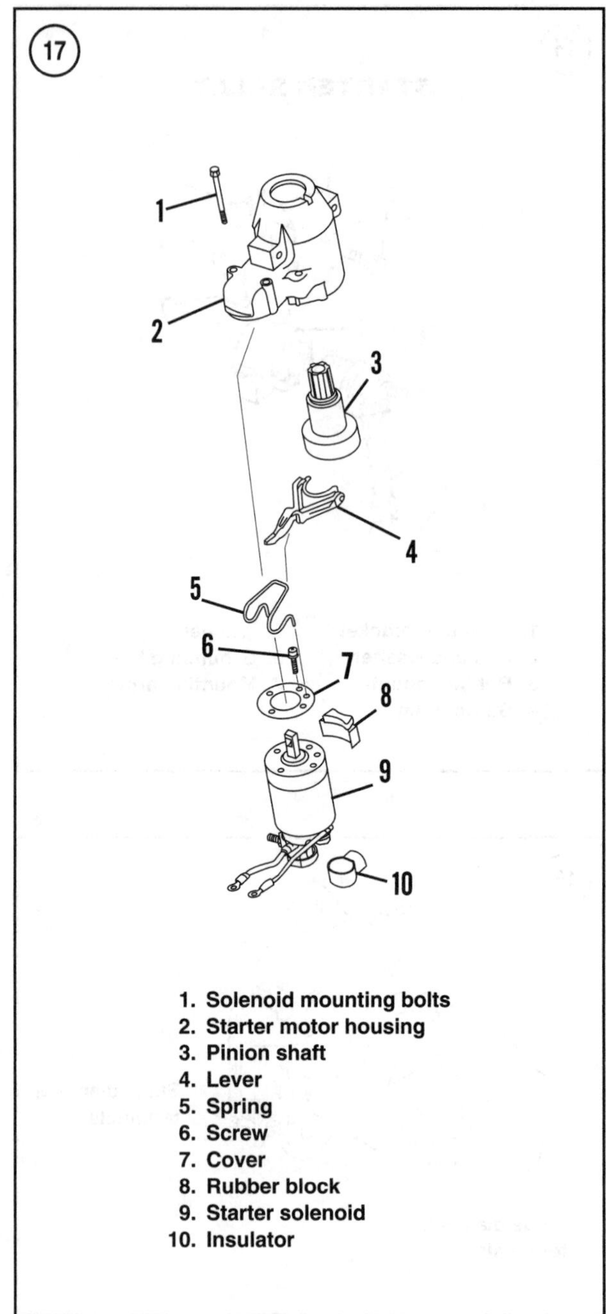

1. Solenoid mounting bolts
2. Starter motor housing
3. Pinion shaft
4. Lever
5. Spring
6. Screw
7. Cover
8. Rubber block
9. Starter solenoid
10. Insulator

2. Install the lever (4, **Figure 17**) into the electric starter motor housing (2). Engage the lever and the pinion shaft and orient the lever with the spring notch facing outward.

3. Position the rubber block (8, **Figure 17**) in the starter relay opening. Carefully insert the relay into its opening in the electric starter motor housing. Ensure the spring (5,

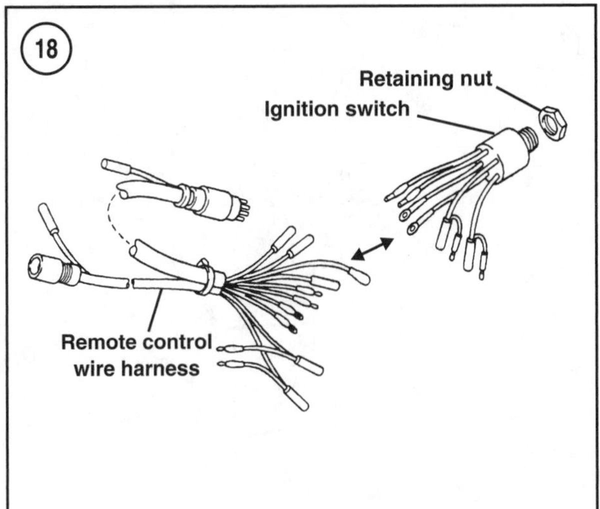

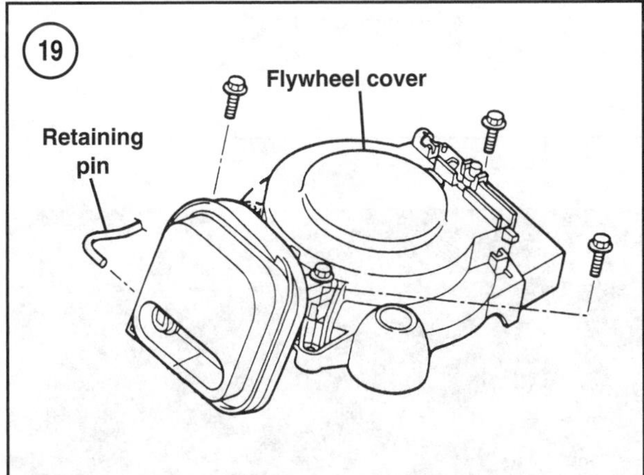

Figure 17) contacts the notch in the lever and the tip of the lever passes through the opening in the solenoid shaft.

4. Hold the solenoid in position and install both bolts (1, **Figure 17**). Tighten both bolts evenly to the specification in **Table 1**. Connect the short cable attached to the starter motor to its starter solenoid terminal. Securely tighten the terminal nut.

5. Install the starter motor following the instructions in this chapter.

Ignition Switch Removal/Installation

Follow Steps 1-8 if the ignition switch is mounted in the remote control or Steps 3-5 if the switch is mounted in the dash.

1. Disconnect both battery cables from the battery terminals. Refer to Chapter Twelve and remove the remote control.

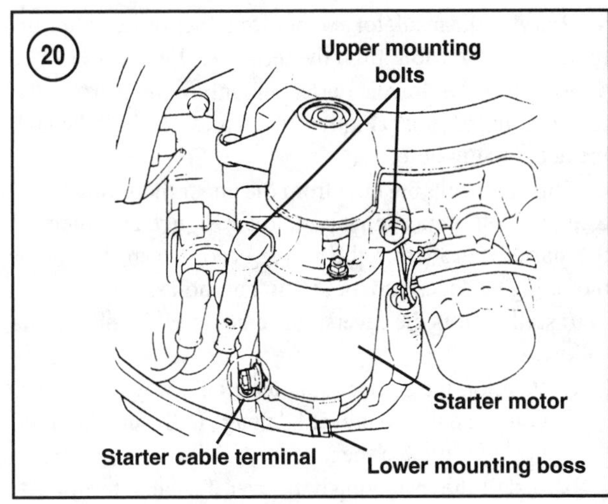

2. Refer to Chapter Twelve and disassemble the remote control to the point the ignition switch leads and retainer (**Figure 18**) are accessible.

3. Disconnect the switch wires from the remote control wire harness.

4. Install the ignition key into the switch and mark the UP side of the switch and ignition key. Remove the ignition key. Note the Mercury or Mariner marking relative to the UP mark.

5. Using the Mercury or Mariner mark on the ignition key, identify the UP side of the replacement ignition switch. Install the replacement ignition switch and securely tighten the retaining nuts.

6. Attach the switch wires to the wire harness. Fully engage the key switch wires into the wire harness connectors. Route the wires and connectors away from moving components.

7. Refer to Chapter Twelve and assemble the remote control. Install the control on the boat.

8. Connect the battery cables to the battery.

Starter Motor Removal and Installation (9.9 [Serial No. OH000057-Prior] and 15 hp Models)

1. Disconnect both battery cables from the battery. Remove all spark plugs and connect the spark plug leads to a suitable engine ground.

2. Remove the flywheel cover (**Figure 19**, typical) as described in Chapter Eight. This step ensures all starter mounting bolts and nuts are accessible.

3. Remove the rubber access plug from the port side of the lower engine cover. The plug is mounted next to the lower mounting boss for the starter motor (**Figure 20**).

4. Remove the insulator and nut from the starter cable terminal. Pull the cable from the terminal (**Figure 20**).
5. Remove the lower starter mounting bolt from the lower mounting boss (**Figure 20**). Access the bolt through the access plug hole.
6. Slip the insulating boot from the upper mounting bolts. Remove both upper mounting bolts (**Figure 20**), then lift the starter motor from the power head. Clean the starter mounting surfaces and mounting bolt holes.
7. Installation is the reverse of removal while noting the following:
   a. Position the starter cable terminal away from other components. To prevent damage to the insulator, do not over tighten the nut.
   b. Install the insulating boot over the cable terminal.
   c. Attach the large ground wire to the upper mounting bolt (**Figure 20**).
   d. Tighten the starter mounting bolts to the specification in **Table 1**.
   e. Route all wires away from moving components.
8. Install the flywheel cover. Install the spark plugs and leads. Clean the terminals and connect the cables to the battery.

Starter Motor Removal and Installation (9.9 hp Models [Serial No OH000058-On])

1. Disconnect both battery cables from the battery. Remove the spark plugs then connect the spark plug leads to a suitable engine ground.
2. Remove the flywheel cover (**Figure 19**, typical) following the instructions in Chapter Eight. This step ensures all starter mounting bolts and nuts are accessible.
3. Remove the nut (2, **Figure 21**) and washer and lift the starter cable (1) from starter motor terminal.
4. Support the starter motor (3, **Figure 21**) while removing both starter mounting bolts (4). Lift the electric starter from the power head.
5. Installation is the reverse of removal while noting the following:
   a. Position the starter cable away from other components. To prevent damage to the insulator, do not over tighten the wire terminal nut.
   b. Install the insulating boot over the large diameter wire terminals.
   c. Tighten the starter mounting bolts to the specification in **Table 1**.
   d. Route all wires away from moving components.
6. Install the flywheel cover. Install the spark plug and leads. Clean the terminals and connect the cables to the battery.

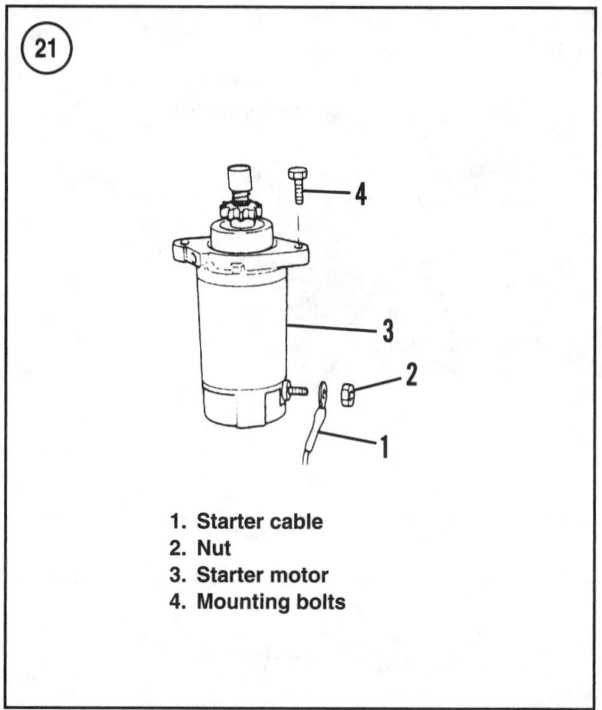

1. Starter cable
2. Nut
3. Starter motor
4. Mounting bolts

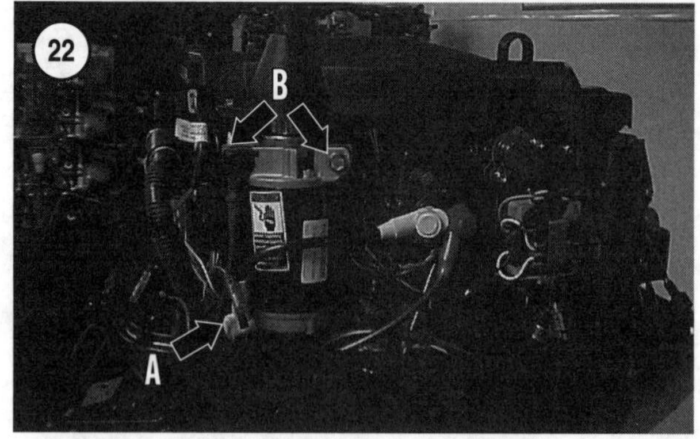

Starter Motor Removal and Installation (25-40 hp Models)

1. Disconnect both battery cables from the battery. Remove the spark plugs and connect the spark plug leads to a suitable engine ground.
2. Remove the flywheel cover (**Figure 19**, typical) following the instructions provided in Chapter Eight. This step ensures all starter mounting bolts and nuts are accessible.
3. Slip the insulating boot (A, **Figure 22**) from the wire terminal then remove the terminal nut. Lift the large wire from the starter motor.
4. Support the starter motor while removing both mounting bolts (B, **Figure 22**). Lift the electric starter motor

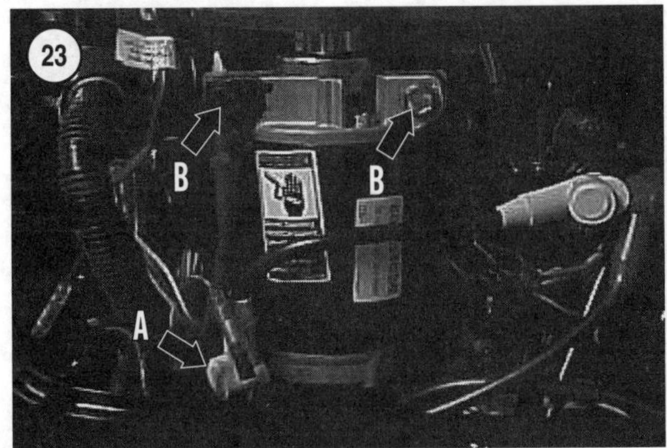

from the power head. Clean the starter mounting surfaces and mounting bolt holes.

5. Installation is the reverse of removal while noting the following:
   a. Connect the large diameter ground wire **(Figure 23)** to the front mounting bolt.
   b. Position the large wire terminal away from other components. To prevent damage to the insulator, do not over tighten the wire terminal nut.
   c. Install all insulating boots over the large diameter wire terminals.
   d. Tighten the starter mounting bolts to the specification in **Table 1**.
   e. Route all wires away from moving components.

6. Install the flywheel cover. Install the spark plugs and leads. Clean the terminals and connect the cables to the battery.

Starter Motor Removal and Installation (50 hp Models [Serial No. OG472132-Prior])

1. Disconnect both battery cables from the battery. Remove the spark plugs and connect the spark plug leads to a suitable engine ground.
2. Remove the nut (2, **Figure 21**) and washer then lift the starter cable (1) from the starter motor terminal.
3. Support the starter motor (3, **Figure 21**) while removing both starter mounting bolts (4). Lift the electric starter from the power head.
4. Installation is the reverse of removal while noting the following:
   a. Position the starter cable terminal away from other components. To prevent damage to the insulator, do not over tighten the wire terminal nut.
   b. Tighten the starter mounting bolts to the specification in **Table 1**.
   c. Route all wires away from moving components.
5. Install the spark plugs and leads. Clean the terminals and connect the cables to the battery.

Starter Motor Removal and Installation (50 hp Models [Serial No. OG472133-On])

1. Disconnect both battery cables from the battery. Remove the spark plugs and connect the spark plug leads to a suitable engine ground.
2. Slip the insulating boot (A, **Figure 23**) from the wire terminal then remove the terminal nut. Lift the large wire from the starter motor.
3. Support the starter motor while removing both mounting bolts (B, **Figure 23**). Lift the electric starter motor from the power head. Clean the electric starter mounting surfaces and mounting bolt holes.
4. Installation is the reverse of removal while noting the following:
   a. Connect the large diameter ground wire to the front mounting bolt.
   b. Position the large wire terminal away from other components. To prevent damage to the insulator, do not over tighten the wire terminal nut.
   c. Tighten the starter mounting bolts to the specification in **Table 1**.
   d. Route all wires away from moving components.
5. Install the spark plugs and leads. Clean the terminals and connect the cables to the battery.

Starter Motor Removal and Installation (75 and 90 hp Models)

1. Disconnect both battery cables from the battery. Remove the spark plugs and connect the spark plug leads to a suitable engine ground.
2. Slip the insulating boot **(Figure 24)** from the wire terminal, then remove the nut **(Figure 25)** from the starter

solenoid terminal. Lift the large wire terminal from the starter solenoid.

3. Remove the lower mounting bolt (**Figure 26**) from the starter motor. Remove the bolt and remove the ground wire from the starter lower cover (**Figure 27**).

4. Disconnect the black and black/white wires (**Figure 24**) from the engine wire harness.

5. Support the electric starter motor while removing both upper mounting bolts (**Figure 28**). Lift the electric starter motor from the engine. Clean the starter mounting surfaces and mounting bolt holes.

6. Installation is the reverse of removal while noting the following:

   a. Connect the large diameter ground wire to the lower cover as indicated (**Figure 27**).

   b. Positon the starter relay wire (**Figure 25**) away from other components. To prevent damage to the insulator, do not over tighten the wire terminal nut.

   c. Tighten the starter mounting bolts to the specification in **Table 1**.

   d. Route all wires away from moving components.

7. Install the spark plugs and leads. Clean the terminals and connect the cables to the battery.

25

26

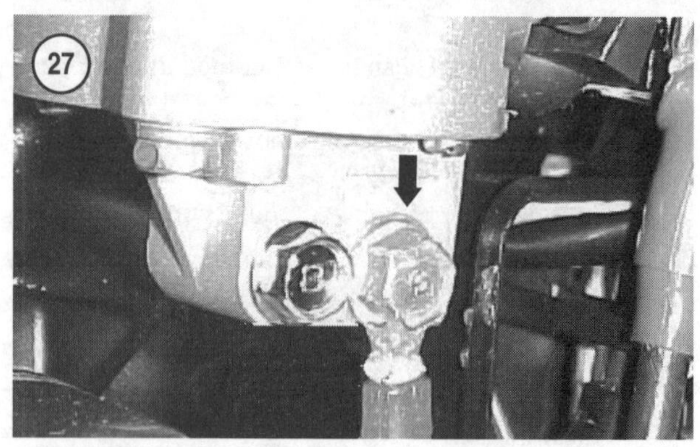

27

28

Starter Motor Disassembly/Assembly (9.9 hp [Prior to Serial No. OH000058], 50 hp [Serial No. OG472133-On] and All 15-40 hp Models)

Refer to **Figure 29** during this procedure.

1. For reference during assembly, place match marks on the starter frame and top and bottom covers (19, **Figure 29**).

2. Pry the cap (1, **Figure 29**) from the armature shaft. Secure the starter motor into a vice with soft jaws. Do not over tighten the vice.

3. Push the pinion stopper toward the starter pinion (**Figure 30**) to expose the locking clip. Carefully pry the locking clip from the armature shaft. Rotate the starter pinion counterclockwise then remove it from the armature shaft. Pull the pinion stopper, spring and washer (3 and 4, **Figure 29**) from the armature shaft.

4. Remove both throughbolts (6, **Figure 29**) then tap the lower cover (9) to free it from the frame (11). Pull the lower cover and brushes from the starter.

5. Tap on the lower end of the armature shaft not the commutator surface with a plastic mallet to free the upper cover (7, **Figure 29**) from the frame (11).

6. Pull the upper cover and washer (7 and 8, **Figure 29**) from the frame assembly (11). Pull the armature from the frame assembly.

STARTER MOTOR (9.9 HP [SERIAL NO. OH000057-PRIOR], 50 HP [SERIAL NO. OG472133-ON] AND ALL 15-40 HP MODELS)

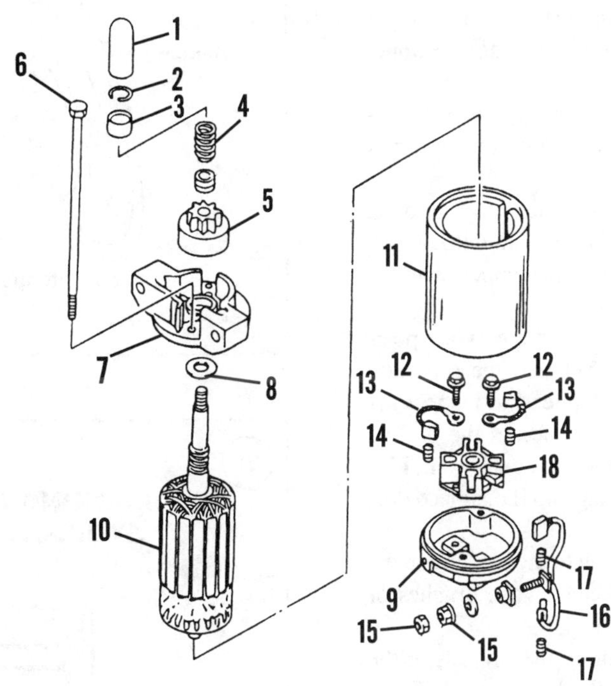

1. Cap
2. Locking clip
3. Pinion stopper
4. Spring
5. Pinion
6. Throughbolts
7. Upper cover
8. Washer
9. Lower cover
10. Armature
11. Frame
12. Screw
13. Negative brush/lead
14. Brush spring
15. Terminal nut
16. Pisitive brush/lead
17. Brush spring
18. Brush plate

7. Remove both screws (12, **Figure 29**), then remove the negative brushes (13) and springs (14) from the brush plate.
8. Remove the nuts (15, **Figure 29** and insulator and remove the positive brushes (16) and springs (17) from the lower cover (9). Pull the brush plate (18, **Figure 29**) from the lower cover (9).
9. Clean the upper cover, lower cover, armature and frame assembly using a quick drying solvent.
10. Inspect all components for worn, damaged or shorted components as described in this section.
11. Place the brush plate (18, **Figure 29**) into the lower cover (9). Align the brush plate in the lower cover (20, **Figure 29**). Install the brush spring (14, **Figure 29**) and negative brushes (13) into in the brush plate (18, **Figure 29**). Install both screws (12, **Figure 20**) through the brush terminals and brush plate (18). Securely tighten the screws.

12. Install both brush springs (17, **Figure 29**) and brushes into the brush plate (18). Place the large terminal and insulator into the opening in the lower cover. Install the washer and nuts. To prevent damage to the insulator and washer, do not over tighten the nuts (15, **Figure 29**).
13. Place the washer (8, **Figure 29**) over the upper end of the armature shaft (10). Apply a light coating of water-resistant grease to the bearing surface in the upper cover (7, **Figure 29**). Slide the armature into the upper cover.
14. Slide the frame assembly (11, **Figure 29**) over the armature (10) and mate the frame assembly to the upper cover (7).
15. Apply a light coating of water-resistant grease to the armature shaft, then thread the starter pinion onto the armature shaft. Place the spring and pinion stopper (3 and 4, **Figure 29**) over the armature shaft .
16. Push the pinion stopper toward the starter while positioning the locking clip (**Figure 31**) into the armature shaft groove. Release the pinion stopper and inspect the locking clip. The clip must be positioned in the groove with the pinion stopper fully over the clip as shown in **Figure 29**. Use pliers to form the locking clip if distorted during installation.
17. Apply a drop or two of engine oil to the bushing in the lower cover. Do not allow oil to contact the brushes or commutator.
18. Ensure all four brushes remain in their recess in the brush plate during installation of the lower cover. Carefully place the lower cover onto the frame and armature. Carefully rotate the lower cover to align the reference marks.
19. Install both throughbolts (6, **Figure 29**). Tighten the bolts to the specification in **Table 1**.

Starter Motor Disassembly/Assembly (9.9 hp Serial No. OH000058-On)

Refer to **Figure 32** during this procedure.

1. For reference during assembly, place match marks on the starter frame and top and bottom covers (**Figure 33**).
2. Secure the electric starter motor into a vice with soft jaws. Do not over tighten the vice.
3. Push the pinion stopper toward the starter pinion (**Figure 30**) to expose the locking clip. Carefully pry the locking clip from the armature shaft. Pull the pinion stopper and spring (2 and 3, **Figure 32**) from the armature shaft. Rotate the starter pinion counterclockwise and remove it from the armature shaft.
4. Remove both throughbolts (17, **Figure 32**), then tap the lower cover (16) to free it from the frame (10). Pull the lower cover and O-ring (15 and 16, **Figure 32**) from the starter. Pull the washer (9, **Figure 32**) from the lower cover or armature shaft.
5. Tap on the lower end of the armature shaft not the commutator surface with a plastic mallet to free the upper cover (5, **Figure 32**) from the frame(10).
6. Pull the upper cover, O-ring and washers (5-7, **Figure 32**) from the frame assembly (10). Pull the armature (8, **Figure 32**) from the frame assembly.

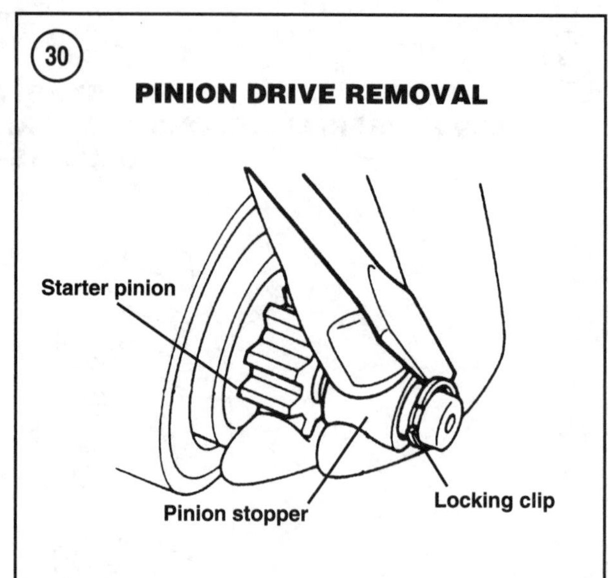

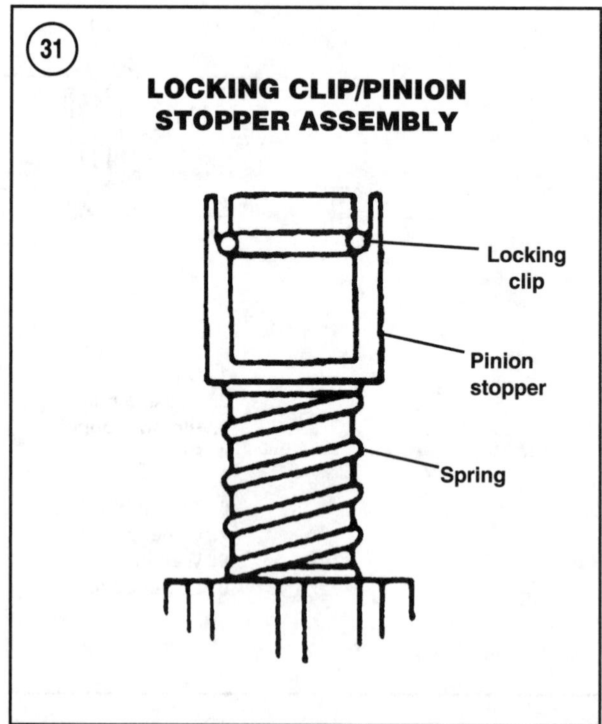

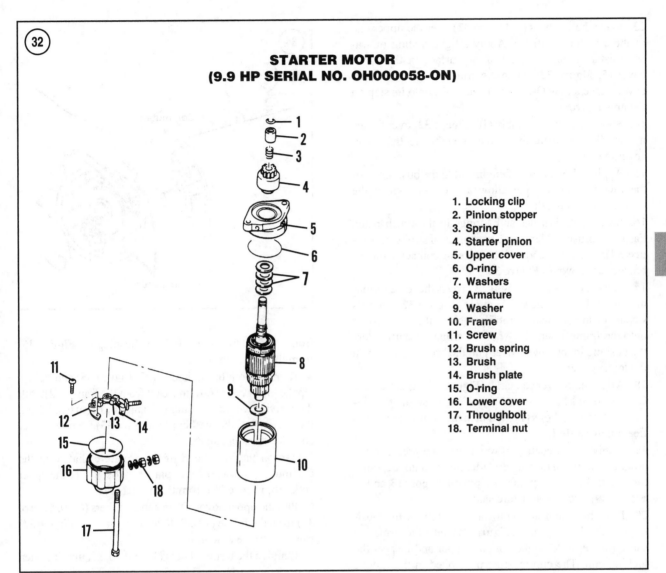

32

STARTER MOTOR
(9.9 HP SERIAL NO. OH000058-ON)

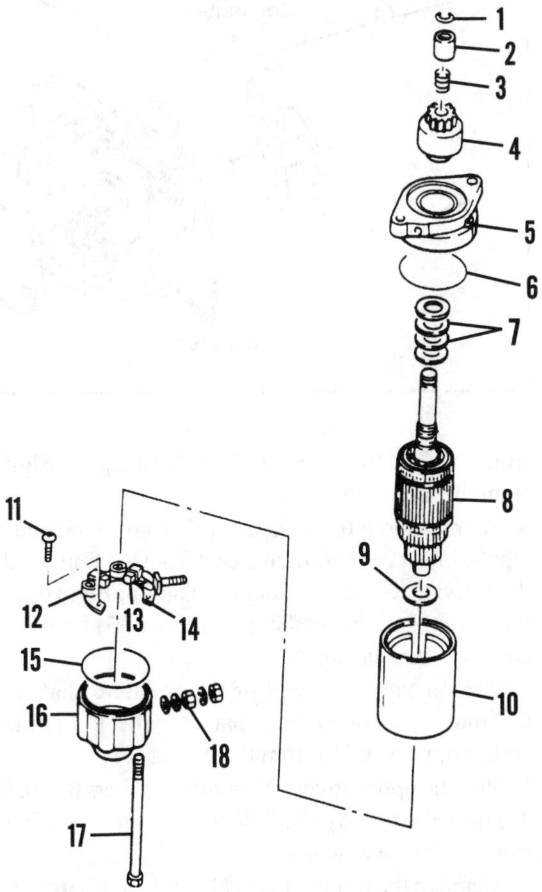

1. Locking clip
2. Pinion stopper
3. Spring
4. Starter pinion
5. Upper cover
6. O-ring
7. Washers
8. Armature
9. Washer
10. Frame
11. Screw
12. Brush spring
13. Brush
14. Brush plate
15. O-ring
16. Lower cover
17. Throughbolt
18. Terminal nut

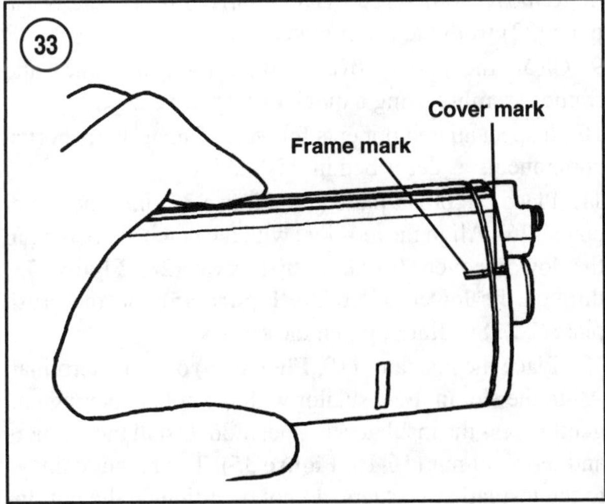

7. Remove the terminal nuts (18, **Figure 32**), then remove all insulating washers from the terminal.

8. Remove both screws (11, **Figure 32**) and lift the brush plate (14) from the lower cover (16).

9. Clean the upper cover, lower cover, armature and frame assembly using a quick drying solvent.

10. Inspect all components for worn, damaged or shorted components as described in this section.

11. Place the brush plate (14, **Figure 32**) into the lower cover (16) with the terminal inserted through its opening. Install both screws (11, **Figure 32**) through the brush plate (14). Securely tighten the screws.

12. Place the insulating washers onto the terminal then install the terminal nut (18, **Figure 32**). To prevent damage to the insulating washers, do not over tighten the nut.

13. Place the washers (7, **Figure 32**) over the upper end of the armature shaft (8). Apply a light coating of water-resistant grease to the bearing surface in the upper cover (5, **Figure 32**). Slide the armature into the upper cover. Place a new O-ring (6, **Figure 32**) onto its step on the upper cover (5).
14. Slide the frame assembly (10, **Figure 32**) over the armature (8) and mate the frame assembly to the upper cover (5).
15. Apply a drop or two of engine oil to the bushing in of the lower cover. Do not allow any oil to contact the brushes or commutator.
16. Install both brushes and springs in the brush plate. Fashion a brush holder from a bent piece of stiff wire (**Figure 34**). Place the ends of the wire in contact with the brushes as shown in **Figure 34**.
17. Place the washer (9, **Figure 32**) over the lower armature shaft. Install a new O-ring (15, **Figure 32**) onto its step in the lower cover. Carefully position the lower cover onto the frame assembly. After the armature shaft enters the bushing in the lower cover pull the brush holder from the lower cover.
18. Align the reference marks (**Figure 33**). Ensure both O-rings (6 and 15, **Figure 32**) remain in position, then install both throughbolts (17). Tighten the bolts to the specification in **Table 1**.
19. Apply a light coating of water-resistant grease to the armature shaft and thread the starter pinion onto the armature shaft. Place the spring and pinion stopper (3 and 4, **Figure 29**) over the armature shaft.
20. Push the pinion stopper toward the starter while positioning the locking clip (**Figure 31**) into the armature shaft groove. Release the pinion stopper and inspect the locking clip. The clip must be positioned in the groove with the pinion stopper fully over the clip as shown in **Figure 31**. Use pliers to form the locking clip if distorted during installation.

Starter Motor Disassembly/Assembly (50 hp Models Prior to Serial No. OG472133)

Refer to **Figure 35** during this procedure.

1. For reference during assembly, place match marks on the starter frame and top and bottom covers (**Figure 33**).
2. Secure the electric starter motor into a vice with soft jaws. Do not over tighten the vice.
3. Push the pinion stopper toward the starter pinion (**Figure 30**) to expose the locking clip. Carefully pry the locking clip from the armature shaft. Pull the pinion stopper and spring (2 and 3, **Figure 35**) from the armature shaft. Rotate the starter pinion counterclockwise and remove it from the armature shaft. Pull the bushing (5, **Figure 35**) from the armature shaft.

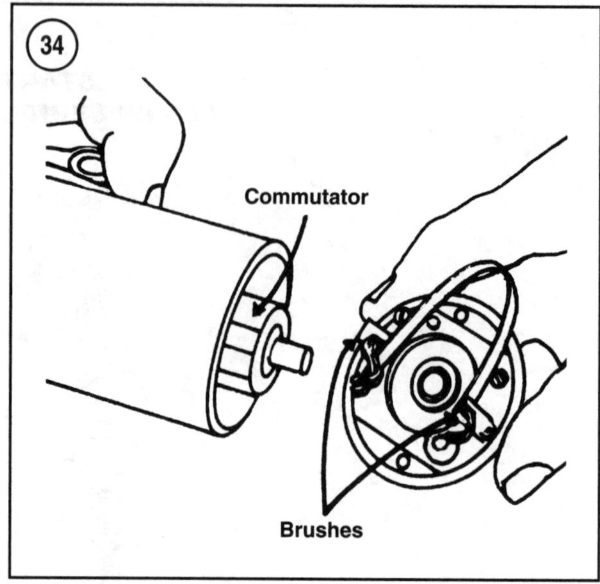

4. Remove both throughbolts (27, **Figure 35**) and lightly tap the lower cover (26) to free it from the frame (12). Pull the lower cover and O-ring (13 and 26, **Figure 32**) from the starter. Pull the washer (25, **Figure 35**) from the lower cover or armature shaft.
5. Tap on the lower end of the armature shaft (not the commutator surface) with a plastic mallet to free the upper cover (6, **Figure 35**) from the frame(12).
6. Pull the upper cover, O-ring and washers (6-10, **Figure 35**) from the frame (12). Pull the armature (11, **Figure 32**) from the frame assembly.
7. Remove the terminal nuts (11 and 16, **Figure 35**), then remove the washers and insulator (17-19, **Figure 35**) from the positive terminal.
8. Remove both screws (28, **Figure 35**) and the brush plate (22) from the lower cover (26).
9. Clean the upper cover, lower cover, armature and frame assembly using a quick drying solvent.
10. Inspect all components for worn, damaged or shorted components as described in this section.
11. Place the brush plate (22, **Figure 35**) into the lower cover (26). Align the terminal with the notched opening in the lower cover. Install both screws (28, **Figure 35**) through the lower cover (26, **Figure 35**) and the brush plate (22). Securely tighten the screws.
12. Place the insulator (19, **Figure 35**) over the terminal. Align the slot in the insulator with the notch opening and gently press the insulator into position. Install the washers and terminal nut (16-18, **Figure 35**). To prevent damage to the insulating washers, do not over tighten the nut. In-

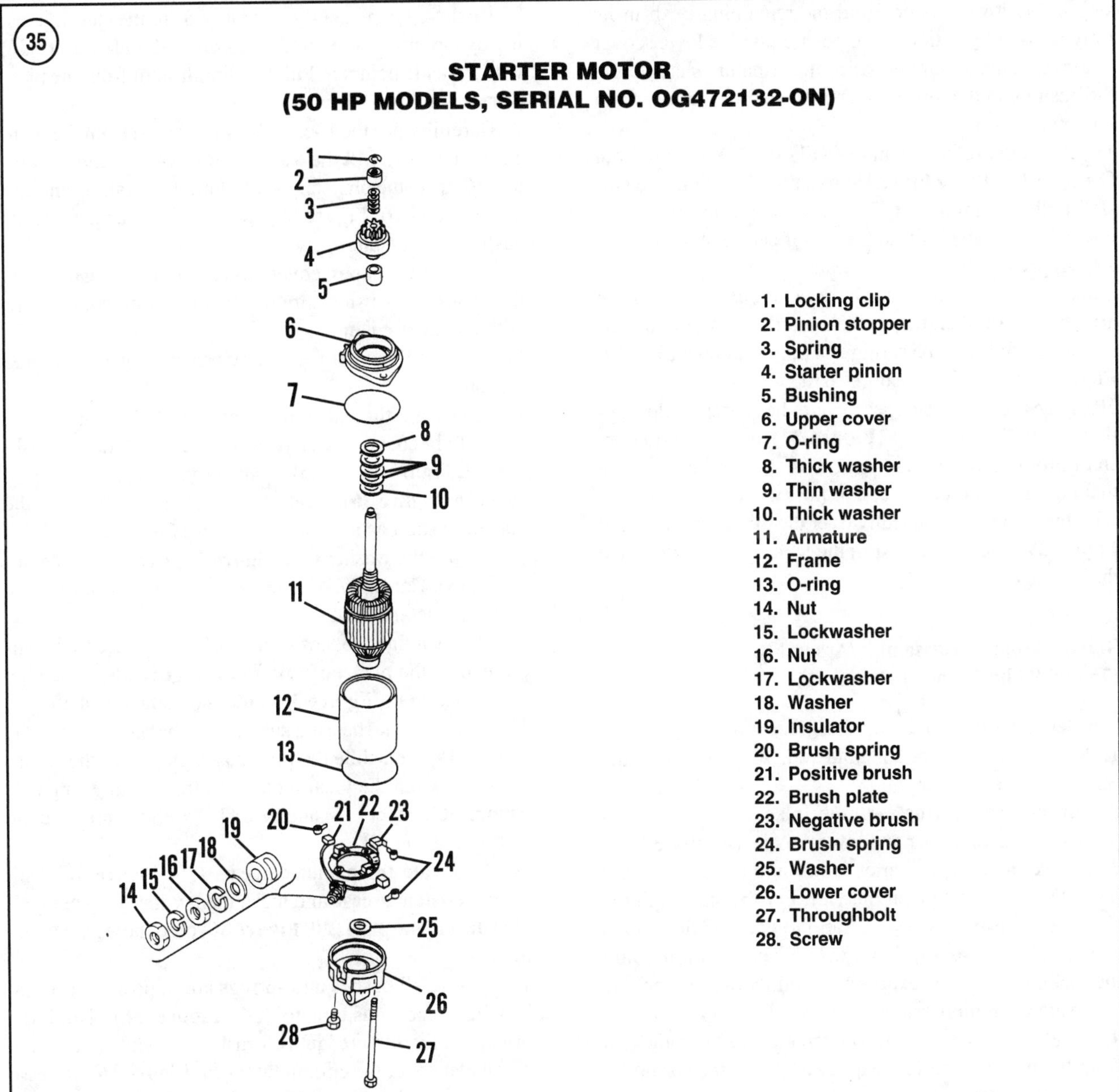

stall the washer and nut (14 and 16, **Figure 35**) during installation of the electric starter motor.

13. Place the washers (8-10, **Figure 35**) over the upper end of the armature shaft (11). Apply a light coating of water-resistant grease to the bearing surface in the upper cover (6, **Figure 35**). Slide the armature into in the upper cover. Place a new O-ring (7, **Figure 35**) onto its step on the upper cover (6).

14. Slide the frame assembly (12, **Figure 35**) over the armature (11) and mate the frame assembly to the upper cover (6).

15. Apply a drop or two of engine oil to the bushing in the lower cover. Do not allow any oil to contact the brushes or commutator.

16. Ensure all three brushes and springs are positioned correctly in the brush plate. Fashion a brush holder from a bent piece of stiff wire (**Figure 34**). Place the ends of the wire in contact with the brushes as indicated in **Figure 34**. Hold the third brush by hand during installation of the cover.

17. Place the washer (25, **Figure 35**) over the lower armature shaft. Install a new O-ring (13, **Figure 35**) onto its

step in the lower cover. Hold the remaining bush in its fully retracted position while positioning the lower cover onto the frame assembly. After the armature shaft enters the bushing in the lower cover pull the brush holder from the lower cover.

18. Align the reference marks (**Figure 33**). Ensure both O-rings (7 and 13, **Figure 35**) remain in position, then install both throughbolts (27). Thread them into the upper cover. Tighten the bolts to the specification in **Table 1**.

19. Apply a light coating of water-resistant grease to the armature shaft. Slip the bushing (5, **Figure 35**) over the armature shaft, then thread the starter pinion onto the armature shaft. Place the spring and pinion stopper (3 and 4, **Figure 29**) over the armature shaft.

20. Push the pinion stopper toward the starter while positioning the locking clip (**Figure 31**) into the armature shaft groove. Release the pinion stopper and inspect the locking clip. The clip must be positioned in the groove with the pinion stopper fully over the clip as indicated in **Figure 29**. Use pliers to form the locking clip if distorted during installation.

Starter Motor Disassembly/Assembly (75 and 90 hp Models)

Refer to **Figure 36** during this procedure.

1. Remove the starter solenoid (26, **Figure 36**) as described in this chapter.
2. For reference during assembly, place match marks on the starter frame, upper and lower covers (**Figure 33**).
3. Secure the electric starter motor into a vice with soft jaws. Do not over tighten the vice. Pry the starter pinion (31, **Figure 36**) downward. Tap the edge of the pinion stopper (1, **Figure 36**) down with a small hammer until the locking clip (2) is exposed. Carefully pry the locking clip from the pinion stopper.
4. Rotate the starter pinion counterclockwise to remove it from the pinion shaft (11, **Figure 36**). Pull the spring (4, **Figure 36**) from the shaft.
5. Remove both screws (39, **Figure 36**) from the lower cover (38). Remove both throughbolts (40, **Figure 36**) then carefully tap the lower cover (38) free from the frame (28). Pull the lower cover (38, **Figure 36**) away from the starter.
6. Using a small punch, tap the plate (35, **Figure 36**) from its groove on the lower end of the armature (29). Pull the brush plate (34, **Figure 36**) from the commutator.
7. Pull the frame and armature (28 and 29, **Figure 36**) from the starter housing (9). Mark the armature side and remove the plate (20, **Figure 36**) from the starter housing (9) or frame (28). Remove the three planetary gears (19, **Figure 36**) from the planetary shaft (18).
8. Remove the planetary assembly from the starter housing by tapping lightly on the pinion shaft (11, **Figure 36**) with a plastic hammer. Pull the pinion shaft from the planetary assembly.
9. Carefully pry the E-clip (12, **Figure 36**) from the planetary shaft (18). Lift the washer and cover (13 and 14, **Figure 36**) from the planetary shaft. Pull the locating ring and gear (15 and 16, **Figure 36**) from the planetary. Slide the bushing off the planetary shaft.
10. Clean the upper cover, lower cover, armature and frame assembly using a mild solvent. Dry all components with compressed air.
11. Inspect all components for worn, damaged or shorted components.
12. Lubricate the entire planetary shaft (18, **Figure 36**) with a light coat of water-resistant grease. Slide the bushing (17, **Figure 36**) over the planetary shaft (18). Place the gear (16, **Figure 36**), locating ring (15) and cover over the planetary shaft as indicated in **Figure 36**.
13. Install the washer (13, **Figure 36**) over the planetary shaft (18). Carefully snap the E-clip (12) into its groove on the planetary shaft (18).
14. Apply a light coat of water-resistant grease to the upper end of the planetary shaft (18, **Figure 36**). Place the pinion shaft (11, **Figure 36**) onto the planetary shaft.
15. Lubricate the bearing surfaces of the pinion shaft (11, **Figure 36**) then slide the pinion assembly into the starter housing. Align the locating tabs on the locating ring (15, **Figure 36**), cover (14) and gear (16) with the notch in the starter housing (9).
16. Lubricate the planetary gears (19, **Figure 36**) with water-resistant grease and mesh them with the larger gear (16). Install the plate (20, **Figure 36**) onto the starter housing (9).
17. Ensure all bushes and springs are in position prior to installing the brush plate (34, **Figure 36**). Hold the brushes fully retracted in the brush plate while sliding the brush plate over the commutator (29, **Figure 36**). Release the brushes only after the brush plate slides into position.
18. Carefully tap the plate (35, **Figure 36**) onto its groove at the lower end of the armature (29). Apply a light coating of water resistant grease to the gear teeth and bearing surfaces of armature.
19. Install the frame (28, **Figure 36**). Hold the armature in the planetary while cautiously sliding the frame assembly over the armature.
20. Rotate the armature (29, **Figure 36**) while inserting its upper end into the planetary assembly. The armature will drop into the opening as the gear teeth on the armature mesh with the planetary gears (19, **Figure 36**).
21. Apply a drop or two of engine oil to the bushing in the lower cover. Align the screw opening in the brush plate

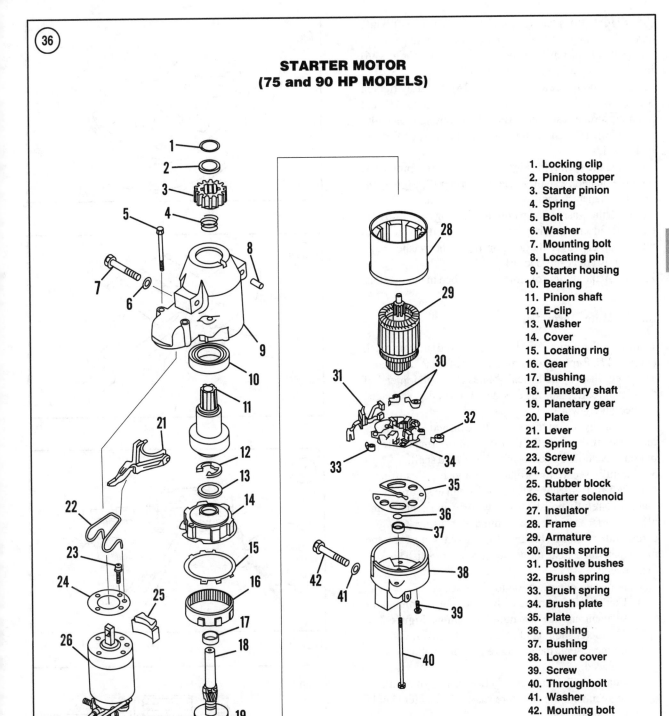

36

STARTER MOTOR
(75 and 90 HP MODELS)

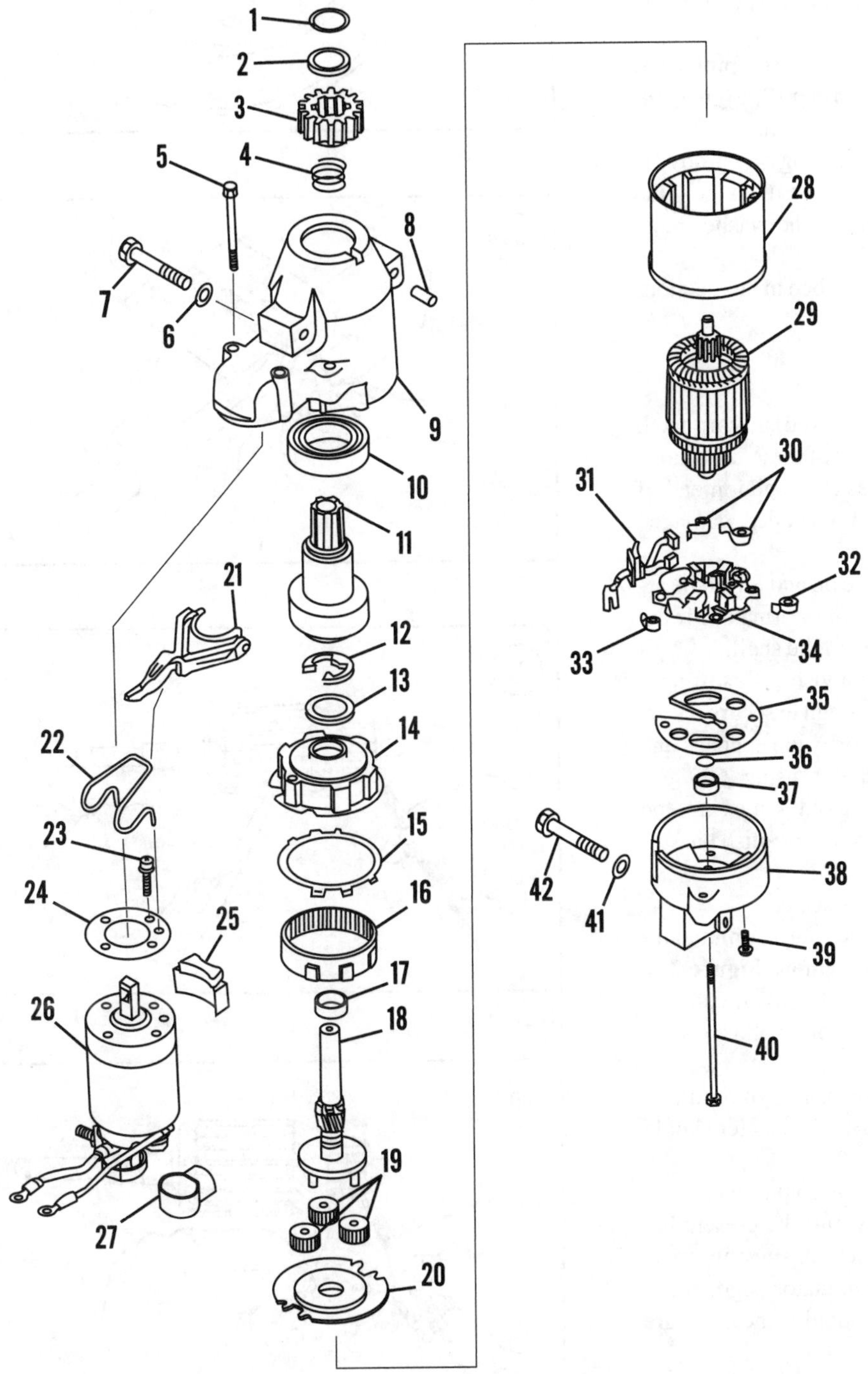

1. Locking clip
2. Pinion stopper
3. Starter pinion
4. Spring
5. Bolt
6. Washer
7. Mounting bolt
8. Locating pin
9. Starter housing
10. Bearing
11. Pinion shaft
12. E-clip
13. Washer
14. Cover
15. Locating ring
16. Gear
17. Bushing
18. Planetary shaft
19. Planetary gear
20. Plate
21. Lever
22. Spring
23. Screw
24. Cover
25. Rubber block
26. Starter solenoid
27. Insulator
28. Frame
29. Armature
30. Brush spring
31. Positive bushes
32. Brush spring
33. Brush spring
34. Brush plate
35. Plate
36. Bushing
37. Bushing
38. Lower cover
39. Screw
40. Throughbolt
41. Washer
42. Mounting bolt

(34, **Figure 36**), plate (35) and lower cover (38) while carefully sliding the lower cover over the brush plate. Fit the insulator portion of the positive brush (31, **Figure 36**) into its groove in the lower cover (38).

22. Install both screws (39, **Figure 36**). Securely tighten the screws. Align all reference marks (**Figure 33**) and aligning structures, then install both throughbolts (40, **Figure 36**). Tighten the throughbolts to the specification in **Table 1**.
23. Slide the spring (4, **Figure 36**) and starter pinion (3) onto the planetary shaft. Place the washer (2, **Figure 36**) onto the planetary shaft with the open end up.
24. Push the washer down until the locking ring groove is exposed. Insert the ring into the groove then pull the washer up and over the locking ring. The washer must completely cover the sides of the ring.
25. Install the starter solenoid as described in this section.

Starter Motor Inspection

1. Inspect the pinion for chipped, cracked or worn teeth (**Figure 37**). Replace the pinion if any of these conditions are noted. Inspect the helical splines at the pinion end of the armature. Replace the armature if corroded, damaged or excessively worn .
2. Repeatedly thread the pinion drive on and off of the armature shaft. Replace the pinion drive or armature if the pinion drive does not turn smoothly on the shaft.
3. Carefully secure the armature in a vise with soft jaws (**Figure 38**). Tighten the vise only enough to secure the armature. Carefully polish away any corrosion deposits and glazed surfaces from the commutator using 600 grit carburundum cloth (**Figure 38**). Avoid removing too much material. Rotate the armature often to polish the surfaces evenly.
4. Calibrate an ohmmeter on the R×1 scale.
   a. Connect the ohmmeter between any commutator segment and the armature lamination (**Figure 39**). The meter should indicate no continuity. If continuity is present, the armature is shorted and must be replaced.
   b. Connect the ohmmeter between any commutator segment and the armature shaft). The meter should indicate no continuity.
   c. Connect the ohmmeter between commutator segments (**Figure 40**). Continuity must be present between any two segments. Repeat this test with the meter connected to each commutator segment. If any segment does not have continuity, the armature must be replaced.
5. Remove the mica particles from the undercut between the commutator segments using a small file (**Figure 41**).

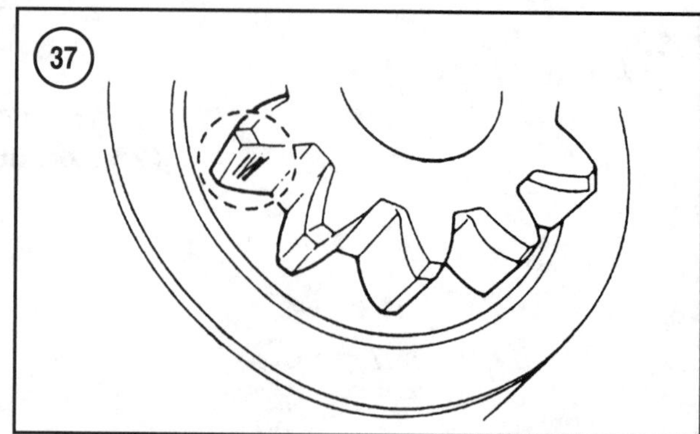

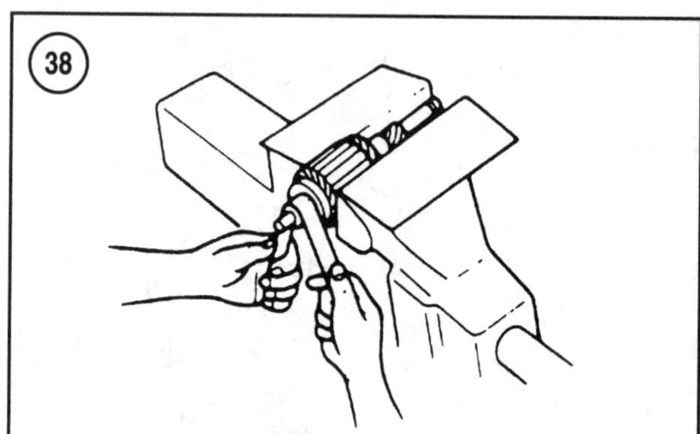

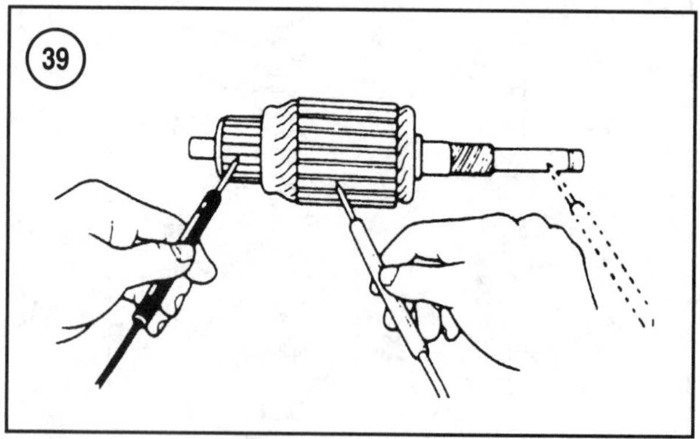

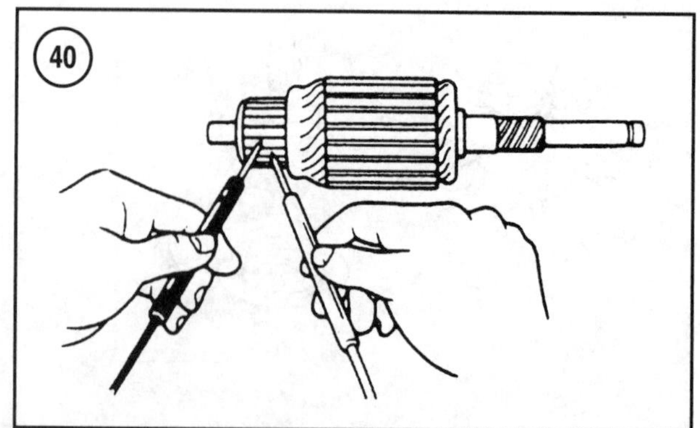

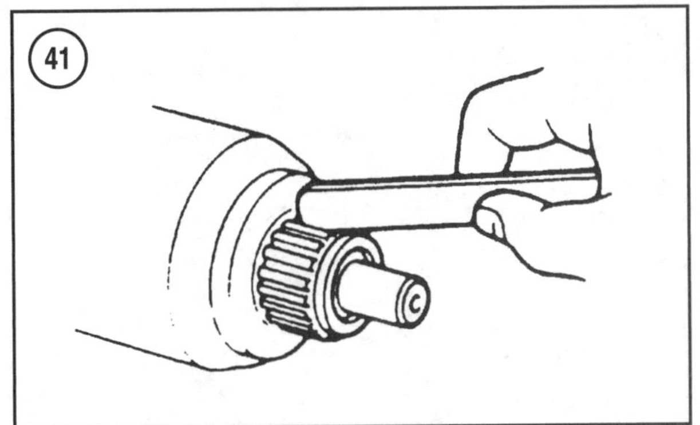

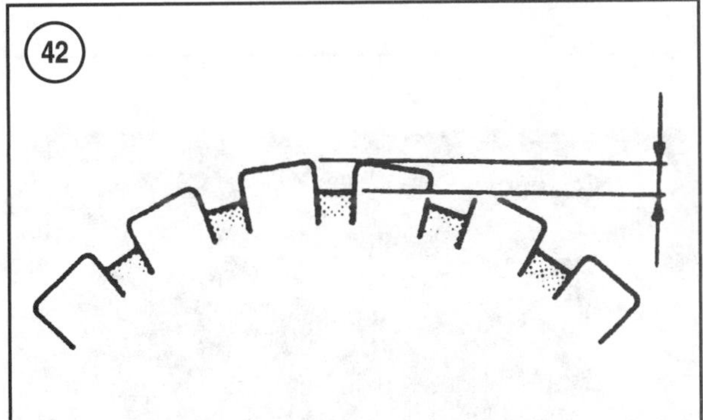

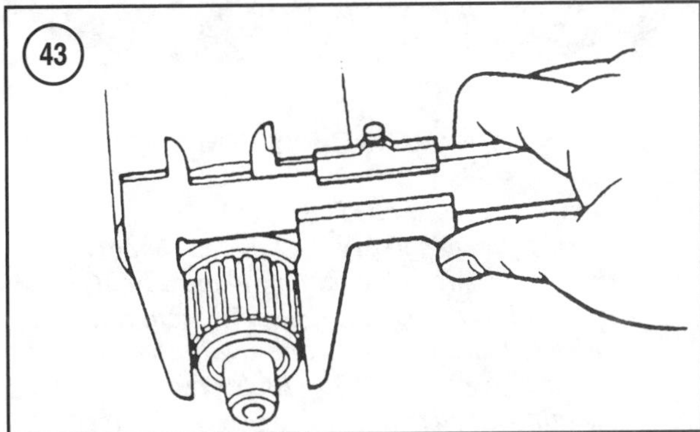

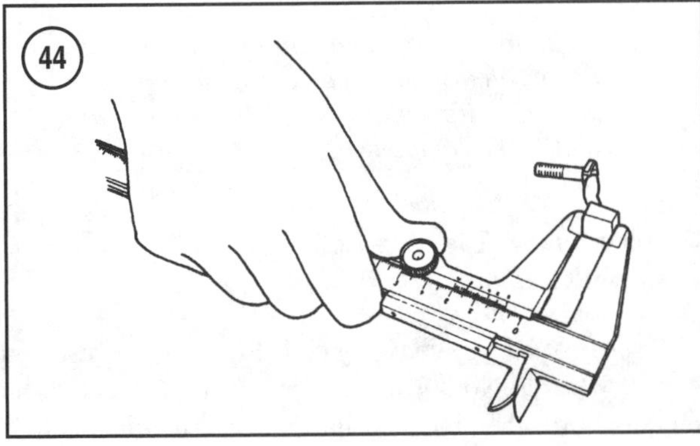

6. Blow away any loose particles using compressed air. Measure the depth of the undercut (**Figure 42**) and compare the depth with the specification in **Table 2**. If necessary, increase the undercut slightly.

7. *9.9 hp (serial No. OH000058-on), 50 hp (prior to serial No. OG472133), 75 hp and 90 hp models*—Measure the commutator diameter (**Figure 43**) at several locations. Replace the armature if the commutator diameter is less than the specification in **Table 2**.

8. Measure the brush length (**Figure 44**). Compare the brush length with the specification in **Table 2**. Replace all brushes if any of them are less than the specification. Replace the complete brush plate if corroded, contaminated, chipped or broken. Inspect the brush springs for corrosion damage or weak spring tension. Replace the springs if any defects are noted.

9. Inspect the magnets in the frame assembly for corrosion or other contamination and clean as required. Inspect the frame assembly for cracked or loose magnets. Replace the frame assembly if it cannot be adequately cleaned or damaged magnets are noted.

10. Inspect the bearing surfaces on the armature and the bushings for discoloration and excessive or uneven wear. Remove and replace any questionable bearings or bushings using a suitable pulling tool and driver. Replace the armature if the bearing surfaces are rough or uneven.

11. On 50 hp models (OG472132-prior), have a reputable machine shop measure the amount of shaft runout or deflection. Compare the amount of runout with the specification in **Table 2**. Replace the armature if excessive runout or deflection is indicated.

Neutral Start Switch Removal/Installation

A neutral start switch (**Figure 45**) is used on all tiller models with electric start.

1. Disconnect the battery cables from the battery. Shift the outboard into NEUTRAL.

2. Disconnect the two neutral switch wires from the engine harness.
3. Remove the switch mounting screws. Remove the switch and mounting plate. Clean the switch mounting surfaces and the cam portion of the shift linkage.
4. Apply a light coat of water-resistant grease to the portion of the shift linkage that contacts the switch plunger.
5. Position the switch onto its mounting bosses with the plunger in contact with the shift linkage. Place the mounting plate onto the switch and install both mounting screws. Securely tighten the screws.
6. Route the switch wires away from moving components. Retain the wires with plastic locking clamps as required. Connect the switch wires to their respective terminals.
7. Connect the cables to the battery. Check for proper operation of the neutral start switch in Chapter Three.

Starter Button

All 9.9-25 hp models with tiller control and electric start are equipped with a tiller handle mounted starter button (**Figure 46**) mounted on the tiller handle. Remove and install the button as follows:

1. Disconnect both cables from the battery.
2. Carefully pry the starter button housing from the throttle shaft portion of the throttle handle.
3. Trace the starter button wires to the starter relay and neutral start switch and disconnect the wires. Feed the wires through their opening in the engine cover to the starter button.
4. Using needlenose pliers, carefully pull the small metal retainer from the starter button housing. Carefully push the starter button from its grooves in the housing. Clean all the starter button housing using soapy water. Thoroughly dry the housing.
5. Apply soapy water to the rubber surfaces of the starter button to assist installation. Carefully push the replacement switch into the housing. Push the metal retainer into the recess in the button housing. Ensure the rounded side contacts the starter button.
6. Route the starter button wires through the opening in the rear of the starter button housing. Feed the wire harness through the opening in the lower engine cover. Clean the terminals then connect the starter button wires to the starter relay and neutral start switch. Retain the wires with plastic locking clamps as required.
7. Carefully snap the starter button housing onto the throttle shaft in the tiller handle.
8. Connect the cables to the battery. Check for proper operation of the neutral start switch as described in Chapter Three.

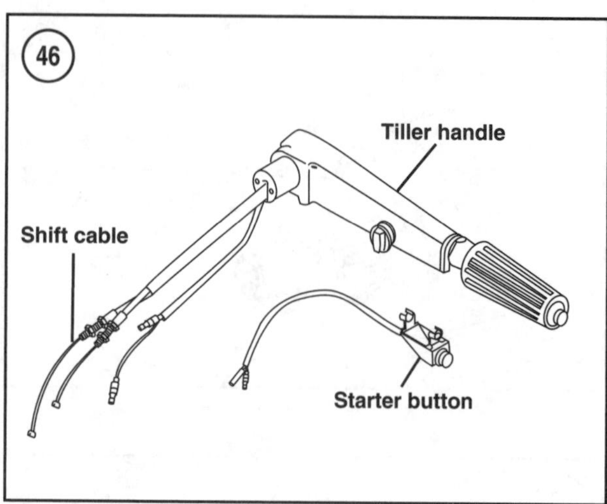

CHARGING SYSTEM

CAUTION
It may be necessary to use an impact driver to remove the battery charge/lighting and ignition charge coil mounting screws. Work carefully and avoid the use of excessive force. The cylinder block can sustain considerable damage if excessive force is used.

NOTE
The battery charge and ignition charge coil appear almost identical on some models. Use the wire colors and illustrations to identify the components.

Battery Charge/Lighting Coil Removal/Installation

A separate battery charging coil (**Figure 47**) is used on 4, 5, 9.9 (serial No. OH000057-prior), 15, 75 and 90 hp models. On other models, the battery charging coil is

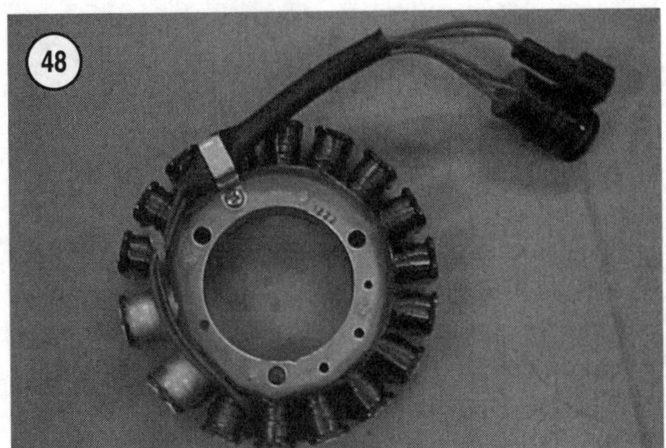

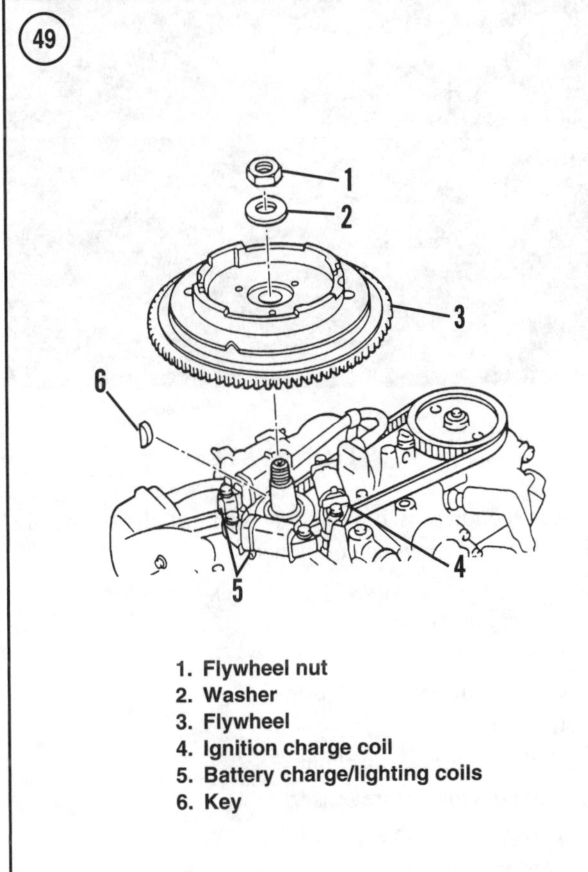

1. Flywheel nut
2. Washer
3. Flywheel
4. Ignition charge coil
5. Battery charge/lighting coils
6. Key

combined with the ignition charge coil as a single unit (**Figure 48**). This section provides instructions for models utilizing a separate battery charge/lighting coil. Refer to *Ignition Charge Coil* in this chapter for removal and installation instructions on other models.

1. Disconnect both cables from the battery. Remove the spark plugs then connect the spark plug leads to a suitable engine ground.

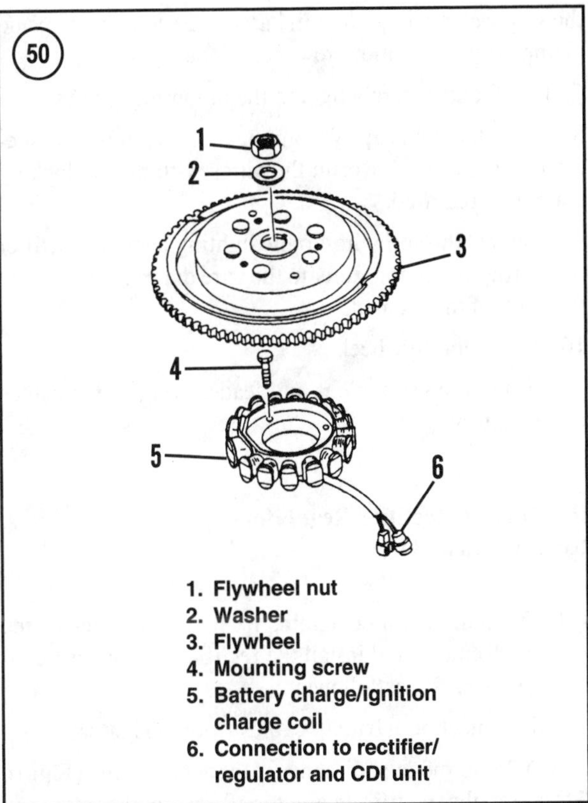

1. Flywheel nut
2. Washer
3. Flywheel
4. Mounting screw
5. Battery charge/ignition charge coil
6. Connection to rectifier/ regulator and CDI unit

2. Remove the flywheel following the instructions in Chapter Eight.
3. Refer to the wire diagrams at the back of the manual to identify the charge/lighting coil wires.

4A. On 4-6 hp models, disconnect the coil wires from the lighting harness or rectifier. Remove both retaining screws and remove the battery charging coil from the cylinder block.

4B. On 9.9 (serial No. OH000057-prior) and 15 hp models, disconnect the battery charge/lighting coil wires from the lighting harness, rectifier or rectifier/regulator. Remove the four retaining screws and remove the battery charge/lighting coil (5, **Figure 49**) from the cylinder block.

4C. On 75 and 90 hp models, disconnect the battery charge coil from the harness leading to the rectifier regulator. Remove the single wire clamp (located near the coil) then remove the three mounting screws (4, **Figure 50**). Lift the battery charging coil from the mounting plate.

5. Clean the battery charge/lighting coil mounting surface. Clean all corrosion or contamination from the mounting screw holes.
6. Place the battery charge/lighting coil in position on the cylinder block or mounting bracket. Route the wires as noted prior to removal. On 75 and 90 hp models, install

the single clamp over the coil harness. Secure the wire and clamp with the clamp screw.

7. Install and securely tighten the mounting screws.

8. Route the wires away from moving components especially the flywheel. Retain the wires with plastic locking clamps as required.

9. Connect the coil wires to the lighting harness, rectifier or rectifier/regulator. Refer to the wire diagrams located at the back of the manual.

10. Install the flywheel.

11. Install the spark plugs and leads. Connect the cables to the battery.

51

52

Rectifier or Rectifier/Regulator Removal/Installation

Refer to the wiring diagrams located at the back of the manual. Remove and install the rectifier or rectifier/regulator (**Figure 51**) as follows:

1. Disconnect both battery cables from the battery.

2. On 25 hp models, disconnect the white wires (**Figure 52**) from the rectifier/regulator. Remove the retaining clamp and the rectifier/regulator mounting bolts are removed.

3. Disconnect all wires leading to the rectifier or rectifier/regulator. Remove the screw and ground wire from the mounting plate if so equipped.

4. Remove the screws retaining the rectifier or rectifier/regulator to the mounting plate and remove the rectifier or rectifier/regulator.

5. Clean, inspect and repair, if necessary, the threads in the mounting plate. Clean all corrosion or contamination from the mounting surface.

6. Carefully route the rectifier or rectifier/regulator unit wires while positioning the unit to the power head. On 25 hp models, install the retaining clamp for the wire terminals prior to installing the mounting screws. Install the mounting screws then tighten them to the specification in **Table 1**. Position the ground wire below the mounting plate screw on models so equipped.

7. Connect all wire harness and battery charge/lighting coil wires to the rectifier or rectifier/regulator. On 25 hp models, connect the white wires (**Figure 52**) to the rectifier/regulator.

8. Connect the cables to the battery. Check for proper charging and ignition system operation immediately after starting the engine.

IGNITION SYSTEM

This section provides removal then installation instructions for the following components:

1. Ignition charge coil.
2. Power source coil.
3. Pulser coil.
4. Crankshaft position sensor.
5. Ignition coil.
6. CDI or engine control unit.
7. Engine temperature sensor.
8. Throttle position sensor.
9. Lanyard switch.
10. Stop switch or button.

Ignition Charge Coil Removal/Installation (4-6 hp Models)

1. Remove the spark plug then connect the spark plug lead to a suitable engine ground.

2. Remove the flywheel following the instructions in Chapter Eight.

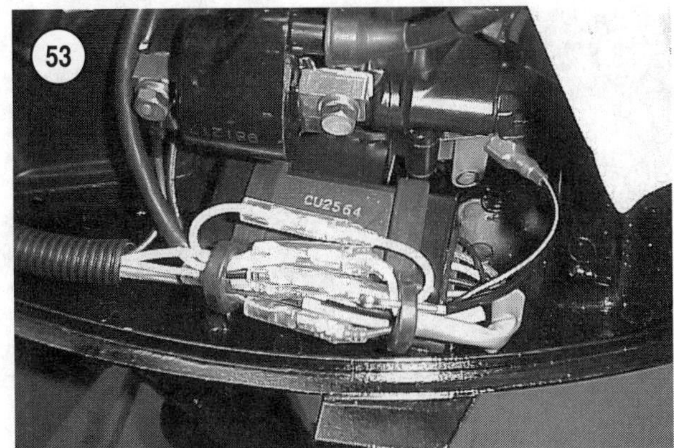

3. Disconnect the black/red and white wires from the CDI unit (**Figure 53**).
4. Remove the single wire clamp and screw from near the ignition charge coil. Remove both mounting screws from the ignition charge coil and cylinder block.
5. Carefully guide the ignition charge coil wires through the opening near the flywheel area in the cylinder block while lifting the ignition charge coil from the cylinder block.
6. Clean all corrosion, debris and contamination from the ignition charge coil mounting surface. Clean the mounting screw holes.
7. Guide the ignition charge coil wires through the opening near the flywheel area in the cylinder block while lowering the coil in position.
8. Install both coil mounting screws. Tighten the screws to 14 in-lb (1.6 N•m). Install the wire retaining clamp and screw. Securely tighten the screw.
9. Connect the black/red and white wires to the CDI unit (**Figure 53**). Route all wires away from moving components.
10. Install the flywheel (Chapter Eight). Install the spark plug and lead.

Ignition Charge Coil Removal/Installation (9.9 [Prior to Serial No. OH000058] and 15 hp Models)

1. Disconnect both cables from the battery. Remove the spark plugs and connect the spark plug leads to a suitable engine ground.
2. Remove the flywheel as described in Chapter Eight.
3. Cut the plastic locking clamp from the wire bundle (**Figure 54**) to access the wire connectors. Disconnect both ignition charge coil wire from the engine control unit harness.
4. Remove both mounting screws and lift the ignition charging coil (4, **Figure 49**) from the power head.
5. Clean all debris, corrosion and contamination from the ignition charging coil mounting surfaces. Clean all corrosion or contamination from the mounting screw holes.
6. Place the ignition charging coil in position on the cylinder block or mounting bracket. Route the wires as ntoed prior to removal. Install and tighten both mounting screws to the specification in **Table 1**.
7. Connect both ignition charging coil wires to the engine control unit harness. Route the wires away from moving components especially the flywheel. Bundle the wires together and retain them with a plastic locking clamp as shown in **Figure 54**.
8. Install the flywheel (Chapter Eight).
9. Install the spark plugs and leads. Connect the cables to the battery.

Ignition Charge Coil Removal/Installation (9.9 hp [Serial No. OH000058-On]-50 hp Models]

On these models the ignition charge coil, battery charge/lighting and power source coil if so equipped are combined into a single component (**Figure 48**). Note the size and location of plastic tie clamps that must be removed and replace them with new clamps during assembly. Apply a light coat of Loctite 222 to the threads of the mounting screws during installation.

1. Disconnect both cables from the battery. Remove the spark plugs then connect the spark plug leads to a suitable engine ground.
2. Remove the flywheel as described in Chapter Eight.
3. Refer to the wire diagrams located at the back of the manual to identify the coil wires.
4. Note all wire routing and disconnect all applicable wires from the CDI or engine control unit, rectifier/regulator and electrothermal valve.
5. Mark the power head indicating the alignment of the coil wire position relative to the power head. This step is

7

important to ensure correct wire routing and phasing of the ignition charging cycles.

6. Remove the mounting screws (4, **Figure 50**) and lift the coil (5, **Figure 50**) from the power head. Clean the battery charge/lighting coil mounting surfaces. Clean all corrosion or contamination from the mounting screw holes.
7. Place the coil in position on the power head. Align the coil with its mounting holes and position its wires as noted in Step 5. Apply Loctite 222 to the threads and evenly tighten the screws to the specification in **Table 1**.
8. Connect all wires to the CDI or engine control unit, rectifier/regulator and electrothermal valve if so equipped.
9. Route all wires away from moving components. Retain the wires with plastic locking clamps as required.
10. Install the flywheel (Chapter Eight).
11. Install the spark plugs and leads and connect the cables to the battery.

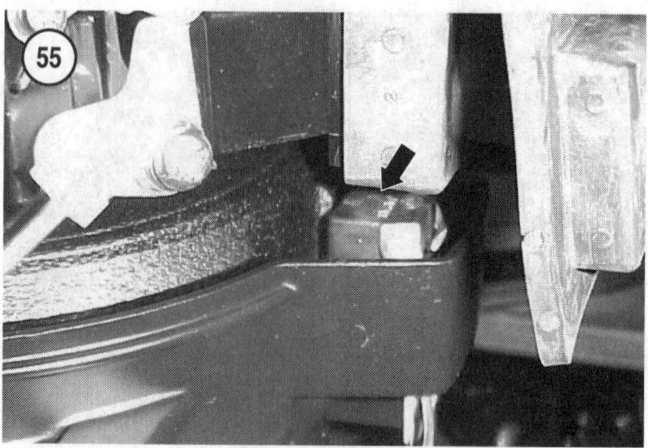
55

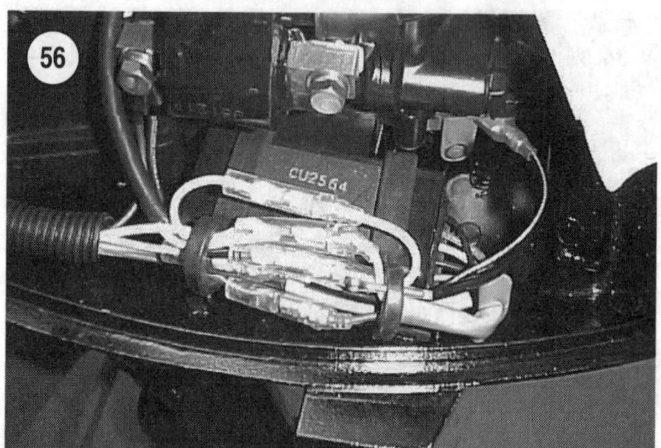
56

Power Source Coil Removal/Installation

The power source coil is integrated into the combination battery/ignition charge coil. The entire component must be replace if any portion of the assembly fails. Refer to *Ignition Charge Coil* in this section for removal and installation instructions.

Pulser Coil Removal/Installation

Pulser coils (**Figure 55**, typical) are used on 4, 5, 9.9 (serial No. OH000058-on) and 50-90 hp models.

Proper operation of the pulser coil requires the correct air gap between the coil and the flywheel. On 9.9 and 50 hp models a 0.030 in. (0.77 mm) feeler gauge is required to position the pulser coil. On other models the pulser coil is not adjustable and is correctly spaced during installation.

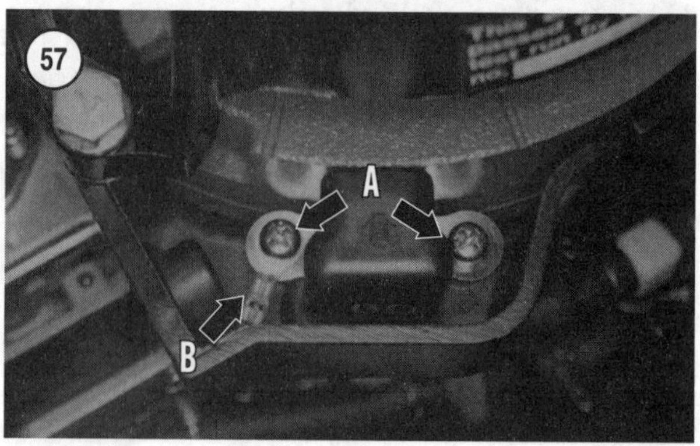

57

4-6 hp models

1. Remove the spark plug and connect the spark plug lead to a suitable engine ground. Remove the manual starter following the instructions in Chapter Ten.
2. Disconnect the red/white wire (**Figure 56**) from the CDI unit harness.
3. Remove the pulser coil retaining screws from the coil (A, **Figure 57**). Route the red/white wire through the rubber grommet located below the coil while removing the coil.
4. Clean the coil mounting surface. Clean corrosion from the mounting screw holes.
5. Guide the red/white wire through the rubber grommet while lowering the pulser coil into position. Install the coil mounting screws (A, **Figure 57**). Attach the ground to the starboard side mounting screw. Securely tighten both mounting screws. Direct the black ground wire (B, **Figure 57**) toward the front of the engine.
6. Connect the red/white wire to the CDI unit wire harness.
7. Install the manual starter (Chapter Ten). Install the spark plug and lead.

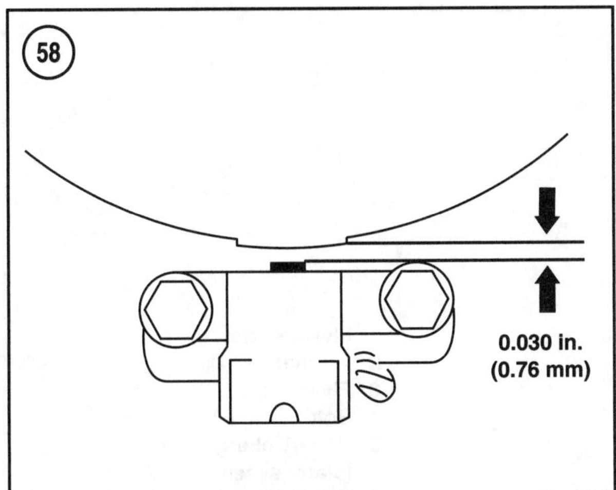

9.9 hp models (serial No. OH000058-on)

The pulser coil is located at the upper front side of the power head near the flywheel.

1. Disconnect both cables from the battery if so equipped. Remove the spark plugs and connect the spark plug leads to a suitable engine ground.
2. On electric start models, remove the flywheel cover following the instructions in Chapter Eight. On manual start models, remove the manual starter following the instructions in Chapter Ten.
3. Disconnect the white/red and black pulser coil wires from the CDI unit harness.
4. Remove the pulser coil mounting screws and washers and remove the pulser coil.
5. Clean the mounting base and threaded holes.
6. Place the pulser coil onto the mounting base. Install both washers and screws. Do not tighten the screws at this time.
7. Connect pulser coil wires to the CDI unit wire harness. Route all wires away from moving components especially the flywheel. Retain the wires with plastic locking clamps as required.

8. Rotate the flywheel until the raised area on the circumference of the flywheel aligns with the protrusion on the pulser coil (**Figure 58**). Insert a 0.030 in. (0.76 mm) feeler gauge between the protrusion and the raised area on the flywheel. Slide the pulser coil toward the flywheel until the feeler gauge is captured. Securely tighten the mounting screws. Check the clearance between the raised area on the flywheel and pulser coil. The feeler gauge must pass between the components with a slight drag.
9. On electric start models, install the flywheel. On manual start models, install the manual starter.
10. Install the spark plugs and leads. Connect the cables to the battery if so equipped.

50 hp models

On 50 hp models the pulser coil (A, **Figure 59**) mounts on the upper port side of the power head near the flywheel.

1. Disconnect both cables from the battery if so equipped. Remove the spark plugs and connect the spark plug leads to a suitable engine ground.
2. Disconnect the pulser coil harness from the engine wire harness.
3. Remove the mounting bolts (B, **Figure 59**) and the pulser coil from its mounting boss. Clean from the pulser coil mounting boss and screw holes.
4. Place the pulser coil onto its mounting boss. Install both washers and mounting bolts (B, **Figure 59**). Do not tighten the bolts at this time.
5. Connect the pulser coil wire harness to its engine wire harness connector. Route all wires away from moving components especially the flywheel. Retain the wires with plastic locking clamps as required.
6. Rotate the flywheel until the larger raised area on the circumference of the flywheel (**Figure 60**) aligns with the

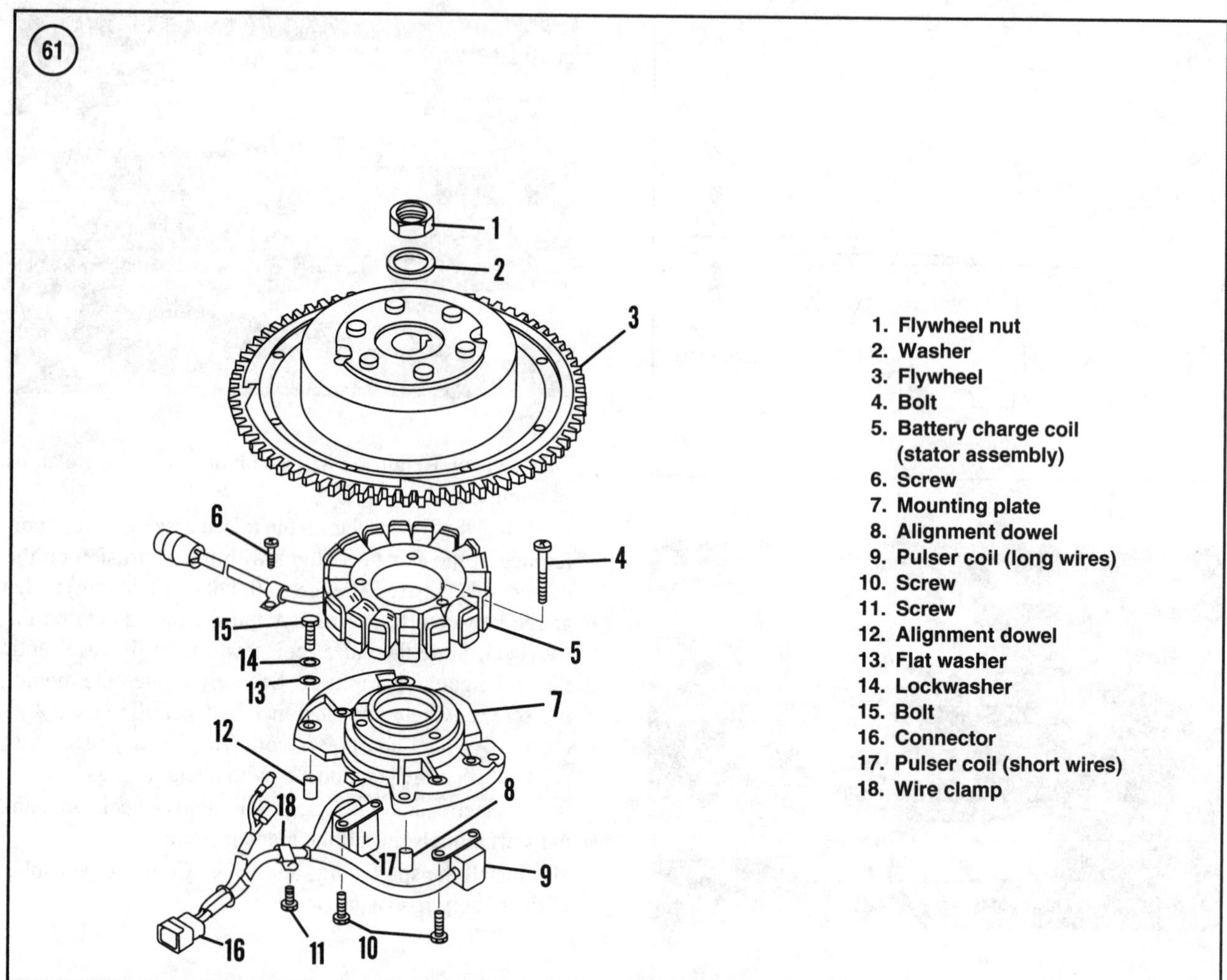

protrusion on the pulser coil (**Figure 58**). Insert a 0.030 in. (0.76 mm) feeler gauge between the protrusion and the raised area on the flywheel. Slide the pulser coil toward the flywheel until the feeler gauge is just captured. Tighten the pulser coil mounting bolts to the specification in **Table 1**. Check the clearance between the raised area on the flywheel and pulser coil. The feeler gauge must pass between the components with a slight drag. Correct as required.

7. Install the spark plugs and leads. Connect the cables to the battery.

75 and 90 hp models

On 75 and 90 hp models the pulser coils (9 and 17, **Figure 61**) are attached to a special mounting plate (7) along with the battery charging coil (5). Access to the pulser coil attaching screws requires removal of the flywheel and battery charging coil.

1. Disconnect both cables from the battery. Remove the spark plugs and connect the spark plug leads to a suitable engine ground.
2. Remove the battery charging coil as described in this chapter.
3. Disconnect the pulser coil harness (16, **Figure 61**) from the engine wire harness. Remove the screw (11, **Figure 61**) and lift the clamp from the mounting plate (7).
4. Mark the mounting plate (7, **Figure 61**) relative to its orientation on the power head. This helps ensure correct wire routing and phasing of the coils during installation.
5. Remove the four screws (13, **Figure 61**) and mounting plate from the power head. Place the alignment dowels (8 and 12, **Figure 61**) into their openings on the power head.
6. Remove the four screws and the pulser coils (9 and 17, **Figure 61**) from the mounting plate. Clean the mounting plate, power head and screw holes.

62

63

64

65

7. Select the pulser coil (18, **Figure 61**) with the shortest length of wire to the clamp (17). Install this pulser coil at the location closest the clamp screw (11, **Figure 61**).

8. Position the pulser coil with the protrusion facing the flywheel (**Figure 58**). Install both screws (10, **Figure 61**) and tighten them to the specification in **Table 1**.

9. Install the pulser coil with the longer length of wire on the opposite location as described in Step 7.

10. Position the clamp (17, **Figure 61**) onto the mounting plate. Install and securely tighten the clamp screw (11, **Figure 61**).

11. Place the mounting plate onto the power head with the reference mark aligned (Step 4). Slip the alignment dowels (8 and 12, **Figure 61**) into the openings in the power head and mounting plate. Install the four flat washers, lock washers and bolts (15, **Figure 61**) and securely tighten them.

12. Install the battery charge coil following the instructions in this section.

13. Connect the harness (16, **Figure 61**) to the engine wire harness. Route all wires away from moving components especially the flywheel.

14. Install the flywheel (Chapter Eight).

15. Install the spark plugs and leads. Connect the cables to the battery.

Crankshaft Position Sensor Removal/Installation

A crankshaft position sensor is used on 9.9 hp (prior to serial No. OH000058) and all 15-40 hp models. The sensor (**Figure 62**) mounts adjacent to the flywheel. The air gap clearance between the sensor and protrusions on the flywheel is not adjustable.

1. Disconnect both cables from the battery if so equipped. Remove the spark plugs then connect the spark plug leads to a suitable engine ground.

2. On manual start models, remove the manual starter as described in Chapter Ten.

3. On electric start models, remove the flywheel cover as described in Chapter Eight.

4. Refer to the wire diagrams located at the back of the manual to identify the wires connected to the crankshaft position sensor. Disconnect the sensor wires **(Figure 63)**.

5. Remove both mounting screws (**Figure 64**) and lift the crankshaft position sensor and wires from the power head. Clean the sensor mounting bosses and screw holes.

6. Align the sensor tip with the flywheel as indicated in **Figure 65**. The protrusions on the flywheel must pass next to the sensor tip as the flywheel rotates.

7. Install both mounting screws (**Figure 64**) and tighten them to the specification in **Table 1**.

8. Connect the sensor wires to the engine wire harness connector. Route all wires away from moving components such as the flywheel and timing belt. Retain the wires with plastic locking type clamps as required.
9. On manual start models, install the manual starter (Chapter Ten).
10. On electric start models, install the flywheel cover (Chapter Eight).
11. Install the spark plugs and leads. Connect the cables to the battery.

Ignition Coil Removal and Installation

1. Disconnect both battery cables from the battery.
2. Refer to the wire diagrams located at the back of the manual to identify the wires connected to the coil (**Figure 66**).
3. Remove the ignition coil from the engine as follows:
   a. On 4-6 hp models, disconnect the wire from the coil terminal (A, **Figure 67**). Remove both mounting bolts (B, **Figure 67**), then lift the coil from the power head.
   b. On 9.9 and 15 hp models, cut the clamp from the wire bundle then disconnect the coil wires. Remove the mounting screw (**Figure 68**), then lift the coil from the engine.
   c. On 25 hp models, disconnect the orange and black/white coil wires (A, **Figure 69**) from the engine wire harness. Remove both mounting bolts (B, **Figure 69**), then lift the coil from the rocker arm cover.
   d. On 30 and 40 hp models, disconnect the coil wire (**Figure 70**) from the engine wire harness. Remove the coil mounting screw, then lift the coil from the cylinder head.
   e. On 50 hp models, remove the screw (A, **Figure 71**), then lift the coil ground wires from the cylinder block. Disconnect the wire connecting the ignition coil to the engine wire harness. Remove both mounting screws (B, **Figure 71**), then lift the coil from the power head
   f. On 75 and 90 hp models, disconnect the wire connecting the ignition coil to the engine wire harness. Remove the screw (A, **Figure 72**), then lift the coil ground wires from the cylinder head. Remove both mounting screws (B, **Figure 72**), then lift the ignition coil from the cylinder head.
4. Clean from the coil mounting surfaces. Thoroughly clean the coil and ground wire screw holes.
5. Refer *Spark Plug Cap* in Chapter Three to determine if cap or wire removal is required. Remove the cap or wire as described in Chapter Three.

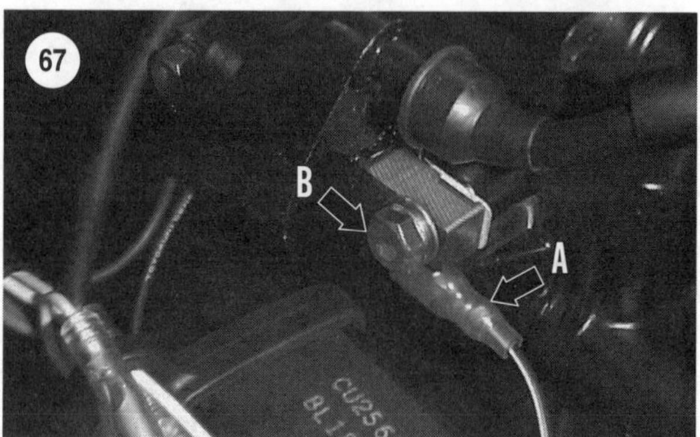

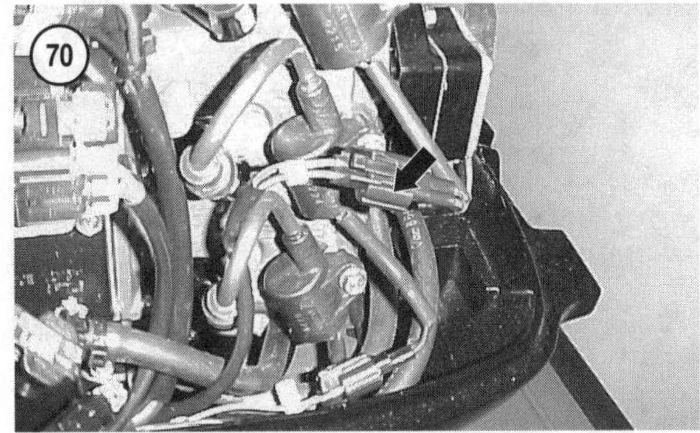
70

A
B
B
71

B
B
A
72

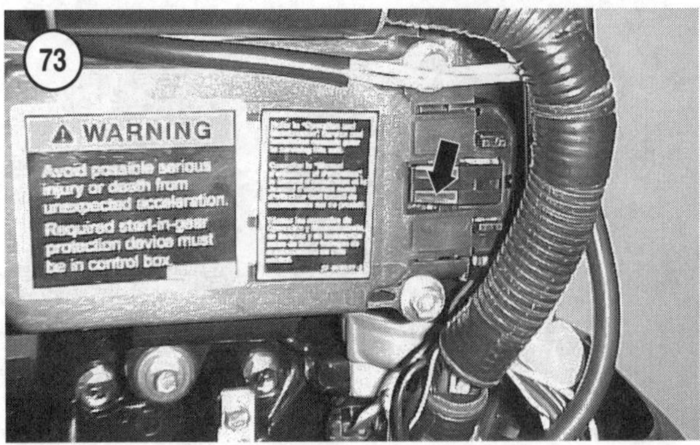
WARNING
Avoid possible serious injury or death from unexpected acceleration.
Required start-in-gear protection device must be in control box.
73

6. Installation is the reverse or removal while noting the following:

   a. Connect all coil ground wires to the common terminal or harness connection.
   b. Install the spark plug cap as described in Chapter Three.
   c. Tighten the ignition coil mounting screws to the specification in **Table 1**.
   d. Route all wires away from moving components. Retain the wires with plastic locking clamps as required.
   e. On 50-90 hp models, install all coil ground wires to the ground terminal. Securely tighten the ground screw.

7. Connect the cables to the battery if so equipped.

CDI and Engine Control Unit Removal/Installation

1. Disconnect both cables from the battery if so equipped.
2. Note of all wire attaching points and routing to ensure proper connections during assembly.
3. Disconnect and remove the CDI or engine control unit as follows:

   a. On 4-6 hp models, slip the CDI unit from its rubber mounting sleeve. Remove the screws retaining the CDI or engine control unit to the power head
   b. On 25-40 hp models, depress the tab (**Figure 73**), then pull the large connector from each side of the engine control unit. Remove the four mounting bolts and remove the engine control unit.
   c. On 75 and 90 hp models, remove the mounting screws and pull the engine control unit from behind the silencer cover. Push in on the tabs while disconnecting all three harness connectors from the engine control unit.
   d. On all other models, disconnect the wires connected to the CDI or engine control unit or its harness.

4. Inspect and clean all terminal in the wire harness and engine control unit connectors.
5. Clean the CDI or engine control unit and the screw holes.
6. Installation is the reverse of removal while noting the following:

   a. Tighten all mounting screws to the specification provided in **Table 1**.
   b. Securely attach all wire connectors to the CDI, engine control unit and the wire harness.
   c. Securely attach all ground wires if so equipped.

7. Connect the cables to the battery if so equipped.

Engine Temperature Sensor Removal/Installation (25-40 hp, 75 and 90 hp)

1. Disconnect both cables from the battery if so equipped.
2. Disconnect and remove the engine temperature sensor as follows:
   a. On 25 hp models, the engine temperature sensor is located on the upper port side water jacket cover (**Figure 74**). Remove the retaining screw and clamp then carefully pull the sensor from the water jacket. Disconnect the sensor wires.
   b. On 30 and 40 hp models, disconnect the sensor wire (**Figure 75**) from the engine wire harness connector. Using an appropriately sized wrench, unthread the sensor from the water jacket.
   c. On 75 and 90 hp models, pinch the sides of the connector (**Figure 76**) then pull it from the sensor. Remove both mounting bolts, then pull the sensor (**Figure 77**) from its opening.
3. Clean the sensor opening with a suitable solvent. Dry the opening with compressed air.
4. Installation is the reverse of removal while noting the following:
   a. On 25 hp models, securely tighten the retaining clamp. Ensure the clamp does not contact the wires.
   b. On 30-90 hp models, tighten the sensor or its mounting bolts to the specification in **Table 1**.
   c. Route all wires away from moving components.
5. Connect the cables to the battery.

Throttle Position Sensor Removal/Installation

The throttle position sensor (**Figure 78**) mounts to the lower port side of the power head and is operated by the throttle linkage.

1. Disconnect the battery cables from the battery. Place the remote control in the idle position.
2. Disconnect the sensor from the engine harness (**Figure 79**). Cut the plastic tie clamps as required.
3. Remove the sensor mounting screws (**Figure 80**). Remove the sensor from the coupler (**Figure 81**).
4. Position the throttle position sensor onto its mount with the wires exiting toward the front of the engine (**Figure 78**). Rotate the throttle position sensor until the pin (**Figure 82**) aligns with the slot in the coupler (**Figure 81**).
5. Support the sensor while installing the mounting screws (**Figure 80**). Rotate the throttle position sensor clockwise until it reaches the limit of its adjusting slot, then securely tighten the mounting screws.
6. Connect the throttle position sensor wire harness to the engine wire harness connector (**Figure 79**). Route all

74

75

76

77

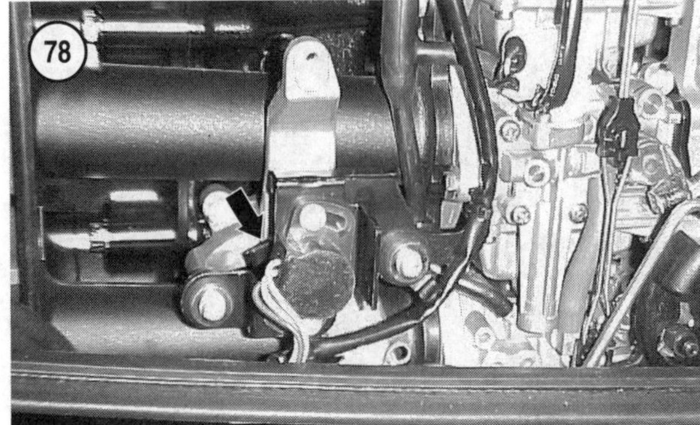
78

79

80

81

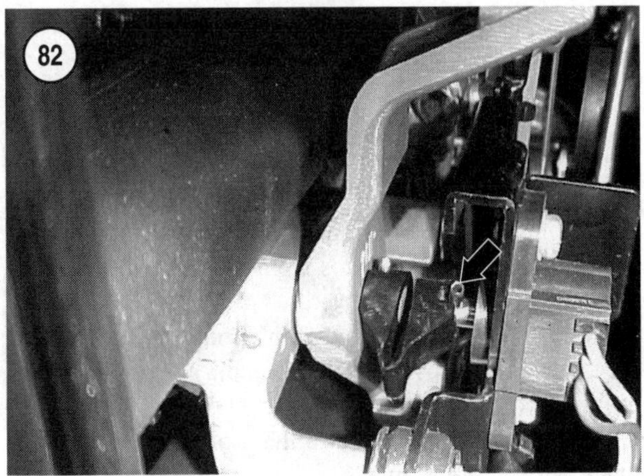
82

wires away from moving components. Install the plastic clamp to retain the wire harnesses.

7. Connect the cables to the battery. Adjust the throttle position sensor as described in Chapter Five.

Lanyard Switch Removal/Installation (Tiller Models)

This section provides instructions for removing and installing the lanyard switch on tiller control models. Refer to Chapter Twelve to remove and install the switch on remote control models. On 4-6 hp models, the lanyard switch is integrated into the stop button. Refer to *Stop Button* in this chapter for removal and installation.

1. Disconnect both cables from the battery if so equipped.
2. Refer to the wire diagrams located at the back of the manual and disconnect the lanyard switch wires.
3. Carefully pry up on the retaining clip while slipping it from the switch. Pull the switch from the lower engine cover.
4. Install the switch with its *run* mark facing up. Slide the switch retaining clip into the groove in the switch.
5. Connect the lanyard switch wires. Route the wires away from moving components. Secure the wires using plastic tie straps.
6. Connect the battery cables to the battery.
7. Start the engine and check for proper switch operation.

Stop Switch or Button Removal/Installation

On 4-6 hp models, the combination stop button and lanyard switch is located on the front side of the lower engine cover (**Figure 83**). On 9.9-40 hp models, this switch is located on the end of the tiller arm grip. This section provides removal and installation for the switch used on 4-6 hp models. Refer to Chapter Twelve for stop switch removal and installation for 9.9-40 hp models.

1. Disconnect the brown stop button wire from the CDI unit. Disconnect the black stop button wire from the ignition coil ground terminal.
2. Hold the button while threading the large plastic retaining nut (**Figure 84**) from the back side of the button. Pull the button and its wires from its opening. Wipe the opening clean.
3. Guide the wires for the button through the opening in the lower engine cover and the retaining nut. Hold the button while securely tightening the retaining nut.
4. Connect the brown wire to the CDI unit. Connect the black wire to the ground connection at the ignition coil. Retain the wires with plastic clamps as required.
5. Check for proper operation of the lanyard and stop switch after starting the engine.

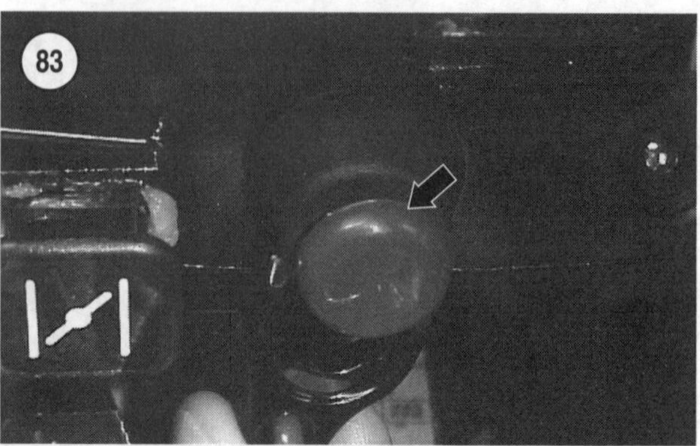

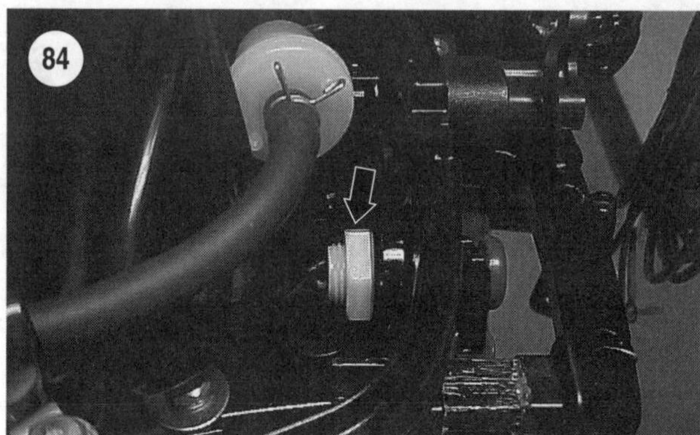

WARNING SYSTEM COMPONENTS

This section provides removal and installation instructions for the following warning system components.

1. Overheat switch.
2. Oil pressure switch.
3. Warning horn.
4. Warning horn driver.
5. Oil pressure light.

Overheat Switch Removal/Installation

An overheat switch is used on all 50 hp models to activate the warning horn and power reduction systems. Remaining 25-90 hp models rely on input from the engine temperature sensor to activate the overheat warning.

1. Disconnect both cables from the battery.
2. Disconnect both overheat switch (**Figure 85**) wires.
3. Remove the retaining bolt and clamp and pull the switch from its opening. Wipe the switch opening clean.
4. Insert the switch fully into its opening. Rotate the switch to position its wires opposite the clamping surfaces. Install the clamp and bolt. Securely tighten the bolt.
5. Connect the switch wires to the engine wire harness then feed the wires into the plastic wrap. Run a band of electrical tape around the switch end of the plastic wire wrap.
6. Connect the cables to the battery.

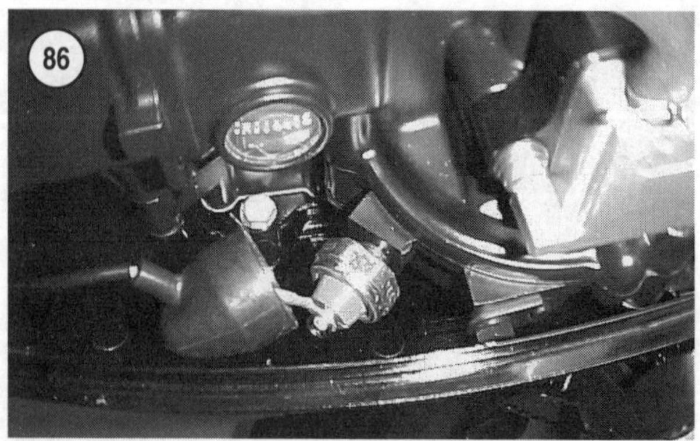

Oil Pressure Switch Removal/Installation

To prevent oil leakage, apply of Loctite pipe sealant to the threaded section of the switch prior to installation.

87

On 4-6 hp models, the switch is located on the lower starboard side of the power head (**Figure 86**).

On 9.9 (serial No. OH000057-prior) and 15 hp models, the switch is located on the upper port side of the power head (**Figure 87**).

On 9.9 hp models (serial No. OH000058-On), the switch is located on the upper starboard side of the power head and below the flywheel (**Figure 88**).

On 25-40 hp models, the switch is located on the upper port side of the power head and next to the oil filter (**Figure 89**).

On 50 hp models, the switch is located on the port side of the power head and next to the ignition coils (**Figure 90**).

On 75 and 90 hp models, the switch is located on the upper port side of the power head and below the flywheel (**Figure 88**).

88

1. Disconnect both cables from the battery if so equipped.
2. On all except 50 hp models, carefully pull the protective boot from the oil pressure switch. Slide the boot down the switch wire.
3. On 50 hp models, pull the wire connector from the switch. On other models, remove the terminal nut and disconnect the wire from the wire terminal.
4. Using an appropriately sized deep socket, remove the oil pressure switch from the power head. Clean all remnants of sealant from the threaded section of the switch. Carefully wipe all sealant from the switch opening in the power head. Do not allow any particles into the opening.
5. Apply a light coating of Loctite pipe sealant to the upper 2/3 of the switch threads. Do not allow any sealant near the opening in the switch.

89

6. Thread by hand the oil pressure switch into the power head. Using an appropriately sized socket, tighten the switch to the specification in **Table 1**.
7. On 50 hp models, push the wire onto the switch terminal. The terminal must have a snug fit. Remove the terminal and squeeze it enough to tighten its fit. Secure the wire with plastic tie clamps to prevent it from loosening.
8. On other models, place the switch wire onto the switch terminal. Install then securely tighten the terminal nut. Carefully slide the protective boot fully over the switch.
9. Route all wires away from moving components.
10. Connect the cables to the battery if so equipped.

90

Warning Horn Removal/Installation

On applications with the key switch mounted in the remote control, the warning horn mounts inside the control. Refer to Chapter Twelve to disassemble the control enough to access the warning horn.

On applications with a dash mounted key switch, the warning horn mounts under the dash near the ignition switch.

On tiller control models the warning horn is located in the tiller support bracket.

Regardless of the mounting location the replacement instructions are similar. Disconnect the terminals and clean them. Remove any fasteners for the horn. Install the horn and connect the wire terminals.

Warning Horn Driver Removal/Installation

The horn driver is used only on 25 hp models with manual start and tiller control and is located at the front starboard side of the power head.

Disconnect the driver from the warning horn and the engine wire harness. Connect the wires for the replacement driver to the engine harness and warning horn. Route all wires away from moving components. Retain them with plastic tie clamps as required.

91

Oil Pressure Light Removal/Installation

The oil pressure light (**Figure 91**) mounts to the lower engine cover or the manual starter bracket. Note the wire routing and disconnect the wires. Remove the retaining nut or clip and pull the light from its opening. Wipe the opening clean then install the replacement light. Install the retaining nut or clip. Securely tighten the nut. Connect the wires to their wire harness connection points. Route all wires away from moving components. Retain the wires with plastic tie clamps as required.

Table 1 TIGHTENING TORQUE

Fastener location	ft-lb.	in-lb.	N•m
Electric starter throughbolts			
9.9 hp			
Serial No. OH000057-prior	–	70	8
Serial No. OH000058-on	–	36	4
15-40 hp	–	70	8
50 hp (serial No. OG472133-on)	–	70	8
75 and 90 hp	–	70	8
Starter relay to starter motor			
75 and 90 hp	–	70	8
Electric starter mounting			
9.9 hp			
Serial No. OH000057-prior	15	180	20
Serial No. OH000058-on	13	156	18
15 hp	15	180	20
25-40 hp	21	256	29
50 hp			
Serial No. OG471232-prior	23	276	31
Serial No. OG471233-on	17	198	22
75 and 90 hp	13	156	18

(continued)

Table 1 TIGHTENING TORQUE (continued)

Fastener location	ft-lb.	in-lb.	N•m
Electric starter mounting bracket			
9.9 hp (serial No. OH000058-on)	13	156	18
50 hp (serial No. OG471232-prior)	17	210	23
ECU mounting			
9.9 hp (serial No. OH000057-prior)	–	70	8
15 hp	–	70	8
25-40 hp	–	45	5
50 hp	–	102	11
75 and 90 hp	–	70	8
CDI unit mounting			
9.9 hp (serial No. OH000058-on)	–	70	8
Rectifier/Regulator mounting			
9.9 and 15 hp	–	70	8
25-40 hp	–	105	12
50 hp	–	102	11
75 and 90 hp	–	70	8
Front component mounting bracket			
9.9 hp (serial No. OH000057-prior)	–	70	8
15 hp	–	70	8
Crankshaft position sensor mounting			
9.9 hp (serial No. OH000057-prior)	–	70	8
15 hp	–	70	8
25-40 hp	–	45	5
Pulser coil			
50 hp	–	45	5
Engine temperature sensor			
30 and 40 hp	–	35	4
75 and 90 hp	–	70	8
Ignition coil mounting			
9.9 and 15 hp	–	70	8
25-50 hp	–	75	9
75-90 hp	–	70	8
Ignition charge coil mounting			
9.9 hp (serial No. OH000057-prior)	–	70	8
15 hp	–	70	8
Combination battery/ignition charging coil			
9.9 hp (serial No. OH000058-on)	–	70	8
25-40 hp	–	85	10
50 hp	–	75	9
75 and 90 hp	–	70	8
Oil pressure switch			
9.9 and 15 hp	–	70	8
25-40 hp	–	50	6
50-75 hp	–	50	6

Table 2 ELECTRIC STARTER MOTOR SPECIFICATIONS

Model	Specification
9.9 hp (serial No. OH000057-prior) and 50 hp (serial No. OG471232-prior)	
Minimum brush length	0.25 in. (6.4 mm)
Minimum commutator undercut	0.03 in. (0.8 mm)
9.9 hp (serial No. OH000058-on)	
Commutator diameter	1.14-1.18 in. (29-30 mm)
Commutator undercut	0.008-0.031 in. (0.2-.08 mm)
Brush length	0.35-0.49 in. (9-12.5 mm)

(continued)

7

Table 2 ELECTRIC STARTER MOTOR SPECIFICATIONS (continued)

Model	Specification
15-40 hp	
Minimum brush length	0.25 in. (6.4 mm)
Minimum commutator undercut	0.03 in. (0.8 mm)
50 hp (serial No. OG471233-on)	
Minimum brush length	0.47 in. (12 mm)
Commutator undercut (mica depth)	0.008-0.031 in. (0.2-0.8 mm)
Minimum commutator diameter	1.22 in. (31 mm)
Maximum armature shaft deflection	0.002 in. (005 mm)
Armature end play	0.002-0.010 in. (0.05-0.25 mm)
75 and 90 hp	
Minimum brush length	0.374 in. (9.5 mm)
Minimum commutator diameter	1.102 in. (28.0 mm)
Minimum commutator undercut	0.008 in. (0.2 mm)

Table 3 BATTERY REQUIREMENTS

Model	Minimum MCA rating	Minimum CCA rating
9.9-25 hp	465	350
30-90 hp		
Above 32° (0° C)	465	750
32° (0° C) and below	1000	750

Table 4 Battery State of Charge

Specific gravity reading	Percentage of charge remaining
1.120-1.140	0
1.135-1.155	10
1.150-1.170	20
1.160-1.180	30
1.175-1.195	40
1.190-1.210	50
1.205-1.225	60
1.215-1.235	70
1.230-1.250	80
1.245-1.265	90
1.260-1.280	100

Table 5 Battery Capacity/Hours of Use

Amperage draw	Hours Of usage	Recharge time approximate
5 amps		
80 amp battery	13.5 hours	16 hours
105 amp battery	15.8 hours	16 hours
15 amps		
80 amp battery	3.5 hours	13 hours
105 amp battery	4.2 hours	13 hours
25 amps		
80 amp battery	1.8 hours	12 hours
105 amp battery	2.4 hours	12 hours

Chapter Eight

Power Head

This chapter provides complete power head repair instructions. Flywheel removal and installation along with break-in instructions are included in this chapter.

Table 1 provides tightening specifications for most power head fasteners. **Tables 2-19** provide tolerances and dimensions for power head components. **Tables 1-19** are at the end of this chapter.

FLYWHEEL REMOVAL AND INSTALLATION

Securely mount the engine to the boat or work bench before removing the flywheel. If removing both the flywheel and power head, remove the flywheel before loosening the power head mounting bolts and nut.

Flywheel removal requires a spanner type wrench or strap wrench and puller. The Mercury part number for these tools is listed in the removal and installation instructions.

WARNING

Wear safety glasses when removing or installing the flywheel or other components of the engine. Never use a hammer without using safety glasses.

WARNING

Disconnect both battery cables, then remove all spark plugs prior to removing the flywheel.

CAUTION

Use only the appropriate tools and instructions to remove the flywheel. Never strike the flywheel with a hard object. The magnets may break and result in poor ignition system performance or potential damage to other engine components.

4-6 hp Models

1. Remove the spark plug and connect the plug lead to a suitable engine ground.
2. Remove the manual starter as described in Chapter Ten.

3. Grip the manual starter with a strap wrench (Mercury part No. 91-24937A1) as shown in **Figure 1**. Loosen the flywheel nut. Remove the three bolts and lift the manual starter pulley (**Figure 1**) from the flywheel. Loosen the flywheel nut until its upper surface is flush with the threaded end of the crankshaft.
4. Thread the three bolts of the puller (Mercury part No. 91-83164M) through the puller plate and into the flywheel as shown in **Figure 2**.
5. Secure the puller with a pry bar while tightening the puller bolt (**Figure 2**). Tighten the center puller bolt until the flywheel pops free from the crankshaft. Remove the flywheel nut and washer, then lift the flywheel from the crankshaft. Wipe all debris and contaminants from the flywheel and crankshaft surfaces.
6. Pull the flywheel drive key from its slot in the crankshaft or flywheel. Inspect the key for wear or damage. Replace the key if bent, worn or damaged.
7. Using gloves, remove all metal filings from the flywheel magnets. Inspect the magnets and flywheel for cracks or corrosion. Clean corroded surfaces with fine sandpaper. Replace the flywheel if deep pitting, cracks or damaged magnets are noted.
8. Place the flywheel key into the crankshaft slot with the rounded side facing inward. Place the flywheel over the end of the crankshaft and align the flywheel key slot with the flywheel key. Lower the flywheel onto the crankshaft taper. Ensure the key enters the slot.
9. Place the washer over the crankshaft and seat it against the flywheel. Thread the flywheel nut onto the crankshaft. Install the manual starter pulley. Tighten the three bolts to the specification in **Table 1**.
10. Engage the strap wrench with the manual starter pulley (**Figure 1**) and tighten the flywheel nut to the specification in **Table 1**.
11. Install the manual starter (Chapter Ten). Install the spark plug and lead.

9.9 (Prior to Serial No. OH000058) and 15 hp Models

1. Disconnect both cables from the battery if so equipped. Remove the spark plugs then connect the spark plug leads to a suitable engine ground.
2. On manual start models, remove the manual starter following the instructions in Chapter Ten.
3. On electric start models, note the wire routing and disconnect the harnesses (1 and 2, **Figure 3**) connecting the flywheel cover to the engine harness. Remove the three mounting bolts (4, **Figure 3**) and pull the pin (3) from the flywheel cover (5). Lift the flywheel cover (5, **Figure 3**) and belt cover (6) from the power head.

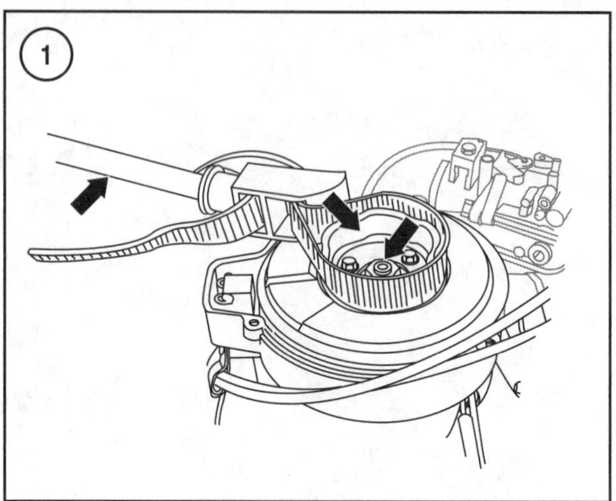

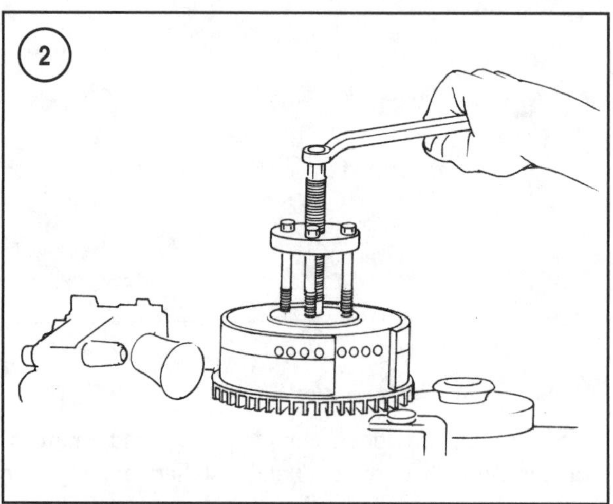

4. Engage the flywheel holding tool (Mercury part No. 91-83163M) with the holes in the flywheel as indicated in **Figure 4**. Using a breaker bar and socket, loosen the flywheel nut until its top surface is flush with the upper end of the crankshaft.

5. Thread the three bolts of the puller (Mercury part No. 91-83164M) through the puller plate and into the flywheel as indicated in **Figure 5**.

6. Secure the puller with a pry bar while tightening the puller bolt. Tighten the bolt until the flywheel pops free from the crankshaft. Remove the flywheel nut (7, **Figure 3**), then lift the flywheel (9) from the crankshaft. Wipe all debris and contaminants from the flywheel and crankshaft surfaces.

7. Pull the flywheel drive key (10, **Figure 3**) from its slot in the crankshaft or flywheel. Inspect the key for wear or damage. Replace the key if bent, worn or damaged.

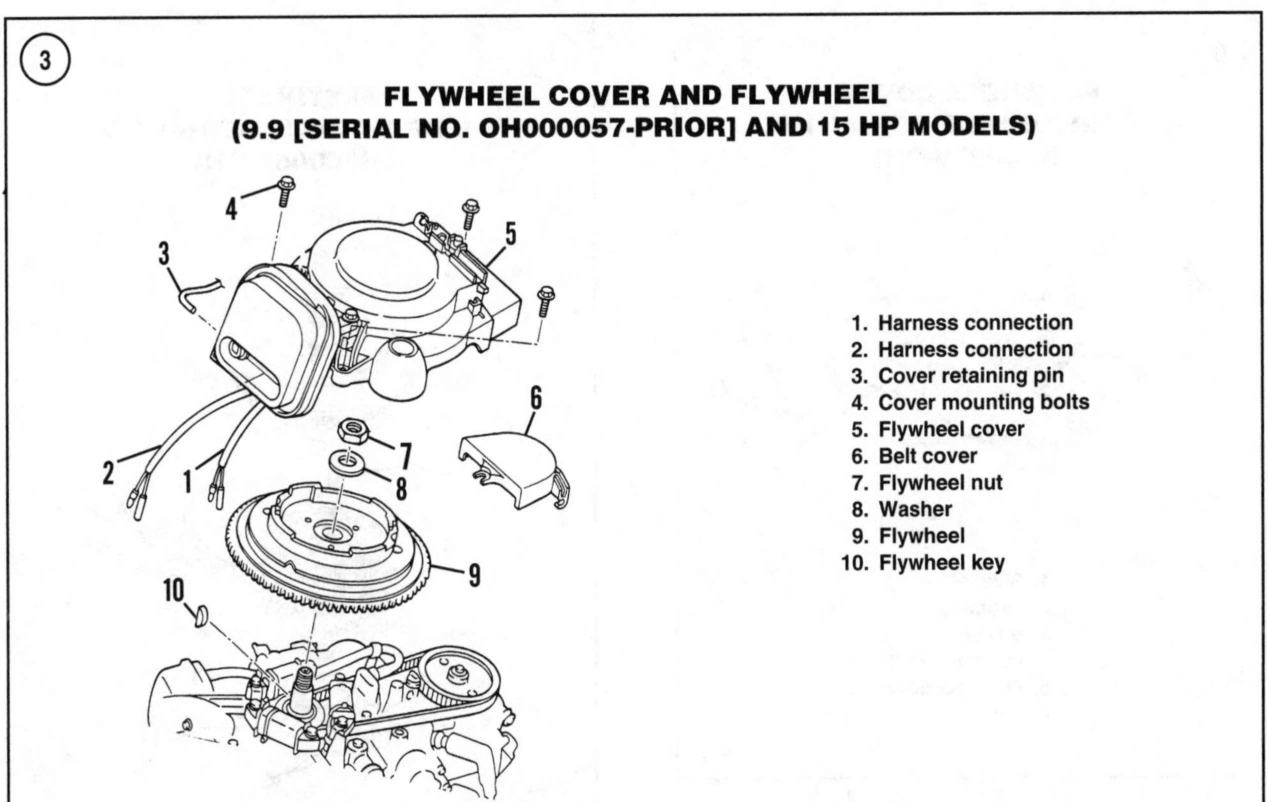

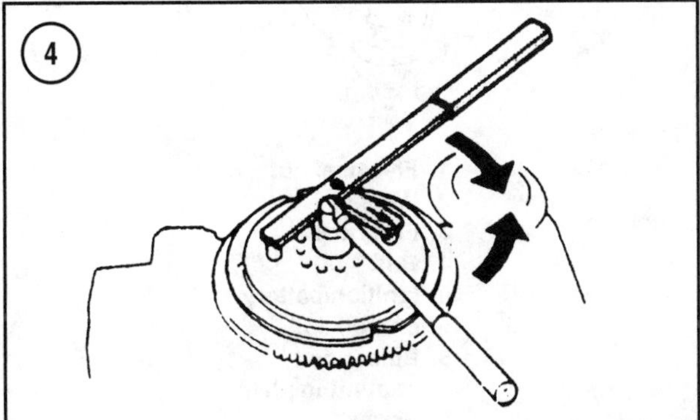

8. Using gloves, remove all metal filings from the flywheel magnets. Inspect the magnets and flywheel surfaces for cracks or corrosion. Remove corrosion using fine sandpaper. Replace the flywheel if deep pitting, cracks or damaged magnets are noted.

9. Place the flywheel key (10, **Figure 3**) into the crankshaft slot with the rounded side facing inward. Place the flywheel (9, **Figure 3**) over the end of the crankshaft and align the flywheel key slot with the flywheel key. Lower the flywheel onto the crankshaft taper. Ensure the key enters the slot.

10. Place the washer (8, **Figure 3**) over the crankshaft and seat it against the flywheel. Thread the flywheel nut (7, **Figure 3**) onto the crankshaft.

11. Engage the flywheel holding tool (**Figure 4**) with the holes in the flywheel. Tighten the flywheel nut to the specification in **Table 1**.

12. On manual start models, install the manual starter (Chapter Ten).

13. On electric start models, place the flywheel cover (5, **Figure 3**) onto the mounting bosses. Align the holes and slide the pin (3, **Figure 3**) through its opening in the flywheel cover. Install all three mounting bolts (4, **Figure 3**). Securely tighten the bolts. Snap the belt cover (6, **Figure 3**) onto the flywheel cover (5). Ensure adequate clearance

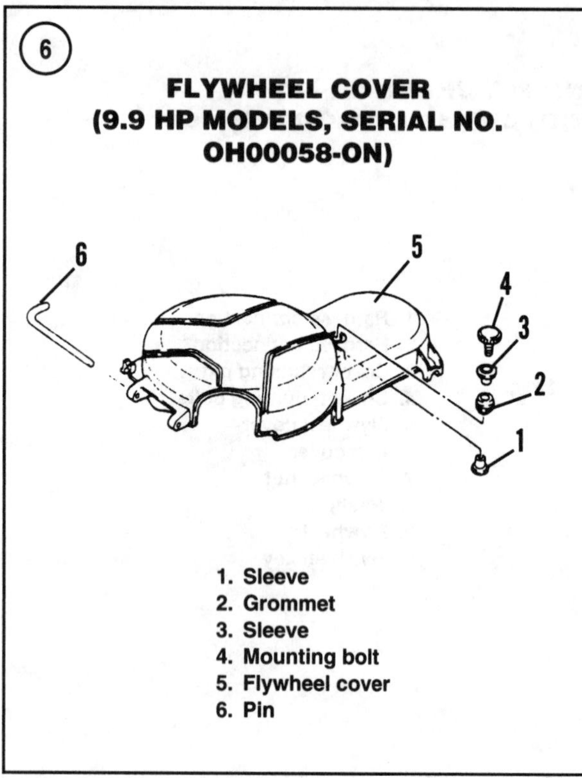

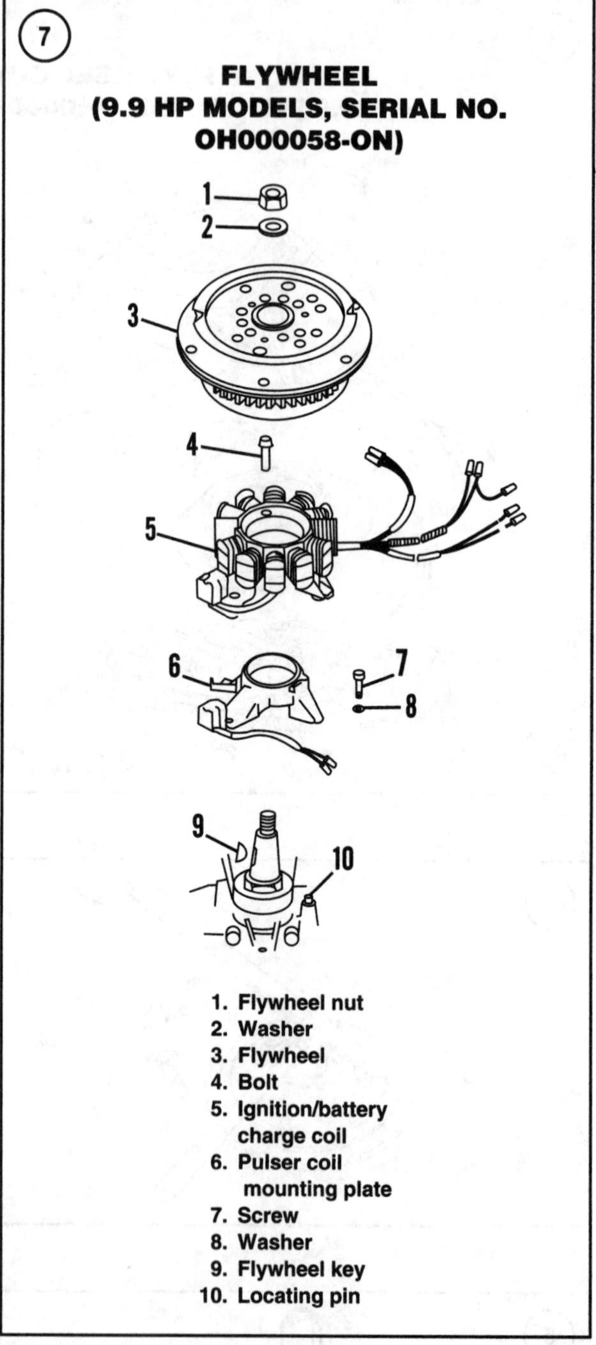

is present between the belt, flywheel and covers. Connect the harness (1 and 2, **Figure 3**) to the engine wire harness. Route all wires away from moving components.

14. Install the spark plugs and leads and connect the cables to the battery if so equipped.

9.9 hp Models (Serial No. OH000058-On)

1. Disconnect both cables from the battery if so equipped. Remove the spark plugs and connect the spark plug leads to a suitable engine ground.
2. On manual start models, remove the manual starter as described in Chapter Ten.
3. On electric start models, remove the mounting bolt (1, **Figure 6**) then pull the pin (6) from the flywheel cover (5). Lift the flywheel cover (5, **Figure 6**) from the power head. Lift the sleeves and grommet (1-3, **Figure 6**) from the flywheel cover or its rear mounting boss.
4. Engage the flywheel holding tool (Mercury part No. 91-83163M) with the holes in the flywheel as shown in **Figure 4**. Using a breaker bar and socket, loosen the flywheel nut until its top surface is flush with the upper end of the crankshaft.
5. Thread the three bolts of the puller (Mercury part No. 91-83164M) through the puller plate and into the flywheel as shown in **Figure 5**. Ensure the larger puller bolt is in direct contact with the crankshaft and the puller and flywheel are parallel before tightening the puller bolt.
6. Secure the puller with a pry bar while tightening the puller bolt. Tighten the center puller bolt until the flywheel pops free from the crankshaft. Remove the flywheel nut and washer (1 and 2, **Figure 7**), then lift the flywheel (3) from the crankshaft. Wipe all debris and contaminants from the flywheel and crankshaft surfaces.

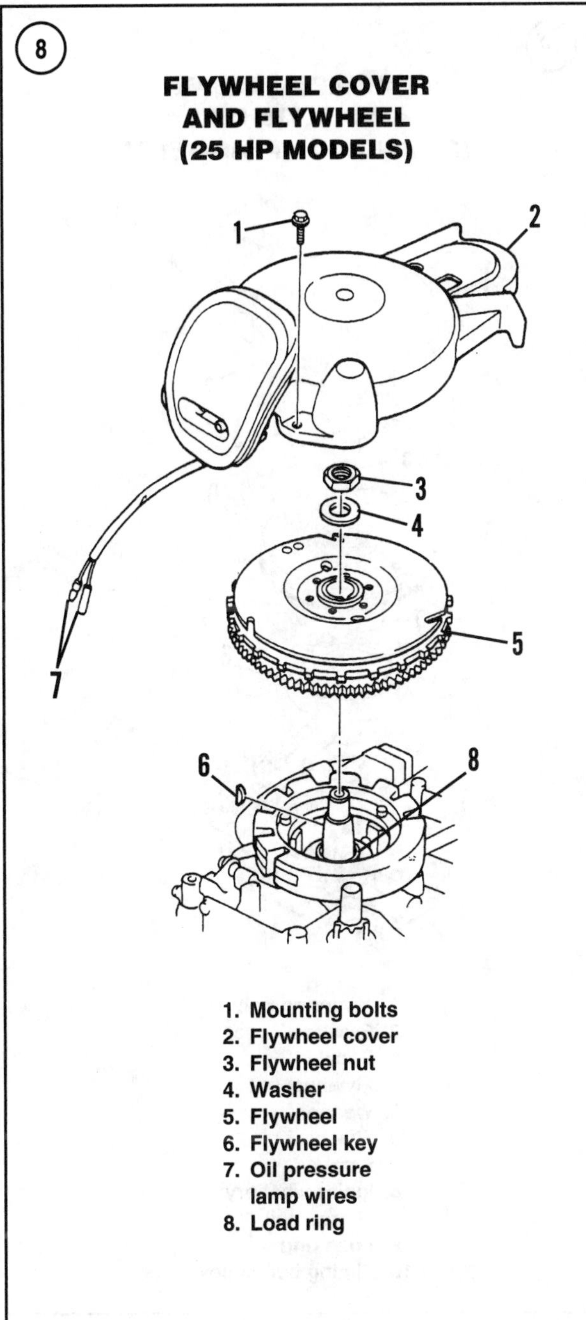

1. Mounting bolts
2. Flywheel cover
3. Flywheel nut
4. Washer
5. Flywheel
6. Flywheel key
7. Oil pressure lamp wires
8. Load ring

7. Pull the flywheel drive key (9, **Figure** 7) from its slot in the crankshaft or flywheel. Inspect the key for wear or damage. Replace the key if bent, worn or damaged.

8. Using gloves, remove all metal filings from the flywheel magnets. Inspect the magnets and flywheel surfaces for cracks or corrosion. Remove corrosion using fine sandpaper. Replace the flywheel if deep pitting, cracks or damaged magnets are noted.

9. Place the flywheel key (9, **Figure** 7) into the crankshaft slot with the rounded side facing inward. Place the flywheel (3, **Figure** 7) over the end of the crankshaft and align the flywheel key slot with the flywheel key. Lower the flywheel onto the crankshaft taper. Ensure the key enters the slot.
10. Place the washer (2, **Figure** 7) over the crankshaft and seat it against the flywheel. Apply a very light coating of engine oil to the threaded section of the crankshaft. Thread the flywheel nut (1, **Figure** 7) onto the crankshaft.
11. Engage the flywheel holding tool (**Figure 4**) with the holes in the flywheel. Tighten the flywheel nut to the specification in **Table 1**.
12. On manual start models, install the manual starter (Chapter Ten).
13. On electric start models, place the grommet and both sleeves (1-3, **Figure 6**) into the bolt opening of the flywheel cover. Place the flywheel cover (5, **Figure 6**) onto the mounting boss. Align the holes and slide the pin (6, **Figure 6**) through its opening in the flywheel cover and front bracket. Snap the pin into its recess at the front starboard side of the flywheel cover. Align the sleeves (1 and 3, **Figure 6**) with the threaded hole in the mounting boss and install the mounting bolt (4, **Figure 6**). Securely tighten the bolts. Ensure adequate clearance is present between the belt, flywheel and cover.
14. Install the spark plugs and leads and connect the cables to the battery if so equipped.

25 hp Models

1. Disconnect both cables from the battery if so equipped. Remove the spark plugs then connect the spark plug leads to a suitable engine ground.
2. On manual start models, remove the manual starter as described in Chapter Ten.
3. On electric start models, disconnect the oil warning lamp wires (7, **Figure 8**) from the engine wire harness. Remove the four mounting bolts (1, **Figure 8**), then lift the flywheel cover (2) from the power head.
4. Engage the flywheel holding tool (Mercury part No. 91-83163M) with the holes in the flywheel as indicated in **Figure 4**. Using a breaker bar and socket, loosen the flywheel nut until its top surface is flush with the upper end of the crankshaft.
5. Thread the three bolts of the puller (Mercury part No. 91-83164M) through the puller plate and into the flywheel as indicated in **Figure 5**. Ensure the larger puller bolt is in direct contact with the crankshaft and the puller and flywheel are parallel before tightening the puller bolt.
6. Secure the puller with a pry bar while tightening the puller bolt. Tighten the center puller bolt until the fly-

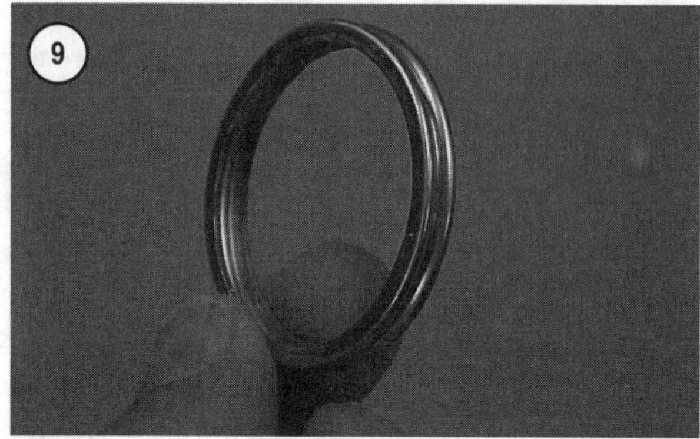

wheel pops free from the crankshaft. Remove the flywheel nut and washer (3 and 4, **Figure 8**) and lift the flywheel (5) from the crankshaft. Remove the load ring (**Figure 9**) from the flywheel or crankshaft surface. Discard the load ring. Wipe all debris and contaminants from the flywheel and crankshaft surfaces.

7. Pull the flywheel drive key (6, **Figure 8**) from its slot in the crankshaft or flywheel. Inspect the key for wear or damage. Replace the key if bent, worn or damaged.
8. Using gloves, remove all metal filings from the flywheel magnets. Inspect the magnets and flywheel surfaces for cracked or corroded surfaces. Remove corrosion using fine sandpaper. Replace the flywheel if deep pitting, cracks or damaged magnets are noted.
9. Place the flywheel key (6, **Figure 8**) into the crankshaft slot with the rounded side facing inward. Install a new load ring (**Figure 9**) over the crankshaft and rest it against the step on the crankshaft. Place the flywheel (5, **Figure 8**) over the end of the crankshaft and align the flywheel key slot with the flywheel key. Lower the flywheel onto the crankshaft taper. Ensure the key enters the slot.
10. Place the washer (4, **Figure 8**) over the crankshaft and seat it against the flywheel. Apply a very light coating of engine oil to the threaded section of the crankshaft. Thread the flywheel nut (3, **Figure 8**) onto the crankshaft.
11. Engage the flywheel holding tool (**Figure 4**) with the holes in the flywheel. Tighten the flywheel nut to the specification in **Table 1**.
12. On manual start models, install the manual starter (Chapter Ten).
13. On electric start models, align the mounting bolts holes with the mounting bosses while placing the flywheel cover on the power head. Install and securely tighten the bolts. Ensure adequate clearance between the belt, flywheel and cover. Connect the oil pressure warning light wires. Route the wires away from moving components.
14. Install the spark plugs and leads and connect the cables to the battery if so equipped.

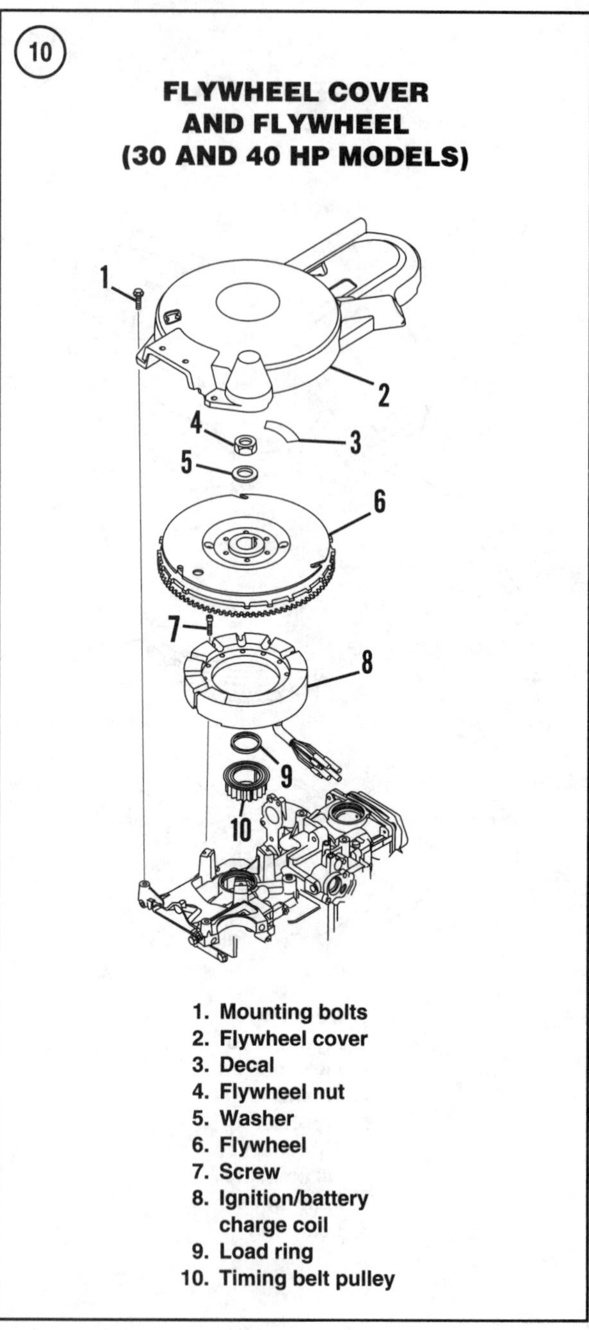

30 and 40 hp Models

1. Disconnect both cables from the battery if so equipped. Remove the spark plugs then connect the spark plug leads to a suitable engine ground.
2. On manual start models, remove the manual starter as described in Chapter Ten.
3. Remove the four mounting bolts (1, **Figure 10**) and lift the flywheel cover (2) from the power head.

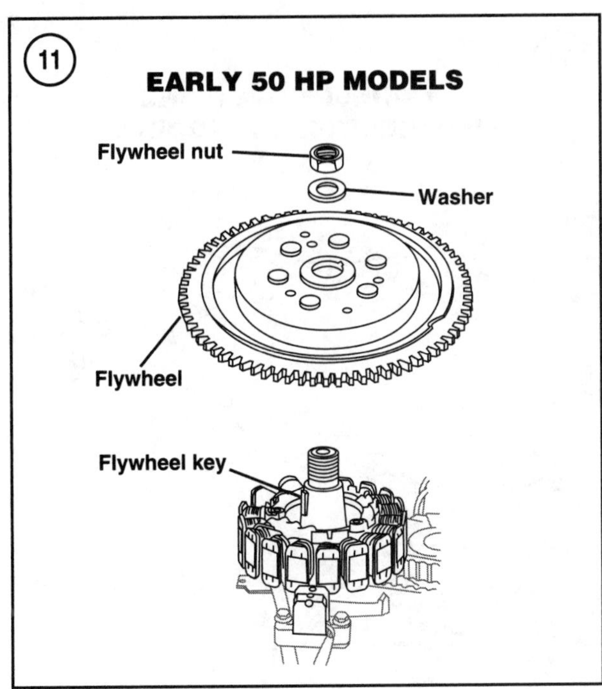

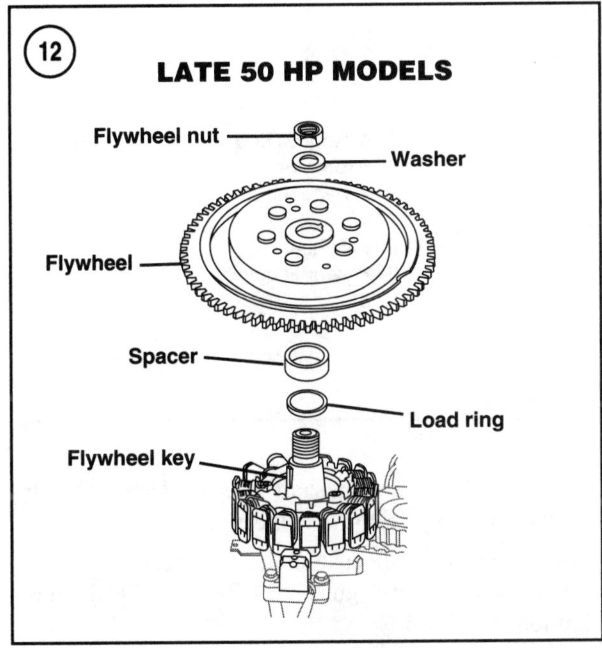

4. Engage the flywheel holding tool (Mercury part No. 91-83163M) with the holes in the flywheel as indicated in **Figure 4**. Using a breaker bar and socket, loosen the flywheel nut until its top surface is flush with the upper end of the crankshaft.

5. Thread the three bolts of the puller (Mercury part No. 91-83164M) through the puller plate and into the flywheel as indicated in **Figure 5**. Ensure the larger puller bolt is in direct contact with the crankshaft and the puller and flywheel are parallel before tightening the puller bolt.

6. Secure the puller with a pry bar while tightening the puller bolt. Tighten the center puller bolt until the flywheel pops free from the crankshaft. Remove the flywheel nut and washer (4 and 5, **Figure 10**), then lift the flywheel (6) from the crankshaft. Remove the load ring (9, **Figure 10**) from the flywheel or crankshaft. Discard the load ring. Wipe all debris and contaminants from the flywheel and crankshaft surfaces.

7. Pull the flywheel drive key from its slot in the crankshaft or flywheel. Inspect the key for wear or damage. Replace the key if bent, worn or damaged.

8. Using gloves, remove all metal filings from the flywheel magnets. Inspect the magnets and flywheel surfaces for cracked or corroded surfaces. Remove corrosion using fine sandpaper. Replace the flywheel if deep pitting, cracks or damaged magnets are noted.

9. Place the flywheel key into the crankshaft slot with the rounded side facing inward. Install a new load ring (**Figure 9**) over the crankshaft and rest it on the pulley (10, **Figure 10**). Place the flywheel (6, **Figure 10**) over the end of the crankshaft and align the flywheel key slot with the flywheel key. Lower the flywheel onto the crankshaft taper. Ensure the key enters the slot.

10. Place the washer (5, **Figure 10**) over the crankshaft and seat it against the flywheel. Apply a very light coating of engine oil to the threaded section of the crankshaft. Thread the flywheel nut (4, **Figure 10**) onto the crankshaft.

11. Engage the flywheel holding tool (**Figure 4**) with the holes in the flywheel. Tighten the flywheel nut to the specification in **Table 1**.

12. On manual start models, install the manual starter (Chapter Ten).

13. On electric start models, align the mounting bolts holes with the mounting bosses while placing the flywheel cover on the power head. Install and securely tighten all four bolts (1, **Figure 10**). Ensure adequate clearance is present between the belt, flywheel and cover.

14. Install the spark plugs and leads and connect the cables to the battery if so equipped.

50 hp Models

Late 50 hp models are equipped with a spacer and load ring (**Figure 9**) under the flywheel. Earlier models do not use the spacer or load ring. Replace the load ring each time the flywheel nut is removed. Refer to **Figure 11** or **Figure 12**.

8

1. Disconnect both cables from the battery. Remove the spark plugs and connect the spark plug leads to a suitable engine ground.

2. Remove both mounting bolts (1, **Figure 13**) and pull the slots (7) from their mounting post. Lift the flywheel cover (6) from the power head. Remove the grommets (2, **Figure 13**) from the flywheel cover.

3. Engage the flywheel holding tool (Mercury part No. 91-83163M) with the holes in the flywheel as indicated in **Figure 4**. Using a breaker bar and socket, loosen the flywheel nut until its top surface is flush with the upper end of the crankshaft.

4. Thread the three bolts of the puller (Mercury part No. 91-83164M) through the puller plate and into the flywheel as indicated in **Figure 5**. Ensure the larger puller bolt is in direct contact with the crankshaft and the puller and flywheel are parallel before tightening the puller bolt.

5. Secure the puller with a pry bar while tightening the puller bolt. Tighten the center puller bolt until the flywheel pops free from the crankshaft. Remove the flywheel nut and washer (3 and 4, **Figure 13**), then lift the flywheel (5) from the crankshaft.

6. On models so equipped, remove the spacer and load ring (**Figure 12**) from the flywheel or crankshaft. Discard the load ring. Wipe all debris and contaminants from the flywheel and crankshaft.

7. Pull the flywheel drive key from its slot in the crankshaft or flywheel. Inspect the key for wear or damage. Replace the key if bent, worn or damaged

8. Using gloves, remove all metal filings from the flywheel magnets. Inspect the magnets and flywheel surfaces for cracked or corroded surfaces. Remove corrosion using fine sandpaper. Replace the flywheel if deep pitting, cracks or damaged magnets are noted.

9. On models without the load ring (**Figure 11**), place the flywheel key into the crankshaft slot with the rounded side facing inward. Place the flywheel (**Figure 11**) over the end of the crankshaft and align the flywheel key slot with the flywheel key. Lower the flywheel onto the crankshaft taper. Ensure the key enters the slot.

10. On models with the load ring (**Figure 12**), place the flywheel key into the crankshaft slot with the rounded side inward. Install a new load ring (**Figure 9**) over the crankshaft and rest it on the pulley or crankshaft. Slide the spacer over the end of the crankshaft and rest it against the load ring. Place the flywheel (**Figure 12**) over the end of the crankshaft and align the flywheel key slot with the flywheel key. Lower the flywheel onto the crankshaft taper. Ensure the key enters the slot.

11. Place the washer (4, **Figure 13**) over the crankshaft and seat it against the flywheel. Apply a very light coating of engine oil to the crankshaft threads. Thread the flywheel nut (3, **Figure 13**) onto the crankshaft.

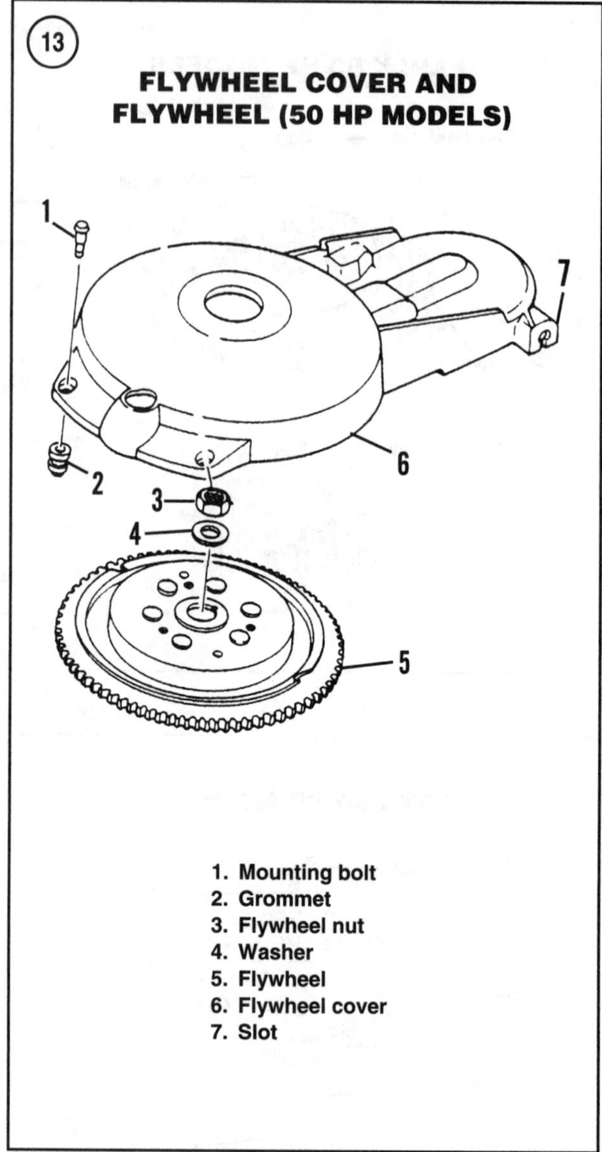

12. Engage the flywheel holding tool (**Figure 4**) with the holes in the flywheel. Tighten the flywheel nut to the specification in **Table 1**.

13. Place both grommets (2, **Figure 13**) into the mounting bolt openings. Align the mounting bolts holes with the mounting bosses while placing the flywheel cover on the power head. Install and securely tighten both mounting bolts (1, **Figure 13**). Snap both slots (7, **Figure 13**) over their mounting posts. Ensure adequate clearance between the belt, flywheel and cover.

14. Install the spark plugs and leads and connect the cables to the battery.

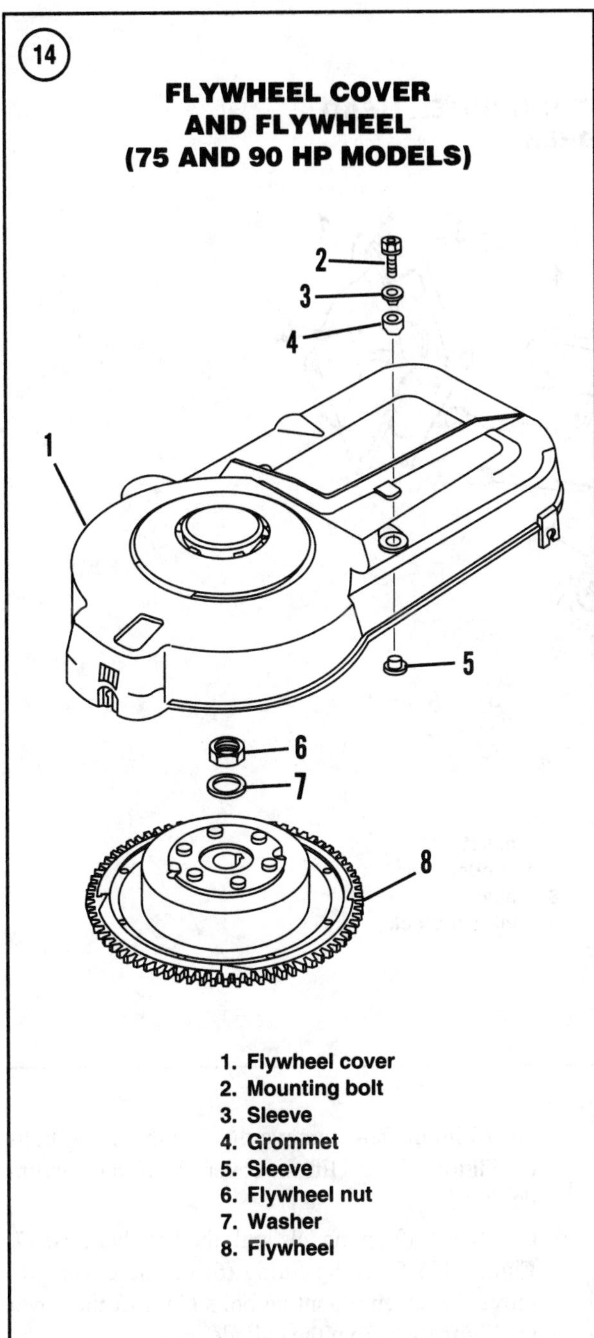

1. Flywheel cover
2. Mounting bolt
3. Sleeve
4. Grommet
5. Sleeve
6. Flywheel nut
7. Washer
8. Flywheel

75 and 90 hp Models

1. Disconnect both cables from the battery. Remove the spark plugs and connect the spark plug leads to a suitable engine ground.

2. Remove both mounting bolts (2, **Figure 14**) and carefully pull the slots at the rear of the cover from their mounting post. Lift the flywheel cover (1, **Figure 14**) from the power head.

3. Engage the flywheel holding tool (Mercury part No. 91-83163M) with the holes in the flywheel as indicated in **Figure 4**. Using a breaker bar and socket, loosen the flywheel nut until its top surface is flush with the upper end of the crankshaft.

4. Thread the three bolts of the puller (Mercury part No. 91-83164M) through the puller plate and into the flywheel as indicated in **Figure 5**. Ensure the larger puller bolt is in direct contact with the crankshaft and the surfaces of the puller and flywheel are parallel before tightening the puller bolt.

5. Secure the puller with a pry bar while tightening the puller bolt. Tighten the center puller bolt until the flywheel pops free from the crankshaft. Remove the flywheel nut and washer (6 and 7, **Figure 14**) and lift the flywheel (8) from the crankshaft. Wipe all debris and contaminants from the flywheel and crankshaft surfaces.

6. Pull the flywheel drive key from its slot in the crankshaft or flywheel. Inspect the key for wear or damage. Replace the key if bent, worn or damaged.

7. Using gloves, remove all metal filings from the flywheel magnets. Inspect the magnets and flywheel surfaces for cracked or corroded surfaces. Remove corrosion using with fine sandpaper. Replace the flywheel if deep pitting, cracks or damaged magnets are noted.

8. Place the flywheel key into the crankshaft slot with the rounded side facing inward. Place the flywheel (8, **Figure 14**) over the end of the crankshaft then align the flywheel key slot with the flywheel key. Lower the flywheel onto the crankshaft taper. Ensure the key enters the slot.

9. Place the washer (7, **Figure 14**) over the crankshaft and seat it against the flywheel. Apply a very light coating of engine oil to the crankshaft threads. Thread the flywheel nut (6, **Figure 14**) onto the crankshaft.

10. Engage the flywheel holding tool (**Figure 4**) with the holes in the flywheel. Tighten the flywheel nut to the specification in **Table 1**.

11. Install the grommet and both sleeves (3-5, **Figure 14**) into the mounting bolt holes. Align the mounting bolts holes with the mounting bosses while placing the flywheel cover on the power head. Install and securely tighten both mounting bolts (2, **Figure 14**). Snap both slots at the rear of the cover over their mounting post. Ensure adequate clearance is present between the belt, flywheel and cover.

12. Install the spark plugs and leads and connect the cables to the battery.

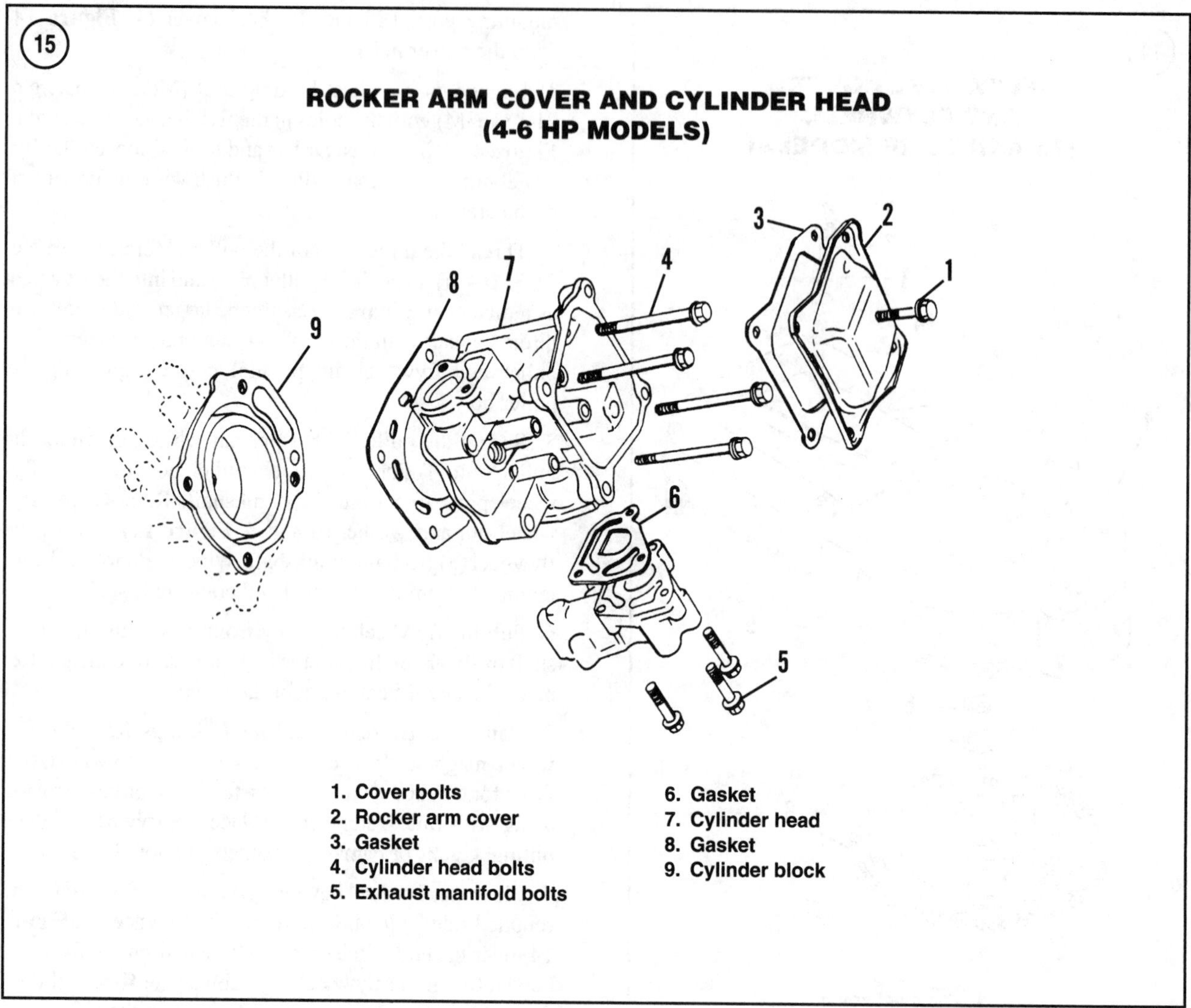

Rocker Arm Cover Removal

1. Disconnect both cables from the battery if so equipped. Remove the spark plugs and connect the spark plug leads to a suitable engine ground.

2. On 9.9-90 hp models, remove the fuel pump as described in Chapter Six.

3. On 9.9-50 hp models, remove the flywheel cover as described in this chapter.

4. Remove the rocker arm cover as follows:

   a. On 4-6 hp models, remove the four cover bolts (1, **Figure 15**) and carefully pry the cover (2) from the cylinder head (7). Remove and discard the gasket (3, **Figure 15**).

   b. On 9.9 and 15 hp models, remove the four mounting bolts (2, **Figure 16**) and lift the cover (3) from the cylinder head.

   c. On 25 hp models, remove the five mounting bolts (1, **Figure 17**) and lift the cover (2) from the cylinder head.

   d. On 30 and 40 hp models, pull the breather hose (7, **Figure 18**) from the fitting (6) on the cover. Remove the seven mounting bolts (3). Lift the cover (1, **Figure 18**) from the cylinder head.

   e. On 50 hp models, pull the breather hose from the fitting on the upper starboard side of the cover. Remove the seven mounting bolts (4, **Figure 19**) and lift the cover from the cylinder head (21).

   f. On 75 and 90 hp models, remove the five bolts (1, **Figure 20**) and lift the spark plug cover from the rocker arm cover (8). Pull the breather hose from the fitting (11, **Figure 20**) on the cover. Remove the 14 bolts (6, **Figure 20**) and pull the rocker arm cover from the cylinder head.

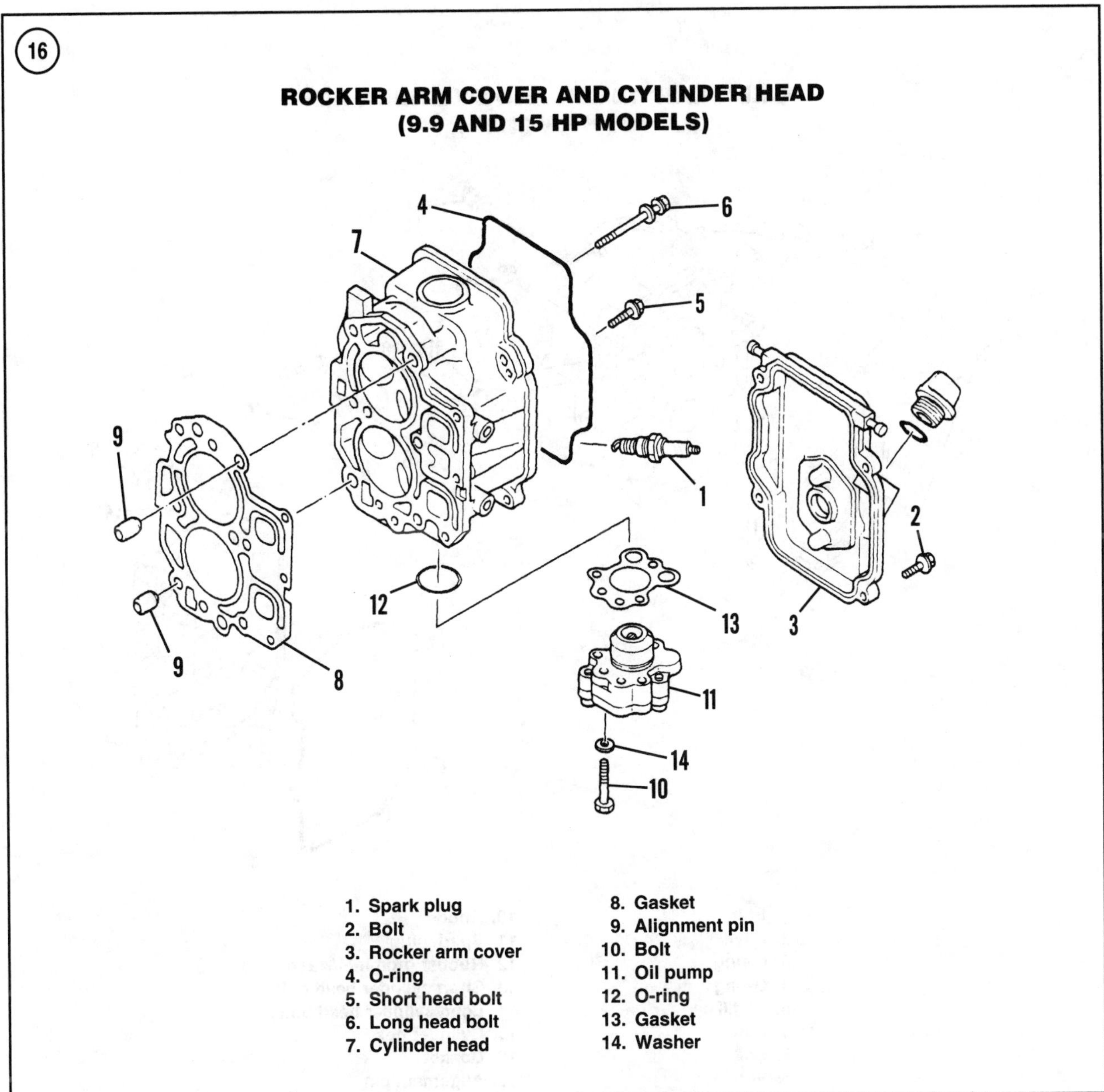

5. Remove and discard the O-ring from the rocker arm cover. On 30-90 hp models, remove the screws and lift the deflector plate from the cover. Using a suitable solvent, thoroughly clean the cover and deflector plate.

Rocker Arm Cover Installation

Refer to **Figures 15-20**.

1. On 30-90 hp models, place the deflector plate onto the cover. Install and securely tighten the deflector plate screws.
2. Place a new gasket, O-ring or seal on the rocker arm cover. Place the cover onto the cylinder head. Install hand tight all cover mounting bolts.
3. On 75 and 90 hp models, apply GM Silicone Sealer (Mercury part No. 92-91600-1) to the seal and the areas around the upper camshaft retainers.
4. Tighten all cover mounting bolts to the specification in **Table 1**. Refer to the following torque sequences.
   a. On 4-15 hp models, refer to **Figure 21**.
   b. On 25 hp models, tighten the bolts following a crossing pattern.

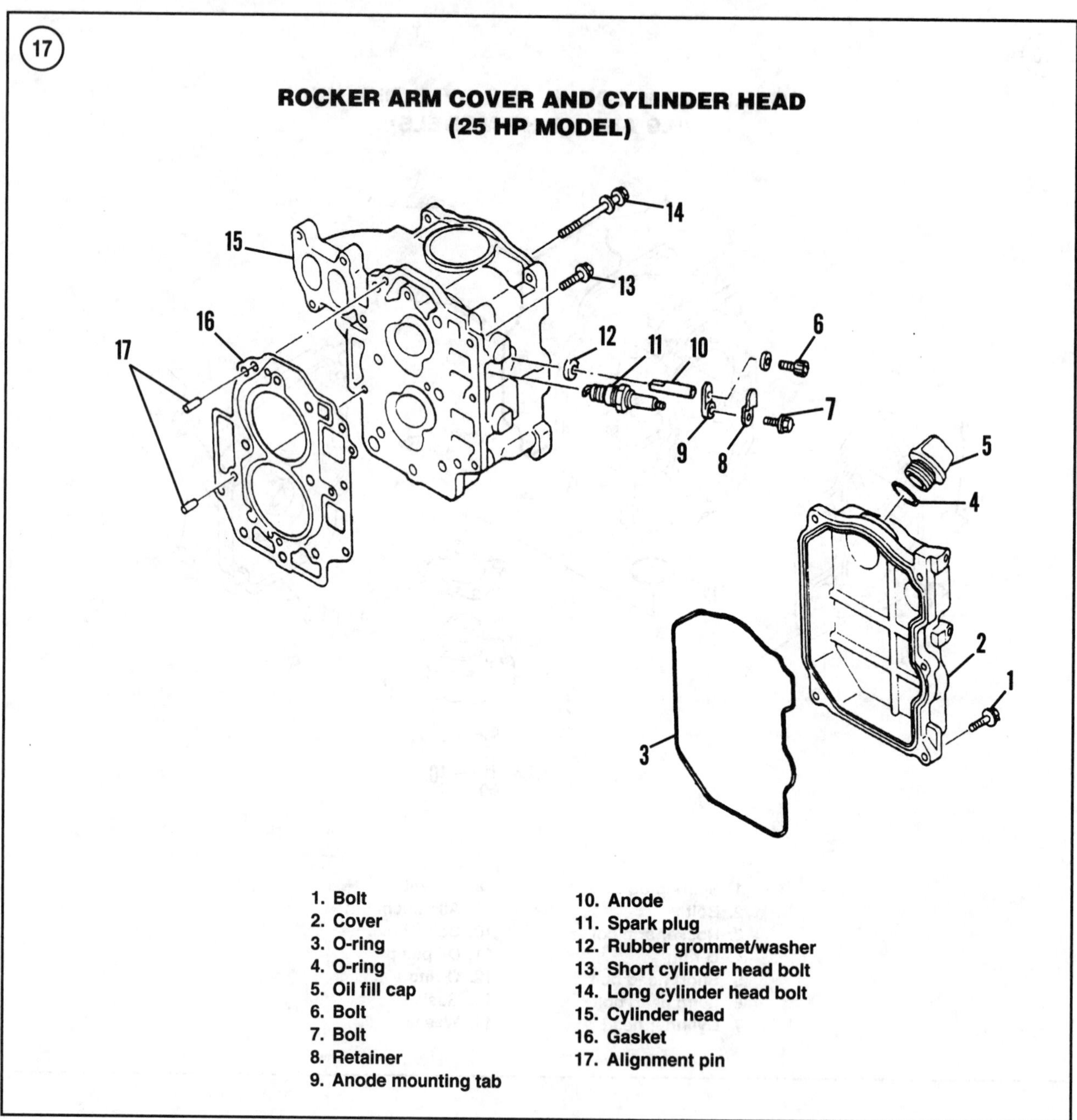

c. On 30-50 hp models, refer to **Figure 22**.

d. On 75 and 90 hp models tighten the bolts in a cross-ing pattern working from the center outward.

5. Install the fuel pump (Chapter Six). Install the fly-wheel cover following the instructions in this chapter.

6. On 30-90 hp models, slip the breather hose over its fit-ting on the cover.

7. Install the spark plugs and leads. Connect the cables to the battery if so equipped.

Timing Belt Removal (All Models)

Refer to **Figures 23-28** as necessary during this proce-dure.

CAUTION

Never rotate the flywheel or camshaft pulley with the timing belt removed or the valves and pistons will be damaged.

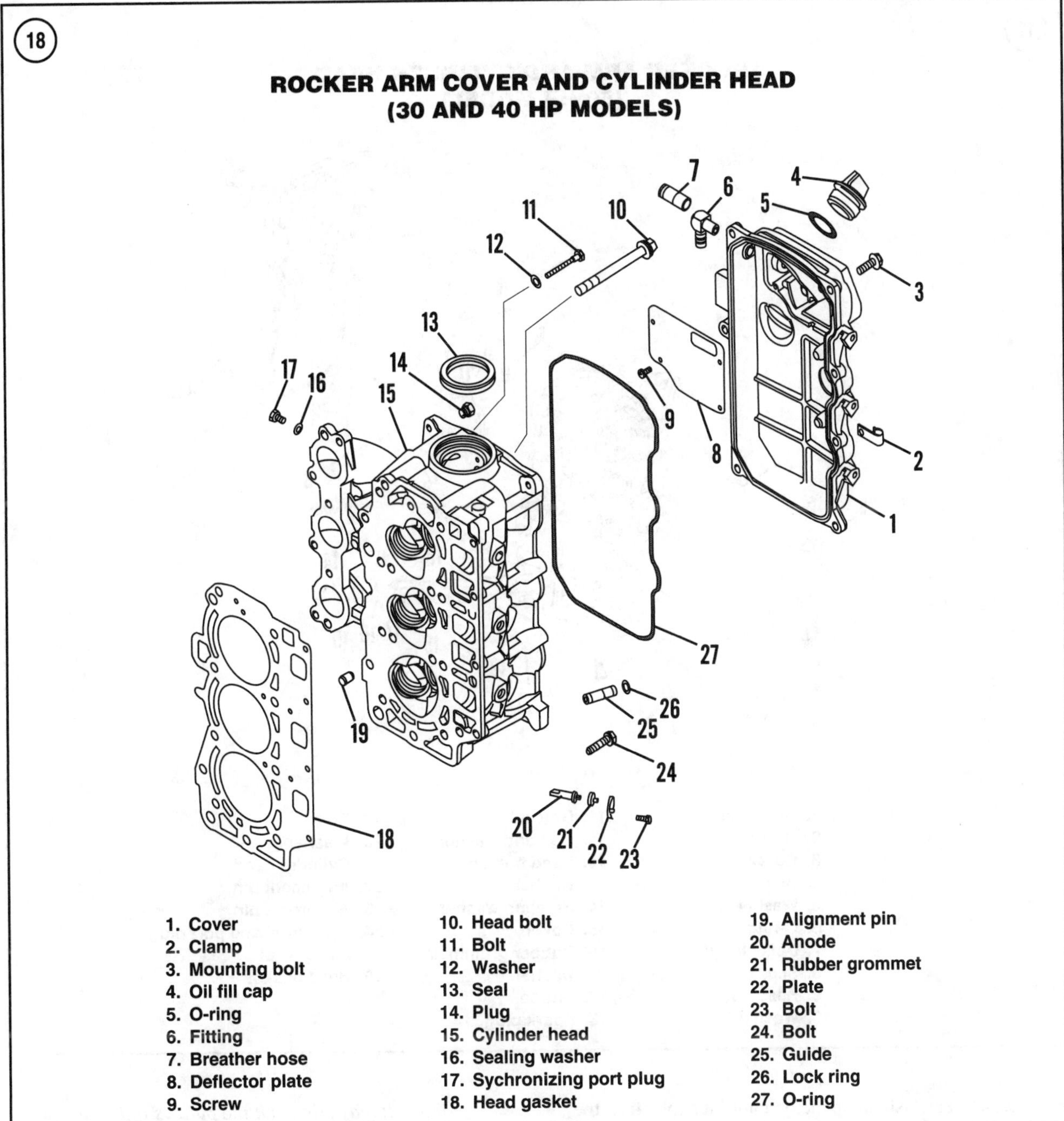

1. Disconnect both cables from the battery if so equipped. Remove the spark plugs and connect the spark plug leads to a suitable engine ground.

2. On manual start models, remove the manual starter as described in Chapter Ten.

3. On electric start models, remove the flywheel cover as described in this chapter.

4. Place the flywheel in the TDC (top dead center) position for No. 1 cylinder.

5. Remove the timing belt as follows:

   a. On 9.9-30 hp models, carefully push up on the belt until it slips off of the camshaft pulley.

   b. On 50 hp models, loosen the pivot bolt (14, **Figure 27**) and adjusting bolt (13) to relieve the belt

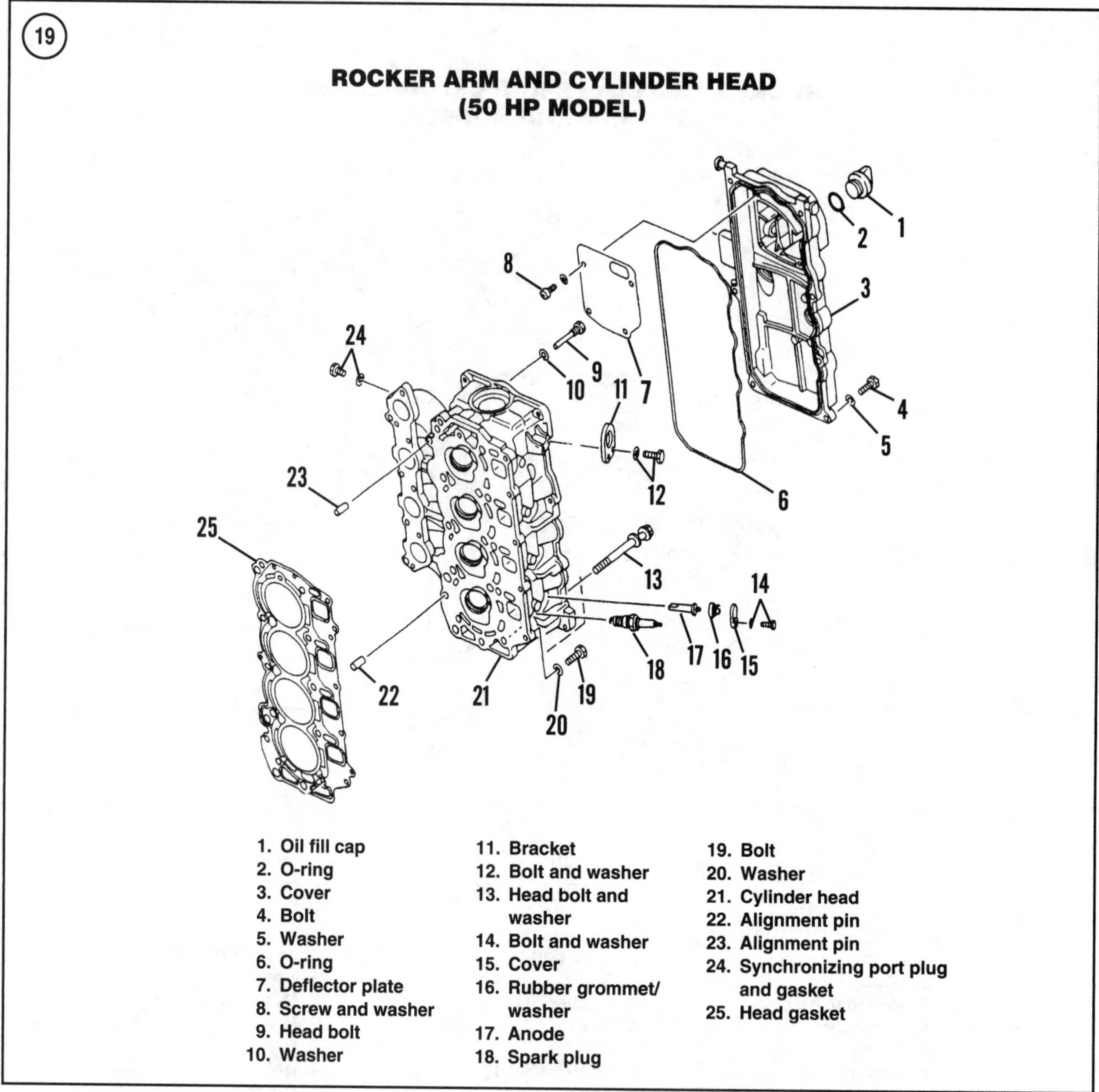

tensioner. Push up on the belt until it slips off of the camshaft pulley.

c. On 75 and 90 hp models, loosen the bolt (18, **Figure 28**) then remove the spring (13) from the tensioner (14). Push up on the timing belt until it slips off of the camshaft pulleys.

6. Do not rotate the flywheel or camshaft pulleys unless the cylinder head is first removed.

CAUTION

Always install the timing belt with the numbers or letters orientated correctly. The timing belt may slip from the pulleys if the belt is installed with the letters upside down. Serious power head damage is likely if the belt slips off with the engine running.

Timing Belt Installation (9.9-40 hp Models)

Refer to **Figures 23-26** as necessary during this procedure.

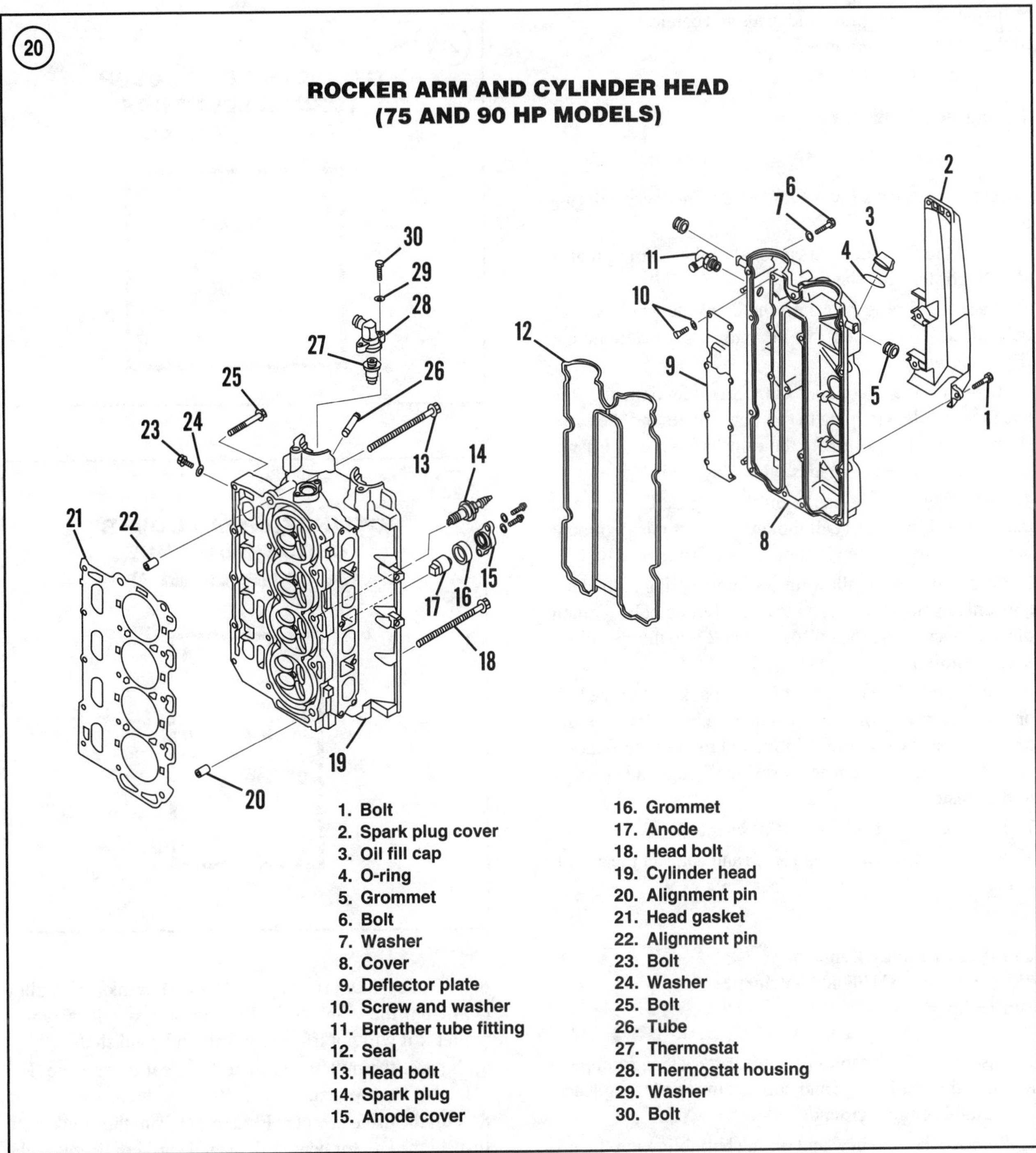

(20) **ROCKER ARM AND CYLINDER HEAD (75 AND 90 HP MODELS)**

1. Align the flywheel and camshaft pulley timing marks at TDC for the No. 1 cylinder. Refer to *Valve Adjustment* in Chapter Five for timing mark alignment.
2. Place the timing belt onto the crankshaft pulley. Install the belt with the numbers or letters positioned correctly.
3. Slip the timing belt over the camshaft pulley.
4. Inspect the timing marks on the camshaft pulley and the flywheel for correct alignment. Correct misalignment before rotating the flywheel or camshaft pulley.
5. On manual start models, install the manual starter (Chapter Ten).
6. On electric start models, install the flywheel cover (this chapter).

7. Install the spark plugs and leads and connect the cables to the battery if so equipped.

Timing Belt Installation (50-90 hp Models)

Refer to **Figure 27** and **Figure 28** as necessary during this procedure.

1. Align the flywheel and camshaft pulley timing marks at TDC for the No. 1 cylinder.
2. Place the timing belt onto the crankshaft pulley. The belt must be oriented so its numbers or letters are right-side-up.
3. Take up the slack on the port side opposite the tensioner while wrapping the timing belt around the camshaft pulleys. Do not rotate the camshaft pulleys. Ensure timing belt properly engages the pulley teeth.
4. Inspect the timing marks on the camshaft pulley and the flywheel for correct alignment. Correct misalignment before rotating the flywheel or camshaft pulley.
5. On 50 hp models, allow the tensioner spring to load the tensioner against the back side of the timing belt. Tighten the tensioner bolts (13 and 14, **Figure 27**) to the specification in **Table 1**.
6. On 75 and 90 hp models, route the back side of the belt on the port side of the tensioner pulley. Tighten the tensioner pulley bolt (18, **Figure 28**) to the specification in **Table 1**. Hook the tensioner spring through the opening in the tensioner.
7. Install the flywheel cover (this chapter).
8. Install the spark plugs and leads and connect the cables to the battery.

Crankshaft Pulley Removal (9.9 [Serial No. OH000057-Prior] and 15 hp Models)

1. Disconnect both cables from the battery if so equipped. Remove the spark plugs and connect the spark plug leads to a suitable engine ground.
2. Remove the flywheel and timing belt following the instructions in this chapter.
3. Refer to Chapter Four and fully loosen all valve adjusting screws.
4. Shift the engine into REVERSE gear then block the propeller from rotating in the counterclockwise direction as viewed from the rear using a block of wood.
5. Using a deep socket, remove the nut (15, **Figure 23**) from the crankshaft.

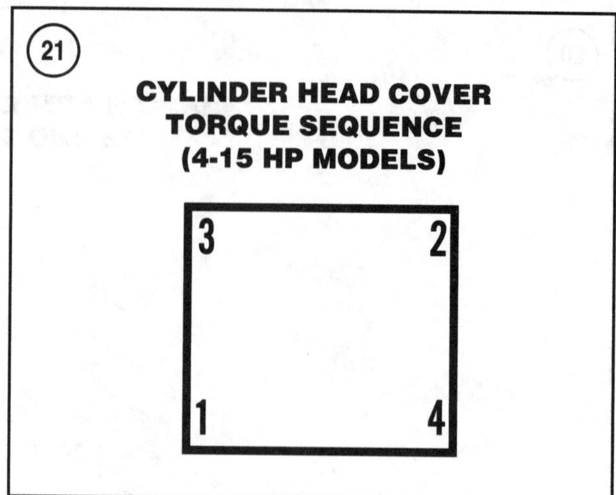

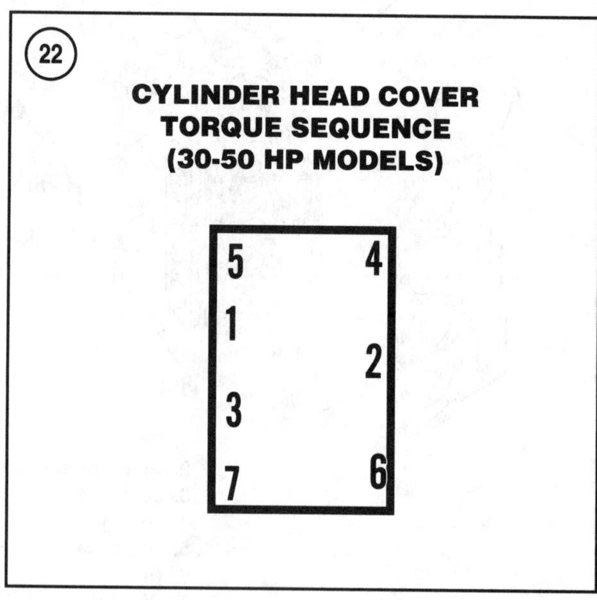

6. Lift the plate (16, **Figure 23**) and crankshaft pulley (17) from the crankshaft. Tap the pulley with a rubber mallet if it will not lift freely from the crankshaft.
7. Inspect the pulley and plate for wear or damage. Replace both components if defects are noted.
8. Pull the drive key (18, **Figure 23**) from the crankshaft. Inspect the key for bent or damaged surfaces. Replace the key if defects are noted.

Crankshaft Pulley Removal (9.9 hp Models [Serial No. OH000058-On])

1. Disconnect both cables from the battery if so equipped. Remove the spark plugs and connect the spark plug leads to a suitable engine ground.

(23)

TIMING BELTS AND PULLEYS
(9.9 HP [SERIAL NO. OH00057-PRIOR] AND 15 HP MODELS)

1. Wire protector
2. Screw
3. Battery charging coil
4. Screw
5. Ignition charging coil
6. Crankshaft position sensor
7. Mounting boss
8. Cylinder block
9. Bolt
10. Washer
11. Timing belt
12. Camshaft pulley
13. Key
14. Washer
15. Nut
16. Plate
17. Crankshaft pulley
18. Key

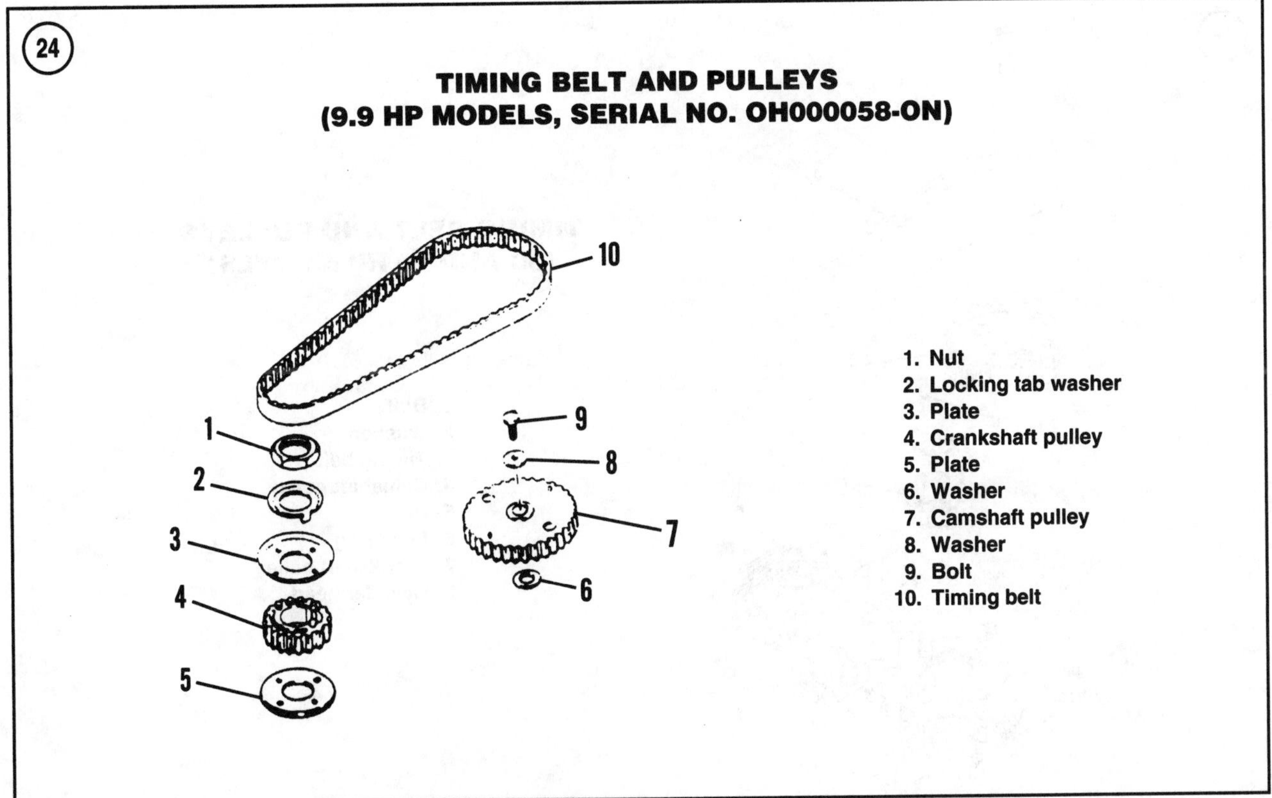

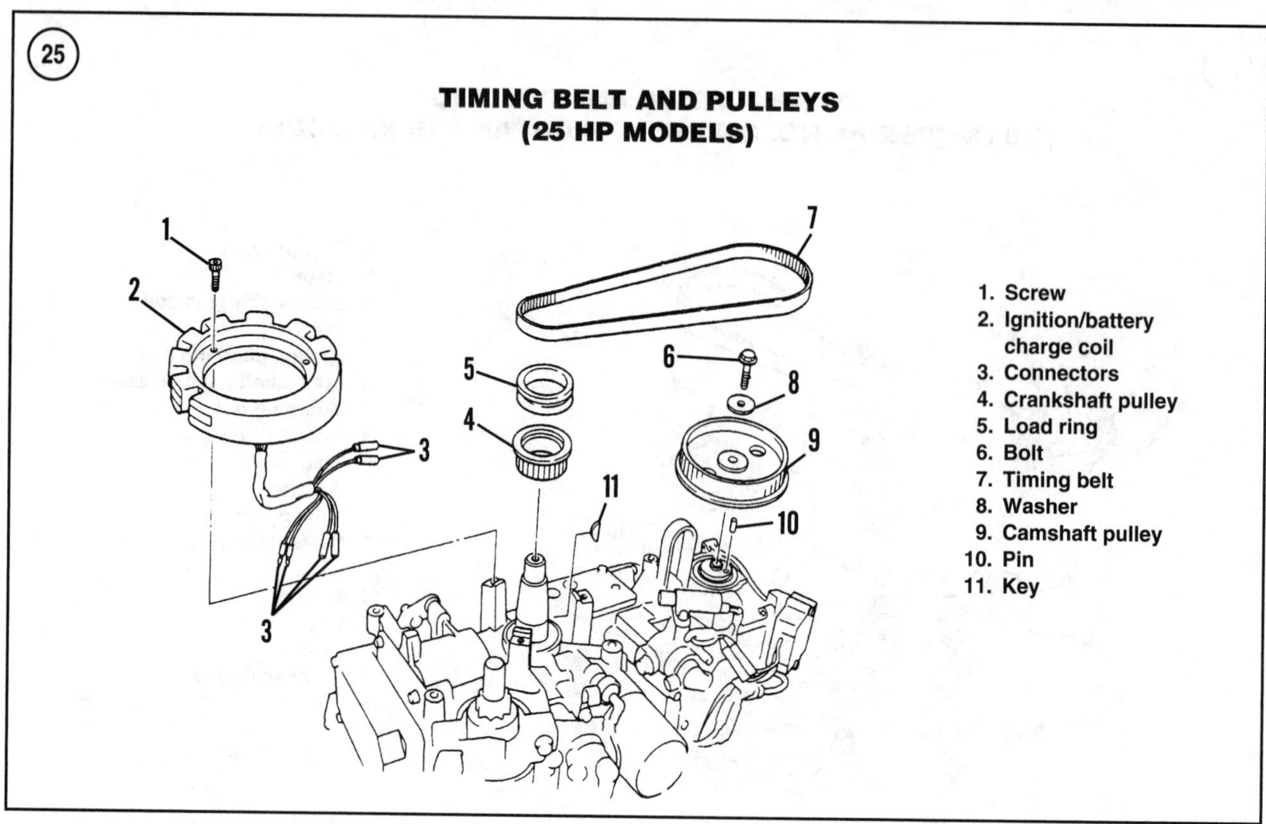
25
TIMING BELT AND PULLEYS
(25 HP MODELS)
1
2
3
4
5
6
7
8
9
10
11
1. Screw
2. Ignition/battery charge coil
3. Connectors
4. Crankshaft pulley
5. Load ring
6. Bolt
7. Timing belt
8. Washer
9. Camshaft pulley
10. Pin
11. Key

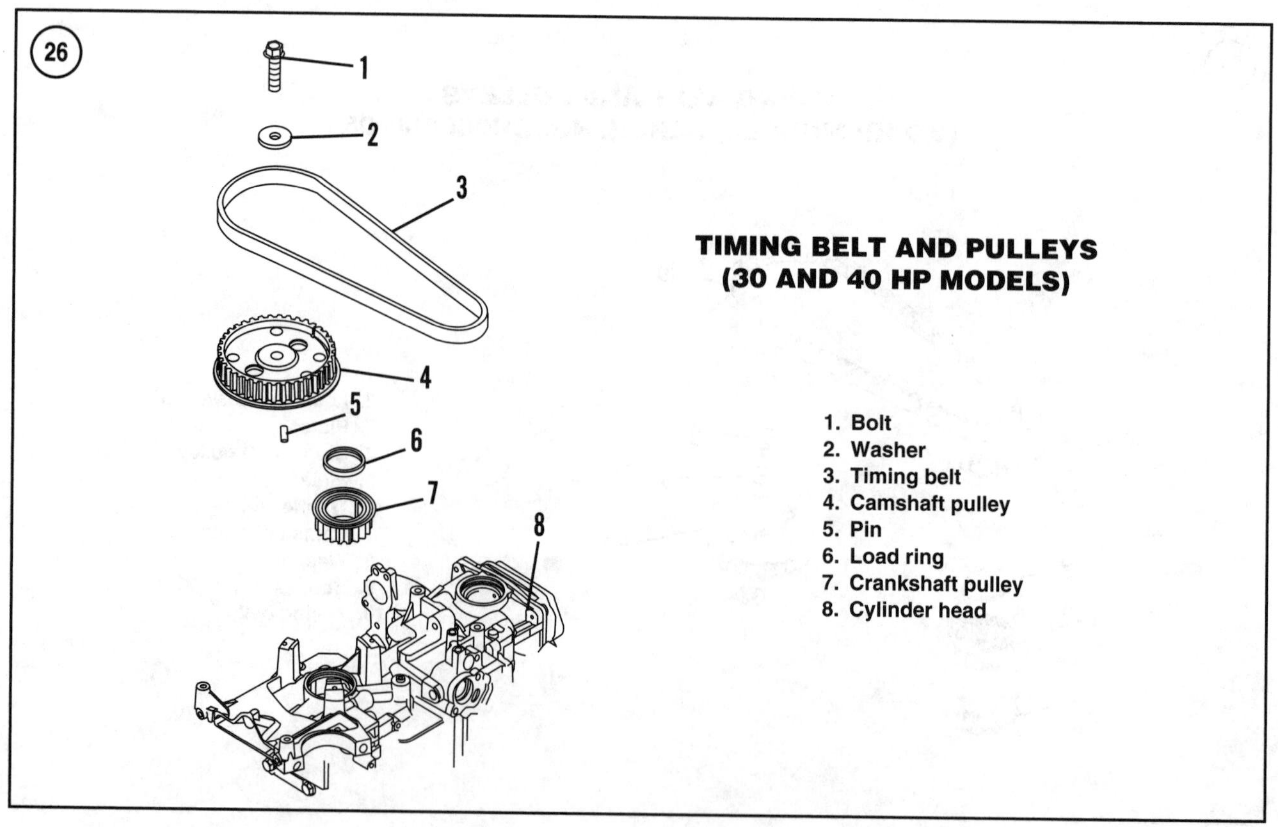
26
TIMING BELT AND PULLEYS
(30 AND 40 HP MODELS)
1
2
3
4
5
6
7
8
1. Bolt
2. Washer
3. Timing belt
4. Camshaft pulley
5. Pin
6. Load ring
7. Crankshaft pulley
8. Cylinder head

TIMING BELT AND PULLEYS (50 HP MODELS)

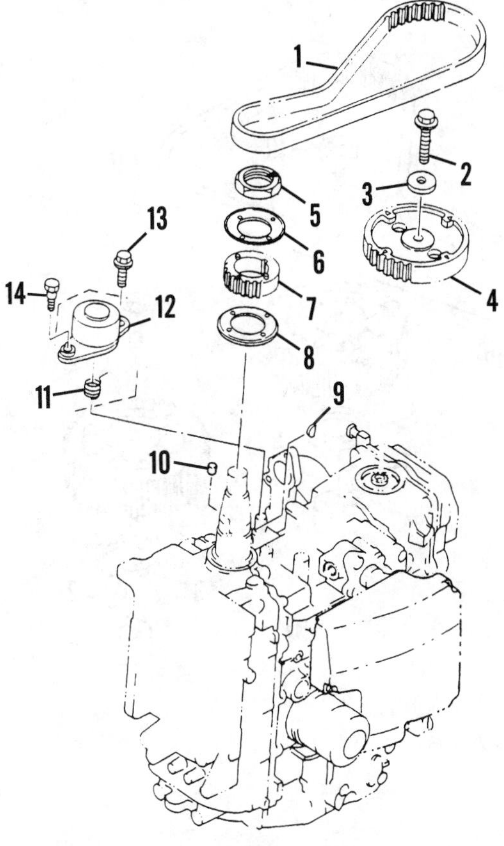

1. Timing belt
2. Bolt
3. Washer
4. Camshaft pulley
5. Nut
6. Plate
7. Crankshaft pulley
8. Plate
9. Key
10. Alignment pin
11. Tensioner spring
12. Tensioner pulley
13. Adjusting bolt
14. Pivot bolt

2. Remove the flywheel and timing belt as described in this chapter.

3. Refer to Chapter Four and fully loosen all valve adjusting screws.

4. Shift the engine into REVERSE gear then block the propeller from rotating in the counterclockwise direction using a block of wood.

5. Bend the locking tab washer (2, **Figure 24**) away from the nut (1). Using a deep socket, remove the nut (1, **Figure 24**) from the crankshaft.

6. Lift the tab washer, plate (2 and 3, **Figure 24**) and crankshaft pulley (4) from the crankshaft. Tap the pulley with a rubber mallet if it will not lift freely from the crankshaft. Lift the lower plate (5, **Figure 24**) from the crankshaft.

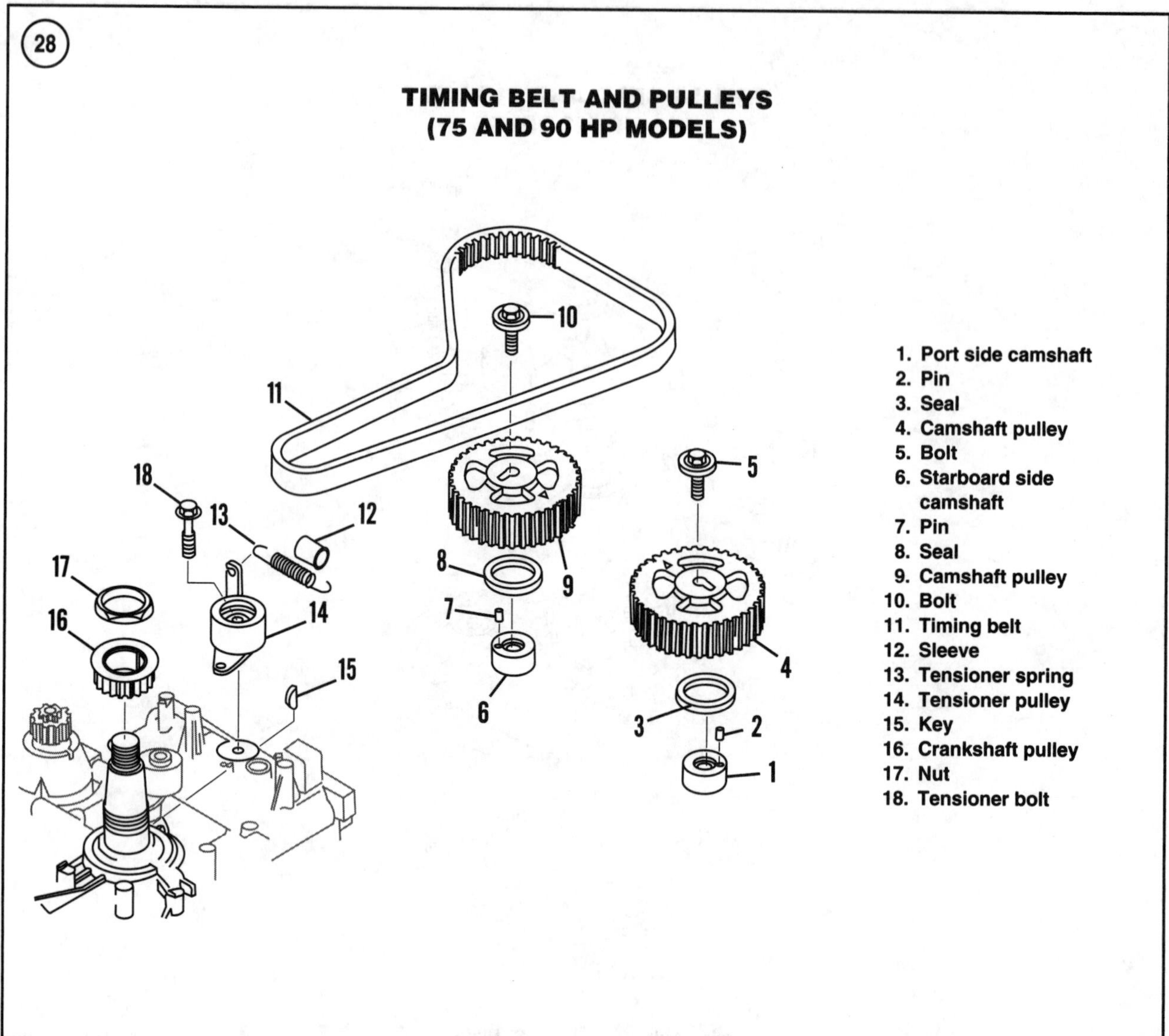

7. Inspect the pulley, plates and locking tab washer for wear or damage. Replace defective components.

8. Pull the drive key from the crankshaft. Inspect the key for bent or damaged surfaces. Replace the key if defects are noted.

Crankshaft Pulley Removal (25-40 hp Models)

1. Disconnect both cables from the battery. Remove the spark plugs and connect the spark plug leads to a suitable engine ground.

2. Remove the flywheel and timing belt as described in this chapter.

3. Lift the crankshaft pulley (4, **Figure 25** or 7, **Figure 26**) from the crankshaft. Tap the pulley with a rubber mallet if it will not freely lift from the crankshaft. Inspect the pulley for wear, cracks or damage. Replace the pulley if any defects are noted.

4. Remove the drive key (11, **Figure 25**) from the crankshaft. Inspect the key for bent or damaged surfaces. Replace the key if defects are noted.

Crankshaft Pulley Removal (50 hp Models)

1. Disconnect both cables from the battery. Remove the spark plugs then connect the spark plug leads to a suitable engine ground.

2. Remove the flywheel and timing belt as described in this chapter.

3. Fully loosen all valve adjusting screws to prevent damage should the flywheel rotate.

4. Thread a flywheel nut onto the crankshaft until it almost bottoms. Thread an additional flywheel nut onto the crankshaft until it contacts the other nut. Hold the lower nut and tighten the upper nut against the first nut.

5. Hold the lower flywheel nut with a wrench to prevent crankshaft rotation. Loosen the crankshaft pulley nut (5, **Figure 27**). Remove both flywheel nuts, then remove the crankshaft pulley nut.

6. Lift the plate (6, **Figure 27**) and crankshaft pulley (7) from the crankshaft. Tap the pulley with a rubber mallet if it will not lift freely from the crankshaft. Lift the lower plate (8, **Figure 27**) from the crankshaft.

7. Inspect the pulley and plate for wear or damage. Replace both components if defects are noted.

8. Pull the drive key (9, **Figure 27**) from the crankshaft. Inspect the key for bent or damaged surfaces. Replace the key if defects are noted.

Crankshaft Pulley Removal (75 and 90 hp Models)

1. Disconnect both cables from the battery. Remove the spark plugs and connect the spark plug leads to a suitable engine ground.

2. Remove the flywheel and timing belt as described in this chapter.

3. Thread a flywheel nut onto the crankshaft until it almost bottoms. Thread an additional flywheel nut onto the crankshaft until it contacts the other nut. Hold the lower nut and tighten the upper nut against the first nut.

4. Hold the lower flywheel nut with a wrench to prevent crankshaft rotation. Loosen the crankshaft pulley retaining nut (17, **Figure 28**). Remove both flywheel nuts, then remove the crankshaft pulley nut.

5. Lift the crankshaft pulley from the crankshaft. Tap the pulley with a rubber mallet if it will not lift freely from the crankshaft.

6. Inspect the pulley and plate for wear or damage. Replace both components if defects are noted.

7. Pull the drive key (15, **Figure 28**) from the crankshaft. Inspect the key for bent or damaged surfaces. Replace the key if defects are noted.

Crankshaft Pulley Installation (9.9 [Serial No. OH000057-Prior] and 15 hp Models)

1. Shift the engine into FORWARD gear and block the propeller from rotating in the clockwise direction using a block of wood.

2. Place the drive key (18, **Figure 23**) into the crankshaft groove with the rounded side facing inward.

3. Place the crankshaft pulley onto the crankshaft with the larger diameter side facing toward the cylinder block. Align the key slot in the pulley with the key and slide the pulley in position.

4. Seat the pulley against the crankshaft, then place the plate onto the pulley with the edge curled away from the cylinder block.

5. Thread the nut (15, **Figure 23**) onto the crankshaft. Tighten the nut to the specification in **Table 1**.

6. Install the timing belt and flywheel as described in this chapter.

7. Adjust the valves as described in Chapter Four.

8. Install the spark plugs and leads and connect the cables to the battery.

8

Crankshaft Pulley Installation (9.9 hp Models [Serial No. OH000058-On])

1. Shift the engine into FORWARD gear, then block the propeller from rotating in the clockwise direction using a block of wood.

2. Place the lower plate (5, **Figure 24**) onto the crankshaft with the curled edge toward the cylinder block.

3. Place the drive key into the crankshaft groove with the rounded side facing inward.

4. Place the crankshaft pulley onto the crankshaft with the *up* mark facing away from the cylinder block. Align the key slot in the pulley with the key, then slide the pulley into position. Engage the protrusions on the bottom of the pulley with the openings in the plate and seat the pulley against the lower plate.

5. Seat the pulley against the crankshaft, then place the plate onto the pulley with the edge curled away from the cylinder block. Engage the protrusions on the top of the pulley with the openings in the plate then seat the upper plate (3, **Figure 24**) onto the pulley.

6. Place the tab of the tab washer (2, **Figure 24**) into the square opening on the upper plate and set the washer against the plate.

7. Thread the nut (1, **Figure 24**) onto the crankshaft. Tighten the nut to the specification in **Table 1**.

8. Bend the tab washer against the one side of the nut to prevent loosening. Do not bend the washer in an area near the tab.
9. Install the timing belt and flywheel (this chapter).
10. Adjust the valves (Chapter Four).
11. Install the spark plugs and leads and connect the cables to the battery.

Crankshaft Pulley Installation (25-40 hp Models)

1. Place the drive key (11, **Figure 25**) into the crankshaft slot with the rounded end facing toward the crankshaft.
2. Place the crankshaft pulley (4, **Figure 25** or 7, **Figure 26**) onto the crankshaft with the larger diameter side facing the cylinder block.
3. Align the key slot with the key and seat the pulley against the step on the crankshaft.
4. Install the timing belt and flywheel (this chapter).
5. Install the spark plugs and leads and connect the cables to the battery.

Crankshaft Pulley Installation (50 hp Models)

1. Place the lower plate (8, **Figure 27**) over the crankshaft with the curled edge facing toward the cylinder block.
2. Place the drive key (9, **Figure 27**) into the crankshaft groove with the rounded side facing inward.
3. Place the crankshaft pulley (7, **Figure 27**) over the crankshaft. Align the key slot in the pulley with the key then slide the pulley into position. Align the protrusions on the bottom of the pulley with the opening in the lower plate (8), then seat the pulley and plate against the crankshaft.
4. Seat the pulley against the crankshaft then place the upper plate (6, **Figure 27**) onto the pulley with the curled edge away from the cylinder block. Align the protrusions on the top of the pulley with the openings in the upper plate. Thread the crankshaft pulley nut (5, **Figure 27**) onto the crankshaft until it just contacts the plate.
5. Thread a flywheel nut onto the crankshaft until it almost bottoms. Thread an additional flywheel nut onto the crankshaft until it contacts the other nut. Hold the lower nut then tighten the upper nut against the first nut.
6. Hold the lower flywheel nut with a wrench to prevent crankshaft rotation. Tighten the crankshaft pulley retaining nut (5, **Figure 27**) to the specification in **Table 1**. Remove both flywheel nuts.
7. Install the timing belt and flywheel (this chapter).
8. Adjust the valves (Chapter Five).
9. Install the spark plugs and leads and connect the cables to the battery.

Crankshaft Pulley Installation (75 and 90 hp Models)

1. Place the drive key (15, **Figure 28**) into the crankshaft groove with the rounded side facing inward.
2. Place the crankshaft pulley over the crankshaft with the larger diameter side facing up. Align the key slot in the pulley with the key, then slide the pulley into position.
3. Thread the crankshaft pulley nut (17, **Figure 28**) onto the crankshaft until it just contacts the plate.
4. Thread a flywheel nut onto the crankshaft until it almost bottoms. Thread an additional flywheel nut onto the crankshaft until it contacts the other nut. Hold the lower nut and tighten the upper nut against the first nut.
5. Hold the lower flywheel nut with a suitable wrench to prevent crankshaft rotation. Tighten the crankshaft pulley retaining nut (17, **Figure 28**) to the specification in **Table 1**. Remove both flywheel nuts.
6. Install the timing belt and flywheel (this chapter).
7. Install the spark plugs and leads and connect the cables to the battery.

Cylinder Head Removal (All Models)

Refer to **Figures 15-20** as necessary during this procedure.

CAUTION
To prevent cylinder head warpage, loosen the cylinder head bolts in the opposite order of the tightening sequence.

1. Remove the carburetors and intake manifold as described in Chapter Six.
2. On 4-6 hp models, remove the power head from the engine as described in this chapter.
3. Remove the timing belt and rocker arm cover following the instructions in this chapter.
4. On 4-6 hp models, remove the three bolts (5, **Figure 15**) from the exhaust manifold and cylinder head.
5. On 75 and 90 hp models, camshaft removal is required to access the cylinder head bolts. Remove the camshafts as follows:
   a. Engage the lugs of the flywheel holding tool (Mercury part No. 91-83163M) with the openings in the camshaft pulleys (4 and 9, **Figure 28**) to prevent camshaft rotation.

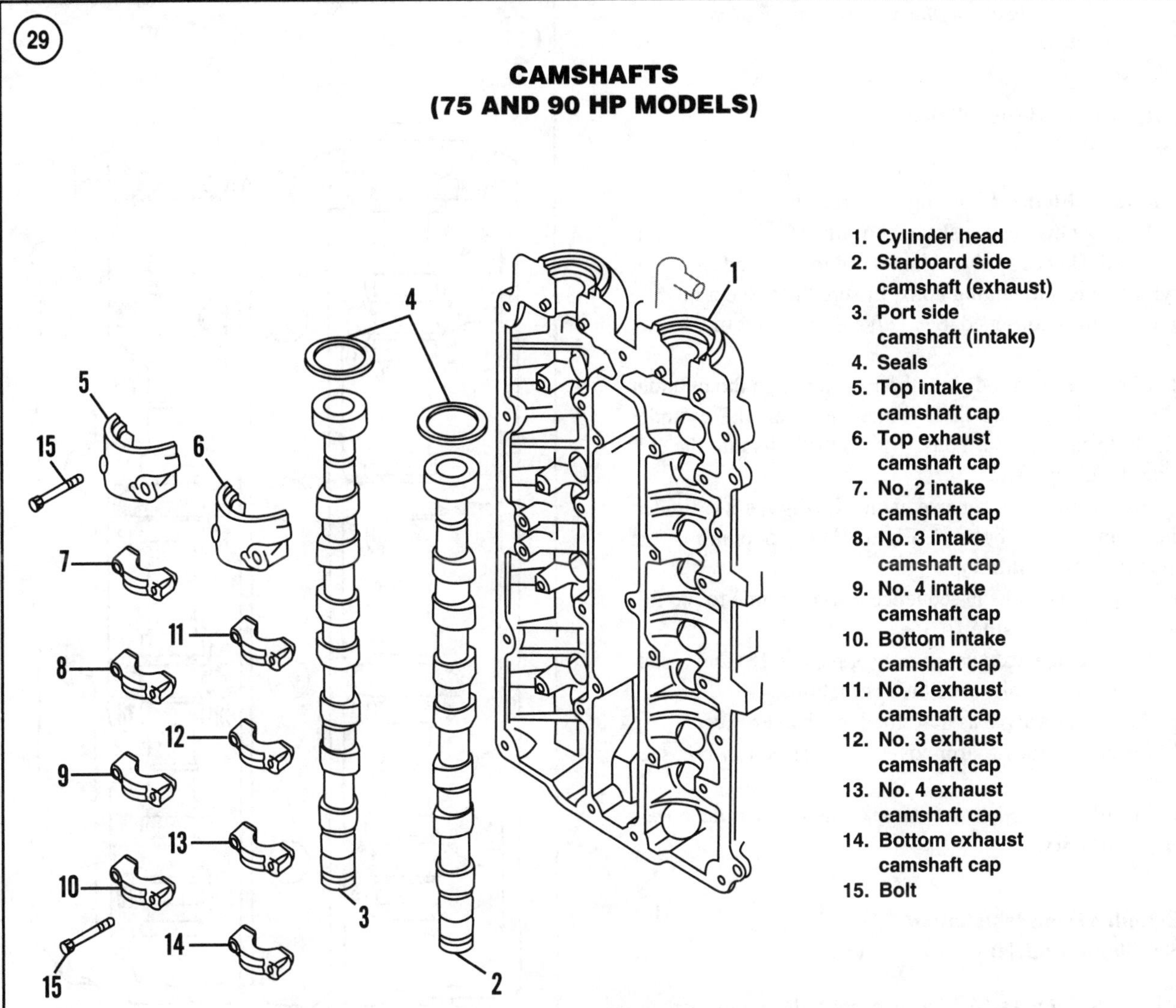

b. Remove the bolts (5, **Figure 28**) and lift the pulleys (4 and 9) and seals (3 and 8) from the camshafts.

c. Mark the location and the up side of each camshaft bearing cap (**Figure 29**). Loosen the bolts 1/4 turn at a time in the opposite of the tightening sequence in **Figure 30**.

d. Support the camshafts while removing each camshaft bearing cap.

e. Mark the location port or starboard, then pull each camshaft from the cylinder head.

6. Loosen the cylinder head bolts 1/4 turn at a time in the opposite order of the tightening sequence until the bolts turn freely. Refer to the following illustrations to determine the tightening torque sequence.

a. **Figure 21**—4-6 hp models.

b. **Figure 31**—9.9-25 hp models.

c. **Figure 32**—30 and 40 hp models.

d. **Figure 33**—50 hp models.

e. **Figure 34**—75 and 90 hp models.

7. Support the head while removing all cylinder head bolts. Pull the cylinder head away from the cylinder block and place it on a clean work surface.

8. Carefully scrape all head gasket material and carbon from the cylinder block and cylinder head mating surfaces (**Figure 35**). Do not gauge or scratch any surface. All gasket surfaces must be absolutely clean.

9. Inspect the cylinder head for warpage following the instructions in this chapter.

CAUTION

On 4-50 hp models the valve adjusting nuts must be fully loosened prior to installing the cylinder head or the valves may be damaged.

Cylinder Head Installation (4-6 hp Models)

Refer to **Figure 15** during this procedure.

1. Place a new head gasket (8, **Figure 15**) onto the cylinder head. Do not apply sealant or oil to the head gasket or cylinder head mounting bolts. Ensure the valve adjusting nuts are fully loosened. See *Valve Adjustment* in Chapter Five.
2. Slide the push rods into their openings in the cylinder block while placing the cylinder head on the cylinder block. Install the four bolts. Thread the bolts into the cylinder block by hand.
3. Following the torque sequence in **Figure 21**, tighten the cylinder head bolts (4, **Figure 15**) to one half of the specification (**Table 1**).
4. Tighten the bolts in sequence a second time to the full specification in **Table 1**.
5. Install a new exhaust gasket (6, **Figure 15**) and install the power head following the instructions.
6. Adjust the valves as described in Chapter Five.
7. Install the rocker arm cover as described in this section.
8. Install the carburetor and intake manifold as described in Chapter Six.

Cylinder Head Installation (9.9-50 hp Models)

Refer to **Figures 16-19** as necessary during this procedure.

1. Position the No. 1 piston at TDC.
2. Make sure that all gasket surfaces are absolutely clean and free of defects. Also make sure that all alignment pins are properly installed in the cylinder block.
3. Install a new cylinder head gasket onto the cylinder block. Make sure all openings in the gasket match the openings in the cylinder block and head.
4. Install the cylinder head onto the cylinder block.
5. Apply a light coat of engine oil to the threads and underside of the head of each head bolt. Thread all bolts into the cylinder block by hand.
6. Tighten the head mounting bolts to one half of the specification in **Table 1** using the correct torque sequence (**Figures 31-33**).
7. Tighten the head mounting bolts a second time in sequence to the full specification in **Table 1**.
8. Install the timing belt as described in this chapter.

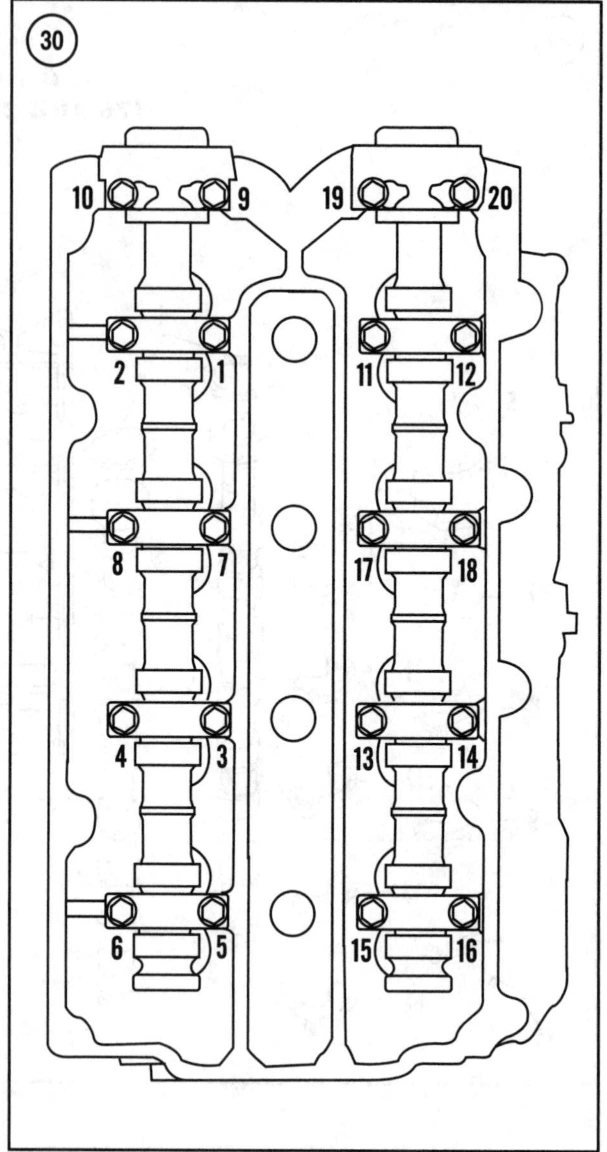

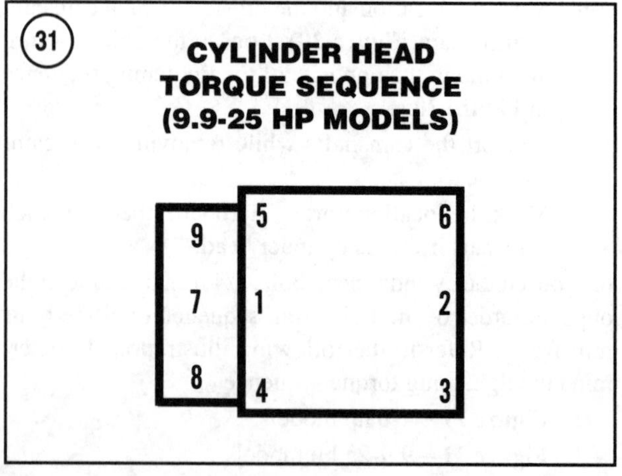

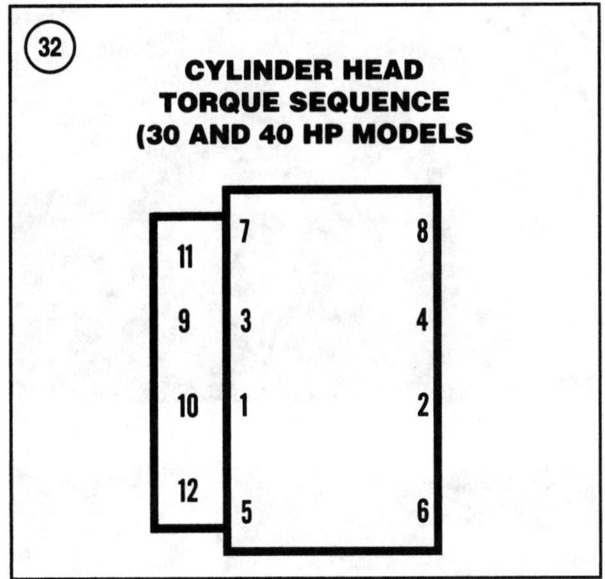

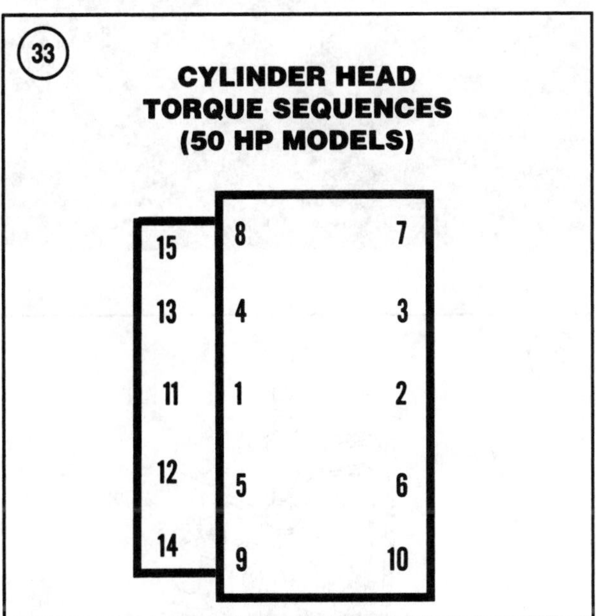

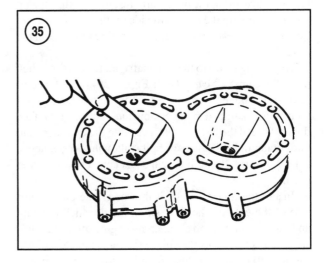

9. Adjust the valves (Chapter Five).

10. Install the rocker arm cover (this chapter).

11. Install the intake manifold and carburetors (Chapter Six).

Cylinder Head Installation (75 and 90 hp Models)

Refer to **Figure 20** during this procedure.

1. Position the No. 1 piston at TDC (**Figure 36**), then rotate the flywheel 90° clockwise. This step is necessary to

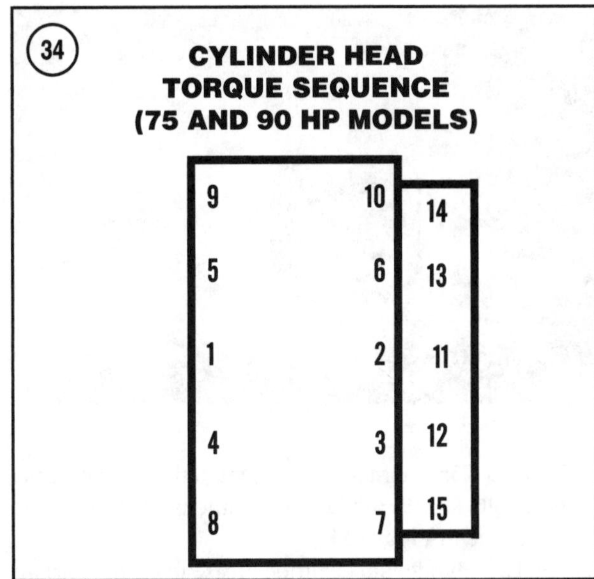

35

prevent piston or valve damage during camshaft installation.

2. Ensure all gasket mating surfaces are absolutely clean and free of defects. Install a new head gasket (21, **Figure 20**) on the cylinder head. Ensure the openings in the gasket match the openings in the cylinder head. All four pistons must be down in their bore.

3. Seat the cylinder head on the cylinder block. Hold the cylinder head in position while threading the bolts through the head and into the block. Do not tighten the bolts at this time.

4. Tighten all cylinder head bolts in the sequence indicated in **Figure 34** to one half the specification in **Table 1**. Tighten all cylinder head bolts a second time in sequence to the full specification in **Table 1**.

8

5. Using a T55 internal torx adapter, tighten each of the 10 mm bolts (13, **Figure 20**) an additional 90° following the sequence in **Figure 34**.

6. Apply molybdenum disulfide grease to each camshaft lobe (**Figure 37**). Identify the exhaust cam by locating its tang (**Figure 38**) or the pink mark. Install the exhaust cam into its cradle on the starboard side on the cylinder head. Position the threaded opening and locating pin hole on the top side.

7. Apply engine oil to the camshaft contact surfaces, then place the camshaft caps (6-14, **Figure 29**) onto the camshaft and cylinder head. Ensure the up side of each cap is facing up. Stamped numbers on the caps usually face down. Thread the bolts for each cap into the cylinder head until finger tight. Tighten the bolts following the sequence (11-19, **Figure 30**) until the caps just contact the cylinder head.

8. Install the intake camshaft into its cradle on the port side of the cylinder head. Position the threaded opening and pin hole on the top side. Apply engine oil to the camshaft contact surfaces then place the camshaft caps (5-10, **Figure 29**) onto the camshaft and cylinder head. Ensure the up side of each cap is facing up. Stamped numbers on the caps usually face down. Thread the bolts for each cap into the cylinder head until finger tight. Tighten the bolts in the sequence (1-10, **Figure 30**) until the caps contact the cylinder head.

9. Tighten all camshaft cap bolts (15, **Figure 29**) in sequence (**Figure 30**) to one half the specification provided in **Table 1**. Next, tighten the bolts a second time in sequence to the full specification in **Table 1**.

10. Place each seal (4, **Figure 29**) over the top of the camshafts with the seal lip facing inward. Push the seals in until they bottom in the bore.

11. Place the pin (2, **Figure 28**) into its opening in the intake camshaft (1). Guide the pin into its opening in the bottom of the port side pulley while lowering the pulley to the camshaft. Install and hand tighten the bolts (5, **Figure 28**). Rotate the pulley until the timing mark faces toward the starboard side.

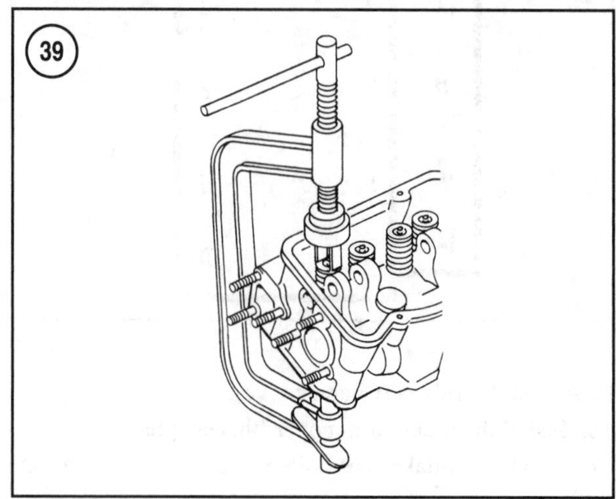

12. Place the pin (7, **Figure 28**) into its opening in the exhaust camshaft (6). Rotate the exhaust camshaft until the pulley (9) can be installed with the timing marks aligned. Guide the pin into its opening on the pulley while lower-

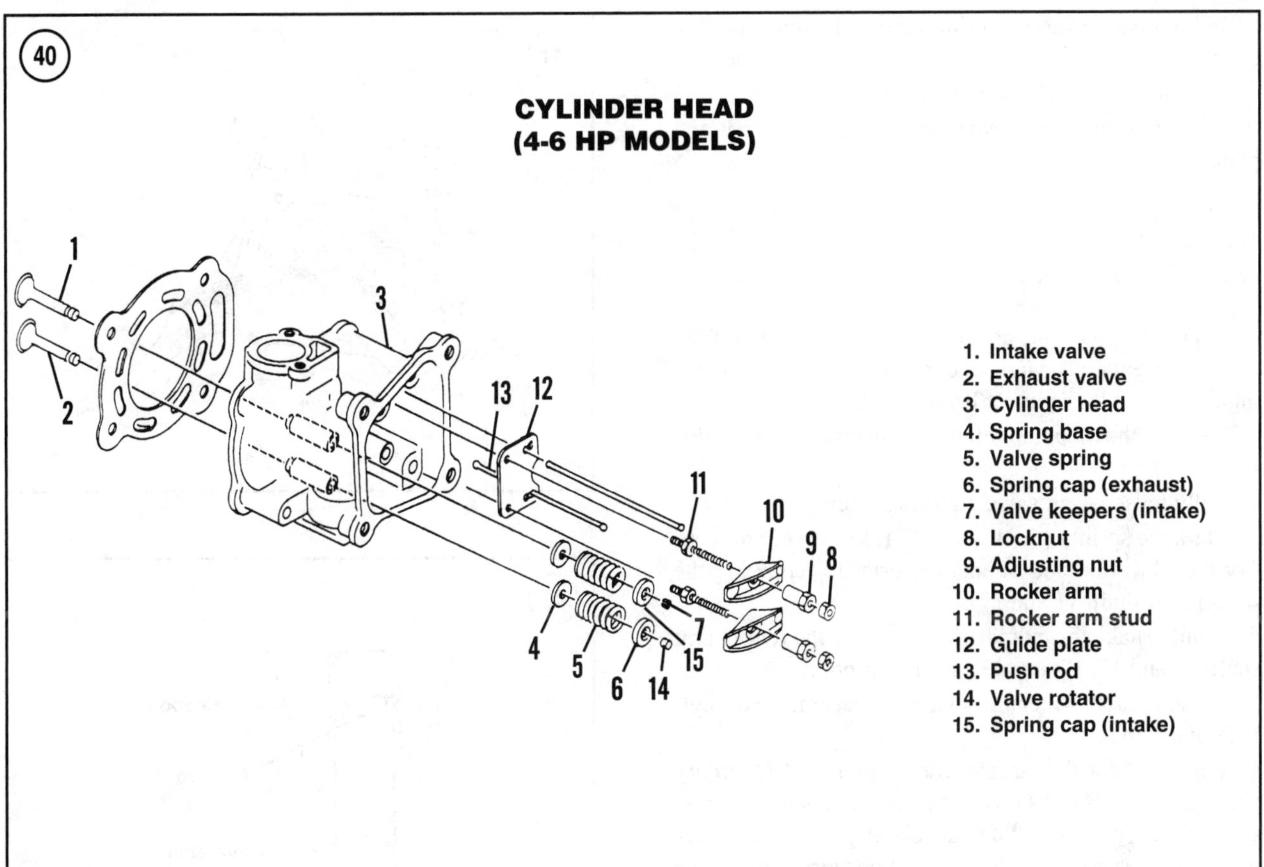

ing the pulley onto the camshaft. Ensure the timing marks perfectly align.

13. Rotate the flywheel 90° counterclockwise until it just reaches TDC for No. 1 cylinder (**Figure 36**).
14. Install the timing belt following the instructions in this chapter.
15. Engage the lugs of the flywheel holding tool (Mercury part No. 91-83163M) with the openings in the camshaft pulleys (4 and 9, **Figure 28**) to prevent camshaft rotation. Tighten each camshaft pulley bolt (5 and 10, **Figure 28**) to the specification in **Table 1**.
16. Adjust the valves following the instructions in Chapter Five
17. Install the rocker arm cover following the instructions provided in this chapter. Install the flywheel as described in this chapter.

WARNING
Valve springs are under considerable tension. The use of makeshift tools or carelessness may allow them and other components to spring free with great force. Use caution and wear protective eye wear when removing components from the cylinder head.

Cylinder Head Disassembly

A valve spring compressor tool (**Figure 39**) is required for cylinder head disassembly on 9.9-90 hp models. Note the location and orientation of each component prior to removal from the cylinder head.

Disassembly (4-6 hp models)

Refer to **Figure 40**. Mark all components prior to removing them from the cylinder head.

1. Remove the oil pump following the instructions in this chapter.
2. Refer to Chapter Five and fully loosen each valve adjusting screw.
3. Mark the springs (5, **Figure 40**) to identify their location and orientation prior to removing them.
4. Select a box end wrench for use as a valve and spring removal tool. The opening in the wrench must be slightly smaller than the valve spring cap.
5. Using the wrench (**Figure 41**) collapse the valve spring. Carefully pull the keepers (**Figure 42**) from the valve stem.

6. Pull the valve spring, spring base and valve from the cylinder head.
7. Repeat Steps 4-6 for the remaining valve.
8. Using a deep socket, remove the rocker arm studs and plate.

Disassembly (9.9 and 15 hp models)

Refer to **Figure 43** to assist with component identification and orientation. Mark all components prior to removing them from the cylinder head.

1. Remove the oil pump following the instructions in this chapter.
2. Fully loosen each valve adjusting screw.
3. Mark the springs (6, 11, 18 and 21, **Figure 43**) to identify their location and orientation prior to removing the rocker arm shafts (1 and 17).
4. Gently shake the cylinder head to slide the rocker arm shafts (1 and 17, **Figure 43**) from their bores.
5. Remove each rocker arm shaft and spacer from the cylinder head.
6. Engage the valve spring compressor tool (Mercury part No. 91-809494A1) with the valve and spring cap as shown in **Figure 39**. Tighten the clamp just enough to remove the keepers from the grooved portion of the valve stem (**Figure 42**).
7. Slowly loosen the clamp, then remove the spring cap 13, **Figure 42**), spring (14) and spring base (16) from the cylinder head. Repeat Steps 6 and 7 for the remaining valves.
8. Engage the lugs of the flywheel holding tool (Mercury part No. 91-83163M) with the openings in the camshaft pulley (**Figure 44**) to prevent camshaft rotation. Remove the bolt and washer, then lift the camshaft pulley, washer and drive key (33, **Figure 43**) from the camshaft.
9. Slip the camshaft from the bottom opening in the cylinder head. Carefully pry the seal (32, **Figure 43**) from the camshaft bore.

Disassembly (25-50 hp models)

Mark all components prior to removal from the cylinder head. Refer to **Figures 45-47** to assist with component identification and orientation.

1. Remove the oil pump as described in this chapter. Place the cylinder head on a clean work bench with the piston side facing down.
2. Loosen each valve adjusting screw.

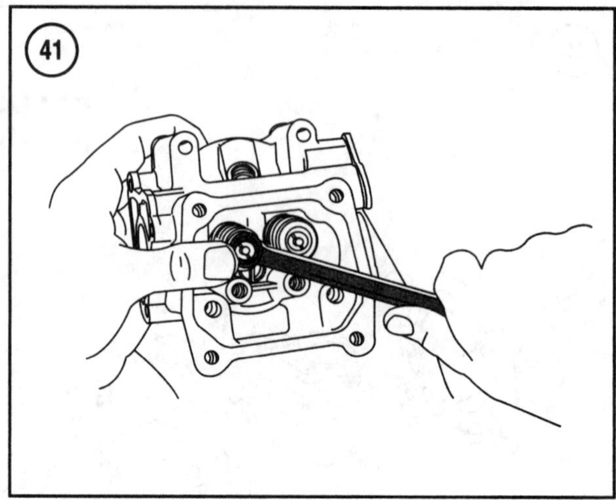

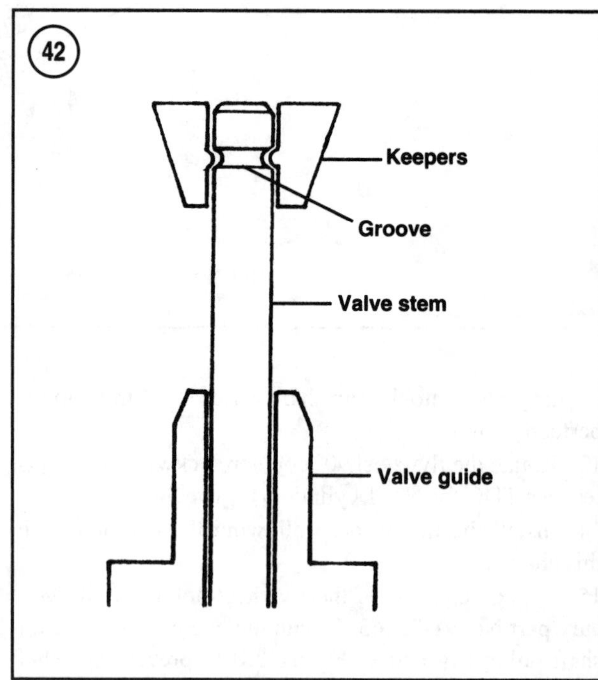

3. Evenly loosen the rocker arm retainer bolts then pull the rocker arm shaft straight up and away from the cylinder head. Remove each rocker arm and retainer from the rocker arm shaft.
4. Engage the valve spring compressor tool (Mercury part No. 91-809494A1) with the valve and spring cap (**Figure 39**). Tighten the clamp just enough to remove the keepers from the grooved portion of the valve stem (**Figure 42**).
5. Slowly loosen the clamp then remove the spring cap , spring and spring base from the cylinder head. Repeat Steps 6 and 7 for the remaining valves.

(43)

CYLINDER HEAD (9.9 AND 15 HP MODELS)

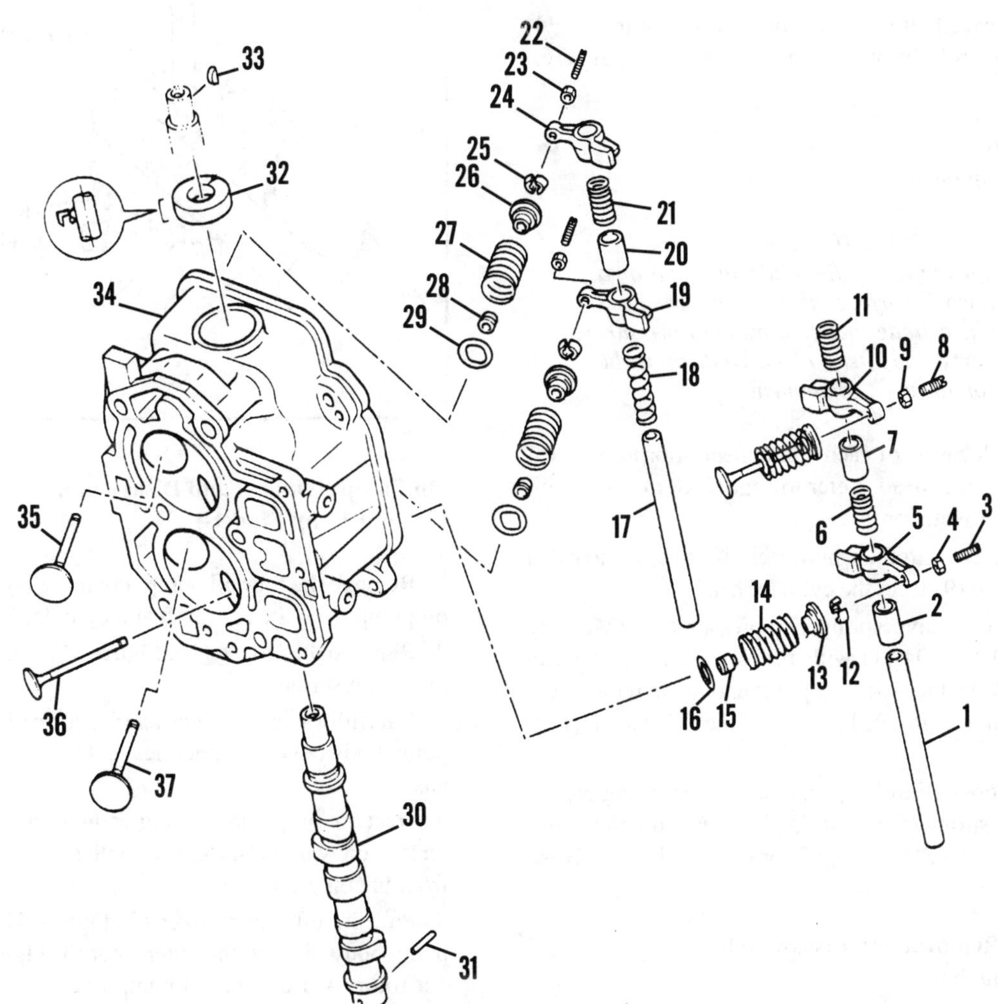

1. Rocker arm shaft (exhaust)
2. Spacer
3. Adjusting screw
4. Locknut
5. Rocker arm (exhaust)
6. Spring
7. Spacer
8. Adjusting screw
9. Locknut
10. Rocker arm (exhaust)
11. Spring
12. Keepers
13. Valve spring cap
14. Spring (exhaust)
15. Seal
16. Spring base (exhaust)
17. Rocker arm shaft (intake)
18. Spring
19. Rocker arm (intake)
20. Spacer
21. Spring
22. Adjusting screw
23. Locknut
24. Rocker arm (intake)
25. Keepers
26. Valve cap
27. Spring (intake)
28. Seal
29. Spring base (intake)
30. Camshaft
31. Oil pump drive pin
32. Seal
33. Pulley drive key
34. Cylinder head
35. Intake valve
36. Exhaust valve
37. Intake valve

8

6. Engage the lugs of the flywheel holding tool (Mercury part No. 91-83163M) with the openings in the camshaft pulley (**Figure 44**) to prevent camshaft rotation. Remove the bolt and washer, then lift the camshaft pulley and washer from the camshaft.

7. Slip the camshaft from the bottom opening in the cylinder head. Carefully pry the seal from the camshaft bore.

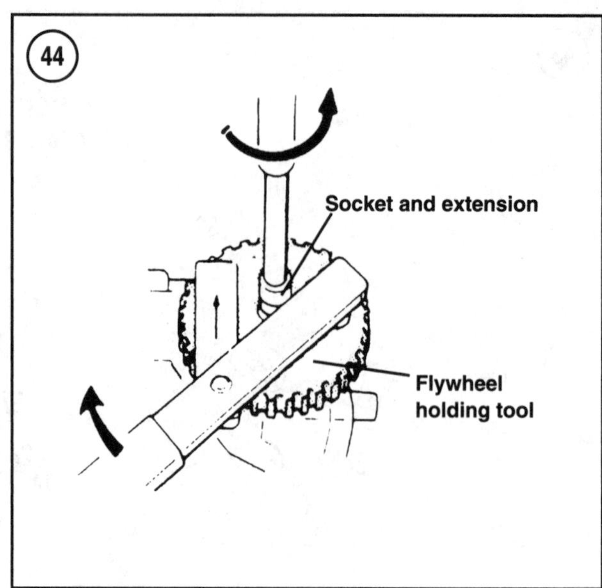

Disassembly (75 and 90 hp models)

> *CAUTION*
> *Arrange the valve lifter and valve pads on a clean work surface as they are removed from the cylinder head. Mark the work surface next to the lifter and pads indicating the location for each component.*

Mark the location of each component prior to removal from the cylinder head. Refer to **Figure 48** to assist with component orientation.

1. Using pliers, carefully pull each lifter (8, **Figure 48**) and valve pad (9) from the cylinder head.

2. Engage the valve spring compressor tool (Mercury part No. 91-809494A1) with the valve and spring cap (**Figure 39**). Tighten the clamp just enough to remove the keepers from the grooved portion of the valve stem (**Figure 42**).

3. Slowly loosen the clamp and remove the spring cap (3, **Figure 48**), spring (5) and spring base (6) from the cylinder head. Repeat Steps 6 and 7 for the remaining valves.

Oil Pump Removal and Disassembly (4-6 hp Models)

1. Remove the power head as described in this chapter.

2. Place the power head on a work bench with the bottom facing up.

3. Remove the bolts and cover (8, **Figure 50**) to access the oil pump components.

4. Lift the outer rotor (5, **Figure 50**) and inner rotor (4) from the oil pump.

5. Pull the drive pin (3, **Figure 50**) from the oil pump drive shaft.

6. Remove the O-ring (6, **Figure 50**) from its groove in the cylinder block. Discard the O-ring.

7. Clean all components in a suitable solvent. Inspect all oil pump components for excessive wear as described in this chapter.

Oil Pump Removal and Disassembly (9.9 and 15 hp Models)

1. Remove the four oil pump mounting bolts and pull the oil pump from the camshaft and cylinder head.

2. Remove the O-ring (10, **Figure 51**) from the oil pump mounting surface.

3. Carefully scrape the gasket (9, **Figure 51**) from the oil pump body (8) or cylinder heade. Discard the O-ring and gasket.

4. Heat the oil pump housing enough to melt the Loctite on the screw threads. Remove both screws (1, **Figure 51**) from the oil pump cover.

5. Pull the oil pump cover (2, **Figure 51**) from the oil pump body (8). Lift the outer rotor (3, **Figure 51**) and inner rotor (4) from the oil pump body. Pull the oil pump shaft (6, **Figure 51**) from the pump body (8). Pull the drive pin (5, **Figure 51**) from the pump drive shaft (6).

6. Lift the O-ring (7, **Figure 51**) from its groove in the pump body (8).

7. Discard the O-ring. Clean all components is a suitable solvent. Inspect all components for excessive wear as described in this chapter.

Oil Pump Removal and Disassembly (25-50 hp Models)

1. Remove the four oil pump mounting bolts and pull the oil pump from the camshaft and cylinder head.

2. Pull the O-ring from the oil pump body (8, **Figure 52**). Discard the O-ring.

45

CYLINDER HEAD (25 HP MODELS)

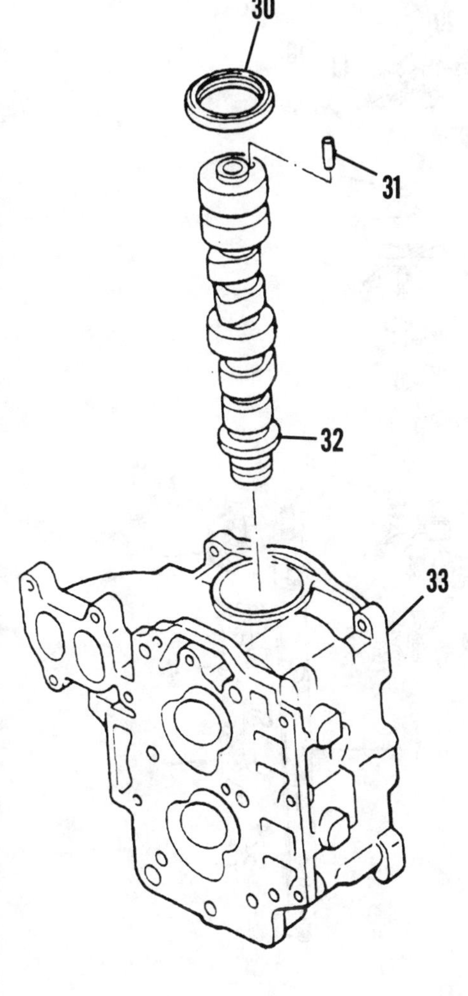

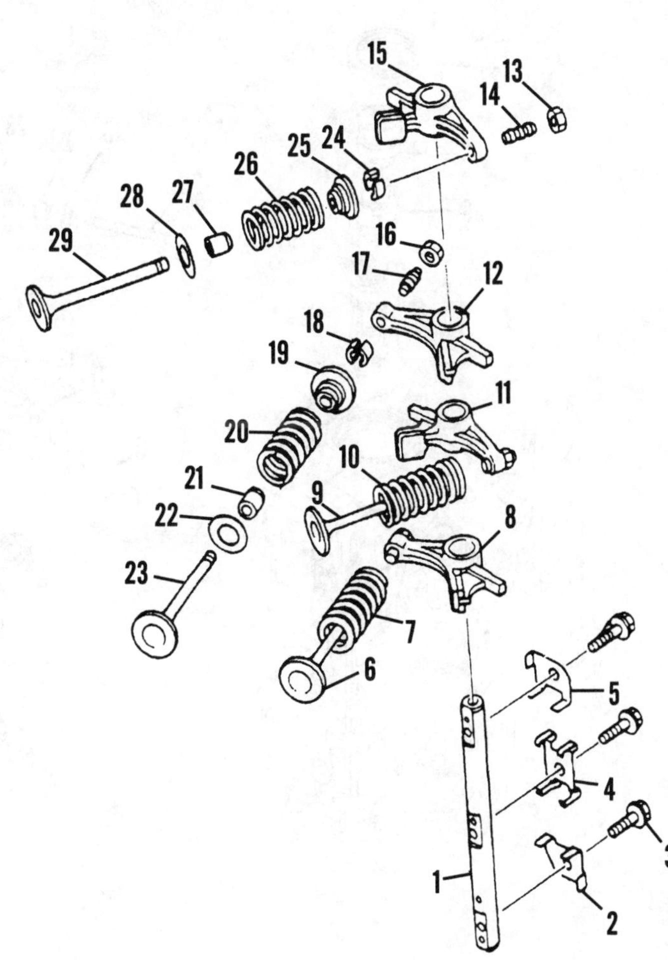

1. Rocker arm shaft
2. Bottom retainer
3. Bolt
4. Middle retainer
5. Top retainer
6. Valve
7. Valve spring
8. Rocker arm
9. Valve
10. Valve spring
11. Rocker arm
12. Rocker arm
13. Locknut
14. Adjusting screw
15. Rocker arm
16. Locknut
17. Adjusting screw
18. Keepers
19. Spring cap
20. Valve spring
21. Seal
22. Spring base
23. Valve
24. Keepers
25. Spring cap
26. Spring
27. Seal
28. Spring base
29. Valve
30. Seal
31. Pin
32. Camshaft
33. Cylinder head

8

46

CYLINDER HEAD
(30 AND 40 HP MODELS)

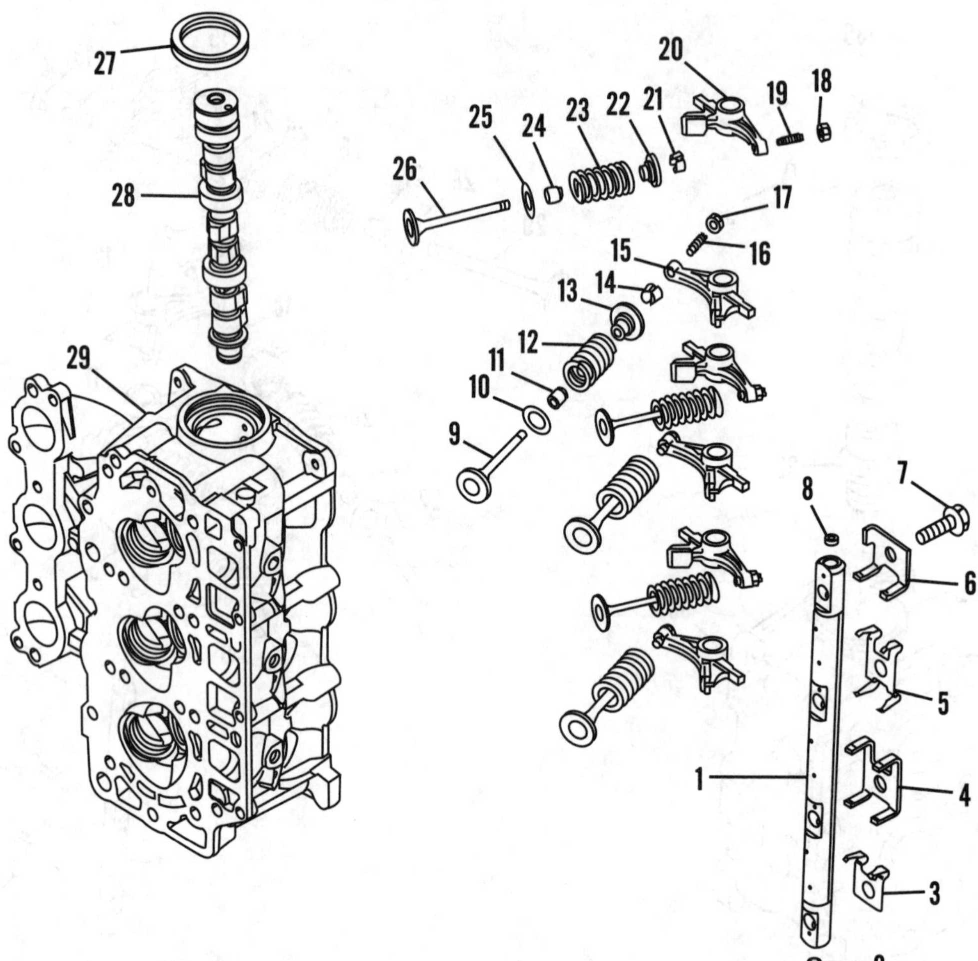

1. Rocker arm shaft
2. Plug
3. Bottom retainer
4. No. 3 retainer
5. No. 2 retainer
6. Top retainer
7. Bolt
8. Plug
9. Valve
10. Spring base
11. Seal
12. Valve spring
13. Spring cap
14. Keepers
15. Rocker arm
16. Adjusting screw
17. Locknut
18. Locknut
19. Adjusting screw
20. Rocker arm
21. Keepers
22. Spring cap
23. Valve spring
24. Seal
25. Spring base
26. Valve
27. Seal
28. Camshaft
29. Cylinder head

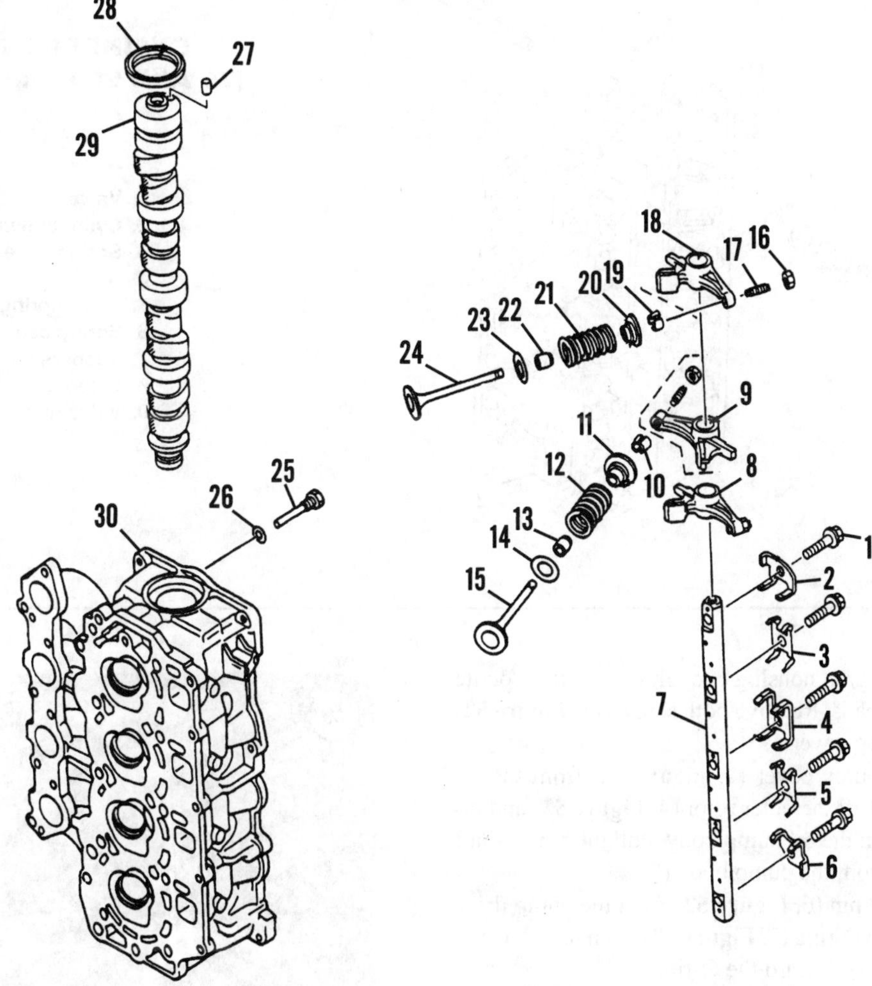

1. Bolt
2. Top retainer
3. No. 2 retainer
4. No. 3 retainer
5. No. 4 retainer
6. Bottom retainer
7. Rocker arm shaft
8. Rocker arm
9. Rocker arm
10. Keepers
11. Spring cap
12. Valve spring
13. Seal
14. Spring base
15. Valve
16. Locknut
17. Adjustment screw
18. Rocker arm
19. Keepers
20. Spring cap
21. Valve spring
22. Seal
23. Spring base
24. Valve
25. Bolt
26. Washer
27. Pin
28. Seal
29. Camshaft
30. Cylinder head

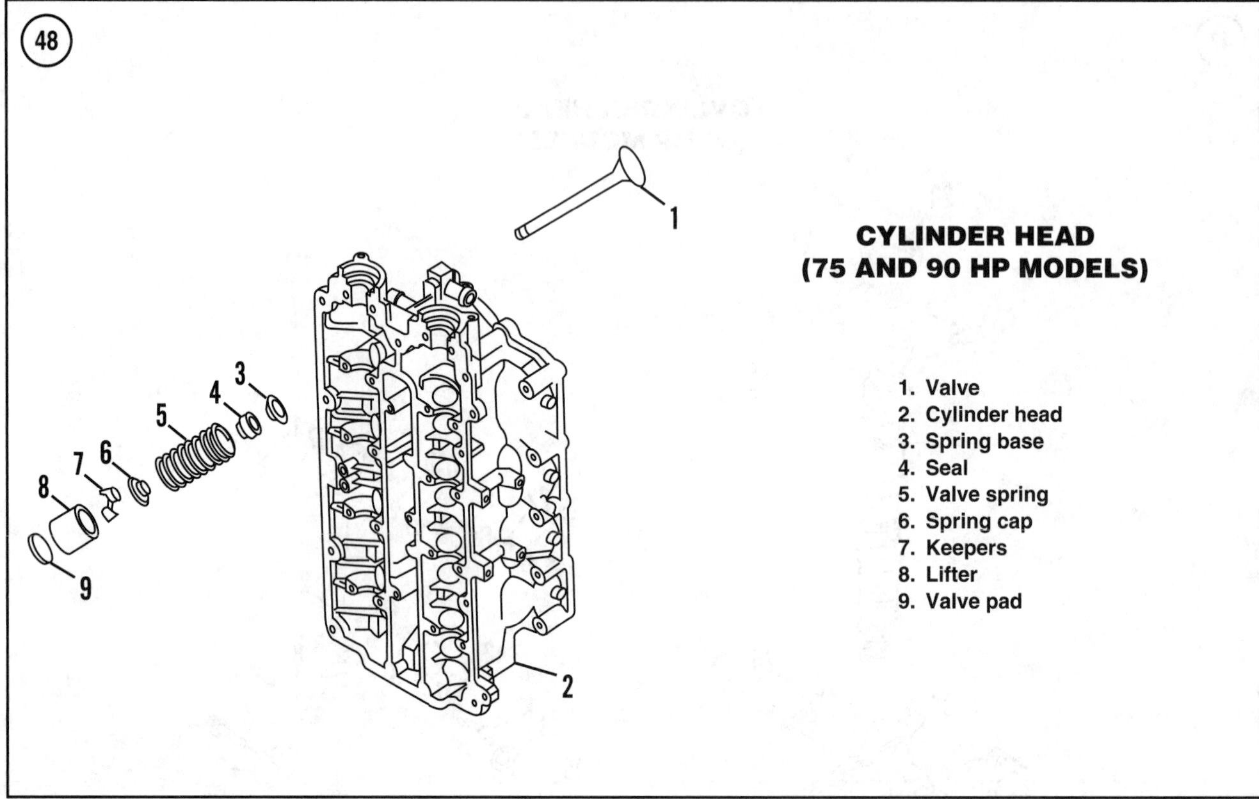

3. Heat the oil pump housing enough to melt the Loctite on the screw threads. Remove both screws (1, **Figure 52**) from the oil pump cover.
4. Pull the oil pump cover (2, **Figure 52**) from the oil pump body (8). Lift the outer rotor (4, **Figure 52**) and inner rotor (5) from the oil pump body. Pull the pump shaft (7, **Figure 52**) from the pump body (8).
5. Pull the drive pin (6, **Figure 52**) from the pump drive shaft (7). Lift the O-ring (3, **Figure 52**) from its groove in the pump body (8).Discard the O-ring.
6. Clean all components using solvent. Inspect all components for excessive wear as described in this chapter.

Oil Pump Removal and Disassembly (75 and 90 hp Models)

1. Remove the power head as described in this chapter. Remove the seal from the boss that surrounds the splined drive shaft bore.
2. Remove the six bolts and remove the oil pump from the power head adapter.
3. Remove the both O-rings from the power head adapter or bottom side of the oil pump.
4. Immerse the oil pump in solvent. Rotate the drive shaft bore to purge all engine oil from the pump. Dry the pump using compressed air. Do not allow the splined section to directing compressed air into the oil passages.
5. Inspect the oil pump mating surfaces for corrosion or cracks and replace as required.

Oil Pump Assembly and Installation (4-6 hp Models)

1. Place the drive pin (3, **Figure 50**) into the slot in the pump drive shaft.

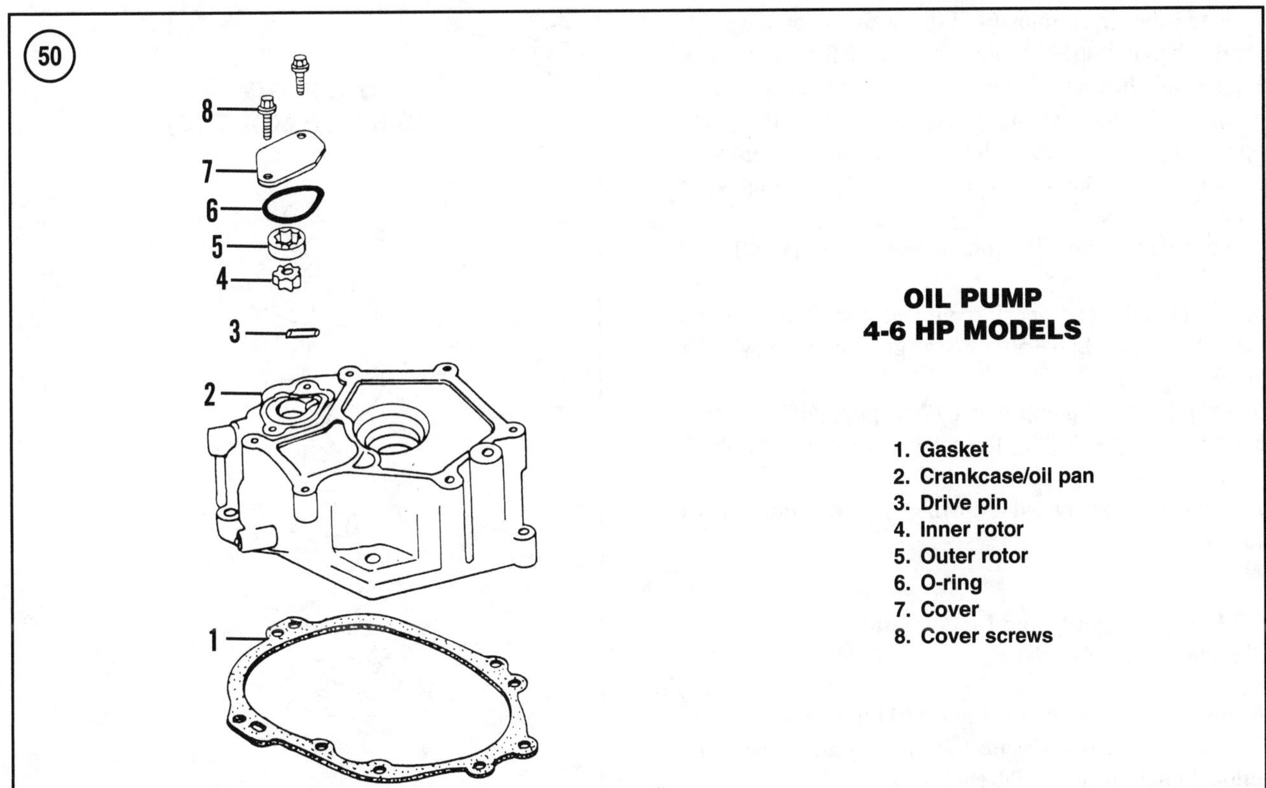
50
8
7
6
5
4
3
2
1
OIL PUMP
4-6 HP MODELS
1. Gasket
2. Crankcase/oil pan
3. Drive pin
4. Inner rotor
5. Outer rotor
6. O-ring
7. Cover
8. Cover screws

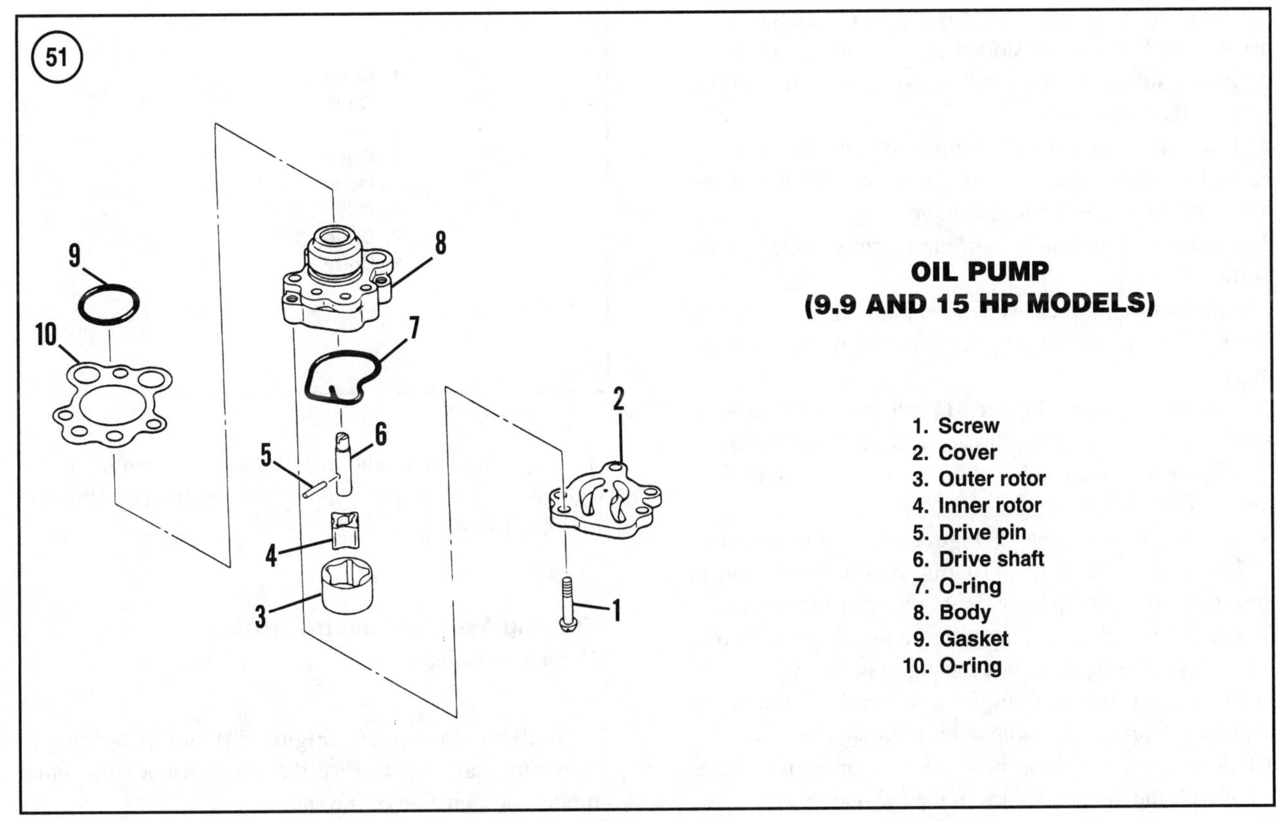
51
9
10
8
7
6
5
4
3
2
1
OIL PUMP
(9.9 AND 15 HP MODELS)
1. Screw
2. Cover
3. Outer rotor
4. Inner rotor
5. Drive pin
6. Drive shaft
7. O-ring
8. Body
9. Gasket
10. O-ring

2. Place the inner rotor (4, **Figure 50**) over the drive shaft. Align the slot in the inner rotor with the drive pin (3, **Figure 50**), then seat the rotor into the oil pump opening.
3. Insert the outer rotor (5, **Figure 50**) into the pump opening. Rotate the rotor until its protrusions align with the inner rotor. The rotor will drop into the opening when properly aligned.
4. Push down on both rotors (4 and 5, **Figure 50**) until seated in the opening.
5. Fill the oil pump opening with engine oil and place a new O-ring (6, **Figure 50**) into the groove in the cylinder block.
6. Install the oil pump cover (7, **Figure 50**) and both cover screws (8). Tighten the cover screws to 70 in.-lb. (8 N•m).
7. Install the power head following the instructions in this chapter.

Oil Pump Assembly and Installation (9.9 and 15 hp Models)

1. Install the drive pin (5, **Figure 51**) into its opening in the pump shaft (6). Ensure the pin protrudes the same amount on each side of the shaft.
2. Slide the pump drive shaft slotted side first into the pump body (8, **Figure 51**).
3. Place the inner rotor (4, **Figure 51**) over the pump drive shaft (6) with the slotted side facing the drive pin. Align the slot in the rotor with the drive pin and seat the rotor in the pump body.
4. Insert the outer rotor (3, **Figure 51**) into the oil pump body. Rotate the rotor until its protrusions align with the inner rotor and drops into the pump body.
5. Push down on both rotors until firmly seated in the body.
6. Fill the oil pump cavity with engine oil. Install a new O-ring (7, **Figure 51**) into the groove on the oil pump body (8).
7. Place the cover (1, **Figure 51**) onto the oil pump body. Apply Loctite 222 to the threads and install both screws (1, **Figure 51**). Tighten the cover screws to the specification in **Table 1**.
8. Install a new gasket (9, **Figure 51**) on the oil pump body. Lubricate the O-ring (10, **Figure 51**) with engine oil and slide it over pump body. Seat the O-ring in the groove.
9. Carefully slide the pump into the opening on the bottom of cylinder head. Rotate the pump body until the slot in the pump drive shaft aligns with the drive pin in the camshaft. Seat the oil pump against the cylinder head.
10. Rotate the oil pump body until its mounting holes align with the threaded holes in the cylinder head.

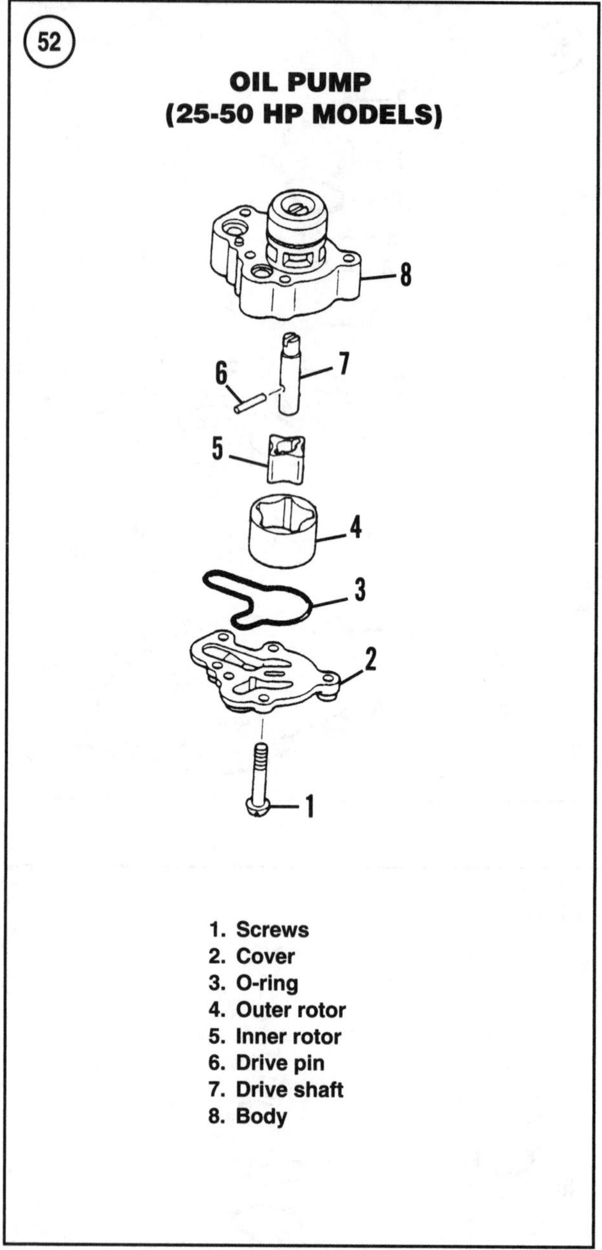

11. Align the gasket and install the four mounting bolts. Tighten the oil pump mounting bolts to the specification in **Table 1**.

Oil Pump Assembly and Installation (25-50 hp Models)

1. Install the drive pin (6, **Figure 52**) into its opening in the pump shaft (7). Ensure the pin protrudes the same amount on each side of the shaft.

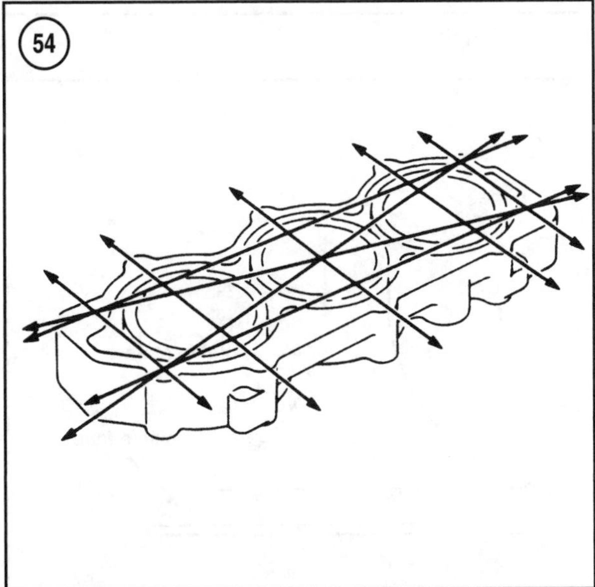

2. Slide the pump drive shaft slotted side first into the pump body (8, **Figure 52**).

3. Place the inner rotor (5, **Figure 52**) over the oil pump drive shaft (7) with the slotted side facing the drive pin. Align the slot in the rotor with the drive pin and seat the rotor in the pump body.

4. Insert the outer rotor (4, **Figure 52**) into the oil pump body. Rotate the rotor until its protrusions align with the inner rotor and drops into the body.

5. Push down on both rotors until firmly seated in the body.

6. Fill the pump cavity with engine oil. Install a new O-ring (3, **Figure 52**) into its groove on the pump body (8).

7. Place the cover (2, **Figure 52**) onto the pump body. Apply Loctite 222 to the threads and install both screws (1, **Figure 52**). Tighten the cover screws to the specification in **Table 1**.

8. Lubricate the three new O-rings with engine oil and place them into the grooves in the pump body.

9. Carefully slide the oil pump into the opening in the bottom of cylinder head. Rotate the pump body until the slot in the oil pump drive shaft aligns with the drive pin in the camshaft and seats against the cylinder head.

10. Rotate the oil pump body until its mounting holes align with the threaded holes in the cylinder head.

11. Pull the pump away from the cylinder head just enough to inspect both small O-rings. Reposition the O-rings if out of position. Install the oil pump mounting bolts then tighten them to the specification in **Table 1**.

Oil Pump Installation (75 and 90 hp Models)

1. Lubricate the new O-rings with engine oil and place them into the grooves in the power head adapter.

2. Pour engine oil into the two openings on the bottom of the oil pump. Rotate the pump shaft to distribute oil throughout the pump. Apply a light coat of water-resistant grease to the splines.

3. Place the oil pump onto the power head adapter.

4. Seat the pump against the power head adapter and install the pump mounting bolts. Tighten the bolts in a crossing pattern to 85 in.-lb. (9.6 N·m).

5. Lubricate the new seal with clean engine oil and carefully place the seal onto the boss surrounding the splined shaft. The larger diameter side of the seal must contact the oil pump.

6. Install the power head as described in this chapter.

INSPECTION

Cylinder Head

1. Scrape all carbon deposits from the combustion chamber using a blunt scraper. Avoid scraping aluminum material from the cylinder head.

2. Pull the valve stem seals (**Figure 53**) from the valve guides.

3. Remove the anode, thermostats and sensors following the instructions in this manual.

4. Thoroughly clean all grease or corrosion from the cylinder head using a solvent suitable for aluminum material.

5. Check for surface warpage by placing a straightedge at various points (**Figure 54**) on the cylinder head mating surface. Hold the straightedge firmly against the head and check the gap at various points along the straightedge

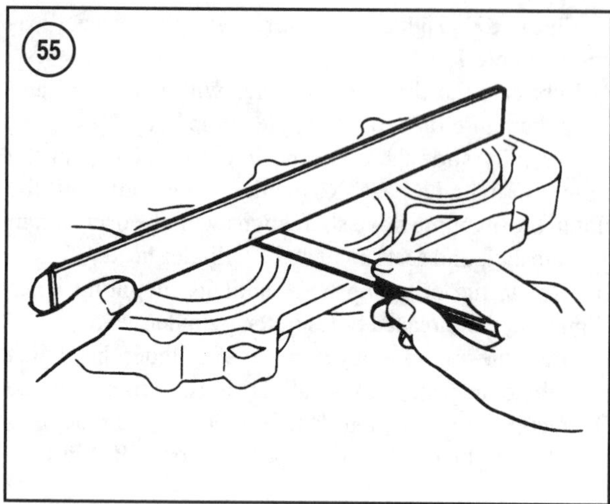

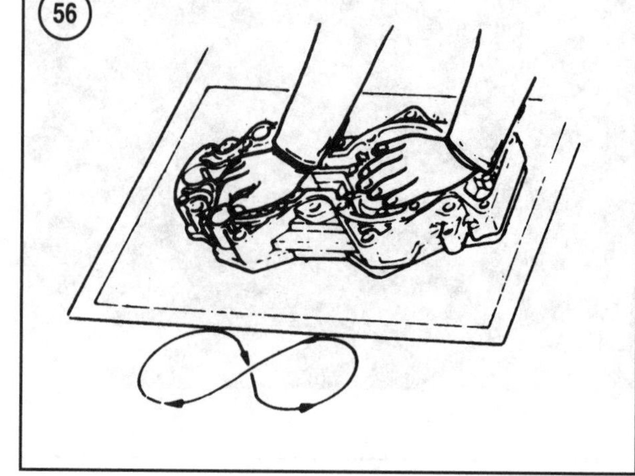

(**Figure 55**) using a feeler gauge. Compare the thickness of the feeler gauge that can be passed under the straightedge with the warpage limit in **Table 19**.

6. Minor warpage can be repared by placing a sheet of 600 grit wet or dry abrasive paper on a surfacing plate. Use slight downward pressure and move the cylinder head in a figure eight motion (**Figure 56**). Stop periodically and check the warpage. Remove only the material necessary to remove the excess warpage.

7. Have a reputable machine shop perform this operation if a surfacing plate is not available. Replace the cylinder head if the warpage is excessive. Do not machine the gasket surface as it can lead to increased compression and difficulty adjusting the valves on some models.

8. Thoroughly clean the cylinder head using hot soapy water and dry with compressed air.

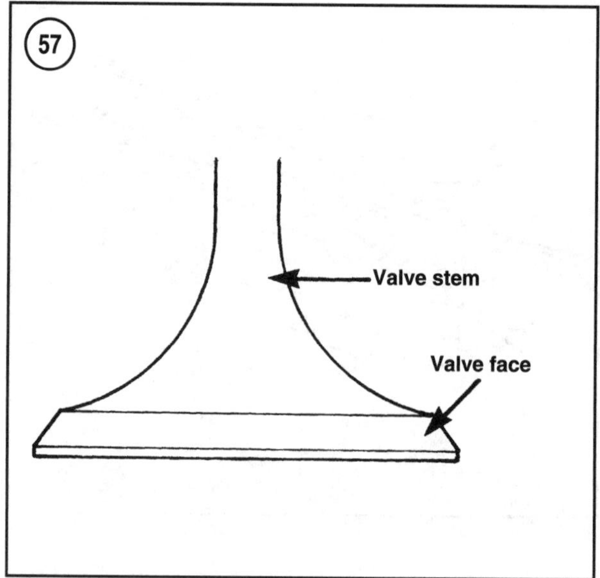

Valves

1. Using a solvent and parts cleaning brush, clean all carbon deposits from the valves. Inspect the valve stem (**Figure 57**) for wear, roughness, cracks, corrosion or damage. Replace the valve if corroded or damaged.

2. Using an accurate micrometer, measure each valve stem (**Figure 58**) along the valve guide contact area. Rotate the valve 90° and repeat the measurement. Record the highest and lowest measurements. Repeat these measurements for the remaining valves. Compare the measurements with the valve stem specification in **Table 15**. Replace the valve if its diameter is below the specification.

3. Mount the valve on V-blocks and position the tip of a dial indicator against the valve stem (**Figure 59**). Observe the amount of needle movement when rotating the valve.

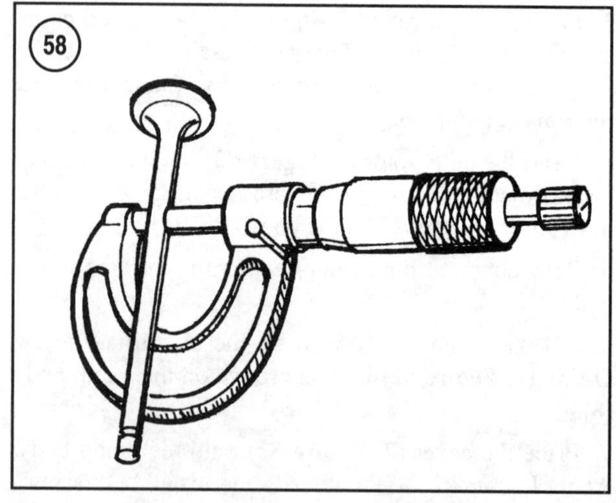

59

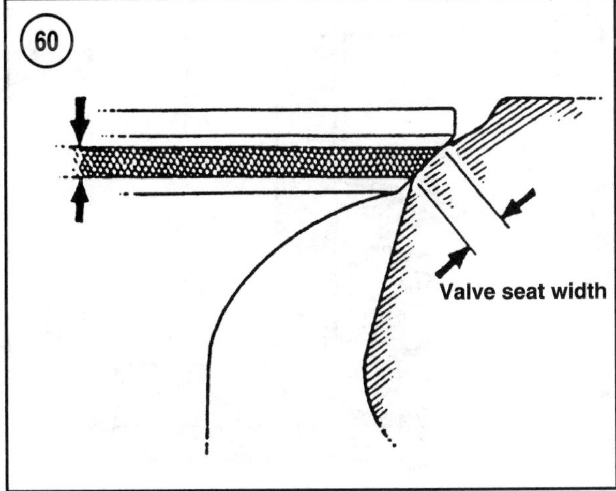

60

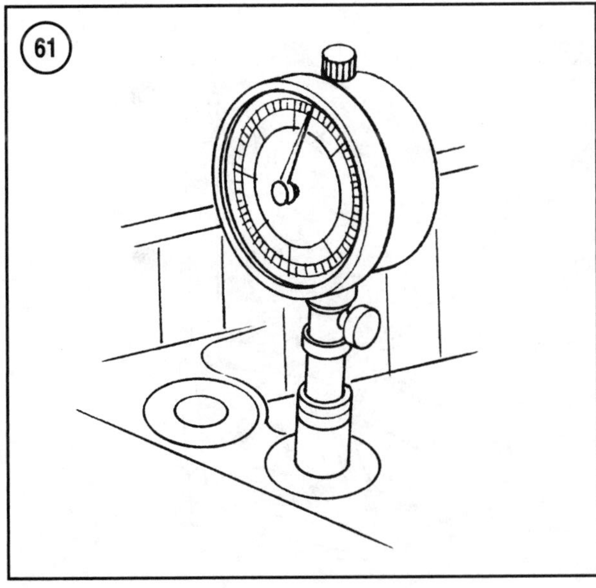
61

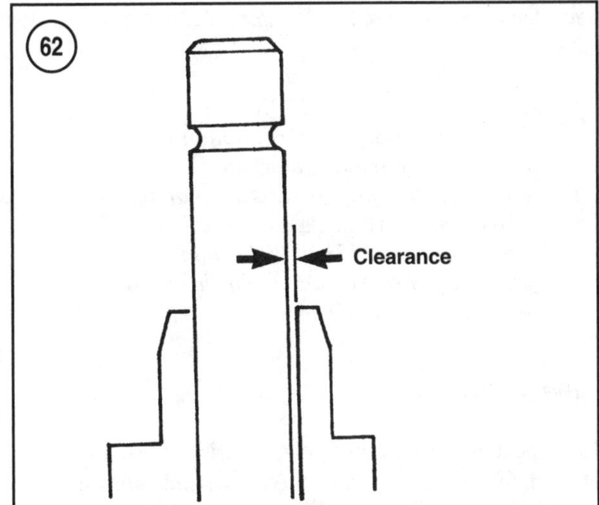

62

Replace the valve if the runout exceeds the specification in **Table 15**.

4. Inspect the valve face (**Figure 57**) for cracked, corroded, damaged or pitted surfaces. Correct valve seating causes a light polished surface on the valve and valve seats.
5. Using a vernier caliper measure the width of the valve seat (**Figure 60**). Compare the measurements with the specification in **Table 15** and **Table 17**.
6. Have the valve and valve seat reconditioned at a machine shop if the valve seat is defective or excessively worn. Cut valve seats to a 45° angle. Cut the first angle on thecombustion chamber side of the seat to 15°. Cut the third angle on the intake side of the seat to 60°.
7. Inspect the valve guide bore for cracked discolored or damaged surfaces. Have the valve guides replaced at a machine shop if damaged or excessively worn.
8. Measure the inner diameter of the valve guide (**Figure 61**) along the entire length of the bore. Rotate the gauge 90° and repeat the measurements. Record the largest and smallest measurements. The valve guide must be replaced if the diameter is not within the specification in **Table 16**.

Valve Guide Clearance

1. Subtract the largest valve stem measurement from the smallest valve guide measurement to determine the lowest valve stem clearance (**Figure 62**).
2. Subtract the smallest valve stem diameter from the largest valve guide diameter to determine the highest valve stem clearance.
3. Compare the results with the specification in **Table 16**. A worn valve stem or valve guide is indicated if excessive clearance is noted. A damaged or improperly installed

valve guide is indicated if the stem clearance is insufficient.

CAUTION
*Improper valve guide installation can lead to poor valve sealing, increased valve wear and potential failure. Ensure that the replacement valve guides are installed to the proper depth on 75 and 90 hp models. Valve guide depth specifications for these models is provided in **Table 16**.*

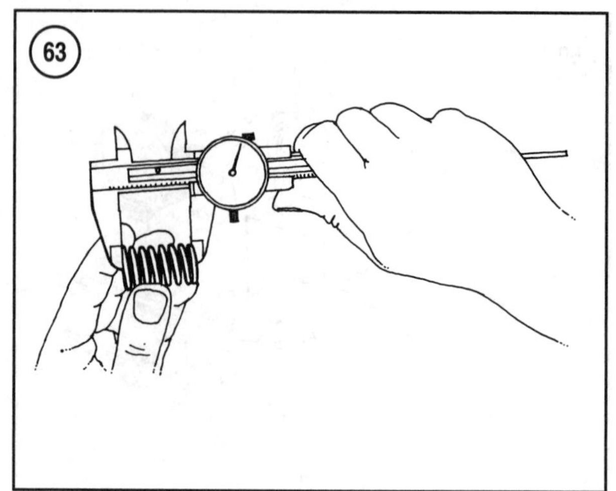
63

Valve Springs

1. Inspect each valve spring for excessive wear, cracks or other damage. Never switch the intake and exhaust valve sprints as the spring tension may differ. Damage to the valve and other components can occur when valve springs are installed on the wrong valve.
2. On all models except 9.9 hp (serial No. OH000058-on), measure the free length of each spring as indicated in **Figure 63**. Compare the measurement with the specification listed in **Table 14**. Replace the spring if incorrect free length is indicated.
3. Using a square, measure the spring for an out of square condition as indicated (**Figure 64**). Compare the measurement with the specification in **Table 14**.

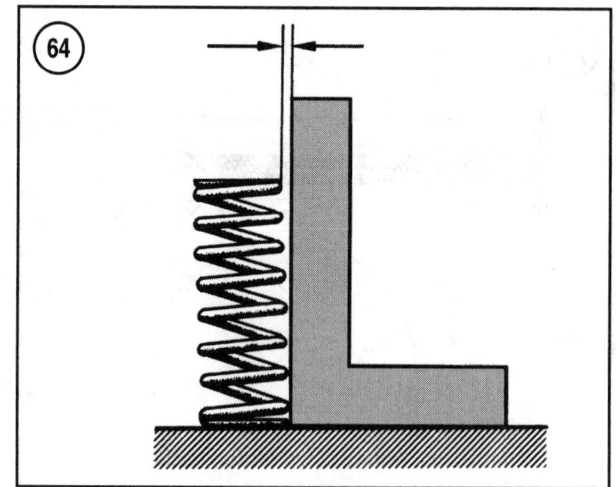
64

The 4-6 hp and 9.9 hp (serial No. OH000058-on) models require spring pressure measurement to determine its condition. This measurement requires a special spring tester (**Figure 65**). Have the spring tested at a qualified machine shop. Spring pressure specifications are provided in **Table 14**.

Rocker Arm and Shaft

A rocker arm and shaft arrangement is used only on 9.9-50 hp models. All 4-6 hp models use a rocker arm supported by a stud.

1. Inspect each rocker arm for worn, corroded, discolored or rough contact surfaces. Replace rocker arms with these or other defects.
2. Using an inside micrometer, measure the inside diameter of each rocker arm (**Figure 66**). Compare the measurement with the specification in **Table 18**. Replace any rocker arm with a measurement greater than the specification.
3. Inspect each rocker arm shaft for worn, corroded or discolored surfaces.
4. Using an outside micrometer measure the shaft diameter at the surfaces contacting the rocker arms (**Figure 67**). Compare the measurements with the specification in **Ta-**

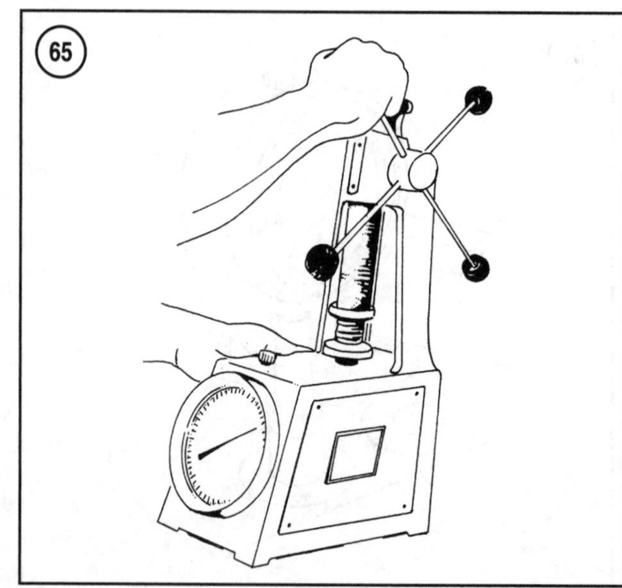
65

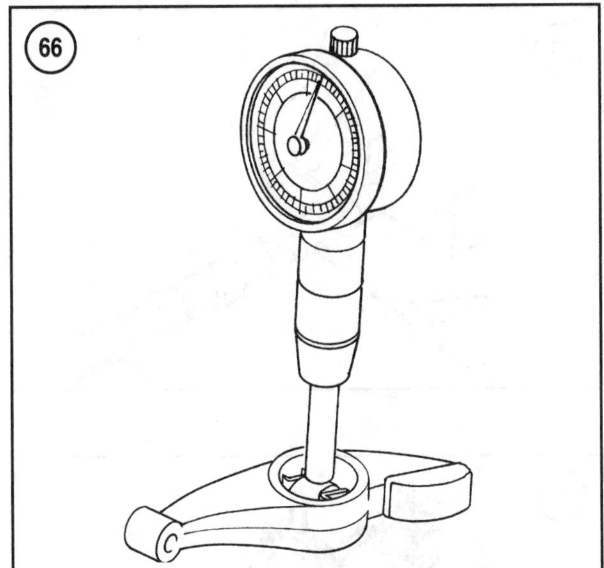

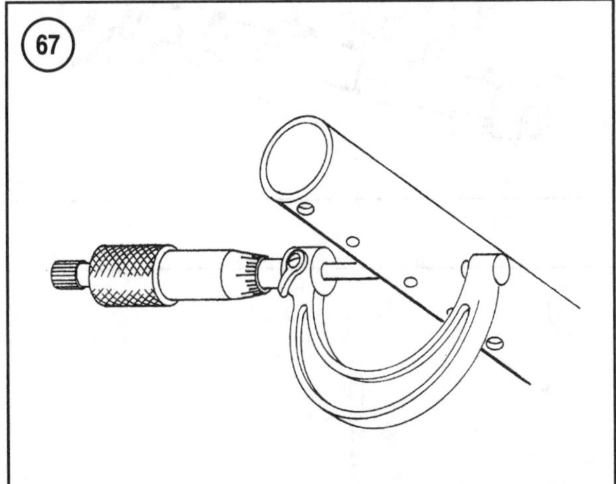

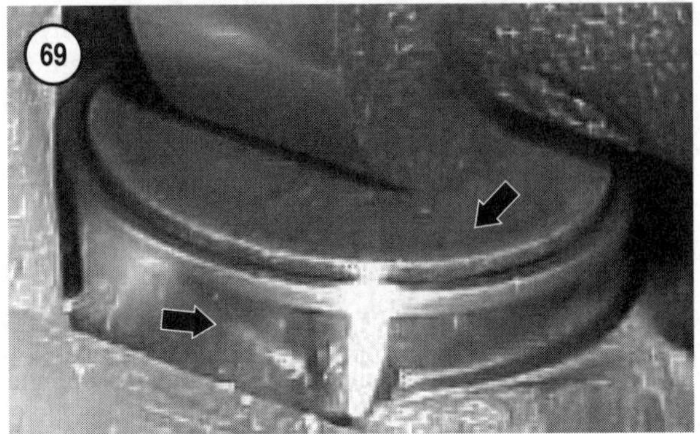

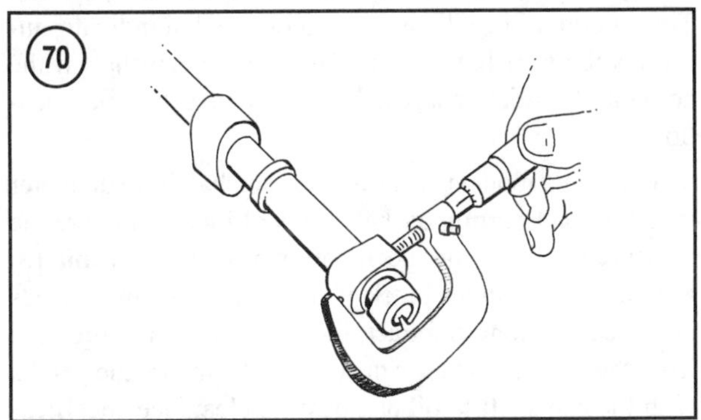

ble 18. Replace the rocker arm shaft if defects are noted or the diameter at the contact surfaces are less than the specification.

Camshaft, Pushrods and Tappets

Inspect the camshaft lobes and journals (**Figure 68**) for wear, cracks or corrosion. Replace the camshaft if any defects are noted.

1. On 4-6 hp models, inspect the pushrods for a bent condition by slowly rolling them across a flat surface. Inspect the end of the rods for roughness, discoloration or excessive wear. Replace the pushrods if bent or defective.
2. On 75 and 90 hp models, inspect then lifters and valve pads (**Figure 69**) for excessive wear or damage. Replace damaged or worn components.
3. Disassembly of the cylinder block is required to access the camshaft or tappets on 4-6 hp models. Refer to *Cylinder Block Repair* in this chapter.
4. Measure the length of each camshaft lobe as indicated in **Figure 70**. Compare the lobe with the specification in **Table 13**. Replace the camshaft if any of the measurements are below the specification.
5. Measure each lobe width at a point 90° from the lobe length measuring points. Compare the lobe width with the

specification in **Table 13**. Replace the camshaft if any of the lobe width measurements are beyond the specification.

6. Measure the camshaft (**Figure 71**) bearing journals. Compare the measurements with the specification. Replace the camshaft if any of your measurements are less than the specifications listed in **Table 13**.

7. On 9.9 hp models (serial No. OH000058-on), place the camshaft on blocks located under the top and bottom journals (**Figure 72**). Securely mount a dial indicator with the plunger directly contacting one of the middle camshaft journals. Observe the dial indicator as the camshaft slowly rotates. Repeat the measurement on all journals. The amount of needle movement on the dial indicator indicates the camshaft runout. Replace the camshaft if the amount of runout on any journal is exceeds the specification.

8. On 2-6 hp models, measure the camshaft bore diameter in the oil pan portion of the cylinder block. Compare the measurement with the specification provided in **Table 13**. Replace the cylinder block if the measurement exceeds the specification. Subtract the camshaft measurement from the bore diameter in the oil pan. Compare the results with the camshaft to oil pan bearing clearance specification listed in **Table 13**). Excessive clearance indicates a worn camshaft or bearing.

9. On 75 and 90 hp models, install all camshaft caps without the camshafts on the cylinder head. Tighten the caps to the specification **Table 1**.

10. On 9.9-90 hp models, use an inside micrometer to measure the diameter of each camshaft bore. Compare these measurements with the specification listed in **Table 13**. Replace the cylinder head if the measurement exceeds the specification.

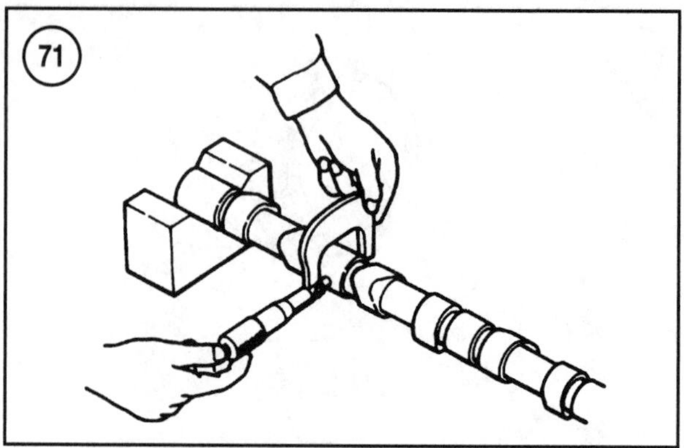
71

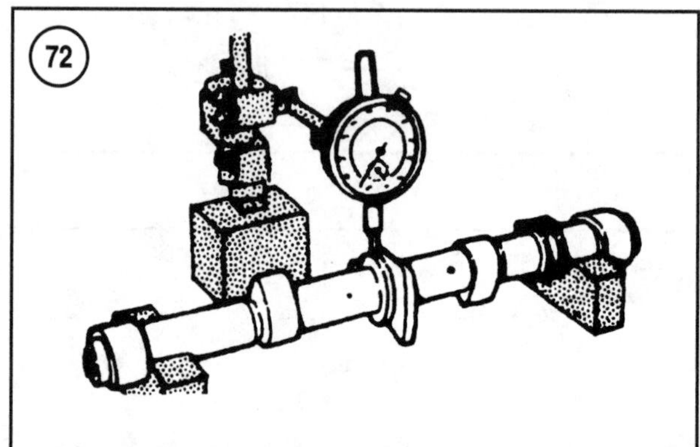
72

Oil Pump

1. Clean all components using solvent and dry them with compressed air. Inspect the components for cracked, discolored or rough contact surfaces. Replace the oil pump if any defects are noted.

2. The oil pump used on 75 and 90 hp models are not serviceable. Replace the oil pump on these models if low oil pressure exists and other causes such as a faulty pressure relief valve or worn bearing are ruled out. On these models the oil pump is located at the power head mounting surface on the midsection. Remove the four bolts and lift the pump from the mount. Install new O-rings on the mounting surface prior to pump installation. Tighten the bolts in a crossing pattern to the specification in **Table 1**.

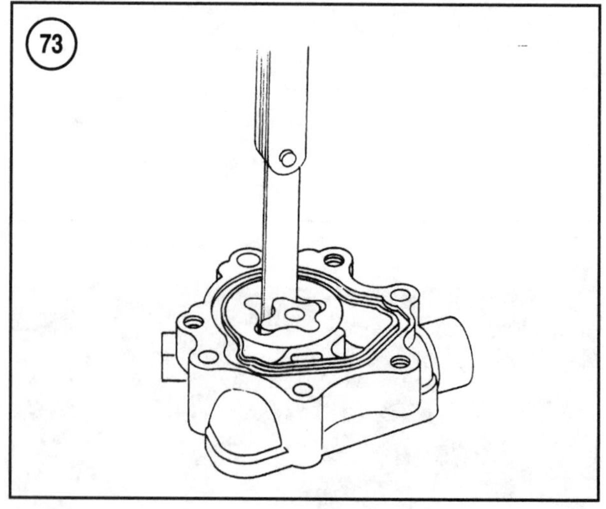
73

3. On all other models, place the inner and outer rotors into the oil pump body or cylinder block opening on 4-6 hp models.

4. Using feeler gauges, measure the clearance between the inner and outer rotors at the point indicated in **Figure 73**. Select the feeler gauge that passes between the rotors with a slight drag. Compare the feeler gauge thickness

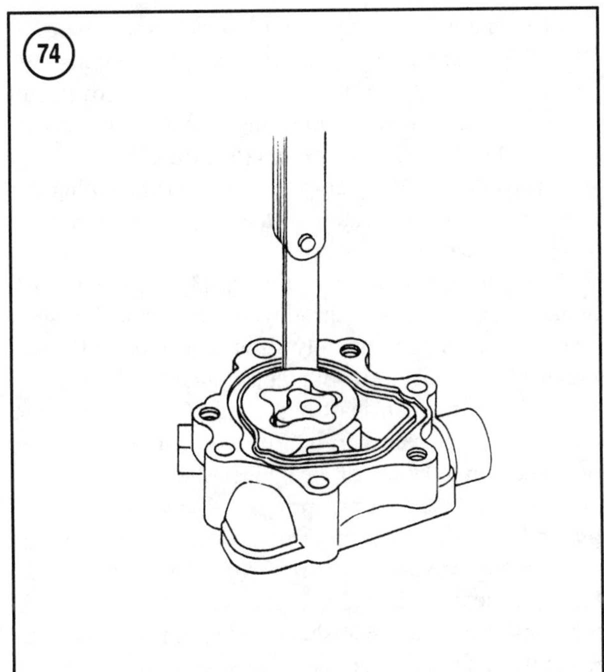

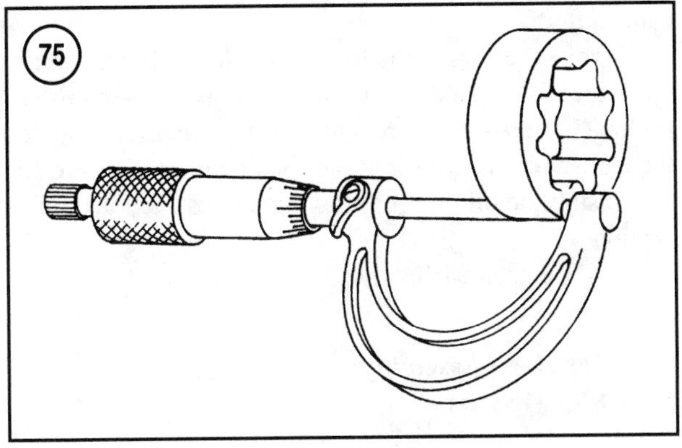

with the specification in **Table 12**. Replace the inner and outer rotors if the clearance exceeds the specification.

5. Place the outer rotor into the oil pump body or cylinder block opening on 4-6 hp models. Using narrow feeler gauges, measure the clearance (**Figure 74**) between the outer rotor and the oil pump body or opening in the cylinder block on 4-6 hp models. Select the feeler gauge that passes between the rotor and oil pump body or cylinder block with a slight drag. Compare the feeler gauge thickness with the specification in **Table 12**. Replace the outer rotor and pump body if the clearance exceeds the specification.

6. On 4-6 hp models, remove the inner and outer rotors from the pump bore. Measure the thickness of the outer rotor (**Figure 75**). Compare the measurement with the

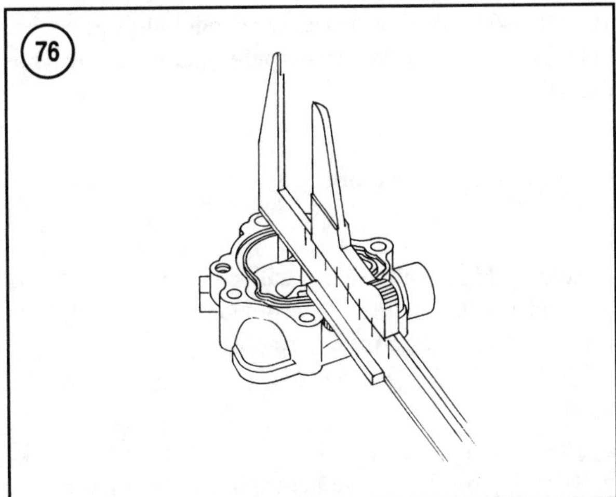

8

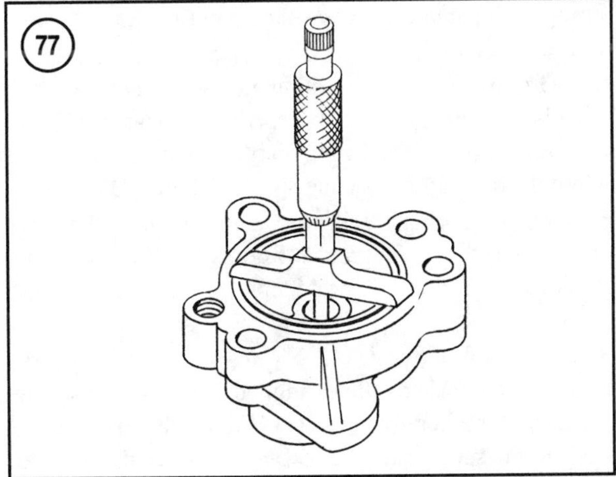

specification listed in **Table 12**. Replace the outer rotor if its measurement is below the specification.

7. Measure the diameter of the pump bore using an inside micrometer or vernier caliper (**Figure 76**). Using a depth micrometer measure the depth of the pump bore (**Figure 77**). Compare the measurements with the specifications in **Table 12**. Replace the cylinder block if either measurement exceeds the specification. Reinstall the outer rotor.

8. On 4-50 hp models, measure the distance from the oil pump mating surfaces or cylinder block surface on 4-6 hp models to the outer rotor. Use an accurate depth micrometer for this measurement. Compare the distance to the specification in **Table 12**.

9. On 9.9-50 hp models, replace the outer rotor if the measurements exceed the specification. Measure the depth with the new outer rotor. Replace the oil pump body if the depth is still excessive.

10. On 4-6 hp models, excessive depth indicates a worn outer rotor or pump bore. Measure both components as described in this chapter.

Cylinder Head Assembly (4-6 hp Models)

Refer to **Figure 40** to assist with component identification and orientation. Install all components in the location and orientation noted prior to removal.

1. Slide the intake valve (1, **Figure 40**) into the cylinder head.
2. Place the spring base (4, **Figure 40**) then the intake valve spring over the valve stem and seat them against the cylinder head.
3. Place the spring cap (15, **Figure 40**) onto the valve spring with the keeper recess facing outward.
4. Use a box-end wrench as a valve spring installation tool (**Figure 41**). The opening in the wrench must be slightly smaller than the valve spring caps (6 and 15, **Figure 40**). Support the larger diameter side of the valve while depressing the cap and spring (**Figure 41**).
5. While the spring is collapsed, carefully place the keepers into the valve stem groove (**Figure 42**). Slowly release tension on the spring. Repeat Steps 4 and 5 for the exhaust valve.
6. Place the guide plate (12, **Figure 40**) into the cylinder head with the push rod holes aligned. Using a deep socket, install both rocker arm studs (11, **Figure 40**). Tighten the studs to the specification in **Table 1**. Slide both push rods into the cylinder head.
7. Place the rocker arms onto the studs. Align the rocker arm tip with the valve stem. Thread the adjusting nuts (6, **Figure 40**) onto the studs just enough to leave threads for the lock nuts (8). Thread the lock nuts onto the stud until they contact the adjusting nut.

Cylinder Head Assembly (9.9 and 15 hp Models)

Refer to **Figure 43** to assist with component identification and orientation. Install all components in the location and orientation noted prior to removal.

1. Press the new valve stem seal (**Figure 53**) onto the end of the valve guide. Install the No. 1 intake valve into the valve guide.
2. Place the spring base and valve spring over the valve stem. Seat them against the cylinder head. Place the spring cap onto the valve spring with the keeper recess facing outward.
3. Place the valve spring compressor (Mercury part No. 91-809494A1) on the valve and spring cap (**Figure 39**). Tighten the clamp just enough to expose the grooved portion of the valve stem and allow installation of the keepers (**Figure 42**). Install both keepers (**Figure 42**).
4. Slowly loosen the clamp then inspect the spring cap and stem for proper seating of the keepers. Repeat Steps 1-4 for the remaining valves.
5. Position the new seal (32, **Figure 43**) into the opening at the top of the cylinder head with the lip side facing inward. Using an appropriately sized socket, drive the seal into the bore until flush with the cylinder head surface.
6. Lubricate the camshaft bearing surfaces with engine oil and slide the camshaft into its bore with the threaded opening facing the top of the cylinder head.
7. Install the rocker arms, springs and spacers. Apply engine oil to the rocker arm shafts and slide them through the cylinder head bores, springs, spacers and rocker arms.
8. Place the drive key (33, **Figure 43**) into its groove in the camshaft. Place the washer over the camshaft then seat it against the seal. Align the drive key grooves while installing the camshaft pulley on the camshaft. Thread the retaining bolt and washer through the pulley and into the camshaft.
9. Engage the lugs of the flywheel holding tool (Mercury part No. 91-83163M) with the openings in the camshaft pulley (**Figure 44**) to prevent camshaft rotation. Tighten the camshaft pulley bolt to the specification in **Table 1**.
10. Install the oil pump following the instructions in this section.
11. Fully loosen each valve adjusting screw.

Cylinder Head Assembly (25-50 hp Models)

Install all components to the location and orientation noted prior to removal. Refer to **Figures 45-47** as necessary.

1. Press the new valve stem seal (**Figure 53**) onto the end of the valve guide. Install the No. 1 intake valve into the valve guide and seat it against the valve seat.
2. Place the spring base and valve spring over the valve stem. Ensure the wider spring loop spacing is positioned closer to the rocker arm side. Seat the spring and base against the cylinder head. Place the spring cap onto the valve spring with the keeper recess facing outward.
3. Place the valve spring compressor tool (Mercury part No. 91-809494A1) on the valve and spring cap (**Figure 39**). Tighten the clamp just enough to expose the grooved portion of the valve stem and allow installation of the keepers (**Figure 42**). Install both keepers as indicated in **Figure 42**.

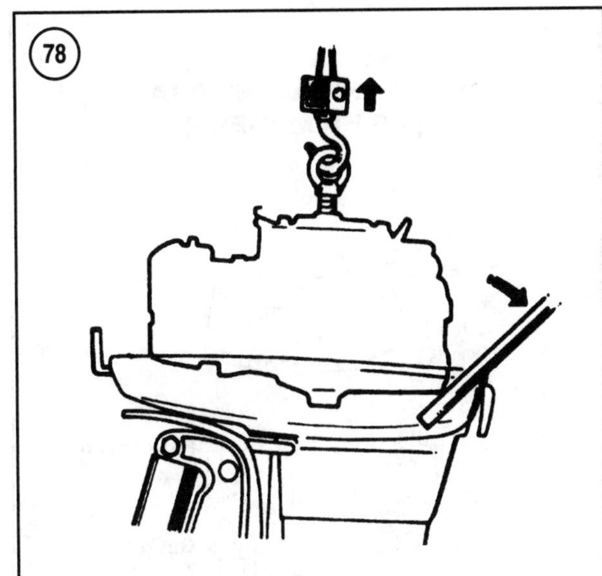

4. Slowly loosen the clamp then inspect the spring cap and stem for proper seating of the keepers. Repeat Steps 1-4 for the remaining valves.

5. Position the new seal into the opening at the top of the cylinder head with the lip side facing inward. Using an appropriately sized socket, drive the seal into the bore until flush with the cylinder head surface.

6. Lubricate the camshaft bearing surfaces with engine oil and slide the camshaft into its bore with the threaded opening facing the top of the cylinder head.

7. Lubricate the rocker arm shaft with engine oil and slide the rocker arms over the shaft. Separate the rocker arms enough to place the retainer against the shaft. Ensure the flat mounting notches face away from the retainers and the arrow mark on the retainers face up.

8. Align the rocker arms with the valve stems and the retainer with the mounting bosses while lowering the rocker arm shaft onto the cylinder head. Thread the retainer bolts into the cylinder head.

9. Evenly tighten the rocker arm shaft retainer bolts to the specification in **Table 1**.

10. Engage the lugs of the flywheel holding tool (Mercury part No. 91-83163M) with the openings in the camshaft pulley (**Figure 44**) to prevent camshaft rotation. Tighten the camshaft pulley bolt to the specification in **Table 1**.

11. Install the oil pump following the instructions in this section.

12. Fully loosen each valve adjusting screw.

Cylinder Head Assembly (75 and 90 hp Models)

CAUTION
Install the valve lifter and pads into the same cylinder bore as noted prior to removal.

Refer to **Figure 48** to assist with component orientation.

1. Press the new valve stem seal (**Figure 53**) onto the end of the valve guide. Install the No. 1 intake valve into the valve guide and seat it against the valve seat.
2. Place the spring base (3, **Figure 48**) over the valve spring with the larger diameter side facing the cylinder head. Slide the valve spring (5, **Figure 48**) over the valve stem and seat the spring and base against the head. Place the spring cap (6, **Figure 48**) onto the valve spring with the keeper recess facing outward.
3. Place the valve spring compressor tool (Mercury part No. 91-809494A1) on the valve and spring cap (**Figure 39**). Tighten the clamp just enough to expose the grooved portion of the valve stem and allow installation of the keepers (**Figure 42**). Install both keepers as indicated in **Figure 42**.
4. Slowly loosen the clamp and inspect the spring cap and stem for proper seating of the keepers. Repeat Steps 1-4 for the remaining valves.
5. Place the valve pad (9, **Figure 48**) into its opening in the lifter (8). Lubricate the lifter with engine oil and slide it over the valve stem. Carefully push the lifter and pad into its bore until the back side of the pad just contacts the valve stem. Repeat this step for the remaining pads and lifters.

POWER HEAD REMOVAL

Inspect the engine to locate the fuel supply hose, throttle and shift cable connections, battery cable connections and trim system connections. Most hoses and wires must be removed if performing a complete power head disassembly. Disconnect only the hoses, wires and linkage required for power head removal. Disconnect the remaining hoses and wires after removing the power head.

Use the diagrams of the fuel and electrical systems to assist with hose and wire routing. Take pictures or make a drawing of all wire and hose connections *before* beginning the removal process.

Secure the proper lifting equipment (**Figure 78**) before attempting to remove the power head. It is easy to lift 15 hp and smaller engines with some assistance. Larger engines require an overhead hoist. A completely assembled

79

power head may weigh over 200 lb (90 kg). Use assistance when lifting or moving any power head.

Lifting hooks (**Figure 79**) are provided on 25-50 hp models. A special lifting tool (Mercury part No. 91-83164M) in required on 75 and 90 hp models.

WARNING
The power head may abruptly separate from the midsection during removal. Avoid using excessive lifting force.

CAUTION
Use care when lifting the power head from the midsection. Corrosion may form at the power head and midsection mating surfaces and prevent easy removal. To help prevent damage to the mating surfaces, avoid using sharp objects to pry the assemblies apart

Power Head Removal (4-6 hp Models)

1. Drain the engine oil as described in Chapter Four.
2. Disconnect the neutral start mechanism and remove the manual starter following the instructions in Chapter Ten.
3. Remove the gearcase following the instructions in Chapter Nine.
4. Disconnect the fuel supply hose, choke linkage and throttle cables.
5. Disconnect the stop button wires, battery cables if so equipped and oil pressure warning light wires.
6. Remove all six power head mounting bolts, then lift the power head (**Figure 80**) from the midsection.
7. Place the power head on a suitable work surface. Remove the gasket (**Figure 80**) from the midsection or bottom of the power head.

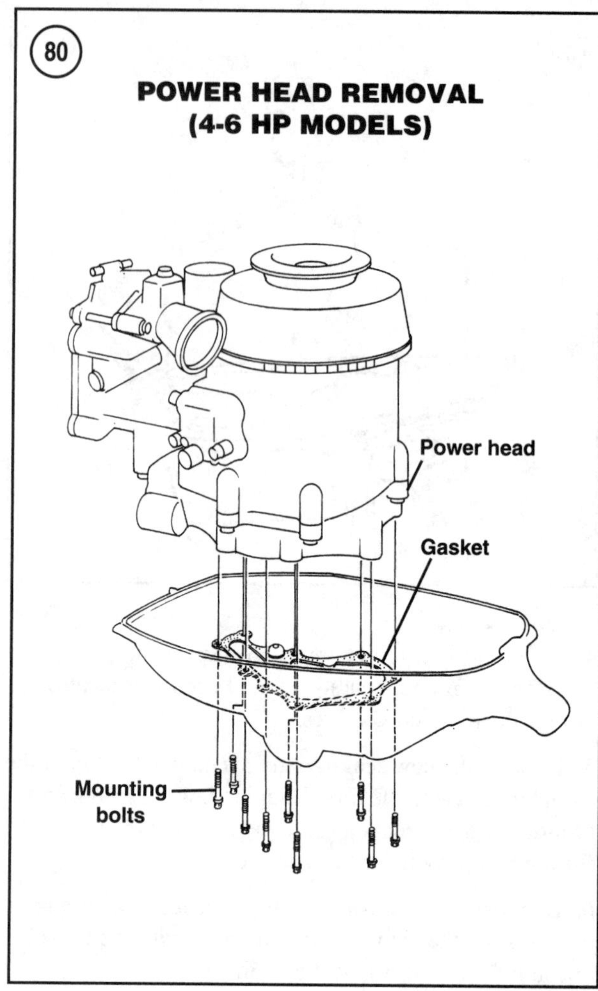

80
POWER HEAD REMOVAL (4-6 HP MODELS)

8. Clean the mating surfaces on the midsection and power head. Replace the drive shaft housing if deep pits, cracks or broken surfaces are noted.

Power Head Removal (9.9 and 15 hp Models)

1. Drain the engine as described in Chapter Four.
2. Remove the dipstick (1, **Figure 81**). Remove the bolts and nuts and remove the covers from the port and starboard side of the drive shaft housing.
3. On remote control models, perform the following:
   a. Disconnect the throttle and shift cables.
   b. Disconnect the battery cables from the battery and the engine.
   c. Disconnect the remote control harness from the engine harness.
4. On tiller control models, perform the following:

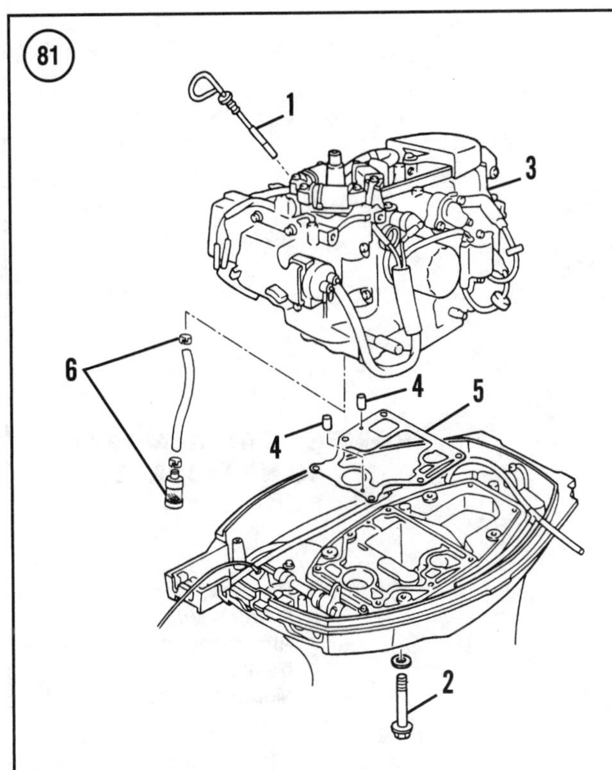

POWER HEAD REMOVAL (9.9 AND 15 HP MODELS)

1. Dipstick
2. Mounting bolt
3. Power head
4. Alignment pins
5. Gasket
6. Oil pickup tube

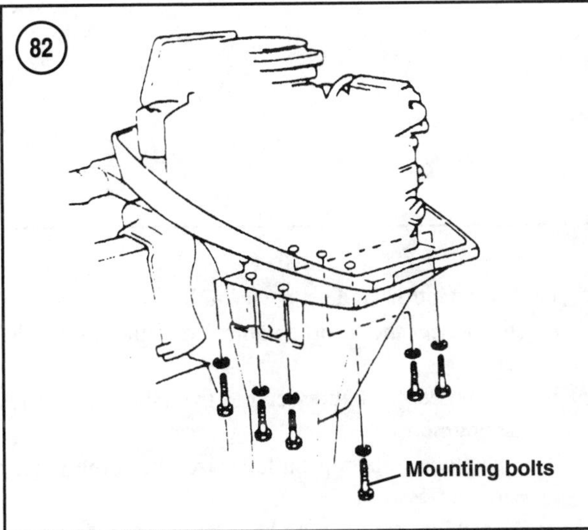

a. Disconnect the throttle cables from the throttle lever.
b. Disconnect the battery cables if so equipped from the battery and the engine.
c. Disconnect the stop button wires from the engine wire harness.
d. Disconnect the oil pressure warning light from the engine wire harness.
e. Disconnect the choke linkage.
f. Disconnect the neutral start switch and starter switch leads on electric start models.

5. Remove the gearcase following the instructions in Chapter Nine.

6. Disconnect the fuel supply hose.

7. On manual start models, remove the manual starter and disconnect the neutral start mechanism following the instructions in Chapter Ten.

8. On electric start models, remove the flywheel cover following the instructions in this chapter.

9. Remove all six engine mounting bolts and washers (**Figure 82**) then lift the power head from the midsection. Place the power head on a suitable work surface.

10. Remove the power head gasket (5, **Figure 81**) from the midsection or bottom of the power head. On 9.9 hp (serial No. OH000057-prior) and 15 hp models, remove the additional gasket and deflector plate from the midsection.

11. Place clean shop towels in the midsection openings to prevent contaminants from entering the oil pan. Carefully scrape all gasket material from the power head mounting surface.

12. Inspect the mating surfaces on the midsection and power head for pits or damage. Replace damaged or de-

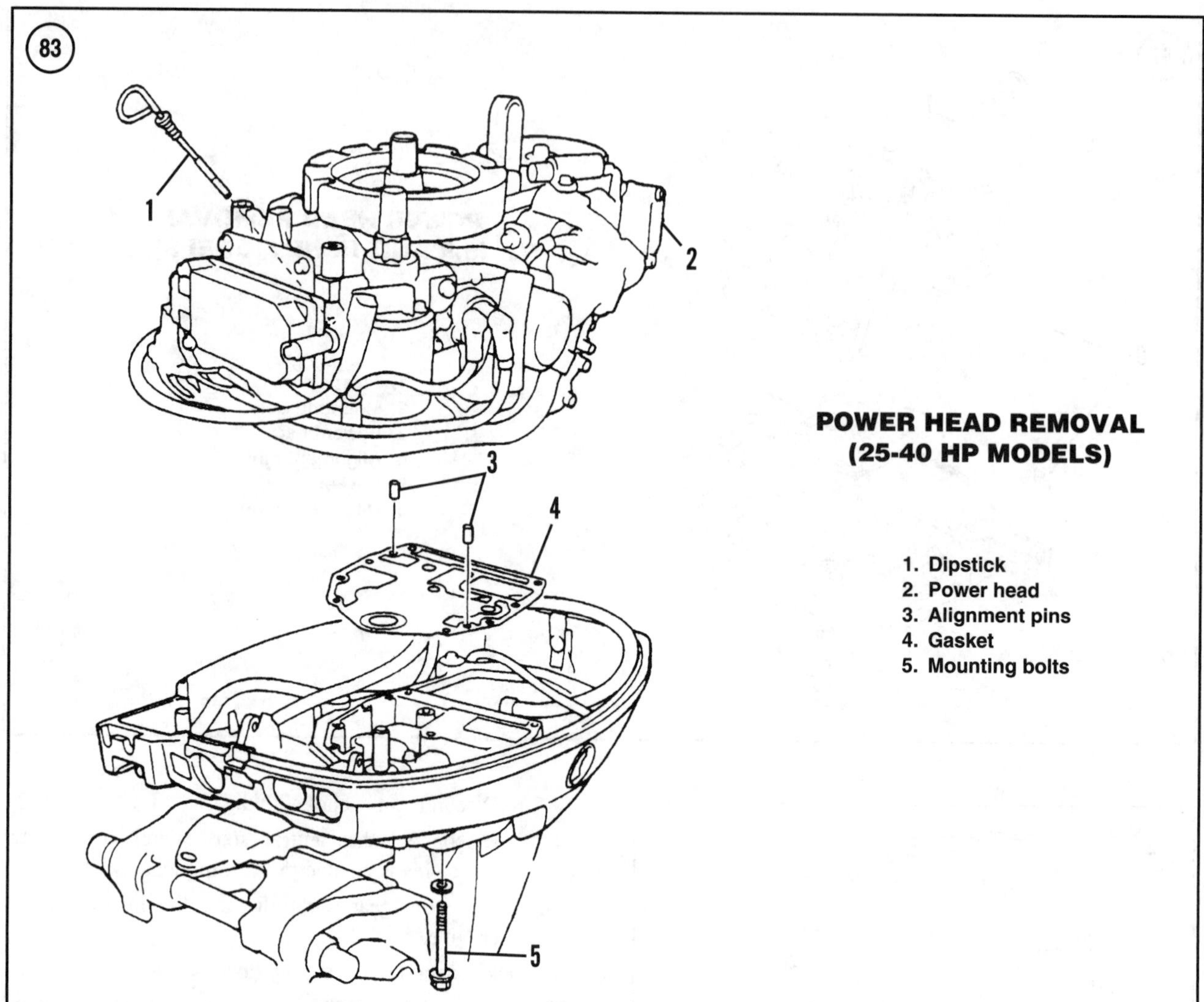

fective components. Oil and water leakage is likely if these surfaces are damaged.

Power Head Removal (25-40 hp Models)

1. Remove the covers from the port and starboard sides of the drive shaft housing.
2. Drain the engine following as described in Chapter Four.
3. Remove the dipstick (1, **Figure 83**).
4. On remote control models, perform the following:
   a. Disconnect the throttle and shift cables.
   b. Disconnect the battery cables from the battery and engine.
   c. Disconnect the remote control harness from the engine harness.
5. On tiller control models, perform the following:
   a. Disconnect the throttle cables from the throttle lever.
   b. Disconnect the battery cables from the battery then the engine.
   c. Disconnect the stop button wires from the engine wire harness.
   d. Disconnect the warning horn wires from the engine wire harness.
   e. Disconnect the neutral start switch and starter switch leads on electric start models.
6. Remove the gearcase following the instructions in Chapter Nine.
7. Disconnect the fuel supply hose.
8. On manual start models, remove the manual starter and disconnect the neutral start mechanism following the instructions in Chapter Ten.

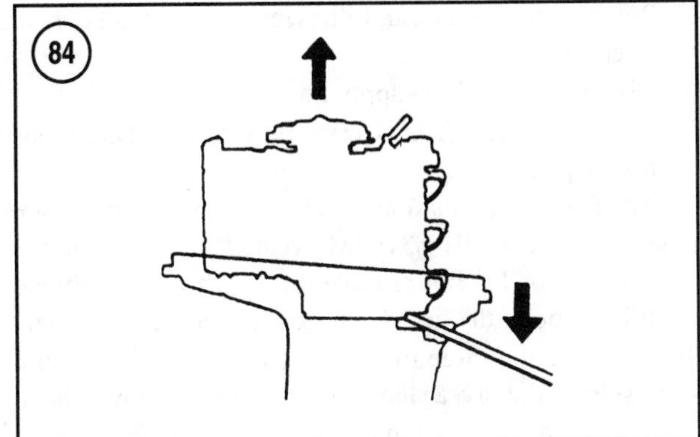

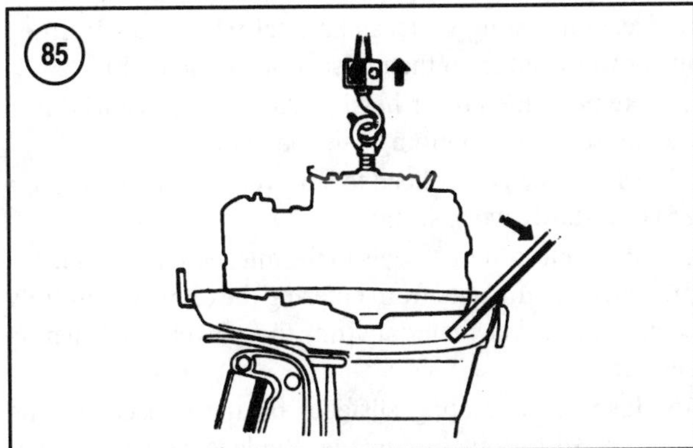

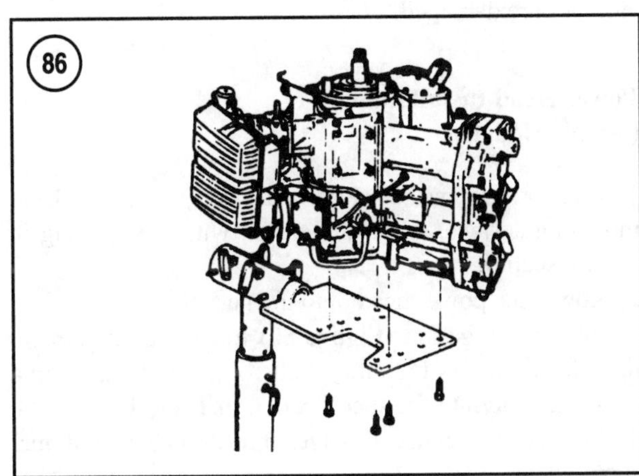

9. On electric start models, remove the flywheel cover following the instructions in this chapter.

10. Remove all eight engine mounting bolts and washers (5, **Figure 83**). Pry the power head loose from the midsection (**Figure 84**).

11. Attach a suitable overhead hoist to then lifting hook. Using a block of wood, keep the power head and midsection mating surfaces parallel while slowly lifting the power head from the midsection (**Figure 85**).

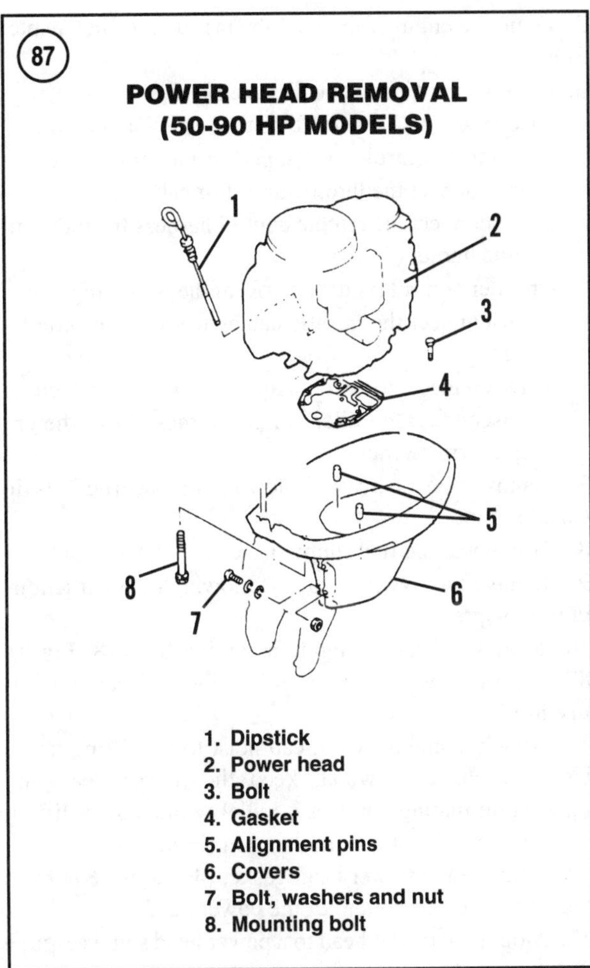

1. Dipstick
2. Power head
3. Bolt
4. Gasket
5. Alignment pins
6. Covers
7. Bolt, washers and nut
8. Mounting bolt

12. Remove the power head gasket (4, **Figure 83**) from the midsection or bottom of the power head.

13. Mount the power head to a power head stand (**Figure 86**) or a sturdy work surface.

14. Place clean shop towels in the midsection openings to prevent contaminants from entering the oil pan. Carefully scrape all gasket material from the power head mating surfaces.

15. Inspect the mating surfaces on the midsection and power head for pits or damage. Replace damaged or defective components. Oil and water leakage is likely if these surfaces are damaged.

Power Head Removal (50 hp Models)

1. Remove the bolt, washer and nut (7, **Figure 87**) and pull the covers from the port and starboard sides of the drive shaft housing.

2. Drain the engine following the instructions in Chapter Four.
3. Remove the dipstick (1, **Figure 87**).
4. Disconnect both cables from the battery and engine.
5. On remote control models, perform the following:
   a. Disconnect the throttle and shift cables.
   b. Disconnect the remote control harness from the engine harness.
6. On tiller control models, perform the following:
   a. Disconnect the throttle cables from the throttle lever.
   b. Disconnect the shift linkage from the shift selector.
   c. Disconnect the tiller control harness from the engine wire harness
7. Remove the gearcase following the instructions in Chapter Nine.
8. Disconnect the fuel supply hose.
9. Remove the flywheel cover following the instructions in this chapter.
10. Remove all eight engine mounting bolts (8, **Figure 87**). Pry the power head loose from the midsection (**Figure 84**).
11. Attach a suitable overhead hoist to the lifting hook. Using a block of wood, keep the power head and midsection mating surfaces parallel while slowly lifting the power head from the midsection (**Figure 85**).
12. Remove the power head gasket (4, **Figure 87**) from the midsection or bottom of the power head.
13. Mount the power head to a power head stand (**Figure 86**) or a sturdy work surface.
14. Place clean shop towels in the midsection openings to prevent contaminants from entering the oil pan. Carefully scrape all gasket material from the power head mating surface.
15. Inspect the mating surfaces on the midsection and power head for pits or damage. Replace damaged or defective components. Oil and water leakage is likely if these surfaces are damaged.

Power Head Removal (75 and 90 hp Models)

1. Remove the bolt, washer and nut (7, **Figure 87**) then pull the covers from the port and starboard sides of the drive shaft housing.
2. Drain the engine following the instructions in Chapter Four.
3. Remove the dipstick (1, **Figure 87**).
4. Disconnect both cables from the battery and engine.
5. Disconnect the throttle and shift cables. Disconnect the remote control harness from the engine harness.
6. Remove the gearcase following the instructions in Chapter Nine.
7. Disconnect the fuel supply hose.
8. Remove the flywheel cover following the instructions in this chapter.
9. Attach the combination flywheel removal/ lifting tool (Mercury part No. 91-83164M) to the flywheel using the included bolts. Do not remove the flywheel nut. Thread the lifting hook fully into the threaded opening of the tool.
10. Remove the three mounting nuts and washers from each side of the drive shaft housing. Pry the power head loose from the midsection (**Figure 84**).
11. Attach a suitable overhead hoist to then lifting hook. Using a block of wood, keep the power head and midsection mating surfaces parallel while slowly lifting the power head from the midsection (**Figure 85**).
12. Remove the power head gasket (4, **Figure 87**) from the midsection or bottom of the power head.
13. Mount the power head to a power head stand (**Figure 86**) or a sturdy work surface.
14. Place clean shop towels in the midsection openings to prevent contaminants from entering the oil pan. Carefully scrape all gasket material from the power head mating surfaces.
15. Inspect the mating surfaces on the midsection and power head for pits or damage. Replace damaged or defective components. Oil or water leakage is likely if these surfaces are damaged.

Power Head Installation (4-6 hp Models)

1. Place a new gasket (**Figure 80**) on the power head mounting surface. Align the gasket with the opening in the midsection.
2. Lower the power head onto the gasket.
3. Inspect the gasket (**Figure 80**) for proper alignment, then install the six mounting bolts. Tighten the bolts in a crossing pattern to the specification in **Table 1**.
4. Connect the choke linkage, throttle cables and fuel supply hoses.
5. Connect the stop button wires, battery cables if so equipped and oil pressure warning light wires.
6. Install the gearcase following the instructions in Chapter Nine.
7. Install the manual starter and connect the neutral start mechanism following the instructions in Chapter Ten.
8. Fill the power head with oil following the instructions in Chapter Four.
9. Perform all applicable adjustments following the instructions in Chapter Five.

Power Head Installation (9.9 and 15 hp Models)

1. Remove the shop towels from the openings in the midsection. Look into the oil pan and check for contamination. Flush the pan as required.
2. Install both aligning pins (4, **Figure 81**) into their holes in the midsection.
3. Install the power head gasket and plate as follows:
   a. On 9.9 hp (serial No. OH000058-on), install the power head gasket (5, **Figure 81**) onto the midsection. Align the pins with their holes in the gasket. Ensure the dipstick and pickup tube (1 and 6, **Figure 81**) openings in the gasket match the openings in the midsection.
   b. On 9.9 hp (serial No. OH000057-prior) and 15 hp models, install the first gasket (5, **Figure 81**) onto the aligning pins. Align the metal deflector plate with the gasket and seat it against the gasket. Align the second gasket with the deflector plate and seat it against the plate. Align the dipstick and pickup tube (1 and 6, **Figure 81**) openings in the gasket with the openings in the midsection.
4. Align the oil pickup tube (6, **Figure 81**) with its opening in the gasket while slowly lowering the power head onto the midsection.
5. Align the pins with their openings in the bottom of the power head.
6. Install the six mounting bolts and washers (**Figure 82**) into the power head. Tighten the bolts in a crossing pattern to the specification in **Table 1**.
7. Install the covers on the port and starboard sides of the drive shaft housing. Securely tighten the cover bolts. Install the oil dipstick (1, **Figure 81**).
8. On electric start models, install the flywheel cover following the instructions in this chapter.
9. On manual start models, install the manual starter and connect the neutral start mechanism (Chapter Ten).
10. On remote control models, perform the following:
    a. Connect the throttle and shift cables.
    b. Connect the battery cables to the engine and battery.
    c. Connect the remote control harness to the engine harness.
11. On tiller control models, perform the following:
    a. Connect the throttle cables to the throttle lever.
    b. Connect the battery cables to the engine then the battery
    c. Connect the stop button wires to the engine wire harness.
    d. Connect the oil pressure warning light to the engine wire harness.
    e. Connect the choke linkage to the carburetor.
    f. Connect the neutral start switch and starter switch leads on electric start models.
12. Connect the fuel supply hose.
13. Install the gearcase (Chapter Nine).
14. Fill the oil pan with oil (Chapter Four).
15. Perform all applicable adjustments (Chapter Five).

Power Head Installation (25-40 hp Models)

1. Remove the shop towels from the openings in the midsection. Look into the oil pan and check for contamination. Flush the pan as required.
2. Install both aligning pins (3, **Figure 83**) into their holes in the midsection.
3. Install the power head gasket and plate as follows:
4. Place the power head gasket (4, **Figure 83**) onto the midsection. Align the pins (3, **Figure 83**) with their holes in the gasket. Ensure the openings in the gasket and midsection align.
5. Using an overhead hoist, lift the power head from the work surface. Keep the power head mating surface parallel with the midsection mating surface while lowering the power head onto the midsection.
6. Align the pins with their openings at the bottom of the power head.
7. Install the eight mounting bolts and washers (5, **Figure 83**) into the power head. Tighten the bolts in a crossing pattern to the specification in **Table 1**.
8. Install the covers on the port and starboard sides of the drive shaft housing. Securely tighten the cover bolts. Install the dipstick (1, **Figure 83**).
9. On electric start models, install the flywheel cover following the instructions in this chapter.
10. On manual start models, install the manual starter and connect the neutral start mechanism (Chapter Ten).
11. On remote control models, perform the following:
    a. Connect the throttle and shift cables.
    b. Connect the battery cables to the engine and battery.
    c. Connect the remote control harness to the engine harness.
12. On tiller control models, perform the following:
    a. Connect the throttle cables to the throttle lever.
    b. Connect the battery cables to the engine and the battery if so equipped.
    c. Connect the stop button to the engine wire harness.
    d. Connect the warning horn to the engine wire harness.
    e. Connect the neutral start switch and starter switch leads on electric start models.
13. Connect the fuel supply hose.
14. Install the gearcase (Chapter Nine).

15. Fill the oil pan with oil (Chapter Four).
16. Perform all applicable adjustments (Chapter Five).

Power Head Installation (50 hp Models)

1. Remove the shop towels from the openings in the midsection. Look into the oil pan and check for contamination. Flush the pan as required.
2. Install both aligning pins (5, **Figure 87**) into their holes in the midsection.
3. Place the power head gasket (4, **Figure 87**) onto the midsection. Align the openings in the gasket and midsection.
4. Using an overhead hoist, lift the power head from the work surface. Keep the power head mating surface parallel to the midsection mating surface while lowering the power head onto the midsection.
5. Align the pins with their openings at the bottom of the power head.
6. Install the eight mounting bolts (8, **Figure 87**) into the power head. Tighten the bolts in a crossing pattern to the specification in **Table 1**.
7. Install the covers on the port and starboard sides of the drive shaft housing. Securely tighten the bolts (7, **Figure 87**). Install the oil dipstick (1, **Figure 87**).
8. Install the flywheel cover following the instructions in this chapter.
9. On remote control models, perform the following:
   a. Connect the throttle and shift cables.
   b. Connect the remote control harness to the engine harness.
10. On tiller control models, perform the following:
   a. Connect the throttle cables to the throttle lever.
   b. Connect the shift linkage to the shift selector.
   c. Connect the tiller control harness to the engine wire harness.
11. Connect the battery cables to the engine and battery.
12. Connect the fuel supply hose.
13. Install the gearcase (Chapter Nine).
14. Fill the oil pan with oil (Chapter Four).
15. Perform all applicable adjustments (Chapter Five).

Power Head Installation (75 and 90 hp Models)

1. Remove the shop towels from the openings in the midsection. Look into the oil pan and check for contamination. Flush the pan as required.
2. Install both aligning pins into their holes in the midsection.

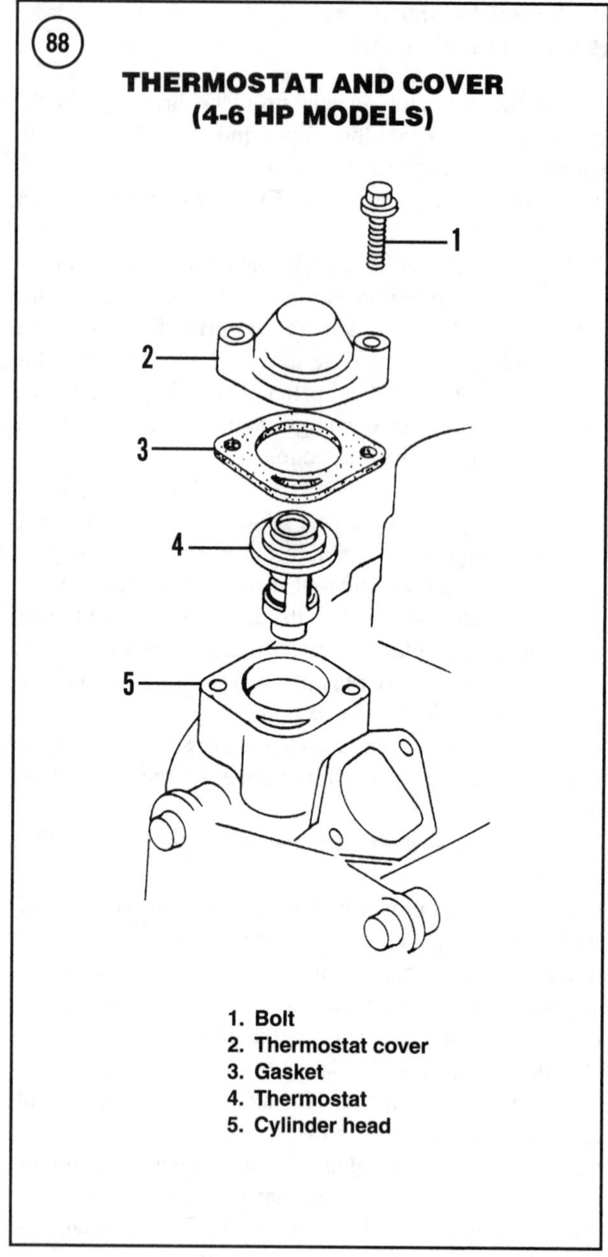

1. Bolt
2. Thermostat cover
3. Gasket
4. Thermostat
5. Cylinder head

3. Attach the combination flywheel removal tool/lifting hook (Mercury part No. 91-83164M) to the flywheel with the included bolts. Do not remove the flywheel nut. Thread the lifting hook fully into the threaded opening.
4. Place the power head gasket (4, **Figure 87**) onto the midsection. Align the pins (5, **Figure 87**) with their holes in the gasket. Align the openings in the gasket and midsection.
5. Using an overhead hoist, lift the power head from the work surface. Keep the power head mounting surface parallel to the midsection mating surface while lowering the

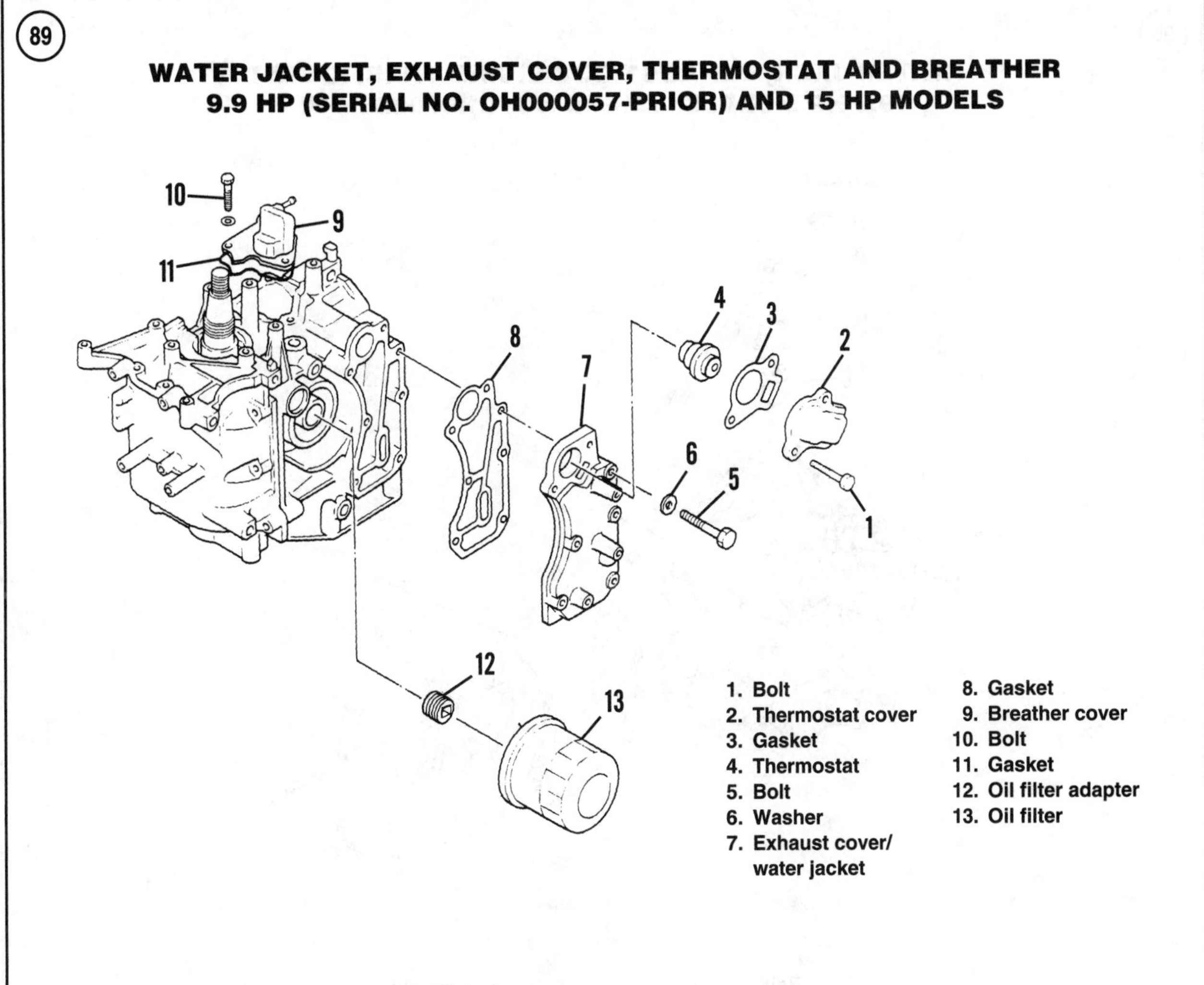

power head onto the midsection. Align the mounting studs with the holes in the midsection.

6. Align the pins with the holes in the bottom of the power head.

7. Install the six mounting washers and nuts onto the mounting studs. Tighten the nuts in a crossing pattern to the specification in **Table 1**.

8. Install the covers on the port and starboard sides of the drive shaft housing. Securely tighten the fasteners (7, **Figure 87**). Install the dipstick (1, **Figure 87**).

9. Install the flywheel cover following the instructions in this chapter.

10. Connect the throttle and shift cables to the power head.

11. Connect the remote control harness to the engine harness.

12. Connect the battery cables to the engine and battery.

13. Connect the fuel supply hose.

14. Install the gearcase (Chapter Nine).

15. Fill the oil pan with oil (Chapter Four).

16. Perform all applicable adjustments (Chapter Five).

Thermostat and Water Pressure Relief Valve

This section provides removal and installation instructions for the thermostat and water pressure relief valve. A water pressure relief valve is used only on 75 and 90 hp models. Thermostats are used on all models. Mounting location for these components vary by model.

On 4-6 hp models, the thermostat is located beneath a cover on the top of the cylinder head (**Figure 88**).

On 9.9 hp (serial No. OH000057-prior) and 15 hp models, the thermostat is located beneath under a cover on the port side water jacket (**Figure 89**).

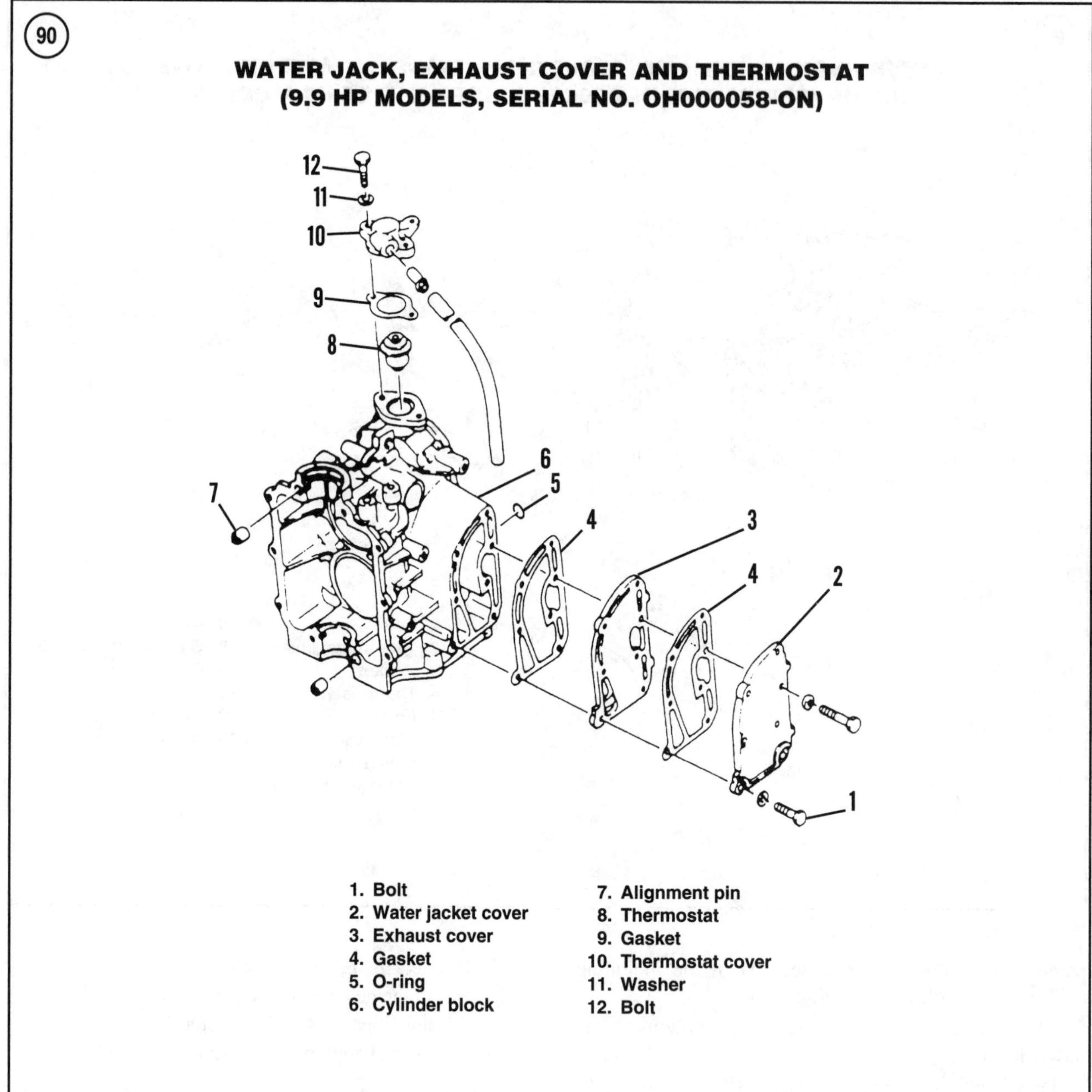

On 9.9 hp models (serial No. OH000058-on), the thermostat is located beneath a cover on the top and rear side of the cylinder block (**Figure 90**).

On 25-50 hp models, the thermostat is located beneath a cover on the port side water jacket (**Figures 91-93**).

On 75 and 90 hp models, the thermostat is located beneath a cover on the top side of the cylinder head (**Figure 20**). The water pressure relief valve is located beneath a cover on the lower side of the starboard water jacket (**Figure 94**).

Thermostat removal

1. Disconnect the cables from the battery if so equipped.
2. On 4-6 hp models, remove the bolt (**Figure 95**) and remove the throttle wheel from the thermostat cover.
3. On 9.9-90 hp models, remove the two bolts from the cover.
4. Lift the thermostat cover from the power head. Carefully tap the cover loose with a rubber mallet if it does not easily pull free.

WATER JACKET, THERMOSTAT AND BREATHER (25 HP MODELS)

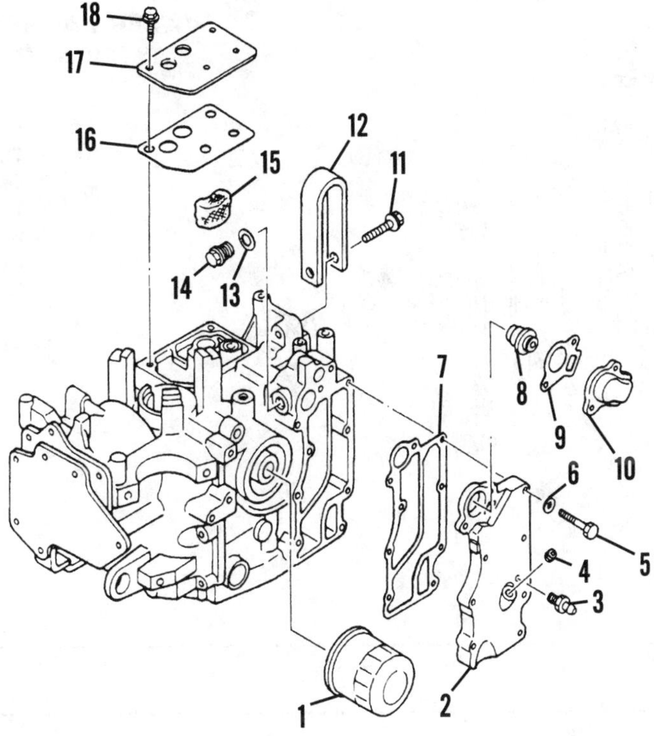

1. Oil filter
2. Exhaust cover/ water jacket
3. Engine temperature sensor
4. Plug
5. Bolt
6. Washer
7. Gasket
8. Thermostat
9. Gasket
10. Thermostat cover
11. Bolt
12. Lifting hook
13. Sealing washer
14. Plug
15. Breather element
16. Gasket
17. Breather plate
18. Bolt

5. Using needlenose pliers, pull the thermostat from the opening.
6. Carefully scrape all gasket material from the thermostat cover and power head. Clean all corrosion, scale or other contamination from the thermostat cover, thermostat and thermostat opening.
7. Test the thermostat as described in Chapter Three.

Thermostat installation

1. Carefully slide the thermostat into the opening with the spring side facing inward. Seat the thermostat against the step in the opening.
2. On 4-6 hp models, install the throttle wheel and bolt (**Figure 95**) onto the thermostat cover.
3. Place a new gasket on the thermostat cover. Slip the bolts through the holes to help retain the gasket.
4. Apply a very light coat of water-resistant grease to the bolt threads and install the cover over the thermostat.
5. Inspect the gasket for correct alignment, then install the bolts. Tighten both bolts evenly to the specification in **Table 1**.
6. Route any hoses attached to the cover away from moving components.
7. Clean the terminals and connect the cables to the battery if so equipped.

92

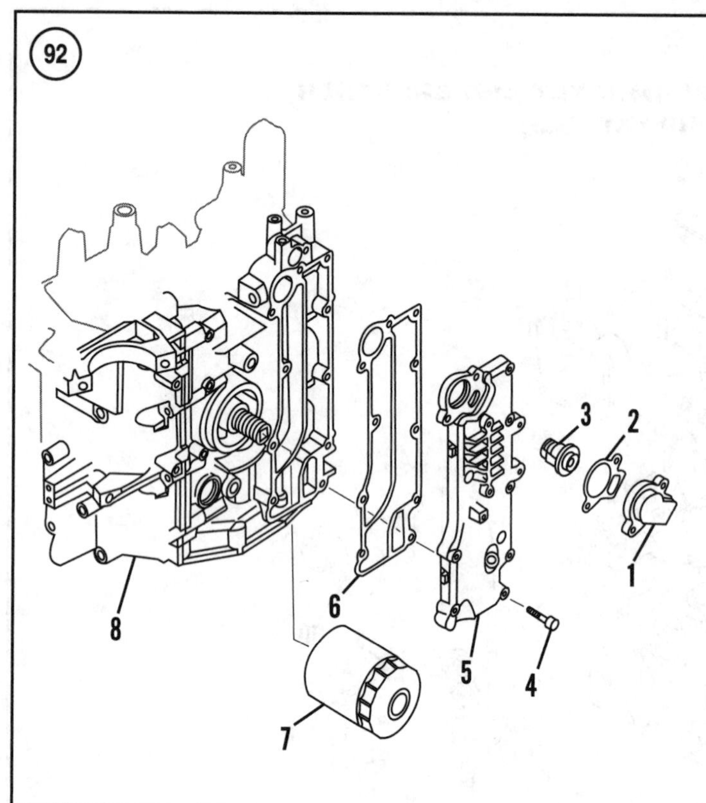

WATER JACKET AND THERMOSTAT (30 AND 40 HP MODELS)

1. Thermostat cover
2. Gasket
3. Thermostat
4. Bolt
5. Exhaust/water jacket
6. Gasket
7. Oil filter
8. Cylinder block

93

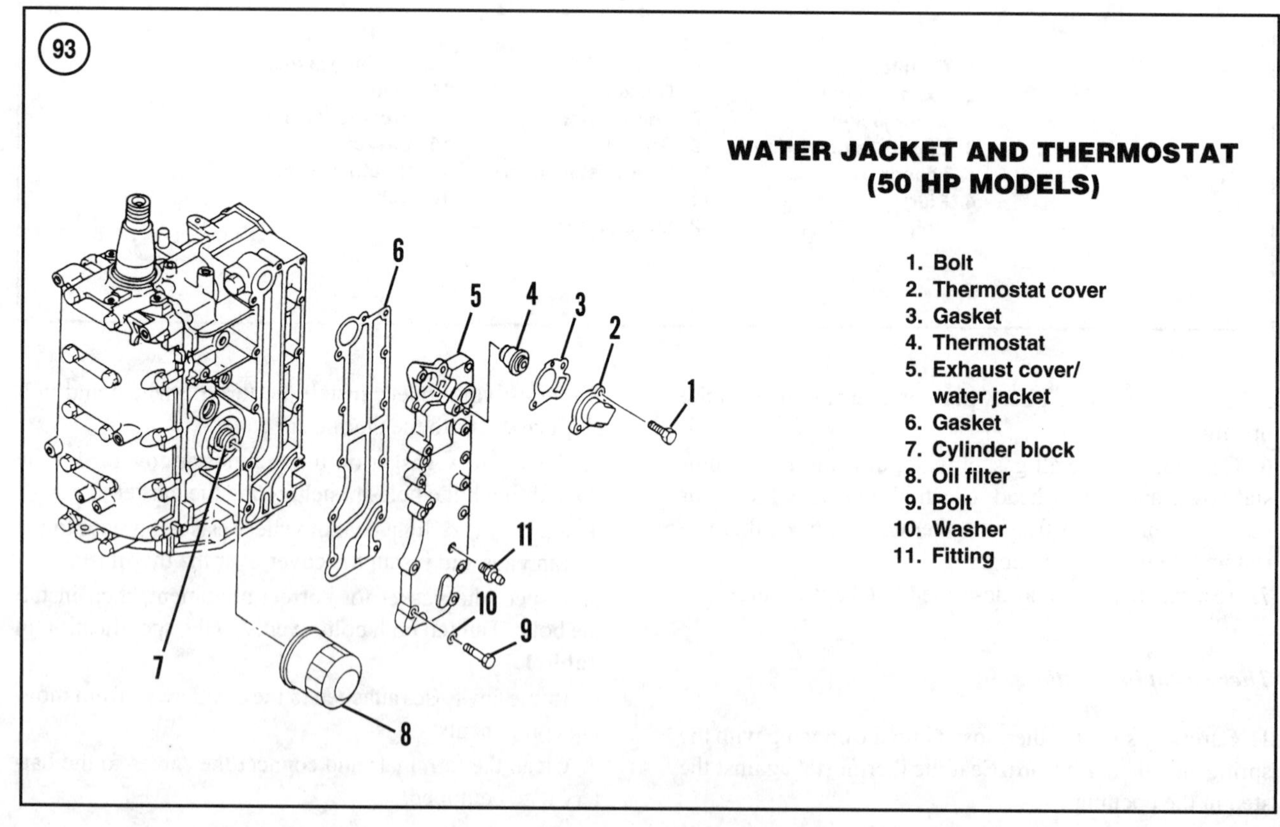

WATER JACKET AND THERMOSTAT (50 HP MODELS)

1. Bolt
2. Thermostat cover
3. Gasket
4. Thermostat
5. Exhaust cover/ water jacket
6. Gasket
7. Cylinder block
8. Oil filter
9. Bolt
10. Washer
11. Fitting

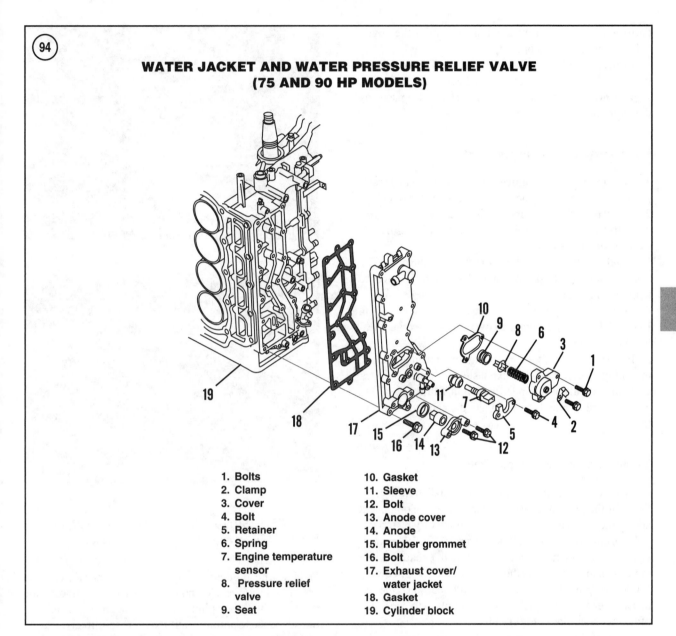

94

WATER JACKET AND WATER PRESSURE RELIEF VALVE (75 AND 90 HP MODELS)

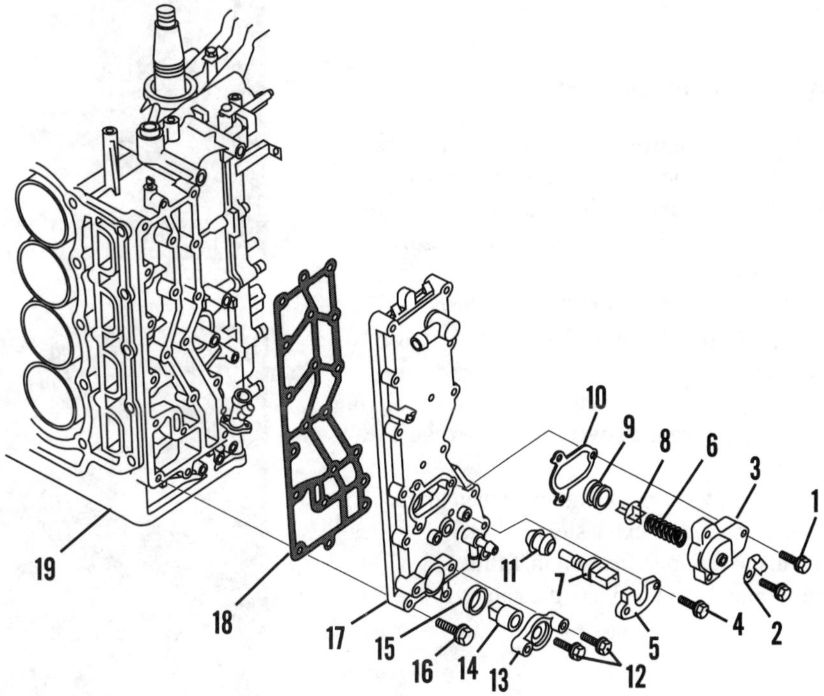

1. Bolts
2. Clamp
3. Cover
4. Bolt
5. Retainer
6. Spring
7. Engine temperature sensor
8. Pressure relief valve
9. Seat
10. Gasket
11. Sleeve
12. Bolt
13. Anode cover
14. Anode
15. Rubber grommet
16. Bolt
17. Exhaust cover/water jacket
18. Gasket
19. Cylinder block

95

Water pressure relief valve removal

1. Disconnect the cables from the battery.

2. Remove both bolts (1, **Figure 94**) and clamp (2), then pull the cover (3) away from the power head. Tap the cover loose with a rubber mallet if it does not easily pull away.

3. Pull the spring and valve (6 and 8, **Figure 94**) from the opening. Carefully pull the seat (9, **Figure 94**) from the exhaust/water jacket cover (17).

4. Carefully scrape all gasket material (10, **Figure 94**) from the cover and exhaust/water jacket cover. Clean all

corrosion, scale or other contamination from the cover, valve, spring, seat and opening.

5. Inspect the valve and seat (8 and 9, **Figure 94**) for worn, broken or missing sections. Inspect the spring (6, **Figure 94**) for corroded or broken surfaces. Replace any defective components.

Water pressure relief valve installation

1. Install the seat (9, **Figure 94**) into the exhaust/water jacket cover. Lock the groove on the seat into the opening.
2. Install one of the X shaped ends of the valve (8, **Figure 94**) into the seat opening. Place the spring (6, **Figure 94**) over the other X shaped end.
3. Install a new gasket (10, **Figure 94**) onto the cover (3). Slide the bolts (1, **Figure 94**) and clamp into the cover to help retain the gasket (10).
4. Align the spring recess in the cover with the spring (6, **Figure 94**) while pushing the cover onto the exhaust/water jacket cover.
5. Inspect the gasket for correct alignment then thread the mounting bolts into the exhaust/water jacket cover. Tighten the bolts to the specification in **Table 1**.
6. Clean the terminals and connect the cables to the battery.

Exhaust Cover and Water Jacket

This section provides removal and installation instructions for the exhaust cover and water jacket. Component appearance, usage and mounting locations vary by model.

On 9.9 hp (serial No. OH000057-prior) and 15 hp models, the combination water jacket and exhaust cover mounts on the port side of the cylinder block (**Figure 89**).

On 9.9 hp models (serial No. OH000058-on), the exhaust cover and water jacket cover mounts to the port side of the cylinder block (**Figure 90**).

On 25-50 hp models, the combination exhaust cover and water jacket cover mounts to the port side of the cylinder block (**Figure 91-93**).

On 75 and 90 hp models, the combination exhaust cover and water jacket cover mounts to the starboard side of the cylinder block (**Figure 94**).

Exhaust/water jacket cover removal

1. Disconnect the cables from the battery if so equipped.
2. On 25-40, 75 and 90 hp models, disconnect the engine temperature sensor from the engine wire harness.
3. On models with a cover-mounted thermostat, remove the thermostat following the instructions in this section.

4. On 75 and 90 hp models, remove the water pressure relief valve following the instructions provided in this section.
5. Note the tightening sequence numbers (**Figure 96**) cast into the cover. Gradually 1/4 turn at a time loosen the cover retaining bolts in the opposite order of the tightening sequence. Continue until the bolts spin freely.
6. Mark the mounting location for each bolt then remove them from the cover.
7. Locate the pry points at the top and bottom of the cover (**Figure 97**). Using a blunt screwdriver, carefully pry water jacket and exhaust cover loose. Lift the cover from the cylinder block (**Figure 98**).
8. Carefully scrape all carbon and gasket material from the cover mating surfaces and exhaust passages. Clean all corrosion, scale or other contamination from the exposed water passages.
9. Inspect the cover for holes or other signs of leakage and distorted or damaged surfaces. Replace the cover if any defects are noted.

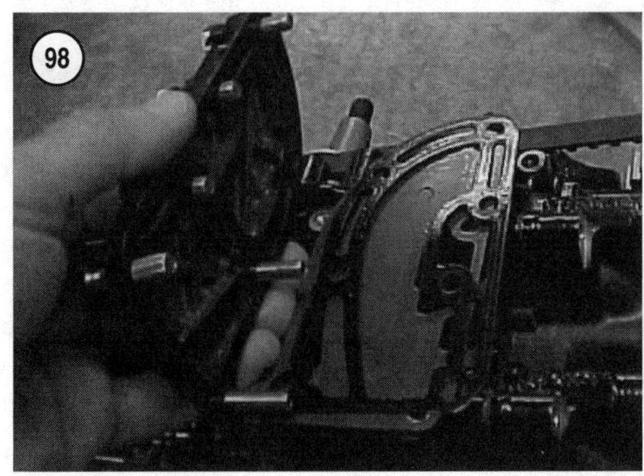

10. Using a properly sized thread chaser, clean all corrosion or contaminants from the threaded holes for the cover mounting bolts. Inspect the threaded holes for damaged threads. Install a thread insert if damaged threads will not clean up with the chaser.

Exhaust/water jacket cover installation

1. Carefully place the cover and new gasket onto the cylinder block.
2. Apply a very light coating of water-resistant grease to the threads then install all mounting bolts finger tight. Inspect the gasket and plate for proper alignment.
3. Tighten the bolts in the sequence cast into the cover to half the tightening torque specification in **Table 1**. Tighten the bolts a second time in sequence to the full tightening torque specification.
4. On 25-40, 75 and 90 hp models, connect the engine wire harness connection to the engine temperature sensor. Route all wires away from moving components.
5. Install the thermostat following the instructions in this section.
6. On 75 and 90 hp models, install the water pressure relief valve following the instructions in this section.
7. Clean the terminals and connect the cables to the battery.
8. Start the engine and inspect the cover for water or exhaust leakage.

Cylinder Block Disassembly and Assembly

Always make notes, drawings and photographs of all external power head components *before* beginning disassembly.

Correct hose and wire routing is important for proper engine operation. An incorrectly routed hose or wire may interfere with linkage movement and result in a dangerous loss of throttle control. Hoses or wires may be damaged if allowed to contact sharp or moving parts. Other components such as fuel pumps can be mounted in two or more positions.

Mark the up and forward direction before removing any components. If possible remove a cluster of components sharing common wires or hoses. This will reduce the time required to disassemble and assemble the power head. This method also reduces the chance of improper connections during assembly.

Use muffin tins or egg cartons to organize the fasteners as they are removed. Mark all fasteners to ensure they are installed in the correct location during assembly.

Disassembly (4-6 hp models)

8

Refer to **Figure 99** to assist with component identification and orientation.

1. Remove the flywheel following the instructions in this chapter.
2. Remove the carburetor and intake manifold following the instructions in Chapter Six.
3. Remove all electrical and ignition components following the instructions in Chapter Seven.
4. Remove the cylinder head following the instructions in this chapter.
5. Place the power head on a work surface with the flywheel side facing down. Remove both bolts and pull the lower oil seal housing from the power head. Remove the gasket from the cylinder block or seal housing. Clamp the oil seal housing in a vice with soft jaws. Using a slide hammer, pull the seals from the housing.
6. Loosen all nine bolts (1, **Figure 99**) retaining the oil pan to the cylinder block following a crossing pattern. Remove the bolts when they spin freely. Locate the pry points (**Figure 97**) near the mating surfaces. Using two blunt tip screwdrivers, carefully pry the oil pan from the cylinder block. Remove then discard the oil pan gasket (11, **Figure 99**).
7. Remove the oil pump following the instructions under *Cylinder Head* in this chapter. Remove the bolts and clamps and lift the oil pickup tube and screen (17, **Figure 99**) along with the pressure relief valve components (12-16) from the oil pan. Carefully pry the lower crankshaft seal (35, **Figure 99**) from the oil pan. Remove the thrust washer (19, **Figure 99**) from the crankshaft (24).
8. Pull the camshaft (22, **Figure 99**) from the cylinder block (38). Pull both tappets (23, **Figure 99**) from the cylinder block. Inspect and measure the camshaft (**Figure**

CYLINDER BLOCK
(4-6 HP MODELS)

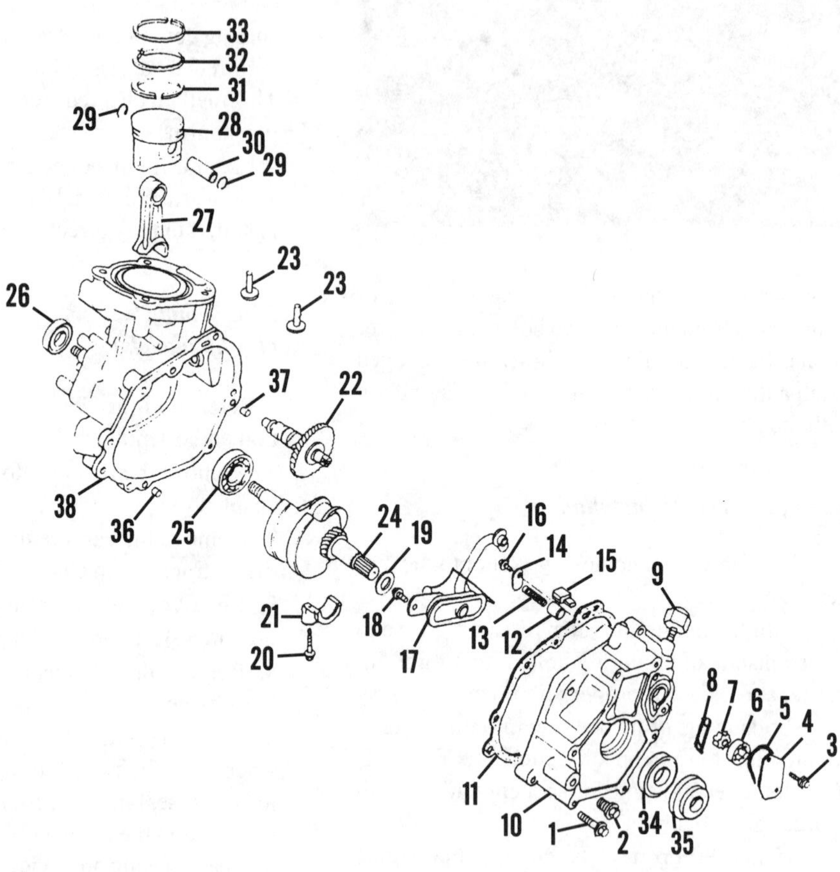

1. Oil pan retaining bolts
2. Plug
3. Bolt
4. Cover
5. O-ring
6. Outer rotor
7. Inner rotor
8. Drive pin
9. Oil pressure switch
10. Oil pan
11. Oil pan gakset
12. Oil pressure relief valve
13. Spring
14. Plate
15. Plunger
16. Bolt
17. Oil pickup tube
18. Bolt
19. Thrust washer
20. Connecting rod bolt
21. Connecting rod cap
22. Camshaft
23. Tappets
24. Crankshaft
25. Ball bearing
26. Upper crankshaft seal
27. Connecting rod
28. Piston
29. Locking ring
30. Piston pin
31. Oil control ring
32. Second compression ring
33. First compression ring
34. Oil seal
35. Oil seal and spacer
36. Alignment pin
37. Alignment pin
38. Cylinder block

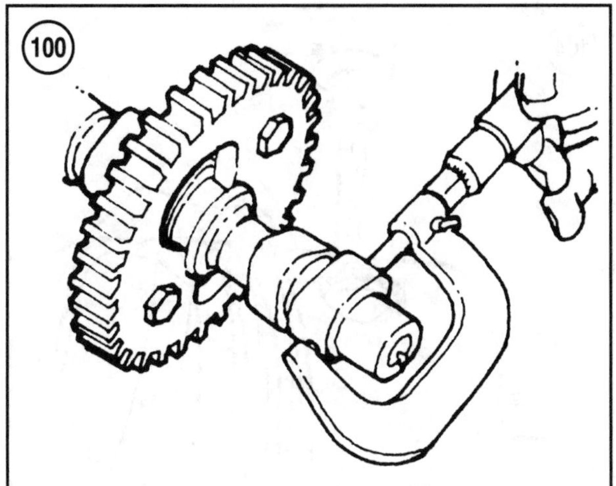

(100)

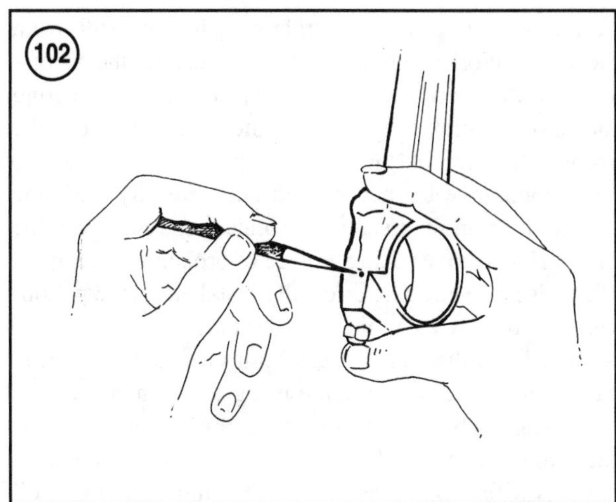

(102)

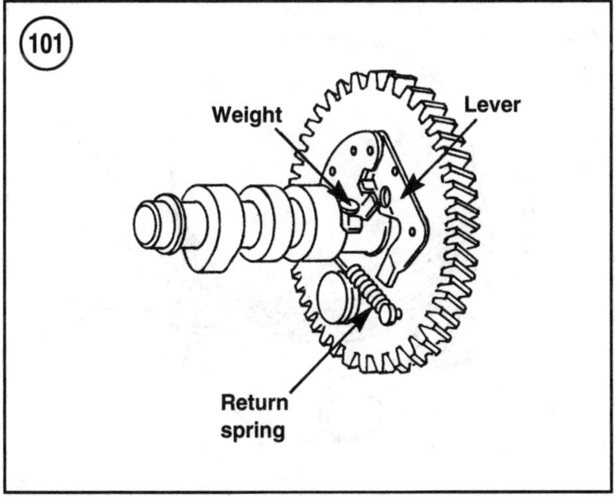

(101)

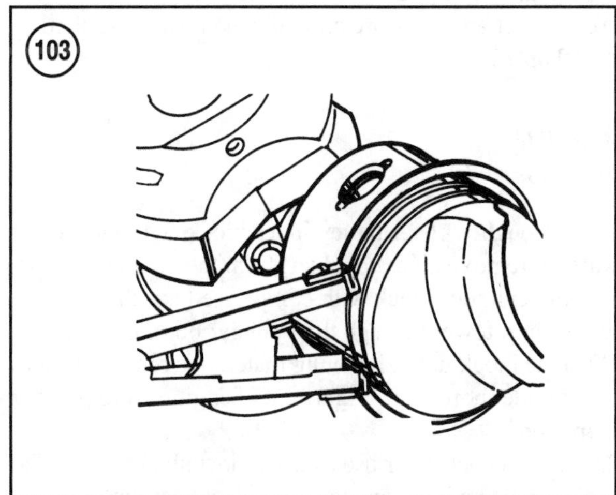

(103)

100) and tappets as described under *Cylinder Head* from this chapter.

9. Inspect the spring, weight and lever (**Figure 101**) of the compression relief mechanism for free movement. Replace any binding, worn or damaged components.

10. Mark the side of the connecting rod and rod cap (**Figure 102**) prior to removal. Slowly loosen 1/4 turn at a time both connecting rod bolts (20, **Figure 99**). Remove the bolts and lightly tap the rod cap (21, **Figure 99**) to free it from the connecting rod.

11. Push up on the lower end of the connecting rod to remove the piston and rod (27 and 28, **Figure 99**) from the cylinder block.

12. Thread the flywheel nut onto the crankshaft just enough to protect the threads. Place the cylinder block on the table of a press with the threaded end of the crankshaft facing up. Support the crankshaft while lightly pressing on the crankshaft. Continue until the crankshaft is free from the cylinder block.

13. Carefully pry the upper seal (26, **Figure 99**) from the cylinder block.

14. Remove the ball bearing (25, **Figure 99**) from the cylinder block only if it must be replaced. Refer to *Inspection* in this chapter to determine the need for replacement. Remove the bearing as follows:

a. Engage the jaws of a slide hammer or suitable puller with the inner bore of the bearing.
b. Using short hammer strokes, pull the bearing from the cylinder block.

15. Remove the two screws from the top side of the cylinder block, then lift the breather cover and gasket from the block. Pull the breather tubes and washers from the opening.

16. Using a ring expander, remove both compression rings (32 and 33, **Figure 99**) from the piston (**Figure 103**).

Carefully remove the oil control ring (31, **Figure 99**) from the piston. Work carefully to prevent damage to the piston.

17. Mark the top side of both the piston and connecting rod. Using a pick or scribe, pry the lock rings from the grooves (**Figure 104**) in the piston pin bore.

18. Support the connecting rod and carefully push the piston pin from the piston and connecting rod. Clean the piston ring grooves using a piece of broken ring (**Figure 105**). Use only the ring originally installed on the piston.

19. Thoroughly clean the cylinder block with hot soapy water. Clean other components using clean solvent. Clean carbon from the piston dome using a stiff non metallic parts cleaning brush and solvent. Blow air through all passages to remove all debris, water or solvent. Dry all components with compressed air. Apply a light coating of oil to the piston, piston pin, cylinder bore, bearings, connecting rod and crankshaft to prevent corrosion.

20. Inspect and measure all components as described in this chapter.

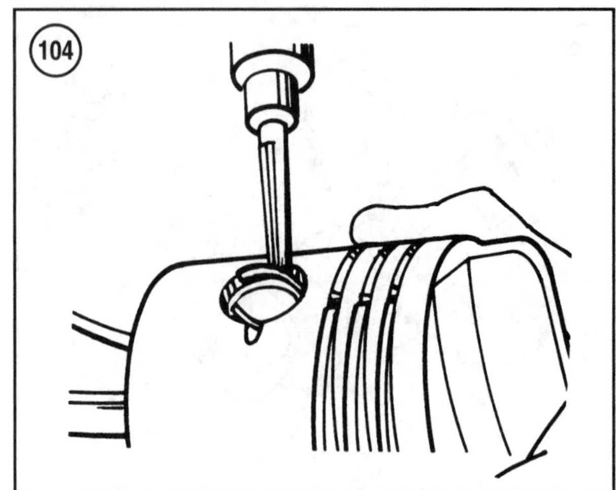

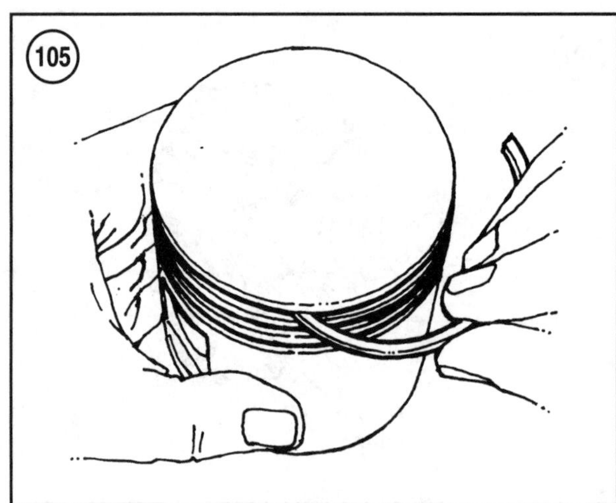

Assembly (4-6 hp models)

1. Thoroughly clean the cylinder block with hot soapy water to remove all material left from the honing process. Dry the cylinder block with compressed air, then wipe a white shop towel through the cylinder bore. Continue to clean the block until all honing material is removed. Coat the cylinder bore with a light coat of engine oil to prevent corrosion.

2. Select a socket for use as a seal installation tool. The socket must be large enough to contact near the outer diameter of the upper crankshaft seal (26, **Figure 99**) yet not contact the seal bore during installation. Install the seal as follows:
   a. Place the new seal into the opening with the lip or spring side facing toward the oil pan.
   b. Gently drive the seal into the opening until it bottoms.
   c. Apply engine oil to the seal lip.

3. Use a large diameter socket or section of tubing as a bearing installation tool. The tool must be large enough to contact the outer race of the ball bearing (25, **Figure 99**) yet not contact the cylinder block during bearing installation. Install the bearing and crankshaft as follows:
   a. Lubricate the bearing and its bore in the cylinder block with engine oil.
   b. Place the new ball bearing into its bore with the numbered side facing out.
   c. Position the cylinder block on the table of a press.
   d. Press the bearing into the bore until it seats in the bore.
   e. Pass the threaded side of the crankshaft through the bearing.
   f. Place a straightedge across the oil pan gasket surface to assist with gauging the depth of crankshaft installation.
   g. Press on the drive shaft side of the crankshaft until the timing gear surface is approximately 0.032 in. (0.7 mm) below the oil pan gasket surface.

4. Assemble the piston and rod assembly as follows:
   a. Align the piston pin bores in the piston and connecting rod. The 3H6 mark on the connecting rod must face up. The triangle mark on the piston must face toward the camshaft when the piston is installed.
   b. Lubricate the piston pin bores with engine oil, then push the piston pin into the piston and connecting rod.
   c. Using needlenose pliers, install new C type lock rings into the groove on each side of the piston pin

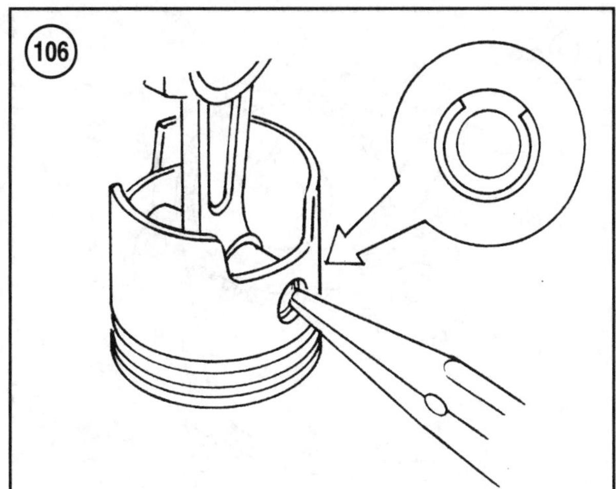

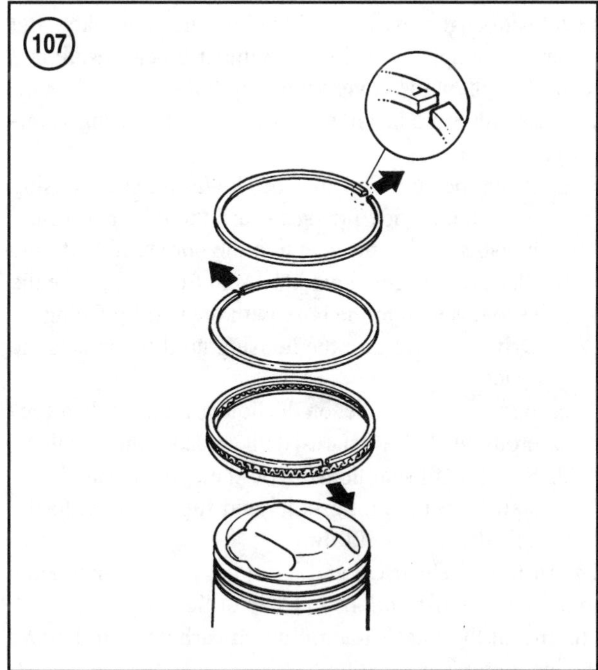

bore (**Figure 106**). Ensure the lock rings span the notched part of the groove and firmly seats in the groove.

d. Carefully install the new rails and spacers of the oil ring onto the lower ring groove as indicated in **Figure 107**.

e. Identify the lower compression ring (32, **Figure 99**) by the 2N or N mark on the ring. This mark must face up. Using a ring expander, open the new ring just enough to pass over the piston crown. Release the ring into the middle groove.

f. Identify the upper compression ring (33, **Figure 99**) by the 1N mark on the ring. This mark must face up.

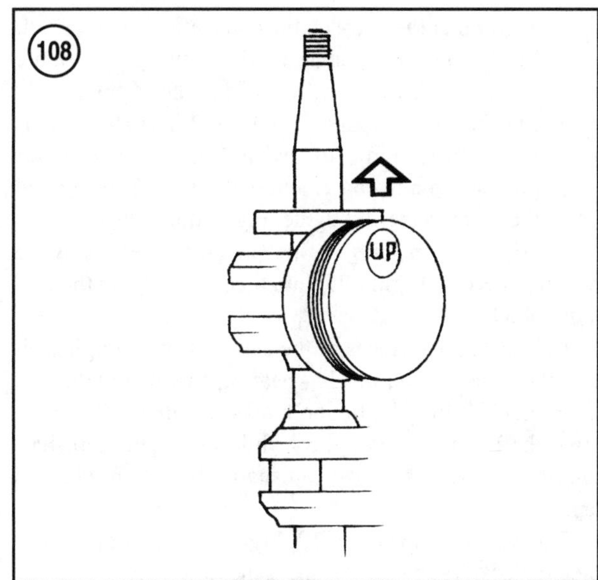

Install the new ring into the top ring groove as described in substep e.

g. Align the ring gaps as indicated in **Figure 107**. Ensure no ring gap aligns with other ring gaps or the piston pin bores.

h. Coat the piston and rings with a light coat of engine oil.

5. Install the piston and rods onto the crankshaft as follows:

a. Slide a ring compressor (or Mercury part No. FT2997) over the piston and rings. Tighten the compressor enough to fully compress the rings yet allow the piston to slide within the compressor. Coat the cylinder walls and crankshaft surfaces with engine oil.

b. Install the connecting rod and piston into the cylinder block from the cylinder head side.

c. Ensure the up mark on the piston and rod face toward the flywheel side of the crankshaft (**Figure 108**). Rotate the crankshaft until the connecting rod bearing surface is closest to the piston.

d. Hold the ring compressor firmly against the cylinder block then gently drive the piston into the bore. Stop and check for adequate ring compression if any resistance is detected.

e. Guide the connecting rod to its bearing surface on the crankshaft. Align the mark on the connecting rod and rod cap and install the cap on the rod. Thread the new rod bolts through the rod cap and into the connecting rod. Do not tighten the bolts at this time.

f. Verify that the mark on the connecting rod face out. Verify that the triangle mark on the piston dome faces toward the camshaft side of the engine.
g. Evenly tighten both rod bolts (20, **Figure 99**) to half the specification provided in **Table 1**. Check for proper cap and rod alignment, then evenly tighten the bolts to the full tightening torque.

6. Lubricate them with engine oil then carefully place both tappets (23, **Figure 99**) into their openings in the cylinder block.
7. Lubricate all surfaces of the camshaft with engine oil and place the camshaft into its bearing bore within the cylinder block. Align the timing marks (**Figure 109**) on the crankshaft and camshaft gears while sliding the camshaft into the block. Ensure the camshaft lobes align with the tappets.
8. Place the thrust washer (19, **Figure 99**) over the end of the crankshaft and seat it against the timing gear.
9. Use a socket as a seal installation tool. The socket must be large enough in diameter to contact near the outer edge of the crankshaft seal (34, **Figure 99**) yet not contact the seal bore the oil pan during installation. Install the seal as follows:
a. Place the new seal into the bore with the lip side facing toward the crankshaft side of the oil pan.
b. Carefully drive the seal into the bore until it bottoms.
c. Apply engine oil to the seal surface and the crankshaft bearing surface in the oil pan.

10. Install the pickup tube, screen clamps and pressure relief valves in the oil pan. Securely tighten the clamp screws. Tighten the oil pressure relief valve bolt to the specification in **Table 1**.
11. Install the oil pan as follows:
a. Clean the oil pan mating surfaces.
b. Ensure the locating pins (36 and 37, **Figure 99**) are in position on the cylinder block and place the new gasket (11, **Figure 99**) on the cylinder block.
c. Guide the crankshaft and camshafts into their openings while installing the oil pan to the cylinder block. Check for proper gasket alignment, then thread the bolts (1, **Figure 99**) through the pan and into the cylinder block. Do not tighten the bolts at this time.
d. Tighten the bolts in a crossing pattern to 1/3 of the torque specification in **Table 1**. Again tighten the bolts in a crossing pattern to 2/3 of the specification. Tighten the bolts a third time to the full tightening torque specification.

12. Install the oil pump components following the instructions provided under *Cylinder Head Repair* from this chapter.

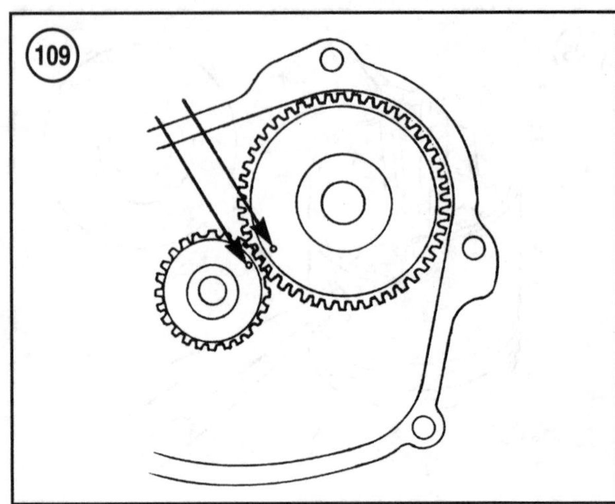

13. Position the washers, breather tubes, gasket and cover on the upper side of the cylinder block. Install and securely tighten the cover mounting bolts.
14. Assemble and install the lower oil seal housing as follows:
a. Place the first seal into the lower oil seal housing with the lip side facing toward the tube part of the housing. Drive the seal into the bore until bottoms.
b. Place the spacer against the seal first seal. Place the second seal into the bore with the seal lip facing in. Drive the seal into the housing until it contacts the spacer.
c. Install a new gasket on the housing and apply a generous bead of water-resistant grease to the seal lips.
d. Seat the oil seal housing on the cylinder block. Install both mounting bolts and tighten them to the specification in **Table 1**.

15. Install all electrical and ignition system components following the instructions in Chapter Seven.
16. Install the intake manifold and carburetor following the instructions in Chapter Six.
17. Install the cylinder head following the instructions in this chapter.
18. Install the flywheel following the instructions in this chapter.

Disassembly (9.9-90 hp models)

Refer to **Figures 110-115** as necessary during this procedure.

1. Remove the cylinder head as described under *Cylinder Head* in this chapter..
2. Remove the crankshaft pulley as described under *Cylinder Head* in this chapter.

CYLINDER BLOCK
(9.9 HP [SERIAL NO. OH000057-PRIOR] AND 15 HP MODELS)

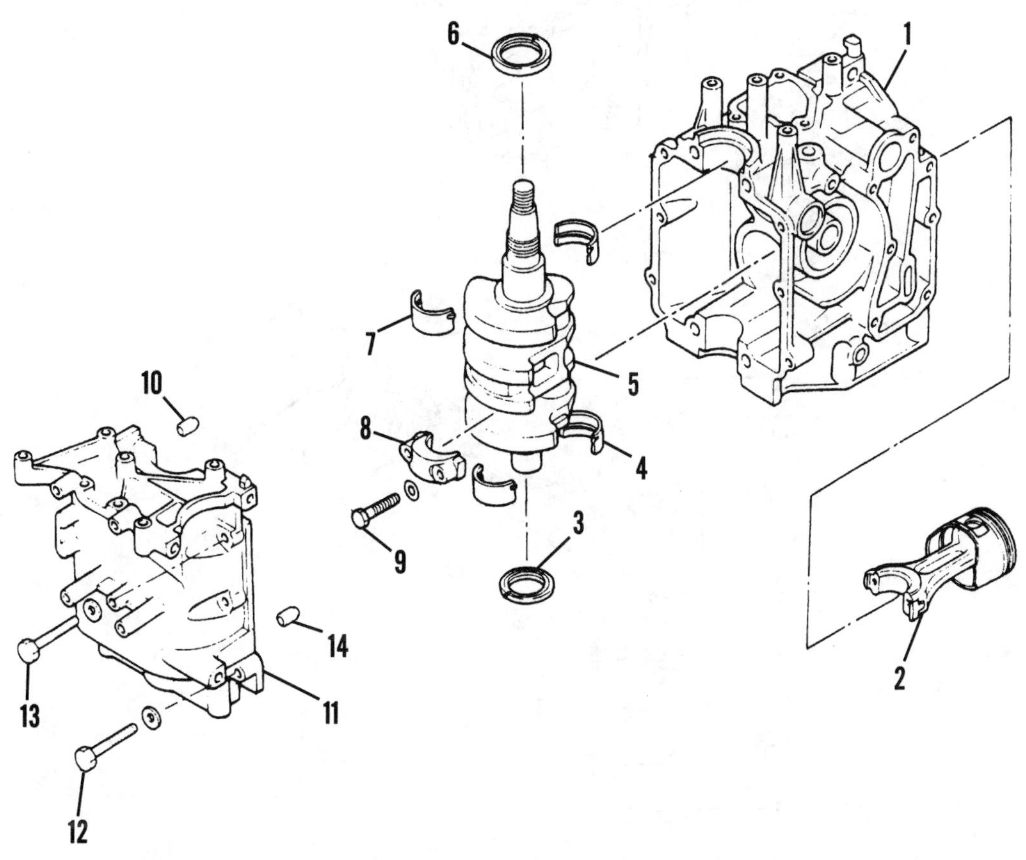

1. Cylinder block
2. Piston and rod
3. Crankshaft seal
4. Main bearing
5. Crankshaft
6. Crankshaft seal
7. Main bearing
8. Rod cap
9. Connecting rod bolt
10. Alignment pin
11. Crankcase cover
12. Bolt and washer
13. Bolt and washer
14. Alignment pin

(111)

CYLINDER BLOCK (9.9 HP MODELS, SERIAL NO. OH000058-ON)

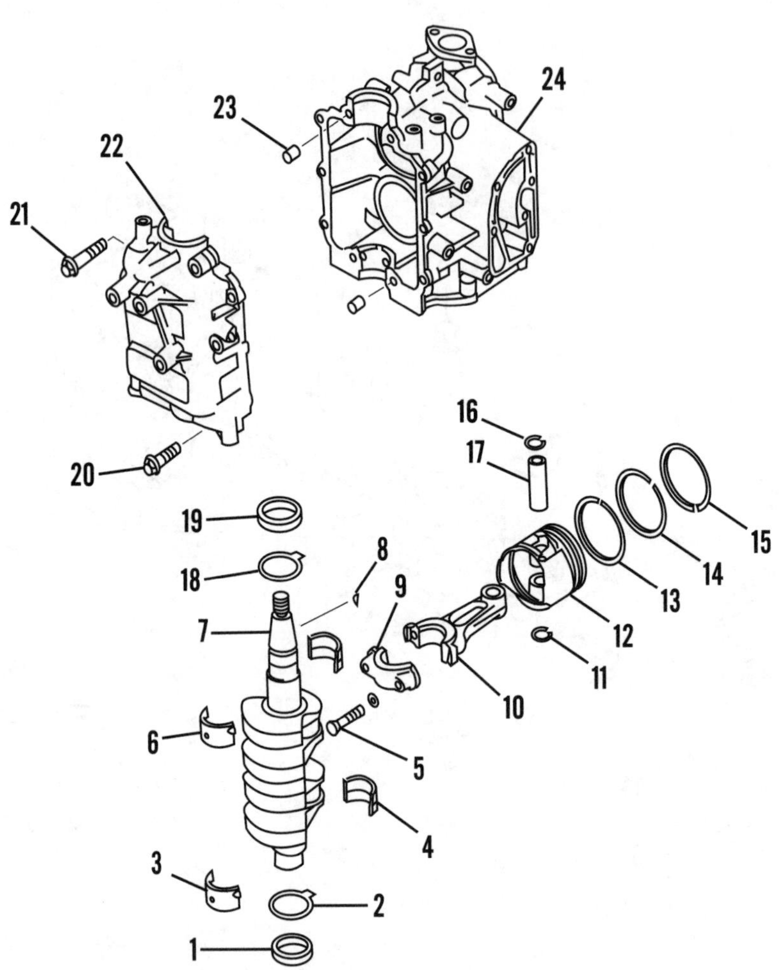

1. Crankshaft seal
2. Lower thrust spacer
3. Lower main bearing)
4. Lower main bearing
5. Connecting rod bolt
6. Upper main bearing
7. Crankshaft
8. Drive key
9. Rod cap
10. Connecting rod
11. Lock ring
12. Piston
13. Oil control ring
14. Second compression ring
15. Top compression ring
16. Lock ring
17. Piston pin
18. Upper thrust spacer
19. Crankshaft seal
20. Bolt
21. Bolt
22. Crankcase cover
23. Alignment pin
24. Cylinder block

(112)

CYLINDER BLOCK (25 HP MODELS)

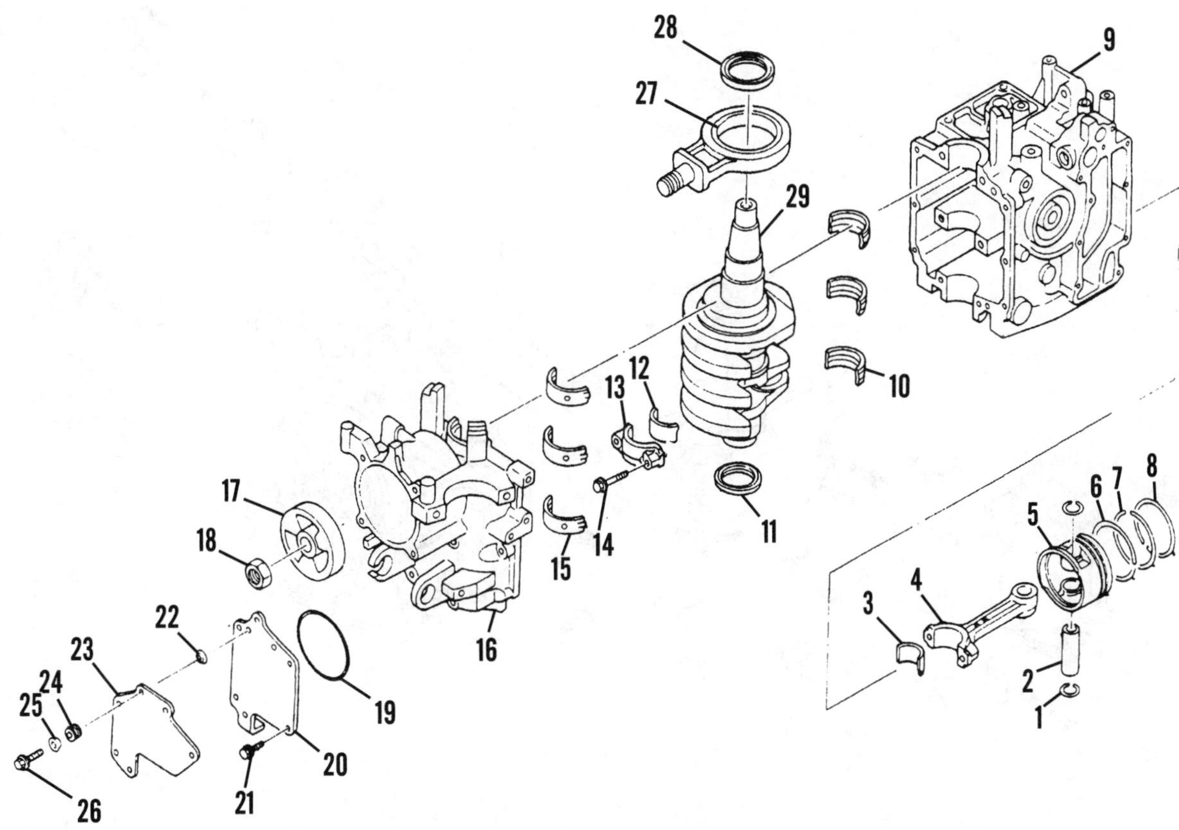

1. Lock ring
2. Piston pin
3. Rod bearing
4. Connecting rod
5. Piston
6. Oil control ring
7. Second compression ring
8. Top compression ring
9. Cylinder block
10. Main bearing
11. Crankshaft seal
12. Rod bearing
13. Rod cap
14. Rod bolt
15. Main bearing
16. Crankcase cover
17. Balance piston
18. Balnce piston nut
19. O-ring
20. Cover
21. Bolt
22. Sleeve
23. Bracket
24. Grommet
25. Sleeve
26. Bolt
27. Connecting rod
28. Crankshaft seal
29. Crankshaft

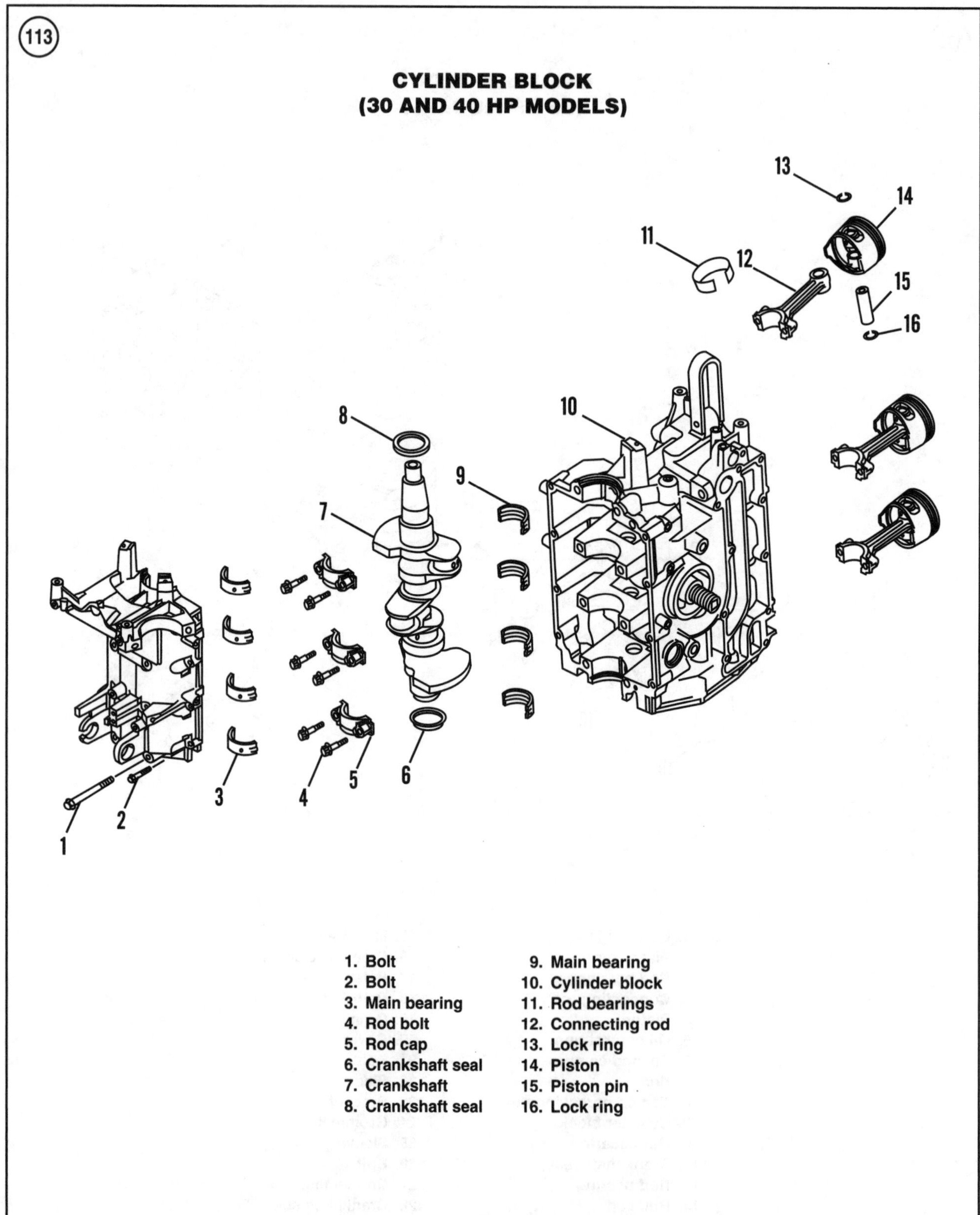
113
CYLINDER BLOCK
(30 AND 40 HP MODELS)
1. Bolt
2. Bolt
3. Main bearing
4. Rod bolt
5. Rod cap
6. Crankshaft seal
7. Crankshaft
8. Crankshaft seal
9. Main bearing
10. Cylinder block
11. Rod bearings
12. Connecting rod
13. Lock ring
14. Piston
15. Piston pin
16. Lock ring

CYLINDER BLOCK (50 HP MODEL)

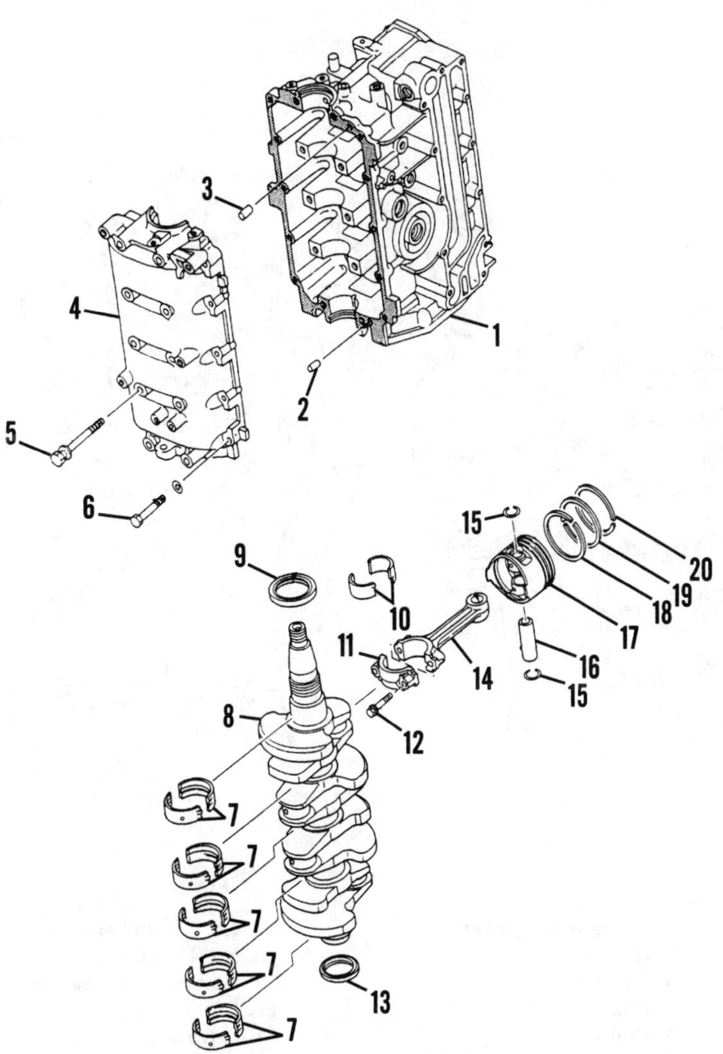

1. Cylinder block
2. Alignment pin
3. Alignment pin
4. Crankcase cover
5. Bolt
6. Bolt
7. Main bearing
8. Crankshaft
9. Crankshaft seal
10. Rod bearings
11. Rod cap
12. Rod bolt
13. Crankshaft seal
14. Connecting rod
15. Lock ring
16. Piston pin
17. Piston
18. Oil control ring
19. Second compression ring
20. Top compression ring

8

(115)

CYLINDER BLOCK (75 AND 90 HP MODELS)

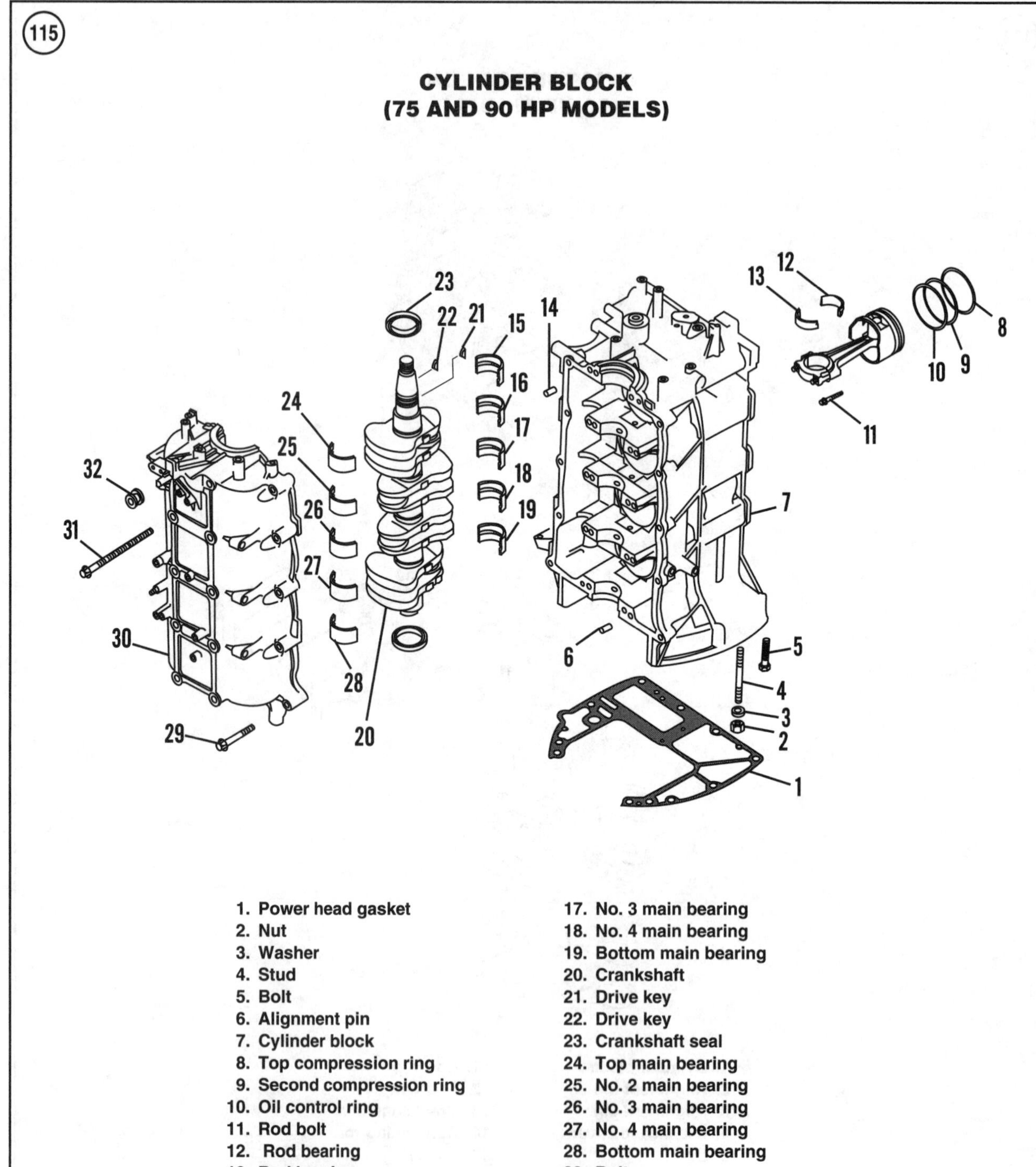

1. Power head gasket
2. Nut
3. Washer
4. Stud
5. Bolt
6. Alignment pin
7. Cylinder block
8. Top compression ring
9. Second compression ring
10. Oil control ring
11. Rod bolt
12. Rod bearing
13. Rod bearing
14. Alignment pin
15. Top main bearing
16. No. 2 main bearing
17. No. 3 main bearing
18. No. 4 main bearing
19. Bottom main bearing
20. Crankshaft
21. Drive key
22. Drive key
23. Crankshaft seal
24. Top main bearing
25. No. 2 main bearing
26. No. 3 main bearing
27. No. 4 main bearing
28. Bottom main bearing
29. Bolt
30. Crankcase cover
31. Bolt
32. Grommet

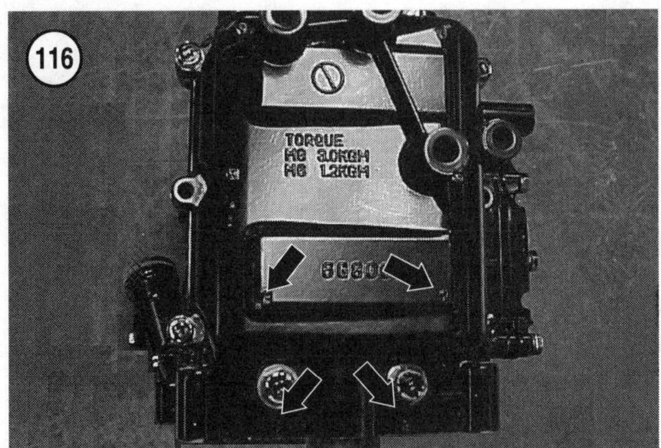

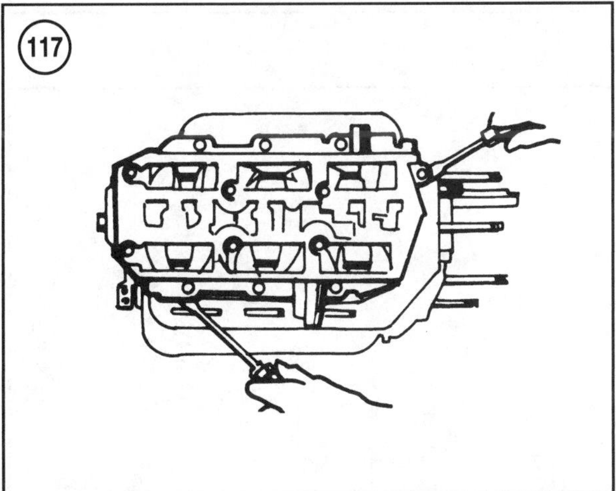

3. Remove all electrical components following the instructions in Chapter Seven.

4. Remove any remaining fuel system components following the instructions in Chapter Six.

5. Remove the exhaust/water jacket covers and thermostat following the instructions in this chapter.

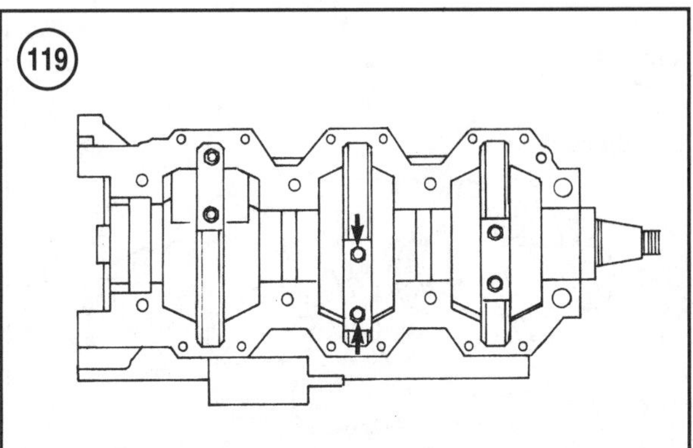

6. Remove the oil filter or screen following the instructions in Chapter Four.

7. On 25 hp models, remove the balance piston as follows:
   a. Remove the bolts (21, **Figure 112**), then lift the cover and O-ring (19 and 20) from the cylinder block.
   b. Using a breaker bar and socket, remove the balance piston retaining nut (18, **Figure 112**).
   c. Pull the balance piston (17, **Figure 112**) from its connecting rod (27).

8. On 9.9 hp (serial No. OH000057-prior), 15 hp, and 25 hp models, remove the breather housing or cover from the cylinder block. Refer to **Figure 89** or **Figure 91**. Thoroughly clean the housing or element with a solvent.

9. Locate the torque sequence numbers cast into the crankcase cover (**Figure 116**). Loosen the crankcase cover bolts 1/4 turn at a time in the reverse order of the tightening sequence until all bolts turn freely.

10. Locate the pry points (**Figure 97**) at the top and bottom corners of the cover. Carefully pry the cover from the crankcase (**Figure 117**). Check for additional bolts if difficult removal is encountered.

11. Note the seal lip direction then remove the crankshaft seals from the top and bottom of the crankshaft (**Figure 118**).

12. Note the location of each main bearing insert, then remove them from the crankshaft or crankcase cover. Arrange the bearing inserts so they will not become switched with other bearing inserts.

13. Remove one piston and rod assembly at a time. Mark the cylinder number on the side of the connecting rod and rod cap (**Figure 102**) prior to removal. Remove the piston and connecting rod as follows:
   a. Using white paint, highlight the UP mark on each piston dome. Verify the cylinder mark on the side of each connecting rod and cap (**Figure 102**).
   b. Evenly loosen 1/4 turn at a time the connecting rod bolts (**Figure 119**) until they spin freely. Lightly tap

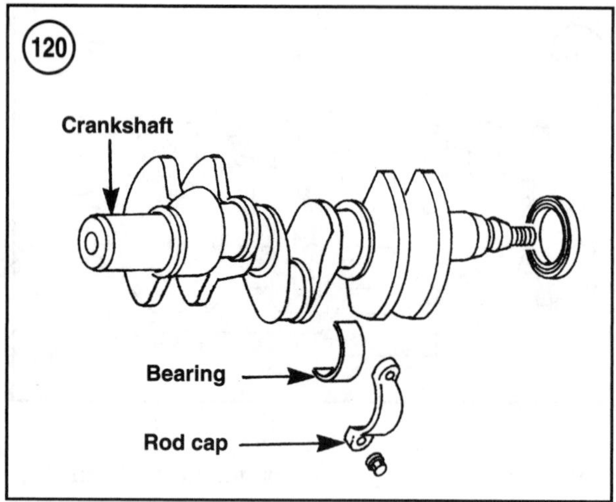

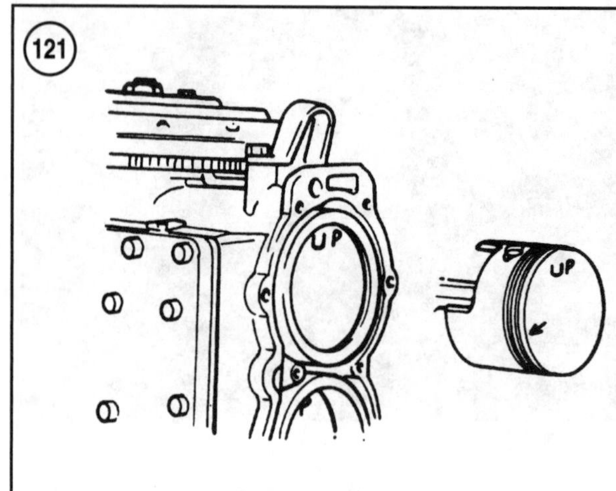

the rod cap (**Figure 120**) to free it from the crankshaft and connecting rod.

c. Remove the rod cap from the crankshaft and connecting rod. Remove the insert bearing (**Figure 120**) from the connecting rod or crankshaft.

d. Scrape the carbon ridge from the top of the cylinder bore with a small knife. Work carefully and avoid scratching the cylinder wall. Using a wooden dowel, push the piston and rod from the cylinder head end of the bore (**Figure 121**).

e. Align the tab on the back side of the bearing with the notch, then install the insert bearings (2 and 3, **Figure 122**) into the connecting rod and rod cap. Align the markings made prior to removal (**Figure 102**) then install the cap to the rod. Install the rod bolts (1, **Figure 102**) to retain the components. Mark the cylinder number on the rod cap (**Figure 123**) and remove each piston and rod assembly.

14. Using a ring expander, remove the upper two compression rings from the piston (**Figure 103**). Carefully pull the oil control ring (lower rails and spacer) from the piston. Work carefully to prevent damage to the piston.

15. Carefully pull the crankshaft from the cylinder block. Note the location of each main bearing insert, then remove them from the cylinder block. Arrange the insert bearings so they cannot become switched with other bearings.

a. On 9.9 hp models (serial No. OH000058-on), mark the up side and mounting location, then remove the thrust spacers (2 and 18, **Figure 111**) from the crankshaft.

b. On 25 hp models, mark the up side, then lift the balance piston connecting rod (27, **Figure 112**) from the crankshaft (29).

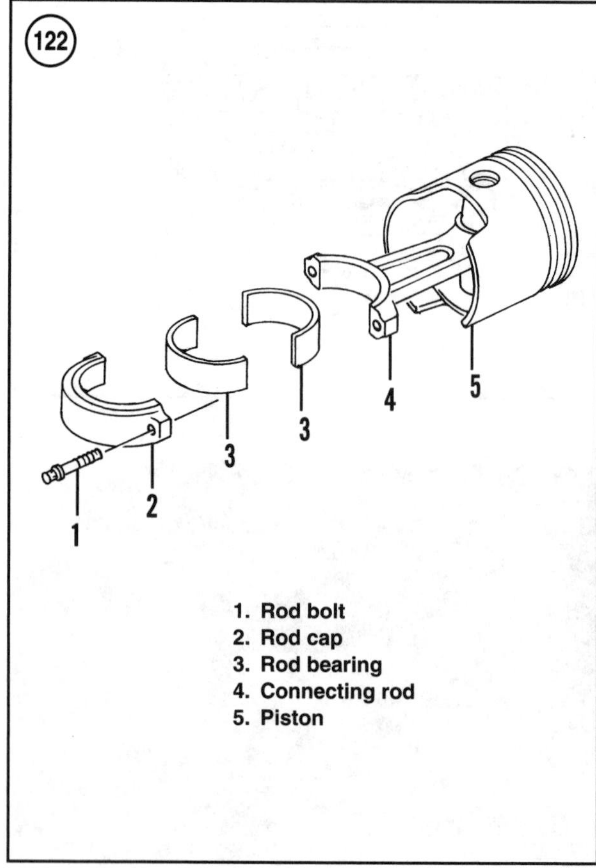

16. Remove the oil filter threaded adapter on models so equipped. Remove the oil filter housing on engines not equipped with a spin-on type oil filter.

17. Do not remove the connecting rod on 75 and 90 hp models. The piston and rod assembly must be replaced as an assembly if either the connecting rod or piston is defec-

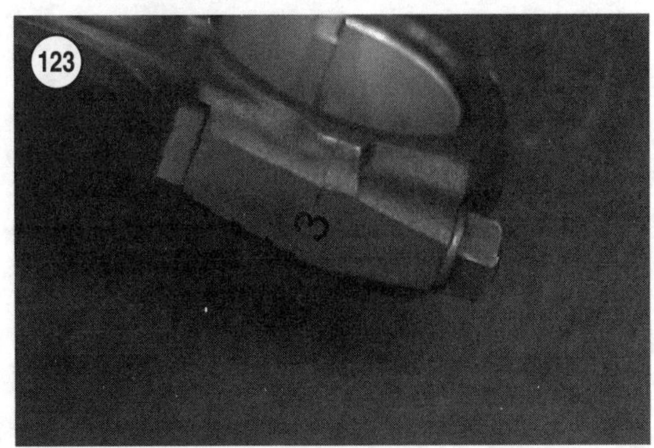

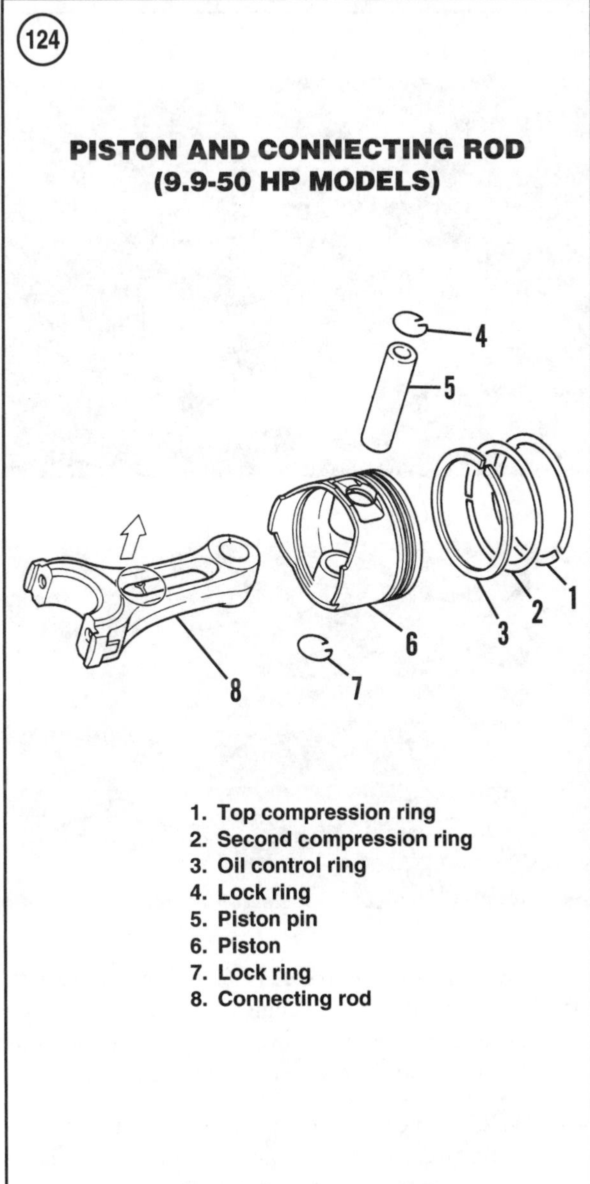

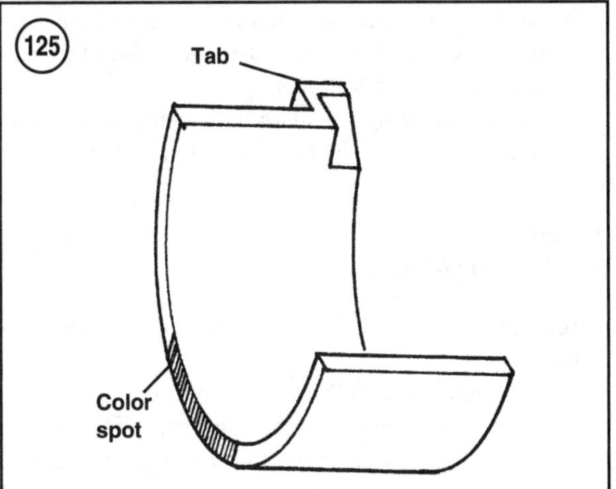

tive or excessively worn. Refer to *Inspection* in this chapter to determine the need for replacement.

18. Disassemble the connecting rod and piston on 9.9-50 hp models as follows:

a. Mark the top side of the piston and connecting rod (**Figure 124**).

b. Using a suitable pick or scribe, pry the lock rings (**Figure 104**) from the grooves in the piston pin bore.

c. Use a deep socket or section of tubing as a piston pin removal and installation tool. The tool must be slightly smaller in diameter than the piston pin (**Figure 124**). Refer to **Table 3** to determine the piston pin diameter.

d. Support the connecting rod and carefully push the piston pin from the piston and connecting rod.

e. Clean the piston ring grooves using a piece of broken ring (**Figure 105**). Use only the ring originally installed on the piston.

19. Thoroughly clean the cylinder block with hot soapy water. Clean other components with clean solvent. Clean carbon from the piston dome with a stiff non metallic parts cleaning brush and solvent. Dry all components with compressed air. Apply a light coat of oil to the piston, piston pin, cylinder bore, bearings, connecting rod and crankshaft to prevent corrosion.

20. Inspect all components following the instructions provided under *Inspection* in this chapter.

21. Note the color spot on the side of each insert type bearing (**Figure 125**). Order replacement bearings for the crankshaft main and connecting rods noting the following:

a. Note the cylinder number for each pair of connecting rod bearings.

   b. Note the main bearing number and its location (cylinder block side or crankcase cover side) for each crankshaft main bearings.
   c. Refer to *Bearing Selection* in this chapter to determine the color of the bearing (**Figure 125**).

Assembly (9.9-90 hp models)

Refer to **Figures 110-115** as necessary during this procedure.

1. Check main bearing clearance as follows:
   a. Clean all oil from the main bearings, cylinder block and crankcase cover prior to installing the bearings. Install the bearings into the cylinder block and crankcase cover. Align the tabs on the bearings (**Figure 125**) with the notches in the cylinder block and crankcase cover. Make sure the correct color bearing is installed at each position in the cylinder block and crankcase cover. On 75 and 90 hp models, install the larger thrust bearing into the third bearing position.
   b. Carefully install the crankshaft into the cylinder block.
   c. Place a section of Plastigage across each main bearing journal (**Figure 126**). Install the crankcase cover on the cylinder block. Thread all crankcase bolts into the cover and cylinder block. Do not rotate the crankshaft.
   d. Tighten the crankcase cover to half the specification provided in **Table 1** following the sequence cast into the cover (**Figure 116**). Tighten the bolts a second time in sequence to the full specification in **Table 1**. Loosen the crank case bolts 1/4 turn at a time in the reverse order of the tightening sequence. Remove the bolts then lift the cover from the cylinder block.
   e. Measure each main bearing clearance by comparing the width of the Plastigage to the marks on the Plastigage envelope. Compare the clearance to the main bearing oil clearance specification in **Table 8**. Refer to *Bearing Selection* in this section if incorrect clearance is indicated. Install the correct bearings into the cylinder block and crankcase cover.
   f. Pull the crankshaft from the cylinder block and clean the Plastigage from the crankshaft and bearing.
2. Install the crankshaft as follows:
   a. Apply engine oil to the crankshaft main bearings.
   b. On 9.9 hp models (serial No. OH000058-on), place the thrust spacers (2 and 18, **Figure 111**) onto the top and bottom ends of the crankshaft with the grooved side (**Figure 127**) facing the crankshaft. Coat the spacers with engine oil. Guide the tab on the spacers into the groove in the cylinder block as the crankshaft is lowered into position.
   c. On 25 hp models lubricate the balance piston connecting rod with clean engine oil. Slide the connecting rod onto the crankshaft with the *up* mark facing

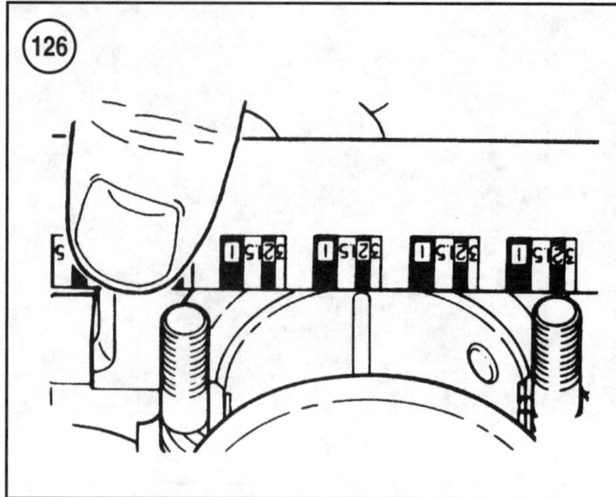
126

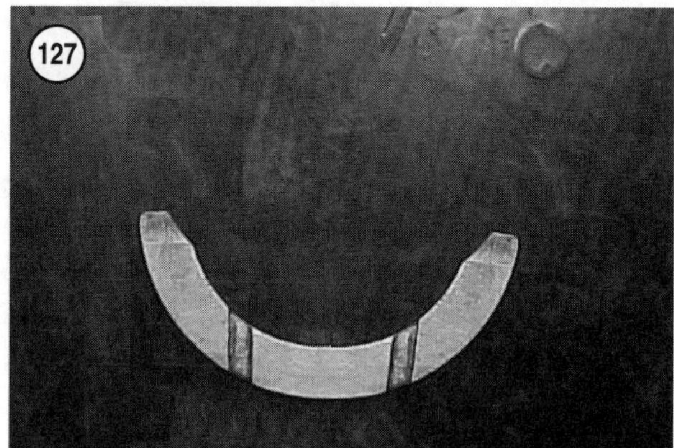
127

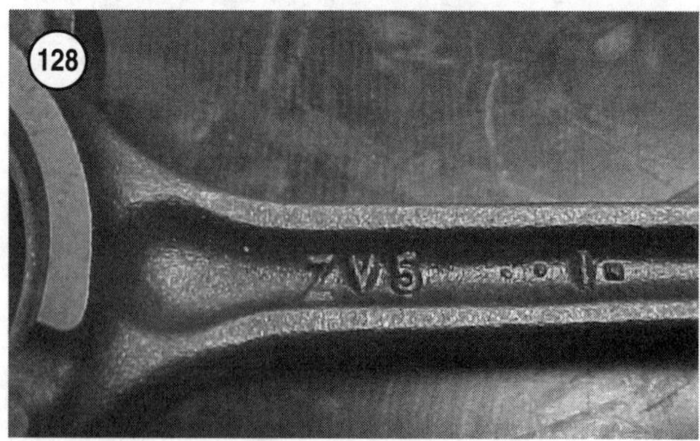

128

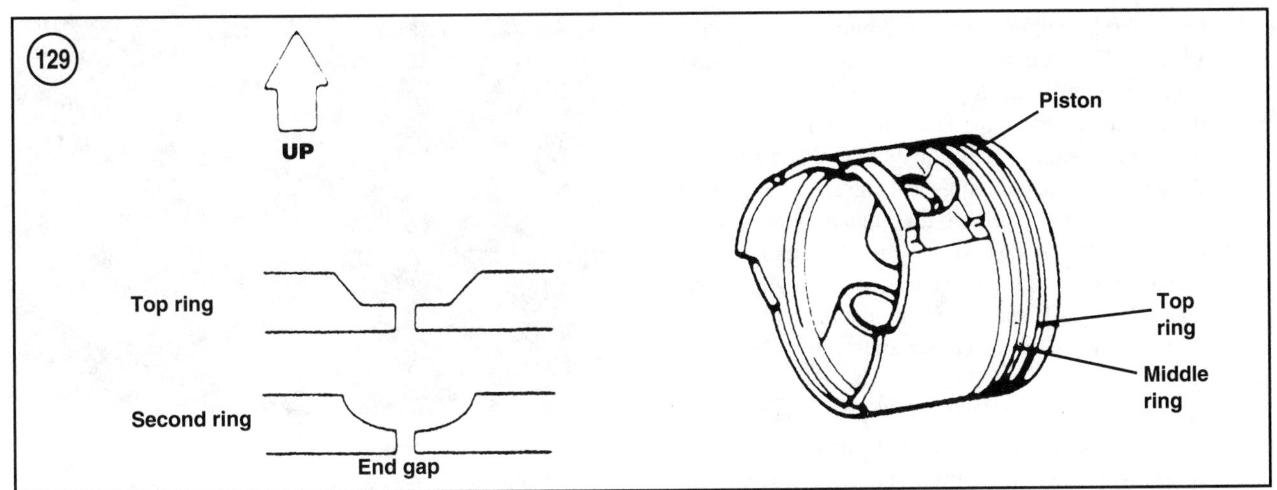

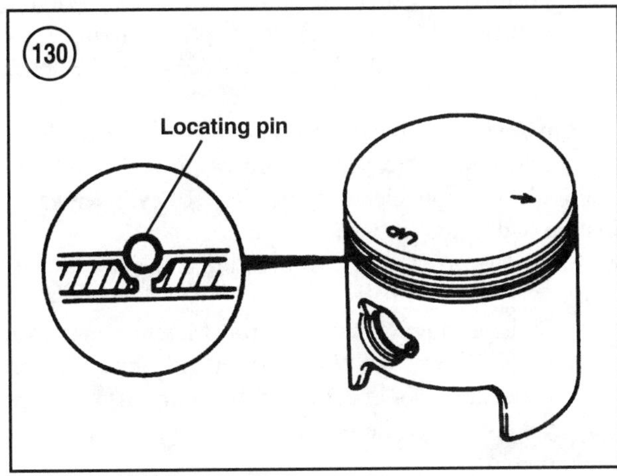

the flywheel end of the crankshaft. Guide the balance piston connecting rod into the cylinder block as the crankshaft is installed into the block.

d. Align the flywheel side of the cylinder block and crankshaft and lower the crankshaft into the cylinder block. Ensure the crankshaft fully seats against the cylinder block main bearings.

e. Slowly rotate the crankshaft to check for free movement. Remove the crankshaft and check for proper bearing seating and installation if binding or rough movement is detected.

3. Apply engine oil to the seals and carefully slide the upper and lower seals onto the crankshaft (**Figure 118**) with the lip side facing toward the crankcase. Seat the seals fully their bores in the cylinder block.

4. Assemble the piston and rod assembly, 9.9-50 hp models only, as follows:

a. Align the piston pin bores in the piston and connecting rod. On 9.9 (serial No. OH000057-prior) and 15 hp models, the *66M-00* mark must face down. On 9.9 hp models (serial No. OH000058-on) the *6G8-03* mark must face up. On 25-50 hp models, the Y mark on the connecting rod (**Figure 128**) must face the same direction as the *up* mark on the piston dome.

b. Lubricate the piston pin bores with engine oil, then push the piston pin into the piston and connecting rod.

c. Using needlenose pliers, install a new C ring into the groove on each side of the piston pin bore (**Figure 106**). Ensure the C rings span the notched part of the groove and firmly seat in the groove.

5. Install the piston rings as follows:

a. On 9.9 hp (serial No. OH000057-prior) and 15 hp models, identify the top side of both compression rings (1 and 2, **Figure 124**) by the *N* mark near the end gap. This mark must face up after assembly. Install the new rails and spacers of the oil ring onto the lower ring groove as indicated in **Figure 107**. Using a ring expander, open the new rings just enough to pass over the piston crown. Release the rings into the groove on the piston.

b. On 9.9 hp models (serial No. OH000058-on), identify the top and second rings by the shape of the end gap (**Figure 129**). The open end of the gap must face the top of the piston after installation. Using a ring expander, open the new rings just enough to pass over the piston crown. Release the rings into the groove on the piston (**Figure 129**). Rotate the top and second rings until they align with the locating pins in the ring groove (**Figure 130**). Install the new rails and spacers of the oil ring onto the lower ring groove as indicated in **Figure 107**.

8

c. On 25-90 hp models, the first compression ring (8, **Figure 112**) is thinner than the second compression ring (7). Identify the top side of each ring by the *T* mark near the end gap. These marks must face the top of the piston after installation. Using a ring expander, open the new rings just enough to pass over the piston crown. Release the rings into the groove on the piston. On 25 and 50 hp models, identify the upper oil ring rail by the notch at the end gap. Place both oil ring rails and the spacer into the bottom ring groove. Ensure the spacer separates the rails.

6. Align the ring gaps as follows:
   a. On 9.9 (serial No. OH000057-prior) and 15 hp models, position the end gap on the top compression ring with a point approximately 50° toward the port side of the *UP* marking on the piston crown. Position the end gap on the second compression ring approximately 50° toward the starboard side of the *UP* mark on the piston crown. Position the gap of the upper oil ring rail to the port side of the piston. Position the gap of the bottom oil rail ring to the starboard side of the piston. Align the gap on the rail spacer to the bottom side of the piston.
   b. On 9.9 hp models (serial No. OH000058-on), align the end gaps on both upper compression ring with the locating pins in the ring grooves (**Figure 130**). Position the gap in the upper oil ring rail approximately 30° from the starboard side of the *up* marking on the piston crown. Position the gap on the lower oil rail spacer 180° from the gap on the top oil ring rail. Position the gap in the oil ring rail spacer to the starboard side of the piston midway between the upper and lower rail gaps.
   c. On 25-40 hp models, position the gap of the top compression ring 50° from the port side of the *up* mark on the piston crown. Position the gap of the second compression ring 50° from the starboard side of the *up* mark. On the oil ring, position the gap in the upper rail over the ring locating pin in the ring groove and the lower rail on the starboard side of the piston. Position the gap in the oil ring spacer opposite the *up* mark on the piston crown.
   d. On 50 hp models, position the end gap of the top compression ring on the port side of the piston and the gap of the second ring approximately 50° starboard from the gap of the upper ring. Position the gap of the upper oil ring rail over the locating pin in the ring groove. Position the gap of the lower oil ring rail 180° from the upper rail. Place the gap in the oil ring spacer midway between the rail gaps.
   e. On 75-90 hp models, position the second compression ring so its gap is approximately 45° starboard of the *up* mark on the piston crown. Position the upper ring gap 180° from the gap in the second ring. Position the gap of the oil ring upper rail 45° to the port side of the *up* mark on the piston crown. Position the gap of the lower rail 180° from the upper rail.

131

7. Run a white shop cloth through the cylinder to check for debris. Repeat the cleaning process until the cloth remains clean. Apply clean engine oil to the cylinder walls, pistons and piston rings.

8. Install the piston and rods onto the crankshaft as follows:
   a. Slide a ring compressor (or Mercury part No. FT2997) over the No. 1 piston and rings. Tighten the compressor enough to fully compress the rings yet still allow the piston to slide through the compressor.
   b. Have an assistant help retain the crankshaft in the cylinder block during piston installation. Rest the power head on the side to allow access to the cylinder head and crankcase cover mating surfaces. Carefully rotate the crankshaft until the No. 1 crankpin is at the bottom of its stroke.
   c. Pass the No. 1 piston into the cylinder block from the cylinder head side. Ensure the *up* marks on the piston and rod face toward the flywheel side of the crankshaft (**Figure 108**). Guide the connecting rod toward the crankshaft during piston installation.
   d. Hold the ring compressor firmly against the cylinder block and gently drive the piston into the bore until the piston dome is slightly below the cylinder head mating surface. Stop and check for adequate ring compression and or improper ring alignment if any resistance is detected.
   e. Install the bearing inserts into the connecting rods and rod caps. Make sure the bearing tabs (**Figure 125**) are properly aligned with the notches in the connecting rods and rod caps.

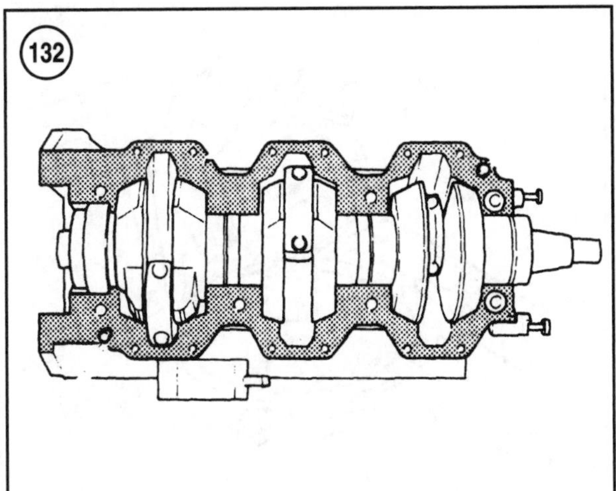

f. Align the marks on the connecting rod and rod cap (**Figure 102**) install the cap on the rod. Install, but do not tighten the bolts at this time.

g. Repeat these steps for the other pistons and connecting rods. Position the crankpin at the bottom of its stroke prior to piston installation.

9. Check the connecting rod bearing clearance as follows:

a. Remove the rod cap for the No. 1 cylinder.

b. Place a section of Plastigage on the crankpin. Install the rod cap and bolts. Tighten the rod bolts in two steps to the specification provided in **Table 1**. Do not rotate the crankshaft.

c. Remove the bolts and rod cap. Determine the connecting rod oil clearance by comparing the width of Plastigage with the mark on the Plastigage envelope. Compare the clearance with the connecting rod oil clearance specification in **Table 7**.

d. Refer to *Bearing Selection* in this chapter if the incorrect bearing clearance is noted. An excessively worn crankpin or connecting rod is likely if the correct bearings are installed, but incorrect clearance is noted. Replace worn or damaged components and check the clearance again.

e. Apply engine oil to the crankshaft and bearings and install the rod cap and new connecting rod bolts. Check for proper rod cap-to-connecting rod alignment. Correct as required. Tighten the connecting rod bolts in two steps to the specification in **Table 1**. On 75 an 90 hp models, tighten the bolts an additional 90° after reaching initial torque specification in **Table 1**.

f. Repeat these steps for the remaining cylinders.

10. Install the crankcase cover as follows:

a. Clean all oil residue or other contamination from the crankcase cover and cylinder block mating surface.

b. Apply a light even coat of Loctite Master Gasket 514 (Mercury part No. 92-12654-2) to the mating surface of the crankcase cover (**Figure 131**). Coat the entire mating surface, but do not allow sealant to flow into the bolts holes (**Figure 132**).

b. Inspect the crankshaft main bearings inserts and thrust washer tab (2 and 18, **Figure 111**) for proper alignment. Inspect the crankshaft seals for correct placement then place the crankcase cover onto the cylinder block.

c. Install the crankcase cover bolts finger tight.

d. Tighten the crankcase cover to half the specification provided in **Table 1** following the sequence cast into the cover (**Figure 116**). Tighten the bolts a second time in sequence to the full specification in **Table 1**. On 75 and 90 hp models, tighten the crankcase cover bolts an additional 60° after the initial torque specification is attained (**Table 1**).

e. Rotate the crankshaft while checking for smooth rotation. Disassemble the cylinder block and check for incorrectly installed or improper clearances if binding is noted.

11. On 25 hp models, install the balance piston and cover as follows:

a. Apply engine oil to the balance piston bore and balance the piston.

b. Place the balance piston (17, **Figure 112**) into the bore and over the threaded end of the connecting rod (27). Thread the balance piston nut (18, **Figure 112**) onto the connecting rod until it contact the piston (17).

c. Have an assistant support the cylinder block while tightening the nut. Tighten the balance piston nut to the specification in **Table 1**.

d. Install a new O-ring (19, **Figure 112**) on the cover or cylinder block and place the cover over the balance piston opening. Install the cover bolts (21, **Figure 112**) then tighten them to the specification in **Table 1**.

12. Install the threaded oil filter adapter for models with a spin on filter into the cylinder block. Tighten the adapter to the specification in **Table 1**.

13. On 9.9 hp (serial No. OH000057-prior), 15 hp, and 25 hp models, install the breather housing or cover into the cylinder block. Refer to **Figure 89** or **Figure 91** to assist with the breather housing, cover component orientation.

14. On 9.9 hp models with a serviceable oil filter, install the filter housing on the cylinder block. Tighten the housing retaining bolts to the specification in **Table 1**.

15. Install the oil filter following the instructions in Chapter Four.
16. Install the exhaust/water jacket cover and thermostat. On 75 an 90 hp models, install the water pressure relief valve. Follow the instructions in this chapter.
17. Install the crankshaft pulley following the instructions in this chapter.
18. Install all electrical and ignition system components following the instructions in Chapter Seven.
19. Install the cylinder head, timing belt and flywheel following the instructions in this chapter.
20. Install the fuel system components following the instructions in Chapter Six.

INSPECTION

Measurement of the power head components requires precision measuring equipment. Have a marine repair shop or machine shop perform the measurements if access is unavailable or are unfamiliar with the required equipment.

All components must be clean and dry before measuring. Keep the components at room temperature for several hours before measuring them.

Cylinder Block Inspection

1. Inspect the cylinder bores for cracks or deep grooves. Deep grooves or cracks in the cylinder bores indicate damage that cannot be repaired by boring and installing oversize pistons. Replace the cylinder block or have a sleeve installed if a cracked or deeply scratched cylinder bore is found. Contact a qualified marine dealership or machine shop to locate a source for block sleeving.
2. Inspect the mounting surfaces for the power head, exhaust/water jacket cover and crankcase cover for cracks or damage. Replace the cylinder block if cracks, deep scratches or gouging is noted
3. White powder-like deposits in the combustion chamber usually indicate water is entering the combustion chamber. Inspect the cylinder walls and cylinder head thoroughly for cracks if this type of deposit is noted. Inspect the head gasket and mating surfaces for discolored areas. Discolored or corroded sealing surfaces indicate a likely source of leakage. Replace any defective or suspect components.
4. Inspect all bolt holes for cracks, corrosion or damaged threads. Use a thread chaser to clean the threads of corrosion or sealant. Pay particular attention to the cylinder head bolt holes. Damaged threads can often be repaired by installing a threaded insert.

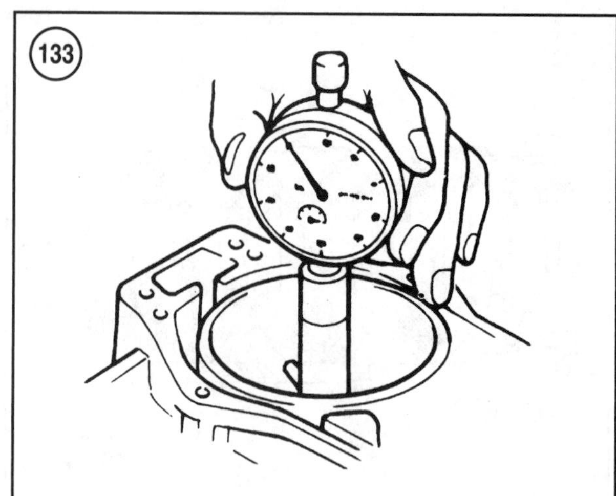

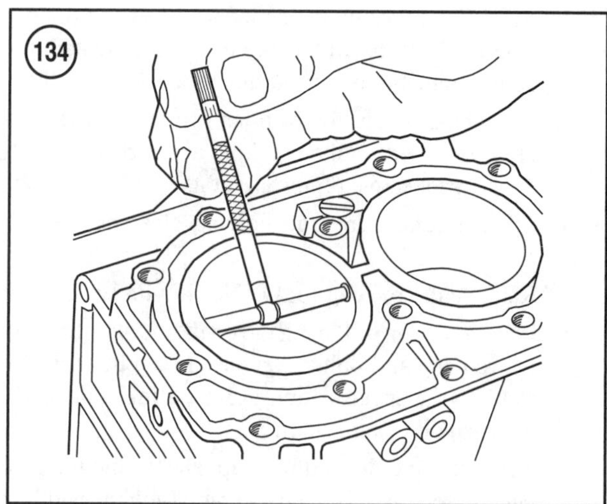

5. Clean and inspect all bolts, nuts and washers. Replace any bolts or nuts with damaged threads or a stretched appearance. Replace damaged or cup-shaped washers.
6. Inspect the alignment pins and pin holes for bent pins or damaged openings. Replace damaged pins or components with damaged pin holes.

NOTE
The cylinder block and crankcase cover are a matched assembly. Replace the entire assembly if either portion requires replacement.

7. Have the cylinder bore lightly honed at a marine repair shop or machine shop before taking any measurements. A heavier honing is required if the cylinder bore is glazed or aluminum deposits are present.
8. Use either a dial (**Figure 133**) or spring type (**Figure 134**) cylinder bore gauge to measure the cylinder bore.

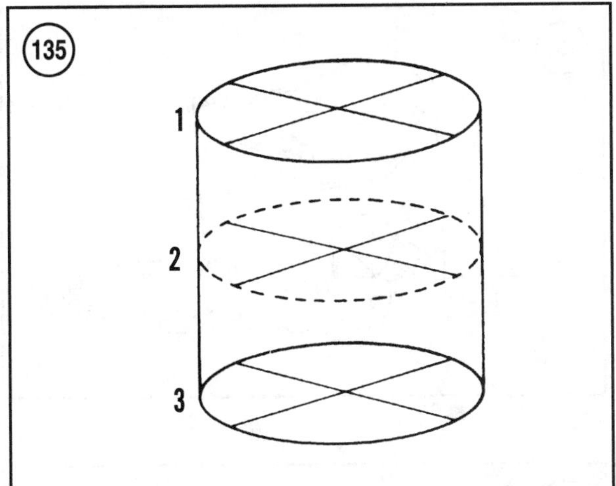

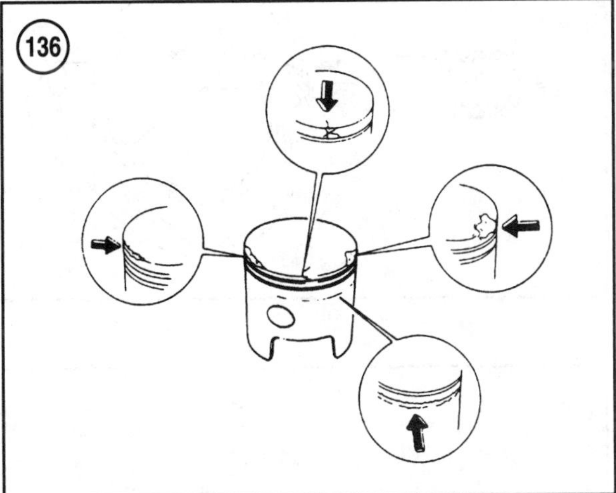

a. On 4-6 hp models, measure the cylinder bore diameter at 1/4, 1/2, and 3/4 down from the cylinder head mating surface.

b. On 9.9-50 hp models, measure the cylinder bore diameter at 0.8 in. (20 mm), 1.6 in. (40 mm) and 2.4 in. (60 mm) down from the cylinder head mating surface.

c. For 75 and 90 hp models, measure the cylinder bore diameter at 0.8 in. (20 mm), 2.8 in. (70 mm) and 4.7 in. (120 mm) down from the cylinder head mating surface.

9. Take the measurements at 90° (**Figure 135**) apart at all three depths. Record all six measurements.

10. Compare the measurements with specification in **Table 2**. A prior repair to the power head may have required boring and the installation of an oversize piston. A second oversize piston is available for 9.9-40 hp models. Measure the pistons to determine if oversize components have been installed. Use the oversize piston and bore specification listed for the oversize components.

11. Have the cylinder bored to the next oversize diameter and install oversize pistons if excessive bore diameter is indicated. Replace the cylinder block or have a sleeve installed if the bore diameter exceeds the specification in **Table 2**. Contact a marine dealership or machine shop for cylinder boring or sleeving.

12. Subtract the smallest cylinder diameter from the largest diameter to determine the cylinder taper from the top to the bottom of the bore. Compare the result with the maximum cylinder taper specification in **Table 2**.

13. Subtract the smallest cylinder bore diameter at a given depth with the diameter at the same depth 90° apart to determine the out-of-round measurement. Compare the result with the maximum out-of-round specification in **Table 2**.

14. Have the cylinder bored and install the oversize piston if the taper or out-of-round exceeds the specification. Replace the cylinder block or have a sleeve installed if oversize pistons are not available in the required size. 8

15. Repeat the cylinder bore measurements for all cylinders.

Piston and Rings Inspection

1. Inspect the piston for eroded surfaces at the edge of the dome, cracks near the ring grooves, cracks or missing portions in the piston dome (**Figure 136**). Inspect for erosion in the ring groove and scoring or scuffing on the piston skirt.

2. Inspect the piston pin for worn, discolored or scrubbed appearance. Inspect the lock ring groove for damage or erosion. Replace the piston if any of these defects are noted.

3. Replace the rings if the piston is removed from the cylinder. Low compression, high oil consumption an other problems may surface if used rings are installed.

4. Refer to **Table 3** to determine the measuring point on the piston. Using an outside micrometer, measure the diameter of the piston at a point 90° from the piston pin bore and at the specified distance from the bottom of the skirt. (**Figure 137**).

5. Compare the diameter to the specification in **Table 3**. Replace the piston if the diameter is below the specification.

6. Measure the piston diameter for the remaining pistons.

7. Perform this measurement on 4-50 hp models. Using an inside micrometer measure the piston pin bore diameter at both openings (**Figure 138**). Compare the diameters with the specification provided in **Table 3**.

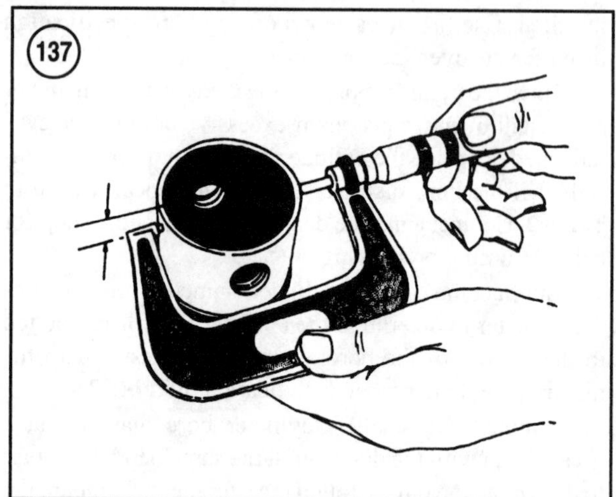
137

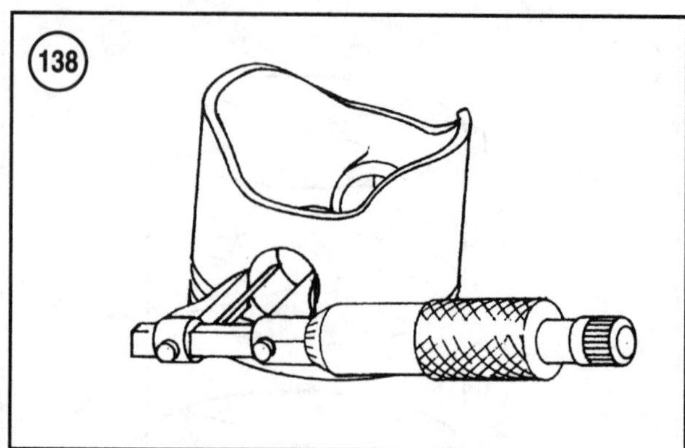
138

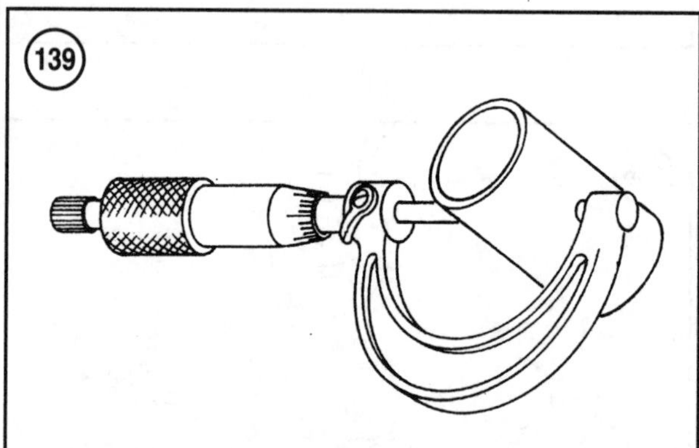
139

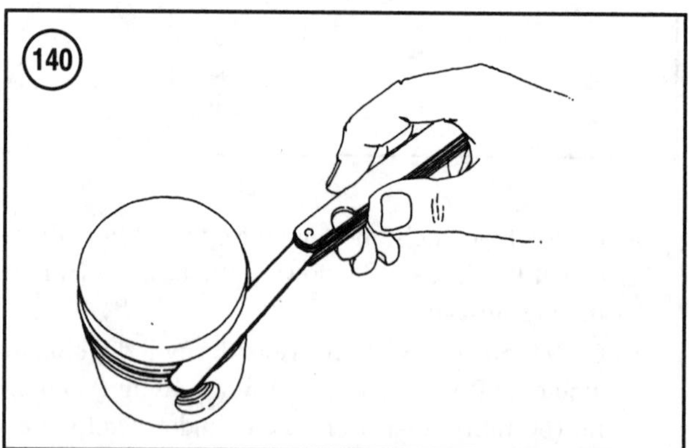
140

8. Repeat this measurement for the remaining pistons. Replace any piston with an excessive pin bore diameter.
9. Measure the piston pin diameter (**Figure 139**) at the piston and rod contact areas along the length of the pin. Compare the measurement with the specification in **Table 3**.
10. Repeat this measurement for the remaining cylinders. Replace any piston pin with a diameter below the specification.
11. On 4-6 hp models, subtract the smallest piston pin diameter from the largest pin bore diameter to determine the clearance.
12. Compare the results with the specification in **Table 3**. Replace the piston and pin if incorrect clearance is indicated.
13. Temporarily install new rings into the piston ring grooves as described in this chapter. Using a feeler gauge, measure the piston ring side clearance as indicated in **Figure 140**. Select the feeler gauge that passes between the ring and the ring groove with a light drag.
14. Compare the thickness of the feeler gauge with the specification in **Table 6**. Replace the piston if incorrect clearance is indicated.

Piston-to-Cylinder Clearance

1. Perform this calculation for each cylinder using the recorded piston and cylinder bore diameters. Subtract the piston diameter from the largest measured cylinder bore diameter for the given cylinder. The results indicate the largest clearance (**Figure 141**).
2. Subtract the piston diameter from the smallest cylinder bore diameter for the given cylinder. The results indicate the smallest clearance. Compare the largest and smallest clearance with the specification in **Table 4**.
3. Excessive clearance indicates excessive cylinder bore diameter or below minimum piston diameter. Inadequate clearance indicates a bore diameter that is too small or too large of a piston diameter. Replace the piston or bore the cylinder to the next oversize to correct the clearance.

Ring End Gap

1. Using a piston without rings (**Figure 142**), push a new piston ring into the cylinder bore to a depth of 0.8 in. (20

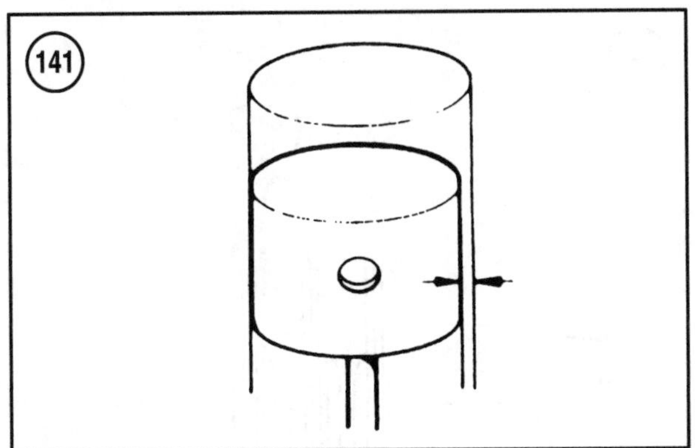

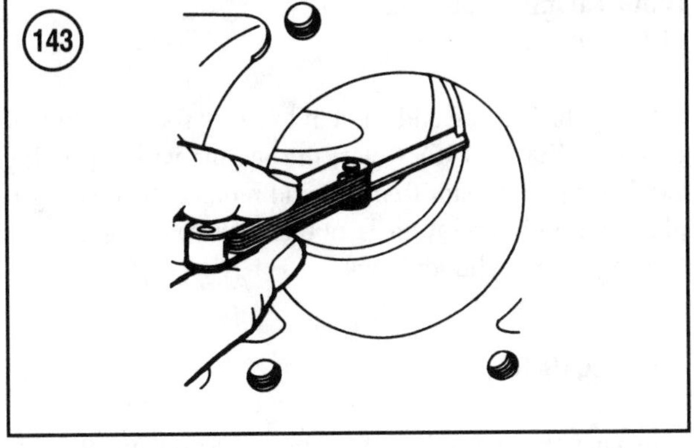

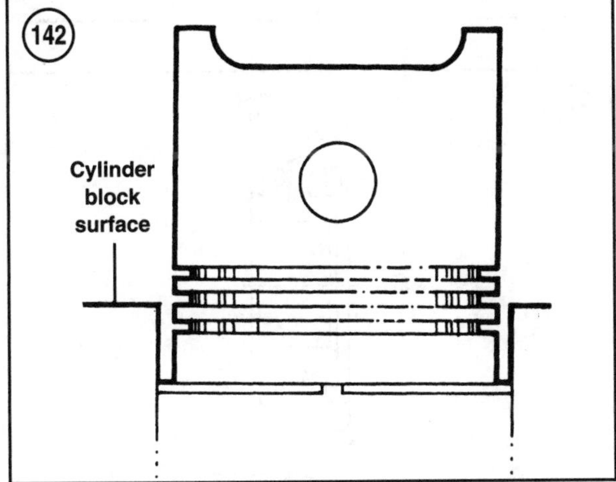

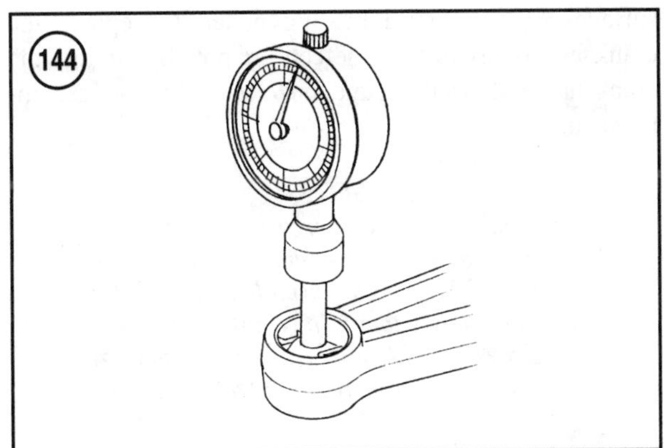

mm) from the cylinder head side of the cylinder block surface.

2. Using feeler gauges, measure the width of the ring gap (**Figure 143**). Select a feeler gauge that passes through the gap with a slight drag.

3. Compare the thickness of the feeler gauge with the specification in **Table 5**. Measure the cylinder bore diameter if and incorrect gap is indicated.

4. Install a new ring if the cylinder bore measures correctly. Continue until a correct ring gap is found.

5. Repeat this measurement for all rings on the piston. Tag these rings to ensure they are installed on the correct piston into the correct selected cylinder.

Connecting Rod Inspection

NOTE

Some minor surface corrosion, glaze-like deposits or minor scratches can be removed with crocus cloth or 320 grit carburundum. Polish the surfaces enough to remove the deposits.

1. Inspect the connecting rod(s) for bent condition, discoloration and worn or damaged bearings surfaces. Replace the connecting rod if any defects are noted.

2. On 4-6 hp models, measure the diameter of the piston pin bore (**Figure 144**). Compare the diameter with the specification in **Table 7**. Replace the connecting rod if and incorrect diameter is indicated.

3. On 4-6 hp models, install the connecting rod on the crankshaft as described in this chapter. It is not necessary to install the crankshaft into the cylinder block to perform this measurement.

4. Using feeler gauges, measure the clearance between the connecting rod and the side of the crankshaft journal (**Figure 145**).

5. Compare the clearance with the specification in **Table 6**. Replace the connecting rod if incorrect clearance is noted, measure the side clearance again. Replace the crankshaft if incorrect side clearance persists.

Ball Bearing Inspection (4-6 Models)

Grasp the bearing and move it to check for axial and radial play (**Figure 146**). Rotate the bearing while applying axial and radial load. Remove and replace the bearing if play or rough operation is noted. Otherwise, leave the bearing in the cylinder block.

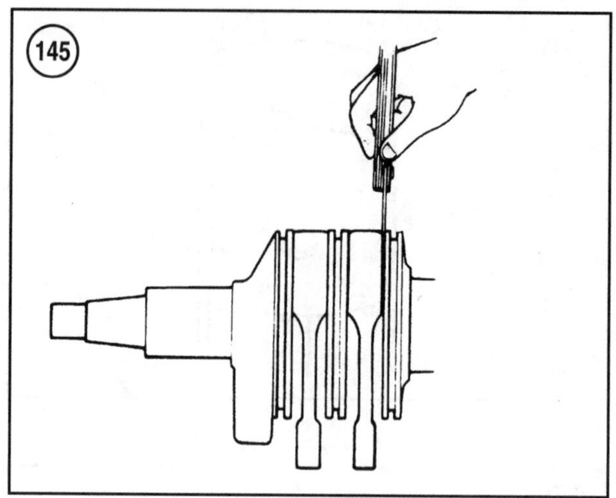

Crankshaft Inspection

Inspect the crankshaft for cracks, corrosion etching, bluing or discoloration. Also check for rough or irregular surfaces or transferred bearing material. Replace the crankshaft if any of these defects are noted. Grinding the crankshaft and installing undersize bearings is not recommended.

NOTE
Some minor surface corrosion, deposits or minor scratches can be removed with crocus cloth or 320 grit carburundum. Polish the surfaces only enough to remove the deposits. Excessive polishing can remove damage from the connecting rod and crankshaft surfaces.

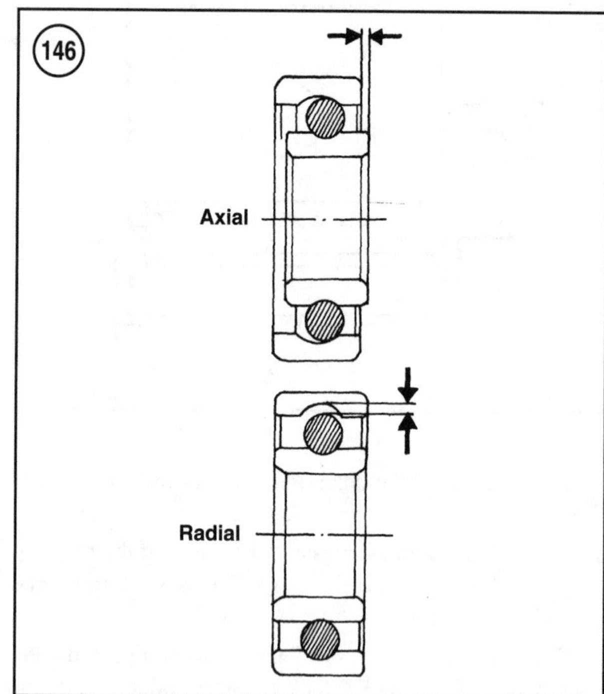

Measure the crankpin diameter on 4-6, 75 and 90 hp models.

1. Using an outside micrometer, measure the journal diameter for the No. 1 crankpin (**Figure 147**). Record the measurement then repeat the measurement of the journals for No. 2-4 connecting rods.
2. Compare the measurements with the specification provided in **Table 8**.
3. Replace the crankshaft if the measurement is below the specification.
4. Retain the measurements for use in bearing selection.
5. On 4-6 hp models, measure the diameter of the crankshaft at the oil pan end of the crankshaft. Compare the measurement with the specification in **Table 8**.
6. Using an inside micrometer, measure the diameter of the crankshaft bearing surfaces in the oil pan. Compare the diameter with the specification in **Table 8**. Replace the cylinder block if the diameter exceeds the specification.
7. Subtract the crankshaft diameter from the bearing diameter to determine the bearing clearance. Compare the results with the bearing clearance specification in **Table 8**. A worn bearing or crankshaft is indicated if excessive clearance is present. Measure all components before replacing any components.

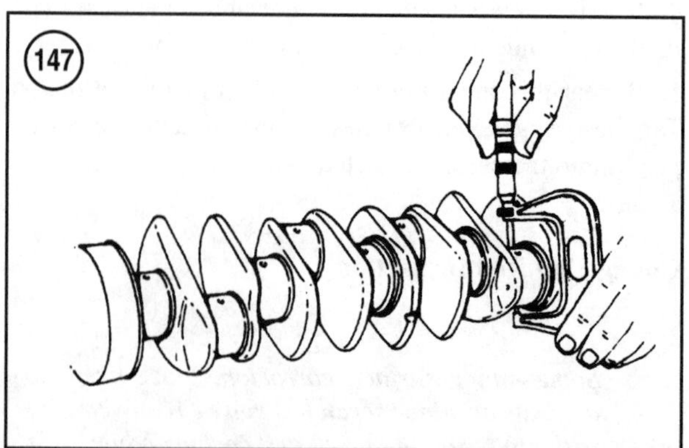

148

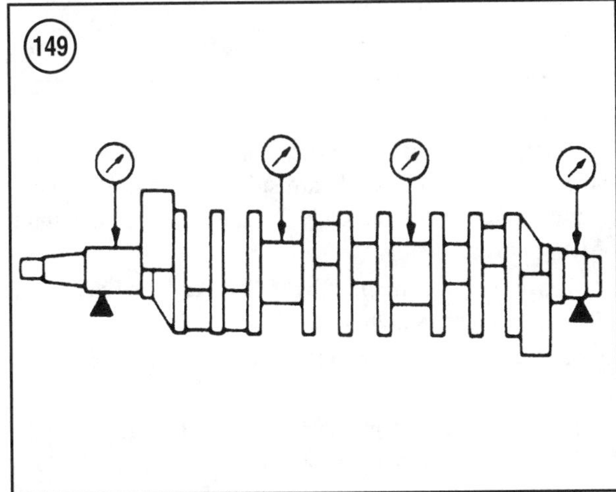

149

8. On 75 and 90 hp models, measure the five main bearing journal diameters (**Figure 148**). Record the journal diameters for use in bearing selection.

9. Compare the main bearing journal diameter with the specification in **Table 8**. Replace the crankshaft if any main bearing journal diameters are below the specification.

10. Thrust spacers inspection is required on 9.9 hp models (serial No. OH000058-on). Inspect the thrust spacer (**Figure 127**) for worn, discolored or rough surfaces. Replace the thrust spacer if wear is visible, rough surfaces are felt or discoloration is noted.

11. Support the crankshaft on the top and bottom main bearing journals with V-blocks or a balance wheel.

12. Position a dial indicator at a remaining main bearing journal (**Figure 149**) or other parallel bearing surface.

13. Observe the dial indicator movement while slowly rotating the crankshaft. Repeat the measurement with the indicator at each main bearing surface.

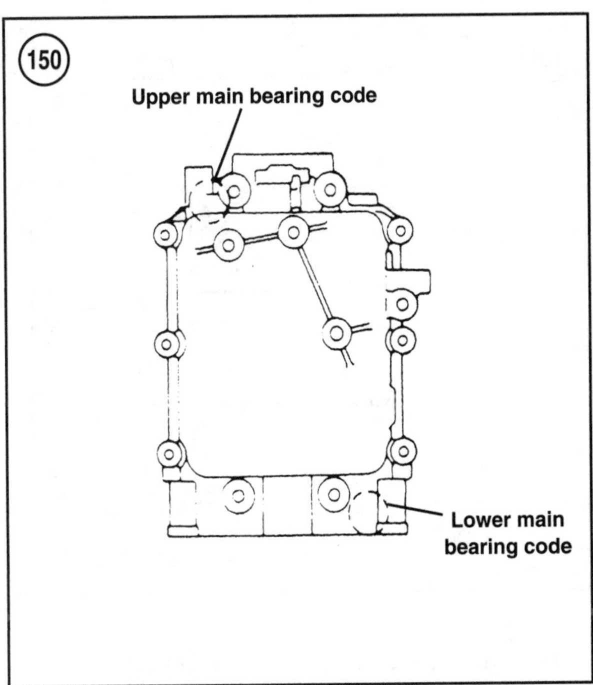

150

14. Compare the crankshaft runout to the specification in **Table 8**. Replace the crankshaft if runout exceeds the specification.

Balance Piston and Balance Piston Bore Inspection (25 hp Models)

1. Measure the balance piston diameter using an outside micrometer. Compare the balance piston diameter with the specification in **Table 3**. Replace the balance piston if the diameter is below the specification.

2. Measure the balance piston bore in the crankcase cover using an accurate inside micrometer.

3. Compare the bore diameter with the specification in **Table 2**.

4. Replace the cylinder block if the diameter exceeds the specification.

Bearing Selection (9.9-90 hp Models)

Select the main bearings by reading the bearing codes on the upper and lower sides of the crankcase cover (**Figure 150**). The upper A, B or C mark indicates the bearing code for the upper main bearing. The lower A, B, or C mark indicates the bearing code for the lower main bearing. Record the mark and refer to **Table 10**. Install the bearing with the color stain listed in the table. Excessive

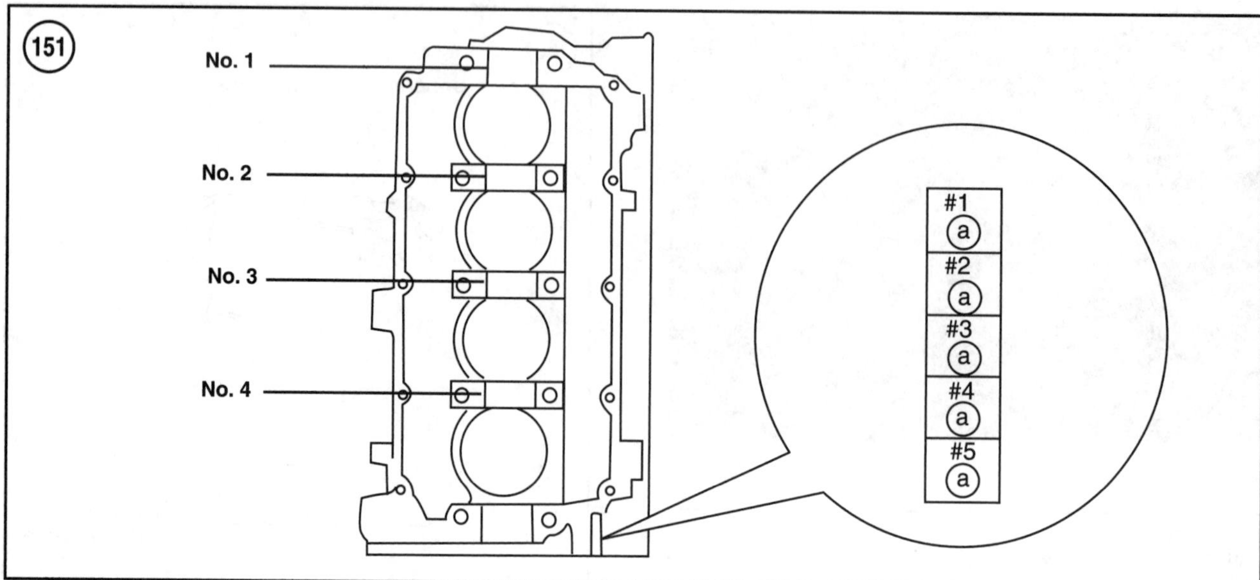

main bearing oil clearance with a new correct color bearing indicates excessive crankshaft wear.

Main Bearing Selection (25-50 hp Models)

Select the main bearings by reading the bearing codes on the lower port side of the crankcase cover (**Figure 151**). The first upper code is the code for the upper main bearing. The second code is the code for the No. 2 main bearing and so on. Record the A, B or C marking then refer to **Table 10**. Install the bearing with the color code listed in the table. Excessive main bearing clearance with a new correct color bearing indicates excessive crankshaft wear.

Main Bearing Selection (75 and 90 hp Models)

Select the main bearings by reading number codes stamped into the crankshaft and cylinder block (**Figure 152**) and using the recorded crankshaft measurements.

1. Determine the crankshaft main journal diameter by reading the code for the No. 1 (top) journal (**Figure 152**).
   a. Multiply the number stamped into the crankshaft by 0.001. Add the results to the base measurement of 47.9.
   b. Record the results as the *crankshaft main journal diameter.*
   c. Read the codes and perform the calculation for the remaining four main bearing surfaces. Record all results.
2. Determine the main bearing bore diameter by reading the codes stamped in starboard side of the cylinder block (**Figure 152**). Read the code for the top or No. 1 main bearing bore.
   a. Multiply this number by 0.001. Add the results to a base measurement of 54.0.
   b. Record the results as the main bearing bore diameter.
   c. Read the codes and perform the calculations for the remaining four main bearing bores. Record all results.
3. Subtract the crankshaft main journal diameter from the main bearing bore diameter and refer to **Table 10**.
4. Install bearings with the indicated color code in the specified location. Install the bearing with the oil groove only in the cylinder block side. Repeat the calculation and bearing selection for the remaining locations.
5. Excessive main bearing clearance with new and correct color bearings indicates excessive crankshaft wear. Measure the crankshaft and check all calculations before replacing the crankshaft. Inadequate oil clearance indicates incorrect bearing selection or improperly installed components.

Connecting Rod Bearing Selection (9.9-50 hp Models)

On 9.9 and 15 hp models, select the crankpin bearings by the oil clearance measurement. Excessive oil clearance with new bearings installed indicates excessive crankshaft wear.

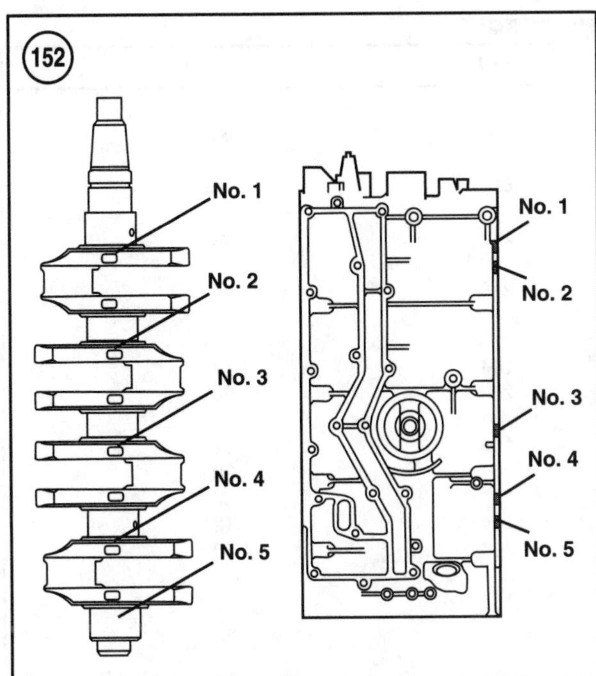

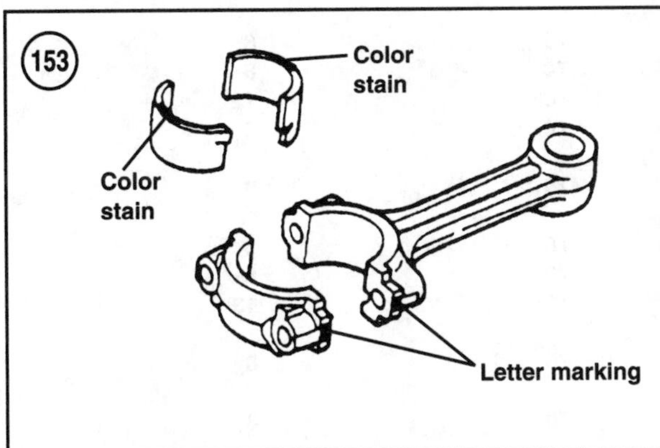

On 25-50 hp models, select the crankpin bearings by refering to the letter code stamped on the side of the connecting rod (**Figure 153**). Record the letter code for the rod, then refer to **Table 9**. Install bearings with the color indicated for the specified rod. Read the code and select bearings for the remaining connecting rods. Excessive oil clearance with new and correct color bearings indicates a damaged rod or excessive crankshaft wear.

Connecting Rod Bearing Selection (75 and 90 hp Models)

Select the connecting rod bearings by measuring the connecting rod oil clearance with new yellow coded bearings installed in the specified connecting rod. Refer to *Cylinder Block* to install new yellow bearing, then measure the oil clearance. Perform the measurements for the remaining connecting rods. Record all test results.

Refer to **Table 11** to determine the color code of bearing and installation locations for the clearance measured with yellow bearings. Record the bearing color code and installation location for each connecting rod.

Engine Break-In

Perform the break-in procedure any time internal components of the power head are replaced. During the first few hours of running, many of the components of the power head must avoid full load until fully seated. Failure to properly break in the engine can result in power head failure, decreased performance, shorter engine life and increased oil consumption.

Full break-in is achieved in approximately 10 hours of running time. Increased oil consumption can be expected during the this period. Check the oil *frequently* during break-in. Refer to Chapter Four. Check and correct the tightness of all external fasteners during the break-in period.

1. During the first hour of the break-in period, do not exceed 3500 rpm or half throttle. Do not run over a few minutes at a given throttle setting.
2. During the second hour of operation, advance the engine to full throttle for a period of one minute to two minute intervals. Otherwise run the engine at 1/4 throttle or 4500 rpm or less during the second hour.
3. During the next eight hours, operate the engine at full throttle for a maximum of 5 minutes at a time. Otherwise run the engine at any throttle settings below full throttle.

Tables 1-19 are located on the following page.

Table 1 TIGHTENING TORQUE

Fastener location	ft-lb.	in-lb.	N•m
Rocker arm cover			
All models	–	70	8
Spark plug cover			
75 and 90 hp	–	66	7.5
Rocker arm studs			
4-6 hp	18	216	24
Cylinder head bolts			
4-6 hp	18	216	24
9.9 hp			
Serial No. OH000057-prior			
6 mm bolts	–	104	12
8 mm bolts	22	264	30
Serial No. OH000058-on			
6 mm bolts	–	106	12
8 mm bolts	22	264	30
15 hp			
6 mm bolts	–	104	12
8 mm bolts	22	264	30
25-50 hp			
6 mm bolts	–	106	12
9 mm bolts	35	–	47
75 and 90 hp			
8 mm bolts	20.6	247	28
10 mm bolts	24.3[1]	292[1]	33[1]
Thermostat cover			
4-6 hp	–	70	8
9.9 and 15 hp	–	70	8
25-50 hp	–	106	12
75 and 90 hp	–	70	8
Breather cover			
4-6 hp	–	70	8
9.9 hp (serial No. OH000057-prior)	–	70	8
15 hp	–	70	8
25 hp	–	115	13
Breather tube fitting			
75 and 90 hp	–	70	8
Water pressure valve cover			
75 and 90 hp	–	70	8
Exhaust cover			
4-6 hp	–	70	8
9.9 hp			
Serial No. OH000057-prior	–	70	8
Serial No. OH000058-on	–	106	12
15 hp	–	70	8
25-90 hp	–	106	12
Oil pump cover			
4-6 hp	–	31	3.5
9.9 and 15 hp	–	39	4
25-40 hp	–	70	8
50 hp	–	66	8
75 and 90 hp	–	70	8
Oil pump mounting			
9.9-40 hp	–	70	8
50 hp	–	68	8
75 and 90 hp	–	84	10
Oil pickup tube			
4-6 hp	–	31	4
75 and 90 hp	–	100	11

(continued)

Table 1 TIGHTENING TORQUE (continued)

Fastener location	ft-lb.	in-lb.	N•m
Oil filter adapter fitting			
9.9-90 hp	30	–	40
Oil filter housing			
9.9 hp (serial No. OH000058-on)	–	70	8
Oil pressure relief valve bolt			
4-6 hp	–	70	8
Crankcase cover			
9.9 hp			
Serial No. OH000057-prior			
6 mm bolts	–	104	12
8 mm bolts	22	264	30
Serial No. OH000058-on			
6 mm bolts	–	106	12
8 mm bolts	22	264	30
15 hp			
6 mm bolts	–	114	13
8 mm bolts	22	264	30
25-50 hp			
6 mm bolts	–	106	12
8 mm bolts	22	264	30
75 and 90 hp			
8 mm bolts	20.6	247	28
10 mm bolts	14[2]	168[2]	19[2]
Balance piston cover			
25 hp	–	115	13
Oil pan			
4-6 hp			
6 mm bolts	–	80	9
8 mm bolts	18.5	222	25
Oil seal housing			
4-6 hp	–	70	8
Connecting rod bolts/nuts			
4-6 hp	–	106	12
9.9 hp			
Serial No. OH000057-prior	16.2	194	22
Serial No. OH000058-on	–	106	12
15 hp	16.2	194	22
25-50 hp	12.5	150	17
75 and 90 hp	–	70[1]	8[1]
Balance piston nut			
25 hp	116	–	157
Power head mounting			
4-6 hp	–	70	8
9.9 hp			
Serial No. OH000057-prior	22	264	30
Serial No. OH000058-on	15	186	21
15 hp	22	264	30
25-50 hp	28	–	38
75 and 90 hp			
Bolts	20	240	27
Nuts	35	–	47
Crankshaft pulley nut			
9.9 hp			
Serial No. OH000057-prior	30	–	40
Serial No. OH000058-on	17	204	23
15 hp	30	–	40
75 and 90 hp	195	–	265

(continued)

8

Table 1 TIGHTENING TORQUE (continued)

Fastener location	ft-lb.	in-lb.	N•m
Camshaft pulley nut/bolt			
9.9 and 15 hp	–	115	13
25-50 hp	28	–	38
75 and 90 hp	44	–	60
Camshaft retainer			
25-50 hp	–	57	6.4
75 and 90 hp	–	150	17
Rocker arm retainer			
25-50 hp	–	160	18
Flywheel cover			
25-90 hp	–	45	5.1
Pulser coil mounting plate			
50 hp	–	75	8.5
Timing belt tensioner			
50 hp			
Pivot bolt	–	70	8
Adjusting bolt	18.4	221	25
75 and 90 hp	29	–	40
Flywheel nut			
9.9 hp			
Serial No. OH000057-prior	81	–	110
Serial No. OH000058-on	72	–	100
15 hp	81	–	110
25-50 hp	116	–	157
75 and 90 hp	140	–	190
Manual starter pulley			
4-6 hp	–	70	8

1. Tighten these bolts an additional 90° after all bolts are tightened to the listed torque.
2. Tighten these bolts an additional 60° after all bolts are tightened to the listed torque.

Table 2 CYLINDER BORE SPECIFICATIONS

Model	Specification
4-6 hp models	
Standard bore diameter	2.323-2.325 in. (59.00-59.06 mm)
Oversize bore diameter	2.343-2.344 in. (59.51-59.56 mm
Maximum cylinder taper	0.003 in. (0.076 mm)
Maximum cylinder out of round	0.003 in. (0.076 mm)
9.9 hp models	
Serial No. OH000057-prior	
Standard bore diameter	2.3228-2.3236 in. (59.00-59.02 mm)
First oversize bore diameter	2.3327-2.3335 in. (26.25-59.27 mm)
Second oversize bore diameter	2.3425-2.3433 in. (59.50-59.52 mm)
Maximum cylinder taper	0.003 in. (0.076 mm)
Maximum cylinder out of round	0.003 in. (0.076 mm)
Serial No. OH000058-on	
Standard bore diameter	2.323-2.326 in. (59.00-59.08 mm)
First oversize bore diameter	2.333-2.344 in. (59.25-59.53 mm)
Second oversize bore diameter	2.343-2.346 in. (59.51-59.59 mm)
Maximum cylinder taper	0.003 in. (0.076 mm)
Maximum cylinder out of round	0.003 in. (0.076 mm)
15 hp models	
Standard bore diameter	2.3228-2.3236 in. (59.00-59.02 mm)
First oversize bore diameter	2.3327-2.3335 in. (26.25-59.27 mm)
Second oversize bore diameter	2.3425-2.3433 in. (59.50-59.52 mm)
Maximum cylinder taper	0.003 in. (0.076 mm)

(continued)

Table 2 CYLINDER BORE SPECIFICATIONS (continued)

Model	Specification
15 hp models (continued)	
Maximum cylinder out of round	0.003 in. (0.076 mm)
25 hp models	
Standard bore diameter	2.5591-2.5596 in. (65.00-65.015 mm)
First oversize bore diameter	2.5689-2.5695 in. (65.025-65.265 mm)
Second oversize bore diameter	2.5787-2.5793 in. (65.50-65.515)
Maximum balance piston bore diameter	3.742 in. (95.045 mm)
Maximum cylinder taper	0.003 in. (0.076 mm)
Maximum cylinder out of round	0.003 in. (0.076 mm)
30 and 40 hp models	
Standard bore diameter	2.5591-2.5596 in. (65.00-65.015 mm)
First oversize bore diameter	2.5689-2.5695 in. (65.025-65.265 mm)
Second oversize bore diameter	2.5787-2.5793 in. (65.50-65.515)
Maximum cylinder taper	0.003 in. (0.076 mm)
Maximum cylinder out of round	0.003 in. (0.076 mm)
50 hp models	
Standard bore diameter	2.4804-2.4809 in. (63.00-63.015 mm)
Oversize bore diameter	2.5000-2.5005 in. (63.50-63.515 mm)
Maximum cylinder taper	0.003 in. (0.076 mm)
Maximum cylinder out of round	0.003 in. (0.076 mm)
75 and 90 hp models	
Standard bore diameter	3.1102-3.1110 in. (79.000-79.020 mm)
Oversize bore diameter	3.1200-3.1208 in. (79.250-79.270 mm)
Maximum cylinder taper	0.003 in. (0.076 mm)
Maximum cylinder out or round	0.003 in. (0.076 mm)

Table 3 PISTON SPECIFICATIONS

Model	Specification
4-6 hp	
Measuring point	0.2 in. (5 mm) from the bottom of the skirt
Standard piston diameter	2.319-2.321 in. (58.91-58.954 mm)
Oversize piston diameter	2.339-2.341 in. (59.4-59.462 mm)
Piston pin diameter	0.6291-0.6299 in. (15.99-16.000 mm)
Piston pin bore diameter	0.6300 in. (16.002 mm)
Piston pin to pin bore clearance	0.0001-0.0015 in. (0.0025-0.038 mm)
9.9 hp	
Serial No. OH000057-prior	
Measuring point	0.2 in. (5 mm) from the bottom of the skirt
Standard piston diameter	2.3209-2.3214 in. (58.950-58.965 mm)
First oversize piston diameter	2.3307-2.3313 in. (59.2-59.215 mm)
Second oversize piston diameter	2.3405-2.3411 in. (59.450-59.465 mm)
Piston pin diameter	0.5510-0.5512 in. (13.996-14.0 mm)
Serial No. OH000058-on	
Measuring point	0.4 in. (10 mm) from the bottom of the skirt
Standard piston diameter	2.3209-2.3215 in. (58.950-58.965 mm)
First oversize piston diameter	2.333 in. (59.258 mm)
Second oversize piston diameter	2.343 in. (59.50 mm)
Piston pin diameter	0.5510-0.5512 in. (13.996-14.0 mm)
15 hp	
Measuring point	0.2 in. (5 mm) from the bottom of the skirt
Standard piston diameter	2.3209-2.3214 in. (58.950-58.965 mm)
First oversize piston diameter	2.3307-2.3313 in. (59.2-59.215 mm)
Second oversize piston diameter	2.3405-2.3411 in. (59.450-59.465 mm)
Piston pin diameter	0.5510-0.5512 in. (13.996-14.0 mm)
25 hp	
Measuring point	0.2 in. (5 mm) from the bottom of the skirt

(continued)

8

Table 3 PISTON SPECIFICATIONS (continued)

Model	Specification
25 hp (continued)	
Standard piston diameter	2.5771-2.5577 in. (64.950-64.965 mm)
First oversize piston diameter	2.5669-2.5675 in. (65.200-65.215 mm)
Second oversize piston diameter	2.5768-2.5773 in. (65.450-65.465 mm)
Piston pin diameter	0.6285-0.6287 in. (15.965-15.970 mm)
Minimum balance piston diameter	3.735 in. (94.883 mm)
30 and 40 hp	
Measuring point	0.2 in. (5 mm) from the bottom of the skirt
Standard piston diameter	2.5771-2.5577 in. (64.950-64.965 mm)
First oversize piston diameter	2.5669-2.5675 in. (65.200-65.215 mm)
Second oversize piston diameter	2.5768-2.5773 in. (65.450-65.465 mm)
Piston pin diameter	0.6285-0.6287 in. (15.965-15.970 mm)
50 hp	
Measuring point	0.2 in. (5 mm) from the bottom of the skirt
Standard piston diameter	2.4783-2.4789 in. (62.950-62.965 mm)
Oversize piston diameter	2.4980-2.4986 in. (63.450-63.465 mm)
Piston pin diameter	0.6285-0.6287 in. (15.965-15.970 mm)
75 and 90 hp	
Measuring point	0.51 in. (13 mm) from the bottom of the skirt
Standard piston diameter	3.1074-3.1082 in. (78.928-78.949 mm)
Oversize piston diameter	3.1172-3.1180 in. (79.178-79.199 mm)

Table 4 PISTON TO CYLINDER BORE CLEARANCE

Model	Specification
4-6 hp	0.001-0.0057 in. (0.025-0.145 mm)
9.9-50 hp	0.0014-0.0026 in. (0.035-0.065 mm)
75 and 90 hp	0.0028-0.0031 in. (0.070-0.080 mm)

Table 5 PISTON RING END GAP

Model	Specification
4-6 hp	
Top ring	0.006-0.019 in. (0.15-0.48 mm)
Middle ring	0.012-0.027 in. (0.30-0.68 mm)
Oil ring	0.008-0.023 in. (0.20-0.58 mm)
9.9 hp	
Serial No. OH000057-prior	
Top ring	0.006-0.012 in. (0.15-0.30 mm)
Middle ring	0.012-0.020 in. (0.30-0.50 mm)
Oil ring	0.008-0.028 in. (0.20-0.70 mm)
Serial No. OH000058-on	
Top ring	0.006-0.012 in. (0.15-0.30 mm)
Middle ring	0.006-0.012 in. (0.15-0.30 mm)
Oil ring	0.008-0.028 in. (0.20-0.70 mm)
15-50 hp	
Top ring	0.006-0.012 in. (0.15-0.30 mm)
Middle ring	0.012-0.020 in. (0.30-0.50 mm)
Oil ring	0.008-0.028 in. (0.20-0.70 mm)
75 and 90 hp	
Top ring	0.006-0.012 in. (0.15-0.30 mm)
Middle ring	0.028-0.035 in. (0.70-0.90 mm)
Oil ring	0.008-0.028 in. (0.20-0.70 mm)

Table 6 PISTON RING SIDE CLEARANCE

Model	Specification
4-6 hp	
Top ring	0.0015-0.0038 in. (0.038-0.097 mm)
Middle ring	0.0012-0.0034 in. (0.030-0.086 mm)
Oil ring	0.0004-0.0081 in. (0.010-0.206 mm)
9.9 hp	
Serial No. OH000057-prior	
Top ring	0.0016-0.0031 in. (0.04-0.08 mm)
Second ring	0.0012-0.0028 in. (0.03-0.07 mm)
Serial No. OH000058-on	
Top ring	0.0016-0.0031 in. (0.04-0.08 mm)
Second ring	0.0012-0.0031 in. (0.03-0.08 mm)
15 hp	
Top ring	0.0016-0.0031 in. (0.04-0.08 mm)
Second ring	0.0012-0.0028 in. (0.03-0.07 mm)
25 hp	
Top ring	0.0008-0.0024 in. (0.02-0.06 mm)
Second ring	0.0012-0.0031 in. (0.03-0.08 mm)
30 and 40 hp	
Top ring	0.0008-0.0024 in. (0.02-0.06 mm)
Second ring	0.0008-0.0024 in. (0.02-0.06 mm)
50 hp	
Top ring	0.0016-0.0031 in. (0.04-0.08 mm)
Second ring	0.0012-0.0031 in. (0.03-0.08 mm)
75 and 90 hp	
Top ring	0.0008-0.0031 in. (0.020-0.080 mm)
Middle ring	0.0012-0.0028 in. (0.030-0.070 mm)
Oil ring	0.0012-0.0059 in. (0.030-0.150 mm)

8

Table 7 CONNECTING ROD SPECIFICATIONS

Model	Specification
4-6 hp	
Bearing clearance	0.002- 0.0034 in. (0.051-0.863 mm)
Side clearance	0.008-0.027 in. (0.203-0.69 mm)
Piston pin bore diameter	0.6303-0.6311 in. (16.009-16.03 mm)
9.9 and 15 hp	
Connecting rod bearing clearance	0.0008-0.0018 in. (0.021-0.045 mm)
25-50 hp	
Connecting rod bearing clearance	0.0008-0.0020 in. (0.020-0.052 mm)
75 and 90 hp	
Connecting rod bearing clearance	0.0009-0.0014 in. (0.023-0.035 mm)

Table 8 CRANKSHAFT SPECIFICATIONS

Model	Specification
4-6 hp	
Maximum crankshaft runout	0.000-0.0019 in. (0-0.048 mm)
Standard crank pin diameter	1.1775-1.179 in. (29.91-29.94 mm)
Diameter at oil pan end	0.9825-0.983 in. (24.955-24.97 mm)
Bearing diameter in oil pan	0.985 in. (25.019 mm)
Crankshaft-to-oil pan bearing clearance	0.0006-0.0019 in. (0.0152-0.048 mm)
9.9 hp	
Serial No. OH000057-prior	
Maximum crankshaft runout	0.0008 in. (0.020 mm)
	(continued)

Table 8 CRANKSHAFT SPECIFICATIONS (continued)

Model	Specification
9.9 hp	
Serial No. OH000057-prior (continued)	
Main bearing oil clearance	0.0004-0.0015 in. (0.011-0.039 mm)
Serial No. OH000058-on	
Maximum crankshaft runout	0.0008 in. (0.020 mm)
Main bearing oil clearance	0.0002-0.0017 in. (0.005-0.043 mm)
15 hp	
Maximum crankshaft runout	0.0008 in. (0.020 mm)
Main bearing oil clearance	0.0004-0.0015 in. (0.011-0.039 mm)
25 hp	
Maximum crankshaft runout	0.0012 in. (0.03 mm)
Main bearing oil clearance	0.0005-0.0017 in. (0.012-0.044 mm)
30 and 40 hp	
Maximum crankshaft runout	0.0018 in. (0.046 mm)
Main bearing oil clearance	0.0005-0.0017 in. (0.012-0.044 mm)
50 hp	
Maximum crankshaft runout	0.0012 in. (0.03 mm)
Main bearing oil clearance	0.0005-0.0017 in. (0.012-0.044 mm)
75 and 90 hp	
Maximum crankshaft runout	0.0012 in. (0.03 mm)
Main bearing oil clearance	0.0009-0.0017 in. (0.024-0.044 mm)
Minimum main bearing journal diameter	1.8887 in. (47.972 mm)
Minimum crank pin (connecting rod journal) diameter	1.7311 in. (43.971 mm)

Table 9 CRANKSHAFT/CONNECTING ROD BEARING SELECTION

Model	Main or rod bearing code	Bearing color code
9.9-50 hp	A	Blue
	B	Black
	C	Brown

Table 10 MAIN JOURNAL BEARING (75 AND 90 HP MODELS)

Calculated diameter	Cylinder side bearing (color code) (without oil groove)	Crankcase side bearing (color code) (without oil groove)
6.023-6.026	Green	Yellow
6.027-6.034	Blue	Green
6.035-6.042	Blue	Blue
6.043-6.049	Red	Blue
6.050-6.058	Red	Red

Table 11 CONNECTING ROD BEARING CODES

Measured oil clearance	Piston side (color code)	Rod cap side (color code)
0.0009-0.0013 in. (0.023-0.035 mm)	Yellow	Yellow
0.0014-0.0016 in. (0.036-0.042 mm)	Yellow	Green
0.0017-0.0019 in. (0.043-0.049 mm)	Green	Green
0.0020-0.0022 in. (0.050-0.057 mm)	Green	Blue
0.0023-0.0025 in. (0.058-0.065 mm)	Blue	Blue
0.0026-0.0028 in. (0.066-0.071 mm)	Blue	Red

Table 12 OIL PUMP SPECIFICATIONS

Model	Specification
4-6 hp	
Inner-to-outer rotor clearance	0.0-0.006 in. (0-0.19 mm)
Outer rotor-to-cylinder block clearance	0.005- 0.009 in. (0.127- 0.228 mm)
Outer rotor-to-cylinder block depth	0.0008-0.0035 in. (0.020-0.09 mm)
Outer rotor thickness	0.235-0.236 in. (5.994-5.97 mm)
Pump bore diameter	0.909-0.9099 in. (23.09-23.11 mm)
Pump bore depth	0.236-0.238 in. (6.0-6.06 mm)
9.9 and 15 hp	
Inner-to-outer rotor clearance	0.0008-0.0059 in. (0.02-0.15 mm)
Outer rotor-to-pump body clearance	0.0024-0.0043 in. (0.06-0.11 mm)
Outer rotor-to-pump body depth	0.0008-0.0028 in. (0.02-0.07 mm)
25-40 hp	
Inner-to-outer rotor clearance	0.0047 in. (0.12)
Outer rotor-to-pump body clearance	0.0035-0.0059 in. (0.09-0.15 mm)
Outer rotor-to-pump body depth	0.0012-0.0031 in. (0.03-0.08 mm)
50 hp	
Inner-to-outer rotor clearance	0.0047 in. (0.12)
Outer rotor-to-pump body clearance	0.0012-0.0059 in. (0.03-0.15 mm)
Outer rotor-to-pump body depth	0.0012-0.0031 in. (0.03-0.08 mm)

Table 13 CAMSHAFT SPECIFICATIONS

Model	Specification
4-6 hp	
Intake lobe height	1.038-1.047 in. (26.37-26.594 mm)
Exhaust lobe height	1.038-1.047 in. (26.37-26.594 mm)
Camshaft diameter at oil pan end	0.550 in. (13.970 mm)
Bearing diameter in the oil pan	0.5515 in. (14.008 mm)
Camshaft-to-oil pan bearing clearance	0.0008-0.002 in. (0.2-0.050 mm)
Maximum camshaft to oil pan bearing clearance	0.0027 in. (0.069 mm)
9.9 hp	
Serial No. OH000057-prior	
Intake lobe length	0.941-0.945 in. (23.90-24.00 mm)
Intake lobe width	0.785-0.789 in. (19.95-20.05 mm)
Exhaust lobe length	0.942-0.946 in. (23.92-24.02 mm)
Exhaust lobe width	0.785-0.789 in. (19.95-20.05 mm)
Camshaft diameter at oil pump end	0.7077-0.7083 in. (17.975-17.991 mm)
Camshaft diameter at pulley end	0.6289-0.6293 in. (15.973-15.984 mm)
Camshaft bore diameter (cylinder head)	0.7087-7094 in. (18.0-18.018 mm)
Serial No. OH000058-on	
Intake lobe length	0.966-0.970 in. (24.541-24.641 mm)
Intake lobe width	0.793-0.797 in. (20.137-20.237 mm)
Exhaust lobe length	0.968-0.972 in. (24.578-24.678 mm)
Exhaust lobe width	0.794-0.798 in. (20.178-20.278 mm)
Maximum camshaft runout	0.004 in. (0.1 mm)
15 hp	
Intake lobe length	0.941-0.945 in. (23.90-24.00 mm)
Intake lobe width	0.785-0.789 in. (19.95-20.05 mm)
Exhaust lobe length	0.942-0.946 in. (23.92-24.02 mm)
Exhaust lobe width	0.785-0.789 in. (19.95-20.05 mm)
Camshaft diameter at oil pump end	0.7077-0.7083 in. (17.975-17.991 mm)
Camshaft diameter at pulley end	0.6289-0.6293 in. (15.973-15.984 mm)
Camshaft bore diameter (cylinder head)	0.7087-0.7094 in. (18.0-18.018 mm)
25-40 hp	
Intake lobe length	1.2161-1.220 in. (30.89-30.99 mm)
Exhaust lobe length	1.2161-1.2173 in. (30.89-30.99 mm)

(continued)

8

Table 13 CAMSHAFT SPECIFICATIONS (continued)

Model	Specification
25-40 hp (continued)	
Intake lobe width	1.0216-1.0255 in. (25.95-26.05 mm)
Exhaust lobe width	1.0216-1.0255 in. (25.95-26.05 mm)
Camshaft diameter at bearing surfaces	1.4541-1.4549 in. (36.935-36.955 mm)
Camshaft bore diameter (cylinder head)	1.4567-1.4577 in. (37-37.025 mm)
50 hp	
Intake lobe length	1.2161-1.220 in. (30.89-30.99 mm)
Exhaust lobe length	1.2134-1.2173 in. (30.82-30.92 mm)
Intake lobe width	1.0216-1.0255 in. (25.95-26.05 mm)
Exhaust lobe width	1.0216-1.0255 in. (25.95-26.05 mm)
Camshaft diameter at bearing surfaces	
At top camshaft bearing surface	1.4541-1.4549 in. (36.935-36.955 mm)
At lower three bearing surfaces	1.4537-1.4545 in. (36.925-36.945 mm)
Camshaft bore diameter (cylinder head)	1.4567-1.4577 in. (37.000-37.025 mm)
75 and 90 hp	
Intake lobe length	1.465-1.472 in. (37.22-37.38 mm)
Exhaust lobe length	1.453-1.459 in. (36.90-37.06 mm)
Intake lobe width	1.178-1.184 in. (29.92-30.08 mm)
Exhaust lobe width	1.178-1.184 in. (29.92-30.08 mm)
Camshaft diameter at bearing surfaces	0.9827-0.9835 in. (24.96-24.98 mm)
Camshaft bore diameter (cylinder head)	0.984-0.985 in. (25-25.021 mm)

Table 14 VALVE SPRING SPECIFICATIONS

Model	Specification
4-6 hp	
Free length	
Intake	1.260 in. (32 mm)
Exhaust	1.260 in. (32 mm)
Compressed pressure	
@ open height 0.709 in. (18 mm)	31 lb. (14 kg)
@ closed height 0.965 in. (24.5 mm)	17 lb. (7.7 kg)
Out of square limit	0.043 in. (1.1 mm)
9.9 hp	
Serial No. OH000057-prior	
Free length	
Intake	1.354 in. (34.4 mm)
Exhaust	1.354 in. (34.4 mm)
Out of square limit	0.043 in. (1.1 mm)
Serial No. OH000058-on	
Compressed pressure	
closed height of 0.96 in. (24.4 mm)	19.8-22.0 lb. (8.9-9.9 kg)
Out of square limit	0.043 in. (1.1 mm)
15 hp	
Free length	
Intake	1.354 in. (34.4 mm)
Exhaust	1.354 in. (34.4 mm)
Out of square limit	0.043 in. (1.1 mm)
25-50 hp	
Free length	
Intake	1.490-1.569 in. (37.85-39.85 mm)
Exhaust	1.490-1.569 in. (37.85-39.85 mm)
Out of square limit	0.067 in. (1.7 mm)
75 and 90 hp	
Free length	
Intake	2.057 in. (52.25 mm)
Exhaust	2.057 in. (52.25 mm)
Out of square limit	0.10 in. (2.6 mm)

Table 15 VALVE SPECIFICATIONS

Model	Specification
4-6 hp	
Face width	
Intake	0.102 in. (2.59 mm)
Exhaust	0.102 in. (2.59 mm)
Valve diameter	
Intake	0.980-0.988 in. (24.89-25.09 mm)
Exhaust	0.941-0.949 in. (23.90-24.10 mm)
Minimum valve margin	
Intake	0.028 in. (0.71 mm)
Exhaust	0.047 in. (1.19 mm)
Standard seat width	
Intake	0.031 in. (0.78 mm)
Exhaust	0.031 in. (0.78 mm)
Maximum seat width	
Intake	0.0707 in. (1.79 mm)
Exhaust	0.0707 in. (1.79 mm)
Valve stem diameter	
Intake	0.2149-0.2157 in. (5.46-5.48 mm)
Exhaust	0.2133-0.2142 in. (5.42-5.44 mm)
Maximum stem runout	0.0006 in. (0.0152 mm)
9.9 hp	
Serial No. OH000057-prior	
Face width	
Intake	0.079-0.124 in. (2.00-3.14 mm)
Exhaust	0.079-0.124 in. (2.00-3.14 mm)
Valve diameter	
Intake	1.098-1.106 in. (27.9-28.1 mm)
Exhaust	0.862-0.870 in. (21.9-22.1 mm)
Seat width	
Intake	0.024-0.031 in. (0.6-0.8 mm)
Exhaust	0.024-0.031 in. (0.6-0.8 mm)
Valve margin	
Intake	0.020-0.035 in. (0.5-0.9 mm)
Exhaust	0.020-0.035 in. (0.5-0.9 mm)
Stem diameter	
Intake	0.2156-0.2161 in. (5.475-5.490 mm)
Exhaust	0.2150-0.2156 in. (5.460-5.475 mm)
Maximum stem runout	0.0006 in. (0.0152 mm)
Serial No. OH000058-on	
Face width	
Intake	0.079-0.124 in. (2.00-3.14 mm)
Exhaust	0.079-0.124 in. (2.00-3.14 mm)
Valve diameter	
Intake	1.020-1.028 in. (25.9-26.1 mm)
Exhaust	0.862-0.870 in. (21.9-22.1 mm)
Seat width	
Intake	0.024-0.031 in. (0.6-0.8 mm)
Exhaust	0.024-0.031 in. (0.6-0.8 mm)
Valve margin	
Intake	0.020-0.035 in. (0.5-0.9 mm)
Exhaust	0.020-0.035 in. (0.5-0.9 mm)
Stem diameter	
Intake	0.2156-0.2161 in. (5.475-5.490 mm)
Exhaust	0.2150-0.2156 in. (5.460-5.475 mm)
Maximum stem runout	0.0006 in. (0.0152 mm)
15 hp	
Face width	
Intake	0.079-0.124 in. (2.00-3.14 mm)
Exhaust	0.079-0.124 in. (2.00-3.14 mm)

(continued)

Table 15 VALVE SPECIFICATIONS (continued)

Model	Specification
15 hp (continued)	
Valve diameter	
Intake	1.098-1.106 in. (27.9-28.1 mm)
Exhaust	0.862-0.870 in. (21.9-22.1 mm)
Seat width	
Intake	0.024-0.031 in. (0.6-0.8 mm)
Exhaust	0.024-0.031 in. (0.6-0.8 mm)
Valve margin	
Intake	0.020-0.035 in. (0.5-0.9 mm)
Exhaust	0.020-0.035 in. (0.5-0.9 mm)
Stem diameter	
Intake	0.2156-0.2161 in. (5.475-5.490 mm)
Exhaust	0.2150-0.2156 in. (5.460-5.475 mm)
Maximum stem runout	0.0006 in. (0.0152 mm)
25-40 hp	
Face width	
Intake	0.079-0.124 in. (2.00-3.14 mm)
Exhaust	0.079-0.124 in. (2.00-3.14 mm)
Valve diameter	
Intake	1.256-1.264 in. (31.9-32.1 mm)
Exhaust	1.020-1.028 in. (25.9-26.1 mm)
Seat width	
Intake	0.035-0.043 in. (0.9-1.1 mm)
Exhaust	0.035-0.043 in. (0.9-1.1 mm)
Valve margin	
Intake	0.020-0.035 in. (0.5-0.9 mm)
Exhaust	0.020-0.035 in. (0.5-0.9 mm)
Stem diameter	
Intake	0.2156-0.2161 in. (5.475-5.490 mm)
Exhaust	0.2150-0.2156 in. (5.460-5.475 mm)
Maximum stem runout	0.0006 in. (0.0152 mm)
50 hp	
Face width	
Intake	0.079-0.124 in. (2.00-3.14 mm)
Exhaust	0.079-0.124 in. (2.00-3.14 mm)
Valve diameter	
Intake	1.177-1.185 in. (29.9-30.1 mm)
Exhaust	1.020-1.028 in. (25.9-26.1 mm)
Seat width	
Intake	0.035-0.043 in. (0.9-1.1 mm)
Exhaust	0.035-0.043 in. (0.9-1.1 mm)
Valve margin	
Intake	0.020-0.035 in. (0.5-0.9 mm)
Exhaust	0.020-0.035 in. (0.5-0.9 mm)
Stem diameter	
Intake	0.2156-0.2161 in. (5.475-5.490 mm)
Exhaust	0.2150-0.2156 in. (5.460-5.475 mm)
Maximum stem runout	0.0006 in. (0.0152 mm)
75 and 90 hp	
Face width	
Intake	0.079-0.096 in. (2-2.43 mm)
Exhaust	0.090-0.107 in. (2.28-2.71 mm)
Valve diameter	
Intake	1.142-1.150 in. (29-29.20 mm)
Exhaust	0.945-0.953 in. (24-24.20 mm)
Seat width	
Intake	0.014-0.022 in. (0.35-0.55 mm)
Exhaust	0.014-0.022 in. (0.35-0.55 mm)

(continued)

Table 15 VALVE SPECIFICATIONS (continued)

Model	Specification
75 and 90 hp (continued)	
Valve margin	
Intake	0.018-0.026 in. (0.45-0.65 mm)
Exhaust	0.026-0.033 in. (0.65-0.85 mm)
Stem diameter	
Intake	0.2352-0.2358 in. (5.975-5.990 mm)
Exhaust	0.2346-0.2252 in. (5.960-5.975mm)
Maximum stem runout	0.001 in. (0.03 mm)

Table 16 VALVE GUIDE SPECIFICATIONS

Model	Specifications
4-6 hp	
Standard valve guide bore diameter	
Intake	0.2165 in. (5.499 mm)
Exhaust	0.2165 in. (5.499 mm)
Maximum valve guide bore diameter	
Intake	0.2180 in. (5.539 mm)
Exhaust	0.2191 in. (5.567 mm)
Valve stem-to-valve guide clearance	
Intake	0.0008-0.0017 in. (0.020- 0.043 mm)
Exhaust	0.0018-0.0028 in. (0.045-0.072 mm)
9.9-50 hp	
Guide bore diameter	
Intake	0.2165-0.2170 in. (5.500-5.512 mm)
Exhaust	0.2165-0.2170 in. (5.500-5.512 mm)
Valve stem-to-valve guide clearance	
Intake	0.0004-0.0015 in. (0.010-0.037 mm)
Exhaust	0.0010-0.0020 in. (0.025-0.052 mm)
75 and 90 hp	
Guide bore diameter	
Intake	0.2364-0.2369 in. (6.005-6.018 mm)
Exhaust	0.2364-0.2369 in. (6.005-6.018 mm)
Valve stem-to-valve guide clearance	
Intake	0.0006-0.0017 in. (0.015-0.043 mm)
Exhaust	0.0012-0.0023 in. (0.030-0.058 mm)
Valve guide height	
Intake	0.45 in. (11.5 mm)
Exhaust	0.45 in. (11.5 mm)

Table 17 VALVE SEAT SPECIFICATIONS

Model	Specification
4-6 hp	
Standard valve seat width	
Intake	0.031 in. (0.78 mm)
Exhaust	0.031 in. (0.78 mm)
Maximum valve seat width	
Intake	0.069 in. (1.75 mm)
Exhaust	0.069 in. (1.75 mm
9.9 and 15 hp	
Valve seat width	
Intake	0.024-0.031 in. (0.6-0.8 mm)
Exhaust	0.024-0.031 in. (0.6-0.8 mm)

(continued)

Table 17 VALVE SEAT SPECIFICATIONS

Model	Specification
25-50 hp	
Valve seat width	
Intake	0.035-0.043 in. (0.9-1.1 mm)
Exhaust	0.035-0.043 in. (0.9-1.1 mm)
75 and 90 hp	
Valve seat width	
Intake	0.014-0.022 in. (0.35-0.55 mm)
Exhaust	0.014-0.022 in. (0.35-0.55 mm)

Table 18 ROCKER ARM AND SHAFT SPECIFICATIONS

Model	Specification
9.9 and 15 hp	
Rocker arm bore diameter	0.5118-0.5125 in. (13.13.018 mm)
Rocker arm shaft diameter	0.5095-0.5099 in. (12.941-12.951 mm)
25-50 hp	
Rocker arm bore diameter	0.6299-0.6306 in. (16-16.018 mm)
Rocker arm shaft diameter	0.6288-0.6296 in. (15.971-15.991 mm)

Table 19 WARPAGE LIMITS

Model	Maximum warpage
4-6 hp	
Cylinder head	0.0012 in. (0.030 mm)
9.9-90 hp	
Cylinder head	0.004 in. (0.10 mm)

Chapter Nine

Gearcase

This chapter provides gearcase removal, repair and installation instructions.

Failure of the gearcase is usually the result of impact with underwater objects or lack of gearcase maintenance. Proper maintenance is essential for proper operation and durability. Gearcase maintenance instructions are provided in Chapter Four.

Special tools and accurate measuring devices are required to remove, position and install many of the gearcase components. The use of makeshift tools may result in irreparable damage to the housing or internal components of the gearcase. Part numbers for these tools are included in the repair instructions. Contact a Mercury or Mariner dealership to purchase these special tools. Some dealerships will rent or loan special tools.

Improper repair can result in extensive and expensive damage to the gearcase. Have a reputable marine repair shop perform the repair if access to the required tools and measuring devices is unavailable.

GEARCASE OPERATION

The gearcase transfers the rotation of the vertical drive shaft (**Figure 1**) to the horizontal propeller shaft. The forward and reverse gears along with the sliding clutch (**Figure 1**) transfer the rotational force to the propeller shaft. The shift selector and linkage moves the clutch.

The pinion and both driven gears (**Figure 1**) rotate anytime the engine is running. A sliding clutch (**Figure 1**) engages the propeller with either the forward or reverse gear.

When neutral is desired (**Figure 1**) the propeller shaft remains stationary as the gears rotate. No propeller thrust is delivered.

When forward gear is desired, (**Figure 1**) the sliding clutch is moved with the shift mechanism to the forward gear. The propeller shaft rotates in the direction of the forward gear as the clutch dogs or raised bosses engage the gear. This provides the clockwise propeller shaft rotation direction necessary for forward thrust.

When reverse gear is desired (**Figure 1**), the sliding clutch is moved by the shift shafts and linkage toward the reverse gear. The propeller shaft rotates in the direction if the reverse gear as the clutch dogs engage the gear. This provides the counterclockwise propeller shaft rotation necessary for reverse thrust.

GEARCASE IDENTIFICATION

All 9.9-15 and 30-50 hp models are available with an optional gearcase. The optional gearcase is larger than the standard gearcase. Engines with the optional gearcase require different components and repair procedures than engines with a standard gearcase. This section provides information that assists with identifying the gearcase used on the various models.

To identify the gearcase, measure the diameter of the gearcase (**Figure 2**) at the propeller shaft end and refer to the following information.

4-6 hp Models

The optional gearcase is not available on these models. The gearcase used on these models contains a 13 tooth pinion gear along with 28 tooth forward and reverse gears to deliver a 2.15:1 final drive ratio.

9.9 and 15 hp Models

Models with the standard gearcase are equipped with a 2.6 in. (66 mm) gearcase. This gearcase contains a 13 tooth pinion gear along with 26 tooth forward and reverse gears to provide a 2:1 final drive ratio.

Models with the optional gearcase use a 3.375 in. (86 mm) gearcase. The larger gearcase contains a 12 tooth pinion gear along with 29 tooth forward and reverse gears to provide a 2.42:1 final drive ratio.

25 hp Models

An optional gearcase is not available for this model. A 3.44 in. (87 mm) diameter gearcase is used on all models. This gearcase contains a 12 tooth pinion gear along with 29 tooth forward and reverse gears to provide a 2.42:1 final drive ratio.

30 and 40 hp Models

Models with the standard gearcase use a 3.44 in. (87 mm) gearcase. The standard gearcase contains a 13 tooth

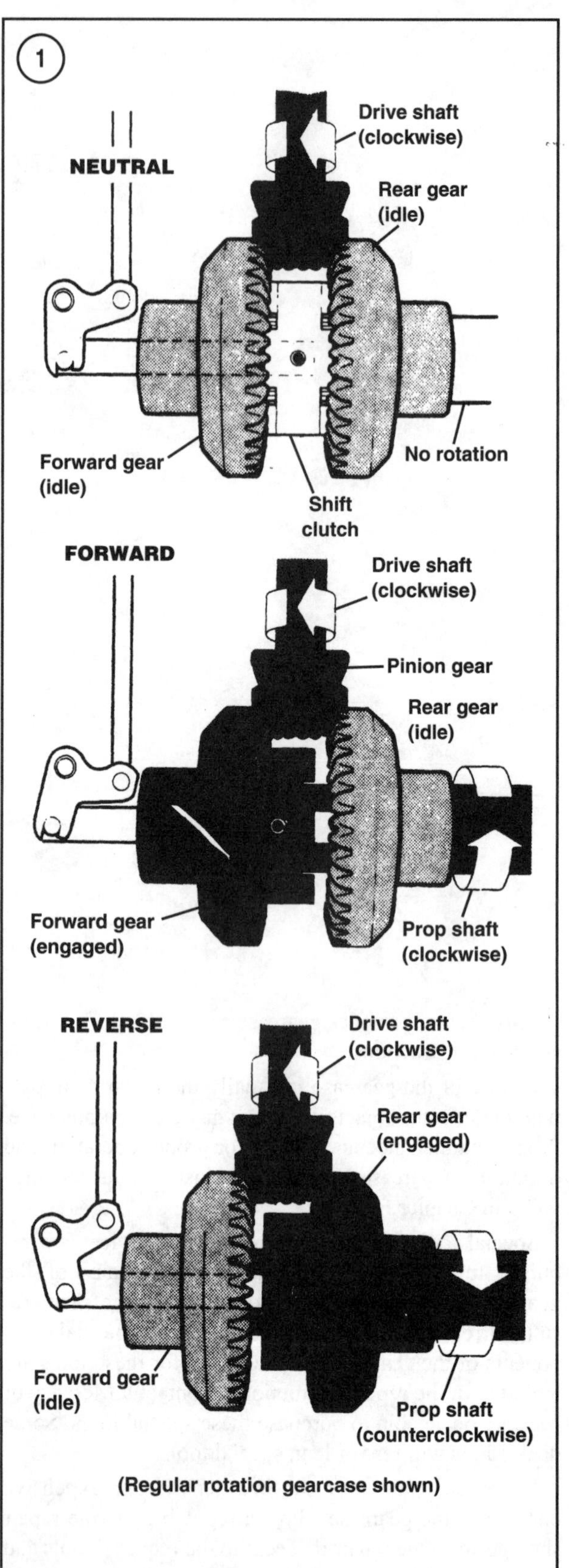

(Regular rotation gearcase shown)

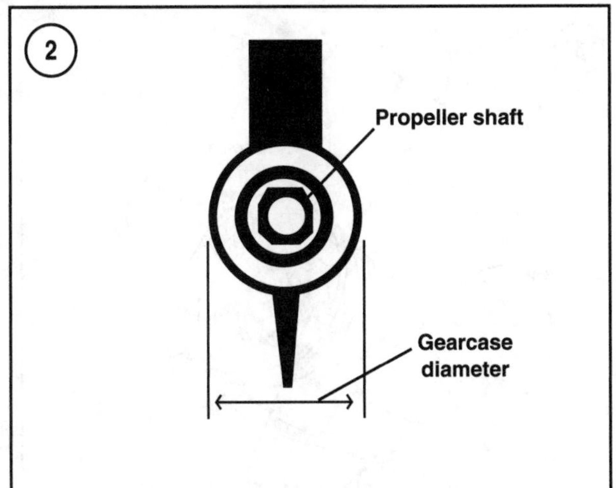

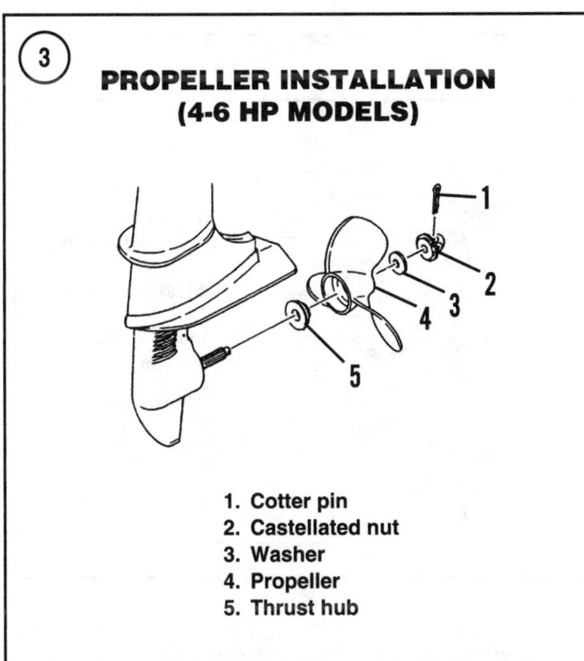

PROPELLER INSTALLATION (4-6 HP MODELS)

1. Cotter pin
2. Castellated nut
3. Washer
4. Propeller
5. Thrust hub

pinion gear along with 26 tooth forward and reverse gears to provide a 2:1 final drive ratio.

Models with the optional gearcase use a 4.25in. (108 mm) gearcase. The larger gearcase contains a 13 tooth pinion gear along with 30 tooth forward and reverse gears to provide a 2.3:1 final drive ratio.

50 hp Models

Models with the standard gearcase use a 3.44 in. (87 mm) gearcase. All 1995 and 1996 model standard size gearcases contain a 13 tooth pinion gear along with 26

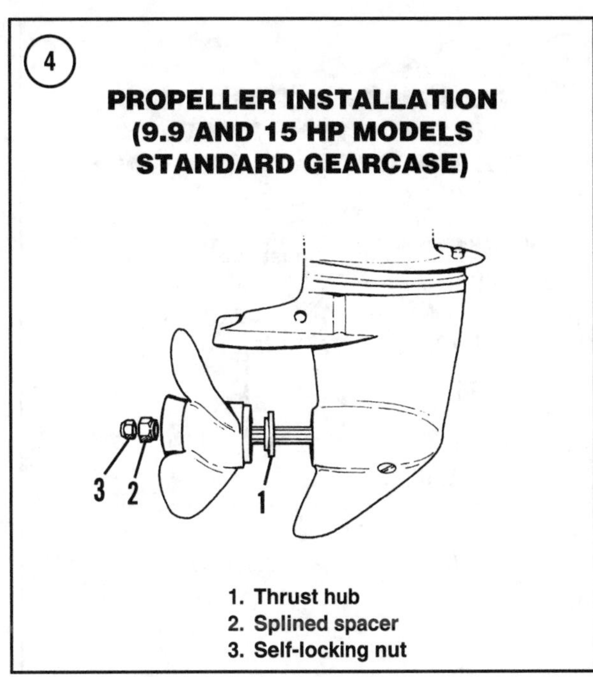

PROPELLER INSTALLATION (9.9 AND 15 HP MODELS STANDARD GEARCASE)

1. Thrust hub
2. Splined spacer
3. Self-locking nut

9

tooth forward and reverse gears to provide a 2:1 final drive ratio. All 1997-on models with the standard size gearcases contain a 12 tooth pinion and a 22 tooth forward and reverse gear to provide a 1.83:1 final drive ratio.

Models with the optional gearcase use a 4.25 in. (108 mm) gearcase. The larger gearcase contains a 13 tooth pinion gear and 30 tooth forward and reverse gears to provide a 2.3:1 final drive ratio.

75 and 90 hp Models

An optional larger gearcase is not available for these models. A 3.44 in. (108 mm) diameter gearcase is used on this model. This gearcase contains a 14 tooth pinion gear and 29 tooth forward and reverse gears to provide a 2.07:1 final drive ratio.

PROPELLER

On 4-6 hp models, the propeller is held the propeller shaft with a cotter pin, castellated nut and washer (1-3, **Figure 3**). The thrust hub (5, **Figure 3**) is located on the propeller shaft forward of the propeller.

On all 9.9 and 15 hp models with the standard gearcase, the propeller is held on the propeller shaft with a splined spacer and self-locking propeller nut (2 and 3, **Figure 4**). The thrust hub (1, **Figure 4**) is located on the propeller shaft forward of the propeller. The smaller diameter side of the thrust hub faces the propeller.

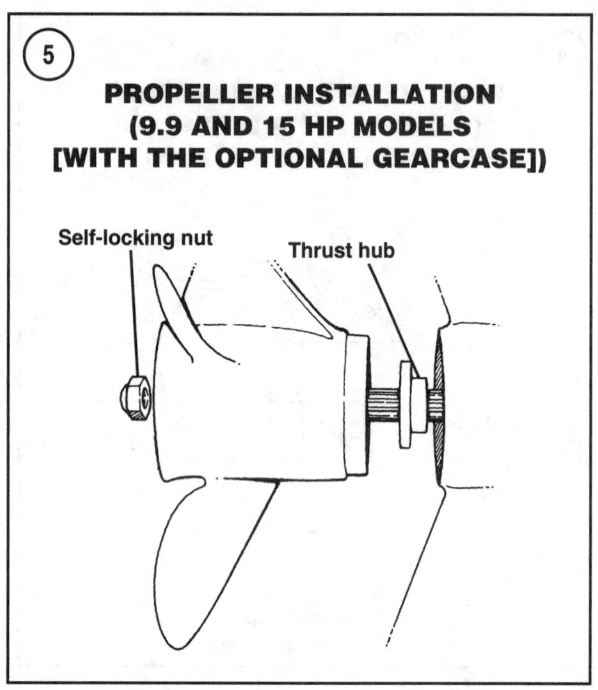

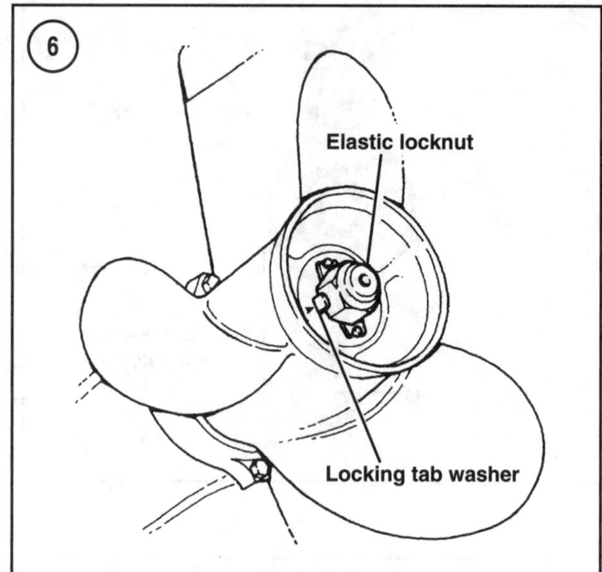

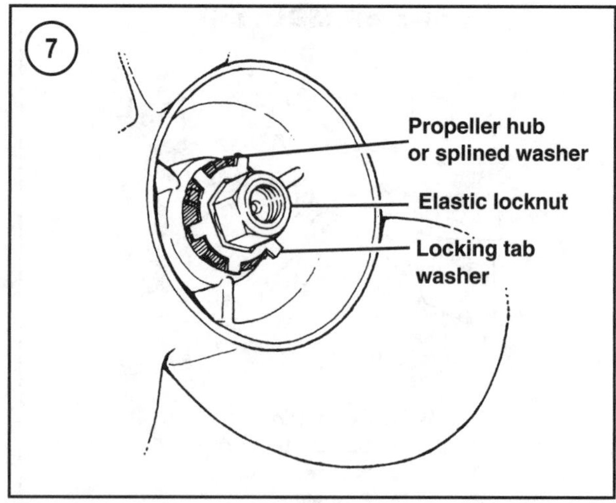

On all 9.9 and 15 hp models with the optional gearcase, the propeller is held on the propeller shaft with a self-locking propeller nut (**Figure 5**). Neither a locking tab, cotter pin or washer is used on this gearcase. The thrust hub is located on the propeller shaft forward of the propeller. The smaller diameter side of the thrust hub faces the gearcase.

On all 25-50 hp models, the propeller is held on the propeller shaft with an elastic locknut and locking tab washer (**Figure 6**). A splined washer, elastic locknut and locking tab washer (**Figure 7**) are also used. Some models use a propeller equipped with the Flo-Torq II hub (2, **Figure 8**). The Flo-Torq hub replaces the rubber shock absorbing hub used on other propellers. The thrust hub (1, **Figure 8**) is located on the propeller shaft forward of the propeller. The tapered inner diameter of the thrust hub faces the gearcase.

On all 75 and 90 hp models, the propeller is held on the propeller shaft with a splined propeller hub or washer, elastic locknut and locking tab washer (**Figure 7**). Some models use a propeller equipped with the Flo-Torq II hub (2, **Figure 8**). The Flo-Torq II hub replaces the rubber shock absorbing hub used on other propellers. The thrust hub (1, **Figure 8**) is located on the propeller shaft and forward of the propeller. The tapered inner diameter of the thrust hub faces the gearcase.

CAUTION

The use of excessive force can damage the propeller, propeller shaft and other internal gearcase components. Have a marine repair shop or propeller repair shop remove the propeller if unable to remove the propeller.

Propeller Removal/Installation (Cotter Pin and Castellated Nut)

A cotter pin and castellated nut is used to secure the propeller on 4-6 hp models. Remove and install the propeller as follows:

1. Remove the spark plug. Connect the spark plug lead to a suitable engine ground.

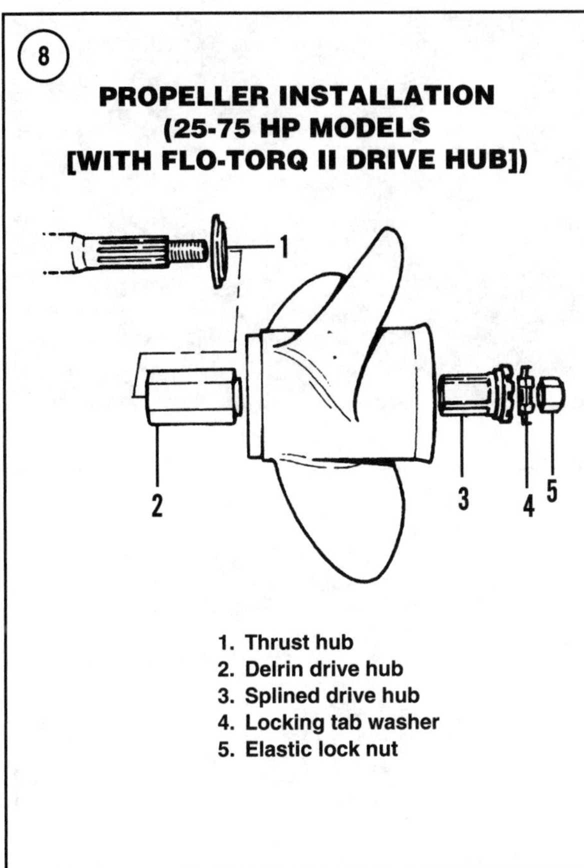

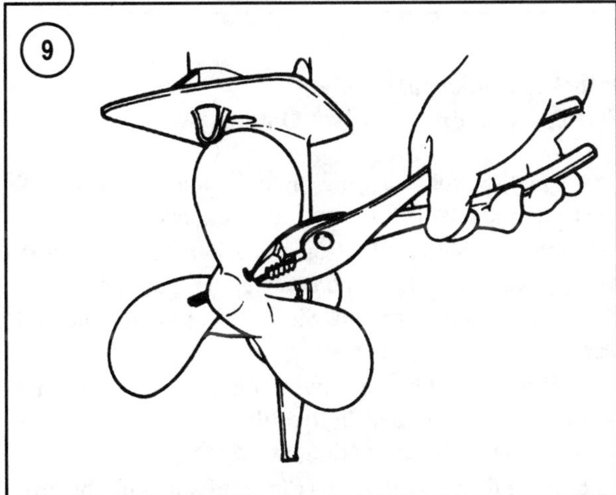

2. Shift the engine into NEUTRAL. Straighten the ends of the cotter pin and pull it from the castellated nut and propeller shaft (**Figure 9**).

3. Place a block of wood between the propeller blade and the antiventilation plate (**Figure 10**). Loosen the propeller nut in a counterclockwise direction.

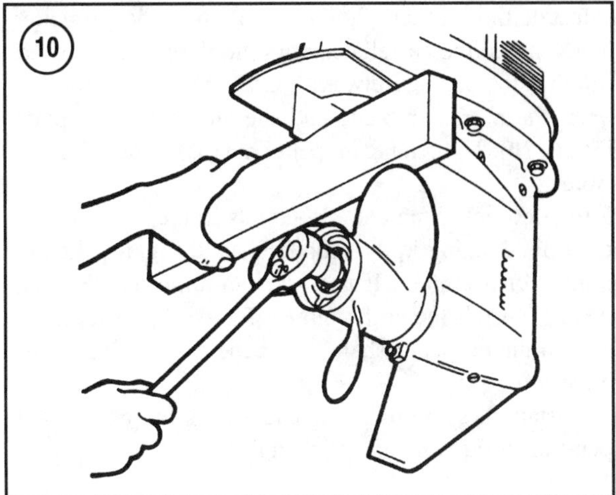

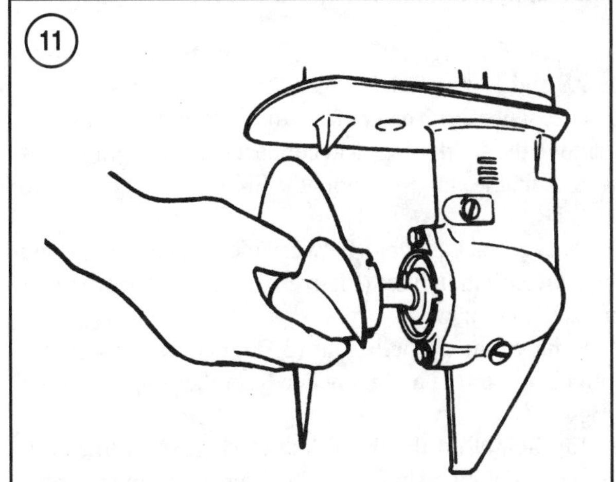

4. Remove the propeller nut and washer (2 and 3, **Figure 3**) then pull the propeller from the propeller shaft (**Figure 11**).

5. Tap lightly on the thrust hub (5, **Figure 3**) to free it from the propeller shaft. Clean all corrosion and grease from the propeller shaft splines, propeller shaft threads and the thrust washer.

6. Apply a coat of Quicksilver 2-4-C Marine Lubricant (Mercury part No. 92-825407A12) or a good quality water-resistant grease to the exposed surfaces of the propeller shaft except the threads.

7. Slide the thrust hub (5, **Figure 3**) over the propeller shaft with the larger diameter side facing the gearcase. Align the splined inner diameter of the propeller (4, **Figure 3**) with the splines of the propeller shaft and slide the propeller fully onto the propeller shaft. Ensure the propeller seats against the thrust washer (5, **Figure 3**).

8. Install the washer (2, **Figure 3**) over the propeller shaft. Thread the castellated nut onto the propeller shaft with the slots facing outward. Place a block of wood between the propeller blade and the antiventilation plate (**Figure 10**). Tighten the propeller nut to the specification **Table 1**.
9. Inspect the alignment of the slots in the nut with the cotter pin opening in the propeller shaft. Tighten the nut an additional amount if necessary to align the slot and opening. Install the cotter pin (1, **Figure 3**) through the slot and the propeller shaft, then bend over both ends of cotter pin.
10. Install the spark plug and lead. Check for proper shift operation before operating the engine.

Propeller Removal/Installation (Splined Spacer and Self-Locking Propeller Nut)

A splined spacer and self locking propeller nut is used on 9.9 and 15 hp models with a standard gearcase.

1. Disconnect both cables from the battery if so equipped. Remove the spark plugs and connect the spark plug leads to a suitable engine ground. Shift the engine into NEUTRAL.
2. Place a block of wood between the propeller blade and the antiventilation plate (**Figure 10**). Loosen the propeller nut counterclockwise.
3. Remove the propeller nut (3, **Figure 4**) and pull the splined spacer (2) and propeller from the propeller shaft (**Figure 12**).
4. Tap lightly on the thrust hub (5, **Figure 3**) to free it from the propeller shaft. Pull the thrust hub from the propeller shaft (**Figure 13**). Clean all corrosion and grease from the propeller shaft splines, propeller shaft threads and the thrust washer.
5. Apply a coat of Quicksilver 2-4-C Marine Lubricant (Mercury part No. 92-825407A12) or a good quality water-resistant grease to the exposed surfaces of the propeller shaft except the threads.
6. Slide the thrust hub over the propeller shaft with the larger diameter side facing the gearcase (**Figure 13**). Slide the propeller fully onto the propeller shaft. Ensure the propeller seats against the thrust washer (1, **Figure 4**).
7. Install the splined spacer (2, **Figure 4**) over the propeller shaft. Seat the spacer against the propeller.
8. Thread the propeller nut onto the propeller shaft with the rounded side facing outward. Place a block of wood between the propeller blade and the antiventilation plate (**Figure 10**). Tighten the self-locking propeller nut to the specification in **Table 1**.
9. Install the spark plugs and leads and connect the cables to the battery if so equipped.

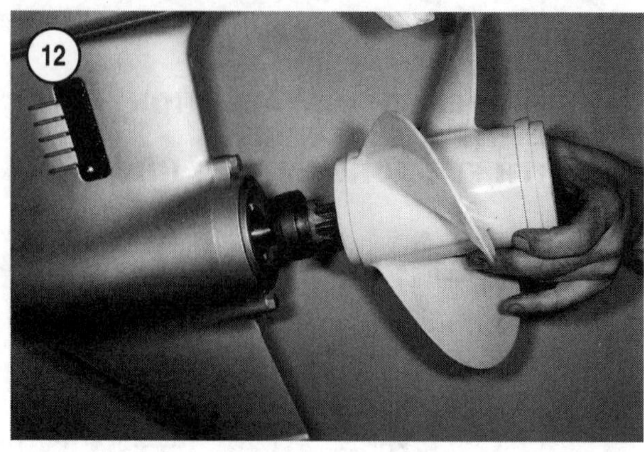

12

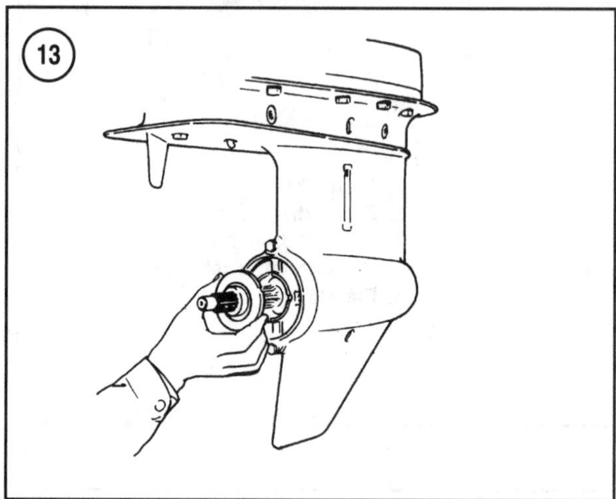

13

Propeller Removal/Installation (Self-Locking Propeller Nut Only)

This method for attaching the propeller is used on 9.9 and 15 hp models with the optional gearcase.

1. Disconnect both cables from the battery if so equipped. Remove the spark plugs and connect the spark plug leads to a suitable engine ground. Shift the engine into neutral gear.
2. Place a block of wood between the propeller blade and the antiventilation plate (**Figure 10**). Loosen the propeller nut in a counterclockwise direction.
3. Remove the propeller nut (**Figure 5**) and pull the propeller from the propeller shaft (**Figure 12**).
4. Tap lightly on the thrust hub (**Figure 5**) to free it from the propeller shaft. Pull the thrust hub from the propeller shaft (**Figure 13**). Clean all corrosion and grease from the propeller shaft splines, propeller shaft threads and the thrust washer.
5. Apply a coat of Quicksilver 2-4-C Marine Lubricant (Mercury part No. 92-825407A12) or a good quality wa-

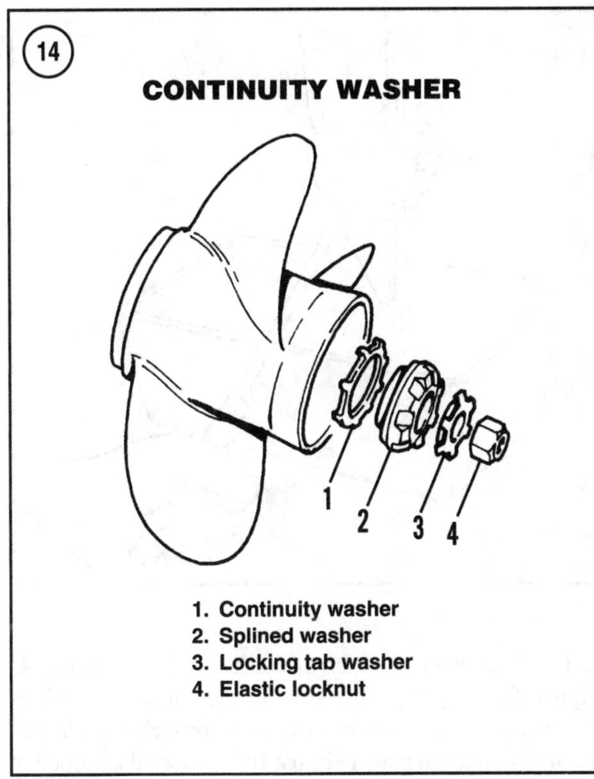

ter-resistant grease to the exposed surfaces of the propeller shaft except the threads.

6. Slide the thrust hub over the propeller shaft with the larger diameter side facing the propeller (**Figure 13**). Slide the propeller fully onto the propeller shaft. Seat the propeller against the thrust washer.

7. Thread the propeller nut onto the propeller shaft with the rounded side facing outward. Place a block of wood between the propeller blade and the antiventilation plate (**Figure 10**). Tighten the propeller nut to the specification in **Table 1**.

8. Install the spark plugs and leads and connect the cables to the battery if so equipped.

Propeller Removal/Installation (Elastic Lock Nut and Locking Tab Washer)

This method of attaching the propeller is used on 25-50 hp models with a standard gearcase.

1. Disconnect both cables from the battery if so equipped. Remove the spark plugs and connect the spark plug leads to a suitable engine ground. Shift the engine into neutral gear.

2. Carefully bend the tabs of the washer away from the propeller nut. Place a block of wood between the propeller blade and the antiventilation plate (**Figure 10**). Loosen the propeller nut in a counterclockwise direction.

3. Remove the propeller nut and pull the locking tab washer (**Figure 6**) from the propeller shaft. Pull the propeller from the propeller shaft (**Figure 12**).

4. Tap lightly on the thrust hub to free it from the propeller shaft. Pull the thrust hub from the propeller shaft (**Figure 13**). Clean all corrosion and grease from the propeller shaft splines, propeller shaft threads, elastic lock nut and the thrust washer.

5. Apply a coat of Quicksilver 2-4-C Marine Lubricant (Mercury part No. 92-825407A12) or a good quality water-resistant grease to the exposed surfaces of the propeller shaft except the threads.

6. Slide the thrust hub over the propeller shaft with the tapered inner diameter facing the gearcase. Slide the propeller fully onto the propeller shaft. Seat the propeller against the thrust washer.

7. Place the locking tab washer over the propeller shaft with the bent ends facing outward. Align both notches in the washer with the locating bosses on the rear of the propeller.

8. Thread the propeller nut onto the propeller shaft with the rounded side facing outward. Place a block of wood between the propeller blade and the antiventilation plate (**Figure 10**). Tighten the propeller nut to the specification in **Table 1**.

9. Inspect the alignment of the locking tabs and the flat surfaces of the elastic lock nut (**Figure 6**). Tighten the nut an additional amount if necessary to align two of the tabs with the nut. Carefully bend the tabs against the flat surfaces of the nut.

10. Install the spark plugs and leads and connect the cables to the battery if so equipped.

Propeller Removal/Installation (Splined Washer, Elastic Locknut and Locking Tab Washer)

This method of attaching the propeller is used on some 25-50 hp models with the optional gearcase along with 75 and 90 hp models.

1. Disconnect both cables from the battery if so equipped. Remove the spark plugs and connect the spark plug leads to a suitable engine ground. Shift the engine into NEUTRAL.

2. Carefully bend the tabs of the locking tab washer (3, **Figure 14**) away from the splined washer (2).Place a block of wood between the propeller blade and the antiventilation plate (**Figure 10**). Loosen the propeller nut in a counterclockwise direction.

9

3. Remove the elastic locknut and pull the locking tab washer and splined washer (2 and 3, **Figure 14**) from the propeller shaft. Lift the continuity washer (1, **Figure 14**) from the propeller. Pull the propeller from the propeller shaft (**Figure 12**).
4. Tap lightly on the thrust hub to free it from the propeller shaft. Pull the thrust hub from the propeller shaft (**Figure 13**). Clean all corrosion and grease from the propeller shaft splines, propeller shaft threads, continuity washer, elastic lock nut and the thrust washer.
5. Apply a coat of Quicksilver 2-4-C Marine Lubricant (Mercury part No. 92-825407A12) or a good quality water-resistant grease to the exposed surfaces of the propeller shaft except the threads.
6. Slide the thrust hub over the propeller shaft with the tapered inner diameter facing the gearcase. Slide the propeller fully onto the propeller shaft. Seat the propeller against the thrust washer.
7. Install the continuity washer (1, **Figure 14**). Slide the splined washer (2, **Figure 14**) onto the propeller shaft with the tab slots facing outward. Align the splines in the washer with the splines of the propeller shaft then seat the splined washer against the continuity washer and the propeller. Check for proper seating of the continuity washer against the stepped portion of the splined washer.
8. Place the locking tab washer (3, **Figure 14**) over the propeller shaft with the open end facing outward. Seat the locking tab washer against the splined washer.
9. Thread the propeller nut onto the propeller shaft with the rounded side facing outward. Align the nut with the hexagon shaped opening in the locking tab washer as the nut seats against the washer.
10. Place a block of wood between the propeller blade and the antiventilation plate (**Figure 10**). Tighten the propeller nut to the specification in **Table 1**.
11. Inspect the alignment of the locking tabs and tab slots in the splined washer. Tighten the nut an additional amount if necessary to align two of the tabs with the washer. Carefully bend the tabs down into the tab slots.
12. Install the spark plugs and leads and connect the cables to the battery if so equipped.

Propeller Removal/Installation (Flo-Torq II Hub)

This method of attaching the propeller is used on some 25-50 hp models with the optional gearcase along with 75 and 90 hp models.

1. Disconnect both cables from the battery if so equipped. Remove the spark plugs and connect the spark plug leads to a suitable engine ground. Shift the engine into NEUTRAL gear.

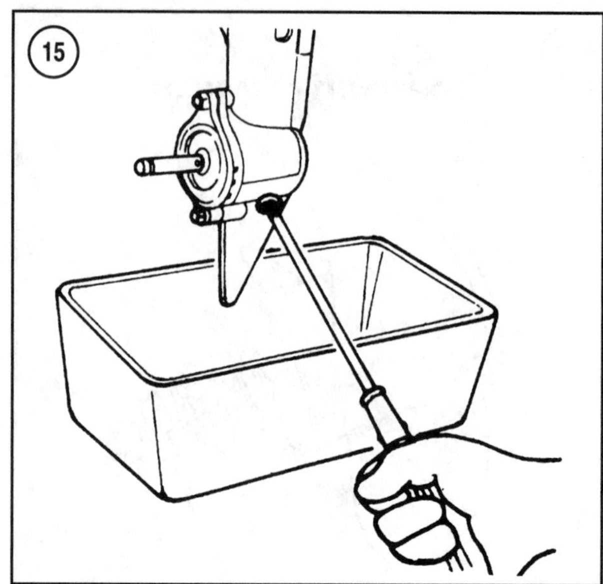

2. Carefully bend the tabs of the locking tab washer (4, **Figure 8**) away from the slots in the splined drive hub (3).Place a block of wood between the propeller blade and the antiventilation plate (**Figure 10**). Loosen the propeller nut in a counterclockwise direction.
3. Remove the elastic locknut and pull the locking tab washer (4, **Figure 8**) from the propeller shaft. Pull the propeller from the propeller shaft (**Figure 12**). Pull the splined drive hub (3, **Figure 8**) from the propeller.
4. Tap lightly on the thrust hub (1, **Figure 8**) to free it from the propeller shaft. Pull the thrust hub from the propeller shaft (**Figure 13**). Pull the delrin drive hub (2, **Figure 8**) from the bore of the propeller. Drive the hub out of the propeller through the propeller nut side if necessary.
5. Clean all corrosion and grease from the propeller shaft splines, propeller shaft threads, splined drive hub, elastic locknut and the thrust washer. Inspect the delrin drive hub for worn, cracked or soft surfaces. Replace the drive hub if any questionable conditions exist.
6. Insert the smaller diameter side of the delrin drive hub (2, **Figure 8**) into the opening on the forward side of the propeller. Align the hub with the propeller bore then press it firmly into the propeller by hand. Apply a coat of Quicksilver 2-4-C Marine Lubricant (Mercury part No. 92-825407A12) or a good quality water-resistant grease to the exposed surfaces of the propeller shaft except the threads.
7. Slide the thrust hub (1, **Figure 8**) over the propeller shaft with the tapered inner diameter facing the gearcase. Slide the propeller over the propeller shaft. Seat the delrin drive hub (2, **Figure 8**) against the thrust hub (1). Align the splines of the drive hub (3, **Figure 8**) with the splines

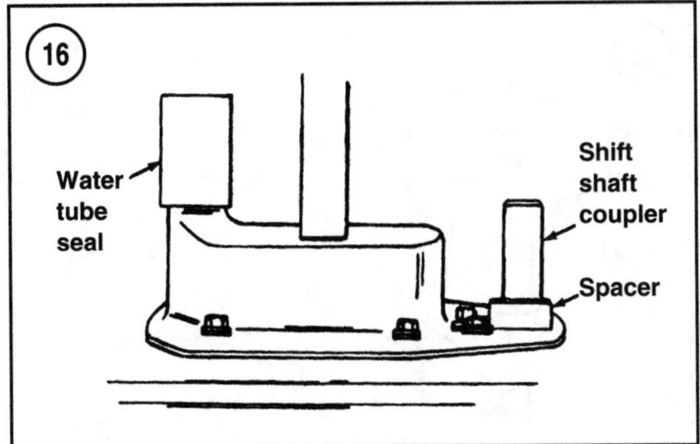

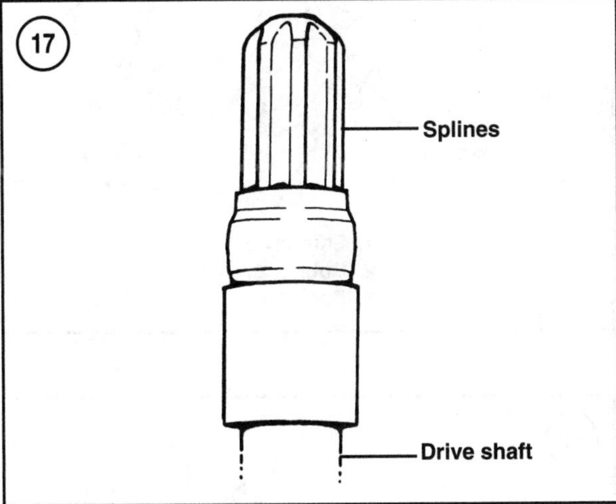

of the propeller shaft. Slide the drive hub (3, **Figure 8**) onto the propeller shaft. Rotate the propeller until the four slots in the delrin drive hub align with the four raised ridges of the splined drive hub. Seat the drive hub against the propeller.

8. Place the locking tab washer (4, **Figure 8**) over the propeller shaft with the open end facing outward. Seat the locking tab washer against the splined drive hub.

9. Thread the elastic locknut onto the propeller shaft with the rounded side facing outward. Align the nut with the hexagon shaped opening in the locking tab washer as the nut seats against the washer.

10. Place a block of wood between the propeller blade and the antiventilation plate (**Figure 10**). Tighten the propeller nut to the specification in **Table 1**.

11. Inspect the alignment of the locking tabs and tab slots in the splined drive hub (3, **Figure 8**). Tighten the nut an additional amount if necessary to align two of the tabs with the washer. Carefully bend the tabs down into the tab slots.

12. Install the spark plugs and leads and connect the cables to the battery if so equipped. Check and correct the propeller nut tightening torque after operating the engine.

GEARCASE REMOVAL AND INSTALLATION

To help prevent injury *always remove the propeller, spark plugs and both battery cables prior to removing the gearcase*. Refer to *Propeller Removal and Installation* in this chapter.

It is always easier to work on a clean engine. Clean the exterior of the gearcase and drive shaft housing before removing the gearcase.

Routine water pump maintenance requires removal of the gearcase. It is a good practice to change the gearcase lubricant anytime the gearcase is removed.

Always drain the lubricant (**Figure 15**) prior to removing the gearcase. It is far easier to properly position the gearcase drain openings with the gearcase mounted on the engine than with the gearcase mounted to a work bench. Follow the gearcase drain and fill procedure in Chapter Four.

CAUTION

Avoid directing pressurized water at exposed seals or exhaust openings. Pressurized water can blow past seals and contaminate the gearcase lubricant or damage the seal. Pressurized water can reach the internal power head components if directed into the exhaust openings.

After gearcase removal, clean from the drive shaft, shift shaft and gearcase mating surfaces. Dirt or debris left on the shaft can contaminate the gearcase lubricant as external seals or covers are removed.

Inspect the grommet or seal connecting the water tube to the water pump (**Figure 16**) for damage or deterioration. Apply grease to the grommet prior to installation of the gearcase.

Inspect the water tube for bent, corroded or cracked surfaces. Replace the water tube if defects are noted. Ensure the dowels or locating pins are properly positioned in the gearcase or drive shaft housing upon installation.

Apply Quicksilver 2-4-C Marine Lubricant (Mercury part No. 92-825407A12) or other good quality water resistant grease to the splines of the drive shaft (**Figure 17**) prior to gearcase installation.

CAUTION

Never apply grease to the top of the drive shaft or fill the splines of the crankshaft with grease. The grease may cause a hydraulic

9

lock on the shaft that can cause failure of the power head and the gearcase. Apply only a light coat of lubricant to the splines.

CAUTION
Use caution if using a pry bar to separate the gearcase from the drive shaft housing. Remove all fasteners before attempting to pry the gearcase from the drive shaft housing. Use a blunt pry bar and locate a pry point near the front and rear mating surfaces. Apply moderate heat to the gearcase to drive shaft housing mating surfaces if corrosion prevents easy removal.

CAUTION
Work carefully when installing the upper end of the drive shaft into the crankshaft. The lower seal on the crankshaft may dislodge or become damaged by the drive shaft. Never force the drive shaft into position. Rotate the drive shaft clockwise as viewed from the top to align the drive shaft and crankshaft spines.

Removal (4-6 hp Models)

Two bolts secure the gearcase to the drive shaft housing on these models. One is located at the rear of the antiventilation plate just behind the water screen. The other bolt is located near the forward edge of the gearcase just below the gearcase mating surfaces.

1. Remove the spark plug then connect the spark plug lead to a suitable engine ground.
2. Remove the propeller and attaching hardware following the instructions in this chapter.
3. Shift the engine into REVERSE gear. Place the engine in the full tilt position the engage the tilt lock mechanism.
4. Carefully pry the rubber grommet (2, **Figure 18**) from the starboard side of the drive shaft housing. Using a felt tip marker, mark the mating surfaces of the upper and lower shift shafts (**Figure 19**). This step helps ensure correct shift adjustment after installing the gearcase.
5. Loosen the bolt (3, **Figure 18**) to free the shift shafts from the clamp.
6. Support the gearcase and remove both gearcase retaining bolts.
7. Carefully tug or pry the gearcase from the drive shaft housing. Pull the gearcase straight from the drive shaft housing to prevent damage to the shift shaft, lower crankshaft seals and water tube.

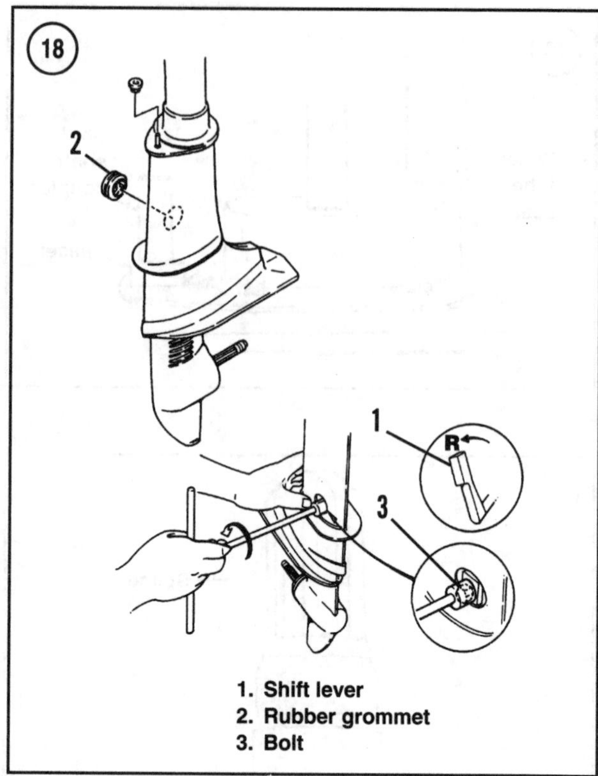

1. Shift lever
2. Rubber grommet
3. Bolt

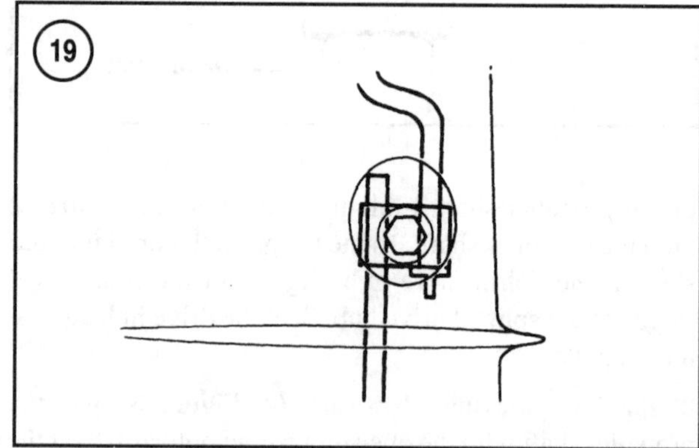

8. Place the gearcase in a suitable holding fixture or securely clamp the skeg in a bench vise. Use wooden blocks or padded jaws to prevent damage to the skeg.

Installation (4-6 hp Models)

CAUTION
Never rotate the propeller shaft to align the drive shaft with the crankshaft. The water pump impeller can suffer damage leading to overheating of the engine.

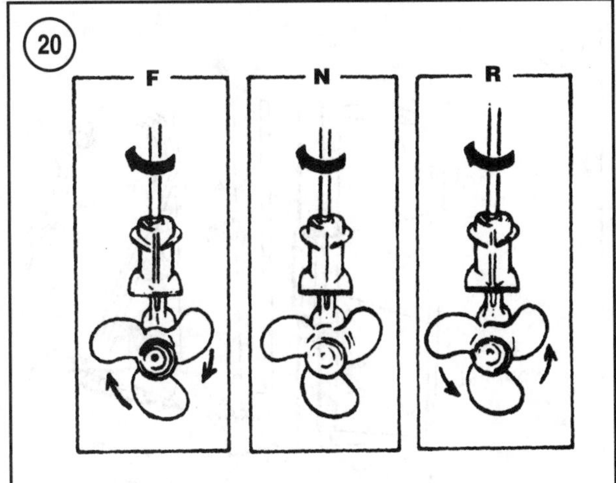

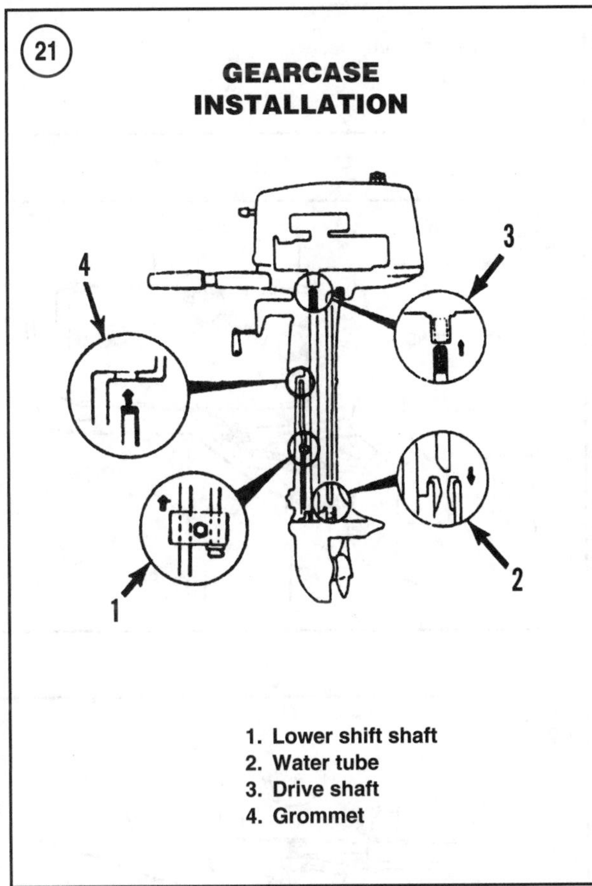

1. Push down the shift shaft until reverse gear is engaged. Rotate the drive shaft clockwise as viewed from the top to check for proper engagement. The propeller shaft rotates counterclockwise (**Figure 20**) if reverse gear is engaged.
2. Apply a light coat of water-resistant grease to the splines of the drive shaft.

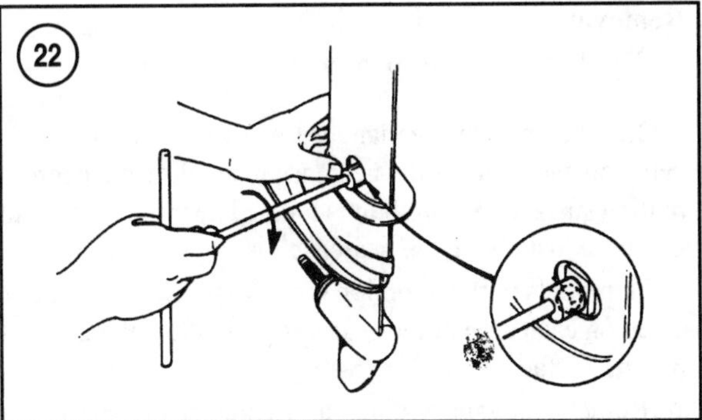

3. Carefully slide the drive shaft into its opening (3, **Figure 21**). Guide the lower shift shaft through the rubber grommet in the drive shaft housing (4, **Figure 21**).
4. Keep the gearcase and drive shaft housing mating surfaces parallel while aligning the bolt holes in the gearcase with the holes in the drive shaft housing. Also note the following:
   a. Align the water tube in the drive shaft housing with the water tube sealing grommet (2, **Figure 21**) while sliding the gearcase into position.
   b. Guide the lower and upper shift shafts into the connector (1, **Figure 21**) as the gearcase is installed.
5. If the housings will not mate up refer to the following instructions.
   a. Drop the gearcase slightly, then rotate the drive shaft clockwise a slight amount.
   b. Repeat Steps 3 and 4 until the drive shaft engages the crankshaft. When properly aligned the gearcase mates fully with the drive shaft housing.
   c. Align the water tube with the grommet each time installation is attempted.
6. Hold the gearcase in position while installing both mounting bolts. Tighten the bolts to the specification provided in **Table 1**.
7. Align the marks on the upper and lower shift shafts with the shift shaft connector. Securely tighten the shift shaft connector (**Figure 22**).
8. Check and adjust the shift linkage following the instructions in Chapter Five. Snap the rubber grommet (2, **Figure 18**) into its opening on the starboard side of the drive shaft housing.
9. Fill the gearcase with lubricant following the instructions in Chapter Four. Install the propeller following the instructions in this chapter.
10. Install the spark plug and lead. Check for correct cooling and shifting system operation immediately after starting the engine.

Removal (9.9 and 15 hp Models)

On models with the standard gearcase, one bolt is located on each side of the gearcase just below the gearcase mating surface. A third bolt is located near the front of the gearcase just above the gearcase mating surface.

On models with the optional gearcase, two bolts are located on each side of the gearcase just below the gearcase mating surface.

1. Remove the spark plugs and connect the spark plug leads to a suitable engine ground. Disconnect both cables from the battery if so equipped.
2. Remove the propeller and attaching hardware as described in this chapter.
3. Shift the engine into NEUTRAL. Place the engine in the full tilt up position then engage the tilt lock mechanism.
4. Using a felt tip marker, mark the lower shift shaft where it aligns with a reference point (**Figure 23**) on the drive shaft housing. This helps ensure quicker shift adjustment after installing the gearcase.
5. Prevent the shift shaft coupling from rotating and loosen the jam nut (**Figure 24**). Rotate the shift shaft coupling counterclockwise to disconnect the shift shafts (**Figure 25**). Loosen the nut to free the reverse hold-down clamp and linkage from the lower shift shaft.
6. Support the gearcase and remove the gearcase retaining bolts.
7. Carefully tug or pry the gearcase from the drive shaft housing. Pull the gearcase straight from the drive shaft housing to prevent damage to the shift shaft, lower crankshaft seals or water tube.
8. Place the gearcase in a suitable holding fixture or securely clamp the skeg in a bench vise. Use wooden blocks or padded jaws to prevent damage to the skeg.

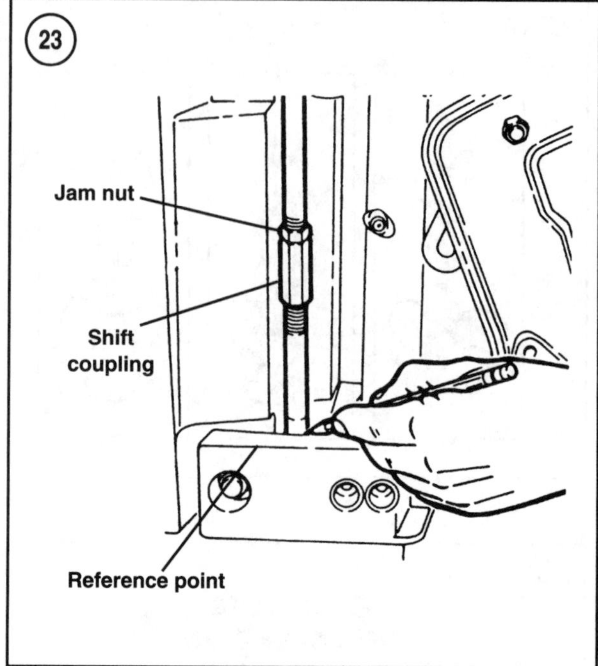

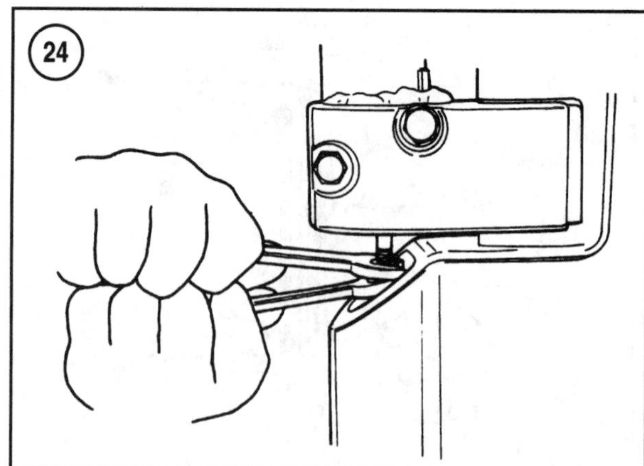

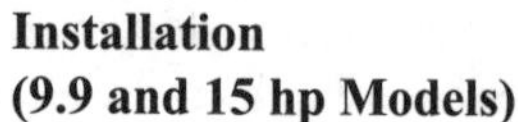

Installation (9.9 and 15 hp Models)

CAUTION
Never rotate the propeller shaft to align the drive shaft with the crankshaft. The water pump impeller can suffer damage leading to overheating of the engine.

1. Remove the spark plugs and connect the spark plug leads to a suitable engine ground. Place the engine in the full tilt position. Engage the tilt lock mechanism. Place the shift selector in the NEUTRAL position.

2A. *Standard gearcase.*

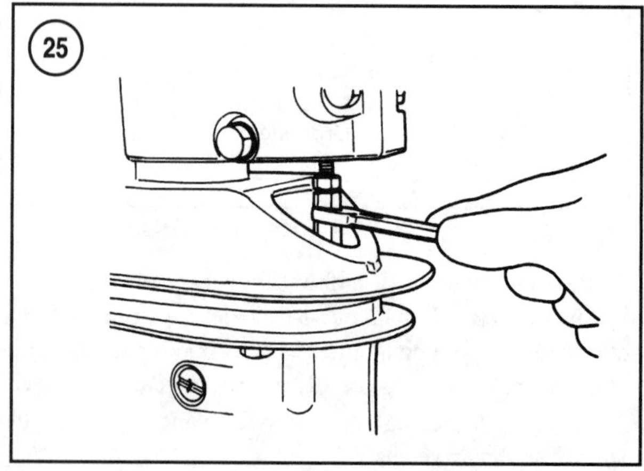

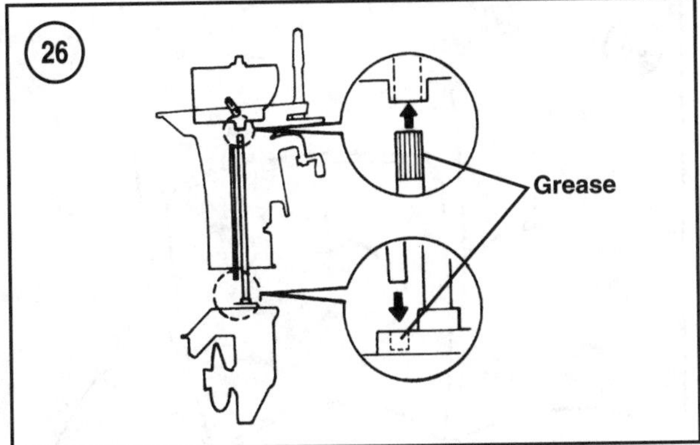

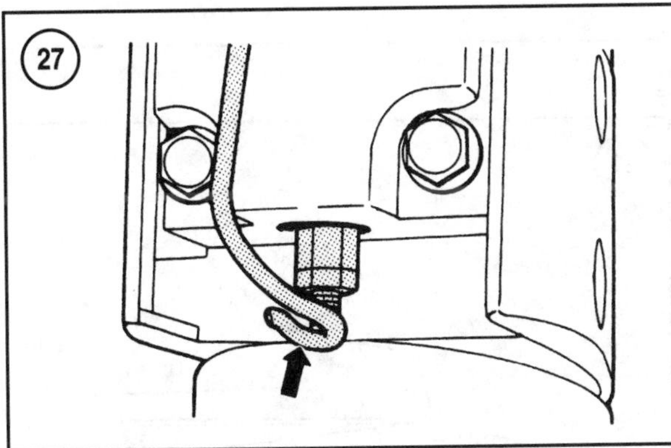

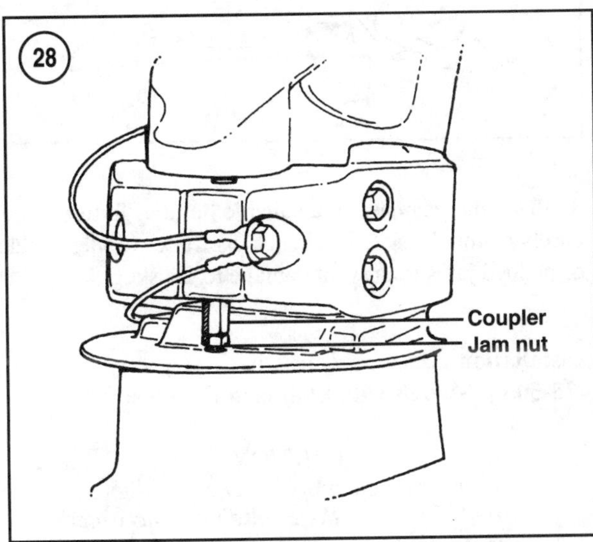

a. Pull up on the shift shaft until the FORWARD gear is engaged. Rotate the drive shaft clockwise to check for proper engagement. The propeller shaft will turn clockwise (**Figure 20**) if the forward gear is engaged.

b. Rotate the lower shift shaft clockwise until it stops.

c. Rotate the shift shaft two complete turns counterclockwise.

d. Rotate the shift shaft counterclockwise enough to align the offset end as closely as possible to the drive shaft.

2B. *All other models*—Push down on the shift shaft until the gearcase is in NEUTRAL. Rotate the drive shaft clockwise to check for proper engagement. The propeller shaft will stop rotating (**Figure 20**) when in NEUTRAL. Verify neutral by spinning the propeller shaft. It must spin freely.

3. Apply a light coat of water-resistant grease to the splines of the drive shaft and to the water tube grommet (**Figure 26**).

4. Carefully slide the drive shaft and shift shaft into the drive shaft housing. Guide the lower shift shaft through the reverse hold down linkage (**Figure 27**) while sliding the gearcase into position.

5. Keep the gearcase and drive shaft housing mating surfaces parallel while aligning the mounting bolt holes in the gearcase with their holes in the drive shaft housing.

6. Align the water tube (**Figure 26**) with the water tube sealing grommet in the water pump.

7. Align the lower shift shaft with the shift shaft coupling (**Figure 28**) as the gearcase is installed.

8. The gearcase mates to the drive shaft housing when the drive shaft and crankshaft splines align. If the housings will not mate refer to the following instructions.

a. Drop the gearcase slightly and rotate the drive shaft clockwise a slight amount.

b. Repeat Steps 4-8 until the drive shaft splines engage the crankshaft splines. When properly aligned the gearcase will mate to the drive shaft housing.

c. Align the water tube with the grommet each time installation is attempted.

9. Hold the gearcase in position and install the mounting bolts. Tighten the bolts to the specification in **Table 1**.

10. Thread the shift shaft connector onto the lower shift shaft until the mark on the lower drive shaft made prior to gearcase removal aligns with its reference mark (**Figure 23**). Prevent the shift shaft coupling from rotating while you securely tightening the jam nut against the coupling (**Figure 24**).

11. Place the reverse hold down clamp (**Figure 29**) onto the lower shift shaft. Install the bolt into the clamp. Do not tighten the bolt at this time.

12. Adjust the shift and reverse hold down linkage following the instructions in Chapter Five.

13. Fill the gearcase with lubricant following the instructions in Chapter Four. Install the propeller following the instructions in this chapter.

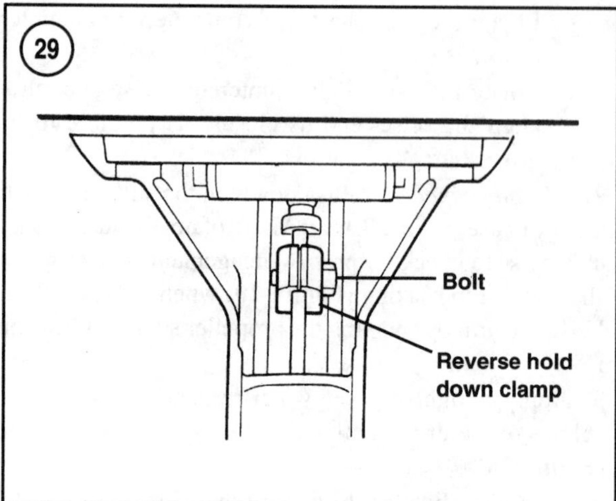

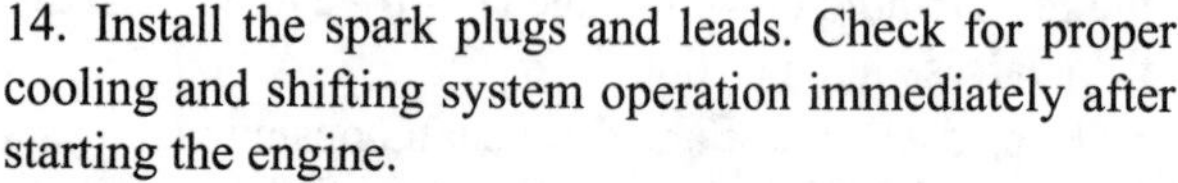

14. Install the spark plugs and leads. Check for proper cooling and shifting system operation immediately after starting the engine.

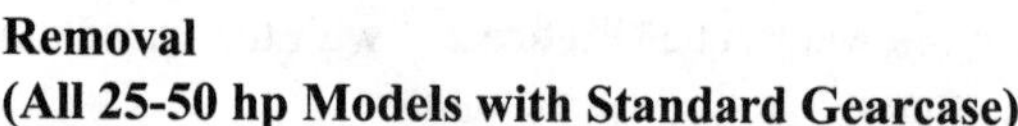

Removal
(All 25-50 hp Models with Standard Gearcase)

This gearcase attaches to the drive shaft housing with five mounting bolts. Two mounting bolts are located on each side of the gearcase just below the gearcase mating surface. A fifth bolt is located at the back of the gearcase inside the trim tab mounting cavity.

1. Remove the spark plugs and connect the spark plug leads to a suitable engine ground. Disconnect both cables from the battery if so equipped.

2. Remove the propeller and attaching hardware following the instructions in this chapter.

3. Shift the engine into NEUTRAL. Place the engine in the full tilt position and engage the tilt lock mechanism.

4. Using a felt tip marker, mark the position of the trim tab (**Figure 30**) for reference during installation. Remove the bolt (**Figure 31**) and remove the trim tab.

5. The shift shaft connector is located just forward of the power head. Carefully pry up on the connector (**Figure 32**) and push the bellcrank toward the starboard side of the engine. Slide the pin on the arm from the hole in the shift shaft.

6. Support the gearcase and remove the five gearcase mounting bolts (**Figure 33**).

7. Carefully tug or pry the gearcase from the drive shaft housing. Pull the gearcase straight from the drive shaft housing to prevent damage to the shift shaft, lower crankshaft seals and water tube.

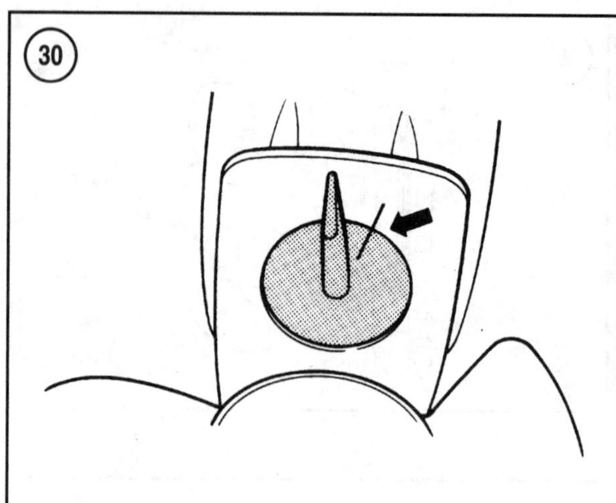

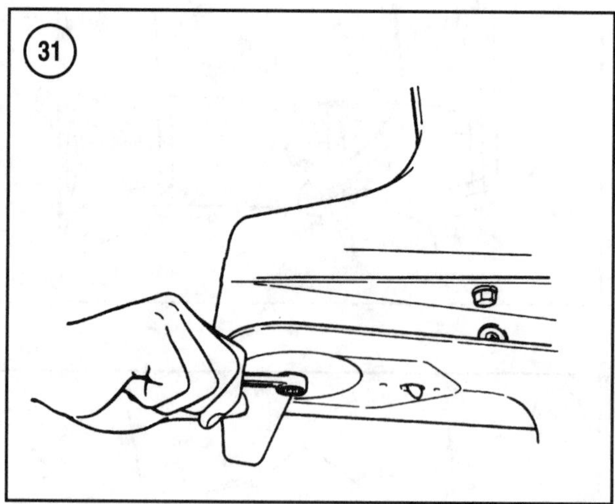

8. Place the gearcase in a suitable holding fixture or securely clamp the skeg in a bench vise. Use wooden blocks or padded jaws to prevent damage to the skeg.

Installation
(25-50 hp Models with Standard Gearcase)

CAUTION
Never rotate the propeller shaft to align the drive shaft with the crankshaft. The water pump impeller can suffer damage that leads to overheating of the engine.

1. Place the engine in the full tilt position. Engage the tilt lock mechanism. Place the shift selector in NEUTRAL.

2. Push the shift shaft up or down as necessary to put the gearcase in NEUTRAL. The propeller shaft will turn freely if the gearcase is in neutral.

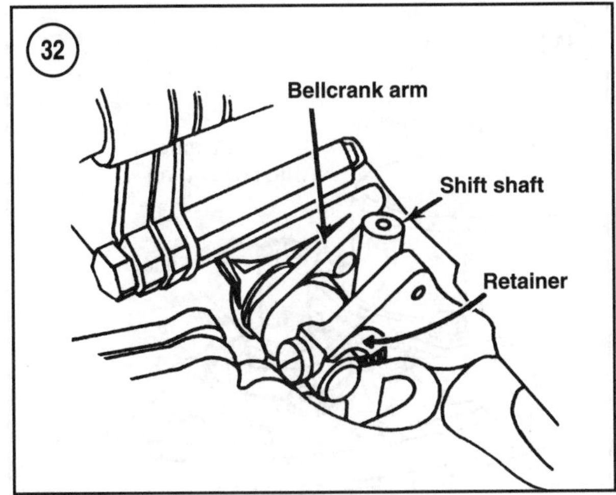

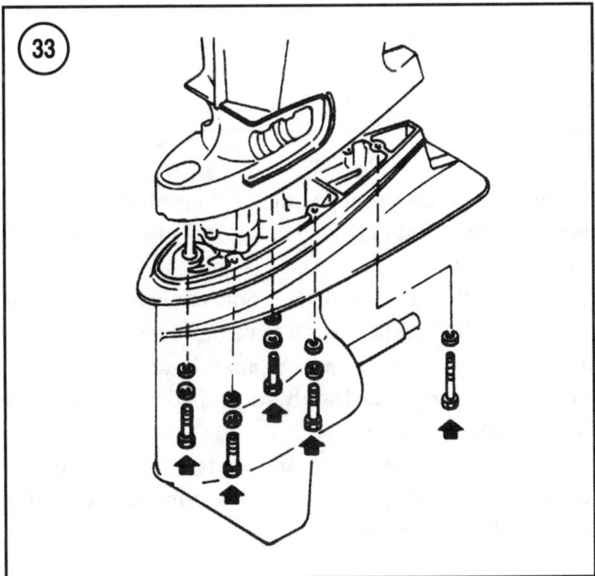

3. Apply a light coat water-resistant grease to the splines of the drive shaft and to the water tube grommet (**Figure 26**).

4. Carefully slide the drive shaft and shift shaft into the drive shaft housing. Guide the shift shaft through its opening in the lower engine cover and the gearcase into position.

5. Keep the gearcase and drive shaft housing mating surfaces parallel while aligning the mounting bolt holes in the gearcase with the holes in the drive shaft housing.

6. Align the water tube (**Figure 26**) with the sealing grommet of the water pump while sliding the gearcase into position.

7. The gearcase will mate to the drive shaft housing if the drive shaft and crankshaft splines align. If the housings will not mate refer to the following instructions.

   a. Drop the gearcase slightly then rotate the drive shaft clockwise a slight amount.
   b. Repeat Steps 4-7 until the drive shaft splines engage the crankshaft spline.
   c. Align the water tube with the grommet each time installation is attempted.

8. Hold the gearcase in position and install the mounting bolts Tighten the bolts to the specification in **Table 1**.

9. Install the trim tab and align the marks (**Figure 30**). Install the trim tab bolt (**Figure 31**). And tighten it to the specification in **Table 1**.

10. Align the upper end of the shift shaft with the pin on the bellcrank (**Figure 32**). Slide the bellcrank toward the shift shaft until the pin fully engages the shift shaft. Push down on the retainer (**Figure 32**) until the locking clip portion of the retainer snaps over the horizontal shift linkage.

11. Adjust the shift and reverse hold down linkage (25 hp models) following the instructions in Chapter Five.

12. Fill the gearcase with lubricant following the instructions in Chapter Four. Install the propeller following the instructions in this chapter.

13. Install the spark plugs and leads. Check for proper cooling and shifting system operation immediately after starting the engine.

Removal (25, 30-50 hp [Optional Gearcase], 75 and 90 hp Models

The gearcase attaches to the drive shaft housing with four mounting bolts and one nut. Two mounting bolts and washers are located on each side of the gearcase. They are located just below the gearcase mating surface. The nut is located at the back of the gearcase just forward of the trim tab.

1. Remove the spark plugs and connect the spark plug leads to a suitable engine ground. Disconnect both cables from the battery if so equipped.
2. Remove the propeller and attaching hardware following the instructions in this chapter.
3. Shift the engine into FORWARD. Place the engine in the full tilt position and engage the tilt lock mechanism.
4. Support the gearcase and remove the five gearcase fasteners (**Figure 33**).
5. Carefully tug or pry the gearcase from the drive shaft housing. Pull the gearcase straight from the drive shaft housing to prevent damage to the shift shaft, lower crankshaft seals and water tube.

6. Pull the shift shaft coupler and spacer (**Figure 34**) from the lower shift shaft.
7. Place the gearcase in a suitable holding fixture or securely clamp the skeg in a bench vise. Use wooden blocks or padded jaws to prevent damage to the skeg.

Installation (25 hp, 30-50 hp [Optional Gearcase], 75 and 90 hp Models)

CAUTION
Never rotate the propeller shaft to align the drive shaft with the crankshaft. The water pump impeller can suffer damage leading to overheating of the engine.

1. Place the engine in the full tilt position. Engage the tilt lock mechanism. Place the shift selector in the FORWARD gear position.
2. Carefully rotate the shift shaft (**Figure 35**) until forward gear engages. Rotate the drive shaft clockwise to check for proper forward gear engagement.
3. Apply a light coating of water-resistant grease to the splines of the drive shaft and to the water tube grommet (**Figure 36**).
4. Apply a light coating of water-resistant grease to the splines of the lower shift shaft (**Figure 37**). Place the spacer (**Figure 34**) over the lower shift shaft. Without rotating the lower shift shaft, align the coupling splines with the lower shift shaft splines. Slide the coupling onto the lower shift shaft as indicated (**Figure 34**).
5. Carefully slide the drive shaft into the crankshaft (**Figure 36**). Guide the upper shift shaft (**Figure 38**) onto the lower shift shaft coupling (**Figure 34**) while sliding the gearcase in position.
6. Keep the gearcase and drive shaft housing mating surfaces parallel while aligning the bolt holes in the gearcase with the holes in the drive shaft housing.
7. Align the water tube (**Figure 36**) with the grommet in the water pump while sliding the gearcase into position.
8. The gearcase will mates to the drive shaft housing when the drive shaft and shift shaft splines align. If the housings will not mate refer to the following instructions.
   a. Drop the gearcase slightly then rotate the drive shaft clockwise a slight amount.
   b. Have an assistant move the shift lever just enough to align the shift shafts.
   c. Repeat Steps 5-8 until the drive shaft engages the crankshaft.
   d. Align the water tube with the grommet each time installation is attempted.

34

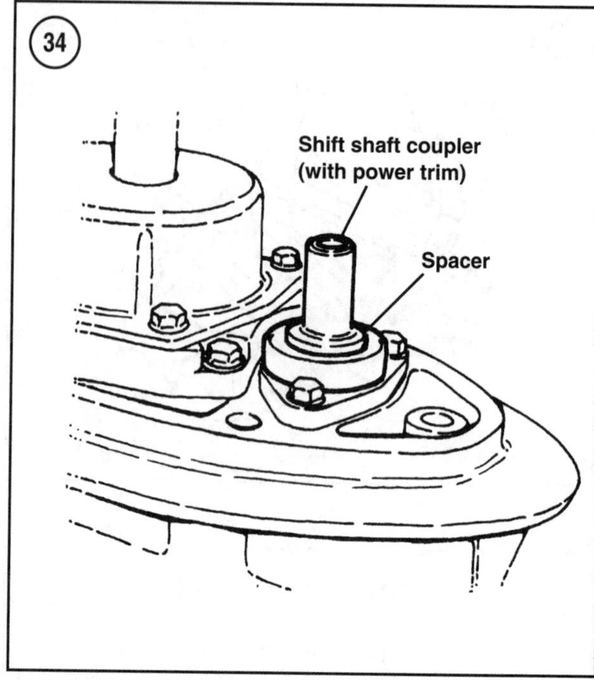

9. Hold the gearcase in position and install the mounting bolts, washers and nut. Tighten the bolts to the specification in **Table 1**.
10. Adjust the shift and reverse hold down linkage (25 hp models) following the instructions in Chapter Five.
11. Fill the gearcase with lubricant following the instructions in Chapter Four. Install the propeller following the instructions in this chapter.
12. Install the spark plugs and leads. Check for proper cooling and shifting system operation immediately after starting the engine.

WATER PUMP

Replace the impeller, seals, O-rings and all gaskets anytime the water pump is serviced. Never reinstall questionable parts. Doing so may compromise the reliability of this vital component.

Disassembly (4-6 hp Models)

Refer to **Figure 39** to assist with component identification and orientation.

1. Drain the gearcase lubricant as described in Chapter Four. Remove the gearcase as described in this chapter. Using a solvent, clean all corrosion and carbon deposits from the exposed portion of the drive shaft.

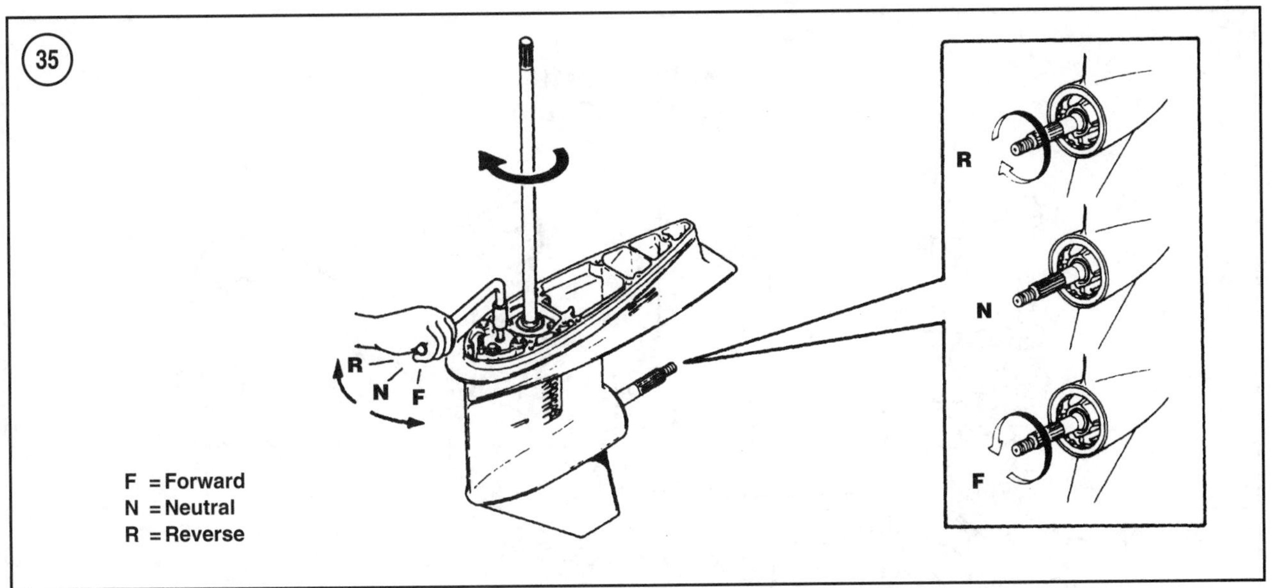

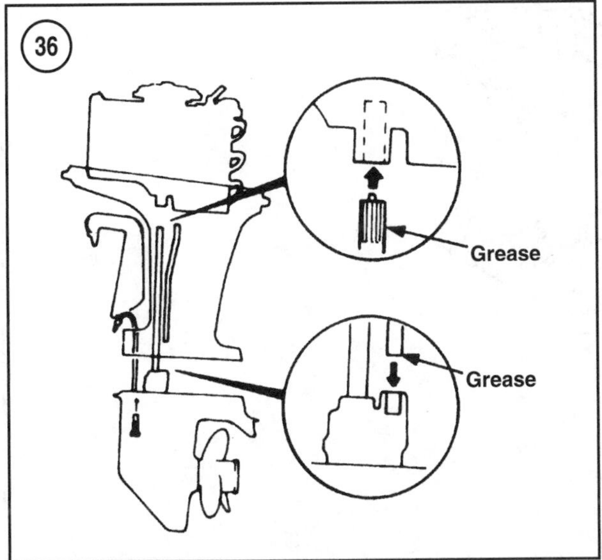

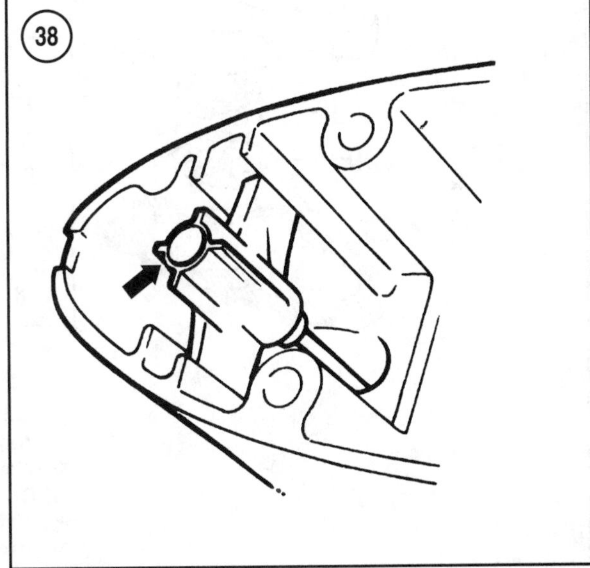

2. Carefully pry the water tube grommet (2, **Figure 39**) from the water pump body (3). Remove the four bolts and washers (1, **Figure 39**) and remove the water pump body (3) from the gearcase. Pull the water tube grommets and tube (4 and 5, **Figure 39**) from the water pump body and inlet screen.

3. Carefully pry the water pump impeller (**Figure 40**) away from the wear plate. Slide the impeller (7, **Figure 39**) from the drive shaft. Pry the impeller from the water pump insert (6, **Figure 39**) if it remains in the water pump body. Working from the drive shaft opening, push the insert from the water pump body (**Figure 41**).

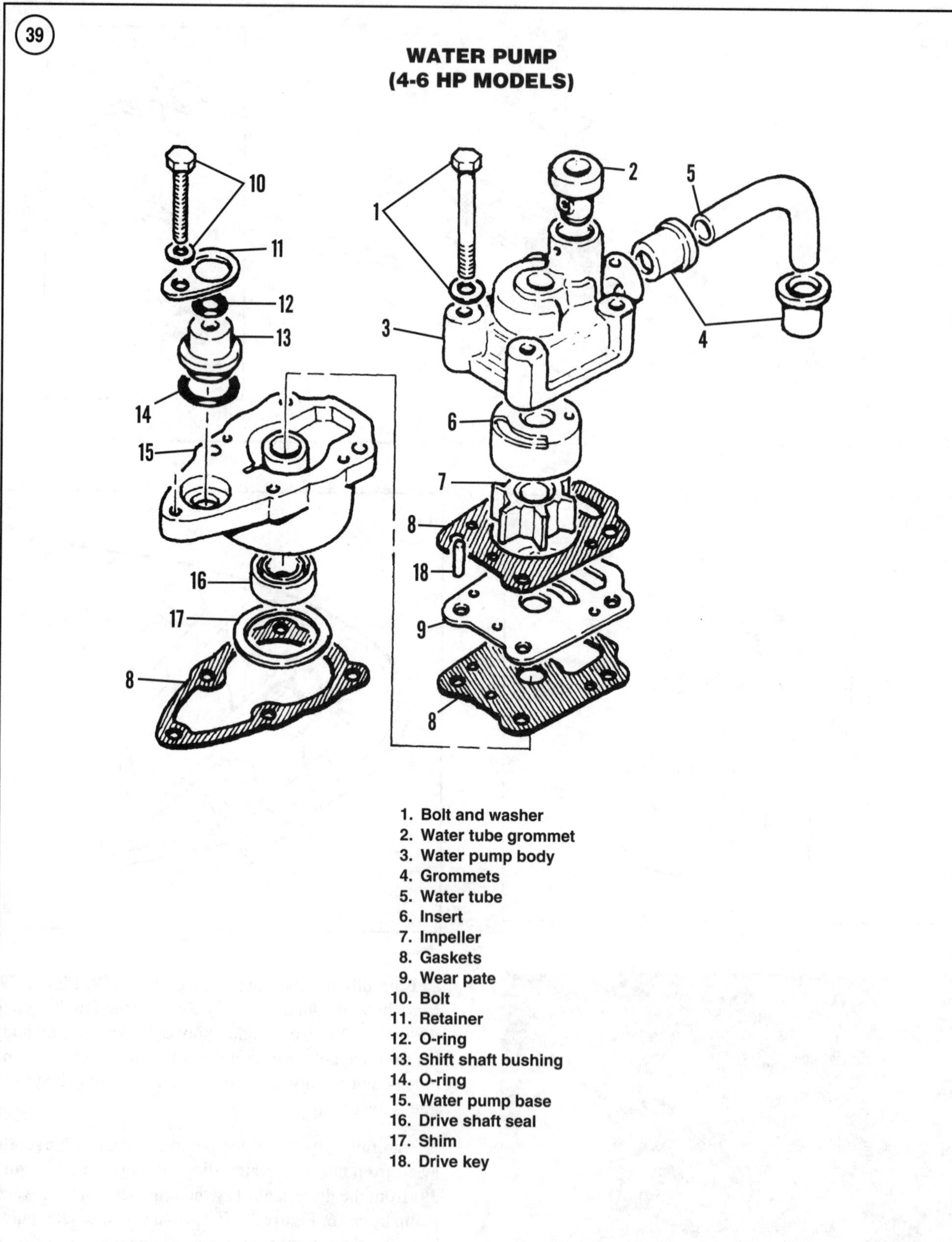
39
WATER PUMP
(4-6 HP MODELS)
10
11
12
13
14
15
16
17
8
1
2
3
4
5
6
7
8
18
9
8
1. Bolt and washer
2. Water tube grommet
3. Water pump body
4. Grommets
5. Water tube
6. Insert
7. Impeller
8. Gaskets
9. Wear pate
10. Bolt
11. Retainer
12. O-ring
13. Shift shaft bushing
14. O-ring
15. Water pump base
16. Drive shaft seal
17. Shim
18. Drive key

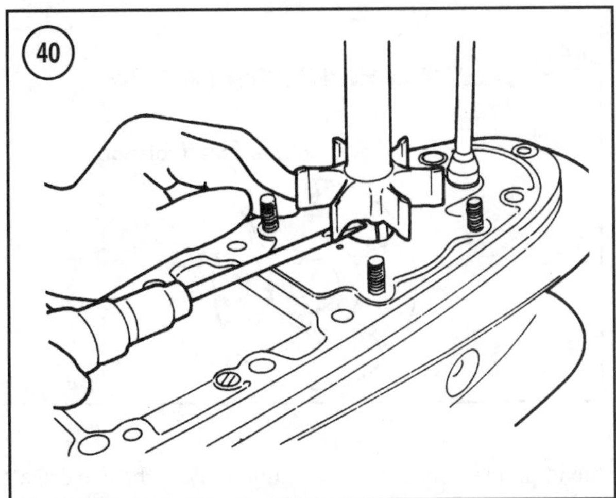

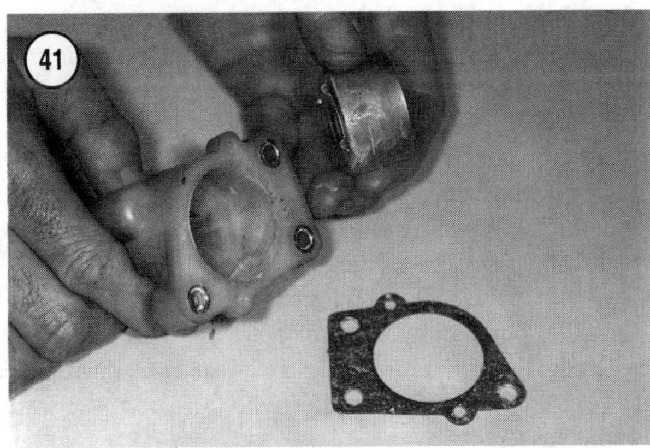

4. Pull the drive key from the drive shaft (**Figure 42**). Lift the gasket (8, **Figure 39**) from the wear plate. Lift the wear plate and gasket (8 and 9, **Figure 39**) from the water pump base.

5. Remove the water pump base (15, **Figure 39**) only if removing the drive shaft or shift shaft, resealing the gearcase or if it is damaged.

6. Remove the bolt and washer (10, **Figure 39**) then lift the retainer, O-rings and bushing (11-14, **Figure 39**) away from the water pump base (15). Pull the shift shaft from the gearcase

7. Carefully pry the water pump base from the gearcase using two blunt screwdrivers. Remove the gasket (8, **Figure 39**) from the bottom of the water pump base (15) or gearcase.

8. Working carefully to avoid damaging the water pump base, carefully pry the drive shaft seal (16, **Figure 39**) from the water pump base.

9. Clean all water pump and shift shaft components using solvent. Carefully scrape gasket remnants from all components. Inspect all water pump components for wear or damage as outlined in this chapter.

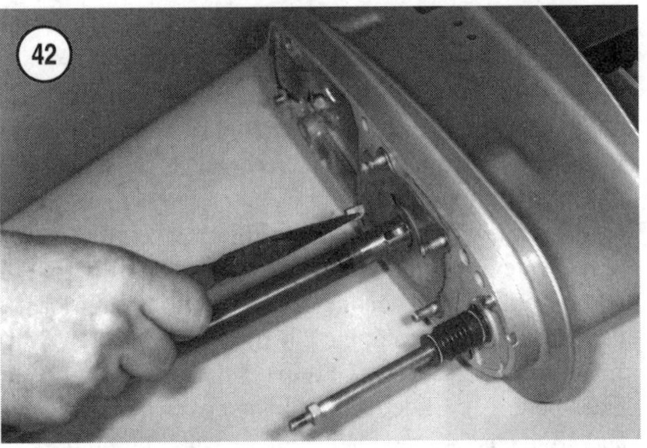

Assembly (4-6 hp Models)

CAUTION
To prevent water and gear lubricant leakage always replace gaskets, seals and O-rings once they are removed or disturbed.

NOTE
Thoroughly clean all corrosion or other deposits from the exposed portion of the drive shaft prior to installing any water pump components. The impeller must slide freely along the length of the shaft.

Refer to **Figure 39** to assist with component identification and orientation.

1. Use a socket or section of tubing as a seal installation tool. The tool must contact the outer diameter of the seal but not the seal bore in the water pump base.

2. Apply Loctite 271 (Mercury part No. 92-809819) to the outer diameter of the water pump seal prior to installing into the water pump base. Position the seal (16, **Figure 39**) into the opening at the bottom of the water pump base with the lip side facing out. Using the installation tool, push the seal into the bore until it bottoms. Apply a bead of Quicksilver 2-4-C Marine Lubricant (Mercury part No. 825407A12) to the lip of the seal.

3. Place the new gasket (8, **Figure 39**) onto the bottom of the water pump base (15). Gasket sealing compound is not required. Guide the water pump base over the drive shaft and position the base and gasket onto the gearcase.

4. Apply 2-4-C Marine Lubricant to the large diameter O-ring (14, **Figure 39**), then place it into the bushing (13) mating surface of the water pump base (15). Slide the shift

9

shaft into the water pump base with the tapered lower end facing the propeller side.
5. Seat the bushing (13, **Figure 39**) against the water pump base, then place the retainer (11) over the bushing. Install the bolt and washer (10, **Figure 39**) and tighten to the specification in **Table 1**.
6. Align the tab on the insert (6, **Figure 39**) with its recess in the water pump body (3). Press the insert fully into the body. Apply a light coating of 2-4-C Marine Lubricant to the exposed surfaces of the insert.
7. Install the gaskets (8, **Figure 39**) on each side of the wear plate (9). Slide the wear plate over the drive shaft and align gaskets and plate with the water pump base.
8. Apply 2-4-C Marine Lubricant to the drive key (18, **Figure 39**) and install it into position on the drive shaft.
9. Slide the impeller over the drive shaft. Align the slot in the impeller hub with the drive key and push the impeller down against wear plate. If reusing the original impeller install it so the vanes curl in a counterclockwise direction (**Figure 43**). Flip the impeller if required.
10. Install the grommet (2, **Figure 39**) into the water tube. Install both grommets and the water tube (4 and 5, **Figure 39**) into the water pump body. Arrange the water tube to point down as shown in **Figure 39**.
11. Place the water pump body (15, **Figure 39**) over the drive shaft. Slide it down until it contacts the impeller. Rotate the drive shaft clockwise while pushing down on the water pump body.
12. Continue rotating the drive shaft until the impeller fully enters the water pump body. Align the water tube grommet with the water screen while seating the water pump body against the gaskets and wear plate.
13. Install the four bolts and washers (1, **Figure 39**) and tighten evenly to the specification in **Table 1**.
14. Install the gearcase as described in this chapter. Fill the gearcase with lubricant (Chapter Four). Check for proper cooling system operation and correct any problems before operating the engine.

Disassembly
(9.9 and 15 hp Models with Standard Gearcase)

Refer to **Figure 44**.
1. Drain the gearcase lubricant (Chapter Four). Remove the gearcase as described in this chapter.
2. Pull the water tube guide (1, **Figure 44**) from the water tube seal (2). Remove the four bolts (3, **Figure 44**) lift the water pump body (4) from the gearcase. Pull the water tube guide (2, **Figure 44**) from the water pump body (4).
3. Carefully pry the water pump impeller (**Figure 40**) away from the wear plate. Slide the impeller (6, **Figure 44**) and both nylon washers (5) from the drive shaft. Pry

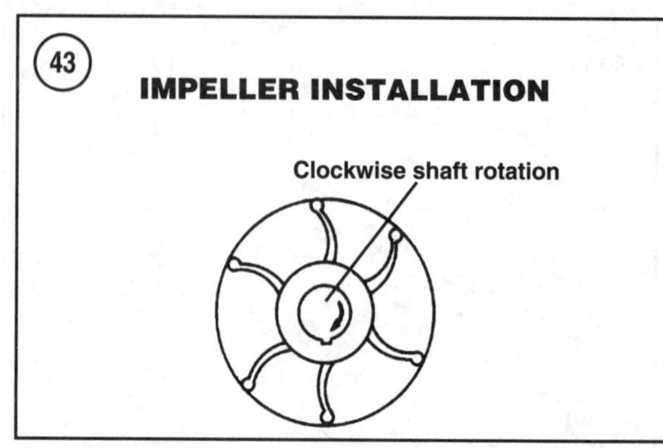

the impeller from the water pump body or the drive shaft. Pull the drive key from the drive shaft (**Figure 42**).
4. Lift the wear plate and gasket (8 and 9, **Figure 44**) from the water pump base.
5. Remove the water pump base only if removing the drive shaft or shift shaft, resealing the gearcase or if it is damaged.
6. Remove the bolt and washer (12, **Figure 44**) and carefully pry the water pump base away from the gearcase. Pull the water pump base, water inlet tube (16, **Figure 44**) and shift shaft from the gearcase
7. Remove the gasket (9, **Figure 44**) from the bottom of the water pump base or gearcase.
8. Remove the screw (15, **Figure 44**) and pull the retainer (14), grommet (13) and water tube (16) from the water pump base.
9. Working carefully to avoid damaging the water pump base, carefully pry the drive shaft seals (10, **Figure 44**) from the water pump base.
10. Thread the shift cam from the lower end of the shift shaft and slide the shaft from the water pump base. Remove the quad ring seal (11, **Figure 44**) from the water pump base.
11. Clean all water pump and shift shaft components using solvent. Carefully scrape gasket remnants from all components. Inspect all water pump components for wear or damage as described in this chapter.

Assembly
(9.9 and 15 hp Models with Standard Gearcase)

CAUTION
To prevent water and gear lubricant leakage always replace gaskets, seals and O-rings if removed or disturbed.

NOTE
Thoroughly clean corrosion or other deposits from the drive shaft prior to installing

WATER PUMP (9.9 AND 15 HP MODELS STANDARD GEARCASE)

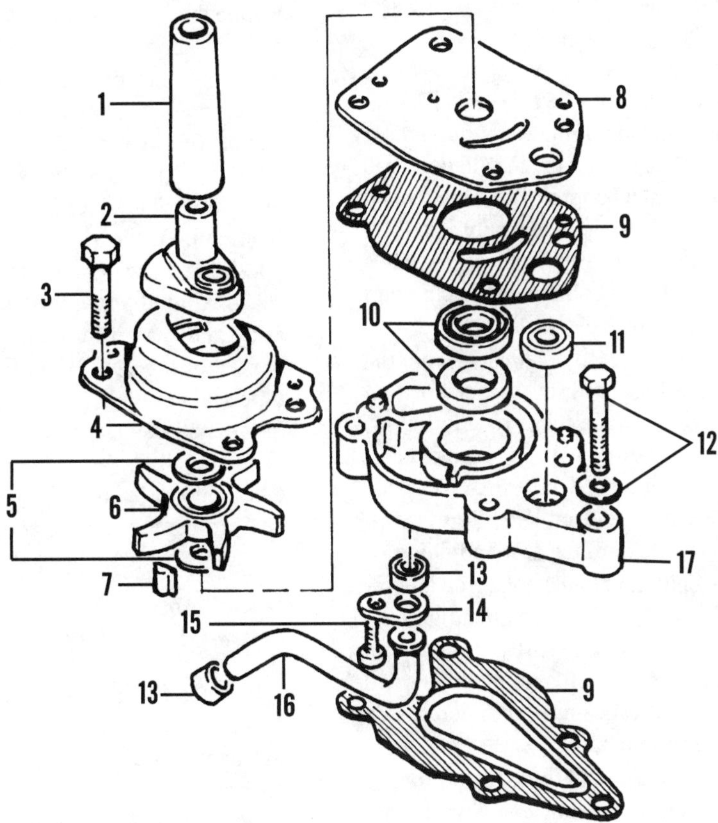

1. Water tube guide
2. Water tube seal
3. Bolt
4. Water pump body
5. Nylon washers
6. Impeller
7. Drive key
8. Wear plate
9. Gasket
10. Drive shaft seals
11. Quad ring seal
12. Bolt and washer
13. Grommet
14. Retainer
15. Screw
16. Water tube
17. Pump base

any water pump components. The impeller must slide freely along the length of the shaft.

Refer to **Figure 44**.

1. Use a socket or section of tubing as a seal installation tool. The tool must contact the outer diameter of the seal but not the seal bore in the water pump base.
2. Apply Loctite 271 (Mercury part No. 92-809819) to the outer diameter of both seals. Position the first seal (10, **Figure 44**) into the opening at the top of the water pump base with the lip side facing inward. Using the installation tool, push the seal into the bore until it bottoms. Place the second seal into the opening with the seal lip facing outward. Push the seal into the bore until it contacts the first seal. Apply a bead of Quicksilver 2-4-C Marine Lubricant (Mercury part No. 825407A12) to the lip surface of the seals.
3. Press the water tube grommet (13, **Figure 44**) into the bottom of the water pump base with the larger opening facing out. Slide the end of the water tube (16, **Figure 44**) with the sharper bend into the grommet. Slide the retainer (14, **Figure 44**) over the water tube. Secure the water tube to the water pump base with the screw (15, **Figure 44**). Align the water tube to face toward the rear and down.
4. Apply 2-4-C Marine Lubricant to the quad rind and install it (11, **Figure 44**) onto the shift shaft opening at the top of the water pump base. Slide the shift shaft through the opening, then thread the shift cam onto the lower end of the shift shaft. Rotate the cam until the tapered side faces the rear of the water pump base.
5. Place the new gasket (9, **Figure 44**) onto the bottom of the water pump base (17). Gasket sealing compound is not required. Guide the water pump base over the drive shaft then lower the shift shaft into its opening. Position the tapered side of the cam toward the rear of the gearcase. Guide the water tube into the grommet above the water screen while lowering the base to the gearcase.
6. Seat the water pump base against the gearcase and install the bolt and washer (12, **Figure 44**). Tighten the bolt to the specification in **Table 1**.
7. Apply a light coating of 2-4-C Marine Lubricant to the inner surfaces of the water pump body (4, **Figure 44**).
8. Slide the gasket (9, **Figure 44**) and wear plate (8) over the drive shaft and shift shaft. Align these components with the water pump base.
9. Slide the lower nylon washer (5, **Figure 44**) over the drive shaft and seat it against the wear plate. Apply 2-4-C Marine Lubricant to the drive key then place the drive key (7, **Figure 44**) into position on the drive shaft.
10. Slide the impeller over the drive shaft. Align the slot in the impeller hub with the drive key and push the impeller down against wear plate. If reusing the original impeller ensure the vanes curl to a counterclockwise direction (**Figure 43**). Flip the impeller if required. Slide the second nylon washer (5, **Figure 44**) over the drive shaft. Position the washer against the impeller.
11. Place the water pump body (4, **Figure 44**) over the drive shaft and slide it down until it contacts the impeller. Rotate the drive shaft clockwise while pushing on the water pump body.
12. Continue rotating the drive shaft until the impeller fully enters the water pump body and the body seats against the wear plate.
13. Install the four bolts (3, **Figure 44**) into the water pump body and base. Tighten the bolts evenly to the specification in **Table 1**.
14. Slide the water tube seal (2, **Figure 44**) over the drive shaft. Align the seal with its opening on the water pump body and snap it into position. Apply 2-4-C lubricant to the water tube guide (1, **Figure 44**) and onto the water tube seal (2).
15. Install the gearcase following the instructions in this chapter. Fill the gearcase with lubricant (Chapter Four). Check for proper cooling system operation and correct any problems before operating the engine.

Disassembly (9.9 and 15 hp Models with Optional Gearcase)

Refer to **Figure 45** during this procedure.

1. Drain the gearcase lubricant following the instructions in Chapter Four. Remove the gearcase as described in this chapter.
2. Pull the water tube guide/seal (1, **Figure 45**) from water pump body (3). Slide the drive shaft seal (2, **Figure 45**) from the drive shaft. Remove the four bolts, then lift the water pump body (3, **Figure 45**) from the gearcase. Pull the O-ring (5, **Figure 45**) from the water pump body.
3. Carefully pry the water pump impeller (**Figure 40**) away from the wear plate. Slide the impeller (7, **Figure 45**) and both nylon washers (6) from the drive shaft. Pull the drive key from the drive shaft (**Figure 42**).
4. Lift the wear plate and gasket (9 and 10, **Figure 45**) from the gearcase. Discard the gasket. Clean all gasket material from the gearcase.
5. Remove the insert (4, **Figure 45**) from the water pump body (3) only if it must be replaced. Refer to *Inspection* in this chapter. Working from the drive shaft opening, carefully drive the insert from the body using a suitable punch.
6. Clean all water pump and shift shaft components with a suitable solvent. Carefully scrape gasket remnants from all components. Inspect all water pump components for wear or damage following the instructions provided in this chapter.

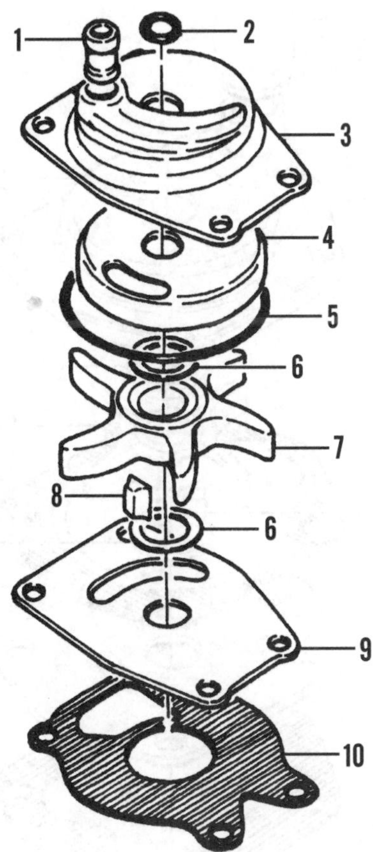

Assembly (9.9 and 15 hp Models with Optional Gearcase)

CAUTION
To prevent water and gear lubricant leakage replace all gaskets, seals and O-rings if removed or disturbed.

NOTE
Thoroughly clean all corrosion or other deposits from the exposed portions of the drive shaft prior to installing any water pump components. The impeller must slide freely along the length of the shaft.

Refer to **Figure 45** during this procedure.

1. Align the raised tab on the circumference of the insert (4, **Figure 45**) with the notch in the inner diameter of the water pump body (3). Press the insert into the body until fully seated.
2. Apply a light coating of 2-4-C Marine Lubricant to the inner surface of the water pump insert (4, **Figure 45**). Fit the O-ring (5, **Figure 45**) over the exposed end of the insert. The O-ring must contact the insert (4, **Figure 45**) and water pump body (3).
3. Slide the gasket (10, **Figure 45**) and wear plate (9) over the drive shaft. Align these components with the opening in the gearcase.
4. Slide the lower nylon washer (6, **Figure 45**) over the drive shaft and seat it against the wear plate. Apply 2-4-C Marine Lubricant to the drive key (8, **Figure 45**) and install it onto the flat surface of the drive shaft with the rounded side of the key facing outward.
5. Slide the impeller over the drive shaft. Align the slot in the impeller hub with the drive key and push the impeller down against wear plate. If reusing the original impeller the vanes must curl in a counterclockwise direction (**Figure 43**). Flip the impeller if required. Slide the second nylon washer (6, **Figure 45**) over the drive shaft. Position the washer against the impeller.
6. Place the water pump body (3, **Figure 45**) over the drive shaft and slide it down until it contacts the impeller. Align the water pump body with the water tube opening toward the rear of the gearcase. Rotate the drive shaft clockwise while pushing down on the water pump body.
7. Continue rotating the drive shaft until the impeller fully enters the water pump body and the body seats against the wear plate. Ensure the O-ring (5, **Figure 45**) remains in position on the body and insert.
8. Apply Loctite 271 (Mercury part No. 92-809819) to the threads of the water pump bolts. Install the four bolts into the water pump body and gearcase. Tighten the bolts evenly to the specification in **Table 1**.

9. Apply 2-4-C Marine Lubricant to the drive shaft seal (2, **Figure 45**) and slide it over the drive shaft. Lightly seat the seal against the water pump body.
10. Install the water tube guide/seal (1, **Figure 45**) over its fitting on the water pump body.
11. Install the gearcase as described in this chapter. Fill the gearcase with lubricant (Chapter Four). Check for proper cooling system operation and correct any problems before operating the engine.

Disassembly (25-50 hp Models with Standard Gearcase)

Refer to **Figure 46** to assist with component identification and orientation.

1. Drain the gearcase lubricant following the instructions in Chapter Four. Remove the gearcase following the instructions in this chapter.
2. Pull the water tube guide/seal (1, **Figure 46**) from water pump body (2). Remove the four bolts, then lift the water pump body (2, **Figure 46**) from the gearcase.
3. Carefully pry the water pump impeller (**Figure 40**) away from the wear plate. Slide the impeller (4, **Figure 46**) and both nylon washers (3) from the drive shaft. Pull the drive key from the drive shaft (**Figure 42**).
4. Lift the wear plate (7, **Figure 46**) and both gaskets (6 and 8, **Figure 46**) from the gearcase. Discard the gaskets. Clean all gasket material from the gearcase, water pump body and the wear plate.
5. Clean all water pump and shift shaft components using solvent. Carefully scrape gasket remnants from all components. Inspect all water pump components for wear or damage following the instructions in this chapter.

Assembly (25-50 hp Models with Standard Gearcase)

CAUTION
To prevent water and gear lubricant leakage replace all gaskets, seals and O-rings if removed or disturbed.

NOTE
Thoroughly clean all corrosion or other deposits from the exposed portions of the drive shaft prior to installing any water pump components. The impeller must slide freely along the length of the shaft.

Refer to **Figure 46** to assist with component identification and orientation.

1. Apply a light coat of 2-4-C Marine Lubricant to the inner surface of the water pump body (2, **Figure 46**).

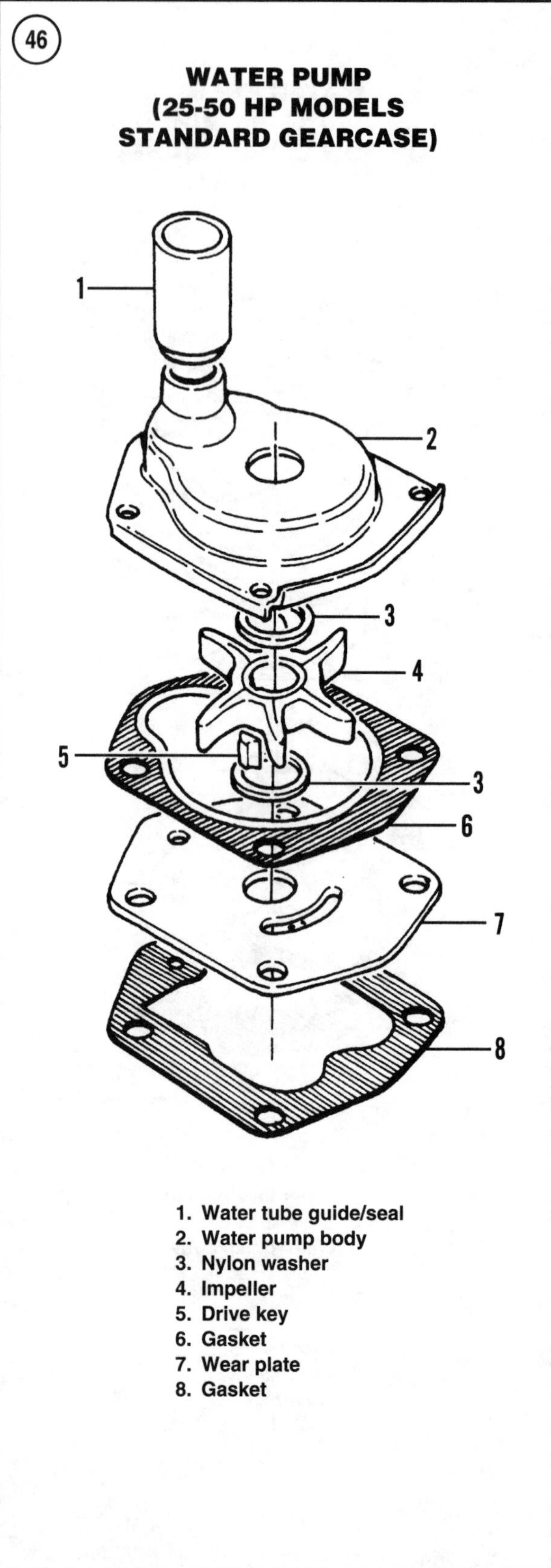

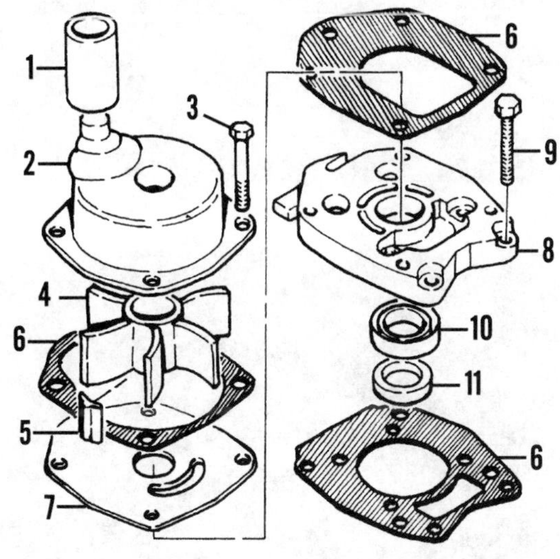

1. Water tube guide/seal
2. Water pump body
3. Bolt
4. Impeller
5. Drive key
6. Gasket
7. Wear plate
8. Water pump base
9. Bolt
10. Large diameter seal
11. Small diameter seal

2. Slide the gasket (8, **Figure 46**) and wear plate (7) over the drive shaft. Align these components with the opening in the gearcase.

3. Slide the lower nylon washer (3, **Figure 46**) over the drive shaft and seat it against the wear plate. Apply 2-4-C Marine Lubricant to the drive key (5, **Figure 46**) and install it onto the flat surface of the drive shaft with the rounded side of the key facing outward.

4. Slide the impeller over the drive shaft. Align the slot in the impeller hub with the drive key and push the impeller down against wear plate. If reusing the original impeller the vanes must curl in a counterclockwise direction (**Figure 43**). Flip the impeller if required. Slide the second nylon washer (3, **Figure 46**) over the drive shaft. Position the washer against the impeller.

5. Install the gasket (6, **Figure 46**) onto the water pump body with raised sealing bead facing the body. Place the water pump body (2, **Figure 46**) over the drive shaft and slide it down until it contacts the impeller. Align the water pump body with the water tube opening toward the rear of the gearcase. Rotate the drive shaft clockwise while pushing down on the water pump body. 9

6. Continue rotating the drive shaft until the impeller fully enters the water pump body and the body seats against the wear plate. Ensure the gasket (6, **Figure 46**) remains in position against the water pump body (2).

7. Apply Loctite 271 (Mercury part No. 92-809819) to the threads of the water pump bolts. Install the four bolts into the water pump body and gearcase. Tighten the bolts evenly to the specification in **Table 1**.

8. Install the water tube guide/seal (1, **Figure 46**) over its fitting on the water pump body.

9. Install the gearcase as described in this chapter. Fill the gearcase with lubricant (Chapter Four). Check for proper cooling system operation and correct any problems before operating the engine.

Disassembly (30-50 hp with Optional Gearcase, 75 and 90 hp Models)

Refer to **Figure 47** during this procedure.

1. Drain the gearcase lubricant as described in Chapter Four. Remove the gearcase as described in this chapter.

2. Pull the water tube guide/seal (**Figure 48**) from water pump body (2). Remove the four bolts (3, **Figure 47**) and lift the water pump body from the pump base (**Figure 49**).

3. Carefully pry the water pump impeller (**Figure 40**) away from the wear plate. Slide the impeller from the drive shaft (**Figure 50**). Pull the drive key from the drive shaft (**Figure 42**).
4. Lift the wear plate from the water pump base (**Figure 51**). Carefully scrape the gaskets (6, **Figure 47**) from the wear plate and water pump body (2).
5. Remove the water pump base only if removing the drive shaft, replacing the seals or if it is damaged. Remove the six mounting bolts (9, **Figure 47**) and carefully pry the water pump base (8) away from the gearcase. Remove the gasket from the gearcase (**Figure 52**) or water pump base.
6. Working carefully to avoid damaging the water pump base, carefully pry the drive shaft seals (10 and 11, **Figure 47**) from the water pump base.
7. Clean all water pump and shift shaft components using solvent. Carefully scrape gasket remnants from all components. Inspect all water pump components for wear or damage following the instructions in this chapter.

Assembly (30-50 hp with Optional Gearcase, 75 and 90 hp Models)

CAUTION
To prevent water and gear lubricant leakage replace all gaskets, seals and O-rings when they are removed or disturbed.

NOTE
Thoroughly clean all corrosion or other deposits from the exposed portions of the drive shaft prior to installing any water pump components. The impeller must slide freely along the length of the shaft.

Refer to **Figure 47** during this procedure.
1. Use a socket or section of tubing as a seal installation tool. The tool must contact the outer diameter of the seal, but not the seal bore in the water pump base.
2. Apply Loctite 271 (Mercury part No. 92-809819) to the outer diameter of both seals prior to installing them into the water pump base. Position the smaller diameter seal (10, **Figure 47**) into the opening at the bottom of the water pump base with the lip side facing inward. Push the seal into the bore until it bottoms. Place the second seal into the opening with the seal lip or spring side facing outward. Push the seal into the bore until it contacts the first seal. Apply a bead of Quicksilver 2-4-C Marine Lubricant (Mercury part No. 825407A12) to the lips of the seals.
4. Place the new gasket (6, **Figure 47**) on the gearcase with the sealing bead side facing up (**Figure 52**). Gasket sealing compound is not required. Guide the water pump base over the drive shaft seal side down and place the base onto the gearcase (**Figure 53**). Position the base with its protruding side facing the rear of the gearcase.

49

50

5. Seat the water pump base against the gearcase. Apply Loctite 271 (Mercury part No. 82-809819) to the threads of the six mounting bolts (9, **Figure 47**). Install the bolts then tighten them evenly to the specification in **Table 1**.
6. Apply a light coating of 2-4-C Marine Lubricant to the inner surface of the water pump body (2, **Figure 47**).
7. Slide the gasket (6, **Figure 47**) and wear plate (7) over the drive shaft. Align these components with the water pump base.
8. Apply 2-4-C Marine Lubricant to the drive key (5, **Figure 47**) and install it into position on the drive shaft.
9. Slide the impeller over the drive shaft (**Figure 50**). Align the slot in the impeller hub with the drive key and push the impeller down against wear plate. If reusing the original impeller the vanes must curl in a counterclockwise direction (**Figure 43**). Flip the impeller if required.
10. Install a new gasket (6, **Figure 47**) onto the water pump body (2) with the sealing bead facing the body.
11. Place the water pump body over the drive shaft (**Figure 49**) and slide it down until it contacts the impeller. Ro-

tate the drive shaft clockwise while pushing down on the water pump body.

12. Continue rotating the drive shaft until the impeller fully enters the water pump body and the body seats against the wear plate. Ensure the gaskets (6, **Figure 47**) remain in position.

13. Apply Loctite 271 to their threads then install the four bolts (3, **Figure 47**) into the water pump body and base. Tighten the bolts evenly to the specification in **Table 1**.

14. Apply 2-4-C Marine Lubricant to the water tube guide/seal (1, **Figure 47**) and push it onto the water pump body (2).

15. Install the gearcase following the instructions provided in this chapter. Fill the gearcase with lubricant (Chapter Four). Check for proper cooling system operation and correct any problems before operating the engine.

GEARCASE

Replacement of gears, bearings or drive shaft usually require accurate positioning of the gears within the gearcase. Proper gear alignment is essential for quiet op-

eration and long gear life. Special tools and measuring instruments are required to check gear alignment. Purchase or rent the special tools from a Mercury or Mariner dealership.

Some of the gearcases use shims to position bearings and gears. Note the location and thickness of all shims as they are removed. Using a micrometer, measure and record the thickness each shim or spacer thickness as they are removed from the gearcase Tag or place them in an envelope. Note the shim location within the gearcase on the envelope or tag.

9

Use pressurized water to thoroughly clean the external surfaces of the gearcase prior to disassembly. Pay particular attention to the bearing carrier area as debris can easily become trapped in hidden recesses. This step helps prevent debris from contaminating the bearings during disassembly.

Mount the gearcase in a suitable holding fixture or a sturdy vise. Use padded jaws or wooden blocks to protect the gearcase. Clamp the gearcase on the skeg when using a vise. Have an assistant provide additional support for the gearcase when removing large or tight fasteners.

CAUTION

When using heat to assist removal of components, keep the flame away from the seals and O-rings. Never heat the housing to the point that the finish is burned. Continually move the flame around the mating surface to apply even heating. Excessive use of heat can distort or melt the gearcase.

NOTE

To assist with removal of the propeller shaft bearing carrier, use a torch to apply heat to the gearcase near the bearing carrier mating surface. Continually move the flame to apply even heat.

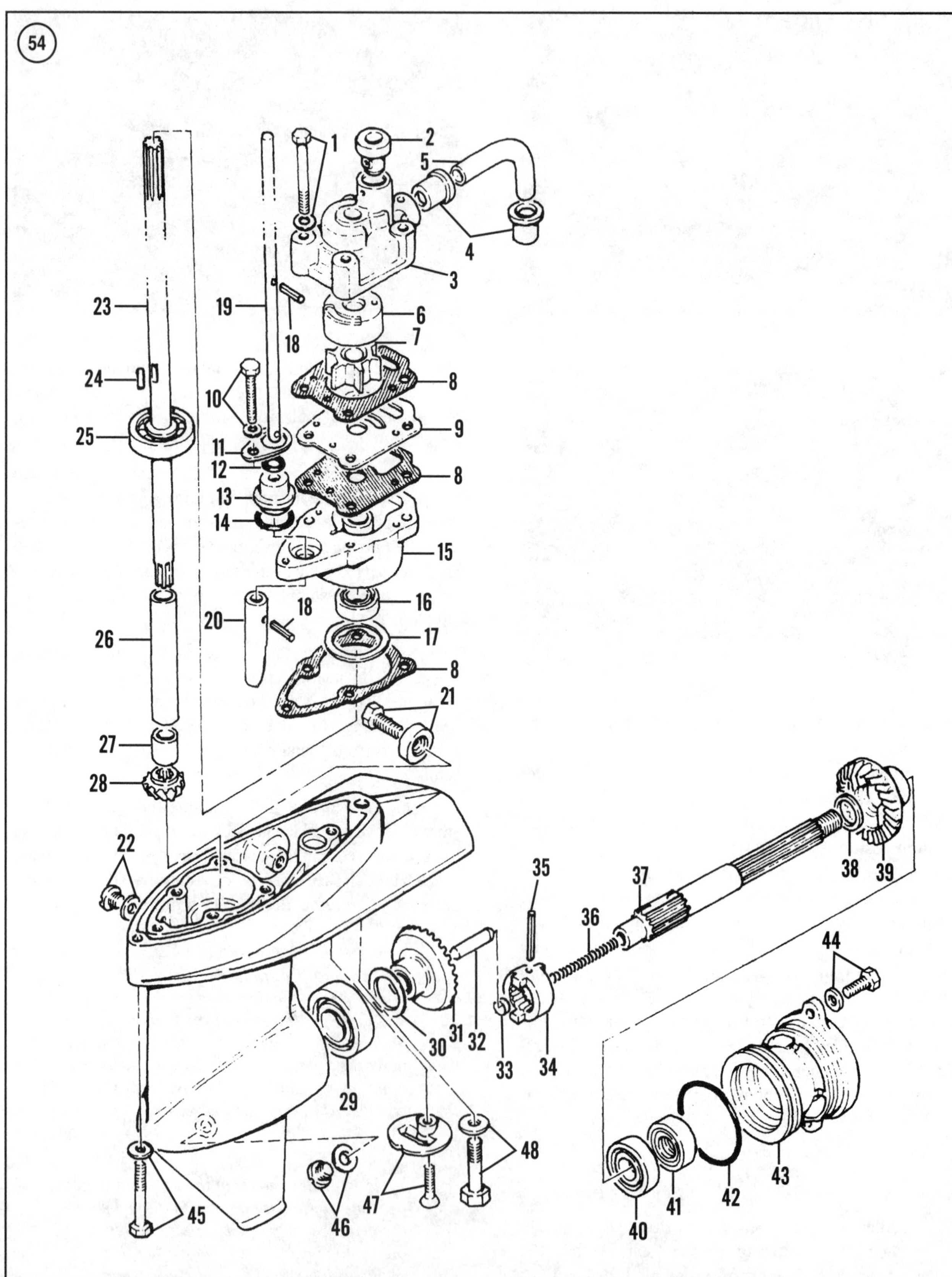
54
1
2
5
4
3
23
19
6
18
7
24
8
10
25
9
11
12
8
13
14
15
16
18
20
17
26
8
21
27
28
22
35
37
38
39
36
44
31
32
30
33
34
29
48
47
46
45
43
42
41
40

GEARCASE (4-6 HP MODELS)

1. Bolt and washer
2. Water tube grommet
3. Water pump body
4. Water tube grommet
5. Water tube
6. Insert
7. Impeller
8. Gasket
9. Wear plate
10. Bolt and washer
11. Retainer
12. O-ring
13. Bushing
14. O-ring
15. Water pump base
16. Seal
17. Shim
18. Roll pin
19. Shift shaft
20. Shift cam
21. Anode and bolt
22. Vent plug and gasket
23. Drive shaft
24. Drive key
25. Ball bearing
26. Sleeve (some models)
27. Drive shaft bearing
28. Pinion gear
29. Forward gear bearing
30. Shim
31. Forward gear
32. Cam follower
33. Guide
34. Clutch
35. Cross pin
36. Spring
37. Propeller shaft
38. Thrust washer
39. Reverse gear
40. Bearing
41. Seal
42. O-ring
43. Bearing carrier
44. Bolt and washer
45. Mounting bolt and washer
46. Fill/drain plug and gasket
47. Water screen and screw
48. Mounting bolt and washer

55

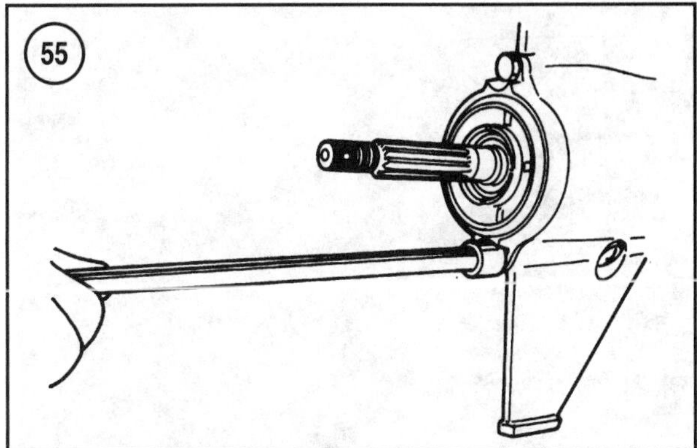

56

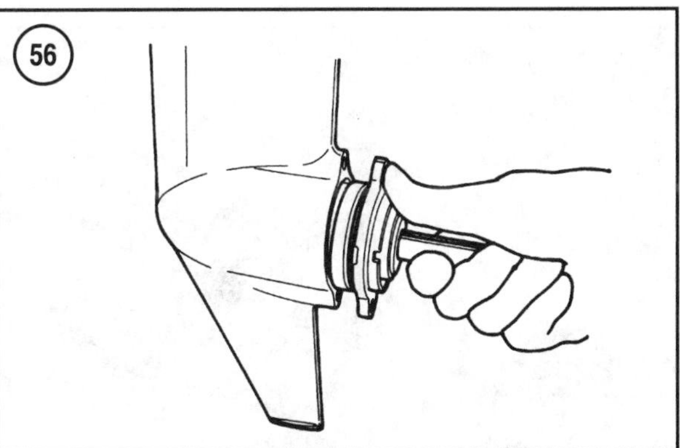

Disassembly (4-6 hp Models)

Refer to **Figure 54** to assist with component identification and orientation.

1. Disassemble the water pump as described in this chapter.

2. Remove both bearing carrier retaining bolts (**Figure 55**), then pull the propeller shaft and bearing carrier from the gearcase (**Figure 56**). Carefully pry the carrier from the gearcase (**Figure 57**) if it cannot be removed by hand.

3. Slide the propeller shaft from the gear side of the bearing carrier. Pull the reverse gear and thrust washer (A and B, **Figure 58**) from the carrier. Remove the O-ring (C, **Figure 58**) from the bearing carrier. Discard the O-ring. Carefully pry the gear from the bearing carrier with two screwdrivers (**Figure 59**) if it cannot be removed by hand.

4. If the gear cannot be removed by prying, clamp the carrier into a vice with soft jaws. Attach the jaws of a slide hammer to the gear (**Figure 60**). Use short hammer strokes to remove the gear from the carrier.

5. Remove the ball bearing from the carrier as follows:

   a. Clamp the bearing carrier into a vice with soft jaws.

9

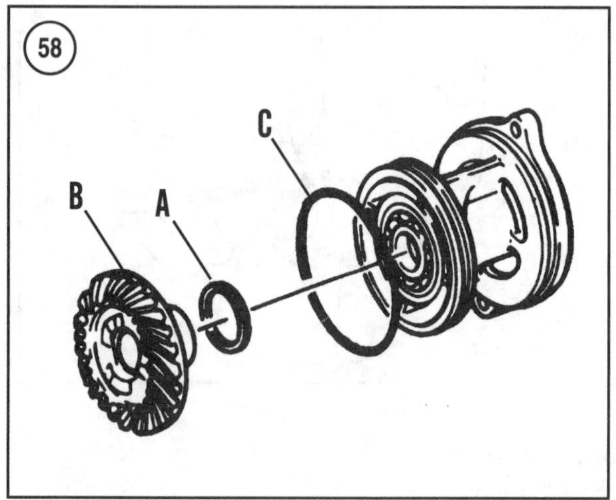

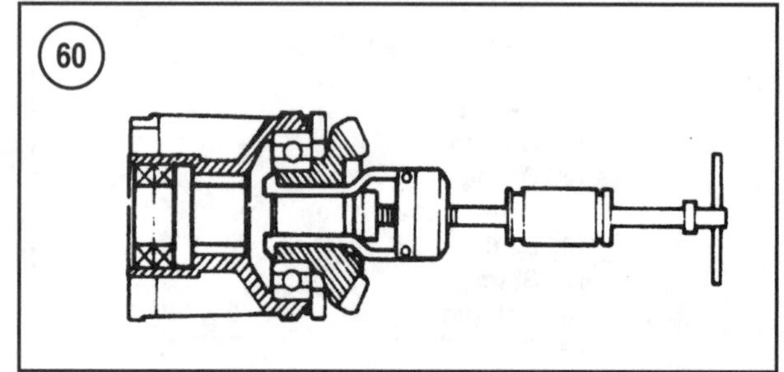

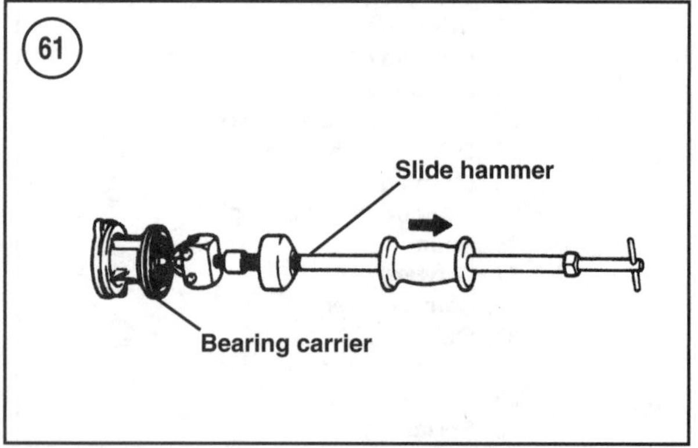

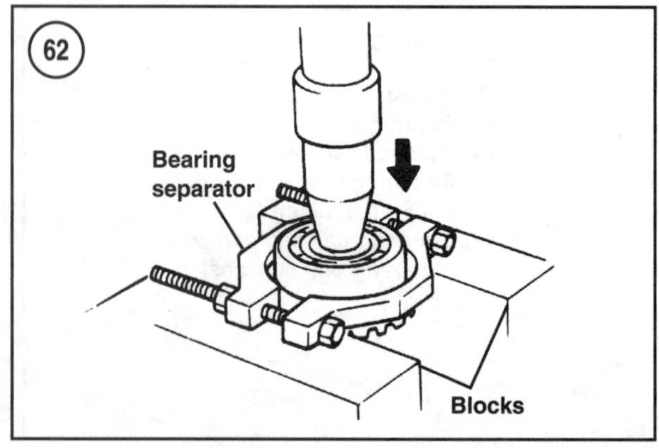

b. Pass the jaws of a slide hammer (**Figure 61**) through the bore of the bearing.

c. Use short hammer strokes to remove the bearing from the carrier.

6. If the ball bearing is seized to the reverse gear, remove it as follows:

a. Position a bearing separator between the ball bearing and the reverse gear (**Figure 62**).

b. Use a socket or section of tubing with a diameter slightly smaller than the inner bore of the bearing as a driver.

c. Place the bearing separator and gear onto a press with no restrictions under the gear. Block the sides of the separator to ensure adequate travel for the gear.

d. Place the socket or section of tubing against the hub of the gear. Press the gear from the bearing (**Figure 62**).

7. Clamp the bearing carrier in a vice with the bearing side facing up. Engage the jaws of a slide hammer (**Figure**

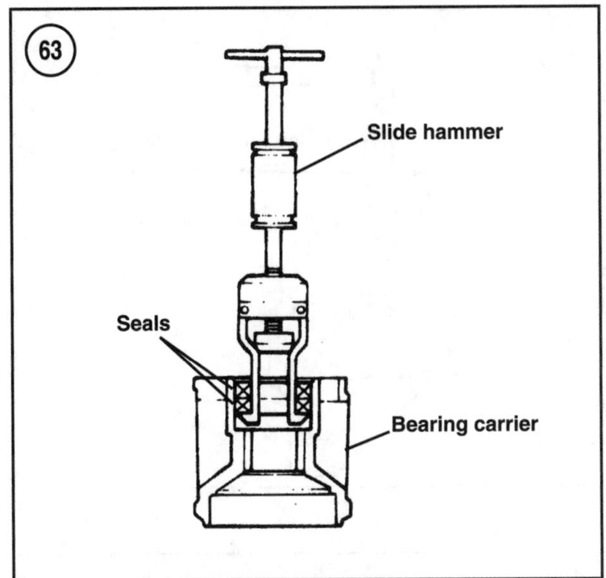

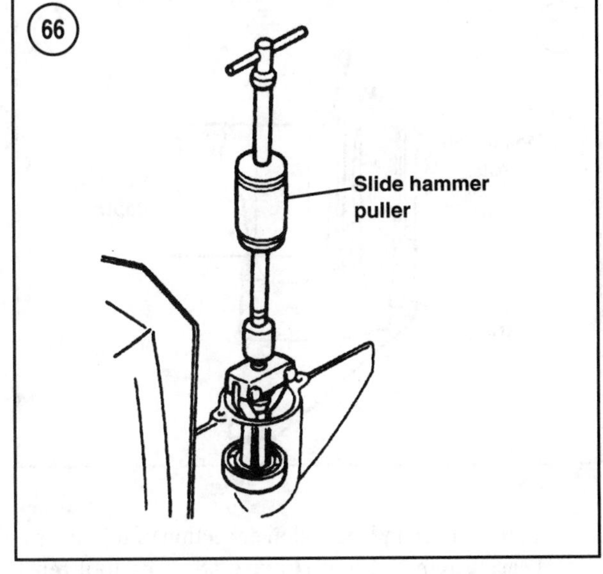

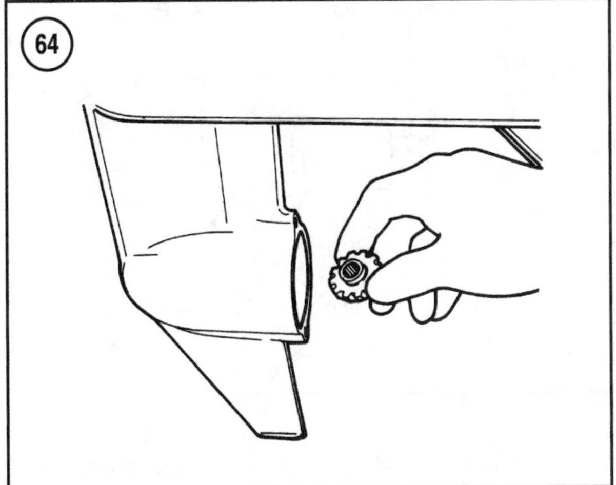

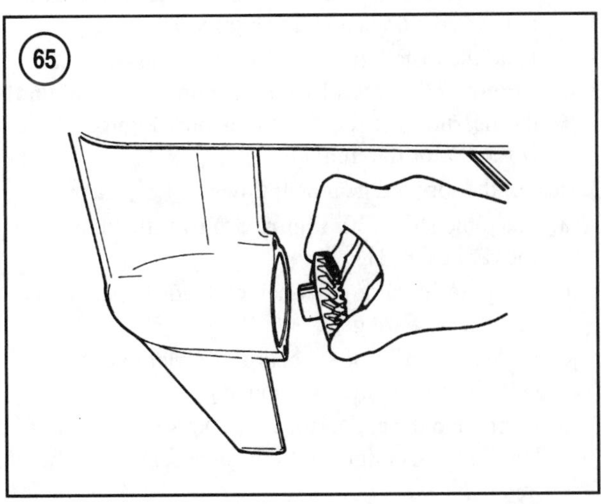

63) with the inner seal. Remove both seals using short hammer strokes. Discard the seals.

8. Pull straight up on the drive shaft and slide it from the gearcase. Reach into the gearcase opening and remove the pinion gear (**Figure 64**), then pull the forward gear from the housing (**Figure 65**). Retain the shim (30, **Figure 54**) from the forward gear (31) or bearing (29).

9. If the forward gear cannot be removed by hand perform the following:
   a. Secure the housing into a gearcase holding bracket or a vice with soft jaws.
   b. Pass the jaws of a slide hammer through the propeller shaft opening in the gear.
   c. Remove the gear using short hammer strokes.

10. Remove the forward gear bearing only if it or the housing must be replaced. Refer to *Inspection* in this chapter to determine the need for replacement. Remove the forward gear bearing as follows:
   a. Pass the jaws of a slide hammer through the gear bore of the bearing (**Figure 66**).
   b. Remove the bearing using short hammer strokes.

11. Remove the drive shaft lower bearings only if they must be replaced. Remove the drive shaft bearings as follows:
   a. Select a section of tubing or an extension of sufficient width and length for use as a measuring rod.
   b. Insert the rod into the drive shaft bore until it contacts the top of the drive shaft bearing (**Figure 67**).
   c. Make a mark on the rod even with the gearcase mating surface.
   d. Record this depth for use during bearing installation.

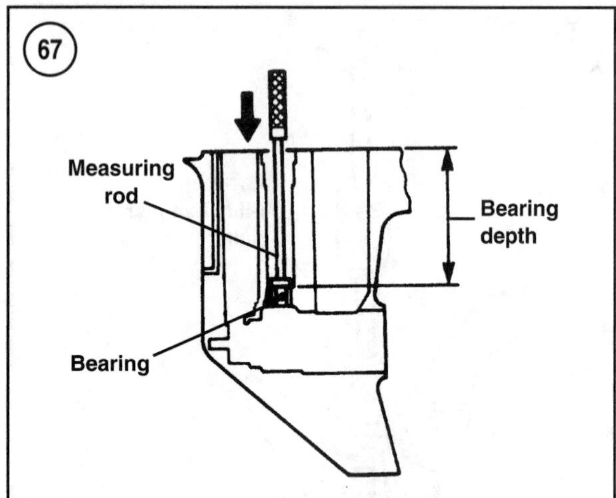

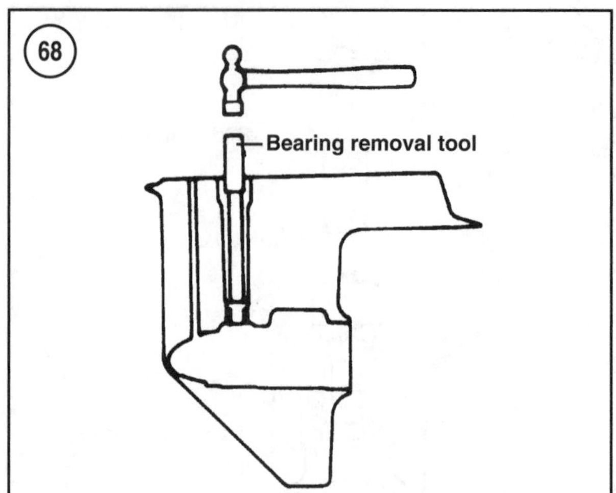

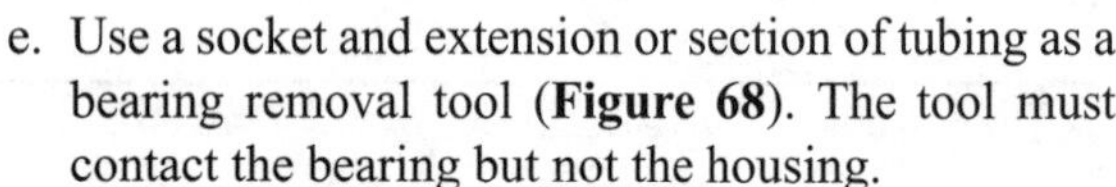

e. Use a socket and extension or section of tubing as a bearing removal tool (**Figure 68**). The tool must contact the bearing but not the housing.
f. Seat the tool firmly against the bearing. Carefully tap the bearing into the gearcase opening.

12. Place the cam follower portion of the propeller shaft (**Figure 69**) against a solid object such as a vice. Push the propeller shaft against the object to push the cam follower into the shaft. Maintain the pressure while driving the cross pin (35, **Figure 54**) from the clutch. Slowly relieve the pressure, then slide the clutch, cross pin, spring, guide and follower (32-36, **Figure 54**) from the propeller shaft.
13. Remove the screw and pull the water screen (47, **Figure 54**) from bottom of the antiventilation plate.
14. Remove the bolt and pull the anode (21, **Figure 54**) from the starboard side of the gearcase.
15. Clean and inspect all components as described in this chapter.

Assembly (4-6 hp Models)

Refer to **Figure 54** during this procedure.

1. Install a new forward gear bearing (29, **Figure 54**) into the housing as follows:
   a. Place the bearing into the housing with the numbered side facing the rear of the housing.
   b. Use a large socket or section of tubing as a bearing installation tool. The tool must be large enough to contact the outer edge of the bearing but not contact the housing during installation.
   c. Hold the installation tool firmly against the bearing (**Figure 70**) and drive the bearing fully into the housing.
2. Install the drive shaft bearing as follows:

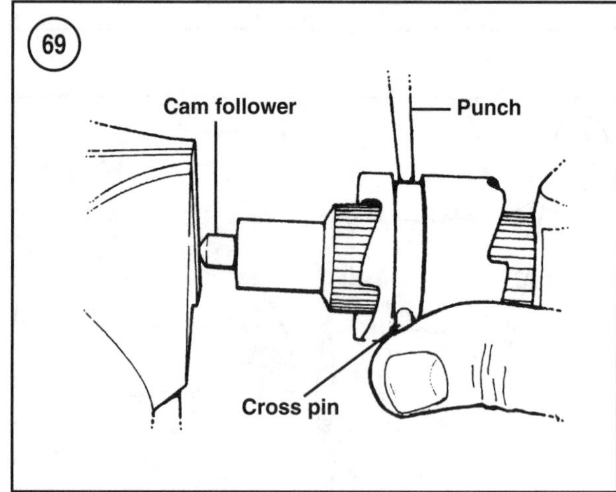

   a. Use a socket and extension or section of tubing as a bearing installation tool.
   b. Slide the bearing into the drive shaft bore with the numbered side facing up (**Figure 71**).
   c. Hold the installation tool firmly against the bearing (**Figure 71**). Carefully tap the end of the tool until the bearing just reaches the depth (**Figure 71**) recorded prior to removal.
3. Install the forward gear as follows:
   a. Place the shim (30, **Figure 54**) over the hub of the forward gear (31).
   b. Temporarily slide the unassembled propeller shaft into the forward gear.
   c. Slide the unassembled bearing carrier over the propeller shaft and into the housing.
   d. Gently tap the end of the propeller shaft with a rubber mallet. Continue until the gear seats in the bearing.

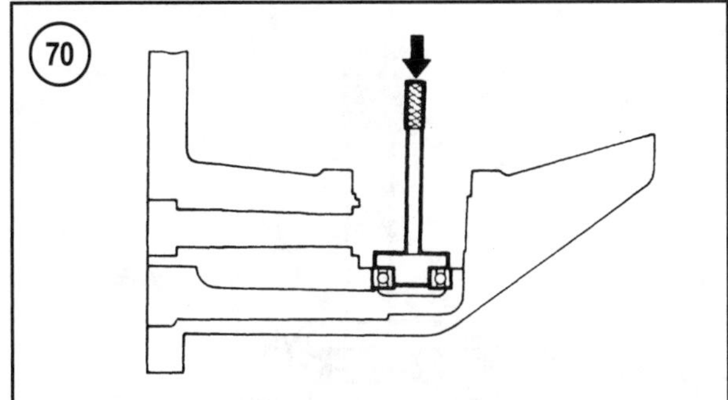

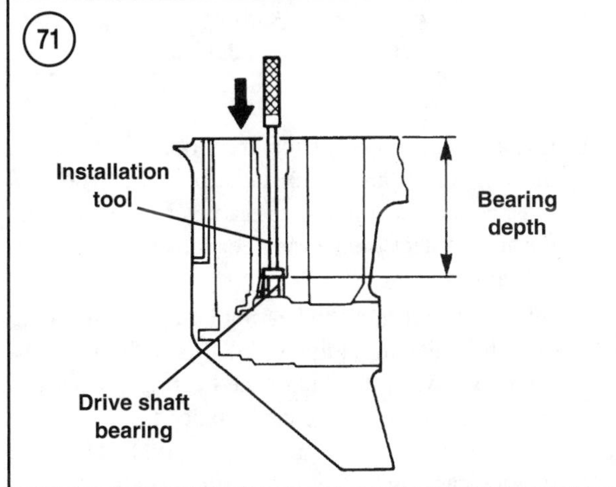

e. Remove the bearing carrier and propeller shaft.

4. Install the drive shaft and pinion gear as follows:
   a. Place the pinion gear into the housing. Mesh the pinion gear teeth with the forward gear teeth and align the gear with the drive shaft bearing.
   b. Slide the drive shaft through its bore and bearings. Slowly rotate the drive shaft to align the drive shaft and pinion gear splines.
   c. Place the shim (17, **Figure 54**) over the end of the drive shaft and rest it against the bearing portion of the drive shaft.
5. Assemble and install the propeller shaft as follows:
   a. Align the cross pin hole in the side of the clutch (34, **Figure 54**) with the slot in the propeller shaft while sliding it over the splines of the propeller shaft.
   b. Slide the spring (36, **Figure 54**) into the bore at the forward end of the propeller shaft.
   c. Insert a ¼ in. socket extension into the opening. Push in on the extension to compress the spring enough to slide a pin punch or scribe through the cross pin openings (**Figure 72**).

   d. Support the pin punch or scribe while carefully driving the cross pin into the clutch until it is flush with the clutch surfaces.
   e. Apply 2-4-C Marine Lubricant to the guide (33, **Figure 54**) and cam follower (32) and install them into the bore at the end of the propeller shaft.
   f. Position the gearcase with the drive shaft pointing up. Slide the propeller shaft clutch side first fully into its bore in the forward gear. Slide the thrust washer (38, **Figure 54**) over the propeller shaft. Seat the washer against the shoulder on the shaft.

9

6. Install the propeller shaft seals into the bearing carrier as follows:
   a. Place the bearing carrier on a flat surface with the larger opening gear side facing up.
   b. Use a socket and extension or section of tubing as a seal installation tool.
   c. Place the first seal into its bore with the lip side facing down. Using the installation tool, gently drive the seal into the bore until it bottoms.
   d. Place the second seal into its bore opening with the lip side facing up. Using the installation tool gently drive the seal into the bore until it contacts the first seal.
   e. Apply a thick coat of 2-4-C Marine Lubricant to the both seal lips.
7. Install the ball bearing into the bearing carrier as follows:
   a. Use a large socket or section of tubing as an installation tool for the ball bearing.
   b. Place the bearing carrier on the table of a press with the gear side facing up.
   c. Position the ball bearing in the carrier with the numbered side facing up. Place the installation tool against the bearing.
   d. Press the bearing into the carrier (**Figure 73**) until it bottoms.

8. Lubricate the new large diameter O-ring (42, **Figure 54**) with 2-4-C Marine Lubricant. Place the O-ring over the bearing carrier. Rest the O-ring on the stepped surface near the reverse gear side of the carrier.
9. Apply gearcase lubricant to its hub, then carefully push the reverse gear into the bearing carrier.
10. Position the gearcase with the drive shaft pointing up. Rotate the drive shaft clockwise while sliding the bearing carrier and reverse gear into the gearcase.
11. Align the bolt tabs with the threaded holes in the housing then thread both bolts and washers (44, **Figure 54**) into the carrier and housing. Tighten the bolts (**Figure 55**) to the specification in **Table 1**.
12. Install the water screen (47, **Figure 54**) into the antiventilation plate with the notched side facing forward. Install and securely tighten the screw.
13. Install the anode and bolt (21, **Figure 54**). Tighten the anode bolt to the specification in **Table 1**.
14. Install the shift shaft and water pump as described in this chapter.

Disassembly (9.9 and 15 hp Models with Standard Gearcase)

Refer to **Figure 74** to assist with component identification and orientation. Removal of the bearing carrier (44, **Figure 74**) requires a special tool. Purchase or rent this tool (part No. 91-13664) from a Mercury or Mariner dealership.

1. Disassemble the water pump as described in this chapter.
2. Slide the carrier removal tool over the propeller shaft (**Figure 75**). Engage the slots of the tool over the struts in the carrier. Turn the tool clockwise until the carrier is free of the gearcase. Pull the propeller shaft and bearing carrier from the gearcase.
3. Slide the propeller shaft from the gear side of the bearing carrier. Pull the reverse gear (43, **Figure 74**) from the bearing carrier (44).
4. If the gear cannot be removed by prying, clamp the carrier into a vice with soft jaws. Attach the jaws of a slide hammer to the gear (**Figure 60**). Use short hammer strokes to remove the gear from the carrier.
5. Clamp the bearing carrier in a vice with the smaller diameter side facing up. Attach the jaws of a slide hammer (**Figure 63**) to the inner seal. Remove both seals using short hammer strokes.
6. Remove the propeller shaft bushing (46, **Figure 74**) only if it must be replaced. Refer to *Inspection* in this chapter. Remove the bushing as follows:
   a. Clamp the bearing carrier in a vise with the threaded side facing up.

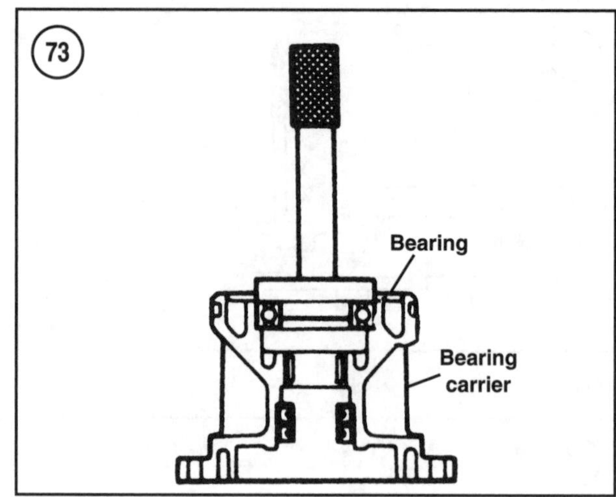

   b. Use a socket and extension or section of tubing as a bushing removal and installation tool. The tool must contact near the outer diameter of the bushing but not contact the bearing carrier bore during removal.
   c. Insert the tool into the bearing carrier until it contacts the bushing (**Figure 76**). Mark the tool at a point even with the end of the bearing carrier. Remove the tool. Measure the distance from the mark to the bushing contact surface. Record this bushing depth measurement for use during installation.
   d. Seat the bushing removal tool firmly against the bushing and carefully drive the bushing from the carrier.
7. Disassemble the propeller shaft as follows:
   a. Pull the cam follower (38, **Figure 74**) from the propeller shaft (42).
   b. Rest the propeller shaft on the slightly open jaws of a vise.
   c. Rotate the propeller shaft to position the grooved end of the cross pin to the bottom of the slightly open vise jaws.
   d. Using a pin punch, drive the grooved pin (**Figure 77**) from the clutch. Remove the clutch and spring (39 and 41, **Figure 74**) from the propeller shaft.
8. Remove the drive shaft and gears from the gearcase as follows:
   a. Pull straight up on the drive shaft and slide it from the gearcase.
   b. Reach into the gearcase then remove the pinion gear (**Figure 64**).
   c. Pull the thrust washer (33, **Figure 74**) from the gearcase or pinion gear. Remove the thrust washer (21, **Figure 74**) from the drive shaft bore.

d. Reach into the gearcase and pull the forward gear and bearing from the housing (**Figure 78**).

9. Remove the drive shaft bushing and sleeve assembly (23 and 24, **Figure 74**) only if the bushing, bearing (32) or the housing must be replaced. Refer to *Inspection* in this chapter. Remove the bushing as follows:

a. Thread a bushing removal tool onto the end of the a slide hammer (**Figure 79**).

b. Engage the tool with the bottom edge of the drive shaft bushing and sleeve (**Figure 79**).

c. Remove the bearing using short hammer strokes. Remove the sleeve (24, **Figure 74**) from the gearcase using the same method if it remains in the housing.

10. Remove the lower drive shaft bearings only if they must be replaced. Refer to *Inspection* in this chapter. Remove the drive shaft bearings as follows:

a. Remove the lubrication sleeve (25, **Figure 74**) from the drive shaft bore.

b. Use a section of tubing or an extension of sufficient width and length as a measuring rod.

c. Insert the rod into the drive shaft bore until it contacts the top of the drive shaft bearing (**Figure 67**).

d. Make a mark on the rod even with the gearcase-to-drive shaft housing mating surface.

e. Record this depth for use during bearing installation.

f. Use a socket and extension as a bearing removal tool (**Figure 68**).

g. Seat the tool firmly against the bearing. Carefully tap the bearing into the gearcase opening.

11. Attach the jaws of a slide hammer puller to the rear of the forward bearing race (**Figure 80**). Remove the bearing race using short hammer strokes.

12. Remove the tapered roller bearing (35, **Figure 74**) from the forward gear (37) only if it must be replaced. Remove the bearing as follows:

a. Engage a bearing separator between the bearing and the forward gear (**Figure 81**).

b. Place the bearing separator and gear onto a press. Block the sides of the separator to ensure adequate travel for the gear.

c. Place a socket or section of tubing against the hub of the gear. Press on the socket or tubing to remove the gear from the bearing.

13. Remove the bushing (36, **Figure 74**) only if it must be replaced. Refer to *Inspection* in this chapter. Remove the bushing as follows:

a. Measure the distance from bearing side of the gear to the bushing. Record this distance for use during installation.

b. Place the gear teeth side down on the table of a press.

c. Ensure adequate clearance exists under the gear and press the bushing from the forward gear.

14. Remove the screws and pull the anode and water screen (28 and 41, **Figure 74**) from the antiventilation plate.

15. Clean and inspect all components as described in this chapter.

Assembly (9.9 and 15 hp Models with Standard Gearcase)

Refer to **Figure 74** as required during this procedure. Bearing carrier installation requires a special tool. Rent or purchase this tool (part No. 91-13664) from a local Mercury or Mariner dealership.

1. Install the anode (28, **Figure 74**) into the bottom of the antiventilation plate. Tighten its screw to the specification in **Table 1**. Install the water screen (41, **Figure 74**) and securely tighten the retaining screw.

2. Install the forward bearing race as follows:

a. Place the forward bearing race in its bore at the front of the gearcase with the larger inner diameter facing outward.

b. Use a large socket or section of tubing as an installation tool. The tool must contact the outer diameter of the bearing race, but not the housing during installation.

c. Seat the installation tool firmly against the bearing race (**Figure 82**). Drive the bearing race into its bore until it bottoms.

3. Install the lower drive shaft bearing as follows:

a. Use a socket and extension as a bearing installation tool. The tool must contact the outer diameter of the bearing, but not the drive bore during installation.

b. Align the bearing with its drive shaft bore opening with the numbered side facing up or toward the water pump mounting surface.

c. Seat the installation tool firmly against the bearing (**Figure 83**). Frequently stop and measure the bearing depth while carefully driving the bearing into its bore. Drive the bearing to the exact depth recorded prior to removal.

4. Align the tab with the recess in the drive shaft bore while sliding the lubrication sleeve (25, **Figure 74**) into the drive shaft bore. Seat the sleeve fully in the bore.

5. Install the drive shaft sleeve and bushing (23 and 24, **Figure 74**) as follows:

a. Use a socket and extension or section of tubing as a sleeve and bushing installation tool.

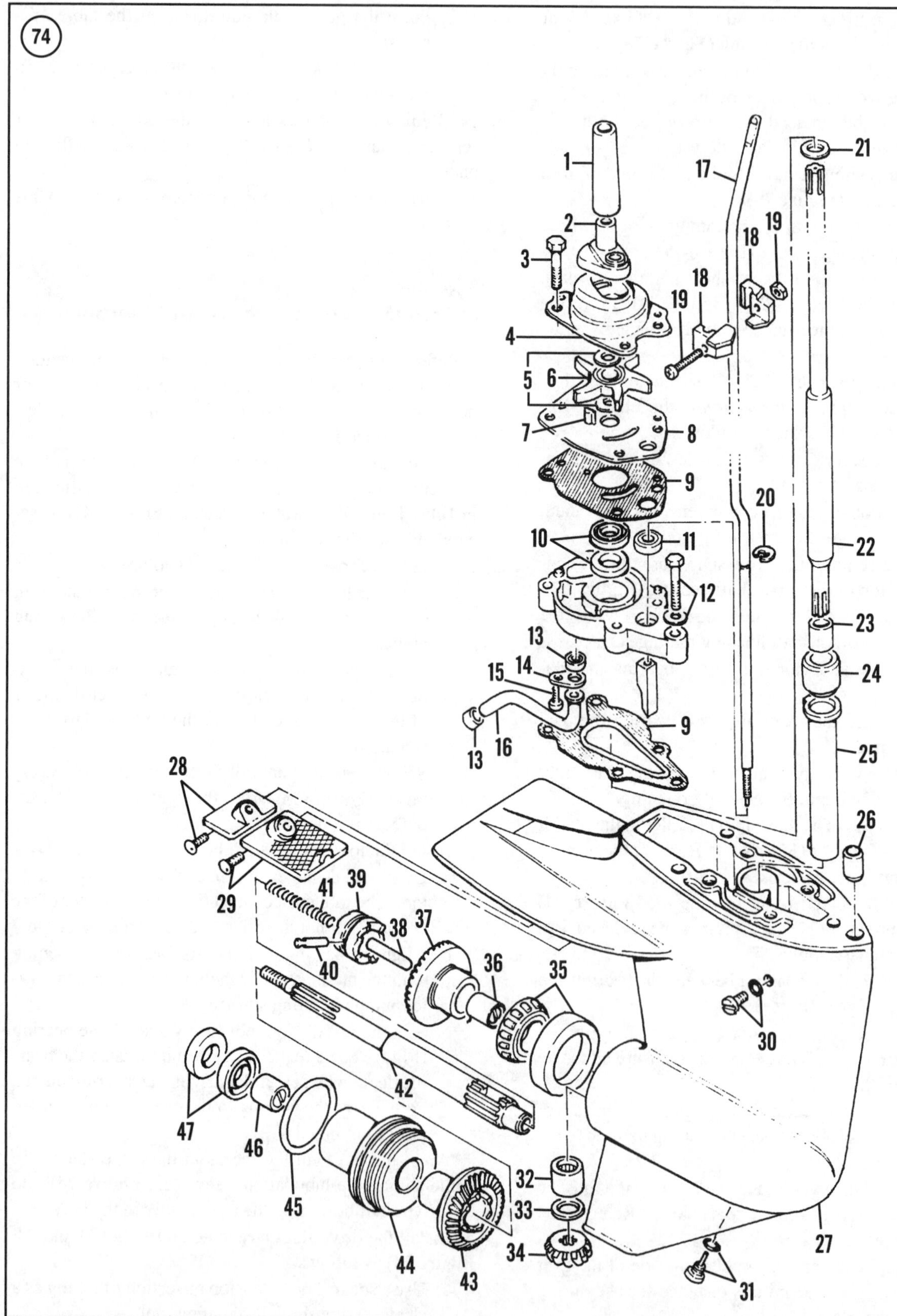
74
1
2
3
4
5
6
7
8
9
10
11
12
13
14
15
16
17
18
19
20
21
22
23
24
25
26
27
28
29
30
31
32
33
34
35
36
37
38
39
40
41
42
43
44
45
46
47

GEARCASE (9.9 AND 15 HP MODELS STANDARD GEARCASE)

1. Water tube guide/seal
2. Drive shaft seal
3. Bolt
4. Water pump body
5. Nylon washer
6. Impeller
7. Drive key
8. Wear plate
9. Gasket
10. Drive shaft seals
11. Quad ring seal
12. Bolt and washer
13. Grommet
14. Retainer
15. Screw
16. Water tube
17. Shift shaft
18. Clamp
19. Bolt and nut
20. E-clip
21. Thrust washer
22. Drive shaft
23. Bushing
24. Sleeve
25. Lubrication sleeve
26. Locating pin
27. Gearcase housing
28. Anode and bolt
29. Water screen and bolt
30. Level/vent plug and washer
31. Drain/fill plug and washer
32. Drive shaft bearing
33. Thrust washer
34. Pinion gear
35. Forward bearing and race
36. Propeller shaft bushing
37. Forward gear
38. Cam follower
39. Clutch
40. Cross pin
41. Spring
42. Propeller shaft
43. Reverse gear
44. Bearing carrier
45. O-ring
46. Bushing
47. Propeller shaft seals

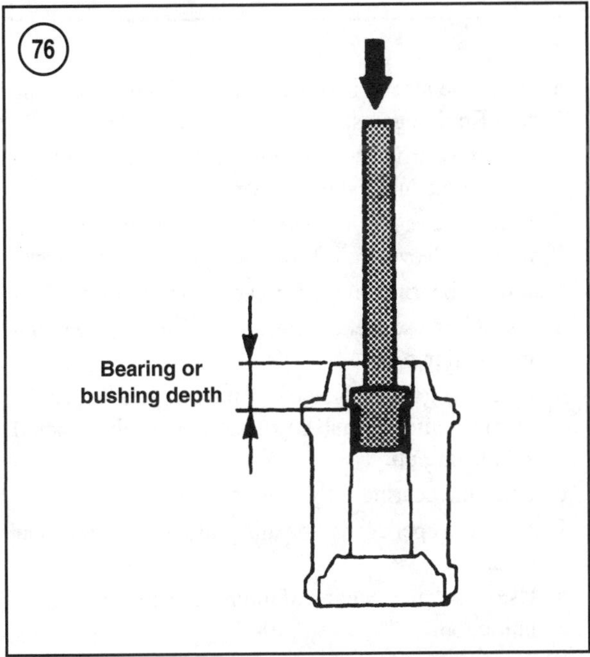

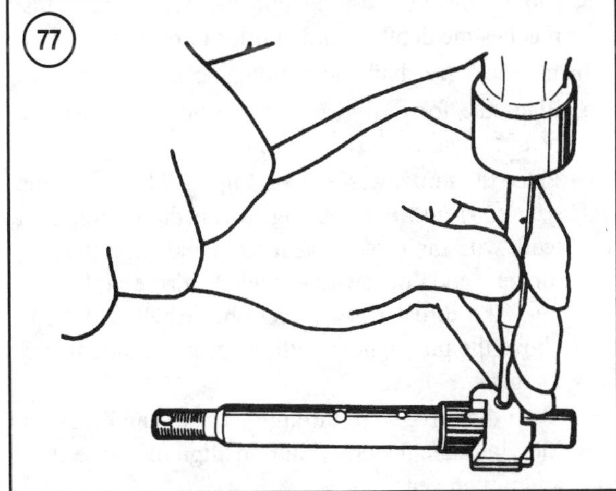

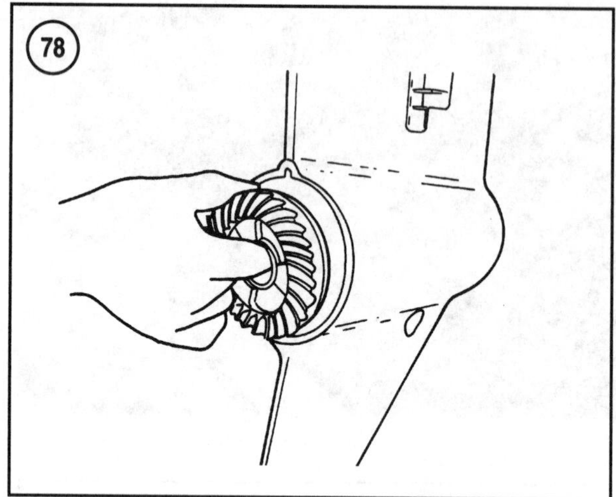

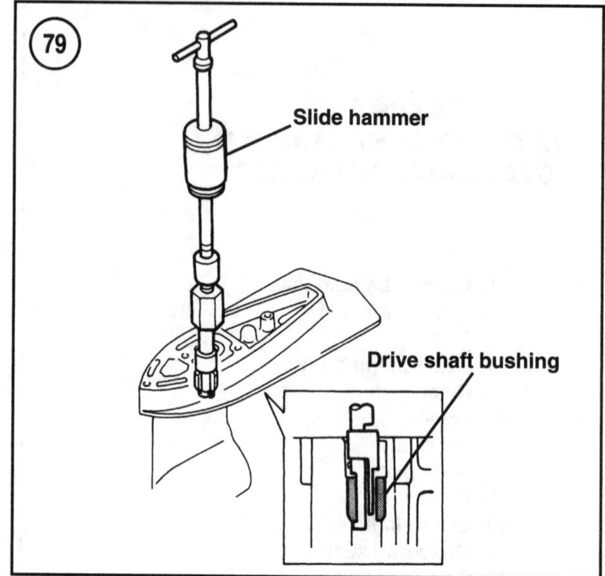

b. Place the sleeve into the drive shaft bore. Seat the tool firmly against the sleeve (**Figure 84**).

c. Carefully drive the sleeve into the bore until it seats against the lubrication sleeve.

d. Using the same tool, carefully drive the bushing into the sleeve until flush with the sleeve surface.

6. Install the bearing on the forward gear as follows:

a. Use a large socket or section of tubing as a bearing installation tool.

b. Place the gear teeth side down on a press. Place the bearing onto the hub of the gear with the tapered side facing up.

c. Press the bearing fully onto the gear.

7. Install the propeller shaft bushing into the forward gear as follows:

a. Use a socket or section of tubing as a bushing installation tool.

b. Place the bushing in the gear. Seat the bushing installation tool firmly against the bushing.

c. Slowly tap the bushing into the gear until it just reaches the depth recorded prior to removal.

8. Install the drive shaft and pinion gear as follows:

a. Place the forward gear into the housing. Seat the bearing against the bearing race.

b. Place the thrust washer (33, **Figure 74**) and pinion gear (34) into the housing. Mesh the pinion gear teeth with the forward gear teeth and align the pinion gear and thrust washer with the drive shaft bearing. The thrust washer must be installed directly above the pinion gear with the grooved side facing the gear.

c. Slide the drive shaft through its bore and bearings. Slowly rotate the drive shaft to align the drive shaft and pinion gear splines.

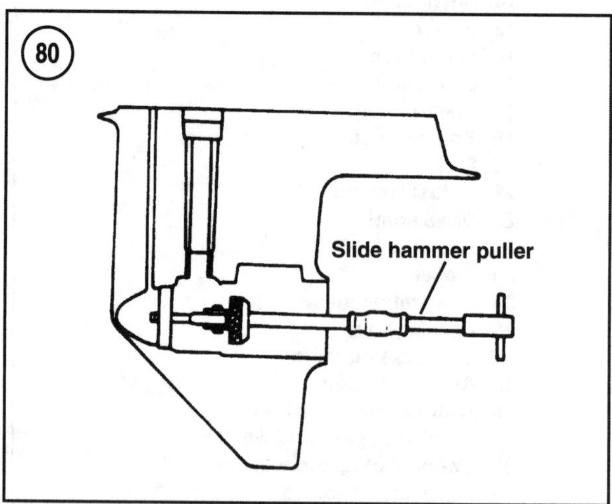

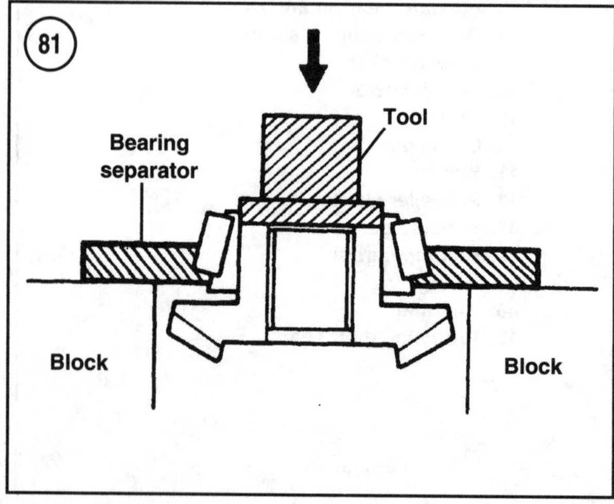

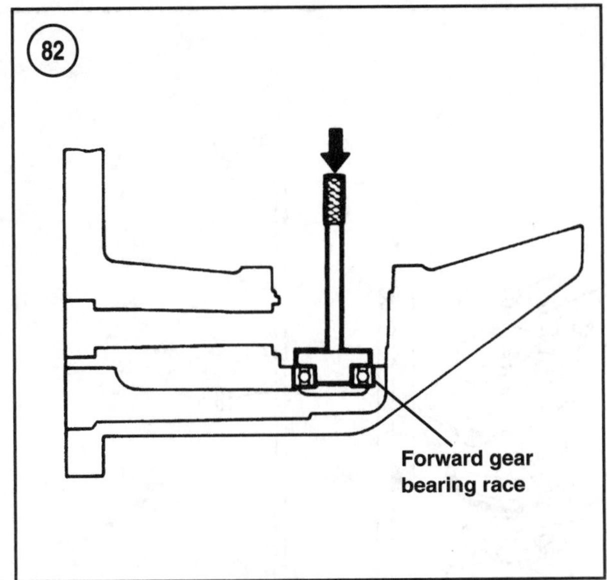

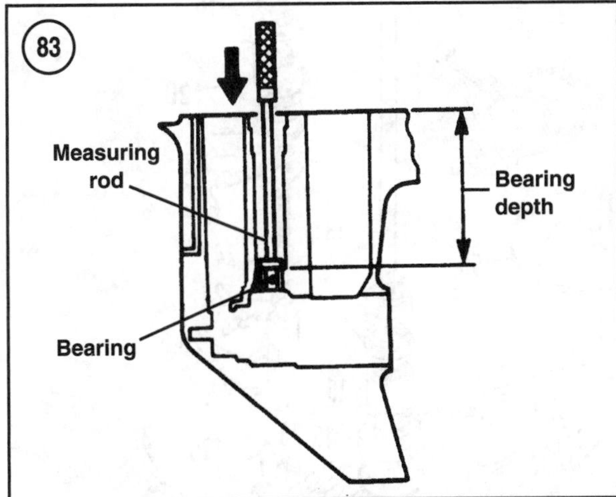

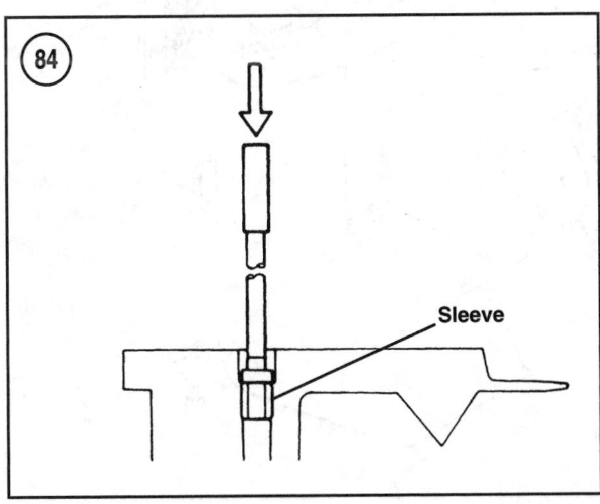

d. Place the thrust washer over the end of the drive shaft and rest it against the bushing and sleeve (23 and 24, **Figure 74**).

9. Assemble and install the propeller shaft as follows:
   a. Align the cross pin hole in the side of the clutch (39, **Figure 74**) with the slot in the propeller shaft. Slide the clutch onto the propeller shaft.
   b. Slide the spring (41, **Figure 74**) into the bore at the forward end of the propeller shaft.
   c. Insert a 1/4 in. socket extension into the opening. Push in on the extension to compress the spring enough to slide a pin punch through the cross pin hole (**Figure 72**).
   d. Place the non-grooved end of the cross pin into its opening in the clutch. Carefully drive the cross pin into the clutch until it is flush with the clutch surfaces.
   e. Apply Quicksilver 2-4-C Marine Lubricant to the shift cam follower and install it into the propeller shaft with its pointed end facing out.

10. Position the gearcase with the drive shaft pointing up. Slide the propeller shaft clutch side first fully into in the forward gear.

11. Install the propeller shaft bushing into the bearing carrier as follows:
   a. Place the bearing carrier on a press with the threaded side facing up.
   b. Align the bushing with its bore in the carrier.
   c. Carefully press the bushing into the bearing carrier using a suitable driver. Stop frequently to check the depth of the bushing. Continue pressing until the bushing is at the depth recorded during disassembly.

12. Install the seals into the bearing carrier as follows.
   a. Place the bearing carrier on a flat surface with the threaded side facing down.
   b. Use a socket and extension or section of tubing as a seal installation tool.
   c. Apply a light coat of type 271 Loctite (Mercury part No. 92-809819) to the outer diameter of both seals and the seal bore in the carrier.
   d. Place the first seal into its bore with the lip side facing down. Using the installation tool, gently drive the seal into the bore until its surface is below the bore opening.
   e. Place the second seal into the bore with the lip side facing up. Using the installation tool, gently drive the seal into the bore until its surface is below the bore opening.
   f. Apply a thick coat of 2-4-C Marine Lubricant to the both seal lips.

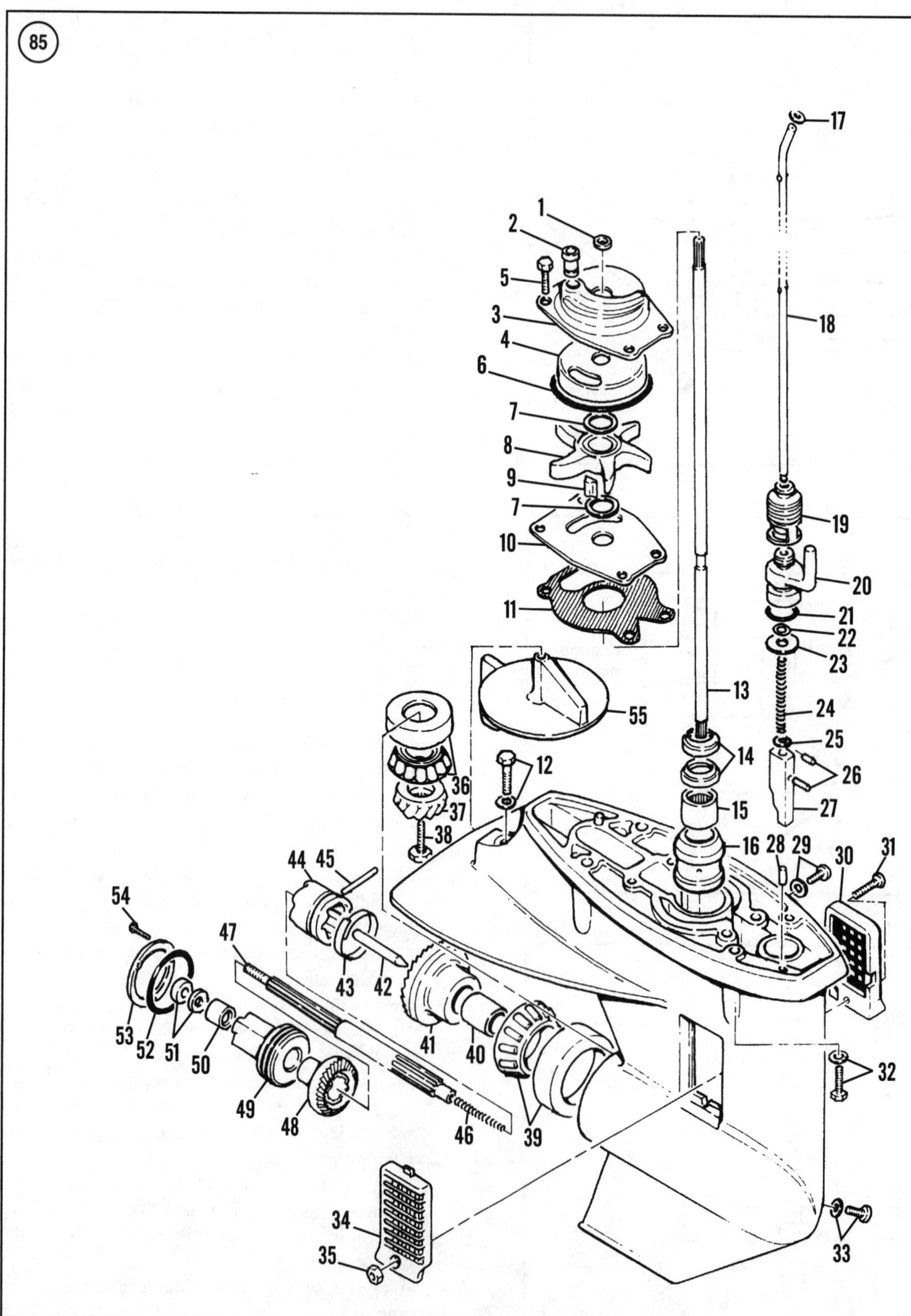
85
1
2
3
4
5
6
7
8
9
7
10
11
12
13
14
15
16
17
18
19
20
21
22
23
24
25
26
27
28
29
30
31
32
33
34
35
36
37
38
39
40
41
42
43
44
45
46
47
48
49
50
51
52
53
54
55

GEARCASE (9.9 AND 15 HP MODELS OPTIONAL GEARCASE)

1. Drive shaft seal
2. Water tube guide/ seal
3. Water pump body
4. Insert
5. Bolt
6. O-ring
7. Nylon washer
8. Impeller
9. Drive key
10. Wear plate
11. Gasket
12. Trim tab bolt
13. Drive shaft
14. Drive shaft seals
15. Drive shaft upper bearing
16. Sleeve
17. Washer
18. Shift shaft
19. Boot
20. Shift shaft bushing
21. O-ring
22. Washer
23. Washer
24. Spring
25. Washer
26. Roll pin
27. Shift cam
28. Alignment pin
29. Level/vent plug and washer
30. Water screen
31. Screw
32. Mounting bolt and washer
33. Drain/fill plug and washer
34. Water screen
35. Nut
36. Tapered roller bearing and race
37. Pinion gear
38. Pinion nut or bolt
39. Forward bearing and race
40. Bushing
41. Forward gear
42. Cam follower
43. Cross pin retainer spring
44. Clutch
45. Cross pin
46. Spring
47. Propeller shaft
48. Reverse gear
49. Bearing carrier
50. Bearing
51. Propeller shaft seals
52. O-ring
53. Bearing carrier retainer
54. Screw
55. Trim tab

13. Place the O-ring (45, **Figure 74**) into its groove on the bearing carrier (44). Apply a generous coat of 2-4-C Marine Lubricant to the O-ring and bearing carrier threads.
14. Slide the reverse gear fully into the carrier.
15. Rotate the drive shaft clockwise while sliding the bearing carrier over the propeller shaft and into the housing. Thread the carrier by hand counterclockwise into the housing.
16. Slide the carrier removal tool over the propeller shaft (**Figure 75**). Engage the slots of the tool over the struts in the carrier. Tighten the carrier to the specification in **Table 1**.
17. Install the shift shaft and water pump following the instructions in this chapter.

Disassembly (9.9 and 15 hp Models with Optional Gearcase)

Refer to **Figure 85** to assist with component identification and orientation. Removal of the bearing carrier (49, **Figure 85**) requires a special tool. Purchase or rent this tool (part No. 91-93843-1) from a Mercury or Mariner dealership.

1. Disassemble the water pump as described in this chapter.
2. Remove the three screws (54, **Figure 85**) and lift the bearing carrier retainer (53) from the gearcase opening. Slip a small screwdriver under the O-ring (52, **Figure 85**) and lift it from the bearing carrier (49).
3. Slide the carrier removal tool over the propeller shaft (**Figure 75**). Engage the slots of the tool over the struts in the carrier. Turn the tool clockwise until the carrier is free from the gearcase. Pull the propeller shaft and bearing carrier from the gearcase.
4. Slide the propeller shaft from the gear side of the bearing carrier. Pull the reverse gear (48, **Figure 85**) from the bearing carrier (49).
5. If the gear cannot be removed by prying, clamp the carrier into a vice with soft jaws. Pass the jaws of a slide hammer through the propeller shaft opening of the gear (**Figure 60**). Use short hammer strokes to remove the gear from the carrier.
6. Clamp the bearing carrier in a vice with the smaller diameter side facing up. Engage the jaws of a slide hammer (**Figure 63**) with the inner seal. Remove both seals using short hammer strokes.
7. Remove the propeller shaft bearing (50, **Figure 85**) only if it must be replaced. Remove the bearing as follows:
    a. Clamp the bearing carrier in a vise with the threaded side facing up.

b. Use a socket and extension or section of tubing as a bearing removal and installation tool. The tool must contact the outer diameter of the bearing cage, but not the bearing carrier bore during removal.

c. Insert the tool into the bearing carrier until it contacts the bearing (**Figure 76**). Mark the tool at a point even with the end of the bearing carrier. Remove the tool and measure the distance from the mark to the bearing contact surface. Record this bushing depth measurement for use during installation.

d. Seat the bearing removal tool firmly against the bearing cage, then carefully drive the bearing from the carrier.

8. Disassemble the propeller shaft as follow:

a. Slip the tip of an awl under the cross pin retainer spring (**Figure 86**). Wind the spring from the clutch.

b. Push the cam follower portion of the propeller shaft against a solid object (**Figure 66**).

c. Using a punch, push the cross pin (45, **Figure 85**) from the clutch and propeller shaft.

d. Slide the clutch from the propeller shaft.

d. Pull the cam follower (42, **Figure 85**) from the propeller shaft (47).

9. Remove the drive shaft and gears from the gearcase as follows:

a. Clamp the drive shaft (13, **Figure 85**) in a vice with soft jaws.

b. Remove pinion gear retaining fastener (38, **Figure 85**).

c. Pull straight up on the drive shaft and slide it from the gearcase.

d. Reach into the gearcase opening and remove the pinion gear (37, **Figure 85**) and tapered roller bearing (36). Pull the forward gear and bearing from the housing (**Figure 78**).

10. Using a depth micrometer, measure the distance from the gearcase surface to the top drive shaft seal (**Figure 87**). Record this seal depth measurement for use during assembly. Pull both seals from the drive shaft bore using the bearing and seal removal tool (Mercury Part No. 91-27780) as indicated in **Figure 88**.

11. Remove the lower drive shaft bearing race (36, **Figure 85**) only if it must be replaced. Use Mercury part No. 91-31229A-7 or an equivalent bearing and sleeve removal tool.

12. Remove the upper drive shaft bearing (15, **Figure 85**) only if it must be replaced. Remove the bearing as follows:

a. Use a section of tubing or an extension of sufficient width and length as a measuring rod.

86

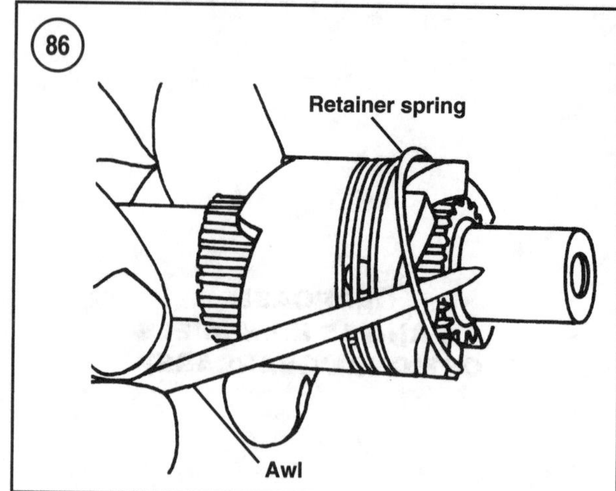

87

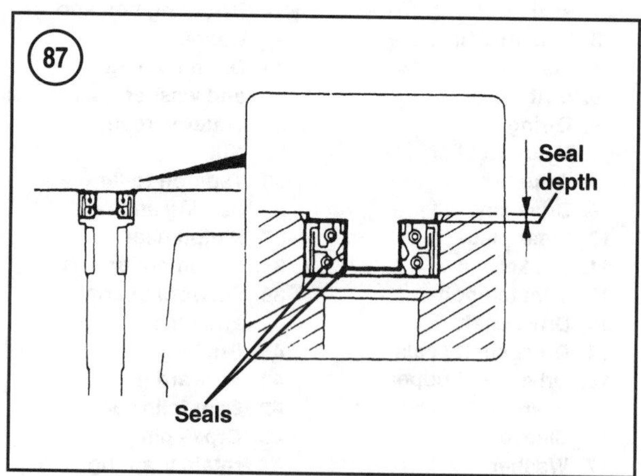

b. Insert the rod into the drive shaft bore until it contacts the top of the drive shaft bearing (**Figure 67**).

c. Make a mark on the rod even with the gearcase-to-drive shaft housing mating surface.

d. Record the length of rod from the mark to the bottom to determine bearing depth. Record this depth for use during bearing installation.

e. Thread a bushing and bearing removal tool onto the end of the a slide hammer (**Figure 79**).

f. Engage the tool with the bottom edge of the drive shaft bearing (**Figure 79**). Remove the bearing using short hammer strokes.

13. Engage the jaws of a slide hammer puller to the rear surface of the forward bearing race (**Figure 80**). Remove the bearing race using short hammer strokes.

14. Remove the tapered roller bearing (39, **Figure 85**) from the forward gear (41) only if it must be replaced. Remove the bearing as follows:

a. Insert the knife edge of a bearing separator between the bearing and the forward gear (**Figure 81**).

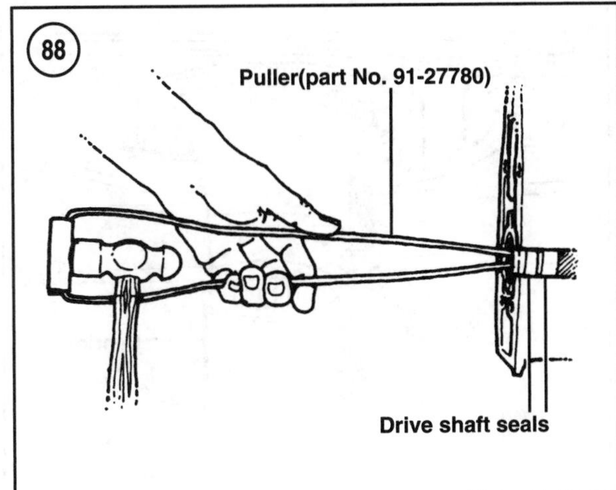

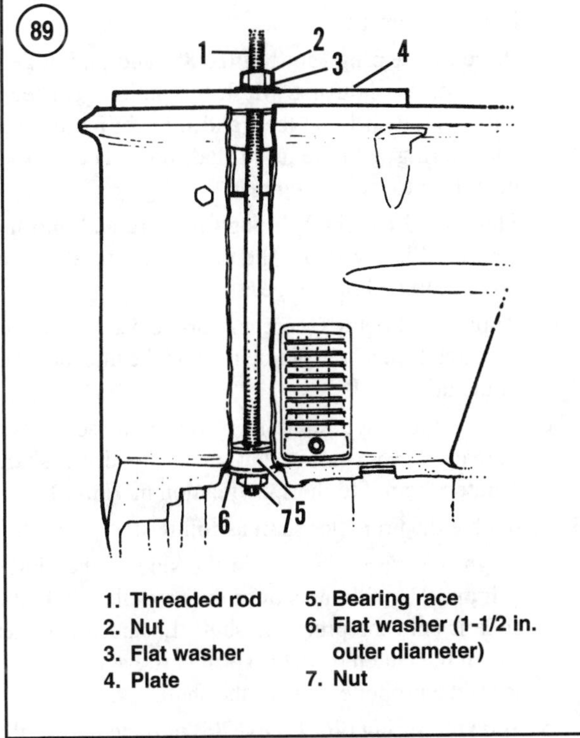

1. Threaded rod
2. Nut
3. Flat washer
4. Plate
5. Bearing race
6. Flat washer (1-1/2 in. outer diameter)
7. Nut

b. Use a socket or section of tubing with a diameter slightly smaller than the hub of the gear as a removal tool.
c. Place the bearing separator and gear onto a press. Block the sides of the separator to ensure adequate travel for the gear.
d. Place the removal tool against the hub of the gear and press the gear from the bearing.

15. Remove the bushing (40, **Figure 85**) only if it must be replaced. Remove the bushing as follows:

a. Measure the distance from the bearing side gear surface to the bushing. Record the bearing depth measurement for use during installation.
b. Use a socket and extension as a bushing removal tool. Place the gear teeth side down on a press. Seat the removal tool against the bushing.
c. Press the bushing from the forward gear.

16. Pull straight up on the shift shaft (18, **Figure 85**) and slide it from the gearcase. Remove the large diameter O-ring (21, **Figure 85**) from the shift shaft bushing/retainer. Disassemble the shift shaft if any of its components are worn or faulty. Disassemble the shift shaft as follows:

a. Mark the shift cam (27, **Figure 85**) and shift shaft (18) mating surfaces to ensure correct orientation during assembly.
b. Using a small pin punch, drive the pin (26, **Figure 85**) from the shift cam (27) and shift shaft (18). Pull the cam from the shaft.
c. Drive the smaller pin (26, **Figure 85**) from the shift shaft (18). Slide the spring, washers, bushing and boot (19-24, **Figure 85**) from the shift shaft.

17. Remove the screw and nut (31 and 35, **Figure 85**) and pull the water screens (34) from each side of the gearcase.
18. Clean and inspect all components as described in this chapter.

Assembly (9.9 and 15 hp Models with Optional Gearcase)

Refer to **Figure 85** to assist with component identification and orientation. Installation of the bearing carrier (49, **Figure 85**) requires a special tool. Purchase or rent this tool (part No. 91-93843 1) from a Mercury or Mariner dealership.

1. Slip the tab on the top of each water screen into the recesses on each side of the gearcase. Push both screens into their opening. Place the nut (35, **Figure 85**) into the starboard side screen. Install the screw (31, **Figure 85**) into the nut on the starboard side screen. Securely tighten the screw.
2. Install the forward bearing race as follows:
   a. Place the forward gear bearing race bore at the front of the gearcase with the larger inner diameter facing outward.
   b. Use a large socket or section of tubing as a bearing race installation tool.
   c. Seat the installation tool firmly against the bearing race (**Figure 82**). Drive the bearing race into its bore until it bottoms.
3. Install the lower drive shaft bearing as follows:
   a. Select a 1-1/2 in. diameter washer (6, **Figure 89**), and the remaining items listed on **Figure 89**.

b. Place the bearing race (5, **Figure 89**) into the drive shaft bore with the larger opening facing toward the gears.
c. Arrange the threaded rod, washers and plates as indicated in **Figure 89**. Hold the threaded rod (1, **Figure 89**) while tightening the nut (2). Continue to tighten the nut until the lower race contacts the shoulder in the drive shaft bore.

4. Install the upper drive shaft bearing as follows:
   a. Use a socket and extension or section of tubing as a bearing installation tool.
   b. Place the sleeve into the drive shaft bore with the numbered side facing up. Seat the tool firmly against the sleeve (**Figure 84**).
   c. Stop frequently for measurement while carefully driving the sleeve into the bore. Stop when the bearing just reaches the depth recorded prior to removal.
   d. Inspect the bearing to ensure its placement is just below the oil hole in the side of the bore (**Figure 90**). Correct the depth if required.
5. Assemble the bearing on the forward gear as follows:
   a. Use a large socket or section of tubing for use as a bearing installation tool.
   b. Place the gear teeth side down on the table of a press. Place the bearing onto the hub of the gear with the tapered side facing up.
   c. Seat the bearing installation tool on the inner race of the bearing. Press the bearing fully onto the gear.
6. Install the propeller shaft bushing into the forward gear as follows:
   a. Use a socket or section of tubing as a bushing installation tool.
   b. Place the bushing in its opening in the gear. Seat the bushing installation tool firmly against the bushing.
   c. Slowly tap the bushing into the gear until it just reaches the depth recorded prior to removal.
7. Install the drive shaft seals as follows:
   a. Use a socket and extension or section of tubing as a seal installation tool.
   b. Apply Loctite type 271 to the outer diameter of both seals prior to installation.
   c. Place the first drive shaft seal into the drive shaft bore with the lip side facing down.
   d. Using the tool, slowly drive the seal into the bore until its top surface is just below the gearcase surface.
   e. Place the second seal into the drive shaft bore with the lip or spring side facing up.
   f. Using the tool, slowly drive both seals into the bore until they just reach the depth recorded prior to removal.
8. Install the drive shaft and pinion gear as follows:

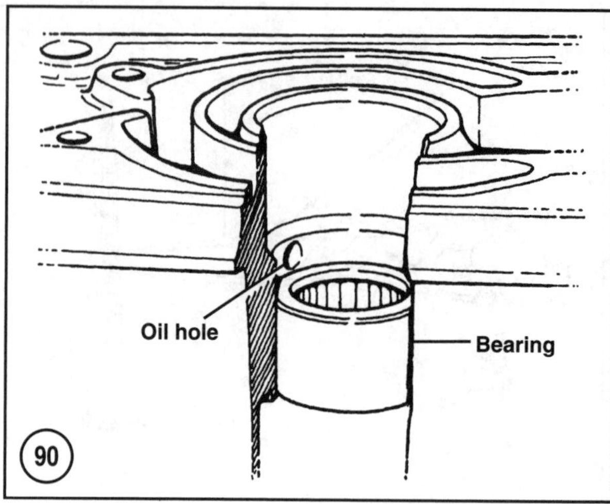

   a. Place the forward gear into the housing. Seat its bearing against the race.
   b. Place the bearing (36, **Figure 85**) and pinion gear (37) into the housing. Mesh the pinion gear teeth with the forward gear teeth and align the pinion gear and bearing with the drive shaft bore. The bearing must fit into its bearing race.
   c. Slide the drive shaft through its bore and into the bearing. Slowly rotate the drive shaft to align the drive shaft and pinion gear splines.
   d. Apply 271 Loctite (Mercury Part no. 92-809819) to the threads of a new pinion nut and the threaded end of the drive shaft.
   e. Clamp the drive shaft in a vise with soft jaws. Thread a *new* pinion nut onto the drive shaft. Tighten the nut to the specification in **Table 1**.
9. Assemble the propeller shaft as follows:
   a. Align the cross pin hole in the side of the clutch (**Figure 91**) with the slot in the propeller shaft and slide it onto the propeller shaft. Ensure the longer end of the clutch from the spring groove to the dogs faces the propeller side of the shaft.
   b. Slide the spring (46, **Figure 85**) into the bore at the forward end of the propeller shaft.
   c. Insert a quarter inch socket extension into the opening. Push in on the extension to compress the spring enough to slide a pin punch through the cross pin hole (**Figure 72**).
   d. Place the cross pin into in the clutch. Support the pin punch and carefully push the cross pin into the clutch. Ensure the ends of the cross pin are flush with the clutch surfaces.
   e. Carefully wind the cross pin retainer (43, **Figure 85**) onto the grooved part of the clutch (44). Ensure

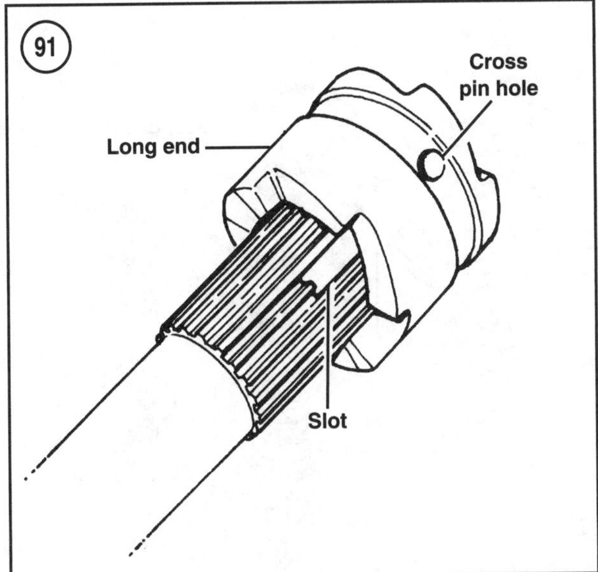

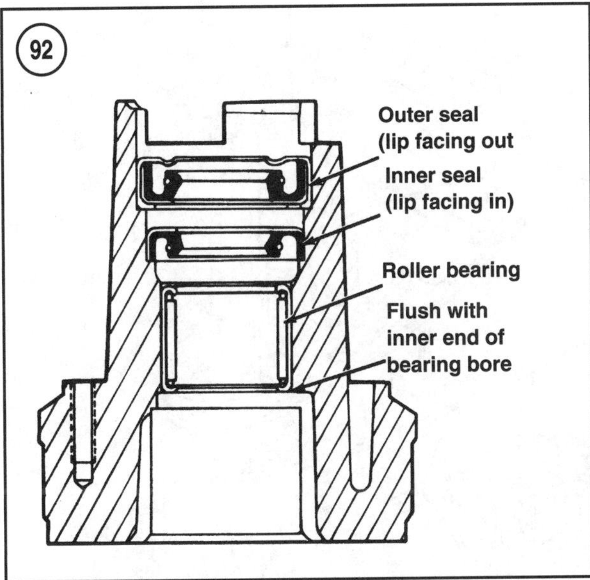

the spring loops lay flat on the clutch and pass over each end of the cross pin.

f. Apply Quicksilver 2-4-C Marine Lubricant to the shift cam follower and install the follower into the propeller shaft with the pointed side facing out.

10. Position the gearcase so the drive shaft is pointing up. Slide the propeller shaft into the gearcase and into the forward gear.

11. Install the propeller shaft bearing into the bearing carrier as follows:

a. Place the bearing carrier on the press with the threaded side facing up.

b. Position the propeller shaft bearing in the carrier with the numbered side facing up.

c. Using a suitable driver, begin pressing the bearing into the carrier, stopping frequently to check the depth of the bearing. Press the bearing into the carrier until the inner end of the bearing is even with the edge of its bore (**Figure 92**).

12. Install the seals into the bearing carrier as follows:

a. Place the bearing carrier on a flat surface with the threaded side facing down.

b. Use a socket and extension or section of tubing as a seal installation tool.

c. Apply a light coat of 271 Loctite (Mercury part No. 92-809819) to the outer diameter of both seals and the seal bore in the carrier.

d. Place the smaller diameter seal into its bore opening with the lip facing down. Gently drive the seal into the bore until it seats against the shoulder in the carrier.

e. Place the larger diameter seal into the opening with the lip side facing up. Gently drive the seal into the bore until it seats on the shoulder in its bore.

f. Apply a thick coat of 2-4-C Marine Lubricant to the both seal lips and the threads of the bearing carrier.

13. Slide the reverse gear fully into the carrier.

14. Rotate the drive shaft clockwise while sliding the bearing carrier over the propeller shaft and into the housing. Thread the carrier by hand counterclockwise into the housing.

15. Slide the carrier removal and installation tool (Mercury part No. 91-93843-1) over the propeller shaft (**Figure 75**). Engage the slots of the tool over the struts in the carrier. Tighten the carrier to the specification in **Table 1**.

16. Apply 2-4-C Marine Lubricant to the O-ring (52, **Figure 85**) and install it into its groove in the bearing carrier.

17. Place the bearing carrier retainer (53, **Figure 85**) onto the bearing carrier. Align the screw holes then install the three screws (54, **Figure 85**). Tighten the screws to the specification in **Table 1**.

18. Assemble and install the shift shaft as follows:

a. Slide the shift shaft boot (19, **Figure 85**) over the bottom end of the shift shaft (18) with the smaller opening facing up.

b. Slide the bushing, washers, spring and O-rings onto the shaft in the order indicated (20-25, **Figure 85**).

c. Carefully drive the pin (26, **Figure 85**) into the shift shaft.

d. Place the shift cam over the bottom end of the shift shaft. Align the reference marks made prior to disassembly, then drive the pin (26, **Figure 85**) through the shift cam and shift shaft.

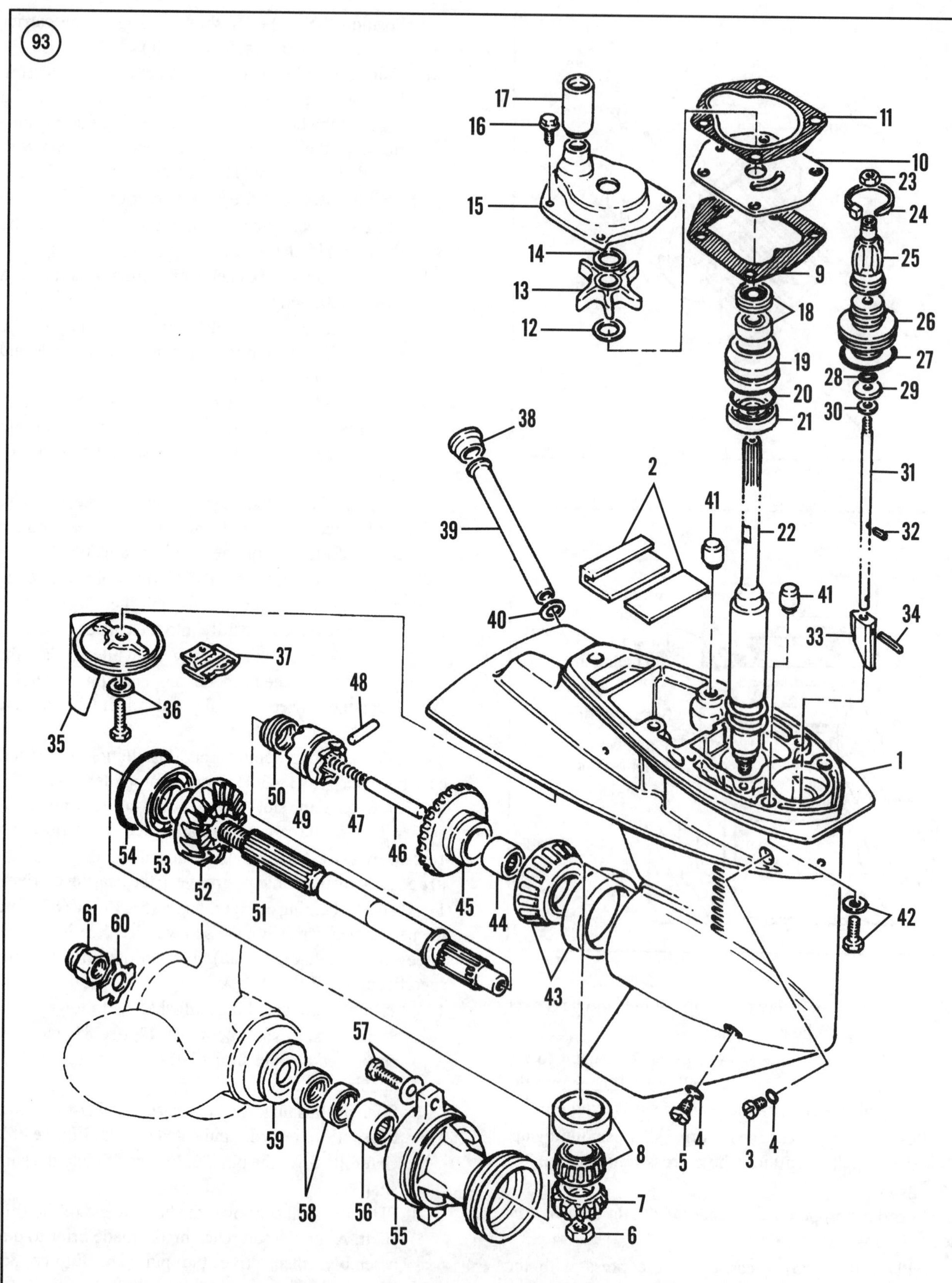
93
1
2
3
4
5
6
7
8
9
10
11
12
13
14
15
16
17
18
19
20
21
22
23
24
25
26
27
28
29
30
31
32
33
34
35
36
37
38
39
40
41
42
43
44
45
46
47
48
49
50
51
52
53
54
55
56
57
58
59
60
61

GEARCASE (25-50 HP MODELS STANDARD GEARCASE)

1. Gearcase housing
2. Water dam and seal
3. Level/vent plug
4. Sealing washer
5. Drain/fill plug
6. Pinion nut
7. Pinion gear
8. Tapered roller bearing and race
9. Gasket
10. Wear plate
11. Gasket
12. Nylon washer
13. Impeller
14. Nylon washer
15. Water pump body
16. Bolt
17. Water tube guide/ seal
18. Drive shaft seals
19. Seal carrier
20. O-ring
21. Ball bearing
22. Drive shaft
23. Jam nut
24. Plastic locking clamp
25. Boot
26. Bushing
27. O-ring
28. O-ring
29. Washer
30. Washer
31. Shift shaft
32. Pin
33. Shift cam
34. Pin
35. Trim tab
36. Bolt and washer
37. Auxiliary water screen
38. Plug
39. Water tube
40. Seal
41. Alignment pin
42. Mounting bolt and washer
43. Forward bearing and race
44. Propeller shaft needle bearing
45. Forward gear
46. Cam follower
47. Spring
48. Cross pin
49. Clutch
50. Cross pin retainer spring
51. Propeller shaft
52. Reverse gear
53. Ball bearing
54. O-ring
55. Bearing carrier
56. Needle bearing
57. Bolt and washer
58. Propeller shaft seals
59. Thrust hub
60. Locking tab washer
61. Propeller nut

94

19. Apply a light coat of 2-4-C Marine Lubricant to the O-ring surfaces of the shift shaft. Slide the shift shaft assembly into its bore with the tapered side of the shift cam facing the rear of the gearcase. Seat the bushing (20, **Figure 85**) against its step in the shift shaft bore.

20. Install the shift shaft and water pump following the instructions in this chapter.

Disassembly (25-50 hp Models with Standard Gearcase)

CAUTION
When using heat to assist with the removal of components, make sure to keep the flame away from the seals or O-rings. Never heat the housing to the point that the finish is burned. Continually move the flame around the mating surface to apply even heating. Excessive use of heat can distort or melt the gearcase.

NOTE
To assist with removal of the propeller shaft bearing carrier, use a torch to apply heat to the gearcase near the bearing carrier mating surface. Continually move the flame to apply even heat. Remove the flame then try removing the bearing carrier.

Refer to **Figure 93** to assist with component identification and orientation.

1. Disassemble the water pump following the instructions in this chapter.

2. Remove both bearing carrier retaining bolts and washers (57, **Figure 93**), then pull the propeller shaft and bearing carrier from the gearcase (**Figure 94**). Carefully pry the carrier from the gearcase (**Figure 95**) if it cannot be removed by hand. Remove the O-ring (54, **Figure 93**) from

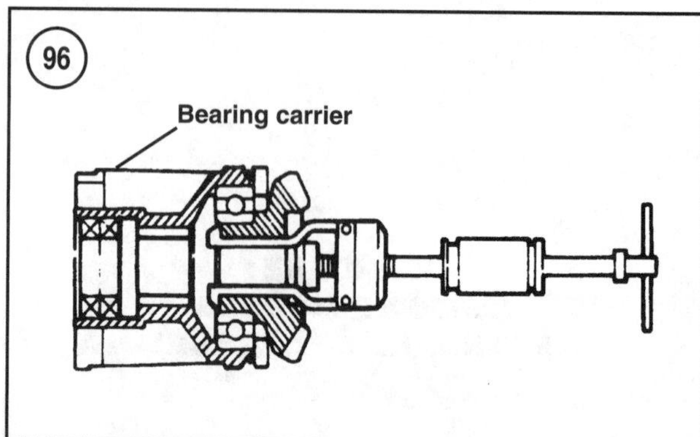

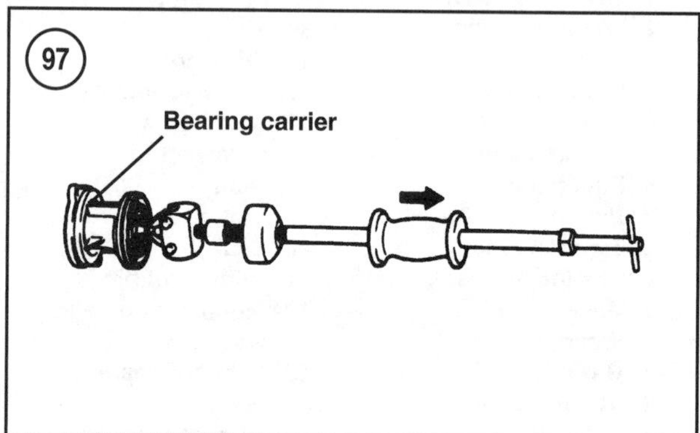

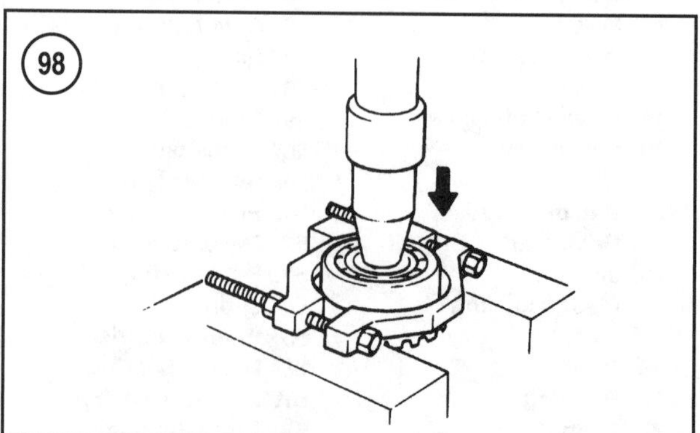

the bearing carrier (55). Slide the propeller shaft from the bearing carrier.

3. Remove the reverse gear and bearing (52 and 53, **Figure 93**) from the bearing carrier only if they must be replaced. Remove the reverse gear and bearing as follows:
4. Pass the jaws of a slide hammer through the gear (**Figure 96**). Use short hammer strokes to remove the gear from the carrier.
5. Remove the ball bearing from the carrier as follows:
   a. Clamp the bearing carrier into a vice with soft jaws.
   b. Pass the jaws of a slide hammer (**Figure 97**) through the bearing.
   c. Use short hammer strokes to remove the bearing from the carrier.
6. If the ball bearing remains on the reverse gear remove it as follows:
   a. Insert the knife edge of a bearing separator between the ball bearing and the reverse gear (**Figure 98**).
   b. Use a socket or section of tubing with a diameter slightly smaller than the inner bore of the bearing as a driver.
   c. Place the bearing separator and gear onto a press. Block the sides of the separator to ensure adequate travel for the gear.
   d. Place the driver against the hub of the gear and press the gear from the bearing (**Figure 98**).
7. Using a pry bar, carefully pry both seals from the bearing carrier (**Figure 99**). Work carefully and avoid any contact with the seal bore portion of the carrier.
8. Remove the propeller shaft needle bearing only if it must be replaced. Remove the bearing as follows.
   a. Clamp the bearing carrier in a vice with soft jaws with the gear and bearing opening facing up.
   b. Use a socket and extension or section of tubing as a bearing removal tool.
   c. Insert the tool into the bearing carrier until it contacts the bearing (**Figure 76**). Mark the tool at a point even with the end of the bearing carrier. Remove the tool and measure the distance from the mark to the bearing contact surface. Record this bushing depth measurement for use during installation.
   d. Seat the bearing removal tool firmly against the bearing cage and carefully drive the bearing from the carrier.
9. Disassemble the propeller shaft as follows:
   a. Slip the tip of an awl under the cross pin retainer spring (**Figure 86**) and wind the spring from the clutch.

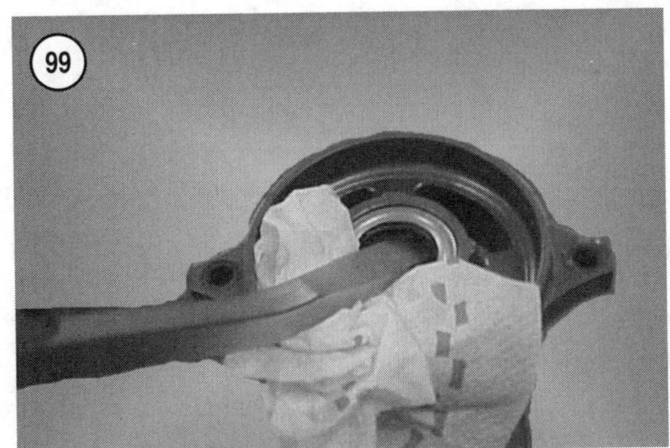

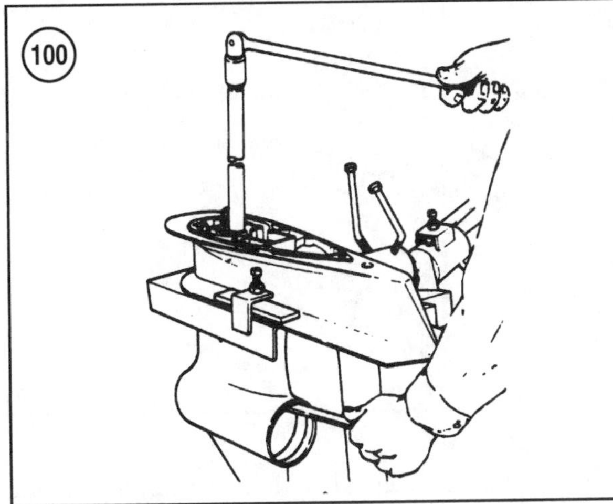

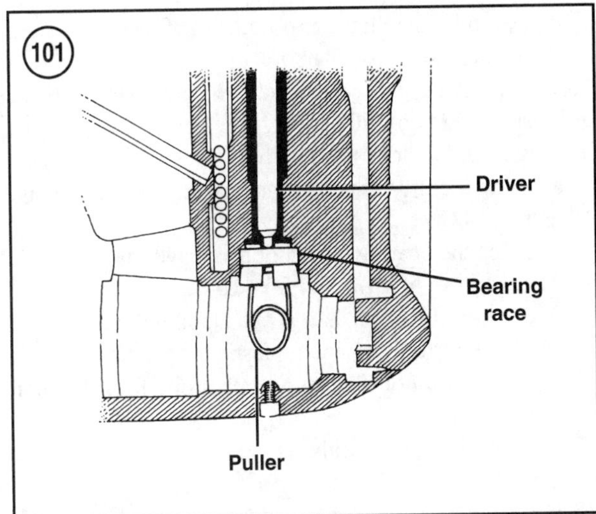

b. Push the shift cam follower portion of the propeller shaft against a solid object (**Figure 69**).

d. Using a suitable punch, push the cross pin (48, **Figure 93**) from the clutch and propeller shaft.

c. Slide the clutch from the propeller shaft.

d. Pull the cam follower and spring (46 and 47, **Figure 93**) from the propeller shaft (51).

10. Remove the drive shaft and pinion gear as follows:

a. Place the drive shaft splined adapter (Mercury part No. 91-83180M) onto the top of the drive shaft.

b. Hold the pinion nut (**Figure 100**) and turn the drive shaft counterclockwise until the pinion nut is loose. Remove the pinion nut from the drive shaft.

c. Pull straight up on the drive shaft (22, **Figure 93**) to free it from the pinion gear. Lift the drive shaft and seal carrier from the housing. Slide the seal carrier (19, **Figure 93**) from the upper end of the drive shaft.

11. Pull the pinion gear and tapered roller bearing (7 and 8, **Figure 93**) from the housing. Pull the forward gear and bearing (43 and 45, **Figure 93**) from the gearcase opening.

12. Engage the jaws of a slide hammer puller with the forward gear bearing race (**Figure 80**). Remove the bearing race using short hammer strokes.

13. Remove the tapered roller bearing (43, **Figure 93**) from the forward gear (45) only if it must be replaced.

a. Insert the knife edge of a bearing separator between the bearing and the forward gear (**Figure 81**).

b. Place the bearing separator and gear onto a press. Block the sides of the separator to ensure adequate travel for the gear.

c. Place a suitable driver against the hub of the gear. Press on the driver to remove the gear from the bearing.

14. Remove the bearing (44, **Figure 93**) only if it must be replaced. Remove the bushing as follows:

a. Measure the distance from the hub side of the gear to the bearing. Record the bearing depth measurement for use during installation.

b. Use a socket and extension or section of tubing as a bearing removal tool. Place the gear teeth side up on the table of a press. Seat the removal tool against the bearing.

c. Press the bearing from the forward gear.

15. Remove the tapered bearing race (8, **Figure 93**) from the housing only if it must be replaced. Remove the bearing race as follows:

a. Engage the puller tool (Mercury part No. 91-825200a-1) with the bearing race (**Figure 101**).

b. Guide the driver (Mercury part No. 91-13779) through the drive shaft bore. Insert the tip of the driver (**Figure 101**) into the puller tool opening.

c. Carefully tap on the exposed end of the driver until the race falls from its bore.

16. Remove the ball bearing (21, **Figure 93**) from the drive shaft (22) only if it must be replaced. Remove the bearing from the drive shaft as follows:

a. Slide the drive shaft into a bearing separator (**Figure 102**).
b. Place the bearing separator and drive shaft over the open jaws of a vice (**Figure 102**).
c. Support the drive shaft while tapping the upper end of the drive shaft with a plastic hammer.
d. Continue until the drive shaft drops from the ball bearing.

17. Carefully pry both seals (18, **Figure 93**) from the seal carrier (19).

18. Grip the upper end of the shift shaft (31, **Figure 93**) with locking pliers. Pull straight up and lift the shift shaft assembly from the housing. Disassemble the shift shaft as follows:

a. Thread the jam nut (23, **Figure 93**) from the upper end of the shaft.
b. Cut the plastic type clamp (24, **Figure 93**) and pull the boot (25) from the shift shaft bushing (26). Slide the bushing, O-rings and washers (26-30, **Figure 93**) from the shift shaft (31).
c. Using a pin punch, carefully drive both pins (32 and 34, **Figure 93**) from the shift shaft.
d. Pull the shift cam (33, **Figure 93**) from the shift shaft (31).

19. Lift the water dam and seal (2, **Figure 93**) from the gearcase. Carefully pry the auxiliary water screen from the antiventilation plate.

20. Remove the plug (38, **Figure 93**) and inspect the water tube (39) for blockage. Clean as required.

21. Clean and inspect all components following the instructions provided in this chapter.

Assembly
(25-50 hp Models with Standard Gearcase)

Refer to **Figure 93** to assist with component identification and orientation.

1. Carefully snap the auxiliary water screen (37, **Figure 93**) into the antiventilation plate. Install the plug (38, **Figure 93**) into its opening.

2. Install the forward bearing race as follows:

a. Place the forward gear bearing race into its bore at the front of the gearcase with the larger inner diameter facing outward.
b. Use a large socket or section of tubing as a bearing race installation tool.

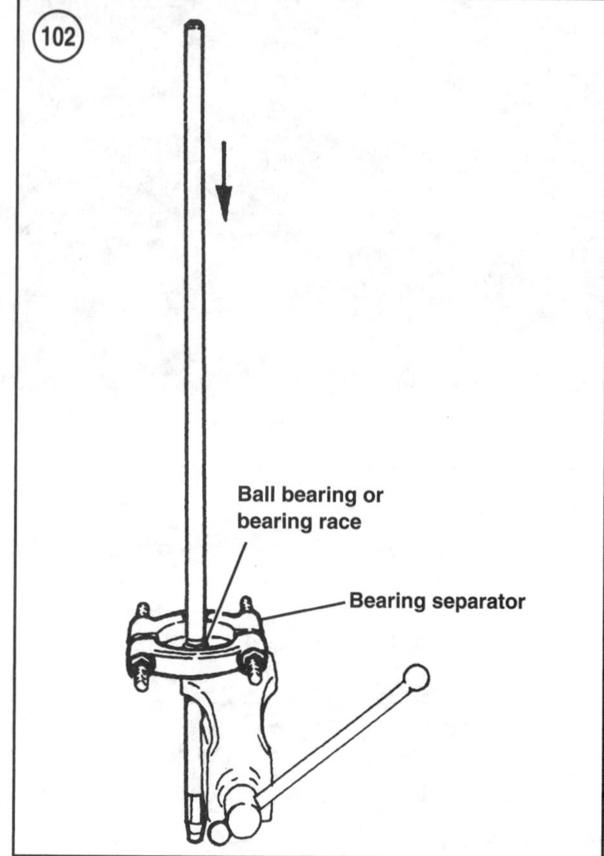

c. Seat the installation tool firmly against the bearing race (**Figure 82**). Drive the bearing race into its bore until it bottoms.

3. Install the lower drive shaft bearing as follows:

a. Select a washer (6, **Figure 89**) with the same diameter as the bearing race, and the remaining items listed in **Figure 89**.
b. Place the bearing race (5, **Figure 89**) into the drive shaft bore with the larger opening facing toward the gears.
c. Arrange the threaded rod, washers and plates as shown in **Figure 89**. Hold the threaded rod (1, **Figure 89**) and tighten the nut (2) until the race contacts the shoulder in the drive shaft bore.

4. Install the upper drive shaft bearing as follows:

a. Slide the ball bearing over the upper end of the drive shaft.
b. Slide the drive shaft through the opening of a bearing separator. Thread the used pinion nut onto the threaded end of the drive shaft enough to protect the threads.
c. Place the bearing separator onto the table of the press with the threaded end facing up. Press on the

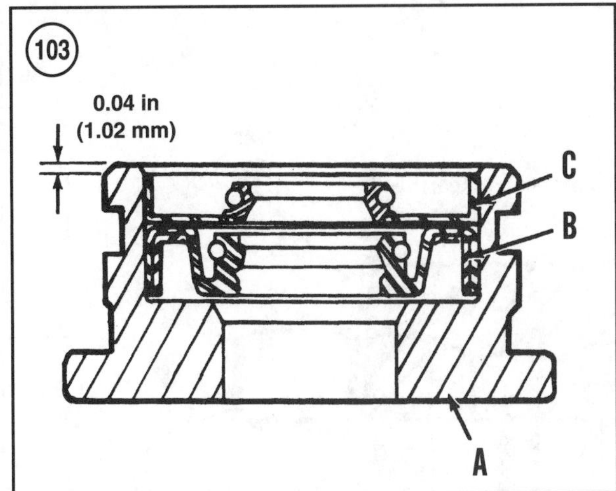

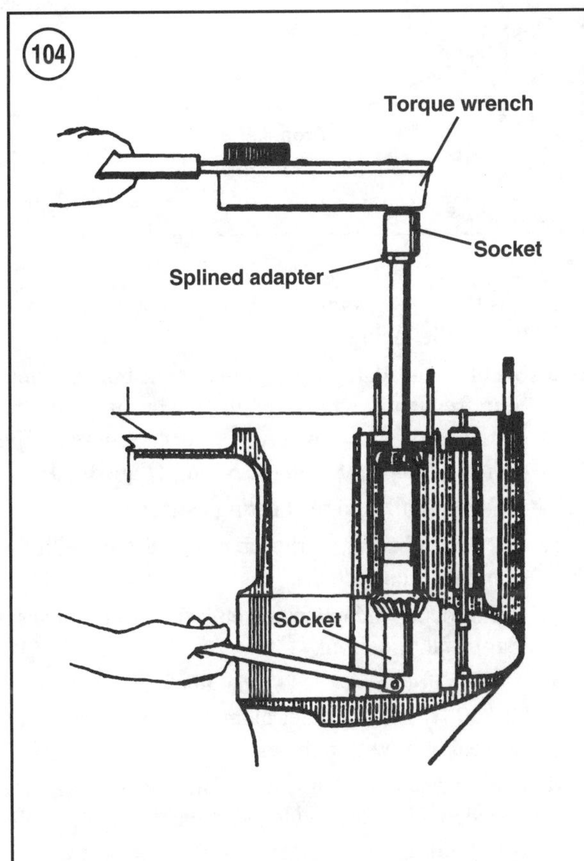

pinion nut until the bearing just seats against its step on the drive shaft. Remove the pinion nut.

5. Install the tapered roller bearing on the forward gear as follows:
   a. Use a large socket or section of tubing as a bearing installation tool.
   b. Place the gear teeth side down on the table of a press. Place the bearing onto the hub of the gear with the tapered side facing up.
   c. Seat the bearing installation tool on the inner race of the bearing. Press the bearing fully onto the gear.
6. Install the needle bearing into the forward gear as follows:
   a. Use a socket or section of tubing as a bearing installation tool.
   b. Install the bearing into its opening in the hub side of the gear. Seat the bearing installation tool firmly against the bearing.
   c. Slowly tap the bearing into the gear until it reaches the depth recorded prior to removal.
7. Install the drive shaft seals into the carrier (A, **Figure 103**) as follows:
   a. Use a socket and extension or section of tubing as a seal installation tool.
   b. Apply 271 Loctite to the outer diameter of both seals prior to installation.
   c. Place the thicker seal (B, **Figure 103**) into its bore with the lip side facing down.
   d. Slowly drive the seal into the bore until its top surface is below surface of the carrier.
   e. Place the thinner seal (C, **Figure 103**) into the drive shaft bore with the lip side facing up.
   f. Slowly drive both seals into the bore until the thinner seal reaches a depth of 0.04 in. (1.02 mm) as shown in (**Figure 103**).
8. Install the drive shaft and pinion gear as follows:
   a. Place the forward gear into the housing. Seat its bearing against the race.
   b. Place the bearing (8, **Figure 93**) and pinion gear (7) into the housing. Mesh the pinion gear teeth with the forward gear teeth and align the pinion gear and bearing with the drive shaft bore. The bearing must fit into its bearing race.
   c. Slide the drive shaft through its bore and into the bearing. Slowly rotate the drive shaft to align the drive shaft and pinion gear splines.
   d. Apply 271 Loctite (Mercury part No. 92-809819) to the threads of a new pinion nut and the threaded end of the drive shaft.
   e. Thread the pinion nut onto the drive shaft. Place the drive shaft splined adapter (Mercury part No. 91-83180M) onto the top end of the drive shaft.
   f. Hold the pinion nut (**Figure 104**) and turn the drive shaft to tighten the pinion nut. Tighten the nut to the specification in **Table 1**.
9. Assemble the propeller shaft as follows:
   a. Align the cross pin hole in the side of the clutch with the slot in the propeller shaft. Slide the clutch onto

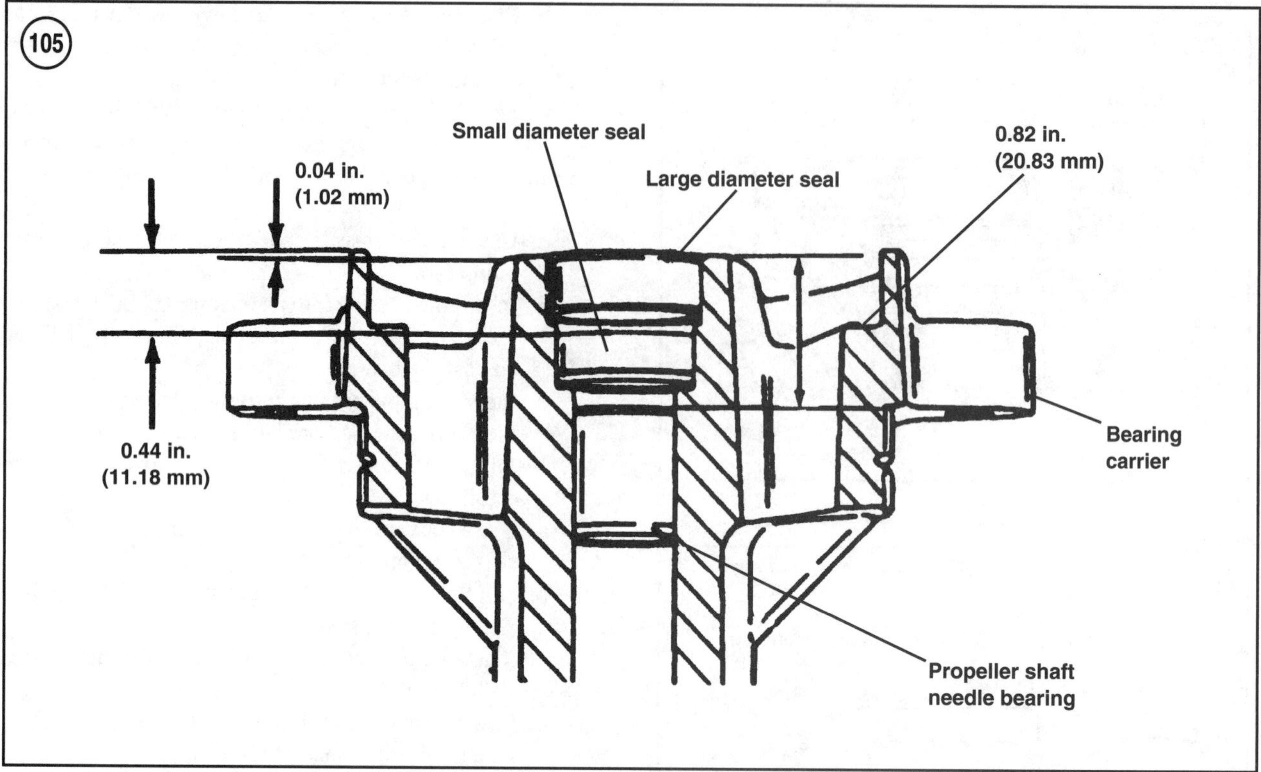

the propeller shaft. Ensure the tapered end of the clutch faces the propeller side of the propeller shaft.

b. Slide the spring (47, **Figure 93**) into the bore at the forward end of the propeller shaft.
c. Insert a quarter inch socket extension into the opening. Push in on the extension to compress the spring enough to slide a pin punch through the cross pin hole (**Figure 72**).
d. Place the cross pin into its opening in the clutch. Support the pin punch or scribe while carefully pushing the cross pin into the clutch. Ensure the ends of the cross pin flush with the clutch surfaces.
e. Carefully wind the cross pin retainer (50, **Figure 93**) onto the grooved part of the clutch (49). Ensure the spring loops lay flat on the clutch and pass over each end of the cross pin.
f. Apply Quicksilver 2-4-C Marine Lubricant to the shift cam follower and install it into the propeller shaft, with its pointed side facing out.

10. Position the gearcase with the drive shaft pointing up. Slide the propeller shaft clutch side first fully into in the forward gear.

11. Install the propeller shaft bearing into the bearing carrier as follows:

a. Place the bearing carrier on a press with the gear side facing down.
b. Position the bushing in the carrier with the numbered side facing up.
c. Seat the installation tool firmly against the bearing. Stop frequently while pressing the bushing into the carrier to the depth recorded prior to removal. The proper depth is 0.82 in. (20.8 mm) (**Figure 105**).

12. Install the seals into the bearing carrier as follows:

a. Place the bearing carrier on a flat surface with the gear side facing down.
b. Use a socket and extension or section of tubing as a seal installation tool.
c. Apply a light coat of 271 Loctite (Mercury part No. 92-809819) to the outer diameter of both seals and the seal bore within the carrier.
d. Place the smaller diameter seal into its bore with the lip side facing down. Gently drive the seal into the bore until it seats against its step in the carrier.
e. Place the larger diameter seal into the opening with the lip side facing up. Gently drive the seal into the bore until it reaches a depth of 0.04 in. (1.02 mm) as indicated in **Figure 105**.
f. Apply a thick coat of 2-4-C Marine Lubricant to the both seal lips.

13. Install the bearing (53, **Figure 93**) onto the reverse gear (52) as follows:

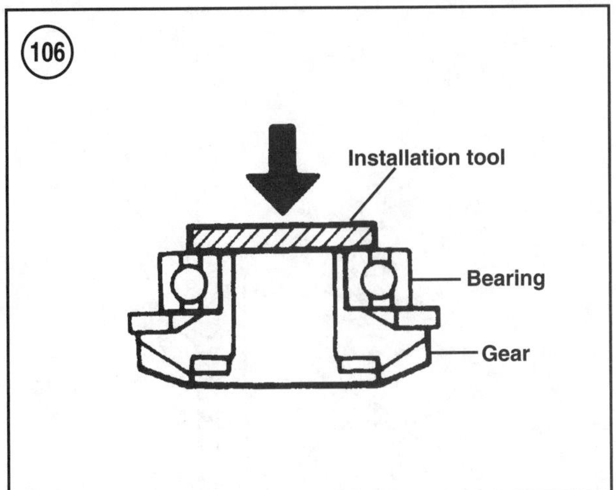

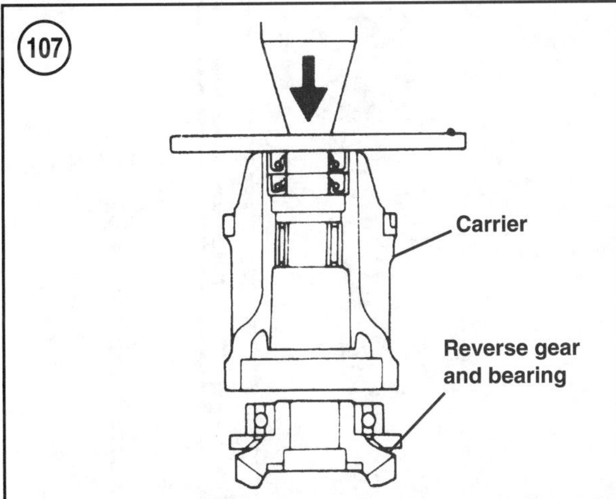

a. Use a large socket, plate or section of tubing as an installation tool. The tool must contact only the inner race of the bearing (**Figure 106**) during installation.

b. Place the reverse gear teeth side down on a press. Place the ball bearing onto the hub of the gear with the numbered side facing up.

c. Align the installation tool with the inner bearing race and press the bearing fully onto the gear.

14. Install the reverse gear and bearing into the bearing carrier as follows:

a. Place the reverse gear teeth side down on a press (**Figure 107**).

b. Place the carrier over the ball bearing.

c. Place a piece of wood or flat plate onto the rear side of the carrier for protection, then press the carrier fully onto the bearing.

15. Slide the O-ring (54, **Figure 93**) onto the bearing carrier. Ensure the O-ring seats in its groove. Rotate the drive shaft clockwise while sliding the bearing carrier over the propeller shaft and into the housing. Align the bolt holes in the carrier with the threaded holes in the housing.

16. Install both bolts and washers (57, **Figure 93**) into the carrier and housing. Tighten the bolts to the specification in **Table 1**.

17. Push in on the propeller shaft and pull up on the drive shaft. Gently rotate the drive shaft back and forth. Correct assembly allows a clicking sound or feel as the drive shaft rotates. The clicking noise indicates some gear lash is present. Disassemble the gearcase and verify all bearing races are seated if gear lash is not detected.

18. Assemble and install the shift shaft as follows:

a. Slide the shift cam (33, **Figure 93**) over the bottom end of the shift shaft. Align the pin openings and drive the pin (34, **Figure 93**) fully into the shift cam and shift shaft. Drive the second pin (32, **Figure 93**) into the shift shaft until it protrudes the same amount on each side of the shaft.

b. Slide the small washer, larger washer and O-ring (28-30, **Figure 93**) over the shift shaft. Lubricate its inner bore with 2-4-C Marine Lubricant, then slide the shift shaft bushing (26, **Figure 93**) over the upper end of the shift shaft with the smaller diameter side facing up.

c. Place the larger opening of the boot (25, **Figure 93**) over the top of the bushing (26). Secure the boot to the bushing with a plastic tie clamp (24, **Figure 93**). Thread the jam nut onto the shift shaft.

d. Lubricate the O-ring (27, **Figure 93**), then place it into the groove in of the bushing (26).

e. Slide the shift shaft assembly into its bore with the tapered side of the shift shaft facing the rear of the gearcase.

f. Press the shift shaft bushing fully into its bore.

19. Lubricate the O-ring (20, **Figure 93**) with 2-4-C Marine Lubricant then place it in the groove on the seal carrier (19). Apply a generous coat of 2-4-C Marine Lubricant to the seal lips in the carrier.

20. Slide the carrier (19, **Figure 93**) over the drive shaft with the seal opening facing the gearcase. Press down on the seal carrier until it fully seats in the drive shaft bore.

21. Install the water dam and seal (2, **Figure 93**) into its recess at the top of the gearcase.

22. Assemble the water pump following the instructions in this chapter.

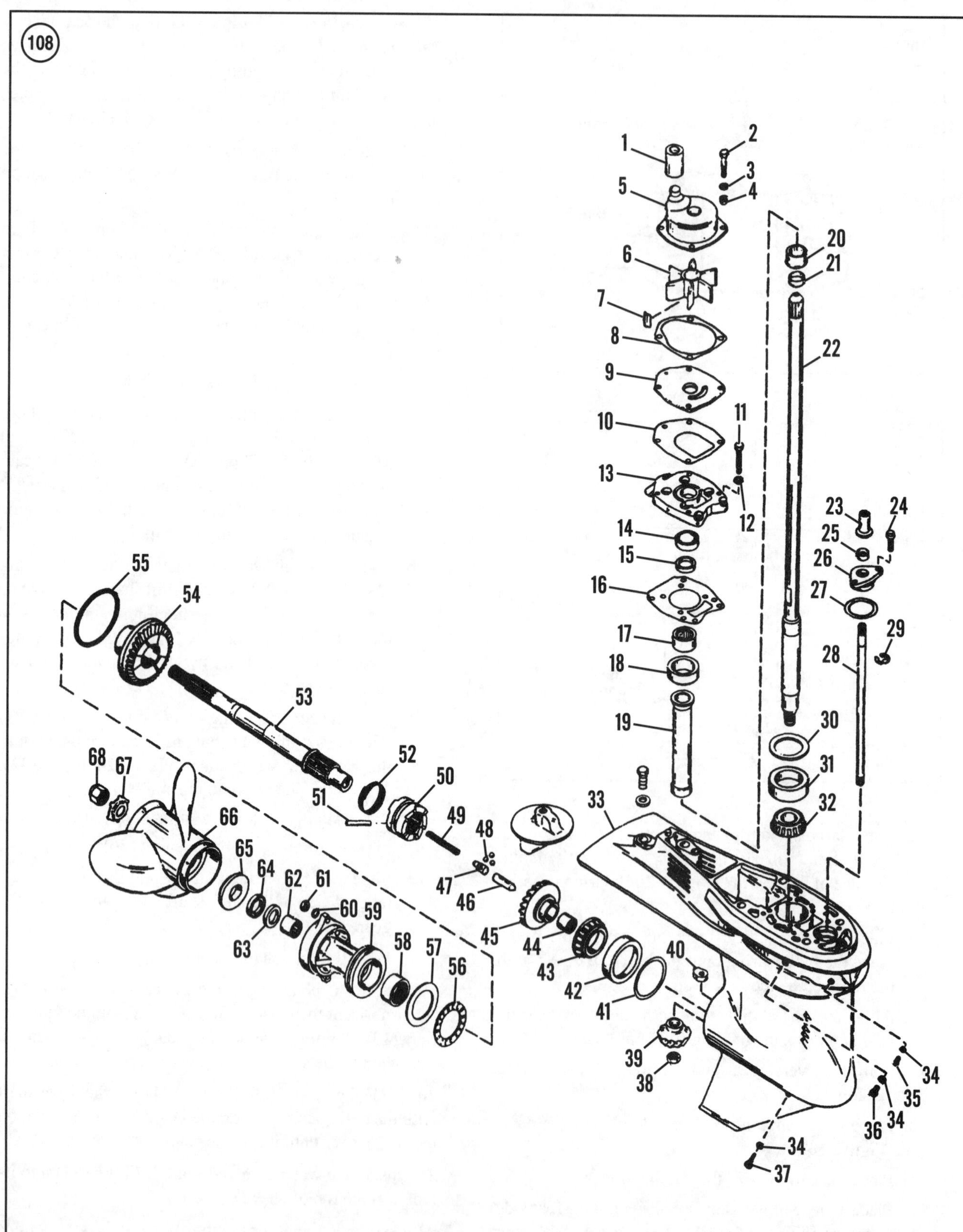
108
1
2
3
4
5
6
7
8
9
10
11
12
13
14
15
16
17
18
19
20
21
22
23
24
25
26
27
28
29
30
31
32
33
34
35
36
37
38
39
40
41
42
43
44
45
46
47
48
49
50
51
52
53
54
55
56
57
58
59
60
61
62
63
64
65
66
67
68

GEARCASE
(30-50 HP MODELS
[WITH OPTIONAL GEARCASE]
AND 75 AND 90 HP MODELS)

1. Water tube guide/seal
2. Bolt
3. Washer
4. Sleeve
5. Water pump body
6. Impeller
7. Drive key
8. Gasket
9. Wear plate
10. Gasket
11. Bolt
12. Washer
13. Water pump base
14. Seal
15. Seal
16. Gasket
17. Drive shaft upper bearing
18. Bearing sleeve
19. Drive shaft sleeve
20. Bearing race
21. Seal
22. Drive shaft
23. Shift shaft coupling
24. Bolt
25. Shift shaft seal
26. Shift shaft bushing
27. O-ring
28. Shift shaft
29. E-clip
30. Shim
31. Bearing race
32. Tapered roller bearing
33. Housing
34. Sealing washer
35. Level/vent plug
36. Level/vent plug
37. Drain/fill plug
38. Pinion nut
39. Pinion gear
40. Shift cam
41. Shim
42. Bearing race
43. Forward gear bearing
44. Needle bearing
45. Forward gear
46. Cam follower
47. Connector
48. Balls
49. Spring
50. Clutch
51. Cross pin
52. Cross pin retainer
53. Propeller shaft
54. Reverse gear
55. O-ring
56. Thrust bearing
57. Bearing race
58. Roller bearing
59. Bearing carrier
60. Washer
61. Nut
62. Needle bearing
63. Inner seal
64. Outer seal
65. Thrust hub
66. Propeller
67. Tab washer
68. Propeller nut

109

110

Disassembly (30-50 hp [Optional Gearcase], 75 and 90 hp Models)

Refer to **Figure 108** to assist with component identification and orientation.

1. Disassemble the water pump following the instructions in this chapter.
2. Remove both bearing carrier retaining nuts and washers (60 and 61, **Figure 108**), then pull the propeller shaft and bearing carrier from the gearcase (**Figure 94**). Carefully pry the carrier from the gearcase (**Figure 95**) if it cannot be removed by hand. Remove the O-ring (55, **Figure 108**) from the bearing carrier (59). Slide the propeller shaft from the bearing carrier.
3. Remove the needle bearing or roller bearing (58 and 62, **Figure 108**) from the bearing carrier (59) only if they must be replaced. Disassemble the bearing carrier as follows.
   a. Secure the bearing carrier in a vise with soft jaws. Carefully pull the reverse gear (**Figure 109**) from the carrier.
   b. Note which side faces the reverse gear, then remove the thrust bearing (**Figure 110**) and bearing race (**Figure 111**).

9

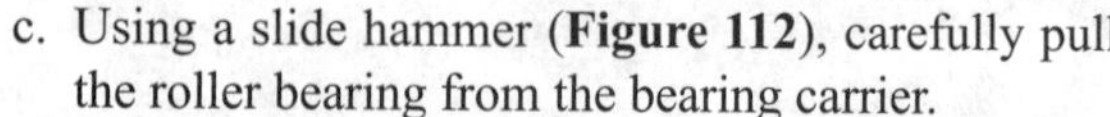

c. Using a slide hammer (**Figure 112**), carefully pull the roller bearing from the bearing carrier.
d. Using a pry bar, carefully pry both seals from the bearing carrier (**Figure 99**).
e. Using a depth micrometer, measure the depth of the needle bearing in the bearing carrier (**Figure 113**). Record this measurement for use during assembly.
f. Use a socket and extension or section of tubing as a bearing removal tool.
g. Carefully drive the bearing from the carrier (**Figure 114**).

4. Disassemble the propeller shaft as follows:
   a. Hook a small screwdriver under one loop of the cross pin retainer then carefully wind the retainer from the clutch (**Figure 115**).
   b. Push the follower end of the propeller shaft against a solid object, then push the cross pin from the clutch and propeller shaft (**Figure 116**).
   c. Pull the clutch from the front of the propeller shaft (**Figure 117**).
   d. Slide the cam follower, ball bearings, connector and spring (46-49, **Figure 108**) from the propeller shaft.
5. Remove the drive shaft and pinion gear as follows:
   a. Use splined drive shaft adapter (Mercury part No. 91-56775) on 30-50 hp models. Use the larger adapter (Mercury part No. 91-8-4776A 1) for 75 and 90 hp models. Slip the adapter onto the top end of the drive shaft.
   b. Hold the pinion nut (38, **Figure 108**) and turn the drive shaft counterclockwise to loosen the pinion nut. Remove the pinion nut from the drive shaft.
   c. Pull straight up on the drive shaft (22, **Figure 108**) to free it from the pinion gear. Lift the drive shaft from the housing.
6. Pull the pinion gear and tapered roller bearing (32 and 39, **Figure 108**) from the housing. Pull the forward gear and bearing (43 and 45, **Figure 108**) from the gearcase opening.

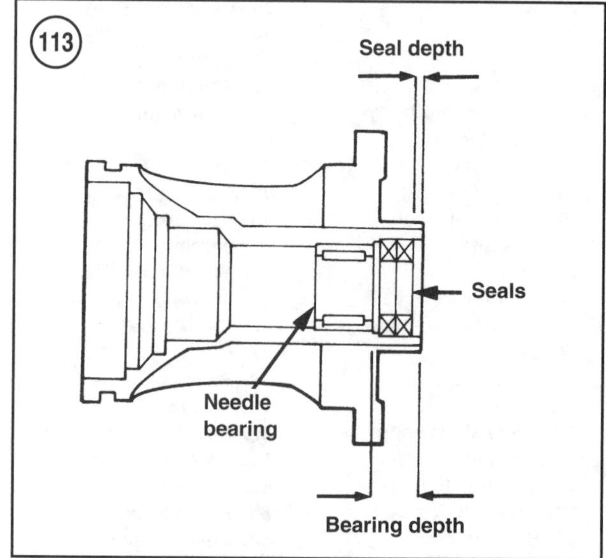

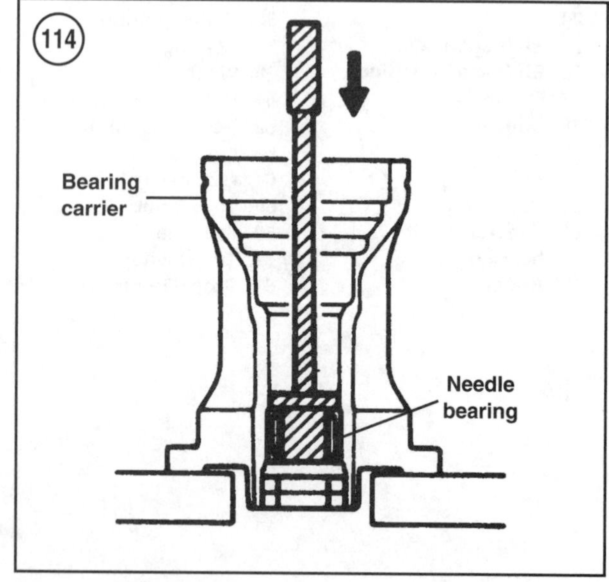

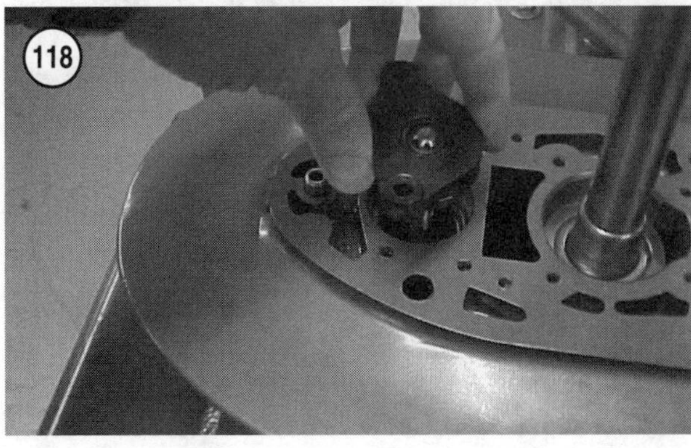

7. Engage the jaws of a slide hammer puller with the rear surface of the forward gear bearing race (**Figure 80**). Remove the bearing race using short hammer strokes.
8. Remove the tapered roller bearing (43, **Figure 108**) from the forward gear (45) only if it must be replaced. Remove the bearing as follows:
   a. Insert the knife edge of a bearing separator between the bearing and the forward gear (**Figure 81**).
   b. Use a socket or section of tubing with a diameter slightly smaller than the hub of the gear as a removal tool.
   c. Place the bearing separator and gear onto a press. Block the sides of the separator to ensure adequate travel for the gear.
   d. Place the removal tool against the hub of the gear and press the gear from the bearing.
9. Remove the bearing (44, **Figure 108**) only if it must be replaced. Remove the bushing as follows:
   a. Measure the distance from the hub side of thegear surface to the bearing. Record this bearing depth measurement for use during installation.
   b. Use a socket and extension or section of tubing as a bearing removal tool. Place the gear teeth side up on a press. Seat the removal tool against the bearing.
   c. Press the bearing from the forward gear.
10. Remove the tapered bearing race and shim (30 and 31, **Figure 108**) from the housing only if it must be replaced. Remove the bearing race as follows:
   a. Attach the puller tool (Mercury part No. 91-14308A 1) to the bearing race (**Figure 101**).
   b. Guide the driver through the drive shaft bore. Insert the tip of the driver (**Figure 101**) into the puller tool opening.
   c. Carefully tap on the exposed end of the driver until the race falls from its bore.
11. Remove the bearing race and seal (20 and 21, **Figure 108**) from the drive shaft (22) only if it is must be replaced. Special tools are required to install the seal and race. Remove the bearing from the drive shaft as follows:
   a. Slide the drive shaft through the opening in the bearing separator and adjust the separator until it contacts the edge of the race (**Figure 102**).
   b. Place the bearing separator and drive shaft over the open jaws of a vice (**Figure 102**).
   c. Support the drive shaft while tapping the upper end of the drive shaft with a plastic hammer.
   d. Continue until the drive shaft drops from the bearing race.
12. Remove and disassemble the shift shaft as follows:
   a. Remove both bolts and carefully pry the shift shaft bushing from the gearcase (**Figure 118**).

b. Pull the shift shaft from the gearcase (**Figure 119**). Remove the E-clip (29, **Figure 108**) from the shift shaft.

c. Reach into the gearcase with needlenose pliers to remove the shift cam (**Figure 120**) from the gearcase.

d. Pry the seal (25, **Figure 108**) from the bushing. Remove the O-ring (27, **Figure 108**) from the bushing or shift shaft bore.

13. Remove the drive shaft upper bearing and sleeve (17 and 18, **Figure 108**) as follows:

a. Attach the special puller (Mercury part No. 91-83165M) or other suitable puller to the bottom side of the bearing sleeve (**Figure 121**).

b. Use a socket or section of tubing as a bearing removal tool. Place the sleeve over the open jaws of a vice.

c. Place the tool in firm contact with the bearing (17, **Figure 108**) then drive the bearing from the sleeve.

d. Lift the drive shaft sleeve (19, **Figure 108**) from the drive shaft bore.

14. Clean and inspect all components following the instructions in this chapter.

119

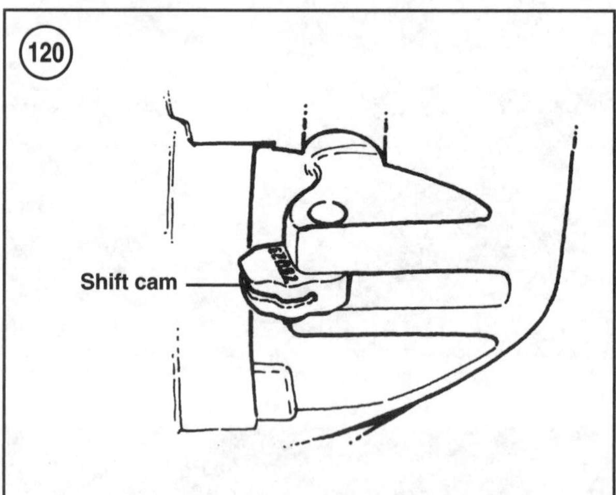

120

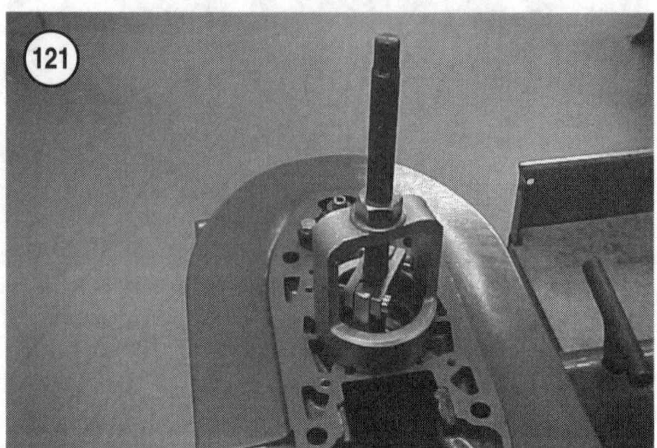
121

Assembly (30-50 [Optional Gearcase], 75 and 90 hp Models)

CAUTION

Serious damage to internal gearcase components can occur if the thrust bearing slips from the bearing carrier during installation. Do not force the carrier into position until verifying all components are in position.

Refer to **Figure 108** to assist with component identification and orientation.

1. Assemble and install the shift shaft and shift cam as follows:

a. Apply Loctite 271 (Mercury part No. 92-809819) to its outer diameter and place the shift shaft seal (25, **Figure 108**) into the shift shaft bushing with the seal lip side facing up.

b. Push the seal fully into the shift shaft bushing (26, **Figure 108**). Apply 2-4-C Marine Lubricant to the O-ring (27, **Figure 108**) and place it into its groove in the bushing (26).

c. Snap the E-clip (29, **Figure 108**) into its groove in the shift shaft (28). Position the shift cam into the gearcase (**Figure 120**). On 30-50 hp models the numbered side of the cam must face downward. On 75 and 90 hp models the numbered side must face up.

d. Align the hole in the cam with the shift shaft bore. Slide the shift shaft into the housing and through the shift cam. Slide the shift shaft bushing over the shift shaft and into its bore in the housing.

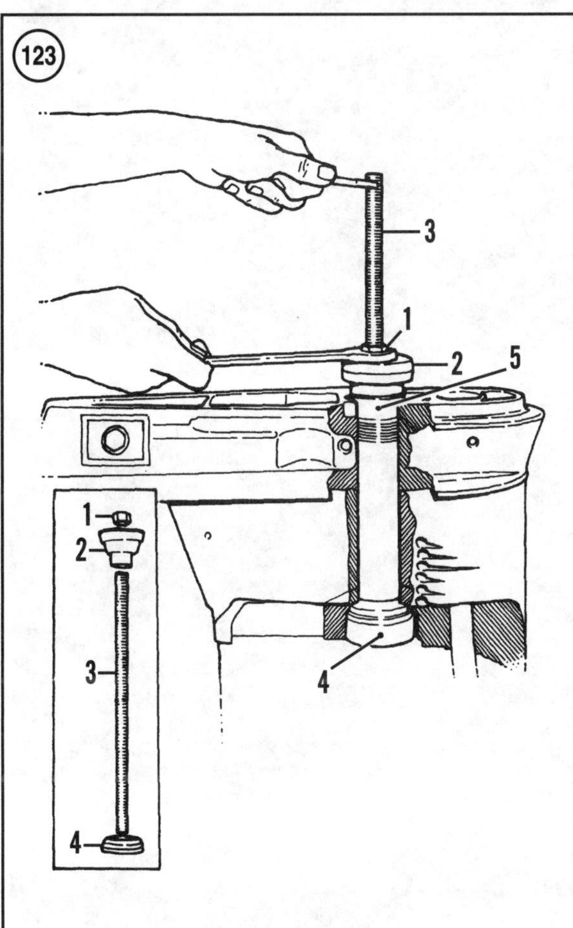

1. Nut (part No. 11-241546)
2. Mandrel (from kit part No. 91-31229)
3. Threaded rod (part No. 91-21229)
4. Mandrel (from kit part No. 91-14309A-1)
5. Bearing/sleeve (tapered end down)

   e. Apply 271 Loctite to the threads and install both bolts (24, **Figure 108**). Tighten the bolts to the specification in **Table 1**.

2. Install the forward bearing race as follows:
   a. Place the forward gear bearing race in its bore at the front of the gearcase with the larger inner diameter facing outward.
   b. Use a large socket or section of tubing as a bearing race installation tool. Place the shim and bearing race into the housing.
   c. Seat the installation tool firmly against the bearing race (**Figure 82**). Drive the bearing race into its bore until it bottom.

3. Install the upper drive shaft bearings and sleeves using bearing installation tools (Mercury part No. 91-14309A-1).
   a. Slide the plastic drive shaft sleeve (19, **Figure 108**) fully into the drive shaft bore.
   b. Apply gearcase lubricant to all surfaces of the bearing sleeve (18, **Figure 108**). Place the sleeve into the drive shaft bore. Position the bearing installation guide onto the sleeve with the larger diameter facing up (**Figure 122**). Carefully tap the guide until it contacts the housing.
   c. Place the new bearing (17, **Figure 108**) into the sleeve with the numbered side facing up. Position the guide onto the bearing and carefully tap the top of the guide (**Figure 122**) until it contacts the gearcase.
   b. Place the bearing race onto the threaded mandrel (4, **Figure 123**). Place the shims onto the top of the bearing race. Install the threaded rod (3, **Figure 123**) through the guide (2) and drive shaft bore. Thread the rod fully into the mandrel.
   e. Tighten the nut (1, **Figure 123**) on the threaded rod until the bearing race is fully seated. Remove the installation tools.

4. Have a machine shop or local Mercury or Mariner dealership install the bearing race and seal (20 and 21, **Figure 108**). Special tools and procedures are required to crimp the race to the shaft.

5. Install the drive shaft and pinion gear as follows:
   a. Place the forward gear into the housing. Seat its bearing against the race.
   b. Place the bearing (32, **Figure 108**) and pinion gear (39) into the housing. Mesh the pinion gear teeth with the forward gear teeth, then align the pinion gear and bearing with the drive shaft bore. The bearing must fit into its bearing race.
   c. Slide the drive shaft through its bore and into the bearing. Slowly rotate the drive shaft to align the drive shaft and pinion gear splines.

124

126

125

127

d. Apply 271 Loctite (Mercury part No. 92-809819) to the threads of a new pinion nut and the threaded end of the drive shaft.

e. Ensure the stepped side of the pinion nut (**Figure 124**) faces the pinion gear then thread the new pinion nut onto the drive shaft.

f. Place the drive shaft splined adapter (Mercury part No. 91-56775 or 91-804776A-1) onto the drive shaft. Attach a socket and torque wrench to the splined adapter. While holding the pinion nut securely, turn the drive shaft clockwise and tighten the pinion nut to the specification in **Table 1**.

6. Check the pinion gear height as follows:

a. Place the lower portion and bearing of the drive shaft preload tool (Mercury part No. 91-14311A 2) over the drive shaft (**Figure 125**).

b. Place the thrust washer onto the bearing (**Figure 126**). Install the spring and the remaining parts of the tool onto the drive shaft (**Figure 127**).

c. Tighten both set screws to secure the tool to the drive shaft. Turn the large nut (**Figure 128**) down enough to preload the drive shaft in the *up* direction. Rotate the drive shaft several times to seat the bearings.

128

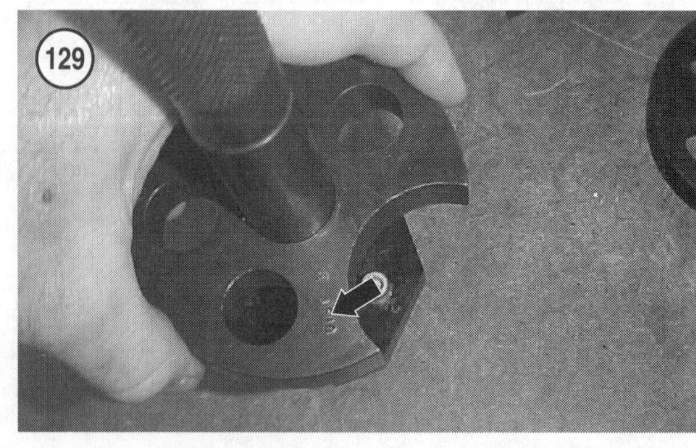
129

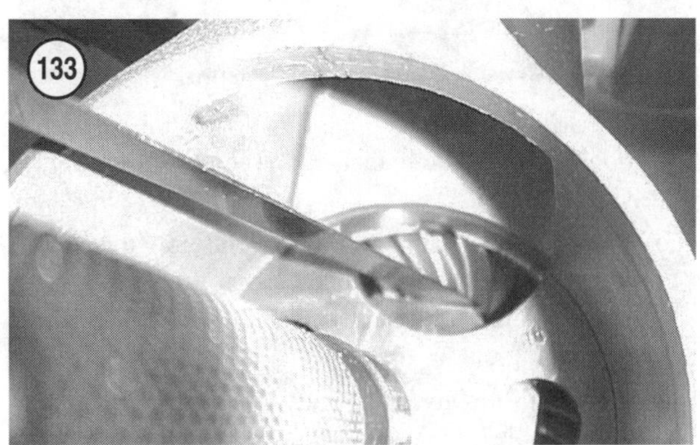

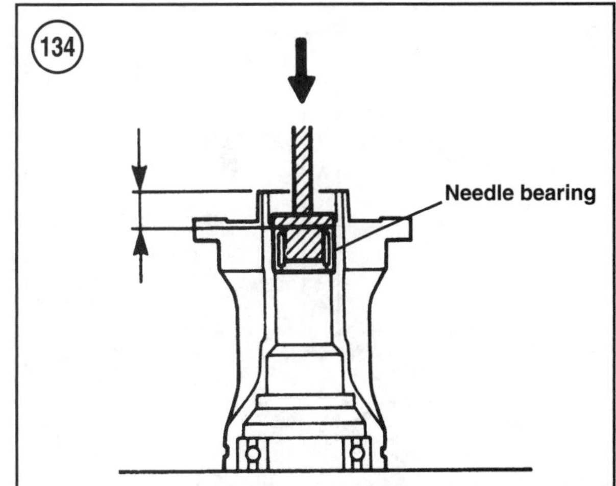

d. Select the disc portion of the shimming tool with the No. 3 stamped into the surface (**Figure 129**). Align the No. 8 gauging surface of the tool (**Figure 130**) with the opening on the disc.

e. Carefully install the shimming tool into the gearcase opening (**Figure 131**). Engage the tool with the needle bearing in the forward gear for alignment. Slowly rotate the tool to align the gauging surface with the pinion gear teeth (**Figure 132**). The gauging surface must be parallel with the pinion gear teeth.

f. Use feeler gauges to measure the clearance between the gauge and the pinion gear teeth (**Figure 133**). The correct clearance is 0.025 in. Change the thickness of the shim pack above the bearing race if the clearance is not correct. Shims of varying thickness are available from a Mercury or Mariner outboard motor dealership.

7. Assemble the bearing carrier as follows:

a. Use a socket and extension or section of tubing as a bearing installation tool.

b. Place the new needle bearing into the bore with the numbered side facing the propeller side of the carrier. Press the bearing into its bore until it reaches the depth (**Figure 134**) noted prior to removal.

c. Apply Loctite 271 (Mercury part No. 92-809819) to the outer diameter of both propeller shaft seals prior to installation. Position the new inner seal into the seal bore with the lip facing the reverse gear side. Place the installation tool firmly against the seal. Drive the seal into the carrier until its surface is below the bore opening.

d. Place the new outer seal onto the inner seal with the lip facing toward the propeller. Place the installation tool in firm contact with the seal. Drive both

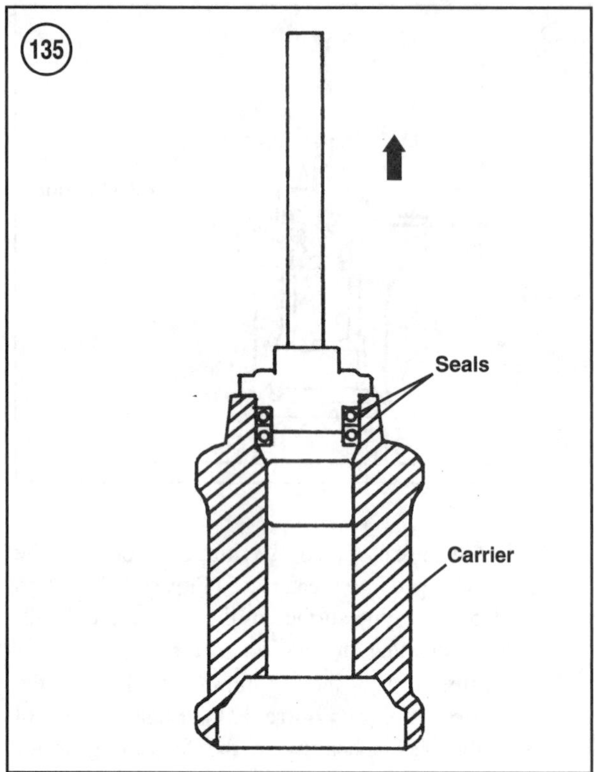

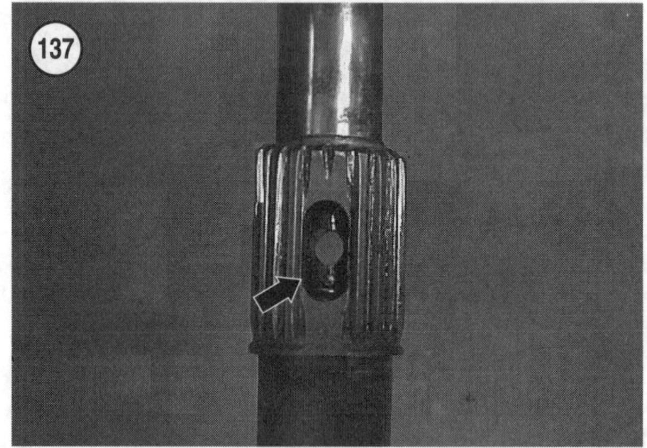

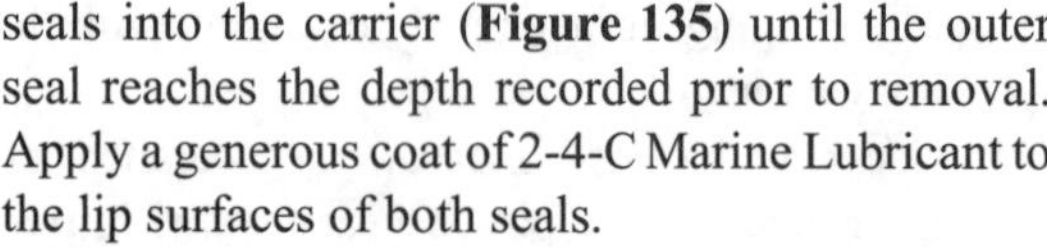

seals into the carrier (**Figure 135**) until the outer seal reaches the depth recorded prior to removal. Apply a generous coat of 2-4-C Marine Lubricant to the lip surfaces of both seals.

e. Apply gearcase lubricant to all surfaces of the roller bearing and its bore in the bearing carrier. Place the bearing into the bore with the numbered side facing toward the reverse gear. Use a large socket or section of tubing as a bearing installation tool. Carefully press the bearing fully into the carrier (**Figure 136**).
f. Place the bearing race (57, **Figure 108**) and thrust bearing (56) onto the bearing carrier. Apply gearcase lubricant to the thrust bearing and install the reverse gear (54, **Figure 108**) onto the bearing carrier. Seat the gear against the thrust bearing.

8. Assemble the propeller shaft as follows:
   a. Slide the spring (49, **Figure 108**) into the propeller shaft. Slide the connector (47, **Figure 108**) into the propeller shaft with the smaller diameter side facing the spring. Align the hole in the connector with the slot in the propeller shaft (**Figure 137**).
   b. Align the cross pin hole in the side of the clutch with the slot in the propeller shaft and slide it onto the propeller shaft (**Figure 117**). Ensure the square dogs of the clutch face the rear of the propeller shaft.
   c. Place all three balls (48, **Figure 108**) into the end of the propeller shaft. Slide the cam follower (46, **Figure 108**) into the propeller shaft with the pointed end facing out.
   d. Push the follower end of the propeller shaft against a solid object to collapse the spring. Slide the cross

139

140

141

142

143

pin through the clutch, propeller shaft and connector (**Figure 138**).

e. Carefully wind the cross pin retainer (52, **Figure 108**) onto the grooved portion of the clutch. Ensure the spring loops lay flat and at least three loops pass over each end of the cross pin (**Figure 139**).

9. Slide the splined end of the propeller shaft into the reverse gear and through the bearing carrier. Ensure the propeller shaft seats against the reverse gear. Maintain pressure to ensure the propeller shaft and reverse gear remain in contact with the bearing carrier during carrier installation.

10. Slide the O-ring (55, **Figure 108**) onto the bearing carrier. Seat the O-ring in its groove. Rotate the drive shaft clockwise while sliding the bearing carrier over the propeller shaft and into the housing. Ensure the *up* mark on the carrier faces up. Align the bolt holes in the carrier with the studs in the housing.

11. Install both nuts and washers (60 and 61, **Figure 108**) into the carrier and housing. Tighten the bolts to the specification in **Table 1**.

12. Check the gear backlash as follows:

a. Refer to Step 6 for instructions and install the preload tool onto the gearcase (**Figure 140**). Spin the drive shaft several revolutions to fully seat the drive shaft bearing.

b. Install a two jaw puller to the carrier and propeller shaft as shown in **Figure 141**. Tighten the puller bolt to 44.0 in.-lb. (5.0 N•m) to load the propeller shaft in the forward direction.

c. Use a backlash indicator tool part No. 91-78473 on 30-50 hp models. Use a tool part No. 91-19660-1 on 75 and 90 hp models. Clamp the tool onto the drive shaft as shown in **Figure 142**.

d. Attach a dial indicator to the gearcase. Align the tip of the indicator with the indicted mark on the backlash indicator tool (**Figure 143**). Align the dial indicator tip with the mark next to the No. 4 on the

9

backlash indicator tool at a 90° angle to the tool (**Figure 144**).

e. Observe the dial indicator while gently rotating the drive shaft in both directions. Loosen the backlash indicator tool then rotate the drive shaft 90°. Reposition the dial indicator and backlash indicator tool, then repeat the measurement. Repeat this step until four measurements are taken. Record the average of the measurements as forward gear backlash.

f. Correct backlash is 0.012-0.019 in. (0.3-0.48 mm) on 30-50 hp models and 0.015-0.022 in. (0.38-0.55 mm) onr 75 and 90 hp models.

13. Correct the gear backlash before installing the gearcase. Disassemble the gearcase enough to access the shims (41, **Figure 108**) beneath the forward bearing race (42). Install thinner or fewer shims to increase the gear backlash. Install thicker or more shims to decrease the gear backlash. Several changes may be required to correct the backlash.

14. Install the water pump following the instructions in this chapter.

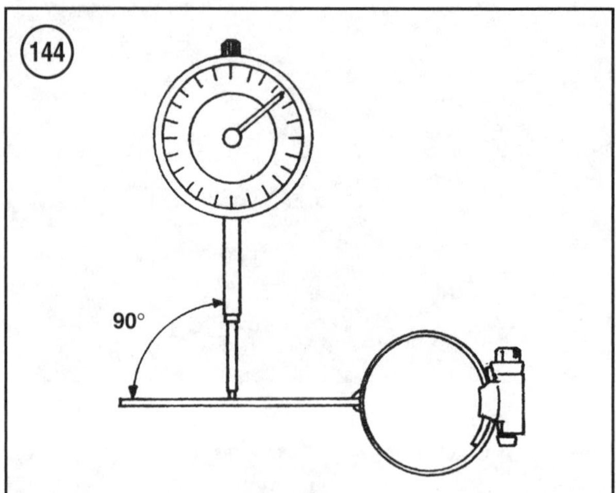

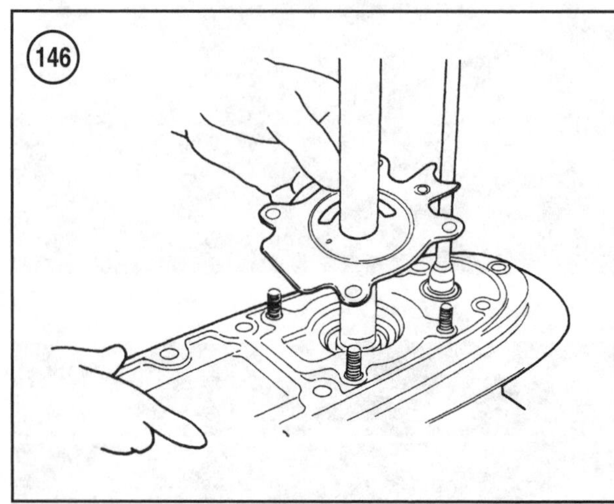

INSPECTION

Never compromise a proper repair by using damaged or questionable components.

Prior to inspection, thoroughly clean all components using clean solvent. Note component orientation prior to cleaning when necessary. Use compressed air to dry all components then arrange them in an orderly fashion on a clean work surface. Never allow bearings to spin while using compressed air to dry them.

Make sure all components are removed, then use pressurized water to clean the gearcase housing. Inspect all passages and crevices for debris or contaminants. Use compressed air to thoroughly dry the gearcase.

WARNING

Never allow bearings to spin when using compressed air to dry them. The bearing may fly apart or explode resulting in personal injury.

Water Pump Inspection

1. Inspect the impeller (**Figure 145**) for brittle, missing or burnt vanes. Squeeze the vanes toward the hub and release the vanes. The vanes should spring back to the extended position. Replace the impeller if damaged, burnt, brittle or stiff vanes are noted.

2. Inspect the water tube, grommets and seals for burned appearance, cracks or brittle material. Replace the water tube, grommets and seals if any defects are noted.

3. Inspect the wear plate (**Figure 146**) for warpage, wear grooves, melted plastic or other damage Replace the wear

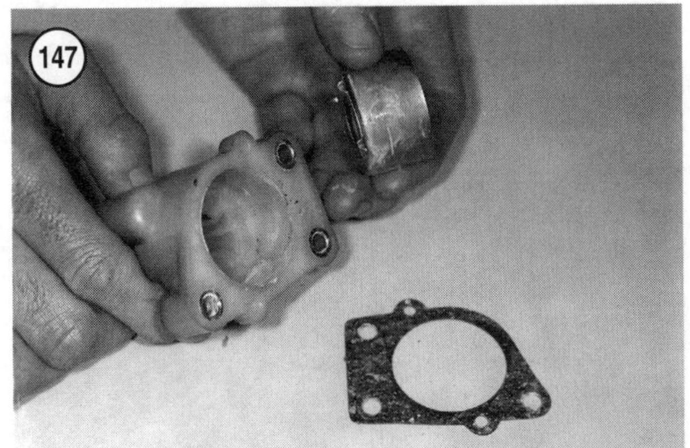

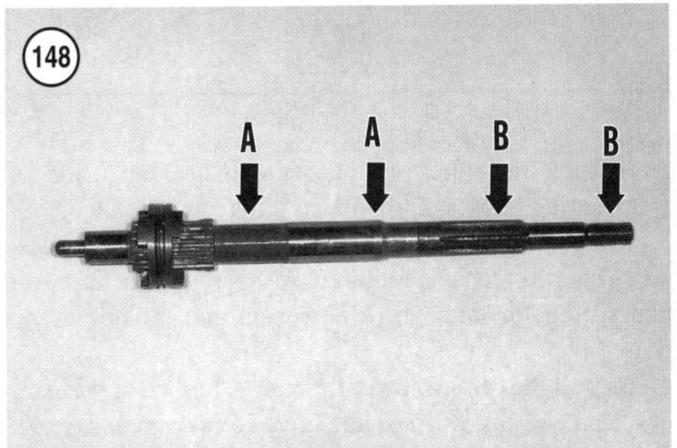

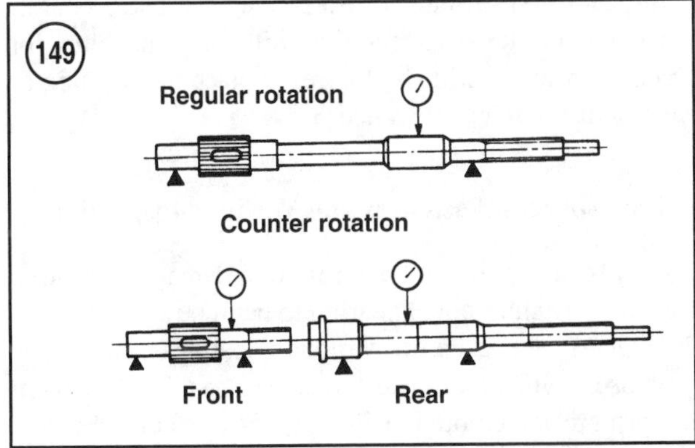

plate if a groove is worn in the plate or any other defects are noted.

4. Inspect the water pump insert (**Figure 147**) for a burned, worn or damaged surface. Replace the water pump body if any defects are noted.

5. Inspect the water pump body for melted plastic or other indications of overheating. Replace the cover and the water pump base if any defects are noted.

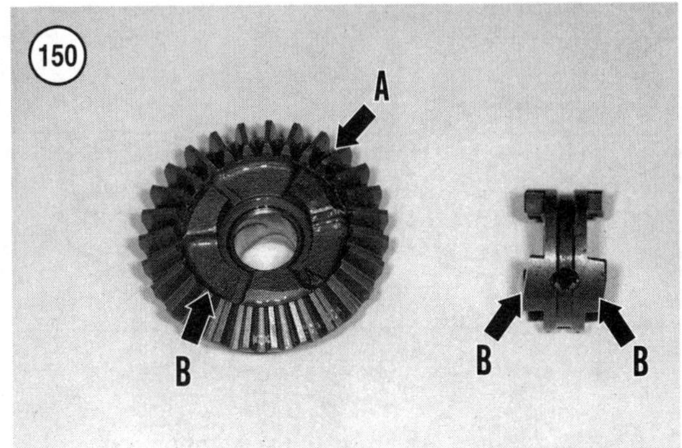

Propeller Shaft Inspection

1. Inspect the propeller shaft for bending, damage or excessively worn areas. Replace the propeller shaft if defects are noted as repair or straightening is not recommended.
2. Position the propeller shaft on V blocks. Rotate the shaft and note if any deflection or wobble is present. Replace the propeller shaft if visible deflection or wobble is noted.
3. Inspect the propeller shaft (A, **Figure 148**) for corrosion, damage or wear. Inspect the propeller shaft splines and threaded area (B, **Figure 148**) for twisted splines or damaged propeller nut threads. Inspect the bearing contact areas at the front and midpoint of the propeller shaft. Replace the propeller if discolored areas, rough surfaces, transferred bearing material or other defects are noted.
4. Inspect the propeller shaft at the seal contact areas. Replace the propeller shaft if deep grooves are worn in the surface.

Place V blocks at the points indicated in **Figure 149**. Use a dial indicator to measure the shaft deflection at the rear bearing support area. Securely mount the dial indicator. Observe the dial indicator movement and slowly rotate the propeller shaft. Replace the propeller shaft if the needle movement exceeds 0.006 in. (0.15 mm).

Gear and Clutch Inspection

1. Inspect the clutch (B, **Figure 150**) and gears for chips, damage, wear or rounded surfaces. Replace the clutch and gears if any of these conditions is found on either component.
2. Inspect the gear for worn, broken or damaged teeth (A, **Figure 150**). Note the presence of pitted, rough or excessively worn highly polished surfaces. Replace all of the gears if any of these conditions are found. This is especially important on engines with high operating hours.

9

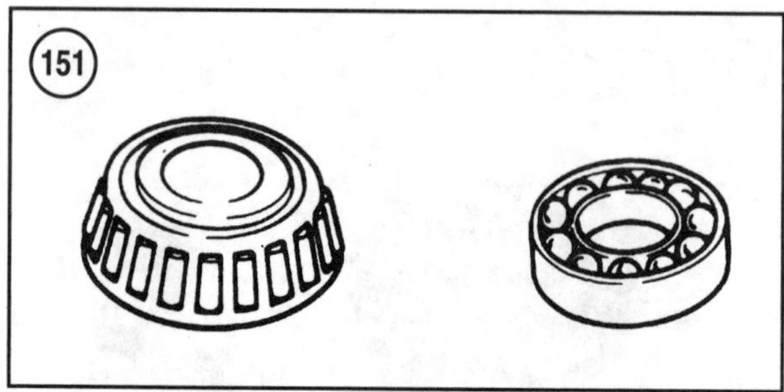
151

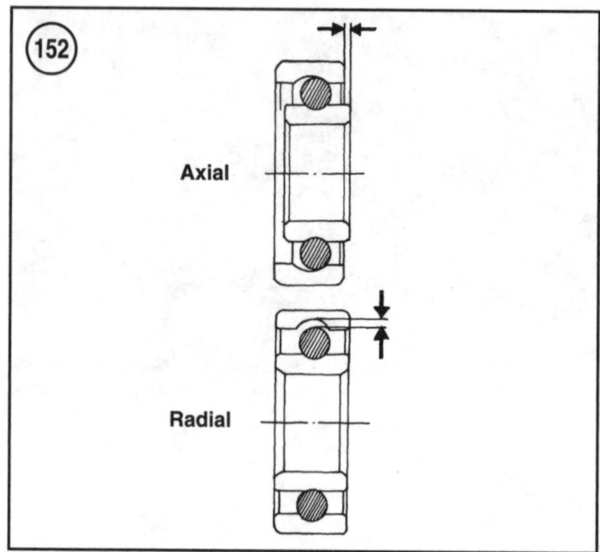

152

NOTE
Replace all gears if any of the gears require replacement. A wear pattern forms on the gears in a few hours of use. The wear pattern is disturbed if a new gear is installed with used gears.

Bearing Inspection

1. Clean all bearings thoroughly in solvent and air dry them prior to inspection. Replace bearings if the gear lubricant drained from the gearcase is heavily contaminated with metal particles. The particles tend to collect inside the bearings.
2. Inspect the roller bearings and bearing races (**Figure 151**) for pitting, rusting, discoloration or roughness. Inspect the bearing race for highly polished or unevenly worn surfaces. Replace the bearing assembly if any of these defects are noted.
3. Rotate ball bearings and note any rough operation. Move the bearing in the directions shown in **Figure 152**. Note the presence of *axial* or *radial* looseness. Replace the bearing if rough operation or looseness is noted.
4. Inspect the needle bearings located in the bearing carrier, forward gear and drive shaft seal and bearing housing. Replace the bearing if flattened rollers, discoloration, rusting, roughness or pitting is noted.
5. Inspect the propeller shaft and drive shaft at the bearing contact area. Replace the drive shaft or propeller shaft along with the needle bearing if discoloration, pitting, transferred bearing material or roughness.

Shift Cam and Related Components Inspection

1. Inspect the bore in the propeller shaft for the presence of debris, damage or excessive wear. Clean debris from the bore.
2. Inspect the clutch spring for damage, corrosion or weak spring tension and replace if defects are noted.
3. Inspect the cross pin for damage, roughness or excessive wear. Replace as required. Inspect the cam follower and spring for damage or corrosion and replace as required.
4. Inspect the cam follower for cracks, broken or worn areas. Replace any worn or defective components.
5. Inspect the shift cam located at the lower end of the shift shaft for wear, chips, cracks or corrosion.

Inspect the shift shaft for excessive wear and a bent or twisted condition. Inspect the shift shaft bushing for cracks or a worn shift shaft bore. Replace the bushing or shift shaft if defects are noted.

Shims, Spacers, Fasteners and Washers Inspection

1. Inspect all shims for bent, rusted or damaged surfaces. Replace any shim not appearing to be in new condition.
2. Spacers are used in various locations within the gearcase. Some function as thrust bearings. Replace them if worn areas are noted or if bent, corroded or damaged. Use only the correct part to replace them. In most cases they are of a certain dimension and made with a specified material.
3. Replace any locking nut unless it is in excellent condition. Always replace the pinion nut during final assembly.
4. Replace any worn or damaged washers located on the pinion gear. These washers are sometimes used as a thrust loaded surface and are subject to wear.

Table 1 TIGHTENING TORQUE

Fastener location	ft-lb.	in-lb.	N•m
Propeller nut			
4-6 hp	–	150	17
9.9 and 15 hp			
Standard gearcase	–	100	11
Optional gearcase	17	200	23
25-90 hp	55	–	75
Gearcase mounting bolts/nuts			
4-6 hp	–	70	8
9.9 and 15 hp			
Standard gearcase	15	180	20
Optional gearcase	40	–	54
25-90 hp	40	–	54
Trim tab bolt			
9.9 and 15 hp (optional gearcase)	17	204	23
25 hp	16	190	22
30 and 40 hp			
Standard gearcase	16	190	22
Optional gearcase	22	–	30
50 hp			
Standard gearcase	15.8	190	21
Optional gearcase	22	–	30
75 and 90 hp	22	–	30
Anode mounting bolt			
4-6 hp	–	70	8
9.9 and 15 hp (standard gearcase)	–	30	3.4
30 and 40 hp (optional gearcase)	–	60	6.8
50 hp (optional gearcase)	–	60	6.8
75 and 90 hp	–	60	6.8
Propeller shaft bearing carrier			
4-6 hp	–	70	8
9.9 and 15 hp			
Standard gearcase	85	–	115
Optional gearcase	80	–	109
25 hp	19	225	25
30 and 40 hp			
Standard gearcase	19	225	25
Optional gearcase	25	–	34
50 hp			
Standard gearcase	19	225	25
Optional gearcase	25	–	34
75 and 90 hp	25	–	34
Bearing carrier retainer			
9.9 and 15 hp (optional gearcase)	–	65	7
Water pump base			
9.9 and 15 hp (standard gearcase)	–	50	6
30 and 40 hp (optional gearcase)	–	60	7
50 hp (optional gearcase)	–	60	7
75 and 90 hp	–	60	7
Shift shaft bushing retainer/bolt			
4-6 hp	–	70	8
30 and 40 hp (optional gearcase)	–	60	7
50 hp (optional gearcase)	–	60	7
75 and 90 hp	–	60	7
Water pump housing			
4-6 hp	–	70	8
9.9 and 15 hp			
Standard gearcase	–	50	6
Optional gearcase	–	60	7
25-90 hp	–	60	7

(continued)

Table 1 TIGHTENING TORQUE (continued)

Fastener location	ft-lb.	in-lb.	N•m
Water inlet screen-to-gearcase			
4-6 hp	–	70	8
9.9 and 15 hp			
Standard gearcase	–	30	4
Optional gearcase	–	25	3
Gearcase drain/fill plugs			
9.9-90 hp	–	60	7
Pinion gear retaining nut			
25 hp	50	–	68
30 and 40 hp			
Standard gearcase	50	–	68
Optional gearcase	70	–	95
50 hp			
Standard gearcase	50	–	68
Optional gearcase	70	–	95
75 and 90 hp	70	–	95

Chapter Ten

Manual Starter

This chapter provides removal, repair and installation instructions for the manual starter (**Figure 1**). Removal and installation instructions for the neutral start mechanism (**Figure 2**) are included.

Table 1 provides tightening specifications for the manual starter and neutral start mechanisms. **Table 2** provides starter rope length for most models. **Table 1** and **2** are located at the end of this chapter.

REMOVAL, DISASSEMBLY, ASSEMBLY AND INSTALLATION

Cleaning, inspection and lubrication of the internal components are necessary if the manual starter does not engage properly or the starter binds.

Use only the starter rope specified for the outboard. Other types of rope will not withstand the rigorous use and will fail in a short amount of time potentially damaging other components. Contact a Mercury or Mariner dealership to purchase the specified starter rope.

Clean all components except the rope in a solvent suitable for composite or plastic components. Use hot soapy water if a suitable solvent is not available. Dry all components with compressed air immediately after cleaning.

Inspect all components for excessive wear or damage and replace them if defects are noted. Pay particular attention to the starter spring. Inspect the entire length of the spring for cracks or other defects.

Apply a water-resistant grease to all bushings, drive pawls, springs and pivot surfaces during installation of these components. To help ensure smooth operation and prevent corrosion, apply water-resistant grease to the starter spring contact surfaces.

CAUTION

When servicing the manual starter wear suitable eye protection and gloves. The starter spring may unexpectedly release from the housing with considerable force and result in injury. Follow all instructions carefully and wear suitable protection to minimize the risk.

CAUTION

Never use grease containing metal particles or graphite on any manual starter compo-

nents. Its use can cause binding or incorrect operation.

Removal (4-6 hp Models)

On these models the manual starter is mounted to the top of the power head. Refer to **Figure 3**.

1. Remove the spark plug. Connect the spark plug lead to a suitable engine ground. Shift the engine into neutral.
2. Carefully pry the neutral start link from the lever (**Figure 4**).
3. Remove the three mounting bolts and lockwashers (2 and 3, **Figure 3**) then lift the starter from the power head.

Disassembly (4-6 hp Models)

1. Pull the starter handle to the fully extended position. Grasp the starter as shown in **Figure 5** to prevent the sheave (6, **Figure 3**) from rotating. While holding the sheave, slip the knot from its recess in the sheave. Untie the knot and slip the rope and handle from the starter.
2. Allow the sheave to slowly unwind in the starter housing. Pull the rope guide (12, **Figure 3**) from the starter housing (1).
3. Hold down on the drive plate (10, **Figure 3**) and remove the sheave retaining bolt (11). Carefully pull the drive plate (10, **Figure 3**), spring (7), drive pawls (9) and drive pawl springs (8) from the sheave (6).
4. Wear protective eye wear, heavy gloves and protective clothing when removing the spring or sheave. Carefully lift up one end of the sheave and insert a screwdriver under it to prevent the spring from pulling up as the sheave is lifted (**Figure 6**). Carefully lift the sheave (6, **Figure 3**) from starter housing.
5. Note the direction in which the spring (5, **Figure 3**) winds into the spring housing (4) prior to removal. Starting at the inside bent end, carefully remove one loop of the spring at a time. Continue until the entire spring is free from the starter housing.
6. Pull the spring housing (4, **Figure 3**) from the starter housing. Remove the pivot bolt (18, **Figure 3**) and pull the washer (19) and lever (21) from the starter housing.
7. Remove the screw (22, **Figure 3**) and pull the washer, spring and sleeve (23-25, **Figure 3**) from the starter housing. Pull the lock lever (26, **Figure 3**) from the starter housing.
8. Carefully pry the handle block (**Figure 7**) from the handle. Slip the knot from the handle block and pull the rope from the handle and block.

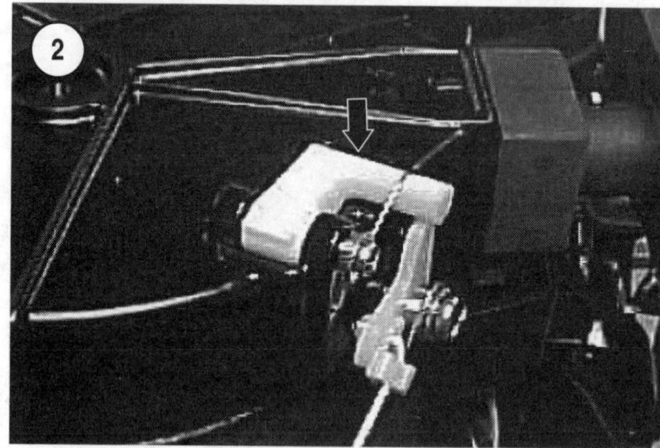

9. Clean all components except the rope in a clean solvent. Inspect all components for worn, or damaged components. Inspect the rope for frayed or damaged areas. Replace any suspect components.

Assembly (4-6 hp Models)

1. Place the spring housing (4, **Figure 3**) into the starter housing with the open end facing out and the tabs in the housing aligned with the notches in the housing. Apply a small amount of water-resistant grease to the surfaces of the spring housing.
2. Hook the small hooked end of the spring into the slot in the housing. Wind the spring in a clockwise direction one loop at a time until its entire length is in the housing. Hook the remaining end of the spring over the raised tab near the center of the starter housing.
3. Apply a light coat of water-resistant grease to the upper surface of the sheave (6, **Figure 3**). Place the center opening of the sheave over the pivot near the center of the starter housing and install the sheave into the starter housing.

3

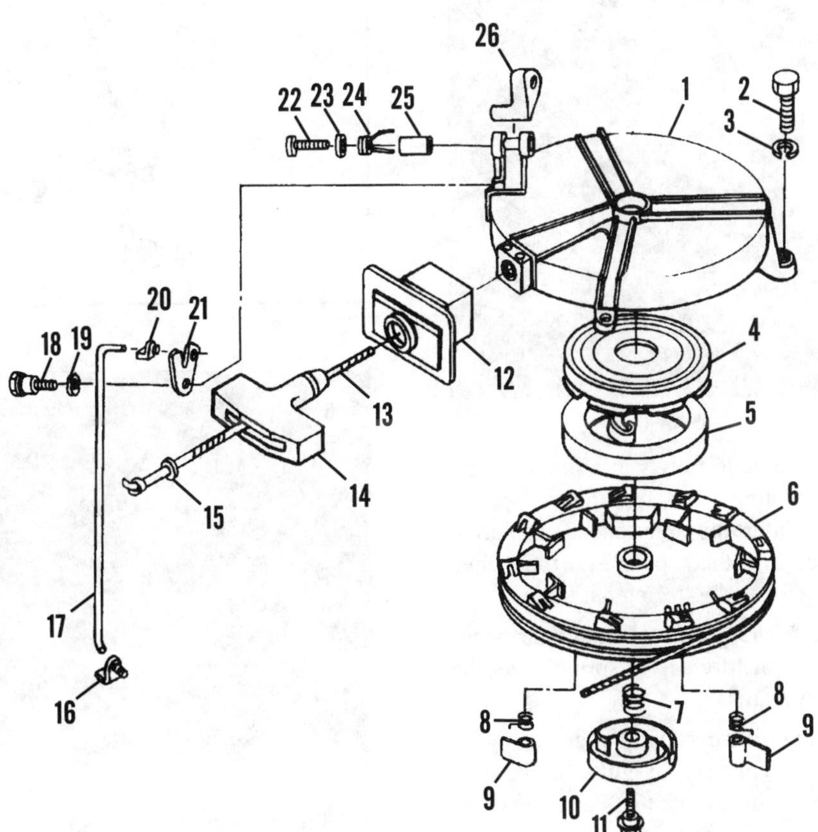

1. Starter housing
2. Bolt
3. Lockwasher
4. Spring housing
5. Starter spring
6. Sheave
7. Spring
8. Drive pawl spring
9. Drive pawl
10. Drive plate
11. Sheave mounting bolt
12. Rope guide
13. Rope
14. Handle
15. Washer
16. Lever
17. Neutral start link
18. Pivot bolt
19. Washer
20. Connector
21. Lever
22. Screw
23. Washer
24. Spring
25. Sleeve
26. Lock lever

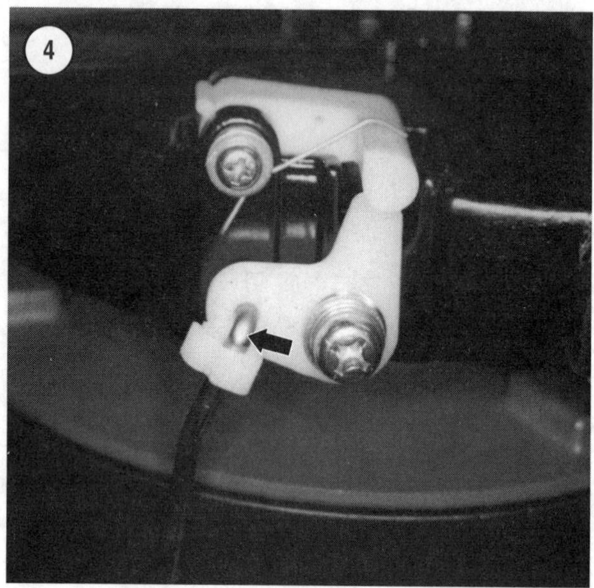

4. Slightly rotate the sheave to fully seat it in the starter housing. Apply a light coating of grease to the drive pawls and drive pawl springs. Insert the coiled end of each drive pawl spring (8, **Figure 3**) into their openings in the sheave with the hooked end of the spring facing outward.

5. Insert both drive pawls (9, **Figure 3**) into their openings in the sheave. Hook the drive pawl springs over the outside edge of the drive pawls.

6. Apply a light coating of water-resistant grease to the inside surfaces of the drive plate (10, **Figure 3**). Place the spring (7, **Figure 3**) into the sheave (7). Place the drive plate (10, **Figure 3**) onto the sheave. Align the opening on the side of the drive plate with the drive pawls (9) while installing the drive plate.

7. Apply Loctite 271 (Mercury part No. 92-809820) to its threads and install the sheave retaining bolt (11, **Figure 3**). Tighten the bolt to the specification in **Table 1**.

8. Slide the rope guide (12, **Figure 3**) onto its raised mounting boss. Cut the replacement rope to the same length as the original rope. Slide the rope through the handle block and the handle (**Figure 7**). Tie a knot in the handle end of the rope then slide the knot into the block. Press the handle block into in the handle.

9. Slip the rope through the rope guide (12, **Figure 3**). Rotate the sheave clockwise to align the rope opening in the sheave with the rope guide. Pass the rope through the rope opening (**Figure 5**), then tie a knot in the end of the rope.

10. Hold light tension on the rope and turn the sheave 2-1/2 turns clockwise . Wind the rope onto the grooved portion of the sheave.

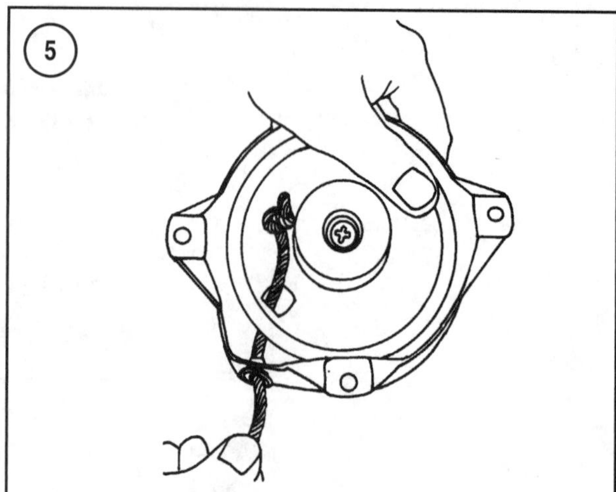

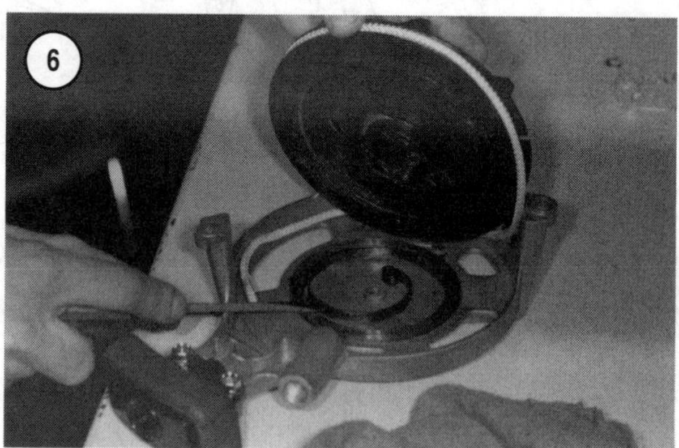

11. Prevent the sheave from rotating while placing the handle end of the rope into the rope notch (**Figure 8**). Hold the rope into the notch and turn the sheave counterclockwise three complete turns.

12. Prevent the sheave from rotating and pull the rope from the notch. Allow the sheave to slowly unwind. Repeat Steps 10 and 11 if the sheave fails to unwind.

13. Lower the lock lever (26, **Figure 3**) into its opening and slide the sleeve (25) through the lever and starter housing.

14. Apply Loctite 271 (Mercury part No. 92-809820) to the threads of the screw (22, **Figure 3**) and install the spring (24), washer (23) and screw. Securely tighten the screw. Place the shorter end of the spring into the hole in the housing (A, **Figure 9**). Hook the longer end of the spring over the lock lever (B, **Figure 9**).

15. Place the lever (21, **Figure 3**), spring and washer (19) onto the starter housing. Apply Loctite 271 to the threads and install the pivot bolt (18, **Figure 3**) into the housing. Securely tighten the screw. Hook one end of the spring

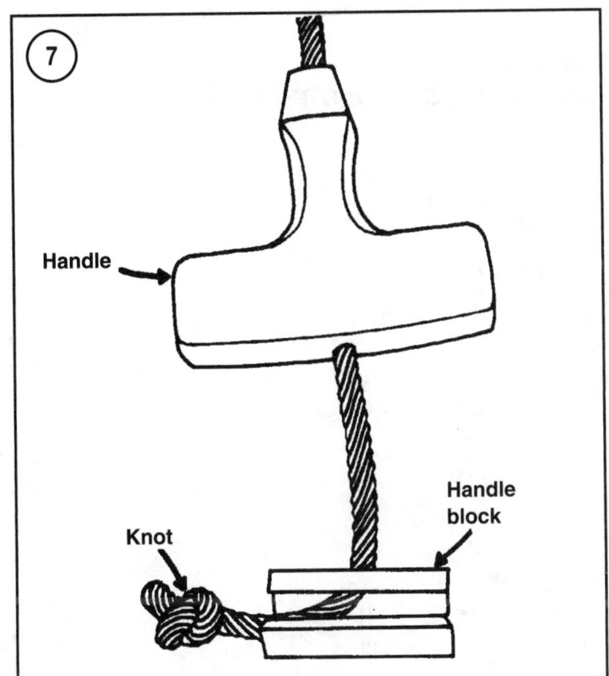

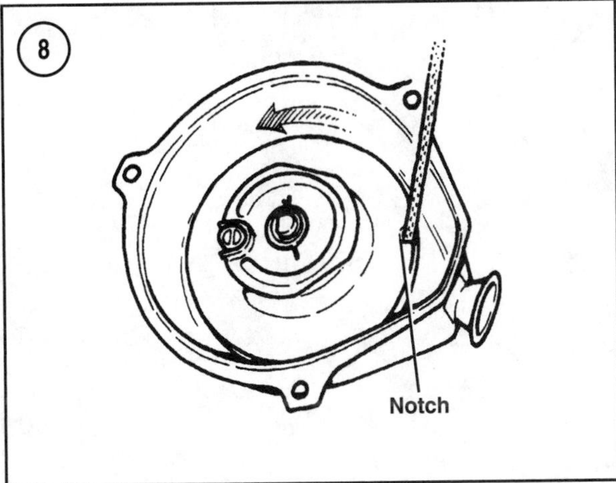

into the opening (C, **Figure 9**)in the starter housing. Hook the other end of the spring onto the lever (D, **Figure 9**).

Installation (4-6 hp Models)

1. Place the manual starter onto its mounting bosses with the starter handle facing forward.

2. Install the three mounting bolts and lockwashers (2 and 3, **Figure 3**). Tighten the bolts to the specification in **Table 1**.

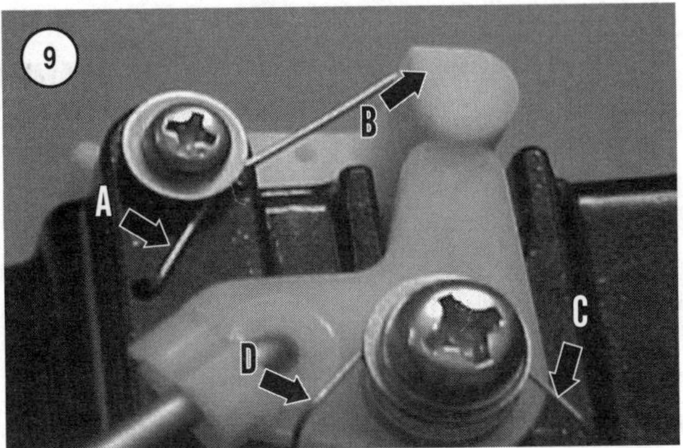

3. Carefully snap the neutral starter link into the connector (20, **Figure 2**) and lever (20). Install the spark plug and lead.
4. Check and adjust the neutral start mechanism following the instructions in Chapter Five.

Removal (9.9 [Serial No. OH000057-Prior] and 15 hp Models)

10

The manual starter is mounted above the flywheel. Refer to **Figure 10**.
1. Shift the engine into neutral.
2. Carefully pry the neutral start cable (4, **Figure 10**) from its groove in the starter housing. Slip the spring (5, **Figure 10**) from its notch then lift the neutral start cable and spring from the starter.
3. Remove both screws (2, **Figure 10**) then tilt the rope guide (3, **Figure 10**) forward.
4. Remove both front mounting bolts (10, **Figure 10**) and the single rear bolt (6). Lift the starter from the power head.

Disassembly (9.9 [Serial No. OH000057-Prior] and 15 hp Models)

1. Rotate the sheave counterclockwise enough to grasp a loop of the starter rope. Hold the sheave securely to prevent rotation. Place the starter rope into the notch provided in the sheave (**Figure 8**). Keep the rope positioned in the notch while *slowly* rotating the sheave clockwise. Continue until all spring tension is relieved.
2. Hold down on the sheave (22, **Figure 10**) and remove the sheave retaining bolt (26) and drive plate (27). Carefully pull the friction spring (28, **Figure 10**) from the sheave (22) and drive pawl linkage (24).

10

MANUAL STARTER
(9.9 [SERIAL NO. OH000057-PRIOR] AND 15 HP MODELS)

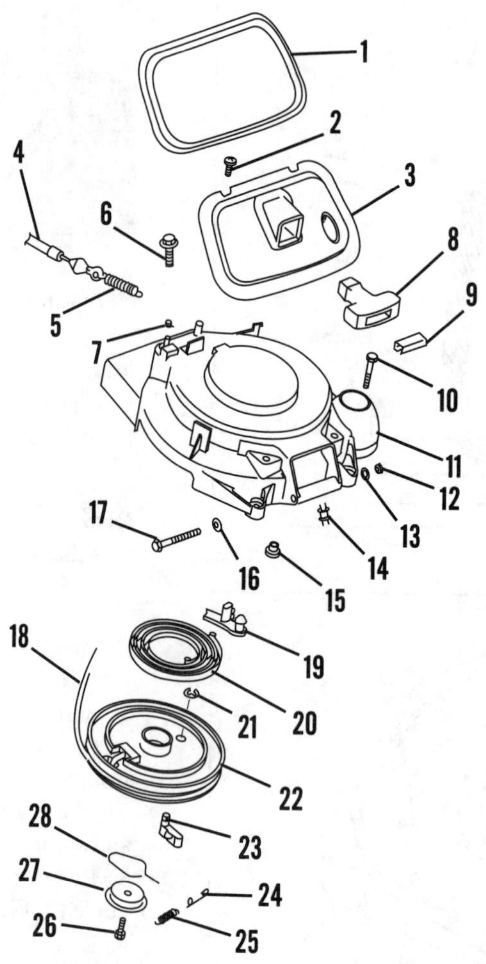

1. Seal
2. Screw
3. Rope guid
4. Neutral start cable
5. Spring
6. Mounting bolt
7. Spring
8. Handle
9. Handle block
10. Mounting bolt
11. Starter housing
12. Nut
13. Washer
14. Grommet
15. Collar
16. Washer
17. Bolt
18. Rope
19. Lock lever
20. Starter spring
21. E-clip
22. Sheave
23. Drive pawl
24. Linkage
25. Spring
26. Sheave retaining bolt
27. Drive plate
28. Friction spring

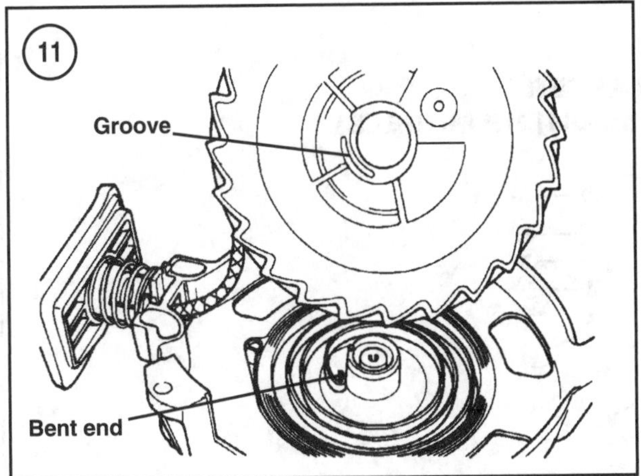

3. Slowly rotate the sheave clockwise until the sheave is free from the starter spring (20).

4. Wear protective eye wear, heavy gloves and protective clothing when removing the spring or sheave. Carefully lift one end of the sheave and insert a screwdriver under it to prevent the spring from pulling up as the sheave is lifted (**Figure 6**). Carefully lift the sheave (22, **Figure 10**) from housing.

5. Note the direction in which the spring (20, **Figure 10**) winds into the spring housing (11) prior to removal. Starting at the inner end, carefully remove one loop of the spring at a time. Continue until the entire spring is free from the starter housing.

6. Carefully pull the drive pawl spring (25, **Figure 10**), linkage (24) from the sheave. Remove the E-clip (21, **Figure 10**) and pull the drive pawl (23) from the sheave.

7. Carefully pry the handle block (**Figure 7**) from the handle. Slip the knot from the handle block and pull the rope from the handle and block.

8. Remove the bolt (17, **Figure 10**) washers (13 and 16) and nut (12) and lift the rope guide (3) from the starter.

9. Note the orientation, then carefully pull the spring (7, **Figure 10**) from the housing (11) and lock lever (19). Gently squeeze the exposed ends of the lock lever (19, **Figure 10**), then push the lever from its opening.

10. Clean all components except the rope in a clean solvent. Inspect all components for worn, or damaged components. Inspect the rope for frayed or damaged areas.

Assembly (9.9 [Serial No. OH000057-Prior] and 15 hp Models)

1. Carefully snap the hooked end of the lock lever (19, **Figure 10**) into the starter housing (11). With the notched end of the lever faces the starboard side of the housing.

2. Install the spring (7, **Figure 10**) over its mounting boss on the rear upper side of the starter housing. Slip the short end of the spring into the small opening in the housing. Slip the longer end of the spring under the projection on the lock lever.

3. Apply a light coat of water-resistant grease to the drive pawl (23, **Figure 10**) and install it into the sheave. Snap the E-clip (21, **Figure 10**) into the groove on the upper end of the drive pawl.

4. Clip the longer end of the linkage (24, **Figure 10**) to the drive pawl (23). Connect one end of the spring (25, **Figure 10**) to the shorter end of the linkage. Place the other end of the spring through the hole in the sheave mounted tab.

5. Place the rope guide (3, **Figure 10**) in position on the starter housing. Guide the bolt and washer (16 and 17, **Figure 10**) through the rope guide and its mounting bosses. Install the other washer and nut (12 and 13, **Figure 10**). Tighten the rope guide retainers to the specification in **Table 1**.

6. Apply a small amount of a water-resistant grease to the areas of the starter housing that contact the starter spring (20, **Figure 10**).

7. Hook the small hooked end of the spring into the slot located in the starter housing near the lock lever. Wind the spring counterclockwise one loop at a time until its entire length is in the housing.

8. Cut the replacement rope to the length specified in **Table 2**. Slide the rope through the handle block and the handle (**Figure 7**). Tie a knot in the handle end of the rope and slide the knot into the block. Press the handle block into the handle.

9. Align the bent end of the spring with the groove on the sheave (**Figure 11**) and lower the sheave into the starter housing.

10. Rotate the sheave slightly counterclockwise to check for spring engagement. Spring engagement is indicated if resistance if felt. Remove the sheave and repeat Ssteps 9 and 10 until spring engagement is detected.

11. Place the pointed end of the friction spring (28, **Figure 10**) through the small loop in the linkage (24). Install the smaller diameter side of the drive plate (27, **Figure 10**) into the friction spring opening while placing it onto the sheave.

12. Apply Loctite 271 (Mercury part No. 92-809820) to sheave retaining bolt threads(26, **Figure 10**). Install and tighten the bolt to the specification provided in **Table 1**.

13. Rotate the sheave clockwise to align the rope opening in the sheave with the rope guide. Pass the rope through the rope guide and sheave (**Figure 5**). Tie a knot in the end of the rope.

(12)

MANUAL STARTER
(9.9 [SERIAL NO. OH00058-ON] HP MODELS)

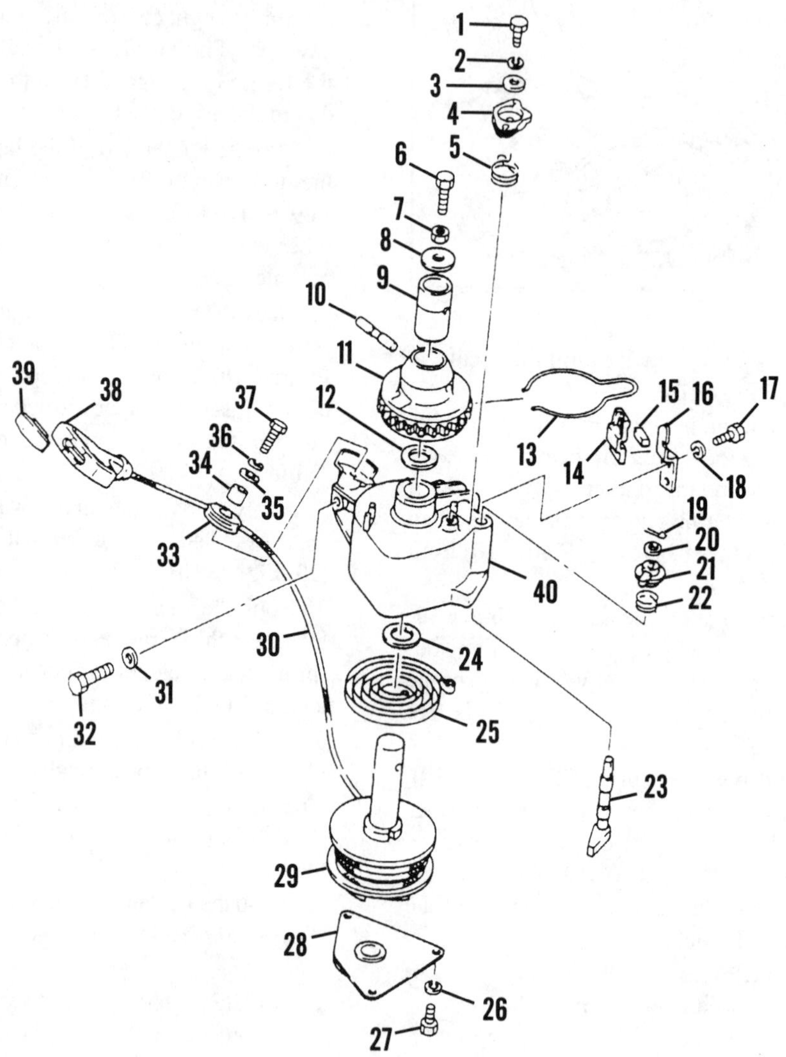

1. Bolt
2. Lockwasher
3. Flat washer
4. Netural start lever
5. Spring
6. Bolt
7. Nut
8. Washer
9. Sleeve
10. Pin
11. Starter pinion
12. Thrust washer
13. Friction spring
14. Block
15. Bumper
16. Bracket
17. Bolt
18. Lockwasher
19. Cotter pin
20. Washer
21. Lever
22. Spring
23. Lock lever
24. Thrust washer
25. Starter spring
26. Lockwasher
27. Screw
28. Cover
29. Starter pulley
30. Rope
31. Washer
32. Bolt
33. Rope guide
34. Sleeve
35. Washer
36. Lockwasher
37. Bolt
38. Handle
39. Plug
40 Starter housing

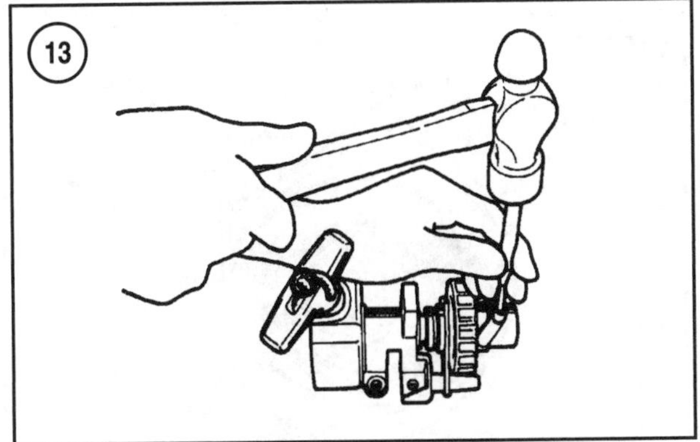

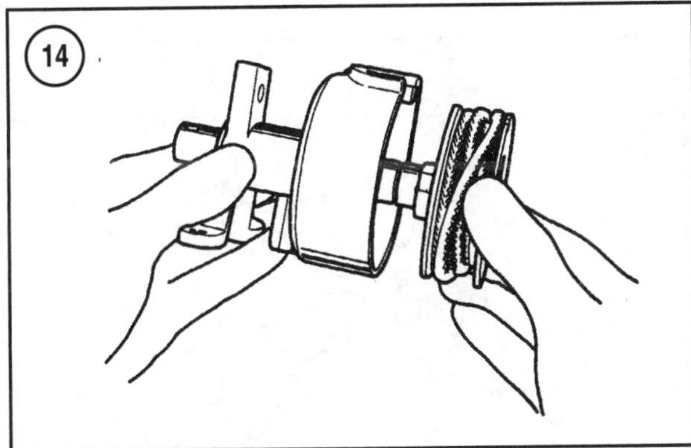

14. Position the rope into the notch in the sheave (**Figure 8**). Hold the rope in the groove (**Figure 8**) and rotate the sheave three full turns in a counterclockwise direction.
15. Prevent the sheave from rotating and pull the rope from the notch. Allow the sheave to *slowly* unwind. Wind the rope into the grooved portion of the sheave. Repeat Steps 13-15 if the sheave fails to unwind.

Installation (9.9 [Serial No. OH000057-Prior] and 15 hp Models)

1. Place the manual starter onto its mounting bosses. Install the mounting bolts (6 and 10, **Figure 10**). Tighten the bolts to the specification in **Table 1**.
2. Swing the rope guide down and install the screws (2, **Figure 10**). Securely tighten the screws.
3. Hook the spring (5, **Figure 10**) into its notch in the starter housing. Pull slightly on the neutral start cable (4, **Figure 10**) and press it into its groove in the housing. Check and adjust the neutral start mechanism following the instructions in Chapter Five. Release the cable.
4. Adjust the neutral start mechanism following the instructions in Chapter Five.

Removal (9.9 hp Models [Serial No. OH000058-On])

The manual starter is mounted forward and below the flywheel. Refer to **Figure 12**.
1. Shift the engine into neutral.
2. Pull the starter rope out approximately 12 in. (30.5 cm). Tie a knot in the rope at the point it exits the manual starter. The knot must be large enough to prevent the rope from retracting into the starter.
3. Carefully pry the plug (39, **Figure 12**) from the handle. Untie the knot and slide the plug and handle from the rope. Carefully slip the neutral start cable from the neutral start lever (4, **Figure 12**).
4. Remove the three mounting bolts from the starboard side of the starter. Carefully lift the manual starter from the engine.

Disassembly (9.9 hp Models [Serial No. OH000058-On])

1. Loosen the nut (7, **Figure 12**), then remove the bolt (6). Drive the pin (10, **Figure 12**) from the spool shaft using a punch and hammer (**Figure 13**). Carefully pull the starter pinion (11, **Figure 12**) and friction spring (13), sleeve (9) and washer (12) from the spool shaft.
2. Hold the manual starter and the end of the rope and untie the knot. Hold firm pressure on the rope while allowing the rope to slowly wind into the housing.
3. Remove the three screws and washers (26 and 27, **Figure 12**), then lift the cover (28) from the starter.
4. Rotate the starter pulley (29, **Figure 12**) three complete turns counterclockwise to disengage the pulley from the starter spring (25).
5. Cover the manual starter assembly with a piece of heavy cloth and carefully slide the spool from the starter housing (**Figure 14**). Unwind the rope from the spool. Untie knot from the rope and pull the rope from the spool.
6. Note the direction the starter spring (25, **Figure 12**) winds prior to removing it from the starter housing. Starting at the inner hooked end of the spring, carefully remove one loop of the spring at a time. Continue until the entire spring is free from the manual starter housing. Remove the thrust washer (24, **Figure 12**) from the starter housing.
7. Remove the cotter pin (19, **Figure 12**) and lift the washer (20), lever (21), and spring (22) from the starter. Remove the lock lever (23, **Figure 12**) from the open end of the starter.
8. Remove the bolt (1, **Figure 12**) and lift the lock washer (2), flat washer (3), neutral start lever (4) and spring (5) from the starter.

9. Remove the bolt (37, **Figure 12**), then lift the washers, sleeves and rope pulley (33-37, **Figure 12**) from the starter housing.
10. Clean all components except the rope using clean solvent. Inspect all components for worn, or damaged components. Inspect the rope for frayed or damaged areas. Replace any suspect components.

Assembly
(9.9 hp Models [Serial No. OH000058-On])

1. Wear protective eye wear and gloves when installing the starter spring (25, **Figure 12**).
2. Wipe a light coat of water-resistant grease to the spring contact surfaces of the starter housing. Place the thrust washer (24, **Figure 12**) into the spring opening. Align the washer with the pinion shaft opening.
3. Install the spring as follows:
   a. When installing a new spring, do not remove the spring retainer until the spring is fully installed. Place the rounded spring end (**Figure 15**) into the notched portion of the starter. Wind the spring in a clockwise direction. Hold the spring firmly in place, then remove the retaining clip.
   b. When a used spring is used, place the rounded spring end (**Figure 15**) into the notched portion of the starter.
4. Carefully wind the spring into the housing clockwise until all loops rest against the housing.
5. Slip the rope through its opening in the starter pulley. Pass the rope through to the bottom side of the pulley. Tie a knot in the end of the rope. Ensure the knot is large enough to prevent the rope from slipping through the hole. Wrap the rope seven complete turns clockwise as viewed from the bottom side around the pulley.
6. Apply a light coat of water-resistant grease to the pinion shaft. Slide the pulley and pinion shaft into the starter housing.
7. Align the bent end of the spring (**Figure 16**) with the groove on the pulley. Carefully slide the spool into the manual starter housing.
8. Rotate the spool clockwise while checking for spring tension. The presence of spring tension indicates the spring and spools are properly engaged. Repeat Step 7 if no spring tension is noted.
9. Place the free end of the rope into the notch in the pulley (**Figure 17**). Apply a light coat of water-resistant grease to the shaft bore portion of the starter pinion (11, **Figure 12**).
10. Slide the washer (12, **Figure 12**) over the pinion shaft. Seat the washer against the starter housing. Slide the sleeve (9, **Figure 12**) over the pinion shaft. Align the pin hole in the sleeve with the pin hole in the pinion shaft. Slide the starter pinion (11, **Figure 12**) over the pinion shaft. Align the slot in the starter pinion with the holes in the sleeve and pinion shaft. Carefully drive the pin (10, **Figure 12**) into the starter pinion, sleeve and pinion shaft. Center the pin is evenly in the pinion shaft.

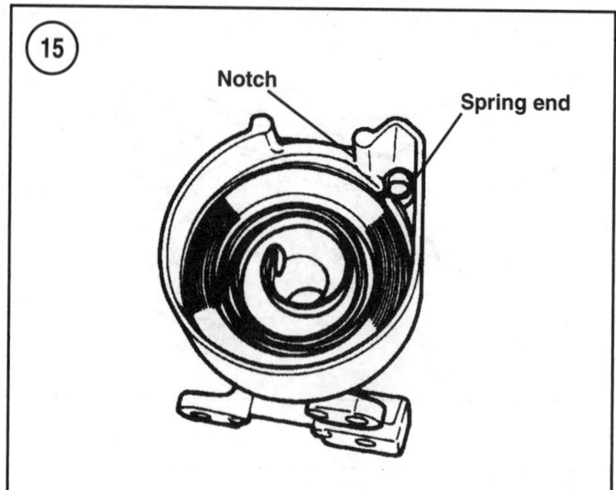

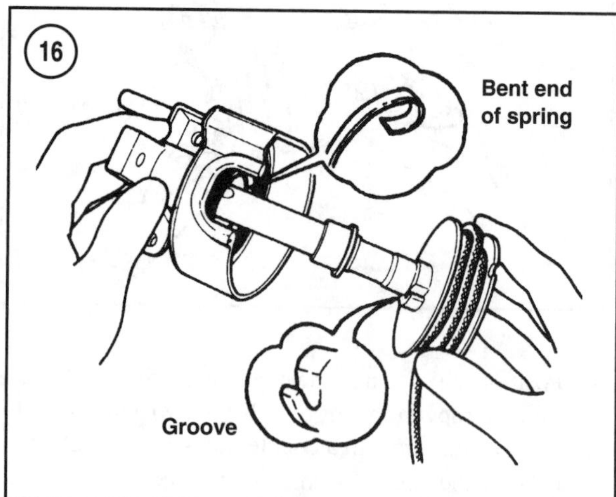

11. Install the nut (7, **Figure 12**) fully onto the bolt (6). Place the washer (8, **Figure 12**) onto the top of the starter. Thread the bolt and nut (6 and 7, **Figure 12**) into the pinion shaft until the bolt contacts the pin. Tighten the pulley retaining bolt to the specification in **Table 1**. Tighten the nut (7) down against the washer (8).

12. Place the friction spring (13, **Figure 12**) onto the starter pinion. Pull about 1 ft. (30.5 cm) of rope free from the starter pulley. Route the end of the rope through the starter housing. Hook the rope into the notch in the pulley (**Figure 8**).

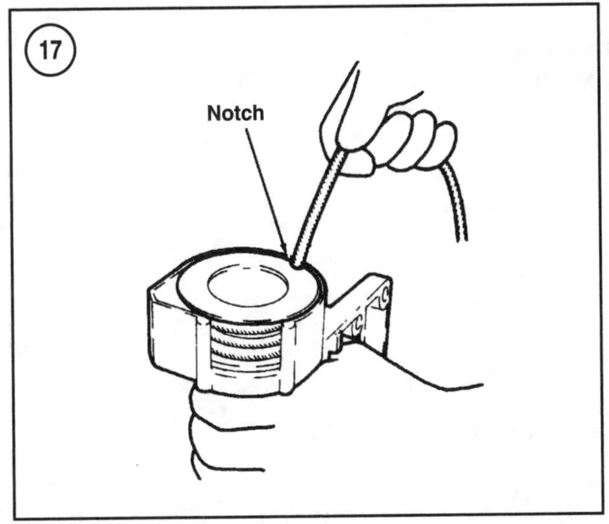

13. Hold the rope in the notch while rotating the starter pulley three complete turns in a clockwise direction as viewed from the open end. Remove the rope from the notch and remove any slack. Tie a knot in the rope at the opening while preventing the pulley from rotating. Ensure the knot is large enough to prevent the rope from winding into the housing.

14. Slip the lock lever (23, **Figure 12**) into its opening in the starter housing. Install the spring and lever (21 and 22, **Figure 12**) onto the housing. Engage the spring with the housing and lever, then install the washer and cotter pin (19 and 20, **Figure 12**). Bend over both legs of the pin.

15. Install the cover (28, **Figure 12**) and the three screws (27). Securely tighten the screws.

16. Install the spring and neutral start lever (4-6, **Figure 12**) onto the starter housing. Engage the spring onto the slots in the lever and the housing. Install the washers and bolt (1-3, **Figure 12**). Securely tighten the bolts.

17. Install the pulley, sleeve, washers and bolt (33-37, **Figure 12**) onto the housing. Securely tighten the bolt.

Installation (9.9 hp Models [Serial No. OH000058-On])

1. Position the manual starter onto the front of the power head and install the mounting bolts. Tighten the bolts to the specification in **Table 1**.

2. Route the end of the rope through the rope guide and starter handle. Slip the rope through the plug (39, **Figure 12**) and tie a knot in the rope. Push the knot into the recessed part of the plug then press the plug into the handle.

3. Pull out slightly on the rope while untying the knot. Allow the rope to slowly wind into the manual starter. Ensure the rope passes next to the rope guide pulley (33, **Figure 12**).

4. Place the end of the neutral start cable into the hole in the neutral start lever (4, **Figure 12**).

5. Adjust the neutral only start cable as described in Chapter Five.

Removal (25-40 hp Models)

The manual starter is mounted above the flywheel. Refer to **Figure 18**.

1. Shift the engine into neutral.

2. Remove the screw and washer (3 and 4, **Figure 18**) from the cable clamp. Remove the locking pin (1, **Figure 18**), then lift the cable end (2) from the manual starter.

3. Remove the four mounting bolts (10, **Figure 18**) and lift the manual starter from the power head.

4. Place the starter top side down on a work surface.

Disassembly (25-40 hp Models)

1. Remove the three screws (30, **Figure 18**) and lift the cover (31) from the starter housing. Pull the cam lever and spring (32 and 33, **Figure 18**) from the starter housing. Lift the lock lever and spring (34 and 35, **Figure 18**) from the starter housing.

2. Pull the starter handle away from the starter until approximately 12 in. (30.5 cm) of rope is exposed. Tie a knot near the rope guide (19, **Figure 18**) to prevent the rope from winding back into the starter. Carefully pry the handle block (17, **Figure 18**) from the handle (16). Loosen the knot and remove the handle and block from the rope. Hold the rope while untying the knot. Allow the rope to *slowly* wind into the starter.

3. Remove the sheave retaining bolt (28, **Figure 18**) and lift the drive plate (27) and spring (29) from the sheave. Remove both E-clips (26, **Figure 18**), then lift the drive pawls (25) and springs (24) from the sheave.

4. Carefully lift the sheave (22, **Figure 18**) and spring plate (20) from the starter housing. Carefully pry the starter spring (21, **Figure 18**) from the sheave.

5. Remove both screws (18, **Figure 18**) and lift the rope guide (19) from the starter housing. Lift the handle rest (15, **Figure 18**) from the starter housing.

6. Remove the bolt (11, **Figure 18**) and lift the washer (12), roller (13) and sleeve (14) from the starter housing.

7. Clean all components except the rope using clean solvent. Inspect all components for worn, or damaged com-

18

MANUAL STARTER (25-40 HP MODELS)

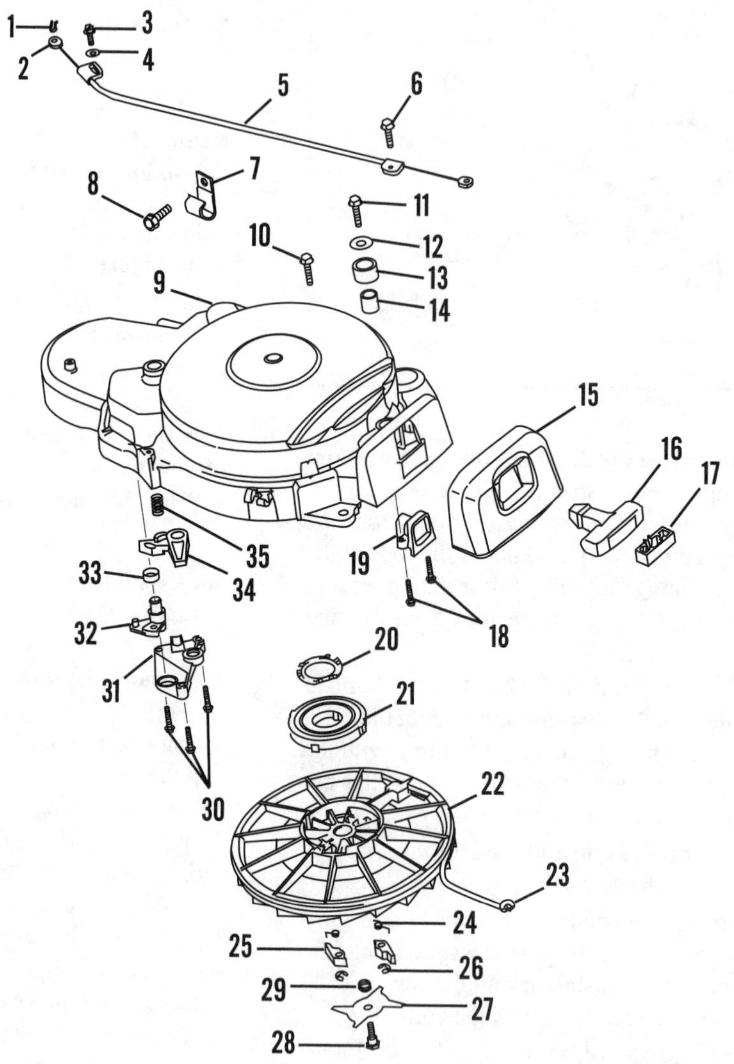

1. Locking pin
2. Cable end
3. Screw
4. Washer
5. Neutral start cable
6. Screw
7. Hose retainer
8. Screw
9. Starter housing
10. Mounting bolt
11. Bolt
12. Washer
13. Roller
14. Sleeve
15. Handle rest
16. Handle
17. Handle block
18. Screw
19. Rope guide
20. Spring plate
21. Starter spring
22. Sheave
23. Rope
24. Drive pawl spring
25. Drive pawl
26. E-clip
27. Drive plate
28. Sheave retaining bolt
29. Spring
30. Screws
31. Cover
32. Cam lever
33. Spring
34. Lock lever
35. Spring

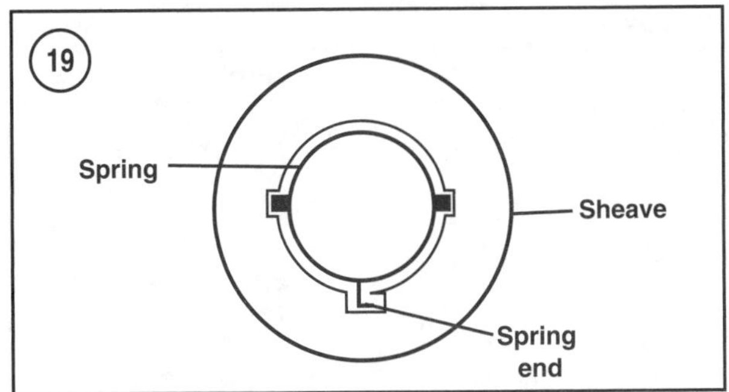

ponents. Inspect the rope for frayed or damaged areas. Replace any suspect components.

Assembly (25-40 hp Models)

1. Install the rewind spring (21, **Figure 18**) into its opening in the sheave (22). Align the exposed end of the spring with the notch in the sheave (**Figure 19**) and seat the bosses fully seated into their openings. Apply water-resistant grease to all surfaces of the spring plate (20, **Figure 18**).
2. Place the spring plate (20, **Figure 18**) into the starter housing with the raised tabs facing the housing. Center the opening in the plate with the retaining bolt hole in the housing. Install the sheave and spring into the starter housing. Ensure the spring plate (20, **Figure 18**) makes direct contact with the spring (21). Rotate the sheave until the raised boss on the spring aligns with its notch in the starter housing and the sheave drops into position.
3. Install the drive pawl springs (24, **Figure 18**) into the sheave. Install both drive pawls (25, **Figure 18**) onto their mounting posts. Engage the ends of the springs over the outside edges of the pawls. Install both E-clips (26, **Figure 18**).
4. Place the spring (29, **Figure 18**) into the sheave. Install the drive plate (27, **Figure 18**) onto the sheave with the X mark facing outward. Align the longer ends of the drive plate tabs with the short tabs of the drive pawls.
5. Apply Loctite 271 (Mercury part No. 92-809820) to the sheave retaining bolt threads (28, **Figure 18**). Install and tighten the bolt to the specification in **Table 1**.
6. Install the rope guide (19, **Figure 18**) and both screws (18). Tighten the screws to the specification in **Table 1**. Install the sleeve, pulley, washer and bolt (11-14, **Figure 18**) onto the starter housing. Securely tighten the bolt. Slide the handle rest over its mounting boss on the starter housing.
7. Rotate the sheave counterclockwise until the starter spring is fully wound. Back off the sheave at least 90° but not more than 1-1/4 revolutions to align the openings. Hold the sheave to prevent it from rotating.
8. Cut the replacement rope to the length in **Table 2**. Route the starter rope through the rope guide and into its opening in the sheave (**Figure 5**). Tie a knot in the end of the rope. Ensure the knot is large enough to prevent it from slipping through the opening. Press the knot into its opening.
9. Grip the rope, then release the sheave. Allow the rope to wind into the starter until approximately 12 in. (30.5 mm) of rope extends from the starter. Tie a knot in the rope to prevent the remaining length from winding into the starter.
10. Slip the remaining end of the rope through the starter handle (16, **Figure 18**) and the hole in the handle block (17). Tie a knot in the end of the rope. Press the knot into its notch in the handle block. Carefully press the handle block into in the handle.
11. Grip the rope, then untie the knot. Allow the rope to slowly wind into the starter.
12. Install the lock lever (34, **Figure 18**) over its mounting post in the starter housing. Install the spring (35, **Figure 18**) over the rounded post on the lock lever. Press the other end of the spring into its recess in the starter housing.
13. Place the spring (33, **Figure 18**) over the pivot point of the cam lever (32). Carefully slide the lever and spring into the opening in the starter housing. Hook one end of the spring over the raised pin of the starter housing and the other end over the cam lever.
14. Apply a light coat of water-resistant grease to the lock lever and cam lever. Align the lever pivot points and install the cover (31, **Figure 18**) on the starter housing. Install all three screws (30, **Figure 18**) tighten them securely.

Installation (25-40 hp Models)

1. Position the manual starter onto its mounting bosses with the handle facing forward. Install the four mounting bolts (10, **Figure 18**) and evenly tighten them to the specification in **Table 1**.
2. Place the cable end (2, **Figure 18**) over its post on the cam lever (32). Install the locking pin (1, **Figure 18**) through the hole in the post to retain the cable end.
3. Retain the cable clamp with its screw and washer (3 and 4, **Figure 18**). Do not tighten the screw at this time.
4. Adjust the neutral start cable following the instructions in Chapter Five.
5. Check for proper operation of the manual starter and neutral start mechanism.

Table 1 TIGHTENING TORQUE

Fastener location	ft-lb.	in-lb.	N•m
Rewind mounting bolts			
4-6 hp	–	70	8
9.9 hp			
Serial No. OH000057-prior			
6x20 mm bolts	–	70	8
6x90 mm bolts	–	30	3
Serial No. OH000058-on	13	156	18
15 hp			
6x20 mm bolts	–	70	8
6x90 mm bolts	–	30	3
25-40 hp	–	62	7
Sheave retaining bolt			
4-6 hp	–	70	8
9.9 hp (serial No. OH000057-prior)	–	52	6
15 hp	–	52	6
25-40 hp	–	135	15
Pulley retaining bolt			
9.9 hp (serial No. OH000058-on)	–	156	18
Lower rewind cover			
9.9 hp (serial No. OH000058-on)	–	43	5
Drive plate retainer			
9.9 hp (serial No. OH000058-on)	–	43	5
Neutral start cable bracket			
9.9 hp (serial No. OH000058-on)	–	43	5
Neutral start cable bracket			
25-40 hp	–	34	4
Rope guide retainer			
9.9 hp			
Serial No. OH000057-prior	–	30	3
Serial No. OH000058-on	–	70	8
15 hp	–	30	3
25-40 hp	–	70	8
Starter pulley to flywheel			
4-6 hp	–	70	8

Table 2 REWIND ROPE LENGTH

Model	Rope Length
4-6 hp	*
9.9 hp	
Serial No. OH000057-prior	71 in. (1800 mm)
Serial No. OH000058-on	*
15 hp	71 in. (1800 mm)
25-40 hp	66 in. (1680 mm)

*Rope length specifications are not provided for these models. Trim the rope to the required length after tying the knot and before installing the rewind starter handle

Chapter Eleven

Power Trim and Midsection

This chapter provides repair instructions for all power trim and midsection components.

Table 1 provides tightening specifications for power trim and manual hydraulic tilt system components. **Table 2** provides tightening specifications for all midsection and tiller control components. **Table 1** and **Table 2** are located at the end of this chapter.

POWER TRIM SYSTEM

Power trim (**Figure 1**) is a factory installed option on all electric start 25-50 hp models. Power trim is standard on all 75 and 90 hp models.

Disassembly, repair and assembly of the hydraulic part of the system requires special service tools and practical experience in hydraulic system repair. Have the hydraulic system repaired at a marine repair facility if access to the required tools is not available or unfamiliar with the repair operations.

Power Trim Relays Removal and Installation

On 25-50 hp models the electric trim motor harness plugs directly into the relays (**Figure 2**).

On 75 and 90 hp models, the trim relays (**Figure 3**) are located beneath the electrical component cover on the front starboard side of the power head. On these models the individual terminals connect the trim relays to the engine and trim motor harness.

25-50 hp models

1. Disconnect both cables from the battery.
2. Trace the trim motor wires to the trim relays. (**Figure 2**).
3. The blue wires connect to the UP relay and the green wires connect to the DOWN relay.
4. Push down on the connector tab and pull the trim harness from the relay. Remove the mounting bolt (**Figure 4**)

and sleeve, then remove the relay from the power head. Remove the rubber grommet from the relay mounting plate. Clean the relay mounting surface and bolt holes.

5. Slip the rubber grommet into its opening on the replacement relay mounting plate. Place the relay onto the power head. Insert the sleeve and bolt into the hole. Securely tighten the mounting bolt.

6. Clean the terminals and carefully plug the trim harness onto the relay. Ensure the locking tab on the connector engages the tab on the relay. Route the wires away from moving components.

7. Clean the terminals and connect the cables to the battery.

75 and 90 hp models

1. Disconnect both cables from the battery.
2. The blue wires connect to the UP relay and the green wires connect to the DOWN relay.
3. Disconnect the wires from the relay.
4. Pull the slots in the rubber relay sleeve from the mounting arms. Clean the relay mounting surface.
5. Align the slots in the rubber relay sleeve with the mounting arms, then push the relay into position.
6. Connect the wires to the replacement relay. Connect the larger diameter wires to the larger diameter terminals on the relay. Verify all terminals do not contact other terminals then securely tighten the terminal nuts. Route the wires away from moving components.
7. Clean the terminals and connect the cables to the battery.

Trim Switch Removal and Installation

1. Disconnect both cables from the battery.
2. The switch is located on the starboard side of the lower engine cover (**Figure 5**). Disconnect the red, blue/white and green/white engine harness wires from the trim switch (**Figure 6**).
3. Carefully slide the retainer clip from the groove in the switch body. Lift the switch from the lower engine cover. Remove the rubber plugs from the unused terminals.
4. Slide the replacement switch into the opening with the switch harness facing downward. Press the switch fully into the opening then insert the locking clip into the switch groove.
5. Connect the red, blue/white and green/white switch wires to the engine wire harness (**Figure 6**). Insert the rubber plugs into unused terminals. Route all wires away from moving components.

6. Clean the terminals and connect the cables to the battery.

Electric Power Trim Motor Removal and Installation

Do not attempt to replace the motor without removing the trim system. Proper alignment of the pump coupler,

fasteners and sealing O-ring is far easier if the trim system is removed. Improper installation can result in water leakage or damage to other trim system components.

NOTE
Always note the orientation of the electric motor and wire harness prior to removing them from the engine. Use a paint dot or piece of tape to mark the wire routing. Never scratch the electric motor or trim housing as it promotes corrosion of the surface.

25 hp and 50 hp (1998-prior) models

Refer to **Figure 7**.

1. Remove the trim system from the engine as described in this chapter.
2. Thoroughly clean from the electric motor and the area surrounding its mating surface to the trim system.
3. Remove the four mounting bolts and lift the electric trim motor (13, **Figure 7**) from the trim system.
4. Pull the O-ring (15, **Figure 7**) from the electric motor and the trim system. Discard the O-ring.
5. Pull the coupler (8, **Figure 7**) from the hydraulic pump or the shaft of the motor.
6. Align the slot in the coupler with the shaft and on the hydraulic pump.
7. Install a new oval shaped O-ring (15, **Figure 7**) onto the trim system. Align the O-ring with the trim system opening.
8. Align the slot on the coupler with the shaft of the electric motor and lower it into position on the trim system. Rotate the motor slightly to align the shaft and coupling then seat the motor against its mounting surface.
9. Lift the electric motor enough to verify correct positioning of the O-ring (15, **Figure 7**). Correct as required. Install the mounting bolts and tighten them evenly to the specifications in **Table 1**. Position the ground wire and washer (14, **Figure 7**) under the front starboard side mounting bolt.
10. Install the trim system following the instructions in this chapter.

All other models

Refer to **Figure 8**. The electric trim motor and fluid reservoir integrate into a single assembly. Open the manual relief valve (**Figure 9**) and tilt the engine if the trim system is inoperative.

1. Remove the trim system from the engine following the instructions provided in this chapter.
2. Thoroughly clean the electric motor and the area surrounding its mating surface to the trim system.
3. Remove the fill plug (14, **Figure 8**) and O-ring (7) from the fluid reservoir. Place the trim system over a suitable container then pour the trim fluid from the reservoir.
4. Remove the four mounting screws (18, **Figure 8**) and lift the trim pump and reservoir assembly (7) from the trim system.

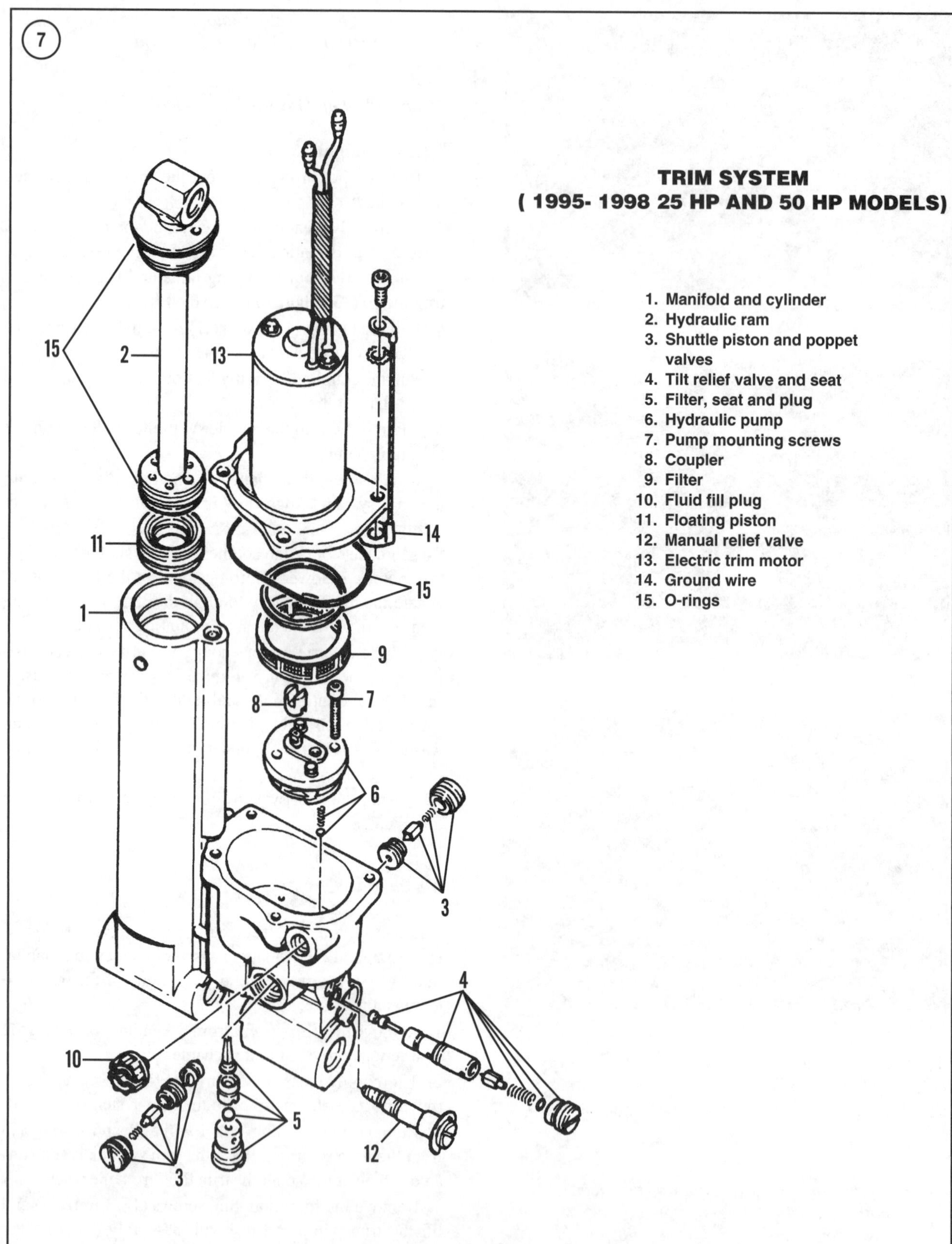
7
TRIM SYSTEM
(1995- 1998 25 HP AND 50 HP MODELS)
1. Manifold and cylinder
2. Hydraulic ram
3. Shuttle piston and poppet valves
4. Tilt relief valve and seat
5. Filter, seat and plug
6. Hydraulic pump
7. Pump mounting screws
8. Coupler
9. Filter
10. Fluid fill plug
11. Floating piston
12. Manual relief valve
13. Electric trim motor
14. Ground wire
15. O-rings
15
2
13
14
11
1
9
8
7
6
3
4
10
5
12
3

8

TRIM SYSTEM (YELLOW FILL PLUG SYSTEMS)

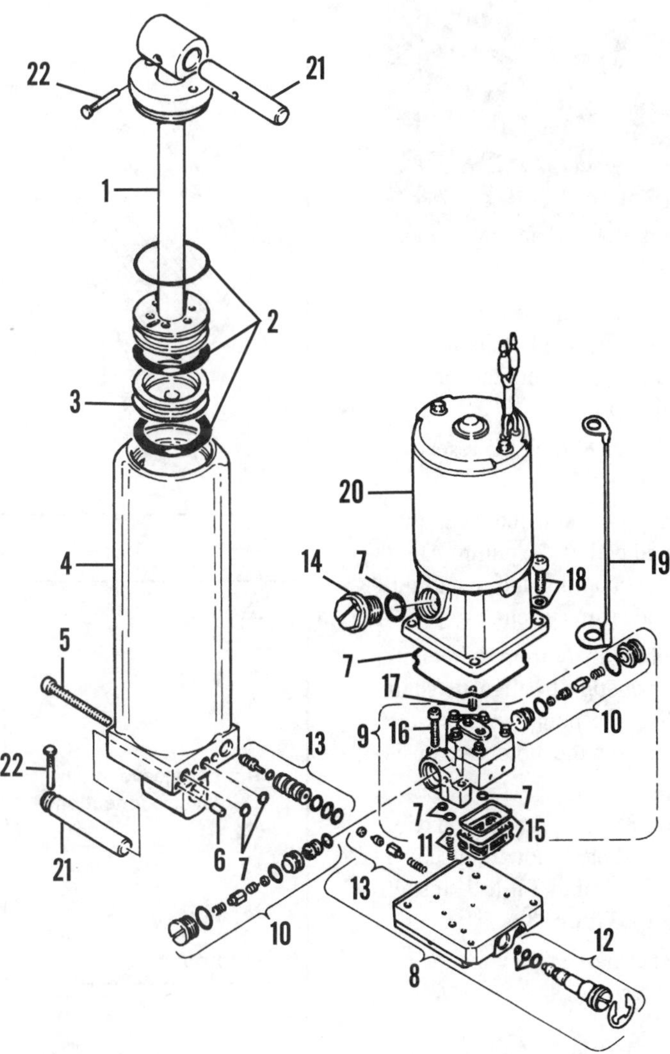

1. Hydraulic ram
2. Shock piston
3. Floating piston
4. Hydraulic cylinder
5. Allen bolts
6. Pins
7. O-rings
8. Manifold
9. Hydraulic pump
10. Poppet valves and shuttle piston
11. Ball and spring
12. Manual relief valve
13. Pilot valve, plunger and housing
14. Fluid fill plug
15. Filter and seal
16. Pump mounting screw
17. Coupling
18. Screw
19. Ground wire
20. Electric trim motor
21. Pivot pin
22. Retaining pin

5. Remove the O-ring (7, **Figure 8**) from the trim system or reservoir. Discard the O-ring. Mark the UP facing side and remove the coupling (17, **Figure 8**) from the electric trim motor shaft or hydraulic pump shaft.

6. Install the new O-ring (7, **Figure 8**) onto the reservoir mating surface.

7. Place the coupler (17, **Figure 8**) into the hydraulic pump shaft closest to the pointed end of the pump. Align the electric motor shaft with the coupling and install the electric motor into position on the trim system.

8. Hold the electric motor slightly away from its mounting surface and turn the motor enough to align its shaft opening with the coupler. Align the pump wires to the starboard side of the system then drop the motor into position.

9. Install the screws (18, **Figure 8**). Place the ground wire (19, **Figure 8**) under the front starboard mounting screw. Tighten the screws to the specification in **Table 1**. Install the O-ring and fill plug (7 and 14, **Figure 8**).

10. Install the trim system on the engine following the instructions provided in this chapter.

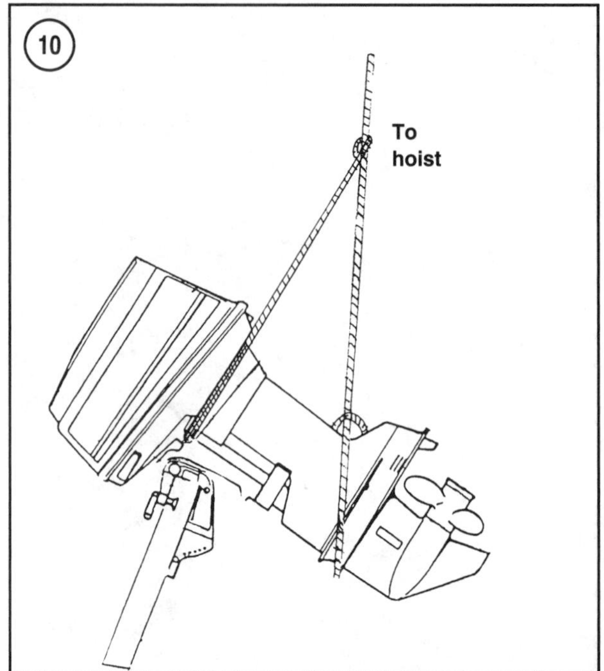

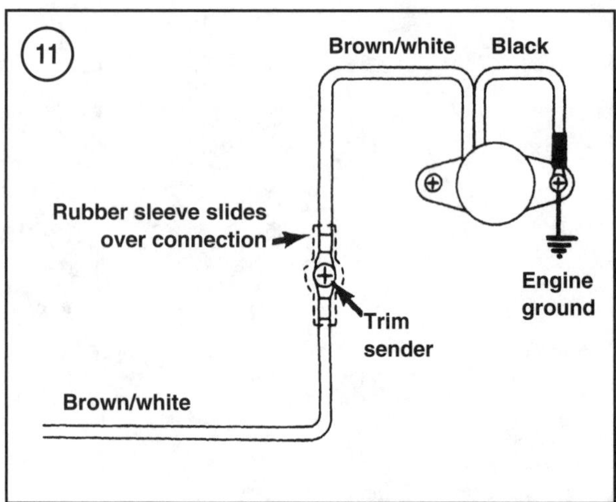

Trim Position Sender Removal and Installation

A trim position sender is installed on some 75 and 90 hp models.

1. Place the engine in the full tilt position. Engage the tilt lock mechanism and support the engine with an overhead hoist (**Figure 10**). Disconnect both cables from the battery.

2. The sensor (**Figure 11**) mounts directly aligned with the upper pivot pin for the trim system.

3. Loosen the screw and disconnect the brown/white trim position sender wire from the wire leading to the gauge.

4. Trace the black sensor wire to its connection to engine ground. Disconnect the wire. Note the direction in which the wires are orientated before removing the sender.

5. Remove both mounting screws and pull mounting strap from the swivel housing. Lift the sender from the swivel bracket. Clean from the sender mounting surface and the slot in the upper pivot pin.

6. Apply a light coating of 2-4-C Marine Lubricant to the slot in the upper pivot pin. Align the protrusion on the sensor with the slot and install the sender into the opening. Rotate the sender until the wires are orientated in the direction noted prior to removal.

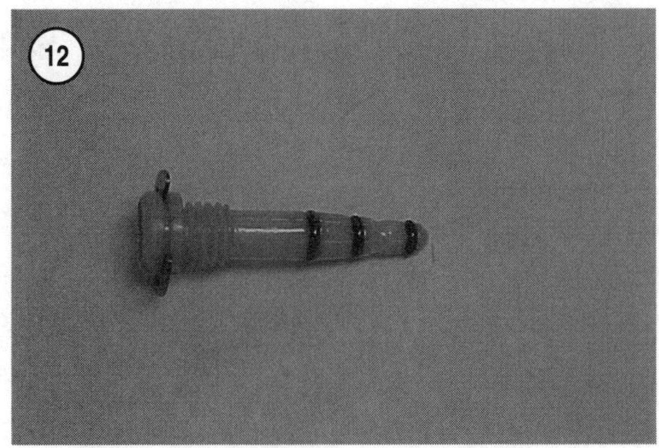

12

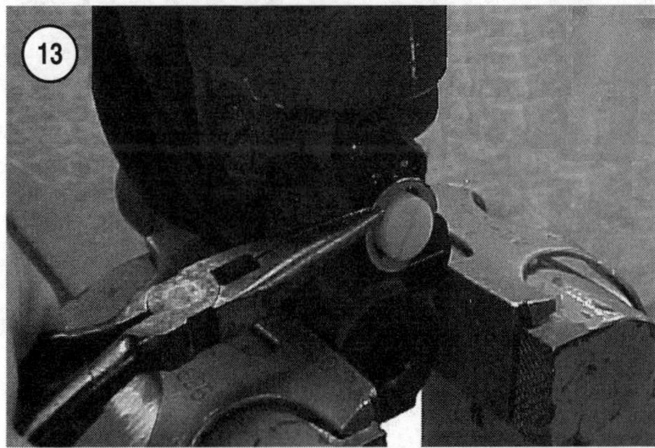

13

7. Slide the sleeve over the terminal and coat the terminals with liquid neoprene after connecting the terminals. Route all wires away from becoming pinched or stretched as the engine tilts and turns. Retain the wire with plastic locking clamps as required. Install the retaining strap and screws. Securely tighten the screws.
8. Clean the terminals and connect the cables to the battery. Disengage the tilt lock mechanism and remove the overhead support.
9. Adjust the sender following the instructions in Chapter Five.

Manual Relief Valve Removal and Installation

Refer to **Figure 7** or **Figure 8**. The valve mounts to the starboard side of the trim system. Access the valve through an opening in the clamp bracket (**Figure 9**).

After removal of the valve, inspect all O-rings (**Figure 12**) for worn, flattened, cut or deteriorated surfaces. Note the size and location of all O-rings prior to removing them from the valve.

Removal of the manual relief valve is simple provided the screwdriver slot end of the valve is intact. If not, heat the tip of a screwdriver and then hold it against the remnants of the valve. The valve material melts into the shape of the screwdriver tip. Allow the material to cool, then use the screwdriver to remove the valve. Never drill the valve out as the machined seating surface for the O-rings usually suffer irreparable damage.

Inspect the O-rings on the valve. Problems may surface when large portions are missing or torn away from the O-rings. They usually migrate to a pressure relief valve or other component within the trim system.

1. Position the engine in the full tilt position. Engage the tilt lock lever and support the engine with an overhead cable (**Figure 10**) or blocks.
2. Locate the manual relief valve through the access hole in the clamp bracket (**Figure 9**). Place a suitable container under the trim system to capture any spilled fluid.
3. Using needlenose pliers, remove the E-clip from the valve (**Figure 13**). Select a screwdriver that fits the screw slot in the valve. Rotate the valve counterclockwise until it can be pulled through the clamp bracket opening.
4. Use a suitable light along with a pick, small screwdriver or tweezers, remove any remnants of the valve or O-ring from the opening. Avoid damaging any of the machined surfaces in the opening.
5. Lubricate the manual relief valve with Dexron II automatic transmission fluid then carefully slide the new O-rings if removed onto the valve. Lubricate the O-rings with Dexron II automatic transmission fluid or its equivalent then install the valve into the opening. Do not tighten the valve at this time.
6. Rotate the valve clockwise until slight resistance is felt. Rotate the valve 1/4 in. the closed direction then 1/8 turn in the open direction. Repeat this process until the manual relief valve is fully seated.
7. Using needlenose pliers, install the E-clip to its groove in the valve (**Figure 13**). Refer to *Filling and Bleeding* in this section and correct the fluid level and purge air from the system.

11

Manual Tilt Removal and Installation

WARNING

Some manual tilt system components are charged with very high pressure nitrogen gas. Do not disassemble any part of the system. Replace a faulty system or have it repaired at a local Mercury or Mariner dealership.

This system is used on 30-50 hp models without power trim.

1. Disconnect both cables from the battery.

2. Place the tilt control lever in the tilt position then raise the engine to the full tilt position. Engage the tilt lock lever then support the engine with an overhead cable (**Figure 10**) or blocks.

3. Carefully pry the ball socket linkage from the lever on the starboard side of the tilt system (**Figure 14**).

4. Remove the upper pivot pin retainer from the lower port side of the pin boss. Using a chisel, drive the retainer down enough to grip it with pliers. Grip the retainer with pliers and pull it from the boss and upper pivot pin.

5. Support the tilt system and drive the upper pivot pin from the swivel bracket and tilt cylinder.

6. Remove the lower pivot pin retainer from the upper port side of the pivot pin boss (**Figure 15**). Using a chisel, drive the retainer up enough to grip the pin with pliers (**Figure 16**). Pull the retainer from the lower pivot pin and mounting boss.

7. Support the tilt system and drive the lower pivot pin (**Figure 17**) toward the port side clamp bracket. Tilt the upper end of the system outward then lift it from the clamp brackets.

8. Clean the pivot pin openings in the clamp brackets and tilt system.

9. Slip the bottom end of the system into position between the clamp brackets. Swing the upper part of the cylinder into position in the swivel bracket.

10. Apply 2-4-C Marine Lubricant to the lower pivot pin and drive into the starboard clamp bracket.

11. Verify the retaining pin opening in the clamp bracket aligns with the groove in the pin. Drive the retaining pin (**Figure 15**) into the opening until fully seated against the clamp bracket.

12. Align the pivot pin openings in the tilt cylinder with the pin openings in the swivel bracket.

13. Lubricate its surfaces with 2-4-C marine lubricant then drive the upper pivot pin into the port side opening.

14. Drive the pin in until flush with the boss surface. Verify the retaining pin opening in the swivel bracket aligns with the groove in the pivot pin. Drive the retaining pin into the opening until fully seated against the pin boss.

15. Carefully snap the tilt linkage onto the ball socket connector on the tilt system. Check for free movement of the lever and full travel of the lever. Adjust the length or connector orientation to correct any faults.

16. Carefully remove the overhead support. Release the tilt lock mechanism the place the engine in the normal running position.

17. Connect the cables to the battery.

14

15

16

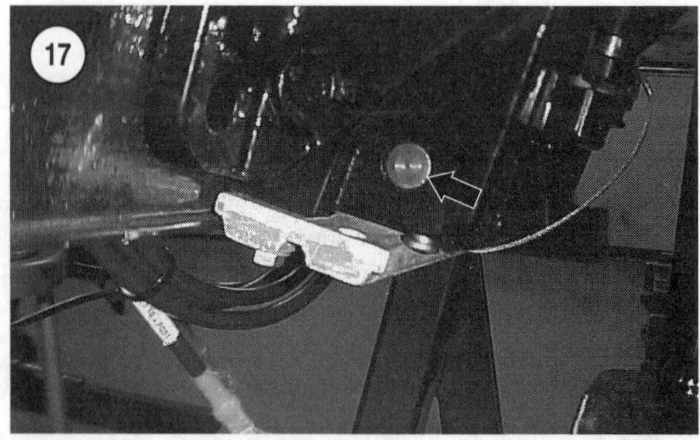
17

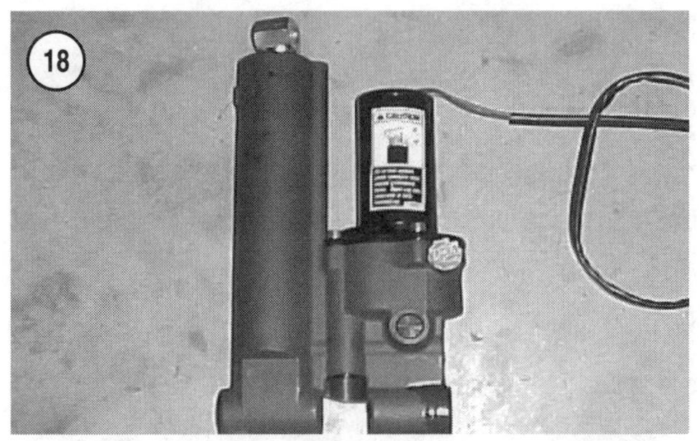

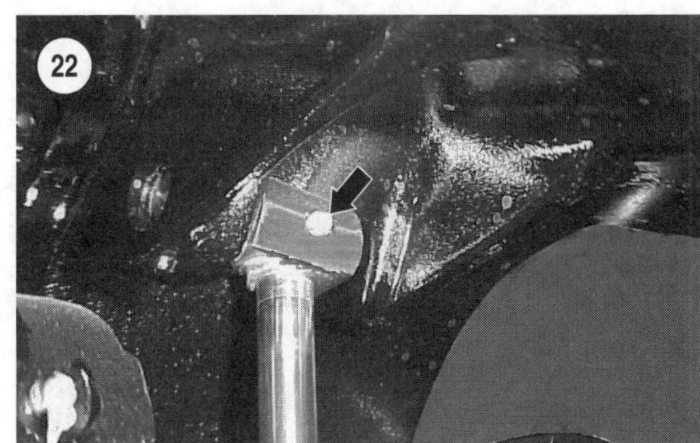

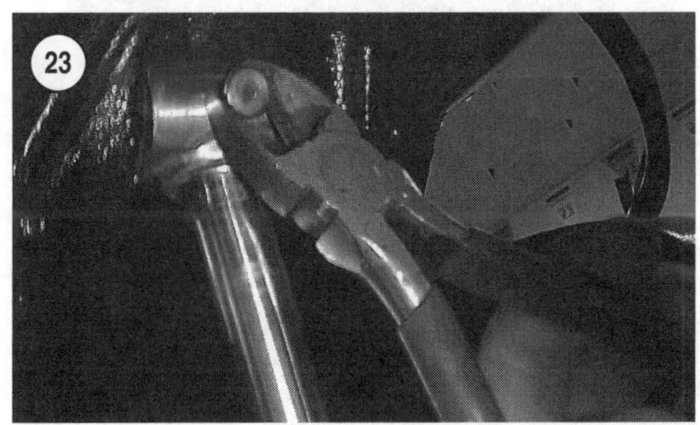

Power Trim Removal and Installation

A small trim system (**Figure 18**) is used on 25 hp and early 50 hp models. All other models are equipped with the larger system (**Figure 19**). Identify the larger and more common system by the yellow fill cap.

1. Position the engine in the full up tilt position. Engage the tilt lock lever then support the engine with an overhead cable (**Figure 10**) or suitable blocks.
2. Disconnect both cables from the battery.
3. Place a suitable container under the trim system to capture any spilled fluid.

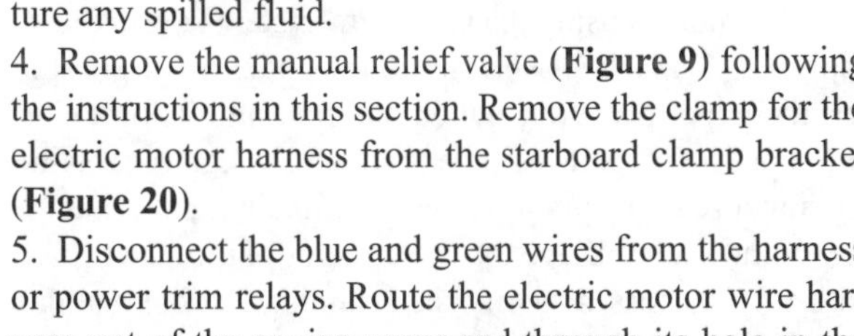

4. Remove the manual relief valve (**Figure 9**) following the instructions in this section. Remove the clamp for the electric motor harness from the starboard clamp bracket (**Figure 20**).
5. Disconnect the blue and green wires from the harness or power trim relays. Route the electric motor wire harness out of the engine cover and through its hole in the clamp bracket.
6. Remove the bolts (**Figure 21**), then drop the large anode from the bottom of both clamp brackets.
7. Remove the retaining pin (**Figure 22**) from the upper end of the hydraulic cylinder. Using a chisel, carefully drive the pin away from its mounting surface. Pull the pin from the end of the cylinder using pliers (**Figure 23**).

8. On 25 and 50 hp models with the small trim system (**Figure 18**), remove the large nuts and washers from the lower ends of the clamp brackets. Support the trim system while carefully driving the lower pivot pin from the clamp brackets and the trim system. Pull the trim system from the engine. Remove the bushings from the pivot pin holes in the clamp bracket and the trim system.
9. On all models using the large trim system (**Figure 19**), remove the retaining pin (**Figure 15**) from the lower port side of the clamp bracket.
10. Support the trim system and drive the lower pivot pin (**Figure 17**) from the clamp bracket and trim system.
11. Swing the top side of the trim system away from the swivel bracket, then lift the system from the clamp brackets.
12. Clean the upper and lower pivot pin holes. Inspect the pivot pins, openings and bushing holes for wear or damage. Replace worn or damaged components.
13. On models with the large system (**Figure 19**), inspect the retaining pin orientation (**Figure 22**). The pin should slope upward as the pin is installed. Incorrect orientation causes the pin to slope downward as the pin is installed. Rotate the pivot end of the hydraulic cylinder until the pin hole slopes upward.
14. On models so equipped, insert the pivot pin bushings in the clamp bracket and trim system. Slide the lower end of the trim system into the clamp brackets, then tilt the upper end back into its upper pin bore. Ensure the fill cap side faces outward. Align the upper pivot pin bores in the cylinder end and the swivel bracket.
15A. On 25 and 50 hp models with the small trim system (**Figure 18**), apply 2-4-C marine lubricant to its surfaces and insert the upper pivot pin grooved side first into its port side opening. Drive the upper pivot pin in until flush with the pin bosses. Align the groove in the upper pivot pin with the retaining pin bore, then insert the pin. Drive the retaining pin in until fully seated.
15B. On models using the large trim system (**Figure 19**), apply 2-4-C Marine Lubricant to the upper pivot pin. Insert the upper pivot pin slotted end first into its port side bore until it enters its cylinder end bore. Align the retaining pin bore in the pivot pin with the retaining pin bore in the cylinder end. Drive the upper pivot pin in until flush with the pin bosses. Verify the retaining pin bores align then insert the pin. Drive the retaining pin in until fully seated.
16A. On 25 and 50 hp models with the small trim system (**Figure 18**), coat the surface of the lower pivot pin with 2-4-C Marine Lubricant. Align the lower pivot pin bores in the clamp brackets and the trim system and slide the lower pin into position. Install the large washer and nuts then tighten them to the specification provided in **Table 1**.

24

25

16B. On models with the larger yellow cap type trim system (**Figure 19**), coat the surface of the lower pivot pin with 2-4-C Marine Lubricant. Align the pin holes in the clamp brackets and trim system then slide the lower pin non grooved end first into its port side opening. Drive the pin in until flush with the clamp bracket (**Figure 17**). Align the retaining pin hole with the groove in the pivot pin and insert the pin. Drive the retaining pin into its opening until fully seated.
17. Route the electric trim motor harness through the starboard clamp bracket. Position the harness clamp on the starboard clamp bracket (**Figure 20**) and install the clamp bolt. Securely tighten the bolt.
18. Route the electric trim motor harness through in the lower engine cover. Connect the wires to the harness or trim relays. Route the wires away from moving components.
19. Refer to *Manual Relief Valve* in this chapter and install the manual relief valve.
20. Disengage the tilt lock mechanism and carefully remove the overhead support. Slowly open the manual relief valve and position the engine in the normal position.
21. Connect the cables to the battery.

22. Correct the fluid level and bleed air from the trim system following the instructions in this chapter.

WARNING
The trim/tilt system creates very high pressure. Always wear eye protection and gloves when servicing the system. Never disconnect any hydraulic lines or remove any fittings without relieving the pressure from the system.

Trim System Disassembly, Inspection and Assembly

Problems with trim systems are almost always the result of debris in the system or damaged O-rings. It is a good practice to replace all O-rings and seals anytime the internal components are removed. Purchase the O-ring and seal kit for the trim system before disassembling the trim system. This reduces the chance of contaminants entering the system while waiting on parts.

Seal and O-ring kits contain numerous sizes and shapes of O-rings. Some of the O-rings have the same diameter, but have a different thickness. To help ensure correct O-ring placement, remove one O-ring at a time. Find the replacement O-ring of the exact diameter and opening size as the one removed. Install the new O-ring or make good notes indicating its exact location.

Scratched or pitted hydraulic cylinder or valve seating surfaces are certain to cause system leak-down or other hydraulic problems. Very fine scratches occur from normal operation and rarely cause hydraulic problems. Scratches deep enough to feel with a fingernail or deep pitting on seating surfaces indicate the need for replacing the affected component.

Note the orientation of all springs, plugs, seats and valves as they are removed. Install all valves and especially springs in the original locations during assembly.

Work only in a clean environment and use lint free shop towels when cleaning all trim system components. Trim systems must operate with very clean fluid.

WARNING
The trim system contains fluid under high pressure. Always use protective eye wear and gloves when working with the trim system. Never remove any components or plugs without first bleeding the pressure off of the system. Follow the instructions carefully and loosen the manual relief valve to relieve the internal pressure.

25 hp and early 50 hp models (small trim system)

A spanner wrench (or Mercury part No. 91-74951) and heat lamp (Mercury part No. 91-63209) are required to completely disassemble the trim system. Refer to **Figure 7** to assist with component identification and orientation.

1. Remove the trim system and trim motor following the instructions in this chapter.
2. Remove the fill plug and pour all trim fluid from the reservoir (**Figure 24**).
3. Clamp the trim system in a vice with soft jaws (**Figure 25**).
4. Engage the pins of the spanner wrench with the openings in the trim cylinder cap (**Figure 26**). Turn the cap counterclockwise to thread the cap from the cylinder. Tap the spanner wrench with a plastic mallet if necessary to loosen the cap.
5. Slowly pull the hydraulic ram from the trim system. Clamp the pivot pin end of the ram in a vice with soft jaws. Slowly loosen the shock piston bolt (**Figure 27**). Remove the springs, ball seats and balls (**Figure 28**) from the piston.
6. Wipe all fluid from the lower end of the hydraulic ram then heat the shock piston with a heat lamp.

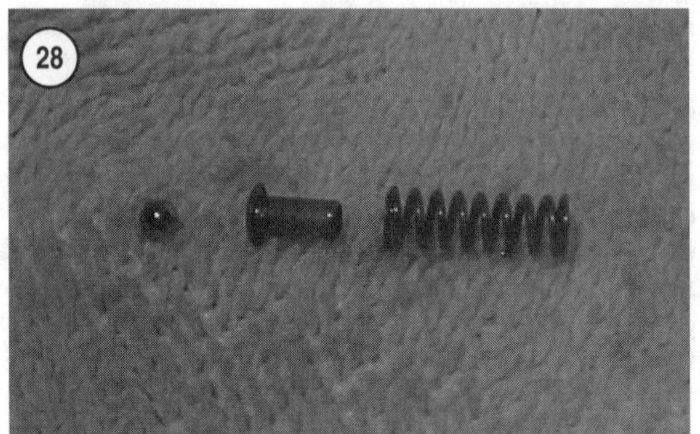

7. Attach the spanner wrench to the opening in the shock piston (**Figure 29**). Rotate the shock piston counterclockwise to remove it from the hydraulic ram. Tap on the spanner wrench with a plastic mallet if required to loosen the piston.

8. Direct the large opening in the cylinder downward into a large bucket half full of shop towels. Using low-pressure compressed air direct air into the manual relief opening (**Figure 30**) to expel the floating piston (**Figure 31**).

9. Remove the large plug (**Figure 32**) from the starboard side of the trim system. Carefully pull the shim spring and poppet valve (**Figure 33**) from the plug opening.

10. Hook a wire into one of the holes in the valve seat and pull the seat (**Figure 34**) and pilot valve from the opening.

11. Remove plug from the lower side of the manifold (**Figure 35**). Push down on the filter tip in the pump opening and pull the ball, filter seat and filter (**Figure 36**) from the manifold.

12. Remove the plug from the rear side of the manifold (**Figure 37**). Pull the spring and poppet valve (**Figure 38**) from the manifold.

13. Remove the plug from the front side of the manifold (**Figure 39**). Pull the spring and poppet valve (**Figure 38**) from the manifold.

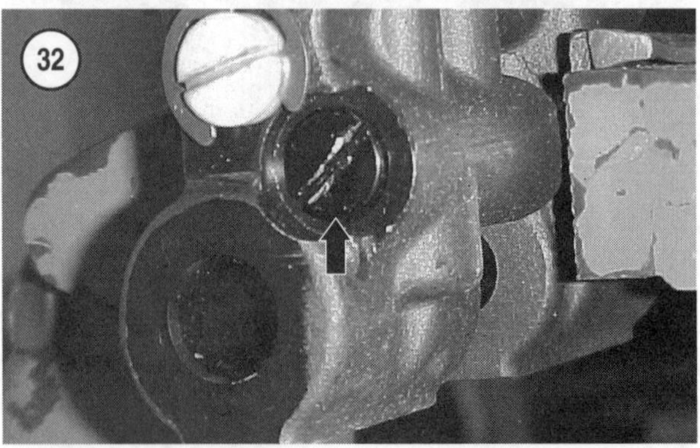

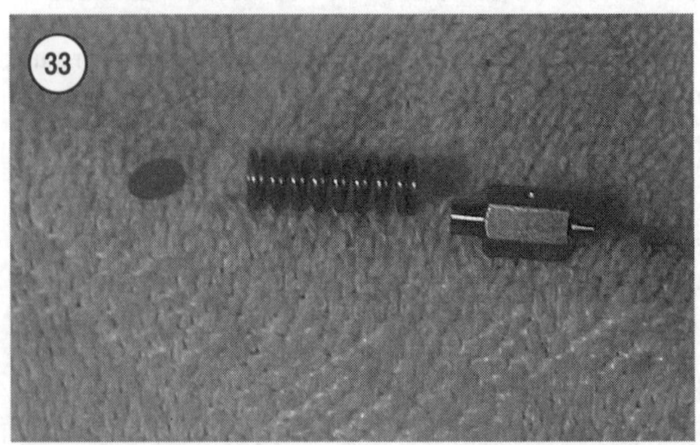

34

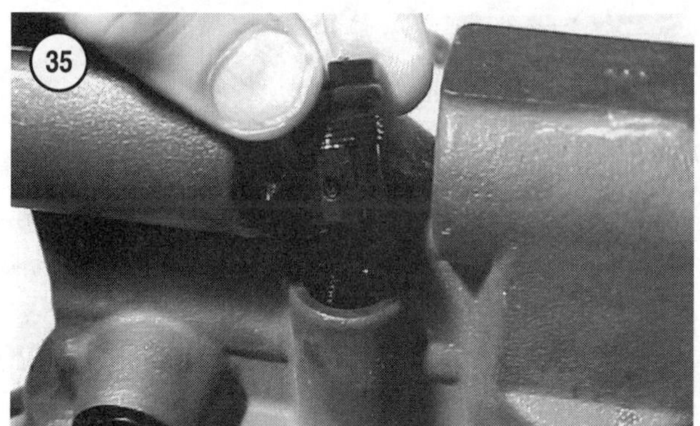

35

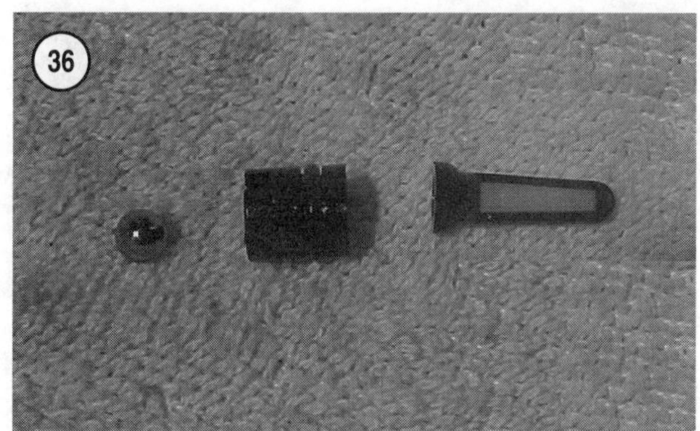

36

37

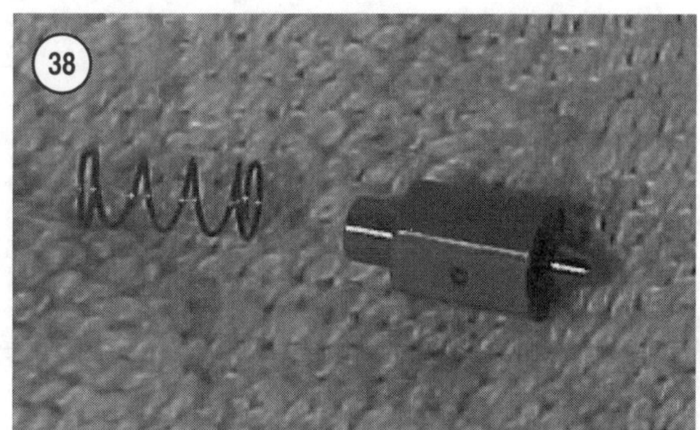

38

39

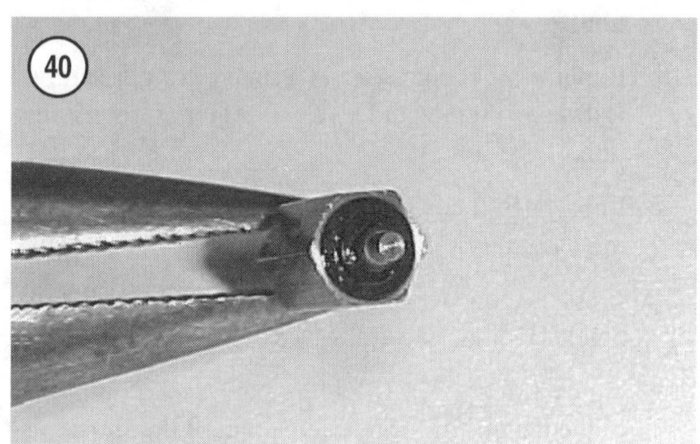

40

14. Inspect the poppet valves for worn or damaged sealing surfaces (**Figure 40**). Replace them if any defects are noted on the sealing surfaces. Pull the wiper (**Figure 41**) from the cylinder cap.

15. Remove the two pump mounting screws (**Figure 42**) and lift the hydraulic pump from the manifold (**Figure 43**). Do not remove the remaining screws or disassemble the hydraulic pump.

16. Lift the O-ring and filter (**Figure 44**) from the manifold. Remove the spring and ball from the pump mounting surface (**Figure 45**) using a suitable pick.

17. Locate the seat in the rear plug opening (**Figure 46**). Insert a small screwdriver or rod through the seat opening (**Figure 47**) and push the shuttle piston and seat (**Figure 48**) out. Push the seat from the rear plug through the front plug opening.

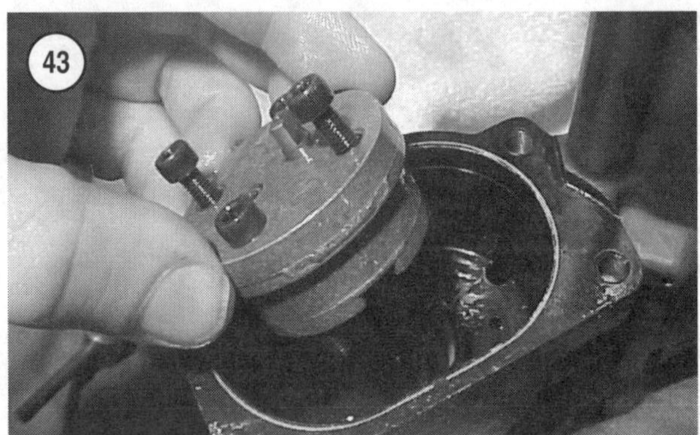

18. Clean all components using clean solvent. Dry the components with compressed air. Direct air through all passages and openings to remove all traces of solvent or debris.

19. Assembly is the reverse of disassembly noting the following:

a. Refer to **Figure 7** to assist with component orientation.

b. Replace all O-rings one at a time during assembly. Lubricate them with Dexron II ATF before installation.

c. Lubricate all components with Dexron II ATF during assembly.

d. Press the new wiper into its bore with the smaller diameter facing outward.

e. Apply Loctite 271 (Mercury part No. 92- 809819) to the threads of the hydraulic ram or the shock piston bolt prior to installing the shock piston.

f. Ensure the open side of the floating piston faces out (**Figure 31**) while pushing it into the cylinder. Push the floating piston to the bottom of the cylinder before installing the hydraulic ram.

g. Fill the hydraulic cylinder 3/4 full of Dexron II ATF prior to installing the hydraulic ram into the cylinder part of the system.

h. Tighten all plugs and fasteners to the specifications in **Table 1**.

20. Install the electric trim motor and trim system following the instructions in this chapter.

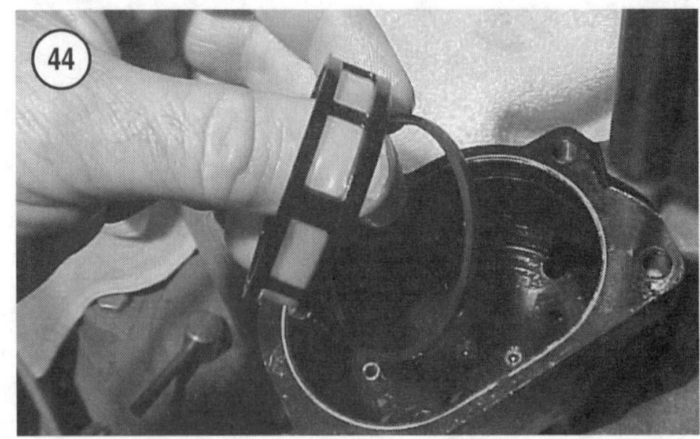

46

47

48

49

50

51

All other models (large trim system)

WARNING

The trim systems contains fluid under high pressure. Always use protective eye wear and gloves when working with the trim system. Never remove any components or plugs without first bleeding the pressure off of the system. Follow the instructions carefully and loosen the manual relief valve to relieve the internal pressure.

1. Remove the trim system and electric trim motor (**Figure 49**) following the instructions in this chapter.
2. Remove the fill plug and pour all trim fluid from the reservoir (**Figure 24**).
3. Clamp the trim system in a vice with soft jaws (**Figure 50**).
4. Remove the rear poppet valve plug (**Figure 51**). Pull the spring and poppet valve (**Figure 52**) from the pump.
5. Remove the front poppet valve plug (**Figure 53**) from the pump. Pull the spring and poppet valve (**Figure 54**) from the opening.

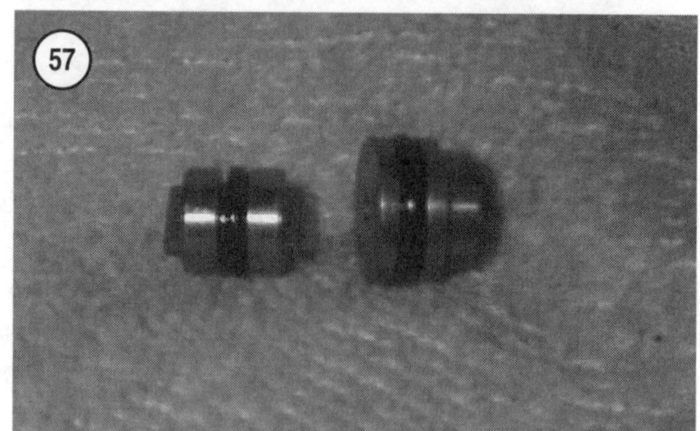

6. Locate the opening in the rear valve seat (**Figure 55**). Insert a small probe or rod through the opening (**Figure 56**) then push the front valve seat and shuttle piston (**Figure 57**) from the pump. Push the rear valve seat from the pump using the shuttle piston bore.

7. Remove both retaining screws (**Figure 58**) from the rear side of the pump. Remove the single screw (**Figure 59**) from the front side, then lift the pump from the manifold (**Figure 60**). Pull the filter (**Figure 61**) from the manifold. Remove the seal and O-ring (**Figure 62**) from the manifold. Remove the ball, then pull the spring (**Figure 63**) from the opening in the reservoir.

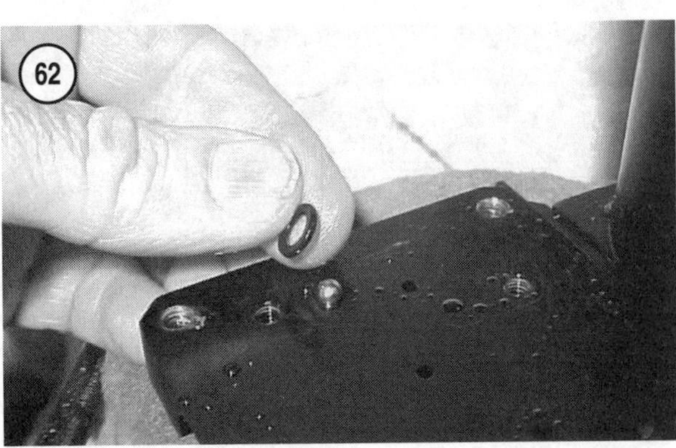

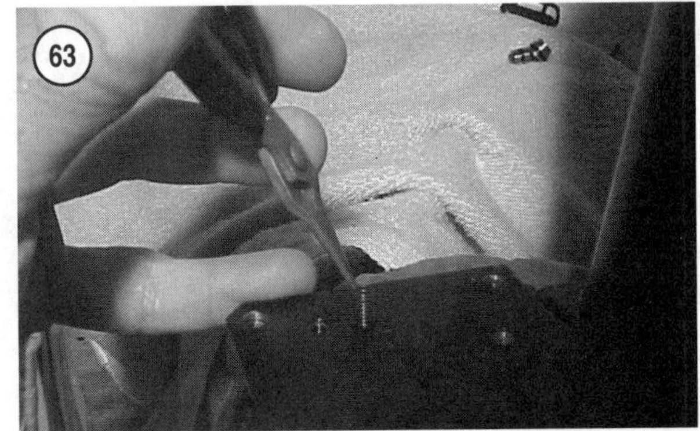

8. Remove both allen bolts (**Figure 64**) from the lower port side of the trim cylinder, then pull the manifold from the cylinder (**Figure 65**).

9. Pull the valve seat and housing (**Figure 66**) from the cylinder. Rest the seat and housing over a slightly open vise, then insert a small rod or probe into the seat opening (**Figure 67**). Push the plunger from the seat and housing (**Figure 68**).

10. Pull the poppet valve from the large opening (**Figure 69**), then pull the spring (**Figure 70**) from the manifold.

66

69

67

70

68

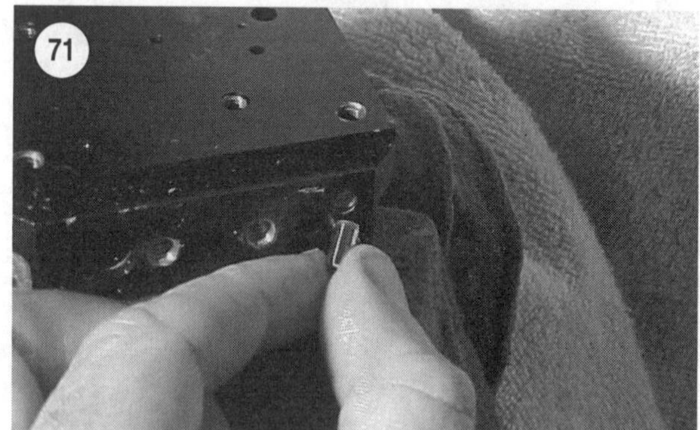

71

Pull both locating pins (**Figure 71**) from the manifold or trim cylinder.

11. Clamp the trim cylinder in a vice with soft jaws. Attach a spanner wrench to the cylinder cap (**Figure 72**). Using the spanner wrench, rotate the cap counterclockwise to remove the cap. Tap the spanner wrench with a plastic mallet if necessary to loosen the cap.
12. Pull the trim ram from the trim cylinder. Direct the large opening of the cylinder into a bucket of shop towels to capture the floating piston. Apply low pressure compressed air to the opening in the cylinder (**Figure 73**) to expel the piston (**Figure 74**).

72

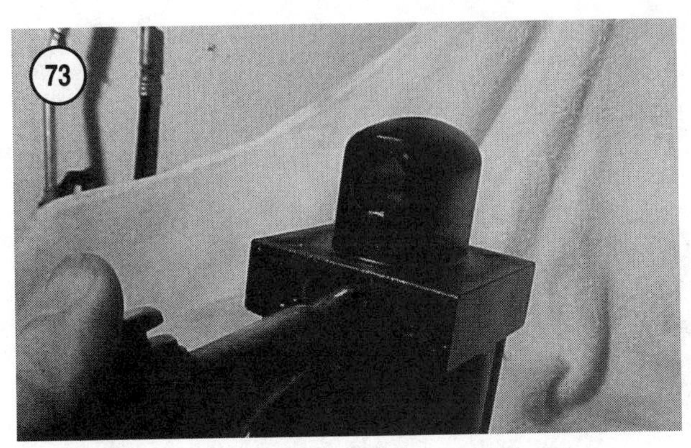

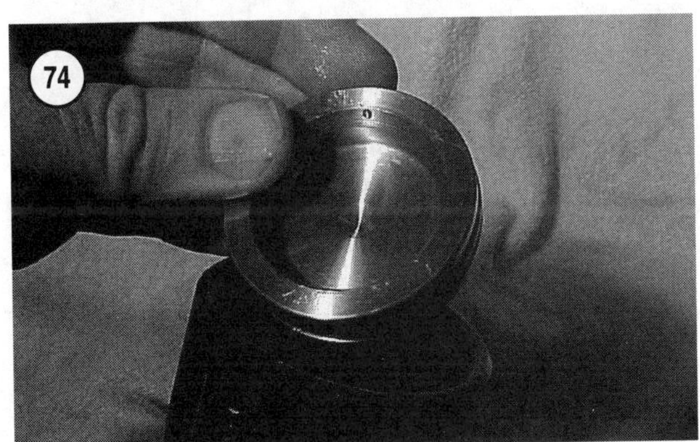

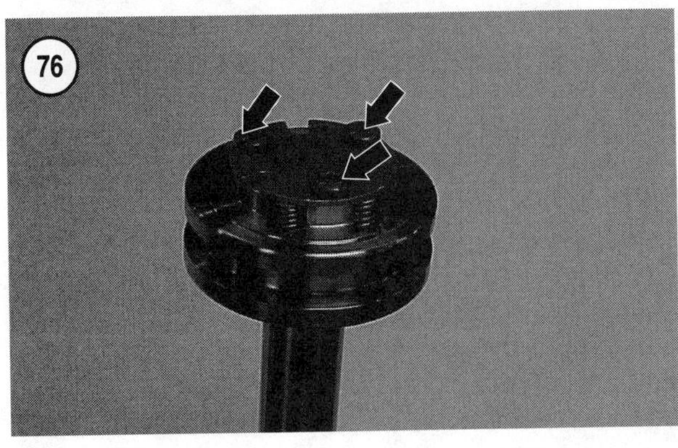

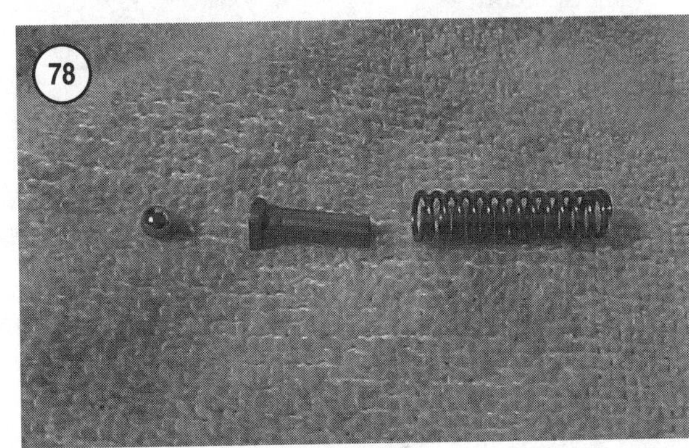

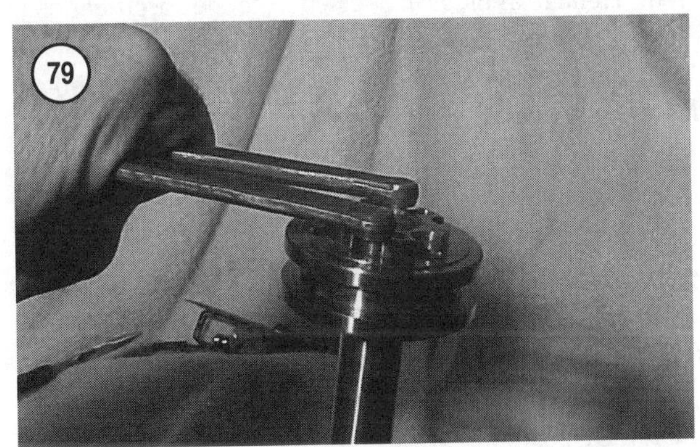

13. Clamp the pivot pin end of the hydraulic ram into a vise with soft jaws (**Figure 75**). Remove the screws (**Figure 76**) retaining the shock valves to the shock piston. Lift the plate from the springs (**Figure 77**). Pull the five springs, valve seats and balls (**Figure 78**) from the shock piston.

14. Wipe all hydraulic fluid from the shock piston. Using a heat lamp, apply heat to the shock piston portion of the hydraulic ram. Attach a spanner wrench to the shock valve (**Figure 79**). Rotate the shock piston counterclockwise to remove it from the ram. Slide the cylinder cap from the ram.

15. Clean all components using clean solvent. Dry the components with compressed air. Direct air through all passages and openings to remove all traces of solvent or debris.

16. Assembly is the reverse of disassembly noting the following:

a. Refer to **Figure 8** to assist with component orientation.
b. Replace all O-rings one at a time during assembly. Lubricate them with Dexron II ATF before installation.
c. Lubricate all components with Dexron II ATF during assembly.
d. Press the new wiper into its bore with the smaller diameter facing outward.
e. Apply Loctite 271 (Mercury part No. 92- 809819) to the threads of the hydraulic ram prior to installing the shock piston.
f. Ensure the open side of the floating piston faces out (**Figure 80**) while pushing it into the cylinder. Push the floating piston to the bottom of the cylinder before installing the hydraulic ram.
g. Fill the hydraulic cylinder 3/4 full of Dexron II ATF prior to installing the hydraulic ram into the cylinder part of the system.
h. Tighten all plugs and fasteners to the specifications in **Table 1**.

17. Install the electric trim motor and trim system following the instructions in this chapter.

FLUID FILLING

Refer to **Figure 7** or **Figure 8** to assist with component identification and orientation. Use Dexron II automatic transmission fluid in both types of trim systems.

1. Open the manual relief valve and position the engine in the full UP position. Engage the tilt lock lever and support the engine with blocks or overhead cable. Close the manual relief valve.
2. Clean the area around the fluid fill plug. Remove the plug and inspect the O-ring on the plug. Replace the O-ring if damaged or flattened.
3. Fill the unit to the lower edge of the threaded fill/check plug opening. Install the fill/check plug and tighten it securely. Remove the supports and disengage the tilt lock lever.
4. Cycle the trim to the full up, then full down positions several times. Stop operating the pump immediately if ventilation of the pump is heard. Ventilation causes a change in the tone of the system as the unit operates.

80

5. Repeat Steps 1-4 if ventilation is detected. Continue until the unit operates to the full up position without ventilation
6. Allow the unit to set in the full up position for several minutes then check the fluid level. Add fluid if required. Securely tighten the fluid fill plug.

AIR BLEEDING

A spongy feel or inability to hold trim under load is a common symptom when air is present in the system. If air is present the engine may tuck under when power is applied and tilt out when the throttle is reduced. Minor amounts of air in the system purge into the reservoir during normal operation. When major components have been removed, a significant amount of air can enter the system. Most air is purged during the fluid filling process. Bleeding the air takes considerably longer if the pump ventilates.

Allow the engine to set for 30 minutes or longer if air remains in the system after filling with fluid. Place the engine in the full tilt position using the manual relief valve. Correct the fluid level then cycle the trim to the full UP and DOWN positions. Again correct the fluid level after sitting 30 minutes.

MIDSECTION

Repairs to the midsection typically involve replacing worn motor mounts, corrosion damaged components or components damaged as the result of impact with underwater objects.

Minor repair to the midsection involve the replacement of easily accessible components such as the lower motor mounts, tilt pin or tilt lock mechanism.

Removal or replacement of major midsection components requires power head and gearcase removal. Power head removal and installation instructions are provided in

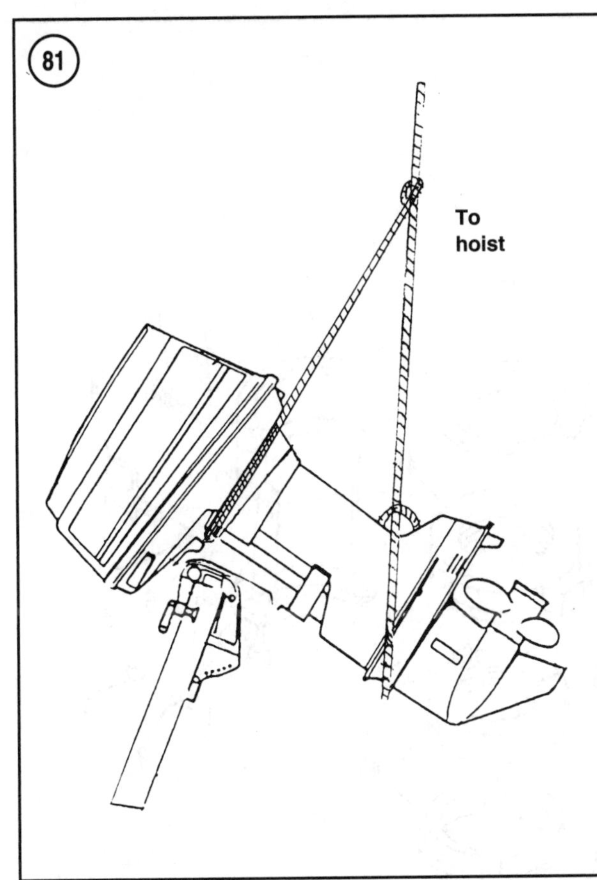

Chapter Eight. Gearcase removal and installation instructions are provided in Chapter Nine.

Tighten all fasteners to the specifications in **Table 2**. **Table 2** is located at the end of this chapter.

WARNING
Never work under any part of the engine without providing suitable support. The tilt lock or hydraulic system may collapse and allow the engine to drop. Support the engine with wooden blocks or an overhead cable before working under the engine.

Clamp Bracket Disassembly and Assembly

Provide overhead support (**Figure 81**) before removing any midsection component. Apply 2-4-C Marine Lubricant (Mercury part No. 92-850736A1) to all pivot points, bushings and sliding surfaces except the steering friction components during assembly. Note the mounting location and orientation of all components prior to removing them from the midsection. To assist with component identification and orientation refer to **Figures 82-87** as necessary.

1. Position the engine in the full tilt position. Support the engine with and overhead cable (**Figure 81**) to prevent the engine from falling as components are removed.
2. Disconnect both cables from the battery if so equipped.
3. Refer to **Figures 82-87** to locate the worn or damaged components. Identify which components must be removed to access the components. Remove the trim or manual hydraulic tilt system following the instructions provided in this chapter prior to removing the clamp bracket or other major components.
4. Note the location and orientation of all fasteners and components prior to removing them. Disassemble the midsection until the selected components are free from the midsection.
5. Clean all corrosion or contaminants from all components. Inspect them for excessive wear or corrosion. Replace all damaged or worn components. Free play or looseness at a pivot point usually indicates significant wear.
6. Refer to **Figures 82-87** during assembly to assist with component orientation.
7. Apply a marine sealant to the engine mounting bolts, washers and transom holes prior to installing them.
8. Tighten all fasteners to the specification in **Table 2**. Install the trim system or manual hydraulic tilt system following the instructions in this chapter.
9. Remove the overhead support (**Figure 81**) and lower the engine. Check for proper operation of the tilt lock, manual tilt or trim system. Binding during tilt or steering movement usually indicates incorrectly installed components or over tightened fasteners. Correct the cause of binding before operating the engine.
10. On models with an adjustable steering friction mechanism, adjust the mechanism as described in Chapter Five.

Drive Shaft Housing Disasembly and Assembly

Provide overhead support (**Figure 81**) before removing any midsection component. Apply 2-4-C Marine Lubricant (Mercury part No. 92-850736A1) to all pivot points, bushings and sliding surfaces during assembly. Note the location and orientation of all components prior to removing them. To assist with component identification and orientation refer to **Figures 88-92**.

1. Remove the gearcase following the instructions in Chapter Nine. Remove the power head following the instructions in Chapter Eight.
2. Remove the mounting screws and pull lower engine cover from the drive shaft housing or power head adapter.
3. Refer to the clamp bracket illustrations (**Figure 82-87**) and the drive shaft housing illustrations (**Figure 88-92**)

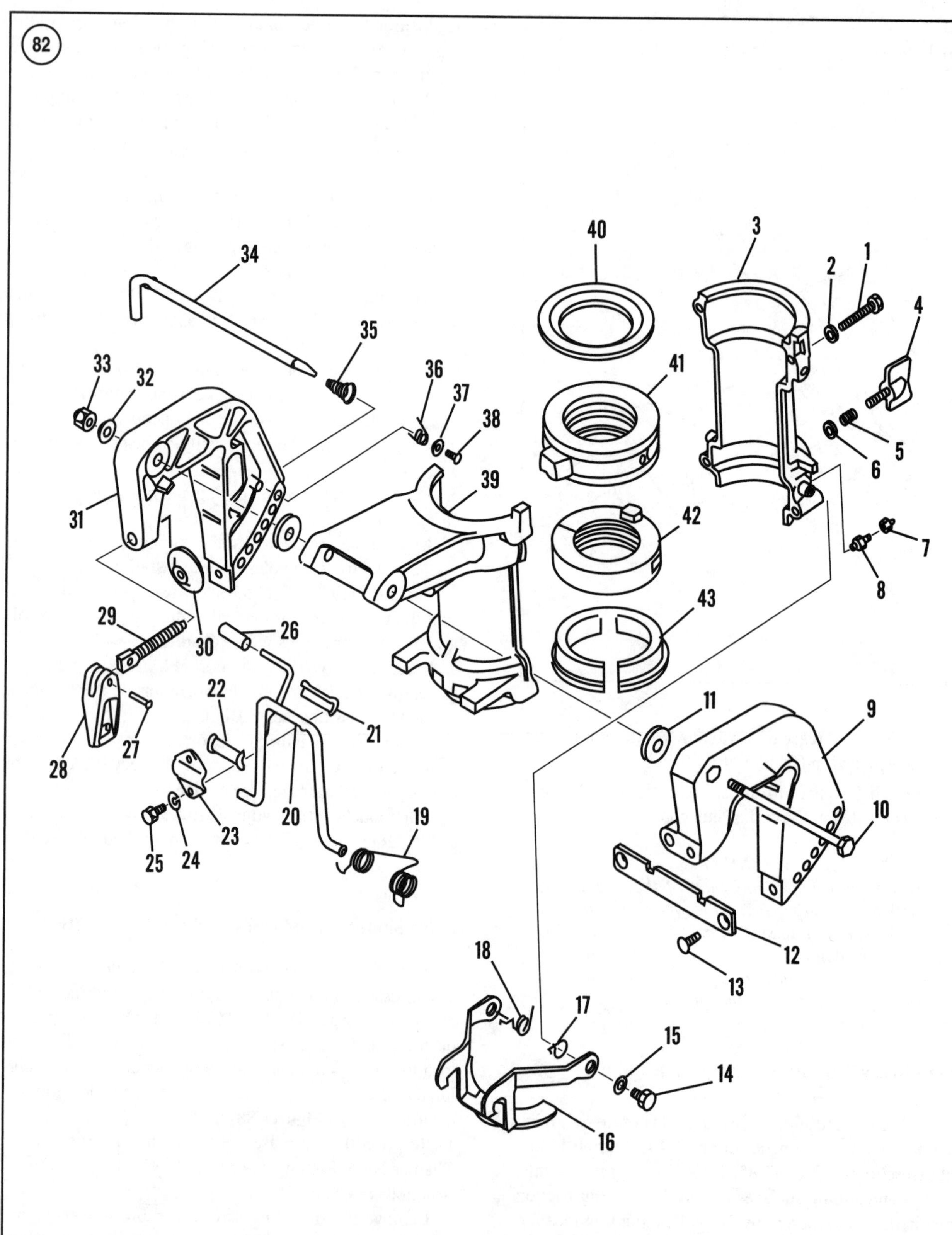
82
1
2
3
4
5
6
7
8
9
10
11
12
13
14
15
16
17
18
19
20
21
22
23
24
25
26
27
28
29
30
31
32
33
34
35
36
37
38
39
40
41
42
43

CLAMP BRACKET (4-6 HP MODELS)

1. Bolt
2. Washer
3. Rear swivel bracket
4. Steering friction screw
5. Spring
6. Washer
7. Cap
8. Grease fitting
9. Port clamp bracket
10. Bolt
11. Washer
12. Plate
13. Screw
14. Bolt
15. Washer
16. Reverse hold down hook
17. Spring
18. Spring
19. Spring
20. Tilt lock lever
21. Sleeve
22. Sleeve
23. Plate
24. Washer
25. Bolt
26. Grip
27. Pin
28. Lever
29. Bolt
30. Pad
31. Starboard clamp bracket
32. Washer
33. Nut
34. Tilt pin
35. Spring
36. Spring
37. Washer
38. Screw
39. Front swivel plate
40. Plate
41. Upper bushing
42. Lower bushing
43. Thrust plates

during component removal and installation. Identify the components required to access the components. Remove the trim or manual hydraulic tilt system following the instructions in this chapter prior to removing the clamp bracket or other major components.

4. Note the location and orientation for all fasteners and components prior to removing them. Disassemble the clamp bracket and mid-section until the components are free from the midsection.

5. Clean all corrosion or contaminants from all components. Inspect them for excessive wear or damage. Replace all damaged or worn components. Free play or looseness at a pivot point usually indicates significant wear. Clean all oil from the oil pan upon removal. Remove all oil pickup tubes, screens and pressure relief valve from the power head adapter. Clean debris from oil screens using a clean solvent. Inspect all gasket mating surfaces for deep scratches or pitting. Replace suspect components to prevent oil, water or exhaust leakage. To help prevent oil or water leakage, replace all O-rings during assembly.

6. Refer to **Figures 82-92** during assembly to assist with component orientation.

7. Apply Loctite Pipe Sealant (Mercury part No. 92-809822) to the threads of hose fittings prior to installing them. Apply a marine sealant to the engine mounting bolts, washers and transom holes prior to installing them. Install new gaskets to the oil pan or adapter plate mating surfaces upon assembly.

8. Tighten all fasteners to the specification in **Table 2**. Install the trim system or manual hydraulic tilt system following the instructions in this chapter.

9. Install the power head following the instructions in Chapter Eight. Install the gearcase following the instructions in Chapter Nine.

10. Remove the overhead support (**Figure 81**) then lower the engine. Check for proper operation of the tilt lock, manual tilt or trim system. Binding during tilt or steering movement usually indicates incorrectly installed components or over tightened fasteners. Correct binding before operating the engine.

11. Check for water or oil leakage after starting the engine. Correct all oil and water leaks prior to operating the engine.

Tiller Control Disassembly and Assembly

1. Disconnect both cables from the battery if so equipped.

2. Note the wire routing and connections and disconnect the stop button or stop switch wires.

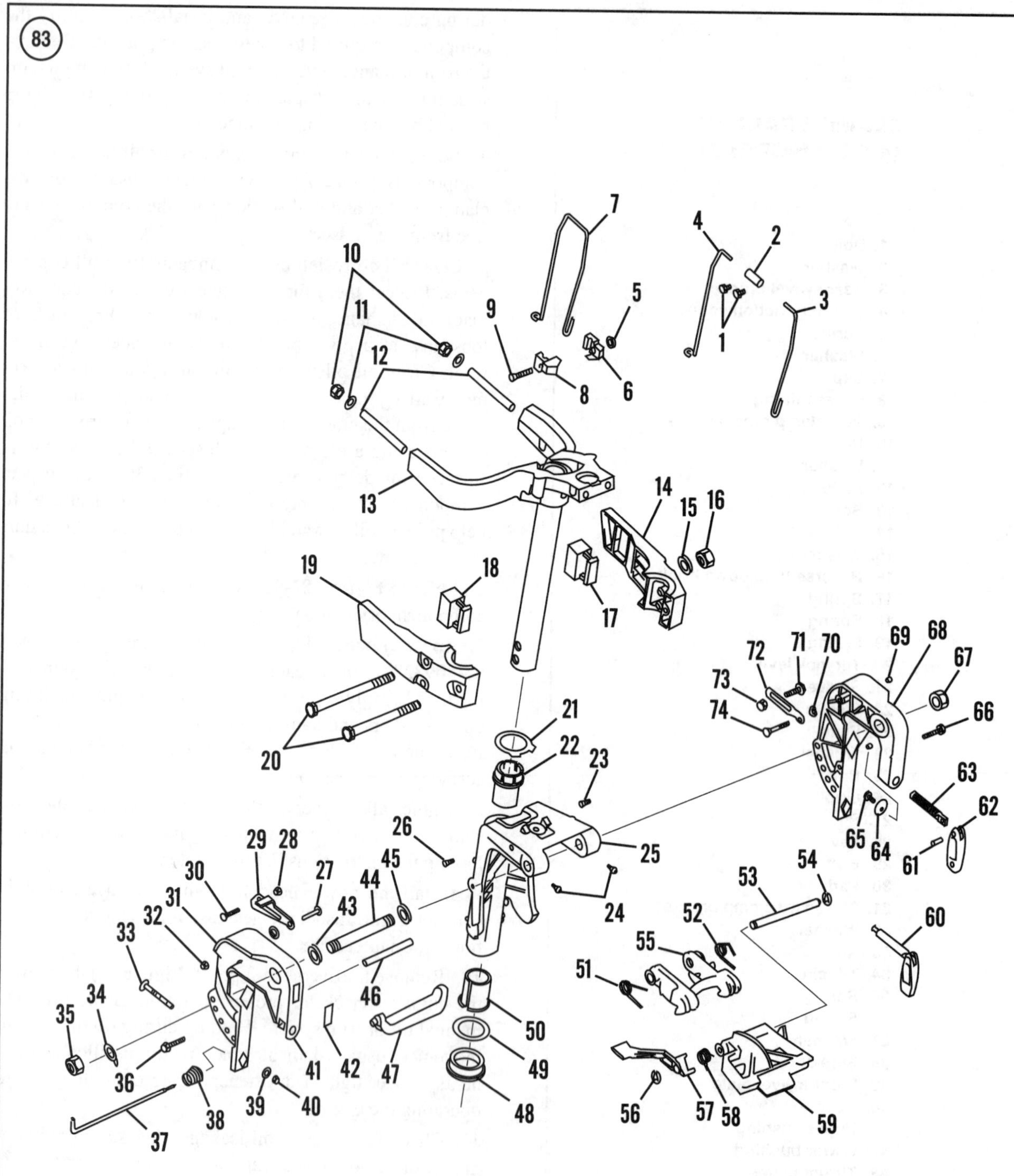
83
1
2
3
4
5
6
7
8
9
10
11
12
13
14
15
16
17
18
19
20
21
22
23
24
25
26
27
28
29
30
31
32
33
34
35
36
37
38
39
40
41
42
43
44
45
46
47
48
49
50
51
52
53
54
55
56
57
58
59
60
61
62
63
64
65
66
67
68
69
70
71
72
73
74

CLAMP BRACKET (9.9 HP [SERIAL NO. OH000057-PRIOR] AND 15 HP MODELS)

1. Screws
2. Retainer
3. Linkage
4. Linkage
5. Nut
6. Clamp
7. Reverse hold down hook
8. Clamp
9. Screw
10. Nuts
11. Washers
12. Sleeves
13. Swivel tube
14. Cover
15. Washer
16. Nut
17. Engine mount
18. Engine mount
19. Cover
20. Bolts
21. Tab washer
22. Sleeve
23. Grease fitting
24. Grease fitting
25. Swivel bracket
26. Grease fitting
27. Screw
28. Nut
29. Tilt lever
30. Screw
31. Starboard clamp bracket
32. Nut
33. Engine mount bolt
34. Clip
35. Nut
36. Screw
37. Tilt pin
38. Spring
39. Washer
40. Nut
41. Clamp screw hole
42. Decal
43. Washer
44. Tilt pin
45. Washer
46. Pin
47. Carry handle
48. Plate
49. O-ring
50. Bushing
51. Spring
52. Spring
53. Pin
54. E-clip
55. Reverse hold down hook
56. E-clip
57. Tilt lever
58. Spring
59. Tilt bracket
60. Thumb screw
61. Pin
62. Lever
63. Screw
64. Pad
65. Screw
66. Bolt
67. Nut
68. Port clamp bracket
69. Grease fitting
70. Wave washer
71. Screw
72. Strap
73. Nut
74. Screw

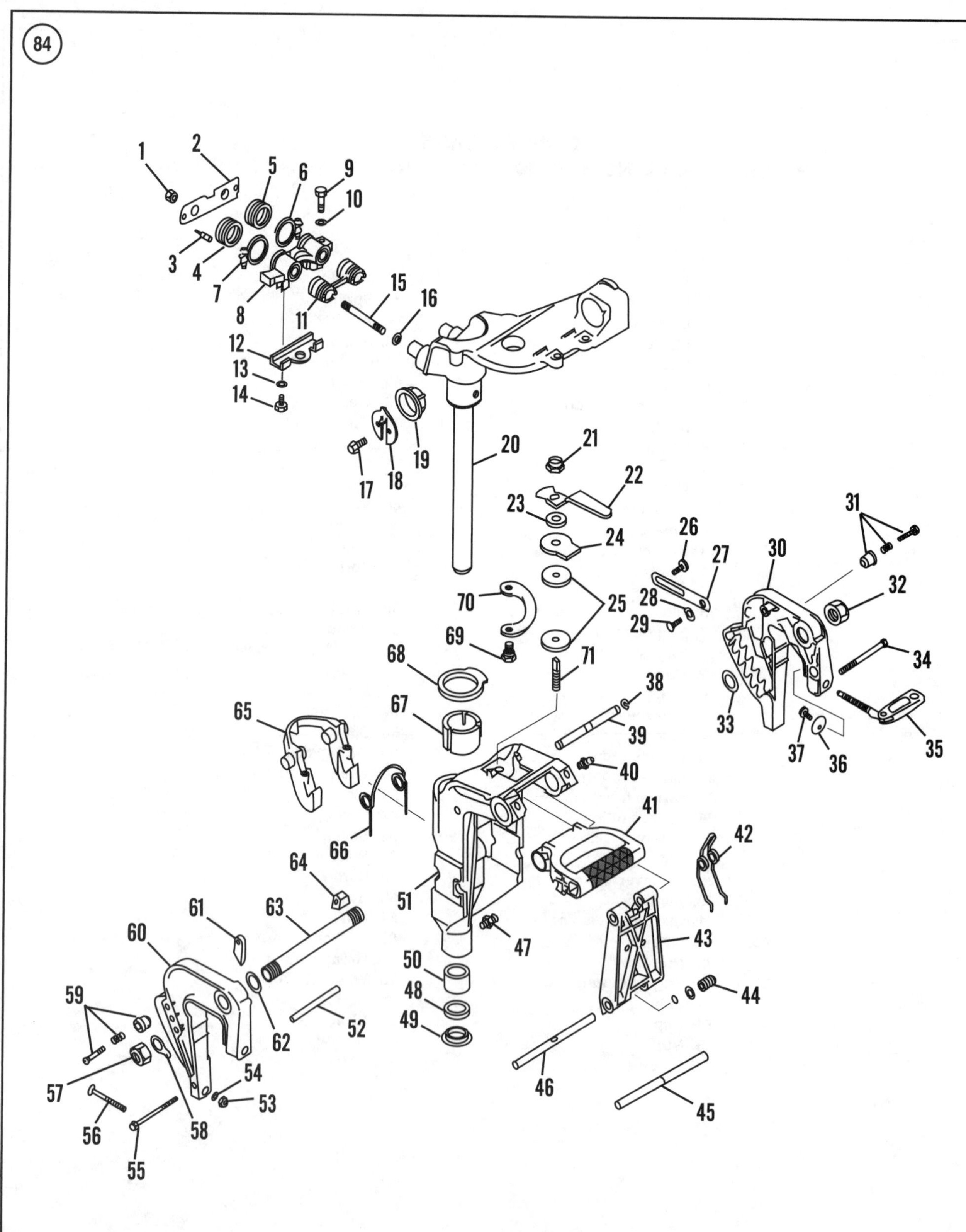
84
1
2
3
4
5
6
7
8
9
10
11
12
13
14
15
16
17
18
19
20
21
22
23
24
25
26
27
28
29
30
31
32
33
34
35
36
37
38
39
40
41
42
43
44
45
46
47
48
49
50
51
52
53
54
55
56
57
58
59
60
61
62
63
64
65
66
67
68
69
70
71

CLAMP BRACKET (9.9 HP MODELS, SERIAL NO. OH000058-ON)

1. Nut
2. Plate
3. Bumper
4. Seal
5. Seal
6. Clamp
7. Clamp
8. Upper mount
9. Bolt
10. Washer
11. Seal
12. Plate
13. Washer
14. Screw
15. Stud
16. Washer
17. Tiller control bolt
18. Plate
19. Bushing
20. Swivel tube
21. Nut
22. Steering friction lever
23. Washer
24. Friction plate
25. Friction washer
26. Screw
27. Tilt stop plate
28. Washer
29. Screw
30. Port clamp bracket
31. Tilt return lever
32. Nut
33. Washer
34. Bolt
35. Thumb screw
36. Pad
37. Screw
38. E-clip
39. Pin
40. Grease fitting
41. Handle
42. Spring
43. Tilt bracket
44. Spring and washer
45. Pin
46. Pin
47. Grease fitting
48. Seal
49. Thrust washer
50. Bushing
51. Swivel bracket
52. Pin
53. Nut
54. Washer
55. Bolt
56. Engine mount bolt
57. Nut
58. Clip
59. Tilt return
60. Starboard clamp bracket
61. Lever
62. Washer
63. Tilt tube
64. Lever
65. Reverse hold down hook
66. Spring
67. Bushing
68. Plate
69. Screw
70. Plate
71. Friction screw

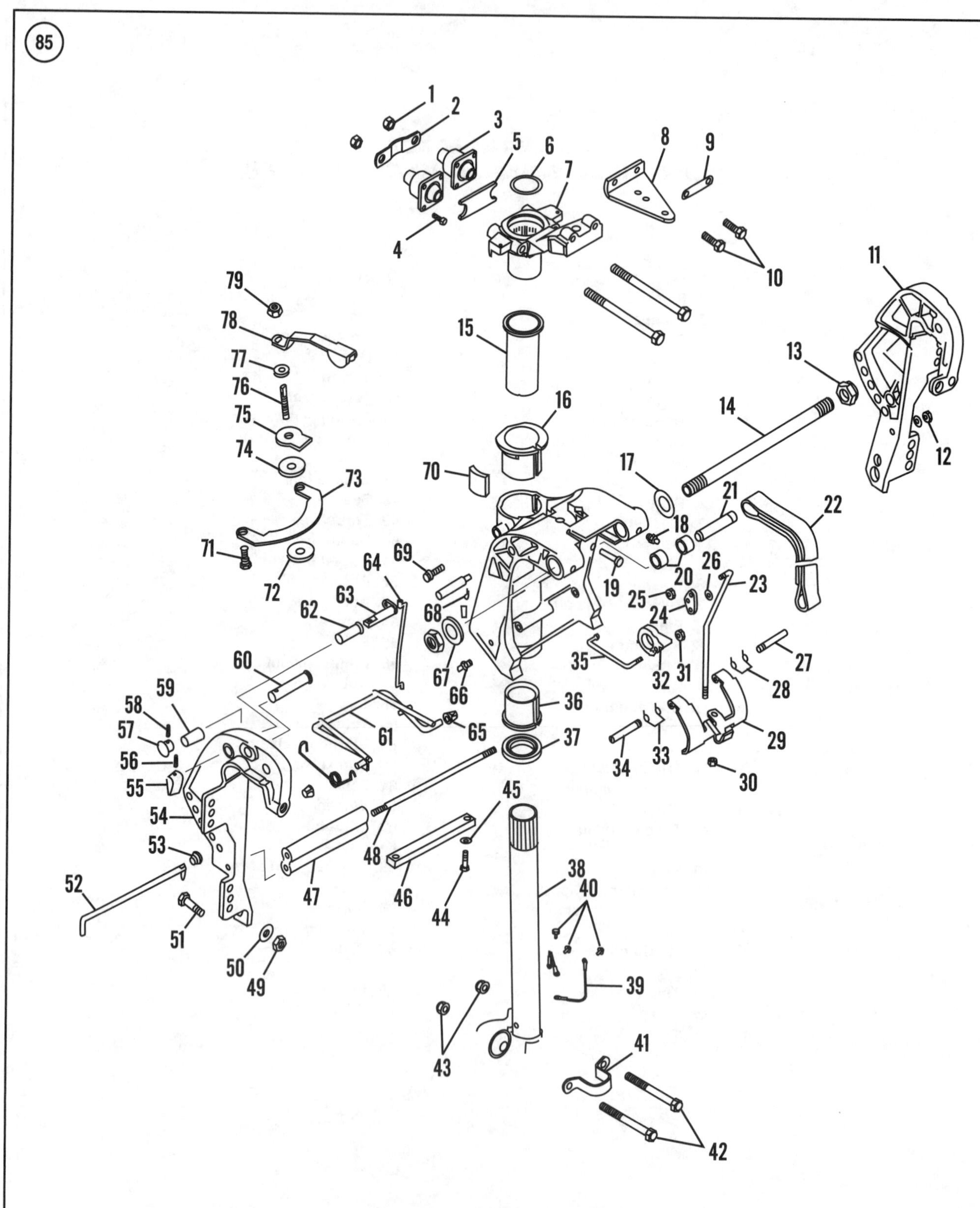
85
1
2
3
4
5
6
7
8
9
10
11
12
13
14
15
16
17
18
19
20
21
22
23
24
25
26
27
28
29
30
31
32
33
34
35
36
37
38
39
40
41
42
43
44
45
46
47
48
49
50
51
52
53
54
55
56
57
58
59
60
61
62
63
64
65
66
67
68
69
70
71
72
73
74
75
76
77
78
79

CLAMP BRACKET (25 HP MODELS)

1. Nut
2. Plate
3. Upper mounts
4. Screw
5. Plate
6. Retaining ring
7. Swivel head
8. Remote steering bracket
9. Locking plate
10. Bolts
11. Port clamp bracket
12. Nut and washer
13. Nut
14. Tilt tube
15. Sleeve
16. Bushing
17. Washer
18. Grease fitting
19. Pin
20. Bushings
21. Pin
22. Strap
23. Reverse hold down linkage
24. Bracket
25. Nut
26. Washer
27. Pin
28. Spring
29. Reverse hold down hook
30. Nut
31. Nut
32. Lever
33. Spring
34. Pin
35. Linkage
36. Bushing
37. Seal
38. Swivel tube
39. Grounding wires
40. Screws
41. Retainer
42. Mount bolts
43. Nuts
44. Bolt
45. Washer
46. Anode
47. Spacer
48. Stud
49. Nut
50. Washer
51. Mounting bolt
52. Tilt pin
53. Spring
54. Starboard clamp bracket
55. Lever
56. Roll pin
57. Grip
58. Roll pin
59. Bushing
60. Tilt lock pin
61. Tilt bracket
62. Bushing
63. Lever
64. Linkage
65. Bushing
66. Grease fitting
67. Washer
68. Locking clip
69. Bolt
70. Friction pad
71. Bolt
72. Washer
73. Plate
74. Washer
75. Friction washer
76. Friction bolt
77. Washer
78. Steering friction lever
79. Nut

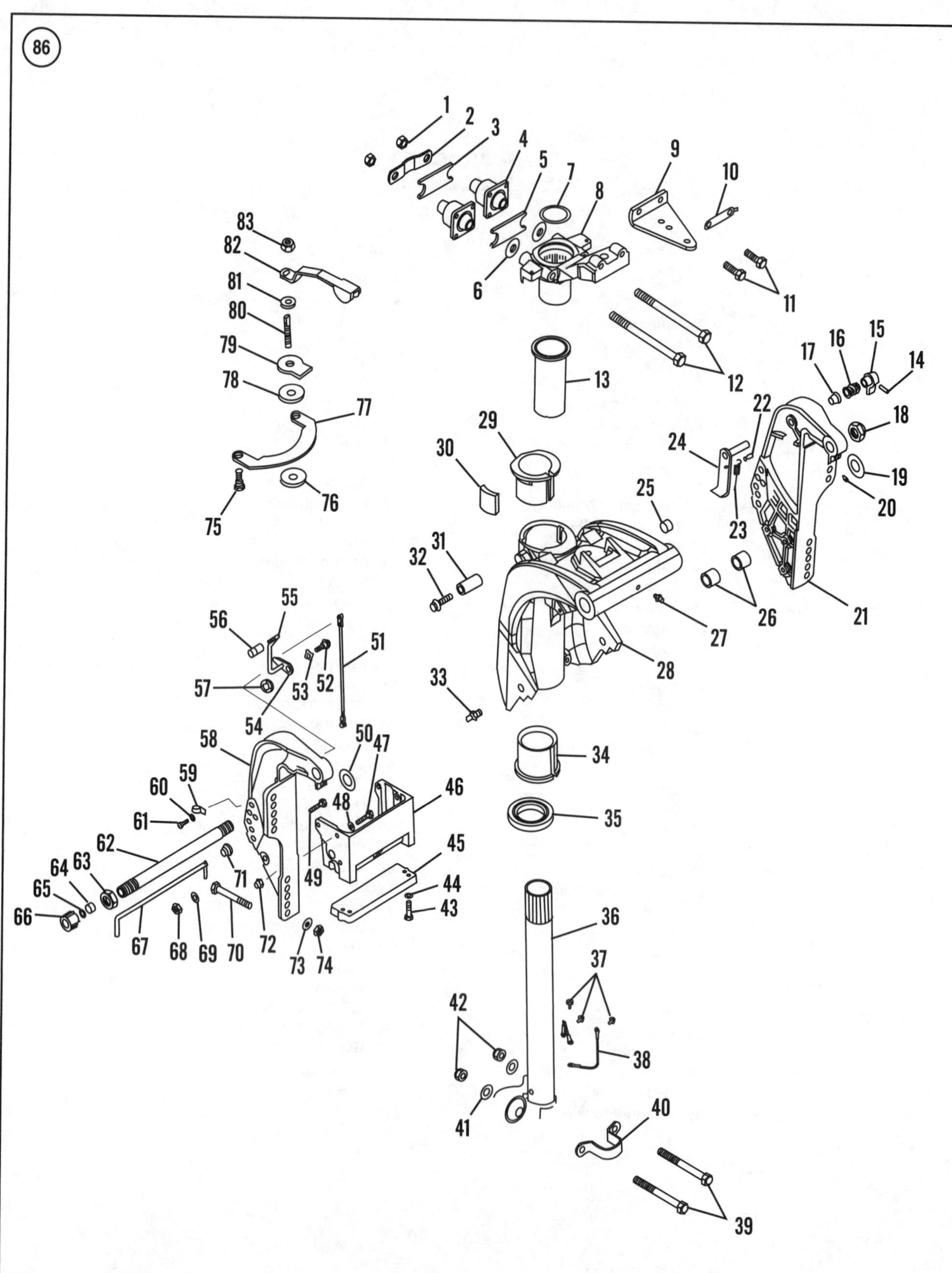
86
1
2
3
4
5
6
7
8
9
10
11
12
13
14
15
16
17
18
19
20
21
22
23
24
25
26
27
28
29
30
31
32
33
34
35
36
37
38
39
40
41
42
43
44
45
46
47
48
49
50
51
52
53
54
55
56
57
58
59
60
61
62
63
64
65
66
67
68
69
70
71
72
73
74
75
76
77
78
79
80
81
82
83

CLAMP BRACKET (30-50 HP MODELS)

1. Nut
2. Strap
3. Bumper
4. Upper mounts
5. Bumper
6. Washer
7. Retaining ring
8. Swivel head
9. Remote steering bracket
10. Locking plate
11. Bolts
12. Mount bolts
13. Sleeve
14. Roll pin
15. Lever
16. Spring
17. Bushing
18. Nut
19. Washer
20. Grease fitting
21. Port clamp bracket
22. Pin
23. Spring
24. Tilt lock
25. Bushing
26. Bushings
27. Grease fitting
28. Swivel bracket
29. Bushing
30. Friction pad
31. Seal
32. Screw
33. Grease fitting
34. Bushing
35. Seal
36. Swivel shaft
37. Screws
38. Grounding wires
39. Lower mount bolts
40. Strap
41. Washer
42. Nut
43. Bolt
44. Washer
45. Anode
46. Clamp bracket support
47. Bolt
48. Washer
49. Screw
50. Washer
51. Manual tilt linkage
52. Pivot bolt
53. Wave washer
54. Tilt lever
55. Tilt linkage
56. Grip
57. Bushing
58. Starboard clamp bracket
59. Clamp
60. Washer
61. Screw
62. Tilt tube
63. Nut
64. Spacer
65. O-ring
66. Cable seal
67. Tilt pin
68. Nut
69. Washer
70. Mounting bolt
71. Spring
72. Nut
73. Washer
74. Nut
75. Bolt
76. Washer
77. Plate
78. Washer
79. Friction washer
80. Bolt
81. Washer
82. Steering friction lever
83. Nut

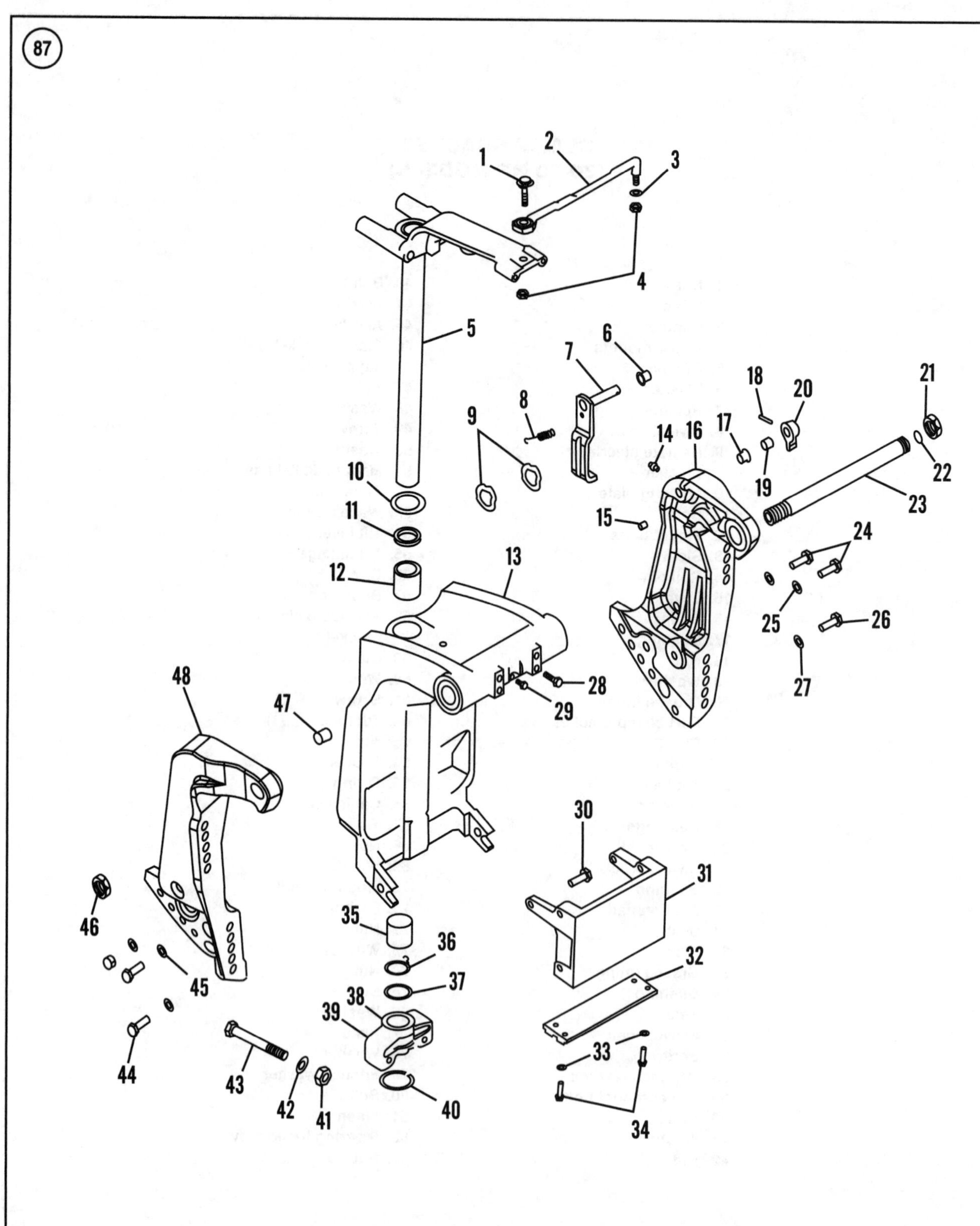
87
1
2
3
4
5
6
7
8
9
10
11
12
13
14
15
16
17
18
19
20
21
22
23
24
25
26
27
28
29
30
31
32
33
34
35
36
37
38
39
40
41
42
43
44
45
46
47
48

CLAMP BRACKET (75 AND 90 HP MODELS)

1. Steering linkage bolt
2. Steering link
3. Washer
4. Nut
5. Swivel tube
6. Bushing
7. Tilt lock lever
8. Spring
9. Wave washer
10. Washer
11. Seal
12. Bushing
13. Swivel bracket
14. Grease fitting
15. Pin
16. Port clamp bracket
17. Bushing
18. Roll pin
19. Spring
20. Lever
21. Nut
22. O-ring
23. Tilt tube
24. Bolts
25. Washers
26. Bolt
27. Washer
28. Bolt
29. Grease fitting
30. Bolt
31. Clamp bracket support
32. Anode
33. Washer
34. Bolt
35. Bushing
36. O-ring
37. Spacer
38. Lower mount bracket
39. Mount bolt hole
40. Retaining clip
41. Nut
42. Washer
43. Mount bolt
44. Bolt
45. Washer
46. Nut
47. Bushing
48. Starboard clamp bracket

88

DRIVE SHAFT HOUSING (4-6 HP MODELS)

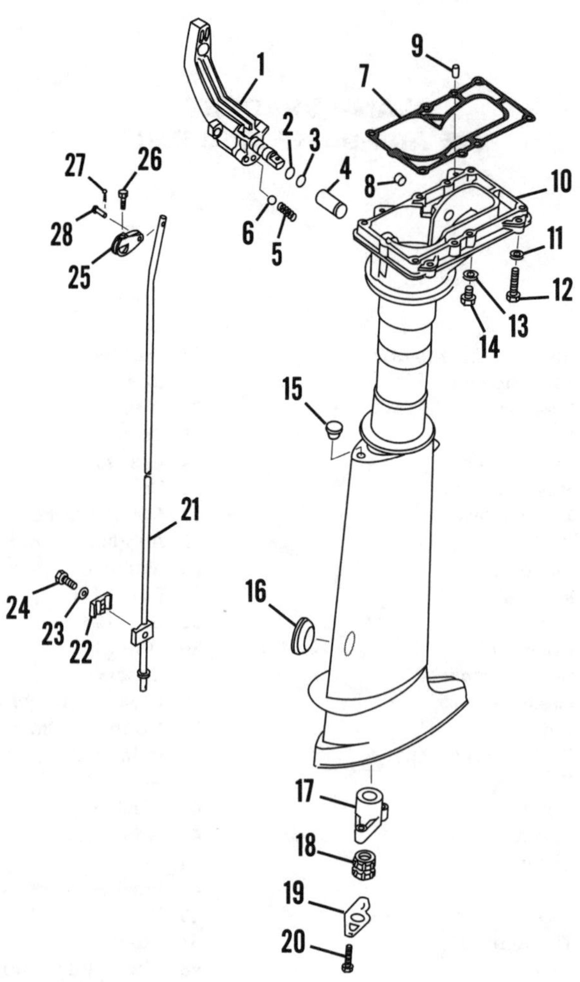

1. Shift selector
2. O-ring
3. O-ring
4. Bushing
5. Spring
6. Detent ball
7. Power head gasket
8. Plug
9. Locating pin
10. Drive shaft housing
11. Washer
12. Bolt
13. Gasket
14. Plug
15. Grommet
16. Grommet
17. Mount
18. Bushing
19. Retainer
20. Bolt
21. Shift shaft
22. Clamp
23. Washer
24. Bolt
25. Lever
26. Screw
27. Locking pin
28. Pin

DRIVE SHAFT HOUSING
(9.9 HP [SERIAL NO. OH000057-PRIOR] AND 15 HP MODELS)

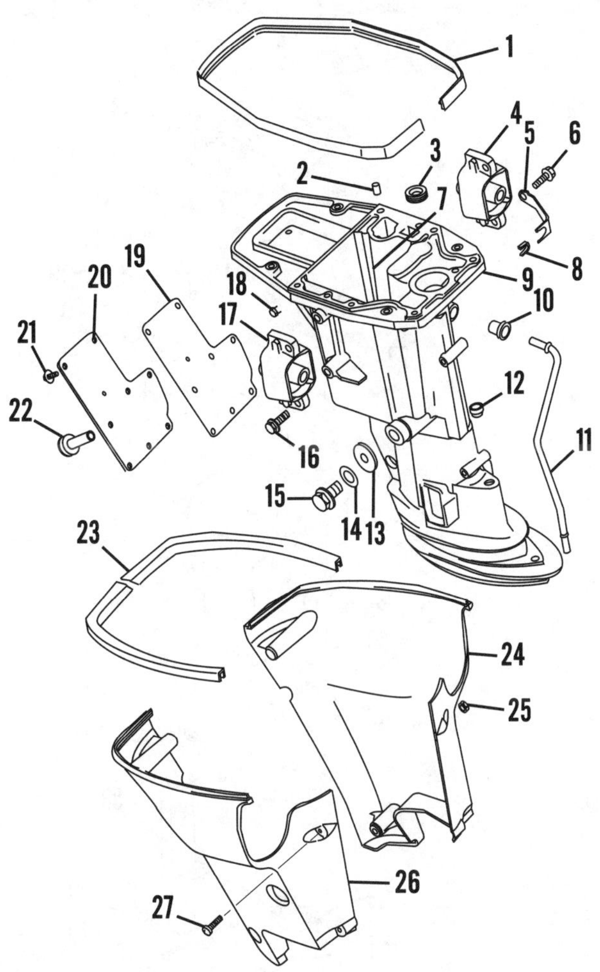

1. Seal
2. Locating pin
3. Seal
4. Upper engine mount
5. Retainer
6. Bolt
7. Oil pan
8. Sleeve
9. Drive shaft housing
10. Grommet
11. Water tube
12. Grommet
13. Sealing washer
14. Washer
15. Oil drain plug
16. Mount bolt
17. Upper mount
18. Plug
19. Gasket
20. Cover
21. Screw
22. Grommet
23. Seal
24. Port drive shaft cover
25. Nut
26. Starboard drive shaft cover
27. Screw

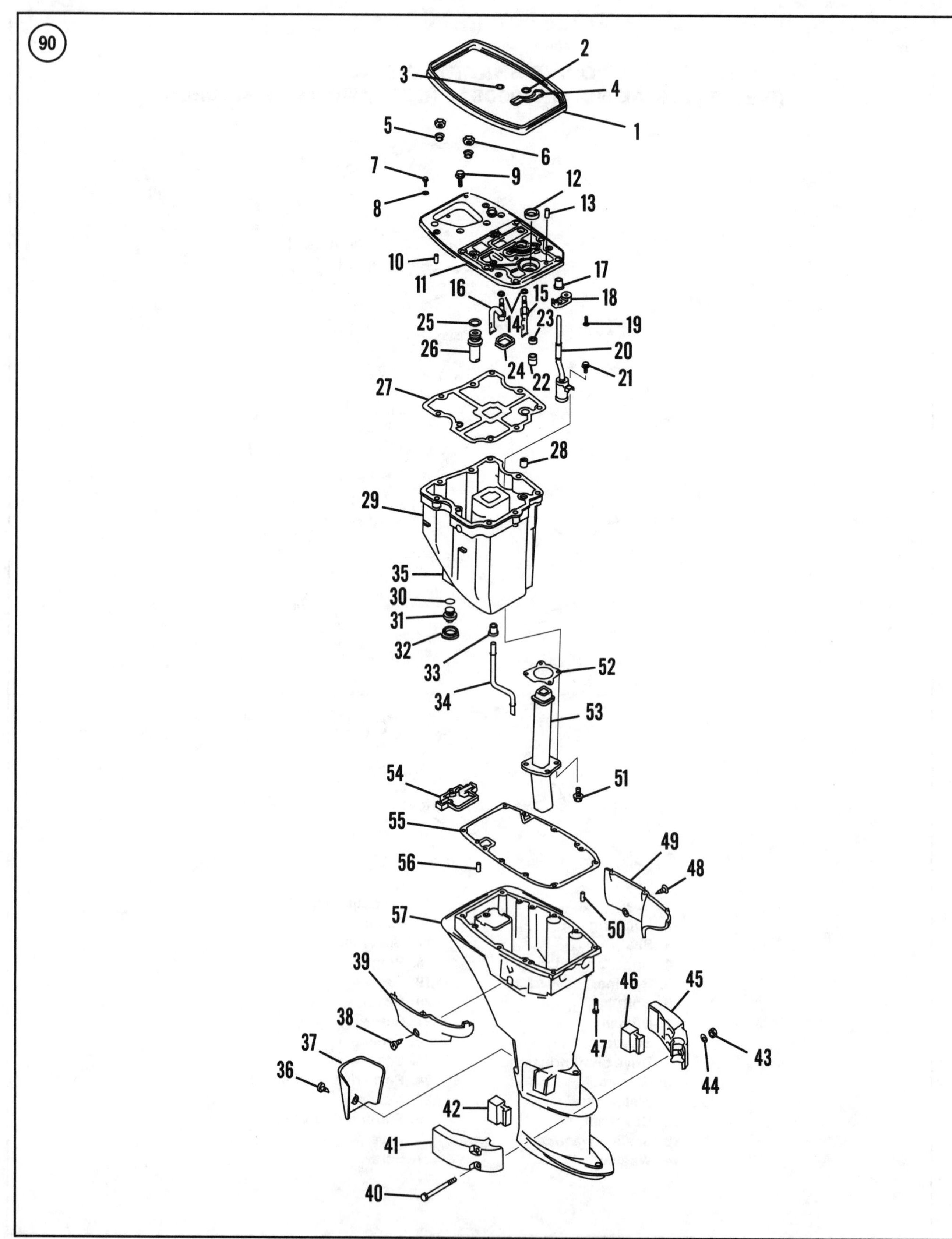
90
1
2
3
4
5
6
7
8
9
10
11
12
13
14
15
16
17
18
19
20
21
22
23
24
25
26
27
28
29
30
31
32
33
34
35
36
37
38
39
40
41
42
43
44
45
46
47
48
49
50
51
52
53
54
55
56
57

DRIVE SHAFT HOUSING (9.9 HP MODELS, SERIAL NO. OH00058-ON)

1. Seal
2. Bumper
3. O-ring
4. Seal
5. Bushing
6. Nut
7. Screw
8. Washer
9. Bolt
10. Locating pin
11. Adapter plate
12. Seal
13. Locating pin
14. Washers
15. Straight discharge tube
16. Curved discharge tube
17. Seal
18. Retainer
19. Screw
20. Oil pickup tube
21. Screw
22. Seal
23. Seal
24. Exhaust seal
25. O-ring
26. Oil pressure relief plug
27. Gasket
28. Seal
29. Oil pan
30. O-ring
31. Oil drain plug
32. Bumper
33. Grommet
34. Water tube
35. Oil drain opening
36. Screw
37. Cover
38. Screw
39. Starboard cover
40. Mount bolt
41. Mount cover/retainer
42. Lower engine mount
43. Nut
44. Washer
45. Mount cover/retainer
46. Lower engine mount
47. Bolt
48. Screw
49. Port cover
50. Locating pin
51. Bolt
52. Gasket
53. Exhaust tube
54. Cover
55. Gasket
56. Locating pin
57. Drive shaft housing

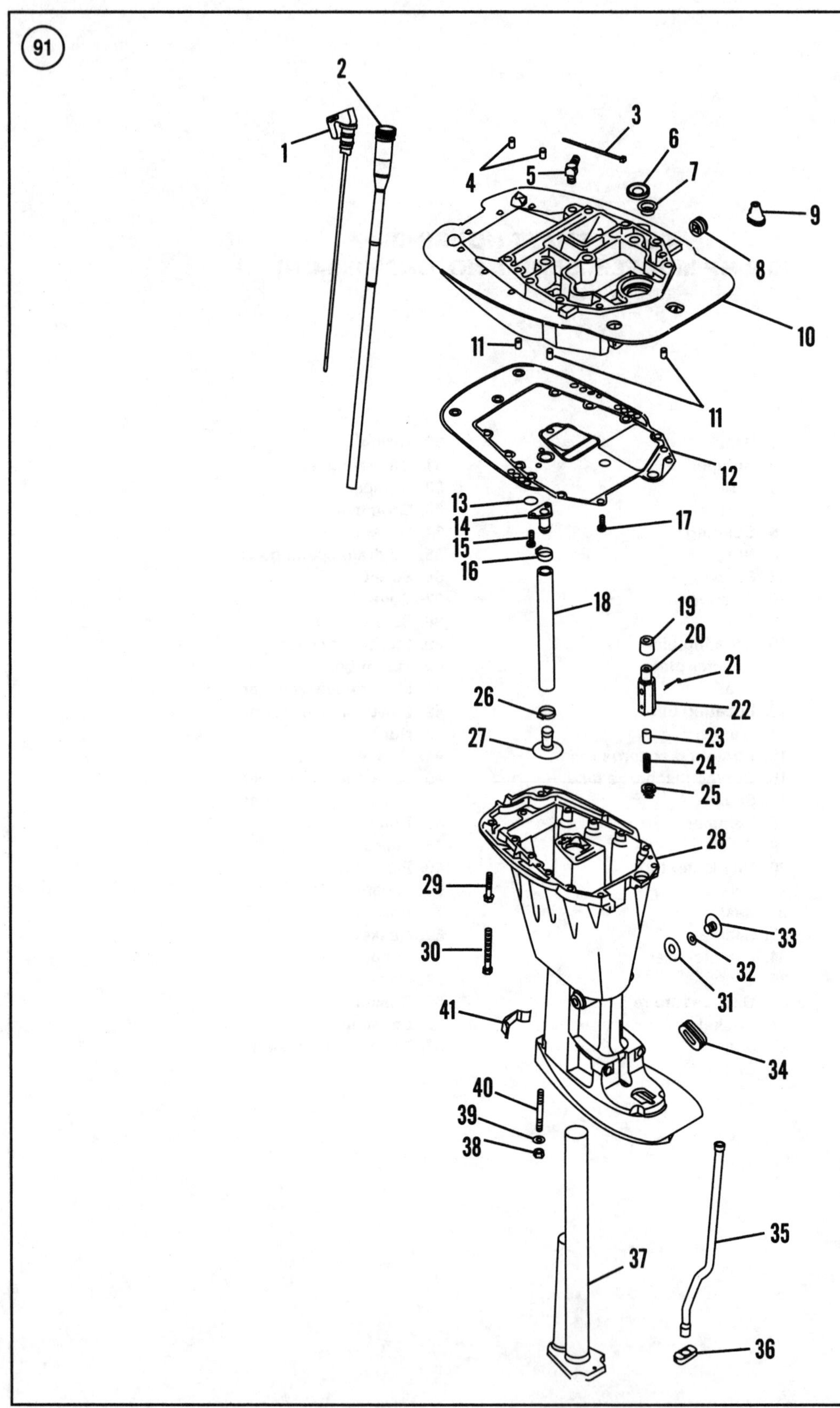
91
1
2
3
4
5
6
7
8
9
10
11
11
11
12
13
14
15
16
17
18
19
20
21
22
23
24
25
26
27
28
29
30
31
32
33
34
35
36
37
38
39
40
41

DRIVE SHAFT HOUSING (25-50 HP MODELS)

1. Dipstick
2. Dipstick tube
3. Plastc locking clamp
4. Locating pin
5. Hose fitting
6. Seal
7. Bushing
8. Plug
9. Grommet
10. Adapter plate
11. Locating pin
12. Gasket
13. O-ring
14. Retainer
15. Screw
16. Clamp
17. Screw
18. Oil pickup tube
19. Deflector
20. Valve opening
21. Cotter pin
22. Valve body
23. Plunger
24. Spring
25. Grommet
26. Clamp
27. Screen
28. Drive shaft housing
29. Bolt
30. Bolt
31. Bumper
32. Sealing washer
33. Oil drain plug
34. Grommet
35. Water tube
36. Tube guide
37. Exhaust tube
38. Nut
39. Washer
40. Stud
41. Bumper

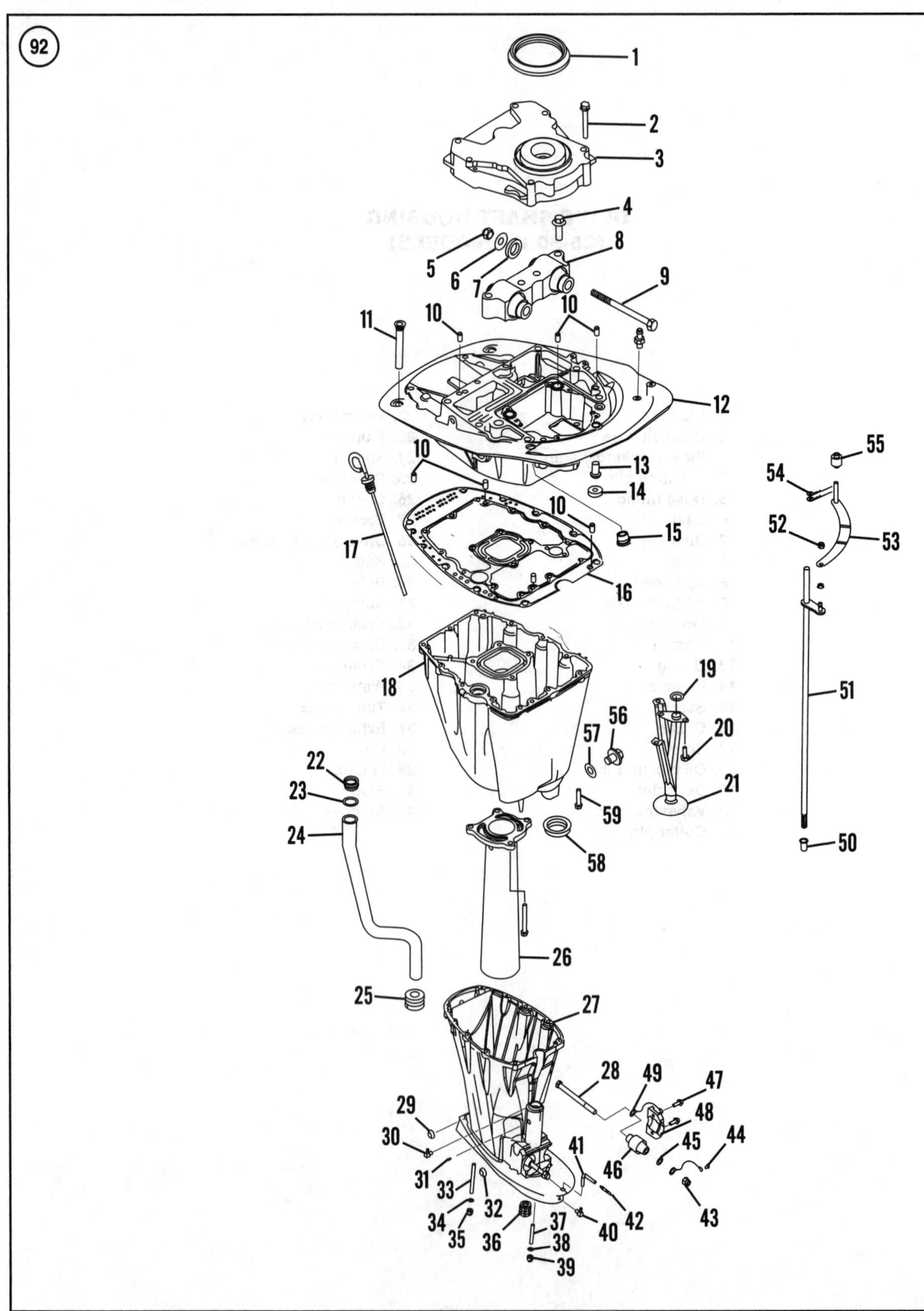
92
1
2
3
4
5
6
7
8
9
10
11
12
13
14
15
16
17
18
19
20
21
22
23
24
25
26
27
28
29
30
31
32
33
34
35
36
37
38
39
40
41
42
43
44
45
46
47
48
49
50
51
52
53
54
55
56
57
58
59

DRIVE SHAFT HOUSING (75 AND 90 HP MODELS)

1. Seal
2. Bolt
3. Oil pump
4. Bolt
5. Nut
6. Washer
7. Washer
8. Upper engine mount
9. Mount bolt
10. Locating pin
11. Check valve
12. Adapter plate
13. Coupler
14. Spacer
15. Grommet
16. Gasket
17. Dipstick
18. Oil pan
19. O-ring
20. Screw
21. Oil pickup tube
22. Grommet
23. Tube flange
24. Water tube
25. Grommet
26. Exhaust tube
27. Drive shaft housing
28. Mount bolt
29. Cap
30. Water hose fitting
31. Alignment pin
32. Cap
33. Stud
34. Washer
35. Nut
36. Drive shaft bushing
37. Stud
38. Washer
39. Nut
40. Speedometer hose fitting
41. Speedometer hose
42. Coupler
43. Nut
44. Grounding wire
45. Washer
46. Lower engine mount
47. Bolt
48. Mount cover/retainer
49. Grounding wire
50. Bushing
51. Shift shaft
52. Nut
53. Lever
54. Locking pins
55. Roller
56. Bolt
57. Washer
58. Seal
59. Bolt

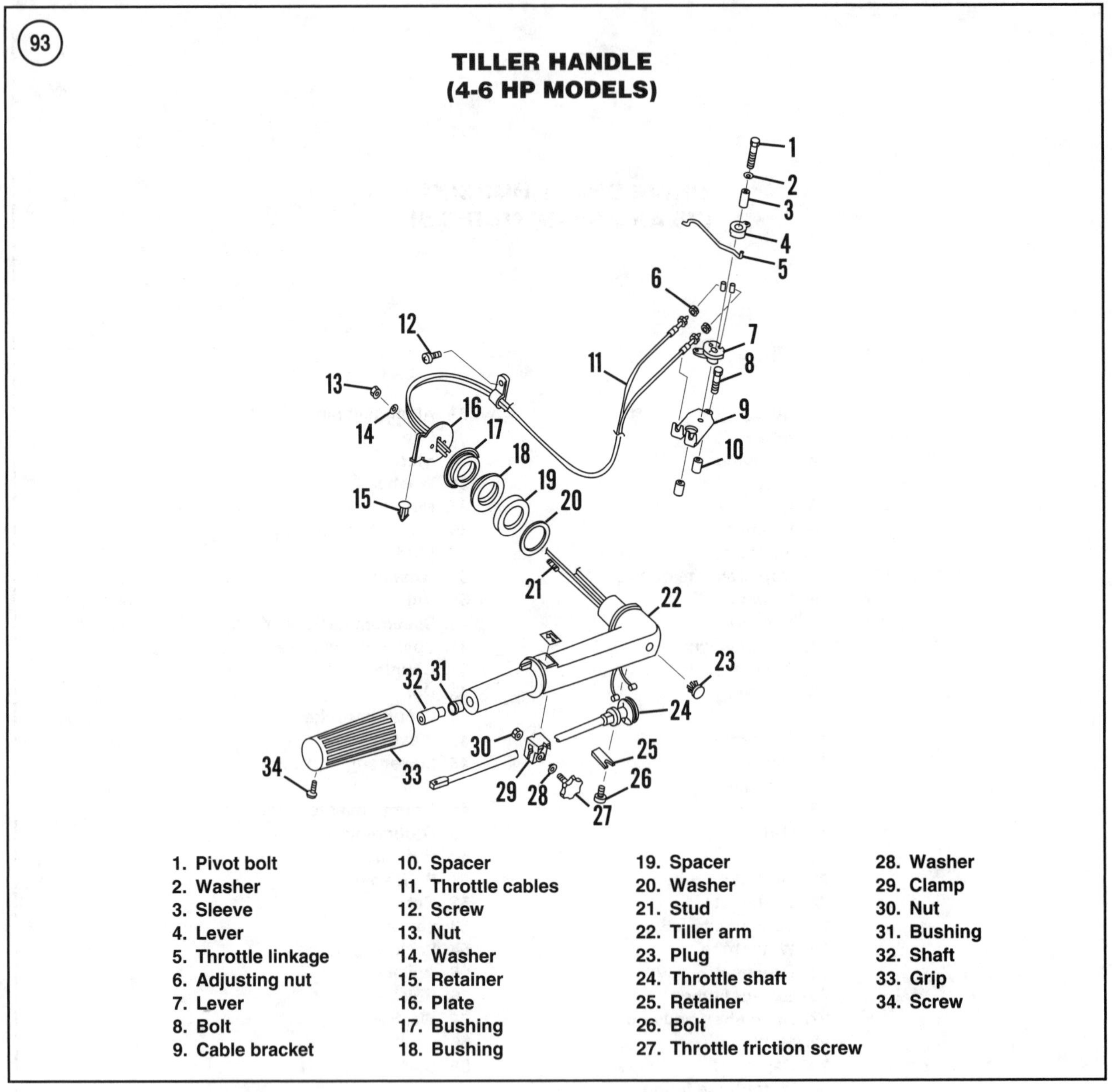

3. Route the wires through in the lower engine cover. Carefully pry the throttle grip from the front of the tiller arm. Slide the stop button/switch from the tiller arm.

4. Disconnect the throttle cables from the throttle lever or wheel.

5. Refer to **Figures 93-95** to determine the location of the tiller control attaching bolts or nuts. Remove the bolts or nuts then pull the tiller arm and cables from the engine.

6. Remove all applicable retainers and pull the throttle shaft from the tiller control. Inspect all components for wear or damage. Replace any worn or damaged components.

7. Assembly is the reverse of disassembly noting the following:
   a. Apply 2-4-C Marine Lubricant to all pivot and sliding surfaces.
   b. Route all wires away from moving components.
   c. Tighten all fasteners to the specification in **Table 2**.

8. Connect the throttle cables to the throttle lever or wheel. Adjust the cables following the instructions in Chapter Five.

9. Connect the cables to the battery if so equipped.

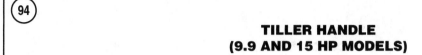

TILLER HANDLE
(9.9 AND 15 HP MODELS)

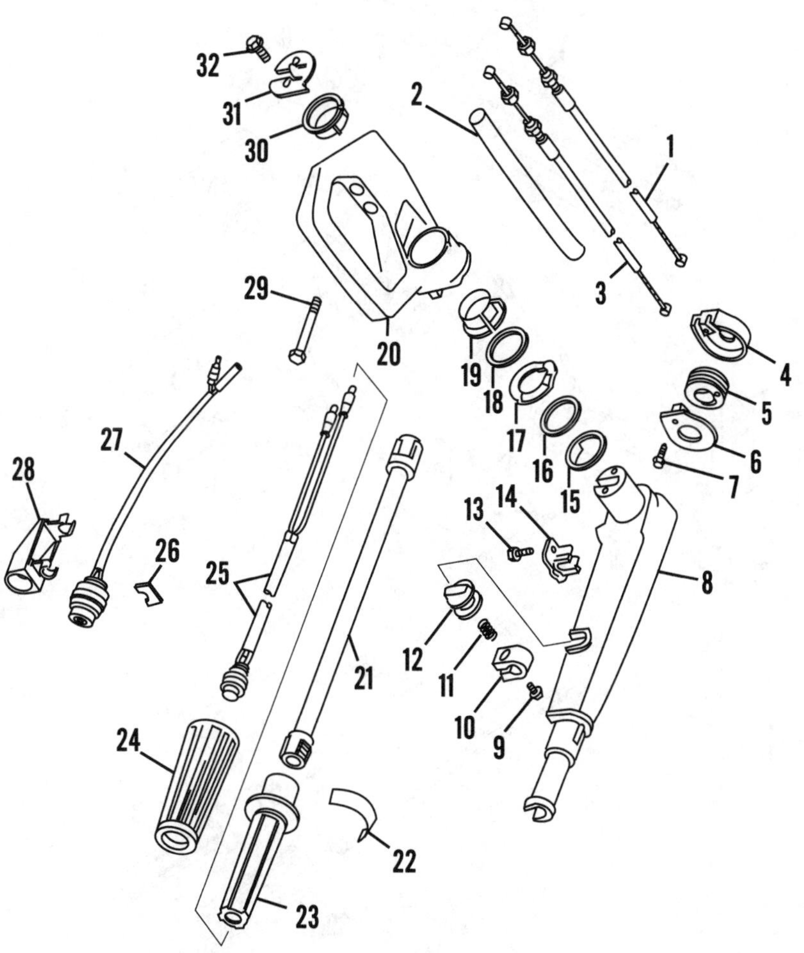

1. Throttle cable
2. Sleeve
3. Throttle cable
4. Cable bracket
5. Spool
6. Cover
7. Screw
8. Tiller arm
9. Screw
10. Clamp
11. Spring
12. Throttle friction screw
13. Bolt
14. Retainer
15. Spacer
16. Washer
17. Plate
18. Washer
19. Bushing
20. Tiller bracket
21. Throttle shaft
22. Decal
23. Handle
24. Grip
25. Stop button
26. Retainer
27. Starter button and harness
28. Button housing
29. Bolt
30. Bushing
31. Retainer
32. Bolt

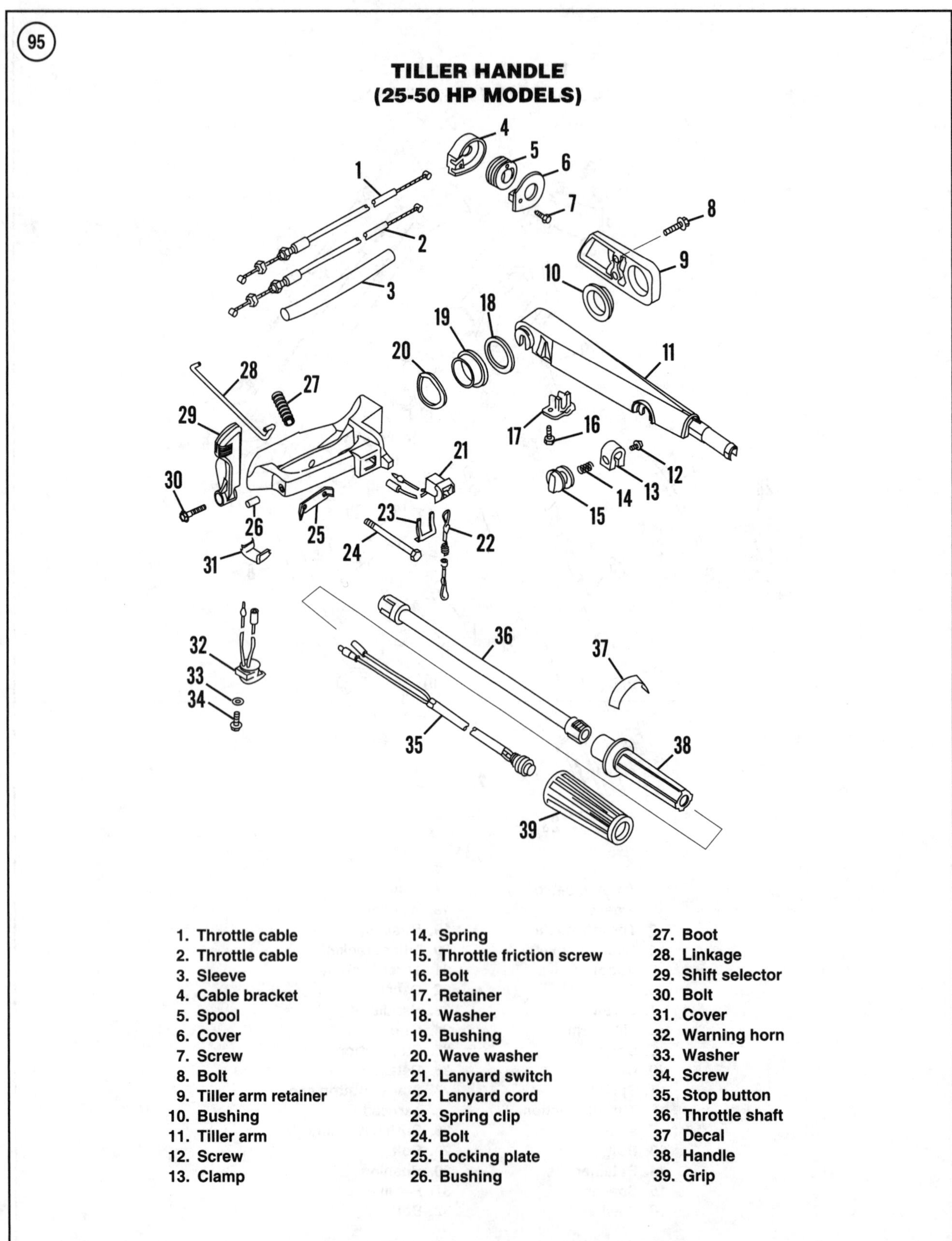

TILLER HANDLE (25-50 HP MODELS)

1. Throttle cable
2. Throttle cable
3. Sleeve
4. Cable bracket
5. Spool
6. Cover
7. Screw
8. Bolt
9. Tiller arm retainer
10. Bushing
11. Tiller arm
12. Screw
13. Clamp
14. Spring
15. Throttle friction screw
16. Bolt
17. Retainer
18. Washer
19. Bushing
20. Wave washer
21. Lanyard switch
22. Lanyard cord
23. Spring clip
24. Bolt
25. Locking plate
26. Bushing
27. Boot
28. Linkage
29. Shift selector
30. Bolt
31. Cover
32. Warning horn
33. Washer
34. Screw
35. Stop button
36. Throttle shaft
37 Decal
38. Handle
39. Grip

Table 1 TIGHTENING TORQUE FOR POWER TRIM COMPONENTS

Fastener location	ft-lb.	in-lb.	N•m
Trim system lower pivot pin			
25 hp	18	216	25
50 hp (standard gearcase)	18	216	25
Gas assist tilt system mounting			
25 hp	18	210	24
Hydraulic cylinder cap			
25-90 hp	45	–	61
Shock piston to ram			
25-40 hp	90	–	122
50 hp			
Standard gearcase	45	–	61
Optional gearcase	90	–	122
75 and 90 hp	90	–	122
Shock relief valve bolt/screws			
25 hp	45	–	61
30 and 40 hp	–	35	4
50 hp			
Standard gearcase	45	–	61
Optional gearcase	–	35	4
75 and 90 hp	–	35	4
Hydraulic pump to manifold			
25 hp	–	70	8
30 and 40 hp	–	68	8
50 hp			
Standard gearcase	–	70	8
Optional gearcase	–	68	8
75 and 90	–	68	8
Fluid reservoir/electric trim motor to manifold			
30 and 40 hp	–	80	9
50 hp (optional gearcase)	–	80	9
75 and 90 hp	–	80	9
Manifold to cylinder (Allen bolts)			
30 and 40 hp	–	97	11
50 hp (optional gearcase)	–	97	11
75 and 90 hp	–	97	11
Poppet valve plugs			
30 and 40 hp	–	120	14
50 hp (optional gearcase)	–	120	14
75 and 90 hp	–	120	14
Lower manifold plug (filter)			
25 hp	–	120	14
50 hp (standard gearcase)	–	120	14
Starboard side plug (tilt relief valve)			
25 hp	–	120	14
50 hp (standard gearcase)	–	120	14
Rear mounted plug (poppet valve)			
25 hp	–	120	14
50 hp (standard gearcase)	–	120	14
Front mounted plug (poppet valve)			
25 hp	–	120	14
50 hp (standard gearcase)	–	120	14
Electric trim motor mounting			
25 hp	–	80	9
50 hp (standard gearcase)	–	80	9

Table 2 TIGHTENING TORQUE FOR MID SECTION COMPONENTS

Fastener location	ft-lb.	in-lb.	N•m
Steering bracket bolt			
9.9 hp (serial No. OH000057-prior)	33	–	44
15-50 hp	33	–	44
Steering link rod			
9.9 hp (serial No. OH000058-on)	20	240	27
25-90 hp	20	240	27
Drive shaft housing cover			
4-6 hp	–	70	8
9.9 hp			
Serial No. OH000057-prior	12	144	16
Serial No. OH000058-on	–	30	3
15 hp	12	144	16
25-50 hp	–	60	7
75 and 90 hp	–	65	7
Exhaust tube to adapter			
9.9 hp (serial No. OH000058-on)	–	80	9
75 and 90 hp	–	100	12
Adapter to oil pan			
9.9 hp (serial No. OH000058-on)	–	90	10
Power head adapter to drive shaft housing			
25-50 hp			
6x120 mm bolts	–	75	9
8x45 mm bolts	28		38
75 and 90 hp	–	100	12
Oil pressure relief valve			
25-50 hp	34	–	46
Tilt tube bolt/nut			
4-6 hp	–	25	2.8
9.9 hp			
Serial No. OH000057-prior	10	120	14
Serial No. OH000058-on	–	97	11
15 hp	10	120	14
25 hp[1]			
30-50 hp[2]			
75 and 90[3]			
Shift selector bolt (tiller models only)			
25-50 hp	–	100	11
Tilt lever/spring retainer			
4-6 hp	–	70	8
Anode (clamp bracket mounted)			
25-90 hp	–	60	6.8
Lower clamp bracket support			
4-6 hp	–	36	4
9.9 hp			
Serial No. OH000057-prior	–	140	16
Serial No. OH000058-on	–	60	7
15 hp	–	60	7
25 hp	28	–	38
30-90 hp	30	–	41
Clamp bracket hex bolt			
25 hp	28	–	38
Tilt control lever (pivot bolt)			
25 hp (gas assist tilt)	–	90	10
30-50 (gas assist tilt)	19	220	25
Rear swivel bracket			
4-6 hp	–	70	8

(continued)

Table 2 TIGHTENING TORQUE FOR MID SECTION COMPONENTS (continued)

Fastener location	ft-lb.	in-lb.	N•m
Tilt lock bolt			
4-6 hp	–	70	8
Tilt stop plate			
9.9 hp			
Serial No. OH000057-prior	–	65	7
Serial No. OH000058-on	–	60	7
15 hp	–	65	7
Tiller arm mounting bracket			
9.9 hp (serial No. OH000057-prior)	33	–	44
15 hp	33	–	44
25-40 hp	35	–	47
50 hp	32	–	43
Tiller arm retaining bolts			
4-6 hp	–	70	8
9.9 and 15 hp	–	50	6
Tiller arm retaining cover			
25-50 hp	–	135	15
Throttle shaft retainer			
9.9 hp			
Serial No. OH000057-prior	–	50	6
Serial No. OH000058-on	–	35	4
15 hp	–	50	6
25-50 hp	–	35	4
Upper engine mount bolts			
9.9 hp			
Serial No. OH000057-prior	15	180	20
Serial No. OH000058-on	18	216	24
15 hp	15	180	20
25-50 hp	50	–	68
75 and 90 hp	55	–	75
Upper engine mount retainer			
9.9 hp			
Serial No. OH000057-prior	33	–	44
Serial No. OH000058-on	–	156	17
15 hp	33	–	44
25-50 hp	–	132	15
75 and 90 hp	25	–	34
Lower engine mount cover			
9.9 hp			
Serial No. OH000057-prior	33	–	44
Serial No. OH000058-on		102	11.5
15 hp	33	–	44
75 and 90	25	–	34
Lower engine mount bolts			
25-50 hp	33	–	44
75 and 90 hp	50	–	68
Reverse lock rod connector			
9.9 hp (serial No. OH000057-prior)	–	50	6
15 hp	–	50	6
Auto pilot friction plate			
25-50 hp	–	70	8

1. Tighten nut until it seats then loosen the nut 1/4 turn.
2. Tighten the nut to 32 ft lb. (43 N•m) then loosen the nut 1/4 turn.
3. Tighten the nut until the tilt tube is secure yet the engine tilts without binding.

11

Chapter Twelve

Remote Control

This chapter provides remote control disassembly and assembly. Many suppliers offer remote controls and the engine may be equipped with any one of them. This chapter provides instructions for the standard side mount remote control (**Figure 1**) and the Commander 3000 panel mount type of control (**Figure 2**). These types are commonly used on Mercury and Mariner outboards. Contact a local marine dealership for parts and information if the engine is equipped with a different type of remote control.

Complete disassembly is not always required to test or replace a failed component. Perform the disassembly steps necessary to access the necessary components or wires. Reverse the steps to assemble and install the remote control.

CABLE REMOVAL AND INSTALLATION

Replace the cables if they are hard to move or excessive play is noted. Replace both cables if either cable requires replacement. Mark the cable mounting points with a felt tip marker prior to removing them from the remote control. This helps ensure the throttle and shift cables are installed to the proper attaching points. To avoid confusion, remove and install one cable at a time.

NOTE

Apply Loctite 242 to the threads of the remote control handle nut or bolt during assembly.

Side Mount Control

1. Disconnect both cables from the battery.
2. Remove the screws, spacers, nuts and washers (**Figure 3**), then pull the remote control away from the boat structure. Lay the control on a suitable surface back side facing up.
3. Carefully pry the small cover (**Figure 4**) down and away from the remote control. Slip the cover tabs from the openings while lifting it from the control.
4. Remove the lower two attaching screws (**Figure 5**) and lift the lower back cover from the remote control.

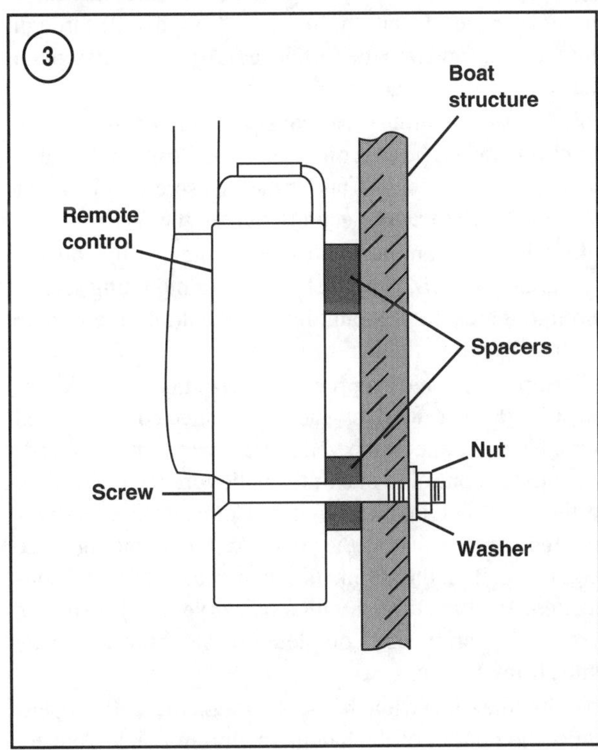

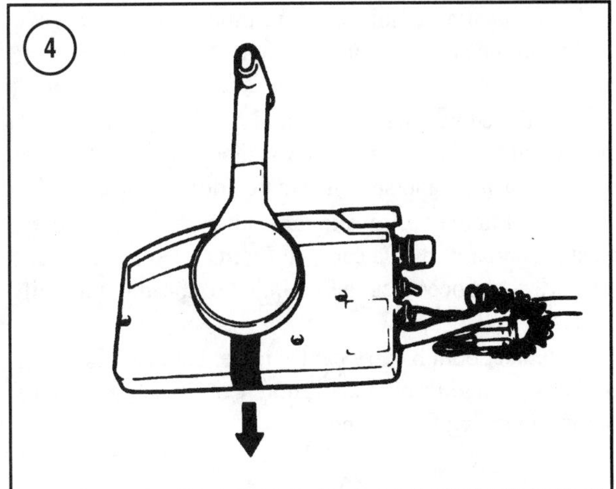

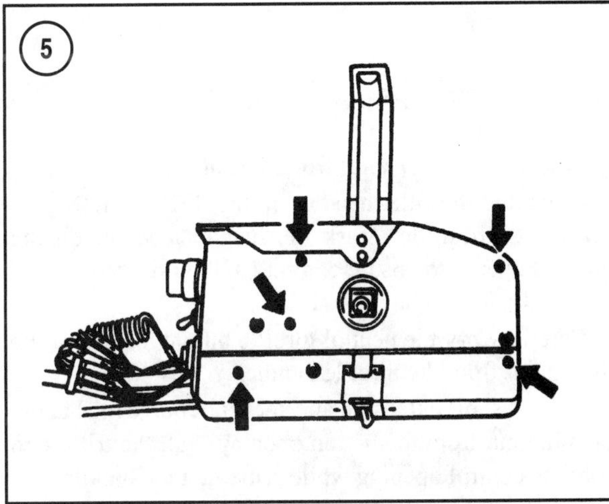

5. Mark the *throttle cable* (**Figure 6**) then remove the small nut and cable retainer from the lever. Disconnect the throttle cable from the lever.

6. Mark the *shift cable* (**Figure 6**) then remove the small nut and cable retainer from the lever. Lift the throttle cable from the lever.

7. Apply a water-resistant grease to the ends of the throttle cable and shift cable (**Figure 6**). Position the pin of the cable retainer (20, **Figure 7**) onto the end of the shift cable. Lower the shift cable barrel into its opening at the rear of the remote control. Align the cable retainer and cable with its attaching points to the shift lever (30, **Figure 7**). Install the cable retainer and nut (20 and 21, **Figure 7**). Securely tighten the nut.

8. Position the pin of the cable retainer (20, **Figure 7**) onto the end of the shift cable. Lower the throttle cable barrel into its recess at the rear of the remote control along with the shift cable. Align the cable retainer and cable

with its attaching points to the throttle lever (28, **Figure 7**). Install the cable retainer and nut. Securely tighten the nut.

9. Install the lower back cover and screws (**Figure 5**). Securely tighten the screws. Slip the tabs of the small cover into the opening and snap it into position (**Figure 4**).

10. Install the control and attaching screws, spacers, washers and nuts as indicated in **Figure 3**. Refer to Chapter Five for procedures then adjust the throttle and shift cables.

11. Connect both battery cables to the battery. Check for proper shift and throttle operation. Correct any problems before operating the engine.

NOTE
Apply Loctite 242 to the threads of the remote control handle nut or bolt during assembly.

Commander 3000 Panel Mount Control

1. Disconnect both cables from the battery.

2. Place the throttle handle in the FORWARD gear full-throttle position. Mark the handle location on the mounting panel to ensure correct handle orientation during installation of the control.

3. Carefully pry the neutral throttle button located at the pivot point from the throttle handle.

4. Using a short extension and socket, remove the handle retaining nut from the button opening. Pull the trim wire from the control opening while removing the handle.

5. Cut the sleeves (28, **Figure 8**) from the yellow/red wires leading into the control. Remove the screws and nuts (14 and 15, **Figure 8**) to disconnect the wires from the control.

6. Carefully pry both plastic covers from the panel mount. Outline the remote control mounting angle on the back side of the boat structure to ensure correct orientation during installation.

7. Remove the four control retaining screws from the external mounting plate then pull the control from the panel.

8. Remove the screw and washer (26 and 27, **Figure 8**) then lift the rear cover (25) from the control.

9. Mark the throttle cable and its attaching point prior to removing it from the control. Remove the screw (20, **Figure 8**) and lift the throttle cable from the throttle lever (20). Note the position of the cable spacers (7, **Figure 8**) while removing the cables.

10. Mark the shift cable and its attaching points prior to removing it from the control. Remove the screw (17, **Figure 8**) then lift the shift cable from the shift lever (16).

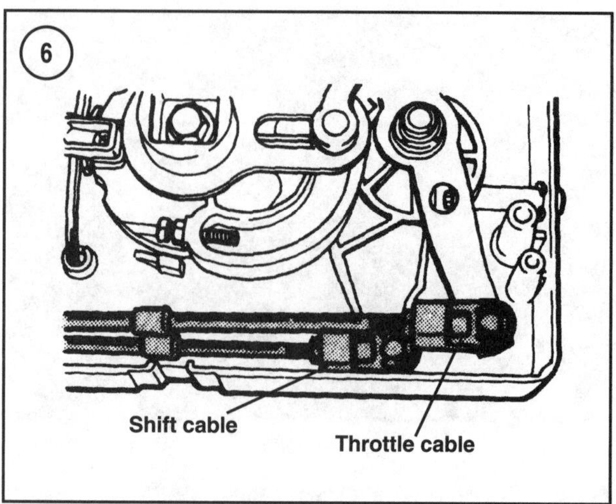

Note the position of the cable spacers (7, **Figure 8**) while removing the cables.

11. Attach the end of the shift cable to the shift lever (16, **Figure 8**). Place the cylinder shaped cable anchor into its recess at the back of the control. Install the screw (17, **Figure 8**) through the cable end and into the shift lever (16). Securely tighten the screw.

12. Install the cable spacer (7, **Figure 8**) into the recess at the back of the control if originally installed. Attach the end of the throttle cable to the throttle lever (20, **Figure 8**). Place the cylinder shaped cable anchor of the cable into its recess at the back of the control along with the shift cable or cable spacer. Install the screw (17, **Figure 8**) through the cable end and into the shift lever (16). Securely tighten the screw.

13. Slip the tab on the rear cover (25, **Figure 8**) into the notch and lower the cover into position. Position the cable anchors in their recesses and install the screw and washer (26 and 27, **Figure 8**). Securely tighten the screw.

14. Align the remote control with the outline on the mounting panel (Step 6). Install the four mounting screws through the external mounting plate and into the remote control. Securely tighten the screws.

15. Slip a section of appropriately sized heat shrink tubing (28, **Figure 8**) over each disconnected yellow/red wire. Connect one of the yellow/red wire terminals leading into the control to one of the yellow/red wires leading to the dash-mounted key switch. Connect the other yellow/red wire terminal to the yellow/red wire leading to the engine. Position the shrink tubing over each terminal connection. Heat the tubing with a hair dryer until it shrinks around the terminals. Completely cover both terminals with shrink tubing.

16. Slip the trim switch harness through the slotted opening at the bottom of the handle mounting point. Connect

(7)

SIDE MOUNT CONTROL COMPONENTS

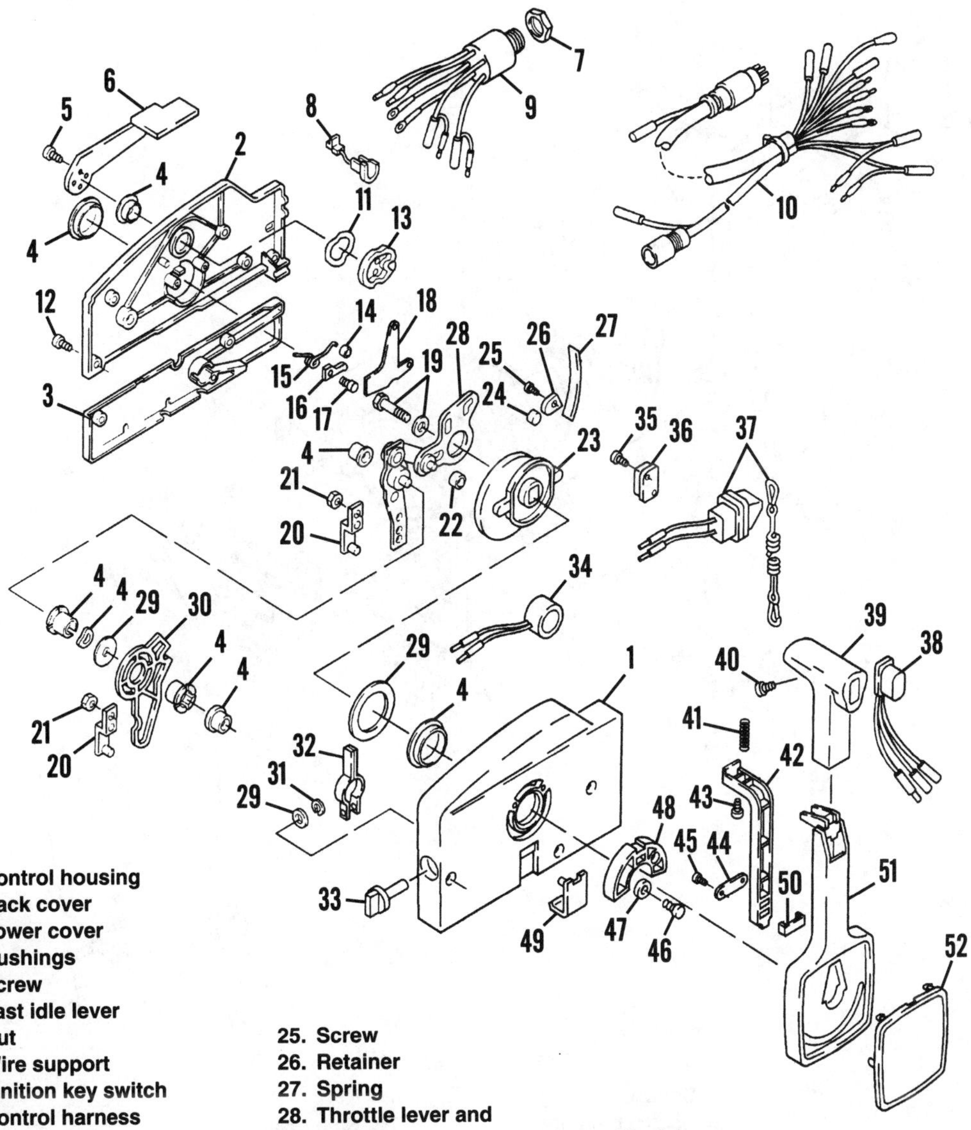

1. Control housing
2. Back cover
3. Lower cover
4. Bushings
5. Screw
6. Fast idle lever
7. Nut
8. Wire support
9. Ignition key switch
10. Control harness
11. Wave washer
12. Screw
13. Fast idle cam
14. Roller
15. Spring
16. Retainer
17. Screw
18. Wire cover
19. Bolt and washer
20. Cable retainer
21. Nut
22. Cam roller
23. Control cam
24. Detent roller
25. Screw
26. Retainer
27. Spring
28. Throttle lever and linkage
29. Washer
30. Shift lever
31. Clip
32. Throttle friction lever
33. Throttle friction screw
34. Warning horn
35. Screw
36. Neutral only start switch
37. Lanyard switch
38. Trim switch
39. Grip
40. Screw
41. Spring
42. Neutral lock lever
43. Screw
44. Bracket
45. Screw
46. Screw
47. Lockwasher
48. Neutral lock bracket
49. Cover
50. Clip
51. Throttle handle
52. Cover

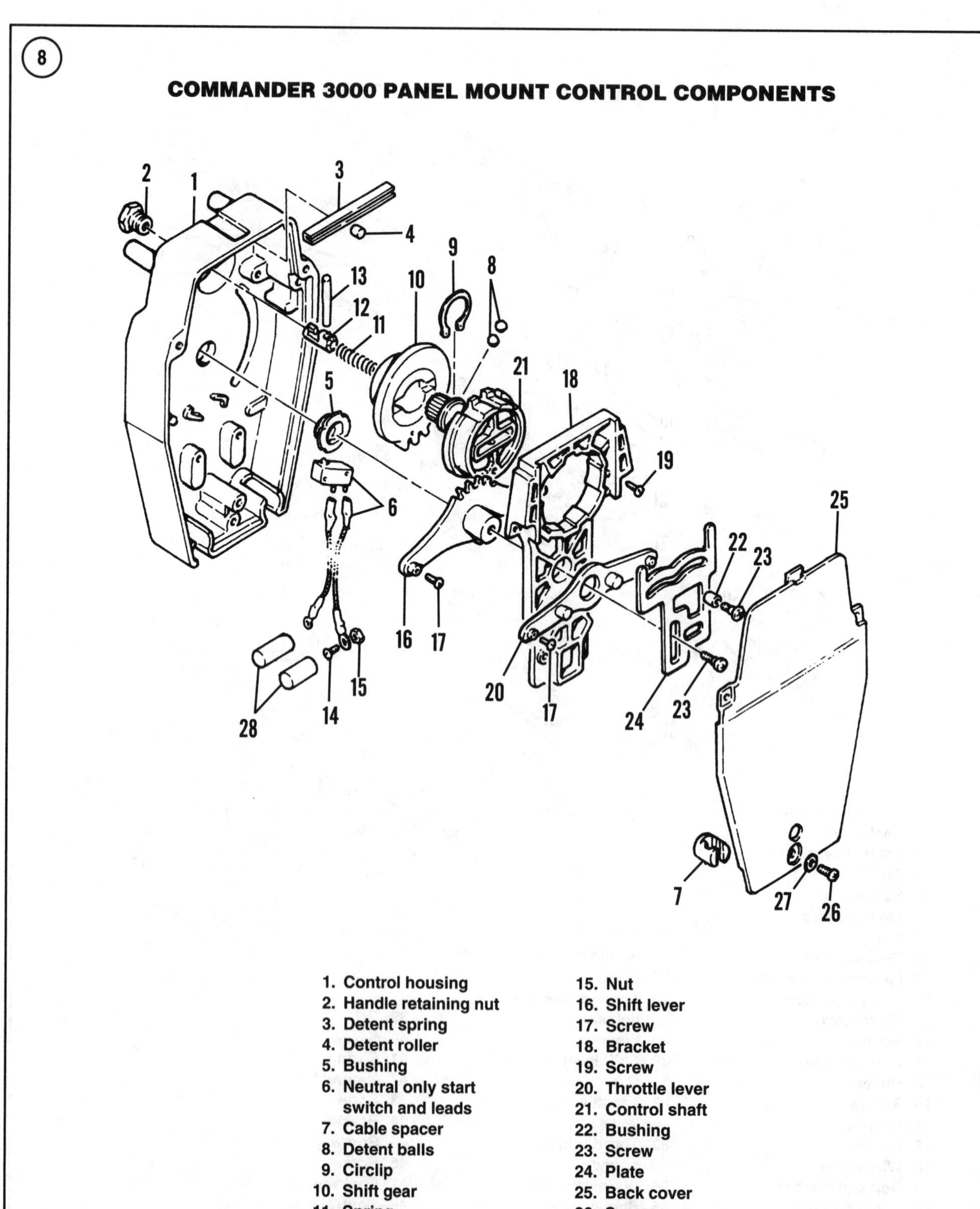

COMMANDER 3000 PANEL MOUNT CONTROL COMPONENTS

1. Control housing
2. Handle retaining nut
3. Detent spring
4. Detent roller
5. Bushing
6. Neutral only start switch and leads
7. Cable spacer
8. Detent balls
9. Circlip
10. Shift gear
11. Spring
12. Neutral throttle shaft
13. Pin
14. Screw
15. Nut
16. Shift lever
17. Screw
18. Bracket
19. Screw
20. Throttle lever
21. Control shaft
22. Bushing
23. Screw
24. Plate
25. Back cover
26. Screw
27. Washer
28. Shrink tubing

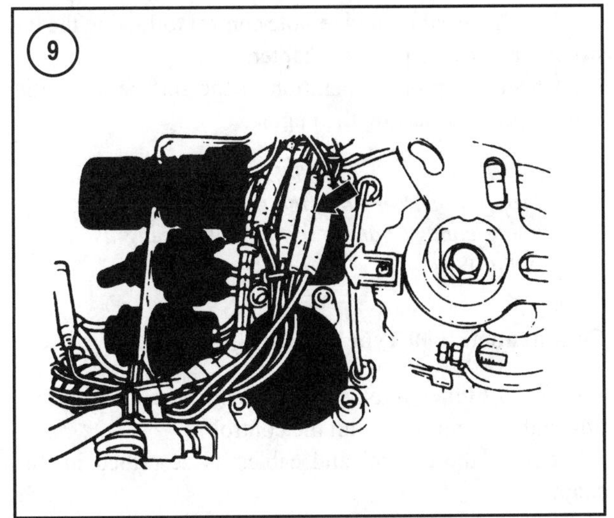

the trim switch connector to its instrument harness connector. Place the plastic bushing into the handle opening with the larger diameter side facing out. Align the raised part of the bushing with the slot in the opening.

17. Align the throttle handle to the mark made prior to removal (Step 2), then slide the handle into its opening. Using an extension and socket, install the retaining nut (2, **Figure 8**) into the handle and throttle shaft. Securely tighten the nut.

18. Carefully slide the shaft of the neutral throttle button into the opening in the retaining nut. Push in until the button locks into the opening.

19. Snap both plastic covers onto the external mounting plate. Place the throttle cable in the neutral position. Adjust the shift and throttle cables following the instructions in Chapter Five.

20. Connect the cables to the battery. Check for proper operation of the shift, throttle and the neutral only start switch. Correct any faults before operating the engine.

CAUTION
Always refer to the owner's manual for specific operating instructions for the remote control. Become familiar with all control functions before operating the engine.

WARNING
A remote control malfunction can lead to lack of shift and throttle control. Never operate an outboard with a control system malfunction. Damaged property, injury or death can result from operating the engine without proper control. Check for proper control system operation before operating the engine or after performing any service or repair to the control system(s).

REMOTE CONTROL DISASSEMBLY AND ASSEMBLY

Although other brands and types of controls use similar components, some significant differences are present. Contact a marine dealership for parts and information on other types of control.

Always mark the orientation of all components prior to removing them. This important step can help ensure proper remote control operation after assembly. Improper assembly can cause internal binding or reversed cable movement.

When complete disassembly is not required to access the faulty component, perform the disassembly steps until the desired component is accessible. Reverse the disassembly steps to assemble the remote control.

Use compressed air to blow debris from the external surfaces prior to disassembling the remote control. Clean all components except electric switches and the warning buzzer using clean solvent. Blow all components dry with compressed air. Inspect all components for damaged or excessive wear. To help ensure correct control operation, replace all worn, damaged or questionable components. Apply water-resistant grease or to all pivot points or sliding surfaces during assembly. Test all electric components when removed to ensure proper operation upon assembly. Chapter Three provides test instructions for electrical components and switches.

NOTE
Apply Loctite 242 to the threads of the remote control handle nut or bolt during assembly.

Side Mount Control

Refer to **Figure 7** to assist with component identification and orientation within the control.

1. Disconnect both cables from the battery.

2. Remove the shift cables from the remote control as described in this chapter.

3. Disconnect the control wire harness from the engine. Route the wire harness away from any boat structure to allow removal of the remote control and wire harness from the boat. Place the control on a clean work surface.

4. Remove the three screws from the back cover (12, **Figure 7**). Lift the back cover (2) from the remote control. Refer to the wire diagrams located at the back of the manual then identify the wires used for the warning horn.. Disconnect the horn wires then lift the warning horn from the remote control. See **Figure 9**.

12

5. Disconnect the wires used for the ignition key switch and the lanyard switch. Remove the retaining nut or clip then slide both switches from the control housing.

6. Disconnect the wires for the neutral start switch (36, **Figure 7**). Note the wire routing and connections and unplug the wires from the wire harness. Remove the mounting screws (35, **Figure 7**) and lift the switch from the control housing.

7. Remove the bolt and washer (19, **Figure 7**) and pull the throttle handle (51) away from the control. Disconnect the trim switch wires from the control harness then pull the throttle handle from the control.

8. Remove the screws (45, **Figure 7**) and lift the bracket (44) from the throttle handle (51). Remove the screw (43, **Figure 7**) and lift the neutral lock lever and spring (41 and 42) from the handle. Pull the clip (50, **Figure 7**) from the handle.

9. Remove the screws and lockwashers (46 and 47, **Figure 7**) and remove the neutral lock bracket from the control.

10. Remove the screw (17, **Figure 7**) and lift the retainer, roller and spring (14-16, **Figure 7**) from the back cover (2). Remove the four screws (5, **Figure 7**), then lift the fast idle lever and bushing (4 and 6) from the back cover. Remove the fast idle cam and wave washer (11 and 13, **Figure 7**) from the back cover.

11. Remove the screw (25, **Figure 7**) then lift the retainer (26), detent roller (24) and spring (27) from the housing.

12. Loosen the throttle friction screw (33, **Figure 7**) and lift the throttle cam and linkage (28, **Figure 7**) along with its bushings, washers and rollers from the control.

13. Lift the shift lever (30, **Figure 7**) and its bushings and washers from the control. Lift the throttle friction lever (32, **Figure 7**) along with its washer (29) and clip (31) from the control. Pull the control cam (23, **Figure 7**) from the control.

14. Wash all grease or contaminants from the control housing and components except electrical components using clean solvent.

15. Assembly is the reverse of disassembly noting the following:

   a. Apply a water-resistant grease to all pivot points and sliding surfaces during assembly.
   b. Connect all wires to the proper terminals on the control harness (10, **Figure 7**).
   c. Route all wires away from moving components.
   d. Securely tighten all bolts and screws. Do not over tighten the throttle friction screw (33, **Figure 7**).

16. Install the cables and remote control following the instructions provided in this chapter.

17. Check for proper operation of the shift and throttle control prior to starting the engine.

NOTE

Apply Loctite 242 to the threads of the remote control handle nut or bolt during assembly.

Commander 3000 Type Control

Refer to **Figure 8** to assist with component identification and orientation within the control.

1. Remove the control and cables as described in this chapter.

2. Remove both screws (23, **Figure 8**) and the bushing (22), then lift the plate (24) from the control. Lift the throttle lever (20, **Figure 8**) from the bracket (18).

3. Remove the screws (19, **Figure 8**) and lift the bracket (18) from the control housing. Pull the control shaft (21, **Figure 8**), shift gear (10) and shift lever (16) from the control housing.

4. Separate the control shaft from the shift gear, then remove the circlip (9, **Figure 8**) from the control shaft. Remove the detent balls (8, **Figure 8**) from the control shaft.

5. Pull the neutral throttle shaft and spring (11 and 12, **Figure 8**) from the control shaft (21). Pull the pin (13, **Figure 8**) from the neutral throttle shaft. Pull the detent spring and bushing (3 and 5, **Figure 8**) from the control housing.

6. Lift the neutral start switch and leads (6, **Figure 8**) from the switch mounting bosses.

7. Wash grease or contaminants from the control housing and components except electrical components using clean solvent.

8. Assembly is the reverse of disassembly noting the following:

   a. Apply a water-resistant grease to all pivot points and sliding surfaces during assembly.
   b. Align the mark on the shift lever (16, **Figure 8**) with the mark on the shift gear (10) during installation.
   c. Install the detent balls (8, **Figure 8**) into their openings in the control shaft.
   d. Route all wires away from moving components.
   e. Securely tighten all bolts and screws.

9. Install the cables and remote control following the instructions provided in this chapter.

10. Check for proper operation of the shift and throttle control prior to starting the engine.

Index

13

R

S

T

V

W

MANUAL START
(9.9 HP MODELS, SERIAL NO. OH000058-ON)

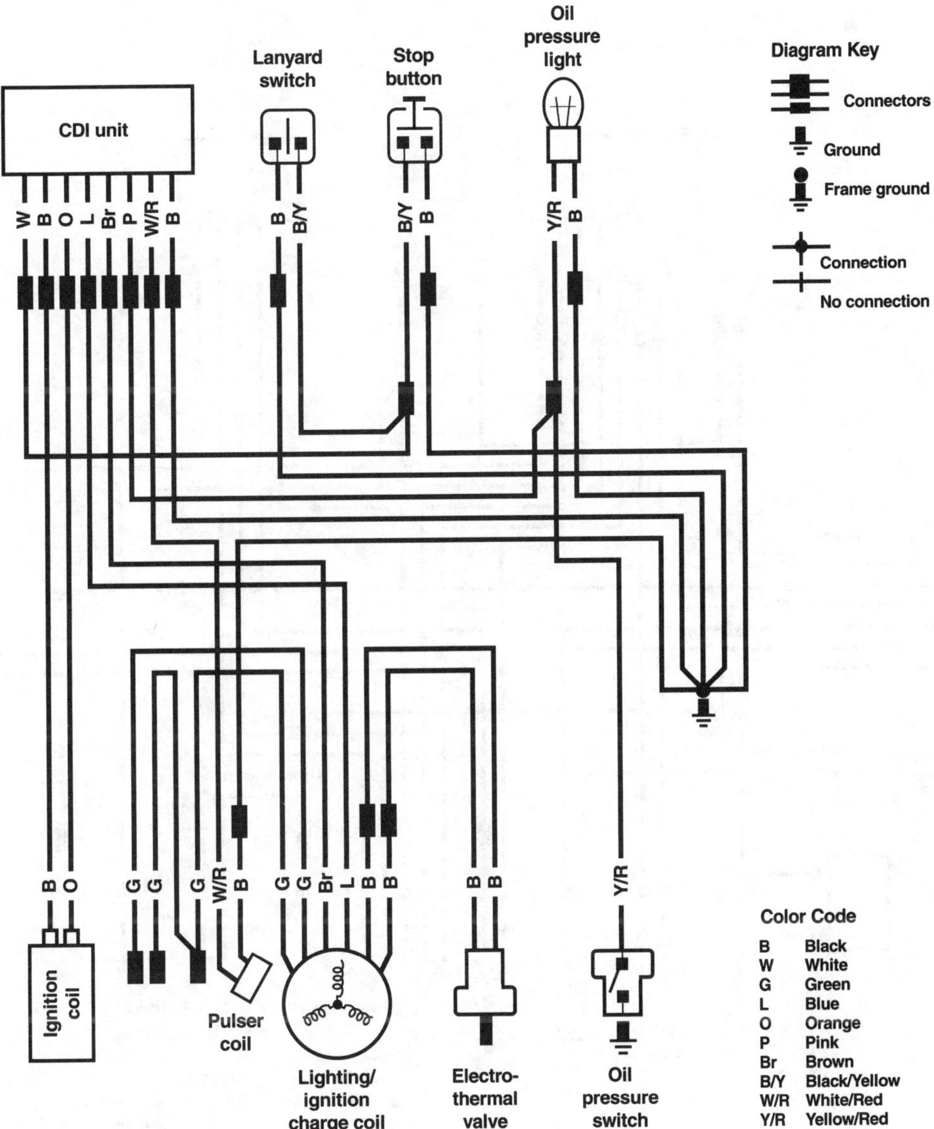

ELECTRIC START
(9.9 HP MODELS, SERIAL NO. OH000058-ON)

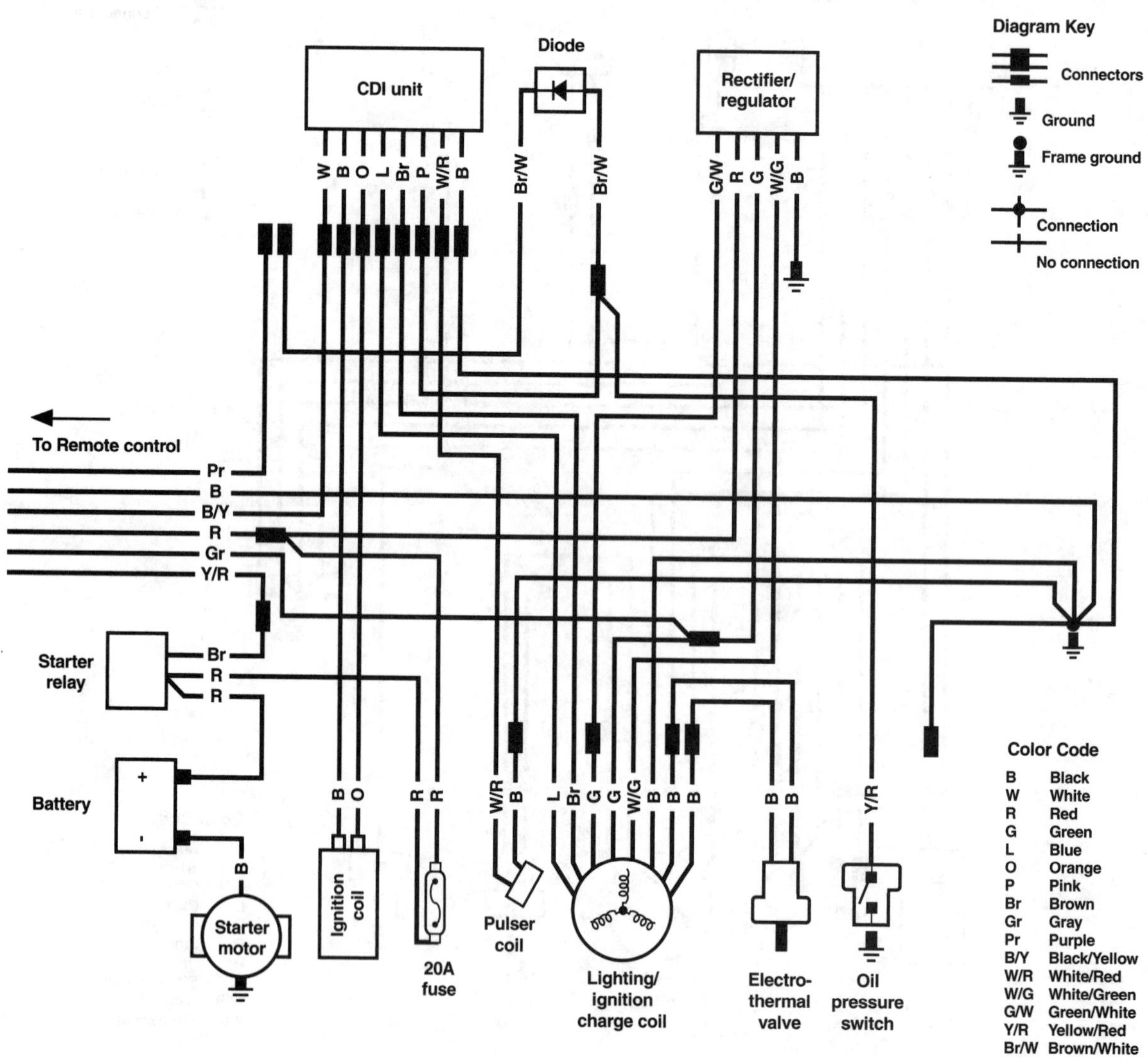

4 AND 5 HP MODELS

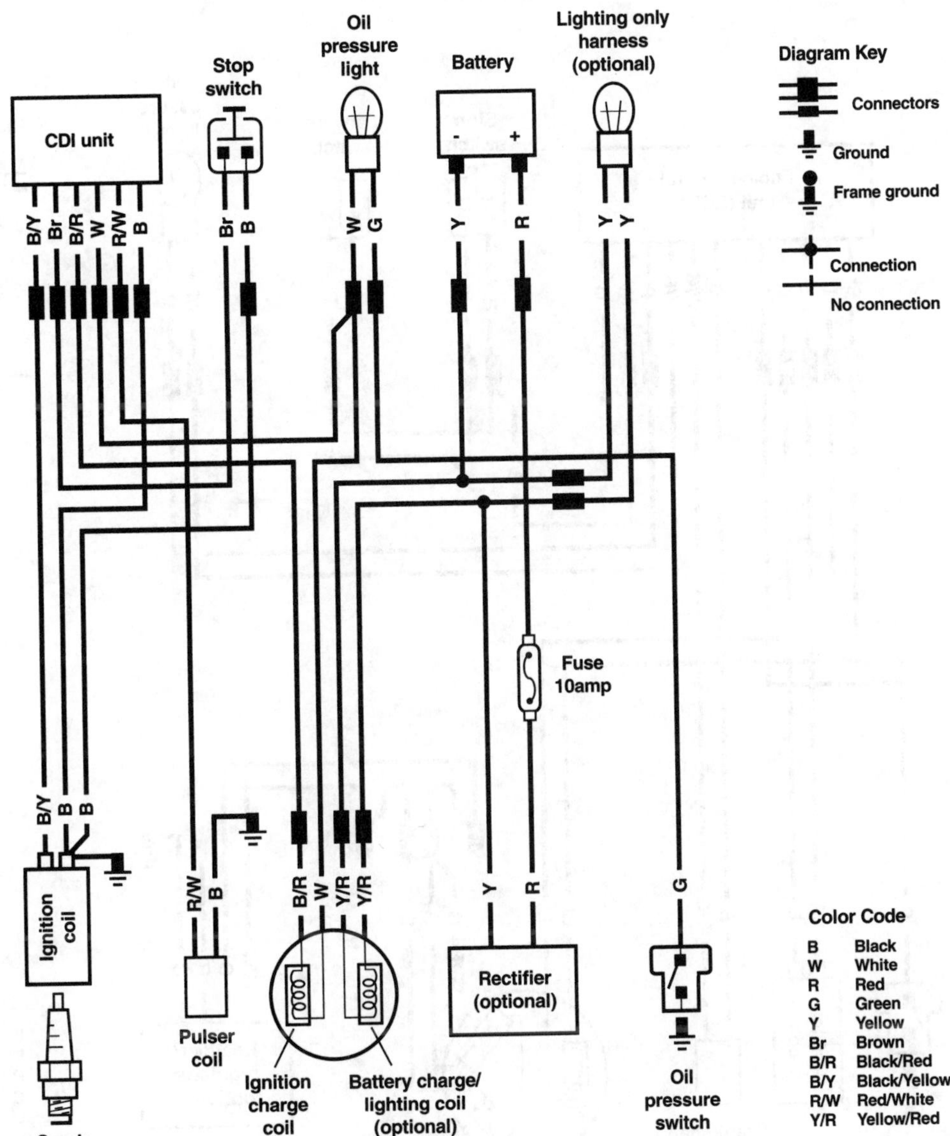

TILLER CONTROL MANUAL START (9.9 HP [SERIAL NO. OH000057-ON] AND 15 HP MODELS)

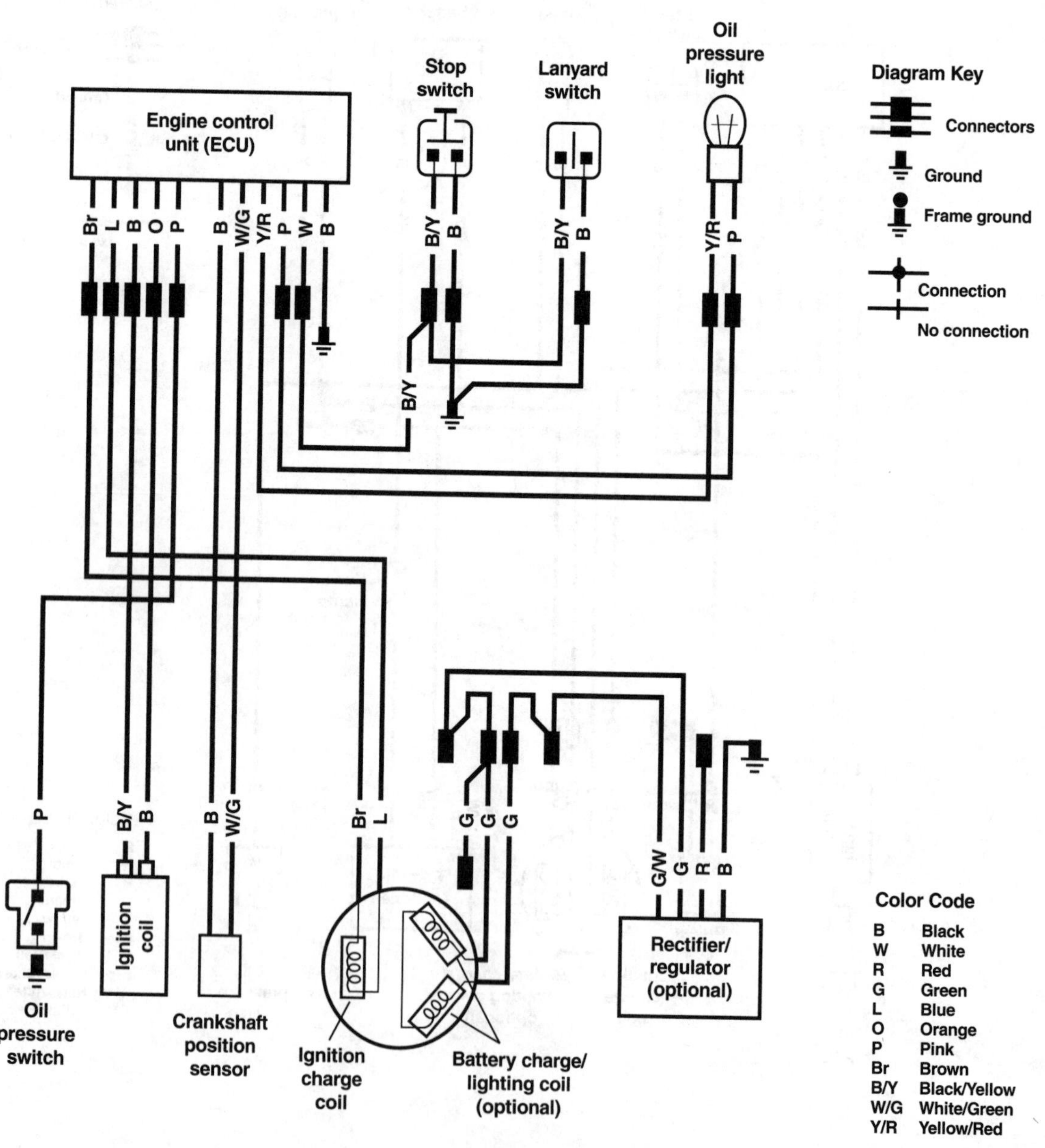

TILLER CONTROL ELECTRIC START (9.9 HP [SERIAL NO. OH00057-PRIOR] AND 15 HP MODELS)

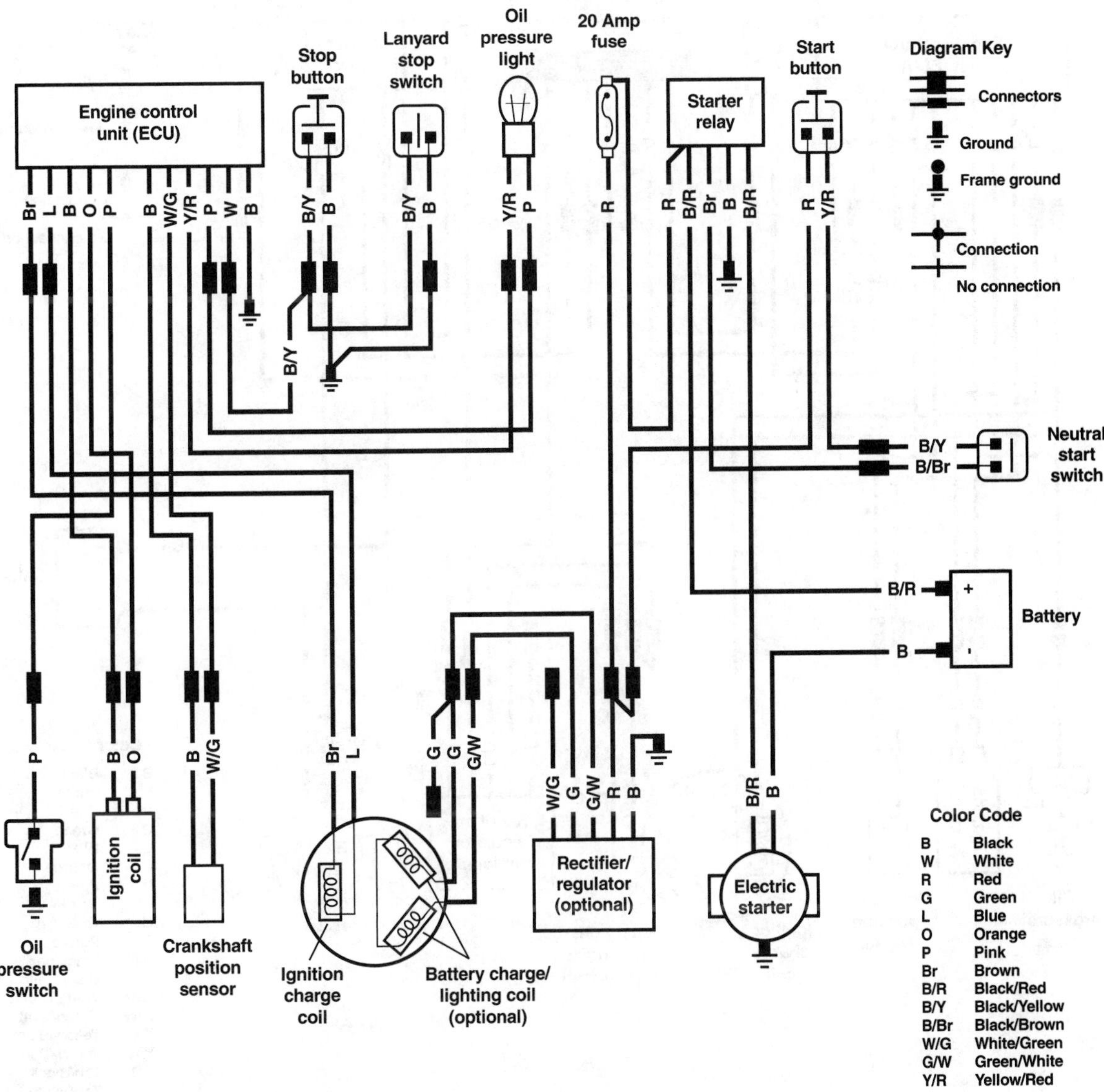

REMOTE CONTROL ELECTRIC START
(9.9 HP [SERIAL NO. OH000057-PRIOR] AND 15 HP MODELS)

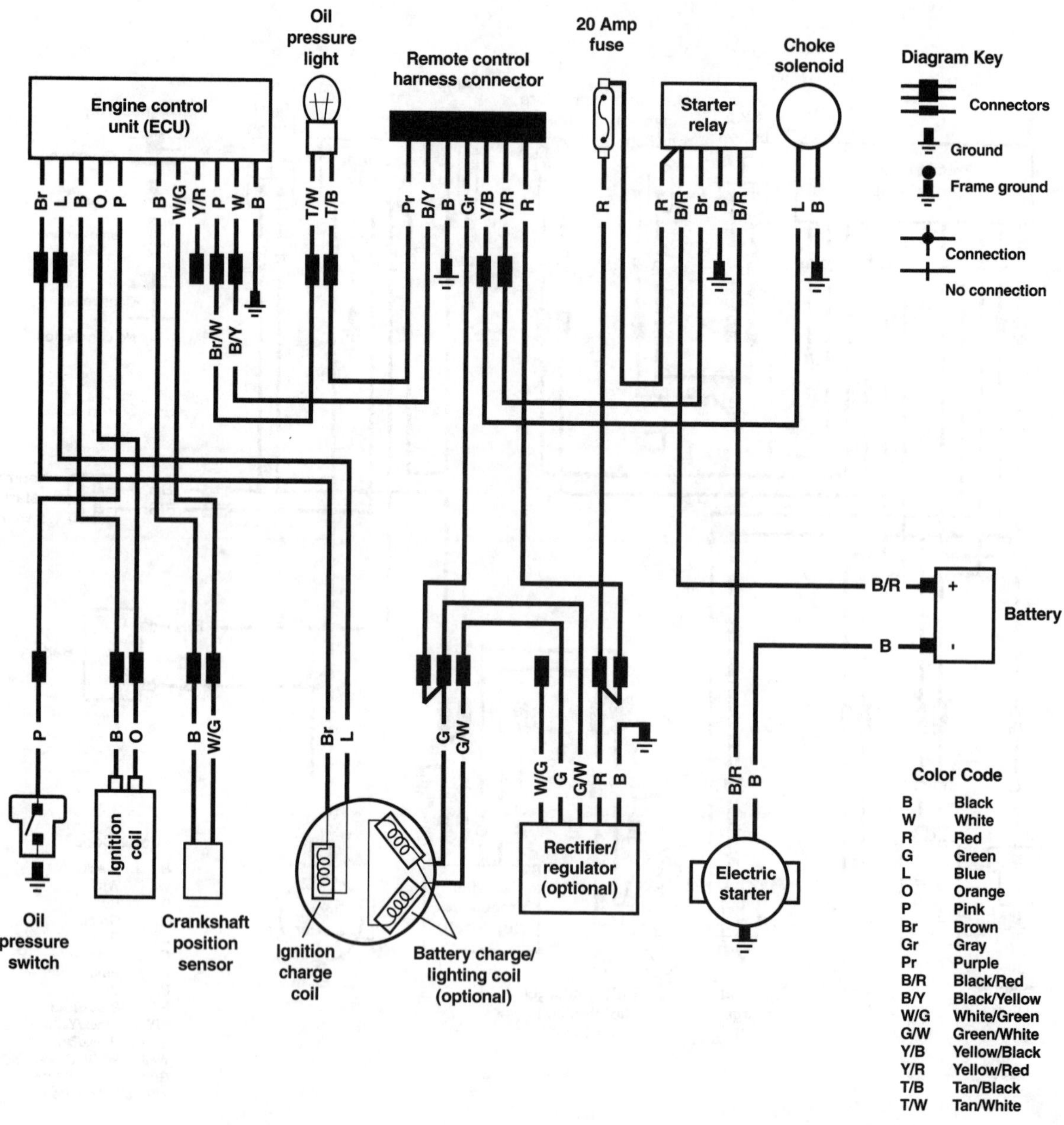

MANUAL START TILLER CONTROL (25 HP MODELS)

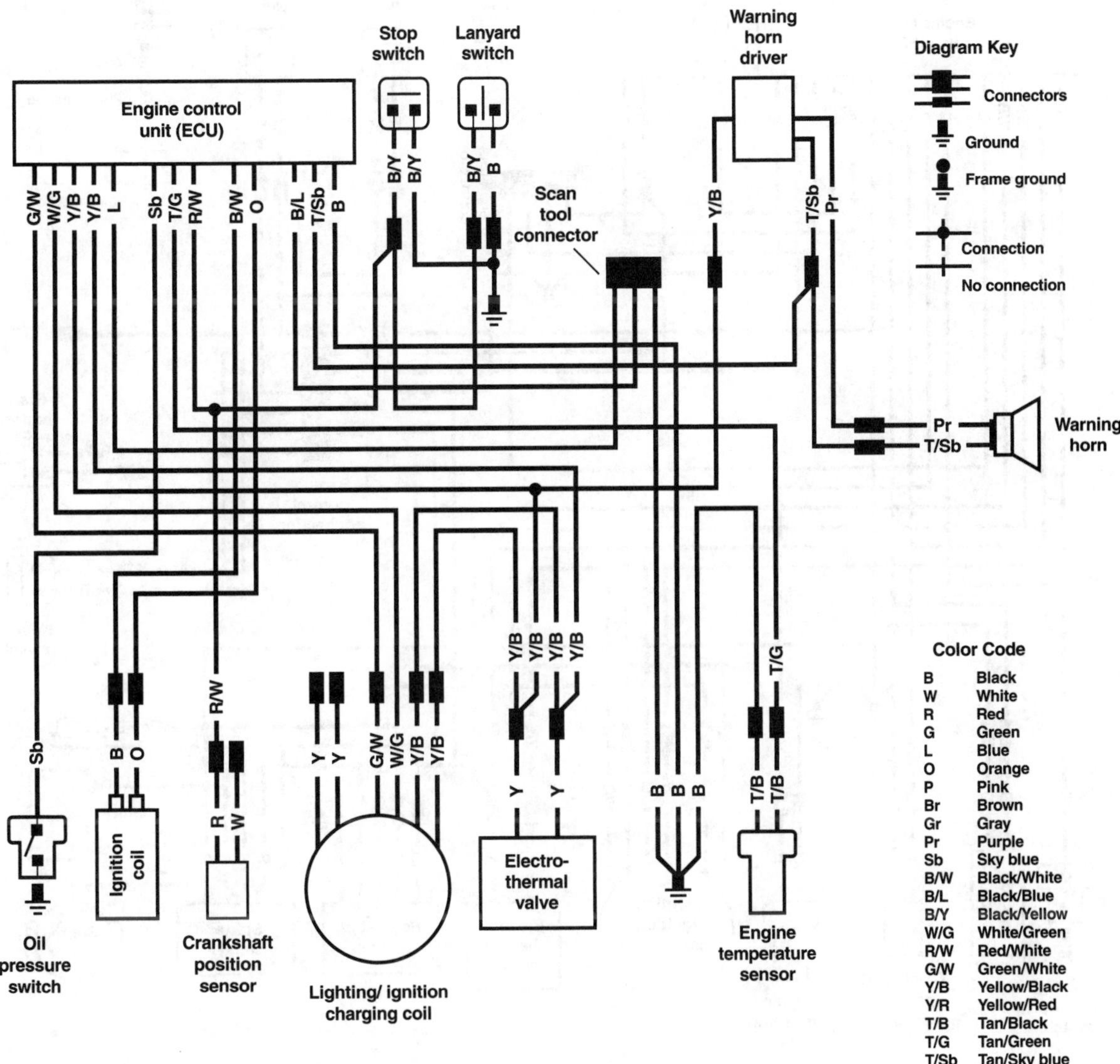

ELECTRIC START TILLER CONTROL
(25 HP MODELS)

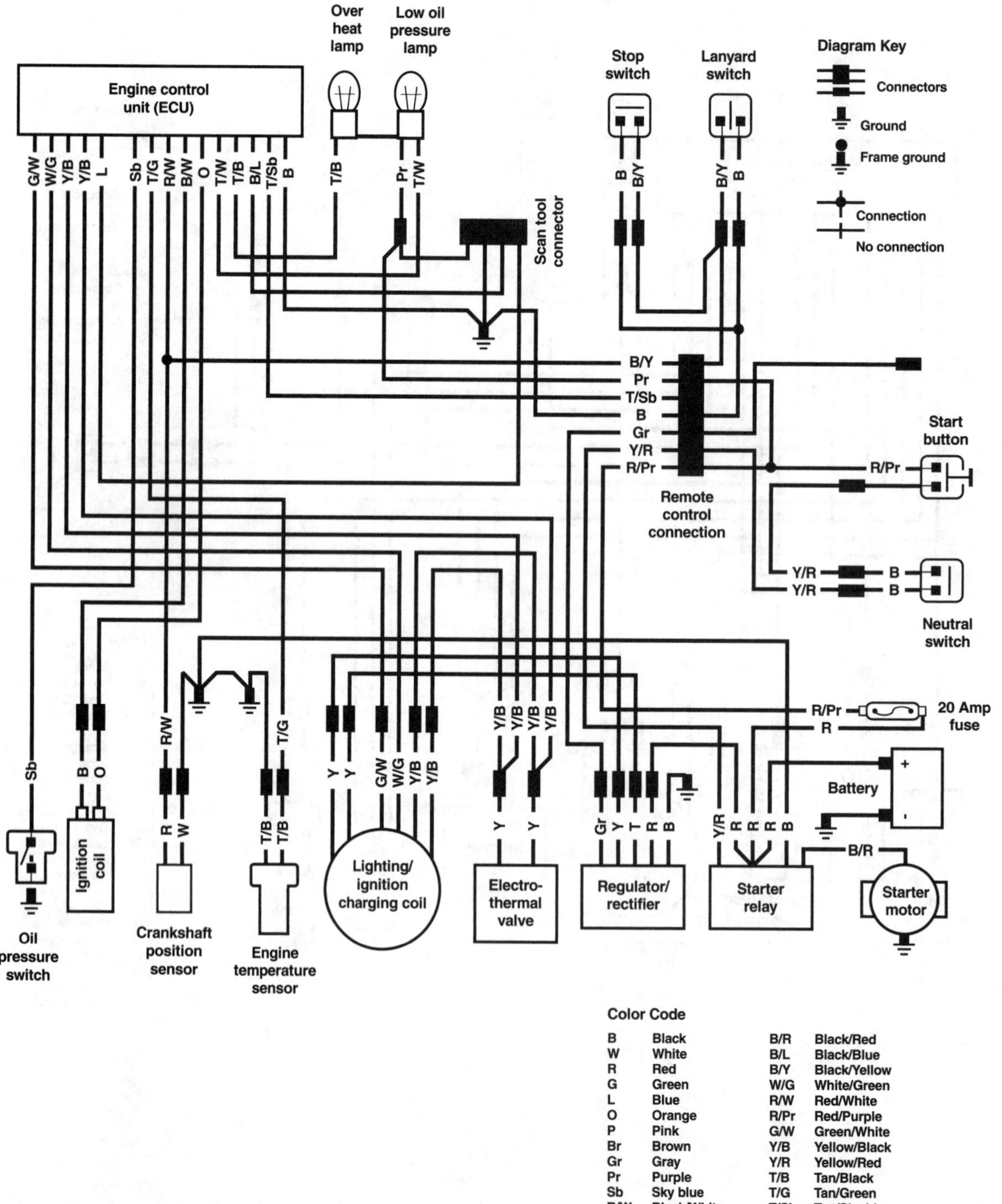

ELECTRIC START REMOTE CONTROL (25 HP MODELS)

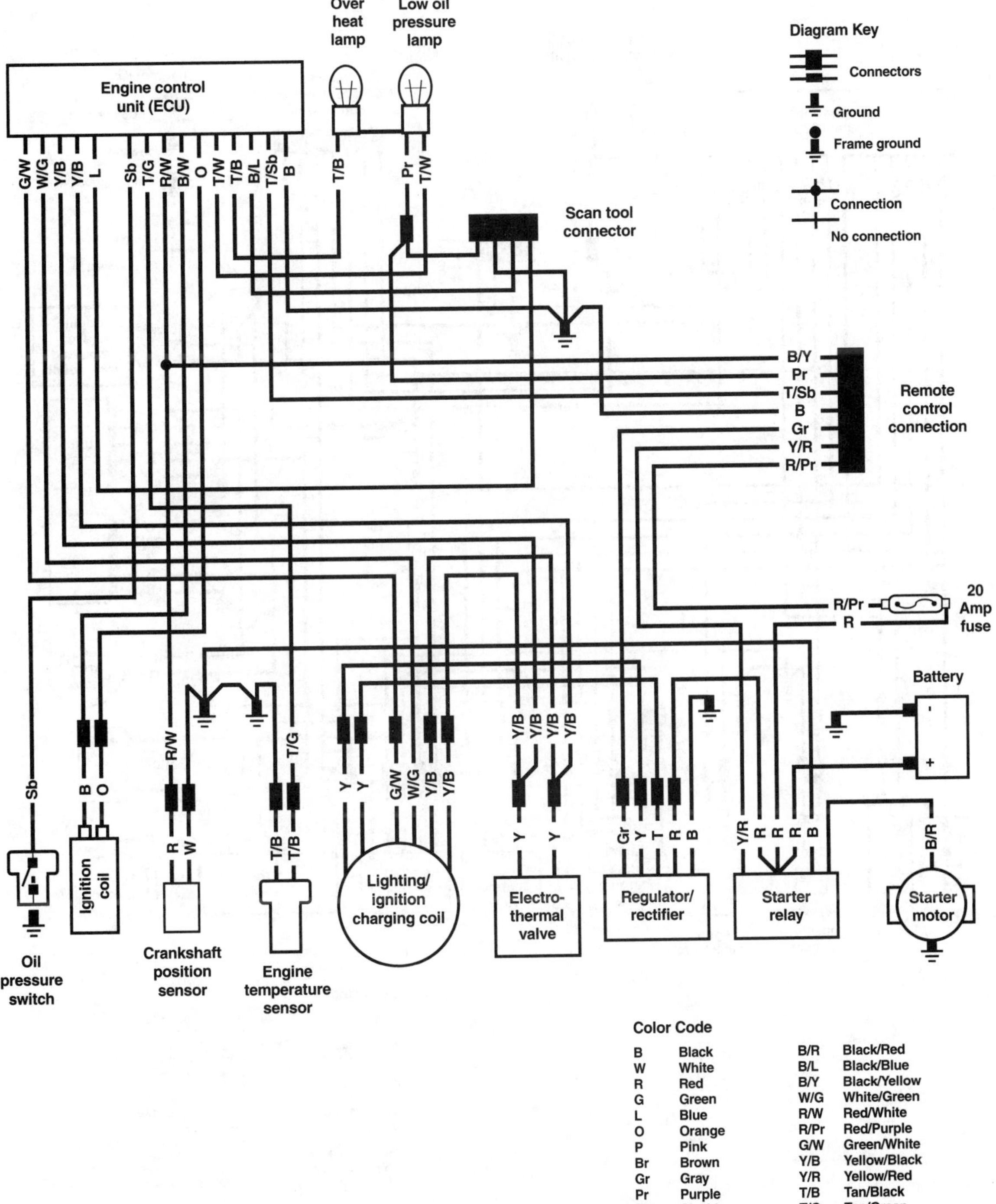

Color Code

B	Black	B/R	Black/Red
W	White	B/L	Black/Blue
R	Red	B/Y	Black/Yellow
G	Green	W/G	White/Green
L	Blue	R/W	Red/White
O	Orange	R/Pr	Red/Purple
P	Pink	G/W	Green/White
Br	Brown	Y/B	Yellow/Black
Gr	Gray	Y/R	Yellow/Red
Pr	Purple	T/B	Tan/Black
Sb	Sky blue	T/G	Tan/Green
B/W	Black/White	T/Sb	Tan/Sky blue

ELECTRIC START, REMOTE CONTROL AND POWER TRIM (25 HP MODELS)

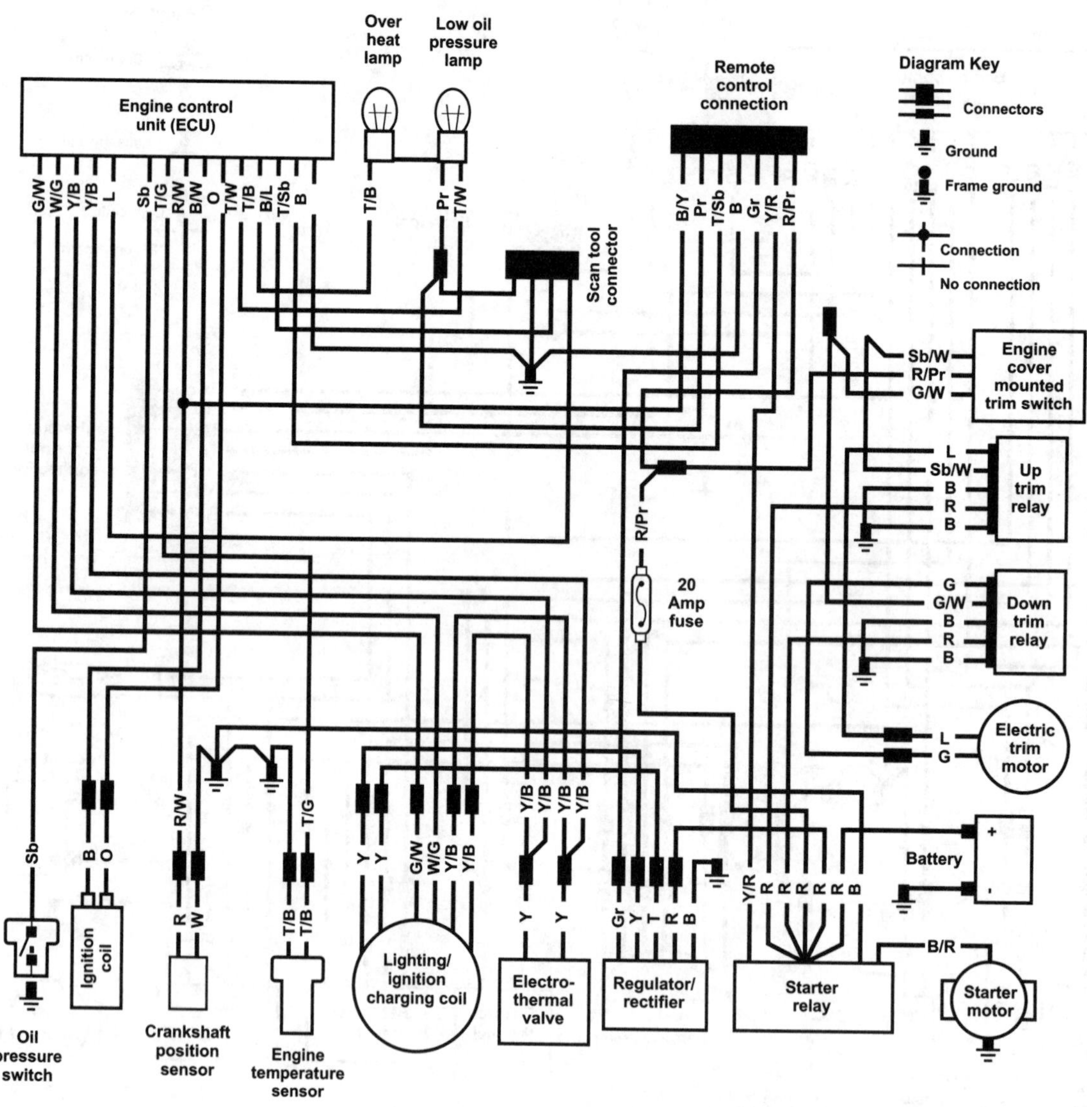

Color Code

B	Black	B/L	Black/Blue
W	White	B/Y	Black/Yellow
R	Red	W/G	White/Green
G	Green	R/W	Red/White
L	Blue	R/Pr	Red/Purple
O	Orange	G/W	Green/White
P	Pink	Y/B	Yellow/Black
Br	Brown	Y/R	Yellow/Red
Gr	Gray	T/B	Tan/Black
Pr	Purple	T/W	Tan/White
Sb	Sky blue	T/G	Tan/Green
B/W	Black/White	T/Sb	Tan/Sky blue
B/R	Black/Red	Sb/W	Sky blue/White

MANUAL START TILLER CONTROL (30 AND 40 HP MODELS)

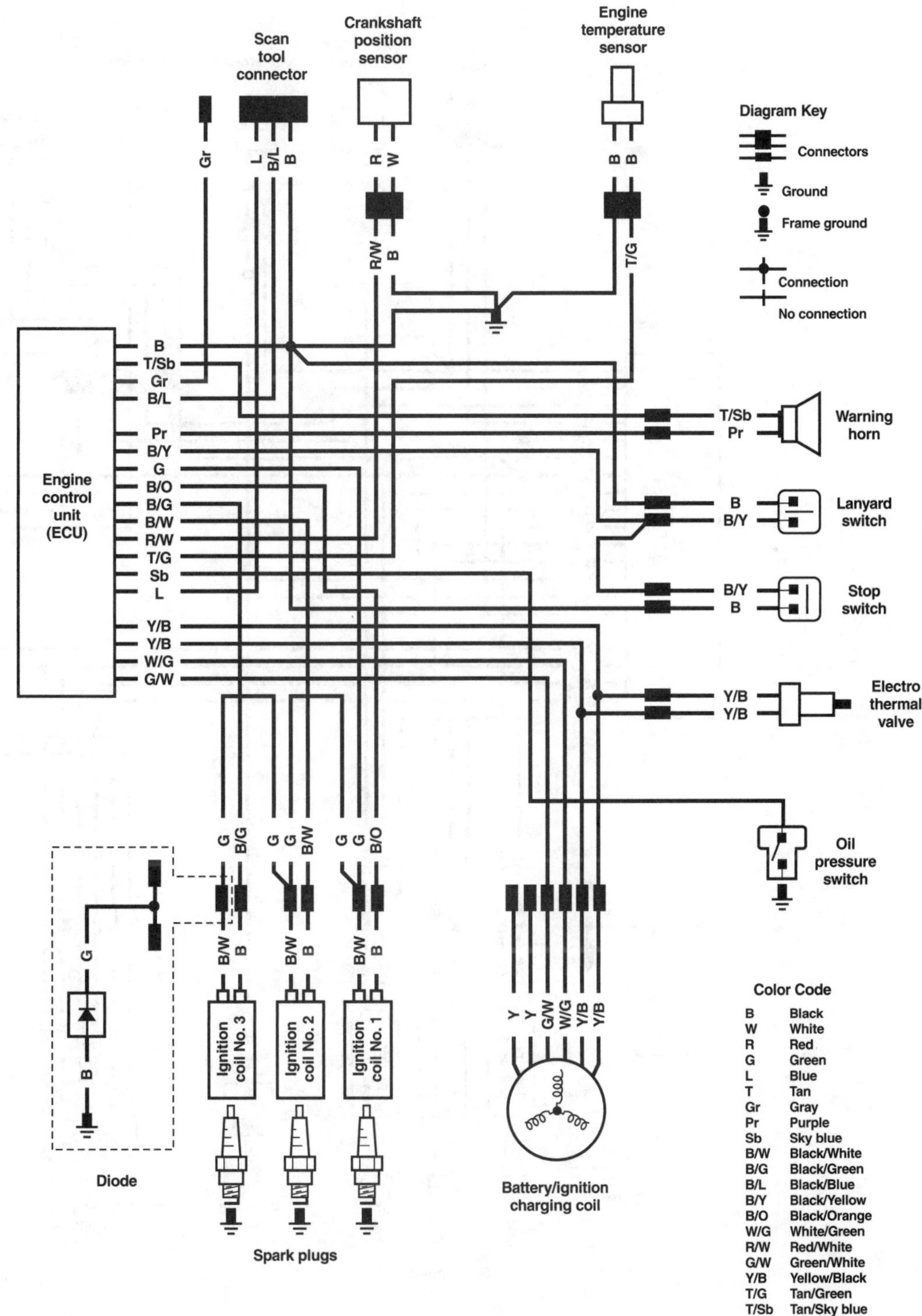

ELECTRIC START, TILLER CONTROL AND POWER TRIM (30 AND 40 HP MODELS)

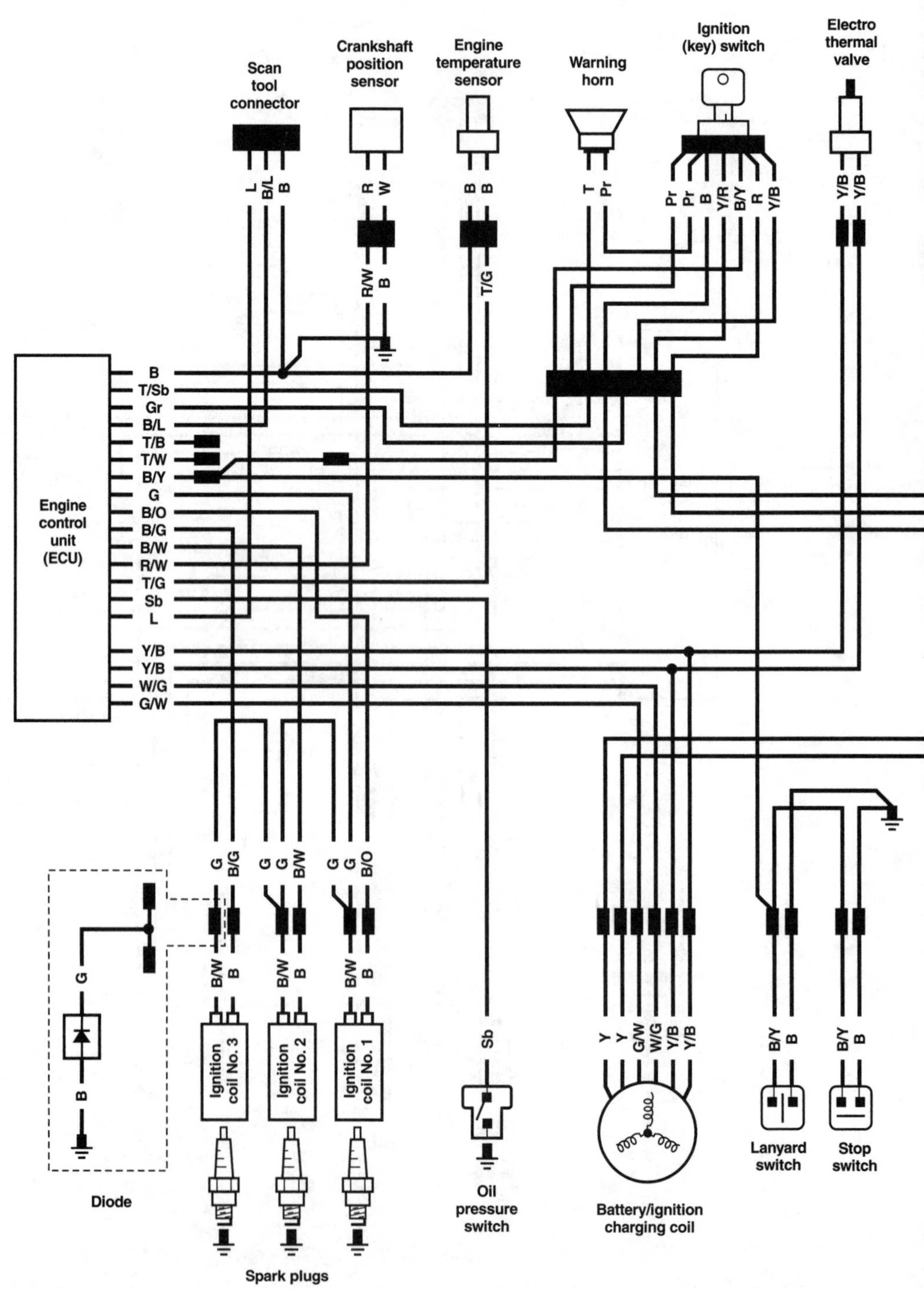

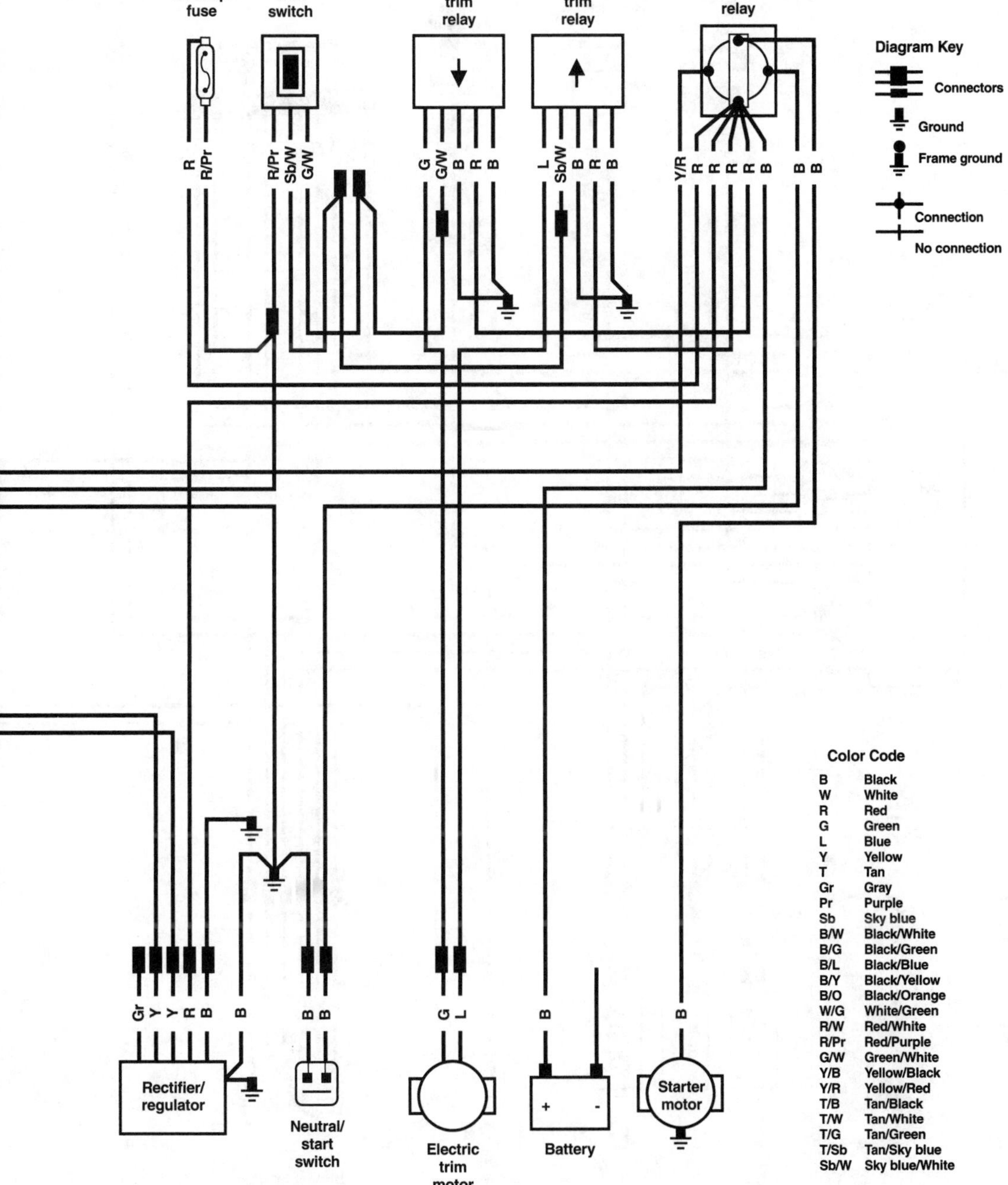

Diagram Key

Connectors

Ground

Frame ground

Connection

No connection

Color Code

B	Black
W	White
R	Red
G	Green
L	Blue
Y	Yellow
T	Tan
Gr	Gray
Pr	Purple
Sb	Sky blue
B/W	Black/White
B/G	Black/Green
B/L	Black/Blue
B/Y	Black/Yellow
B/O	Black/Orange
W/G	White/Green
R/W	Red/White
R/Pr	Red/Purple
G/W	Green/White
Y/B	Yellow/Black
Y/R	Yellow/Red
T/B	Tan/Black
T/W	Tan/White
T/G	Tan/Green
T/Sb	Tan/Sky blue
Sb/W	Sky blue/White

ELECTRIC START, REMOTE CONTROL AND POWER TRIM (30 AND 40 HP MODELS)

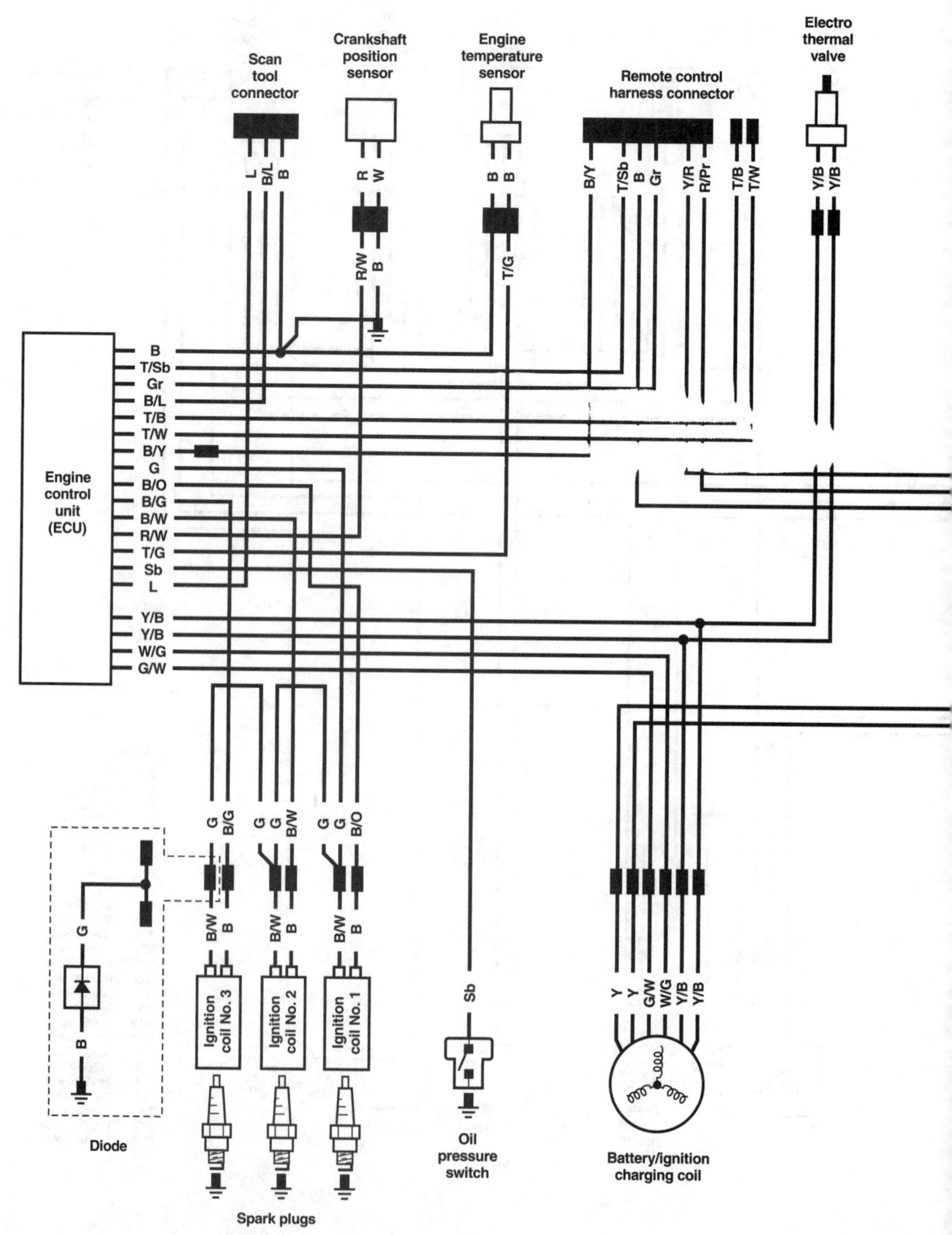

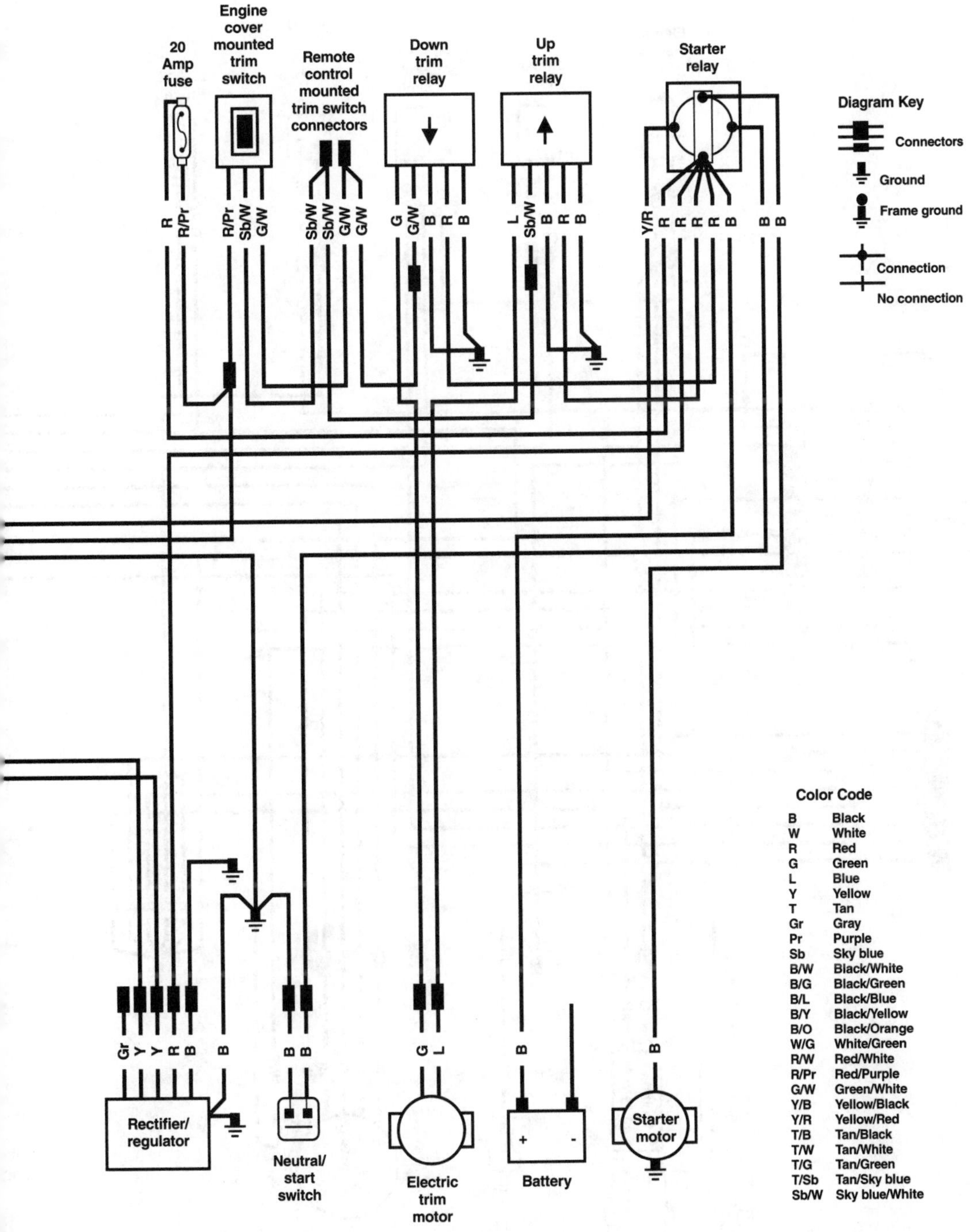

20 Amp fuse

Engine cover mounted trim switch

Remote control mounted trim switch connectors

Down trim relay

Up trim relay

Starter relay

R R/Pr R/Pr Sb/W G/W Sb/W Sb/W G/W G/W G G/W B R B L Sb/W B R B Y/R R R R R B B B

Diagram Key

Connectors

Ground

Frame ground

Connection

No connection

Gr Y Y R B B B B G L B B

Rectifier/ regulator

Neutral/ start switch

Electric trim motor

Battery

+ -

Starter motor

Color Code

B	Black
W	White
R	Red
G	Green
L	Blue
Y	Yellow
T	Tan
Gr	Gray
Pr	Purple
Sb	Sky blue
B/W	Black/White
B/G	Black/Green
B/L	Black/Blue
B/Y	Black/Yellow
B/O	Black/Orange
W/G	White/Green
R/W	Red/White
R/Pr	Red/Purple
G/W	Green/White
Y/B	Yellow/Black
Y/R	Yellow/Red
T/B	Tan/Black
T/W	Tan/White
T/G	Tan/Green
T/Sb	Tan/Sky blue
Sb/W	Sky blue/White

50 HP MODELS

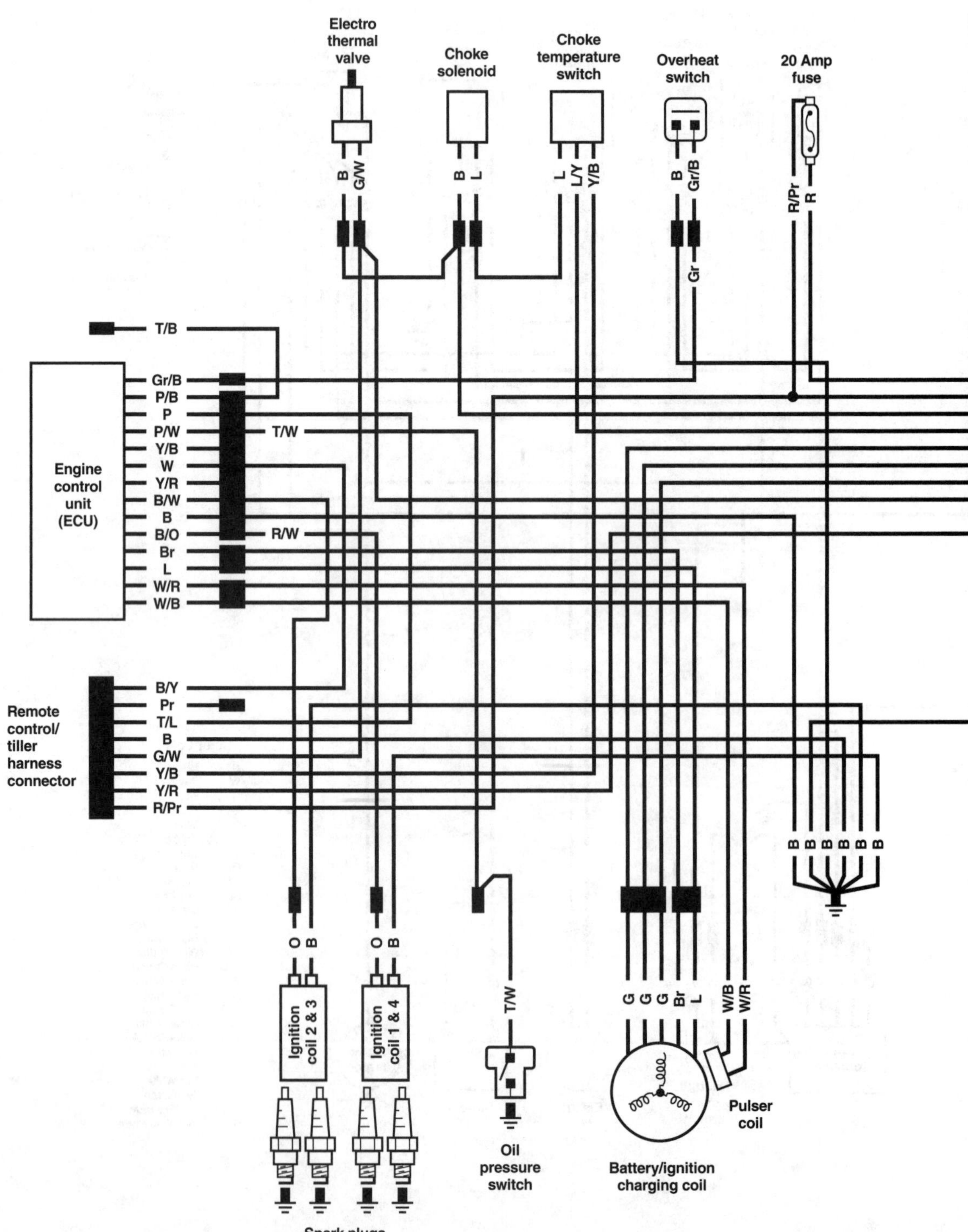
Electro thermal valve
Choke solenoid
Choke temperature switch
Overheat switch
20 Amp fuse
B
G/W
B
L
L
L/Y
Y/B
B
Gr/B
Gr
R/Pr
R
T/B
Engine control unit (ECU)
Gr/B
P/B
P
P/W
Y/B
W
Y/R
B/W
B
B/O
Br
L
W/R
W/B
T/W
R/W
Remote control/ tiller harness connector
B/Y
Pr
T/L
B
G/W
Y/B
Y/R
R/Pr
B
B
B
B
B
B
O
B
O
B
Ignition coil 2 & 3
Ignition coil 1 & 4
T/W
G
G
G
Br
L
W/B
W/R
Pulser coil
Spark plugs
Oil pressure switch
Battery/ignition charging coil

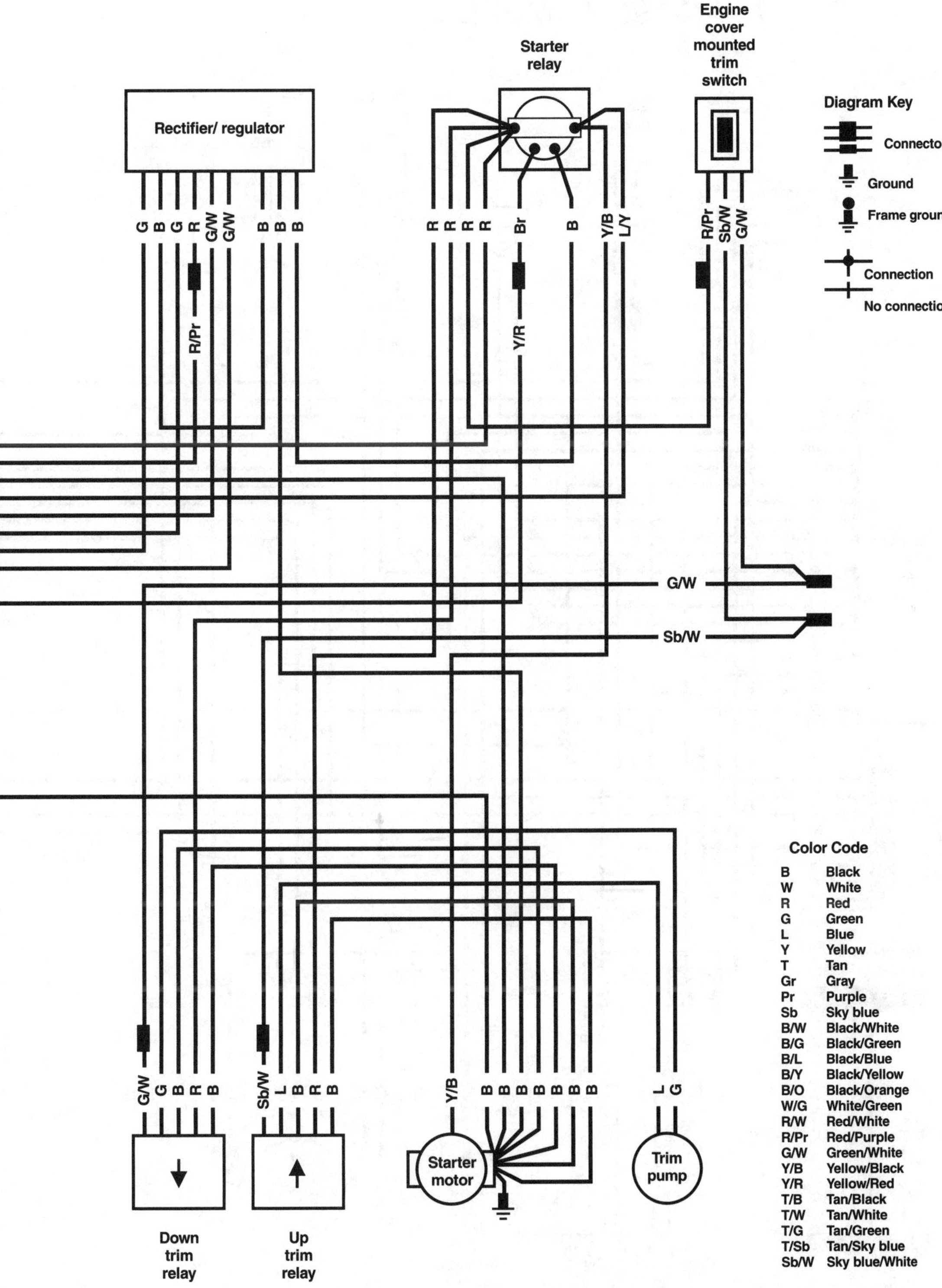

Color Code

B	Black
W	White
R	Red
G	Green
L	Blue
Y	Yellow
T	Tan
Gr	Gray
Pr	Purple
Sb	Sky blue
B/W	Black/White
B/G	Black/Green
B/L	Black/Blue
B/Y	Black/Yellow
B/O	Black/Orange
W/G	White/Green
R/W	Red/White
R/Pr	Red/Purple
G/W	Green/White
Y/B	Yellow/Black
Y/R	Yellow/Red
T/B	Tan/Black
T/W	Tan/White
T/G	Tan/Green
T/Sb	Tan/Sky blue
Sb/W	Sky blue/White

75 AND 90 HP MODELS

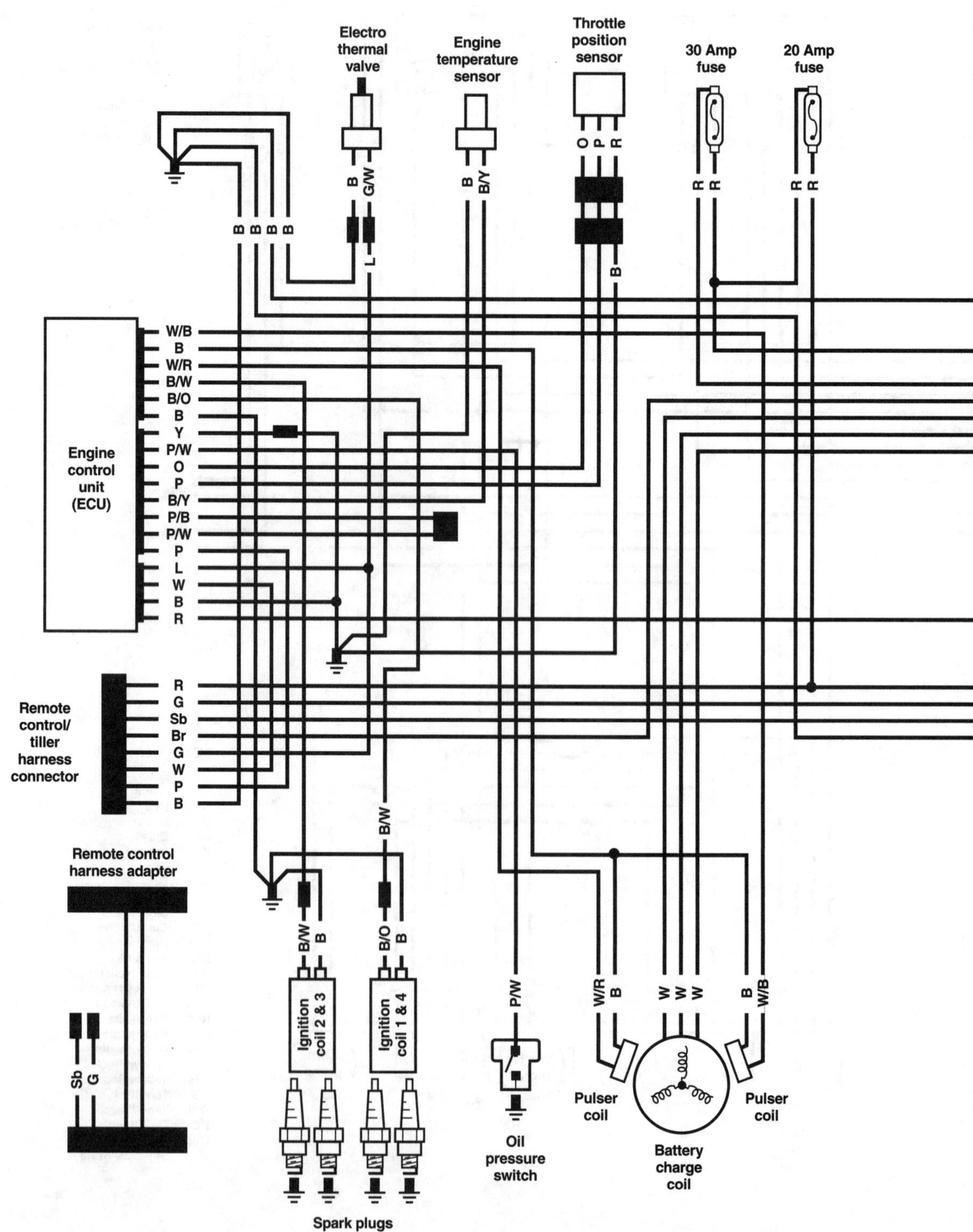

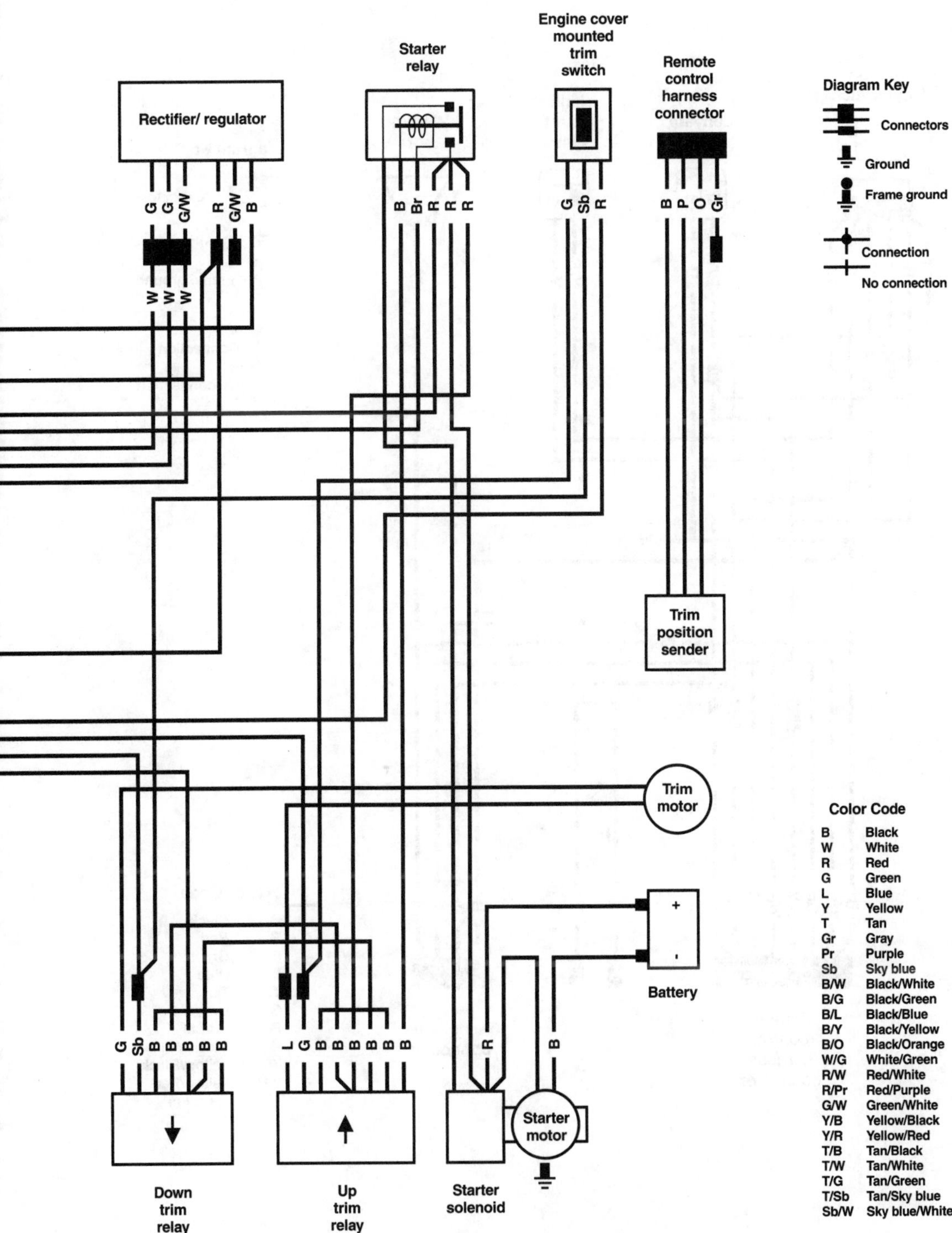

Diagram Key

Connectors

Ground

Frame ground

Connection

No connection

Color Code

B	Black
W	White
R	Red
G	Green
L	Blue
Y	Yellow
T	Tan
Gr	Gray
Pr	Purple
Sb	Sky blue
B/W	Black/White
B/G	Black/Green
B/L	Black/Blue
B/Y	Black/Yellow
B/O	Black/Orange
W/G	White/Green
R/W	Red/White
R/Pr	Red/Purple
G/W	Green/White
Y/B	Yellow/Black
Y/R	Yellow/Red
T/B	Tan/Black
T/W	Tan/White
T/G	Tan/Green
T/Sb	Tan/Sky blue
Sb/W	Sky blue/White

QUICKSILVER REMOTE CONTROL

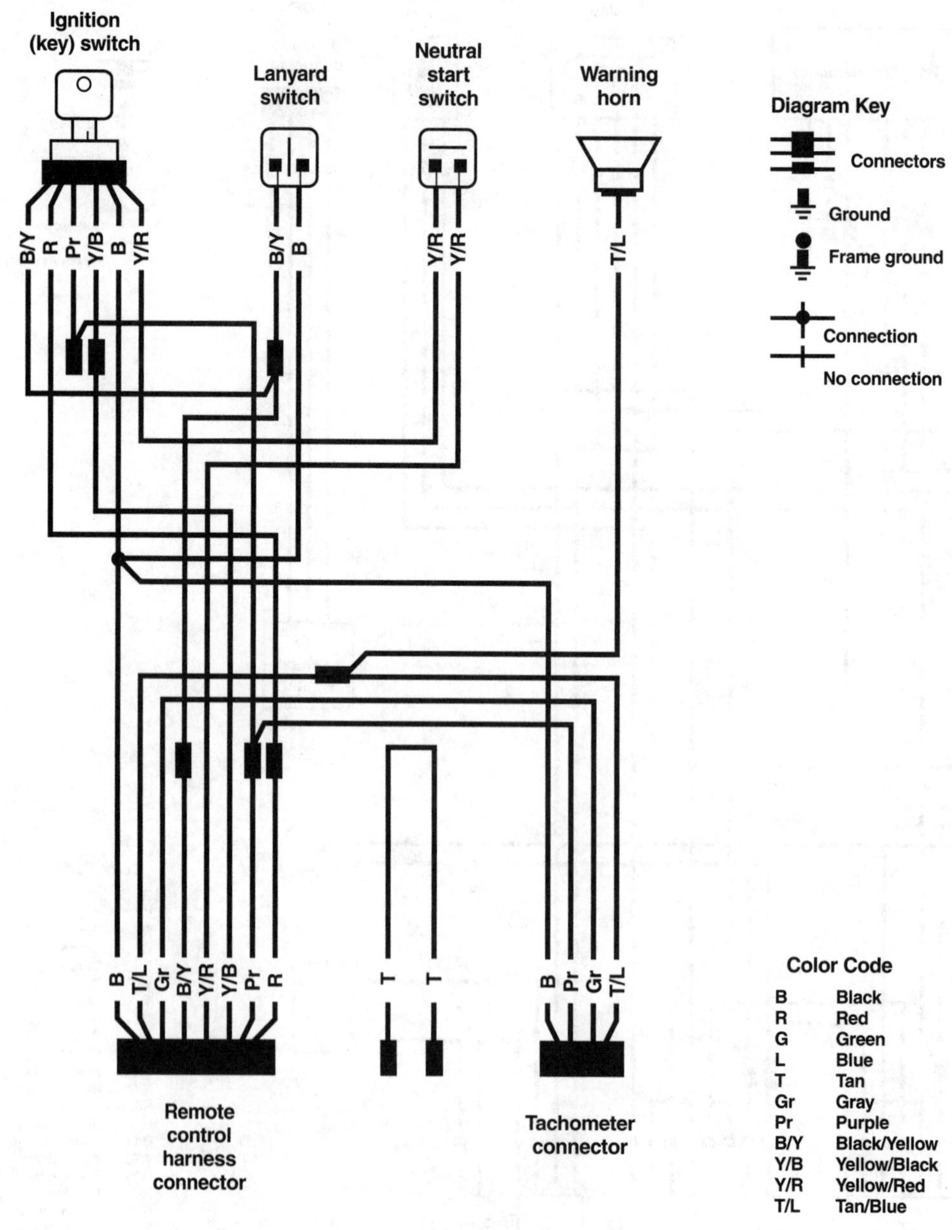